Abram Joseph Ryan

A Crown for our Queen

Abram Joseph Ryan

A Crown for our Queen

ISBN/EAN: 9783337269708

Printed in Europe, USA, Canada, Australia, Japan

Cover: Foto ©Lupo / pixelio.de

More available books at **www.hansebooks.com**

A CROWN

— FOR —

OUR QUEEN

Ave Maria—gratia plena
Dominus tecum,—
Benedicta tu in mulieribus
Et benedictus fructus ventris tui Jesus.

By REV. ABRAM J. RYAN.

BALTIMORE:
PUBLISHED BY JOHN B. PIET & CO.
No. 174 West Baltimore Street
1882.

J. M. J.

TO THE CHILDREN OF MARY,

of

THE CATHEDRAL

of

THE IMMACULATE CONCEPTION,

MOBILE, ALABAMA,

IN MEMORY

Of happy Years of their Spiritual Direction,

IN GRATITUDE

For their many kindnesses, known and unknown,

AND AS A PUBLIC TESTIMONY

To the Virtues

Which made their Sodality

The Fairest Flower

Of one of the most edifying Congregations in the South,

THIS BOOK

IS AFFECTIONATELY DEDICATED

By its Author,

ABRAM J. RYAN.

BILOXI, MISS., Ascension Thursday, 1882.

PREFACE.

THIS book was intended as a "MONTH OF MARY." It would have been published a few months ago had it not been for the illness of the author. However, better late than never, and by the clients of Mary it may be made to suit any month in the year.

At the suggestion of a child of Mary, its title is "A CROWN FOR OUR QUEEN," in which the author has tried to intertwine his own humble thoughts and the remembered ideas of others with the holy truths of faith regarding Mary's place in the plans of God. Would that the crown were worthier of our Queen!

The book substantially contains, in enlarged form, a a series of instructions given every Sunday evening, for several years, to the Children of Mary, of the Cathedral of Mobile, Alabama. Indeed, it belongs to them as much as it does to the author. They inspired it—he only wrote it.

The book closes with some simple little legends published in French, with the approbation of the Bishop of Limoges, and kindly translated by a Child of Mary. The book is dogmatic as well as devotional, for what is devotion but the blooming and blossoming and fruitage of dogma? If it leads a single soul, through Mary, to Jesus, the author will feel that his humble work has God's blessing. He asks for nothing more.

In a work on the Grandeurs of Mary written by

Father D'Argentan, a Capuchin monk of the last century, the author of this book found and used many beautiful thoughts. But if there be a single sentence in this work which is not in perfect accord with Faith and Faith's authoritative expressions—that sentence is here and in advance condemned and repudiated by the author.

A. J. RYAN.

CONTENTS.

	PAGE.
INTRODUCTION	viii
THE IMMACULATE CONCEPTION	xviii
FIRST DAY—The Flower of Mary's Predestination (First Part)	1
SECOND DAY—The Flower of Mary's Predestination (Second Part)	7
THIRD DAY—The Flower of the Promise (First Part)	15
FOURTH DAY—The Flower of the Promise (Second Part)	22
FIFTH DAY—The Flower of the Immaculate Conception (First Part)	29
SIXTH DAY—The Flower of the Immaculate Conception (Second Part)	43
SEVENTH DAY—The Flower of the Birth	56
EIGHTH DAY—The Flower of the Name	67
NINTH DAY—The Flower of the Vow	79
TENTH DAY—The Flower of the Espousals	92
ELEVENTH DAY—The Flower of the Annunciation	105
TWELFTH DAY—The Flower of the Consent	115
THIRTEENTH DAY—The Flower of the Visitation	122
FOURTEENTH DAY—The Flower of the Fear	128
FIFTEENTH DAY—The Flower of the Flight	137
SIXTEENTH DAY—The Flower of the Midnight of Mercy	142
SEVENTEENTH DAY—The Star in the East	149
EIGHTEENTH DAY—The Flower of the Purification	155
NINETEENTH DAY—The Flower of Sorrow and Joy	160
TWENTIETH DAY—The Flower of the Wedding-feast	168

CONTENTS. vii

PAGE

TWENTY-FIRST DAY—The Flower of Mary's Martyrdom (First Part).................173
TWENTY-SECOND DAY—The Flower of Mary's Martyrdom (Second Part)...............180
TWENTY-THIRD DAY—The Flower of Mary's Martyrdom (Third Part).................187
TWENTY-FOURTH DAY—The Flower of the Glory of the Resurrection................195
TWENTY-FIFTH DAY—The Flower of the Glory of the Ascension....................201
TWENTY-SIXTH DAY—The Flower of the Glory of Mary on Pentecost................209
TWENTY-SEVENTH DAY—The Flower of the Joy of Mary's Death.....................215
TWENTY-EIGHTH DAY—Flower of the Glory of Mary's Coronation in Heaven.........221
TWENTY-NINTH DAY—The Flower of Mary's Intercession...........................228
THIRTIETH DAY—The Flower of Mary's Glory in the Church.......................235
THIRTY-FIRST DAY—The Flower of Catholic Devotion to Mary.....................242
LEGENDS..................................251-276

INTRODUCTION.

SHALL we say it? Why not? We might as well, and we must, for it is an alarming fact which, though seen of all, seems to alarm but a few, and these few the watchers on the towers of truth. The humble spirit of Christian faith is on the wane everywhere around us, while the proud spirit of human reason is waxing strong with a giant's strength, gaining the force which faith seems to be losing. Real strength? Not at all. 'Tis only a seeming strength, the effect of falsehood's stimulants, for falsehood is a stimulant, while truth is food. That strength will not last, but the harm it is doing may and will. A servant may don the royal robes of his master, but he is not therefore king.

So falsehood, or if you will, knowledge without faith (they often look and speak alike, as if they were akin), may wear a kingly mantle and crown, and wield a sceptre of authority, and command the fealty which is the right of faith alone; and many may kneel down before the usurper's throne with the tender of their homage; yet none the less, whether they know it or not, are they committing an act of high treason against the majesty of truth, the while they are violating the spiritual laws of their being and betraying the sacred honor of their own reason; for the weakening of faith is a sign of the weakening of reason.

Revelation accepted by faith is the coronation of reason. Revelation rejected for mere human knowledge is reason's enslavement.

Our age possesses (and sooth to say in boastfulness) the gift of pens and of tongues, and of words and of notions, and of guesses and of theories, but it does not possess the gift of true thought. By our age, we mean the children of this generation, "who are wiser in their day than the children of light." It is a talking and not a thinking generation. It has a superficial smartness in its own sphere—intelligent, perhaps, as the word goes, but not intellectual. It chatters—that, and nothing more. To the supernatural it says, "No, begone, I deny and reject you." A few men stand apart from the chatterers who teach them the glory of saying No to anything beyond the limits of their senses and the reach of their comprehension.

These are the philosophers. They are hailed as the liberators of the human mind, and when they die they are buried in Westminsters. They are crowned with laurel, and not with thorns, for their theories. They have no Calvary nor Cross; and it so happens, when they die their graves do not open nor do they rise again. The philosophers are quite different from Christ. They teach, and what? The novel and the uncertain. The uncertain takes with the thoughtless. There is a strange fascination about it. It is a new face with a vague beauty. It charms—so does the serpent.

To the dear old familiar features of truth men grow indifferent. With their knowledge they will "become like God." 'Tis the old temptation of Eden over again. God's word they reject for the serpent's word; divine faith for human knowledge, so called. Tis a new beauty. It wins recognition, loyalty, love. The olden beauty, truth, must retire. She wears the veil of faith. Knowledge, less modest, wears no veil at all. She has a terribly earthly face, fit for sensuous but not for spiritual eyes. Has faith, veiled truth, lost a single one of her charms? Not at all. She cannot. Her's is the half-seen beauty of God. She is the same as ever she was, with a beauty not of earth.

There is something wrong and wanting elsewhere. Where? In the eyes of men's souls. Why? They are growing blind. Why, again? The planets of false knowledge are crossing the disk of the sun of truth. 'Tis dim up there and it is dark down here. So they grope, and creep and crawl, not man like nor reason like, and they no longer walk straight on and upright, with the light of eternity on their lifted brow, for to them the eclipse of truth is total—and they call darkness light. They desire us (how kind and considerate they are!) to give up our faith's certainties for their guesses. They wish us to abandon our truths as the vain dreams of an effete superstition, and to accept their fickle dreams as truths undoubted; and many do. They abandon the truths of revelation, fling away their faith, and they become slaves or dupes of human credulity. They give up Christ for the philosophers. There is no room for Christ in their syllogisms, and so they thrust him away. Well, there was no room for Him, of old, in Bethlehem. But somehow His stable still remains with the Gloria in Excelsis above it. Thitherward, in ceaseless pilgrimage, go the children of light to pray and to adore. Philosophers! that stable is too much for you. It stands;—your syllogisms pass away.

Nature's and Supernature's God was made visible to the world, in human nature, in that stable. The Supernature you deny. At its wonders you superciliously smile. Yourselves mysteries to your own very selves, you scoff at mysteries. Nature is your temple, you the self-ordained priests. Well, priests! listen. Are there not tabernacles in nature's temple closed against you? You come to the gates, but they are locked and you have not the key. Has not nature's temple a Holy of Holies, where dwell the mysterious powers of creation? And you cannot enter there. Facts and phenomena broider the mysterious veil which hangs before it. The broidery you may show, but you cannot lift the veil.

Your motto is: " We reason and we know." But do you reason right? Where is the reason lying back of your first reasoning? Only in your own brain? Then you only make a rope of sand. And how much do you know? Are not the primary elements in nature beyond the reach of your chemistry? And if this be true, as it is, of mere material nature, then what of human nature?

One of your school writes a work on the "Descent of Man." Unwittingly he uses the proper word, "descent." Yes, we (and we know and feel it) descend from something, some one higher, from God himself. And the philosopher substitutes for the glorious truth of man's descent from God, his theory of man's ascent from heaven knows where, in the world that lies beneath us. Error is forced to be logical in order to be self-consistent. Put aside God's creative act, and the truth and high honor of it, and necessarily the honor of man's origin suffers detriment. God lost, in false logic, all is lost in reason's life, not only God's but man's honor.

Now God visibly comes before us in human form and

nature in the Christ—the man—the God, through real birth from a real human mother—Mary. His mother denied, Christ is denied; that is the real, true Christ of God's Scriptures and Man's history. He denied, God is denied. What then? Chaos, darkness, and this life is a horror. Not so cry out the children of light and faith and hope. Christ is the key of every mystery. As man, he touched every human question, and as God he gave to each question full, absolute, infinite answer. Beside Him, as man, stands His mother, beside Him, as God, stands the Eternal Father; beside Him, as Man-God, stand Mary and the Father. Christ is not a philosopher, He is eternal wisdom. He is not a scientist, but He is a Saviour. He is not a mere reasoner, He is a Redeemer, and being that, He is the real reason of all things; and He is the fact which touches with light every fact of human history. And not only that, He is the Truth, away and apart from which all else is false. And not only that, He is the Life, outside of which stretches the land of death.

Philosophers! you give us dead words. The canker worm of hopelessness is within all. The human race is against you. It must believe and hope and love something, and some one above, beyond this earth—God. He stands revealed in Jesus Christ, and Him born of a woman of the race. Jesus Christ is the living answer to all the mysteries of man's nature and man's history.

Scientists need Christ, the Word, the Wisdom, the Alpha and Omega, the Principle and the End, to give true light that enlightens minds to every question connected with nature—else science is a darkness. But what of Christians? Jesus Christ and Mary, His mother, are the living answers to all the questions that touch human nature in its spiritual history; that is, they begin the answer asked and needed by faith and hope and love, which the Church continues to give forever, to all generations.

Any other answer is false. Christ alone, His mother apart, is not the full answer. He and she, in the Christian order, stand first, and together. After them come the apostles, evangelists, the Church, with all her wondrous prerogatives. One by one apostles and evangelists pass away, leaving successors. Jesus and Mary have no successors. The Church remains forever, and speaks to the world each day two names, first names, Jesus and Mary, and they will be the last names of human history. They give revelation and redemption their full meaning. Revelation's truths are announced to us, and the merits of redemption are applied to us by the Church of Jesus Christ—His Church and no other.

When reason meets the Church and hears her voice she has but one of four acts to make:

First—I believe all truth on the word of God, who can neither deceive nor be deceived, authoritatively announced by the Church of Christ, which, because His Church, can never err nor lead to error. This act honors reason by honoring God, and honors Christ by honoring His Church with absolute obedience. It is the Catholic act with an infinite trust and courage in it.

Second—" I deny all." It is the dark, defiant act of the infidel. It is the absolute *No* hurled at revelation. It degrades reason by denying Christ. It is worse than satanic, for the demons believe all and tremble. In hell there are no infidel demons. Fallen angels are innocent of the guilt of infidelity to doctrine. The crime and its dishonor are found only among fallen images of God on earth.

Third—"I doubt." It is the act of the sceptic, halting, hesitating in the presence of the incomprehensible truth, and is an act of craven cowardice.

Fourth—"I protest." It is an act of reason, consciously or unconsciously compromising, where compromise is secret or overt treason to truth. It is an act of weakness unworthy of reason. The act of the weak compromise "I protest," leads to the act of the coward "I doubt," and the act of the coward leads straight into the darkness of the infidels, "I deny all."

"I believe all that the Church teaches," the Roman Catholic act, is the only act of faith which reason can make without debasement, which the free-will can proclaim, crowning itself thereby with the unspeakable honor of union with God's will, and which the heart can approve, for the peace and the hope and the glory of it. It is the only act of faith commensurate with all revelation, the only act worthy of man and worthy of God, the only act that reaches round all truth, the only act that touches that throne in the heavens, where faith will melt into vision. It is the everlasting act of the Holy Church in which each of her countless children has personal share. It ascends to heaven ceaselessly in a thousand thousand beautiful forms. It goes up from the hearts of the innumerable children of Christ's faithful family. Christ's family? Yes. We are His younger brothers and sisters by the adoption of grace. In that family, His mother by nature is ours by grace, and, therefore, next to Him, she holds and must forever hold highest place.

We have not a motherless Christ, neither have we a

motherless Church. What she was to Him she is to His Church, and to each one a mother by adoption. He gave her to us and us to her on Calvary, and He has never taken her away from us, for He never repents of His gifts.

Hence, in our Holy Church she is the Queen-mother. She has the heart of the mother and she wears the crown of the queen. In other churches she is nothing but a name. She was more than a name to Christ. In our Church she is herself, her very self, with all her powers and privileges. In other churches even her name is seldom mentioned, and then sometimes in tones that are cold and indifferent. In the Church of her Son, her name is one of power, sweetness, hope, tenderness, held in honor next to Christ's own adorable name; the very sound of the name of Mary forever thrills the hearts of the children of the Church with the sweetest truth in all creation—God has a mother. Out of that little sentence, as out of a perennial fountain, flows forever the stream of the precious blood of man's redemption; and out of that sentence floats murmured forever, in every crimson ripple of the saving stream, the beautiful truth —God's mother is ours.

The book here presented to those who may please to read its pages, is an humble attempt to set before their minds these two truths and their necessary mutual relations. It is an age of novels and novel readers. What novel can compare in fascinating interest with the New Testament? What romance is like the romance of God's eternal love revealed in Jesus, born of Mary? What drama like the drama of our redemption consummated on Calvary with Christ dying on His cross and His mother standing beneath it? What poetry so sweet, sublime, pathetic and glorious as the poetry of Bethlehem, Nazareth, Calvary, the riven Grave and Mount Olivet?

But alas! the divine scriptures yield before mere human writings. God's words, Christ's history, have lost their charm and interest. They are too serious for a thoughtless generation. Tales of human loves have taken the place of the wonderous story of God's eternal love, all of which manifestly proves the weakening of faith. Outside of the Church, where the beautiful Christ is only half-known, we do not wonder if the human supersedes the divine and the natural takes the precedence of the supernatural. But in Christ's Holy Church, alas, we must wonder if such things be; and such things are. 'Tis sad to say it, and sadder still to know that it is but too true. How many Catholics read the word of God? And yet the Church (though it is falsely denied by her enemies) recommends its perusal, not as necessary, but as useful and edifying. How many Catholics read the lives of the saints, the members of their own spiritual family? The stories of the world's heroes attract; the lives of the heroes of grace are too dry and uninteresting. Ah! the priests know this encroachment of this world's unfaith in the realms of Christ's kingdom. They contend against it with all the might of their zeal, sometimes successfully, but often, alas, with little or no success. And is it to be wondered at if children inherit the uncatholic tastes of their Catholic parents?

Dime novels, periodicals of marked immorality, weekly newspapers, with stories wherein crime is justified, romances where passion is apotheosized, poetries which are pagan in conception and sentiment, are not these, and such like works, found and read in Catholic homes all over the land? Alas, and yes. And the consequence? We know some, God knows more.

Books of piety are too seldom found in Catholic hands. The Church advises, entreats, pleads. The loving children and the loyal listen and obey. The Church goes farther, and puts her ban on books with danger in them to faith and morals, and still too many heed not her prohibitions. 'Tis to their own cost and at their own spiritual peril. Now out of the Church and in the Church, our wild, unruly age needs the strong, true Christ, to restrain its lawless will and to enlighten its darkening mind. The age, like Herod, has banished Christ into exile. No wonder it is in the dark when its light is gone. Ah! if the world would only pray "Hail full of grace, the Lord is with thee!" Exiled by this world, His mother exiled from human churches, Jesus and Mary—Mary and Jesus, together in our Holy Church, would hear the prayer of this generation, and from its sanctuary would bless this agitated age with the peace of the perfect and beautiful faith.

THE IMMACULATE CONCEPTION.

Fell the snow on the Festival's vigil
   And surpliced the city in white.
I wonder who wove the pure flakelets?
   Ask the Virgin—or God—or the Night.

It fitted the Feast: 'twas a symbol,
   And earth wore the surplice at morn,
As pure as the vale's stainless lily
   For Mary the sinlessly born,

For Mary, conceived in all sinlessness.
   And the sun, thro' the clouds of the East,
With the brightest and fairest of flashes,
   Fringed the Surplice of White for the Feast.

And round the horizon hung cloudlets,
   Pure Stoles to be worn by the Feast;
While the earth and the heavens were waiting
   For the beautiful Mass of the Priest.

I opened my window, half dreaming.
   My soul went away from my eyes,
And my heart began saying "Hail Marys,"
   Somewhere up in the beautiful skies,

Where the shadows of sin never rested;
   And the angels were waiting to hear
The prayer that ascends with "Our Father,"
   And keeps hearts and the heavens so near.

And all the day long,—can you blame me?
"Hail Mary," "Our Father," I said,
And I think that the Christ and His Mother
Were glad of the way that I prayed.

And I think that the great, bright Archangel
Was listening all the day long
For the echo of every "Hail Mary"
That soared thro' the skies, like a song,—

From the hearts of the true and the faithful,
In accents of joy or of woe,
Who kissed in their faith and their fervor
The Festival's Surplice of snow.

I listened, and each passing minute,
I heard in the lands far away
"Hail Mary," "Our Father," and near me
I heard all who knelt down to pray

Pray the same as I prayed, and the angel,
And the same as the Christ of our love—
"Our Father," "Hail Mary," "Our Father"—
Winging just the same sweet flight above.

Passed the morning, the noon : came the Even,
The temple of Christ was aflame
With the halo of lights on three altars,
And one wore his own Mother's name.

Her statue stood there ; and around it
Shone the symbolic stars. Was their gleam
And the flow'rets that fragranced her altar,
Were they only the dream of a dream?

Or were they sweet signs to my vision
Of a Truth far beyond mortal ken,
That the Mother had rights in the temple
Of Him she had given to men.

Was it wronging her Christ-son, I wonder,
  For the Christian to honor her so?
Ought her statue pass out of His temple?
  Ask the Feast in its Surplice of snow.

Ah, me! had the pure flakelets voices,
  I know what their white lips would say,
And I know that the lights on her altar
  Would pray with me, if they could pray.

Methinks that the flowers that were fading,
  Sweet virgins that die with the Feast
Like martyrs upon her fair altar,
  If they could, they would pray with the Priest,

And would murmur "Our Father," "Hail Mary,"
  Till they drooped on the altar, in death
And be glad in their dying for giving
  To Mary their last sweetest breath.

Passed the day as a poem that passes
  Through the poet's heart's sweetest of strings;
Moved the minutes from Masses to Masses—
  Did I hear a faint sound as of wings.

Rustling over the aisles and the altars?
  Did they go to her altar and pray?
Or was my heart only a-dreaming
  At the close of the Festival-day?

Quiet throngs came into the temple,
  As still as the flowers at her feet,
And wherever they knelt, they were gazing
  Where the statue looked smiling and sweet.

"Our Fathers," "Hail Mary's" were blended
  In a pure and a perfect accord,
And passed by the beautiful Mother
  To fall at the feet of our Lord.

Low-toned from the hearts of a thousand
  "Our Fathers," "Hail Marys" swept on
To the star-wreathed statue. I wonder
Did they wrong the great name of Her Son,

Her Son and our Saviour—I wonder
  How He heard our "Hail Marys" that night?
Were the words to Him sweet as the music
  They once were, and did we pray right?

Or was it all wrong?—will He punish
  Our lips if we make them the home
Of the words of the great, high Archange
  That won Him to sinners to come?

Ah, me! does He blame my own mother,
  Who taught me a child at her knee,
To say, with "Our Father," "Hail Mary"?
  If 'tis wrong, my Christ! punish but me.

Let my mother, oh, Jesus! be blameless;
  Let me suffer for her if you blame.
Her pure mother's heart knew no better
  When she taught me to love the pure name.

Oh, Christ! of Thy beautiful Mother
  Must I hide her name down in my heart?
But ah! even there you will see it—
  With Thy Mother's name how can I part?

On thy Name all divine have I rested
  In the days when my heart-trials came—
Sweet Christ, like to Thee I am human,
  And I need Mary's pure human name.

Did I hear a voice? or was I dreaming?
  I heard—or I sure seemed to hear—
"Who blames you for loving my Mother
  Is wronging my heart—do not fear.

"I am human e'en here in my heavens,
    What I was I am still all the same,
And I still love my beautiful Mother,—
    And thou, Priest of mine do the same.'

I was happy—because I am human—
    And Christ in the silences heard
"Our Father," "Hail Mary," "Our Father"
    Murmured faithfully word after word.

*   *   *   *   *   *   *   *

Swept the beautiful "O Salutaris"
    Down the aisles—did the starred statue stir?
Or was my heart only a-dreaming
    When it turned from her statue and her?

The door of a white tabernacle
    Felt the touch of the hand of the Priest;
Did he waken the Host from its slumbers
    To come forth and crown the high Feast?

To come forth so strangely and silent,
    And just for a sweet little while,
And then to go back to its prison.
    Thro' the stars did the sweet statue smile?

I knew not, but Mary, the Mother,
    I think almost envied the Priest,
He was taking her place at the altar,—
    Did she dream of the days in the East?

When her hands, and her's only, held Him
    Her Child, in His waking and rest,
Who had strayed in a love that seemed wayward
    This eve to this shrine in the West.

THE IMMACULATE CONCEPTION. xxiii

Did she dream of the straw of the manger
    When she gazed on the altar's pure white?
Did she fear for her Son any danger
    In the little Host, helpless that night?

No, no! she is trustful as He is;
    What a terrible trust in our race!
The Divine has still faith in the Human—
    What a story of infinite grace!

"Tantum Ergo," high hymn of the altar,
    That came from the heart of a saint,
Swept triumph-toned all through the temple,
    Did my ears hear the sound of a plaint?

'Neath the glorious roll of the singing
    To the temple had sorrow crept in?
Or was it the moan of a sinner?
    Oh! Beautiful Host, wilt thou win

In thy little half-hour's Benediction
    The heart of a sinner again?
And, merciful Christ, Thou wilt comfort
    The sorrow that brings Thee its pain.

Came a hush, and the Host was uplifted,
    And It made just the sign of the Cross
O'er the low bended brows of the people.
    Oh, Host of the Holy, thy loss

To the altar and temple and people
    Would make this world darkest of night;
And our hearts would grope blindly on through it,
    For our love would have lost all its light.

"Laudate," what thrilling of triumph!
    Our souls soared to God on each tone,
And the Host went again to its prison,
    For our Christ fears to leave us alone.

THE IMMACULATE CONCEPTION.

Blessed Priest! strange thou art His jailor,
    Thy hand holds the beautiful key
That locks in His prison love's Captive,
    And keeps Him in fetters for me.

*   *   *   *   *   *   *   *

'Twas over—I gazed on the statue,
    "Our Father," "Hail Mary," still came,
And to-night Faith and Love cannot help it,
    I must still pray the same, still the same.

—*Written at Loyola College on the night of Dec. 8, 1880.*

FIRST DAY.

The Flower of Mary's Predestination.

FIRST PART.

"The Lord possessed me in the beginning of His ways, before He made anything, from the beginning. I was set up from eternity, and of old, before the earth was made."—*Prov.*, viii.

HOLY MARY'S month, everywhere with graces blessed, and in our sunny land bright with bloom of countless flowers begins to-day. Let us leave the day of earth whose light is shining like a halo of heaven on her altar, just a little while, to pass across all the days of the Mays of the past, and go back to the unbeginning. Not by reason's light, for, indeed, it is too dim and uncertain, and it is too faint to guide us, for it flickers. Not with the feet of reason, for they too often go astray, nor are they strong enough to climb the slopes that rise to the inaccessible heights where dwelleth in glory the infinite God.

We of the Holy Church, by God's sweet grace in sacraments received and from grand doctrines reflected, have another light, better by far—clear, steady, certain, unfailing—divine Faith.

This light, which "enlightens every man who cometh into this world" (though many there are who will not see its shining), cometh down to us from the bosom of God, and knoweth the way back to its home in the heavens. Let it lead us there to-day. And Faith hath wings to soar to the highest, while reason, left to itself, hath only feet to walk the ways of this valley of shadows and tears; and so on the wings of Faith, and by Faith's pure light guided, we will ascend to the eternities and enter, with worship in our hearts, the very Holy of Holies of God's divine Will, where hidden, until revealed in God's determined days, all the great decrees, vocations and predestinations are shrined waiting for their accomplishment in time.

There, in the very temple of the Trinity, we will find to-day the first flower for the Crown of our Queen —Mary's eternal predestination. And just as by the rays which the sun sends down to earth we lift our eyes aloft to seek the central source of light, but in looking we are dazzled, and but dimly see its splendors; so by the light of Faith which comes to us from heaven, we look up to its divine brightness, and we see surely, but only dimly the mysteries shining in and from it. We see in part but not in whole, with imperfect sight, but if the little that we do see be so wondrous, what must be the wonder of it all when seen by perfect sight?

Here below we apprehend by Faith what reason cannot comprehend. Human philosophy cannot comprehend the mysteries of man, nor can science comprehend the mysteries of this earth, and yet they accept them as facts of knowledge; and that same philosophy mocks the mind which, without comprehending, believes in the mysteries of God, and accepts them as truths of faith. Their motto is "Knowledge"—and that knowledge is but little better than a guess. Our motto is "Faith"—and our faith is a certainty.

Only in the Holy Catholic Church, where Faith is pure and truth is whole and guidance sure, can we rise to the contemplation of the eternal truths and approach, with reverence and understanding, finite yet certain, the mysteries of God and man in heaven and on earth, as we do now.

Whatever was, is, or ever shall be, existed in a true sense in the mind of God from all eternity. Angels and men, heaven and earth, all creations were always in his thoughts. From the unbeginning, God, by voluntary decree, determined to create. Why? "Who hath been his counsellor?" Himself.

Deepest in the infinite life of God lives the principle of love. "God is love," wrote the evangelist of love, to whose care the dying Christ left his sorrowful mother. Did she tell him, I wonder, how to phrase his inspired thought? The law of love is to give. It governs God's images on earth, and it governs Him (we speak humanly) in His heavens.

The law of the highest love is to give the greatest gifts. The greatest gift is life—and greater still, life with intelligence and immortality. In God's mind all creations existed—not one, but many. Who in His mind is the first born of all creation? Who the first fruits of all creation? Jesus Christ. All creations were to revolve for grace and light around the future Christ, like stars around the sun. There came a day in heaven's history when God's will, moved by the power of infinite love, pronounced the first FIAT; and lo! the great throne was surrounded by spirits innumerable, into nine choirs divided, bright, beautiful and glorious, and God was glad. He crowned them all with the gift of free will, for He would not create slaves, who, by coercion, would be obliged to serve Him. He made them the Princes of His Court. and they were happy.

But their free will must be tested—and their fidelity. The test was given. What was it? Who knows? How long did it last? Who can tell?

Many, if not most of the writers on the "Angelic Fall," teach that God revealed to the angel world the creation of this world and our race, and manifested to them the future Christ—God and man, and commanded them to adore Him. There came an hour when a dark storm of pride swept by the throne of God. The mystery of the God-man, eternally hidden in divine decree, flashed on their vision from the far off future (for God strengthened and intensified their spiritual sight to behold the truth of the Incarnation), and they were bidden to believe and to worship in the heavens the future Christ of our earth, the Christ-God in a human form, born as man, in a nature lower than theirs, of a human mother. Right on their vision, and with a suddenness that startled their high intelligences, shone the central mystery of all creation, like a sun rising out of clouds, and gilding the very clouds around it and beneath it with the golden glory of the purest light of heaven. It was the miracle of God in eclipse. The light and the shadows fell on and moved over the angel-world. The clouds that hung round and seemed to dim the brightness of the great mystery, were to test the trust of those spiritual intelligences in the wisdom and the works of their Creator.

Lucifer and his followers would not believe—or believing, would not adore the Man-Christ, their future king, nor honor His mother, their predestined queen. They rejected the brightness of the sun of justice and mercy, because of the clouds around its light. They arose in pride. God in the eclipse of humility they would not have. He was beneath them, and they would not worship. On them fell the awful eclipse of an eternal exile from the light of joy and the joy of light. Thus sin came, the first sin. It rose right beside the Most High. It began—strange mystery—in the spirit of the first and highest of the angels in the aristocracy of creation, who stood nearest to the throne. It was a horror in the heavens only an instant, and the darkness, without a moment's mercy, was swept away out of the sight of God into everlasting darkness. They who stood the trial of their free will and remained faithful were elevated into higher places and confirmed in everlasting grace. Heaven lost not a gleam of its glory. God lost not a joy of His infinite happiness, but the fallen lost all in losing Him.

Will God create again? His first and brightest creatures, the princes of His court, have fallen. Yes, he will. But will he trust the power of free will to the next creation? God will never make creations who would be slaves or machines, and they would be one or the other if bereft of free will.

From the unbeginning he had resolved to create the human race. He would unite together matter immortal and immortal intelligence crowned with the gift of free will. His son was to belong to that race and find a mother in it. It was to be created not only to His image, but to His likeness as well. Adam and Eve were to found the race. He foresaw the race would fall as the angels fell, and yet, notwithstanding this knowledge, he resolved to create the human race. Which resolve, to those who deeply think, instead of being an argument against His goodness, is a wondrous proof in its favor.

Adam was to be made to the image and likeness of the future Christ. Eve, the mother of the race, was to be formed to the image and likeness of Mary, the mother of the Christ of this race; but Adam and Eve must wait. God, in His own appointed time, shall create their dwelling place. In the history of time and earth they will precede Christ and Mary, but in the divine decrees Christ and Mary precede them. Jesus and Mary were not afterthoughts, owing to the foreseen fall. They were God's first thoughts before and notwithstanding the fall. Their predestinations antedated, if I may use the word, all predestinations angelic, human, or the predestinations of those of any other race which God might create. Thus, as Eve was contained in the first Adam, who fell, being part of the same creation, so Mary was contained in the decree of Christ's, the second Adam's predestination, as having, of all creatures first and highest, part in the redemption.

ASPIRATION.

"THE LORD is nigh unto all them that call upon Him; to all that call upon Him in truth. He will do the will of them that fear Him, and He will hear their prayer and save them."—*Psalm* cxliv.

PRAYER.

OUR FATHER and Hail Mary.

SECOND DAY.

The Flower of Mary's Predestination

SECOND PART.

"P..ul, a servant of Jesus Christ, * * * separated unto the Gospel of God, which He had promised before by His prophets in the holy scriptures, concerning the [His] Son, who was made to Him of the seed of David, according to the flesh, who was predestinated the Son of God. * * *."—*Romans, i.*

From the unbeginning, Jesus Christ, The Man of the human race, was predestined to be the Son of God. Therefore, Mary, the woman of the human race, was predestined to be the Mother of the Son of God, by becoming the Mother of Jesus Christ. The two predestinations are inseparable. One cannot be without the other in the decrees of eternity, because one has not been manifested and realized without the other in the days of time. There is no equality between these two first predestinations, because one is the predestination of the Man-God, who is infinite, while the other is the predestination of a finite creature; but each in decree eternal, as in earthly fact, is necessary to the other. We cannot put asunder their predestinations in the will of God no more than we can separate their realizations in the worship of earth.

Jesus Christ, as man, was predestined to possess the divine substance, and to be, therefore, God perfect as well as perfect man. Mary was predestined to form, out of her flesh and blood, the human nature of the Man-Christ, to which the divine nature is to be personally united, and, therefore, by God's will she is made a necessary element in the predestination of Jesus Christ, to be in God's appointed time the Son of God.

It is impossible for God to elevate a human person higher than Mary, who was to become in time, and on earth, the Mother of Him who in the heavens and from all eternity is the Father's only Son; and, therefore, Mary stands amid all creatures solitary in her grandeur, unapproached in the order of grace, and she cannot be judged by the standards with which we judge other creatures. She must be measured by God's standards, and those standards are found in her eternal predestination to be the Mother of the God-Man, Son of the eternal Father and Saviour of the world. We must not forget that. Human personality was not glorified nor exalted, much less divinized by or in Jesus Christ, for though real man He was not a human person.

He left human personality just where and as it was before, and yet every person, in any creation, has and must have personal relations and degrees of relationship with Jesus Christ. That relationship is the test of the moral position of any and every creature. To break its bonds means sin and condemnation; to preserve them means grace and salvation. To make that relationship nearer, dearer, higher, closer, more intimate, marks the various ascending degrees of Christian sanctities. To weaken the bonds and make them less near and dear, less close and intimate, marks the descending grades of human sinfulness.

"I was God's chosen prophet," Isaias exclaims back in the shadows of the old dispensation, and the other prophets re-echo the same, for the gift of prophecy was divided among many. There was succession in their office and order.

"I was Christ's Apostle," cries out St. Peter, and the eleven and his and their successors repeat the same; for the dignity was divided among many. "I was His penitent," exclaims Mary Magdalen, and all the sin-wrecked souls in the world that ever drift on mercy's waves to His feet, the calm and beautiful shore of pardon, sigh the same; for the grace of pardon is distributed among many, and countless is the number of penitents. "I am His disciple," exclaims, in the joy of his heart, the true believer, and innumerable are the voices rising out of every age and nation proclaiming the same; for the grace of discipleship is divided, and many as the sands of the sea are the faithful followers of Christ. "I am His angel," cries out the faithful Michael, in the glory of the heavens, and ten thousand times a hundred thousand voices in the eternal courts re-echo the cry; for angelic dignity is divided, and greater in number and in splendor, brighter than all the stars that arch the aisles of space, are the hierarchies on high.

Prophet, apostle, penitent, disciple here below, angels above, how they fill the earth and the heavens with ceaseless hymns of glory to God and His Christ, the accords of which are as innumerable as the singers in creation's countless choir.

But apart and alone—and though amid—above them all, stands one with a tone in her voice none other can ever borrow; and a tone so true, so sweet, so tender, with such a mystery and meaning in its melody—a human SOLO in creation's choir—Mary of Nazareth, who, in the humility of her glory and in the glory of her humility, exclaims "I AM HIS MOTHER." It is a human voice with a finite tone.

Out of the eternal silence floats something like an echo, from a voice divine, in an infinite tone—from God Himself—"I am His Eternal Father."

"I am His Eternal Father!" "I am His Mother!" Incommunicable words, these. None other, save God and Mary, can pronounce them, for none other holds such personal and natural relationship to Jesus Christ.

He has prophets, apostles, evangelists, penitents, disciples, ministers in creation, beyond the reckoning of man—but He has only one mother, and can never have another.

Thus it is that personality belonging to our human nature, in Mary of Nazareth, has reached an elevation of glory simply, and forever inaccessible. The eternal paternity of the Infinite Father, which is not shared in by the Son or the Holy Ghost, is the first and greatest (if we may use first and greatest where there is nothing secondary or less great) mystery within the Trinity. The divine maternity of Mary of Nazareth is the first and greatest mystery outside of the Trinity. God's power could go no farther. Personality, angelic or human, could rise no higher. Within the Trinity, even to the Eternal Word and the Eternal Spirit, paternity is incommunicable, it belongs to the Father alone. Outside the Trinity, Mary's divine maternity is incommunicable to any finite creature; and, therefore, the predestination of Mary to be the mother of Jesus Christ was, and is, next to the decree of the Incarnation, and by her consent made inseparable from it, the grandest act of infinite wisdom, power, mercy and love conceived in eternity and consummated in time. Such another act will never again be made, for such another act can never again be called for; because, though Mary was a finite, and chosen though still free agent in it, the act itself was infinite, and as such, covers every fact of good or evil in all creation—of good, to better, bless, crown and glorify it; of evil, to remedy, pardon, punish or eternally doom it.

"I am God's Mother" is a declaration beyond and above which there can be but one higher announcement to men, Christ's: "I am your God!" Christ's announcement to angels and men, to all creatures of all creations. "I am your God," and Mary's declaration, "I am His mother," define forever their incommunicable relations to one another and to all creation, while, at the same time, they at once, and forever, fully determine the only true, correct, certain and perfect inner acceptance, and the only correct, certain, true and perfect outward profession of faith in the presence of two truths which are inseparably bound together, and meet, without either greatening or lessening the other, or either absorbing the other, in the one great mystery of the redemption.

There is another being that is not a person, a moral yet visible being that alone can and does present to the eyes of faith these two truths, separate, yet united, with all their evidences, meanings and consequences. That moral being is mystically a virgin and a mother, bringing forth Jesus Christ in the minds and hearts and lives of men, and in the full sight of the world. She is the bride of the Lamb, who, as Mary of Nazareth, alone could say "I am the mother of Jesus," has alone the sacred and exclusive right to say "I am Christ's Church." That Church, by the grace of God to each of us given, is our own Holy Roman Catholic Church.

She, alone, not only realizes, but through all the days of time, livingly perpetuates the Incarnation; and she only by faith can apprehend, and by divinely commissioned infallible authority does and must proclaim, as part of the Incarnation, the mystery of Mary's eternal predestination, with all its everlasting meanings and consequences.

Ah! how the Trinity must have loved her in the act of her predestination. She became daughter of God the Father, mother of God the Son, and spouse of God the Holy Ghost; and through her Son, she, the finite creature, enters into real kinship with each of the divine persons of the Trinity. For Jesus Christ has two origins—one in heaven, as God in the bosom of the Eternal Father, having infinite relations with Father and Holy Ghost—the other on earth, as man in the bosom of His Virgin Mother, who, therefore, becomes lovingly related to the three persons of the Holy Trinity. Take away in fact, or deny in thought, either of these two origins, and Jesus Christ cannot be what he was predestined to be, the Son of God. Mary is to give Him the humanity by which He will become the Saviour of the world, whilst the eternal Father, from all eternity, generates His divinity, which, when united to the humanity received from His mother, will make the world's salvation infinite. Without Mary He would not be man, and could not live, teach, suffer and die for us. Without His eternal Father He would have no divinity, and could He have lived, taught, suffered and died for us, our redemption would be vain.

Jesus Christ is the "first fruit of all creation," as the Scripture says, and He is the sole cause of all predestination and salvation. But Christ is the fruit of the womb of Mary, and she, by the operations of the Holy Ghost, is the cause of Christ's human existence. And as in the decrees of eternity, so in all the glorious work of Christ in time, she stands not by favor but by holiest right with Him and beside Him. He, as man, is her fruit. All the fruit which ever will be produced by Him, belong primarily to Him, but must secondarily belong to her. By the work of the Holy Ghost she gave to the Son of God a new existence, in which existence Jesus Christ, her son, gave to the Father what else the Father never could have received, infinite worship. She made Him man. The Father generated Him God. The Holy Ghost, who terminates the Trinity and within the Trinity is barren (we speak it in reverence), producing no person, becomes infinitely fruitful, outside of the Trinity, in the womb of Mary, when He does produce Jesus Christ, Man and God.

In every work of grace that ever was, or ever will be, Father, Son and Holy Ghost have part. But all grace is from and through Jesus Christ, and Jesus Christ is by Mary; therefore, in every work of grace the mother of the Father's Son Incarnate has also her part; and remember that all these beauties, glories, truths, are contained in the two eternal predestinations of Jesus Christ as the Son of God and of Mary of Nazareth as His mother. All salvation and predestinations come from theirs—and if theirs be inseparable, as inseparable they are, Mary, the mother of Jesus Christ, is an ever-living, everlasting element in all predestinations.

Now did we not do well to leave the earth a little while in order to ascend to the eternities, where we have gathered the fairest flower, on Mary's first day, for the crown of our Queen? Let us come back to her altar again, and first think and then pray.

The greatest writers, men who have sounded the depths of truths, teach that true devotion to the Virgin Mother is a certain sign of predestination. Have we that true devotion? Do we make our lips wings to waft Hail Mary's to heaven? Ah! the Hail Mary came from heaven, but it wants to go back home again. It wants to fly from the sinful world to the sinless heaven, and to bring in its sweet, simple words, our petitions to our King through our Queen. Happy the lips that breathe the Queen's prayer. Blessed the hearts that shrine worship for the Son, love for the mother and homage for the Queen!

Aspiration.

O THE depth of the riches of the wisdom and of the knowledge of God! How incomprehensible are His judgments and how unsearchable His ways! For of Him and by Him and in Him are all things. To Him be glory forever.—*Romans*, xi.

Prayer.

I BELIEVE in God, the Father Almighty, Creator of heaven and earth; and in Jesus Christ, His only Son, our Lord; who was conceived by the Holy Ghost, born of the Virgin Mary; suffered under Pontius Pilate; was crucified, dead and buried; He descended into hell; the third day He arose again from the dead; He ascended into heaven, and sitteth at the right hand of God, the Father Almighty; from thence He shall come to judge the living and the dead. I believe in the Holy Ghost; the Holy Catholic Church; the communion of saints; the forgiveness of sins; the resurrection of the body, and life everlasting. Amen.

THIRD DAY.

The Flower of the Promise.

FIRST PART.

And the Lord God said to the serpent: "I will put enmities between thee and the woman, and thy seed and her seed."—*Gen.*, iii.

WHITHER shall we go to-day to gather another flower for the crown of our Blessed Queen? Yesterday we gathered, in Eternity, the Flower of Mary's Predestination. To-day let us enter the Garden of Eden and find the Flower of the Promise.

Does God ever rest? Never. His Power and Love have ceaseless activities. He is always in action; but His action costs Him no effort.

Does God ever rest? Always. With Him work is rest, and rest is work. He is always creating, and forever resting in His manifold creations. This very hour He is creating souls for this earth; and who knows? mayhap new worlds and other races in the immensity of His Heavens.

Ah, me! men's minds sometimes seem as narrow as their own little horizons. They fain would confine God within the limited circle of their own knowledge. They know the history of the angelic world, dimly and only in part; and they read the story of this world, but only in fragments; and they fain would believe that beyond this and the angel-world God has done nothing. Not a half of what God has done and is doing and will do has been revealed. Reason is always at fault in measuring the immeasurable. Revelation tells us only a tithe of the doings of God. What is sufficient for our soul's salvation Revelation teaches. It seldom goes beyond this; but it sometimes does, and when it does it opens to the wondering eyes of Faith vast, luminous horizons, bright with infinite suggestions of God's power and glory.

How long after the creation and fall of the angels did God wait before He created this our world, and the human race? No one knows. And between these two creations, were there other creations of worlds and beings unknown to us? Who can tell? Beyond our horizons extends the Illimitable. Think you that it is a barren and lifeless waste, without creatures to worship, or voices to praise, or intelligences to glorify the beautiful God?

No, no. God is Power, and the passion of power is to act, and God is Love infinite and the law, and the love of Love is to give life and happiness. Examine a drop of water with the microscope. What do you see? A little world teeming with life. Thousands of living creatures are born, grow, live and die in the little world of a drop of water. Does this not show how God loves to give life?

And even matter that is lifeless—does it not manifest something strangely like unto life in the cohesion of its atoms?

Now lift your eyes aloft at night and gaze on the beautiful stars, and remember that beyond your vision's farthest reach there are bright worlds innumerable. Are they all tenantless? Are any of them, or some of them, or many of them inhabited? We know not—but why may it not be? It may be—why should it not be?

that there are in the heavens stars and planets, other
than ours, peopled by intelligent beings, different from
us in the composition of their natures, and yet like our
race, made to know, love, serve and possess God, with
us, in eternity. It may be that we belong to the lowest
order of intelligent beings, that we are the poor plebians
of the universe. And it may be that this is the reason
why the Son of God, by whom all worlds were made,
wishing to humble Himself to the lowest, descended into
this lowest part of all creation, and became one of our
race by assuming our nature. If it be so, the blood of
the Cross sh d on earth's Calvary benefits whatever is
above us. Does not the Apostle of the Gentiles coming
back to earth from the third heaven, seem to be in
accord with our thought in the first chapter of his
epistle to the Ephesians? Be this as it may, this is the
world in which we are concerned.

"In the beginning God created the heavens and the
earth." Thus begins the story of our world. It is God-
made. Let science, without faith, quibble, quarrel,
theorize, doubt, deny. Let philosophers attribute the
world's creation to chance, to the fortuitous coming
together of atoms, or to any other absurd cause. It is
a way they have. But the moment they deny its divine
creation they fall into puerile absurdities. They destroy
the dignity of the material world. For it has a dignity
of its own. The mark of the hand of its God is bright
and clear and holy on it all. The words of Genesis,
written on the gates of this earth's creation, shine with
a light that never fades; and the same words are written in the traditions of all nations and peoples. Who
made this world? Ask the race that inhabits it. The
human race answers God. That is sufficient. If there

be a few insensate minds, which, discordant among themselves, give other and different answers, why let them rave over their theories. They stand against the race, and the race stands for God as the maker of its dwelling place; and the race is right. Let beliefless science adequately account for the history of a single grain of sand, It cannot, try it never so hard. It is baffled. Science stands on the outside of matter. It never yet has entered into the hidden sanctuary of substance, and it never can. Like the veil which hid the Holy of Holies from the gaze of the people, so around the mysteries of matter hangs a veil which the hand of science can never lift. And yet science would fain have us accept as truths beyond question the mysteries of its philosophies, while it laughs us to scorn for accepting, and with highest reasons, the divine mysteries of the supernatural order. The horizon of knowledge is narrow and bounded by earth. The horizons of faith are as illimitable as the heavens.

"God created the earth:" that makes the mystery of earth's existence beautiful and sublime, and solves the mystery by naming its creator. Slowly, day by day, moved the great Creator in His work. He was building a habitation for the race to which, in the far future, His only begotten Son was to belong. Came the sixth day, and a voice spoke: "Let us make man to our own image and likeness."

Think you that only on the sixth day the voice thus spoke? God had determined the words by voluntary decree of love from all eternity. And the sixth day was Friday. On a future Friday the fallen creation will be redeemed.

"And the Lord God formed man of the dust of the

earth, and He breathed into him the breath of life, and man became a living soul," and He planted a garden in Eden and there placed man, the visible image of the invisible God; and not out of the dust of earth, but out of Adam's side He made the woman for his companion, and He walked with them in the evenings in the garden. He created them immortal and crowned them with supernatural justice. Ah! Eden was then a home of holiest joy and purest happiness. As He had tried the free will and fidelity of the angels, so He gave a test of obedience to our first parents. God tests all His creatures. The angels fell through pride which uprose in disobedience. Man fell through disobedience caused by pride. "You shall be like Gods," said the tempter. In both falls there was high treason against the majesty of God. Of every tree in the garden they might freely eat, except of the tree of the knowledge of good and evil; in eating of it lay the penalty of death. How long did the trial last? It is not known.

And God was wont to walk with them at evening time in the garden of their innocence; and in Adam God beheld the image of the future Christ; and in Eve the image of the mother of His Son, and He was glad. Did God walk with them, in Eden, in holy converse in order to lighten the trial of their obedience and to make them strong to meet the tempter who was to come?

He came at last, and he approached the weaker. Eve was alone. He tempted her insidiously. She hesitated. But when the tempter said "if you eat of the tree you shall be as Gods," she yielded and did eat of the fruit, and gave it also to her husband, and he did eat. Thus, as the angels had fallen, they fell. Ah! the great darkness that swept across their fallen souls! Ah! the wild rush of passions into their hearts! Ah! the awful horror of their guilt! Ah! the unutterable fear to meet the beautiful God! And they hid themselves.

As if, in sooth, to hide would be their crime's concealment! Why the whole universe felt at once the shock of earth's first sin and the crash of the fall. Down crumbled the lofty pillars of the temple of human nature, the glorious pillar of supernatural grace of the soul and the beautiful column of immortality of the body. The temple was in ruins. Adam and Eve were uncrowned and dethroned. The royal, grace-woven, mantle of original justice, the sign of their sovereignty, fell from their souls and bodies; and no wonder, as Scripture says, that they felt themselves naked. Rising, as they did, in rebellion against God's command, material nature threw off its subjection to their sovereignty. Woman, man's equal, was placed under his power, and man became a victim to the strong forces of nature which, by his sin, escaped from his control and scorned his power. Such was the fall of Adam and Eve, and with them, and in them, fell from its high estate the entire human race. So sin entered, and with sin, death. It might have been otherwise. An instant's disobedience darkens forever the history of the race. What will the creator do? Not a moment of mercy nor a sign of hope gave He the angels in their fall. No promise of restoration afar off was theirs. Not a word of love. The high treason was too near the throne; but on them sudden fell a dark, swift, hopeless, everlasting malediction. 'Twas an act of infinite justice. Ah! will mercy come with God when He enters the garden to meet the criminals? Ah, yes! already they are repenting. The first tears have fallen. They are hiding themselves away from the face of God, and by their very hiding they are acknowledging their guilt and its shame.

ASPIRATION.

"O HOW great is the multitude of Thy sweetness, O Lord, which Thou hast hidden for them that fear Thee; which Thou hath wrought for them that hope in Thee, in the sight of the sons of men!"—*Psalm*, xxxi.

PRAYER.

RAISE up, we beseech Thee, O Lord, Thy power, and come, that by Thy protection we may deserve to be rescued from the threatening dangers of our sins and to be saved by Thy deliverance. Amen.

FOURTH DAY.

The Flower of the Promise.

SECOND PART.

"Behold a virgin shall conceive and bear a son, and his name shall be called Emmanuel."—*Isaias*, vii.

INTO the garden which sin had entered came God, at eventide, seeking the sinners. What will He do? When the angels, the princes of creation and of His court fell, there was no mercy. Right beside the throne they had fallen, and swift and sudden on them fell the everlasting malediction. Not the faintest whisper of a far off hope for them was heard in the dark and terrible sentence. The sinners hiding in the garden, conscious of their own guilt, were unconscious of the fact of the other, and first sin, in the higher places, and of the fearful act of justice which had punished it forever.

God called Adam, but, ah! how earth's first sin had changed the very tone of the Creator's voice! It had lost its tenderness. And God called Eve. He questioned both, and each confessed their guilt. Did they then fall down at His feet and weep? Did they plead with piteous prayers for mercy? Who knows? And then God called the serpent to pass his sentence. "I will put enmities between thee and the woman, and between thy seed and her seed. She shall crush thy head and thou shalt lay in wait for her heel." Then to the woman: "I will multiply thy sorrow and conception. In sorrow thou shalt bring forth thy children." Then to the head of our race He spoke: "Cursed is the earth for thy sake. In sorrow shalt thou eat of it all the days of thy life. In the sweat of thy brow shalt thou eat thy bread until thou returnest unto earth; for dust thou art, and unto dust shalt thou return."

Oh, wondrous mercy! God cursed the serpent and He cursed the earth, but He did not curse our first parents, nor did He utter a curse against our race. Why? Because His only Son was to be born in our race.

He looked away from the garden of guilt down the future years. Afar off He saw the "express image" of Himself in the human face of Christ, the second Adam, and in Mary He beheld the second Eve; and with a love surpassing highest thought, because it was infinite, with the very malediction which He pronounced against Satan He mingled mercy's promise.

"I will put enmities between thee and the woman, between thy seed and her seed, and she shall crush thy head." Great is the mystery! the woman was conquered by the tempter, and the tempter will be crushed by the woman. Through the woman came sin to the man, and by the woman will come the Man who is to conquer sin, and the children of the race, though fallen, will become like unto God, "made conformable by grace to the image of the Son of God." Thus the flower of the promise of the woman who was to crush the serpent's head bloomed fair and sweet in the very shadows that fell around the garden of the first sin. The woman is promised first, because the woman first fell, and the flower of promise is twined around the prophecy of her seed—the Messiah.

The history of our race from its fall, begins with the mighty words, "I will put enmities between thee and the woman, and between thy seed and her seed." What woman? One who will be a mother. Whose mother? The mother of Jesus Christ, who will be her seed, and for all who receive Him the seed of eternal life. And her name? Ask all the generations, they call it blessed, they know, honor and love it—Mary.

Ah! name more beautiful than all names save His, at the sound of which "every knee must bend in heaven and on earth," thou wert a hidden glory in eternity, and thou didst shine like a star in the darkness of the fall of our race, and thy rays, pure and bright, gleamed a halo of mercy and hope on the sorrowful souls of our guilty first parents when they passed out of the gate of Eden by the flaming sword of the cherubim guarded, leaving all their happiness there when all their innocence had been lost.

Oh woman, "blessed among women!" the fallen world lifts up its eyes to thee, and in its weeping hails thee as the harbinger of its redemption!

Oh Mother of the Saviour Christ! make haste and meet those who walk "moaning and weeping in this valley of tears." Tarry not long, for the weary world leans towards the future, and is listening for the sweet sound of thy footsteps; for thou wilt bring to its darkness, Christ, the everlasting light, and to its sorrows, Christ, the everlasting joy, and to its places of death, Christ, the everlasting life, and to its sinfulness, Christ, the infinite salvation.

Oh, Mary of the Promise! Heaven does not need thee, for all is joy and blessedness there! Poor earth sighs for thee! Oh, dove of the new covenant, come soon, through the gates of the morning, bearing the olive branch of the peace of God to the world.

But she will tarry long before the earth shall see her face. Here below, the Eden of innocence and happiness was closed forever, and no one yet has passed the cherubim who guards its gates, and no one ever shall. There is a brighter Eden above, whose gates are also closed until He comes who holds, by right, the keys. But His mother must come first.

On went the years into the past, on moved the human race, looking towards the future; wickedness grew apace; corruption defiled the whole world, and God was angry. What will He do? He has called on men to repent and to return to Him in the repentance of their hearts. The patriarch Noah is His preacher. The world will not hear. Then came a day, not two thousand years away from man's last day in Eden, when the fountains of the great deep were broken up and the cataracts of heaven rushed down and whelmed the world in universal deluge. All flesh was destroyed from the face of the earth save Noah and his family, and God made a covenant with him. They carried in the ark with them the memories that came down from the gates of Eden, and when they were dispersed all over the world, wherever they went, they bore with them the tradition of hope. They looked towards the future, and the cry of the world's faith was: "We believe that He will come—the Messiah."

But the woman of Genesis, promised in the garden, must come first. Every cry for Him was a sigh for her. David, the royal poet of the old covenant, sang in loftiest strains inspired, of the glories of the Messiah's reign and the mercies of His redemption. Every song for Christ was a song for Mary, for His mother must come first.

Great prophets arose. They knew the histories of the yesterdays, and with cloudless vision they saw the mysteries of the to-morrows. Isaiah, Ezekiel, Jeremiah and Daniel, the four prophet evangelists of the covenant of figures, cried with a strong voice aloud to the people and the world: "He will come—the Messiah. His day is growing nearer," and the people waited in hope and worshipped Him afar off. But His mother must come first.

The last of the prophets, Malachias, gave the "burden of the word of the Lord to Israel." He predicted, in words that sound impassioned, the glorious, universal and everlasting sacrifice of the coming covenant. But the victim must come first, and before the victim, the victim's mother.

Then there fell a strange hush on Israel. The last of the prophets had spoken and prophecy ceased. Why? The Prophet of Prophets was near at hand. Near at hand? Some hundred years will pass before the Messiah shall appear. Some hundred years seem far enough away from a common event, but hundreds of years are near indeed to the greatest event of earth and the grandest day of time—the coming of the expectation of the nations, Jesus Christ. But Mary must come first.

On went the years. The tread of Roman soldiers had been heard in Judea and Jerusalem. The sceptre of Israel had passed into the hands of strangers, and the banners of Rome had flung their shadows against the holy temple. The east looked towards the west, the west looked towards the east in mysterious expectation. The Messiah is coming. But His mother must come first. The flower of promise that bloomed out of God's words, far back in Eden, will soon blossom in Judea.

Oh, Flower of Promise! thou hast brightened nearly forty centuries. Thou hast filled with thy sweet fragrance the faith and hope of the world. What hand will dare to disentwine thee from the prophecies? Who will dare tear thee away from the history of the Messiah in His coming, or cast thee out of the garden of the Scriptures as if thou wert a worthless weed? And if, Oh, Blessed Queen! I wreathe the flower of promise with the flower of predestination in thy beautiful May-crown, thou knowest that I have done well; while I, O Virgin Queen! do but only, and in humbleness, know that there are ten thousand hands than mine more worthy far to give thy crown a beauty which, alas, mine cannot give.

How blind to the understanding of the supernatural economy of God's grace in this fallen world, are they who do not see the Christ and His Mother walking side by side, step to step together, down the ways of prophecy, their faces towards Bethlehem and Calvary! Is it in some a judicial blindness? Will you fling the flower of the promise of the woman away? Then reject the Messiah and be consistent. The Messiah takes His mother along with Him wheresoever He goeth, wheresoever He manifests Himself. She must be with Him to give him His human meaning. She must be with Him to prove that He is the man with flesh and blood like ours, which flesh shall be bruised and which blood, derived from her, will be shed for this world's redemption. She must be with Him, mysteriously, back of all the figures of the old covenant. She must stand with Him back of the symbols and shadows of the old law, else He is not in figure, nor will He be in reality what His Father predestined Him to be—Jesus Christ, the Son of God.

But what He was predestined to be He must and shall be. His Father's eternal honor is pledged to it by eternal decree. His Father's eternal love is pledged to it by divine decree. His own voluntary acceptance to become, through Mary, the Saviour of the world He must faithfully meet. The entire Holy Trinity, Father, Son and Holy Ghost, will be false to itself, and if so it is the very death of the Deity if the decree be not fulfilled in time, just as it was framed in the eternal counsels. God changeth never His counsels.

And the mother of the Man of Sorrows and God of glory must have her share in both. Her heart will be pierced by the sword as His side will be pierced by the soldier's lance; but her soul, also, must be clothed with the glory of her divine Son. She must drink the chalice with Him, and while He will wear the crown of the Man-God she will wear the mother's crown.

Sweet flower of promise! we have gathered thee from the garden of Eden. Fill our souls again with the fragrance of the innocence we have lost, that so the gates of the Eden of Heaven may be opened by grace unto us to enter in and reign in glory with our queen forever.

Aspiration.

"O Lord, our Lord! how wonderful is Thy name in the whole earth!"—*Psalms*, viii.

Prayer.

O God, who didst ordain Thine only begotten Son to be the Saviour of mankind, and didst command that He should be called Jesus, mercifully grant that we may enjoy in heaven the blessed vision of Him, whose holy name we worship on earth. Amen.

FIFTH DAY.

The Flower of the Immaculate Conception.

FIRST PART.

"One is my dove, my perfect one is but one, she is the only one of her mother, the chosen of her that bore her."—*Canticles*, vi.

IN the year 1849, Pius the IX was driven from Rome and went an exile to Gaeta. It seems that in our days the vicars of Christ must be victims for truth. Though he had given to the Roman people a liberal constitution, and had made many reforms in the government of the Papal States, the liberals became revolutionists and clamored for what could not in honor and principle be granted. 1848 was a year of revolutions all over Europe. The waves of the revolution at last reached Rome and swept furiously over the States of the Church; and, as in all Italian revolutions, the cruel knife of assassination found many a hand ready enough to grasp it and many a victim to fall beneath it. In disguise, the Pope fled secretly from Rome and found refuge in the kingdom of Naples. Then forgetting his own wrongs and sufferings, and thinking only of the glory of God and the good of the Church, he addressed an Encyclical to each of the high prelates of the Church, in regard to the definition of the Immaculate Conception of the blessed Virgin Mary. Questions were proposed to them for answer, as to their own belief and the faith of their flocks, and the traditions of their churches in regard to the conception of Mary. Meanwhile, the revolution raged and ruined. The world needed some gentle, peaceful truth to calm its agitations. What truth more serene than the sinless conception of the holy Virgin?

On the 12th of April, 1850, Pius the IX returned to Rome. Meanwhile his Encyclical had been read by the Bishops all over the earth, and with a wonderful unanimity they desired the definition of the dogma; but the Church, in the world of dogmas, moves slowly, like unto God in the works of creation. Congregations of theologians, of unquestioned piety and of learning unsurpassed, were appointed to study the subject from every point of view, to examine authorities, to search the Scriptures, to inquire into ancient traditions, and to exhaust every source where reason could find reasons of the truth of the immaculateness of Mary's conception; for in building up the grand temple of Catholic dogmas, only the stones hewn by the hand of God from all eternity, and found where He has placed them in time, can be chosen, stones consecrated with the chrism of His love and power and will; for only such stones have the right to be built up into the temple of faith resting on Jesus Christ, the corner stone; and it is not authority alone, nor is it reason alone, that builds the temple by formulating truths into dogmas; but it is authority infallible, united to highest reason, that does the sacred work. Meantime, while the minds of the learned men were studying, examining and discussing the subject, the hearts of the faithful were praying for the object of their desires.

In our Holy Church, as in each of its members, mind and heart together, not either of them separately, form the principle of every spiritual and catholic act, just as the Father and the Son, are the one principle, whence proceeds the Holy Spirit. Years passed on. The Church did not speak. As at the Council of Ephesus, the faithful were filled with a holy impatience, and all over the world they prayed for the day of the definition of the truth. It came at last. On the eighth of December, in the temple of St. Peter's of the Vatican, the mount which is the Thabor of truth and the Calvary of sorrow, was filled with an immense concourse of the faithful and strangers from many lands. Two hundred Bishops from many nations were there, and priests in thousands. The Holy Sacrifice of the Mass was offered with a grandeur of ceremonies unequalled. When the gospel had been sung in Latin and in Greek, a Cardinal, accompanied by Bishop and Archbishop, approached the throne of the Vicar of Christ and thus addressed the Sovereign Pontiff:

"Most Holy Father, the Catholic Church has ardently and long desired that your supreme and infallible judgment will pass upon the Immaculate Conception of the most Holy Virgin Mary, Mother of God, a decision which will bring her an increase of praise, of glory and of veneration. In the name of the Sacred College of Cardinals, in the name of the Bishops of the Catholic world, and in the name of all the faithful, we humbly, and with fervent instance, ask that the universal desires of the Church may be granted in this solemnity of the Conception of the Blessed Virgin. Even now, while we are offering the august Sacrifice of the Altar in this temple consecrated to the Prince of the Apostles, and in the midst of this solemn reunion of the Sacred College, of the Bishops and of the people, deign, Holy Father, to lift up your apostolic voice and proclaim the dogmatic decree of the Immaculate Conception of Mary, and there will be joy in the heavens and gladness on earth."

Such was the petition of the Cardinals, Patriarchs, Archbishops, Bishops, Priests and two hundred millions and more of the faithful. Were they blind? Who will say so? The deepest learning of the world made the petition. Were they deceived? The greatest wisdom on earth made the petition. Was it a petition of wickedness? Wickedness will surely never ask for a dogma which means sinlessness.

But before the Supreme Pontiff accedes to this universal petition he and the petitioners must pray to heaven. So the hymn of the Holy Ghost, the *Veni Creator*, rose in glorious melody from the hearts and lips of all in the temple, and tears of joy trickled down many a face there, with a soundless music of their own. While the echoes of the hymn, rising heavenward, were still faintly sounding high up in the lofty dome, Pius the IX, with great emotion in his voice, read the decree in which it is proclaimed:

"*That it is a dogma of Faith that the Blessed Virgin Mary, from and in the first instant of her Conception, by special grace and privilege from God, in virtue of the merits of Jesus Christ, the Saviour of the human race, was preserved and placed beyond the reach and stain of original sin.*"

Ages ago, in a temple at Ephesus, when Mary's relationship towards Christ had been assailed by Nestorius, the Fathers of the Council vindicated the rights of her divine maternity. On that 8th of December, in St.

Peter's, the Pontiff and Bishops defended the honor of Mary's soul and the integrity of her innocence. Faith kept a feast of joy in the hearts of the faithful. The glory of the joy of faith, like a grand *Te Deum,* swept over the world. Ten thousand temples sounded with song, and twice a hundred thousand altars, in lowly chapels and in cathedrals grand, flamed with lights and shone fair with flowers. And the unbelieving world laughed. Let it laugh. And a part of the unbelieving world sneered. Let them sneer. If the faithful were glad, surely God and His angels were filled with joy.

Think you that the Immaculate Conception of Mary was the invention of a truth that day in St. Peter's temple? Truth cannot be invented. Divine truth is even beyond the reach of mere human discovery. But divine truth is no more beyond the reach of infallible human announcement than it is beyond the reach of human certain acceptance. No one save the prophets, the Apostles and the Church of Christ has received truths of the divine order directly and immediately from God. Since the ascension of Christ, God is still. He never himself breaks His silence. The Church has "the mind of Christ," and as Christ, in the days of His life, only gradually gave forth His revelations, so the Church, which is His human organ of speech on earth, only gradually, and in God's appointed time, gives to the world His announcements of the revealed truths in her possession.

The sun holds as much light on the rim of the eastern horizon in its morning rising as when it reaches the hour of its noon, but greater and brighter grows its light as it ascends the skies. So the Church, when it rose on the horizon of Judea eighteen centuries agone, held all the light of truth in possessing Christ, the eternal light; but only gradually, like our material sun, did it shine with greater splendors as it rose over the world. Nor will its light ever decrease. It shines on the dial of the day of Christ, telling the hours of truth forever, and so shall it shine till it reaches its noonday here below, and then will come the end. The sun of truth has no west where it will go down in shadows. Its west is in the heavens, into whose everlasting light it will triumphant rise. What then is dogma? A new invention? Is it a new invention of light at nine o'clock in the morning, because there shines more light than just after morning's dawn? Is it not the same sun shining? Is it not the same light coming to the earth? Same sun? Yes. Same light? Truly so, the very same, but to our eyes growing brighter, and covering with its increasing brightness more of the heavens and more of the earth. What then are dogmas? They are the TRUTH whose bright light is shining forever in the Church, growing brighter, as the centuries pass, to the eyes of faith, in varied but not contradictory manifestations, and covering with the same increasing light more of the world of mind.

Look at the rainbow which spans the heavens and arches the earth, a sign of bright peace when the tempest has passed away, and learn a lesson. On the clouds shine rays of light. What else? From each drop of water in the cloud, out of each ray, seven different colors are reflected. The seven colors were hidden in each white ray till the rays touched the drops of water in the cloud, and then each ray reveals its hidden beauties to our eyes. So in the Church, there is but one truth, and that is all truth; but like unto the ray with its seven colors, in that one truth are hidden countless truths, until they are reflected on our souls through dogmas defined by infallible authority, and like the rainbow after the storm, they come to bless the hearts of the faithful often, and generally after the tempests of sins and heresies have swept over the fold of Christ and filled His flock with uncertainty and fear.

Music is only a sweet sound, but in that sound, like unto the ray of the sun, seven notes lie hidden until revealed to our ears. The eighth note is but a repetition of the first and the beginning of another seven. So truth has but one sound, and that is the sound of the voice of Christ, but in that sound sleep countless songs of truth unheard until the voice of authority wakes them into the sweet words of divine faith.

Study the unit. All numbers and figures are contained in it. What are tens, hundreds, thousands, millions and more rising above the unit, but it itself manifested in higher and fuller forms? And what are all the fractions lying beneath the unit, but it itself broken into fragments? When the unit affirms itself it grows, it puts on greatness and glory; but when the unit denies itself it decreases, it puts off its power and breaks itself into ignominious fragments. In the unit then are countless affirmations. So in the one truth there are hidden innumerable affirmations. And the unit has the power of denial; when it denies itself it descends beneath itself, and gives up its life as unity.

So when reason, and no matter whose, denies truth in its unity, or any of its affirmations of faith, it descends into regions of deformed fragments and of darkness, and it loses the life by losing the light of truth, and then reason ceases to reason right. Mere religious opinions are fractions of faith, and once reason begins to work at this sinful sum of fractions, there is no telling when it will stop. Dogmas are affirmations of truths, going to make up the whole sum of faith; and as truth is infinite while we are finite, not in this world shall we ever reach the fullness of the sacred sum; not till in the eternities, when we shall behold truth face to face in the vision of the Trinity.

Alas for those who are blind to the clear light of the divine dogmas which shine out of the heaven of truth, like suns for the days and stars for the nights! Alas for those whose eyes look only on the fitful light that flickers across the changeful clouds blown about by the winds of human opinions! Any church (we use the incommunicable name, which belongs to our Church alone, through mere courtesy) that cannot affirm the ancient truths has gone beyond their reach, and away from the light of Christ. Any church that has said its last word and can say no more, has exhausted its life and must die. Its very silence proves that it possesses only dead fragments. When any church ceases to affirm, it begins to deny. When once it has began to deny, by a force which it cannot resist, it will continue to deny, and will lean on denials for its very existence. When it ceases to say YES before the throne of truth, it will begin to say No behind the throne, and sometimes the first low muttered No leads to the loud, last, blasphemous, absolute No. Then dies the very light of truth and the night of darkness comes.

Oh beautiful Church! Bride of the crucified Christ, bearing the heart as well as the mind of Christ, possessing His divine person as well as His powers, thou didst come down from the upper chamber in Jerusalem, where

Mary was praying with thy Apostles, filled as were they with the Paraclete, and while thou didst preach Christ and Him crucified and risen from the grave, thou never didst forget the mother of the Christmas night, the mother of Good Friday, the mother of the Pentecost.

Oh living Church of the everlasting God! Queen of truth, bearing the sceptre of divine authority, wearing the triple crown of faith and hope and charity, with the mercy-clasped sandals of salvation on thy feet, when thou didst stand in Ephesus of old, and didst speak in honor of the name of Mary, thy voice was strong and sweet, but in the temple of St. Peter's thy voice didst rise to triumphant tones when thou didst defend against unbelievers the honor of Mary's sinless soul.

Ah! the olden words of Genesis, in God's malediction of Satan, "I will put enmities between thee and the woman, and between her seed and thy seed," never before received such triumphant confirmation, and the malediction of Satan never before put on such dark and mighty meaning. Out of her glorious Magnificat and into the glorious dogma rang, with their crowning meaning, "All generations will call me blessed." Blessed the lips that announced the great truth, and blessed, in these days, the hearts that hailed with the welcome of faith and joy the glorious dogma. Was it all or only the work of men? No, it was the act of the Son of Mary, through His chosen representatives. Listen!

Had Christ Himself stood in the midst of that assembly, which represented eighteen centuries of doctrine, and had He been asked the question, "Tell us, was the conception of your Mother immaculate?" What would have been His answer? Would He have said *No?* Would He have replied, "Pontiff and Priests, you are troubling yourselves too much about my Mother's honor?" No, no, a thousand times No. Listen. He would have said:

"Pontiff and Priests; and let the whole world hear: My mother was conceived as pure and stainless in time as she was conceived in the divine thought and decree of her and My predestination, in the bosom of the Divinity. You have to-day reached back to My mother's eternal predestination, and our divine act in eternity you have accepted by the light of faith, and by your authority, which is mine, you have affirmed our act in the days of time. You have reached back to the promise of My mother and Me in the garden of Eden, and you have given to that promise, this day, its full authentic meaning.

"Pontiff and Priests, was My mother, Mary of Nazareth, conceived in sin? Who here will dare assert it? No, no! I the Son of God, had the right, because I so willed to humble myself. Did I not do so? Did I not bear every humiliation for you and for all. But I, as the Son of God, could not degrade myself. Had My mother been conceived in sin she would have been the slave of him whose empire I came to destroy; and I, as the eternal Son of God, could not become the son of a slave of Satan. My divinity must be inviolate in My humanity, and therefore the mother who was to clothe My divinity with the clothing of humanity must be immaculate in soul and body; for out of her flesh and blood she is to weave the robes which my divinity must wear. The robes must be stainless. If she were stained by sin, could I, as the Son of God, wear robes with sin's stain on them? Pure as the heavens I came from, and purest of the pure to the touch of My divinity and humanity must she be whose Son I myself predestined myself to be. Did I not, from all eternity, choose Mary of Nazareth to become my mother? Have I not all power? Would I be true to My infinite power if I had not preserved my mother from the contamination of Satan's touch and from the ignominy of his slavery? Am I not infinite love? Have I not proven My love for the world, even unto death? If I gave you a law to love and honor your mothers, must I not myself give you the most perfect example of keeping the law? Must I not love My mother with perfect love, and honor My mother with highest honor, the perfect love and highest honor of God and man? Would I be true to the perfect and infinite love wherewith I must, as God and man, love My mother, and would I not be false to the highest honor of My mother, if, having all power to which nothing is impossible, and an infinite will which nothing can resist, and an infinite love for her, which your thoughts cannot comprehend nor your speech describe, I would permit the fallen angel to glory in My mother's fall? And when I stand before the world with My mother, and with My love for her as her own and only child, proclaim that she is mine, could I leave it in the power of Satan to cry out in defiance: 'Yes, Christ! she is your mother, but she was my slave?' In heaven, that Lucifer would fain become equal to God. Hence he was cast out. No wonder he strives, in hate, to drag My mother down into the mire of sin. No, no, it would be an infamy that would degrade My divinity—it would be an ignominy that would disgrace My humanity—and before the angels in heaven, and men on earth, and demons in hell, it would be the everlasting opprobrium of My mother. And the infinite honor of My eternal Father, whose chosen daughter My mother is, would be shamed that I, His Son, would have a sin-stained mother; and the infinite sanctity of Our own Holy Spirit, whose spouse My mother is, would suffer detriment if, for an instant, My mother's purity had been tarnished by guilt.

"Pontiff and Priests, ye have worshipped Me with highest worship to-day, My mother's feast on earth, in that you have crowned her with an honor than which none can be greater—an honor which has been her's from all eternity, and which you proclaim to earth to-day. Pontiff and priests, this day was foreseen from all eternity, and your proclamation on earth was written from the unbeginning in letters as pure as My mother in the mind of the Father and of the Son and of the Holy Ghost."

Thus would Christ give His own divine testimony to the eternal honor of His mother. Thus would the Father and the Holy Spirit testify. And thus the dogma proclaimed that blessed day, in the grandest temple of faith on earth, is based not only on Scripture's inspired words, not only on the teachings of the holy Fathers, not only on the mystical illuminations of countless saints, not only on the traditions handed down from the beginning, not only on the divine proprieties of things, not only on the clearest, unanswerable reasonings of the minds of men; but it rests on the very reason of God, and on the infinite will that decreed it from the beginning, and on the infinite power that guarded the decree, and on the glorious love, which could not be more glorious, that made the eternal decree a reality in time, in the home of Joachim and Anna.

And now listen. Do not they who deny Mary's sinless conception deny, consciously or unconsciously, her full blessedness? Do they not, knowingly or unknowingly, lift up their voices against her prophecy: "All generations shall call me blessed?" Do they not, let us hope in ignorance, stand by Satan in the garden, and when they read the curse uttered against Satan: "I will put enmities between thee and the woman, and between thy seed and her seed" (the words are absolute), do they not think in fact, if not say in words: "No, there will not be absolute and everlasting enmity. There will be an instant, or more, when the enmity will be suspended or cease. She will be conceived in sin and fall under the power of Satan?" The attribution of such power to Satan involves the withdrawal from Christ's mother of her soul's pure honor, and from God the power to prevent or the will to resist such an indignity. Take away the principle of eternal enmity between the Woman and Satan for one instant, how will the enmity be resumed? To honor the power of Satan so as to make it prevail over Mary, is it not a sort of diabolic worship? And to deny the sinlessness of the Mother of Jesus Christ, is it not a sort of diabolic blasphemy?

Oh, Mary! Virgin, Mother, Queen! we are of the generations who rejoice to call thee blessed—blessed in thy predestination, blessed in the promise, and thrice blessed in thy holy and Immaculate Conception. To-day we twine the flower of thy sinless conception in thy crown. But, ah! it is too fair a flower to lend its beauty to but only one day. To-morrow, oh Queen of spotless purity, we will look on the beauty of this spotless flower, that we may fill our hearts with its mystical fragrance. We, who have been conceived in sin and brought forth in sorrow, lift up our souls in praise to God for having by His preventing grace, preserved at least one of our race—thee, oh Mary! from stain of sin; and we magnify God, who hath done this thing for thee; and we worship God because He hath placed thee outside of the darkness of sin, and hath established thee in the full sunshine of His infinite grace.

And, oh! though sinless, thou wilt have pity on us sinners. Pray for us sinners "now and at the hour of our death," that we may in our own measure fulfill the prophecy and share thy privilege—that like unto thee, there shall be enmities between our souls and Satan forever and forever.

Aspiration.

Blessed art thou, O Virgin Mary, by the Lord, the most high God, above all women upon the earth. Thou art all fair, O Mary, and there is no stain of sin in thee.

Prayer.

Oh, God! who, by the Immaculate Conception of the Virgin, didst prepare a worthy habitation for Thy Son, we beseech Thee that as Thou didst, through the foreseen death of Thy same Son, preserve her from all stain, so Thou wilt also grant that we may reach Thee cleansed through her intercession.

SIXTH DAY.

The Flower of the Immaculate Conception.

SECOND PART.

"Come and hear, all ye that fear God, and I will tell you what great things He hath done for my soul."—*Psalm*, lxv.

To-day let us gaze again upon the spotless purity of this beautiful flower. There are three Edens—the Eden of Genesis, the Eden of grace, and the Eden of glory. The first was an Eden of perfect happiness until innocence was lost; the second is an Eden of perfect grace, in which innocence is regained; the third is an Eden of perfect glory, where innocence, restored by grace, is forever crowned. The first was a material garden, bright with the beauty of all natural beautiful things; the second is the mystical garden of the Church, full of the spiritual beauties of supernatural grace; the third is the Eden of heaven, radiant with the ineffable beauties of everlasting glory.

Before the closed gate of the earthly Eden stands the angel of God's justice, with sword of flame, guarding the gate and barring entrance through it. That first perfect happiness, with innocence lost, never has been and never shall be found again here below. Before the ever-open gate of the mystical Eden of grace, the Holy Church, stands the angel of God's mercy, bidding those who are laden with sorrow and burdened by sin to come and enter. At the narrow gate of the Eden of glory, heaven, as sentinel stands the high Archangel of

God's sanctity, guarding entrance through it against all souls defiled. In the first Eden, amid the falling ruins of perfect happiness and innocence, God promised the Redeemer and the Woman. In the second Eden of grace, the Redeemer, Jesus Christ, the Son of God, and the woman, Mary of Nazareth, His mother, appear in fulfillment of the promise; and their relations, each to the other, are as inseparable in the Eden of grace as they were in the garden of the promise. In the third Eden, heaven, Jesus Christ is sitting at the right hand of His Father, in glory, King, as man, over all creations, while with Him, Mary of Nazareth, by right of her royal, divine motherhood, reigns queen over all creatures. And why? Because her Immaculate Conception was, in the divine will, a necessary part of the predestination of Jesus Christ as Son of God, the Redeemer, and therefore King of all creations. It was by God's eternal ordaining, the first preparation for the kingdom of grace, the perfect fulfillment of the promise, the necessary prelude to the foundation of the Church, and to the wonderful history of the Sacraments; and more than that, the very beginning on earth of all man's future glories in heaven.

What then is the Immaculate Conception? It is the restoration, in Mary, of the lost perfect innocence of the earthly paradise; it is the divine dowering of Mary with all the supernatural perfections of Eve in her innocence and before her fall; and still more than that, because sinlessly conceived she is to make true, by conceiving Christ, the very words of Satan to Eve: "Ye shall be as Gods," for Christ, her Son, is our Saviour—God, and by His grace we become partakers of His divinity, and become like unto God.

Mark you, we were made to God's image; the image was not lost by sin, for the image, like the indelible character of baptism, could not be destroyed; but we were also made to His likeness. By the first sin that likeness was destroyed. In the Immaculate Conception of Mary, that lost likeness is restored perfectly to her; if we can so speak (it is against grammar, but in harmony with truth), *more perfectly* in Christ; and in Christ born of her the likeness is restored by grace, but less perfectly to us.

She is the most perfect human person ever made by God (remember her Son, Jesus Christ, is not a human but a divine person); but the perfection of her personality rests on her Immaculate Conception. In what does highest human perfection consist? In the total absence of all sinfulness, and in the presence and possession of all graces.

What said the Angel of the Annunciation to her? "Hail! full of grace!" Therefore, her soul was full of grace, and, therefore, in her soul sin never had a place; but had she been conceived in sin, sin would have had a place in her, and would have emptied her soul of the very grace which is the greatest of all—the absence of the sin original, which is the root of all sinfulness, and the cause of all sins.

These are the proprieties, the reasons and the glories of the Immaculate Conception. All of them? Not half; yet enough. But what is the meaning of the Immaculate Conception? Conception and death are the two terms of every human life. In conception, life begins. In death, life ends. In conception, the soul is united to the substance which is to form the human body, and the moment of that union is the first instant of the life of man. Before the actual union of soul and body we cannot properly say that the child has been conceived, or has begun to live, though there is a something, in mystery hidden, disposing itself little by little, and no one knows how long, for the conditions necessary to the receiving of the soul. So, after the actual separation of the soul from the body we cannot say that man lives, or that even he is man, though something of him remains—his corpse, which little by little returns, by its own corruption, unto dust, while the soul has passed into eternity. How is it possible that an infant can be a sinner in its conception, that is to say, in the instant when its soul is united to its body? The infant is incapable of sin, and yet it is infected with the contagion of the sin of our first parents. Why? Because though thousands of years afar from the hour of the first fall,—the moment it is conceived into it flows the sin-stained blood of Adam. For Adam was not only the first; but, because the first, he was the universal man. All humanity was contained in him. When he fell, all humanity fell with him, and this is why every child of his race is born fallen from grace and in sin; so that every child, his in conception, can be called an innocent criminal—innocent, because personally the child has done no wrong, but criminal, because the child is involved originally in the sin of him who, in himself, germinally contained the entire human race. Thousands of oak trees are contained in one single acorn, and if there be a flaw in the acorn, it will be reproduced in every tree that grows from it.

Whence, then, to each person of our fallen race comes the stain of sin? Does it come from the soul, or does it come from the body? Not from the soul; because the soul is created directly by God and comes pure from His hands. Not from the body; because the body is not capable before animation of having any part in sin. How then comes the stain? The soul is innocent, and the unanimated body is incapable of sin. This is how. The instant soul and body unite, their union produces a child of Adam; and to be a child of Adam is to inherit in person, with his blood, his sin, and with his sin its penalties for soul and body. In Adam we all have sinned, and on account of sin we die.

If the blessed Virgin Mary sinned in Adam, she was certainly conceived in sin. Did she sin in Adam? Was she, like the rest of the race, involved in the fall from grace? There is no better place to answer the question than the very scene of the primal guilt.

Go we now there. Eve fell—Adam fell, Satan conquered. But God came into that garden. What are His words? They breathe malediction against Satan, and promise benediction to the race in some future day. "I will put enmities between thee and the woman, and between thy seed and her seed." Mark, He says "I will." That means the future. Will God ever do anything, in any future, that He has not decreed to do from all eternity? No; and why? Because if He would, it would be because He would have a new thought. God cannot have new thoughts. His thoughts are as old as Himself—eternal. Therefore, that enmity between the woman and Satan is from all eternity. It is not a new thought, it is an eternal decree. If eternal, the enmity must be always. If she were conceived in sin the enmity would not be always, it would cease awhile. Then God, if He lets the enmity cease for an instant, in time, between the woman, Mary of Nazareth, and the evil spirit, would contradict and contravene, here below, His very own eternal decree. Will He do it? No; why? Because He cannot do it. Why? Because an eternal truth would become an eternal lie. With God all things are possible save one; and that is self-contradiction.

No, no, the common laws that rule every person of Adam's race do not govern the person of Mary. All women conceive children by men. She conceives her child by the operation of the Holy Ghost. All women bring forth in sorrow. She brought forth in gladness. All die in pain. She died what could scarcely be called a death. The separation of her soul from her body was a rapture. All bodies return to dust and await the day of resurrection. Her pure body was translated to heaven. As in her conceiving Christ, so in her own conception she stands outside and above the general law, an eternal exception.

Many, in ignorance, imagine that our Holy Church, in proclaiming the truth of Mary's Immaculate Conception, teaches that Mary's body, as well as her soul, was created directly by God. Let us have pity on ignorance, when it cannot help itself. But who can respect that ignorance which, by examining, can correct itself, and will not? If God himself had created her body, as well as her soul, she would not belong to the human race at all. Then her Son, Christ, would not belong to the race. Then, in no real sense, would He be man. Nor could He call himself the Son of Man.

Now, who are they who deny the truth of Mary's Immaculate Conception? What is their character for learning and piety? They are those who imagine (mark you, *imagine*, for they have no settled beliefs; they are not nourished by the manna of faith divine, and they try to satisfy their soul's hunger—do they ever satisfy it? God help them if they can, with the husks of human opinions) that by covering the conception of Mary with the cloak of original sin, they are placing a crown of greater glory on the head of Jesus Christ. Foolish men, and blind! Christ would tear such crown in twain and trample it under His feet. His glory is her glory, and her ignominy is His ignominy.

Of all the moments of her life, its first instant was its supremest. For that first instant was to tell for her or against her forever. It was to be the criterion of the very character of her soul. If conceived in sin, she would be placed in the position and possibility of never seeing God face to face; and more, if sin touched her, and she was an instant under the power of Satan, God, by His sanctity, was obliged to look upon her with infinite hatred, and to hold her in abomination. Could such a thing be? And the Son of God, who was to be her son sixteen years afterwards, would have been obliged to regard His own future mother with detestation. No, no; a conception in sin of God's Mother would be an infinite horror. It is as abhorrent to the Divinity of the Son as it would be unworthy of the human personality of His Mother Mary. But why say more?

Our Holy Church has defined the dogma as God had decreed its truth. Mary, in her conception and birth, is a living sacrament—she being, on earth, the living outward sign of the greatest grace to creature ever given. God's power could not go farther. In her person, God made the greatest act of divine love for our race that even He could make; the greatest, save the greater one of assuming in her our human nature. And these grand acts of eternal love are inseparable from one another.

Not very far from Jerusalem lived Joachim, of the royal tribe of Juda, with Anna, his saintly spouse. They were rich in flocks. They divided their riches into three parts: the first for the temple and the ministers of the altar; the second for the poor; and the third for themselves. They were faithful to the law.

Sacred Scripture does not mention even their names; nor does Scripture say one word about the conception and birth of Mary. A veil of mysterious silence hangs around these two great mysteries. Remember that the inspired writers have not written a single word or omitted to write a single thing without the special direction of the Holy Spirit. Not a word about her conception; not a word about her birth; not a word about her childhood; not a word about her life in the temple; not a single word until in the Gospel of St. Matthew we read: "And Jacob begat Joseph, the husband of Mary, of whom was born Jesus, who is called the Christ." And then not another word until in the first chapter of the Gospel of St. Luke we read: "The angel Gabriel was sent from God unto a city of Galilee, named Nazareth, to a virgin espoused to a man whose name was Joseph, and the name of the virgin was Mary."

What is the meaning of this mysterious silence, for the silences of the Scriptures have meanings as well as its written words?

Around the Eternal Father of the Eternal Son what a silence hangs like a holy veil. He stays in the eternal silences, and in infinite silence He speaks His Eternal Word. So the Mother of that Eternal Word Incarnate wears on earth the mantle of silence until the Angel of the Annunciation comes. For Mary, as the Mother of the Son of God, is to bear a strange resemblance to His Eternal Father. Hence the silence that veils her birth and first years.

Ah! how many there are, outside our Holy Church, who read the Scriptures and make great boast of their knowledge, and yet read its words divine all in vain and miss their deepest meanings! But since the marriage day of Joachim and Anna years went by; twenty years, says St. Jerome; forty years say others; and they bore the opprobrium of barrenness. No child came to bless their union, and a childless marriage was a humiliation among their people. But they waited and they prayed, and they hoped against hope.

Never is the effect of grace more evident and powerful than when nature is powerless. Was not Isaac, the Patriarch, born of Sara, who was barren? Was not Jacob, his son, born of Rebecca, who was barren? Was not Joseph born of Rachel, who was barren? Was not Samuel, the prophet, born of Anna, who was barren? Was not Sampson, that miracle of strength, born of a barren mother? Was not John the Baptist, than whom, by the testimony of Christ, none greater was ever born of woman, born of Elizabeth when she was aged and barren? Strange mystery! but with God all things are possible, and when nature is powerless, He loves to manifest His own power; and is there not a strange resemblance between barrenness and virginity, since both are equally without fruit?

The prayers of Joachim and Anna were heard at last. St. Jerome says that the angel Gabriel announced to each of them separately that God would answer their prayers; and the glorious answer was the Immaculate

Conception of Mary in the womb of Anna. It was a natural, and not a supernatural conception. The name Joachim signifies the Preparation of the Lord, and Anna signifies grace. Was the immaculateness of Mary's conception revealed to them? Some writers think so. And now, from the sinless soul of Mary, in her mother's womb, ascended to God acts of worship greater than the angels' adorations; for, remember, her sinless soul had at once the fullness of reason and the illumination of all the graces of the Holy Spirit. All the perfections of the soul of Eve in the instant of her creation were in the soul of Mary in the first moment of her conception. The light of perfect understanding, the strength of perfect love, the perfect union of her will with the Divine Will, all these, and more, were there. In the first instant of her conception her soul was self-conscious, and while she was corporally united to Anna, her mother, her soul at once became intimately united to God, in a union that was never to be broken. The life of her soul reached an almost infinite intensity.

Never had God been praised as she was silently praising Him then. Never had God been so loved as her sinless soul was loving Him. Faith, hope and charity, in perfection, filled her soul; and every instant was a perfect act of each; and as the hours and the days and the months went by, and her mother waited for the moment of the birth of the child she bore, that child was giving more glory to God than all the angels in heaven. Only one was to give to God a greater glory; and He was to be her Son, Jesus Christ.

Did the angels in heaven know of the mystery? Did God reveal it to them in reward for their fidelity in the day of their trial? And if He did, how they must have longed for the coming of their Queen! Oh! sinless soul, next to the human soul of thy future Son, most beautiful! all pure! most glorious! perfect with all perfections! full of all graces! sweet hope of the hopes of the world! we salute thee in the mystery of thy Immaculate Conception! we bless thee for the blessings thou hast received from on high! And, oh Immaculate, we bless thee more for the blessed Christ whom thou wilt bring to us in the day when thou shalt say from the depths of thy all pure soul: "Behold the handmaiden of the Lord, be it done unto me according to His word."

Is there any need to go back to the past and ask the saints of old to give their testimony? No need indeed; but still it might edify; for the words of saints bear the seal of their sanctities. Read the ancient liturgy containing the Masses of St. James and of St. Mark, the Evangelist. In the first, Mary is saluted as "most holy, most glorious, immaculate, altogether outside the ranks of sinners." In the other, Mary is called "most holy, immaculate and blessed, ever Virgin Mother of God." Listen to St. Hyppolitus, Bishop and Martyr, nigh seventeen hundred years ago. He salutes Mary as Immaculate. And old Origen calls her "the Holy and Immaculate Mother of the Immaculate;" as if he were drawing a parallel between the purity of the Mother and the purity of the Son. Hear the words of Gregory, the wonder worker of Neo-Cæsaria: "An angel without a body was sent to a Virgin pure and Immaculate. He, who had never known sin, was sent to her who was spotless and without the corruption of sin." Let Cyprian, the great Archbishop, speak from his throne in Carthage: "Mary is like the rest of mortals in nature, but not in sin."

Fifteen hundred years ago, St. Epiphanius, Bishop, not in preaching, but in prayer, exclaims: "Thou art full of grace, Oh thrice Blessed Virgin, and, after God, thou dost excel all creatures! In entering this world thou art more beautiful than the Cherubim and Seraphim." Would she have been more beautiful than those highest of the angels, had she ever been stained with original sin? Listen to the great St. Augustine, the prince of the doctors of the Church, in his discussion with the heretic Pelagius: "When there is question of sin, on account of the honor of the Lord, the Virgin Mary is out of the question." And so, from age to age, saint passes down to saint one grand unbroken testimony to the truth of the mystery of the Immaculate Conception; and in the halls of holy councils echoed the word, Mary's word, "Immaculate." True, here and there, at times, rose a voice of hesitation, of uncertain sound, and sometimes of doubt; but not, all along the line, one single great voice of plain denial. Religious orders, confraternities, universities, cathedrals, kingdoms, all adown the centuries, placed themselves under the protection of Mary of the Immaculate Conception; and all these traditions, of the same universal belief, blended with the words of Scripture, expressed themselves on that eighth of December, eighteen years ago, in the solemn definition of the dogma.

And was it not singularly appropriate that these United States, free from all tyranny, and the home of all the natural rights born with men, should be placed under the special patronage of Mary Immaculate, who was free from all the tyranny of sin, and whose soul, by her Immaculate Conception, became the sanctuary of all the supernatural rights of grace? Oh, Mary Immaculate! guard with loving care this country dedicated to thee. Let thy purity keep it pure. Watch over its institutions. As thou art the refuge of all sinners, this country is the refuge of the exile and the oppressed; guide it ever in the ways of peace; let it never forget its high vocation to teach the nations of the world, by word and example, the principles of well regulated liberty and reverence for the rights of man! Let not its prosperity be its ruin! Many, alas! of its children, who know not what they do, are walking in uncertain paths, which are dark and lead them away from truth! Mother of all! pray for us and plead for them, that we, thy children, may love and honor thee more and more, and love and adore thy adorable Son with more fervent faith; and that they who are wandering in error's path may, through thy intercession, return to the one fold of the true Shepherd, who is thy only Son forever, and our Saviour Jesus Christ.

ASPIRATION.

"Cry with joy to God, all the earth.

"Sing ye a psalm to His name; give glory to His prais

"Say unto God: How terrible, Oh Lord! are Thy works; in the multitude of Thy strength Thy enemies shall lie to Thee!"—*Psalm*, lxv.

PRAYER.

ALMIGHTY and everlasting God, vouchsafe, we beseech Thee, that as we venerate with festal-solemnity the stainless virginity of the purest of Virgins, Mary; so thro' her intercession we may attain into purity both of mind and body.

SEVENTH DAY.

The Flower of the Birth.

"I am the mother of fair love, and of fear, and of knowledge, and of holy hope. In me is all grace of the way and of the truth; in me is all hope of life and of virtue."—*Eccl.*, xxiv.

Let us go, in the spirit of faith and love, to-day to the thrice blessed home where the Immaculate Queen of the blessed was born.

Tread softly, for we are to enter a new Eden of perfect innocence and highest grace. In reverence let us go in, as if we were passing through the gate of a sanctuary, where a sanctity incomparable is hiding in a holy tabernacle.

Eighty days have passed since the birth of Mary. For a man child, as we read in Leviticus, the law ordained forty days of purification for the mother, and twice forty days for a maid child.

Anna went to the temple and offered two doves on the altar, one a burnt offering and the other a sin offering. She is purified, according to the law; she returns home, praising the God of her fathers, and her soul is filled with the peace of a great gladness.

On the face of the aged Joachim there shines a light as if it were a gleam of joy reflected from the heavens. The old man is thinking of the past. Strangely through his memory move the words of a hundred prophecies. Dim presentiments about his child fill his soul; and somehow, if he does not know all, he seems to feel the glory of her future. The words of Isaias: "The Lord Himself shall give you a sign. Behold, a virgin shall conceive and bring forth a son, and his name shall be called Emmanuel," have set him dreaming; and, somehow, while he gazes on the face of his little Mary, he scarcely knows why, the words of Jeremias: "The Lord hath created a new thing in the earth, a woman shall compass a man," seem to put on meanings new and very near to him.

In Anna's arms the infant is nestling; and the mother looks, as only mothers can look, with her heart in her eyes, upon her offspring. She, too, was a-dreaming, as she gathered her child to her breast in the clasp of love; and, like all mother's dreams, hopes and fears, desires and doubts, met in her soul, and yet did not destroy its peace.

Ah, yes! this is a holy place. If not the Lord, the Mother of the coming Lord is here, a little infant. How frail it seems! What a far-off look in its eyes! What a fair and beauteous face! How perfect the beauty of its body. No wonder in the soul within it the beauty of perfect grace is reigning. Look how the little hands are clasped, as if in prayer! but the lips move not. Nearly three months old now, with a perfect self-conscious soul from the first instant of conception,—but the body must grow, little by little, like the rest of children. There must be nothing startling, nothing extraordinary in the child's external life. She must be just like any other child; for the secret of her coming into this world, and why she came, must not yet be revealed.

How hidden everything is about the child! In her veins, even now, is flowing the very blood which Christ will take into His humanity, and which, derived pure from her, the all-pure, and united to His divinity, will become infinite in mercy and in merits when it flows for us in the day of Calvary. God makes no sign. His future mother is a frail little infant. Ah! how the Father, Son and Holy Ghost, in infinite love, must have watched over the predestined child! How Gabriel, her guardian angel, must have hovered near her!

How all the angels of heaven (for surely now they know of the mystery of Mary of Nazareth) must have glorified the Eternal in the contemplation of this, the most beautiful creature of all the Creation! And the world went on just the same as ever; the world that was losing the instincts of the supernatural, waiting, it is true, for the coming of the Messiah, but, indeed, little dreaming that His Mother had already come. It was all so still. No one saw, no one heard, no one knew of the mystery hidden in the dwelling of Joachim and Anna. It is God's way. He moves in His great designs strongly but sweetly. He made no noise when He created the heavens and earth, and He was stiller than ever at the cradle of Mary. Do not all grand and beautiful things move towards their purposes and reach their perfections in the silences?

Who hears the flowers growing, or the grasses, or the trees? Who hears the earth moving? Who hears the stars marching, like bannered hosts, through the heavens? Is not nature, when it moves in harmony, always still? Only when its elements are thrown out of order, and their forces clash, comes the din of confusion.

So in the world of supernature, the Spiritual and the Divine move on in a harmony beautiful as a hymn, heard in the heavens clearly, but too sweet to be heard by human sense; praiseful of God and peaceful for man. It is only when the weak will and strong passions of the human heart rise in rebellion against the laws of grace that the tumult comes in which God can never dwell.

But around Mary fell, from the first, the stillness and the peace of God. Why? Because her will was in perfect harmony with God's decrees and designs. Because, from the first moment of her life she was in perfect accord with the eternal will. Indeed, a mystery of silence folded all her life. What great strengths have their homes in the silences! Ask the world's thinkers, and they will tell you that their deepest thoughts, and best, came to them, like stars, in the silences of the nights. Ask the world's singers, and they will tell you that their grandest songs came sounding through their souls in the stillnesses of the dark. Enter the monasteries, back of whose closed gates live men gifted with glorious speech, and they have long hours of silences; and through those hours their feet walk faster towards God. Go into the convents of the virgins ot the Church. They, too, have their hours and days of silence, in which the whisper of a word cannot be heard, and their hearts, like the lilies of the valley, are growing and whitening in the silence. Enter a Catholic church, without a single worshipper or with thousands crowded, what a silence?

The spell of the silence of the Tabernacle falls on them all. And that Tabernacle-silence; how mysterious, and yet how mighty? In the half-hour Mass in the morning what a silence comes down upon the Altar when the priest reaches the moment of consecration, when infinite love and infinite power hide themselves in the stillness of a little white host? And the church itself, what a silence she keeps about the deposit of Christ's revelations in her possession. How the years pass—she the while listening to human discussions, with the quiet patience of Christ at Pilate's tribunal, before she rises and proclaims her dogmas.

Human churches, like the men who founded them, are noisy. In them is the everlasting chatter of discordant tongues about changeable opinions. They are always talking, and at random. The Church of Christ inherits the stillness as well as the speech of Christ, and she never says an unnecessary word.

How still are the rays of the sun that bring to us the light of heaven. In their coming they make no noise, but when they do come they clothe the world with robes of glory. So Mary was to bring to us the light of the sun of justice. Heard ye ever the snow-flakes falling? Silently they fall, and they weave a virgin-veil for earth. So the Virgin of virgins came silently, to weave out of her pure flesh the veil of Christ's humanity. How silently in the bosom of nature, where poor earth is as a virgin, is she, unknown to us, giving birth, like a fruitful mother, to emeralds, pearls, amethysts, diamonds and a hundred other beautiful children of clay?

Only those elements which are like man's variable will and restless passions make din and discord here below; the sea, with its stormy waves; the air, with its changeful winds; the rivers, with their rise and fall and noisy flow; the clouds, with their lightnings and thunders; fire, with its angry violences; and in the brute creation, those animals only which, in voice and ferocity, seem to symbolize the destructive power of sin in man.

Have we strayed away from the little Mary in the arms of Anna? Not at all. We have never left the holy chamber. Look! the infant has fallen asleep. Let us not awake her! Speak low, No! pray low. Oh! infant, in whose heart the blood of our Redeemer is even now beating, dream your dreams divine, but dream in pity, too, and in love of us poor sinners! Come now from the sleeping child to the Altar where her Christ, and ours, is sleeping in the Eucharist.

It is the eighth of September, the Feast of the Nativity. This month the sun passes, in the zodiac, out of the sign of the lion into the sign of the virgin. So into her was to pass, and over us was to shine forever, the sun of justice; and the sign of the lion, which is the sign of that evil one, "who goeth about like a roaring lion, seeking whom he may devour," would be subjected forever to the sign of the virgin in the zodiac of the heaven of grace.

According to a tradition, from the beginning, Mary was born on the eighth day of September. Listen to St. Ambrose. The eighth day, or octave, is not a day of time. It is a day of eternity. "The octave is the crowning of our hope." Our time is reckoned by weeks, and the week has but seven days. When the week ends we begin one again, and count from the first to the seventh day. Beyond the seventh we do not pass, and thus the eighth day is not in the measurement of time, and the day that passes beyond the calendar of the week of time is of eternity. See you not the mystical reason why the octave should be her birthday, for with her birthday dawned the eternal day of Christ. The dawn came first; the sun is coming soon. So, back in the far ages, our Holy Church commemorates Mary's nativity on the eighth day of September. What other church celebrates it? The Greek church; yes. What other? None. If they celebrate the birth of Christ on Christmas day, why not celebrate the nativity of Christ's Mother? Does ever the sun of nature come without the dawn? and, in supernature's heavens, the sun of justice has, necessarily, his Aurora. If you keep the birth of the sun of justice in the noon of Christmas night, why not keep the feast of the dawn of the sun, in Mary's birth, in September? Ah! you want the sun, but you disdain its dawn! Have your way, but it is neither nature's nor supernature's way. We follow the way of both—the Catholic way.

Look! the priest is coming to the Altar, with the chalice and the bread. He is going to sing the Mass. Was it wrong for her to have been born? Is it then wrong to celebrate her birthday? Do you not keep the birthdays of the great and the illustrious, who were often, alas, great sinners? Do you not keep the birthday of your own mothers, and can you let the birthday of the Mother of Christ pass as any other common day, and all unnoticed? Go on! priest of the Son of Mary, and celebrate the sacrifice of Him who was sin's victim, and is our Saviour and Mary's son.

Ah! Holy Church, thou art beautiful in thy mind, for the light of truth is shining ever there; and thou art beautiful in thy heart, for the love of Christ is ever throbbing there; and thou art beautiful in thy memory of the holy ones of God, writing their names on the brows of all thy days; keeping feasts in their honor, but, above all, holding in eternal remembrance, at the Altar of the victim, His Mother's holy name.

Listen to the first words of the Mass in honor of Mary's nativity: "*Thy birth, oh Virgin Mary! Mother of the Son of God, has announced joy to all the world, because thou hast brought forth the Sun of Justice, Jesus Christ, our God, who, taking away malediction, gave benediction, and confounding death, gave unto us eternal life.*"

Are they not true, true as very Scripture? Do they honor or dishonor Christ, her son? From the lips of the priest they ascend to the heavens. Is Christ angry? Are the words a sin against Him? Is He afraid to hear His Mother praised, lest He might, thereby, lose a part of His glory? Why then did He make her so glorious? Why did He make her His Mother? Can He ever be jealous of her who conceived Him, gave Him birth, nursed Him, watched over His childhood, and stood at the foot of His cross? Has she not the right to be forever remembered as His Mother, and, if remembered, forever praised on earth? Priest, sing the *Gloria!* The song belongs to Him, but it was not sung until He had become hers. It belongs to both. Now go to the Gospel side, and sing the Gospel of the day.

Listen! "The book of the generation of Jesus Christ, the son of David, the son of Abraham." Abraham begot Isaac; and Isaac begot Jacob, and Jacob begot Judas and his brethren," and down a long and glorious ancestry of patriarchs, prophets, princes and kings, from name to name, moves the inspired pen of Matthew, Apostle and Evangelist, until it pauses thus: "And Jacob begot Joseph, the husband of Mary, of whom was born Jesus, who is called the Christ." The moment her name is written, His, the Christ's, is linked to it. Such was His and her ancestry.

But she was to have but one descendant, Jesus Christ our Saviour. She closes the "Book of the Generation of Jesus Christ." Take her name away, then take His. But she herself was, and is, the living book of the generation of Christ. How? Listen! In God was infinite and eternal thought. He expressed that thought in His Eternal Word—His only Son. But this thought, eternally conceived in the mind of God and eternally expressed, remained hidden in the Trinity. No one saw it, no one heard, no one knew it, save the three Divine persons. God willed to speak this Word outside of Himself and eternity, in time, and God willed to write this Word in a living book, that it might be heard and read forever. Mary received the secret thought of God and the invisible Word. Through her it was spoken in time and became Incarnate. In her pure flesh it was written and became visible. She does not express the Word as the Father does, but she bears it written in herself, and she makes it visible in the humanity of Jesus Christ, her son, to all the world.

While I am writing these words, the dawn of day is beginning to gild the eastern horizon, and to glimmer over the waves of the Gulf of Mexico. The waves, only a hundred yards away from where I write, are just waking from sleep. Last night they were very still. Not a wave sang or moaned on the pure, white shore, and now they seem glad for the coming of the day. Far out on the waters, the sails of the fishing boats have welcomed the beautiful dawn. I am thinking of Mary, not as the star of the sea, but I am thinking of her birth, as the dawn of the everlasting day of Christ. Perhaps, the sweetest hour of the day is that of the Aurora, *aurea hora,* golden hour, which banishes the darkness of the night and brings the light of the day. Out there, on the moss-veiled trees, the birds are beginning to sing their morning prayers. Light to the waking waves and joy to the wakened wild birds, the fair Aurora brings. Why? The waves and the birds know why. The sun, in his glory, will soon be born out of the heart of the Aurora. What a virginal light it is! The Aurora is the day's virgin, and, while it is the pure child created by the coming sun, it seems to be the mother that brings forth the sun, which gives to the day its golden hours, to the earth its fairest beauties, and to the heavens its wondrous glory.

So Mary, in her birth, is the virgin created by the Son of God. In a little while the virgin, because she is a virgin, will become His Mother; and as the sun of day, when he rises above the horizon, does not destroy the light of dawn, but gathers its beautiful light into his own splendors and carries it with him up into the heavens; so when the Sun of Justice, clothed with the splendors of His Eternal Father, will rise over the world, He will gather into His glory and blend with His infinite light, as He ascends on high, the fair, sweet light of His Mother Mary.

And as the Aurora came before the sun, and follows the sun wheresoever he shineth, inseparable from his last rays as from his first, so the Virgin Mother, in her pure human light, will follow and be mingled with the light of Him who "enlightens every one that cometh into the world."

Oh fair light! oh sweet light! oh gentle light! shine on our days! Shine o'er our ways forever! and, as thou wert the beautiful dawn of Christ in this world, be the dawn of the day of thy children's blessed eternity.

Aspiration.

All the glory of the King's daughter is within, in golden borders,—clothed round about with vanities. After her virgins shall be brought to the King. They shall be brought with gladness and rejoicing. They shall be brought into the temple of the King.

Prayer.

Vouchsafe, O Lord, we beg of Thee, to grant us, Thy servants, the gift of heavenly grace; that as in the childbirth of the Blessed Virgin, our salvation began, we may obtain an increase of peace.

EIGHTH DAY.

The Flower of the Name.

"I came out of the mouth of the Most High; the first-born before all creatures. I made, that in the heavens there should rise light that never faileth, and as a cloud I covered all the earth. I dwelt in the highest places, and My throne is in a pillar of a cloud."

THERE is mystery in names. All objects come to our understanding through their different names. The objects themselves are more than mere names, but they must be named in order to be clearly known, though when named, they may not be fully known. Names distinguish things each from the other. Names are the titles of things. What is nameless is unknown, and has no real existence for us. The nameless is a nothing. Names are symbols that cannot be separated from their objects without producing confusion in speech as well as chaos in the mind. Each object owns, in its own right, its own name, and cannot be robbed of it. The lily is a lily, and the rose is a rose, and each must keep its own exclusive title in order to be known. All speech is based primarily on nouns, which are names of objects. This is the fundamental part of every language, and the other parts of speech have meanings only as they refer to names. But names of intelligent beings are greater than names of mere material things; because the higher the object in the ascending scale of creation, the greater the name. The name of God is supreme and incommunicable. He alone can bear it.

Angels in heaven have each their particular name, the mark of their individuality in the angelic world. Some of their names, by revelation, we know, and each of their names has a special, exclusive meaning of its own. Michael, the prince of the heavenly hosts, Raphael, Gabriel, are not only named in heaven, but their names are known on earth. In the human race, each child of Adam has his own especial name.

In the Christian order, we each receive our name in baptism, as in the old covenant days the Hebrews received theirs on the day of circumcision. Unlike the angels, we have family names, for we are the offspring of human generation, having fathers and mothers. Not so the angels. They have special names, but the name of the particular choir in the heavenly hierarchy to which they belong corresponds to our family name. Think as you please, we and our names go together, and is it strange? our names will last longer than ourselves. When the souls of men have gone to eternity and their bodies to the resting place of the dead, their names still live; some a little while, some a longer while, some for ages, and a few forever. Our merit or demerit passes into our names, remains there, and lasts after we have passed away

Human history is a necrology. From the days of Adam until yesterday, it is names, and the name of the dead that give life to the record of human events. Mortal men are made immortal by their names; and, ah! fallen from our first estate, though we are, what glorious names have been written in the annals of our race. Beyond the Messiah's day, out of the days of the law of nature, Adam, Abel, Seth, Abraham, Isaac, Jacob, Joseph, then Moses, Aaron, Miriam, Joshua, Esther,

David, Solomon, Isaias, Jeremias, Ezechiel, Daniel, Zacharias, Malachy and others not here named, God's instruments in the order of providence. And in the outer world, lying in the darkness of idolatry, conquerors, poets, philosophers, whose names are living still, and who, in their day and way, unconsciously furthered the designs of God; and all to prepare the world for the coming of Him whose name is above all names, Jesus Christ. But before His name is written on the first page of the New Testament, we read the name of Mary. Her name was the morning star that shone before the sun of His name rose on the horizon of human history.

His earthly name, Jesus Christ, is as incommunicable as His name in eternity, the Eternal Word; and it was His Mother who, giving Him his humanity, gave Him, according to the angel's word, the adorable name, Jesus. "And thou shalt call His name Jesus." His name is the light of the world, but He would not have borne that name had not His Mother borne Him.

In the eclipses of your souls, and, ah! their shadows fáll on all, and when you cry for less of dark and more of bright, do you not call on the name of Jesus, the eternal light? His Mother gave Him His name. Can you forget that?

His name is a name of strength, and when you are weak and passion is strong, and you feel yourselves unequal to cope with the power of evil, do you not have recourse to the power of the name of Jesus? Well, His Mother named Him so. Always remember that. And His name is Truth, and Hope, and Love, and Everlasting Life; and His name Jesus has infinite beautiful meanings besides. The evangelists named Him Christ; and asked, before His passion, "Art thou Christ?" He answered the High Priest: "Thou hast said it." But His greater name, His Saviour name, is Jesus! and His Mother gave it to Him.

In your sins and in your sorrows, do you fall down before the Saviour Jesus, and plead for the mercy He never refuses? Do you breathe His name as if it were the very breath of the life of your souls? Remember that the mother who bore Him named Him, and love and honor His Mother's name. And His Mother's name is Mary, and, next to His, that name is the highest and the holiest.

Thousands bear the Virgin Mother's name and glorify it by their virtues, but many, alas, are named with her name who are not worthy to bear it. In no Mary on earth, does, or can, the name mean what it means in her. And what does it mean in her? It has depths we cannot fathom. It has heights we cannot touch. It has beauties beyond the reach of words, no matter how beautiful. It has glories beyond the reach of loftiest thought. It has real meanings of relations to Christ, which never have been and never can be told. It has mystical meanings of relations to the Father and the Holy Spirit beyond our comprehension. It has spiritual meanings of relations with the angelic world and with ours, which nor man nor angel can adequately describe. It is, in a sense, an eternal name, for the name was appointed to her in the eternal decree of her predestination. St. Peter Damian says, that the name of Mary came directly out of the treasury of the Divinity.

Father, Son and Holy Ghost decreed the name from all eternity. It was praised and glorified by the angels from the beginning of the world. It is the name of alliance between heaven and earth, and God and man;

not in the infinite sense in which the name of Jesus Christ bears that title, but in the highest and holiest sense which the name of a finite creature can reach. It is a name fragrant with all spiritual sweetnesses. It is a mirror which reflects more of the light of the name of Jesus Christ than all the rest of creation. It is the everlasting accord of the name of Jesus. They have sounded together from all eternity, Jesus and Mary, the divine note and the human note, in the glorious hymn of God's mercy. Sound either apart, and the music is false. Each note is in need of the other in the true song of redemption.

Her name is the pure and sacred vase which contains the chrism of the name of Christ. Her name is the holy lamp of the wisest of virgin of virgins, which burns with the divine oil of the name of Christ. Her name is a crown in which are intertwined all human perfections, all spiritual grace and glories only inferior to God's. Her name is a garden, "a closed garden," full of flowers, which bloom with the beauty of God. Her name is a pure fountain, high up on the loftiest mountains of the sanctities, whence flows to us, and over the world forever, the holy stream of Christ's most precious blood, with salvation in its every crimson drop. Her name is the mysterious tree, with one root in the Trinity and the other on earth, in Joachim and Anna, which has produced the fruit of eternal life, Jesus Christ. Her name is like the "burning bush," which Moses saw, growing on sinless ground and flaming with the light of the name Jesus. Her name is like the ark of the new covenant, with the manna of the name of Christ within it.

Her name is the pure, white, finite shore that girdles the sea of the infinite. Her name is the golden cloud, floating in the heavens and over the earth, with not one dark spot on it, and filled with the splendors of the Divinity. Her name is like the pillar of fire that goes before the chosen people, guiding them across the bleak deserts of time, to the land of eternal promise—it, the pillar, and the name of Jesus the fire that flames around it. Her name is like the dove of the deluge, bearing the olive branch of the peace of the name of Christ across the angry waters to all who are in the ark of salvation. Her name is the beautiful gate that opens into the temple of grace. Her name is the holy, mysterious veil that hangs before the Holy of Holies, where dwells the living name of Christ.

Her name is like a valley, where the flowers of the graces of the name of Christ bloom forever in the bright spring-tide and summer-days of Mercy. Her name is the star, with never shadow on it, that shines the highest and the brightest in the heavens of faith and hope and love, to which the magnet of the heart of every storm-tossed mariner on the sea of life is turned, the polar star of heaven, with the light of Jesus in it, to guide their way and lead them to the eternal haven. Her name is the glorious rainbow of peace and hope, spanning all the days of time, from the garden of Eden to the valley of judgment, on which the light of the Sun of Justice shines forever reflected, and beneath which walk the generations who love the name and keep the law of her Divine Son.

From the beginning of the Church, all down the centuries until this very day, true faith has bound together the names of Jesus and Mary, as they were bound together in the great decree of mercy in eternity; as their persons were bound together in the promise in

Eden, and as they were bound together in the bond of the birth in Bethlehem, the bond of blood, and as they were bound together on the hill of Calvary, in the bond of sorrow. Separate one name from the other, and the mystery of the Incarnation is a broken thing. The name of Jesus leans on the name of Mary for its human meaning, as much and as really as the name of Jesus leans on the name of the Eternal Father for its divine meaning.

No wonder that the name of Mary sounds round the altar of her Son in our Holy Church. Say the Apostles Creed. First is named God, the Father; then Jesus Christ, His only Son, "who was conceived by the Holy Ghost, born of the Virgin Mary." His name is linked to the Father's, the Holy Ghost's name to His, and to the Holy Ghost is linked the name of the Virgin Mary. So the Christian Creed binds the names together. Can that Church be called Christian that will break the holy circle of the four names? No. In the Greek Church, and the others of Eastern rites, they keep, as we, the names forever united in their liturgies as in their creeds. And if the Creed be right, we and they are right. Alas! for the so-called churches who have banished the name of Mary from their services; or who, if they speak her name, do it in halting tone and bated breath. The New Testament is, in highest sense, the everlasting "Religious Service" of man's redemption, and the prelude to it is ever the same, it begins with the name of Mary, of whom was born Christ.

Oh! Holy Church, thou art the living New Testament, not written by human hands, but formed by the Holy Spirit; thou art the speaking New Testament, and wheresoever thou goest, thou art true to all the truth of redemption, which is human and divine, and which comes to the world with two inseparable names impressed upon it, names which are the signs of heaven and of earth—Jesus and Mary!

Truths must be revealed to be believed, and beliefs must be taught to be accepted; but faiths must have festivals. In what Church, outside of ours, is feast kept in honor of the Holy Name of Mary? In none. No wonder, then, our Holy Church has feasts besides her Sundays. Must the "communion of saints" lie in the Creed, a mere, cold dogma, to be read with the eyes and accepted by the mind,—only that and nothing more? No, no, the truly, fully Christian heart needs something more. Dogmas must have days of festival, when they clothe themselves with earthly beauty, and thus appeal to faith's high and holy emotions; and holy names, as well, must have their holy-days. The calendar of the Church is spiritual, not secular. The world keeps feasts of great events and of names which it considers great, and it is well; but we, we celebrate events still greater, and commemorate names by sanctity made immortal; and next to the name of the all-holy, Jesus Christ, what reason can forbid feast in honor of His purest Mother Mary? So, scattered through the months of the year, are days set apart to honor the Mother who has honored all the days of time. In each of the feasts in which she receives the homage of our honor, beside her stands Christ, who alone claims our adoration; while in every feast of His in which He demands our supreme worship, she stands beside Him and claims her honors as His Mother.

In the spring-tide, when the sun, greatening in brightness and growing in warmth, announces the coming of the flowers, we keep the feast of the Angelical Annunciation. When summer, like a queen, assumes all her splendors in the month of August, we celebrate the feast of Mary's glorious assumption and coronation. When autumn comes, and men are gathering the fruits of the year, we commemorate, in September, the festival of the nativity of Mary, who was the purest fruit of prophecy and promise. In the mid of winter, when nature looks like death, we keep, with Mary, in Bethlehem, the great festival of the birth of the Giver of that life that never dies; and strewn between these greater festivals, are other days, blessed and bright in their dedication to the blessed Mary.

But days pass—their life is only twenty-four hours; they do not last. But temples last; monuments last; orders of men and women last; hymns last. Go through every country in Europe; look upon those grand temples built in the ages of faith; call them dark, if you will, it is the fashion, and ignorance is imitative, but show us in modern days brighter monuments. Show us grander art. Match by modern skill, if you can, the magnificence of those minsters conceived in the heart and built by the hands of true faith. You cannot do it. Your age is too material. It is the age of factories, not the age of temples. It has lost the instincts of spiritual beauty; it is building the material on the ruins of the spiritual. It is an age of reason; yes, but a reason growing materialized and forgetting how to believe. It worships in the workshop of man, not in the temple of God. These eyes that guide this pen have looked, in a wonder passing all words, upon those monuments whose histories are ages and ages; and how many of them bear the name of the Blessed Virgin Mary? It is beyond our reckoning. From the marble stones hidden in humility deep down in the ground; and, like unknown saints, forming the unseen foundation, up to where the cross, on lofty tower, kisses the skies, comes the evidence of the veneration of the people for the name of Mary. Enter the grand aisles leading up to the Christian's Holy of Holies. At either side altars stand, like sleepless sentinels, to guard the sacramental presence in its own special shrine; and sure you are to find an altar dedicated to Mary there, and sometimes her own altar is, like herself, the altar-mother where her Son in the Eucharist rests.

The stories of the joys and sorrows, the triumphs and tears of souls innumerable, seem still to live in the silences of those glorious temples. Every stone you tread on has its memories. If the feast days pass, the temples last. It was a rule of the Cistercians to dedicate all their churches and chapels and monasteries to the Blessed Virgin Mary. In our Holy Church there is nothing dead. Its truths spring into eternal life in dogmas, its devotion makes itself visible in the material structure of glorious temples; but it goes farther, and enshrines its thoughts and love of Christ and Mary in the holy hymns of Christian poesy. Open the Breviary of the priest and the Missal of the Altar; and read. Out of the hearts of her children, some known but most of them unknown, sound songs thrilling with adoration of Christ and honor of Mary. These songs of music, all spiritual, live on the lips of the priests, and ascend to heaven, breathed by faith, all over the world, day and night; for the Church that is forever preaching is forever praying, and the Church that is forever praying is forever singing Christ's and Mary's praises. But songs, after all, are only words. Love of Christ and Mary calls for living hymns, and has them. Count, if you can, the religious associations of men and women who are living prayers and living songs of praise.

Enter the monasteries, where men of highest faith abide. Go into the cells of those self-made prisoners. They have preferred the slavery of Christ to the freedom of the world. They are aiming at perfection. Ask them how they are striving to reach it, and they will surely tell you this: "Here we love and adore Christ, and here we love and honor His holy mother, Mary." That is the secret, as well as solace, of their lives.

Enter the gates of a hundred thousand convents, where, like " doves in the clefts of the rocks," dwell the virgins of the Church. They lead the life of purity and prayer. Ask them what brought them there. Ask them what keeps them there. Ask them why their faces wear that look, common to them all, of such unworldly peace. They will tell you: LOVE OF GOD. Ask them who is their model. They will tell you, as if the very name were a prayer: the Blessed Virgin Mary. Mary is living her olden life over again in them. They are virgins like her, but like her, they are mothers too, spiritual mothers, who, by their sacrifices and prayers, are bringing forth Christians into the Church, as Mary brought forth Christ into the world.

Oh! holy name of Mary, how thou art glorified in our Holy Church! True, thou art crowned queen in the heavens, but still thou art living with us on earth, in the beautiful vows of our virgins. The bishops and priests of the Church, under the Pontiff-chief, are the guard of honor of the names of Jesus and Mary.

Christ had a Virgin Mother. Christ has a virgin Church, and the virgin Church must have priests who will be the virgin fathers of souls. From the Pontiff down to the humblest soldier-priest in the ranks of that guard of honor, faith in Christ the Adorable and love of Mary the Immaculate are the only watchword of all the days, and the battle-call and the triumph-cry. That watchword never changes. 'Tis forever ringing down the ranks.

What though sometimes a traitor deserts? Another soldier takes his place, and leaves no break in the line; and high over the ranks float, side by side, the glorious ensign of Jesus Christ and the beautiful banner of Mary. March on, true soldiers of the cross! You never can halt here below. The enmity between Satan and the woman lasts forever, and between her seed and his seed. In battle for Christ, you battle for her. Jesus and Mary watch the everlasting conflict. March on in the bravery of faith, in the confidence of hope, in the enthusiasm of love; and fadeless crowns of victory shall grace your brows, when, stainless as the hour they were placed in your hands, and wreathed with a thousand glories, you enter in triumph the gates of heaven and lay at the feet of the Eternal Father the standard of Jesus Christ and the banner of Mary.

ASPIRATION.

HOLY MARY, Mother of God! pray for us sinners now and at the hour of our death.

PRAYER.

GRANT, we beseech Thee, Almighty God, that Thy faithful, who rejoice beneath the name and protection of the ever Blessed Virgin Mary, may, by her holy intercession, be delivered from all earthly evils, and reach the eternal joys of heaven.

NINTH DAY.

The Flower of the Vow.

"Hearken, O daughter, and see, and incline thy ear and forget thy people and thy father's house. And the King shall greatly desire thy beauty, for He is the Lord thy God and Him they shall adore."—*Psalm*, xliv.

CALMLY went on the days in the home of Joachim and Anna.

It was the happiest home earth ever had. What cared the holy couple about the great noisy world without them? They never had mingled in it much; and now since Mary had come to bless the evening of their days,—and the mornings and evenings of all days;—and they had a beautiful world of their own, little thought they of the great world lying without. A journey to Jerusalem, a visit to the Temple on the Feast days of the Law,—a brief stay, and a hurried return were the only things to interrupt the quietness of their life.

They had been childless so long that Jerusalem wondered much when it heard of Mary's birth. They would ask Joachim about his little child; but unlike the aged, Joachim was not garrulous. He kept his own counsel. His words were few, and his questioners saw that somehow he seemed shy of speaking about her. Two years passed away. The child had begun to speak. I wonder what was the first word lisped by the child's pure lips? Seldom did the feet of strangers or visitors pass the threshold of that secluded home. But, betimes some would come. But whoso came, went away in wonderment of her beauty; and somehow they were moved by a something in her face and ways and words difficult to divine. It was as if they had caught a glimpse of Heaven, or seen an angel in earthly form. They went their way carrying in their hearts the memory of the lovely child. And so Jerusalem heard of her wondrous beauty and began to busy itself about the child's future. Marriage was the dream of the maidens of Judea,—as marriage is the dream of most of their Christian sisters. To be the mother of the Messiah,—to bring forth Him who was to be King of Kings forever and to save their nation,—this was the unspoken thought and intense desire of their hearts. And who could blame the Hebrew maidens whose souls were the shrine of a desire so pure and holy? But ah! how little they and their priests knew of the ways of God! Their idea of the Messiah was carnal. They looked for Him coming in the pomp of secular glory. The clearness of the meanings of prophecy had grown dim. True, they read or heard read the words, but their spiritual significations were hidden from their minds.

Joachim belonged to one of the priestly orders,—so around the temple courts where, after the evening sacrifice had been offered, the priests and their children congregated, there was frequent talk of Joachim's designs about his beautiful child. Is it curious or not, that world-talk seldom touches God's thoughts? Little did those talkers know the future of Joachim's Mary. In her home there was a stillness about her like the silence in the Holy of Holies. She spoke not often; and when she did, her voice was very low as if she were afraid to let it speak,—lest it might tell some secrets hidden as yet down in her heart,—and its tones were tremulous with a sweetness indefinable. And how she loved her holy parents; nor was child ever loved as she was loved by them. She learned the prayers prescribed by the Law. In morning and evening times she would kneel down beside her mother, with her face lifted like an angel's, towards the heavens, and pray as none had ever prayed before. Did the angels hush their songs in heaven when the breath of her prayer ascended? Did new, strange glories, never by the hosts of heaven seen before, gleam from the face of the All-beautiful God, as He listened to the child-prayers of His future mother? And did the Father feel a divine impatience for the coming of the hour when He was to send Gabriel, the Angel of the Throne, with His prayer to the Virgin?

Sometimes, as quietly as the sunshine, she would steal away into the garden that surrounded the house,—and breathe her prayers where the flowers were blooming and the roses were resting,—but sweeter the breath of her lips than the breath of their leaves. Ah! happy flowers that heard her prayers! Ah! blessed roses that felt the touch of her pure hand!

How mysteriously shy the little child was growing day after day, as if she were hiding a mystery in her soul!

In the long, calm evenings, resting on her mother's breast,—still as a Host upon an altar, she would listen with a rapt attention even in her far-off look to her father's voice while he spoke of the history of their race and explained the prophecies announcing the coming of the Messiah. And when he would speak in tones full of pathos of the growing wickedness of even the chosen people and of the fearful, wide-spread idolatries of all the nations, the little child would nestle closer in her mother's arms with such a look of infinite pity in her eyes. And she would ask questions of strangest kind that made them marvel much. And when he would speak of the days of the exile in Egypt; and of Bethlehem, the birth-place of David his royal ancestor and of Jerusalem where factions were dividing men and almost breaking to fragments the old inherited faith, she would sometimes startle, as if strange presentiments, like clouds across skies, were moving over her soul. Who will ever know how much she knew in those the first days of her life? And who will ever know if what, she did know, was in her soul clear as a ray or dim as a shadow?

They sometimes saw the mist of tears in her eyes,—and they wondered why. In her sleep they heard her sometimes sigh,—and they were sad.

But she often smiled and then the very light of heaven shone upon her face. Only Joachim and Anna and the child Mary in that humble home? No more?

Ah no! The Archangel of the Throne, Gabriel, hovered unseen round his ward, with ceaseless vigilance;—and hosts of other angels were with him there. That home was a very Heaven, for its Queen was there. She had not won her crown as yet,—but she will surely win it. Did she ever see them? If she did, she made no sign. And, meantime, her sinless soul was ascending higher and still higher in the immense sphere of grace.

Those were still days on earth. The mystery kept its hiding place. But those were grand days in Heaven. To the clear vision of the angels, as from the Face of God, come new revelations of glory hour after hour in the cycles of eternity,—so to them came from the soul of Mary, day after day, new unfoldings of ineffable beauties.

And so went on the days. Did you ever see a golden cloud in the summer sky, full of water by the heavens purified, and all wrapped round with the robes of the sun? And in its waters floats the very life of the flowers of the earth. And the cloud bends low in love for the earth. And it opens its heart and the rain comes down with the warmth and the light of the sun in its every drop. And they fall on the flowers and on the trees and the humble grasses,—when lo! a new life comes into them all. And though they were nearly a-dying, they brighten again and are filled with joyous, abounding life, by the beautiful baptism of Nature. So, in those days, Mary's soul was the golden cloud that had risen on high from the earth, robed with the rays of the Sun of Justice,—and containing the very waters of life eternal. Wait awhile,—and the golden cloud will open its bosom,—and bend down to earth again, and out of it will come, the pure human-divine drops of the mercy of the blood of Jesus Christ.

It was a long day in the ending of summer. She was never demonstrative,—but all that day she was hovering around her parents. Her very heart seemed to be going out of her to them. A new strange expression shone on her face. And it was a day of many questions too, about God and the Messiah. She looked as if she were going to reveal something. They remarked it wonderingly. But the day passed,—and not a word. When the twilight's shadows fell around their home, Joachim and Anna and Mary entered the garden. She was holding her father's hand. They went into the garden to pray.

With their faces towards the Temple they said together the evening's prayers;—and ah! how fervent were their blended voices when they besought the God of their fathers to remember the Promise and send the Messiah!

The prayer over,—then spoke the voice of the child in trembling way. Her hand was resting in her father's hand. She asked them to give their consent to her desire to dedicate herself by the vow of virginity forever to the service of God. They did not feel surprised. It was as if they had expected it. Silence fell between them just a little while. Ah! how deep and full of mystery is silence! Did the flowers listen for her father's answer? There was listening in heaven then such as had never been before. At last, Joachim spoke,—and his voice was firm; and he with Anna gave full and glad consent. Like the Eternal Father's: "Let light be made:" was Joachim's words to Mary: "Child! let it be so." But like the Eternal Father in Creation,—though swift to give his glad consent,—he moved slowly to fulfill it. He must wait awhile. He must lay the matter before the High Priest, and the priests of the Temple. Their consent was necessary. And that night a wondrous spiritual happiness filled that home. Joachim fell a-dreaming about the olden words of prophecy. Anna's soul was full of joy. And the second great ecstacy after the Immaculate Conception was filling Mary's soul with rapture. And the expectant world went on just the same as ever,—not knowing that the second step in the Redemption was made, on earth—and by the feet of a little child.

A few days afterwards Joachim turned his face towards the Holy-City. He sought the High Priest and placed his child's desire before him. He assembled the priests. Zacharias, the father of the future John the Baptist was present,—and so also was the aged Simeon. The High Priest laid the request of Joachim before them. He told them it was the desire of Joachim's child,—and that she was not yet three years old. Some of the priests objected on account of the tenderness of her age. But up rose Simeon,—and he spoke almost like a Christian priest, as if he were inspired. His words moved all in the assembly, and all gave consent to receive the child Mary.

Joachim returned to his home, and brought the glad tidings of a great joy to Mary. And now Anna begins to make preparations for her child's departure. Human sorrow and spiritual joy often live together in the same heart. It is a mystery hard to be understood by worldlings. But God's saints know it. To part with her child was a grief beyond words;—but to give her to God and His service was a joy—the greatest of her life. Joachim was man; and though he could not feel, as the mother felt; still a quiet, deep pain lay on his heart shadowing the gladness that was in it for giving his Mary to God. September passed. They quietly kept the third birth-day of their child. October came and went with falling leaves and fading flowers. Closer and closer grew the bonds of tenderest human love between those three hearts as nearer and nearer drew the hour of separation. A part of our October and November formed the eighth month of the Hebrew year. In November, Joachim and Anna, accompanied, by many of their kinfolks who were in amaze at Joachim's folly, went up to Jerusalem, with Mary.

And no one else? St. Germanus, the Patriarch of

Constantinople, describing that journey to Jerusalem, says that hosts of unseen angels surrounded and accompanied Mary. The world may laugh at this as a fable. Let it laugh. For us are the testimonies of the saints. They presented her to Zachary the father of John the Baptist.

And before the Altar of Perfumes she silently made the vow of virginity. Did the Royal Prophet, her ancestor sing to her across the ages: *"Hearken O Daughter,—and consider, and incline thine ear, and forget thy people and thy father's house, and the King shall love thee for thy beauty; for He is thy Lord and worship thou Him?"

Did the singer of the song of mystical love, chaunt for her Presentation-Feast when he sings: †"Rise up my Love, my fair one, and come away, for lo! the winter is past, and the rain is over and gone; the flowers appear on the earth, the time of the singing of birds is come, and the voice of the turtle-dove is heard in our land."

The vow was made. Then the temple sounded with gladsome song. Aged priests, young levites, all the assembled people, Joachim and Anna swelled the canticle with their voices. Mary's lips were moving in silent prayer.

Then came the parting moment. She knelt before her parents for their blessing,—and then arose. She clasped her arms around their neck,—first Joachim's. He was weeping tears of sorrow and of joy. And then she clasped her arms around her mother,—and lingered longer in her embrace; while from the eyes of Mary fell such tears as are seldom shed. They are the most tenderly human who have gone deepest into the divine.

---

* *Psalm*, xlv.   † *Cant.*, ch. 2.

Her parents went away; she remained the little prisoner of divine love in the Holy Temple.

Her vow was the coronation of her Immaculate Conception.

Ah! child of grace! these words I write have set my heart a-dreaming and wakened memories of far off happy days! And there are eyes, that will read my words unworthy, sure, of thee; and when they read them, they too will look from the page before them back to olden, golden days, of which they formed a part with me. Sweet St. Mary's of the Barrens in Missouri's wilds! thy children never can forget thee! Ah! well do they remember thy Presentation Feast when thou didst dedicate thyself to God. The great High Altar, in that seven Altared Church was radiant every year with lights and fragranced with flowers; and the setting sun shone through the western window, the while thy Litany sounded before the Benediction. And then the names of many who yearned to be priests of Thy only Son were placed in the silver heart hanging from thy statue's neck in promise made to thee that they, like thee, would leave their fathers' house and dedicate themselves to the service of the Temple!

Ah me! how many names were shrined within that silver heart! Many are dead and gone;—but a few are living still; and who would have thought, that long gone evening when my poor name was given into thy keeping, that I, so unworthy, would dare to dream of weaving a crown in thy honor?

Farther from the world—nearer to God. Now began the hidden, unrevealed life of Mary in the Temple. Around it with its courts and surroundings there was a circumference of half-a mile.

The High Priest did not live there. He had a dwelling of his own in Jerusalem. But many priests and levites did live within its precincts. The Scriptures and many holy Doctors give us to understand, that near and around the Temple, within the walls, dwelt devout women in cells apart, separated from the men whose duty it was to pray before the gate of the Tabernacle, to assist at the sacrifices of the morning and evening—to meditate on the law of God night and day, and to make the vestments of the priests. According to the testimony of St. Ambrose, St. Cyril of Alexandria, Origen and others, only widows and maidens were admitted and allowed to live within the Temple's precincts. And all this was a shadow of the consecrated cloisters of the virgins of our Holy Church. In those days, the aged widow Anna, was a dweller in the Temple. The High Priest appointed those who were to take charge of and train the young maidens. They were taught to sing the canticles of the Lord. Their every day was regulated as to their duties. Like the nuns of our Holy Church they lived in separate cells. The rules were strict. To be dismissed from the Temple-service was considered an ignominy. It was a world within a world,—a world of peace and prayer and silence and song and gentle labor.

Into that world went Mary. Her cell, according to tradition, was the nearest to the Holy of Holies. And with her went God and His angels. The Temple was her solitude. In the din of the noisy world God's voice is but faintly and vaguely heard. The world is a loud talker but a very poor thinker. It lives on words—very poor food,—and on noises,—very poor music. It does not understand that solitude is the home of great thoughts and aspirations. It will not see, that even mere human greatness makes a solitude for itself amid the little littlenesses around it in order to achieve future triumphs. But so it is.

But sanctity which is the greatest greatness, even still more, has need of solitude, for growth. Read the lives of the saints. Even while in perpetual action,—and while in conflict with the world around them,—their souls were solitaries. They lived within themselves a wondrous separated life, even when in daily contact with the tumult all about them. Our Holy Church, in inner life, is as much a hermit to-day, as when with cross in hand she began the pilgrimage of time.

Mary spent eleven years in the Temple. Meanwhile Joachim and Anna died and "went to their fathers." She was alone,—an orphan in the world. The Temple was her only home,—and the Eternal her only Father; and the Priests of the Old Covenant became the guardians of the Mother of the Christ of the New Dispensation. Beautiful, by her sinlessness in the supernatural order, her natural beauty went on towards its perfection day by day. She was a living picture of God's beauty on earth.

Her companions loved her,—and in their love there was a strange reverence for her person. When they sang together the canticles of the Lord, her pure voice sounded like an angel's.

And she was the humblest one of them all. She was the mystery of the Temple. Many ancient writers and holy Fathers tell us that in her cell,—she held converse with the angels,—and that they were wont to bring her food. This, will you say, is only a beautiful imagination? And why only that? Ordinary laws,—common rules are for all of the children of our race, because we are ordinary. But hers was an uncommon life—and her destiny extraordinary. Canisius says that once she prolonged her prayers to the hour of midnight, when through the Temple's silence sounded the words: "Thou shalt bring forth My Son." And she rose and in wonder, went to her cell.

Christian imagination, glowing with the light of Faith and full of Faith's inspirations, can never conceive the superhuman facts in which her life in the Temple was folded.

In the material world around us what innumerable beauties are lying unrevealed. We see Nature's surface but not her sanctuaries. And if what we do see fill our eyes with rapture, do we not know that all that visible beauty is a veil concealing the invisible beauty beneath it.

Yes,—"in the world of Nature, as in Super-Nature's realms, there is that which no eye can see,—nor heart conceive, nor human mind understand." And of every human life given to God, the same is true. We read the lives of the saints,—but never know but half. And her life, the saint of saints,—the Mother of the life of the Christ of the saints, of it we know only the least little part. And why? Because in her life, the greater part is above and beyond any imitation. It was a life unique, absolutely exceptional,—a life that could not be lived by any one but Mary. And this is why her Temple-life of eleven years has not been revealed to us. It is inimitable,—and therefore gives no outward sign. It is strangely like the life of God before the Creation. God's was a life unknown and of infinite silence until He spoke:—"Fiat Lux:" "Let there be light." And Mary's life before Redemption was a life unknown,—

and silent,—till she broke its silence in answer to the angel: "Fiat mihi:" "Be it done unto me according to thy word."

Ah! Child of Grace! while thou didst pray in all the days of those eleven years for the coming of the Messiah, thou didst also breathe thy all-fervent prayers for the sinners He was coming to save. Pray on,—sweet child; and ah! 'tis joy to know that we too here gathered in thy honor had a place in thy heart and a part in thy prayers;—and who knows? a deeper place and a greater part, because we wreathe to-day in thy queenly crown the beautiful Flower of Thy Vow.

Aspiration.

"Thy kingdom come. Thy will be done on earth as it is in heaven!"

Prayer.

May the humanity of Thy only begotten Son be our succor, O Lord; that Jesus Christ, our Lord, who, when born of a Virgin, did not diminish, but did consecrate the integrity of His Mother, and may the same humanity adorable, deliver us from our sins and make our petitions acceptable.

TENTH DAY.

The Flower of the Espousals.

"I have chosen to be an abject in the house of my God, rather than to dwell in the tabernacles of sinners."—*Psalm*, lxxxiii.

THERE was Feast in the Temple courts. Sweet melodies of many harps were sounding, and voices of holy widows and innocent maidens were chanting canticles of joy. Many lights were glowing on the Altar of Perfumes. And in the Temple and around it gladness was reigning everywhere. What feast? Only a Birthday Feast. The sun of the eighth of September shone in a sky all-cloudless, all day long. Came the High Priest,—the priests of inferior order and the Levites to grace the Feast with their presence, and to bless the day with their blessings. On that day Mary was fourteen years old. It was her Birthday Feast. Zachary and his spouse, holy Elizabeth were there. And Simeon came, and many of the kinfolks of the Child. For eleven years, Simeon had watched Mary, with now and then strange presentiments which he could hardly define.

With a shyness, that puzzled many, she listened to their congratulations. There were holy faces there, and saintly souls and hearts with grace's high consecrations (for we must not think that the grand Old Covenant had no saints in its Vesper time) but amid them all, like a dream of God, moved Mary in her beauty. In that covenant of beautiful shadows how many wonderful women, figures of her, had come and gone, and left to Israel memories of virtues and of grace! Miriam, Ruth, Judith, Esther, the mother of the Machabees and others are the glories of that olden Dispensation. But Mary was its crown.

There was that in her face, that day, which was in none other there,—a something indescribable; and in her eyes an infinite calm; and in her voice the very tones of heaven's music; and in her every movement an unconscious grace, which, somehow, wove a spiritual spell on all who looked upon her. "How like an angel!" they whispered low to one another.

But,—"all the glory of the King's daughter is from within."

Her wondrous, natural beauty was but the transparent veil through which shone the interior, ineffable beauty of her soul, that, for fourteen years, in constant and closest union with God, had far surpassed the transcendent sanctities of all the angels; and was rising, hour by hour, up towards the inaccessible heights of God's supremest grace.

In after days, that Birthday Feast was long remembered, with new and added meanings, by those who had come to celebrate it.

All day long the Feast was kept until the hour of evening-sacrifice. Then to the Temple all repaired: and the evening-song was sung,—and the sacred censor was swung, while the white smoke of the Sacrifice ascended from the altar. Begun in joy and with gladsome song, that day closed in the hush of holy prayer. All had gone, but Mary still knelt and prayed. The Spirit of God was on her. Silence filled the Temple with its own strange holiness. The shadows,—and did they tremble? folded her kneeling form. Strange emotions moved through her heart. "Coming events cast their shadows before;"—and, somehow, she felt, as if the gates of her Eden in the Temple were about to open for her to pass through, and to move on to some other act of God in the which she was to take part. In her cell, that night, she held long converse with her angel. He bade her follow the wishes of the priests, revealed to her a secret of Eternity and bade her not to fear.

The priests held council about the child. What to do with her was the question that disturbed them. The last words of Joachim, and the dying pathetic pleadings of Anna lay on their minds.

When she leaves the Temple, in whose charge will they place her? In spite of her vow they decided to give her in marriage.

But to whom? She was of the royal race of David; where find for her in his line a fitting companion? They had not long to think,—nor far to go. There was a man named Joseph who belonged to the royal line and had the same ancestor. "And he was a just man." He was getting on into age; and the priests had often wondered why he had never chosen a bride from among the fair daughters of Sion.

Though his ancestors had been prophets, princes and kings he was only a poor carpenter; but his were the riches, better than those of earth, of great graces. He lived up in Nazareth, loved and respected by all who knew him. A tall, stately man,—very silent, with a singular tranquillity about him, he was wont to be seen in the Temple, on the Feasts of the Law, presenting his humble offerings to the altar, with the mild look of one of the ancient patriarchs; and he was pointed out to the people as a model of the faithfullest observance of all the sacred ordinances.

He lived alone a life of daily toil. Why he had never married, no one knew. He had his own secret; and he kept his own counsel. He was known of all for his knowledge of the words of the Lord, for his deep faith in the promises; for his love of His chosen race; but above all for his humility. When he came to the Temple,—not into the first seats did he enter,—but down near the Temple's door he might be seen, sometimes standing,—sometimes kneeling and sometimes prostrate in prayer.

Of his ancestry he did not speak. He belonged to none of the various conflicting, noisy sects into which, unfortunately, the Hebrews had become divided. Apart from them all he stood, bewailing their enmities towards one another, and sighing over the olden Faith that was a-breaking into fragments. This was the man,—"the just man" selected by the priests to lead to the Altar of Marriage Mary of the Temple.

The High Priest summoned her to his presence; and after prayer—for those old Hebrews believed—(and some of them with greater faith than many Christians) that prayer brought light from heaven in difficulties and doubts,—Mary was told of the decision of the Priests.

She made no dissent. She simply obeyed, for she, too, had her secret, and kept her own counsel.

And then they sent for Joseph to come to Jerusalem.

Any command that went to him from the Temple was as if it came from God. Down to the Holy-City he came; and they offered him the Virgin Mary for his bride. He heard their proposal,—nor did he seem surprised; and made the promise to take her into his keeping. Little did the priests of the Temple know what strange mysteries, from them hidden, they were touching. It is always so. Men,—and at times those who seem the most unlikely, work out God's secret designs. And God never had a more secret and mysterious design over any creature, than He had over Mary. Joseph had a part in that design,—though what and how great a part he did not know.

The Hebrew Prophets had foretold the Messiah's coming; and now the last of the Hebrew priests, unknown to themselves, are preparing His way. It was the law that the Hebrew maidens should be married from their father's house. Mary had no home but the House of God,—the Holy Temple. Hence, and is there not a mystery in it? her marriage with Joseph was celebrated in the Temple, the sacred house of the olden promise and later prophecies.

The day came at last. Accompanied by his and Mary's kinfolks Joseph went down to the Temple. The marriage canticles, with the accompaniment of many harps rang gladly through the holy place. Before one of the priests (many think Zachary the father of John the Baptist) stood Joseph and Mary. The priest lifted up his hands towards the heavens, and prayed over them; and then with the beautiful Hebrew ritual he united Joseph and Mary in the holiest marriage earth ever knew,—a marriage which was to veil with secrecy the purest mystery and the deepest of all time,—the conception and birth of Jesus Christ.

How near we sometimes are to God's mysterious works without knowing it! We almost touch Him when He is at His great works;—and we are unconscious of

His presence. He passes right before our eyes and we see Him not. Who, in that Temple, that day dreamed in looking on the face of Mary, of the Woman of Genesis. Yet there stood the Woman of Genesis, forty centuries old by promise, in the form of a maiden a little more than fourteen years of age. There stood the "Virgin" of Isaias' prophecy; there stood the living realization of all the predictions,—a pure, young girl, in the mystery of a human marriage which was to conceal a more mysterious marriage in her womb,—the espousals of human nature to divine nature in Jesus Christ, her Son.

Back in the eternal predestinations lay the strange vocation of Joseph. He was to be the Eternal Father's visible shadow on earth,—and like a shadow, he was to shroud, for a time, the earthly conception and birth of the Son of God; as the eternal generation of the same is hidden forever in the glory of the bosom of the Father. Holy Joseph! sacred shadow of God! "the virtue of the Most High will overshadow" Mary in the time of her Divine Conception; and thou shalt be the shadow to shield her honor and that of her Divine Offspring in the face of the world.

Sorrow is the sister of joy,—and they walk the world closer together than many think. For:

"Tears are the Vespers of Gladness,—
Life's Matin-Laudate scarce ends
Ere a psalm all a-thrilling with sadness
From the lips of the singer ascends."

The Temple was to lose its angel-child. How lonesome it would look without her! Ah! through all those eleven years, how she had grown to be almost a necessary part of the holy service! In a sense unknown to them, she was a necessary part. Somehow the Temple would not be the same. It would be as sad as a sky that loses its brightest star. Far brighter than the lights on the altars was the light in the temple of Mary's soul. Never mind! Temple! your child will come back, and bring before your altar the Light of the World! Tears in the eyes of the saintly widows,—tears in the eyes of the priests,—tears in the eyes of the young maidens,—when with her hand in Joseph's she passed through the gate of the Temple, and wept as many another bride has wept in leaving her father's house. Because she was perfect she was most human. Our nature lost the perfection of its humanity when it lost divine grace. Hence it is hard, rough, ungentle, untender. Its tears fall when they ought not to fall; and it does not weep when it ought to weep. As Christ was most human because He was divine; so His Mother was most human because she was perfect and sinless. So Mary mingled her tears with those of her companions in the Temple when the hour of her departure came.

The Temple's loss was Nazareth's gain. It was a journey of three days to Joseph's humble home. They left Jerusalem and pursued their way by the city of Naim,—along the valleys at the foot of Mount Hermoin, and by Mount Thabor. As was the custom, Joseph and Mary were met on their entrance into Nazareth, by young maidens who sang canticles of joy and praise to God. If the virtues of Joseph had won the reverence of Nazareth,—the singular beauty of Mary, at once, charmed the hearts of all.

And now began her life as St. Joseph's spouse. There is no mere make-believe in any of God's works. He may hide much back of what He does,—but what He does is always real.

So the marriage of Joseph and Mary was a real, true and valid marriage. The alliance was sincere on the part of both. They each had made a vow of perpetual virginity to God,—and their very marriage was a mutual contract for the preservation of their virginities. Mary knew, by inspiration, that it was not the will of God, and that it would never be the will of Joseph to cause detriment to her virginity. In marriage there are three goods, as theologians say,—Sacrament (a mystery), Fidelity and Offspring. But the last is not essential either to the reality or validity of marriage. How many holy marriages there are—sacramentally and in beautiful fidelities, which are not blessed with children? The absence of the child, by no means, disproves the reality of the marriage,—it simply shows the incompleteness of the alliance.

But in the marriage of Joseph and Mary there was to be, by miracle, not through Joseph, but through the Holy Spirit the most glorious offspring,—Jesus Christ. In the old law when the oldest son of a family died without issue, the second brother espoused the widow and to the first born child the name of his deceased brother was given; and this for the purpose of preserving the direct line of descent of the ancestors of the Messiah. But does it not seem that it was also by a great mystery?

Mark,—this law is accomplished to the very letter.

For St. Joseph espouses Mary,—and we can well say he dies without a child of his own, for the vow of virginity which he had taken was a beautiful, mysterious death, by which of his own will, he laid down the life of his body,—and became carnally dead. Then came the Holy Spirit treating Joseph as an elder brother dead, became the spouse of Mary, who else would be humanly childless,—and in her conceived Jesus Christ the Son of God whom Mary brought forth for our redemption.

To whom as His Father will Jesus Christ be attributed?

Not to the Holy Ghost, for He was not His Father, as He did not produce Christ out of His Divine substance. The glorious title will be and must be given to the Eternal Father alone together with Mary the true Mother. But in the world Jesus Christ will be called the Son of Joseph because He will be born of her who was Joseph's spouse. "Is He not the son of the carpenter:"—they said. Did not Mary His Mother, with deep mystery in her word, say to Christ: "Thy Father and I have sought Thee sorrowing?" Oh! glorious mystery, Joseph bears on earth to Christ the incommunicable name—Father!

Origen says that the Holy Spirit rendering Mary fruitful of Christ honored Joseph with the name of Father. Shadow-name!—sweet and beautiful cast on earth by the light of the substantial Name of the Eternal Father, concealing from men and demons the glorious mystery of the Incarnation, how Faith rests, and dreams, and prays and adores in thy presence,—as they of the Old Covenant did before the veil that hid the mysteries of the Holy of Holies.

Ah! the mysterious relations between Christ's reputed Father on earth and His real Father in Heaven! Who can describe or understand them? But between St. Joseph and the Holy Ghost there are also intimate relations. They were both spouses of Mary,—Joseph the visible and the Holy Spirit the invisible spouse. She was to bring forth a son who would be visible and invisible at the same time and always;—as man visible,—as God invisible;—and because her Son was to be visible and corporal, she had a visible and corporal spouse,—"the just man"—Joseph; and because her Son was to be invisible and purely spiritual in His Divine substance, she had an invisible and purely spiritual spouse,—the Holy Ghost.

And thus St. Joseph, like a sacred shadow, hides the Paternity of the Eternal Father,—conceals the Divine action of the Holy Ghost, invests Jesus Christ with a seeming human parentage;—and what else.

He stands before the world as Mary's necessary protector. Had she in the Temple been found with child;—or had she, out of the Temple, remaining in the eyes of the world a virgin, given birth to Jesus Christ,—think you they would take her at her word and believe her testimony? Think you when brought before the tribunal, where mercy hushed, and sternest justice gave decree, they would listen to her piteous cry: "Oh, no! my child is not of man,—it is born of the Holy Ghost! condemn me not to death?" No—no,—there was little of mercy in that law to which the Promise of Mercy gave all its meanings. They would have dragged her out of the gates of the Holy City,—to the great wide plain,—they would have taken up the stones of malediction to hurl them at the outcast; they would have cursed her, in the awful stoning, with the terrible curses of the Law,—until she fell dead before them; they would have branded her child Jesus with the dark ban of illegitimacy; and they would have regarded the greatest act of God's love as the darkest crime against the Law.

It was Joseph's vocation to be the shield of her honor, and the defender of her purity,—and to stand between her and the stones of curse. It was a mighty vocation,—but a mournful one. And besides, the Divine Conception of Christ and His miraculous birth needed a human witness, apart from the Mother; a witness of character unimpeachable,—of testimony which, perforce, must be taken and believed; and whose word stood higher, among priests and people, than the word of Joseph "the Just man?"

But he was so mild and gentle and silent. The gentlest are the bravest. What hidden forces are folded in the quiet, still cloud? On Calvary the gentle John was braver than all his co-Apostles. He stood by the cross, whence they fled. No wonder the dying Christ left His Mother in charge of such gentle bravery! Look on the quiet-faced water. What powers it conceals? Fire makes it brave and strong, and clothes it with an almost natural omnipotence; and then the great steamers cleave the waves, and brave the storms and sail across the seas; and then the long trains are borne over continents, by the gentle power of little drops of water, made strong by the furnace-fires in the locomotive. The gentlest Faith is always the most fearless. So Joseph stood between the Old Dispensation and the New Covenant to guard the honor of the Woman of the Promise, and to defend the Divine legitimacy of her Child, by standing before men in the position of His earthly father.

But more still! Listen. And let us pray! Oh adorable Bosom of the Father Eternal! Thou art the first Principle of the Blessing of all Thy creatures! We adore Thee with all the Faith of our hearts, for having given unto us Thy own, only Son with all His Divinity!

Oh Virginal Bosom of Mary! Purest Breasts of Virgin-Mother! we glorify thee, as the second principle of our Redemption, for having given unto us, the same Eternal Son, in His holy Humanity! And blessed hands of Joseph, we honor you as the third source of our Salvation, for did not thy hands labor and toil, day by day, and year on year to nourish and strengthen and bring to perfection the Humanity of our Saviour!

He is the Word of the Eternal Father, begotten without effort;—but thy toils and labors for thirty years, procuring His earthly food, did give strength to Him and preserve His human life

Only a year did He draw nourishment from Mary's breast;—and all the rest of His years His life while thou didst live, went on nourished by the fruit of thy daily toil!

And in Nazareth there was an earthly Trinity,—as in Heaven a Trinity Divine. In Heaven three invisible persons,—and one God. In Nazareth three visible persons,—and one God,—Jesus Christ.

Through Mary's Espousals with Joseph, he was brought into closer relations with the Trinity and with the history of Redemption than any other saint. He stood nearest to the source of all grace. He was the shadow that hid the source. His was the heart, which, next to Mary the Virgin Mother, drew from the source the deepest stream of grace.

No wonder, that in our day, St. Joseph has been proclaimed by the Church,—her universal Patron. For Mary the Mother of Christ her Son is, by right, the mother of the Church, the mystical Bride of her Son.

And as Joseph was the foster-father of Jesus Christ, because he was the Spouse of the Mother of Jesus, is, by right, the Foster-father of the universal Church. And thus over the Church St. Joseph is united with the Holy Spirit as they were united in regard to the Blessed Virgin.

Holy Joseph! there are sorrows still before you, but God will give you light and strength! And Virgin Mother! thou wilt bless thy children to-day who weave into thy Crown the mysterious Flower of thy Espousals!

ASPIRATION.

THE just shall flourish like a palm tree, he shall grow up like the cedar of Libanus, planted in the honor of the Lord,—in the courts of the house of our God. It is good to give praise to the Lord,—and to sing to Thy name O Most High!

PRAYER.

VOUCHSAFE, Oh Lord! that we may be helped by the merits of Thy most Holy Mother's Spouse: that what of ourselves we cannot obtain, may be given unto us through his intercession!

ELEVENTH DAY.

The Flower of the Annunciation.

"Hail, full of grace;—the Lord is with thee."

NAZARETH was a little city in lower Galilee, built on the slope of a rocky hill, faces the southeast and surrounded by mountains. There began the new life of Mary in marriage with Joseph,—a marriage uncarnal, consecrated by two virginities,—a marriage of the sinless soul to the holiest soul in all Judea,—a marriage of purest heart to a heart more pure than any other known of God or man.

Nazareth had a poor reputation in and around Jerusalem. Among the people there was a by-word: "Can any good come out of Nazareth?" In that city of the taunting by-word, Mary and Joseph were dwelling. And by and by out of that city was to come the Infinite Goodness Himself.

The Ark of the Covenant was constructed in the desert-solitudes. It was made of the incorruptible wood of the beautiful Acacia tree, and it was covered on all sides with plates of purest gold. Over the Ark stood two Cherubim, with their faces turned towards each other and their wings expanded and joined so as to cover the propitiatory, which was the place of the special presence of Jehova among His people. There was not only the mercy-seat,—but also the place of giving responses.

Joseph and Mary in their life at Nazareth were like the Cherubim, with their pure faces turned towards each other,—the wings of their virginities expanded,—and joined together to cover the great mystery of the Ark of the New Alliance. The Ark of the Covenant of shadows was no longer in existence. Solomon's grand Temple lasted only thirty-three years, when it was plundered by Sesoc, King of Egypt, who pillaged Jerusalem, and carried away all the treasures of the Temple. The Temple was finally burnt by Nabuchodonosor.

So the old Ark has passed away. Waiting in Nazareth like its Cherubim were Joseph and Mary for the coming of the Living Ark of this world's salvation.

From morning to night Joseph toiled in his shop adjoining his humble home. Patient,—and very silent and shy was he in his work-a-day life. When evening came and closed his labors, how often did he pass from his shop into the house, weary of heart and tired of hand, for the world drove hard bargains with the poor carpenter. For himself he cared not. Little or nothing would suit him;—but rough, poor food did not seem to him fitting nourishment for the young and tender Mary.

She, too, knew no hours of idleness. In the Temple she had been taught all the necessary and ornamental arts of labor peculiar to females. Young maidens and mothers would come to her to assist them in making their garments. Those gentle lips could not say—"No."

She would graciously lend them her labor; and many a mother's face brightened when the garment made by Mary's hands was brought home. She was the Angel of the little city, but no one ever dreamed that poor, little, wicked Nazareth was contained, among its three thousand inhabitants, the very Queen of the Angels.

What prayers of pure hearts blended and holy voices mingled went up from Joseph's home to God! The contact of saints makes each more saintly. The blending of two rays of light, gives each to the other, a greater brightness.

How long, oh! Lord! how long! the nations, by a strange universal instinct, are growing more expectant. Among all the nations,—a tradition is twined through their histories and poetries and religions, that a virgin would bring forth a great Saviour. In Rome, the Sibyls had written in their mystery-books that a God would be born of a spotless virgin.

Far in India it was taught that a pure ray of light would come from heaven, shine on a virgin—and in her produce a God.

In the wild woods of Gaul the Druid priests offered homage to the future virgin that would bring forth. And strange to say, about a hundred years before the birth of Christ, the Pontiff of the Carnati, a celtic tribe inhabiting the country between the river Loire and the Seine, in the presence of the druids, the kings and princes of the place, solemnly erected in a grotto of the sacred forest a statue of a Virgin holding in her lap a divine infant, who was to reign in peace over all the world. Thus the memory of the Woman of the Promise followed the race in all its wanderings from the Gates of Eden.

Gone were the chill winds of February and came the warmer breath of March. The heart of the Spring was beginning to beat under the grasses, and the trees and the flowers and the vines.

Spring is a virgin but soon becomes a mother. Already her new-born children were coming forth in their first, fresh beauty all around Nazareth. And the skies became brighter and the birds came back and sang with joy while they made their nests. It had been a hard winter with Joseph,—and he welcomed, with gladness in his heart, the birth of the fair sweet Spring, for it gave him more vigor and brought him more work.

The 25th day of March dawned. Sts. Chrysostom and Augustin tell us that it was a Friday;—in order that, as Adam was created on Friday, the sixth day, so on the same day of the week Mary might conceive the second Adam. St. Bernard says that it was early in the morning so that the Sun of Super-nature might begin to shine in the bosom of Mary together with the material sun in nature's sky. Joseph was working in his shop. In her chamber Mary was kneeling in prayer.

Pray on! thou sinless virgin. The sound of the hammer in Joseph's hand,—for he has much to do to-day, reaches thy ears but does not distract thy heart. It is beating to-day with a strange, new, higher, excessive, ecstatic love. How thy lips pant with the wondrous strength of thy prayer! Pray on, thou purest one;—for nor you, nor earth, nor heaven will ever forget this all-blessed day.

Up in the eternal Heavens there was rapture in the Angel-world. A new look of beauty never before seen had come into the Father's face,—and the Son wore it too and the Holy Spirit: only in the Father it was a look of Power and peace; and in the Son,—the while the angels marvelled,—it was the glorious look of a divine humility,—and in the Holy Ghost a look of preparation.

The angels had not forgotten how the Unchangeable seemed always to put on a look of change before all the great works He wrought outside of Himself. It was a mystery to them,—that seeming changefulness in the great Unchangeable.

But such a look as shone on them this day they had never seen before. And they fell down before the throne in the holy hush of worship;—for they knew that God was going to speak.

Gabriel, the Archangel of the Throne, whose name signifies the "Strength of God,"—and also as testifies one of the Bishops of the Council of Ephesus,—it means God and man,—the guardian Angel of Mary, is summoned before the Throne, and receives from God a commission which he must bring to Nazareth and deliver to Mary. Gabriel went. "Was there silence then a half-an-hour in Heaven?"

Suddenly a bright light shines around Mary and fills her humble apartment with glory. She lifts her eyes; and lo! Gabriel, her angel, appears before her in human form, radiant with the very light which he brought from the Throne.

One instance of glory's silence,—the while they heard the sound of the Carpenter's hammer in the shop,—and he saluted her:

"Hail, full of grace, the Lord is with thee; blessed art thou among women." Angels had communed with her before,—but never in words like those. "And she was troubled and wondered in her mind what manner of salutation this might be." What does it mean? rushed the troublous question over her soul.

"And the angel said to her: Fear not Mary; for thou hast found grace with God. And behold thou shalt conceive in thy womb, and bring forth a Son and thou shalt call His name Jesus. He shall be great and shall be called the Son of the Most High; and the Lord God shall give unto Him the throne of David his father; and He shall reign over the house of Jacob forever, and of His Kingdom there shall be no end." Did a great fear creep into her heart, the while the angel spake these words? Her virgin-vow rose pure and white before her. And she said: "How can this be because I know not man?" Then said the angel: "The Holy Ghost shall come upon thee; and the power of the Most High shall overshadow thee; therefore, also, the holy thing that shall be born of thee shall be called the Son of God." The very calm of God came down on her soul. Doubts and darknesses faded away. Ineffable light filled her whole being. Her heart was wrapped into highest ecstacy. The waves of God's wondrous love rolled under her feet and bore her out,—out—far and farther across the bright waters of Mercy's infinite sea,—and she walked its glorious waters, in the intense rapture of humility. She only said: "Behold the Handmaid of the Lord; be it done unto me according to thy word." And the angel departed from her. She listened a moment,—only the hammer of Joseph was heard as he still worked on,—unconscious of the great mystery announced to Mary and hidden so near him.

Is it not always so? God passes near us,—almost touches us, working the works of grace,—but in His coming and going He is so still that we know not of His presence till He has passed us by and gone.

Gabriel the ambassador of Mercy returned to the angel-land;—and never had heaven kept Feast of greater joy.

How wonderful are the divine ways. In Eden the

fallen angel of darkness, in serpent form, accosted Eve; and announced to her that if she and her companion would eat of the fruit of the forbidden tree, they would become as Gods. And she fell through pride.

In Nazareth an angel of light appears and announces to Mary that she has been chosen to become the mother of God. She hesitates on account of her vow of virginity. Her doubts removed by the angel's words,—she consents and rises to the highest dignity in all creation on the wings of the humblest words: "Behold the handmaid of the Lord." And, at once, the Holy Ghost came upon her; and the power of the Most High overshadowed her,—and in the pure substance of her sinless body, she conceived the sacred humanity of Jesus Christ.

"Hail full of Grace, the Lord is with thee, blessed art thou among women." The words are the salutation of the Eternal Father. And more, they imply a prayer sent by Him to Mary, through the angel, asking her consent to become the Mother of His Son on earth. Absolutely Mary could have refused. There was no coercion of her will. She was never more free than in that annunciation hour,—and no will ever rose to such glory of its freedom than hers when meeting the great, Free will of God, she seemed almost to share in its infinite Freedom when she gave consent to the mystery of Redemption in her person. The law of Promise began with the Woman of Genesis, whose seed was to be in everlasting enmity with the seed of the serpent.

The New Covenant begins historically with that Woman's name,—Mary of whom was to be born the Christ; and when she is fifteen years of age, Heaven salutes her: "Hail full of Grace;"—and she conceives the Christ. Hail full of grace! a salutation,—and a prayer given and made by the eternal Father. The eternal Son in human form, in after days will also give to the world a salutation—and a prayer,—" Our Father! who art in Heaven."

" Hail full of grace" preceded; and had to precede the "Our Father who art in Heaven." And why? Beyond the days of Mary and of Christ,—the race had no right to call God,—Father. It was obliged to wait until God's Son became the human brother of every one of the children of Adam. How did he become our brother? Because Mary was His human mother. The Fatherhood of our God, rests in our brotherhood with His Son, Jesus Christ,—and that brotherhood rests on the motherhood of Mary. You cannot separate one from the other. In eternity as in time they are forever and inseparably interlinked.

Who then will dare to blame the children of the eternal Father and the brothers of the eternal Son incarnate, when they salute on earth and from earth Mary who was first so saluted by Heaven. "Hail full of grace" was Heaven's first prayer and salutation to Mary. And who will challenge either our words or our motives, when, from hearts and lips we echo the salutation back to Heaven? Those first words,—the PRINCIPIUM of all the words of the New Covenant,—because they are the first words, will give the tone of their truth and the meaning of their divine melody to every single word that will ever fall from the lips of Christ.

Came the evening of the day. The tired Joseph entered the house. Did he mark the new look that had come into the face of Mary?

They sat side by side at their humble table and partook of their scanty evening meal. Joseph was too weary to hold much converse. Mary was mysteriously shy. She knew all,—and Joseph knew nothing. Down in her throbbing heart slept the great Mystery. What must she do? Speak and tell all? No,—no,—she is going to be the Mother of the Saviour;—and she must be like His Eternal Father. Her lips must be silent, while her heart hides the divine secret. They knelt and prayed together fervently and long. Then Joseph rose up and went to his own apartment and soon was sleeping a peaceful sleep. Mary lingered yet awhile; then retired to her small, humble room, with emotions that cannot be even conceived. For from the hour of the angel's visit,—and her consent, her inner life was ecstacy! And yet, withal, a shadow hung over her soul;—she began to feel a great fear of Joseph.

What would he do when the mystery would come to his knowledge? Would he send her away, by disbelieving her word? Ah! the terror that swept across her ecstacy! But she trusted in the Father of Him she had conceived;—and closed her eyes in holy rest.

O Mary holy Virgin! It was thy consent that brought us the Christ of our Salvation. We praise and glorify thee forever, as the hand maid, whose pure hand opened the gates between time and eternity,—between the finite and Infinite, to let the Redeemer enter the world!

Ah! holy Joseph! there are days of sorrow before thee. 'Tis always so. Wherever God passes a shadow falls. The anguish of doubt will come to thee. But the doubt will pass away;—and then will come long days and nights of sorrow and of suffering; but God will give thee strength, and Mary consolation.

Aspiration.

"Grace is poured abroad in thy lips. Therefore hath God blessed thee forever. Because of truth and meekness and justice; and thy right hand shall conduct thee wonderfully."—*Psalm*, xliv.

Prayer.

O God, who wast pleased that thy Word, at the message of an angel, should take flesh in the womb of the blessed Virgin Mary: grant to us thy suppliants, that we who believe her to be truly the Mother of God may be assisted by her intercessions with thee.

TWELFTH DAY.

The Flower of the Consent.

"Be it done unto me according to thy will."—*Luke*, 1.

THERE be those, (nor are they small in numbers, though they are exceeding small in knowledge) who ignorantly think, and as ignorantly teach, that the will of Mary had nothing to do with the great mystery of their salvation. To their mind (how shallow such mind must be?) the Virgin all-pure was only a tool in the hands of God,—a passive instrument to be employed for a great divine purpose,—and then to be flung aside, out of the way of Christ's works. They must have a singular idea of the honor of God's character,—and a low idea of the dignity of God's creatures, and more particularly of the glory of her who is the highest of pure creatures. Let them have their little notions. We have higher thoughts of God and therefore higher thoughts of all His creatures, for in our holy Church, we have "the mind of Christ,"—and we judge all things by the standards of truth divine.

God can say YES; and God can say NO,—and either word from His lips is infinite and immutable. We are made in His image and to His likeness. And we like Him can say *Yes;* and like Him can say *No.* Free will is the crown of His creatures.

And we can say *yes* or *no* even to God Himself,—but our *yes* or *no* is finite and changeable. In all God's worlds of created intelligences,—there is not,—nor can there be coercion.

Coercion is a chain; it means slavery and slaves. It is beneath God to accept enforced service. Worship forced from slaves would be ignominy to God. He never can belie or undo His creative act. In that act He gives every intelligence free will. Free will is a crown worn by the princes of God.

True,—many of them may desecrate the crown by laying it down at the feet of evil. But God is not going to interfere by coercion. He will never press the weight of His omnipotent will on the crowns we wear and thus force us to wear them whether we will or no. His way is to let us have our own way as well as our own will; and His way is best.

He reveals His will to us in laws; He reveals His love to us in graces,—He reveals His mind to us in truth,—and He reveals Himself to us in Jesus Christ the Son of Mary. His laws we may keep or break; His love we may preserve or lose; His truths we may believe or deny; and Himself we may accept or reject. For "our worship must be reasonable,"—and to be so,—it must be free; for ours is "the freedom of the children of God." Such is our high inheritance. Our will must be guided,—not destroyed; strengthened, not broken; persuaded, not coerced. There are so-called churches that teach and preach a cruel, heartless God; that coolly tell God's creatures that many of them have been made by Him to give Him the exquisite happiness of sending them to hell. They tell us that such are doomed from all eternity. Shame on such teachings!

Does the beautiful God exult in the foreordained horrors of His creatures? Then strike out the word Hope from religion;—then efface the word Penance from the pages of Scriptures and the hearts of men. Then change the very name of God;—infinite name signifying GOOD; and write on the gates of Heaven in black, merciless letters:—CRUEL, HEARTLESS, WICKED. Let such be the name of such a God. But away with such blasphemies. We will keep our own God,—and His Christ and His Mother, and His lovingness and His mercy and His tenderness and His infinite pity;—the God of the Infinite, beautiful Heart.

Yes,—and the God-Christ with His human heart that can and does compassionate all our miseries. Who gave the Son of God the gift of a human heart? Mary. Was she forced to give it? Will God accept a forced gift? Never,—for it would be no gift at all. Her free and willing consent was the cause of the creation of that heart in her womb, by the Holy Ghost. Without her consent that heart would never have beat or bled here below.

Was the Son of God forced by the Father to become the Son of Man? Who will sustain such blasphemy? Was Mary forced by the Father to become the Mother of His Son on earth, the Christ? He was free and willing to become her Son,—and she was willing and free to become His Mother. God never made an act more grandly free than the decree of the Incarnation;—and never creature made an act of higher freedom than Mary when in the words which are tremulous with humility she answered the angel: "Behold the handmaid of the Lord." But listen to the firm and powerful words of her consent: "Be it done unto me according to thy word." Is she borrowing the strength of the olden word of the Eternal? "FIAT"—"Let it be done."

The consent sounds like a command. The FIAT of God gave being only to creatures. The FIAT of Mary gives human being and life to God Himself who is infinitely above all creatures. The Fiat of God produced His work out of nothing, the lowest origin that can be. The FIAT of Mary brought her work out of the very bosom of God,—the highest source imaginable. The FIAT of God added nothing to His infinite grandeurs and perfections. The FIAT of Mary as soon as pronounced lifted her up to the supreme dignity of the Mother of the Infinite and clothed her round with all the glorious prerogatives of that incomparable position. The FIAT of God gave Him empire only over creatures who are as nothing in His presence. The FIAT of Mary gave Him dominion over His other Self—His Son in human form.

The FIAT of Mary made His Son God's, inferior in His humanity; and caused to be given to God, in creation, what else He never would have received, an infinite worship.

Thus our race, through the Son of Mary, gives infinite glory to God. The consent of Mary to be the Mother of Jesus, freely asked and freely given, crowns the Finite with an infinite crown.

God's omnipotent power can reach forth no farther. The illimitable touches its limit in Mary. No creature can rise higher. The limited has ascended into the Illimitable.

Mary's pure bosom touches the eternal bosom of the Father. It participates in that Infinite fruitfulness out of which the Eternal Son, the Father's other Self in substance, though in person different,—and produces not by human and natural fecundity, but by power divine, Jesus Christ. Out of the Father's bosom the Son comes the Creator-God.

In Mary's womb the Son is conceived,—the Saviour-God. The Father has but one Son;—and the same becomes Mary's;—and through birth from her He will have innumerable brothers by the adoption of grace,—and the roll of the names of them, who become His brothers, and adopted sons of His Father, will reach down to the end of time.

But who can describe all the other mysteries that rose to reign forever on earth and in heaven, out of the consent of Mary?

Nor man,—nor angel,—nor Mary herself.

What a miracle of loving Power and powerful Love!

The Infinite is compassed by and contained in the finite!

The Eternal is going to lead a new life and reckon its length by days of time. The frail body of a virgin maiden bears up the infinite weight of God. "God chooses the weak to confound the strong."

And above all in Mary we have the truest, clearest, fullest, tenderest revelation of the beautifulness of God.

But how can it be? She herself asked the angel the puzzling question.

He only said: "With God nothing shall be impossible;"—answer clear and plain and convincing enough for Faith.

Last night I walked down on the beach to listen to the songs of the sea. Each wave sang a song of its own. I lifted my gaze to the skies, and thousands of stars shown into my upturned eyes. The immense bright, far-off worlds all—all contracted themselves and came down along the innumerable paths of their silvery rays,—and each had its place in my eyes, without losing their brightness or grandeur at all. And I thought again how nature is all the time showing us the ways of the beautiful Supernature. If my eyes can reach and compass and contain in their little circle the bright immensities of the Heavens;—why cannot the grandeurs of the Divinity be contained in the sacred Humanity hidden yet away in the bosom of the Immaculate Mary? The winds had lulled and I looked away over the waves again that were falling asleep; and I wondered how the frail white shore,—only weak sand,—can clasp in its arms the strong and mighty sea and hold it there in its gentle embrace.

And I came to my room where I live with my books; and I began to muse how all the literatures of earth blossom like flowers varied and innumerable out of the few letters of the Alphabet.

And I went over to the piano, to sing a hymn in honor of holy Mary, and I wondered again how all the melodies of music rest on only seven notes. And I thought again, as often before, how in the nature that surrounds and in its works we find so many beautiful types and striking counterparts of the wonders of God's grace in the realms of revelation.

Only greatness can make itself little without losing its dignity. Each drop of water in the sea sleeping out there shrines the light of a thousand stars.

So Mary consenting, shrined in her conception all the uncreated splendors of the Divinity.

Deep as her life had been before it grew deeper day by day.

She was leading, in a far-off way, the life of the Father of Eternity eternally conceiving and begetting His only Son.

After awhile she will bring Him forth. But ah! Pure Virgin! before the Midnight of Christmas, fear will come to you and trouble will encompass you! It is the mystery of this world. It is the law of the Incarnation.

They, who are loved most by God, must suffer most.

But thy soul will rest, like a troubled child on the breast of its mother, in the sweet will of the Eternal Father

ASPIRATION.

"THE rod of Jesse hath blossomed. A Virgin hath brought forth God and man. God hath given peace, reconciling the lowest with the highest in Himself."—*Missal.*

PRAYER.

STRENGTHEN, O Lord, in our minds, we beseech thee, the mysteries of the true faith; that we who confess him was conceived of a virgin to be true God and man, may, by the power of his saving resurrection, deserve to arrive at eternal joy.

THIRTEENTH DAY.

The Flower of the Visitation.

"Arise my love, my beautiful one: and come; my dove in the clifts of the rock, in the hollow places of the wall, show me thy face; let thy voice sound in my ears,—for thy voice is sweet."—*Cant.*, ii.

WHERE the little city of Hebron nestles amid the mountains of Judea there was a holy and a happy home. Zachary an aged priest had long lived there with Elizabeth his holy wife. She was a cousin of Mary of Nazareth. One day Zachary was burning incense in the Temple, while, as was the law, the people were praying without. "And there appeared to him an angel of the Lord standing on the right side of the altar of incense. And when Zachary saw him, he was troubled and fear fell upon him. But the angel said unto him: Fear not Zachary, for thy prayer is heard, and thy wife Elizabeth will bear thee a son and thou shalt call his name John. And thou shalt have joy and gladness; and many shall rejoice at his birth. For he shall be great in the sight of the Lord; and he shall be filled with the Holy Ghost even from his mother's womb." And Zachary said unto the angel: How shall I know this? For I am an old man and my wife is well stricken in years. And the angel answering, said unto him: "I am Gabriel who stand in the presence of God, and am sent to speak unto thee and to show thee these glad tidings. And behold thou shalt be dumb until the day that these things shall be performed, because thou hast not believed my words, which shall be fulfilled in their season."

The people were waiting and had wondered much why he tarried so long in the Temple.

When he came out he could not speak, but only made a sign and then they knew that he had seen a vision in the temple. "And after those days his wife Elizabeth conceived."

Long had they prayed that God would bless them with offspring; and at last their prayer is granted.

But Zachary is speechless. He has lost his voice. How strange, that his child, when he faces the world thirty years afterwards, and when asked who he is, will answer "I am a voice crying in the wilderness."

To that home in the hill-country went Mary of Nazareth; and Scripture tells us that she went in haste.

From Nazareth to Jerusalem it was a long three days' journey. She passed by the Mount of Transfiguration. She passed by Calvary to reach the Holy City bearing the unborn victim. When she saw in the distance or near (or did she cross them?) its dark gray rocks, did their shadows give to her soul the light of presentiments? Or was it more than mere presentiment? Who knows?

The young virgin mother hastens to meet the aged mother.

The one bears the unborn Christ,—the other, His unborn precursor. The aged Elizabeth is the image of the Old Law passing away, which did not produce grace, but only promised and waited for it. Mary represents the New Law,—young and never to grow old, virginally fruitful of sanctity and abounding in ageless grace. The younger hastens to visit the older that truth may meet the Figure 'ere it passes away,—that Substance may face the Shadow, and bless it 'ere it goes. And as Mary's presence, in after days, at the wedding-feast in Cana will be the means of eliciting from Christ the first Manifestation of His glory and the first Miracle of the New Law;—so her going with her unborn Child to Zachary's home brings the last manifestation and the last miracle of the spiritual life of the Old Law in the presanctification of John the Baptist.

She brought Christ into the world (hidden as yet) and now she brings Him to meet (hidden as Himself) and to bless His great Precursor.

What a meeting it must have been between two such mothers of two such children? There will never be such a meeting in this world again.

But let St. Luke describe it.

She entered the house of Zachary, and saluted Elizabeth. "And it came to pass that when Elizabeth heard the salutation of Mary; the infant leaped in her womb, and Elizabeth was filled with the Holy Ghost. And she spoke with a loud voice and said : 'Blessed art thou among women, and blessed is the fruit of thy womb; and whence is this to me that the Mother of my Lord should come to me? For lo! as soon as the voice of thy salutation sounded in my ears, the babe leaped in my womb for joy. And blessed art thou that hast believed, for all these things shall be accomplished which were told thee from the Lord.'"

Listen!—At the sound of the voice of Mary, Elizabeth is filled with the Holy Ghost. Whose voice like her's save Christ's? And that voice is stronger now than ever.

Up in yonder heaven, this peaceful evening, (for there

is a lull in the winds and a holy hush out there on the waves of the gulf.) (I wonder do they know that I am trying to praise the Queen of Heaven and Star of the Sea?) Mary's voice is the sweetest music in the ears of God, and the mighty power of grace for us.

Oh voice above all voices, save the voice of Him who was and is thine forever, plead with the Father for us.

Thy voice has the tones of the voice of His Eternal Son,—and the Father loves to hear them.

Sweeter than all the voices of the angels in melody,—and next to the very voice of God in might!

"Blessed art thou among women" came from the lips of her cousin;—the very words of Gabriel to herself. Zachary stood by the mystery, speechless; as Joseph stood by the greater mystery, silent. Elizabeth, the mother of the Precursor, "filled with the Holy Ghost," is the first after the Archangel Gabriel to give public testimony of an honor above all honors, saving that due to God alone, to the Blessed Virgin Mary. Was she wrong? Was it too much or too great? But,—she was filled with the Holy Ghost. She spoke with His inspiration. It was the Holy Ghost speaking through her aged lips.

Thus Christ and the Precursor met,—and they met through their mothers. Wondrous mystery! too deep in the least of its meanings for any lips to tell, save Mary's.

So let us be still while Mary sings the first and grandest *Te Deum* of Redemption

MAGNIFICAT.

My soul doth magnify the Lord,
And my spirit hath rejoiced in God my Saviour.

Because He hath regarded the humility of His handmaid: for behold from henceforth all generations shall call me blessed.

For He that is mighty hath done great things to me, and holy is His name,

And His mercy is from generation to generation to them that fear Him.

He hath showed might in His arm; He hath scattered the proud in the conceit of their heart.

He hath put down the mighty from their seat; and hath exalted the humble.

He hath filled the hungry with good things; and the rich He hath sent empty away.

He hath received Israel His servant; being mindful of His mercy.

As He spoke to our fathers; to Abraham and to his seed forever.

Thus Mary, in the "ecstacy of humility," chants the first Christian psalm. It was her royal right as queen of her Son's Kingdom. There is no song on key as lofty in all Scripture. It lives an everlasting life in the Vespers of Holy Church. No wonder when it is entoned the people rise to honor its every syllable.

No wonder that in Solemn Vespers, the altar is incensed; for the closed tabernacle contains the very Holy One who was then hidden in her womb.

'Tis a song enshrining all the grandeurs of God, for it contains and expresses the greatest things which God has done in time and eternity, in Heaven and on earth, for His own glory and the happiness of His children. It was the grand human echo of the music of divine mercy then silent in her bosom. For the unborn Child in tones unheard sang the *Magnificat* with His Mother.

The first announcement that the Messiah had come was by His Mother's song.

She remained with her cousin until the Child was born. In her own arms she held Him, Who thirty years afterwards will baptize her own Son. And the Precursor of her child nestled on her bosom.

Eight days afterwards they came to circumcise the Child. Then the speechless Zachary opened his long-closed lips in sudden song.

The harmonies of grace broken by the discord of sin are coming back to earth. Zachary sings his BENEDICTUS. But Mary's *Magnificat* had already entoned the first notes of the eternal hymn of divine Mercy.

Ah me! discords still will come to mar the beauty of the holy hymn. But Mary's voice is ever ready, sweet and tender, if only we plead with her, to bring, by its own power, our voices, our hearts and our lives into the harmony of the eternal hymn again.

ASPIRATION.

"BLESSED art thou among women, and blessed is the fruit of thy womb! And whence is this to me, that the Mother of my Lord should come to me?"—*Luke* i, 42.

PRAYER.

VOUCHSAFE, Lord, we beseech thee, to us thy servants the gift of thy heavenly grace; that as in the childbirth of the blessed Virgin our salvation began, so from the votive solemnity of her Visitation we may obtain an increase of peace.

FOURTEENTH DAY.

The Flower of the Fear.

"Fear not, Mary, for thou hast found grace with God."—Luke, i.

ALL the Feasts of the Old Covenant were historical and memorial. There was not a single day set apart in honor of a divine Truth. The very Sabbath was more a memorial-day of God's rest, than a reminder of His Nature and attributes.

The Pasch, Pentecost, Feast of Tabernacles and others were merely commemorative of the great facts of Hebrew history. But while those festivals borrowed their meanings from the past, they were shadows of a great coming Future. The Feast of Expiation, the only day in the year, when the white-robed High Priest entered the Holy of Holies merely represented the sinfulness of the people, and typically foreshadowed the day of Redemption.

Not so the Feasts of the New Dispensation. The living truth in the beautiful variety and the more beautiful harmony of Dogmas is their primary object,—commemoration is but secondary. What was typical in the Old Law is mystical in the New. For the New Law is an ever present Life,—that of the ever-living Christ. We have, of course, seven signs or symbols called Sacraments; but they are more than signs, they are the supernatural activities of the divine life of Christ in the Church made present and sensible. The old Hebrew Church was a Shadow-Church. Ours is the Church of the divine Substance. The priests and people of the old Dispensation, generally, kept their Shadow-Feasts with wonderful strictness and fidelity, wherein, they have left an example which many Christians would honor themselves by following.

Joseph, always attentive to the strictest observance of the Law, never failed to go down to Jerusalem and to assist with fervor at the services on the great Feasts.

And, always, poor though he was, would he bring his humble offerings to the Temple. The journey was too long for Mary, and besides, to some of the Festivals the Hebrew women were not obliged, by the law, to go. And, further, in most of the towns of Judea there were synagogues which stood instead of the Temple.

So after that 25th of March Joseph went down to celebrate, at least, the latter days of the Paschal Festival. And Mary was left alone,—with her mysterious secret. Joseph's absence, for a single day, was wont to make her sorrowful; but now a change had come over her soul, and the pain of parting was not so great. Not that her pure love for him had diminished. Contrariwise it had increased; but a love of all loves deepest was filling the Virgin-heart:—a mother's love for an unborn Child,—and it,—her very God. Joseph returned from the Feast of the Pasch. Closer and closer together grew their hearts. Mary prayed,—and Joseph marked it,—more frequently and with a fervor that looked like rapture. And in the long-evenings she would ask him to read the old Scriptures and its strange prophecies about the Messiah.

He was a man learned in the Law; and while his outer life was a life of daily toil that seemed scarcely in keeping with much or deep thought:—he, nevertheless, in unknown, inner life, lived more with the great prophets of the past than in the noisy discussions of the present teachers of the Law. How could the Emmanuel be conceived by a Virgin,—and how could a virgin bring Him forth,—as Isaias had predicted;—she would oftimes ask Joseph. She knew the secret. She was hiding it in her heart. Was she trying him by her questions? Was she striving to reach his inner thought? Was she thinking of the day when the mystery, in herself, would be manifested?

Joseph would listen,—and ponder long in silence, as he had done a thousand times before, but he could not solve the mysterious Prophecy.

Did she ever answer him;—or did he ever say to her: "Nothing shall be impossible with God." And, all the while, a great fear like a shadow that folds the hill, was creeping around her heart.

Again Joseph was obliged to go down to the Holy-City for the Feast of Pentecost. Jerusalem, like all other cities, either Hebrew or Christian, when external ordinances are of more importance than interior piety, was gossippy, talkative, curious, questioning. It busied itself about everybody. It had not forgotten the day of the Espousals of the best Hebrew of their race to its most beautiful Maiden. And they would ask Joseph about Mary. His answers were as brief as they were gently given. The High-priest and the priests would express their hopes that God would bless Mary with offspring. No word,—spake he then,—save perhaps: "God's will is best." For none there knew of his vow of virginity. He was the most secret and silent saint that ever lived in this world of vain and useless and commonplace chatter. Home he came again. Up the long, narrow street that led to his dwelling and his shop he walked;—but Mary met him on the humble threshold,—in sooth more like a child and daughter than a woman and his spouse. Did he mark it? She was becoming more like a child day by day? Or were his eyes veiled yet for awhile. May with its flowers,—the angels of the valley passed. June came with her splendors of earth and sky, and the birds were singing vesper-songs up in the bitter-sweet almond-trees,—when:—

Hush and listen. All-day long Joseph had been working in his shop. He was very tired. All day long Mary had been praying in her humble room.

Had she a presentiment. All day long a great fear was folding darkest shadows around her soul;—and she was heart-tired.

Joseph entered. She rose to meet him. Ah! the look that swept like a cloud across his face! Ah! the storm that rushed over her soul!

It was a minute with infinite sorrow in it for both.

In his face suspicion. In her heart terror. In his eyes an awful doubt. On her face the white pallor of an indescribable pain.

His eyes could not deceive him. The hidden mystery stood manifested before him. She was going to be a mother. The signs were there. Has she broken her vow? If not the purest virgin, she must be the vilest outcast. Men are more suspicious than women,—and though he was a saint Joseph was a man,—with a man's temperament.

But to be suspected of sin in that which was the very mystery of sanctity was a blow that fell heavy on her heart;—but to be suspected by him, her husband according to the law, almost broke her heart. If he puts her away; if he denounces her, her unborn Child, who is the Blessing of the world, will bear the brand of an eternal curse. The haunting doubt that lurked in the eyes of Joseph;—his voice that hesitated when he spoke to her; his manner so gentle and simple that now put on a strange constraint;—his cold silence; but above all that look that seemed to mar the very sanctity of his face, filled the soul of Mary with all the terrors of a great overmastering fear. If he only asked a question,— but his lips were sealed. If she could only tell the secret,—but she dare not lift the lid of Mystery. Ah! Mary! before your child has appeared, you begin to live his life. His own people will doubt, and deny His divinity, and crucify Him. Joseph has doubts of your virginity, which is to you, what Divinity is to your unborn Child. His own people will lead Him to crucifixion;—your own Spouse crucifies you on the cross of his doubt. His own people will know not what they do. Did he not pray it: "Forgive them Father, for they know not what they do." Your own Joseph knoweth not what he is doing.

Go to rest, if rest you can to-night, virgin of sorrow, but around thy heart the very hand of Joseph has woven, by his suspicion, a crown of thorns. So they, his people, will weave another for the brow of your Son, and they will look upon Him on Calvary as Joseph, not knowing all, looks upon you to-night,—as a malefactor! Oh! the wondrous silences of God! Why does He not speak just one word in Nazareth? Why does not Gabriel come right down to Joseph, and rebuke him for his doubt? Why does he not descend again to Mary and bring her consolation and give her hope? Let God alone.

THE FLOWER OF THE FEAR. 133

Let Mary suffer all the anguish of fear. Let Joseph suffer all the pangs of doubt. Sorrow like theirs is the shadow of God coming nearer and nearer.

Wait till its darkest folds encircle them. The shadow over the Holy of Holies betokened God's invisible Presence. Such sorrow as theirs is the Holy of Holies that hides the nearest Presence of God.

Next day came. They prayed apart. A wall of separation divided their souls. Joseph went to his shop and worked on in a weary way. Tears were sleeping in eyes; pain was gnawing at his heart. He was standing beneath a great dark cloud. All day long his thoughts were tortures.

What should he do? Denounce Mary? And his ears began to listen to the awful sounds of the cruel stones that would slay his child-spouse. For what else was she but a child? Would he lay his sorrow before the priests of the Temple? Ah! no! Mary was the child of the Temple,—the very angel of Jerusalem. And how the infamy would spread through Judea.

What should he do? What else but pray,—and perhaps some light would come from Heaven. Or, he thought:—"I will put her away privately."

And Mary? It was her hour of agony. If an angel came to Gethsemane in years long after to comfort her Christ; did an angel come to her that day to brighten the darkness around her?

All day long she prayed;—and sorrow gave swift wings to her prayers.

Her heart was whelmed in a sea of grief dark and deep and stormful, but far over the waters,—walking them as her Son will walk the waves of Galilee hereafter,—came the beautiful feet of Peace;—not to her, first, but to Joseph in his sleep.

"Yes,—I will put her away privately." "No one will know of it but my own heart." Came the awful rush of sorrow's torrents through his soul. He prayed and wept himself to sleep. "And behold the angel of the Lord" (was it Gabriel?) appeared to him in his sleep, saying: "Joseph, Son of David, fear not to take unto thee Mary thy wife, for that which is conceived in her, is of the Holy Ghost. And she shall bring forth a son, and thou shalt call His name Jesus; for He shall save His people from their sins."

It was in the first watches of the night. Mary was praying for sleep had fled from her eyes. Came a call,— and Joseph's voice: "Mary!" Never had she been called at such a time and in such a tone before. She went out to meet him. His face was her salutation. The glory of honor and the rapture of adoration blended in his looks. Did he kneel at her feet to adore the "Word made Flesh" tabernacled in her? Yes,—and if she was the first, he was the second Christian. No need of words! Did he try to frame his mistaken doubt in words?

Did they kneel down, and with hearts and voices blended, more closely now than ever, adore together the Word Incarnate?

Ah Joseph! you said in your thoughts: "The fruit of her womb is not my child." The world will call him so; and, with the glory of a divine revenge, Mary, whom you doubted, the child of the Temple, will cry aloud in the Temple, with the same gladness, after sorrow, felt by you, in presence of the doctors of the law and the priests: "Son why hast thou done so to us.

Do you not know that thy Father and I have sought thee sorrowing three days?"

Next day came. And now two know the mystery of the Incarnation: Mary the Mother that is to be, the purest of the pure in Judea; and Joseph the foster-father that is to be,—the most just man in Israel.

"In the mouth of two witnesses every word shall stand." In the testimony of Mary and Joseph the eternal Word will stand in the glory of His truth. For the rest of the world was the expectation of the Messiah.

To Mary and Joseph He was already come. They had and hid His Presence. In after days His priests, sharing the power of Mary His Mother, and the prerogatives of Joseph His foster-father, will mystically yet really conceive Him, by the words of Consecration, on the altar;—and like Joseph His foster-father, will keep care for Him in the tabernacle; and when, needs be, will carry Him into the Egyptian darkness of the dying. Oh! Mary! thou art called our sweet Hope and our Peace, but thou hast become so unto us, by the agony of thy great Fear. For Hope wears the sandals of fear.

We praise thee and bless thee in the clouds of thy sorrow as in the brightness of thy glory! In our fears, —and ah! how many they are; send our angels to us, as came the angel to Joseph, and let hope and holy peace dispel the darkness and bring us the light of earthly and eternal rest!

ASPIRATION.

"I WILL not fear thousands of the people surrounding me. Arise, oh Lord! Save me, oh my God."—*Psalm*, iii.

Prayer.

Pour forth, we beseech thee, O Lord, thy grace into our hearts: that we, to whom the incarnation of Christ thy Son was made known by the message of an angel, may by His passion and cross be brought to the glory of His resurrection.

FIFTEENTH DAY.

The Flower of the Flight.

"Arise, and take the child and His mother and fly into Egpyt, and be there until I shall tell thee."—*Math.*, ii.

In Jerusalem Herod had heard from the wise men of the birth of the new-born King. He feared a rival. He had waited for the return of the men who had come from the East,—but he waited in vain. They had been admonished to return by a different way to their own countries. Jealousy is always cruel,—sometimes savage. Many children had been born in and around Bethlehem about the time of the birth of Christ. Baffled in his desire to discover the new-born King he would not be baulked in his design to destroy him. Jealousy like his has patience to wait. He kept his secret. "I will slay all the children in Bethlehem and the coasts thereof, from two years of age and under," he said in his wicked heart. He bided his time. "I will send my soldiers to do the work," he said to himself. The day had not yet come; but an angel had come to Joseph in sleep and bade him to take the child and his mother and to go down into Egypt. In the night time he rose and took the child and his mother,—and hurried out towards the deserts.

The day of massacre came. Brutal soldiers tore the little children from their mothers' arms and heedless of their wild wailings and hardened against the innocent, pleading faces of the poor infants put them mercilessly to death.

The law of sacrifice the shedding of the blood of Innocence began thus in the New Kingdom. The little King of Sacrifice is hurrying out to the great, bleak deserts,—driven from his home into exile. Joseph bears the frail burden, and carries his God. Mary, her heart overwhelmed with fear, startled by every sound, walks beside the foster father of her child. They are going to Egypt. The way is long and lone and drear. But God gives strength to all who fulfill His great designs. Day by day they traveled on. Across those same deserts from Egypt to Judea had come the Hebrews. In these deserts the Covenant had been made with them by the Lord. In those same deserts, in the first ages of the Church will live anchorites and monks without number,—exiles from the world where the child Christ passed an exile from His own Judea.

Full of memories of the old dispensation and full of memories of the new dispensation are those bleak deserts.

Amid those wildernesses will live men of loftiest lives. No wonder. Christ passed over them; and where He passes grace blossoms into beautiful virtues. In the night the sands of the deserts was their resting-place. Dangers lurked along all their way,—but there are no guardians like the angels. Day followed day and night followed night,—and still on traveled the three exiles to the land of Idolatry. In Egypt they worshipped the sun; and now the Sun of Justice in the wondrous eclipse of a Child's form is about to rise above the horizon of that land.

Hunger and thirst they often suffered. Did angels bring them manna? Their passage across the desert is as silent as the desert itself. Tradition tells us of lofty trees that bent down to give them shade and shelter; and that when they entered Egypt many idols fell in the temples. At last they reached the "land of bondage;—and dwelt in or near Heliopolis. How long they remained in exile we do not know. Joseph the Carpenter worked at his trade procuring daily bread for the Child-God and His Mother.

Meanwhile the Child grew apace and Mary and Joseph rose higher and higher in Sanctity. What sufferings and privations they must have endured? What sorrow was theirs to live under the dark shadow of heathenism! He came unto His own and His own drove Him away. And now He hides in the home of idols. How strangely the first years of Christ are passing! But His Mother is with Him. Mother and Child together,—you cannot separate them without contradicting the closeness of their lives. What mighty adorations of the true God in Child-form came out of the hearts of Mary and Joseph in the land where the very memory and name of the true God had been lost! How the Flower of the Flight bloomed into wonderful spiritual beauties; and all in shadow and in sorrow.

Poor Egypt knew not the glory hidden near the banks of the Nile. How God does hide Himself, and for so long before He makes a sign of His presence and His power! Men are forward whose God is shy. Men are loud and proud whose God is still and humble.

Far away in Jerusalem, if Simeon were still living what must have been his thoughts?

Did he miss the Mother and the Child? Was he waiting for another glimpse of them to bless his eyes? In the Temple regular was the course and order of sacrifice and ceremony. Daily on the altars came and went the shadows typical of the Messias; while the shadow of the Child-Christ, already come and gone for awhile away was reflected on the waters of the Nile.

What spiritual work unknown to the Egyptians was the Christ doing in their land? From the first instant of His birth He was working His Father's will though not in a manifest way. And Mary!—did not virtue go out from her silently yet none the less really in that strange land?

Stars that are never seen are doing silent work all the while in this world of ours. The trees and flowers and fruits and seas know it and feel it. So in Egypt, Jesus, Mary and Joseph were, though hidden, doing wondrous work that will never be known.

Herod died and to Joseph came from heaven thro' an angel a message to return to Judea.

Obscure persons,—the Holy Family was not noticed when they entered Egypt, nor were they missed when they left the place of their exile. Baronius thinks that the flight into Egypt took place in Christ's first year and that He returned when He was nine years of age. Back across the deserts they came again,—enduring privations of hunger and hardship, of weary travel and thirst and of dangers of every kind. The tender feet of Christ are blistered by the scorching sands and for Him to suffer so was a part of the Martyrdom of His Mother; and Joseph suffered, as shall never be known in the charge which was his burden as well as his glory. How few ever travel in spirit those dreary wildernesses! Ah! blessed sands consecrated by the feet of Mary and Jesus and Joseph;—made holy by the passage of Holiness—cry out to the world the mystery of hate that banished them from home, and the mystery of love that brought them back to Nazareth, where Joseph was to sink to rest after a little while, and where Mary was to watch over her child and our Saviour until the day of His manifestation when again human hate would face Divine Law and pursue and persecute the Christ until He would reach the cross on Calvary,—where He would be found with His Mother standing beside Him!

Hate exiled Him. Love brought Him back. Sin, which is hate, exiles us from God. Love brings us back to the Nazareth of grace where, side by side, we find Jesus and His Mother. Mary brought Him back; and ah! is she not forever and ever bringing us back to Him. Let us then fly to her protection and call on her name,— exiles as we are in this valley of tears and she, who brought Him to Nazareth for us, will bring us to His house of grace and to His home of glory in heaven.

ASPIRATION.

"From Egypt have I called thee."

PRAYER.

O God, who wast pleased that thy Word, at the message of an angel, should take flesh in the womb of the blessed Virgin Mary: grant to us thy suppliants, that we who believe her to be truly the Mother of God may be assisted by her intercessions with thee.

SIXTEENTH DAY.

The Flower of the Midnight of Mercy.

"Glory be to God in the highest and peace on earth to men of good will."—*Luke*, ii.

Down in Brazil there is a flower of rarest beauty which blooms only at midnight. It is found far in the heart of the great silent forests. The sun passes over its close-shut leaves in the day;—but when night comes they open and the forests are filled with its sweet perfume.

"The stars were in the middle of their courses:" it was the noon of night. A hush fell around a stable outside of Bethlehem,—like the deep silence that comes over the people in the temple a little while before the moment of the Consecration in the Mass:—For the Holy of Holies was about to enter His creation in visible form. Nine months He had been in it,—but hidden. Joseph and Mary had been obliged to go to Bethlehem to be enrolled, because they belonged to the house and family of David. The order had come from Rome. How many another order will go forth to the world from Christian Rome? So to Bethlehem they came. Up and down the narrow streets they had gone in the closing of the day seeking a shelter for the coming night. But in the city of their royal ancestors there was no place for them in the inn. "He came unto His own and His own received Him not."

Mary's heart sank within her because she knew that His and her hour was nigh. Out towards the cold, bleak plains they went,—plains which were the property of the Temple where the animals to be used in sacrifices were kept and fed by herdsmen and shepherds.

They reached a rude stable hollowed in the rock. They entered. A few animals were there that gazed in mute wonder at the intruders. He was to be born outside of the city of His ancestors. He was to die outside of the city of the Temple. The night grew on apace. All was still. The world slept while the great Waker was coming. Ah! there was wonder in the hearts of the angels that night. They breathlessly awaited the mystery to become visible. Suddenly as a flower exhales its perfumes;—stilly and painlessly as the ray reflects its light, the Virgin brought forth the Word Incarnate; and wrapped the infant God in swaddling clothes and laid Him in a manger. Ah! her rapture as she gazed on the little face! A mother's love and a creature's adoration met in her heart and were blended, in her first look upon the infant. The mother's familiarity and the creature's awful reverence met the mystery. And Joseph fell prostrate in worship intense,—overpowered by the awful responsibility placed upon him,—the charge of Mary the mother and the care of God His own creator,— now his foster child. Not a sound on earth;—but listen, the very angels have left the heavens and they are singing "*Gloria in Excelsis*" up in the starry stillness of the sky. "Glory be to God in the highest." And is this glory? Out on the hills the shepherds were watching the sheep destined for the sacrifices of the Temple. They left the sheep and they found the Shepherd of souls in the stable. For: Lo! the angel of the Lord came upon them and the glory of the Lord shone round about them and they were very much afraid. And the angel said unto them, "Fear not; for behold I bring you good tidings of great joy which shall be to all the people: for unto you is born in the city of David, a Saviour who is Christ the Lord. And this shall be a sign unto you: you shall find the infant wrapped in swaddling clothes and lying in a manger." Was it Gabriel that spoke to them "Fear not," that night of the Lord's coming, the very words that he had said to Mary before she gave her consent to let Him come through her? And suddenly there was with the angel a multitude of the heavenly hosts, praising God and saying: "Glory to God in the highest, and peace on earth to men of good will." And the shepherds said to one another: "Let us go over to Bethlehem and see this thing which has come to pass which the Lord hath made known unto us. And they came in haste and found Mary and Joseph and the infant lying in a manger."

Mark:—first came the tidings in angelic song to those who were watching the sheepfolds that belonged to the Temple for sacrificial purposes. They came and they found in the crib "the Lamb slain from the foundation of the world" in the sweet form of a little babe. But they wondered only. How could they comprehend the mystery of the manger.

Let us go with them. How often we have done so on many a Christmas night! Let us enter. We find as they found Mary and Joseph and the infant;—an earthly Trinity in the stable. Faith still wonders as the shepherds did. And Faith still finds what they did find,—Mary and her child. Kneel down now and adore the infant. The Mother has taken it from the cold crib to her warm bosom. You cannot take the child out of those arms; or from that breast. It is the first altar purer than any altar ever to be in all time. And those arms own that child.

Do you adore? Adoration of Him is veneration of her. Do you praise? Praise of Him is honor for her.

Mother and child together,—united indissolubly forever. In the Promise,—in the Conception and now the bond of birthhood unites them visibly.

In that stable, the haunt of animals, all the mysteries of Redemption begin to meet. Strange! Those mysteries were conceived and decreed amid the splendors of the heavens; and now they are fulfilled in the squalor of a stable. Let God alone. He has come to reverse human standards. He has come to revolutionize all the criteria of this world. Omnipotence becomes powerlessness. Riches eternal become Poverty. Immensity circumscribes itself in an infant's little face and form; and God's highest glory on earth begins in a stable! and it will end on a cross!

End?—Ah no,—it will never end.

Who presides over the Mystery's beginning? Mary, the Child's Mother. And she will preside over all Redemption's mysteries with all the right and power of a mother down to the last. In as true a sense as the word means she is co-redemptress of the human race. Christ is ours because He was hers. She is the human mother of the Father's consubstantial eternal Son. By divine decree from all eternity, and by that decree's accomplishment in time, Mary, Virgin and Mother has become a necessary factor in Christian faith. Therefore she cannot be left out without marring the completeness of Faith.

If the whole wide world keeps Christmas as a day of abounding joy it is because she gave the Christ, who is the joy of Christmas, to the whole world. That stable has multiplied into hundred of thousands of temples. That manger has grown into millions of altars. The Temple means the stable and the altar means the crib. So, in temple and at altar we must find what the shepherds found Mary with her child. Mother and child together. You cannot, dare not part them. The very stable would protest, had it a voice; and the poor, humble straw made consecrate by becoming the first resting place of the Word Incarnate, would protest. And Joseph, and the shepherds and the mother;—but above all the child. Let him stay in His Mother's arms. Next to His Father's bosom, her breast is His place. Wonderful mystery! Who can understand it?

The mother,—a creature, clasps and kisses her creator! Well—is it not a mystery of Love?

Our Holy Church, like the stable, keeps the Mother and Joseph and the child together. In the inn, they were told that there was no room for them. There are so-called churches like the inn. They have no room for Mary and Joseph. They have room only for Christ. His Mother and His foster-father must stay outside the doors, forsooth! Christ and only Him is their cry. There is no such thing as Christ solitary and alone. He is akin to our race on His Mother's side. She is the bond of the kinship,—she, and her blood. Thrust her aside, you must thrust Him away. No—no. He will stay with His Mother and she will stay by Him. And both together will stay with us. Mother and child together.

The Catholic temple or humblest chapel on Christmas night and day represent the stable. We have room for them—Jesus, Joseph, Mary. The rest of the churches represent the inn. They have no room for them. Ah! humble crib thou didst not stay in the stable. Thou hast moved down the centuries and across the world,—and not only on Christmas night and day;—but every hour of time thou, transformed into countless altars, art still presenting to the eyes and heart of faith the story of the stable; and Mary the Mother is always there,—in her own place,—and if she had power to give the Christ birth, which is the grandest power of all, she has all other powers which that contains,—and has them forever.

The birth was, by divine operation on the sinless Mary, without throes of sorrow,—but with throbs of rapture. The sinlessness of the Mother sweetened the humiliation of Christ. He came from the sinless heavens through His sinless Mother to save the sinful world. Can the world forget that Mother? Ought not every child of the human race love Mary with a devotion only inferior to love for God?

And remember, because of being His Mother, Mary became, in a sense the superior of Christ. If He obeyed the law that was passing away,—He, with greater reason, obeyed His Mother, because she had more right to His submission than the law.

The story of that Midnight can never pass away. And Holy Church keeps forever on her altars the echoes of the "*Gloria in Excelsis.*" It was not sung until Mary bent over the babe in the crib,—and now it will be sung forever.

Oh! Holy Mary! thou didst bring forth our Saviour in a poor and squalid stable for all the world. Bring Him forth in our poor souls, by thy prayers and intercessions! As in Holy Church—so in our hearts we will have room for Jesus, Joseph and Mary.

Aspiration.

"A LIGHT shall shine upon us this day: for our Lord is born to us: and he shall be called Wonderful, God, the Prince of peace, the Father of the world to come; of whose reign there shall be no end." —*Is.*, ix.

The Lord hath reigned, he is clothed with beauty: the Lord is clothed with strength, and hath girded himself."—*Psalm*, xcii.

Prayer.

GRANT, we beseech thee, Almighty God, that we who are filled with the new light of thy incarnate Word, may show forth in our works what by faith shineth in our minds.

SEVENTEENTH DAY.

The Star in the East.

"Behold the Lord the Ruler is come; and a kingdom is in his hand, and power and dominion. Give to the king thy judgment, O God; and to the king's son thy justice."—*Mal.*, iii,

TO-DAY a star instead of a flower for the crown of the Queen. To simple, humble shepherds near Bethlehem watching the flocks that belonged to the Temple came first the sign of the Messiah's birth. That sign was supernatural and angelic. The angels that sang the *Gloria* in the heavens that night were the first Apostles proclaiming the first visible Mystery of Jesus Christ. And that the gentle, humble and simple first heard the tidings presaged that in the new Kingdom simplicity and humility and poverty would gain the first and highest favors from the King whose palace, that night, was a stable.

But beyond the boundaries of Judea lay in darkness the great Gentile world. They too will have their sign and that in the heavens. Their hearts were hungry for God,—so hungry that they had thousands of gods from the stones beneath them to the stars above them.

The modern monster,—the atheist had not yet made his appearance. Their gods were material things—things to look upon with their eyes;—to kneel down before with their body—and to touch with their hands.

Their very idols,—Gods in material form curiously hinted at the true God's coming in visible form.

Throughout the East men studied the skies more than the earth, while in the West men gave more attention to the soil beneath their feet. Dreamers from the East,—practical people from the West.

Through those nations dim traditions had floated like fragments of a lost beautiful song—and one of those traditions, they knew not whence it came, was a prophecy that a wonderful star would rise in the heavens to herald the coming of the Expectation of the World. It was transmitted from generation to generation and from age to age. Those ancient peoples had marvellous memory. Their world moved slow. To forget is a signal trait of the busy Moderns.

They have no time to remember. They fling the yesterdays away as soon as the to-day dawns.

The predicted star at last rose in splendor in the heavens—a beacon light to guide the wise men to the crib. One from Persia,—one from Arabia and one from far Ethiopia. It must have appeared long before the angels sent the shepherds to the stable. When they approached Jerusalem the star vanished. Were they deceived? Was their long journey but a folly? Surrounded by their servants they entered Jerusalem in all their oriental splendor. The people gazed at them in wonder and admiration. "Where is he, they asked, who is born King of the Jews? for we have seen his star in the East and have come to adore him?" Had they beside the sign in the sky to guide their way,—a revelation in their heart that the new-born king was God to be adored? Trouble in the heart of Herod,—and trouble in all Jerusalem. The

priests are assembled: Herod puts the question—
"Where will He be born?" "In Bethlehem"—came
the answer.

Leaving Jerusalem the star reappeared. and gladness filled their hearts. From Jerusalem to Bethlehem only six miles. Did the three kings,—the shepherds of the people, pass, on their way to the crib, the shepherds of the Temple's flocks.

The star stopped over where the child was.

"And when they were come in they saw the child with Mary his Mother,—and they adored him and offered to him gold, frankincense and myrrh."

Was the child resting on the Mother's breast,—as on an altar?

Again Mother and child together. Through her they offered their symbolical gifts to the child. Were they wrong? Can we not offer our gifts through her to Him?

When a gift to a child passes across the palm of a mother's hand, it becomes more precious.

How Mary must have wondered at these men from the East? First came simplicity and humility in garb of shepherd. Her ancestor David was a shepherd and had fed his flocks nigh unto the very stable. But the Shepherd David became a King. The Kings came next to adore. They came with their riches, their culture, their power. And these three things which rule the world are still outstripped on the path to truth by simplicity and humility. And always shall be.

At both these comings to Christ, Mary prseides. As the mother of the child-king she was queen in His palace-stable to the wise men as well as to the shepherds.

And when that stable shall be multiplied and transformed into countless temples, she still will be queen to the lofty as well as to the lowly. She still will preside as queen and the gold of all human gifts and the frankincense of prayer and the myrrh of all beautiful virtues will be presented through her to her Son. Kings will lay their crowns,—queens their jewels, soldiers their swords, scholars their culture, poets their songs, orators their eloquence for her Son's sake at her feet. And eyes will bring their tears, and lips will bring their sighs and feet will bring their thorns,—and souls will bring their sorrows, and hearts will bring their anxieties, and hope will bring her fears and love will bring her pangs to the feet of the queen for consolation and relief. The poverties and the royalties will walk side by side to her throne. Fame and failure will kneel together there like brothers. Learning and ignorance with interclasped hands will bow before her throne. The aged bishop and the bright young altar-boy will bend before her as equals. The veiled nun and the broken-hearted penitent will mingle their voices in one chord before her. All these varieties there become unity.

All these differences before her throne become a harmony. Ah—it is only at the feet of Jesus Christ and at the feet of His Mother that all this world's inequalities are transformed into a marvellous equality.

Listen in the evening time and you hear the sound of the blessed beads all around the earth as they pass through the fingers that touch them as gently as if every bead was a rose;—and the Rosary in its form of chain is not a symbol of slavery but a most beautiful sign of the perfect equality of all the children of God.

In the hands of the Supreme Pontiff and in the hands of the aged negro; in the hands of an Empress and in the hands of the poor, unlettered negro girl,—the same sign. Those beads—those Hail Mary's equalize us all and how? Why they lift us up above this world and they place us on the very same lofty plane of prayer. Blessed Beads! beautiful Hail Mary's! Ah the while you crown all the children of thy Son with a beautiful spiritual equality,—you chain us to His throne with better than golden chains.

And better than the gold of the Wise Men is the gold of every bead, and sweeter than the frankincense brought from the East is the precious incense of each Hail Mary.

Let the star of love of Jesus and Mary shine every day in the sky of our souls,—beckoning us to come to the place where the King is resting;—let us bring our beads as our gifts and we shall be sure to find, as the Wise Men did, Him with His Mother. They were told in dream to go back home by another way;—for the cruel and dangerous Herod was plotting against the Child. So from God's temple whither we bring our Rosaries as gifts,—we will always return home another way, with happier souls and more of grace in them and thus escape the spiritual snares which the Herod's of our passions are always planning in our hearts. The star that led the Magi to the Christ crib has disappeared. But ah! another star hath taken its place,—shining forever in the heavens of Faith; Mary herself, with brightness ever increasing. Star of hope shed thy purest rays on the shadows that oftimes gather around us, and we shall like the Wise Men, but with wisdom higher than theirs, follow thy guidance and find the sweet Saviour whom they found a few years here below at the altars of Faith—but in heaven on His throne of glory.

Aspiration.

"We have seen His star in the East and have come with gifts to adore Him."—*Missal.*

Prayer.

O God, who on this day by the leading of a star didst reveal thine only-begotten Son to the Gentiles; mercifully grant, that we who know thee now by faith may be brought to contemplate the beauty of thy majesty.

EIGHTEENTH DAY.

The Flower of the Purification.

"Now dost thou dismiss thy servant, O Lord, according to thy word, in peace. Because mine eyes have seen thy salvation. Which thou hast prepared before the face of all peoples. A light to the revelation of the Gentiles, and the glory of thy people Israel."—*Luke*, ii.

FORTY days after the birth of Jesus, His blessed Mother accompanied by Joseph went up to the Temple for her purification and His presentation.

Sinless as Mary was there was no real need for her compliance with the ceremony of purification as there had been no need of our Lord's subjecting himself to the rite of circumcision. They complied with the requirements of the law in order to leave us an example of obedience. And besides the mystery of her Motherhood and the divinity of the child were in this way to remain unrevealed. Mary the child of the Temple re-enters its gates a Virgin Mother bearing in her arms the everlasting God. Joseph carried the turtle doves as humble offerings. Never had God received such homage in heaven or on earth as when Mary presented her child in the Temple. It was an infinite offering and the little Christ gave to His Father in that hour infinite homage.

Into the Temple, by the inspiration of the Holy Spirit came the aged Simeon, a just man and devout, "who had been waiting for the consolation of Israel."

For it had been revealed to him that before death he would see with his own eyes the Lord's Christ. Mary he had known in the days of her childhood. He had been present at her presentation. A great joy filled his aged heart. He took the child in his trembling arms, and blest God. And then his voice arose in song: "Now thou dost dismiss thy servant, O Lord, according to thy word in peace. Because my eyes have seen thy salvation, which thou hast prepared before the face of all peoples: A light to the revelation of the gentiles, and the glory of thy people Israel."

Simeon blessed them, and said to Mary the Mother: "Behold this child is set up for the ruin and resurrection of many in Israel and for a sign that shall be contradicted; and thy own soul a sword shall pierce that out of many hearts thoughts may be revealed." Simeon read in prophetic vision the whole future history of the child and he tells it to the Mother; for she is to be involved in it,—to be part and portion of it. Anna the prophetess, also entered the Temple and gave thanks to the Lord. There were listeners in the Temple,—but they did not understand Simeon's song and prophecy and Anna's blessing. The wondrous beauty of the young mother, the resemblance between her face and that of the child a-nestling in her arms, the gentleness of Joseph;—all this attracted their attention; but though they were almost touching the mystery of mysteries they knew it not. How often we are face to face with the supernatural and it passes us by unheeded? Are we not surrounded by mysteries, sacraments, facts above nature filling all hours and somehow we seem blind to their presence. Are we not dwelling in the awful every-whereness of God

THE FLOWER OF THE PURIFICATION. 157

from first to last of life half-the-while heedless of the mystery.

So they in the Temple,—the lookers-on in the day of Mary's purification and Christ's presentation stood in the shadow of the supernatural;—but they went their ways merely passing wondering remarks upon Mary and Joseph and the child.

And Mary went her way;—the sharp point of the sword of sorrow entering her heart; but as day follows day it will sink in deeper until her soul shall be transfixed with sorrow.

The Mother of the victim must also be a victim. "The Man of sorrow" must have a mother of sorrow. Few the joys of their lives,—but countless and intense the pangs

She saw, in spirit, every footstep of Christ until the nailing of the feet on Calvary.

No wonder that the sorrowful hasten to the Mother of sorrows! She can compassionate sorrow's every pang because she suffered them all.

And where the Mother of sorrow is with her will be found the Man of Sorrows;—Mother and child together. Seven great mysteries of sorrow divide the days of her life.

The world worships joy,—goes forth to meet it, welcomes it,—walks in its light;—but flies or tries to fly from grief. And yet after all that earth-joy is vain, fleeting and unsatisfying. A ghost of grief haunts the footsteps of every joy.

Only spiritual joys can satisfy the soul,—joys that spring from prayers, graces, sacraments, obediences to God's laws. And these fill the heart with that holy peace which this world can neither give nor take away.

For such souls beside the greatest earthly sorrows the highest spiritual joys can be found interclasping one another. Sorrow was to be one of the most powerful elements in the holiness of the Blessed Virgin. Remember that from the moment of her immaculate conception on up until the moment of her death, her life was ascensional. Every moment she rose higher in sanctity. Her graces and merits were constantly a-multiplying; until she reached heights to no other creature accessible and though finite manifested, more than all other beings combined, the awful sanctity of God himself.

As towards all other creatures her holiness was and is incommunicable. No being ever bore the image and likeness of God as Mary did and does now in heaven. We are His images but imperfect. But in Mary the divine image is perfectly mirrored. Omnipotence cannot create a more perfect spiritual work. And the sign of that spiritual work is sorrow. Her life before Calvary was a martyrdom of suspense and fear and expectation. Her martyrdom on Calvary is only surpassed by that of her Saviour-son. And after Calvary she suffered the martyrdom of waiting. And always in perfect conformity to the will of God.

Sweet is the spiritual fragrance of the flower of the purification. It is a mingling of obedience to the law—of joy in presenting such a child, God's own equal, to God himself and of sorrow for His foretold sufferings.

On the second day of February, Holy Church who is also a virgin mother, keeps the feast of Mary's purification. But all the days of all the years our beautiful Church holds festivals of Purification. The Bride of the Lamb forever, her mission is to purify the world of error and sin. The gates of her temples are ever open that those who may need to be purified may enter and be cleansed. The ceremony of purification never ceases. At the baptismal font,—from the pulpit, in the confessional, on the altar the purifying power is always active.

Blessed are they who needing to be purified come in imitation of Mary, who, though not in need of it went up to the Temple in obedience to the law. And then to each of us the Saviour with the gentleness of a child and the mercy of a God will be presented. Once she presented Him to the Father;—but now her love is to present Him to sinners in the hours of their purification.

ASPIRATION.

"WE have received thy mercy, O God, in the midst of thy temple: according to thy name, O God, so also is thy praise, unto the ends of the earth: thy right hand is full of justice."—*Psalm*, xlvii.

"Great is the Lord, and exceedingly to be praised: in the city of our God, in his holy mountain."—*Ibid.*

PRAYER.

ALMIGHTY everliving God, we humbly beseech thy Majesty, that as thine only-begotten Son was this day presented in the temple in the substance of our flesh; so we also may, with purified hearts, be presented unto thee.

NINETEENTH DAY.

The Flower of Sorrow and Joy.

> "And it came to pass, that after three days they found him in the temple sitting in the midst of the doctors, hearing them and asking them questions. And all that heard him were astonished at his wisdom and his answers. And seeing *him* they wondered. And his mother said to him: Son, why hast thou done so to us? behold, thy father and I have sought thee sorrowing."—*Luke*, ii.

JESUS was twelve years of age. The Paschal feast was approaching. With Mary and Joseph,—and tradition says on foot,—Jesus went up to Jerusalem. Though God and not bound by law, He was a Hebrew and strictly observed the law. What a lesson this to Christians.

They reached the Holy City and performed all things according to the ordinances.

Between Joseph and Mary in His own Temple Jesus knelt down to pray. God on earth in the form of a beautiful boy prays to God in heaven. What a mystery! Too deep for words. The feast closed. And not one in all those multitudes that thronged the Temple knew that in their midst moved the feet of Him who had come to bring salvation. The Feast closed. In the afternoon the worshipers left the city. The men passed out through one gate and the women through another to meet again at night-fall. During this afternoon's journey Joseph and Mary were separated. When they met at the closing of the day where was the child Jesus? With neither.

And a great fear came on Joseph and Mary's heart was filled with a strange terror. Jesus was gone. Whither? The Boy was lost. How and why? How the mystery of His sudden disappearance filled their souls with darkness. Just this morning beside them in the Temple,—so fair, so beauteous, with the very light of heaven in His face to their eyes,—and now gone. He had given no sign. He had said no word. He had let them leave the Temple and the city without Him and without a warning. It was so unlike Him. They turned their faces towards the Holy City. Night came on; but a darker night fell on their souls. Fear and love gave strength to their weary feet. It was very dark. Did Mary think of the Christmas night and its angels when He came to the world? No angels to night and no *Gloria* of joy. Only a dumb, desolate sorrow. It was the first time she was without Him. How they hurried back! Her heart was crying out for her lost child. On the still night air trembled the mother's prayers. The stars shone on the tears that flowed from her grief-filled eyes.

For the waves of a starless sea of sorrow swept stormily over her soul. Ah! mothers with lost children have known griefs similar but never equal to her's. For never a mother had a son like her's. In the dark they reach the city and in the dark they enter it. Where did they spend the rest of that desolate night? Did they go straight to the vestibule of the Temple to wait till the morning would open its gates? Or did they wander up and down the narrow streets seeking in the dark for Him who was their only light?

Dawn in the East and the Temple doors were opened. He was not there. Where had He gone? Had He gone out to Calvary and spent the night amid its gray rocks? The weary search went on. They made inquiries of those they met. And how Mary could describe her child? But no one had seen Him. Another day's search but all in vain. Dawned the third day. Was it an inspiration or was it only the presentiment of a mother's heart that turned their steps towards the Temple?

* * * * That day the teachers of the law were assembled. The Scriptures were in their hands. They were reading and expounding the Law and the Prophets. Suddenly into their midst came a boy fair to look upon with something of more than human beauty in His face. It was unusual for a child thus to come amid their deliberations. But somehow His coming did not seem an intrusion. It was as if He had a right to be there. In their midst He stood listening to them and asking them questions. They wondered at His wisdom and His answers. The promised Messiah of forty centuries,—twelve years of age,—looked into their faces,—with His questions and His answers stirred their souls;—and they, with the Scriptures in their hands, did not recognize Him. The Boy to them was only a wonder. An old Prophet had written His name would be called Wonderful.

Will He now reveal Himself and show unto them that the Wonder in their midst is their very God? No,—He must bide His time.

A silence fell on the Assembly—one of those strange hushes that follow one mystery and precede another.

Footsteps were heard approaching.

Swiftly to where the fair boy stood came Mary and Joseph. It was a second wonder. And the Teachers heard a voice with a mother's pathos in it while the light of joy shone on her face: "Son why hast thou done so to us: behold thy father and I have sought thee sorrowing?" The teachers knew the aged carpenter and they had not forgotten the face of Mary. The Boy and the Mother looked strangely alike. And the Boy spoke: "How is it that you sought Me: do you not know that I must be about my Father's business?" Did the teachers think that the Boy was about Joseph's business,—for had not Mary said: "your Father and I sought thee?" Yes the mystery is not yet to be revealed. Mary took the Boy's fair hand in hers and led Him from the Temple. Her sorrow had blossomed into joy.

"And He went down with them and came to Nazareth and was subject to them. And Jesus increased in wisdom, age and grace before God and man." The sorrow of the three days brightened into the joys of eighteen years. Eighteen years more must the world wait for the Teacher. Why let the world wait? Why give thirty years of His life to His Mother and only three years to the world?

Why this seclusion in Nazareth? Why the silence unbroken by a word to the world resting on those eighteen years? The communings of mother and child are not for the world. They are sacred and secret. Thrice only in public and in the hearing of others He addressed His Mother,—in the Temple where she found Him,—at the wedding feast in Cana and on Mount Calvary.

. But the words that passed between them at home

have been buried in a silence which not one inspired writer has invaded.

But ah! the constant interchange of thought between Jesus and Mary during those eighteen years must be full of the mysteries of human and divine love! How her soul must have been filled with the light of those mysteries which we see only in shadow! It is again for years and years mother and child. Nazareth is more than a city,—it is an argument. Of what? Of the indissoluble bond between Jesus and Mary. And of what else? He was subject to her. He obeyed her. He acknowledged all her rights and powers as His Mother and fulfilled all His duties towards her as her son.

Has He ever annulled His Mother's rights? When?— Once a mother,—a mother forever. He must break the birth-bond,—He must sunder the blood tie before He can compel His Mother to abdicate her rights. He must go against the face of the eternal decree by which He elected to become Mary's child.

Has He ever taken away her power? Why and how? Did He ever reach an hour in His life here below,—or has He reached an hour in His glorified life in heaven when to her, who said: "Be it done unto me according to thy word:" He has said or could say: "What you my Mother ask will not be done according to thy word?" No—no,—the rights, the powers, the privileges of her who is the Mother of the Eternal King will last as long as He reigns. He has never emancipated Himself from the sceptre of His Mother's love. He was subject to her in the earthly Nazareth,—and because her will is perfectly united to the divine will, He is still subject to her in the heavenly Nazareth. * * * *

So sweetly—peacefully and silence-veiled went on the days at Nazareth. In the city there was a synagogue. There on every Sabbath day knelt the Holy Family in prayer. The Christ in silence listened to the readings of the Scriptures; and never did human soul feel such reverence for the divine word as did His. He was in their midst and they knew Him only as the aged carpenter's son. On other days He worked for Joseph was growing feeble. Came a day when Joseph was missed in the synagogue. Only Jesus and Mary came. And so for Sabbath after Sabbath. It was in the order of Providence that the Foster-father should pass away from earth before his Foster-son would face the world. It came at last. Did the Foster-Son anticipate the time and baptize with Christian Baptism the last and greatest Hebrew patriarch?

In the arms of Jesus and Mary he calmly died.

Ah! what a death! They laid him away with his fathers,—and now Jesus and Mary were alone. Their hearts grew closer together. Every day He entered the little shop to toil for His Mother's support. Once she fed Him. Now He feeds her. Often a great fear crept into her heart and whitened her all pure face;—for she knew the day of separation was coming fast.

It came a day of deepest human sorrow to Jesus as well as to Mary. Ah! love wants the face of the loved one to look on. It is so in the glorious heavens where the face of God will be an eternal need eternally gratified. It is so in this sorrowful world where hearts, though they know and are happy to know that they love one another, still want one another's face, and still want to hear the tones of one another's voice. Their loves are not going to part,—that she knows,—

but He is going to take His face away—the face that has been her heaven of human joy for thirty long years. Did Mary's Son kneel down to get His Mother's blessing before He went out alone into the world? For alone He must go to do His mighty work. Or did He ask her consent to go forth and die for the world? Asked or not asked she gave it.

Three years,—awful years for Him with Calvary at the close. The moment came. Mother and Son embraced. They were human and they wept. He turned away from peaceful Nazareth with His face towards the Jordan. Mary entered her humble home. What passed there only angels knew. It was like an agony that separation. Ah Mary! your Jesus is truly lost to you now,—but it must be so because He is going to save the lost. Did angels come to comfort her?

When after a while He will preach to the people,— to His Father in heaven will be ascending from Mary in far off Nazareth the mightiest prayers that ever heaven heard. For her prayers had part in His three years ministry.

Jesus preaching,—Mary, praying—ah me! how could men resist? Oh! Mary crowned in heaven! pray for us with the heart of a Mother and the power of a Queen that we may never resist the graces sent us by thy Son.

Aspiration.

"Send forth thy light and thy truth: they have conducted me, and brought me unto thy holy hill, and into thy tabernacles. And I will go in to the altar of God: to God who giveth joy to my youth."—*Psalm,* xlii.

Prayer.

GRANT, we beseech thee, O Lord, that both the course of the world may be peaceably ordered for us by thy governance, and that thy Church may rejoice in tranquil devotion.

TWENTIETH DAY.

The Flower of the Wedding-feast.

"His Mother said to the waiters: Whatsoever he shall say to you,—do ye."—*Luke* ii, 5.

JESUS went down to the Jordan and was baptized by His cousin John the Baptist. Then He went into the desert; fasted forty days, was tempted by the devil; bade him begone,—and he went; returned from the desert; called a few disciples who followed Him; began to teach in the synagogues and was followed by many; and at last came to Nazareth. What a meeting it must have been when He entered His Mother's home. How soon He returns to her! He had a reason. There is nothing accidental in His life. His mother has a work to do before He separates Himself from her only to meet again on Calvary. Three days after the calling of His first disciples "there was a marriage in Cana" (not far from Nazareth) "and," writes St. John, "the mother of Jesus was there." And Jesus was invited with His disciples to the marriage. Mary, who perhaps presided at the feast, saw, with a woman's quick intuition, that wine was wanting; and said to Jesus: "They have no wine." Simple words,—but strange. Had she ever seen Him exercise His omnipotent power? In the flight to Egypt and return had He procured, out in the bleak desert, food and drink for her and Joseph, by the use of divine power? Her request almost implies as much. And if not, she knew her Son was God. Just as strange was His reply: "Woman, what have I to do with thee: My hour is not yet come." It seemed like a harsh refusal softened only by the reason He gave. His hour had not yet come. But the mother knew her Son better than the guests. Mayhap some said: "He has refused her." She said to the servants: "Whatsoever He saith unto you, do ye." There were six water-pots of stone; and Jesus said to the servants: "Fill the water-pots with water." And they did so. And He said: "Draw out now and bring to the ruler of the feast." And they obeyed. The ruler of the feast tasted the water made wine;—so did the guests;—and a great wonder filled the room. St. John writes: "This beginning of miracles did Jesus in Cana of Galilee, and manifested His glory and His disciples believed in Him." They had listened to the glory of His words,—for no man spake as He; and had followed Him. Now manifest to them is the glory of His power—and they believe in Him. Yes,—there was a reason why His mother should be present at the feast. She had brought Him into this world by miracle. She had given Him that body which enshrined omnipotence and it was but right and fitting that the first exercise of His power should be at her request. Through her the humility of the God-man was first manifested in Bethlehem; and through her the glory of the Man-God, in the beginning of His ministry, is first made manifest at the wedding feast of Cana. But said He not: "My time is not yet come?" And at His mother's simple words: "They have no wine" He anticipates His time, works His first miracle,—shows His power,—displays His glory—and now His disciples believe in Him. To be the cause of the manifestation of His glory is glorious enough:—Oh Mary! but most glorious is it to have been the cause of that first faith which began that day in Cana in the souls of the first few disciples and which will last strong and unshaken as long as this world shall exist! Yes—Mary the Mother of Christ is the mother of the first faith in Him;—and that faith like Mary—will be always a virgin pure from any stain of error;—and always a mother bringing forth in every age innumerable children, down to the consummation of the world. Yes indeed there was a reason,—and more than one, why Jesus should meet His mother at the feast. It was a marriage feast. Marriage is the appointed means whereby our race is perpetuated. Marriage must be holy, and to be so,—must have God's blessing,—and to have it, husband and wife must love one another and have reverence for one another's body. Else marriage loses its purity. That lost,—marriage sinks into degradation. Mary the great Mother of Christ and of His posterity was there as a model for all mothers. Mary the Virgin was there in all the glory of her purity to signify that purity should guard motherhood. The laws of human generation are sacred. Mary is present at the feast held in honor of those laws to attest their sacredness. Ah! how those laws are dishonored! And then? Unhappiness. And then? How often infidelity? And then? How often divorce? Why dishonored? Jesus and His mother were not at the wedding feast. The world was there with its congratulations. Fashion was there with its finery. But grace was absent. No wonder there are so many miserable marriages! No wonder that fretful husbands and complaining wives are met with everywhere and every day! They have missed their wedding-blessing or they have lost it and are not willing to strive by prayer and sacraments to win it back again. Nor need we marvel that this tells on the children, disturbs society, sometimes dishonors the Church and leads to ills temporal and spiritual beyond all reckoning. In the pastorals of nearly all the Bishops the question of marriage holds a prominent place. They are not only teachers of truth but they are the guardians of the sacraments. Faith without the sacraments is a sky without the sun. The Bishops of the Church see that as the world is drifting farther and farther away from the safe moorings of Christ's teachings,—no sacrament is in greater peril of losing its sanctities by moral shipwreck in society than that of matrimony. Entered into too hastily,—a matter of mere human love and sometimes alas! human passion, without the preparation of prayer and the presence of supernatural grace,—marriage is losing its sacredness among the married.

The honor of the faith is often yielded and the laws of Holy Church transgressed in mixed marriages. The children of the same faith should marry together without seeking, and then only for gravest reasons, outside connections.

Over the order of human generation Jesus and Mary must preside that it may have heaven's blessing.

But let us ascend to the order of regeneration where grace reigns over souls.

In that order the feast is everlasting and Jesus with His mother presides. Every holy thought,—every pious desire, every fervent prayer,—every act done for eternity,—every sacrament received and all the other countless things that go to make up the supernatural life have relations to Jesus and His Mother. Where He is,—she is as well; He with His saving mercy, she with her mother-love. In every feast of grace in our souls Jesus and Mary meet.

Oh Mary Queen of heaven pray that sin may never enter our souls to cast a shadow on those sweet interior feasts we keep when Jesus comes in all His love to sanctify them more; and we know He will bring a mother's blessing with Him.

ASPIRATION.

"SON! they have no wine."

PRAYER.

FAVORABLY hear our supplications, O Lord, and graciously protect thy institution which thou hast ordained for the propagation of mankind: that the union made by thy appointment may be preserved by thy aid.

TWENTY-FIRST DAY.

The Flower of Mary's Martyrdom.

FIRST PART.

"And thy own heart a sword shall pierce that out of many hearts thoughts may be revealed."—*Luke* ii, 35.

AMID the splendors of the Transfiguration of Jesus on Mount Thabor, Peter loth to leave the place, cried out in the rapture of his heart: "Oh Lord! it is good for us to be here!" Thabor was a Calvary in the Light. Calvary is a Thabor in the Dark. And loth to leave the mount of mercy,—as He hung on the cross three long hours, let us linger three days amid its mysteries that we may learn more (we never can learn all) of the relations of the Mother of Jesus with His Passion and our Redemption. Two souls were never more united than theirs on Calvary. Two sorrows were never more as one. That union lasted not only during those three hours that passed on Calvary. It lasts forever; for the Passion, at which Mary was not only a spectator but in which as His Mother she was an actor,—is eternal. She had given Him that sacred flesh which was bruised,—that blood which was shed,—that form which was nailed to the cross. The drops of His precious blood that redden the rocks had their far-off sinless fount in the heart of Mary. They began to flow from her heart on the day of the Annunciation,—nine months invisibly till Christmas night came and the Child was born. Then for months He was nursed on her sinless breast and drew the nourishment of His life from her sinless body. The blood was hers no longer. It was His only each drop of it united to Divinity. But still in the beginning it had been hers—and what she gave Him, He gave us for our Redemption. He was her's before He became ours. He became our Saviour as her son as man as really in the temporal order as he was in the eternal order Son of the Father.

From His Mother He received that human life in human body, which He laid down for our salvation. That body, in the eternal decrees, was necessary for our Redemption. From the Eternal Father, by eternal generation, He received (if we can use that word for lack of another) His divinity which made the reparation, wrought through His body, of infinite value. So in the decrees of God Mary was as necessary to the human part of the Passion as was the Father to the divine part. Now the divine and human elements of the Passion are eternal in their effects; and therefore Mary His Mother has part in every effect that flows from the Passion. The history of Christianity is the continuation of the Passion. Christian life finds its roots in His death;—two roots,—one in the human soul and body—the other in His Divinity. The body to His human soul united comes from Mary,—His Divinity, from the Father. Therefore as His Father has,—as He has,—so Mary His Mother has part in every single effect of His Passion. Out of the Passion came the Church and the sacraments; and therefore His mother stands in everlasting relationship with the sacraments and the Church. Every sanctification of soul,—every salvation of sinner,—every sanctity of saint flows from the Passion, and therefore intimately, inseparably, everlastingly related to the Passion, Mary is intimately, indissolubly, and forever connected with the work of the Passion in the soul of every saint and sinner.

The action of the Church is the perpetuation of Christ's Passion. Therefore as in His Passion so in the action of the Church Mary holds by mother's right a necessary place,—and that place highest, next to His. She stands forever by the Cross and she stands forever within the Church. You can no more thrust her out of His Church than you could have thrust her away from the cross. You cannot take the cross and Him without taking her. They go together. They stay together. They do the grand work of this world's salvation together. "What God has placed together you cannot put asunder."

Jesus alone is the Mediator. His Redemption of us is infinite. Mary, sinless as she was, with all her merits could not have atoned for a single sin; could not have saved a single sinner. Christ's Infinite Redemption of sinners is as incommunicable as His Divinity.

But do not the elect co-operate with Jesus in the Redemption of the world? Do they not, as St. Paul writes: "fill up in their bodies that which is lacking of the sufferings of Christ, for His body's sake, which is the Church?" And this co-operation is real and substantial. By His merits have they not acquired the power of meriting? Do not their works satisfy for sins not only for their own sins but for the lesser sins of others, by their union with His? But the co-operation of all the saints together does not and cannot equal the co-operation of Mary.

Their co-operation is but a shadow compared to her's. For her co-operation is based upon her Divine Maternity; and that, in God's decrees, was indispensable. The consent which she gave to the Incarnation involved her consent to the Passion. Her will was in it all as well as God's will. Her will is in it still and will be in it forever. So that in a limited, finite sense we may well and accurately call Mary, His Mother Co-Redemptress. For without her we would not have had Him as our Redeemer. It could have been otherwise if God had willed it otherwise in eternity. He did not so will it. Therefore it is as it is and can never be otherwise than as it is. It was God's free decree. It was realized. Mary is an essential part of that realization;—and remains so forever.— Why,—did He not say it: "My words shall never pass away?" And they have not and never shall. Is not Mary mother of the Word made flesh greater than the words that fell from His lips? Can she ever pass away out of the sight of Faith? Does not Faith demand her everlasting presence as mother to believe and prove that God was man,—man, because, her own son? Is not His mother greater than His words? Why,—she gave Him the very lips that spoke the words? "Never man spake as He"—His very enemies said. And that man was her own and only Son. His words will go down the ages full of grace and truth and light and spiritual life;—and tell me! must the mother who gave Him the lips to speak salvation to all ages retire into the background of history,—to become a mere beautiful memory,—nothing but a name? No—no,—as she stood by the cross for three hours the mother of the Crucified she must stand by His words forever the mother of the Teacher of men. His words are human as His form on the cross was human. His mother proves the humanity of that crucified form and His Mother proves the humanity (if I can so write) of His undying words. His human words are like His human body. It shrined a divine person. They shrine divine thoughts. The body, with its human soul and human lips to speak human words enshrining divine thoughts, came from Mary His Mother. Wherever His words go,—she goes. She is more than a memory,—more than a name. She is the mother of His words as well as of Himself. For their human tone they lean on her, for their divine teachings they lean solely on Him.

The words of the Word-made-Flesh need His mother in person to prove that they are human words as well as they need Himself in person to prove that they are words divine. So therefore, the invisible presences of Jesus and His Mother are justly demanded by the eyes of Faith, as witnesses of His human-divine words wherever they are preached. She witnessed the crucifixion; and she must witness forever the preaching of "Jesus Christ and Him Crucified."

Now listen! all ye who preach His name and words!

Do you give His Mother her rightful and necessary place? Do you take His words into your pulpits and bid His Mother stay outside the doors of your churches? Do you preach "Christ and Him Crucified" without saying a word of her, the witness of His Passion? Do you preach the words of the Word-made-flesh and put the

Mother of that Word Incarnate aside? Then surely is your preaching false,—false to Him because false to her,—false to both, because false to the very Scriptures in your pulpits. It is a wonder that the calm, sweet words of Holy-writ on Scripture's pages do not frown upon you in wrath! Have you not read in the closing of God's Revelations: "And if any man shall take away from the words of the book of this prophecy, God shall take away his part out of the book of life and out of the holy city?"

And if you take away any of the words of the Book —by thrusting aside His Mother,—it is more than taking away words,—it is an offence against Christ Himself personally,—it is a crime against the Word-made-flesh who came to dwell forever amongst us as God—Son of the Eternal Father,—as Man,—Son of Mary, His Mother,—for wheresoever He, through His representatives witnesseth to the Truth she must witness to the Truth of truths that He is man because He is her Son.

Representatives did I say? His true representatives must represent Him and His Mother forever and ever working together for man's salvation.

Alas! there are Maryless, Motherless Churches (so-called.) They will have nothing to do with her,— though from her they receive their Christ. Christ was not Motherless. His true Church—made to His likeness, cannot be Motherless. His Mother is her Mother, for her Son is the head of the Church. Oh! holy Church! re-living the life of Jesus;—clothed with His sanctities,—enshrining His everlasting Presence,—possessing His powers,—infallible witness of His truths,— executor of His will; thou hast not forgotten His last legacy on Calvary to His well-beloved disciples: "Behold thy Mother!" Wherever thou goest and wherever thou preachest "Christ and Him Crucified," thou dost keep forever in the sight of true Faith the Mother who "stood beside the Cross." Thou dost frame the Name of Jesus in the name of Mary as he was fashioned in her sinless womb. Thou art true to Calvary and its Passion;—thou art true to the Son and true to the Mother;—and wherever thou goest—"Jesus and Mary,"—"Mary and Jesus," are sounded by thy lips together and forever,—an everlasting hymn of only two notes of only two names—telling the true and full story of Man's redemption.

Aspiration.

"Be it done unto me according to thy will."

Prayer.

O God, in whose passion, according to the prophecy of Simeon, a sword of grief pierced through the most sweet soul of thy glorious virgin mother Mary: mercifully grant that we who celebrate the memory of her dolors may obtain the happy effect of thy passion.

TWENTY-SECOND DAY.

The Flower of Mary's Martyrdom.

SECOND PART.

"When Jesus saw his Mother and the disciple standing, whom he loved,—he saith to his Mother: Woman,—behold thy Son."—*John* xix, 26.

THE Three Years, on which all the years of human history lean and will forever lean for the light of truth, for grace divine and for salvation were coming to a close. The words that fell from the lips of Christ during those years shine still like heavenly stars above all the horizons of time.

Palm Sunday came and passed with its Hosannas. Monday and Tuesday he taught in the temple, returning to Bethany every evening. His Mother was there. Wednesday night he spent amid the hills alone in prayer. Thursday morning he returned to Bethany. He had asked her consent to His Incarnation. He comes to ask her consent to His Passion,—and to bid her farewell. He knelt to His Mother and begged her blessing. She refused to bless her God and fell on her knees to adore His Divinity. They both remained kneeling and at last each blessed the other. She had given her consent to the crucifixion. She had given her child away to the world. Unutterable human anguish filled her heart,—for by supernatural light she saw every single detail of the awful drama in which Christ was to be the victim. But above all the dark anguish, like the far calm sky above the storm-swept sea and angry clouds, her will was tranquil and her soul was full of such graces as she had never known before. She needed them all to meet her coming desolation.

On Thursday night she was in Jerusalem. It was the Eucharistic night. Did she, in some way, receive her Son's body and blood to give her strength to bear the woes of Good Friday?—Many think she did. Next morning came. Accused, tried, not convicted yet condemned, scourged, crowned with thorns, accompanied by two malefactors, preceded by Roman soldiers, surrounded by a savage crowd whose blasphemies rent and desecrated the air, followed by an immense multitude, some wondering,—some pitying, some weeping but the most clamoring for His death,—Jesus went on His way through the streets to Calvary. John the Virgin and Magdalen the outcast stood by the Mother of the Son of God. The Apostles had fled. Jostled by the crowd Mary stood at the corner of a street by which her Son would pass. He saw her blue mantle. Their eyes met. Ah! what a meeting! One moment,—but it was equal to an age of grief. Higher, darker surged the waves of sorrow in the Mother's soul. Grace held her up. The next moment Jesus fell under the weight of His cross and His Mother's sorrow. He rose again. More savage rose the clamors for His blood. They echoed and re-echoed through the streets of Jerusalem,— but ah! they rang through Mary's heart and filled it with an agony like to His in Gethsemane. And she? She was praying for them all. John, Magdalen, Mary followed the multitudes. They crept up the slopes of Calvary. She saw it all, every detail of the awful crucifixion. Her ears heard every stroke of the hammer driving in the nails. Christ was lifted up on the cross. No wonder the earth was shaken from centre to circumference,—appalled by the murder of its God by men,—and these,—men of His chosen race. But not only the sin-stained earth gave signs of terror;—in the sinless heavens there were portents of sorrow,—as if they knew and felt the infinite horror on Golgotha. Darkness came creeping over the hill;—growing deeper and deeper;—hushing the blasphemies on the lips of the rabble, who now filled with fear rushed away from the cross back to Jerusalem when they heard that strange and awful sounds had issued from the temple and that the veil in the temple had been rent in twain.

In the darkness Mary and Magdalen and John came together to the cross. Mary and John stood. Magdalen crept to her old place,—crouched on the ground;—kissed and kissed the nailed feet;—and mystery of mysteries! the tears of the forgiven outcast mingled with the blood of the Son of God.

Silence came. Seven times was it broken by the dying Saviour. In a tone of infinite pathos rose from his lips: "Father forgive them for they know not what they do." Mary stood beside the cross calm in her illimitable woe;—making in her breaking heart an almost infinite act of almost infinite contrition for the murderers of her Son and for all sinners. Her silent act of contrition ascended to the Father blessed with the prayer of Jesus. But ah! if sinners need a divine Saviour,—do they not need a human, sinless Mother?—Wait awhile. There is silence again. When she became His mother in Bethlehem thirty-three years ago,—it was in joy—in rapture, in ecstasy. His human nature was sinless. But now she is to be made the Mother of all sinners on Calvary; she must suffer the penalty of such motherhood. She will be made their Mother when her soul and body are suffering agonizing throes beyond the reach of thought. When she has reached her closest union with her dying Son in the pangs of her compassion;—when His Passion and her compassion become almost as one, then shall her second motherhood be proclaimed to the world by the dying lips of the world's Redeemer. Silence still. Poor Magdalen is weeping her very heart away—kissing now the nails as if to make them less cruel. The moment of the second maternity came.

"When Jesus therefore saw His Mother and the disciple standing by whom He loved, He saith unto His Mother: 'Woman, behold thy Son.' Then to the disciple: 'Behold thy Mother.'"

Ah! what a transfer from Jesus to John! Has He given His Mother away? Yes. Has He abandoned Her? No. He has given her away to those for whom He is giving away His life. He gives her away and still keeps her. How? The soul that takes Him must take her. The sinner that calls Him Saviour must call the Saviour's Mother his Mother. He gives Himself to sinners as their Saviour;—He gives her to sinners as their Mother. So Jesus and Mary are still together. From Bethlehem to Calvary together. From Calvary's Cross to heaven's crown together. The Mother of the Redeemer is proclaimed by Christ,— Mother of the Redeemed. The Mother of Christ is the Mother of Christians. John the Apostle, on Calvary, becomes the representative of all the posterity of Jesus Christ. Mark the Scripture words: "He said to the beloved disciple: 'Behold thy Mother.'" On Calvary John represented all the beloved disciples of Jesus Christ in the Kingdom that was to last to the end of time. And therefore Mary, by Christ's appointment is made forever the Mother of His disciples.

Ah! Cross of mercy eternal! wherever you are preached; —wherever you are planted,—wherever the sunshine of your salvation is cast;—you are not true to the great Good Friday;—you are not true to Calvary—unless who so preaches or plants you still keeps Mary His Mother standing beside you.

The scene on Calvary on that Good Friday is framed in every day and hour of time. On the Mount, the Cross,—on the cross Jesus Christ; beside the Cross; Mary His Mother. She must be there as part of the picture. If not there,—the picture is false. No—no—if I go in in my sins and sorrows for pardon or comfort to the foot of the Cross of Christ, I find kneeling there a sinner like myself the Magdalen; and I find standing there Mary His Mother. Can I thrust her aside? No—no. It is her place to stand there not only for the three hours in visible form,—but to the eyes of faith forever.

To the eyes of Faith, Magdalen the sinner has her arms around the foot of the Cross forever.

To the eyes of Faith the well-beloved of Christ, representative of His disciples, stands beside his and our Mother. For Good Friday lasts forever. No after day has gone back to it; but it has come to every day of time bringing the Cross and the Christ and the Mother, and the penitent sinner. Will you take the Cross and Him—and reject her? Do not the deepest meanings of God's eternal decrees gather around the Cross on Calvary? Did Mary stand there for nothing? Were her presence and even her posture there meaningless? Who will dare to say so? Were His words to her and John without meaning? John would care for her anyhow,—and the Apostles. When He said to His Mother: "Behold thy son:" could He have meant it literally? No. A literal meaning is nonsense. John was not her son. What else could He mean? Why: His words on Calvary are as wide and deep as His work of mercy on Calvary. They reach beyond that hill and that day,—and the spiritual meaning of the words He spoke will last as long as the work of mercy He accomplished. When to John He said: "Behold thy Mother:" what did He mean? Only John? She was not John's mother. Taken in literal sense His last dying words would be false. Who will dare say so? What then did He mean? He meant it in a spiritual or mystical sense. As He is mystical Head of the Church,—she is the mystical Mother of all the members of the Church. Why?—We are brothers of Christ;—He was her Son; and therefore we are her spiritual children.

In Bethlehem in joy she became the Mother of the Redeemer. On Calvary in the throes of sorrow she became the Mother of the Redeemed.

Oh! Mother of our Redeemer! look down upon us from thy throne in heaven; and as thou didst follow thy own adorable Son from His birth even unto His death; guide us thy children through every day of our lives; and as thou didst stand at the foot of thy Son's Cross, in the hour of His death, be with us in our last hour when we shall commend our spirit into the hands of our eternal Father.

Aspiration.

"Great as the sea is my sorrow."

Prayer.

O God, at whose passion, according to the prophecy of Simeon, a sword of sorrow did pierce through the most sweet soul of the glorious Virgin and Mother Mary; mercifully grant that we, who devoutly celebrate her transfixion and suffering, may, through the mediation of the glorious merits and prayers of all the saints who faithfully stand beneath the cross, obtain the blessed fruit of thy passion.

TWENTY-THIRD DAY.

The Flower of Mary's Martyrdom.

THIRD PART.

"After that he saith to his disciple: Behold thy Mother. And from that hour the disciple took her to his own."—*Luke* xix, 27.

THE dead who had come out of their graves, awakened to life by the death of Christ, were walking through the streets of Jerusalem, seen of many, who awe-struck rushed away to hide themselves from the appalling sight. There was terror in the city,—and a horror indescribable fell over the hearts of all. Jesus still hung on the Cross. The centurion rode down the slopes of Calvary crying out in the darkness through which light had entered his soul: "Truly this was the Son of God."

"When the evening was come there came a rich man of Arimathea, named Joseph, who was also himself one of the disciples of Jesus: he went to Pilate and begged the body of Jesus." "And there came also Nicodemus (who at the first came to Jesus by night) and brought a mixture of myrrh about an hundred pound in weight,"—to embalm the body of the dead Christ. They and their servants found Mary still standing beside the Cross. She as Mother had watched o'er the crib—and she as Mother is guarding the Cross. That body is hers. She had given it its life out of her own life. He has given it away for the sins of the world. She stands there the sinless watcher and the sorrowful weeper over her Son's death.

She saw them coming,—and she waited. They neared the Cross. White as a lily was the face of the Dead; and white as the lily of the Valley was the face of the Mother of the Dead. Poor Magdalen was in her chosen place at the foot of the Cross bathing the dead feet with her tears. John was calm and still beside Mary. His vocation was a high one. Peter was to have charge of the Church; but John was to take care of Mary the Mother of all the disciples of her divine Son.

Against the Cross a ladder was fixed. Joseph and Nicodemus mounted. The crown of thorns is gently loosened from the head and passed down to Mary.

Ah! such a crown and so cruel and for such a King! His blood is on it. That crown can never wither. It never has;—nor shall.

Better thorns than flowers;—for flowers fade. Never mind! the thorns will bloom into immortelles of mercy and love and joy. The nails were loosened in the hands and feet. They are gently letting the body down.

Now Sorrowful Mother! you may kneel down and take Him in your arms again and nestle the poor sacred head upon your breast. He is coming back to you. To whom else would He first come dead who living first came to you? And to you for us? The hands of poor Magdalen are the home of His feet. They seem to be thirsty for her tears. And they rest so sweetly in her hands.

But ah! around that scene hovered unseen hosts of angels. Gabriel of the Annunciation was there strengthening the soul of the Mother in her sorrows,—strengthening her arms to bear the dead Burden.

Not a word was heard;—only Magdalen could not help but wail;—for she could not understand it all. Jesus was dead and her heart was breaking. The Mother's heart was already broken.

What woe was like His Mother's woe? She would have died holding the dead Christ had not God's strong grace held her up. She smoothened the tangled and blood-clotted hair as calmly as she smoothened His hair long ago when He was a child. 'Twas deep joy then. It is deepest sorrow now.

She sits down on the grass,—and the dead Christ is resting in her lap. "He had no place to rest His weary head" in life,—He said it Himself long ago. In death as in birth He rests on His mother. Wait awhile! She is gazing in unutterable grief on the wan, white face. What a long, intense, searching look. Does she read there the names of all the elect? Her grief is brightened. Does she read there the names of all lost souls?

Ah! how her sorrow puts on a darker darkness!

Let her alone. 'Tis the saddest picture this world shall ever look upon. Somehow the outstretched arms will not be closed. Even dead they want to stay wide open with mercy's welcome for all the world.

The mingled myrrh and aloes she, with the others, applies to the wounds. Magdalen embalms the Feet. Poor thing! and did she not know that if His feet were her's, His heart was her's as well? One last look of absolute agony at the dead Face;—the winding sheet is wrapped around the body;—and then Joseph and Nicodemus gently raise the sacred corpse, assisted by John, and wend their way down the slopes of the mount to the tomb in the garden below. Mary and Magdalen walk together,—the sinless and the sinner. Is it not ever so?

It was Joseph's Garden. In it he had built a tomb for himself. It was hewn out of the solid rock. In it no dead had as yet lain. Slowly,—silently they came down from the mount. They reached the sepulchre. It was almost night. The heavens and the earth, awhile ago so stirred with terror, were now as calm and peaceful as the Face of the dead Christ.

In the tomb they laid their burden down. They adored It with profoundest adoration. The Mother looked her last on the shrouded form of her dead Son;— calm with an almost infinite calmness,—sorrowful with an almost infinite sorrow. Her grief was an icy, frozen grief that could not melt into the tears that relieve. Magdalen sobbed as sinners sob after pardon has come;— wept as those do weep who have lost all they love. The great stone was rolled against the door of the sepulchre. The restless Christ had found a place of rest at last. He will not rest even there long. Away from the closed tomb went the mother with a Christ-like calm covering the inner sea of sorrow that was whelming her soul down into depths too deep to fathom, where all was dark as all was deep, for the light of her life was hidden away in the sepulchre. Mary Magdalen could scarcely tear herself away from the grave of Him who had shown such loving mercy to her. But the Mother of the dead Christ was now her Mother also, and when called away by the voice of the sinless Mary,—the Magdalen, like a little child, obeyed. They passed across Calvary on their way to the city. The Paschal moon was shining on the Cross. At its feet again fell Magdalen. She fain would linger there all night long. Ah! it had been a cruel bed of death for her beautiful Christ! The bed was empty;—but though empty she would watch it still.

The Mother kissed the Cross, and bade Magdalen rise and come. They entered the city away in the night. Roman soldiers were already guarding the grave of Christ. And what a night for Mary the Mother!

Every moment,—and every moment was one of intense painful wakefulness,—for her sorrow would not go to sleep,—filled the Mother's heart with desolation.

What if the Roman soldiers would desecrate her Son's grave? What if they would roll away the stone and drag the body forth and maltreat the dead as they had maltreated the living? The light in Mary's soul has gone out. Down in her heart where all was now so dark,—like to Christ's cry upon the Cross,—she cried in agony: "My Son! my Son! why hast thou forsaken me?"—And yet, like Him, she was resigned.

And the night passed on and away. The Sabbath dawned. One by one the scattered Apostles gathered around her. She was their Mother now. Surely Magdalen stole away that day to go up to Calvary. If He was not there, His Cross was there. Did Mary the Mother try to approach the grave that day? Or did she go to the Temple to pray for the crucifiers of her Son? The day wore on. The awful gloom of yesterday hung like a pall 'round that Sabbath. Night came again. "In three days I shall rise again;" the Mother knew the words and knew they would be realized. All that night the words were singing in the heart of Magdalen. * * * Let us pause and think. The Mother stood by the Cross to the last. The Mother received into her own arms the dead Christ taken down from the Cross.

It was her right. The birth-right gave her the death-right. To hold Him in her arms living and dead was her right and her's only. To see that He was fittingly buried was her duty,—a mother's. No doubt,—Joseph of Aramathea asked her consent to accept his sepulchre for her divine Son. From first to last,—from the Annunciation to the burial of her Son her will had its place and her consent its part.

For Mary was not a tool to be used by God for awhile and for a purpose, and then to be flung away as useless. Men work with tools. God works with wills. And as never Creature was more perfect,—or could be, than Mary,—chosen from all eternity to be the Mother of Christ;—so never creature had will as full and free and perfect in its workings as the will of the Blessed Virgin Mary.

In the perfect freedom of her will she is more like God in the infinite freedom of His will than all other created beings. The Father did not force her to become the Mother of His Son. A forced divine motherhood would have been an infinite sacrilege. He chose her one out of all. She could reject or accept the choice, with full, free will,—yet not without asking and knowing the conditions and consequences of such maternity, she accepted it. And from the moment Mary said: "Be it done unto me according to thy will,"—until the last moment of her sinless life, her will was as free as a creature in her finite sphere as God's will is free as a Creator in His infinite sphere. It is the perfect freedom of her will united to the will of God,—more than her perfect intelligence,—that crowns her with her glories. Eve's will yielded to Satan. Hence the Fall. Mary's will yielded to God's,—hence the Redemption.

Her giving her will to God's will gave us our Redeemer. That act of Mary's will last as long as the days of Redemption, and has something to do with every grace of Redemption. It was a finite act with infinite consequences. It was done in a moment,—and it is eternalized.

So two wills govern the Kingdom of the Redeemed;—the will of God and the will of His Mother Mary.

You cannot break the union of these two wills,—the divine and infinite,—God's;—the human and finite,—Mary's. Their accord is eternal. And, therefore, in a finite way but everlastingly, the will of Mary given, for our sakes, to God, in a real, though finite way bears on every day and deed of our Redeemer and Redemption; as in an infinite way on every detail of Redemption bears the will of God who accepted her will and made it His own. You cannot divide the two wills,—God's and Mary's. They began Redemption's work; and the two wills are working together still. If the wills;—the persons who own the wills. Therefore the will of Jesus and the will of Mary,—and therefore the Person of Jesus and the person of Mary can never be separated in any single work of this world's salvation.

And that Saturday night when she was waiting and watching for the Resurrection (for her grace-enlightened intelligence knew it all beforehand) her will was as passive and patient as the dead Christ in His grave.

She would not hasten that glory for even one instant.

Her will was resting in God as peacefully as the dead Christ was resting in His grave.

Though her mother-heart hungered to see His face again; though once long ago she knew that He had worked a miracle, as He Himself said, before His time, for her sake; her prayer before the Resurrection was just like her prayer at the Annunciation: "Let it be done according to Thy will." For her perfect will had risen from height to height until it touched,—transfigured without losing its freedom,—the infinite will of God. And the free "Fiat" of God and the free "Fiat" of Mary met and mingled in free and perfect union.

Ah Mother of the free and perfect will! thy children's wills are weak and wayward,—and their consents to heavenly calls, slow and uncertain;—pray for us, oh holy Mother! that our wills may be as thine, united to God's will always; and that our consent to calls of grace may be as thine prompt and full and fervent and always faithful,—so that we, like thy divine Son, Our Saviour may live only and always "to do the will of our Father who is in heaven."

Aspiration.

"Son! behold thy Mother."

Prayer.

O God! from whom Judas received the punishment of his sin, and the thief the reward of his confession: grant us the effects of thy mercy; that as our Lord Jesus Christ at the time of his passion bestowed on each a different recompense of his merits, so having destroyed the old man in us, he may give us the grace of his resurrection. Who liveth.

TWENTY-FOURTH DAY.

The Flower of the Glory of the Resurrection.

"Peace be to you."—*John* xx, 21.

ROMAN soldiers were guarding the closed grave. The stone was sealed with Pilate's seal. No doubt that with the soldiers were some of the Jews who had assisted at the Crucifixion. The Sabbath night wore on. The dawn was breaking. Suddenly there was a great earthquake; the stone was rolled away; the Keepers of the tomb were struck with terror and rushed away from the garden to the city. Jesus had risen. Mary Magdalen and Mary the mother of James, and Salome had hurried early in the morning to the sepulchre bringing sweet spices to anoint the Dead. In the garden He first appeared to the Magdalen, and sent her the sinner to be the Apostle of His Resurrection to Peter and the others, bidding them meet Him in Galilee. But already because she had the first right to see Him, in His glory, He had appeared to His blessed Mother. She had not gone forth to the grave because He had come to her. And oh! what a meeting between the Risen Christ and Mary! How the soul that on Calvary was overwhelmed with sorrow, was now filled with joy unspeakable! How she worshipped Him in His glory with all a creature's adoration and with all a Mother's love! His glory shone around her as the darkness of

Calvary had gathered about her. She was the first to make the grand act of Faith in His Resurrection. No more sorrow now. Her soul is lifted up into ecstacy. His Face has come back to her again radiant and triumphant. She holds the shining hands in her own. Yes,—this is her own Jesus. And how all the memories of His life from Bethlehem to Calvary melted into that one golden vision before her! No more darkness for her now. The vision of Light she gazed upon flashed its splendors o'er her soul; and new graces without number as without measure filled her heart;—and as Christ had risen from the grave, Mary rose, higher and higher into brightest spiritual spheres beyond the touch of human thought. That body now glorified and risen He had received from her. Those hands, feet, face, heart had been fashioned out of her flesh and blood. The Crucified was her own and the Risen one is her's as well. He is the same Christ. He has not lost His human identity and that human identity springs from her motherhood. Yes,—He has come back changed in appearance,—but not in body. And Risen He is still her's and because her's, our's. The body, which she gave Him,—dying and dead, proved His humanity. And the self-same body rising and risen attests His divinity. The same body received from her proves that Christ was the Son of Man and proves that He is the Son of God. His body is the argument. She who gave the body is necessary to the argument. There is no one living on that Easter Sunday morning to prove that the Risen Saviour was the babe of Bethlehem, except Mary. The Mother of Jesus is the single solitary personal eyewitness to testify that He of whom the Angel says to-day: "He is risen He is not here:"—is the self-same one over whom the Angels sang the *Gloria* thirty-three years ago. Over the lowly crib she bent and claimed the babe as her own. Beside the Cross she stood "the Mother of Jesus" claiming Him as her own. And now beside the open grave she stands—Mother still;—and testifies: "Yes,—He is the same: The Risen Christ was the babe of Bethlehem. I know it;—for I am His Mother."

She has a real and rightful (and for us a necessary) place in the glory of the Resurrection as she had in the mystery of the Crucifixion. She cannot be done without.

Christmas needs her presence not only as a part of the scene and a factor in the Mystery but as a necessity to the argument of Christ's birth. Calvary needs her not only as a figure in the awful scene, and an actor in the mystery but as an argument for the real physical death of the Body Christ received from her. Easter Sunday needs her presence not only as a part of its mystery of glory but as a living witness that the same human body which she brought forth has risen again. It is still in logic as well as in life Jesus and Mary together. And the logic as well as the life of Faith, that rise triumphant with Christ's body out of the open tomb last forever; and the Mother who stood in the shadows of Calvary that passed away, stands and must of right stand for all days before the eyes of believers as an essential element of that Christian Truth which for its divinity rests upon the mystery of the Resurrection. As Good Friday with the shadows that gathered about the death of Jesus comes to every day of time with its Cross and Mary standing beside it;—a Mystery of infinite love and Mercy; so Easter Sunday with its open grave and Risen Saviour comes with its splendors to light up, a mystery of infinite power and glory with Faith and Hope, every day of this world's history;—and we see and must see the Mother standing in the glory of its light that shall never pass away.

For Mary gives the human meaning to every divine mystery. She stands amid them all;—she moves along with them; she places them within our reach. Without her they are not humanly real. Without her they are vague, incomplete, far-off and unapproachable. With her they are definite, complete, near unto us and accessible.

Where any mystery of Christ's life presents itself,—she must present herself as Mother, as witness, and as argument. When Christ rose from the dead He did not cease to be man. He was man transfigured, glorified, victorious, never to die again. As man thus risen, in the which He proved His divinity, Mary did not cease to be His Mother. Nor did her rights as Mother cease.

The mysteries of the life of Jesus are the irrefragable arguments attesting that He is the eternal Truth and as such has the right to the faith of every man. You give your faith to Him as Truth and to the truths He taught. But He,—as The Truth as well as the truths which He announced have their reason in His life's mysteries. All those mysteries are human and divine,—physical and spiritual. And Mary alone is the ever-living—everlasting,—and to the eyes of true Faith,—the everessential element giving earthly reality to the human and physical side of every one of the mysteries of Christ's life.

The mystery of Christ's human priesthood; (for He was not a priest as God) the mystery of Christ's human

Kingship over all men (for only as man is He King of all men); the mystery of Christ's absolute infallible authority as teacher of all men (for it is by the right of His Divine Manhood that He teaches the world),—need Mary and her motherhood as their human reason. Those mysteries lose half their meaning,—or are meaningless; and the truths based on them lose half their evidence—or are evidenceless—if Mary be thrust aside. In the order of Providence she is as necessary to Jesus as He is necessary to us. It is ever and always Jesus and Mary together.

The hand of the human race must rest in the hand of Mary to find beside her and with her, her Son, our Saviour Jesus Christ.

So His glorified Hands and Feet and Face belonged to her as His Mother in the glory of Easter-morn, as truly as they did, when the weak little Hands and Feet and Face of the Babe belonged to her far back in the Christmas midnight at Bethlehem. And the glorified body,—ah! 'tis the same wondrous truth;—her's,—then His;—then our's. Oh Mary, Mother of the Risen Christ! we hail thee in the triumph of thy divine Son, as we bowed in sorrowing love before thee in thy desolation on Calvary! Thou dost stand forever in His glory as thou did'st stand beside Him in the gloom of the Cross. At the crib, at the cross, at the grave thou art His Mother still,—and because His, our ever-blessed Mother. In the heavens where thou art throned Queen Mother of the Victor of death, pray that we, rising from the grave of sin triumphant by penance victorious in hope, may never lose again the eternal life of His holy grace!

Aspiration.

"He is risen,—he is not here."

Prayer.

O God, who on this day, through thine only begotten Son, didst overcome death, and open unto us the gate of everlasting life; as by thy prompting grace thou dost breathe on the desires of our hearts, so do thou ever accompany them with thy help.

TWENTY-FIFTH DAY.

The Flower of the Glory of the Ascension.

"And Jesus coming spoke to them, saying: All power is given to me in heaven and in earth. Going therefore teach ye all nations: baptizing them in the name of the Father, and of the Son, and of the Holy Ghost, teaching them to observe all things whatsoever I have commanded you: and behold I am with you all days, even to the consummation of the world."—*Matthew* xxvii, 18, 19, 20.

WHEN Jesus died on the cross His human soul still united to the Divinity (as was His body in the grave) true to its mission of mercy for all, descended into Limbo. There all the souls of the dead from the beginning (that had been saved before the day of Redemption as we are saved after it by faith and by participating in the merits of Christ) were waiting, in hope, as the world had waited for "the glad tidings of the great joy." Our Good Friday was their Christmas. Adam and Eve, Abel and Seth, Noah and Abraham, Moses and Aaron and generations of the saved from every race and land dwelt there in Rest and Expectation.

Perhaps by angelic revelation they knew, in part, the work of salvation already accomplished by Christ on earth.

Perhaps Joseph the Foster-father had told them the story of Bethlehem and the Messiah and the Mother.

Limbo was a place of life. It was an abode of souls. And if in our world soul seeks soul and mind communicates with mind in interchange of thought; how much more intimate must that interchange be when the senses that help and yet hinder the union of our souls, have been laid aside. When one by one they reached that place of Rest would not each soul there ask each new-coming one tidings of the earth? Our world forgets. The next world remembers. The supernatural world, the Church has the memory as well as the mind of Christ.

And when the soul of the penitent thief, who died before Christ, went straight from its pardon and its cross to their Paradise, did it not Apostle-like announce to them the Mystery of Calvary? The three o'clock of Good Friday filled the earth with darkness but to Limbo brought eternal Light.

How long had they been waiting there and how marvellous must have been the life they led in those realms of Rest!

What activities of hope must have filled that quiet place? What a strange all-spiritual ritual must have ruled their worship?

They knew that Heaven's gates would not be opened until He would come who held the keys.

So they lived on, age after age, a strange, mysterious life, with a hidden history of its own,—beautiful, peaceful, hopeful; for they knew that the God of their fathers remembered, and would surely in His own time, keep His promises.

While the earth, which their spirits had departed from and where their bodies were buried, was full of tumult and iniquity,—their abode was as still as a sacred temple waiting for its Lord to enter its beautiful gates.

He came at last from the dark Friday,—the feast of His death, bringing them a feast of life and Redemption's joy. They were the first to see the soul of Christ,—for the earth had only seen the body that veiled His soul.

The shepherds saw it first. And now His soul goes down to meet the souls of the great shepherds of His people. There was surely a *Gloria in Excelsis* sounding through the beautiful Limbo;—while they worshipped the soul of the Messiah.

What a meeting between the soul of Adam and the soul of the second Adam. Did the soul of Eve sing a *Magnificat* for the glory of her pardon and the fulfillment of the Promise, as the second Eve had sung hers on earth for the glory of her Divine Maternity? And the spirits of the Patriarchs and the Prophets waiting, resting, hoping so long hailed the human soul of Jesus Christ in the joy of profoundest adoration.

The soul of John the Baptist was there. Had he been Christ's precursor there as he had been on earth?

Christ announced to them the accomplishment of the promises in His person, words and works. His preaching to them has not been written. It was soul to soul,—thought to thought,—no word. But if the words that veil his thoughts are so beautiful, how glorious must be the thoughts unveiled?

Three days His body in the tomb by Roman soldiers guarded,—three days His soul in the under-world of Rest surrounded by the souls pre ransomed by His merits.

What a beautiful Feast those three days must have been!

On Easter morn His soul re-ascended to earth, was united to the body—and Christ rose from the dead.

Forty days He remained on earth.

Scripture tells us of ten or more apparitions to His Apostles and disciples. He taught them the mysteries of the Kingdom of God. He gave them the details of the constitution of our Holy Church and the essential laws of the Sacraments. What else was the work of Christ in His risen life?

Are there other worlds inhabited by intelligent creatures, creatures fallen in their trial,—or unfallen? Did Christ ascend to them to announce the work of Mercy and of love wide enough for all the worlds? Did He pass round the earth, to bless beforehand every spot where an altar of Redemption would be raised? His works are always greater than Scripture tells us. St. John says so. May not His Church,—does not His Church fill all creation wherever a creature fallen or unfallen is found? May not the Militant Church on earth be only, as it were, a little diocese of the glorious Church which reaches from end to end of creation? If all creation did not need Redemption,—all creation needed Glorification to complete and perfect it. There are mysteries hidden and secrets unknown in that strange life of the forty days after the Resurrection, which we may dream of (for Faith does not forbid such dreamings) but which, unrevealed, lie far away beyond our narrow, earthly knowledge. And during those days whose history is hidden in silence from us,— somewhat like the days of Nazareth,—what of Mary His Mother? How many times did He appear to her? I wonder did He stay days and nights beside her who had so faithfully stood beside His Cross! Scripture is silent, but there can be no doubt that she had more privileges of His appearance and presence than all or anyone else. Magdalen still clung to her;— but after Easter Morn the name of Mary Magdalen disappears from the sacred record.

The Forty days passed with their known and unknown words and works. He was about to ascend to His Father. There was a Mount called the Mount of Olives, near Jerusalem. Thither went His Apostles with His Mother and many disciples. Jesus approached and they adored Him,—"but some still doubted." "All power is given unto me in heaven and on earth: Go ye therefore and teach all nations,—baptizing them in the name of the Father and of the Son and of the Holy Ghost;—teaching them to observe all things whatsoever I have commanded you; and behold I am with you all days even unto the consummation of the world." His last words these,—and to last forever. They were the commission given to men from Him as Son of Man to whom the Father had given all power, to perpetuate the Kingdom of Truth which He by His life, Crucifixion and Resurrection had founded. Then a bright cloud hid Him from sight. His visible presence disappeared from the world not to reappear until the Day of Judgment. He had come to the world in the noon of night—secretly and silently. He leaves the world in the noon of day publicly and with words of power on His lips. His Mother was there. She was the Mother of the Man to whom all power had been given and who delegated this power to the Apostles. She has her place on Mount Olivet. She is not only a joyous spectator of Christ's Ascension;—she is the Mother of the Ascending One;—and a living part of the Mystery. She is the Mother of Him who had all Power. She is the Mother of Him who gave all Power. Wherever that Power goes;—wherever that Power works; wherever that Power triumphs down to the end of time,—she has her place in its history,—with this difference, that whereas the Apostles were; and their successors were to be only representatives of Christ, Mary was His real Mother,—and as such had a royal right to the Queen's place in His Kingdom.

Who ascended? The Son of Mary who is the Son of God. Who gave the Power for the world's conversion? The Son of Mary who is the Son of the Eternal Father. Can they preach Christ's humanity without preaching Mary's Maternity? No,—no. It is still and still forever, as in the mysteries of Judea, so in the histories of the everlasting kingdom,—Jesus and Mary,—Son and Mother together. Whatever church (so-called through courtesy) keeps her back keeps Him back from the reach of the race redeemed. Their faces, their names, their lives, in time's days as in Eternity's decrees, appear together side by side. If Christianity be the frame out of which the merciful face of Jesus, suffering, risen, ascending and triumphant in heaven looks down forever, livingly, divinely, humanly, on the worshiping world of believers,—the face of Mary must be framed with it to make and keep it human, earthly and of real likeness to ourselves.

If the human heart of Jesus beats back of every grace, law, truth and sacrament for the world's redemption;—the heart of Mary must be felt beating with it in everlasting accord. The heart of the Mother throbs forever in the heart of the Son. Had Christ had an earthly father He would not have been divine,—could not have been true and real God, and His redemption would not and could not have been infinite in power and eternal in effects.

He has but one Father,—the Eternal. But without earthly father He is as truly and really,—and forever, the Son of Mary as He is the Son of God consubstantial with His Father. And therefore as her Son and corporally consubstantial with His Mother,—Mary, in finite degree, as the Father in degree infinite has part and place and power and share down all His reign as King in the endless Kingdom. His Mother must come with Him to prove that He is man,—and of kith and kin to the human race;—as the Eternal Father must go with Him to attest His divine Personality in the Godhead. The Eternal Father and the earthly Mother stand together back of Christ,—spiritually ever present (and Christian logic demands it) back of every word He speaks personally or representatively;—back of every work He does, of Himself or through His plenipotentiaries. The Divine of Christ teaches us through the Human;—the Human of Christ teaches us and can teach us only through Mary, His Mother.

Nor is this mere sentiment. It is clear Christian human reason. And that human reason is founded on the very reason of God Himself foreordaining from all eternity and accomplishing in time, the economy of man's Redemption.

Writing of the Church, St. Paul says: "We have the mind of Christ." And so we have. Christ's body shrined and gave forth Christian life. Christ's mind contains and reflects Christian logic,—not lifeless arguments,—but living reasons. We have His mind and with it we have the living reasons which lie back of, and inform the work of Redemption in all its wonderful outline of love and in its every single detail of mercy.

Into those reasons (man the object of salvation apart) enter four persons,—three Divine,—Father, Son and Holy Ghost;—one human,—Mary, a creature and Christ's Mother. She is necessary to the life of Redemption and she is equally, and just for that reason, necessary to the logic of Christianity. Oh Holy Church! Bride sinless of Him who was and is and will be forever the human-divine Son of the sinless Mary,—thou hast the mind of Christ,—thou dost perpetuate the life of Christ,—and wherever thy voice is lifted thou dost magnify her whom God magnified and whose soul did magnify God,—and thou dost know and thou dost preach to all generations and to all ages the Eternal Fatherhood,—the Eternal Son's Brotherhood,—the over-shadowing of the Holy Spirit,—and Mary's Motherhood,—and thus thou alone dost give to the world the perfect reason of that Faith without which it is impossible to serve God and save our souls.

Aspiration.

"I go to Him who sent me."

Prayer.

Grant, we beseech thee, Almighty God, that we who believe thy only-begotten Son our Redeemer to have this day ascended into the heavens, may ourselves also in mind dwell amid heavenly things.

TWENTY-SIXTH DAY.

The Flower of the Glory of Mary on Pentecost.

"All these were persevering with one mind, in prayer, with the women and Mary the Mother of Jesus."—*Acts* i, 14.

JESUS had promised to send the Holy-Spirit, the Paraclete, to abide with the Apostles and to carry on to its completion the great work of Redemption.

As the Spirit of God had "moved over the face of the waters" in Creation's beginning to infuse into them the principle and germs of creature-life;—as the same Holy Spirit had overshadowed Mary, in the day of the Annunciation, with the vivifying power by and through which she conceived Jesus—creature,—yet also Creator;—so the same Holy Spirit was to overshadow the Virgin Church, with mighty power, to make her truly the spiritual mother of innumerable children.

Ten days passed. The Apostles were gathered together in an upper room in Jerusalem,—and "Mary, the Mother of Jesus" was with them. "Suddenly there came a sound from heaven as of a mighty wind rushing; and there appeared unto them cloven tongues as of fire and it sat upon each of them; and they were all filled with the Holy Ghost."

The Virgin Mother Church had been conceived in the heart of Christ immaculate as His Virgin Mother had been conceived immaculate.

On Pentecost by the coming of the Holy Ghost the Church was born in her divine perfection.

And Mary who had watched over the new-born Christ in Bethlehem, watched over the new-born Church;—and, for fifteen years longer she was still to remain on earth to watch the infant Church in its growth.

Was it merely accidental? Hush! with God in His ways and works there is nothing accidental. Let ignorance be welcome to the false and meaningless word.

Faith says—no. Her stay on earth after the Ascension was not, 'tis true, necessary; but it was providential. God had a reason why she should remain yet awhile longer in the world.

The Mother of Christ was to be to the Church,—not a Teacher,—not an apostle,—but something higher, nearer, dearer, tenderer,—the Mother of the Faithful.

Her very face recalled to their eyes the face of Jesus. Her very presence implied that where and with whom she was her divine Son would be. Her grand graces hung around the cradle of the Church as they had hung around the crib of the Infant Christ. What we reason about from afar off the Apostles and the faithful beheld before them. What was clear sight to them is clear, true syllogism to us. She is a living part of Pentecost's mystery. The mysterious day of Pentecost lasts forever. With it begins,—never to end until the last day of time, the reign of the Holy Ghost with all the rights and royalties of the graces of Sanctification.

And so henceforth it is and it will be always not only Jesus and Mary together,—but Jesus and Mary and the Holy Ghost together;—and where they are the Eternal Father must be. Down from the upper chamber came Peter with the eleven. Peter, the commander-in-chief, by right of rank, stood up and spoke for the rest and gave to the multitudes around him the first battle-cry of Christian faith: "Ye men of Israel, hear these words. Jesus of Nazareth a man approved of God among you by miracles and wonders and signs, which God did by Him in the midst of you, as ye yourselves also know,—Him being delivered by the determinate counsel and fore-knowledge of God, ye have taken and by wicked hands have crucified and slain." The battle-cry is Christ's humanity. And amid the hearers stood Mary His Mother; living, present, visible proof that Christ was Man.

Then rising in his argument to the triumph of Christ's resurrection and to the glory of His Ascension Peter concluded: "Therefore let all the house of Israel know assuredly that God hath made that same Jesus whom you have crucified both LORD and CHRIST."

The Mother was just as necessary to his argument as was God Himself. "Jesus of Nazareth a MAN." Mary is necessary. Jesus of Nazareth,—LORD and CHRIST. The eternal Father is necessary. "Jesus of Nazareth" is the subject of the first sermon of Christianity,— as He will be the subject of Christianity's last sermon;— and the subject of every sermon between the first and the last. Essential to the subject are His eternal Father and His earthly Mother. Either thrust aside, He is not the Christ of Bethlehem—or of Nazareth, or of Calvary, or of the Resurrection, or of the Ascension,—nor is He the Christ preached to the world on Pentecost Sunday. His manhood and her womanhood,—His human sonship and her motherhood stand or fall together.

Where goes the Man goes the Mother. Where the Mother is not there is not, nor can be the true and real

Christ. As long as He lives she lives. Where He works, her Son works,—where He wins, her Son wins; and she, as Mother, has a Mother's incommunicable share in His works and in His triumphs. The Apostles will have successors. His Mother has no successor. Their preaching will give testimony to the Word made flesh. But their testimony needs Mary's sinless body to confirm it and to make it full, clear, true, real and comprehensible.

And above all things, that Sacrament of Sacraments which is the "Mystery of Faith," the blessed Eucharist in which we receive the very body and blood of Christ rests fundamentally on the fact of Christ's humanity which itself rests on the fact of Mary's maternity.

Pentecost was the Birth-day of the Church of Christ. Our Holy Church alone has the right to keep it.

The Peter of Pentecost is preaching still and will preach and teach the world forever. Pope Leo holds his place and his prerogatives. And the sermon is the same as the subject is the same,—the "Man Jesus of Nazareth." His humanity springs from Mary's maternity. The Sermon must lean on the Mother as a star must lean upon a sky. And—"The CHRIST and LORD." The teaching must lean upon the Eternal Father,—as the sun leans against the Heavens.

Peter's Pentecostal argument is Faith's eternal argument. Any thing less is false. Any thing more is wrong. And it is the full and perfect and unanswerable argument. He was brief, terse, brave, pointed. He said it all in a few sentences. He gave to the world the plan of Christian preaching. He had the right to give the plan, for he was the Prince of the Apostles. First point,—the humanity of Jesus of Nazareth. Christ's

Mother proves it. Second point,—the Divinity of Jesus; —the Eternal Father proves it. Oh beautiful Christ!— and Thy Kingdom shall be as wide as the world,—and everlasting shall be Thy reign;—and Thou shalt win victories,—and Thou shalt have triumphs;—and Thou shalt wear crowns of infinite glories. When Thou dost now every day lay them down in heaven at Thy Father's feet;—and when in the end Thou shalt lay down all the trophies of Thy Precious blood at the footstool of Thy Father's throne,—will not the Mother who gave Thee Thy Precious Blood participate, with Thy Eternal Father, in Thy infinite glory? Thou Son of Man and King of men! wilt Thou forget her who made Thee such? Will she not have ever and forever the sacred rights of Thy Mother,—and the royal prerogatives of Queen in Thy Kingdom?

Yes,—yes,—they are her's given to her and never to be taken away.

Let us enter the gates of all the churches.

Ah me! there are many churches differing each from the other, though they each among all assume the glory of being the Church of Christ. Did Christ ever differ from Himself? Is His name a name of contradictions which Faith, violating the protests of truth, must accept? Can He Himself, or through His Church, say one thing to one and contradict it to another? No—no. One Christ,—one Church. But let us enter the doors of the churches which claim to be His.

There are many tests. Let us take but one.

Only one question,—ever so simple. How do you stand towards the Mother of Christ? What is your attitude? Is it one of love and veneration;—or one of indifference, or else one of hostility? That tests your title as Church of Christ. Do you keep the Mother and Son together—Him to adore as your Saviour-God,—her to honor and venerate as the Mother of the God-Saviour. Answer—Yes—or No. And your answer, in the court of human reason as well as before the tribunal of true Christian Faith settles at once and forever the question whether you are of God's divine design or of mere man's false dreaming.

Alas! and yet alas! in the so-called Christian churches we seek but find not Mary, the Mother, of Jesus with her rights and powers. Logically a Maryless church is a Christless church. A church, that does not take the Mother and throne her in her exclusive place has no right to take the Christ whom the world received through her. Mother and Son,—Jesus and Mary together! 'Tis the ceaseless refrain of Redemption's glorious and endless hymn.

Aspiration.

"He is risen,—he is not here."

Prayer.

O God, who on this day, through thine only begotten Son, didst overcome death, and open unto us the gate of everlasting life; as by thy prompting grace thou dost breathe on the desires of our hearts, so do thou ever accompany them with thy help.

TWENTY-SEVENTH DAY.

The Flower of the Joy of Mary's Death.

"My memory is unto everlasting generations."—*Eccl.* xxiv, 28.

PETER, the Chief of the Apostles preached the first sermon; and Peter celebrated the first Mass. At that Mass Mary received the Holy Eucharist; and as many think, the sacred species remained in her incorruptible, with the sacred Presence, from one Communion to another;—so that her heart was all the while the ciborium and the Tabernacle where Jesus mystically dwelt. Her Communions, like her Conception of Jesus, in intensity of love and in unapproachable graces, are simply beyond measure of thought and description of word. Meanwhile,—just as Christ had said: "The disciple is not above the Master;—if they persecuted Me—they will persecute you:"—the Jews rose up in wrath against the new doctrines. The cry of His enemies on Good Friday: "Away with Him; away with Him"—rang out in fierce hatred against His followers. Stephen, a disciple of Gamaliel, was the first to shed his blood and give up his life for Christ. His body fell beneath, but his soul soared above their brutal argument of stones. Peter was put into prison. Chain the chief and his followers will retreat or surrender. Such their thought. They were soon undeceived. An angel came,—as Mary of Agreda writes, sent by the Blessed Virgin,—unbound him, opened the prison doors and set him free. Mary was not teaching,—but she was guarding the Teachers. Had Jesus not said it: "I will not leave you orphans?" As He,—so the Church has a Mother;—and her name is Mary. How she watched its first sufferings,—its sudden growth,—and the beginnings of its glory! The Apostles preached. Mary, the Mother prayed.

And who can measure the power of those prayers? All looked so dark around the young Church. So few against so many. But nothing now was dark to her. She saw it all,—the growing Light around her. She rejoiced with an exceeding joy. Down in her heart she was singing over again with the same music but with new meanings her soul's MAGNIFICAT. For she saw the future,—all,—all,—all,—and the endless glories of the Kingdom of her Son. The Apostles and disciples separated. When soldiers separate,—they are defeated. The soldiers of the Cross separated to conquer. Each went to his own mission and his appointed country to preach, to testify, to die,—and to triumph. They were workers,—and they had no time to write. Human lips—and not a pen were to bring salvation to the nations. Paul was not converted by preaching. Did Mary's prayers convert him? With the Apostle John she went down to Ephesus among the gentiles. So says tradition. After the day of Pentecost Scripture does not mention her name. The olden law of silence gathers around her life again. Yet none the less was she there with all her rights and powers and privileges just as she had lived in the silences of Nazareth. Her marvellous graces could not help but manifest their activities wherever she went. She had never lost the beauty of her maidenhood. The years had come and gone but in appearance she did not grow old. The charm of perpetual youth enhanced her incomparable beauty. The inner beauty of her soul dazzled the eyes of the very angels. It was moving and mounting, every minute, from sphere to higher sphere of grace. It was gaining merits that will forever help to save the souls of sinners and increase the sanctities of the just. The Church in her soul and inner life was perfect from the first; and now she begins to adorn her visible body with that external beauty which never will be lost and never can be borrowed. How much had Mary to do with the external adornment of the Church? Much surely,— though how much none can say.

Will Mary die? Sinless,—can death touch her? Is not death the penalty of sin? She had no sin. Or,—is not death like that of Christ the chosen, vicarious expiation of sin. Mary cannot expiate even a venial sin by her life or death. But she can die to imitate her Son in His vicarious death. And like Jesus she will, though not under the ban of sin bear the burden of death which belongs to the human race.

She went up to Jerusalem. The Mother's eyes craved to behold once more the scenes hallowed by her Son in His life and death. She would fain make the way of the Cross before she went to receive her crown. Her faithful children in the faithful Church will, in after times, imitate her. In lowly chapel and in grand Cathedral pictured forever are the fourteen stations of the Way of the Cross. She knelt at each and prayed at each of them not for herself but for us. The day of her death came,— and the hour. It was a Friday. Even as to the day she will be like unto Jesus. Had the Archangel Gabriel come again to announce the joyful tidings of her death?

For death was a joy to her,—and such a joy—to go and meet her Beloved in the Kingdom of His glory!

St. John of Damascus writes: "By the command of her Son, the Apostles assembled around her, and they had come for this purpose to the city of Jerusalem from the most distant parts of the world."

She strengthens and comforts them. She speaks her last words to them—so strangely like the words of Jesus. He was looking at them through His Mother's eyes. St. Thomas of Villanova writes: "Her eyes turned heavenward,—and with boundless joy and jubilation she resigned to her Son her most blessed spirit." Her life went out in the ecstacy of a Mother's love. And Mary was dead. Thomas alone of the eleven living Apostles (for James had suffered martyrdom) was not present at Mary's death. They bore the dead sinless body to the grave and gently and reverently laid it there. Denis the Areopagite writes that he was present at her death and burial. John of Damascus writes that heaven and earth were filled with joy when Mary's spirit passed away. The Apostle Thomas came at last. They went to her tomb on Sunday,—but her body was not there.

Sinless her body was incorruptible. Being the Mother of the Risen Christ, Mary by special grace and by the power of God with her body, to her sinless soul reunited, anticipated the general resurrection; Christ raised her from the dead and she was assumed into heaven. The law of sin in its consequences never attainted her soul. Why should the law of death in its consequences attaint her body with corruption? She died, it is true, in imitation of her Divine Son,—and like Him she was laid away in a grave. But a sinless body cannot corrupt. It is beyond the reach of that which is death's last and lowest humiliation—the worm of the sepulchre,—and the return to dust. St. Epiphanius treating the question of Mary's death employs these remarkable words: "I do not say that she remained immortal;—nor am I certain that she died."

The Church, however, believes that Mary did undergo the law of death,—not because she was a sinner,—but because her body was human and therefore mortal. Yet none the less was her body endowed with the grace of incorruption. Immaculate soul implies incorruptible flesh. So our holy Church with a true and a perfect and a brave Faith (for the honor of the Son of God Incarnate is involved in the honor of the body that conceived and brought Him forth) holds up to our veneration not only the pure soul of Mary,—but her virgin, human form, as well, that was on earth the first and sacred tabernacle of the Emmanuel. The Truths of Faith flower into beautiful Festivals that their sweet fragrance may fill our hearts as they fill our holy Church. Every Saturday, since the Saturday when the Christ was lying dead in the sepulchre, and only His Mother stood amid the disciples,—her face recalling to their eyes the Face that had disappeared, is devoted to Mary. It is her day in every week of time.

And all through the year there are feast-days in the Church celebrating, in Christ's honor, her privileges, and commemorating, in His honor, the mysteries of His Mother's blessed life. Midway in August we meet the Feast of her Assumption. The whole Catholic world meets, in the spirit of the one Faith, beside her deathbed, watches her passing away, beholds her dead, follows the Apostles whose consecrated hands bore the consecrated Burden,—and kneels down at the grave of the Mother of God; while in tones of joy triumphant floats from the altar the voice of the Priest: "Let us all rejoice in the Lord keeping holy Feast in honor of the Blessed Virgin Mary;"—while across the ages realized in the festival and illustrating its glories come to us the words of old St. Jerome in his sermon on the Assumption: "To all others grace is given in parts;—but to Mary comes the plenitude, of all the graces, that is in Christ." Oh! blessed Mother dying! Pray for all the dying! "Pray for us now and at the hour of our death!" And pray that our bodies like thine may rise in incorruption to be crowned with glory forever in the heavens!

Aspiration.

"My Beloved to me and I to him."—*Canticles.*

Prayer.

Pardon, Lord, we beseech thee, the transgressions of thy servants: that we, who by our own deeds are unable to please thee, may be saved by the intercession of the Mother of thy Son our Lord.

TWENTY-EIGHTH DAY.

Flower of the Glory of Mary's Coronation in Heaven.

"For her thoughts are more vast than the sea and her counsels more deep than the great ocean."—*Eccl.* xxiv, 39.

IT was Sunday on earth. The light of the sun, whose stillness and whose brightness are so strangely like the stillness and the brightness of God, was shining over the grave of Mary. Thither,—and early,—with others went Peter and John as erst they had gone together to the tomb of Christ. For the grave of the sinless one was a holy place. They entered,—they looked,—they wondered and knelt them down to worship the Power of God;—for Mary was not there. Only a moment their wonder lasted. Their quick, intense Faith met the mystery and grasped its reason and its meaning. Heaven had claimed that sinless body for its own. It was too pure to stay. Up there in heaven it had wondrous rights.

The glorified human form of Christ was seated at the right hand of the Most High. In heaven the angels wanted what earth had needed,—Mother and Son together,—for if Mother of men she is Queen of Angels. They have seen her soul, but they want her sinless body; for without soul and body reunited, she is not the Mary of Bethlehem for whom and her babe they had sung that long-gone *"Gloria in Excelsis."*

Heaven wants her in the perfection of her person. That means body as well as soul. Heaven's prayer is God's will.

It was Sunday on earth. Are there days in Heaven's Eternal Day reflecting the light of their glory on our little Earth-days and catching from our days the light of our Faith? Has the Church Triumphant a calendar of Festivals of glory,—the beautiful counterparts of the Feasts of grace in the militant church? Is there a communion of days as well as a communion of saints between heaven and earth? We speak a human thought,—and only speak it half;—for out of human words, alas! we can never weave a perfect royal robe rich and grand and glorious enough to clothe one single divine truth.

Faith's eyes are better than Faith's fingers.

Open ye gates that hide the everlasting Vision!

Ye rest on hinges of mercy. At the breath of a saint's prayer or a sinner's sigh for pardon ye are, every instant, opened. When the soul of the innocent cometh,—when the soul of the penitent cometh ye open and let them enter in.

Oh! beautiful gates! hung on the pillars of God's infinite Love! "Lift ye up your heads! oh ye gates! and be ye lifted up ye everlasting gates!" Who hath come in through you? The King of glory? Who is this King of glory? "The Lord strong and mighty,—the Lord mighty in battle?" Yea,—He hath entered in and is seated at the right hand of His Father.

But again: "Lift up your heads oh ye gates! yea—lift them up ye everlasting gates,"—the "King of glory,—the Lord strong and mighty" will pass through your opening to-day,—and with Him all the angels;—for His

Mother is coming from afar off—is coming "fair as the moon and bright as a sun" to heaven and to earth and to heaven's enemies "terrible as an army set in array!" And the King goes forth surrounded by angels,—followed by the glorified souls of Patriarchs and Prophets to meet the sinless Mary. Ah! once He went forth to become her child and to make her His Mother; but now He goeth forth to meet her on her heavenward way, to bring her through the beautiful gates to her throne and her crown and her glory. Amid such splendors as heaven had never seen,—save at His Ascension; amid such songs of joy triumphant as heaven had never heard, He leads His Mother into the Eternal Courts and presents her to His Eternal Father who crowns her Queen of all Creation, by right of her being Mother of Christ its King. Her place in Heaven corresponded to her place on earth,—the highest. Her privileges and powers and glories in heaven are like her's on earth,— God's Mother's;—and therefore unshared and incommunicable.

She is crowned and throned above all the heavenly hierarchy. The angelic world honors her with profoundest veneration. She is a part of the religion of Glory (if I may so speak) as she is a part of the religion of grace. Her relations to the Trinity are so real and so intimate that she sees deepest into the eternal Beatific Vision; and from its depths draws into her one own heart more raptures of joy ineffable than all the angels together. Religion here below is union with God in grace. Heaven's happiness is union with God in the vision of His glory. Mary, highest in grace here is highest in glory there. She has reached heights so lofty, where union with the Divinity is closest, that they are simply inaccessible to any other created being.

Do the angels adore the Divine Humanity of Jesus Christ? Do they not gaze with joys ever new upon the glorified Face of Him who sits at the Father's right hand? Can they adore that Divine Humanity,—or gaze upon its Face without a thought of Mary the Mother?

No—no. What we reason about,—the angels see clearly, fully and at once. The angels belong to the triumphant church of Christ Triumphant, as we here below and now belong to the militant church of Christ Crucified. Before their sight in the Vision of Glory as before our eyes with their light of Faith Jesus Christ and Mary His Mother are together inseparably and eternally united. What is truth believed on earth is truth seen in heaven. What is fact of Faith in time is flash of glory in eternity. Heaven and earth, like God and man, are alike. But the likeness is dim and marred. Sin's shadow still hangs over the world. But beneath the shadow there is a realm of grace and truth and light and priesthood and sacraments. That realm is inhabited by men and women and children all the world over. It is the realm of Sanctification. The invisible Holy Spirit of God the Father and of God the Son rules it through visible rulers. It is the Holy Church; —herself sinless, yet the Church of sinners; and she is like unto the church in the heavens,—essentially like and can never be otherwise. What is the cause of the likeness, which if removed the likeness will be dim and marred?—Jesus and Mary,—neither from the other apart,—but both together.

Mary, by the power of the Holy Ghost,—her human will uniting with the divine will, made Christ, in all reality and substantially, to the image and likeness of

Man; and by Him and through her, the Holy Spirit still operating, the Church on earth is, in all inner reality and substantially made unto the image and likeness of the Church in heaven.

The "Hail full of Grace" with its mystery sounds through every day of Redemption. We hear the words and believe the mystery. The "Hail ful' of Grace" with its mystery is a part of heaven's eternal hymn. Up there they sing the words and see the mystery in the fulness of its glory. Here and There the words are the same,—and the mystery. There and Here the names shining out of the words are the same,—Mary and Jesus,—giving perfect meaning to the Mystery seen in Glory as they give complete meaning to the mystery believed here below in the days of grace.

If this be a dream,—it was the dream of God from all eternity,—and was made true. If this be poetry,—it is the poetry of eternal love wordless in the heart of God from the unbeginning,—but sung in time and in words of human speech by the Archangel Gabriel in the hour of the Annunciation. That was an eternal hour,— eternal in the song itself which came from eternity and eternal in its echo.

That echo rings true and clear from every pulpit of our Holy Church when the words of the Christ are preached to men. Its mystical music is heard at every altar where the Christ the Word made flesh comes eucharistically to dwell among us. That echo is sounding back of all dogmas—as they come one by one rays out of the sun of Truth, to guide the feet of the Faithful.

That echo is sounding,—a human undertone to the divine music of the Sacraments. That echo can be heard by the grace-quickened ears of Faith wherever grace is a-working,—or battling with evil or winning triumphs.

That echo is heard on the lips of the young and the old and the high and the lowly, who become Gabriel-like in re-announcing from earth to Mary in heaven, in faith and love and trust, the words of the Annunciation.

When that echo dies, Faith in its fullness dies.

When that echo is lost Mary is lost,—and when she is lost the beauty of Jesus is lost,—and the perfect meaning of His mercy.

Mary's coronation in the heavens in highest place and first next to Christ's is but the simple recognition by the Trinity and the angel-world of the privileged position which she held among and above all creatures of every creation.

Around her throne there the angels gather with homages of honor, in the very sight of God,—as we gather around her altars here below in veneration of her blessed name. They adore Christ the King as God-man crowned with the diadem of the Mercy that redeemed the world,—as do we in the Kingdom of Redemption on earth,—which is the Church. And they honor with highest angelic honor Mary the King's Mother and their Queen,—as a part of their eternal worship and of their eternal beatitude. The visible presence of their blessed Queen has added another to their countless glories;—and has added another duty (if so we may speak of duty in heaven) to their other duties.

For they are at her call,—and gloriously imitating in the heavens their King's subjection to her on earth, they obey her behests. She has work for them to do in all creation. And it is new joy for them to do it, for to work for Mary is to work for Jesus.

Ah! in the day of her Coronation she was crowned with a glory next to that of Christ,—but though crowned, her power does not rest, her work does not end;—for her love for her Son the Redeemer throbs in her heart for all the redeemed!

She gave the Saviour to Creation and she must help to sanctify the saved. Infinite Mercy is not hers. That is the attribute of God alone. But Mary possesses that which is next to infinite Mercy,—the power of the Prayer of the Mother of the Infinite.

Over the eternal Church on high she rules as Queen, for she is not the Mother of the angels;—but amid the glories of her Queendom she does not forget our far-off earthly Kingdom of grace of which on Calvary's day she was appointed Mother forever.

ASPIRATION.

"MARY hath chosen the better part."

PRAYER.

PARDON, Lord, we beseech thee, the transgressions of thy servants: that we, who by our own deeds are unable to please thee, may be saved by the intercession of the Mother of thy Son our Lord.

TWENTY-NINTH DAY.

The Flower of Mary's Intercession.

"And all mine are thine,—and thine are mine : and I am glorified in them."—*John* xvii, 10.

HEAVEN is a place of rest,—but heaven is also a place of work. Its rest does not mean idleness. God rests but not in the sense of doing nothing. He is always at work and always in rest. His grand Omnipotence, in this very minute, is governing and preserving worlds already made;—and who knows?—perhaps creating new worlds. But His work is effortless. He wills because He wills and it is done. The angels are in the rapture of the rest. And yet are they not "ministering spirits?" Does not ministering mean working? The souls of the just are at rest; but in heaven do they not make constant supplication for us? Is not supplication work? Jesus Christ throned at His Father's right hand is in the glory of rest;—and yet this very moment is He not governing His Holy Church and through her applying to the children of men the merits of Redemption. And is not that everlasting work? While every day in heaven is a day of rest, heaven has no workless days. Just as the sun and the stars, by laws appointed unto them, work down through the great distances, on our earth with their influences;—so the heavens of Glory, where all is rest, are forever shedding their influences on the Church of Christ. There is a law of communion of suns and stars by which each affects the other. So there is a higher, spiritual law of which nature's law is but a type;—"the communion of saints." What does it mean? Is it only a pretty poetic phrase? It is written in the Apostles' Creed. It is a living dogma; and every dogma is a poem of God's infinite love.

But what does it mean? "There is but one Mediator,—Jesus Christ." Is not His mediatorship sufficient? Yes indeed—and over-sufficient. Is not His infinite love, which is the heart of His infinite omnipotent power which is the hand to make His work of grace full and perfect, sufficient of itself?

Verily yes,—and more than sufficient. Does He need helpers to assist Him down here in the Kingdom of Sanctification?

Verily no. He alone of Himself is sufficient for His work. And yet nevertheless He does not do the work by Himself alone. That work is the work of His own Will. But He has willed that the activities of all the Redeemed in Heaven and on earth should have part and force and power (finite of course) in the great Act of Redemption. And more than that. He brings into His service and to His assistance in the accomplishment of His work the material creation itself. He summons the element of water not only to be a mere sign,—but to be the essential matter of the Sacrament of Baptism,—Chrism for Confirmation; wheat and wine for the Eucharist,—oil for Extreme Unction.

Words of human speech by Himself chosen are to constitute the forms of His sacraments. And words of human speech written in the Scriptures, or spoken by Authority, are His earthly auxiliaries in the battles and victories of Faith. He might have done without such alliance with powers so weak and things so lowly,—but He did not. He did as He willed; and His will was and is that creatures and creation should help Him in the consummation of His work of Mercy. Thus creation helps to redeem itself. Thus creatures of a sinful race assist in repairing and rebuilding the fallen Temple of original grace. Thus Priests, Bishops, Popes are intermediaries between man and man's Mediator. Thus outside of our Holy Church the Bible as read by each, or preached even by self-appointed and commissionless teachers is an intermediary between the human mind and the Mediator. The priests form the House of Christ's Representatives chosen by God and by Holy Church ordained,—and they stand nearest to the People of Christ. The Bishops form the Senate in the Commonwealth of the Faithful. The Roman Pontiff is Supreme Head of the Church, possessing sovereign power in the realms of revealed truth,—a power guarded from every danger of abuse by the prerogative of official Infallibility.

Christ Himself, visibly and personally has done His last work and said His last word in this world. He works through others on earth. So in Heaven the kingdom of glory where He makes infinite mediation for us, Christ also works through others. He works through the choirs of the angels. He works through the souls of the saints. Through their prayers and supplications in the home of glory He worketh in the kingdom of grace here below.

But above them all reigns Mary,—Heaven's Queen

and earth's Mother. If Christ gave to His Apostles "all power in heaven and on earth,"—is not His Mother greater? Are not her prerogatives higher? Has she not power next to the very Omnipotence of God? Did she lose that power on the day of her coronation? Was it not made greater the hour she was crowned Heaven's Queen? Has God taken away her rights? When He crowned her did He not confirm them? Next to her Divine Motherhood is it not her greatest glory to be the mediatrix of sinners? While on earth did she not love God more than all created beings ever did or will or could love Him? And now in heaven has not her love for Him immeasurably increased? Did she not love man, while on earth, more than man could ever be loved except by God Himself? Is not her power equal to her love? And who will draw,—and where,—the line that limits her love?

It cannot be drawn save to say only that it is not infinite. Love and Power,—Power and Love superior to all Loves and Powers,—inferior only to God's. Let the pens of glorious saints and not my pen,—a poor sinner's write of her power.

St Peter Damian writes that all power is given to Mary in heaven and upon earth as even Christ the Almighty is subject to her since she herself gave unto Him a Power which He had not received from God the Father,—the power to die and redeem sinners with His precious blood. St. Bernard, whose devotion to the Blessed Virgin is one of the most striking traits of his wonderful life, preaching on the Feast of her Nativity, says that God has placed expressly in Mary the plenitude of every good, that we may be obliged to receive every gift from the abundance of her's; and that if for us there be any hope of salvation, any grace of Redemption, any right to eternal glory we must recognize that all these things come to us from the Saviour through her.

St. Bernardine of Sienna writes: "From the time in which the Virgin Mary conceived in her chaste womb God's own Son, she obtained a certain jurisdiction or a special authority over the temporal mission of the Holy Ghost, so that no creature has obtained from God either grace or merit save by the dispensation of this holy Mother." Stronger thoughts come out of the heart of the great St. Bernard when he says that not a single grace descends from heaven to earth that does not come through the hands of Mary.

St. Thomas of Aquin, the Angel of the Schools, says: "As the Son intercedes for us with the Father, so the Mother intercedes for us with the Son."

These were saints who thus wrote and spoke,—men of profound learning only equalled by their piety. They were men of lofty reason, of deep, life-long study of God's holy word,—of highest virtues. They manifested the mind as well as the heart of revelation.

They were not the babblers of an hour whose words were only mere sounds, and like sounds, pass away. They were the representatives of truth in the past and teachers of faith for the future.

Their words still ring in truth's own clear and certain tone; but heresy has made too many ears deaf to the "Faith which comes by hearing." And so the words of the saints share the fate of the words of the Saint of saints. They are heard or read but they are not understood;—not because the words are not true-toned or clearly written;—but because inherited error flings a film over the eyes that read; and dulls and deafens the ears that hear, the words of divine Truth.

The minister of error, only a day old in his ministry, who has had a call to preach the Gospel, with no virtues, except perhaps honesty and gentlemanliness; with no study worth the waste of words to measure it, will rise in his pulpit; and one of his first subjects of discourse, if not the very first, is what? An attack against Christ's Church. Against what? The honor we pay to Mary, Christ's Mother.

And he will ring the changes on a word coined by falsehood and accepted by prejudice. And the word? You know it —MARIOLATRY. Gentlemen! take care. It is Christ-like and therefore Christian-like and therefore Catholic,—to honor Christ's Mother. Not to honor her is to dishonor her,—and to dishonor her is surely to dishonor her Son, and to dishonor him is to dishonor His Father.

And pray, who are ye who dare give the lie to nineteen centuries? Are you saints? Are you learned men? If saints, show us your virtues. If learned men, prove to us your wisdom.

Why! the great centuries are choristers singing around the altar of changeless Faith hymns of adoration of Jesus and songs of honor and veneration of Mary.

We in Holy Church are of "the generations (regenerated) who call Mary blessed." And who can be more blessed than the Mother of the infinitely blessed God? False to her is false to Him. Indifferent to her is indifferent to Him. Hostile to her is hostile to Him. Enmity of mind or speech, or of so-called doctrine to her settles the side to be taken by her enemies. The words of Genesis are exceedingly plain. They were spoken to Satan: "I will place enmities between thee and the Woman and between thy seed and her seed." The posterity of Christ is the posterity of Mary the Mother of Christ. He is of the seed of Mary—and like Him so are we. With knowledge or without knowledge they who are against us are against Christ and His Mother, and are on the side of Satan.

Are these words hard? Yes! hard to a faith as flimsy as it is soft (though we ought to call it human fancy rather than divine Faith);—but they are God's words and not ours;—and so we let them stand in all hardness. Catholic Truth in its entirety is a rock that will not be splintered. It braves the blow of the boldest hand; and it defies the rush of the wildest waves; and it smiles, if a rock can smile, at the fury of the darkest storm. Who is the truth that is the Rock? Jesus Christ. And who is the shore on which it leans? Mary—the Mother of God. The Rock and its Shore are ours and ours alone forever.

Aspiration.

"Pray for us now and at the hour of our death."

Prayer.

Hail Mary! full of grace, the Lord is with thee, blessed art thou amongst women, and blessed is the fruit of thy womb, Jesus. Holy Mary, Mother of God, pray for us sinners, now, and at the hour of death. *Amen.*

THIRTIETH DAY.

The Flower of Mary's Glory in the Church.

"And in all these I sought rest and I shall abide in the inheritance of the Lord."—*Eccl.* xxiv, 11.

THE Incarnation of Jesus Christ through Mary is the rehabilitation in grace of the human race. The Church of Christ is the perpetuation of the Incarnation. By the first Man Adam, at the word of the Woman Eve, sin entered into the world. Sin's reparation was to be made by the Man Christ who, at the word of Mary: "Be it done unto me according to thy word," entered into this world. Man and Woman,—Adam and Eve were the causes of our spiritual ruin. Man and Woman,—Christ and Mary,—second Adam and second Eve are the causes of our Redemption. Everywhere on earth and until the end of time the act of the disobedience of our first parents reaches in its consequences of sin for souls and death for bodies. And so everywhere in the world and down to its last day reaches the act of Mary's obedience to the divine will in becoming the Mother of Christ, together with the obedience of Christ in doing His Father's will, in the consequences of grace for the souls and immortality for the bodies of every child of the human race who accepts the Redeemer. The influences of Jesus and Mary move forever alongside the influences of Adam and Eve.

Adam and Eve were two persons united in one act,—it was our ruin. Jesus and Mary are two persons united in one act,—it is our Redemption.

Every day of history will man's heart ask: "Through whom have I lost all right to heaven?" And every heart's answer will be: "Through Adam and Eve." And every day of time each heart will ask: "Through whom shall I recover the right to enter Heaven?" And every heart's question shall have its answer,—Through Jesus and Mary. It is the only true answer. It is the full and perfect answer. Truth gives it,—Faith proclaims it; and the Church of Truth and Faith must realize and illustrate it. Else all is as dark to the questioning world as it was before the mystery of the Infant's birth in Bethlehem. For the mystery of man's regeneration in grace must solve the mystery of man's generation in sin. In the light of the former mystery stand Jesus and Mary. In the darkness of the latter mystery stand Adam and Eve.

Our Holy Church is the mystical Eden in this world, with gates wide open, guarded by the Angel of the Redemption. Who so wills to leave the beautiful spiritual garden may do so. God forces none to stay. But who so desire to return and re-enter cannot do so unless they come to the gates wearing the robes of grace. In the garden are the second Adam and the second Eve,—Jesus and Mary,—for it is theirs to keep and cultivate;—and in our Holy Church we meet them there together.

With us of the true Faith the glory of Jesus is the royal mantle of Mary His Mother;—and her glory is the brightest gem in the crown of Christ.

St. Paul writing to the Ephesians proclaims that

Christ's would be "a glorious Church without spot or wrinkle, or any such thing" and that "it would be holy and without any blemish."

What are the glories of the "glorious Church?"
Her divine truths with their heavenly light? Yes.
Her laws with their sanctifying influences? Yes.
Her sacraments with their supernatural action? Yes.
Her teachings with their divine power over the human mind,—and their infallible certainty? Yes.

Her messages of Mercy, the legacies of His love, to every heart redeemed? Yes.

Sinners in their penances and pardons? Yes.
Saints in the splendors of their sanctities? Yes.
Apostles,—Martyrs, Confessors, Virgins with the supernatural braveries, sufferings, austerities and purities of their lives and deaths? Yes.

For in their persons redeeming grace has conquered their minds with its light, their wills by its law, their hearts with its love.

Ah! Yes they are the living glories of the "glorious Church" whose life is divine. They visibly realize in their persons and reflect on the world, within as well as without the kingdom of grace, the glories of dogmas, and laws and sacraments,—the splendors of Faith and Hope and Charity,—the light of the Christ who lives over again in their lives.

The Church of Christ must have other Christs,— human to prove to the world His divine Christhood. All along the ages she will have her Calvaries to climb; but she must and will have a thousand Thabors up the slopes of which she will lead sinners from the valley of sin to transfigure them on the summit with the splendors of sanctity,—so that the generations of men passing by will see the glory shining; and in the wonder of Faith and with the Faith of wonder, will cry aloud as Peter cried: "Oh Lord it is good for us to be here."

Churches calling yourselves Christian listen!

You must prove your title. How? In your hand you bring us the Scriptures. Well and good. We also have them. In your other hand have you the lives of your Saints? Saints are living scriptures. Do you bring us only words even though they be the words of Christ? They are dead words unless you show us men who have lived them. Life is the logic that proves the power of Christ. He Himself is not in His words. Only His thoughts are there. He Himself in His Church by His grace lives in men, women, children who participate in His sanctity. Show us such if you can.

Read for us the Litany of your Saints! Have you none?

No Saints,—no Christ.

No canonizations,—then no names crowned on earth with the halo of Christ's holiness.

Churches! do you lead your followers only through the valley of ordinary virtues and commonplace duty?

Lift up your eyes! Yonder on the mountains, rising towards the skies the splendors of the "Sun of Justice" are shining on the snow-white purities of lofty Christ-like lives. Do those lives belong to you? Is the white snow up there too cold for the feet of your children? Are the mountains of sanctity too steep and too rugged for them to climb? Are the splendors on their summits too bright and dazzling to your eyes?—Then— move on down in the valley. You know not the mysteries and the meanings of the mountains climbed by Christ,—Calvary, Thabor, Olivet. You are not His

Church. You have no saints. You have no hearts beating with the highest heroisms of Faith.

Not so we of His Holy Church. True,—the most of us walk in the lower valleys of ordinary virtue; but countless is the number of those who have scaled the steeps and reached the summits of holiness. And their glory shines down on our souls, making our way brighter and our hearts braver;—and their glory is their's and yet Christ's, and what is theirs and His is our's. We salute them as we pass, for they are the heroes in the march,—in the battles and in the victories of the soldiers of Jesus Christ. And they hail us as we pass them by with cheering words that give us comfort and courage and heavenly trust on our homeward way.

Human sanctity is the splendor of Divine grace. Where its light gleams there surely shines the moveless sun of changeless Faith. From the Birth-day of the Church until this very evening all down the ages there has been a line of Saints. But above them all, with a brighter glory than they all together possess, and with a greater power, reigns Mary the Mother in the kingdom of her Son. Mother of Christ—Mother of His Church,—such is her place and power and glory.

Is it a wonder that the Church has glorified her in every age? Is it a marvel that blazoned on her banners of battle and sounding in her hymns of triumph the name of Mary is forever united with the name of Jesus?

From the beginning she has held in her keeping the honor of the Mother of Christ. Whoso dared to lift a voice or write a word against Mary, she at once anathematized. And her reason was the simplest,—only this: Whosoever attacks the Mother assaults the Son. Arius attacked the Divinity of Jesus Christ by denying His divine and eternal Sonship,—and therefore attacked the Fatherhood of God.

Arius was anathematized.

Nestorius arose and denied the divine maternity of Mary. The Church has never far-fetched or abstruse reasons for her action. Clear and simple was her reason when she condemned Nestorius. Only this,—Whoso attacks the Mother attacks the Son. Just as simple and clear as her reason against Arius;—he who attacks the Son attacks the Father. Her enemies pass away leaving memories that shame the pages of history. The Church of her divine Son moves on. "All her generations, in the simplicity of their Faith call Mary blessed." It is her own prophecy becoming part of their religion. But in each generation of the children of Faith appear men full of wisdom and learning and mighty in grace who are the special guards of the rights and the honors of the Mother of Christ. Why read the roll of their names? Why quote their words from Jerome and Augustine and Ambrose down to the infallible utterances of Pius the Ninth of but yesterday? The children of the Kingdom hear them from childhood to the grave. The wanderers outside the Kingdom hear them not,—or when they do they will not understand. Look everywhere along the past see you not the beautiful bannered processions,—simply endless, for where one stops another starts, going up to the temples of Jesus to keep the feasts of Mary!

Do you not behold the consecrated Virgin walking side by side with the Magdalen who has come back to the shrine of mercy, through the prayers of Mary? Do you not see ignorance in ungainly hurry jostling learning when she moves with a step that cannot help but be stately though her face does wear the look of Faith's humbleness? And listen! where they move with psalms and hymns and spiritual canticles singing the endless *"Sanctus! Sanctus! Sanctus!"* to the Son, and re-echoing back to Mary His Mother her own glorious Magnificat. From the hall and from the hovel come the singers singing. The robe of the king touches the rag of the beggar man and becomes more beautiful and more royal for the touch. The mantle of the princess floats beside the tatters of the peasant. The Tiara crowned head of the Pope bows where the little altar-boy is kneeling. The Bishop's purple and the priest's black cassock meet before the altars to honor Mary. The Purple and the Black meet there on perfect spiritual equality. Savagery and civilization repeat together the same Our Father and the same Hail Mary. The Indian strolling the forest tells the same beads as the sage in his study. It is all for Mary because it is all for Jesus. Is she not then the Glory of the glories of our Holy Church: and is it not our glory, with our words and with our actions, with our whole hearts and with our whole souls and with all the strength of Faith the truest and of love the tenderest, to glorify the blessed name of Mary in life, in death and in eternity.

ASPIRATION.

"PRAY for us, oh! Holy Mother of God, that we may be made worthy of the promises of Christ."

PRAYER.

POUR forth, we beseech thee, O Lord, thy grace into our hearts, that we, to whom the incarnation of Christ thy Son was made known by the message of an angel, may, by His passion and cross, be brought to the glory of His resurrection, through the same Christ our Lord.

THIRTY-FIRST DAY.

The Flower of Catholic Devotion to Mary.

"Be ye imitators of me as I am of Christ."—*St. Paul.*

WE have gathered Flowers for the Crown of our Mother and Queen from Heaven and from earth;—flowers whose roots are in the eternities,—which bloom in the vases of the Scriptures and blossom in the Dogmas and on the altars of our Holy Church;—their spiritual beauty and their glory and their fragrance filling all the days of time. Let us come back to our poor, little earth to find a fadeless flower growing out of the hearts of the Faithful of Christ,—and cull it,—and twine it in the crown of our Queen. And she will be glad. Christ was devoted to His Mother in life, in death and after death. His Church like Himself is devoted to Mary. That devotion is one of the signs and proofs of its Truth. Jesus was subject to Mary in the days of time and is subject to her in the days of eternity. For He never changes. So His Church subject to Him is subject for His sake to Mary. Both subjections have their reasons in her divine maternity. Subjection is another name for devotion. And Devotion is another name for love. Jesus Christ loved Mary more than He could love all other created beings,—loved her for her incomparable graces,—loved her for her love for Him,—loved her with the infinite love of God for His Mother. So the Church loves Mary,—and must,—in order to be in harmony with the divine heart of Jesus. The measure of the Faith that adores Christ measures the Faith that honors Mary. And the measure of the love that springs from Faith in the Son of God measures the love that is given to His Mother Mary.

Love is the beating heart of Faith,—the lifted look of Faith,—the wide, everlasting embrace of Faith. The heart of the Church beats towards Mary;—the Face of the Church is ever lifted in love's look to the Face of Mary;—and the arms of the Virgin-Mother Church are clasped around the Mother of Jesus in an everlasting embrace. It cannot but be so. It is in the nature of things and in the super-nature of things that it should and must be so.

The children of the true Faith,—not only the sinners but the saints, have announced to the world the glorious ignominy of their slavery to Mary. In the face of the world they hold up their chains,—Rosaries and Scapulars,—chains for their hands and chains for their necks. They openly exhibit the signs of their lofty degradation,—they wear them in the brave pride of the Faith that defies the scorn of this world. They are medals,—golden,—silver, brass or of humbler materials made. But no matter. Her figure is graven on them,—or her name. That alone,—and is it not enough?—makes them precious. They are related to the Crucifix as Mary is related to Jesus. Wherever the Crucifix goes,—and where has it not gone?—they follow. Not because the Crucifix absolutely needs them;—but because the Crucifix lovingly wants them. What the Crucifix means for Christ,—they mean for Mary. They are a part of the adornments that enhance the beauty of the Church,—the Bride of the Lamb.

All round the world the Rosary chains are clanking. All round the world the scapulars are living their mysterious hidden life out of the world's but in heaven's sight. And all the earth over, the outward-worn medal reflects the rays of every sun in every clime. They are the marks of "The Legion of Honor" in the army of Jesus Christ.

Love wants nearness. Her pictures on the temple walls or hung in Christian homes,—and her statues on the altars are sweet and beautiful to the eyes of the Faith that loves her Son.

But they are too far off. Love wants something nearer,—something to touch and hold and possess and wear. And if natural love has her own ingenuities,— supernatural love has her's as well. Blessed the neck that hides the holy scapulars! Blessed the hands that hold the blessed beads! Blessed the heart beating back of the breast where shines the blessed medal! Is it foolish? Well;—it is the folly of Faith. Is it blindness? Let it be called so. It is the blindness of love. Is it superstition? Well;—and in reverence we write it,—it is like the superstition of Christ Himself who wore and would only wear the seamless garment woven by His Mother's pure hands.

If the world laughs at these signs of our Faith;—why let it laugh,—poor blind thing that it is;—for how can it understand the spirit of our Faith?

And if so-called Christians scorn us for what we do in Mary's honor (they doing nothing for her while they pretend to do every thing for Christ, her Son)—why let them scorn,—for scorn like their's does but simply show that we and our Holy Church are Mary-like—and therefore Christ-like.

The inheritance of the saints is the contempt of the world without any belief and the scorn of those who only half-believe. Between non-believers and half-believers there is an alliance not openly proclaimed yet none the less hiddenly existing. For, the enmities between Satan and the woman, and "between his seed and her seed" find,—sad and shameful as it is to say it,—soldiers and standards and weapons not only in the Godless world,— but even in the camps of those who pretend to be the soldiers of Christ. So-called Christian soldiers! the banner of Mary waves over every word of Scripture. On its pure, white folds in red letters of blood is blazoned the name of Jesus. Now—tear—if you dare,—that banner down,—trail it in the dust of the beliefless world's denial, or in the half-cold ashes where the flames of Faith once brightly glowed. Are you not traitors? Take heed,—and have a care! To betray Mary and her honor is to betray Jesus Christ Himself and His honor.

Be on your guard. You may kiss Christ, as Judas did, with the kiss of a pretended love only to deliver Him into the hands of His enemies. And you may kiss your Scriptures where Mary's name is written (I wonder do you?) with a kiss of Faith that falters and half-denies, and with no love at all,—thereby delivering the Mother of your Christ into the hands of unbelievers! And you have done it. It is the sacrilege of your system.

Never mind. Mary was not in the garden of Gethsemane desecrated by the kiss of Judas. But she stood beside the cross of Jesus on Calvary, consecrated by His dying on it and her presence beneath it. You cannot drag her thence. Why,—the very Cross with the infinite dead burden on it would go with her who came up to it with her heart by sorrow broken. And Magdalen, who is crouching there, would even leave His feet and rise to defend the Mother whose prayers had helped to save her soul from ruin;—and with Faith's divine wrath ablaze in her glorious eyes, and in tones ringing with the authority of an Apostle,—she would bid you begone. Or she might tell you where to find the tree, whereon, in the dark, the other traitor hung himself. . . . .

Hard words these! Then let them be hard.

The Church of Truth is built on a rock, firm, strong, moveless,—not soft enough to be splintered. Let other churches than ours, with their soft, shaky, shifting foundations, use soft words in their teachings. It becomes them to do so. But it does not become the Church of Christ.

Christ is King of the Church. Mary is Queen. Their united honors;—His Divine and Infinite, her's human, sinless, perfect, highest,—give the true tone to all true teaching. In the temple of God's truth there is nothing soft in the foundations,—in the pillars,—in the stones of the lofty walls,—in the loftier dome,—in the very cement that helps to hold the temple together. Nor in the voice that fills the temple with Faith's eternal accents is there or can there be a falter or an uncertain tremulousness. Firm, strong, certain, true,—ringing as the clarion rings marshalling the ranks for the battle with falsehoods,—sounding as loud trumpets sound clear, triumphant in the hour of Faith's victories and Truth's definitions,—are the voices of the leaders of the hosts of the Lord. Jesus and Mary!—Son and Mother!— go sounding together down the long cross-bannered lines of the close-serried columns.

It was so from the dawn of the day of perfect Truth;

and it will be so to the last Vespers of the day of perfect Faith. Adoration of Jesus necessarily implies Love of Mary. Love implies honor. Honor implies Devotion. Devotion means more than mere profession of Love and Honor of Mary's person and name. It has a higher meaning? What?

Your own hearts feel and your own lips pronounce it;—imitation of Mary's virtues.

"Imitate Mary"—do you doubtingly ask?

"Imitate Mary"—I certainly answer.

Her privileges are beyond you. Her prerogatives are, in a true sense, like God's, incommunicable. Not so her virtues. You cannot touch the sun. It is too far off. But you can catch its rays and see and walk by their light.

Mary's virtues are the rays shining out of her grace-filled, sinless heart. The rays reach sinners as well as saints. Every virtue that has a name she possessed in perfectness. And we can possess them all—though in imperfectness. She will surely help us. Is she not "The Refuge of Sinners" as well as "Queen of all the Saints?" Is she not "The Help of the Weak"—as well as the "Strength of the Strong?"

And she will aid us for the asking.

What virtues do we need the most—the most just now—to give our living testimony to Jesus Christ?

The answer is plain and simple.

We need to be faithful in the possession and practice of those virtues, which the world without God, and Christians of only half-faith, are boldly denying or are forgetting or are almost losing in this our day and generation.

What are these virtues? First,—the chief of all the

virtues,—Faith. The world has boldly ostracized divine Faith. And Christian Churches have chained Faith with the fetters of human opinion. To the world Faith is an outlaw,—in those so-called churches Faith is a slave. The world has reasoned away Revelation. Science has found a Calvary on which to put to death the very name of God. Science is blaspheming still. Faith can wait,—and waiting pray: " Forgive them for they know not what they do."

Men calling themselves Christians have been trying to uncrown Christ by their efforts to uncrown His Holy Church. Their Faith grows weak as their human opinions grow strong.

Their teachers are not dogmatic. They have shuffled off, as if they were slavery's shackles, the bonds of Faith, to wear the manacles of man's opinions. And they think that they are free, confounding the "liberty of the children of God" who believe all and are free, with truth's freedom, with the license of the children of men who believe what they please and so believing can never be free from human error.

We in Holy Church in our times must confront the conspirators against Religion.

How? By our Faith firm, practical, loyal.

Christ is the object of our Faith. Who ought to be our Model? Whose Faith was first and firmest and fullest? Whose Faith was clearest and most certain and perfect?—Whose? You have pronounced her name—Mary's.

It is an age whose idol is pride,—national pride,—race-pride,—individual pride,—pride of mind,—pride of heart,—pride of will. It laughs at the past and boasts of itself. It believes in bravado. It worships force. It points to its material prosperity as if that were the very consecration of its genius. It mocks at the very word—humility,—and looks down in scorn on the humble.

To that pride we must oppose humility.

And who our Model? You have called her name,—Mary. "My soul doth magnify the Lord and my spirit hath rejoiced in God my Saviour; because He hath regarded the humility of His handmaid." They are lowly words graven on lofty gates through which the Son of God did enter this world.

But why speak of her other virtues?

Their story can never be fully told.

All virtues ascend towards one,—their Queen. Her name divine Love,—love of God and love of man.

The mystery of Mary's love for God and man is simply beyond the reach of thought. We bow in silence before it as we would bend in worship before a tabernacle with its hidden miracle of Eucharistic love. Mary! Mother! Queen! we kneel in silence before thy altar. Our thoughts fly away from speech. Our souls are still,—too still for aught but a breathless, soundless prayer. Thou art listening to it down in our hearts!—Let us love Jesus with Mary's love.

ASPIRATION.

HAIL Holy Queen, Mother of Mercy! our life and sweetness and our hope!

PRAYER.

OUR Father who art in heaven, hallowed be thy name; thy kingdom come; thy will be done on earth as it is in heaven. Give us this day our daily bread; and forgive us our trespasses, as we forgive them who trespass against us; and lead us not into temptation; but deliver us from evil. *Amen.*

Hail, Mary, full of grace, the Lord is with thee; blessed art thou amongst women; and blessed is the fruit of thy womb, Jesus. Holy Mary, Mother of God, pray for us sinners, now, and at the hour of our death. *Amen.*

THE following Legends translated from the French,—and as naively translated as they were simply written, will close; and with their child-like simplicity will crown the "Crown for our Queen." Legends, sometimes, are based on facts;—but, perhaps, are more frequently, the beautiful imaginings of Faith. For, though Faith is the unquestioning assent of reason to truth, divinely taught—it, still, can, while believing, imagine many beautiful things which, like golden sun-lit clouds, float across the horizons of Truth;— and make the skies of Faith so beautiful. May I say it? I think I may. Legends in unison with Truth are the poetries of Faith. Legends are to the heart somewhat what doctrines are to reason. Irreligion has no legends; nor has Protestantism. We have. So,—just as they were written;— and just as they have been translated by a child-like heart,— they close and crown my humble work.

A. J. R.

LEGEND OF THE FAMILY OF THE BLESSED VIRGIN.

STOLLON also called Nathan, a virtuous Israelite, a descendant of the tribe of Levi and the priestly family of Aaron,—espoused in the first century before Christ a young Jewish maiden called Emerentiana. She was descended from the tribe of Juda and the royal race of David. They lived in Nazareth, a small town in lower Galilee beautifully situated on the summit of a hill. From their union blessed by Heaven three girls were born,—Mary, whose husband was Cleophas, and whose sons were those disciples of Jesus, called in Scripture "brothers of Christ;" Sobe, mother of St. Elizabeth who was to receive in her old age a visit from her young relative the Virgin Mary; and lastly St. Anne destined by God to carry in her womb, as in a couch perfumed by roses and lilies, her whom He had chosen to become His Mother! A great wonder attended the birth of Anne, and revealed to her parents the precious charge confided to their care and affection. A noble resident of Nazareth who was blind from his birth, inspired by God asked to be led to the child's cradle; taking her two little hands in his own, he said in a trembling voice: "Child of the Most High open my eyes that I may see the glories of heaven." His prayer was immediately granted and the first object which met his eyes was the sweet countenance of Anne smiling at his happiness. St. Anne espoused St. Joachim, like her of royal race. According to the prophecy the Messiah was to come from the tribe of Juda and the family of David. Joachim and Anne were called by Providence to realize the words of the oracles, in having for child the Mother of the Redeemer. Anticipating the distinctive character of the law of grace, the care of the poor, and the ritual of the house of the Lord, Joachim and Anne had divided their fortune into three equal parts: one destined for the relief of the poor, the other for the temple to contribute to the grandeur of its feasts; and with the third they lived very frugally.

LEGEND OF THE NATIVITY OF THE BLESSED VIRGIN.

A PIOUS solitary whose life was unknown to men living in a desert heard every year on the night of the eighth of September angelic harmonies coming from heaven. Surprised at this miracle he prayed the Lord to reveal to him what was the meaning of this heavenly melody. An angel appeared to him and said: "The immaculate Virgin Mother of God was born this very night, men forget but the angels celebrate her Nativity in heaven." Since this secret was given to the world the Catholic Church celebrates the eighth of September the day when the Virgin of Juda was born, and as that day is the Hebrew Sabbath it is not strange that Saturday has been consecrated in a special manner to Mary. Pious authors who have written the life of the Blessed Virgin do not agree as to the place of her birth. Some say she was born in Jerusalem, others in Nazareth in a house belonging to St. Anne's parents. However it may be, in that moment of ineffable joy Joachim and Anna were filled with gratitude, and a voice from heaven was heard saying: "Blessed art thou in this world O my well-beloved! a heavenly choir thrilled with transports of joy, assists at thy birth:—may the Holy Ghost repose in thee! Heaven and earth will submit to thy power, and the angels will serve thee as their Queen." It is not without a profound mystery, writes a chronicler, that Mary appeared on earth at the time of year when the grapes begin to redden and ripen—and when the grateful laborer sees his hopes at last realized; the vine whose sweet fruits are gathered in autumn—is it not Mary herself the sweet vintage giving joy to the world—expected by the patriarchs, announced by the prophets. On the anniversary of a loved mother children who love and respect their parents offer her the double tribute of their gratitude and affection.

Let us never fail to give Mary the tender token of our filial piety, and she will rejoice and reward her children.

LEGEND OF MARY'S INFANCY.

SOMETIME after the birth of the Blessed Virgin St. Joachim and St. Anne gave a banquet in their house at Nazareth at which were present the priests and chiefs of the synagogue and temple. Mary was presented to the priests who called down on her all the blessings of heaven. Afterwards they called her by her name *Mary*, which the angels had given her.

St. Anne brought Mary to the temple and renewed her vow of consecrating her to the Lord when she would reach her third year. Mary, enjoying all the fullness of her reason without showing any outward sign, interiorly ratified the promise. At that instant a light was seen surrounding the mother and her child. Mary concealed all her privileges, appearing always like a little child, she never was impatient nor did she cry over trifles so common at her age, but in her humility she concealed her admirable disposition, weeping often for the sins of men, in order to obtain their forgiveness and to hasten the coming of the Redeemer. Mary unlike all children was not deprived of the power of speech during the first months of her life, nevertheless she remained more than a year before uttering a word, and before using so dangerous a gift she entreated God to assist her, that she might not say anything to displease or offend Him. St. Bernard poetically calls her, "The Immaculate Lily exhaling the odor of Hope."

During this period of her life St. Anne would have the the Blessed Virgin stand beside her and holding in her lap the Scriptures, would have Mary follow with her eyes her hand while she pointed out to her the words of the Sacred Scriptures; thus initiating the little Mary into their mysteries. Sculptors and painters have often produced in their art this tradition. The picture of the calm face of Anne and pure features of Mary awakens in our soul memories of childhood's first impressions. How priceless are the beautiful beliefs which bring back to the memory only the days of candor and peace. Holy religion of childhood, the heart that is false to thee is alas! guilty, but the heart that despises thee is a heart unhappy indeed!

LEGEND OF THE PRESENTATION OF MARY IN THE TEMPLE OF JERUSALEM.

THE time of parting from their darling child having come, St. Joachim and St. Anne said to each other—"Let us go to the temple with our Mary and give her to God according to our promise." Taking with them a few maidens of their tribe they departed. On their way to the temple they stopped to rest and Joachim pressing his darling child to his heart said to her with ineffable tenderness : "My child I will never see thee more." The holy child had on a blue robe and mantle, her little arms and neck were covered with flowers. Having arrived at the gate of the temple Mary without assistance mounted the fifteen steps which led to the house of God. Anne and Joachim watched her with anxiety, thinking that never again would their lonely hours be brightened by the presence of their sweet and gentle child. Mary was received by the high priest Zachary, who was to watch with so much care over the Virgin of Juda. Joachim offered a lamb as sacrifice, and while the victim was being consumed and the smoke of the holocaust ascended heavenwards, Anne and Mary remained in a precinct of the temple reserved for women. An altar was then erected and Mary knelt on the steps with Joachim and Anna. The priest cut off a few of her tresses and placed them in a thurible. The couple renewed the vow they had made of consecrating her to God. Mary then offered herself to God with such fervor that never since the beginning of the world had there ever been so pure an oblation. Zachary placed on her head a veil, and leading her to a place in the temple where she was met by six maidens the priest gave the child to one of the matrons of the temple and went away. Mary then turning towards her parents, and falling on her knees asked their blessing which they gave her. Joachim and Anna departed in great sorrow for their only child. The prophetess Anne presented Mary to her companions. At night Mary was led to the cell prepared for her—the one nearest to the Holy of Holies. The attendant retired leaving Mary alone with her God, alone with the angels watching near the sanctuary. She who was to become the immaculate sanctuary of the Divinity; the Ark of the new alliance; the virginal propitiatory from which the Lord was to announce his pardon to the guilty world. The cherubims cover her already with their wings and greet her as the "Mother of the Redeemer."

LEGEND OF MARY'S ESPOUSALS.

THE young maidens who were brought up in the house of God only remained until the age of fourteen years. The high priest would then solemnly announce to them this news; and tell them to return to their parents to become faithful spouses and happy mothers after having been obedient and submissive maidens. All of Mary's companions who like her had attained that age obeyed the priest's order. Mary alone modestly declared she could not obey. The high priest knowing the vow she had made to the Lord found himself in the alternative of annulling a sacred engagement or of authorizing a usage against the custom of the Hebrews. Not willing to decide such a question alone he convoked a council of the principal men of the people and the doctors of the Law. They all began to pray. Their High Priest went to the altar to be enlightened from on high. Suddenly a voice from the Propitiatory was heard saying: "The oracle of Isaiah must be fulfilled. There will rise a branch from out the roots of Jesse and a flower will bloom from the stem. Let all the family of David lay each their rod in the temple, and the one whose branch will bloom will be the chosen one to espouse the Blessed Virgin."

The command of God was made known by the sound of trumpets; heralds went all through the city proclaiming the command; and rumor brought the tidings into the confines of Judea. All the young descendants of the family of David came to deposit their rods near the altar. They offered sacrifices to the Lord. But the next day none of the rods had blossomed. The high priest again consulted the God of light and truth. He was answered as the father of David was answered by the prophet Samuel: "Here are not all your sons." Immediately new search was made and one named Joseph was found who had not appeared in the Temple with those of his tribe.

The priests sent for him. Joseph came. When he was brought into the presence of the priests they gave him the testing rod on which they wrote his name; it was then laid near the altar and the following day it was found covered with flowers. Mary was called, and she appeared in the midst of the assembly with her modest grace, her angelic beauty. On learning of the prodigy she adored the mysterious designs of the Lord and as a sign of consent placed her pure hand in the hand of the poor artisan. What a moment for the holy patriarch, how unworthy he deemed himself, with what respect he received from the hands of the High Priest the Lily of Israel, and with what joy he heard from Mary that from her earliest infancy she had consecrated herself to God; he who had made a similar vow. Before leaving the temple, where she had spent such happy hours, she bade farewell to her companions, her superiors and the holy old priest Zachary. Mary left in sadness, but her sorrow was softened by the knowledge of accomplishing the will of God.

LEGEND OF THE NATIVITY.

In the vast empire governed by Augustus, the clashing of swords was heard no more. He had quelled seditions in Rome, and revolutions in the world. After waiting more than four hundred years, God at last announced in low, solemn tones the word of eternal peace, and celestial messengers were soon to sing the grand "*Gloria in Excelsis Deo, et in terra pax,*" sublime summary of the religion that the God-man will give to the universe to redeem it.

Mary enclosed some wearing apparel for the child Jesus in a coffer, which she carried with her to Bethlehem. Nazareth, destined to possess so long the God hidden from its eyes, was not to see Him born. That honor was reserved for Bethlehem, the city of David, the smallest of all the towns in Judea, as the prophet Michaes had foretold. The Emperor of Rome in ordering a census of all his subjects, was to be an unconscious agent in realizing the prophecy, foretold many centuries before, in bringing back to Bethlehem, whence they came, St. Joseph and the most holy Virgin.

The journey lasted several days. The holy patriarch procured a small animal used to fatigue and eating very little. It was bitter cold in the valleys, surrounded by mountains. The homes were few and uncomfortable, the road was filled with people, but the angels walked before them and lightened by their pious hymns their sufferings. The holy travelers arrived at Bethlehem on Saturday at sunset. They sought in vain for lodgings, no one would receive them. Mary knew by revelation all these refusals, but to practice humility and patience, she followed her spouse from door to door.

It was nine o'clock at night; Joseph, not knowing where to direct his steps in this inhospitable town, went with Mary towards a grotto outside the walls of the city, where shepherds, during stormy days, would come and seek shelter As soon as they entered this miserable place, they went on their knees, thanking God for the double gift of poverty and humility which He deigned to give them. They both took a little food. The Blessed Virgin filled a crib with straw and hay on which the infant God was to rest. The beast of their travels and an ox that was in the stable were placed so as to warm by their breath that cold and damp couch. All these preparations finished, Saint Joseph retired to pray. The hours went by, and night had completed half of its course when the Saviour of the world was born. Mary wrapped Him in swaddling clothes, and after embracing Him as her son she adored Him as her God. She then placed Him on the straw, when suddenly the stable was filled with a marvellous light. Saint Joseph, contemplating his God in the form of a little child, wept tears of joy and kissed the little hands which seemed to open as if to caress him. Joseph and Mary are thus models of all real worshipers of Jesus; after them come the shepherds. Warned by the angels, they fly to the stable and pay to the new-born child their simple and humble worship; they return full of joy to the care of their flocks, praising and blessing God for what they had heard and seen. And Mary was keeping all these things and treasuring them in her heart.

LEGEND OF THE MAGI.

THE birth of Christ so hidden and humble, was signalized by different wonders. At Jerusalem all the writings of the Saducees were scattered here and there through the temple. In Rome, one of the fountains which watered the city bore to the Tiber for a whole day wavelets of pure and limpid oil. A statue of Jupiter crumbled to dust. And the Emperor Augustus saw above the Capitolian Mount a woman bearing in her arms a little child. Three Magi who were watching and praying on Mount Victory, saw a new star in the heavens shining with wondrous light. They were descendants of Seth, and knew that a resplendent star would one day rise in the heavens to announce the birth of the Saviour. On perceiving the prophetic sign they were filled with joy and announced the glad tidings to the other wise men who like them were awaiting the coming of a divine King. The happy Magi who were favored by the celestial vision were called Gaspard, Melchoir, and Balthazar; and though young they were renowned for their profound wisdom and knowledge. The miraculous star, came shining nearer and nearer: and lo! they saw in the midst of its rays a child of heavenly beauty bearing on its head in a halo of light the form of a cross. At the same time they heard these words: "Go to the country of Judea; there you will find the King who has been promised, and who has just been born." The Magi descended the mountain and began their journey towards Palestine. The star preceded them. Mounted on the dromedaries of Madian they carried to the Lord the riches of their country. When they reached Jerusalem the star disappeared. "Where," they asked, "is the new-born King of the Jews; for we have seen His star in the East and we have come to adore Him." The priest opening the Book of the Prophets, said to them: "In Bethlehem of Juda the Messiah is to be born."

The ambitious Herod fearing the loss of his throne, exacted a promise from the Magi to return to Jerusalem and tell him where they had found the Child, that he also might go and adore Him. The Magi departed joyous and confident. The star which had guided them towards Jerusalem reappeared and led them to the place where they found the Child with Mary its Mother. Prostrating themselves before the Infant they adored Him, then opening their treasures they offered Him gold, frankincense and myrrh. The most Holy Virgin touched by their faith placed her son in the arms of Gaspard the oldest of the three: then taking the veil which enveloped her person, she gave it to him. The Magi bowed down, and their hearts were filled with gladness and gratitude for the Virgin's gift.

LEGEND OF THE PRESENTATION AND THE INFANCY OF THE LORD.

THE time having come for Mary to perform the ceremony of Purification and to present her Son to the priests, the Holy Family left Bethlehem and went down to Jerusalem. The cold was so excessive that it made the Infant weep. Affected by His sufferings, the Blessed Virgin used the power God had given her over creatures and changed the rigorous weather into a mild one for her infant Son—but she never made use of this supernatural power in her own favor. Arrived at the Holy City, she enters the temple with Saint Joseph, carrying in her arms her Divine Son, that celestial treasure, all the wealth and happiness of the world. "O Eternal Father," says she, "Creator of the universe, Behold thy Divine Son and well-beloved, whom you have made my own. I give Him to thee now to accomplish thy divine will." She then gave to the priests the five sheckels demanded by law,—fruit of the labor of Saint Joseph, and two doves, the gift of poverty. The old man Simeon had received interiorly the promise of not dying before seeing with his own eyes the consolation of Israel. Warned by the spirit of God he entered the temple at the same time that Mary was entering with the Infant. The dazzling rays which emanated from that glorious circle attracted the attention of the people, and whilst the other witnesses of that scene remained unmoved, Simeon is not mistaken by this marvel and recognizes in the child the desire of his old age, and the Rest of his heart. He approaches with delight the Blessed Virgin, who placed the Infant in his arms. He then recites in a touching voice the hymn *Nunc Dimitis*, the last which was to come from his lips. Simeon then predicted to Mary that her soul would be pierced with a sword of sorrow! These words, which were a prophecy of Calvary and its unutterable sorrows, begin the martyrdom of the celestial Queen by lifting the veil which hid from her view the most heart-rending mysteries. Hereafter the gentle Mother of the Saviour will have to suffer. The prophetess Anna, who had been Mary's directress, was also inspired to go to the temple at that hour of peace. On recognizing the gentle Virgin and at sight of the miraculous light which surrounded the divine Infant, her eyes filled with tears, and after having adored her Lord, animated with a holy enthusiasm she began to speak of His glory to all those who were expecting the redemption of Israel. Nevertheless Mary in her humility shone like a celestial rose. Saint Joseph then distributed the presents which the Magi had given them. One half he gave for the decoration of the temple, and the other half destined for the rearing of the poorest maidens brought up in the house of the Lord. The poor had already received theirs. All which being accomplished, the Holy Family went back to Nazareth. Jerusalem, the grand, the populous, the noisy city, was not to become the home of the poor artisan whom Jesus was to call Father. The days and months went by rapidly in that solitary and blessed home. After having enjoyed the return of spring, winter came, and with it the anniversary of the birth of Christ. The wind blew with violence, the most-holy Virgin, holding her child on her bosom was warming Him with her maternal breath. Suddenly two angels appeared in Mary's humble home : " It is the first year of the Redeemer's birth," said they with their melodious voice, "we come to bring Him an offering," and prostrating themselves before the Child they offered Him a small cross. His Mother grew pale on seeing this sign, but Jesus received it smiling. Immediately the walls of the holy house of Nazareth shone like a palace of heaven, and the two angels slowly reascended towards the empyrean amid a shower of lilies and roses of fire, which in falling were consumed like burnt incense at the feet of the Virgin.

SOJOURN OF THE HOLY FAMILY IN EGYPT.

SYRA was the first of the towns of Egypt which the Holy Famiy entered. The descendants of Pharaoh who lived in the time of Joseph, had built a temple in which were all the gods, objects of their superstitious worship. The exiles sought shelter under the portico of the majestic edifice; but hardly had the child Jesus placed His foot in the temple than all the idols, by a sudden impulse, fell down with a great noise. The priest who had charge of the temble had them replaced on their pedestal but the following night they fell down again. This commotion was spread throughout Egypt, whose soil was covered by the " débris " of the mutilated idols. It is thus that carried in the arms of its Mother the Infant God triumphed over the devil and strewed on this pagan earth a harvest rich with blessings, which will bloom in silence, peopling this earth with angels whose life will recall the life of the angels of heaven.

Leaving Syra, our holy travelers advanced towards the East, in the interior of the country, where the inhabitants of a burgess offered them hospitality, according to the patriarchal traditions, which they had faithfully continued to practice. The family which welcomed them to their hearth was celebrating a wedding; but joy, the faithful handmaiden of all such feasts, was not seen on the face of the partakers. Beneath the crown of roses which decked her young brow, the bride had felt a strange sensation. Her tongue refused to articulate a sound, she had suddenly become dumb. The bright smiles had been replaced by stupor and horror on the lips of the guests.

But this afflicted woman had drawn near to Mary. She was contemplating with an ineffable look of tenderness the marvellous chiid sleeping on the bosom of the stranger. His ineffable grace, His innocent charms moved deeply every heart. Taking the infant Jesus from the arms of the Virgin, she embraced It with respect and tenderness, and while the daughter of Egypt bestows on the Eternal Word these demonstrations of love her tongue is loosed, she suddenly recovers her voice and speech.

In another town of Egypt, a child who was possessed by the devil, took from the child Jesus a robe which he had and placed it on his head. Immediately the demon left the pagan child. His father being present said: "It is possible that this child may be the Son of God, because since he has been here all of our idols have been overthrown." The poor exiles lived then in Heliopolis. The wretched hovel in which they lived is often pointed out to travelers.

LEGEND OF THE RETURN FROM EGYPT.

BEFORE the massacre of the innocents, St. Elizabeth hid her son John the Baptist in a grotto whose entrance could not be discovered by the agents of Herod. The angels revealed his place of security to the Blessed Virgin, who gave thanks to the Lord for it.

The hour of Divine vengeance was near for King Herod. He was seized with a violent fever, worms gnawed his entrails, causing him horrid pains; he uttered despairing shrieks; his whole being was a prey to unutterable suffering. He died from so much tortures, carrying to his grave the curse of the Jews and the indelible stain of innocent blood. An angel then appeared to St. Joseph telling him his exile was ended. The holy patriarch went immediately to Mary and announced the glad tidings.

They gave their tools and few articles to Jesus to distribute among the poor of their neighborhood, and many were the words of comfort and hope spoken to them by their friends when bidding them good-bye. Mary mounted a beast similar to the one that had brought her into Egypt. She held the child Jesus in her arms—and Joseph walked before them.

When they arrived at the border of the desert they met St. John the Baptist, clothed in his garment of camel's hair. He shared some roots with them which was all he could offer them for their meals. The precursor's joy was indescribable on seeing the child Jesus, but it was of short duration. Immediately after resting a few hours the holy travelers crossed the Jordan leaving St. John in the desert. He was scarcely eight years old and lived alone in the desert, his father and mother being both dead.

St. Joseph had taken the road to Bethlehem, thinking to continue to Jerusalem and live there; but an angel had warned him that Archelaus, a son of Herod, reigned in Juda. He continued on to Nazareth which was governed by another man. When they returned to their country the Infant Jesus mingled with all the children. One day helping St. Joseph with his work the Divine Child cut his hand—the wood was red with His blood. The Blessed Virgin was called out to Him. The Child reassured her with a sweet smile, but she perceived a small cross on the wood He had been cutting. She turned away her head to hide the tears that silently fell down her pale cheeks. The cross is a present of the Child Jesus to us, and when He gives it to us dyed with His blood, cut by Himself—we ought to receive it with gratitude, embrace it with joy,—as being a token of Christ's sufferings and of an eternal love.

JESUS LOST AND FOUND.

THE grand feast of the Pasch brought back every year Joseph and Mary to Jerusalem. Being twelve years of age Jesus accompanied by His parents and friends went to celebrate this great day. The days of this feast over, Mary and Joseph with a few of their companions returned to Nazareth. According to the Hebrew custom the men walked together and the women followed with their children. Joseph thinking that Jesus had remained with His mother did not feel uneasy at His absence, and Mary not seeing Him near her, thought that the Jesus-God had gone with Joseph. At night they all stopped at the same place to rest. The Blessed Virgin on seeing St. Joseph asked immediately for the child Jesus. Joseph was troubled at that question, and answered in an anxious voice: "I thought He was with you?" Perceiving their sorrow, His parents looked for Him among the crowd that was with them; not finding Him they went back to Jerusalem asking every one they met if they had seen the Child Jesus. Mary would say describing Him, "His beautiful hair falls to His shoulders, His features are faultless, His smile angelic and His look divine." "Poor mother!" they would answer looking at her with compassion, "perhaps later you will find your Son so gentle and beautiful." The two travelers met in Jerusalem a woman who told them she had seen such a Child asking her for alms, and afterwards saw Him in the hospital consoling the poor and the sick. Mary went to the temple thinking to find Him there and saw Him with the doctors of the law conversing and propounding the most difficult questions with great wisdom, and astonishing the people with His answers. Mary looked at her Son and with a low plaintiveness spoke to Him the words written in the Gospel. Preserving the majesty of God Jesus answered in a grave and solemn voice: "Why do you seek me? Did you not know that I must be about my Father's business."

He followed His parents, and when Mary found herself in a quiet place she fell on her knees before Him and asked His blessing. Jesus then consoled her, and told her more fully than ever before the mysteries of His heart.

DEATH OF ST. JOSEPH.

THE Blessed Virgin seeing that her chaste spouse was about to die asked her Divine Son to aid her to soothe his last moments. The Child Jesus promised her not only to assist him in his agony but to raise him to such a rank in heaven that the angels would be struck with admiration. Assisted by these two lights, Jesus and Mary, the last hours of

Joseph resembled more the dawn of a new life than the evening of a life passing away.

Before sleeping the sleep of the just Joseph went once more to the temple to pray. "Merciful God," he prayed, "author of all consolation, prostrate at Thy feet I adore Thee, my life is passing away, sovereign Judge of mortals, hear my last prayer. Illuminate the path that must lead me to Thee and send your angels to take my soul and carry it to the bosom of Abraham."

Thus did Joseph pray, when he returned to Nazareth he died in the arms of Jesus and Mary. Jesus on seeing him whom He had so lately called father lying still and cold, tenderly embraced him. Mary prepared him for the burial, and the next day the holy remains of the descendant of the Kings of Juda were deposited in a vault given him by a wealthy man. He was not embalmed like the rich Hebrews, with aromas of great price and perfumes from Arabia, but he carried into his tomb a glorious immortality. Many Saints believe that the holy body of Joseph, sanctified before his birth, did not undergo corruption, but was reunited to his soul when Jesus ascended into Heaven.

MATER ADMIRABILIS.

IN a convent situated on the Pincian hill in Rome, there is a little sanctuary in the midst of the cloister containing a beautiful fresco painting of the Virgin. The pilgrim who comes to pray before this beautiful representation of the Maiden of the temple of Jerusalem feels a religious calm steal over him which seems to emanate from this graceful image. The Virgin is sitting down weaving linen; near her to the right is a distaff and on the left is a vase containing a lily whose fragile form seems to bend towards Mary. That lily seeks Mary, she raises her eyes in order to look upon its beauty, and she inhales its virginal perfume.

Here in a few words is the origin of *Mater Admirabilis*, which title she has merited by the wonderful prodigies which have happened at the foot of this painting. It was in the month of May, 1844, during the nuns' recreation to whom belongs this beautiful monastery, whilst they were celebrating with great pomp the grandeurs and mercies of Mary (then a great custom in Rome), the superioress was called away to the parlor. On seeing her place vacant one of the nuns exclaimed: "Ah! if the Blessed Virgin could come and take her place and preside at our recreation." At that moment an artist who had come to Mount Trinity to finish her studies in painting fixed her eyes on a recess in the wall opposite to the place occupied by the superioress. She saw in a moment by a flash of genius the work she was to paint with such perfection. "Do you wish me," said she, "to make the Blessed Virgin come in the place of our mother?" "Yes, yes," was echoed by all, "let the Blessed Virgin descend and come into our midst!" The first of June the artist commenced her work, which was to be completed by the middle of July—but alas! instead of the lily of the valley which the artist had promised, they saw with horror an illuminated figure draped in a black robe and a yellow veil. This horrified all those who were admitted to judge of the work. That appearance was caused by the fresh lime upon which the picture was painted. The poor artist herself recoiled with horror. When the drapery was removed which had concealed the painting for three weeks, and they saw the Madonna in all her innocent beauty, cries of joy were heard. Later the Sovereign Pontiff Pius IX prayed before the *Mater Admirabilis* and solemnly blessed the painting. That benediction brought on so many miracles that the Madonna became a place of pilgrimage where we learn from Mary the secret of self-abnegation, humility and devotion.

LEGEND OF MARY'S TRIALS.

THE bright young years which came one by one to crown the Virgin blessed with the first flowers of maidenhood, increased the infirmities of her parents. St. Joachim felt the presentiment of sorrow and prepared himself by many virtuous acts to end worthily his long career fraught with so many beautiful virtues. When his end drew near he sent for Mary; she left the temple and came to Nazareth. She had just completed her eleventh year and for the first time since her entrance in the temple she went to visit her parents. But that joy was troubled by the pain of knowing that she was to see her father only to bid him a last adieu. Joachim embraced her tenderly and lifting his drooping hands, he placed them on her head. At that moment the Patriarch saw the angels surrounding their glorious Queen and guarding her. In the transport of his gratitude the happy old man commenced a hymn of thanksgiving but it died away on his lips. Calmly he passed away. After helping her mother to render the last services to the dead, she returned to the temple weeping. A year after she returned to Nazareth to receive her mother's dying blessing. The Blessed Virgin predestined to become by excellence the mother of orphans, was to be an orphan herself in order to know the inexpressible sadness of those who have no parents to guide and support them. When she returned to the temple the holy priest Zachary (spouse of St. Elizabeth) received her with tenderness and promised her to be a father to her. Mary bowed her head in gratitude and promised to obey him in all things. The demon jealous of the great virtue which distinguished Mary, and not able to make her commit the least sin, breathed the spirit of jealousy into the hearts of her companions. Under that fatal influence they reproached her bitterly for imaginary faults and succeeded in turning against her some of the priests of the temple. Mary listened gently to the reproofs of her superiors; she opposed only meekness and silence to these unjust accusations, and humbling herself before God she prayed for those who accused her. The demon vanquished by this heroic patience abandoned his work; the innocence of Mary was proclaimed and the young maidens called her Queen of Virgins, when suddenly an angel descended into the midst of the maidens saying: "The words you have just uttered will not be meaningless, they will be the fulfilling of the prophecy." At sight of the heavenly messenger, the young maidens filled with fear, fell prostrate. When they rose up the angel was gone but Mary knelt in peaceful prayer.

JOAN OF ARC AND THE DIVINE EUCHARIST.

JOAN OF ARC, the humble shepherdess, the gentle victim, the heroic martyr, had a most tender and innocent devotion to Mary. The greatest pleasure of her infancy was to make crowns for our "Lady of Domrémy."

Nothing prepares us to receive worthily the Blessed Eucharist as devotion to the Lord's Mother. When Joan arrived at the age in which she began to understand the divine gifts she prepared herself by fervent prayer to make her first Communion worthily; and it left in her pure soul a memory of peace that never passed away. Henceforth the Holy Eucharist became the sun of her young life and the supreme strength of her last moments. See the heroine advancing towards Orleans with an army composed of only four or five thousand men to rescue that faithful city from the English besiegers. In the morning Joan's soldiers arranged an altar in the camp; and under the dew of heaven, before the kneeling troops the angel of France received that day in Holy Communion the contract of her mysterious alliance. She breaks through the enemy's ranks, she pursues them, forces them to admit their defeat; yet not even then does the heroine lose anything of her piety and fervor even in the midst of carnage. She is seen mingling with the children in the Church of the Franciscans going to the Holy Table and receiving her Adorable Lord. Joan after saving France by victories was doomed to become an innocent victim and to suffer an awful martyrdom.

Her love for the Eucharist far from weakening when she was bound in chains only increased. Vainly does she entreat the Judges to allow her to go to Mass and receive Communion. Nothing is more touching than to see the poor captive kneeling near the church door before which she has to pass to go to the tribunal. The door remains closed, but her faith penetrates the walls and her soul unites itself with the God of the Tabernacle. The most unjust of sentences condemns the heroic young maiden to be burnt alive as a heretic and apostate; her whose faith was so vivid and pure. What does she ask her executioners at that last moment, a respite, a moment's grace? No! no! What she entreats, what she begs with heart-rending words is for the Holy Eucharist. When at last she receives Him at her last hour, her face is illumined by a heavenly light and Joan receives in this supernatural union with her Jesus in the Sacred Host grace and strength to die resigned. Brought to the public square she is bound to her funeral pyre. It is lighted by the cruel executioners. The flames ascend, ascend! The moment she feels the scorching fire the poor victim shudders and asks for some holy water. Water, water, she cries! It was the cry of nature and it was her last. Heaven opens to receive her; her Calvary becomes a Thabor, and from that temple of fire a voice pure like that of an angel is heard saying—"My saints have not deceived me, my mission came from God." The martyr then gave a last dying look towards the image of her crucified Saviour; then drooped her virgin head! She gave one cry—"*Jesus!*" All was over. . . . The pure soul of Joan had flown to Heaven.

LEGEND OF OUR LADY OF LOURDES.

WE find at Lourdes a little child very simple, knowing nothing but how to say her Rosary, which she was always repeating at all hours whilst tending her sheep, such are the instruments God loves to use when he wishes to create wonders, because their humble weakness does not obscure His divine transparency. It was Thursday, the eleventh of February, 1858. It was bitter cold at the Soubiron's (Bernadette's parents.) Her father was a miller at Lourdes, and her mother attended to their household, the fireplace had no fire in it, the meal hour was past, and there was no wood to prepare anything to eat. The mother says to Mary her second daughter, "go and get some wood on the banks of the Gave." Bernadette asked her mother permission to go with her sister and Joan Abadie their little neighbor. They descended to the prairie which extends below the city following the course of the current,—Bernadette less active and weaker than the others lingers in the rear. Arriving at Massabielle's grotto she thought she heard a noise, suddenly a gust of wind swept past her with irresistible power. It is doubtless a storm thought the child, but the impetuous rolling of that noise continued, and raising her head, she remains, spellbound, transfixed, dazzled by the sight which met her eyes and fell on both knees. The grotto before which Mary and Joan were picking wood, in an excavation in the form of a recess which crowned the rock, was standing in the midst of a celestial light, a lady of dazzling beauty! her veil and robe were as white as snow, her girdle half knotted around the body was the color of the heavens, and on each of her feet which reposed on a rock, bloomed a mystical golden rose, an alabaster rosary hung between her crossed hands, but her lips remained immovable. Instead of saying the rosary the Queen of Virgins seemed to listen to the immortal echo of the Angelical salutation and the music of Bernadette's prayers who being magnetized, dazzled, commenced to recite humbly her rosary. When she came to the last *Gloria Patri* the apparition disappeared. The child went home very nervous, and the other children had not seen or heard anything. Her mother listened to her story, fearing that perhaps she was the dupe of an illusion. Nevertheless, the next day she consented to the child's entreaties to return to the grotto. The apparition came again, the child obeying the advice of her companions, threw some holy water on the apparition—to be certain it was no demon. But the Virgin approached nearer to the grotto smiling on Bernadette, she fell on her knees and taking her rosary she recited them with angelical fervor. When she finished, the apparition disappeared. The young visionary returned to the grotto on the 18th February accompanied by two pious ladies of Lourdes. The Blessed Virgin appeared again and asked her to come to the grotto during fifteen consecutive days. Bernadette promised her to do so, and the Blessed Virgin promised her not happiness in this world but in the other. The child had to overcome many difficulties, to bear many trials, but she kept her promise, and every time she went to the grotto she was followed by a curious crowd, who were anxious to see that child of earth, who, when transfigured by prayer, resembled an angel; the apparition was seen by Bernadette alone.

The august Queen was preparing a new surprise for her protégée. On the 23d of February she called her by name and confided a secret to her which concerned only herself. "Now," she added, "you will tell the priest to have a chapel built here." After having said these words she disappeared, and poor little Bernadette felt very sorry and her face lost its angelic look. Mary's little ambassadress went without loss of time to the pastor of Lourdes. He, wishing to test her words, asked as a proof that a twig on which the Blessed Virgin placed her foot should bloom. The next day Bernadette told the Blessed Virgin of this; the Apparition smiled, and in answer to her only confided another secret. Some time after this, to the great astonishment of the multitude, they saw Bernadette walking on her knees repeating these words: "Penance, penance!" As for the rose tree it remained sterile. Mary was reserving a greater wonder to prove her appearance in those unknown regions. The Virgin appeared a fourth time to the child, revealed a third and last secret, and said to her:—"Go and drink, wash yourself in the fountain, and eat the grass which grows in the grotto." The child directs her steps towards the river Gave, but the hand of the Apparition points to the right of the grotto: the same barren place where on the eve Bernadette had walked on her knees. The child obeys, but finding no trace of water digs the soil with her fingers and nails, the hole fills with muddy water. Bernadette feels sick at sight of the water, nevertheless she obeys, drinks of the water and eats the grass growing at the foot of a rock. All these things being accomplished the Virgin cast a look of satisfaction on the child and disappears.

The next day Bernadette went to the grotto accompanied by an immense crowd, but the most Holy Virgin did not appear. This was the second time that Bernadette was deprived of her presence, though the gentle sovereign was not present her work progressed and the fountain impelled from the mysterious depths by an invisible force comes bubbling on the soil to the surprise of the dazzled multitude. Whilst each one commented in their own way about these marvels, a laborer, who had lost the sight of his right eye, came to the fountain and washed himself in the water and immediately regained his sight. This first miracle was followed by many others. The fifteen visits to the grotto were ended, and yet on the 25th of March Bernadette went again. She had a presentiment of the joy which was reserved for her. Arrived at the rock of Massabielle the little visionary fell on her knees, the apparition showed itself to her charmed looks, just as ever an ineffable light is seen about her whose splendor is without limit, whose gentleness is infinite. Bernadette, contemplating her in ecstacy, asks her three times: "Madam, I pray you tell me whom are you and what is your name." At the third question of the child the apparition opens its arms and inclines a little to the earth to show to the world her virginal hands filled with blessings. Crossing them again with incomparable fervor she pronounces those solemn words—"*I am the Immaculate Conception.*" Having said these words she disappears in a luminous cloud and the child finds herself with the crowd in front of a lonely rock. But the crowd soon knelt on these rugged stones sanctified by Mary's presence. A beautiful statue of the Apparition has been placed in the rustic recess where the Blessed Virgin appeared to the child.

LEGEND OF THE IDIOT OF THE WOODS.

AMONG the legends which are said of Mary there is perhaps none so touching as the history of Salaün called the idiot of the woods. He was idiotic but of a holy idiocy which has a place in paradise. It is believed that in the beginning of the XIV century was born a being frail, sickly and poorly endowed by nature, fortune also frowned on him, his parents were poor country people who lived off the fruits of their labor, they dwelt in a hovel situated in Lower Brittany, not very far from the town of Lesleven. When their child was old enough to attend school they sent him to the neighboring village, but all he learnt to remember were these two words, "*Ave Maria.*" His parents died leaving him penniless; he begged his bread from the people and lived in a wood near a fountain shaded by a large oak tree. It was at the foot of this tree that Salaün stretched on the ground would sleep. Although very ignorant he was very pious, and every morning he went to Lesleven to hear Mass, and whilst the priest was raising the sacred Host during the elevation he repeated ceaselessly "*Ave Maria.*" On coming out of church he would ask for alms, saying in his peculiar language, "Salaün would eat bread if he had some, '*Ave Maria.*'" The children who heard him continually repeating the same words would run after him crying out, "Salaün the fool," but the older ones would give him in the name of God the nourishment he so much needed. He would then go to his woods, and seated by the fountain would saturate his bread in the water and at each mouthful would repeat "*Ave Maria.*" Sometimes he would get up on his tree and swinging himself to and fro on its branches would incessantly repeat, "*Ave Maria,*" and the neighboring echoes would answer the blessed refrain of poor Salaün "*Ave Maria.*" In winter he braved all the inclemencies of the weather and never left his retreat. A few charitable persons, touched with his sufferings, offered him an asylum in their house, but he would never accept. He was never heard to utter one complaint; never was offended at the injuries he would receive; never would steal, and always looked contented. The wolves and wild animals which roamed the forest never tried to molest him. The all-powerful Virgin whose name was always on his lips chained their sanguinary instincts. After living forty years that solitary life he fell sick. As he did not appear at his accustomed place in church, the people of Lesleven went to his retreat in search of him and found him by his fountain. They begged him to let them carry him to their house where he would be nursed, but all their entreaties he refused, declaring that he would die where he had lived, but he asked them to send him the pastor of Lesleven to hear his confession. The good priest came immediately. After piously confessing all his sins poor Salaün gave his pure soul to the Blessed Virgin whom he had so often invoked and slept in the Lord. He was buried with great simplicity, but wonderful to say some time after his death the people saw a beautiful lily all in bloom growing on his grave, bearing on each petal the words "*Ave Maria.*" The news spread far and wide, and counts, barons, ladies, simple villagers all came to contemplate the beautiful flower. But after the lily had bloomed its brightest it began to fade, then every one wished to see how the lily grew. Pushing aside the clay from around the plant they discovered that its roots rested in the mouth of the fool Salaün. The duke of Brittany, hearing of this surprising fact, ordered a chapel built near the fountain under the name of "Our Lady of Folgoët, or The Fool of the Woods." This forest sanctuary became a place of frequent pilgrimages.

THE END.

www.ingramcontent.com/pod-product-compliance
Lightning Source LLC
Chambersburg PA
CBHW021957220426
43663CB00007B/849

OEUVRES
DE
J. RACINE

NOUVELLE ÉDITION

REVUE SUR LES PLUS ANCIENNES IMPRESSIONS
ET LES AUTOGRAPHES

ET AUGMENTÉE

de morceaux inédits, des variantes, de notices, de notes, d'un lexique des mots
et locutions remarquables, d'un portrait, de fac-simile, etc.

PAR M. PAUL MESNARD

TOME SIXIÈME

PARIS
LIBRAIRIE DE L. HACHETTE ET Cie
BOULEVARD SAINT-GERMAIN, N° 77

1865

REMARQUES

SUR LES

OLYMPIQUES DE PINDARE

ET SUR

L'ODYSSÉE D'HOMÈRE

NOTICE.

Les traductions que nous avons données à la fin du tome précédent ne sont pas tout ce qui nous reste des studieux exercices qui ont été pour Racine l'apprentissage de son art, et la préparation des œuvres de son génie. On trouve aussi parmi ses manuscrits, à la Bibliothèque impériale, des cahiers qui renferment ses *Remarques sur les Olympiques* et *sur l'Odyssée* et des extraits qu'il avait faits de plusieurs auteurs anciens, ou sacrés, ou profanes. En outre, l'on a conservé un assez grand nombre des annotations dont il avait coutume de couvrir les marges de ses livres, soit au temps de sa jeunesse, soit plus tard. Nous parlerons d'abord de ses *Remarques sur Pindare* et *sur Homère*, qui sont, avec les traductions, les seules parties de ces études qu'il convienne de reproduire sans en rien retrancher. Quant aux *Extraits* et aux *Livres annotés*, que, dans quelques parties, il suffira de faire connaître un peu plus sommairement, nous réservons pour une autre notice ce que nous avons à en dire.

Les *Remarques sur les Olympiques* se trouvent écrites de la main de Racine dans un cahier[1] de format in-8º, dont le cartonnage vert paraît ancien, et où elles ont cinquante-sept pages. Elles y sont précédées de cinquante pages d'*Extraits* de Virgile, d'Horace, de Pline l'ancien, et de Cicéron, qui ont une pagination à part.

Le manuscrit des *Remarques sur les dix premiers livres de l'Odyssée* est également un cahier in-8º, avec un cartonnage semblable. Ce cahier[2] ne contient pas autre chose; il a cent vingt-six pages.

L'écriture grecque de ces deux cahiers est aussi nette, aussi jolie, on peut le dire, que la française. On y remarque quelques simples et faciles ligatures ou abréviations. L'accentuation est généralement très-correcte.

M. Aimé-Martin a, dans son édition de 1825, publié le premier ces deux études. Sans en vouloir exagérer la valeur, nous pensons

---

[1]. Bibliothèque impériale, Fonds français, nº 12890.
[2]. *Ibidem*, nº 12891.

comme lui qu'elles méritaient de ne pas être condamnées à l'oubli : on lui a certainement su gré de les avoir recueillies ; mais il est regrettable qu'il ait laissé, dans sa transcription, se glisser un certain nombre d'erreurs qu'une lecture plus attentive des manuscrits lui aurait fait éviter.

Racine a lui-même daté ses *Remarques sur les Olympiques* et ses *Remarques sur l'Odyssée*, les secondes du mois et de l'année[1] (avril 1662), les premières du jour et du mois seulement (1ᵉʳ mars) ; mais il est difficile de mettre en doute que celles-ci soient pareillement de 1662. Les deux cahiers se ressemblent beaucoup ; tous deux, nous l'avons dit, sont de format in-8°, et reliés dans un cartonnage vert. On trouve, il est vrai, quelques différences dans les marques du papier ; mais l'écriture est bien du même temps, et le travail est du même genre. On peut remarquer aussi que Racine compare quelques traits de la description des Champs Élysées dans Homère et dans Pindare ; et ce rapprochement, il le fait deux fois, en commentant le quatrième livre de l'*Odyssée*, comme en commentant la seconde *Olympique* : cela ne peut-il au moins confirmer l'opinion qu'il étudiait les deux poëtes dans le même temps ?

Ce temps était celui où il se trouvait à Uzès, et où il ne laissait guère entrevoir dans ses lettres à ses jeunes amis qu'il fît de ses loisirs un emploi si studieux. Mais nous avons déjà, nous appuyant tout au moins sur de grandes vraisemblances, rencontré d'autres traces des travaux sérieux qui l'occupaient à cette époque[2]. Que la jeunesse de Racine ait été nourrie des plus fortes études, n'est-ce pas depuis longtemps comme un lieu commun ? Ce qu'on répète à ce sujet demeure toutefois un peu vague, quand on ne l'appuie pas sur des preuves. Nous en avons de très-certaines ici, comme dans quelques-uns des livres annotés, dont la date connue est plus ancienne encore ; elles sont telles que, de nos jours, les jeunes gens du même âge les plus chargés de couronnes scolaires pourraient bien se croire ignorants, s'ils venaient à se comparer à cet élève de Port-Royal. A ce point de vue, et comme témoignages de la connaissance étendue, et voisine de l'érudition, que Racine eut de bonne heure de l'antiquité, ces notes de jeunesse sont assez dignes d'attention pour qu'on n'accuse pas d'un soin trop minutieux les éditeurs qui les ont recueillies. Nous allons avoir à dire jusqu'à quel point on peut leur reconnaître un autre prix ; et nous verrons s'il n'y a pas là une distinction à faire entre les deux études que nous croyons l'une comme l'autre du temps d'Uzès.

---

1. Pour les *Remarques* sur le livre V, il a même marqué le jour (19 avril).
2. Voyez notre tome V, p. 444.

Admettant qu'elles sont en effet de la même année, nous avons dû placer celle qui est du mois de mars avant celle qui est du mois d'avril, et par conséquent commencer par les *Remarques sur les Olympiques*.

Racine a été poëte lyrique dès qu'il a tenté de l'être ; et il ne lui a manqué, ce semble, que de le tenter plus tôt et plus souvent pour mériter la même gloire dans l'ode que dans la tragédie. Ces seuls mots : « Racine commentant Pindare, » donnent donc tout d'abord une grande idée, que ne remplit assurément pas la lecture de ses *Remarques*. Reconnaissons qu'en général, et sans faire d'exception pour aucun des autres travaux analogues de notre poëte, sous quelque forme qu'ils nous aient été conservés, il s'est contenté, dans ses études sur les auteurs qu'il commentait, d'attention, d'exactitude et de bon sens, et n'a point eu de hautes visées. Les habitudes de critique modeste dans lesquelles il s'est toujours renfermé ont, chez un si grand esprit, quelque chose qui ne déplaît pas. Nous ne dirons pas cependant qu'il n'y ait là rien à regretter, et nous ne voudrions pas nier le désappointement où l'on tombe, lorsqu'au lieu d'un vif sentiment des beautés poétiques de Pindare, on ne trouve sous une telle plume que des explications littérales, et des traductions des vieux commentaires. Est-ce donc que ces odes admirables n'auraient pas dit à Racine autre chose que ce qu'elles disaient à de froids scoliastes? Heureusement une explication moins invraisemblable s'offre sans peine. Lorsque Racine a annoté les auteurs anciens, il n'a écrit que ce qui lui était utile à lui-même, soit pour se rendre maître de leur texte, soit pour graver dans sa mémoire les principaux traits ou le dessein général de leurs ouvrages; mais comment se pourrait-il que sous ce commentaire si prosaïquement consciencieux, son génie de poëte n'en eût pas en même temps et tacitement fait un autre qui sans doute le transportait d'enthousiasme, et éveillait en lui toutes les puissances de la Muse? Ce commentaire-là, il ne nous l'a donné que dans ses poésies, toutes nourries du miel qu'il avait dérobé à l'antiquité. Là se retrouvera plus tard cet éclat, qu'on cherche en vain dans ses *Remarques* : après la fumée viendra la flamme. Car nous pouvons appliquer à Racine les vers d'Horace qu'il cite lui-même à la première page de ses *Remarques sur l'Odyssée :*

.... *Ex fumo dare lucem*
Cogitat, ut speciosa dehinc miracula promat[1].

Voilà le lecteur assez averti de ce que sont les *Remarques sur Pin-*

---

1. *Art poétique,* vers 143 et 144.

dare : uniquement une preuve de solide instruction chez un jeune homme destiné à devenir un grand poëte. C'est dans ce sens qu'il faut tâcher de se rendre compte de son travail.

Racine a commenté les quatorze *Olympiques*. Cette étude atteste beaucoup de connaissance de la langue grecque. Il ne serait sans doute pas difficile, aujourd'hui que bien des obscurités de Pindare ont été éclaircies, de relever chez son jeune commentateur des explications erronées de plus d'un passage. Cependant son intelligence d'un texte si difficile est remarquable, surtout quand on tient compte du peu de secours qu'il avait à sa disposition. Si celui d'une traduction latine a pu quelquefois ne lui être pas inutile, il est aisé de voir que le plus souvent il savait s'en passer. Il a plutôt consulté les scolies, qu'évidemment il lisait avec facilité, et dont à chaque page de ses *Remarques* il expose les différentes interprétations. Allons au-devant d'un doute qu'on pourrait élever. Il s'est conservé un exemplaire de l'édition de Pindare publiée à Saumur, en 1620, par Benoît (1 volume in-4°), qui porte la signature de Racine, et dont les marges sont chargées de notes de sa main, se rapportant non-seulement aux *Olympiques*, mais aussi à plusieurs autres odes du lyrique grec ; nous donnerons ci-après les notes de ce volume. L'édition de Benoît, outre sa paraphrase latine, a un commentaire dans la même langue. Racine se serait-il aidé de ce commentaire, dans ses *Remarques*, au lieu de s'adresser directement aux scoliastes ? On se tromperait en le supposant. Benoît a fait quelques emprunts aux vieilles scolies ; mais Racine en a fait de bien plus nombreux, que par conséquent il n'a point puisés là. Au surplus, après quelque examen, il nous a paru certain que Racine, lorsqu'il écrivait les *Remarques sur les Olympiques*, ne connaissait pas encore l'édition de 1620, qui lui eût permis de rectifier plus d'une erreur ; nous allons dire celle qu'il avait alors sous les yeux.

Parmi les éditions qui donnent les scolies, on en compte plusieurs antérieures à 1662 ; il semble donc qu'on pourrait hésiter entre elles. Mais le texte des vers transcrits par Racine dans son cahier est décisif. Nous avons comparé ce texte avec ceux qu'ont publiés Calliergi à Rome en 1515, et Brubach à Francfort en 1542, tous deux contenant les scolies. Sans entrer dans des détails qu'on jugerait ici hors de leur place, nous dirons qu'en plusieurs passages ces textes diffèrent assez de celui qu'a suivi Racine, pour qu'on n'attribue pas seulement ces différences à quelques erreurs de transcription. Il n'en est pas de même du texte publié en un volume in-4° par Paul Estienne ; nous ne parlons pas de celui de 1612, mais de celui de 1599. Jusque dans ses particularités les plus notables, il est d'accord avec le texte du manuscrit de Racine : d'où l'on peut conclure avec certitude qu'il est celui dont notre auteur s'est servi pour son travail. L'édition dont nous parlons a pour titre : ΠΙΝΔΑΡΟΥ ΟΛΥΜΠΙΑ, ΠΥΘΙΑ, ΝΕΜΕΑ, ΙΣΘΜΙΑ, μετὰ ἐξηγήσεως παλαιᾶς πάνυ ὠφελίμου, καὶ σχολίων ὁμοίων.... *Adjuncta est interpretatio latina ad verbum. Anno M.D.XCIX.* Nous avertissons ceux qui voudraient faire comme nous la comparaison des deux textes, que pour celui du manuscrit de Racine, il faut se servir de notre édition, qui y est conforme, et non de celle de M. Aimé-Martin, qui a trouvé bon, comme nous nous en sommes assuré, de suivre l'édition de Schmid (in-4°, Wittenberg, 1616), ou quelque réimpression de cette même édition.

Les *Remarques sur les dix premiers livres de l'Odyssée* ont plus d'étendue que les *Remarques sur les Olympiques*. Le commentaire y est surtout moins sèchement explicatif, et répond davantage à ce qu'on doit attendre de Racine, qui y a trouvé plus d'occasions de montrer son goût déjà très-sûr, la délicatesse et la finesse de son esprit : soit qu'un texte plus facile le laissât plus libre d'apprécier les beautés du poëte, au lieu de se renfermer dans l'explication du sens, soit qu'il eût une prédilection particulière pour cet antique récit, abondante et profonde source du roman et du poëme dramatique, et où tout lui paraissait, comme il le dit, « admirable et divertissant. » L'auteur des *Remarques sur l'Odyssée* ne fût-il pas connu, on lirait encore avec plaisir cette fidèle et vive analyse, tant d'excellentes observations littéraires, tant de saines réflexions morales, dont la naïveté d'expression a ici un charme particulier, parce qu'elle met le commentateur tout à fait en harmonie avec son poëte. C'est dans un tel esprit qu'il faudrait toujours pouvoir traduire l'*Odyssée* ou en parler. Ces *Remarques* sont aussi fort curieuses par les nombreux rapprochements que Racine y a faits de vers d'Homère avec des passages d'auteurs très-divers : ils attestent combien sa mémoire était facile, son instruction déjà étendue, ses lectures et ses études variées. En tête de la première page du manuscrit, on lit cette note de Louis Racine : « On voit que mon père, dans sa jeunesse, étoit tout plein d'Héliodore, qu'il cite souvent. » Plusieurs passages d'Homère, en effet, le lui rappellent si à propos qu'on en croit plus volontiers la tradition, qui veut qu'il l'ait su par cœur. Il parait encore qu'il avait beaucoup lu l'*Argenis* de Barclay. C'étaient là ses amusements; mais ses *Remarques* le montrent en même temps très-versé dans les grands auteurs de l'antiquité, et Louis Racine aurait pu constater aussi ses nombreuses citations de Virgile, d'Horace, de Pline, de Cicéron. Un peu plus bas, dans la même page, il ajoute : « Quand mon père a écrit ces *Remarques*, en 1662, il avoit vingt-deux ans ; il étoit à Uzez. — Comme le nom de Télémaque n'étoit pas alors si connu qu'aujourd'hui, il écrit toujours *Telemachus*, au lieu qu'il écrit *Pisistrate;* mais il écrit *Menelaüs, Penelopé.* » Pour être entièrement exact, il faut dire que Racine n'est pas toujours d'accord avec lui-même, et que son manuscrit, à côté de *Telemachus*, donne quelquefois *Télémaque*. Nous avons partout laissé les noms tels qu'il les a écrits, sans corriger les variations.

Parmi les anciennes éditions du texte grec de l'*Odyssée*, il nous a paru assez difficile, et peut-être n'est-il pas très-nécessaire, d'indiquer celle dont Racine a fait usage pour ce travail. C'est une de celles où l'on trouve une version latine; car il parle quelque part de cette version. Nous avons particulièrement remarqué le texte de l'édition in-16 donnée par Jean Crespin (*e typographia Joannis Crispini Atrebatii*, 1567), comme presque partout conforme à celui qui est cité dans les *Remarques*. S'il y a quelques différences, elles sont très-légères, et de telle nature qu'on peut les attribuer à des inadvertances de Racine.

On trouvera plus loin des notes que Racine a écrites sur les marges d'un exemplaire de l'*Iliade*. Moins développées que ses *Remarques sur l'Odyssée*, elles nous ont cependant paru offrir aussi un assez grand intérêt.

REMARQUES

SUR LES OLYMPIQUES DE PINDARE.

1ᵉʳ mars [1662 １].

ODE I.

A HIÉRON,

VAINQUEUR A LA COURSE DU CHEVAL CÉLÈTES.

Ἄριστον μὲν ὕδωρ.

Il appelle l'eau le plus excellent de tous les éléments, pour deux raisons : 1° à cause que d'elle se forment les autres ; car l'air se fait d'une eau subtilisée, la terre d'une eau condensée, et le feu, se faisant de l'air devenu plus subtil, tire aussi par conséquent son origine de l'eau ; 2° parce que l'eau et l'humidité est ce qui est le plus nécessaire aux animaux vivants, et inanimés, car nous vivons de ce que la terre produit : or les semences ne peuvent pousser sans humidité.

Ὁ δὲ
Χρυσὸς, αἰθόμενον πῦρ
Ἅτε διαπρέπει νυ-
κτὶ, μεγάνορος ἔξοχα πλούτου.

L'or éclate autant par-dessus les richesses qu'un feu allumé

1. Voyez la *Notice*, p. 4.

éclate au milieu de la nuit. Il appelle les richesses [1] μεγάνορα πλοῦτον, parce que ceux qui sont riches font les grands hommes, ou parce que les richesses font de grandes choses. Un commentateur dit que Pindare a suivi son inclination naturelle en louant les richesses [2].

> Μηκέθ' ἁλίου σκόπει
> Ἄλλο θαλπνότερον
> Ἐν ἀμέρᾳ φαεινὸν ἄστρον,
> Ἐρήμας δι' αἰθέρος.

Ne cherchez point d'astre plus échauffant ni plus brillant que le soleil durant le jour, lorsqu'il éclaire l'air désert.

Les uns disent que ἔρημος veut dire, en cet endroit, chaud et ardent, en sorte que personne n'ose aller à l'air, qui est par conséquent désert; d'autres disent que la mer a des poissons, et la terre les autres animaux qui l'habitent, mais qu'aucun d'eux ne fait sa demeure dans l'air; enfin d'autres disent qu'il veut dire par là que l'air est calme, tranquille et sans nuages; quelques-uns disent qu'il entend la sphère du feu [3].

> Δρέπων μὲν
> Κορυφὰς ἀρετᾶν ἄπο πασᾶν·
> Ἀγλαΐζεται δὲ καὶ
> Μουσικᾶς ἐν ἀώτῳ,
> Οἷα παίζομεν φίλαν
> Ἄνδρες ἀμφὶ θαμὰ
> Τράπεζαν.

Il dit qu'Hiéron étoit élevé au sommet de toutes les vertus, et qu'il en recueilloit le fruit, et qu'il se plaisoit aux fleurs et aux douceurs de la musique, ou bien qu'il se plaisoit aux odes, qui sont la fleur de la musique. Or, quand un prince se plaît aux exercices de la musique, qui sont des exercices de paix, c'est une marque que son royaume est paisible. Tels que sont, dit-il, les chants que nous jouons souvent autour de

---

1. Racine avait d'abord écrit : « l'opulence. »
2. Un des scoliastes dit en effet : τῆς ἑαυτοῦ φύσεως φιλοχρημάτου τυγχανούσης, « sa nature étant amie de la richesse. »
3. Nous ne trouvons rien dans les scolies qui nous paraisse tout à fait semblable.

sa table amie, parce que la musique n'est jamais si agréable qu'à l'issue du festin. Il appelle la table *amie*, parce qu'on n'y appelle que des amis, ou bien à cause qu'elle noue les amitiés.

> Ἀλλὰ Δωρίαν ἀ-
> πὸ φόρμιγγα πασσάλου
> Λάμβαν'.

Mais prends ton luth dorien du clou où il est attaché. Il l'appelle dorien, parce que des trois harmonies, dorienne, phrygienne et lydienne, la dorienne ou la dorique étoit la plus grave.

> Σύτο, δέμας
> Ἀκέντητον ἐν δρόμοισι παρέχων,
> Κράτει δὲ προσέμιξε δεσπόταν
> Συρακόσιον ἱπποχάρμαν
> Βασιλῆα.

Il loue le cheval d'Hiéron, qui, courant sans attendre l'éperon, menoit son maître à la victoire, savoir Hiéron, roi de Syracuse, qui aimoit les chevaux.

> Ἦ θαῦμα τὰ πολλά·
> Καί πού τι καὶ βροτῶν φρένα
> Ὑπὲρ τὸν ἀληθῆ λόγον
> Δεδαιδαλμένοι ψεύδεσι ποικίλοις
> Ἐξαπατῶντι μῦθοι.

Après avoir conté la fable de Pélops, à qui les Dieux rendirent une épaule d'ivoire après que Cérès eut mangé la sienne : Il y a, dit-il, beaucoup de choses merveilleuses, et cependant des fables embellies de divers mensonges trompent et divertissent l'esprit humain beaucoup plus que de véritables discours.

> Χάρις δ' ἅπερ ἅπαντα τεύ-
> χει τὰ μείλιχα θνατοῖς,
> Ἐπιφέροισα τιμὰν,
> Καὶ ἄπιστον ἐμήσατο πιστὸν
> Ἔμμεναι τὸ πολλάκις.

Par cette grâce qui rend tout agréable aux hommes, et qui donne le prix aux choses, il entend la grâce de la poésie.

> Ἁμέραι δ' ἐπίλοιποι,
> Μάρτυρες σοφώτατοι.

Mais les jours de l'avenir sont des juges sages et infaillibles.

> Ἔστι δ' ἀνδρὶ φάμεν
> Ἐοικὸς ἀμφὶ Δαιμόνων κα-
> λά.

Il sied bien à un homme, ou il est juste que l'homme parle toujours bien des Dieux.

> Ἐμοὶ δ' ἄπορα, γαστρίμαργον
> Μακάρων τιν' εἰπεῖν.
> Ἀφίσταμαι. Ἀκέρδεια λέλογχε
> Θαμινὰ κακαγόρως.

Il dit cela après avoir réfuté la fable que Pélops avoit été mis en pièces par les Dieux, pour être mangé : il dit seulement que Pélops fut enlevé par Neptune au palais de Jupiter, pour lui servir d'échanson, comme après lui Ganymède.

> Ἀλλὰ γὰρ κατα-
> πέψαι μέγαν ὄλβον οὐκ ἐδυ-
> νάσθη· κόρῳ δ' ἕλεν
> Ἄταν ὑπέροπλον.

Il parle de Tantale, que les Dieux avoient honoré plus qu'aucun homme; mais il ne put digérer ce grand bonheur, et il s'attira un malheur infini par son dégoût. Il fait allusion aux viandes, qui nuisent beaucoup à l'estomac, lorsqu'il ne les sauroit digérer. Quelques-uns entendent par ce dégoût l'orgueil et l'insolence. Il marque par là qu'un homme qui ne peut digérer son bonheur se perd souvent.

> Εὐφροσύνας ἀλᾶται·
> Ἔχει δ' ἀπάλαμον βίον
> Τοῦτον, ἐμπεδόμοχθον.

Il décrit la misère de Tantale, qui, voulant détourner de sa tête cette pierre qui est pendue sur lui, ne sauroit avoir de joie, et mène une vie toujours pénible.

> Ἀθανάτων ὅτι κλέψας
> Ἁλίκεσσι συμπόταις
> Νέκταρ ἀμβροσίαν τε
> Δῶκεν, οἷσιν ἄφθιτον
> Θέσσαν.

Les uns expliquent cela en disant que Tantale découvrit les mystères des Dieux ; d'autres disent que c'étoit un naturaliste qui voulut découvrir la nature du soleil.

Εἰ δὲ θεὸν
Ἀνήρ τις ἔλπεταί τι λαθέ-
μεν ἔρδων, ἁμαρτάνει.

Celui-là se trompe qui croit faire quelque chose au desçu[1] des Dieux.

Τοὔνεκα προῆκαν υἱὸν
Ἀθάνατοί οἱ πάλιν
Μετὰ τὸ ταχύποτμον
Αὖθις ἀνέρων ἔθνος.

Les Dieux punissent Tantale en la personne de son fils, en le renvoyant parmi les hommes, qui meurent bientôt.

Πρὸς εὐάνθεμον δ' ὅτε φυὰν
Λάχναι νιν μέλαν γένειον ἔρεφον,
Ἑτοῖμον ἀνεφρόντισεν γάμον.

Il appelle la jeunesse florissante. Il dit que Pélops chercha un mariage qui se présentoit. L'histoire est qu'Œnomaüs étoit si fort épris de la beauté de sa fille qu'il ne croyoit pas que personne la méritât. Il ne la donnoit qu'à cette condition que son amant la devoit enlever[2] à la course d'un char. Il étoit derrière le char avec une pique ; et quand son chariot, qui étoit le plus vite du monde, avoit atteint l'autre, il perçoit de sa lance l'amant de sa fille. Il en avoit déjà tué treize quand Pélops eut recours à Neptune, lequel, selon quelques-uns, gagna le cocher d'Œnomaüs afin qu'il laissât courir Pélops avec Hippodamie ; mais, selon Pindare, Neptune donna à Pélops un char d'or[3], tiré par des chevaux ailés.

Ἄγχι δ' ἐλθὼν
Πολιᾶς ἁλὸς οἷος ἐν ὄρφνᾳ,

---

1. M. Aimé-Martin a imprimé « au-dessus, » ce qui, dans ce passage, n'a point de sens. Il y a dans le manuscrit : *au desceu*, c'est-à-dire, « à l'insu. »
2. *Enlever* est écrit au-dessus de *atteindre*, qui est effacé.
3. Racine avait écrit d'abord d'*argent*.

>Ἄπυεν βαρύκτυπον
>Εὐτρίαιναν.

Il appelle la mer chenue, ou parce que c'est le premier et le plus ancien des éléments, ou à cause que sa continuelle agitation la fait blanchir [1].

>Ὁ μέγας δὲ κίνδυ-
>νος ἄναλκιν οὐ φῶ-
>τα λαμβάνει. Θανεῖν δ' οἷσιν ἀνάγκα,
>Τί κέ τις ἀνώνυμον γῆρας ἐν σκότῳ
>Καθήμενος ἕψοι μάταν, ἁπάντων
>Καλῶν ἄμμορος;

Puisque aussi bien il faut mourir, pourquoi consumer une vieillesse inconnue dans les ténèbres, dénué de vertu et d'honneur?

>Ἀρεταῖσι μεμαλότας υἱούς.

Il eut des enfants adonnés à la vertu.

>Τύμβον ἀμφίπολον
>Ἔχων πολυξενωτάτῳ πα-
>ρὰ βωμῷ.

Il a un sépulcre tout environné de la multitude des pèlerins.

>Ὁ νικῶν δὲ λοιπὸν ἀμφὶ βίοτον
>Ἔχει μελιτόεσσαν εὐδίαν,
>Ἀέθλων γ' ἕνεκεν.

Ou parce que cette victoire est le comble de l'honneur, ou parce qu'il n'a plus besoin de combattre davantage, ayant une fois vaincu.

>Τὸ δ' ἀ-
>εὶ παράμερον ἐσλὸν,
>Ὕπατον ἔρχεται παν-
>τὶ βροτῷ.

Les hommes oublient les biens qu'ils ont reçus [2] par le

---

1. Cette remarque n'est pas tirée des scolies.
2. Il y a dans le manuscrit : *receu*, sans accord.

passé, et ne goûtent bien que ceux qui leur viennent de jour en jour. Ou : le bien qui nous arrive sans discontinuer est le souverain bien. Ou : le bien qui nous arrive après l'avoir bien souhaité est le bien qui nous plaît davantage[1] : comme Hiéron, qui a vaincu après avoir fait tous ses efforts pour vaincre.

> Πέποιθα δὲ ξένον
> Μή τιν' ἀμφότερα
> Καλῶν τε ἴδριν ἄλλον, καὶ δύ-
> ναμιν κυριώτερον,
> Τῶν γε νῦν, κλυταῖσι δαιδα-
> λωσέμεν ὕμνων πτυχαῖς.

Je suis certain que je ne louerai jamais personne qui soit plus savant et plus vertueux qu'Hiéron. Ou bien : jamais personne ne vous louera avec plus de connoissance et plus de force que moi.

> Θεὸς, ἐπίτροπος ἐ-
> ὼν, τεαῖσι μήδεται,
> Ἔχων τοῦτο κῆδος, Ἱέρων,
> Μερίμναισιν.

Cela s'entend ou du dieu protecteur d'Hiéron, ou du dieu de la poésie.

> Ἐπ' ἄλλοι-
> σι δ' ἄλλοι μεγάλοι· τὸ δ' ἔσχατον κορυ-
> φοῦται βασιλεῦσι.

Les uns excellent en une chose, les autres en une autre ; mais les rois excellent souverainement aux choses où les autres n'excellent que médiocrement. Ou bien : la puissance des rois est le souverain degré d'honneur.

> Μηκέτι
> Πάπταινε πόρσιον.

Ne souhaitez rien davantage que la gloire que vous venez d'acquérir aux jeux ; ou bien : que la dignité que les Dieux vous ont donnée.

> Εἴη σέ τε τοῦτον

---

[1] Ces différents sens sont proposés par les scoliastes.

Ὑψοῦ χρόνον πατεῖν, ἐμέ
Τε τοσσάδε νικαφόροις
Ὁμιλεῖν, πρόφαντον σοφίαν καθ' Ἑλ-
λανας ἐόντα παντᾶ.

Puissiez-vous cependant jouir de la gloire où vous êtes élevé; et moi puissé-je[1] jouir de la conversation des braves comme vous, me rendant fameux parmi les Grecs par ma sagesse. Le sens est qu'autant qu'Hiéron est heureux d'être vainqueur et d'être roi, autant Pindare se croit-il heureux de converser avec des héros comme lui, et de chanter leurs louanges.

Cet Hiéron étoit si beau, si brave et si généreux, qu'il passa pour un prodige. Théocrite lui a adressé quelques églogues[2].

ODE II.

A THÉRON, TYRAN OU ROI D'AGRIGENTE,

VAINQUEUR A LA COURSE DU CHARIOT.

Ἀναξιφόρμιγγες ὕμνοι,
Τίνα θεὸν, τίν' ἥρωα,
Τίνα δ' ἄνδρα κελαδήσομεν;

Il appelle les chansons reines des instruments, parce qu'on compose les chansons, et puis on y accommode le luth.

Γεγωνητέον ὀπὶ
Δίκαιον ξένον
Ἔρεισμ' Ἀκράγαντος,
Εὐωνύμων τε πατέρων
Ἄωτον, ὀρθόπολιν.

Il appelle Théron la fleur de ses illustres parents, parce

---

[1]. Racine écrit *puissay ie*. Voyez le *Lexique de Corneille*, tome I, p. LXXXVII.

[2]. Racine confond ici Hiéron I avec Hiéron II.

qu'il étoit de la race de Cadmus. Il le loue aussi d'être le conservateur de sa ville.

Αἰών τ' ἔφε-
πε μόρσιμος, πλοῦτόν
Τε καὶ χάριν ἄγων
Γνησίαις ἐπ' ἀρεταῖς.

Le temps et la destinée a comblé leurs vertus de richesses et de bonheur.

Τῶν δὲ πεπραγμένων,
Ἐν δίκᾳ τε καὶ παρὰ δίκαν,
Ἀποίητον οὐδ' ἂν
Χρόνος, ὁ πάντων πατὴρ,
Δύναιτο θέμεν ἔργων τέλος·
Λάθα δὲ πότμῳ σὺν εὐδαίμονι γένοιτ' ἄν·
Ἐσθλῶν γὰρ ὑπὸ χαρμάτων,
Πῆμα θνάσκει παλίγκοτον δαμασθέν.

Il dit cela à cause que Théron avoit été en guerre avec Hiéron. Le temps ne sauroit pas empêcher que cela n'ait été fait ; mais le bonheur et la joie présente doit faire oublier tous ces malheurs.

Ἕπεται δὲ λόγος εὐθρόνοις
Κάδμοιο κούραις, ἔπα-
θον αἳ μεγάλα. Πένθος
Δὲ πιτνεῖ βαρὺ
Κρεσσόνων πρὸς ἀγαθῶν.

Il fait venir là l'histoire des filles de Cadmus, parce que Théron étoit de cette race. Elles furent donc toutes malheureuses ; mais après elles devinrent immortelles, comme Sémélé et Ino.

Ἦ τοι
Βροτῶν γε κέκριται
Πεῖρας οὔ τι θανάτου,
Οὐδ' ἀσύχιμον ἀμέραν
Ὁπότε παῖδ' Ἀλίου
Ἀτειρεῖ σὺν ἀγαθῷ
Τελευτάσομεν.
Ῥοαὶ δ' ἄλλοτ' ἄλλαι
Εὐθυμιᾶν τε μέτα καὶ
Πόνων ἐς ἄνδρας ἔβαν.

Il appelle les Journées filles du Soleil; il y en a qui expliquent ce vers, ἀσύχιμον ἁμέραν, pour le jour de la mort, parce qu'elle finit tous nos travaux.

> Οὕτω δὲ Μοῖρ', ἅ τε πατρώϊον
> Τόνδ' ἔχει τὸν εὔφρονα πότμον
> Θεόρτῳ σὺν ὄλβῳ
> Ἐπί τι καὶ πῆμ' ἄγει
> Παλιντράπελον ἄλλῳ χρόνῳ.

Il revient à Théron, dont la race a été heureuse, et puis après malheureuse, et ensuite est retournée à son premier bonheur.

> Τὸ δὲ τυχεῖν,
> Πειρώμενον ἀγωνίας
> Παραλύει δυσφρόνων.
> Ὁ μὰν πλοῦτος ἀρεταῖς
> Δεδαιδαλμένος
> Φέρει τῶν τε καὶ τῶν
> Καιρὸν, βαθεῖαν ὑπέχων
> Μέριμναν ἀγροτέραν.

Les richesses qui sont ornées de la vertu supportent aisément la bonne et la mauvaise fortune. C'est ce qu'a dit élégamment Sapho[1] :

« Πλοῦτος ἄνευ ἀρετῆς οὐκ ἀσινὴς πάροικος ·
Ἡ δὲ ἐξ ἀμφοτέρων κρᾶσις εὐδαιμονίας ἔχει
Τὸ ἄκρον. »

Callimachus a eu la même pensée en ces vers :

« Οὔτ' ἀρετῆς ἄτερ ὄλβος ἐπίσταται ἄνδρας ἀέξειν,
Οὔτ' ἀρετὴ ἀφένοιο, δίδου δ' ἀρετήν τε καὶ ὄλβον. »

> Ἀστὴρ ἀρίζηλος, ἀλαθινὸν
> Ἀνδρὶ φέγγος.

---

1. Ces vers de Sapho, et les suivants, de Callimaque, ont été cités aussi par un des scoliastes; et c'est à lui que nous devons la connaissance des premiers. Les vers de Callimaque sont les deux derniers (95 et 96) de l'*Hymne I, à Jupiter*.

L'un avec l'autre[1], dit-il, est un astre brillant, et le véritable ornement d'un homme.

> Εἰ δέ μιν ἔχει
> Τις, οἶδε τὸ μέλλον,
> Ὅτι θανόντων μὲν ἐν-
> θάδ' αὐτίκ' ἀπάλαμνοι φρένες
> Ποινὰς ἔτισαν. Τὰ δ' ἐν τᾷδε Διὸς ἀρχᾷ
> Ἀλιτρὰ κατὰ γᾶς δικά-
> ζει τις, ἐχθρᾷ λόγον φράσας ἀνάγκᾳ.

Il représente la justice de l'autre monde, où sont punis les crimes de celui-ci. Ἐχθρᾷ, parce qu'on n'y juge point par amis, mais selon les actions. *Comm.*[2]

> Ἴσον δὲ νύκτεσσιν αἰεὶ,
> Ἴσα δ' ἐν ἀμέραις ἅλι-
> ον ἔχοντες, ἀπονέστερον
> Ἐσλοὶ νέμονται βίο-
> τον, οὐ χθόνα ταράσσον-
> τες ἀλκᾷ χερῶν,
> Οὐδὲ πόντιον ὕδωρ
> Κεινὰν παρὰ δίαιταν· ἀλ-
> λὰ παρὰ μὲν τιμίοις
> Θεῶν οἵ τινες ἔχαι-
> ρον εὐορκίαις,
> Ἄδακρυν νέμονται
> Αἰῶνα· τοὶ δ' ἀπροσόρα-
> τον ὀχχέοντι[3] πόνον.

1. M. Aimé-Martin a mis : « l'un ou l'autre. » — Racine paraît avoir écrit d'abord *et*, au lieu de *avec*.

2. Tel est le texte du manuscrit. M. Aimé-Martin a mis : « les actions commises. » Mais il nous paraît évident que *Comm.* est une abréviation du mot *Commentaire*, et signifie que l'explication proposée est tirée d'un scoliaste. On lit en effet dans les scolies (édition de Paul Estienne, p. 140) : τὸ δὲ ἐχθρᾷ, διότι οὐδεὶς ἐκεῖ φίλος, ἀλλ' ἕκαστος ἐκ τῶν ἔργων δικαιοῦται καὶ κατακρίνεται, « il dit ἐχθρᾷ, *ennemie*, parce que là il n'y a point d'ami, mais que chacun est jugé et condamné d'après ses actions. »

3. Le manuscrit porte : οἰχέοντι. Tel est aussi le texte de l'édition de Paul Estienne (1599). Les autres éditions ont ὀχέοντι, ou ὀχχέοντι, les seules formes légitimes. Οἰχέοντι est sans doute une faute d'impression dans le texte de 1599 ; nous la signalons parce

Il montre la différence des bons qui vivront[1] toujours en l'autre monde sans travail et sans affliction, sans labourer la terre et sans naviguer[2] sur la mer, ou, comme d'autres expliquent, sans se battre sur la terre et sans se battre sur la mer.

> Ὅσοι δ' ἐτόλμασαν ἐς τρὶς
> Ἑκατέρωθι μείναντες
> Ἀπὸ πάμπαν ἀδίκων ἔχειν
> Ψυχάν, ἔτειλαν Διὸς
> Ὁδὸν παρὰ Κρόνου τύρ-
> σιν· ἔνθα μακάρων
> Νᾶσον ὠκεανίδες
> Αὖραι περιπνέουσιν· ἄν-
> θεμα δὲ χρυσοῦ φλέγει,
> Τὰ μὲν χερσόθεν ἀπ' ἀ-
> γλαῶν δενδρέων,
> Ὕδωρ δ' ἄλλα φέρβει·
> Ὅρμοισι τῶν χέρας ἀνα-
> πλέκοντι καὶ στεφάνοις.

Il parle ici des plus parfaits qui ont persévéré dans la vertu, et qui, marchant par la voie de Jupiter, sont arrivés aux Îles des Bienheureux, où brillent des fleurs dorées, tant celles qui viennent dessus les arbres que celles que l'eau nourrit, comme les roses, etc.

Quelques-uns ont cru qu'il entendoit parler de la métempsycose en la personne de ceux qui ont persévéré dans la vertu partout où ils ont été, c'est-à-dire dans une condition ou dans une autre; mais il semble qu'il ne veuille parler que de ceux qui dans l'une et l'autre fortune ont toujours été également vertueux; et cela vient mieux au discours qu'il a tenu auparavant de ces diverses fortunes. Car, dit-il, ces esprits fiers et intraitables, ἀπάλαμνοι, qui ont abusé de leur fortune, sont punis. Ceux qui se sont honnêtement gouvernés ne sont point tourmentés; mais ceux qui ont gardé leur âme toujours inviolable à l'injustice, en quelque état qu'ils aient été, et qui ont

---

que c'est une des preuves que ce texte est celui sur lequel Racine a travaillé.

1. Au lieu de « qui vivront, » il y a « qui vivent » dans l'édition de M. Aimé-Martin.

2. Racine a écrit : *naviger*.

suivi la voie de Jupiter, c'est-à-dire le chemin des héros et des Dieux, ceux-là vont dans les Îles heureuses. Homère les décrit comme Pindare, 4 *Odys*.[1].

> Ὃς Ἕκτορ' ἔσφαλε, Τροίας
> Ἄμαχον ἀστραβῆ κίο-
> να.

Il parle d'Achille, qui vainquit Hector, la colonne inébranlable de Troie.

> Πολλά μοι ὑπ' ἀγκῶ-
> νος ὠκέα βέλη
> Ἔνδον ἐντὶ φαρέτρας
> Φωνᾶντα συνετοῖσιν· ἐς
> Δὲ τὸ πᾶν ἑρμηνέων
> Χατίζει.

Il dit que ses flèches, c'est-à-dire ses vers, se font bien entendre aux savants, mais qu'ils ont besoin d'interprète pour être entendus du peuple.

> Σοφὸς ὁ πολ-
> λὰ εἰδὼς φυᾷ·
> Μαθόντες δὲ, λάβροι
> Παγγλωσσίᾳ, κόρακες ὣς,
> Ἄκραντα γαρύετον
> Διὸς πρὸς ὄρνιχα θεῖον.

Il dit que celui-là est véritablement sage qui est naturellement savant : cela s'entend de la poésie plus que de pas une autre science ; car il veut dire qu'il n'y a point de bon poète que ceux qui le sont naturellement, et qu'au contraire ceux qui ne le sont que par étude sont comme des corbeaux qui croassent méchamment au prix du divin oiseau de Jupiter, qui est l'aigle.

> Φίλοις ἄνδρα μᾶλλον
> Εὐεργέταν πραπίσιν ἀ-
> φθονέστερόν τε χέρα.

---

[1]. *Odyssée*, livre IV, vers 563-568.

Il dit qu'aucune ville n'a mis au monde depuis cent ans un homme plus obligeant et plus libéral que Théron.

> Ἀλλ' αἶνον ἔβα κόρος
> Οὐ δίκᾳ συναντόμενος, ἀλ-
> λὰ μάργων ὑπ' ἀνδρῶν,
> Τὸ λαλαγῆσαι θέλων,
> Κρύφον τε θέμεν ἐσλῶν κακοῖς
> Ἔργοις.

L'envie et l'insolence attaque la gloire de Théron, et excite de méchants hommes à le troubler, afin d'étouffer ses belles actions sous leurs crimes. Quelques parents [de] Théron[1], envieux de sa gloire, firent la guerre contre lui.

ODE III.

AU MÊME THÉRON.

> Καλλιπλοκάμῳ θ' Ἑλένᾳ.

Hélène aux beaux cheveux.

> Ὕμνον ὀρθώσας ἀκαμαντοπόδων
> Ἵππων ἄωτον.

Faisant un hymne à la louange de ses chevaux infatigables à la course.

> Διχόμηνις ὅλον χρυσάρματος
> Ἑσπέρας ὀφθαλμὸν ἀντέφλεξε μῆνα.

La pleine lune sur un char d'or montroit tout son visage sur le soir. Il l'appelle διχόμηνις, parce qu'elle coupe le mois en deux.

> Ἀλλ' οὐ καλὰ δένδρε' ἔθαλλε
> Χῶρος ἐν βάσσαις Κρονίου Πέλοπος.
> Τούτων ἔδοξε
> Γυμνὸς αὐτῷ κᾶπος ὀξεί-
> αις ὑπακουέμεν αὐγαῖς ἀλίου.

---

1. Ses cousins, Capys et Hippocrate, suivant le scoliaste.

La plaine d'Élide, étant dépouillée d'arbres, étoit sujette aux violentes ardeurs du soleil.

> Εἰ δ' ἀριστεύει μὲν ὕδωρ, κτεάνων
> Δὲ χρυσὸς αἰδοιέστατον·
> Νῦν γε πρὸς ἐσχατιὰν Θή-
> ρων ἀρεταῖσιν ἱκάνων, ἅπτεται
> Οἴκοθεν Ἡρακλέος στηλᾶν. Τὸ πόρσω
> Δ' ἔστι σοφοῖς ἄβατον,
> Κἀσόφοις. Οὐ μὴν διώξω. Κεινὸς εἴην.

Comme l'eau est le plus excellent des éléments, et l'or le plus précieux des métaux, aussi Théron ayant remporté la plus belle victoire, qui est celle des jeux olympiques, il est au plus excellent degré d'honneur ; et par ses vertus domestiques il va jusqu'aux colonnes d'Hercule, au delà desquelles ni sage ni ignorant ne peut aller. Je ne passe donc point plus outre, c'est-à-dire je ne le louerai pas davantage ; car je l'entreprendrois vainement.

ODE IV.

A PSAUMIS DE CAMÉRINE,

VAINQUEUR AU CHARIOT.

> Ἐλατὴρ ὑπέρτατε βροντᾶς
> Ἀκαμαντόποδος
> Ζεῦ· (τεαὶ γὰρ ὧραι, etc.)

Il appelle le tonnerre infatigable à la course, pour faire allusion aux chevaux qui courent aux jeux olympiques. Il dit que les heures appartiennent à Jupiter, ou parce qu'il est le maître du temps, ou bien il entend par là les cinq années qui sont le terme des jeux olympiques, dédiés à Jupiter.

> Ξείνων δ' εὖ πρασσόντων, ἔσαναν
> Αὐτίκ' ἀγγελίαν
> Ποτὶ γλυκεῖαν ἐσλοί.

Les gens de bien sont ravis quand ils entendent dire que leurs amis ont fait quelque chose de beau.

Δέχευ χαρίτων ἕκα-
τι τόνδε κῶμον,
Χρονιώτατον φάος εὐρυ-
σθενέων ἀρετᾶν.

Reçois cet hymne en action de grâces, lequel fera vivre longtemps la mémoire des vertus ; car les belles actions sont étouffées, si la poésie ne les chante.

Ἐπεί μιν
Αἰνέω μάλα μὲν
Τροφαῖς ἑτοῖμον ἵππων,
Χαίροντα δὲ ξεινίαις πανδόκοις,
Καὶ πρὸς ἡσυχίαν φιλόπολιν
Καθαρᾷ γνώμᾳ τεθραμμένον.

Car il y a des gens qui aiment leur ville ; mais ils n'aiment pas le repos comme Psaumis.

Οὐ ψεύδεϊ τέγξω
Λόγον. Διάπειρά τοι
Βροτῶν ἔλεγχος.

Je ne souillerai point mon discours de mensonge, en louant sans doute un homme déjà âgé d'avoir remporté le prix ; car l'expérience fait connoître les hommes, comme elle a fait connoître Erginus, un des Argonautes, qui sembloit déjà vieux, [et[1]] ne laissa pas de vaincre à la course, quoique les femmes de Lemnos se moquassent de lui.

Χαλκοῖσν δ' ἐν ἔντεσι νικῶν
Δρόμον, ἔειπεν Ὑψιπυλείᾳ,
Μετὰ στέφανον ἰών·
Οὗτος ἐγώ, ταχυτᾶτι
Χεῖρες δὲ καὶ ἦτορ ἴσον.

Tel que vous me voyez, dit-il à Hypsipyle[2], fille de Thoas,

---

1. Racine avait d'abord écrit : « qui étant déjà vieux, » ce qui explique l'omission de *et*.
2. Dans le manuscrit : *Hypsipile*.

pour qui se faisoient ces jeux à son tombeau, mes mains et mon corps répondent encore à la vitesse de mon esprit[1]; c'est-à-dire, si je fais de grands desseins, j'ai de la force assez pour les mettre en exécution.

> Φύονται δὲ καὶ νέοις
> Ἐν ἀνδράσι πολιαὶ
> Θαμὰ, καὶ παρὰ τὸν ἁλικίας
> Ἐοικότα χρόνον.

Ou parce que souvent les vieillards sont encore jeunes et vigoureux, ou parce qu'en effet les cheveux blanchissent souvent avant la vieillesse.

ODE V.

AU MÊME PSAUMIS,

VAINQUEUR EN TROIS COURSES.

> Αἰεὶ δ' ἀμφ' ἀρεταῖσι, πόνος δαπά-
> να τε μάρναται πρὸς
> Ἔργον κινδύνῳ κεκαλυμμένον.
> Εὖ δὲ ἔχοντες, σοφοὶ καὶ πολί-
> ταις ἔδοξαν ἔμμεν.

Il parle, ou de la victoire que Psaumis a remportée, ou bien de ce que Psaumis a rebâti de nouveau sa ville, Camérine.

> Σωτὴρ ὑψινεφὲς Ζεῦ,
> . . . .
> Ἱκέτας σέθεν ἔρχομαι, Λυδίοις
> Ἀπύων ἐν αὐλαῖς,
> Αἰτήσων πόλιν εὐα-
> νορίαισι τάνδε κλυταῖς
> Δαιδάλλειν· σέ τ', Ὀ-

---

[1]. Cette traduction ne se justifie pas aussi bien avec la ponctuation adoptée par M. Aimé-Martin, pour les deux derniers vers grecs, d'après des éditions plus récentes.

λυμπιόνικε, Ποσει-
δανίοισιν ἵπποις
Ἐπιτερπόμενον, φέρειν γῆρας εὔ-
θυμον, ἐς τελευτὰν,
Υἷῶν, Ψαῦμι, παρισταμένων. Ὑγί-
εντα δ' εἴ τις¹ ὄλβον
Ἄρδει, ἐξαρκέων κτεάτεσσι, καὶ
Εὐλογίαν προστιθεὶς, μὴ ματεύ-
σῃ θεὸς γενέσθαι.

Il prie Jupiter d'orner la ville de Psaumis, en lui donnant d'illustres habitants, et de donner à Psaumis une vieillesse heureuse, ayant toujours ses enfants auprès de lui ; et puis il loue ceux qui, jouissant d'une forte santé, se contentent de ce qu'ils ont, et tâchent seulement d'être en bonne réputation, et il dit qu'en cet état ils ne doivent point souhaiter d'être dieux.

ODE VI.

A AGÉSIAS SYRACUSAIN.

Χρυσέας ὑποστάσαντες εὐ-
τειχεῖ προθύρῳ θαλάμου
Κίονας, ὡς ὅτε θαητὸν μέγαρον,
Πάξομεν. Ἀρχομένου δ' ἔργου πρόσωπον
Χρὴ θέμεν τηλαυγές.

Comme quand on bâtit quelque beau logis², on embellit le vestibule de colonnes dorées : ainsi, quand on commence un ouvrage, il y faut donner une face éclatante.

Τίνα κεν φύγοι ὕμνον
Κεῖνος ἀνήρ, ἐπικύρσας ἀφθόνων
Ἀστῶν ἐν ἱμερταῖς ἀοιδαῖς ;

1. Dans le manuscrit, il y a : δέ τις. Ce ne peut être qu'un lapsus. L'édition de 1599 a : δ' εἴ τις. C'est ainsi que dix vers plus haut Racine s'est trompé en écrivant : ἰκέθας, pour ἰκέτας.
2. Dans l'édition de M. Aimé-Martin : « un beau logis. »

Parce que d'ordinaire les habitants d'une même ville sont envieux l'un contre l'autre.

>Ἀκίνδυνοι δ' ἀρεταὶ
>Οὔτε παρ' ἀνδράσιν, οὔτ' ἐν ναυσὶ κοίλαις
>Τίμιαι. Πολλοὶ δὲ μέ-
>μνανται, καλὸν εἴ τι ποναθῇ.

C'est ce qu'Hésiode dit aussi :

« Τῆς δ' ἀρετῆς ἱδρῶτα Θεοὶ προπάροιθεν ἔθηκαν[1]. »

>Ποθέω στρατιᾶς
>Ὀφθαλμὸν ἐμᾶς, ἀμφότερον,
>Μάντιν τ' ἀγαθὸν[2],
>Καὶ δουρὶ μάρνασθαι....

Il fait dire cela à Adraste, lorsqu'il perdit Amphiaraüs, Thébain, que la terre engloutit avec son char, lorsqu'il alloit être tué avec ses compagnons.

>Ἅ τοι, Ποσειδάονι μι-
>χθεῖσα Κρονίῳ, λέγεται
>Παῖδ' ἰοπλόκαμον Εὐάδναν τεκέμεν,
>Κρύψαι δε παρθενίαν ὠδῖνα κόλποις.

Il parle de Pitané, fille d'Eurotas, d'où est venue la race d'Agésias ; car Pitané eut Évadné, de laquelle Apollon eut Iamos, qui fut le premier de cette race. Tous ceux qui naissoient d'une mère avant qu'elle fût mariée s'appeloient παρθένιοι.

>Ὑπ' Ἀπόλλωνι γλυκεί-
>ας πρῶτον ἔψαυσ' Ἀφροδίτας.

Il parle d'Évadné, qui fut connue par Apollon.

>Ἐν θυμῷ πιέσας
>Χόλον οὐ φατὸν ὀ-
>ξείᾳ μελέτᾳ.

---

1. *Opera et Dies*, vers 287. Le scoliaste cite ce vers.
2. Racine a écrit : μάντιν τε ἀγαθόν, leçon qui n'est pas dans le texte de 1599.

Il parle d'Æpitus, roi de Phésane[1], en Arcadie, qui retira chez lui Évadné, encore enfant. Il étoit donc fort en colère, la voyant grosse. Il alla consulter l'oracle d'Apollon à Delphes, qui lui apprit qu'Apollon étoit celui qui l'avoit engrossée[2]. Et cependant Évadné accoucha d'un enfant sous un buisson.

> Ἁ δὲ φοινικόκροκον
> Ζώναν καταθηκαμένα,
> Κάλπιδά τ' ἀργυρέαν,
> Λόχμας ὑπὸ κυανέας
> Τίκτε θεόφρονα κοῦρον.

Apollon lui rendit Lucine favorable : ainsi elle accoucha d'un enfant ; mais la douleur l'ayant forcée de le mettre à terre, deux dragons aux yeux bleus vinrent, et le nourrirent avec grand soin par l'ordre des Dieux, lui donnant l'innocent venin des abeilles pour nourriture. Cependant le Roi, étant revenu de Delphes, demanda où étoit l'enfant d'Évadné et d'Apollon, lequel devoit être un grand prophète, lui et sa race : personne n'en savoit rien.

> Ἀλλ' ἐγ-
> κέκρυπτο γὰρ σχοίνῳ βατίᾳ τ' ἐν ἀπει-
> ράτῳ, ἴων ξανθαῖσι καὶ παμπορφύροις
> Ἀκτῖσι βεβρεγμένος ἁβρὸν
> Σῶμα.

De là vient que sa mère le nomma Iamos[3].

> Τερπνᾶς δ' ἐπεὶ
> Χρυσοστεφάνοιο λάβεν
> Καρπὸν ἥβας.

Il appelle la jeunesse couronnée d'or, ou à cause sans doute que c'est le plus bel âge de la vie, ou à cause que les cheveux sont blonds et ne blanchissent pas encore.

> Τιμῶντες δ' ἀρετὰς,

---

1. Racine a écrit : « Æpilus, roi de Bessane. » Mais ce ne peuvent être que des lapsus.
2. Il y a dans le manuscrit : *engrossie*.
3. Dans le manuscrit : « Iamis. »

SUR LES OLYMPIQUES DE PINDARE. 29

Ἐς φανερὰν ὁδὸν ἔρχονται. Τεκμαίρει
Χρῆμ' ἕκαστον. Μῶμος δ' ἐξ
Ἄλλων κρέμαται φθονεόντων.

Chaque action témoigne de la vertu d'un homme, et les hommes qui sont vertueux marchent par un chemin découvert, ou parce que la vertu ne se cache point, ou à cause qu'elle est glorieuse.

Ἐσσὶ γὰρ ἄγγελος ὀρθὸς,
Ἠϋκόμων σκυτάλα Μοισᾶν, γλυκὺς
Κρητὴρ ἀγαφθέγκτων ἀοιδᾶν.

Il parle à un musicien, qu'il appelle l'ambassadeur des Muses.

Ἀδύλογοι
Δέ μιν λύραι μολπαί τε γινώσκοντι. Μὴ
Θραύσοι χρόνος ὄλβον ἐφέρπων.

Il loue Hiéron, qu'il dit être connu[1] des lyres et des chansons.

Ἀγαθαὶ δὲ πέλον-
τ' ἐν χειμερίᾳ νυκτὶ θοᾶς
Ἐκ ναὸς ἀπε-
σκίμφθαι δύ' ἄγκυραι.

Il dit allégoriquement qu'il est bon dans une tempête d'avoir deux ancres pour assurer un vaisseau; aussi il est bon à Agésias d'être citoyen de deux villes, de Syracuses, et dans l'Arcadie.

1. Dans l'édition de M. Aimé-Martin : *comme*, au lieu de *connu*.

ODE VII.

A DIAGORAS,

Πύκτῃ, VAINQUEUR AU COMBAT DE MAIN.

Il commence par une belle comparaison qu'il fait d'une coupe pleine de vin à un poëme qu'il appelle le nectar des Muses.

> Φιάλαν ὡς εἴ τις ἀ-
> φνειᾶς ἀπὸ χειρὸς ἑλὼν,
> Ἔνδον ἀμπέλου καχλάζοι-
> σαν δρόσῳ δωρήσεται
> Νεανίᾳ γαμβρῷ προπίνων
> Οἴκοθεν οἴκαδε, πάγ-
> χρυσον, κορυφὰν κτεάνων,
> Συμποσίου τε χάριν, κᾶδός τε τιμά-
> σας ἑὸν, ἐν δὲ φίλων
> Παρεόντων, θῆκέ μιν ζα-
> λωτὸν ὁμόφρονος εὐνᾶς·
> Καὶ ἐγὼ νέκταρ χυτὸν,
> Μοισᾶν δόσιν, ἀθλοφόροις
> Ἀνδράσιν πέμπων, γλυκὺν καρ-
> πὸν φρενός γ' ἱλάσκομαι.

Tout de même qu'un homme riche, prenant à la main une coupe pleine de vin, la porte à son gendre, et lui donne le plus précieux de ses meubles, tant pour l'honneur du festin que pour honorer son alliance, et le fait estimer heureux de ses amis pour l'amitié qui est entre le gendre et le beau-père : aussi je porte maintenant un nectar tout pur, lequel est un don des Muses, et le doux fruit de mon esprit, afin de réjouir nos vainqueurs.

> Ὁ δ' ὄλβιος, ὃν
> Φᾶμαι κατέχοντ' ἀγαθαί,
> Ἄλλοτε δ' ἄλλον ἐποπτεύει Χάρις ζω-
> θάλμιος, ἁδυμελεῖ
> Θ' ἅμα μὲν φόρμιγγι, παμφώ-
> νοισί τ' ἐν ἔντεσιν αὐλῶν.

Celui-là est heureux qui est en bonne réputation ; mais il y en a peu qui soient honorés et loués par la poésie, laquelle immortalise les hommes et leur donne une vie florissante. Il y en a qui entendent ce mot de Χάρις pour la Fortune.

> Ὑμνέων παῖδ' Ἀφροδίτας,
> Ἀελίοιό τε, νύμφαν
> Ῥόδον.

Il est ordinaire à Pindare de donner aux villes le nom des nymphes qui ont été appelées comme elles, et d'en faire des divinités.

> Ἀδόντα Δίκᾳ.

Un homme qui plaisoit à la justice, c'est-à-dire un homme juste.

> Ἀμφὶ δ' ἀνθρώ-
> πων φρεσὶν ἀμπλακίαι
> Ἀναρίθμητοι κρέμανται·
> Τοῦτο δ' ἀμάχανον εὑρεῖν,
> Ὅ τι νῦν καὶ ἐν τελευ-
> τᾷ φέρτατον ἀνδρὶ τυχεῖν.

Il dit cela à cause que Tlépolémus, aïeul de Diagoras, avoit tué le frère de sa mère : en suite de quoi l'oracle lui ordonna de quitter son pays, et de venir à Rhode, où il régna heureusement.

> Αἱ δὲ φρενῶν ταραχαὶ
> Παρέπλαξαν καὶ σοφόν.

Ainsi la colère avoit emporté Tlépolémus.

> Ἔνθα ποτὲ
> Βρέχε Θεῶν βασιλεὺς ὁ μέγας
> Χρυσαῖς νιφάδεσσι πόλιν.

Ainsi Homère a dit de la même ville de Rhode :

> « Καί σφι θεσπέσιον πλοῦτον κατέχευε Κρονίων[1]. »

Ensuite il décrit tout à fait bien la naissance de Pallas.

---

1. *Iliade*, livre II, vers 670. Ce vers est cité dans les scolies.

Lorsque Vulcain, dit[-il], avec une hache d'airain fit sortir Minerve de la tête de Jupiter :

> Πατέρος Ἀθαναία κορυφὰν κατ' ἄκραν
> Ἀνορούσασ' ἀλάλα-
> ξεν ὑπερμάκει βοᾷ·
> Οὐρανὸς δ' ἔφριξέ νιν καὶ Γαῖα μάτηρ.

Alors le Soleil, φαυσίβροτος[1], commanda aux Rhodiens de bâtir[2] en l'honneur de Pallas; et le vénérable Prométhée, c'est-à-dire la Prévoyance, y mit les vertus et la joie. La vénération qu'on a pour les Dieux en prévoyant le bien et le mal qu'ils nous peuvent faire produit dans les cœurs la vertu et la joie[3]; mais ils oublièrent de porter du feu pour le sacrifice, et firent des sacrifices sans feu. Le commentaire ne dit point à quelle cause Pindare dit cela.

Jupiter leur versa donc une pluie d'or :

> Κείνοισι μὲν ξαν-
> θὰν ἀγαγὼν νεφέλαν,
> Πολὺν ὗσε χρυσόν.

Et Pallas leur donna l'art d'exceller par-dessus tous les autres hommes dans les ouvrages des mains, ἀριστοπόνοις χερσί; car on eût vu dans leurs rues des statues qui sembloient être animées.

> Ἔργα δὲ ζωοῖσιν ἑρπόν-
> τεσσί θ' ὁμοῖα κέλευθοι
> Φέρον· ἦν δὲ κλέος
> Βαθύ.

En effet, les Rhodiens ont inventé l'art de la sculpture. Quelques-uns croient que ç'a été Dédale. Pindare parle peut-être ici de ces statues qu'on faisoit marcher, et dont il est parlé dans Platon, ce me semble, *in Conv.*[4].

> ...... Δαέντι δὲ καὶ σοφία
> Μείζων ἄδολος τελέθει.

1. « Qui éclaire les mortels. »
2. Il y a de plus dans le grec : βωμόν, « un autel. »
3. Ce sens est tiré des scolies.
4. Dans le manuscrit, il y a : *in Conu.*, ce qui ne peut signifier que : *in Convivio*. M. Aimé-Martin a mis : « *in Conus*, » attribuant ainsi

Quelque adroit que soit un homme, néanmoins il est toujours beaucoup plus habile quand il est instruit, et est moins sujet à manquer : comme les Rhodiens, qui étoient naturellement adroits, furent encore instruits par Minerve.

> Φαντὶ δ' ἀνθρώπων παλαιαὶ
> 'Ρήσιες.

C'est-à-dire les poëtes, sans doute, qui étoient les historiens de ce temps. Et en effet c'est une fable qu'il rapporte pour montrer la raison pour laquelle Rhodes est consacrée au Soleil. Rhodes, dit-il, étoit au fond de la mer, et ne paroissoit pas encore, lorsque les Dieux firent le partage de la terre entre eux ; mais le Soleil étant absent, personne ne se souvint de lui, et ils laissèrent ce dieu pur et chaste sans aucune ville.

Il appelle le Soleil ἁγνὸν θεόν, parce qu'il purifie tout de ses rayons. A son retour, Jupiter vouloit recommencer les partages, mais le Soleil ne voulut pas, et dit qu'il voyoit au fond de la mer[1] une fort belle île, et qu'il la prenoit pour lui. Il commanda donc à la parque Lachésis de confirmer les partages, et aux Dieux de jurer qu'ils ne les violeroient point, mais que cette ville lui seroit éternellement consacrée : ce qui fut fait ; et cette île sortit de la mer toute fertile, et le Soleil la prit pour lui.

> Ἔχει τέ μιν ὀ-
> ξειᾶν ὁ γενέθλιος ἀκτίνων πατὴρ,
> Πῦρ πνεόντων ἀρχὸς ἵππων.

Et là, c'est-à-dire dans cette île, ayant couché avec une nymphe du même nom, il en eut sept enfants fort sages et de bon esprit, dont l'un eut trois enfants, lesquels ayant habité cette île, donnèrent leurs noms aux lieux où ils habitèrent. C'est là qu'on fait des jeux en l'honneur de Tlépolémus, qui accompagna les Rhodiens au siége de Troie, où il mourut ; et

---

à Platon un dialogue tout à fait nouveau. — Racine donne son souvenir comme incertain. Le passage qu'il croyait avoir lu dans *le Banquet* est dans le *Ménon*, p. 97 de l'édition de Henri Estienne.

1. Dans l'édition de M. Aimé-Martin : « au bord de la mer. »

Diagoras, dit-il, y a été couronné deux fois, et quatre fois aux jeux isthmiens, deux fois à Némée et à Athènes. Le fer, *i.* (*c'est-à-dire*) la lance[1], qui est le prix des jeux d'Argos, le connoît bien. Cette expression est belle et hardie. Il est connu en Arcadie, à Thèbes et en Béoce, à Ægine et à Pellane, où il a vaincu six fois; et la pierre où l'on écrit le nom des vainqueurs, à Mégare, ne connoît que lui. Après avoir compté toutes ses victoires, il invoque Jupiter[2], afin qu'il rende Diagoras aimé de ses citoyens et des étrangers.

>'Επεὶ ὕβριος ἐχθρὰν
>'Οδὸν εὐθυπορεῖ,
>Σάφα δαεὶς, ἅτε οἱ πατέρων
>'Ορθαὶ φρένες ἐξ ἀγαθῶν
>"Εχραον.

C'est-à-dire qu'il a appris de ses pères à révérer les Dieux. Sa ville, dit-il, a souvent été en réjouissances pour les victoires qu'il a acquises.

>"Εχει
>Θαλίας καὶ πόλις. 'Εν
>Δὲ μιᾷ μοίρᾳ χρόνου
>"Αλλοτ' ἀλλοῖαι διαιθύσσουσιν αὖραι.

En un moment les vents changent, et les choses prennent toute une autre face; car Diagoras, qui, peu de temps auparavant, avoit eu de l'affliction, se voit maintenant glorieux; ou bien, en un sens contraire. C'est sans doute ce Diagoras dont parle Gellius[3], qui eut trois enfants, excellents en trois différentes luttes, qu'il vit vaincre tous trois en un même jour aux jeux olympiques; et comme ses enfants, ayant mis leur couronne sur sa tête, le baisoient en présence de tout le peuple, il expira entre leurs mains. Cicéron en parle aussi au [livre] I. des *Tusculanes*[4].

1. Ici χαλκός n'est pas la *lance*, mais le *bouclier d'airain*, ἀσπὶς χαλκῆ, dit le scoliaste. La couronne et le bouclier étaient les prix des jeux d'Argos.
2. Il y a dans le manuscrit : « il invoque *à* Jupiter. »
3. *Noctes Atticæ*, livre III, chapitre xv.
4. Chapitre xlvi.

ODE VIII.

A ALCIMÉDON ET TIMOSTHÈNE, athlètes, et MILÉSIAS, maître des athlètes.

>Ἄλλα δ' ἐπ' ἄλλον ἔϐαν
>Ἀγαθῶν· πολλαὶ δ' ὁδοὶ
>Σὺν Θεοῖς εὐπραγίας.

Les uns sont heureux en une chose, les autres en une autre, et il y a plusieurs chemins pour devenir heureux quand on a les Dieux favorables. Il dit cela parce que l'un avoit vaincu aux jeux olympiques, et l'autre aux néméens, comme il ajoute.

>Ἦν δ' ἐσορᾶν καλός· ἔργῳ
>Τ' οὐ κατ' εἶδος ἐλέγχων.

Il parle d'Alcimédon, qui étoit beau à voir, et qui ne déshonoroit point sa beauté par ses actions. C'est ce qu'Hector reproche à Pâris, au [livre] III. de l'*Iliade* [1] :

« Δύσπαρι, εἶδος ἄριστε, γυναιμανές. »

Et il dit un peu après : Les Grecs croient que tu es un homme de conséquence,

« . . . . Οὕνεκα καλὸν
Εἶδος ἔπ'· ἀλλ' οὐκ ἔστι βίη φρεσὶν, οὐδέ τις ἀλκή [2]. »

Après il parle d'Égine [3], où le peuple étoit fort humain aux étrangers : c'étoit le pays d'Alcimédon.

>Ἔνθα σώτειρα, Διὸς Ξενίου
>Πάρεδρος, ἀσκεῖται Θέμις,
>Ἔξοχ' ἀνθρώπων. Ὅ τι γὰρ
>Πολὺ, καὶ πολλὰ ῥέπει,
>Ὀρθᾷ διακρίνειν φρενὶ μὴ παρὰ καιρὸν
>Δυσπαλές.

---

1. Vers 39. — 2. Vers 44 et 45. — 3. Racine écrit *Égyne*.

Il dit que la Justice, laquelle est comme l'assistante et la conseillère de Jupiter l'Hospitalier, est révérée là plus que partout ailleurs; car ce n'est pas, dit-il, une chose aisée de garder l'équité et la mesure dans une si grande foule de gens[1], en parlant du peuple de cette ville ou des étrangers qui y abordoient, voulant dire qu'il est bien difficile, parmi tant d'étrangers, de les contenter tous, et de recevoir chacun selon son mérite. Et il ajoute après :

>Τεθμὸς δέ τις ἀθανάτων
>Καὶ τάνδ' ἁλιερκέα χώραν
>Παντοδαποῖσιν ὑπέστασε ξείνοις
>Κίονα δαιμονίαν.

Ç'a été un arrêt des Dieux que ce pays fût tout environné de la mer, afin que ce fût le refuge et comme la colonne de tous les étrangers, de quelque pays qu'ils fussent. Puissent-ils jamais ne se lasser d'une si belle pratique!

>Ὁ δ' ἐπαντέλλων χρόνος
>Τοῦτο πράσσων μὴ κάμοι·
>. . . . .
>Τερπνὸν δ' ἐν ἀνθρώποις ἴσον ἔσσεται οὐδέν.

Il n'y a rien qui plaise également à tout le monde. Les uns aiment une chose, les autres une autre. Si on loue deux personnes également, il y en aura quelqu'un[2] de jaloux. Aussi, si je loue Milésias, je crains, dit-il,

>Μὴ βαλέτω με λίθῳ τραχεῖ φθόνος,

je crains que l'envie ne me jette des pierres.

>Κουφότεραι γὰρ ἀπειράτων φρένες.

Les gens sans expérience sont d'ordinaire foibles et légers d'esprit. Il dit cela au sujet de Milésias, qui étoit le maître de ces deux jeunes athlètes, et qui lui-même avoit souvent com-

---

1. Racine a suivi le sens que donne une des scolies publiées dans l'édition de 1599.
2. Nous avons déjà plusieurs fois fait remarquer cet emploi du masculin après le mot *personne*. Voyez le *Lexique*.

battu. Celui, dit-il, qui sait[1] les choses par expérience est plus capable de montrer aux autres :

Διδάξασθαι δέ τοι,
Εἰδότι ῥαίτερον. Ἄγνω-
μον δὲ τὸ μὴ προμαθεῖν.

C'est une chose ridicule d'enseigner sans avoir appris ; mais celui-ci peut enseigner beaucoup mieux que personne comment il faut vaincre ; et on peut dire qu'il a vaincu en Alcimédon, puisque la gloire du disciple rejaillit[2] sur le maître ; cet Alcimédon, qui a vaincu quatre jeunes hommes, et qui les a fait retourner avec honte et n'osant pas seulement ouvrir la bouche, mais se tenant clos et couverts, et cherchant des chemins détournés, comme font les vaincus.

Ὃς τύχᾳ μὲν δαίμονος, ἀ-
νορέας δ' οὐκ ἀμπλακών,
Ἐν τέτρασι παίδων ἀπεθήκατο γυίοις
Νόστον ἔχθιστον, καὶ ἀτιμοτέραν
Γλῶτταν, καὶ ἐπίκρυφον οἶμον.

Il étoit, dit-il, favorisé des Dieux ; mais il n'étoit pas privé de force et de courage.

Sa victoire a donné à son père une joie de père[3], et une nouvelle force pour résister à la vieillesse :

Πατρὶ δὲ πατρὸς ἐνέπνευσεν μένος
Γήραος ἀντίπαλον.
Ἀΐδα τοι λάθεται,
Ἄρμενα πράξας ἀνήρ.

Il revient à Alcimédon. Un homme, dit-il, qui fait de belles actions ne songe point à la mort[4], et ne s'en soucie point. Cela me fait souvenir des Blepsiades, ses ancêtres, dont il faut que je recueille la mémoire ; car voilà la sixième victoire

1. Dans l'édition de M. Aimé-Martin : « qui fait. »
2. Racine écrit *rejallit*.
3. Ce n'est ici ni le scoliaste ni la traduction latine de 1599 qui ont induit Racine en erreur. Dans la phrase qu'il a mal traduite, πατρὶ πατρὸς signifie « à l'aïeul. »
4. M. Aimé-Martin a mis : « à la morale. »

qui est entrée dans leur famille ; et cela les rendra encore plus glorieux.

>Ἔστι δὲ καί τι θανόντεσσιν μέρος
Κἄννομον ἑρδόμενον.

Les morts ont aussi leur légitime, c'est-à-dire la gloire qui les suit après leur mort.

Καταχρύπτει δ' οὐ κόνις
Συγγόνων κεδνὰν χάριν.

La terre qui les couvre n'empêche pas qu'ils ne prennent part[1] à la gloire de leurs descendants. Ainsi, lorsque Iphion, un des ancêtres d'Alcimédon, apprendra sa victoire de la Renommée ou de l'Ambassade, fille de Mercure, car il en fait un personnage,

Ἑρμᾶ δὲ θυγατρὸς ἀκούσας Ἰφίων
Ἀγγελίας,

il contera cette nouvelle à Callimachus, un autre de ses ayeuls[2]. Cependant je prie les Dieux de le conserver en santé, et que la déesse Némésis ne s'oppose point à sa félicité.

ODE IX.

A ÉPHARMOSTUS.

Il appelle les Muses ἑκαταβόλους, parce que leurs chansons s'étendent fort loin ; Δία τε φοινικοστερόπαν, Jupiter aux rouges éclairs.

Οὔ-
τοι χαμαιπετέων λόγων ἐφάψῃ
Ἀνδρὸς ἀμφὶ παλαίσμασι
Φόρμιγγ' ἐλελίζων.

1. Au lieu de *part*, il y a ici *pas* dans le manuscrit ; et à la ligne suivante, *Alcimendo*, pour *Alcimédon*.
2. M. Aimé-Martin a corrigé *ayeuls* en *aïeux*.

SUR LES OLYMPIQUES DE PINDARE.

Il ne faut pas se servir de discours bas et rampants[1] en chantant les victoires d'Épharmostus, citoyen d'Oponte, capitale des Locres.

>   Ἐγὼ δέ τοι φίλαν πόλιν
>   Μαλεραῖς ἐπιφλέγων ἀοιδαῖς,
>   Καὶ ἀγάνορος ἵππου θᾶσσον
>   Καὶ ναὸς ὑποπτέρου παντᾷ
>   Ἀγγελίαν πέμψω ταύταν,
>   Εἰ σύν τινι μοιριδίῳ παλάμᾳ
>   Ἐξαιρέτων[2] Χαρίτων νέμομαι
>   Κᾶπον· κεῖναι γὰρ ὤπασαν
>   Τὰ τέρπν'. Ἀγαθοὶ δὲ
>   Καὶ σοφοὶ κατὰ δαίμον' ἄνδρες
>   Ἐγένοντο.

Pour l'honneur de cette ville, et pour la faire éclater[3] par mes chansons illustres, je veux répandre partout la victoire d'Épharmostus, et en faire voler la nouvelle plus vite qu'un cheval léger, ou qu'un navire ailé, pourvu que je sois assisté des Grâces; car les grands hommes sont tels par le secours des Dieux. Autrement Hercule auroit-il pu résister tout seul contre trois dieux, contre le trident de Neptune, l'arc d'Apollon et la verge de Pluton?

>   Οὐδ' Ἀΐδας ἀκι-
>   νήταν ἔχε ῥάβδον,
>   Βρότεα σώμαθ' ᾇ κατάγει
>   Κοίλαν πρὸς ἀγυιὰν
>   Θνασκόντων[4].

Dans la rue ténébreuse, c'est-à-dire dans la sombre demeure des morts.

>   Ἀπό μοι λόγον
>   Τοῦτον, στόμα, ῥίψον.

---

1. Racine a suivi le sens donné par une scolie et par la traduction latine de l'édition de 1599.

2. Ἐξαιρέτων, au lieu de ἐξαίρετον, est la leçon de notre manuscrit et de l'édition de 1599.

3. *Éclater*, au sens de *briller*, « pour faire briller cette ville, faire éclater sa gloire. » Voyez plus bas, p. 45, ligne 1.

4. Racine a écrit par mégarde Θνησκόντων, au lieu de Θνασκόντων,

Pindare se repent d'avoir parlé de ces dissensions des Dieux, comme d'une chose qui leur est injurieuse.

> Ἐπεὶ τόγε λοιδορῆσαι
> Θεοὺς, ἐχθρὰ σοφία· καὶ
> Τὸ καυχᾶσθαι παρὰ καιρὸν
> Μανίαισιν ὑποκρέκει.

C'est une mauvaise sagesse de mal parler des Dieux, et c'est une espèce de fureur de faire gloire de cette impiété. Ὑποκρέκει veut dire *approche*, comme quand on accorde un instrument on cherche le son de l'oreille, et on approche du vrai ton. Cet endroit est beau contre ceux qui font les esprits forts.

> Μὴ νῦν λαλάγει τὰ τοι-
> αῦτ'. Ἔα πόλεμον, μάχαν τε πᾶσαν,
> Χωρὶς Ἀθανάτων.

Il faut laisser là les dissensions des Dieux; ou plutôt : il ne faut point admettre de dissension entre les Dieux. Il faut plutôt faire l'éloge d'Oponte, ville ancienne, où Deucalion et Pyrrha s'établirent lorsque le déluge fut passé.

> Ἄτερ
> Δ' εὐνᾶς ὁμόδαμον
> Κτισάσθαν λίθινον γόνον·
> Λαοὶ δ' ὀνόμασθεν.

Mais il quitte ce sujet comme trop commun, pour en traiter un autre.

> Αἴνει δὲ παλαιὸν
> Μὲν οἶνον, ἄνθεα δ' ὕμνων
> Νεωτέρων.

C'est ce que dit Homère, au [livre] I. de l'*Odyssée*[1]. Il décrit donc la généalogie de la ville d'Oponte, qui venoit d'une fille de Jupiter; car Jupiter enleva Protogénée, femme de Locrus, et lui fit un enfant, de peur que Locrus ne mourût sans enfant. Cette charité de Jupiter est fort plaisante.

---

que veut le dialecte de Pindare, et qui est la leçon de 1599 et en général des diverses éditions.

1. Vers 351 et 352. — On verra plus bas, p. 64, que Racine a noté ces mêmes vers dans ses *Remarques sur l'Odyssée*.

Μὴ καθέλοι μιν αἰ-
ὼν, πότμον ἐφάψας,
Ὀρφανὸν γενεᾶς. Ἔχε
Δὲ σπέρμα μέγιστον
Ἄλοχος.

Jupiter la ramena à son mari, lequel, croyant que c'étoit son enfant, l'appela du nom de son grand-père maternel, Opuns, fils de Deucalion.

Ὑπέρφαντον ἄνδρα μορφᾷ
Τε καὶ ἔργοισι.

Cet enfant fut un homme extraordinaire pour sa beauté et pour ses actions. Il habita la ville d'Oponte, et force étrangers se rangèrent auprès de lui; mais il honora surtout Ménœtius, père de Patrocle. Pindare fait cette digression pour embellir son sujet, qui seroit trop stérile d'ailleurs; et il parle de la valeur de Patrocle, qu'il montra contre les Mysiens, leur résistant seul avec Achille. Depuis ce temps-là, Achille l'aima et lui commanda de ne se mettre jamais en bataille qu'auprès de lui. Patrocle étoit citoyen d'Oponte.

Ἐξ οὗ Θέτιος γό-
νος οὐλίῳ μιν ἐν ἄρει
Παραγορεῖτο, μήποτε
Σφετέρας ἄτερθε ταξιοῦσθαι
Δαμασιμβρότου αἰχμᾶς.

Achille lui dit ces paroles dans Homère[1]:

« Μὴ σύγ' ἄνευθεν ἐμεῖο λιλαίεσθαι πολεμίζειν
Τρωσὶ φιλοπτολέμοισιν· ἀτιμότερον δέ με θήσῃς. »

Il souhaite une grande éloquence pour dignement louer les victoires d'Épharmostus.

Εἴην
Εὑρησιεπὴς ἀναγεῖσθαι
Προσφόρος ἐν Μοισᾶν δίφρῳ·

1. *Iliade*, chant XVI, vers 89 et 90. Ces vers sont cités dans une des scolies. Racine, reproduisant une faute de l'édition de 1599, a écrit ἀτιμώτερον.

> Τόλμα δὲ καὶ ἀμφιλαφὴς δύναμις
> Ἕσποιτο.

Plût à Dieu que je pusse inventer de belles paroles pour chanter dans le chariot des Muses, c'est-à-dire au style des Muses, qui marche comme dans un char roulant, au lieu que la prose marche à pied; et que la hardiesse me suivît avec l'abondance et la fécondité! car l'un ne suffit pas sans l'autre.

Il parle des diverses victoires qu'il a remportées comme garçon et comme homme.

> Ἄργει τ' ἔσχεθε κῦδος ἀν-
> δρῶν· παῖς δ' ἐν Ἀθάναις.
> . . . .
> Ὡραῖος ἐὼν καὶ
> Καλὸς, κάλλιστά τε ῥέξας.

Étant beau garçon et ayant fait de fort belles choses. Il parle de ses autres victoires, et conclut ainsi :

> Τὸ δὲ φυᾷ κράτιστον ἅπαν.
> Πολλοὶ δὲ διδακταῖς
> Ἀνθρώπων ἀρεταῖς κλέος
> Ὤρουσαν ἑλέσθαι.
> Ἄνευ δὲ Θεοῦ, σεσιγα-
> μένον γ', οὐ σκαιότερον χρῆ-
> μ' ἕκαστον.

Tous les commentateurs sont fort empêchés de dire le sens de ces deux derniers vers, qui sont en effet fort obscurs. Il dit donc que ce qui est naturel est toujours le meilleur. Plusieurs ont voulu acquérir de la gloire par des qualités[1] qu'ils avoient apprises ou empruntées de l'art; mais les choses qui se font autrement que par la nature (car Dieu ne veut dire autre chose que la nature) doivent plutôt être ensevelies dans le silence que publiées. Cela se doit appliquer à toutes sortes de sciences, soit à la poésie, soit aux jeux, et ainsi du reste. C'est pourquoi il ajoute que chacun doit s'appliquer aux choses où il a plus de disposition naturelle.

> Ἐντὶ γὰρ ἄλλαι
> Ὁδῶν ὁδοὶ περαίτεραι.

1. Racine avait d'abord écrit *avantages*.

Μία δ' οὐχ ἅπαντας ἄμμε θρέψει
Μελέτα. Σοφίαι μὲν αἰπει-
ναί.

La sagesse est difficile à obtenir; je crois qu'il entend la perfection : il y a plusieurs sciences différentes, mais il est difficile d'y être parfait. Il conclut en s'exhortant lui-même : puis donc que tu as ce don-là, c'est-à-dire que tu es naturellement savant et bon poëte, loue hardiment Épharmostus, publie que c'est un homme héroïque,

Εὔχειρα, δεξιόγυιον, ὁρῶν-
τ' ἀλκάν.

C'est-à-dire qui porte sa générosité empreinte dans ses yeux, qui a les yeux guerriers et courageux.

ODE X.

A AGÉSIDAMUS,

JEUNE GARÇON LOCRIEN DE LA PROVINCE DES ÉPIZÉPHYRIENS,

LUTTEUR.

Car les Locres étoient divisés en trois provinces, les Épizéphyriens, qui confinoient avec l'Italie ; les Ozoles avec l'Étolie; et les Épicnémides avec l'Eubœe. Il commence cette ode par un ressouvenir. Il avoit promis à Agésidamus de faire une ode pour lui, et l'avoit oublié. Il lui en veut payer l'usure, et c'est pourquoi il accompagne cette ode d'une autre petite.

Muses, dit-il, montrez-moi en quel endroit de mon esprit[1] j'ai laissé Agésidamus[2], car j'ai oublié que je lui devois un

---

[1]. M. Aimé-Martin a mis : « en quel endroit de mon écrit. »
[2]. Par inadvertance, Racine a écrit *Archidamus,* que M. Aimé-Martin a conservé.

poëme; et toi, Vérité, fille de Jupiter, garantis-moi du blâme d'avoir manqué de parole à un ami.

> Ἀλλὰ σὺ καὶ θυγάτηρ
> Ἀλάθεια Διὸς,
> Ὀρθᾷ χερὶ [1] ἐρύκετον ψευδέων
> Ἐνιπὰν ἀλιτόξενον.

Il est vrai que j'ai été longtemps sans m'acquitter; mais je me mettrai à couvert[2] en payant l'intérêt. Je veux donc absorber cette dette, et composer un hymne en sa faveur et en celle de son pays : c'est ce que veut dire le mot de κοινόν[3]; car la ville des Zéphyriens aime la vérité, et ils sont affectionnés aux Muses et à la guerre :

> Μέλει τέ σφισι Καλλιόπα
> Καὶ χάλκεος Ἄρης.

Hercule a bien été mis en fuite en se battant contre Cycnus, fils de Mercure, qui tuoit tous les passants, et de leurs têtes vouloit bâtir un temple; et si Agésidamus....[4], il faut qu'il en rende grâce à Iolas, son maître d'exercice, comme Patrocle à Achille; car les instructions et les exemples des autres font souvent parvenir au comble de la gloire, pourvu qu'on soit outre cela secouru de Dieu.

> Θήξας δέ κε φῶτ' ἀρετᾷ, ποτὶ
> Πελώριον ὥρμασε κλέος ἀ-
> νήρ, Θεοῦ σὺν παλάμᾳ.
> Ἄπονον δ' ἔλαβον χάρμα παῦροί τινες,
> Ἔργων πρὸ πάντων βιότῳ φάος.

Peu de gens acquièrent du bonheur sans peine, et ont fait

---

1. Racine a écrit χειρί. Toutes les éditions, celle de 1599, comme les autres, donnent χερί.
2. Racine avait mis d'abord : « mais je me justifierai. »
3. Ce mot est au vers 15, que Racine n'a pas transcrit.
4. Évidemment quelques mots sont restés au bout de la plume de Racine, tels que ceux-ci : « et si Agésidamus *n'a pas, comme Hercule, essuyé des défaites.* » Nous avons remplacé les mots omis par des points. La phrase, telle que l'a conservée M. Aimé-Martin, est inintelligible.

éclater leur vie et leurs actions. Il raconte l'inimitié d'Hercule avec Augéas, dont il avoit nettoyé l'écurie. Augéas ne lui vouloit point donner sa récompense ; mais il fut bien puni.

Καὶ μὰν
Ξεναπάτας Ἐπειῶν βασιλεὺς ὄπιθεν
Οὐ πολλὸν ἴδε πατρίδα πολυκτέανον
Ὑπὸ στερεῷ πυρὶ πλαγαῖς τε σιδάρου
Βαθὺν εἰς ὀχετὸν ἄτας ἵζοισαν ἑὰν πόλιν.

Il vit sa ville réduite dans un abîme de misères ; car, ajoute-t-il, il n'est pas aisé de se réconcilier avec des puissances offensées :

Νεῖκος δὲ κρεσσόνων [1] ἀποθέσθ᾽ ἄπορον.

Hercule tua donc Augée, roi de Pise ou d'Élide ; et ayant amassé là toute son armée, il y dédia un temple à Jupiter, son père, et y institua les jeux olympiques, ayant dressé une grande place, pour ce dessein, sur le bord du fleuve Alphée [2]. A cette première institution les Parques se treuvèrent, et le Temps,

Ὅ τ᾽ ἐξελέγχων μόνος
Ἀλάθειαν ἐτήτυμον
Χρόνος.

C'est-à-dire que le Destin vouloit que ces jeux fussent immortels, et avec lui le Temps[3], qui l'a appris ensuite aux siècles suivants.

Il fait mention de ceux qui furent victorieux à la première fois ; et parce que ces jeux se célébroient au clair de la lune, lorsqu'elle étoit pleine, il dit :

Ἐν δ᾽ ἕσπερον ἔφλεξεν εὐώπιδος
Σελάνας ἐρατὸν φάος.

1. Ici encore Racine a substitué à la forme poétique la forme ordinaire en prose : κρεισσόνων à κρεσσόνων. Voyez ci-dessus, p. 39, note 4, et p. 44, note 1.

2. Ce lieu fut aussi nommé Δωδεκάθεος, à cause des douze dieux principaux. (*Note de Racine.*)

3. Racine avait d'abord mis : « C'est-à-dire qu'on ne se souvient plus qui est-ce qui s'y treuva, et il n'y eut que la Destinée et le Temps. »

Ou bien, c'est-à-dire seulement que ces jeux-là se célébroient le 15. du mois. En suite des jeux, tout le temple retentissoit d'applaudissement[1]; et suivant cette coutume, nous faisons des hymnes en l'honneur de Jupiter Foudroyant. Et les vers qui ont été inventés à Thèbes bien du temps après, c'est-à-dire les vers lyriques, accompagnent, ou répondent à la flûte; et ces vers ne sont pas moins agréables au vainqueur qu'un fils légitime l'est à son père vieux et mourant. Cette comparaison est fort bien exprimée.

> Ἀλλ' ὥστε παῖς ἐξ ἀλόχου πατρὶ
> Ποθεινὸς ἥκοντι νεότατι
> Τὸ πάλιν ἤδη[2], μάλα δέ τοι θερ-
> μαίνει φιλότατι νόον·
> Ἐπεὶ πλοῦτος ὁ λα-
> χὼν ποιμένα ἐπακτὸν ἀλλότριον,
> Θνάσκοντι στυγερώτατος.

Car il n'y a rien de plus fâcheux [pour] qui se meurt, que de laisser son bien en la puissance d'un étranger. Autant est-il déplaisant à un homme qui a fait de belles choses, de mourir sans être honoré de louanges.

> Καὶ ὅταν καλὰ ἔρξας, ἀοιδᾶς ἄτερ,
> Ἀγησίδαμ', εἰς Ἀΐδα σταθμὸν
> Ἀνὴρ ἵκηται, κενεὰ πνεύσας,
> Ἔπορε μόχθῳ βραχύ τι τερπνόν.

Ce n'est pas un grand plaisir; mais il n'en va pas de même de vous; car les Muses répandront votre gloire partout.

> Τὶν δ' ἁδυεπής τε λύρα
> Γλυκύς τ' αὐλὸς ἀνα-
> πάσσει χάριν· ἔχοντι δ' εὐρὺ κλέος
> Κόραι Πιερίδες Διός.

Et à votre sujet je loue aussi la ville de Locres.

---

1. Il y a ainsi le singulier dans le manuscrit.
2. Racine a mis un astérisque devant ἥκοντι, et écrit en marge : « qui redevient enfant. » Il a suivi le sens donné par la traduction latine de l'édition de 1599.

Μέλιτι [1]
Δ' εὐάνορα πόλιν καταβρέχων.

Et vous surtout, Agésidamus, que j'ai vu victorieux,

Ἰδέᾳ τε καλὸν
Ὥρᾳ τε κεκραμένον,

doué de beauté et de jeunesse, laquelle a rendu Ganymède immortel par l'ordre de Vénus,

ἅ τ' ἀναι-
δέα Γανυμήδει τὸν θάνατον [2] ἄ-
λαλκε, σὺν Κυπρογενεῖ.

Il appelle la Mort impudente, parce qu'elle ne respecte personne.

ODE XI.

AU MÊME AGÉSIDAMUS,

τόκος, L'INTÉRÊT.

Il commence par une belle comparaison de la poésie avec les vents et la pluie :

Ἔστιν ἀνθρώποις ἀνέμων ὅτε πλεῖστα
Χρῆσις· ἔστιν δ' οὐρανίων ὑδάτων
Ὀμβρίων, παίδων νεφέλας.
Εἰ δὲ σὺν πόνῳ τις εὖ πράσσοι, μελιγάρυες ὕμνοι
Ὑστέρων ἀρχαὶ λόγων τέλλεται,
Καὶ πιστὸν ὅρκιον μεγάλαις ἀρεταῖς.

Les poëmes sont cause qu'on parle longtemps après des belles actions, et sont un gage fidèle des grandes vertus; et les victoires olympiques sont celles à qui les louanges doivent être moins enviées :

Ἀφθόνητος δ' αἶνος Ὀλυμπιονίκαις
Οὗτος ἄγκειται.

1. Racine a écrit en marge : « le miel de la poésie. »
2. En marge : « Mort impudente. »

C'est moi qui sais donner de telles louanges, et un homme instruit des Dieux, comme moi, produit toujours de belles pensées :

Ἐκ θεοῦ δ' ἀνὴρ σοφαῖς ἀνθεῖ ἐσαεὶ πραπίδεσσιν.

C'est pourquoi je compose cet hymne à votre louange et en l'honneur de votre ville, ô Agésidamus. Puis, adressant son discours [au chœur] des Muses : Vous pouvez hardiment, leur dit-il, aller en cette ville, et vous y réjouir ou y danser ; je vous réponds que ses citoyens ne sont pas ennemis des étrangers, ni ignorants des belles choses.

Ἔνθα συγκωμάξατ'. Ἐγγυάσομαι
Μή μιν, ὦ Μοῖσαι, φυγόξενον στρατὸν,
Μηδ' ἀπείρατον καλῶν,
Ἀκρόσοφον δὲ καὶ αἰχματὰν ἀφίξεσθαι. Τὸ γὰρ
Ἐμφυὲς οὔτ' αἴθων ἀλώπηξ
Οὔτ' ἐρίβρομοι λέοντες
Διαλλάξαιντο ἦθος.

Il appelle le renard αἴθων, ou à cause qu'il est vif, ou plutôt à cause qu'il est roux. Il dit que le renard ne quitte point sa finesse, et le lion son courage, parce qu'il a loué ce peuple d'être adroit et d'être courageux.

ODE XII.

A ERGOTÉLÈS D'HIMÈRE, VILLE DE SICILE,

VAINQUEUR A LA LONGUE COURSE.

Il invoque la Fortune, qu'il appelle fille de Jupiter Libérateur, afin qu'elle prenne sous sa protection la ville d'Himère.

Τὶν γὰρ ἐν πόντῳ κυβερνῶνται θοαὶ
Νᾶες, ἐν χέρσῳ τε λαιψηροὶ πόλεμοι,
Κἀγοραὶ βουλαφόροι· αἵ γε μὲν ἀνδρῶν
Πόλλ' ἄνω, τὰ δ' αὖ κάτω
Ψεύδη μεταμώνια τέμνοι-
σαι, κυλίνδοντ' ἐλπίδες.

SUR LES OLYMPIQUES DE PINDARE.

Il compare nos espérances aux navires qui coupent des apparences trompeuses comme des flots, tantôt en haut et tantôt en bas; et cette comparaison est parfaitement bien exprimée.

> Σύμβολον δ' οὔπω τις ἐπιχθονίων
> Πιστὸν, ἀμφὶ πράξιος ἐσ-
> σομένας, εὗρεν θεόθεν.
> Τῶν δὲ μελλόντων τετύφλωνται φράδαι.

C'est ce qu'Horace a rendu en ces paroles, liv. III, *ode* XXIX[1] :

> *Prudens futuri temporis exitum*
> *Caliginosa nocte premit Deus;*
> *Ridetque si mortalis ultra*
> *Fas trepidat....*

Pindare poursuit cette matière et ajoute :

> Πολλὰ δ' ἀνθρώποις παρὰ γνώμαν ἔπεσεν,
> Ἔμπαλιν μὲν τέρψιος. Οἱ δ' ἀνιαραῖς
> Ἀντικύρσαντες ζάλαις,
> Ἐσλὸν βαθὺ πήματος ἐν μι-
> κρῷ πεδάμειψαν χρόνῳ.

Horace, liv. I, *ode* XXXIV[2] :

> *. . . . Valet ima summis*
> *Mutare, et insignem attenuat Deus,*
> *Obscura promens. Hinc apicem rapax*
> *Fortuna cum stridore acuto*
> *Sustulit; hic posuisse gaudet.*

Pindare dit tout cela au sujet d'Ergotélès, qui, ayant été banni de Candie, son pays, durant des troubles, s'étoit venu habiter à Himère, et avoit remporté le prix des jeux olympiques. Aussi il ajoute, en s'adressant à lui, que s'il fût demeuré toujours en son logis, comme un coq qui ne se bat que sur son fumier, il n'auroit rien fait d'illustre, et la gloire de ses pieds, c'est-à-dire sa vitesse, se fût flétrie.

> Υἱὲ Φιλάνορος, ἤτοι καὶ τεά κεν,
> Ἐνδομάχας ἅτ' ἀλέκτωρ,
> Συγγόνῳ παρ' ἑστίᾳ

1. Vers 29-32. — 2. Vers 12-16.

Ἀκλεὴς τιμὰ κατεφυλλορόησε ποδῶν,
Εἰ μὴ στάσις ἀντιάνειρα
Κνωσίας ἄμερσε πάτρας.

Au lieu qu'à présent, ayant vaincu aux jeux olympiques et aux autres jeux, vous avez honoré Himère, où sont les bains des Nymphes, et y vivez comme en votre propre pays.

ODE XIII.

A XÉNOPHON CORINTHIEN,

VAINQUEUR A LA COURSE DU CHARIOT ET AUX CINQ JEUX.

Il appelle Corinthe ἀγλαόκουρον, c'est-à-dire pleine de belles filles ou de beaux garçons; il dit que la police y règne.

Ἐν τᾷδε δ' [1] Εὐνομία ναίει, κασίγνη-
ταί τε, βάθρον πολίων
Ἀσφαλὴς Δίκα, καὶ ὁμό-
τροπος Εἰράνα, ταμίαι
Ἀνδράσι πλούτου, χρύσεαι
Παῖδες εὐβούλου Θέμιτος.
Ἐθέλοντι δ' ἀλέξειν Ὕβριν, Κόρου
Ματέρα θρασύμυθον.

Ce n'est pas l'Insolence qui est mère de la Saturité[2], mais la Saturité qui est mère de l'Insolence.
Homère[3] :

Τίκτει τοι Κόρος Ὕβριν, ὅταν κακῷ ὄλβος ἕποιτο.

1. Racine a écrit ἐν τᾷδ', au lieu de ἐν τᾷδε δ', que donne l'édition de 1599, comme toutes celles qui n'ont pas ἐν τᾷ γάρ.
2. *Injuriam Saturitatis matrem*, dit la traduction latine de l'édition de 1599. C'est ce mot *Saturitas* qui a suggéré à Racine celui de *Saturité*, au lieu de *Satiété*. La remarque par laquelle il redresse la parole de Pindare est empruntée à une scolie, où le vers Τίκτει τοι Κόρος.... est également cité.
3. C'est sur la foi du scoliaste que Racine attribue ce vers à Homère; mais il est de Théognis. C'est le vers 53 dans les *Sentences*

SUR LES OLYMPIQUES DE PINDARE.

C'est-à-dire que ces deux filles de Thémis, la Justice et la Paix, bannissent l'Insolence, mère, ou plutôt fille de la Saturité[1].

Ἄμαχον δὲ κρύψαι τὸ συγγενὲς ἦθος.

Il dit cela au sujet des Corinthiens qui ne démentoient point leur bon naturel, ou il s'entend lui-même, disant que c'est son naturel de louer les excellents hommes.

Πολλὰ δ' ἐν
Καρδίαις ἀνδρῶν ἔβαλον
Ὧραι πολυάνθεμοι ἀρ-
χαῖα σοφίσμαθ'. Ἅπαν δ' εὑρόντος ἔργον.

Le temps a mis au jour beaucoup de belles inventions des anciens; mais quoiqu'elles soient maintenant communes, toutefois la gloire en appartient aux inventeurs. Les Corinthiens avoient trouvé les poids, les mesures, et beaucoup d'autres choses. Pindare dit ici que ce sont eux qui ont inventé les danses en rond, qu'il appelle dithyrambes. Il dit qu'ils ont aussi trouvé l'art de brider les chevaux et de les conduire, et d'avoir mis les premiers un double aigle[2] dans les temples des Dieux. Il dit aussi que les sciences et l'art militaire y fleurissent:

Ἐν δὲ Μοῖσ' ἁδύπνοος,
Ἐν δ' Ἄρης ἀνθεῖ νέων
Οὐλίαις αἰχμαῖσιν ἀνδρῶν.

Il invoque Jupiter, afin qu'il soit favorable à ses hymnes et aux louanges de Xénophon, lequel a vaincu et a remporté les cinq prix : ce qui n'étoit jamais arrivé à un homme seul.

Οὐκ
Ἀντεβόλησεν τῶν ἀνὴρ
Θνατὸς οὔπω τις πρότερον.

de ce poëte (*Theognidis Megarensis Sententiæ. Parisiis, M. D. LXXIX. Apud Joannem Bene-natum*).

1. Racine a écrit : « fille de l'Oisiveté. » Mais ce ne peut être qu'un lapsus. Son intention a été sans doute de répéter le mot *Saturité*.
2. Dans l'édition de M. Aimé-Martin, on a imprimé *aide*, au lieu d'*aigle*.

Il raconte le grand nombre de ses autres victoires, et dit à la fin qu'il est aussi malaisé de les compter toutes que de compter le gravier de la mer. Cette hyperbole est démesurée. Aussi il ajoute que la médiocrité est une bonne chose, et qu'il est bon de la connoître et de la suivre partout, c'est-à-dire qu'il n'en veut pas dire davantage.

> Ἔπεται δ' ἐν ἑκάστῳ μέτρον. Νοῆ-
> σαι δὲ καιρὸς ἄριστος.

Il se jette sur les louanges de Corinthe et de ses anciens habitants, comme de Sisyphe, qu'il appelle adroit comme un dieu, de Médée, et de Bellérophon, qui, voulant monter le cheval Pégase, n'en pouvoit venir à bout, jusqu'à ce que Pallas lui en donna en dormant une bride, qu'il appelle φίλτρον ἱππεῖον[1], laquelle étoit d'or, δαμασίφρονα χρυσόν.

Car les Dieux rendent aisé ce qui paroissoit hors d'espérance :

> Πληροῖ δὲ Θεῶν δύναμις καὶ τὰν παρ' ὅρκον
> Καὶ παρὰ ἐλπίδα κού-
> φαν κτίσιν γ'.

En effet, le généreux Bellérophon ayant mis cette bride à la bouche du cheval ailé, il sauta dessus tout armé, et lui faisoit faire la volte ; et il alla dessus faire la guerre aux Amazones, à la Chimère et aux Solymes. Je ne dirai rien de sa mort, et cela sans doute à cause qu'elle n'étoit pas glorieuse pour Bellérophon, qui tomba de dessus le cheval Pégase, et se rompit la cuisse.

Horace dit, *ode* xi, liv. IV[2] :

> *Terret ambustus Phaeton avaras*
> *Spes; et exemplum grave præbet ales*
> *Pegasus, terrenum equitem gravatus*
>   *Bellerophontem;*
> *Semper ut te digna sequare....*

Homère décrit bien au long l'histoire de Bellérophon, au [livre] VI. de l'*Iliade*[3], en la personne de son petit-fils Glaucus,

---

1. Ce mot est accentué semblablement dans l'édition de 1599.
2. Vers 25-29. — 3. Vers 155-205.

SUR LES OLYMPIQUES DE PINDARE.

qui s'alloit battre contre Diomède; et c'est aussi au sujet de Glaucus que Pindare en parle, disant que Glaucus se glorifioit parmi les Troyens d'être petit-fils de Bellérophon; et il fait cela pour imiter Homère.

> Τὸν δ' ἐν Οὐλύμπῳ φάτναι
> Ζηνὸς ἀρχαῖαι δέχονται.

Il parle du cheval Pégase, car il fut changé en astre, et Aratus dit que même parmi les astres il y en a quelques-uns qui s'appellent des ânes[1]. Mais, dit-il, je m'arrête trop hors de mon sujet, ayant entrepris de louer les Corinthiens et de prêter ma main aux Muses, ἀγλαοθρόνοις, pour les louer : Μοίσαις ἔβαν ἐπίκουρος. Il loue donc les diverses victoires des Corinthiens, et s'engage de louer celles qu'ils remporteront encore. Puis il finit priant Jupiter qu'il donne de l'agrément à ses vers[2], et qu'il les fasse estimer.

> Ἀλλὰ κούφοισιν ἐχνεῦσαι ποσί,
> Ζεῦ, τέλει, αἰδῶ διδοὺς
> Καὶ τύχαν τερπνῶν γλυκεῖαν.

Il dit κούφοισιν ποσί, c'est-à-dire qu'il finisse son hymne en sorte que personne n'y treuve à redire et n'en soit choqué.

ODE XIV ET DERNIÈRE DES OLYMPIQUES.

A ASOPICHUS D'ORCHOMÈNE,

VAINQUEUR A LA COURSE.

Il adresse tout son discours aux Grâces qui résidoient à Orchomène, ville de Bœoce, d'où étoit Asopichus. Céphisus est un fleuve qui y passe. Il les prie d'assister favorablement à cette chanson qu'il fait pour Asopichus.

> Καφησίων ὑδάτων λαχοῖσαι,

---

1. Cette remarque appartient à un des scoliastes.
2. Racine a suivi le sens donné par une scolie.

REMARQUES

Αἴ τε ναίετε καλλίπωλον ¹ ἕδραν,
Ὦ λιπαρᾶς ἀοίδιμοι βασίλειαι
Χάριτες Ὀρχομενοῦ,
Παλαιγόνων Μινυᾶν ἐπίσκοποι,
Κλῦτ', ἐπεὶ εὔχομαι.

Minyus fut le premier roi d'Orchomène, fils de Neptune.

Σὺν γὰρ ὑμῖν τὰ τερπνὰ καὶ τὰ γλυκέα
Γίνεται πάντα βροτοῖς,
Εἰ σοφὸς, εἰ καλὸς, εἴ τις ἀγλαὸς
Ἀνήρ. Οὔτε γὰρ Θεοὶ
Σεμνᾶν Χαρίτων ἄτερ
Κοιρανέοντι χοροὺς,
Οὔτε δαῖτας· ἀλλὰ πάντων
Ταμίαι ἔργων ἐν οὐρανῷ,
Χρυσότοξον θέμεναι
Παρὰ Πύθιον Ἀπόλλωνα θρόνους,
Ἀέναον σέβοντι πατρὸς
Ὀλυμπίοιο τιμάν.

Il dit qu'elles sont assises auprès d'Apollon. En effet, à Delphes, elles étoient placées à sa main droite, parce qu'elles président aux sciences et aux vers comme lui. Il ajoute leurs noms :

Πότνι' Ἀγλαΐα, φιλησίμολπέ
Τ' Εὐφροσύνα, Θεῶν κρατίστου παῖδες,
Ἐπάκοοι νῦν, Θαλία τε ἐ-
ρασίμολπε, ἰδοῖσα τόνδε
Κῶμον ἐπ' εὐμενεῖ τύχᾳ
Κοῦφα βιβῶντα.

Parce que cet hymne étoit une chanson à danser; et il ajoute ensuite qu'il est sur un ton lydien. Ensuite il s'adresse à la Renommée, qu'il appelle Écho, et lui dit qu'elle aille aux Enfers devers Cléodamus, le père d'Asopichus, pour lui raconter la victoire de son fils :

Μελαντειχέα δόμον
Φερσεφόνας ἴθι, Ἀχοῖ.

Ce mot de μελαντειχής est fort expressif pour décrire l'En-

---

1. Racine a écrit en marge : « Noble par ses chevaux. »

fer, comme si ses murailles étoient toutes noircies de fumée. Au reste, il y avoit deux Orchomènes, l'une en Arcadie, l'autre en Bœoce, qui est celle-ci, que l'on appeloit le séjour des Grâces, parce que ce fut là où on leur sacrifia la première fois.

FIN DES ODES OLYMPIQUES.

REMARQUES

SUR L'ODYSSÉE D'HOMÈRE.

Avril 1662[1].

Horace loue le commencement de ce poëme dans son *Art poétique*, et dit qu'Homère est bien éloigné de la conduite de ces poëtes qui font de grandes promesses à l'entrée de leur ouvrage, et qui donnent après cela du nez en terre : au lieu qu'Homère commence modestement, et montre ensuite de grandes choses[2].

Homère laisse Ulysse dans l'île de Calypso durant tous les quatre premiers livres, et il ne le fait paroître qu'au cinquième.

---

1. Voyez la *Notice*, p. 4.
2. Au verso du premier feuillet, Racine a transcrit les vers 140-152 de l'*Épître aux Pisons* :

> *Quanto rectius hic qui nil molitur inepte!*
> « *Dic mihi, Musa, virum, captæ post tempora Trojæ,*
> *Qui mores hominem multorum vidit et urbes.* »
> *Non fumum ex fulgore, sed ex fumo dare lucem*
> *Cogitat, ut speciosa dehinc miracula promat,*
> *Antiphatem Scyllamque et cum Cyclope Charybdim.*
> . . . .
> *Semper ad eventum festinat; et in medias res,*
> *Non secus ac notas, auditorem rapit; et quæ*
> *Desperat tractata nitescere posse, relinquit;*
> *Atque ita mentitur, sic veris falsa remiscet,*
> *Primo ne medium, medio ne discrepet imum.*

Cependant il parle de ce qui passoit[1] entre les Dieux au sujet d'Ulysse, et décrit l'état où étoit sa maison à Ithaque.

Ulysse est toujours persécuté de Neptune, et toujours sous la protection de Pallas, et il n'y a que ces deux divinités qui soient opposées l'une à l'autre dans l'*Odyssée*, au lieu que dans l'*Iliade* tous les Dieux sont divisés en deux partis. Et l'on voit même que tout se passe fort doucement entre Neptune et Pallas, qui n'ose pas ouvertement résister aux desseins de son oncle, comme on voit au livre XIIIe, où elle le dit en propres termes à Ulysse[2], qui se plaignoit qu'elle l'avoit abandonné depuis la prise de Troie.

LIVRE PREMIER.

Les Dieux s'assemblent. Jupiter prend sujet de parler de la mort d'Égisthe[3], qu'Oreste venoit de tuer pour venger la mort d'Agamemnon son père; et il dit ces belles paroles :

Ὦ πόποι, οἷον δή νυ Θεοὺς βροτοὶ αἰτιόωνται.
Ἐξ ἡμέων γάρ φασι κάκ' ἔμμεναι· οἱ δὲ καὶ αὐτοὶ
Σφῇσιν ἀτασθαλίῃσιν ὑπὲρ μόρον[4] ἄλγε' ἔχουσιν. [Vers 32-34.]

Car, dit-il, n'avions-nous pas envoyé Mercure à Égisthe pour lui dire de ne point épouser Clytemnestre, et de ne point tuer Agamemnon, s'il ne vouloit être tué lui-même? Et cependant il s'est attiré tout cela, en dépit même du destin, c'est-à-dire de nos volontés.

1. M. Aimé-Martin a corrigé « ce qui passoit » en « ce qui se passoit. » Mais il ne faut ici rien changer au manuscrit. Racine s'est servi d'une ancienne locution : voyez le *Lexique*. Nous aurions mieux fait nous-même, dans un autre endroit (tome IV, p. 619, note 3), de ne pas ajouter entre crochets *se* devant *passoit*.
2. Vers 341-343.
3. Dans le manuscrit : *Égyste*, et cinq lignes plus loin : *Égysthe*.
4. Racine a écrit, comme en général les anciennes éditions, ὑπὲρ μόρον, en deux mots. Au premier vers, il a mis par mégarde οἷα, au lieu de οἷον. Cette leçon fautive ne peut nous apprendre de quelle édition il s'est servi : nous ne l'avons vue dans aucune.

Ὣς ἔφαθ᾽ Ἑρμείας· ἀλλ᾽ οὐ φρένας Αἰγίσθοιο
Πεῖθ᾽ ἀγαθὰ φρονέων· νῦν δ᾽ ἀθρόα πάντ᾽ ἀπέτισε. [Vers 42 et 43.]

Pallas prend occasion de plaindre Ulysse, qui est malheureux, dit-elle, sans l'avoir mérité; car Calypso le retient et veut qu'il l'épouse, l'amusant par des paroles douces et amoureuses, pour lui faire oublier son pays.

Αὐτὰρ Ὀδυσσεὺς,
Ἱέμενος καὶ καπνὸν ἀποθρώσκοντα νοῆσαι
Ἧς γαίης, θανέειν ἱμείρεται. [Vers 57-59.]

Il exprime par là combien est puissant l'amour du pays, puisqu'un héros et un esprit aussi fort qu'Ulysse ne souhaite autre chose que de voir seulement la fumée de son pays, et puis mourir, quoiqu'il fût dans une île si belle, comme nous verrons au V° livre. Virgile a imité en la personne de Vénus la harangue de Pallas, [livre] I, *En.*[1].

Τέκνον ἐμὸν, ποῖόν σε ἔπος φύγεν ἕρκος ὀδόντων. [Vers 64.]

Homère se sert souvent de cette façon de parler, qui est belle, et qui marque bien qu'une parole lâchée ne se peut plus rappeler.

Pallas prie Jupiter d'envoyer Mercure à Calypso, et cependant elle s'en vient à Ithaque, où elle treuve tous les amants de Penelopé qui jouoient aux dés devant la porte, tandis que leurs valets apprêtoient le souper. Télémaque, au contraire, étoit dans la maison, triste et affligé, ayant toujours son père dans l'esprit, et soupirant après son retour. Il voit Pallas sous la figure d'un étranger, et se fâche qu'on la fasse si longtemps attendre à la porte. Il va au-devant d'elle, et la prend par la main. C'est une belle chose de voir comment l'hospitalité est exercée dans l'*Odyssée*, et la vénération avec laquelle on y reçoit tous les étrangers[2]. C'est ce qu'on voit bien au long au livre VII°, dans l'île des Phéaques, où Ulysse est reçu comme un roi, sans qu'on le connût; et au livre XIV°, où il est reçu par son fermier, sous la figure d'un pauvre vieil homme. Et

---

1. *Énéide*, livre I, vers 229-253.
2. Cette phrase a été omise par M. Aimé-Martin.

SUR L'ODYSSÉE D'HOMÈRE.

lorsqu'il remercie son fermier du bon traitement qu'il lui fait, voilà ce que répond Eumeüs :

Ξεῖν', οὔ μοι θέμις ἔστ', οὐδ' εἰ κακίων σέθεν ἔλθοι,
Ξεῖνον ἀτιμῆσαι· πρὸς γὰρ Διός εἰσιν ἅπαντες
Ξεῖνοί τε πτωχοί τε [1].

Peut-être Homère, étant errant comme il étoit, et n'ayant point de pays certain, a voulu être bien reçu dans les pays étrangers. Et la première chose qu'on dit à un étranger lorsqu'il entre dans un logis, c'est qu'on le prie de manger, et qu'on l'écoutera après. C'est ce que fait ici Télémaque à son étranger : il prend ses armes, et les serre avec celles de son père ; il le fait asseoir auprès de lui, lui fait laver les mains, et le fait mettre à table. Voilà l'ordre de tous les festins d'Homère. Après que tout est préparé, une servante vient, qui donne à laver avec une aiguière dorée, tenant dessous un grand bassin d'argent ; après on se met à table. Celle qui a soin de la dépense sert toutes sortes de pains et de fruits sur la table :

Σῖτον δ' αἰδοίη ταμίη παρέθηκε φέρουσα,
Εἴδατα πόλλ' ἐπιθεῖσα, χαριζομένη παρεόντων. [Vers 139 et 140.]

Ce mot d'αἰδοίη fait voir que c'étoit quelque femme âgée. Le cuisinier met après les viandes :

Δαιτρὸς δὲ κρειῶν πίνακας παρέθηκεν ἀείρας
Παντοίων [vers 141 et 142],

et met en même temps des coupes d'or auprès de chacun. Il semble qu'Homère fait couvrir ses tables de viandes toujours grossières. Voyez *Apol. pour Hérodote*, 2. *partie* [2]. Ainsi,

---

1. *Odyssée*, livre XIV, vers 56-58.
2. Cette phrase est écrite en interligne. Le livre d'Henri Estienne, auquel Racine renvoie, a pour titre : *L'Introduction au traité de la conformité des merueilles anciennes auec les modernes, ou Traité preparatif à l'*Apologie pour Herodote. *A Geneue. L'an* M.D.LXVI (1 volume in-8). Dans la *seconde partie*, au *chapitre* XXVIII (*Comment nos predecesseurs estoyent grossiers en plusieurs actes*), on lit, p. 365 : « Encor de nostre temps il y a eu plusieurs desquels Galien se pourroit mocquer à aussi bon droit qu'il se mocque de ceux qui fai-

dans l'*Iliade*, au 2. livre[1], Agamemnon sert un bœuf aux chefs de l'armée; Achille sert un mouton aux principaux d'entre eux qui le vont voir[2], et à Priam tout de même[3]. Et l'on ne voit guère d'autres viandes que des bœufs, des moutons, des chèvres, des porcs et des agneaux. Mais ce mot παντοίων marque ici qu'il y en avoit de plusieurs sortes. Enfin il leur fait verser à boire par un héraut : c'étoit sans doute quelque sorte de valet de pied, ou bien des gens dont on se servoit pour faire des messages, ou des gens qui portoient quelque marque particulière comme des hérauts, à cause qu'on fait comme une espèce de société et d'alliance quand on boit ensemble.

Κῆρυξ δ' αὐτοῖσιν θάμ' ἐπῴχετο οἰνοχοεύων. [Vers 143.]

Ce n'est pas qu'il y admet[4] encore d'autres valets, comme on voit par ce vers :

Κοῦροι δὲ κρητῆρας ἐπεστέψαντο ποτοῖο. [Vers 148.]

Ils couronnoient de vin des coupes, c'est-à-dire qu'ils les emplissoient. La première chose qu'on faisoit, c'étoit de boire en l'honneur des Dieux, comme de Jupiter l'Hospitalier et de quelques autres dieux, et même de ses meilleurs amis, lorsqu'ils étoient morts ou absents, comme on voit partout dans Homère et dans d'autres auteurs. Ainsi dans Héliodore[5],

---

soyent l'amour à la Penelope d'Homère, de ce qu'ils mangeoyent les grans vilains pourceaux et donnoyent à leurs seruiteurs les petits cochons. » Ce passage est celui que Racine a eu sans doute en vue. — Était-ce dans la bibliothèque de son oncle, le vicaire général, qu'il avait pu trouver l'*Apologie pour Hérodote*? Depuis trois ans et demi qu'il était sorti de Port-Royal, le jeune Racine s'était bien émancipé dans ses lectures.

1. Vers 402 et suivants.
2. *Iliade*, livre IX, vers 207 et suivants.
3. *Iliade*, livre XXIV, vers 621 et suivants.
4. Tel est le texte du manuscrit. On s'attendrait à une double négation : « Ce n'est pas qu'il n'y admet; » ou plutôt : « n'y admette. »
5. Au chapitre v des *Éthiopiques* (livre II), p. 101 de l'édition de Lyon, M.DC.XVI (1 volume in-8).

Calasiris, devant que souper avec Cnémon, boit en l'honneur des Dieux, et aussi, dit-il, en l'honneur de Théagène et de Chariclée, qui méritent bien cet honneur. Cette cérémonie consistoit à répandre quelque goutte de vin, et puis après d'en boire un peu; c'est [ce] que les Grecs appellent λείβω, et les Latins *libo*, c'est-à-dire *leviter degusto*. Cela s'observoit inviolablement au commencement des festins; et si Homère l'omet ici, il faut attribuer cela à l'importunité de tous ces amoureux qui mettoient le trouble partout. Sur la fin du festin, un musicien chantoit. Après qu'on avoit levé les tables, on chantoit encore, ou bien on dansoit : c'est ce que font ici tous ces importuns.

> Αὐτὰρ ἐπεὶ πόσιος καὶ ἐδητύος ἐξ ἔρον ἕντο
> Μνηστῆρες, τοῖσιν μὲν ἐνὶ φρεσὶν ἄλλα μεμήλει,
> Μολπή τ' ὀρχηστύς τε· τὰ γάρ τ' ἀναθήματα δαιτός. [Vers 150-152.]

Car ce sont là, dit-il, les embellissements d'un festin. Pour Telemachus, il avoit d'autres choses à songer; et pendant que le musicien touche son luth, il entretient Pallas, et il lui dit que ces gens-là ont bon temps, parce qu'ils se divertissent aux dépens d'autrui.

> Τούτοισιν μὲν ταῦτα μέλει, κίθαρις καὶ ἀοιδή,
> Ῥεῖ', ἐπεὶ ἀλλότριον βίοτον νήποινον ἔδουσιν. [Vers 159 et 160.]

Puis il lui demande ce qu'on demandoit d'abord à un étranger :

> Τίς, πόθεν εἶς ἀνδρῶν; πόθι τοι πόλις, ἠδὲ τοκῆες;
> Ὁπποίης δ' ἐπὶ νηὸς ἀφίκεο; [Vers 170 et 171.]

Après il demande si elle est des anciens amis de la maison, parce qu'on avoit encore plus d'égard à eux; et il dit ces belles paroles à la louange d'Ulysse :

> Ἠὲ νέον μεθέπεις, ἢ καὶ πατρώϊός ἐσσι
> Ξεῖνος; ἐπεὶ πολλοὶ ἴσαν ἀνέρες ἡμέτερόν δῶ
> Ἄλλοι, ἐπεὶ καὶ κεῖνος ἐπίστροφος ἦν ἀνθρώπων. [Vers 175-177.]

Il faisoit du bien aux hommes, c'est-à-dire qu'il les traitoit toujours bien. Pallas lui répond qu'elle s'appelle Mentès de Taphe; et que lui et Ulysse sont amis de père. Elle l'assure qu'Ulysse n'est pas mort, et qu'il reviendra assurément à Ithaque. Et puis elle dit à Télémaque, pour lui donner du courage, qu'il ressemble tout à fait à Ulysse :

Αἰνῶς γὰρ κεφαλήν τε καὶ ὄμματα καλὰ ἔοικας
Κείνῳ. [Vers 208 et 209.]

Après Homère décrit parfaitement le caractère d'un jeune homme, en la personne de Telemachus, qui souhaiteroit d'être plutôt le fils de quelque homme riche qui lui eût laissé beaucoup de bien, que non pas d'Ulysse, qui lui a laissé une maison qui s'en va en ruine à cause de l'insolence des amants de Penelopé.

Ὣς δὴ ἔγωγ' ὄφελον μάκαρός νύ τευ ἔμμεναι υἱὸς
Ἀνέρος, ὃν κτεάτεσσιν ἑοῖς ἔπι γῆρας ἔτετμε.
Νῦν δ' ὃς ἀποτμότατος γένετο θνητῶν ἀνθρώπων. [Vers 217-219.]

Pallas le console, et lui demande qui sont tous ces gens-là qui font tant d'insolences chez lui; et elle lui fait cette demande afin de l'irriter encore davantage. Télémaque dit qu'Ulysse avoit fait une fort bonne maison, tandis qu'il demeuroit à Ithaque; mais qu'à présent on ne savoit ce qu'il étoit devenu, et qu'il étoit mort sans faire parler de lui. Il vaudroit bien mieux, dit-il, qu'il fût mort glorieusement devant Troie; les Grecs lui auroient dressé un tombeau, et la gloire en seroit revenue à son fils. Après il parle de tous ces rivaux qui font ensemble l'amour à sa mère.

Ἡ δ' οὔτ' ἀρνεῖται στυγερὸν γάμον, οὔτε τελευτὴν
Ποιῆσαι δύναται· τοὶ δὲ φθινύθουσιν ἔδοντες
Οἶκον ἐμόν. Τάχα δή με διαρραίσουσι καὶ αὐτόν. [Vers 249-251.]

Il fait voir là la prudence de Penelopé, qui, ayant ce mariage en horreur, ne les rebute pas pourtant tout à fait, de peur qu'ils ne s'emportent aux dernières extrémités. Pallas répond que si Ulysse revenoit au logis au terrible état où elle l'a vu quelquefois, il leur feroit d'étranges noces.

Ἀλλ' ἤτοι μὲν ταῦτα Θεῶν ἐν γούνασι κεῖται. [Vers 267.]

Ce vers est assez fréquent dans Homère, pour marquer la

providence des Dieux, de qui dépend toute chose[1]. Après elle conseille à Telemachus d'assembler le lendemain tous les rivaux, et de leur dire hardiment que chacun s'en aille chez soi, et qu'il dise à sa mère que si elle se veut marier, elle s'en aille chez ses parents, qui lui feront tel avantage qu'ils voudront ; qu'après cela il aille chercher qui lui apprendra des nouvelles de son père : si on lui dit qu'il vit encore, qu'il ait patience ; que, s'il est mort, il lui fasse des funérailles, et qu'il tâche après de se défaire de tous ces importuns, *sive dolo*, *sive palam*. Car vous n'êtes plus enfant, dit-elle,

Οὐδέ τί σε χρὴ
Νηπιάας ὀχέειν, ἐπεὶ οὐκ ἔτι τηλίκος ἐσσί. [Vers 296 et 297.]

Ne voyez-vous pas, dit-elle, quelle gloire s'est acquise Oreste en vengeant la mort de son père ?

Καὶ σὺ, φίλος (μάλα γάρ σ' ὁρόω καλόν τε μέγαν τε)
"Ἄλκιμος ἔσσ', ἵνα τίς σε καὶ ὀψιγόνων εὖ εἴπῃ. [Vers 301 et 302.]

Telemachus la remercie de ses conseils, et lui veut faire un présent avant qu'elle s'en aille ; mais elle remet cela à une autre fois ; car jamais Homère ne laisse sortir un étranger qu'on ne lui donne un présent, afin qu'il se souvienne de celui qui l'a reçu à sa maison, et que ce soit à l'avenir une marque de leur amitié. Aussitôt Pallas s'envole comme un oiseau, lui inspirant dans l'âme de la hardiesse et du courage.

Ὑπέμνησέν τέ ἑ πατρὸς
Μᾶλλον ἔτ' ἢ τὸ πάροιθεν. [Vers 321 et 322.]

Et lui s'aperçoit bien que c'est une divinité, et il va trouver les rivaux.

Τοῖσι δ' ἀοιδὸς ἄειδε περικλυτὸς, οἱ δὲ σιωπῇ
Εἴατ' ἀκούοντες. [Vers 325 et 326.]

Ce vers exprime bien l'attention qu'on a dans une grande assemblée lorsque quelque musicien chante. Celui-ci chantoit

---

1. Racine a écrit : « de qui dépend toutes choses. » — Avant ces mots, le texte de M. Aimé-Martin est *de Dieu*, et non *des Dieux*. Le singulier est aussi la première leçon du manuscrit ; *s* et *x* ont été ensuite ajoutés : est-ce de la main de Racine ?

le retour des Grecs après la prise de Troie. Là-dessus vient Penelopé, qui descend de sa chambre; car elle demeure toujours dans une chambre d'en haut, toute seule avec ses servantes, et n'a point de communication avec ses amants, si ce n'est qu'elle descend quelquefois pour voir ce qui se passe dans le logis, comme présentement pour entendre ce musicien; et elle n'entre jamais dans la salle, mais se tient toujours à l'entrée, ayant deux servantes à ses côtés, telle qu'elle est dépeinte en cet endroit:

Κλίμακα δ' ὑψηλὴν κατεβήσατο οἷο δόμοιο,
Οὐκ οἴη, ἅμα τῇγε καὶ ἀμφίπολοι δύ' ἕποντο.
Ἡ δ' ὅτε δὴ μνηστῆρας ἀφίκετο δῖα γυναικῶν,
Στῆ ῥα παρὰ σταθμὸν τέγεος πύκα ποιητοῖο,
Ἄντα παρειάων σχομένη λιπαρὰ κρήδεμνα·
Ἀμφίπολος δ' ἄρα οἱ κεδνὴ ἑκάτερθε παρέστη. [Vers 330-335.]

Homère lui fait toujours tenir un voile ou un mouchoir devant ses joues, pour montrer qu'elle pleuroit presque toujours son mari. Elle dit en pleurant à ce musicien qu'il prenne un autre sujet, parce que celui-là est trop douloureux pour elle. Mais Telemachus, qui veut commencer à prendre quelque autorité dans la maison, et qui est bien aise même qu'on chante la gloire de son père, afin d'entretenir le deuil et l'affection[1] de Penelopé pour son mari, dit qu'elle laisse faire ce musicien. Car, dit-il, ce n'est pas sa faute si vous pleurez; mais il s'en faut prendre aux Dieux qui font les faveurs qu'il leur plaît aux hommes d'esprit, en les inspirant. Outre cela, dit-il, les hommes n'aiment rien plus qu'une nouvelle chanson:

Τὴν γὰρ ἀοιδὴν μᾶλλον ἐπικλείουσ' ἄνθρωποι,
Ἥτις ἀκουόντεσσι νεωτάτη ἀμφιπέληται. [Vers 351 et 352.]

C'est-à-dire qu'en matière de poésie les plus nouvelles sont toujours les plus estimées. Mais, poursuit Telemachus, remontez à votre appartement, ayez soin de votre ménage, et laissez l'entretien aux hommes, et à moi surtout, qui suis le maître du logis:

Ἀλλ' εἰς οἶκον ἰοῦσα τὰ σαυτῆς ἔργα κόμιζε,

---

1. M. Aimé-Martin a mis *affliction*, au lieu d'*affection*.

Ἱστόν τ' ἠλακάτην τε, καὶ ἀμφιπόλοισι κέλευε
Ἔργον ἐποίχεσθαι· μῦθος δ' ἄνδρεσσι μελήσει. [Vers 356-358.]

Ce qu'elle fait; et elle s'en va avec ses femmes, où elle pleure continuellement son mari, jusqu'à ce que Minerve lui envoie un peu de sommeil.

Cependant ses amants font grand bruit, et chacun voudroit bien coucher auprès d'elle. Telemachus leur dit qu'ils se taisent, et qu'ils écoutent ce musicien, qu'il appelle Θεοῖς ἐναλίγκιος αὐδήν [vers 371].
Et il leur dit que le lendemain ils s'assemblent, afin qu'il leur déclare sa volonté, et qu'ils s'en aillent tous chacun chez soi : sinon qu'il implorera la vengeance des Dieux. Ils se mordent tous les lèvres de rage, admirant la hardiesse de Telemachus. Antinoüs lui dit qu'il est un hardi discoureur, ὑψαγόρην [vers 385], et qu'il seroit bien marri qu'un homme comme lui fût roi d'Ithaque, comme l'a été son père. Telemachus répond : Je le voudrois bien être, moi, si les Dieux m'en faisoient la grâce : croyez-vous qu'il y ait du mal à l'être ? Au contraire, dès qu'on est roi, on fait une maison riche, et on se fait honorer ; mais le soit qui voudra : au moins je le veux être de ma maison et de la famille qu'Ulysse m'a laissée. Eurymachus répond que cela est en la disposition des Dieux de faire un roi ; puis il lui demande quel étoit cet étranger. Telemachus répond que c'étoit Mentès, prince des Taphiens.

Ὣς φάτο Τηλέμαχος, φρεσὶ δ' ἀθανάτην θεὸν ἔγνω. [Vers 420.]

Après ils se mettent tous à danser et à chanter jusqu'à la nuit, et alors chacun s'en retourne coucher chez soi. Telemachus se retire en haut à son appartement, où il avoit une fort belle chambre.
Sa gouvernante Euryclée porte un flambeau devant lui. C'étoit une vieille fille que Laërte avoit achetée fort jeune, et qu'il aimoit beaucoup, et comme sa femme.

Εὐνῇ δ' οὔποτ' ἔμικτο· χόλον δ' ἀλέεινε γυναικός. [Vers 433.]

Elle avoit nourri Telemachus tout petit, et elle l'aimoit plus que toutes les autres femmes. Elle ouvre donc la porte de sa chambre. Il s'assit, et se déshabille, et donne ses habits à Euryclée, qui les plie, et les pend à un portemanteau tout près de son lit. Ensuite elle s'en va, et ferme la porte; et Telemachus demeure seul dans son lit, et songe toute la nuit à exécuter tout ce que lui a dit Pallas. Ainsi Homère décrit les moindres particularités.

LIVRE II.

Ἦμος δ' ἠριγένεια φάνη ῥοδοδάκτυλος Ἠώς. [Vers 1.]

C'est le vers qui est le plus fréquent dans Homère, et il exprime admirablement le lever de l'Aurore. Héliodore l'applique à Chariclée [1].

Βῆ δ' ἴμεν ἐκ θαλάμοιο, Θεοῖς [2] ἐναλίγκιος ἄντην. [Vers 5.]

Il décrit Telemachus, qui sort de sa chambre aussitôt qu'il est habillé. Il appelle les Grecs à l'assemblée, et il vient lui-même, ayant un javelot à la main,

Οὐκ οἶος, ἅμα τῷγε δύω κύνες ἀργοὶ ἕποντο [vers 11],

pour montrer sans doute qu'il étoit en équipage de chasseur; et aussitôt il dit que Pallas lui donna une grâce tout à fait haute :

Θεσπεσίην δ' ἄρα τῷγε χάριν κατέχευεν Ἀθήνη. [Vers 12.]

Tout le monde l'admiroit, dit-il; et il s'alla seoir à la place de son père, et les vieillards se levèrent devant lui, parce que les vieillards étant plus sages que les jeunes gens [3], le reconnoissoient pour le successeur de son père. Un vieillard nommé Égyptius,

Ὃς δὴ γήραϊ κυφὸς ἔην καὶ μυρία ᾔδη [vers 16],

et de plus dont l'un de ses enfants avoit suivi Ulysse et avoit

---

1. Au chapitre VII des *Éthiopiques* (livre III), p. 136.
2. Il y a Θεοῖς dans le manuscrit de Racine; la leçon ordinaire est Θεῷ.
3. Racine a mis par mégarde : « que les jeunes ans. »

été dévoré par Polyphème, et dont un autre faisoit l'amour à Penelopé, commence à parler, et demande qui est-ce[1] et à quel dessein on a convoqué l'assemblée ; car, dit-il, depuis le départ d'Ulysse nous ne nous sommes point assemblés ; mais qu'on dise librement pourquoi nous sommes assemblés à présent. Telemachus répond, et auparavant un héraut lui donne un sceptre à la main. Homère a cette coutume de mettre toujours un sceptre à la main des princes qu'il fait haranguer ; sans doute que cela donnoit plus de grâce et plus de majesté. Ainsi dans le [livre] 2. de l'*Iliade*[2], parlant d'une assemblée, il appelle les princes σκηπτοῦχοι[3] βασιλῆες ; et il dit qu'Agamemnon se leva pour parler ayant un sceptre à la main :

Ἀνὰ δὲ κρείων Ἀγαμέμνων
Ἔστη, σκῆπτρον ἔχων[4].

Et il parle de la dignité de ce sceptre, disant que Vulcain l'avoit fait pour Jupiter, lequel l'avoit donné à Mercure, et Mercure aux ancêtres d'Agamemnon :

Τῷ ὅγ' ἐρεισάμενος ἔπεα πτερόεντα προσηύδα[5].

Et dans le troisième de l'*Iliade*, Anténor parlant d'Ulysse lorsqu'il vint à Troie en ambassade avec Menelaüs : Lorsqu'il se leva, dit-il, pour haranguer, il avoit les yeux fichés contre terre, et tenoit son sceptre immobile sans le remuer, ni par devant ni derrière lui, comme feroit un ignorant ; mais, etc.

Σκῆπτρον δ' οὔτ' ὀπίσω οὔτε προπρηνὲς ἐνώμα,
Ἀλλ' ἀστεμφὲς ἔχεσκεν ἀΐδρεϊ φωτὶ ἐοικώς·
Φαίης κεν ζάκοτόν τινα ἔμμεναι, ἄφρονά θ' αὔτως[6].

Telemachus donc répond, et décrit bien au long l'insolence de ces jeunes gens qui mangent tout son bien, et les conjure par les Dieux d'avoir égard à ce que diront les peuples voi-

---

1. Racine écrit constamment : « esce. »
2. Vers 86.
3. Il y a encore là un lapsus dans le manuscrit : σκηπροῦχοι, pour σκηπτοῦχοι.
4. *Iliade*, livre II, vers 100 et 101. — 5. *Ibidem*, vers 109.
6. *Iliade*, livre III, vers 218-220.

sins, et de craindre la colère des Dieux mêmes, de peur qu'ils ne les abandonnent à cause de leurs méchantes actions.

Λίσσομαι ἠμὲν Ζηνὸς Ὀλυμπίου ἠδὲ Θέμιστος,
Ἥτ' ἀνδρῶν ἀγορὰς ἠμὲν λύει ἠδὲ καθίζει. [Vers 68 et 69.]

La Justice, dit-il, convoque et termine les assemblées, c'est-à-dire qu'elle autorise tout ce qui s'y passe, à cause qu'un corps a toujours plus d'égard à la justice que des particuliers. Enfin il leur dit qu'il aimeroit mieux que ce fût eux qui mangeassent tout chez lui, et que peut-être ils lui rendroient tout un jour; mais que c'étoit des jeunes gens et des étrangers dont on ne pourroit jamais avoir raison.

Ὣς φάτο χοώμενος, ποτὶ δὲ σκῆπτρον βάλε γαίῃ,
Δάκρυ' ἀναπρήσας· οἶκτος δ' ἕλε λαὸν ἅπαντα. [Vers 80 et 81.]

C'étoit une marque d'affliction ou de colère de jeter son sceptre à terre, après avoir parlé, au lieu de le rendre aux hérauts. Ainsi, au [livre] I. de l'*Iliade*, après qu'Achille a parlé contre Agamemnon, il jette encore son sceptre par terre:

Ποτὶ δὲ σκῆπτρον βάλε γαίῃ
Χρυσείοις ἥλοισι πεπαρμένον, ἕζετο δ' αὐτός[1].

Et c'étoit comme une marque qu'on ne vouloit pas parler davantage. Ici tout le monde demeure muet:

Ἔνθ' ἄλλοι μὲν πάντες ἀκὴν ἔσαν, οὔτέ τις ἔτλη
Τηλέμαχον μύθοισιν ἀμείψασθαι χαλεποῖσιν. [Vers 82 et 83.]

Il n'y a qu'Antinoüs qui étoit le plus insolent, à cause qu'il étoit d'une des meilleures maisons et qu'il aspiroit à la royauté, comme on voit dans la suite. Il dit donc à Telemachus que ce n'est pas leur faute, mais celle de sa mère, qui les tient toujours en haleine, et qui est, dit-il, la plus adroite femme qu'on ait jamais vue; qu'elle les a amusés longtemps en leur disant qu'elle vouloit faire un grand voile pour Laërte, le père d'Ulysse, afin de l'ensevelir:

Μή τίς μοι κατὰ δῆμον Ἀχαιϊάδων νεμεσήσῃ,
Αἴκεν ἄτερ σπείρου κεῖται πολλὰ κτεατίσσας. [Vers 101 et 102.]

Sans doute que le voile de la sépulture étoit toujours donné

---

1. *Iliade*, livre I, vers 245 et 246.

au père par ses enfants. Antinoüs dit donc qu'ils attendoient qu'elle eût fait; qu'elle y travailloit en effet le jour, mais qu'elle défaisoit tout la nuit : ce qu'ils reconnurent ensuite. Et ils lui firent achever ce voile malgré elle. Il dit donc à Telemachus qu'il la renvoie chez son père, et qu'il lui ordonne de se marier, au lieu d'employer tous ces artifices pour nous tromper :

Τὰ φρονέουσ' ἀνὰ θυμὸν ἅ οἱ πέρι δῶκεν Ἀθήνη
Ἔργα τ' ἐπίστασθαι περικάλλεα καὶ φρένας ἐσθλὰς,
Κέρδεά θ' οἶ' οὔπω τίν' ἀκούομεν οὐδὲ παλαιῶν,
Τάων αἳ πάρος ἦσαν ἐϋπλοκαμῖδες Ἀχαιαὶ,
Τυρώ τ', Ἀλκμήνη τε, ἐϋπλόκαμός τε Μυκήνη,
Τάων οὔτις ὁμοῖα νοήματα Πηνελοπείῃ
Ἤδη. [Vers 116-122.]

On voit par là qu'Homère a voulu donner en Penelopé le caractère d'une femme tout à fait sage, aussi bien que d'un homme parfaitement adroit en Ulysse. Mais, dit Antinoüs, elle ne considère pas que nous vous ruinons pendant qu'elle nous amuse de la sorte :

Μέγα μὲν κλέος αὐτῇ
Ποιεῖτ', αὐτὰρ σοί γε ποθὴν πολέος βιότοιο. [Vers 125 et 126.]

Car nous ne sortirons point de votre logis jusqu'à ce que quelqu'un de nous l'emmène pour son épouse. Telemachus répond à cela qu'il n'a garde de faire sortir du logis celle qui l'a mis au monde et qui l'a nourri :

Ἀντίνο', οὔπως ἐστὶ δόμων ἀέκουσαν ἀπῶσαι,
Ἥ μ' ἔτεχ', ἥ μ' ἔθρεψε. [Vers 130 et 131.]

Car d'un côté, dit-il, mon père vit peut-être encore.

Ἐκ γὰρ τοῦ πατρὸς κακὰ πείσομαι, ἄλλα δὲ δαίμων
Δώσει, ἐπεὶ μήτηρ στυγερὰς ἀρήσετ' Ἐρινὺς,
Οἴκου ἀπερχομένη· νέμεσις δέ μοι ἐξ ἀνθρώπων
Ἔσσεται. [Vers 134-137.]

On voit là un bel exemple du respect que les enfants doivent avoir pour leur mère : car y avoit-il [rien] de plus juste[1], ce semble, que de faire sortir Penelopé de la maison d'Ulysse,

---

1. Il y a dans le manuscrit : « n'y avoit-il de plus juste? »

qu'on croyoit mort, afin qu'elle se mariât, et qu'elle n'achevât pas la ruine de sa maison? Cependant Telemachus dit que cette parole ne sortira jamais de sa bouche. Mais vous-même, dit-il, sortez de ma maison, et allez faire bonne chère ailleurs : sinon, et si vous aimez mieux manger tout mon bien, mangez. Pour moi, j'invoquerai la vengeance des Dieux, comme dans la dernière extrémité :

Κείρετ'· ἐγὼ δὲ Θεοὺς ἐπιδώσομαι αἰὲν ἐόντας
Αἴ κέ ποτε Ζεὺς δῶσι παλίντιτα ἔργα γενέσθαι. [Vers 143 et 144.]

Telle étoit la confiance qu'on avoit aux Dieux. En effet, Jupiter lui envoie un bon augure de deux aigles qui se battent au milieu de leur assemblée. Un bon vieillard, nommé Halitherses Mastorides, enseigne ce que cet augure veut dire, et intimide tous ces jeunes gens; mais Eurymachus lui dit qu'il aille deviner à ses enfants[1] ; car, dit-il, tous oiseaux ne font point augure :

Ὄρνιθες δέ τε πολλοὶ ὑπ' αὐγὰς ἠελίοιο
Φοιτῶσ', οὐδέ τε πάντες ἐναίσιμοι. [Vers 181 et 182.]

Il lui dit donc de se taire, et Telemachus aussi, tout grand discoureur qu'il est, μάλα περ πολύμυθον ἐόντα [vers 200]; et qu'il songe seulement à renvoyer Penelopé chez son père, ou à voir manger tout son bien jusqu'à ce qu'elle se marie.

Ἡμεῖς δ' αὖ ποτιδέγμενοι ἤματα πάντα
Εἵνεκα τῆς ἀρετῆς ἐριδαίνομεν, οὐδὲ μετ' ἄλλας
Ἐρχόμεθ', ἅς ἐπιεικὲς ὀπυιέμεν ἐστὶν ἑκάστῳ. [Vers 205-207.]

Eh bien, dit Telemachus, n'en parlons plus; mais au moins faites-moi donner un vaisseau, afin que j'aille chercher des nouvelles de mon père, afin que je puisse prendre mes mesures là-dessus. Alors Mentor, le plus fidèle des amis d'Ulysse, dit ces belles paroles : Il ne faut plus qu'un roi traite ses peuples avec douceur, puisqu'on ne se souvient plus d'Ulysse, et que tant de gens qui sont ici ne détournent pas seulement de paroles tous ces jeunes gens de leur dessein :

---

1. Ce membre de phrase a été omis dans l'édition de M. Aimé-Martin.

Μή τις ἔτι πρόφρων ἀγανὸς καὶ ἤπιος ἔστω
Σκηπτοῦχος βασιλεὺς, μηδὲ φρεσὶν αἴσιμα εἰδώς,
Ἀλλ' αἰεὶ χαλεπός τ' εἴη καὶ αἴσυλα ῥέζοι,
Ὡς οὔτις μέμνηται Ὀδυσσῆος θείοιο
Λαῶν οἷσιν ἄνασσε, πατὴρ δ' ὡς ἤπιος ἦεν. [Vers 230-234.]

Mais Liocritus, un des jeunes gens, lui dit des injures, et se moque de tout cela et d'Ulysse même, quand il seroit de retour. Ainsi l'assemblée est rompue, et chacun s'en va de côté et d'autre. Mais Telemachus va sur le bord de la mer, et se lavant les mains, invoque Pallas :

Κλῦθί μοι, ὃς χθιζὸς θεὸς ἤλυθες ἡμέτερον δῶ. [Vers 262.]

Pallas vient à lui sous la figure de Mentor, et elle l'excite par les louanges de son père :

Τηλέμαχ', οὐδ' ὄπιθεν κακὸς ἔσσεαι, οὐδ' ἀνοήμων,
Εἰ δή τοι σοῦ πατρὸς ἐνέστακται μένος ἠΰ,
Οἷος ἐκεῖνος ἔην τελέσαι ἔργον τε ἔπος τε. [Vers 270-272.]

Mais si vous n'êtes pas son fils, c'est-à-dire si vous ne lui ressemblez pas, vous ne viendrez pas à bout de votre entreprise.

Παῦροι γάρ τοι παῖδες ὁμοῖοι πατρὶ πέλονται·
Οἱ πλέονες κακίους, παῦροι δέ τε πατρὸς ἀρείους. [Vers 276 et 277.]

Mais je vous connois, dit-elle, et espérez tout, principalement avec un ami paternel comme moi, qui vous suivra partout. En effet, Pallas protégea toujours Ulysse.

Τοῖος γάρ τοι ἑταῖρος ἐγὼ πατρώϊός εἰμι. [Vers 286.]

Mais allez : faites provision de vivres, et moi je vous treuverai un vaisseau et des compagnons.

Telemachus s'en va chez lui, et y treuve tous ces jeunes gens, qui s'apprêtoient à souper. Antinoüs le prend par la main, et le prie de souper avec eux. Telemachus dit qu'il songe plutôt à se venger d'eux, et arrache sa main de celle d'Antinoüs. Les autres se moquent de lui; et lui monte en haut, en une chambre où étoient toutes les provisions du logis, comme de l'or et de l'airain, des habits, ἅλις τ' εὐῶδες ἔλαιον [vers 339], et de l'excellent vin qu'on gardoit depuis longtemps pour le retour d'Ulysse :

Ἐν δὲ πίθοι οἴνοιο παλαιοῦ ἡδυπότοιο
Ἕστασαν, ἄκρητον θεῖον ποτὸν ἐντὸς ἔχοντες,
Ἐξείης ποτὶ τοῖχον ἀρηρότες, εἴποτ' Ὀδυσσεὺς
Οἴκαδε νοστήσειε καὶ ἄλγεα πολλὰ μογήσας. [Vers 340-343.]

Tout cela étoit à la garde d'Euryclée, à qui Telemachus demande tout ce qu'il lui faut, et le meilleur vin, dit-il, après celui qu'on garde pour mon père. Elle pleure; mais il lui [ordonne[1]] d'apprêter tout, et de ne point dire son départ devant onze ou douze jours, à moins qu'elle ne [l'] apprenne d'ailleurs,

Ὡς ἂν μὴ κλαίουσα κατὰ χρόα καλὸν ἰάπτῃ. [Vers 376.]

Ce qu'elle lui promet, et elle prépare tout; et lui s'en retourne en bas avec tous ces jeunes gens pour couvrir son dessein. Pallas cependant, sous la figure de Telemachus, amasse des gens et treuve un vaisseau.

Δύσετό τ' ἠέλιος σκιόωντό τε πᾶσαι ἀγυιαί. [Vers 388.]

Homère décrit ainsi le soleil couché dans les villes, disant que les rues étoient devenues obscures; et il le fait justement coucher, afin qu'on ne voie point Pallas, qui monte son vaisseau en mer, et l'équipe[2]. Après elle endort tous les jeunes gens, qui s'en vont chacun chez soi; elle avertit Telemachus que tout est prêt. Il la suit, et fait apporter ses provisions : ils s'embarquent. Pallas fait venir un vent favorable; le vaisseau s'avance en pleine mer; et ceux qui étoient dedans boivent en l'honneur des Dieux, et surtout de Pallas :

Ἐκ πάντων δὲ μάλιστα Διὸς γλαυκώπιδι κούρῃ. [Vers 433.]

C'est là l'épithète ordinaire de Minerve; et, comme disoient nos vieux traducteurs, « Minerve aux yeux pers » : c'est entre le bleu et le vert, car ce n'est pas bleu tout à fait, comme on voit par ce passage de Cicéron, [livre] I, *de Nat. Deorum*[3] :

1. Ici Racine a sauté un mot : *dit, ordonne, commande ?*
2. Dans l'édition de M. Aimé-Martin : « et l'équipage. »
3. *De Natura Deorum*, livre I, chapitre xxx.

Cæsios oculos Minervæ, cæruleos Neptuni. On voit cette couleur dans les yeux de chat : d'où vient que quelques-uns l'ont appelée *felineus color ;* mais beaucoup mieux dans ceux d'un lion : de là vient que les poëtes ont donné ces yeux-là à Minerve, qui étoit une guerrière. En un mot, ce sont des yeux entre le bleu et le vert, mais des yeux forts[1], reluisants et perçants. Et souvent on n'appelle Minerve que de ce nom-là, γλαυκῶπις, comme d'un nom honorable. Ainsi elle le témoigne elle-même[2], lorsqu'elle dit à Junon, tandis que Jupiter étoit en colère contre elle, au [livre] 8. de l'*Iliade*[3] :

Ἔσται μὰν ὅτ' ἂν αὖτε φίλην γλαυκώπιδα εἴπῃ.

Junon au contraire, qui étoit d'une humeur plus posée et plus majestueuse, est appelée βοῶπις, aux yeux de bœuf. Ce sont de grands yeux bleus qui ont beaucoup de majesté : aussi Homère ajoute toujours βοῶπις πότνια Ἥρη. Enfin Vénus, qui n'étoit point guerrière et qui ne tenoit pas tant sa gravité, mais qui au contraire étoit d'une humeur gaie et toute[4] amoureuse, est appelée ἑλικῶπις, ou ἑλικοβλέφαρος, aux yeux ou aux prunelles noires, ou, si l'on veut, aux yeux petillants, et, comme a dit Homère, ὄμματα μαρμαίροντα : ce qui exprime admirablement de certains yeux qui ne peuvent se tenir en place, et qui ont toujours un mouvement adroit et lascif. Catulle appelle cela *ebrios ocellos*[5], et nous disons quelquefois *des yeux fripons. Atque ipsa in medio sedet voluptas,* dit un ancien épigramme[6]. Mais pour revenir à la couleur des yeux

1. Racine a écrit « des yeux forts, reluisants..., » et non, comme on lit dans l'édition de M. Aimé-Martin, « des yeux fort reluisants. »
2. Dans le manuscrit, par suite d'un lapsus, il y a « lui-même. »
3. Vers 373.
4. Il y a ainsi *toute* dans le manuscrit.
5. *Carmen* XLV, vers 11.
6. Qui commence : *O blandos oculos et inquietos ;* ce qui revient au grec. (*Note de Racine.*) — Racine a fait le mot *épigramme* du genre masculin. On trouvera l'épigramme qu'il cite au tome I, p. 646, de l'*Anthologie* de Burmann (*Anthologia veterum epigrammatum et poema-*

de Vénus, Homère les fait noirs, et tous les anciens aussi ; et on voit que la plupart des beautés de l'antiquité ont été ainsi qualifiées.

LIVRE III.

Ἠέλιος δ' ἀνόρουσε λιπὼν περικαλλέα λίμνην
Οὐρανὸν ἐς πολύχαλκον, ἵν' Ἀθανάτοισι φανείη
Καὶ θνητοῖσι βροτοῖσιν ἐπὶ ζείδωρον ἄρουραν. [Vers 1-3.]

Ce marais ne peut être autre chose que la mer, qui est en effet un assez beau marais. (Au [livre] 5., ἀνεδύσατο λίμνης, parlant d'Ino[1].) Ils arrivent à Pyle, et sacrifient aux Dieux en prenant terre. Pallas dit à Telemachus qu'il ne doit point être honteux, mais demander librement à Nestor des nouvelles de son père.

Ψεῦδος δ' οὐκ ἐρέει· μάλα γὰρ πεπνυμένος ἐστί. [Vers 20.]

Il ne vous dira point de fausseté, dit-elle ; car il est fort sage. Telemachus lui demande conseil.

Μέντορ, πῶς τ' ἄρ' ἴω ; Πῶς τ' ἄρ προσπτύξομαι αὐτόν ; [Vers 22.]

tum, 2 volumes in-4°, Amsterdam, 1759), livre III, *épigramme* CCXII. La voici telle qu'elle y est donnée :

> *O blandos oculos et inquietos,*
> *Et quadam propria nota loquaces!*
> *Illic et Venus, et leves Amores,*
> *Atque ipsa in medio sedet voluptas.*

—Suivant Burmann, elle est d'Alcimus. On l'attribue à Pétrone dans les commentaires du *Satyricon* : voyez à la page 353 de l'édition de cet ouvrage publiée à Genève en 1624 (1 volume in-4°), la note 4 sur un passage du chapitre LXXXVI (c'est le chapitre CXXVI dans les plus récentes éditions). Ce peut bien être là que Racine avait lu cette épigramme, car on voit par un autre passage des *Remarques sur l'Odyssée* qu'il lisait alors Pétrone.

1. Cette phrase que nous avons mise entre parenthèses est en interligne dans le manuscrit. Ἀνεδύσατο λίμνης est au vers 337 du livre V de l'*Odyssée*. Il s'agit de la déesse des mers, Ino, comme le dit Racine. M. Aimé-Martin a bizarrement altéré ce passage, qu'on lit ainsi dans son édition : « Au cinquième livre, ἀνεδύσατο λίμνης ; partant d'Ino, ils arrivent à Pyle. »

Cicéron rapporte ce vers-là, *lib. IX, ep.* 8, *ad Attic.*: *Hic ego vellem habere Homeri illam Minervam simulatam Mentori, cui dicerem :* Μέντορ, etc. Et la raison pourquoi Telemachus demande conseil,

Οὐδέ τί πω μύθοισι πεπείρημαι πυκινοῖσιν·
Αἰδὼς δ' αὖ νέον ἄνδρα γεραίτερον ἐξερέεσθαι. [Vers 23 et 24.]

Je n'ai pas, dit-il, encore assez d'expérience pour parler. Homère nous apprend par là qu'un jeune homme ne doit pas s'ingérer de parler, puisque Telemachus, qui étoit un prince si bien né, appréhende de parler ; et, dit-il, ce n'est pas honnête à un jeune homme d'interroger un vieillard. Mais Pallas le rassure par ces belles paroles :

Τηλέμαχ', ἄλλα μὲν αὐτὸς ἐνὶ φρεσὶ σῇσι νοήσεις,
Ἄλλα δὲ καὶ δαίμων ὑποθήσεται. Οὐ γὰρ ὀΐω
Οὔ σε θεῶν ἀέκητι γενέσθαι τε τραφέμεν τε. [Vers 26-28.]

Dites, dit-elle, ce qui vous viendra dans la pensée, et quelque bon démon vous inspirera le reste. Commencez, et Dieu achèvera ; car vous ne lui êtes pas indifférent.

Ὣς ἄρα φωνήσασ' ἡγήσατο Παλλὰς Ἀθήνη
Καρπαλίμως, ὁ δ' ἔπειτα μετ' ἴχνια βαῖνε θεοῖο. [Vers 29 et 30.]

Pallas lui montra le chemin ; et lui, marchoit sur les pas de cette déesse. Ils viennent treuver Nestor à une assemblée.

Ἔνθ' ἄρα Νέστωρ ἧστο σὺν υἱάσιν. Ἀμφὶ δ' ἑταῖροι
Δαῖτ' ἐντυνόμενοι κρέα ὦπτων, ἄλλα δ' ἔπειρον. [Vers 32 et 33.]

Il étoit assis avec ses enfants, et ses domestiques (ou ses amis) préparoient le souper. D'abord qu'ils virent ces étrangers, ils vinrent tous en foule à eux, les prirent par les mains et les firent asseoir, après les avoir salués :

Οἱ δ' ὡς οὖν ξείνους ἴδον, ἀθρόοι ἦλθον ἅπαντες
Χερσίν τ' ἠσπάζοντο καὶ ἑδριάασθαι ἄνωγον. [Vers 34 et 35.]

Et surtout Pisistrate, l'aîné des enfants de Nestor, qui les prend et les fait mettre à table. Homère fait paroître tous les enfants de Nestor fort bien nourris, pour montrer qu'un père sage instruit bien ses enfants. Ainsi, dans l'*Iliade*, Antilochus, son fils, étoit un des plus braves, et grand ami d'Achille : aussi y mourut-il[1]. Pisistrate donc leur présente à boire, et les avertit de boire en l'honneur de Neptune ; car ce festin est à son honneur ; et il dit un peu devant que c'étoit sur le bord de la mer.

Πάντες δὲ Θεῶν χατέουσ' ἄνθρωποι. [Vers 48.)

Tout le monde, dit Pisistrate, a besoin des Dieux, et par conséquent doit les honorer. Mais il donne la coupe à Pallas la première, parce, dit-il, étranger, que vous paroissez le plus âgé, l'autre étant de mon âge. Pallas fait une prière à Neptune, et puis après donne la coupe à Telemachus.

Ὣς ἄρ' ἔπειτ' ἠρᾶτο, καὶ αὐτὴ πάντα τελεύτα. [Vers 62.]

Elle pria ainsi, dit-il, et elle-même accomplit tout ce qu'elle demandoit à Neptune ; ou bien, elle accomplit toute la cérémonie des libations. Ils soupent, et après Nestor leur demande qui ils sont. Telemachus lui répond, et avec assurance, car Pallas lui en inspiroit :

Θαρσήσας · αὐτὴ γὰρ ἐνὶ φρεσὶ θάρσος Ἀθήνη
Θῆχ', ἵνα μιν περὶ πατρὸς ἀποιχομένοιο ἔροιτο,
Ἠδ' ἵνα μιν κλέος ἐσθλὸν ἐν ἀνθρώποισιν ἔχῃσιν. [Vers 76-78.]

Il lui demande des nouvelles de son père, et l'en conjure par son père même, s'il en a jamais reçu quelque service à la guerre de Troie :

Λίσσομαι, εἴ ποτέ τοί τι πατὴρ ἐμὸς ἐσθλὸς Ὀδυσσεὺς
Ἢ ἔπος ἠέ τι ἔργον ὑποστὰς ἐξετέλεσσε
Δήμῳ ἐνὶ Τρώων, ὅθι πάσχετε πήματ' Ἀχαιοί. [Vers 98-100.]

Car rien ne lie si bien l'amitié que d'avoir enduré de la misère ensemble. En effet, Nestor commence à lui parler de la guerre de Troie, et dit qu'ils y ont tant souffert de maux que,

---

1. Nous reproduisons le texte du manuscrit. Il faut sans doute remplacer : « y mourut-il, » par « mourut-il devant Troie. » (Voyez le livre IV de l'*Odyssée*, vers 188.) Racine paraît avoir omis quelques mots dans la phrase.

quand il seroit cinq ans entiers à en parler toujours, il ne pourroit pas tout dire. Il lui raconte ce qui se passa au retour des Grecs, et comme ils se séparèrent les uns des autres. C'est là le caractère qu'Homère donne à Nestor, de parler beaucoup, et de rapporter des histoires de son vieux temps. Nous voyons dans l'*Iliade* que, quand il y a quelque différend, Nestor se produit toujours, et leur dit qu'ils se taisent tous, et qu'il est plus expérimenté qu'eux : aussi avoit-il vu trois siècles. Homère a pratiqué encore cela dans quelques autres vieillards, comme dans Phénix, au [livre] 9. de l'*Iliade*; dans le fermier d'Ulysse, à la fin de l'*Odyssée*, etc. Nestor dit que jamais ils ne furent d'avis différents, lui et Ulysse :

Ἔνθ' ἤτοι εἵως μὲν ἐγὼ καὶ δῖος Ὀδυσσεὺς
Οὔτε ποτ' εἰν ἀγορῇ δίχ' ἐβάζομεν, οὔτ' ἐνὶ βουλῇ,
Ἀλλ' ἕνα θυμὸν ἔχοντε, νόῳ καὶ ἐπίφρονι βουλῇ
Φραζόμεθ', Ἀργείοισιν ὅπως ὄχ' ἄριστα γένηται. [Vers 126-129.]

Cela montre que deux hommes sages discordent rarement quand il s'agit du bien public.

Οἱ δ' ἦλθον οἴνῳ βεβαρηότες υἷες Ἀχαιῶν. [Vers 139.]

Il parle d'une assemblée des Grecs, où tout se passa fort mal et avec désordre, et dit que les Grecs étoient chargés de vin.

Νήπιος, οὐδὲ τὸ ᾔδη ὃ οὐ πείσεσθαι ἔμελλεν·
Οὐ γάρ τ' αἶψα θεῶν τρέπεται νόος αἰὲν ἐόντων. [Vers 146 et 147.]

Agamemnon vouloit persuader aux Grecs de demeurer jusqu'à ce qu'ils eussent fait des sacrifices à Pallas. Mais, dit-il, il ne savoit pas qu'il ne leur persuaderoit jamais cela, les Dieux ne le voulant pas permettre, parce qu'ils étoient irrités contre eux ; et l'esprit des Dieux ne se change pas si aisément.

Νύκτα μὲν ἀέσαμεν χαλεπὰ φρεσὶν ὁρμαίνοντες
Ἀλλήλοις. Ἐπὶ γὰρ Ζεὺς ἤρτυε πῆμα κακοῖο. [Vers 151 et 152.]

Nous passâmes la nuit en dormant, nous voulant du mal les uns aux autres ; car Jupiter préparoit aux Grecs un grand orage de malheurs.

Ἐστόρεσεν δὲ θεὸς μεγακήτεα πόντον. [Vers 158.]

Ce vers exprime bien le calme et la tranquillité de la mer. Il dit donc que quelques-uns, du nombre desquels il étoit, s'embarquèrent, et qu'ils eurent un retour assez heureux ; mais que les autres, avec Agamemnon et Ulysse, demeurèrent. Les autres revinrent enfin, à ce que j'ai ouï dire, et Agamemnon même, qui a été tué et vengé après par son fils.

Ὡς ἀγαθὸν καὶ παῖδα καταφθιμένοιο λιπέσθαι
Ἀνδρός. [Vers 196 et 197.]

Tant il est bon de laisser un fils après soi. Et vous, mon enfant, qui êtes beau et grand, ayez du courage, afin que la postérité parle bien de vous :

Καὶ σὺ, φίλος, μάλα γάρ σ' ὁρόω καλόν τε μέγαν τε,
Ἄλκιμος ἔσσ', ἵνα τίς σε καὶ ὀψιγόνων εὖ εἴπῃ. [Vers 199 et 200.]

Telemachus dit qu'il voudroit bien faire parler de lui, mais qu'il est trop foible, étant seul contre tant d'hommes. Ah ! dit Nestor, ils seroient tous bien punis si Pallas vous aimoit autant que votre père ; car je n'ai jamais vu les Dieux aimer si ouvertement un homme :

Οὐ γάρ πω ἴδον ὧδε Θεοὺς ἀναφανδὰ φιλεῦντας,
Ὡς κείνῳ ἀναφανδὰ παρίστατο Παλλὰς Ἀθήνη. [Vers 221 et 222.]

Telemachus dit que cela n'est pas aisé, quand les Dieux mêmes s'en mêleroient ; et aussitôt Pallas prend la parole : Qu'osez-vous dire, Telemachus ?

Ῥεῖα θεός γ' ἐθέλων καὶ τηλόθεν ἄνδρα σαώσαι. [Vers 231.]

Il est aisé à un dieu de sauver un homme, en quelque extrémité[1] qu'il soit.

Ἀλλ' ἤτοι θάνατον μὲν ὁμοίϊον οὐδὲ Θεοί περ
Καὶ φίλῳ ἀνδρὶ δύνανται ἀλαλκέμεν. [Vers 236 et 237.]

Ce n'est pas, dit-elle, que les Dieux puissent sauver un homme de la mort, lorsque son heure est venue une fois.

Telemachus change de discours, et dit qu'il veut demander

---

1. M. Aimé-Martin a mis : « En quelque endroit. »

autre chose à Nestor, puisqu'il passe tous les hommes en science et en sagesse; car il a vu trois générations d'hommes.

Ὥστε μοι Ἀθανάτοις ἰνδάλλεται εἰσοράασθαι. [Vers 246.]

De sorte que je le respecte et que je le regarde comme un dieu. Cela montre le respect qu'on doit avoir pour les vieillards. Il lui demande donc comment s'est passée[1] la mort d'Agamemnon. Ainsi Homère décrit ce qui s'est passé après la mort d'Achille, où finit son *Iliade*, tantôt par la bouche de Nestor, tantôt par celle de Menelaüs, et par celle d'Ulysse même.

Nestor décrit comme Égisthe, étant amoureux de Clytemnestre, tâchoit de la corrompre; mais cette femme refusoit d'abord une action si déshonnête, car elle étoit bien conseillée, φρεσὶ γὰρ κέχρητ' ἀγαθῇσι[2], ayant auprès d'elle un musicien, ἀοιδὸς ἀνήρ[3], à qui Agamemnon l'avoit fort recommandée. Mais Égisthe emmena ce musicien dans une île déserte, où il le laissa en proie aux oiseaux; et alors cette femme se laissa aller.

Τὴν δ' ἐθέλων ἐθέλουσαν ἀνήγαγεν ὅνδε δόμονδε,
Πολλὰ δὲ μηρί' ἔκηε Θεῶν ἱεροῖς ἐπὶ βωμοῖς,
Πολλὰ δ' ἀγάλματ' ἀνῆψεν ὑφάσματά τε χρυσόν τε
Ἐκτελέσας μέγα ἔργον, ὃ οὔποτε ἔλπετο θυμῷ. [Vers 272-275.]

Et il fit bien des sacrifices aux Dieux, mit des couronnes sur leurs statues, et leur fit plusieurs autres dons, étant venu à bout d'une chose qu'il n'espéroit pas pouvoir jamais faire. Cela montre le transport d'un homme amoureux. Cependant, dit-il, je revenois avec Agamemnon et Menelaüs, son frère; mais Apollon ayant tué de ses flèches Phrontis, le pilote de Menelaüs, qui étoit le plus habile de tous les hommes à gouverner un vaisseau quand la tempête étoit violente, Menelaüs demeura derrière, et fut emporté en Égypte; et ainsi Égisthe eut la commodité de tuer Agamemnon : ce qui est plus amplement décrit au XIe livre[4]. Égisthe régna sept ans du-

---

1. *Passé*, sans accord, dans le manuscrit.
2. Vers 266. — 3. Vers 267.
4. *Odyssée*, livre XI, vers 408-433.

rant, après quoi il fut tué par Oreste. J'ai remarqué qu'Homère ne dit jamais expressément qu'Oreste ait tué sa mère, et qu'il évite cela comme une chose odieuse ; mais il le dit ouvertement ici :

Ἤτοι ὁ τὸν κτείνας δαίνυ τάφον Ἀργείοισιν
Μητρός τε στυγερῆς καὶ ἀνάλκιδος Αἰγίσθοιο. [Vers 309 et 310.]

Il fit un banquet pour la sépulture de sa mère et du lâche Égisthe. Oreste étant jeune avoit été envoyé par sa sœur Électra dans la Phocide, afin qu'il ne fût pas tué par Égisthe. Il n'en revint que douze ans après, selon quelques-uns, et sept, selon Homère.

Nestor conseille à Telemachus de n'être pas longtemps hors de son logis.

Καὶ σὺ, φίλος, μὴ δηθὰ δόμων ἄπο τῆλ' ἀλάλησο,
Κτήματά τε προλιπὼν ἄνδρας τ' ἐν σοῖσι δόμοισι
Οὕτω ὑπερφιάλους, μήτοι κατὰ πάντα φάγωσι. [Vers 313-315.]

Mais il dit qu'il aille voir auparavant Menelaüs, lequel est nouvellement revenu de bien loin, et d'une mer dont les oiseaux mêmes ne pourroient pas revenir en un an, car elle est vaste et horrible à voir. Ce n'est pourtant que la Méditerranée ; car Menelaüs n'avoit été qu'en Égypte, et les héros d'Homère n'ont jamais vu l'Océan, ni même les Romains devant César, qui y monta le premier pour passer en Angleterre. Alors ils se mettent à table, et font des libations à Neptune et aux autres dieux. Pallas leur dit qu'ils se hâtent, et qu'il ne faut pas être trop longtemps à table quand on y est pour faire des libations, parce que ces choses-là sans doute se devoient faire avec révérence. Nestor les retient à coucher, et dit que tant qu'il vivra, il ne souffrira pas que le fils d'un tel homme qu'Ulysse couche sur le plancher d'un vaisseau. Après moi, mes enfants auront encore soin de bien traiter les hôtes :

Ἔπειτα δὲ παῖδες ἐνὶ μεγάροισι λίπωνται,
Ξείνους ξεινίζειν ὅστις κ' ἐμὰ δώμαθ' ἵκηται. [Vers 354 et 355.]

Pallas lui dit qu'elle lui sait bon gré ; mais, pour éviter de coucher au logis de Nestor, elle dit qu'ayant le plus d'autorité parmi les compagnons de Telemachus, il faut qu'elle les aille treuver, et que dès le matin elle ira chez les Caucons, où on lui doit une dette qui n'est pas nouvelle ni petite; car les vieilles dettes sont les meilleures :

Ἔνθα χρεῖός μοι ὀφέλλεται, οὔτι νέον γε
Οὐδ' ὀλίγον. [Vers 367 et 368.]

Puis elle lui recommande Telemachus, et elle s'en va, pareille à un aigle, c'est-à-dire terrible comme une aigle[1] :

Φήνῃ εἰδομένη · θάμβος δ' ἔλε πάντας ἰδόντας. [Vers 372.]

Les Latins traduisent *ossifraga* : c'est une espèce d'aigle qui est carnassier et qui brise les os; car Pline en rapporte de six espèces, liv. X, c. 3.

Aussitôt Nestor prend Telemachus par la main, et dit qu'il doit être un jour quelque chose de grand, puisque les Dieux l'accompagnent si visiblement :

Εἰ δή τοι νέῳ ὧδε Θεοὶ πομπῆες ἕπονται. [Vers 376.]

Car assurément, dit-il, c'est là la fille de Jupiter, Pallas. Nestor lui fait un vœu de lui sacrifier une génisse bien saine, large de front, et qui n'est pas encore domptée, et de lui verser de l'or entre les cornes. C'étoit là un des plus augustes sacrifices. Pallas l'écouta. Après Nestor ramène tous ses gendres et ses enfants à son logis, les fait asseoir chacun selon son rang, et puis il remplit une coupe de vin qu'on gardoit depuis onze ans; et ils en boivent tous en l'honneur de Pallas.

Après quoi ils se vont tous coucher. Nestor retient Telemachus, et fait coucher son fils Pisistrate auprès de lui, car il n'étoit pas encore marié; et lui couche dans un appartement d'en haut avec sa femme. Dès le matin il se lève, et se vient seoir sur de belles pierres blanches et reluisantes qui étoient devant sa porte. Là s'étoit assis Neleüs, son père; et Nestor s'y assoit présentement, portant un sceptre à la main; et autour de lui s'arrangeoient tous ses enfants, dont Homère nomme six.

---

1. Racine a écrit ainsi, dans cette même phrase, d'abord *un aigle*, puis *une aigle*.

Telemachus y vient aussi avec Pisistrate, qui fait le sixième. Nestor commande à ses enfants d'aller, les uns querir une génisse à la campagne, les autres querir les compagnons de Telemachus, les autres d'aller querir l'orfévre, afin de faire le sacrifice, et aux autres enfin de donner ordre au dîner.

Ὣς ἔφαθ'. Οἱ δ' ἄρα πάντες ἐποίπνυον. [Vers 430.]

Il est aussitôt obéi. La génisse vient, les compagnons de Telemachus, et l'orfévre,

Ὅπλ' ἐν χερσὶν ἔχων χαλκήϊα πείρατα τέχνης,
Ἄκμονά τε σφύραν τ' ἐϋποίητόν τε πυράγρην [vers 433 et 434],

ayant dans les mains ses instruments, son enclume, son marteau et ses tenailles. Il ne se peut rien voir de mieux réglé que toute la famille de Nestor. On voit que chacun fait son office : l'un tient la coignée, l'autre le vase pour recevoir le sang. Nestor tient une aiguière; il invoque Minerve, coupe du poil dessus la tête de la génisse, et puis les jette dans le feu avec de la farine salée, que les Latins appellent *mola* (d'où vient *immolo*), les Grecs, οὐλοχύτης.

Aussitôt Thrasymède, son fils, lui donne un grand coup de hache sur le cou, et la tue; les filles et les femmes font un grand cri, ὀλόλυξαν[1]. Héliodore dit la même chose en un sacrifice de cent bœufs. Aussitôt, dit-il, qu'on donna les coups de hache, ὠλόλυξαν αἱ γυναῖκες, ἠλάλαξαν οἱ ἄνδρες[2]. La femme de Nestor s'appeloit Eurydicé, fille de Clymenus. On fait cuire les viandes, c'est-à-dire les membres de cette génisse découpés; on couvroit les cuisses de la coiffe, c'est-à-dire de la peau qui couvre les intestins, *omentum*. Cependant la belle Polycaste, la dernière des filles de Nestor, lave Telemachus : après quoi il reprend ses habillements.

Ἔκ ῥ' ἀσαμίνθου βῆ δέμας Ἀθανάτοισιν ὁμοῖος. [Vers 468.]

Après le dîner, Nestor commande à ses enfants d'accommoder un chariot pour Telemachus : ce qu'ils font. Telemachus y monte, et Pisistrate aussi, qui prend les rênes à la

1. Vers 450.
2. *Éthiopiques*, chapitre VIII (livre III), p. 141.

main. Il fouette les chevaux, et [ils] partent; ils vont coucher à Phères, où Dioclès, fils d'Alphée, les reçoit; et le lendemain, à soleil couchant, ils arrivent à Lacédémone.

Μάστιξεν δ' ἐλάαν. Τὼ δ' οὐκ ἄκοντε πετέσθην. [Vers 484.]

Ce vers exprime bien des chevaux qui vont légèrement, et il est fréquent dans Homère.

Les livres de l'*Odyssée* vont toujours de plus beau en plus beau, comme il est aisé de reconnoître, parce que les premiers ne sont que comme pour disposer aux suivants; mais ils m'ont paru[1] tous admirables et divertissants.

LIVRE IV.

Ils descendent chez Menelaüs, lequel étoit occupé à faire les noces de son fils et de sa fille, dont l'une étoit Hermione, fille d'Hélène[2]; car Hélène, dit Homère, n'eut plus d'enfant après la belle Hermione :

'Ελένη δὲ Θεοὶ γόνον οὐκέτ' ἔφαινον,
'Επειδὴ τὸ πρῶτον ἐγείνατο παῖδ' ἐρατεινὴν
'Ερμιόνην, ἣ εἶδος ἔχε χρυσῆς 'Αφροδίτης. [Vers 12-14.]

Menelaüs l'avoit promise à Pyrrhus, fils d'Achille, lorsqu'ils étoient devant Troie, quoiqu'elle eût déjà été accordée à Oreste, qui s'en vengea depuis, et tua Pyrrhus dans le temple d'Apollon : après quoi il la reprit pour son épouse. Mais Homère ne parle point qu'Oreste y fût intéressé[3]. Il dit donc que Menelaüs envoyoit sa fille à Pyrrhus. Et il marioit à une fille de Sparte son fils Mégapenthès, qui lui étoit né d'une concubine. Il étoit donc en festin, où jouoit un musicien, tandis que

---

1. Dans l'édition de M. Aimé-Martin : « mais ils n'ont pas tous paru. »
2. Racine écrit tantôt *Élène*, tantôt *Hélène*.
3. Certainement le jeune Racine ne se doutait pas du parti qu'il allait, peu d'années après, tirer de cette histoire, qui devint le sujet de son premier chef-d'œuvre.

deux danseurs dansoient à la cadence. Dans ce temps-là ces deux jeunes princes parurent à sa porte. Un des domestiques de Menelaüs lui vient demander s'il les fera entrer, ou s'il les envoyera chez quelque autre.

Τὸν δὲ μέγ' ὀχθήσας προσέφη ξανθὸς Μενέλαος [vers 30],

comme s'il se fâchoit qu'on lui fît cette demande. En effet, il répond : Je vous ai toujours vu assez sage jusques ici ; mais, à ce que je vois, vous ne savez ce que vous dites. Moi qui ai été reçu si favorablement dans tous les pays étrangers, je refuserois ma maison à personne ! mais détachez leurs chevaux, et faites-les venir, afin qu'ils soupent : ce qu'on fait, et on observe toutes les cérémonies ordinaires dans Homère. Il faut, leur dit Menelaüs, que vous soyez nés de quelques princes :

Ἐπεὶ οὔ κε κακοὶ τοιούσδε τέκοιεν. [Vers 64.]

Sur la fin du souper, Telemachus dit tout bas au fils de Nestor qu'il considère la maison de Menelaüs, combien elle est riche, étant toute brillante d'airain[1], d'or, d'ambre, d'argent et d'ivoire, et comme il est dit un peu devant,

Ὥστε γὰρ ἠελίου αἴγλη πέλεν ἠὲ σελήνης. [Vers 45.]

Mais Telemachus va plus loin, et dit qu'on la prendroit pour le palais de Jupiter :

Ζηνός που τοιήδε γ' Ὀλυμπίου ἔνδοθεν αὐλή. [Vers 74.]

Menelaüs l'entend bien, et lui dit qu'il n'y a point de comparaison avec l'éternelle demeure de Jupiter :

Ἤτοι Ζηνὶ βροτῶν οὐκ ἄν τις ἐρίζοι. [Vers 78.]

Mais, dit-il, je voudrois n'en avoir pas la troisième partie, et n'avoir pas perdu tant d'amis, surtout Ulysse. Il dit qu'il a erré en Chypre, dans la Phénicie, l'Égypte, l'Éthiopie, et la Libye, où les agneaux naissent avec des cornes, et où les

---

1. Racine écrit : *d'erain*.

brebis portent trois fois l'an : si bien que ni roi ni pâtre ne manquent jamais de lait, ni de fromage, ni de chair :

Ἔνθα μὲν οὔτε ἄναξ ἐπιδευὴς οὔτε τι ποίμην
Τυροῦ καὶ κρειῶν, οὐδὲ γλυκεροῖο γάλακτος. [Vers 87 et 88.]

Il dit, en un mot, ce qui s'est passé chez lui durant cela ; et ainsi, dit-il, je ne fais plus autre chose que de pleurer tous mes amis, mais surtout Ulysse, que j'aimois principalement. Il dit cela à cause de la ressemblance qu'il treuvoit dans son fils avec lui. Cela tire les larmes des yeux de Telemachus, qui se cache de son manteau : ce que Menelaüs aperçoit bien. Telemachus songe s'il lui parlera de son père, ou s'il l'en laissera parler le premier. Cependant Hélène descend de son appartement ; Homère décrit admirablement son arrivée ; et, sans mentir, c'est un plaisir de voir comme il s'entend à faire une description. Il remarque les plus petites choses, et les fait toutes paroître devant les yeux : ainsi on croit voir arriver Penelopé avec toute sa modestie, quand il décrit qu'elle vient ; tout de même quand Telemachus se va coucher. Et ici on voit Hélène paroître avec éclat et avec majesté, quoiqu'il la décrive en ménagère.

Ἐκ δ' Ἑλένη θαλάμοιο θυώδεος ὑψορόφοιο
Ἤλυθεν, Ἀρτέμιδι χρυσηλακάτῳ εἰκυῖα. [Vers 121 et 122.]

Parce qu'elle vient à la négligence, il la compare à Diane. Une de ses femmes, nommée Adreste, lui apporte un siége ; l'autre, nommée Alcippe, met un carreau dessus :

Τάπητα φέρεν μαλακοῦ ἐρίοιο. [Vers 124.]

Phylo, l'autre, apporte devant elle un vase d'argent pour tenir la laine, en grec τάλαρον : d'où, selon Plutarque[1], les Romains ont pris le nom de *Talassio*, chanson nuptiale,

---

1. *Vie de Romulus*, chapitre xv. « La plupart des autheurs.... estiment que c'est un admonestement pour aduertir les nouuelles maryées à penser de faire leur besongne, qui est de filer ce que les Grecs appellent *Talassia*. » (*Traduction d'Amyot*, tome I, p. 47 de l'édition de Lausanne, 1572.) — Voyez aussi les *Questions romaines* de Plutarque, chapitre xxxi.

comme pour avertir les femmes d'avoir soin du ménage. Ce vase lui avoit été donné avec beaucoup d'autres présents par Alcandra, dame égyptienne, et il étoit bordé d'or. Phylo le met donc au pied[1] de sa maîtresse, tout rempli de laine, et dessus étoit étendue sa quenouille garnie d'une laine violette. Hélène s'assoit sur son siége, où il y avoit aussi un marchepied ; car Homère décrit toujours tous les siéges avec un marchepied, quand c'étoient des siéges honorables, comme Junon en promet un au Sommeil, ayant besoin de lui afin qu'il endorme Jupiter. Je te donnerai, dit-elle, un beau siége d'or qui sera incorruptible, et fait des mains de Vulcain ; mais comme si ce n'étoit pas assez, elle ajoute :

Ὑπὸ δὲ θρῆνυν ποσὶν ἧσει,
Τῷ κεν ἐπισχοίης λιπαροὺς πόδας εἰλαπινάζων[2],

afin que vous y mettiez vos pieds délicats tout à votre aise. En cet état, Hélène parle à son mari. On voit bien qu'autrefois les dames ne faisoient pas tant de façons qu'elles en font à présent. Et elles vivoient assez familièrement, comme Hélène qui fait apporter avec elle tout son ouvrage, devant de jeunes hommes qu'elle n'avoit jamais vus. Néanmoins elle dit à son mari qu'elle se trompe fort si ce n'est Telemachus, tant il lui ressemble : sans doute que c'est à cause qu'il ressembloit à son père. Et si Hélène le devine devant son mari, c'est que les femmes font plus de réflexion et examinent les nouveaux venus avec curiosité ; car c'est leur coutume. Menelaüs avoue qu'elle a raison :

Κείνου γὰρ τοιοίδε πόδες, τοιαίδε τε χεῖρες,
Ὀφθαλμῶν τε βολαὶ, κεφαλή τ', ἐφύπερθέ τε χαῖται. [Vers 149 et 150.]

Virgile dit : *Sic oculos, sic ille manus, sic ora ferebat*[3] ; mais Homère est plus particulier, et ce tour des yeux, ὀφθαλμῶν βολαί, est tout à fait expressif. Aussi, dit Menelaüs, cela m'a fait souvenir et parler d'Ulysse, et j'ai remarqué que cela l'a

---

1. Il y a ainsi dans le manuscrit : « au pied, » et non « aux pieds. »
2. *Iliade*, livre XIV, vers 240 et 241.
3. *Énéide*, livre III, vers 490.

fait pleurer. Le fils de Nestor répond pour lui, parce qu'il est mieux séant qu'un tiers dise qui il est. Il est vrai que c'est lui, dit-il; mais il est sage, et ne veut pas se vanter devant vous, que nous écoutons comme un dieu :

Νεμεσσᾶται δ' ἐνὶ θυμῷ,
Ὧδ' ἐλθὼν τὸ πρῶτον, ἐπεσβολίας ἀναφαίνειν
Ἄντα σέθεν. [Vers 158-160.]

Et Nestor m'a envoyé pour l'accompagner, et il est venu vous demander des nouvelles de son père, dont l'absence lui est insupportable, et le fait souffrir beaucoup. Menelaüs s'écrie aussitôt :

Ὦ πόποι, ἦ μάλα δὴ φίλου ἀνέρος υἱὸς ἐμὸν δῶ
Ἵκεθ', ὃς εἵνεκ' ἐμεῖο πολεῖς ἐμόγησεν ἀέθλους. [Vers 169 et 170.]

La reconnoissance de Menelaüs paroît par ces paroles. J'avois résolu, dit-il, de l'aimer plus que personne, et de l'emmener hors d'Ithaque, lui et sa famille, et son peuple, et de lui donner une de mes villes, afin que nous vécussions ensemble.

Οὐ δέ κεν ἡμᾶς
Ἄλλο διέκρινεν φιλέοντέ τε τερπομένω τε,
Πρίν γ' ὅτε δὴ θανάτοιο μέλαν νέφος ἀμφεκάλυψεν. [Vers 178-180.]

Mais quelque dieu nous a envié ce bien-là, et l'a privé de son retour. Ces paroles tendres les font pleurer tous quatre,

Ὣς φάτο. Τοῖσι δὲ πᾶσιν ὑφ' ἵμερον ὦρσε γόοιο.
Κλαῖε μὲν Ἀργείη Ἑλένη Διὸς ἐκγεγαυῖα,
Κλαῖε δὲ Τηλέμαχός τε καὶ Ἀτρείδης Μενέλαος,
Οὐδ' ἄρα Νέστορος υἱὸς ἀδακρύτω ἔχεν ὄσσε. [Vers 183-186.]

Car il se souvenoit de son frère Antilochus, et il dit à Menelaüs : Croyez-moi, changeons de discours; car je n'aime pas de pleurer après (*ou* durant) le souper,

Οὐ γὰρ ἔγωγε
Τέρπομ' ὀδυρόμενος μεταδόρπιος [vers 193 et 194];

mais demain au matin, tant que vous voudrez; car je n'empêche point qu'on pleure les morts, vu que c'est là leur récompense :

Τοῦτό νυ καὶ γέρας οἶον ὀϊζυροῖσι βροτοῖσι
Κείρασθαί τε κόμην, βαλέειν τ' ἀπὸ δάκρυ παρειῶν. [Vers 197 et 198.]

Menelaüs loue son discours, et dit ces belles paroles :

Ῥεῖα δ' ἀρίγνωτος γόνος ἀνέρος ᾧτε Κρονίων
Ὄλβον ἐπικλώσῃ γαμέοντί τε γεινομένῳ τε. [Vers 207 et 208.]

Tel qu'est Nestor, à qui Dieu a fait la grâce de vieillir longtemps et agréablement dans sa maison, et d'avoir des enfants également sages et vaillants. Ainsi ils lavent les mains et soupent ; et pour leur faire oublier leur affliction, Hélène jette dans leur vin une drogue d'une herbe qui ôte toute la douleur et la colère :

Νηπενθές τ' ἄχολόν τε, κακῶν ἐπίληθον ἁπάντων [vers 221],

de sorte qu'après cela un homme auroit passé tout le jour sans pleurer, quand il verroit mourir ou sa mère [ou son père], et qu'on tueroit cruellement son frère, ou même son fils à ses yeux. Quelques-uns croient que cette herbe, qui a été appelée *nepenthes*, n'est autre que la buglose ; au moins Pline dit qu'elle a les mêmes qualités. Voici ce que Pline en dit l. XXV, c. 3, où il la décrit : *Homerus quidem, primus doctrinarum et antiquitatis parens, multus alias in admiratione Circes, gloriam herbarum Ægypto tribuit;* et un peu après : *Nobile illud nepenthes oblivionem tristitiæ veniamque afferens, et ab Helena utique omnibus mortalibus propinandum;* il en parle encore l. XXI, c. 21 [1]. Homère dit donc que cette herbe, avec plusieurs autres, avoit été donnée à Hélène par Polydamna, princesse égyptienne.

Τῇ πλεῖστα φέρει ζείδωρος ἄρουρα et 230.]
Φάρμακα πολλὰ μὲν ἐσθλὰ μεμιγμένα, πολλὰ δὲ λυγρά. [Vers 229

Plutarque [2] applique ce passage à la lecture des poëtes, où

---

1. *Nepenthes illud prædicatum ab Homero.* Dans d'autres éditions ce passage est au chapitre xci; et le précédent au chapitre v du livre XXI.
2. *Comment le jeune homme doit écouter les poëmes*, chapitre 1.

il y a beaucoup de bonnes choses à prendre, et beaucoup de mauvaises. Homère dit qu'en Égypte chacun y est fort habile médecin, car ils descendent tous de Pæon. Aussi les Égyptiens passoient partout pour des devins et des enchanteurs, comme on voit dans le Calasiris d'Héliodore; cet auteur assure qu'Homère étoit Égyptien, et le prouve[1].

Puis elle leur parle, et leur dit ces mots qui sont fréquents dans Homère :

Ἀνδρῶν ἐσθλῶν παῖδες (ἀτὰρ θεὸς ἄλλοτ' ἐπ' ἄλλῳ 237],
Ζεὺς ἀγαθόν τε κακόν τε διδοῖ· δύναται γὰρ ἅπαντα) [vers 236 et

pour montrer que la misère et le bonheur n'ôtent et n'ajoutent rien à la vertu d'un homme, puisque ce sont des choses que Dieu donne à qui il veut. Hélène loue Ulysse, et surtout lorsqu'il se lacéra lui-même, et que, déguisé en gueux, δέκτῃ [vers 248], il entra dans Troie, où il fit grand ravage.

Et elle dit qu'elle s'en réjouissoit, desirant alors de revenir avec son premier mari, et déplorant le jour que Vénus l'avoit emmenée à Troie; car elle fait l'honnête femme, et veut dire qu'elle avoit été enlevée par force. Menelaüs dit que ce fut bien autre chose lorsqu'ils étoient enfermés dans ce grand cheval de bois, où il fermoit la bouche à tous ceux qui vouloient répondre à Hélène, qui, par je ne sais quel instinct, les appeloit tous, en contrefaisant la voix de leurs femmes. Telemachus dit alors : Et le pis, c'est que tout cela ne lui a servi de rien :

Ἄλγιον· οὐ γάρ οἵ τι τάγ' ἤρκεσε λυγρὸν ὄλεθρον. [Vers 292.]

Après ils se vont tous coucher. Du matin Menelaüs se lève, et vient demander à Telemachus le sujet de son voyage. Il le lui conte tout au long, comme à Nestor. Menelaüs, indigné de l'impudence de tous ces beaux amoureux, dit :

Ὦ πόποι, ἦ μάλα δὴ κρατερόφρονος ἀνδρὸς ἐν εὐνῇ
Ἤθελον εὐνηθῆναι ἀνάλκιδες αὐτοὶ ἐόντες. [Vers 333 et 334.]

Ainsi, dit-il, lorsqu'une biche vient mettre ses petits dans

---

[1] *Éthiopiques*, chapitre VIII (livre III), p. 154 et 155.

la tanière d'un lion tandis qu'il en est dehors, le lion revient après, qui les maltraite et les tue, tant la mère que les petits :

Ὡς δ', ὁπότ' ἐν ξυλόχῳ ἔλαφος κρατεροῖο λέοντος
Νεβροὺς κοιμήσασα νεηγενέας γαλαθηνοὺς,
Κνημοὺς ἐξερέῃσι καὶ ἄγκεα ποιήεντα
Βοσκομένη, ὁ δ' ἔπειτα ἑὴν εἰσήλυθεν εὐνήν,
Ἀμφοτέροισι δὲ τοῖσιν ἀεικέα πότμον ἐφῆκεν. [Vers 335-339.]

Rien ne sauroit être mieux dit que cette comparaison, et cela vient bien à de certaines gens qui veulent débaucher des femmes dont les maris valent bien plus qu'eux.

Alors, pour venir à Ulysse, il raconte tous ses voyages, et les maux qu'il endura pour n'avoir pas sacrifié aux Dieux.

Οἱ δ' αἰεὶ βούλοντο Θεοὶ μεμνῆσθαι ἐφετμέων. [Vers 353.]

Il dit donc qu'il étoit dans une petite île, à une journée de l'Égypte, qu'on appelle le Phare, et que là il alloit mourir de faim, lui et son monde, étant réduit à pêcher quelques poissons pour vivre ; mais qu'Inothée, nymphe marine, fille de Protée, au moins, dit-elle, on le dit :

Τόνδε τ' ἐμόν φασιν πατέρ' ἔμμεναι, ἠδὲ τεκέσθαι. [Vers 387.]

Elle lui dit qu'il aille treuver ce Protée, qui vient tous les jours dormir la méridienne, là auprès, avec tous ses veaux marins. Enfin elle lui donne les mêmes avis que Cyrené en donne à son fils Aristée, au [livre] 4. des *Géorgiques ;* car Virgile a traduit cette fable mots pour mots, sinon que Virgile fait cacher Protée dans un coin, et ici Inothée donne trois peaux de ces gros poissons à Menelaüs, afin qu'il se cache dessous avec deux de ses amis. Car Protée comptoit son troupeau chaque jour ; et Menelaüs dit qu'ils n'eussent pu durer, à cause de la puanteur de ces peaux. Mais Inothée leur boucha les narines d'ambrosie,

Ἡδὺ μάλα πνείουσαν, ὄλεσσε δὲ κήτεος ὀδμήν. [Vers 446.]

Protée lui demande enfin ce qu'il veut ; il dit : Οἶσθα, γέρον[1], *Scis, Proteu.* Protée donc lui dit la cause de ses malheurs, et

---

1. Vers 465.

dit qu'il faut qu'il retourne sacrifier sur le bord du Nil, Διπε-τέος ποταμοῖο[1], qui coule de Jupiter, c'est-à-dire du ciel[2], à cause qu'on ignoroit sa source. Menelaüs lui demande des nouvelles de ses amis, s'ils sont tous revenus en leur pays. Protée dit qu'il lui en dira, mais qu'il ne sera pas longtemps sans pleurer :

Οὐδέ σέ φημι
Δὴν ἄκλαυτον ἔσεσθαι, ἐπὴν εὖ πάντα πύθηαι. [Vers 493 et 494.]

En effet, il dit qu'il y a deux des principaux chefs qui ont péri dans leur retour, et qu'il y en a encore un qui est vivant en un endroit de la mer. Le premier est Ajax, dont il décrit la mort, non pas selon Virgile, qui le fait tuer par Pallas[3]; mais il dit que Neptune, irrité d'une parole impie d'Ajax, qui s'étoit vanté d'échapper de la mer malgré tous les Dieux, le jeta de son trident contre un rocher, où il périt. Après il conte [qu']Agamemnon revint à son pays, et baisa la terre natale :

Καὶ κύνει ἁπτόμενος ἣν πατρίδα, πολλὰ δ' ἀπ' αὐτοῦ
Δάκρυα θερμὰ χέοντ', ἐπεὶ ἀσπασίως ἴδε γαῖαν. [Vers 522 et 523.]

Mais un espion d'Égisthe le vit, et le courut dire à son maître, qui lui ayant fait un festin, le tua comme un bœuf à l'étable :

Ὥς τίς τε κατέκτανε βοῦν ἐπὶ φάτνῃ. [Vers 535.]

Alors Menelaüs ne vouloit plus vivre, d'affliction, et se rouloit sur le sable en pleurant.

Αὐτὰρ ἐπεὶ κλαίων τε κυλινδόμενός τ' ἐκορέσθην [vers 541]

(c'est une façon de parler fort ordinaire à Homère), « après que je fus soûlé de pleurer. » Ainsi Menelaüs dit au commencement de ce livre :

Ἄλλοτε μέν τε γόῳ φρένα τέρπομαι, ἄλλοτε δ' αὖτε
Παύομαι. Αἰψηρὸς δὲ κόρος κρυεροῖο γόοιο. [Vers 102 et 103.]

---

1. Vers 477.
2. Dans le manuscrit : « *i.* [*id est*] du ciel. »
3. *Énéide*, livre I, vers 39 et suivants.

C'est une espèce de plaisir de pleurer, et Homère ne dit jamais autrement, sinon : il pleura à cœur joie ; mais, dit-il, on se soûle bientôt de ce plaisir-là. Protée raconte la vengeance d'Oreste, et enfin il lui dit qu'Ulysse est dans l'île de Calypso, et lui dit que pour lui il ne mourra point à Argos, à cause qu'il est mari d'Hélène et gendre de Jupiter.

> Ἀλλά σ' ἐς Ἠλύσιον πεδίον καὶ πείρατα γαίης
> Ἀθάνατοι πέμψουσιν (ὅθι ξανθὸς Ῥαδάμανθυς,
> Τῇ περ ῥηΐστη βιοτὴ πέλει ἀνθρώποισιν·
> Οὐ νιφετός, οὔτ' ἄρ χειμὼν πολὺς, οὔτε ποτ' ὄμβρος,
> Ἀλλ' αἰεὶ ζεφύροιο λιγυπνείοντας ἀήτας
> Ὠκεανὸς ἀνίησιν, ἀναψύχειν ἀνθρώπους)·
> Οὕνεκ' ἔχεις Ἑλένην, καί σφιν γαμβρὸς Διός ἐσσι. [Vers 563-569.]

Pindare décrit amplement les Champs Élysiens, *ode* 2, et dit la même chose qu'Homère : Ἔνθα μακάρων νᾶσον ὠκεανίδες αὖραι περιπνέουσιν[1]. Mais j'ai remarqué qu'Homère n'en bannit pas tout à fait l'hiver, mais il dit qu'il n'y en a guère. Et il le dit avec raison, car l'hiver est absolument nécessaire pour faire cette diversité de saisons qui est beaucoup plus agréable qu'un printemps éternel, pourvu que le froid ou le chaud ne soient pas excessifs.

> Ὣς εἰπὼν, ὑπὸ πόντον ἐδύσατο κυμαίνοντα. [Vers 570.]

Hæc Proteus, et se jactu dedit æquor in altum[2].

Menelaüs achève son récit, et offre des présents à Telemachus, et surtout trois chevaux ; mais il le remercie de ses chevaux, et il dit qu'il les garde pour son plaisir (Horace, l. 1., *ep.* 7[3]) : Car vous régnez dans un pays où il y a abondance de souchet ou jonc (*cyperus*), d'orge, de blé et d'aveine ; mais à Ithaque il n'y a point de prés ni de lieu pour exercer les chevaux ; elle n'est bonne qu'aux chèvres, et avec tout cela elle en est plus agréable :

> Αἰγίβοτος, καὶ μᾶλλον ἐπήρατος ἱπποβότοιο. [Vers 606.]

---

1. Voyez ci-dessus, p. 20.
2. Virgile, *Géorgiques*, livre IV, vers 528.
3. Livre I, *épître* VII, vers 40-43. — Racine a mis par mégarde : *livre* 2, au lieu de *livre* 1.

Il dit cela par l'amour qu'on a pour la patrie. Aussi Menelaüs en rit, et lui promet d'autres présents, et même une coupe, qui est le plus beau meuble de son logis. Telemachus dit qu'au reste il demeureroit un an entier avec lui sans songer à son pays ni à ses parents, tant il se plaît à l'entendre; mais qu'il n'ose pas faire longtemps attendre sa compagnie, qui l'attend à Pyle.

Menelaüs lui dit:

Αἵματος εἶς ἀγαθοῖο, φίλον τέκος. [Vers 611.]

Homère laisse Telemachus chez Menelaüs jusqu'au retour d'Ulysse, et il revient au logis d'Ulysse, et décrit l'étonnement qu'eurent tous ces jeunes gens quand ils surent que Telemachus étoit parti. Homère fait qu'ils l'apprennent fort naturellement d'un d'entre eux, qui lui avoit apprêté son vaisseau : c'est Noémon, fils de Phronius, qui demande à Antinoüs s'il ne sait point quand il reviendra; et il dit qu'il a vu monter avec lui un guide qui étoit ou un dieu ou Mentor,

Μέντορα ἠὲ θεὸν, τῷ δ' αὐτῷ πάντα ἐῴκει. [Vers 654.]

Mais, dit-il, ce qui m'étonne, c'est que j'ai vu hier Mentor ici. Ils sont tous fort surpris, et cela leur fait quitter tous leurs jeux :

Μνηστῆρες δ' ἄμυδις κάθισαν, καὶ παῦσαν ἀέθλων. [Vers 659.]

Surtout Antinoüs enrage, et Homère dit bien cela :

Μένεος δὲ μέγα φρένες ἀμφιμέλαιναι
Πίμπλαντ', ὄσσε δέ οἱ πυρὶ λαμπετόωντι εἴκτην. [Vers 661 et 662.]

Il fait dessein d'aller au-devant et de le tuer, et ils louent tous ce dessein; mais un héraut qui étoit avec eux, nommé Médon, le découvre à Penelopé. Elle lui demande d'abord qu'est-ce que veulent ces jeunes gens : N'iront-ils jamais ailleurs, dit-elle, et n'ont-ils point de honte de manger tout ce qu'il y a ici? N'avez-vous pas appris de vos pères quel a été Ulysse, et avec quelle douceur il les a gouvernés, sans jamais maltraiter personne, ni d'action, ni de parole en public? Cependant les rois peuvent aimer et haïr qui bon leur semble :

Ἥτ' ἐστὶ δίκη θείων βασιλήων
Ἄλλον κ' ἐχθαίρῃσι βροτῶν, ἄλλον κε φιλοίη. [Vers 691 et 692.]

Ce n'est pas tout, dit Médon, ils veulent tuer votre fils à son retour de Pyle.

Elle, qui ne savoit pas seulement qu'il fût parti, tombe en foiblesse, et s'afflige pitoyablement, se jetant par terre et ne se voulant pas seoir sur des siéges, οἴκτρ' ὀλοφυρομένη[1]. Toutes ses femmes pleuroient aussi, mais tout bas, μινύριζον[2], pour montrer que ce n'étoit pas par une simple complaisance. Alors Penelopé fait des plaintes fort touchantes sur le malheur de sa maison, qui lui a fait perdre son mari, et bien plus son fils. Elle veut envoyer avertir Laërte, afin qu'il voie ce qu'il y a à faire; mais Euryclée lui dit qu'elle n'afflige pas à ce point ce bon vieillard :

Μηδὲ γέροντα κάκου κεκακωμένον. [Vers 754.]

Et elle lui raconte ce qui s'est passé entre Telemachus et elle. Cela la console; et se lavant les mains, et prenant une robe pure, καθαρὰ χροΐ εἵμαθ' ἑλοῦσα[3], elle fait une supplication à Pallas, dont elle est exaucée. Cependant ces jeunes gens font bruit, et quelques-uns croient que Penelopé s'apprête à se marier; mais ils étoient bien loin de leur compte. Antinoüs leur dit qu'ils exécutent leur dessein sans bruit et sans discours :

Δαιμόνιοι, μύθους μὲν ὑπερφιάλους ἀλέασθε. [Vers 774.]

Aussi Sénèque dit[4] : *Ira quæ tegitur nocet*. Ils préparent donc un vaisseau. Cependant Penelopé ne veut point manger, et songe toujours à son fils, tel qu'un lion songe, dans une foule de gens, pour se garder d'être enfermé. Elle s'endort, et Pallas lui envoie l'idole d'Iphthime, son amie, pour la con-

---

1. Vers 719. — 2. *Ibidem*.
3. Vers 759.
4. *Médée*, vers 153.

soler. Cet[1] idole lui dit de ne point craindre, et que son fils reviendra,

Οὐ μὲν γάρ τι θεοῖς ἀλιτήμενός ἐστιν. [Vers 807.]

Penelopé lui répond, à demi endormie, et rêvant à demi, ce qu'Homère dit fort bien : Dormant agréablement aux portes des songes :

Ἡδὺ μάλα κνώσσουσ' ἐν ὀνειρείῃσι πύλῃσι. [Vers 809.]

Comment, dit-elle, ne m'affliger point, n'ayant plus Ulysse, et voyant mon fils qui s'en est allé?

Οὔτε πόνων εὖ εἰδὼς, οὔτ' ἀγοράων. [Vers 818.]

L'idole lui dit qu'elle se rassure, et qu'il a pour guide Pallas; mais elle ne lui dit pas si son mari vit encore ou non :

Κακὸν δ' ἀνεμώλια βάζειν. [Vers 837.]

Les autres vont attendre Telemachus à Asteris, petite île entre Ithaque et Samos.

LIVRE V.

19 avril.

Homère revient à Ulysse, et laisse là sa femme et son fils. Les Dieux s'assemblent, et Pallas obtient son retour. Il commence par la description du matin :

Ἠὼς δ' ἐκ λεχέων παρ' ἀγαυοῦ Τιθωνοῖο
Ὤρνυθ'. [Vers 1 et 2.]

Pallas déplore la misère d'Ulysse, que Calypso tient captif. Jupiter envoie aussitôt Mercure dire à cette nymphe qu'elle le renvoie. Mercure part avec cet équipage qui lui est ordinaire. Voici comme Homère le dépeint :

Αὐτίκ' ἔπειθ' ὑπὸ ποσσὶν ἐδήσατο καλὰ πέδιλα,

---

1. Il y a *cet*, et non *cette*, dans le manuscrit. Voyez le *Lexique*.

Ἀμβρόσια, χρύσεια· τά μιν φέρον ἠμὲν ἐφ' ὑγρὴν,
Ἠδ' ἐπ' ἀπείρονα γαῖαν, ἅμα πνοιῇς ἀνέμοιο.
Εἵλετο δὲ ῥάβδον, τῇ τ' ἀνδρῶν ὄμματα θέλγει,
Ὧν ἐθέλει, τοὺς δ' αὖτε καὶ ὑπνώοντας ἐγείρει. [Vers 44-48.]

Et voici comme Virgile l'a traduit mot à mot au [livre] 4. de l'*Énéide*[1] :

Primum pedibus talaria nectit
Aurea, quæ sublimem alis, sive æquora supra,
Seu terram, rapido pariter cum flamine portant.
Tum virgam capit : hac animas ille evocat Orco
Pallentes, alias sub tristia Tartara mittit;
Dat somnos, adimitque, et lumina morte resignat.

Virgile a encore traduit la suite, et raconte, aux mêmes termes qu'Homère, de la façon que Mercure part du ciel : ils le comparent tous deux à un plongeon; mais Virgile a ajouté cette belle fiction du mont Atlas, où il le fait reposer :

Heic primum paribus nitens Cyllenius alis
Constitit; hinc toto præceps se corpore ad undas
Misit[2].

Il arrive dans l'île de Calypso :

Ἠπειρόνδε
Ἤϊεν· ὄφρα μέγα σπέος ἵκετο, τῷ ἔνι Νύμφη
Ναῖεν ἐϋπλόκαμος. [Vers 56-58.]

Cette île s'appelle autrement Ogygie; au moins Pline dit que plusieurs ont cru qu'Homère l'appeloit ainsi. *Calypso, quam Ogygiam appellasse Homerus existimatur*[3]. Elle est devers l'Italie, près des Locres, qui en sont une province. Ce qu'Homère appelle ici du mot de caverne n'en étoit pas une sans doute; mais c'étoit quelque grande grotte que la nature avoit faite, et que Calypso avoit ornée pour en faire son palais. Ainsi les nymphes de la mer logeoient véritablement dans des grottes, mais ces grottes étoient riches et comme enchan-

---

1. Vers 239-244.
2. *Énéide*, livre IV, vers 252-254.
3. Livre III, chapitre x. Le texte de Pline est : « *Altera Calypsus (insula), quam Ogygiam appellasse*, etc. »

tées, comme on peut voir au [livre] 4. des *Géorgiques*[1], où Virgile en fait la description. Celle de Calypso étoit bien agréable, si on croit Homère; car en voici la situation : Il y avoit, dit-il, tout autour de cette grotte une belle forêt pleine d'arbres verts, d'aune, de peuplier et de cyprès odoriférant; et là nichoient des oiseaux à grandes ailes, τανυσίπτεροι[2], ou qui volent les ailes étendues; il nomme des hiboux, des éperviers et des corneilles à la langue large, τανύγλωσσοί τε κορῶναι[3], et quelques oiseaux marins, ce qui montre que c'étoit un désert tout à fait retiré, et qui avoit quelque chose d'affreux : ce qui est agréable sans doute, quand cela est adouci par quelques autres objets, comme de la vigne, des fontaines et des prairies, qu'Homère y met encore :

Ἡ δ' αὐτοῦ τετάνυστο περὶ σπείους γλαφυροῖο
Ἡμερὶς ἡβώωσα, τεθήλει δὲ σταφυλῇσι.
Κρῆναι δ' ἑξείης πίσυρες ῥέον ὕδατι λευκῷ,
Πλησίαι ἀλλήλων τετραμμέναι ἄλλυδις ἄλλη.
Ἀμφὶ δὲ λειμῶνες μαλακοὶ ἴου ἠδὲ σελίνου
Θήλεον. [Vers 68-73.]

Σέλινον est ce qu'on appelle en latin *apium*, du persil; c'est une herbe de jardin, et qui n'est pas champêtre : ainsi ces prés-là doivent s'entendre aussi pour des jardins. Et on peut dire que cette belle île étoit en partie inculte et sauvage, et en partie cultivée, ce qui fait un beau mélange. Aussi il ajoute qu'un dieu même l'auroit admirée avec plaisir :

Ἔνθα κ' ἔπειτα καὶ ἀθάνατός περ ἐπελθὼν
Θηήσαιτο ἰδών, καὶ τερφθείη φρεσὶν ᾗσιν. [Vers 73 et 74.]

C'est ce que fit Mercure, et après l'avoir admirée tout son loisir, ἐπειδὴ πάντα ἑῷ θηήσατο θυμῷ[4], il entra dans la grotte de Calypso, et elle le reconnut aussitôt; car, dit-il, les Dieux se connoissent bien les uns les autres, quand ils demeureroient en des lieux fort éloignés. On peut appliquer cela aux personnes de condition, lesquelles ont d'ordinaire quelque marque avantageuse qui les fait reconnoître. Il ne treuva pas Ulysse; car il

---

1. Vers 363-374. — 2. Vers 65.
3. Vers 66. — 4. Vers 76.

étoit allé pleurer tout seul sur le bord de la mer. Homère le décrit admirablement :

Οὐδ' ἄρ' Ὀδυσσῆα μεγαλήτορα ἔνδον ἔτετμεν,
Ἀλλ' ὅγ' ἐπ' ἀκτῆς κλαῖε καθήμενος· ἔνθα, πάρος περ
Δάκρυσι καὶ στοναχῇσι καὶ ἄλγεσι θυμὸν ἐρέχθων,
Πόντον ἐπ' ἀτρύγετον δερκέσκετο, δάκρυα λείβων. [Vers 81-84.]

On ne peut pas mieux décrire un affligé. Il étoit assis, dit-il, sur le rivage de la mer, où il nourrissoit sa douleur de larmes, de gémissements et d'inquiétudes, versant des pleurs dans la mer, où il avoit les yeux toujours attachés. Il semble qu'on voit un homme qui cherche la solitude pour pleurer, et qui regarde la mer à cause de la passion qu'il a pour son retour. Ainsi Virgile dit des Troyennes, au [livre] 5. de l'*Énéide* :

*Cunctæque profundum
Pontum adspectabant flentes*[1].

Cependant la nymphe Calypso interroge Mercure qui l'avoit treuvée travaillant à une toile, et chantant avec une agréable voix; et il dit la même chose de Circé, livre X :

Κίρκης δ' ἔνδον ἄκουον ἀειδούσης ὀπὶ καλῇ
Ἱστὸν ἐποιχομένης μέγαν, ἄμβροτον· οἷα θεάων
Λεπτά τε καὶ χαρίεντα καὶ ἀγλαὰ ἔργα πέλονται[2],

faisant, dit-il, une grande toile, et incorruptible, tels que sont les ouvrages des Déesses, qui ne font rien que de délicat, d'agréable et d'éclatant. Il dit encore que de cette grotte sortoit une odeur de cèdre et de quelque autre bois odoriférant, qui brûloient dedans. Virgile a compris tout cela en ces trois vers, parlant de Circé :

*Assiduo resonat cantu, tectisque superbis
Urit odoratam nocturna in lumina cedrum,
Arguto tenues percurrens pectine telas*[3].

1. *Énéide*, livre V, vers 614 et 615.
2. *Odyssée*, livre X, vers 221-223.
3. *Énéide*, livre VII, vers 12-14.

Mais Homère ne dit pas que ce fût pour éclairer; car il dit que ce bois brûloit au foyer :

Πῦρ μὲν ἐπ' ἐσχαρόφιν μέγα καίετο, τήλοθι δ' ὀδμή, etc. [Vers 59.]

Il semble qu'Homère a voulu dire que cette île n'étoit habitée que de Calypso, car il ne parle point des habitants. Elle demande donc à Mercure ce qu'il veut : Car, dit-elle, vous ne veniez pas souvent ici. Elle le fait manger, et puis après il lui répond ainsi :

Εἰρωτᾷς μ' ἐλθόντα, θεὰ, θεόν. [Vers 97.]

Vous m'interrogez, dit-il, moi qui suis dieu, et vous déesse; c'est-à-dire vous savez bien ce que j'ai dans l'esprit; car, comme il a dit devant que les Dieux se connoissent bien les uns les autres :

Οὐ γάρ τ' ἀγνῶτές γε θεοὶ ἀλλήλοισι πέλονται [vers 79],

il veut dire ici qu'ils lisent chacun dans leurs pensées : c'est-à-dire, vous m'interrogez, moi qui lis dans votre âme, et vous qui lisez dans la mienne, et qui savez aussi bien que moi tout ce qui se passe entre les Dieux. Mais je vous le dirai pourtant, puisque Jupiter m'a donné cette commission bien malgré moi; car qui se plairoit à passer un si grand espace de mer, où il n'y a point d'hommes qui fassent des sacrifices? On diroit que les temples fussent autant d'hôtelleries pour les Dieux, et que pour cette raison c'est autant que si Mercure disoit qu'il n'a bu ni mangé depuis qu'il est parti du ciel. Mais, dit-il, il ne faut pas qu'aucun des Dieux ait la pensée de désobéir à Jupiter. On voit en plusieurs endroits de l'*Iliade* combien Jupiter étoit absolu, et comme Junon et Neptune son frère l'appréhendoient. Et ainsi on peut dire que l'empire des Dieux étoit monarchique[1].

Il lui dit donc que Jupiter veut qu'elle renvoie Ulysse. Cette parole la fait tressaillir, ῥίγησεν [vers 116], ce qui marque qu'elle aimoit beaucoup Ulysse.

---

1. Isocrate, *Nicocl.* Λέγεται καὶ τοὺς Θεοὺς ὑπὸ τοῦ Διὸς βασιλεύεσθαι. (*Note de Racine.*) — Voyez le *Nicoclès* d'Isocrate, chapitre VI, à la page 32 de l'édition d'Henri Estienne (1593).

En effet, elle répond que les Dieux sont inhumains et jaloux plus que personne, puisqu'ils ne veulent jamais souffrir que les Déesses aiment des hommes :

Σχέτλιοί ἐστε, Θεοὶ, ζηλήμονες ἔξοχον ἄλλων,
Οἵτε Θεαῖς ἀγάασθε παρ' ἀνδράσιν εὐνάζεσθαι
Ἀμφαδίην, ἥ τις τε φίλον ποιήσετ' ἀκοίτην. [Vers 118-120.]

Ainsi, dit-elle, quand l'Aurore prit Orion pour mari, vous lui portâtes envie, jusqu'à ce que la chaste Diane l'eût tué de ses flèches. Ainsi, quand Cérès aux beaux cheveux coucha avec Jason pour satisfaire son amour :

Ὦ θυμῷ εἴξασα, μίγη φιλότητι καὶ εὐνῇ [vers 126],

Jupiter ne fut pas longtemps sans en être averti, et le tua d'un coup de foudre. Vous êtes fâchés[1] tout de même que j'aie auprès de moi un homme que j'ai sauvé de la mort, lorsque Jupiter brûla son vaisseau, où tous ses compagnons périrent; car je le recueillis ici, et l'ai nourri avec grand soin, et l'ai aimé.

Τὸν μὲν ἐγὼ φίλεόν τε καὶ ἔτρεφον, ἠδὲ ἔφασκον
Θήσειν ἀθάνατον καὶ ἀγήραον ἤματα πάντα. [Vers 135 et 136.]

Mais puisqu'il n'est pas permis aux Dieux mêmes de désobéir à Jupiter, eh bien ! qu'il s'en aille; car pour le renvoyer je n'ai point de vaisseau, mais je l'assisterai de mes conseils. Mercure dit qu'elle fait bien, et s'envole aussitôt. Elle va chercher Ulysse, qu'elle treuve en cet état où il étoit, et qu'Homère décrit encore plus exactement :

Τὸν δ' ἄρ' ἐπ' ἀκτῆς εὗρε καθήμενον· οὐδέ ποτ' ὄσσε
Δακρυόφιν τέρσοντο· κατείβετο δὲ γλυκὺς αἰὼν
Νόστον ὀδυρομένῳ, ἐπεὶ οὐκέτι ἥνδανε Νύμφη.
Ἀλλ' ἤτοι νύκτας μὲν ἰαύεσκεν καὶ ἀνάγκῃ
Ἐν σπέσσι γλαφυροῖσι παρ' οὐκ ἐθέλων ἐθελούσῃ·
Ἤματα δ' ἐν πέτρῃσι καὶ ἠϊόνεσσι καθίζων [vers 151-156],

et le reste de ce qu'il a dit auparavant.

Ses yeux, dit-il, n'étoient jamais secs, et les plus beaux de

---

1. *Fâché*, sans accord, dans le manuscrit.

ses jours se consumoient à soupirer pour son retour : car la Nymphe ne lui pouvoit plaire, ou, comme je crois, la Nymphe n'agréoit pas son retour. Mais il passoit les nuits avec elle qui le vouloit, quoiqu'il ne le voulût pas, et il alloit pleurer tout le jour sur le rivage et sur des rochers. Calypso lui dit qu'il ne pleure plus, et qu'il se fasse un petit vaisseau de branches d'arbres, et qu'elle le pourvoira de tout ce qu'il lui faut. Ulysse tremble de peur, ῥίγησεν[1]; car il croit qu'elle lui prépare quelque autre mauvais tour, et il veut qu'elle lui jure le contraire. Calypso sourit,

Χειρί τε μιν κατέρεξεν, ἔπός τ' ἔφατ', ἔκ τ' ὀνόμαζεν·
ᾟ δὴ ἀλιτρός γ' ἐσσὶ, καὶ οὐκ ἀποφώλια εἰδώς. [Vers 181 et 182.]

Vous êtes un rusé, dit-elle, et il n'est pas aisé de vous tromper. Après elle le rassure, et jure même par le Styx[2], qui est, dit-elle, le plus grand et le plus terrible jurement des Dieux, qu'elle ne songe point à lui faire mal, mais qu'elle ne lui veut que ce qu'elle se voudroit à elle-même, si elle étoit dans une pareille extrémité :

Καὶ γὰρ ἐμοὶ νόος ἐστὶν ἐναίσιμος, οὐδέ μοι αὐτῇ
Θυμὸς ἐνὶ στήθεσσι σιδήρεος, ἀλλ' ἐλεήμων. [Vers 190 et 191.]

Après elle le ramène à sa grotte, et le fait asseoir sur le même siége d'où Mercure venoit de se lever. Elle le fait servir à table de viandes telles qu'en mangent les hommes.

Νύμφη δ' ἐτίθει πάρα πᾶσαν ἐδωδὴν,
Ἔσθειν καὶ πίνειν, οἷα βροτοὶ ἄνδρες ἔδουσιν. [Vers 196 et 197.]

Elle s'assit vis-à-vis de lui, et ses servantes lui servent l'ambrosie et le nectar. Cela montre que l'ambrosie n'étoit pas une viande dont les hommes pussent manger, parce qu'ils n'étoient pas immortels, et que la nature des Dieux étoit tout à fait différente de celle des hommes. C'est ce qu'on voit plus clairement dans ce bel endroit de la blessure de Vénus, au [livre] 5. de l'*Iliade*[3] ; car Homère dit qu'il n'en coula pas du sang, mais une certaine liqueur pareille au nectar, les

---

1. Vers 171. — 2. Racine écrit *Stix*.
3. Vers 334-343.

Dieux ne se nourrissant pas d'une nourriture commune aux hommes. Calypso lui dit alors : Ulysse, vous voulez donc vous en aller? faites ce que vous voudrez, mais assurez-vous que vous aurez bien à souffrir devant que d'arriver chez vous : au lieu que vous seriez ici à votre aise, et vous seriez immortel, quoique vous ayez tant d'envie de revoir votre femme, après qui vous soupirez tous les jours. Toutefois je ne crois point lui céder en rien, soit pour le corps, soit pour l'esprit ; car une femme mortelle ne disputeroit pas de la beauté et de la taille du corps avec des déesses. — Je sais tout cela, répond Ulysse, et que la sage Penelopé vous est beaucoup inférieure en beauté et en majesté, ou en riche taille :

Εἶδος ἀκιδνοτέρη μέγεθός τ' εἰς ἄντα ἰδέσθαι·
Ἡ μὲν γὰρ βροτός ἐστι, σὺ δ' ἀθάνατος καὶ ἀγήρως. [Vers 217 et 218.]

Avec tout cela, je souhaite passionnément de voir le jour de mon retour ; et s'il faut que je souffre, je souffrirai, ayant l'âme assez patiente ; car j'ai déjà beaucoup souffert, et je veux bien souffrir encore cela :

Τλήσομαι, ἐν στήθεσσιν ἔχων ταλαπενθέα θυμόν·
Ἤδη γὰρ μάλα πόλλ' ἔπαθον καὶ πόλλ' ἐμόγησα
Κύμασι καὶ πολέμῳ· μετὰ καὶ τόδε τοῖσι γενέσθω. [Vers 222-224.]

On voit là un beau caractère d'un esprit fort et résolu qui ne craint point les traverses. Le soleil se couche, et alors se retirant tous deux au fond de la grotte,

Τερπέσθην φιλότητι, παρ' ἀλλήλοισι μένοντε. [Vers 227.]

Dès le matin Ulysse s'habille, et Calypso lui met elle-même de fort beaux habits ; puis elle lui donne une hache à manche d'olivier, une scie, et le mène en un endroit de l'île où il y avoit force[1] arbres secs, qu'il coupe pour en faire son vaisseau. Calypso lui donne encore un vilebrequin et des clous, tant Homère est exact à décrire les moindres particularités :

---

1. Racine a écrit *forces*. C'était une faute alors comme aujourd'hui. Nous l'aurions attribuée ici à une simple distraction, si nous ne l'avions retrouvée quelques pages plus loin, et dans les lettres que Racine écrivait à peu près dans le même temps.

ce qui a bonne grâce dans le grec, au lieu que le latin est beaucoup plus réservé, et ne s'amuse pas à de si petites choses. La langue sans doute est plus stérile, et n'a pas des mots qui expriment si heureusement les choses que la langue grecque ; car on diroit qu'il n'y a rien de bas dans le grec, et les plus viles choses y sont noblement exprimées. Il en va de même de notre langue que de la latine ; car elle fuit extrêmement de s'abaisser aux particularités, parce que les oreilles sont délicates et ne peuvent souffrir qu'on nomme des choses basses dans un discours sérieux, comme une coignée, une scie et un vilebrequin. L'italien, au contraire, ressemble au grec, et exprime tout, comme on peut voir dans l'Arioste, qui est en son genre un caractère tel que celui d'Homère.

Enfin Ulysse bâtit adroitement son vaisseau ; et on apprend de là qu'il n'est point messéant à un grand homme de savoir faire les plus petites choses, parce que la nécessité les rend souvent très-importantes, comme en cette occasion, où vraisemblablement Ulysse n'auroit pu sortir de cette île déserte, s'il n'eût su lui-même se faire un vaisseau aussi bien que le plus habile charpentier du monde, comme dit Homère. Il travailla durant trois jours, et au quatrième tout fut fait, et le monta en mer avec des leviers, μοχλοῖσιν[1]. Tout le bâtiment de ce vaisseau est décrit par le menu. Calypso le pourvoit de vivres et lui envoie un vent favorable ; et il part et met les voiles au vent. Il s'assit sur la poupe, et gouverne adroitement le timon, sans souffrir que le sommeil lui fermât les yeux, observant les Pléiades, et le Boote, qui se couche tard, et l'Ourse, qu'on appelle le Chariot, qui est là auprès, et qui regarde l'Orion, et qui est la seule qui ne se mouille point dans les eaux de l'Océan. Il navigua sept jours durant, et au huitième il aperçut la terre de Phéaque, qui paroissoit de loin, sur cette mer obscure, sous la forme d'un bouclier. Mais par malheur, comme Junon dans Virgile[2], Neptune le voit en revenant d'Éthiopie, par terre sans doute, car il le vit de la montagne de Solyme.

Et comme il étoit fort irrité contre lui à cause qu'il avoit

1. Vers 261.
2. *Énéide*, livre I, vers 34 et suivants.

aveuglé Polyphème son fils, il se fâche fort, et le veut persécuter devant qu'il arrive aux Phéaques, où le destin vouloit qu'il se sauvât. Aussitôt il amasse les nues et frappe la mer avec son trident, excitant toutes les tempêtes, et couvrant de nuages la mer et la terre :

> Ὀρώρει δ' οὐρανόθεν νύξ·
> Σὺν δ' Εὖρός τε Νότος τ' ἔπεσε, Ζέφυρός τε δυσαὴς,
> Καὶ Βορέης αἰθρηγενέτης, μέγα κῦμα κυλίνδων. [Vers 294-296.]

Pline a remarqué[1] qu'Homère n'admettoit que ces quatre vents, et que l'antiquité n'en connoissoit point davantage. Il dit que depuis quelques-uns en ajoutèrent huit ; mais il dit que la meilleure opinion est celle qui les réduit au nombre de huit, dont voici les noms. Il y en a deux dans chacune des quatre parties du ciel. *Ab oriente æquinoctiali Subsolanus, ab oriente brumali Vulturnus : illum Apeliotem, hunc Eurum Græci nominant. A meridie Auster seu Notus, et ab occasu brumali Africus.... Ab occasu æquinoctiali Favonius sive Zephyrus, ab occasu solstitiali Corus.... A septentrionibus Septentrio, interque eum et exortum solstitialem Aquilo, Aparctias dicti et Boreas*[2]. Quoi qu'il en soit, Virgile a suivi Homère en cet endroit, l. 1. de l'*Énéide :*

> *Una Eurusque Notusque ruunt, creberque procellis*
> *Africus*[3],

et nomme peu après le Zéphyre,

> *Eurum ad se Zephyrumque vocat*[4].

Il l'a aussi copié dans la suite :

> Καὶ τότ' Ὀδυσσῆος λύτο γούνατα καὶ φίλον ἦτορ·
> Ὀχθήσας δ' ἄρα εἶπε πρὸς ὃν μεγαλήτορα θυμόν. [Vers 297 et 298.]
>
> *Extemplo Æneæ solvuntur frigore membra;*
> *Ingemit*[5].

---

1. Livre II, chapitre XLVII.
2. Nous donnons ce passage de Pline tel que Racine l'a écrit.
3. *Énéide*, livre I, vers 85 et 86.
4. *Ibidem*, vers 131.
5. *Ibidem*, vers 92.

Τρὶς μάκαρες Δαναοὶ καὶ τετράκις, οἳ τότ' ὄλοντο
Τροίῃ ἐν εὐρείῃ, χάριν Ἀτρείδῃσι φέροντες. [Vers 306 et 307.]

O terque quaterque beati
Queis ante ora patrum Trojæ sub mœnibus altis
Contigit oppetere [1] *!*

Car, dit-il, il faut que je meure maintenant d'une mort sans honneur :

Νῦν δέ με λευγαλέῳ θανάτῳ εἵμαρτο ἁλῶναι. [Vers 312.]

Il dit qu'un vent le vint pousser avec violence, lorsqu'il faisoit ces plaintes.

Talia jactanti [2], etc.

Mais Ulysse tombe loin de sa frégate, et revient à grand peine dessus les eaux.

Mais quoiqu'il fût noyé d'eau, il n'oublia pas sa frégate :

Ἀλλ' οὐδ' ὣς σχεδίης ἐπελήθετο, τειρόμενός περ [vers 324],

mais il remonta dessus, τέλος θανάτου ἀλεείνων [3]. On fuit toujours tant qu'on peut le dernier passage de la mort, et on ne se rend qu'à l'extrémité.

Τὴν δ' ἐφόρει μέγα κῦμα κατὰ ῥόον ἔνθα καὶ ἔνθα. [Vers 327.]

Il décrit l'agitation de ce petit vaisseau, qu'il compare à des petites ronces qu'un vent d'automne promène par les campagnes, et qui se roulent l'une avec l'autre. Ainsi, dit-il, les vents promenoient ce vaisseau :

Ἄλλοτε μέν τε Νότος Βορέῃ προβάλεσκε φέρεσθαι,
Ἄλλοτε δ' αὖτ' Εὖρος Ζεφύρῳ εἴξασκε διώκειν. [Vers 331 et 332.]

On peut appliquer cela à une ville ou à une république agitée de plusieurs partis, comme a fait Horace dans l'ode qui commence : *O navis, referent in mare te novi Fluctus* [4].

Mais Ino Leucothée, fille de Cadmus, καλλίσφυρος [5], aux beaux talons, eut pitié d'Ulysse, et mit la tête hors de l'eau,

---

1. *Énéide*, livre I, vers 94-96. — 2. *Ibidem*, vers 102.
3. Vers 326. — 4. Livre I, *ode* xiv. — 5. Vers 333.

et même se vint asseoir dans son vaisseau. Elle lui dit de se mettre en nage jusqu'au port des Phéaques, et lui donne un ruban de sa tête pour le soutenir; elle rentre après dans la mer. Ulysse prend cela pour une tentation de quelque dieu ennemi, et se résout de demeurer dans son vaisseau tant qu'il pourra. Mais Neptune pousse contre[1] un flot violent, horrible ; et comme un grand [vent] dissipe un monceau de paille, qu'il fait voler çà et là, aussi tous les ais de ce vaisseau se dissipent. Et alors Ulysse se dépouille, et étendant sous sa poitrine ce ruban, il se met à nage, χεῖρε πετάσσας[2]. Neptune, le voyant en cet état, se croit assez vengé, et chasse ses chevaux vers Ægues, où il avoit un temple. Mais Pallas, qui craignoit la présence de son oncle, vient alors au secours d'Ulysse, bouche le chemin des autres vents, et les fait demeurer coi, et permet au seul Boréas de souffler et de fendre les flots, afin qu'Ulysse les puisse traverser. Il est deux jours entiers à nager et à voir toujours la mort devant les yeux :

Πολλὰ δέ οἱ κραδίη προτιόσσετ' ὄλεθρον. [Vers 389.]

Au troisième[3], il aperçoit la terre à grand peine, et en s'élevant de dessus les flots.

Ὡς δ' ὅταν ἀσπάσιος βίοτος παίδεσσι φανείη
Πατρὸς, ὃς ἐν νούσῳ κεῖται κρατέρ' ἄλγεα πάσχων,
Δηρὸν τηκόμενος, στυγερὸς δέ οἱ ἔχραε δαίμων,
Ἀσπάσιον δ' ἄρα τόν γε θεοὶ κακότητος ἔλυσαν·
Ὡς Ὀδυσῆ' ἀσπαστὸν ἐείσατο γαῖα καὶ ὕλη. [Vers 394-398.]

Cette comparaison est tout à fait belle et bien naturelle, car il n'est rien de plus doux que de voir revenir un père d'une longue maladie, où sa vie étoit désespérée, tout de même que de voir le port après la tempête. Aussi il se hâte tant qu'il peut de nager; mais quand il est un peu avancé, il entend un bruit impétueux et voit que c'est de l'eau qui bat contre des rochers escarpés, au lieu du port qu'il pensoit trouver. Alors

---

1. Racine a-t-il oublié d'écrire le complément de la préposition, ou a-t-il employé absolument l'expression *pousse contre?*
2. Vers 374.
3. Racine a écrit : « au 3ᵉ, » c'est-à-dire *au troisième jour.* M. Aimé-Martin a mis : « Au troisième livre. »

il perd courage et se plaint misérablement, reconnoissant bien que Neptune est irrité contre lui ; et une vague l'alloit pousser contre ce rocher, où il eût été brisé sans doute, si Pallas ne lui eût mis dans l'esprit de se prendre des mains à ce rocher, et de s'y tenir jusqu'à ce que la vague se fût brisée : ce qu'il fait, et Homère le dit admirablement :

Ἀμφοτέρῃσι δὲ χερσὶν ἐπεσσύμενος λάβε πέτρης,
Τῆς ἔχετο στενάχων, εἵως μέγα κῦμα παρῆλθε. [Vers 428 et 429.]

On diroit qu'on le voit attaché avec les ongles à ce rocher ; mais le reflux de la vague l'arrache de là, et l'emporte bien loin dans la mer. Toute la peau de ses mains s'en va en lambeaux, comme, quand un poulpe est retiré de sa coquille, une infinité de petites pierres s'attachent à ses bras. C'est un poisson dont la peau est tendre et qui a plusieurs pieds : *polypus*. Et alors le pauvre Ulysse étoit perdu, si Pallas ne lui eût inspiré de sortir de l'eau où il étoit plongé, et de suivre la vague qui se fendoit du côté du rivage. Et il arrive à l'embouchure d'un fleuve qui se déchargeoit dans la mer, et où on pouvoit prendre terre. Ulysse lui fait cette prière :

Κλῦθι, ἄναξ, ὅς τ' ἐσσί· πολύλλιστος δέ σ' ἱκάνω,
Φεύγων ἐκ πόντοιο Ποσειδάωνος ἐνιπάς.
Αἰδοῖος μέν τ' ἐστὶ καὶ ἀθανάτοισι Θεοῖσιν,
Ἀνδρῶν ὅστις ἵκηται ἀλώμενος.... [Vers 445-448.]

C'est ce que Sénèque a traduit dans les vers qu'il fit durant son exil, en ces mots : *Res est sacra miser*[1]. Et ce sentiment est d'autant plus beau qu'il est imprimé dans les cœurs par la nature même. Ainsi, dit Ulysse, je viens à vos eaux et à vos genoux : à vos eaux, σόν τε ῥόον, comme à un fleuve, σά τε γούνατ' [vers 449], comme à un dieu. Et ainsi on peut traiter les fleuves d'une et d'autre façon.

Ἀλλ' ἐλέαιρε, ἄναξ, ἱκέτης δέ τοι εὔχομαι εἶναι. [Vers 450.]

On révéroit les suppliants, et on ne permettoit pas qu'on

---

[1]. Voyez dans la collection Lemaire, au tome IV des *OEuvres philosophiques de Sénèque*, la IVe des épigrammes qui lui sont attribuées. Dans les anciennes éditions ces épigrammes sont intitulées : *Epigrammata super exilio*.

les touchât. Cela se voit partout dans l'histoire, soit aux asiles, soit aux temples, soit aux palais, soit aux statues des princes. Aussi, dit Homère, ce fleuve arrêta son cours et retint ses flots, rendant tout paisible afin qu'il se poussât à bord, ce qu'il fait. Et alors il plie les deux genoux et laisse aller ses mains robustes.

Ἁλὶ γὰρ δέδμητο φίλον κῆρ,
Ὤδεε δὲ χρόα πάντα. [Vers 454 et 455.]

Et l'eau de la mer, θάλασσα πολλή [vers 455], lui couloit par le nez et par la bouche,

Ὁ δ' ἄπνευστος καὶ ἄναυδος
Κεῖτ' ὀλιγηπελέων· κάματος δέ μιν αἰνὸς ἵκανεν. [Vers 456 et 457.]

A la fin, il revient à lui et jette le ruban d'Ino dans le fleuve, comme elle lui avoit commandé; le fleuve emporte ce ruban dans la mer, et la Nymphe le vient reprendre. La fiction de ce ruban est tout à fait belle ; car il est vraisemblable que ce ruban ou ce linge, qui couvroit la tête d'une déesse marine, pouvoit soutenir un homme sur l'eau, et cela donne [à] Homère le moyen de faire paroître Ulysse dans toutes ces extrémités où on croit toujours qu'il va périr : ce qui suspend l'esprit et fait un fort bel effet. Aussi rien ne peut être mieux décrit qu'Ulysse flottant entre la vie et la mort, trois jours durant, comme il fait. Il ne sait ici s'il doit passer la nuit dans le fleuve, dont il craint la fraîcheur trop grande, ou dans un bois tout proche, où il a peur des bêtes farouches, qui pourroient le surprendre en dormant. Néanmoins il choisit le dernier, et va dans ce bois, et treuve deux arbres, l'un d'olivier sauvage, et l'autre d'olivier, tous deux nés d'un même endroit, et si étroitement serrés qu'ils ne pouvoient être pénétrés ni par le souffle des vents, ni par le soleil, ni par la pluie :

Τοὺς μὲν ἄρ' οὔτ' ἀνέμων διάει μένος ὑγρὸν ἀέντων,
Οὐδέ ποτ' ἠέλιος φαέθων ἀκτῖσιν ἔβαλλεν,
Οὔτ' ὄμβρος περάασκε διαμπερές· ὣς ἄρα πυκνοὶ
Ἀλλήλοισιν ἔφυν ἐπαμοιβαδίς. [Vers 478-481.]

Là il dresse un lit de feuilles en grande abondance, et assez même pour couvrir trois hommes dans le plus grand froid de l'hiver. Il se couche dessus, et se couvre avec quantité de ces feuilles, comme un tison caché sous la cendre en quelque maison écartée :

Ὡς δ' ὅτε τις δαλὸν σποδιῇ ἐνέκρυψε μελαίνῃ,
Ἀγροῦ ἐπ' ἐσχατιῆς, ᾧ μὴ πάρα γείτονες ἄλλοι,
Σπέρμα πυρὸς σώζων.... [Vers 488-490.]

Pallas l'endort,

Ἵνα μιν παύσειε τάχιστα
Δυσπονέος καμάτοιο, φίλα βλέφαρ' ἀμφικαλύψας. [Vers 492 et 493.]

LIVRE VI.

Tandis qu'il dort, Minerve s'en va à la ville des Phéaques. C'est une île autrement dite Corfou, *Corcyra*, sur la mer Ionie, entre l'Épire et la Calabre. Elle s'appeloit encore Schérie; mais les Phéaques, qui logeoient auparavant près des Cyclopes, dont ils étoient tourmentés, vinrent, sous la conduite de Nausithoüs, habiter cette île. Nausithoüs s'appeloit autrement Phéax, et étoit fils d'une nymphe nommée Phéacie, fille d'Asope, que Neptune engrossa[1]. Il avoit bâti une ville, dit Homère, dressé des temples aux Dieux et divisé les terres à chacun. Après quoi il mourut; et son fils Alcinoüs régnoit présentement. Homère dit que ce peuple étoit loin des peuples ingénieux :

Ἑκὰς ἀνδρῶν ἀλφηστάων. [Vers 8.]

Cependant il les représente pour les plus ingénieux hommes du monde. Ils ne recevoient point les étrangers chez eux que pour les renvoyer en leur pays quand l'orage les avoit jetés contre leur côte : ce qu'ils faisoient charitablement, comme ils firent à Ulysse; mais ils n'étoient adroits que de la main et pour les exercices du corps, car c'étoit un proverbe parmi

---

1. Racine avait écrit *engrossit :* voyez ci-dessus, p. 28, note 2. Dans le manuscrit on a corrigé *engrossit* en *engrossa*. Mais la correction, qui laisse encore parfaitement distinguer les lettres *it*, n'est sans doute pas de la main de Racine.

les Grecs et dans Platon[1] : *Alcinoï apologus*, pour des contes à perte de vue, à cause de ceux qu'Ulysse leur fait, se jouant d'eux comme d'hommes grossiers. Néanmoins il y a trois ou quatre personnages qui n'étoient pas bêtes, de la manière qu'ils sont ici dépeints : tels qu'Alcinoüs, sa femme Arété, sa fille Nausicaa, un musicien et quelques vieillards. Minerve va donc chez Alcinoüs lorsque tout le monde étoit couché, et vient dans la chambre de Nausicaa :

Βῆ δ' ἴμεν ἐς θάλαμον πολυδαίδαλον, ᾧ ἔνι κούρη
Κοιμᾶτ' Ἀθανάτῃσι φυὴν καὶ εἶδος ὁμοίη [vers 15 et 16],

et auprès d'elle deux servantes belles comme les Grâces :

Πὰρ δὲ δύ' ἀμφίπολοι, Χαρίτων ἄπο κάλλος ἔχουσαι [vers 18] ;

car les Grâces étoient les servantes de Vénus. Elles étoient donc couchées contre la porte, qui étoit bien fermée ; mais Minerve entra dedans, comme le souffle du vent, et parut à Nausicaa sous la figure d'une de ses compagnes. Elle lui dit qu'elle est bien négligente de laisser là ses beaux habits sans les laver ; cependant on vous mariera bientôt, et alors il faut que vous soyez bien vêtue, car cela est honorable, et cela réjouit le père et la mère :

Ἐκ γάρ τοι τούτων φάτις ἀνθρώπους ἀναβαίνει
Ἐσθλή · χαίρουσιν δὲ πατὴρ καὶ πότνια μήτηρ. [Vers 29 et 30.]

Allez donc demain les laver et demandez un chariot à votre père, car les bains sont éloignés. Elle disoit cela pour faire en sorte qu'Ulysse, qui étoit tout nu, eût quelques habits, et parût honnêtement devant Alcinoüs ; car elle lui dit de laver aussi les habits de ses frères, qui la doivent mener aux noces. Aussitôt Minerve s'en retourne au ciel empyrée, qu'Homère décrit ainsi[2] :

1. *République*, livre X, au commencement du mythe d'Er l'Arménien.
2. Sur un des feuillets de son manuscrit, qui précède les remarques sur le livre V, Racine a écrit la note suivante : « Description du ciel par Homère, p. 65. (*C'est à la page 65 du manuscrit que se trouvent les mots :* « ciel empyrée, » *auxquels cette note de Racine se rapporte.*) Plutarque dit à ce sujet, dans la *Vie de Périclès :* « Les

Ἀπέβη γλαυκῶπις Ἀθήνη
Οὔλυμπόνδ', ὅθι φασὶ Θεῶν ἕδος ἀσφαλὲς αἰεὶ
Ἔμμεναι, οὔτ' ἀνέμοισι τινάσσεται, οὔτε ποτ' ὄμβρῳ
Δεύεται, οὔτε χιὼν ἐπιπίλναται· ἀλλὰ μάλ' αἴθρη
Πέπταται ἀννέφελος, λευκὴ δ' ἐπιδέδρομεν αἴγλη·
Τῷ ἔνι τέρπονται μάκαρες Θεοὶ ἤματα πάντα. [Vers 41-46.]

Aussitôt l'Aurore paroît dans son beau char : ἔΰθρονος[1]. Nausicaa admire son songe, et pour l'exécuter elle vient treuver sa mère et son père : l'une étoit auprès du feu, avec ses servantes, filant des laines de pourpre, et l'autre s'en alloit à l'assemblée avec les principaux des Phéaciens. Dès qu'elle [le] voit, elle lui tient ce discours, qui est tout à fait naïf et propre à une jeune fille. Elle l'appelle son papa, quoiqu'elle fût déjà à marier :

Πάππα φίλ', οὐκ ἂν δή μοι ἐφοπλίσσειας ἀπήνην
Ὑψηλήν, εὔκυκλον. [Vers 57 et 58.]

Il semble qu'elle commande, mais il faut imputer cela à l'affection des pères pour leurs enfants. Elle lui dit donc :

« poëtes mettent nos esprits en trouble et en confusion par leurs
« folles fictions, lesquelles se contredisent à elles-mêmes, attendu
« qu'ils appellent le ciel où les Dieux habitent, séjour très-assuré,
« et qui point ne tremble, et n'est point agité des vents, ni of-
« fusqué des nuées, ains est toujours doux et serein, et en tout
« temps également éclairé d'une lumière pure et nette, comme
« étant telle habitation propre et conuenable à la nature souuerai-
« nement heureuse et immortelle. Et puis ils les décriuent eux-
« mêmes pleins de dissensions et inimitiés, de courroux et autres
« passions, qui ne conuiennent pas seulement à hommes sages et de
« bon entendement. » Il dit cela sur le nom d'*Olympien* qui fut
donné à Périclès à cause de son éloquence, et dit qu'il le méritoit
bien mieux pour avoir toujours conservé ses mains pures de sang,
ce qui lui fit dire en mourant qu'aucun Athénien n'avoit porté
le deuil à son occasion; et ce sentiment de Plutarque est parfaitement beau. » — Racine s'est servi de la traduction d'Amyot : voyez le tome I, p. 308, de l'édition des *Vies des hommes illustres* (2 volumes in-8º, à Lauzanne, par Jean le Preux, MDLXXII). Le passage cité est à la fin de la *Vie de Périclès*.

1. Vers 48.

Vous voulez que vos habits soient bien propres quand vous paroissez en public. Tout de même j'ai cinq frères qui sont bien aises quand ils vont au bal d'avoir des habits honnêtes ; j'ai soin de tout cela, dit-elle ; car elle n'ose pas nommer le nom du mariage :

Ὡς ἔφατ'· αἴδετο γὰρ θαλερὸν γάμον ἐξονομῆναι
Πατρὶ φίλῳ· ὁ δὲ πάντα νόει. [Vers 66 et 67.]

Mais il se douta bien de tout, et commanda qu'on lui attelât un chariot, ce qui est exécuté, et sa mère lui met des viandes dans une corbeille, et du vin dans une peau de chèvre, et lui donne aussi de l'huile dans une lampe d'or, afin qu'elle se frottât elle et ses servantes. Elle monte sur le chariot, prend[1] les rênes et le fouet ; ses mulets courent aussitôt, et elle arrive aux bains, où ses servantes laissent paître les chevaux le long du rivage. Cependant elles lavent tous leurs habits dans le bain, qui étoit de l'eau du fleuve, et après les étendent au soleil sur le gravier du rivage. Elles se lavent et se frottent d'huile, et dînent ensuite. Après elles jouent à la balle ; c'est comme aujourd'hui à la raquette : elle jetoit une balle, et c'étoit à qui la retiendroit. Cependant on chantoit, et il semble que l'on jouât à la cadence ; car il dit que Nausicaa commença la chanson, et il la compare à Diane. Telle qu'est Diane, dit-il, qui se plaît aux flèches sur une montagne, ou sur le haut Taygète ou sur l'Érymanthe, se plaisant à poursuivre les chevreuils et les biches légères. Et autour d'elle les Nymphes champêtres, filles de Jupiter, se jouent :

Τῇ δέ θ' ἅμα Νύμφαι, κοῦραι Διὸς αἰγιόχοιο
Ἀγρονόμοι παίζουσι· γέγηθε δέ τε φρένα Λητώ·
Πασάων δ' ὑπὲρ ἥγε κάρη ἔχει ἠδὲ μέτωπα,
Ῥεῖα δ' ἀριγνώτη πέλεται, καλαὶ δέ τε πᾶσαι. [Vers 105-108.]

Voilà la traduction de Virgile, au [livre] 1. de l'*Énéide*[2] :

Qualis in Eurotæ ripis aut per juga Cynthi
Exercet Diana choros : quam mille secutæ
Hinc atque hinc glomerantur Oreades ; illa pharetram

---

1. Racine par mégarde a écrit : *prenne*, au lieu de *prend*.
2. Vers 498-503.

Fert humero, gradiensque Deas supereminet omnes;
Latonæ tacitum pertentant gaudia pectus :
Talis erat Dido.

Il faut que ce soit de cet endroit que parle Pline, p. 630 : [*Apelles*] *pinxit Dianam sacrificantium virginum choro mistam, quibus vicisse Homeri versus videtur idipsum describentis*[1].

Ὡς ἥγ' ἀμφιπόλοισι μετέπρεπε παρθένος ἀδμής. [Vers 109.]

Mais lorsqu'elle étoit prête à s'en aller, Minerve, voulant qu'Ulysse s'éveillât et qu'il vît cette belle fille, εὐώπιδα κούρην[2], afin qu'elle le conduisît à la ville, s'avisa de cette invention. La princesse jeta la balle à ses servantes; mais elle les manqua, et la balle tomba dans le fleuve. Ces filles firent un grand cri, et Ulysse s'éveilla. Il songe d'abord en quel pays il est venu : il ne sait s'il est parmi des barbares et des insolents, ou des hommes civils aux étrangers et craignant Dieu. Il ne sait non plus s'il a ouï la voix des Nymphes ou de quelques filles. Pour s'en éclaircir, il va droit à elles, et arrache quelques branches pour couvrir sa nudité.

Il s'en va vers elles comme un lion farouche, ὀρεσίτροφος[3], et hardi, ἀλκὶ πεποιθώς, qui, après avoir enduré le vent et la pluie, s'en va tout furieux chercher à manger :

Ὅστ' εἶσ' ὑόμενος καὶ ἀήμενος· ἐν δέ οἱ ὄσσε
Δαίεται· αὐτὰρ ὁ βουσὶν ἐπέρχεται, ἠδ' ὀίεσσιν,
Ἡὲ μετ' ἀγροτέρας ἐλάφους· κέλεται δέ ἑ γαστὴρ,
Μήλων πειρήσοντα καὶ ἐς πυκινὸν δόμον ἐλθεῖν. [Vers 131-134.]

Ainsi vint Ulysse parmi ces filles, tout nu qu'il étoit, car la nécessité l'y forçoit; mais il leur parut terrible, étant tout couvert de l'écume de la mer. Et elles s'enfuirent toutes, qui deçà, qui delà, le long de la rivière. La seule Nausicaa demeura ferme :

---

1. Livre XXXV, chapitre x (dans d'autres éditions, chapitre xxxvi). La page indiquée par Racine nous fait connoître l'édition dont il s'est servi : c'est l'édition in-folio de Lyon, MDLIII.
2. Vers 113. — 3. Vers 130.

Τῇ γὰρ Ἀθήνη
Θάρσος ἐνὶ φρεσὶ θῆκε, καὶ ἐκ δέος εἵλετο γυίων·
Στῆ δ' ἄντα σχομένη. [Vers 139-141.]

Car c'est une marque d'un esprit bien né de n'être point si timide ; et c'est ce que Barclay exprime fort bien en la personne du petit Polyarque, qui étoit avec une troupe d'enfants de son âge. J'ai oublié les paroles ; c'est vers les derniers livres[1]. Ainsi, au [livre] 8. de l'*Énéide*, Pallas, fils d'Évandre, vient hardiment, *audax*[2], au-devant d'Énée. Ulysse doute s'il doit embrasser ses genoux ou s'il lui fera de loin un discours flatteur et obligeant, afin qu'elle lui donne quelque habit. Ce dernier avis lui semble plus honnête, craignant que cette belle fille ne se fâchât s'il lui alloit embrasser les genoux.

Αὐτίκα μειλίχιον καὶ κερδαλέον φάτο μῦθον. [Vers 148.]

En effet cette harangue est une des plus belles pièces d'Homère et des plus galantes. Elle est tout à fait propre à un esprit délicat et adroit comme Ulysse, pour gagner quelque crédit auprès de cette belle inconnue.

La voici :

Γουνοῦμαί σε, ἄνασσα· θεός νύ τις, ἢ βροτός ἐσσι.
Εἰ μέν τις θεός ἐσσι, τοὶ οὐρανὸν εὐρὺν ἔχουσιν,
Ἀρτέμιδί σε ἔγωγε, Διὸς κούρῃ μεγάλοιο,
Εἶδός τε μέγεθός τε φυήν τ' ἄγχιστα ἐΐσκω. [Vers 149-152.]

Voici comme Virgile l'a imité, [livre] 1. *Én.*[3] :

O! quam te memorem, virgo? namque haud tibi vultus

---

1. L'ouvrage de Barclay qui avait laissé à Racine ce souvenir est, comme on sait, l'*Argenis*. Le passage, dont il ne se rappelait pas les paroles textuelles, est au livre IV. Les voici : *Video puerorum aliquot chorum, intra se simplici temeritate ludentium. Propius ego accessi, si illo forte cœtu itineris mei causam* (Polyarchum) *offenderem.... Non auctore, non indice illic opus. Tot heroum scilicet stirpem satis efficax natura monstravit. Alii rustico vel puerili metu diffugiunt, aut timide, pectore toto aversi, me reflexis intuentur cervicibus. Restitit ille, nihil territus inassueti hominis vultu.* (Io. Barclaii Argenis, Amstelodami, ex officina Elzeviriana, anno M.DC.LIX, p. 372.)

2. Vers 110. — 3. *Énéide*, livre I, vers 327-329.

Mortalis, nec vox hominem sonat : o dea certe;
An Phœbi soror, an Nympharum sanguinis una?

Mais comme il n'y avoit guère d'apparence que ce fût une déesse, Ulysse se contente d'en douter, et la cajole comme fille ; car il ne faut pas que les louanges soient excessives, et il vaut mieux dire à un homme qu'il est un grand homme que de lui dire qu'il est un dieu ; car le dernier passe pour une pure flatterie.

Εἰ δέ τίς ἐσσι βροτῶν, τοὶ ἐπὶ χθονὶ ναιετάουσι,
Τρισμάκαρες μέν σοί γε πατὴρ καὶ πότνια μήτηρ,
Τρισμάκαρες δὲ κασίγνητοι· μάλα πού σφισι θυμὸς
Αἰὲν ἐϋφροσύνῃσιν ἰαίνεται, εἵνεκα σεῖο,
Λευσσόντων τοιόνδε θάλος χορὸν εἰσοιχνεῦσαν.
Κεῖνος δ' αὖ περὶ κῆρι μακάρτατος ἔξοχον ἄλλων,
Ὅς κέ σ' ἐέδνοισι βρίσας οἶκόνδ' ἀγάγηται. [Vers 153-159.]

Cette expression est tout à fait belle. Ah! dit-il, quelle joie pour vos parents, lorsqu'ils voient une si belle fille paroître dans la danse comme une fleur qui brille par-dessus toutes les autres[1]! car c'est là que la beauté éclate, chacune ayant soin de se parer. Mais plus heureux, dit-il, celui qui vous épousera, en vous chargeant d'une dot immense! pour dire qu'elle méritoit beaucoup : Car, dit-il, je n'ai encore rien vu de si beau, ni homme ni femme, et je suis saisi de vénération :

Σέβας μ' ἔχει εἰσορόωντα. [Vers 161.]

Telle ai-je vu une jeune plante de laurier qui croissoit auprès de l'autel d'Apollon à Délos, il n'y a pas longtemps ; car j'ai été là, et j'étois suivi de beaucoup de peuple dans ce voyage, qui m'a tant coûté de maux. Il marque en passant qu'il est une personne de conséquence, afin qu'elle l'écoute mieux. J'admirai, dit-il, ce beau rejeton, et je le regardai longtemps, car je n'en avois point vu sortir de terre un si beau ; et je vous admire tout de même, et n'ose pas m'appro-

---

1. Racine a écrit : « *un* fleur qui brille par-dessus *tous* les autres. » On peut s'étonner de cette double inadvertance, qui reproduit le genre latin de *flos*.

cher de vos genoux, quoique je sois fort affligé. Il lui conte ce qu'il a souffert sur la mer, et lui dit :

Ἀλλὰ, ἄνασσ', ἐλέαιρε, σὲ γὰρ κακὰ πολλὰ μογήσας
Ἐς πρώτην ἱκόμην. [Vers 175 et 176.]

Car c'est comme une obligation plus forte d'assister un étranger qui s'est adressé à nous tous les premiers. Et voilà le vœu qu'il fait pour elle :

Σοὶ δὲ Θεοὶ τόσα δοῖεν, ὅσα φρεσὶ σῇσι μενοινᾷς,
Ἄνδρα τε καὶ οἶκον, καὶ ὁμοφροσύνην ὀπάσειαν
Ἐσθλήν· οὐ μὴν γὰρ τοῦγε κρεῖσσον καὶ ἄρειον
Ἢ ὅθ' ὁμοφρονέοντε νοήμασιν οἶκον ἔχητον,
Ἀνὴρ ἠδὲ γυνή· πόλλ' ἄλγεα δυσμενέεσσι,
Χάρματα δ' εὐμενέτῃσι· μάλιστα δέ τ' ἔκλυον αὐτοί. [Vers 180-185.]

Je souhaite que les Dieux vous donnent tout ce que vous desirez : un mari, une famille, et une bonne intelligence ; car il n'y a rien de plus beau que quand une femme et un mari sont d'accord. Quand ils se haïssent, il leur arrive toute sorte de maux, et toute sorte de biens quand ils s'aiment ; et ils le reconnoissent eux-mêmes fort bien, ou plutôt, comme je crois, les Dieux mêmes les favorisent de plus en plus lorsqu'ils s'entendent bien l'un avec l'autre.

La princesse lui répond ces paroles obligeantes :

Ξεῖν' (ἐπεὶ οὔτε κακῷ, οὔτ' ἄφρονι φωτὶ ἔοικας),
Ζεὺς δ' αὐτὸς νέμει ὄλβον Ὀλύμπιος ἀνθρώποισιν,
Ἐσθλοῖς ἠδὲ κακοῖσιν, ὅπως ἐθέλῃσιν ἑκάστῳ·
Καί πού σοι τάδ' ἔδωκε, σὲ δὲ χρὴ τετλάμεν ἔμπης. [Vers 187-190.]

Ces paroles sont belles et sont ordinaires dans Homère, pour ne pas mépriser un homme parce qu'il est en un pauvre état, parce que le bonheur et le malheur viennent à chacun selon que Dieu les distribue. Elle lui apprend en quel pays il est, et qui elle est elle-même. En même temps elle appelle ses servantes, et leur dit : Faut-il s'enfuir pour voir un homme ? il n'y en a point d'assez hardi pour venir comme ennemi dans le pays des Phéaques ; car ils sont trop aimés des Dieux. Mais celui-ci est un malheureux qu'il faut bien traiter ; car tous les étrangers et les pauvres viennent de la part de Jupiter, et il leur faut donner, pour peu que ce soit. Ces servantes s'approchent, et mènent Ulysse sur le bord du fleuve, sous un ombrage, et apportent de l'huile pour le frotter. Mais Ulysse leur dit de se retirer, parce qu'il auroit honte de paroître nu devant des filles : ce qu'elles font, et elles le redisent à leur maîtresse. Alors Ulysse se lave, et fait en aller[1] toute l'écume et toutes les ordures de la mer, dont son corps et sa tête étoit couverte. Et après qu'il s'est bien lavé, et qu'il a mis sur son dos la casaque que la princesse lui avoit fait donner, Minerve répand autour de lui une nouvelle beauté, et le fait paroître plus grand et plus gros à proportions. Elle fait descendre sur ses épaules ses beaux cheveux noirs bouclés ; car il dit qu'ils étoient de la couleur d'hyacinthe, qui passe pour noire. Homère répète cette fiction en deux ou trois endroits, et Virgile l'a imitée au [livre] 1. de l'*Én*. Voici comme ils parlent tous deux :

Τὸν μὲν Ἀθηναίη θῆκεν Διὸς ἐκγεγαυῖα,
Μείζονά τ' εἰσιδέειν καὶ πάσσονα· καδδὲ κάρητος
Οὔλας ἧκε κόμας, ὑακινθίνῳ ἄνθει ὁμοίας.
Ὡς δ' ὅτε τις χρυσὸν περιχεύεται ἀργύρῳ ἀνὴρ
Ἴδρις, ὃν Ἥφαιστος δέδαεν καὶ Παλλὰς Ἀθήνη
Τέχνην παντοίην, χαρίεντα δὲ ἔργα τελείει.
Ὡς ἄρα τῷ κατέχευε χάριν κεφαλῇ τε καὶ ὤμοις.
Ἕζετ' ἔπειτ', ἀπάνευθε κιών, ἐπὶ θῖνα θαλάσσης,
Κάλλεϊ καὶ χάρισι στίλβων· θηεῖτο δὲ κούρη. [Vers 229-237.]

Restitit Æneas, claraque in luce refulsit,
Os humerosque deo similis ; namque ipsa decoram
Cæsariem nato genitrix, lumenque juventæ
Purpureum, et lætos oculis afflarat honores :
Quale manus addunt ebori decus ; aut ubi flavo
Argentum, Pariusve lapis, circumdatur auro[2].

Virgile est plus court, mais il paroît aussi plus délicat, et il met tout l'embellissement d'Énée aux cheveux, au teint du visage et à l'éclat des yeux, au lieu qu'Homère se contente de dire qu'Ulysse parut plus grand et plus gros, et que ses che-

---

1. M. Aimé-Martin a remplacé *en aller* par *disparoître*.
2. *Énéide*, livre I, vers 588-593.

veux descendirent sur sa tête. Il est vrai qu'il dit après : κάλλεϊ καὶ χάρισι στίλβων. Virgile finit comme Homère :

Obstupuit primo aspectu Sidonia Dido [1].

Mais ici Nausicaa dit à ses servantes : Ce n'est point contre la volonté [des Dieux] que cet étranger est venu ici. D'abord il paroissoit un homme de néant, mais maintenant il est beau comme un dieu. Ah! plût à Dieu que j'eusse à [2] mari semblable à lui ! ou bien, plût à Dieu que je le pusse appeler mon mari, et qu'il voulût demeurer ici ! mais donnez-lui à boire et à manger : ce qu'elles font, et Ulysse mange avec avidité, ἁρπαλέως [3]; car il n'avoit pas mangé de longtemps. Cependant Nausicaa replie tous ses habits et se prépare à s'en aller. Elle monte à son chariot, et dit à Ulysse qu'il la suive. Tant que nous serons dans la campagne, venez derrière mon chariot avec mes femmes ; mais lorsque nous arriverons près du port, où le peuple tient son assemblée sur de grandes pierres cavées exprès, et où l'on travaille à l'équipage des vaisseaux, car c'est là toute leur étude, et les Phéaques ne s'appliquent point à l'arc ni au carquois, mais seulement aux voiles et aux rames, j'appréhende leur médisance cruelle, car le peuple est insolent ; et peut-être quelqu'un d'eux diroit méchamment : Qui est ce bel et grand étranger qui suit Nausicaa ? Où l'a-t-elle trouvé ? Sans doute qu'il sera son mari. Ne l'a-t-elle point sauvé de quelque naufrage ? Ou bien, n'est-ce point quelque dieu qui lui soit venu du ciel durant qu'elle faisoit ses prières? Et elle l'aura toute sa vie pour mari. Aussi bien méprise-t-elle tous ceux de ce pays qui la recherchent en grand nombre, et tous fort nobles. On voit là une peinture admirable des discours d'une populace qui s'ingère dans toutes les actions des grands.

Aussi Nausicaa dit-elle qu'elle fuit ces bruits-là : Et ce me

---

1. *Énéide*, livre I, vers 613.
2. C'est bien là le texte. Racine a-t-il par mégarde écrit *à* pour *un*? ou bien faut-il prendre *à* dans le sens de *pour*? — M. Aimé-Martin a ainsi modifié ce passage : « que j'eusse un mari comme lui. »
3. Vers 250.

seroient des outrages, dit-elle, car je treuverois moi-même fort mauvais qu'une fille fréquentât des hommes sans le consentement de son père et de sa mère, et devant qu'être mariée publiquement. C'est pourquoi nous treuverons sur le chemin l'agréable bois de Pallas où est la métairie et les beaux jardins de mon père : demeurez-y jusqu'à ce que je sois arrivée dans la ville et au palais de mon père ; et quand vous jugerez que nous [y] sommes, entrez dans la ville et demandez le logis de mon père : il est aisé à connoître, et un enfant vous y mèneroit, car il n'y en a point de pareil dans l'île des Phéaques. Quand vous serez entré, avancez-vous dans la salle, où vous treuverez ma mère assise près du feu, contre un pilier, où elle file des laines de pourpre avec ses femmes. Vous y verrez mon père, qui est auprès d'elle dans son trône.

Τῷ ὅγε οἰνοποτάζει, ... ἀθάνατος ὥς. [Vers 309.]

Mais passez-le, et allez embrasser les genoux de ma mère, et assurez-vous que si elle vous veut une fois du bien, vous reverrez vos amis et votre maison, si loin que vous en soyez. Cela dit, elle fouette ses mulets, qui courent et plient les jambes adroitement :

Εὖ δὲ πλίσσοντο πόδεσσιν. [Vers 318.]

Mais elle les gouvernoit sagement, afin que ses femmes et Ulysse la pussent suivre, et les fouettoit avec art :

Νόῳ δ' ἐπέβαλλεν ἱμάσθλην. [Vers 320.]

Le soleil se couche, et ils arrivent au bois sacré de Pallas, où Ulysse invoque la Déesse et lui reproche de l'avoir abandonné.

Δός μ' ἐς Φαίηκας φίλον ἐλθεῖν, ἠδ' ἐλεεινόν. [Vers 327.]

Elle l'exauce, mais elle n'ose pas se découvrir à lui, αἴδετο γάρ ῥα πατροκασίγνητον[1], qui étoit grandement irrité contre lui.

---

1. Vers 329 et 330.

LIVRE VII.

Nausicaa arrive à la maison de son père, et ses frères viennent à l'entour d'elle et détachent ses mulets, et la descendent du chariot. Elle va à sa chambre, où sa nourrice lui allume du feu. Cependant Pallas a soin d'Ulysse, et afin que personne ne le voie et ne l'importune par des injures ou par des interrogations hors de saison, elle répand autour de lui un nuage épais. C'est ce que Virgile a imité au [livre] 1. *Én.*[1], où Vénus en fait autant à Énée. Et il l'a encore imité en faisant venir Vénus au-devant d'Énée pour lui apprendre des nouvelles de Carthage[2], comme ici Homère fait que Pallas vient à la rencontre d'Ulysse sous la figure d'une jeune fille qui portoit une cruche d'eau. Ulysse lui demande : Mon enfant, ne sauriez-vous m'enseigner la maison d'Alcinoüs? Oui, dit-elle, étranger, mon père, je vous la puis bien montrer, car le logis de mon père est tout contre. Il ne se peut rien de plus beau que la justesse et l'exactitude d'Homère : il fait parler tous ses personnages avec une certaine propriété qui ne se trouve[3] point ailleurs; car on diroit qu'il diversifie son style à chaque endroit, tant il garde bien le caractère des gens. Ulysse, par exemple, parle simplement à cette fille, et cette fille lui répond avec naïveté. En d'autres endroits, Ulysse et les autres parlent en héros, et ainsi du reste. Pallas lui dit donc qu'elle le mènera : Mais allez, dit-elle, sans rien dire à personne, et ne regardez personne non plus; car les Phéaques n'aiment pas volontiers les étrangers :

Οὐ γὰρ ξείνους οἵδε μάλ' ἀνθρώπους ἀνέχονται,
Οὐδ' ἀγαπαζόμενοι φιλέουσ', ὅς κ' ἄλλοθεν ἔλθοι. [Vers 32 et 33.]

Ils n'aiment que la marine, et Neptune leur en a donné l'art, et leurs vaisseaux vont plus vite que l'aile d'un oiseau

---

1. *Énéide*, livre I, vers 411-413.
2. *Ibidem*, vers 314 et suivants.
3. Racine, dans ces *Remarques*, écrit ordinairement ce verbe par *eu;* mais pourtant nous avons plusieurs fois déjà rencontré, comme ici, la diphthongue *ou*.

et que la pensée. C'est le naturel des hommes de ce métier d'être brutaux et de n'avoir point de civilité. Et cela tourne davantage à la louange d'Ulysse, qui a été si bien reçu de ces gens-là. Il marche derrière Pallas, sans que personne le voie, à cause de ce nuage qui l'environnoit. Ulysse admire le port et les vaisseaux qui y étoient en bel ordre; il admire les grands logis de ces héros et les places et les murailles hautes et environnées de fossés.

Miratur molem Æneas, magalia quondam;
Miratur portas, strepitumque, et strata viarum [1].

Enfin voilà, dit Pallas, la maison d'Alcinoüs; vous y treuverez ces rois ou ces princes divins, διοτρεφέας [2], qui sont à table; mais entrez et ne craignez rien. Un homme hardi réussit toujours mieux dans toutes les occasions, fût-il étranger :

Μηδέ τι θυμῷ
Τάρβει· θαρσαλέος γὰρ ἀνὴρ ἐν πᾶσιν ἀμείνων
Ἔργοισιν τελέθει, εἰ καί ποθεν ἄλλοθεν ἔλθοι. [Vers 50-52.]

Vous y trouverez d'abord la reine Arété, qui est de la même race qu'Alcinoüs, car Neptune engendra premièrement Nausithoüs, de Péribée, la plus belle des femmes, laquelle étoit fille du brave Eurymédon, qui commanda autrefois aux géants; mais il fit périr ce peuple farouche et se perdit luimême :

Ἀλλ' ὁ μὲν ὤλεσε λαὸν ἀτάσθαλον, ὤλετο δ' αὐτός. [Vers 60.]

Nausithoüs régna sur les Phéaques et eut deux fils : Rhexenor et Alcinoüs; mais le premier fut tué par Apollon, étant nouveau marié et sans enfants mâles, ἄκουρον ἐόντα [3]; mais il laissa Arété, fille unique, qu'a épousée Alcinoüs et qu'il honore plus que femme ne peut être honorée sur la terre. Voici l'idée d'une grande princesse qui est aimée et révérée de tout le monde :

Καί μιν ἔτισ' ὡς οὔτις ἐπὶ χθονὶ τίεται ἄλλη,
Ὅσσαι νῦν γε γυναῖκες ὑπ' ἀνδράσιν οἶκον ἔχουσιν·
Ὡς κείνη περὶ κῆρι τετίμηταί τε καὶ ἔστιν

---

1. *Énéide*, livre I, vers 421 et 422. — 2. Vers 49. — 3. Vers 64.

Ἔκ τε φίλων παίδων, ἔκ τ' αὐτοῦ Ἀλκινόοιο,
Καὶ λαῶν, οἵ μίν ῥα, θεὸν ὡς, εἰσορόωντες,
Δειδέχαται μύθοισιν, ὅτε στείχησ' ἀνὰ ἄστυ.
Οὐ μὲν γάρ τι νόου γε καὶ αὐτὴ δεύεται ἐσθλοῦ,
Οἷσίν τ' εὖ φρονέῃσι, καὶ ἀνδράσι νείκεα λύει. [Vers 67-74.]

Que si elle vous veut du bien, espérez que vous reverrez bientôt votre pays. Aussitôt Minerve s'en alla à Athènes, εὐρυάγυιαν[1], à la maison d'Érechtée, roi d'Athènes, dont les filles souffrirent la mort pour leur patrie, selon Cicéron[2]. Ulysse arriva à la maison d'Alcinoüs, dont voici la description toute entière ; car elle mérite bien d'être copiée mot à mot :

Αὐτὰρ Ὀδυσσεὺς
Ἀλκινόου πρὸς δώματ' ἴε κλυτά· πολλὰ δέ οἱ κῆρ
Ὥρμαιν' ἱσταμένῳ, πρὶν χάλκεον οὐδὸν ἱκέσθαι·
Ὥστε γὰρ ἠελίου αἴγλη πέλεν, ἠὲ σελήνης,
Δῶμα κάθ' ὑψερεφὲς μεγαλήτορος Ἀλκινόοιο.
Χάλκεοι μὲν γὰρ τοῖχοι ἐρηρέδατ' ἔνθα καὶ ἔνθα,
Ἐς μυχὸν ἐξ οὐδοῦ· περὶ δὲ θριγκὸς κυάνοιο·
Χρύσειαι δὲ θύραι πυκινὸν δόμον ἐντὸς ἔεργον·
Ἀργύρεοι δὲ σταθμοὶ ἐν χαλκέῳ ἕστασαν οὐδῷ,
Ἀργύρεον δ' ἐφ' ὑπερθύριον, χρυσέη δὲ κορώνη.
Χρύσειοι δ' ἑκάτερθε καὶ ἀργύρεοι κύνες ἦσαν,
Οὓς Ἥφαιστος ἔτευξεν ἰδυίῃσι πραπίδεσσιν,
Δῶμα φυλασσέμεναι μεγαλήτορος Ἀλκινόοιο,
Ἀθανάτους ὄντας καὶ ἀγήρως ἤματα πάντα.
Ἐν δὲ θρόνοι περὶ τοῖχον ἐρηρέδατ' ἔνθα καὶ ἔνθα,
Ἐς μυχὸν ἐξ οὐδοῖο διαμπερές· ἔνθ' ἐνὶ πέπλοι
Λεπτοὶ ἐΰννητοι βεβλήατο, ἔργα γυναικῶν.
Ἔνθα δὲ Φαιήκων ἡγήτορες ἑδριόωντο,
Πίνοντες καὶ ἔδοντες· ἐπηετανὸν γὰρ ἔχεσκον.
Χρύσειοι δ' ἄρα κοῦροι ἐϋδμήτων ἐπὶ βωμῶν
Ἕστασαν, αἰθομένας δαΐδας μετὰ χερσὶν ἔχοντες,
Φαίνοντες νύκτας κατὰ δώματα δαιτυμόνεσσι.
Πεντήκοντα δέ οἱ δμωαὶ κατὰ δῶμα γυναῖκες [vers 81-103],

dont les unes travailloient à moudre le blé μήλοπα[3], i. (c'est-à-dire) couleur de pomme, les autres faisoient des toiles plus déliées que les feuilles d'un peuplier ; et on voyoit dégoutter

---

1. Vers 80. — 2. *Tusculanes*, livre I, chapitre XLVIII.
3. Vers 104.

la teinture où l'on mouilloit ces voiles. Autant que les Phéaques excellent sur les autres hommes dans l'art de conduire les vaisseaux, autant leurs femmes excellent-elles à faire des toiles :

Πέρι γάρ σφισι δῶκεν Ἀθήνη
Ἔργα τ' ἐπίστασθαι περικαλλέα καὶ φρένας ἐσθλάς. [Vers 110 et 111.]

Ensuite il vient à la description du jardin, qui est un des beaux endroits de l'*Odyssée*. Virgile n'en fait point lorsqu'il décrit la maison de Didon[1]. On peut dire que c'est à cause que Didon étoit à Carthage depuis peu de temps, et qu'un jardin n'est pas sitôt dans sa perfection.

Mais les jardins d'Alcinoüs ont été fameux dans toute l'antiquité. Virgile, au [livre] 2. des *Géorgiques :*

Pomaque, et Alcinoï silvæ[2].

Voici donc la description qu'en fait Homère, et que le Tasse a voulu imiter dans le palais d'Armide[3] :

Ἔκτοσθεν δ' αὐλῆς μέγας ὄρχατος ἄγχι θυράων
Τετράγυος· περὶ δ' ἕρκος ἐλήλαται ἀμφοτέρωθεν.
Ἔνθα δὲ δένδρεα μακρὰ πεφύκει τηλεθόωντα,
Ὄγχναι, καὶ ῥοιαὶ, καὶ μηλέαι ἀγλαόκαρποι,
Συκαῖ τε γλυκεραὶ, καὶ ἐλαῖαι τηλεθόωσαι.
Τάων οὔποτε καρπὸς ἀπόλλυται, οὐδ' ἐπιλείπει,
Χείματος, οὐδὲ θέρευς, ἐπετήσιος· ἀλλὰ μάλ' αἰεὶ
Ζεφυρίη πνείουσα τὰ μὲν φύει, ἄλλα δὲ πέσσει.
Ὄγχνη ἐπ' ὄγχνῃ γηράσκει, μῆλον δ' ἐπὶ μήλῳ,
Αὐτὰρ ἐπὶ σταφυλῇ σταφυλή, σῦκον δ' ἐπὶ σύκῳ.
Ἔνθα δέ οἱ πολύκαρπος ἀλωὴ ἐρρίζωται·
Τῆς ἕτερον μὲν θειλόπεδον λευρῷ ἐνὶ χώρῳ
[Τέρσεται ἠελίῳ· ἑτέρας δ' ἄρα τε τρυγόωσιν,][4]
Ἄλλας δὲ τραπέουσι· πάροιθε δέ τ' ὄμφακές εἰσιν,
Ἄνθος ἀφιεῖσαι, ἕτεραι δ' ὑποπερκάζουσι.
Ἔνθα δὲ κοσμηταὶ πρασιαὶ παρὰ νείατον ὄρχον
Παντοῖαι πεφύασιν, ἐπηετανὸν γανόωσαι [vers 112-128],

c'est-à-dire des parterres ornés de fleurs continuelles ; et il y

---

1. *Énéide*, livre I, vers 637 et suivants.
2. Vers 87. — 3. *La Jérusalem délivrée*, chant XVI, stances x et xi.
4. Ce vers est omis dans le manuscrit.

avoit encore deux fontaines, dont l'une se répandoit par tout le jardin, et l'autre alloit par-dessous la cour du logis auprès de la porte, où toute la ville venoit querir de l'eau.

Τοῖ᾽ ἄρ ἐν Ἀλκινόοιο Θεῶν ἔσαν ἀγλαὰ δῶρα. [Vers 132.]

Ulysse, après avoir tout admiré dans son âme, entre [dans] la salle, où les plus apparents des Phéaques étoient à table, et faisoient une libation en l'honneur de Mercure,

Ὧ πυμάτῳ σπένδεσκον, ὅτε μνησαίατο κοίτου. [Vers 138.]

La raison de cela étoit sans doute qu'il avoit le pouvoir d'endormir et de réveiller, lorsqu'il vouloit, avec sa verge, comme Homère le dit au commencement du 5. livre, et Virgile au 4. [livre] :

Dat somnos, adimitque[1].

Ulysse entre donc, toujours environné de cette obscurité qui le rendoit invisible ; il se va jeter aux genoux d'Arété, et alors ce nuage miraculeux se dissipe, et tout le monde est effrayé de voir un homme devant eux. Ulysse fait sa prière à Arété, la conjurant par le nom de son père, qu'il avoit fort bien retenu, de faire [en] sorte qu'on le renvoie chez lui ; et, attendant sa réponse, il étoit dans la cendre pour la toucher davantage, jusqu'à ce que le vieillard Echeneüs, qui étoit le plus ancien,

Καὶ μύθοισι κέκαστο, παλαιά τε πολλά τε εἰδώς [vers 157],

dit à Alcinoüs qu'il a tort de laisser un étranger à terre : Faites-le asseoir, et commandez qu'on verse du vin en l'honneur de Jupiter, qui accompagne les suppliants, lesquels sont en vénération, et faites apporter à souper à cet étranger. Alcinoüs prend Ulysse par la main et le fait asseoir dans un beau siége, d'où il fait lever le jeune Laodamas, son fils, qui étoit assis près de lui, et qu'il aimoit plus que tous les autres. Ulysse mange donc ce qu'on lui apporte ; et cependant Alcinoüs dit à Pontonoüs, son héraut, qu'il donne du vin à tout le monde, afin qu'on boive en l'honneur de Jupiter ; et après que cha-

1. *Énéide*, livre IV, vers 244.

cun a bu autant qu'il a voulu, Alcinoüs dit que chacun s'en aille coucher chez lui, et que demain au matin ils viennent en bonne compagnie, afin que nous traitions, dit-il, cet étranger, et que nous donnions ordre pour son retour, afin qu'on le remène chez lui sans aucun danger, et qu'après cela il reçoive tout ce que les Parques lui ont destiné :

Ἔνθα δ' ἔπειτα
Πείσεται ὅσσα οἱ Αἶσα Κατακλῶθές τε βαρεῖαι
Γεινομένῳ νήσαντο λίνῳ, ὅτε μιν τέκε μήτηρ. [Vers 196-198.]

Que si c'est quelqu'un des Dieux qui soit descendu du ciel, il en arrivera ce qu'il leur plaira ; car d'ordinaire les Dieux nous apparoissent visiblement quand nous leur faisons des hécatombes, et mangent avec nous ; et quelquefois ils se déguisent en forme de voyageurs, et après se découvrent à nous, car nous sommes leurs alliés, aussi bien que les Cyclopes et les Géants. L'on diroit qu'Homère a pris ce beau sentiment dans les livres de Moïse, que les Dieux prennent quelquefois la figure des voyageux[1] pour éprouver l'hospitalité de ceux qui les servent, et qui sont favorisés d'eux, comme on voit par l'histoire d'Abraham.

Ulysse rejette bien loin cette pensée d'Alcinoüs. Ayez d'autres sentiments, dit-il, car je ne suis point semblable aux Immortels qui habitent le ciel, ni de corps, ni d'esprit,

Ἀλλὰ θνητοῖσι βροτοῖσιν·
Οὕς τινας ὑμεῖς ἴστε μάλιστ' ὀχέοντας ὀϊζὺν
Ἀνθρώπων, τοῖσίν κεν ἐν ἄλγεσιν ἰσωσαίμην [vers 210-212];

et je puis dire même que j'ai plus souffert que personne. Mais permettez-moi de souper à mon aise, tout affligé que je suis ; car rien n'est plus impudent qu'un ventre affamé :

Οὐ γάρ τι στυγερῇ ἐπὶ γαστέρι κύντερον ἄλλο
Ἔπλετο, ἥτ' ἐκέλευσεν ἕο μνήσασθαι ἀνάγκῃ,
Καὶ μάλα τειρόμενον, καὶ ἐνὶ φρεσὶ πένθος ἔχοντα. [Vers 216-218.]

Notre langue ne souffriroit pas dans un poëme héroïque cette façon de parler, qui semble n'être propre qu'au burles-

---

1. C'est ainsi que Racine a écrit ici.

que : elle est pourtant fort ordinaire dans Homère. En effet, nous voyons que dans nos poëmes, et même dans les romans, on ne parle non plus de manger que si les héros étoient des dieux qui ne fussent pas assujettis à la nourriture : au lieu qu'Homère fait fort bien manger les siens à chaque occasion, et les garnit toujours de vivres lorsqu'ils sont en voyage. Virgile en fait aussi mention, quoique plus rarement qu'Homère, et il ne le fait que dans des occasions importantes, comme au [livre] 1er, après le naufrage, Énée tua des cerfs qu'il donna à ses gens, qui en avoient bien besoin ; ensuite le souper de Didon, où cette princesse devient amoureuse : et c'est ce qui lui fait dire au [livre] 4e, pour éviter les répétitions :

Nunc eadem, labente die, convivia quærit [1] ;

au 3e, le dîner des Harpies ; au 5e, en l'honneur d'Anchise ; au 7e, pour accomplir la prophétie :

Heus ! etiam mensas consumimus [2] *!*

et au 8e, le sacrifice d'Évandre. Voilà, ce me semble, tous les endroits où il est parlé de manger dans Virgile. Mais dans Homère il [en] est fait mention presque partout, et plus encore dans l'*Odyssée* que dans l'*Iliade*, parce qu'ici Homère ne parle presque que d'affaires domestiques, au lieu que l'*Iliade* est pour les actions publiques. En cet endroit, on recommence par trois fois à boire, à l'occasion d'Ulysse et des libations qu'on faisoit aux Dieux ; en suite de quoi chacun se va coucher. Ulysse demeure seul, et Arété et Alcinoüs auprès de lui. Arété reconnoît le vêtement que sa fille lui avoit donné, et qu'elle-même avoit fait de ses mains. Elle lui demande donc qui le lui a donné : Ne dites-vous pas que vous avez [été] jeté par l'orage en ce pays-ci? Et Ulysse lui répond, et lui dit de quel pays il vient. Il y a assez loin d'ici une île qu'on appelle Ogygie, où demeure la nymphe Calypso, fille d'Atlas,

Δεινὴ θεός· οὐδέ τις αὐτῇ
Μίσγεται, οὔτε Θεῶν, οὔτε θνητῶν ἀνθρώπων.
Ἀλλ' ἐμὲ τὸν δύστηνον ἐφέστιον ἤγαγε Δαίμων
Οἶον. [Vers 246-249.]

1. Vers 77. — 2. Vers 116.

Il conte de quelle manière il a vécu là sept ans durant, toujours en affliction :

Εἵματα δ' αἰεὶ
Δάκρυσι δεύεσκον, τά μοι ἄμβροτα δῶκε Καλυψώ [vers 259 et 260];

enfin de quelle façon elle le renvoya, les périls étranges qu'il courut sur la mer, comme il arriva à leur île, comme il s'endormit toute une nuit et jusqu'au soleil couchant du lendemain. Ce fut alors que je vis votre fille, qui paroissoit comme une déesse parmi ses femmes.

Τὴν ἱκέτευσ'· ἡ δ' οὔτι νοήματος ἤμβροτεν ἐσθλοῦ,
Ὡς οὐκ ἂν ἔλποιο νεώτερον ἀντιάσαντα
Ἐρξέμεν· αἰεὶ γάρ τε νεώτεροι ἀφραδέουσιν. [Vers 292-294.]

Elle me traita plus charitablement que je n'eusse attendu d'une jeune personne; car les jeunes gens sont presque toujours légers d'esprit.

Alcinoüs dit qu'elle a eu tort néanmoins de ne le pas amener avec elle, vu qu'il s'étoit adressé à elle toute la première. Ulysse l'excuse, et dit qu'elle[1] n'a pas voulu venir avec lui, craignant, dit-il, que [vous] n'en eussiez quelque déplaisir :

Δύσζηλοι γάρ τ' εἰμὲν ἐπὶ χθονὶ φῦλ' ἀνθρώπων. [Vers 307.]

Nous sommes, dit-il, naturellement jaloux, nous autres hommes. Mais Alcinoüs lui répond qu'il n'est pas si prompt à se fâcher, et que l'honnêteté est toujours belle :

Ἀμείνω δ' αἴσιμα πάντα. [Vers 310.]

Il entend, comme je crois, la civilité. Après tout, on voit, par cette action d'Ulysse, combien il faut éviter de donner aucun soupçon, et d'éviter[2] plutôt la compagnie d'une femme que de mettre sa réputation en danger. Il est vrai que ce fut Nausicaa elle-même qui donna ce sage conseil à Ulysse; et Ulysse le trouve si juste qu'il ne veut pas souffrir que son père lui impute pour cela le moindre reproche d'incivilité, parce que la civilité n'est pas préférable à l'honnêteté et au soin de la ré-

1. Dans le manuscrit : *il*.
2. Racine a sans doute cru avoir dit plus haut *il importe*, ou *il convient*, au lieu de *il faut*.

putation. Aussi Alcinoüs, admirant la sagesse d'Ulysse : Bien loin, dit-il, d'avoir quelque ombrage de vous, je voudrois que vous voulussiez de ma fille, tel que vous êtes :

Αἲ γάρ, Ζεῦ τε πάτερ, καὶ Ἀθηναίη, καὶ Ἀπολλον,
Τοῖος ἐὼν, οἷός ἐσσι, τά τε φρονέων ἅ τ' ἐγώ περ,
Παῖδά τ' ἐμὴν ἐχέμεν, καὶ ἐμὸς γαμβρὸς καλέεσθαι,
Αὖθι μένων· οἶκον δὲ ἐγὼ καὶ κτήματα δοίην [vers 311-314],

pourvu que vous y demeurassiez volontiers, car jamais personne ne vous retiendra ici malgré vous, Dieu m'en garde ! Demain je donnerai ordre à votre retour, et vous serez remené en votre pays, si loin qu'il soit, quand il seroit plus éloigné que l'Eubœe, qu'on dit être la plus éloignée de ce pays. Cependant nos vaisseaux y ont mené Rhadamante, pour y voir le fils de la terre Tityus, et l'ont ramené chez lui en un jour. Ulysse se réjouit à cette nouvelle ; après on lui dit que son lit est fait, et qu'il vienne coucher : ce qu'il fait, et tous les autres aussi.

LIVRE VIII.

Dès le matin, Alcinoüs et Ulysse se lèvent, et s'en vont à l'assemblée ; et Pallas, déguisée en héraut, va appeler tout le monde par la ville, et leur inspire de bons sentiments pour Ulysse, et le fait paroître plus beau lui-même, et lui donne l'art de vaincre dans tous les jeux où les Phéaques l'éprouveroient. Alcinoüs ouvre l'assemblée, et exhorte le peuple à préparer un vaisseau et à élire cinquante-deux jeunes hommes pour reconduire Ulysse ; et cependant il prie les principaux et les plus anciens, qu'il appelle σκηπτοῦχοι βασιλῆες[1], de venir à son logis, afin de festoyer cet étranger : Et que personne n'y manque, dit-il. Faites venir aussi le divin chantre Démodocus, à qui Dieu a donné la grâce de chanter agréablement tout ce qu'il veut :

Τῷ γάρ ῥα Θεὸς περιδῶκεν ἀοιδὴν
Τερπνὴν, ὅππῃ θυμὸς ἐποτρύνῃσιν ἀείδειν. [Vers 44 et 45.]

1. Vers 41.

A l'heure même, on va équiper le vaisseau, et puis tout le monde vient chez Alcinoüs, jeunes et vieux :

Πολλοὶ δ' ἄρ' ἔσαν νέοι, ἠδὲ παλαιοί. [Vers 58.]

Alcinoüs fait tuer une douzaine de brebis et sangliers, ou plutôt des porcs, ἀγριόδοντας ὕας[1], et deux bœufs. Le héraut amène le chantre. Il semble qu'Homère se soit voulu dépeindre sous la personne de ce chantre, s'il est vrai qu'il étoit aveugle, comme on dit : Car les Muses, dit-il, l'aimoient uniquement et lui avoient donné du bien et du mal. Elles l'avoient privé de la vue, et lui avoient donné l'art de bien chanter :

Κῆρυξ δ' ἐγγύθεν ἦλθεν, ἄγων ἐρίηρον ἀοιδόν·
Τὸν πέρι Μοῦσ' ἐφίλησε, δίδου δ' ἀγαθόν τε κακόν τε·
Ὀφθαλμῶν μὲν ἄμερσε, δίδου δ' ἡδεῖαν ἀοιδήν. [Vers 62-64.]

Le héraut lui donne un siége, θρόνον ἀργυρόηλον[2], au milieu de la salle, contre un pilier où étoit pendu un luth, qu'il lui met entre les mains, et met une table auprès de lui, garnie de viandes et de vin, afin qu'il bût quand il voudroit. Sur la fin du dîner, il commence à chanter :

Μοῦσ' ἄρ' ἀοιδὸν ἀνῆκεν ἀειδέμεναι κλέα ἀνδρῶν,
Οἴμης, τῆς τότ' ἄρα κλέος οὐρανὸν εὐρὺν ἵκανε·
Νεῖκος Ὀδυσσῆος καὶ Πηλείδεω Ἀχιλῆος. [Vers 73-75.]

C'étoit la coutume de ce temps-là de toucher le luth et de chanter tout ensemble ; et les chansons ordinaires étoient la louange des belles actions. Ainsi, au [livre] 9. de l'*Iliade*, Homère représente agréablement Achille qui jouoit du luth, lorsque les principaux des Grecs le vinrent voir dans sa tente. Il semble que les autres poëtes aient tenu cela au-dessous de leurs héros, car ils ne leur donnent jamais cette qualité, qui étoit néanmoins affectée des grands hommes, comme Cicéron remarque de Thémistocle, qui, ayant déclaré en bonne compagnie qu'il n'en savoit pas jouer, *habitus est indoctior*[3]. Cela convient fort bien à Achille, pour le divertir durant tout le temps qu'il demeuroit seul dans son vaisseau.

---

1. Vers 60. — 2. Vers 65.
3. *Tusculanes*, livre I, chapitre II.

Τὸν δ' εὗρον φρένα τερπόμενον φόρμιγγι λιγείῃ,
Καλῇ, δαιδαλέῃ, ἐπὶ δ' ἀργύρεος ζυγὸς ἦεν·
Τὴν ἄρετ' ἐξ ἐνάρων, πτόλιν Ἠετίωνος ὀλέσσας.
Τῇ ὅγε θυμὸν ἔτερπεν, ἄειδε δ' ἄρα κλέα ἀνδρῶν.
Πάτροκλος δέ οἱ οἶος ἐναντίος ἧστο σιωπῇ,
Δέγμενος Αἰακίδην, ὁπότε λήξειεν ἀείδων [1].

Et lorsqu'il vit entrer Ulysse et les autres chefs de l'armée grecque, il se leva, αὐτῇ σὺν φόρμιγγι [2].

Mais ici Homère, par un bel incident, et pour surprendre davantage l'esprit du lecteur, fait chanter la guerre de Troie, qui étoit une chanson, dit-il, dont la gloire montoit déjà jusqu'au ciel. Il l'a déjà fait chanter dans la maison d'Ulysse ; mais c'est quelque chose de plus étonnant qu'on la chante parmi les Phéaques. Virgile, qui a voulu imiter cette invention, a mis des tableaux à Carthage où Énée voit la guerre de Troie :

Quæ regio in terris nostri non plena laboris [3] *?*

Le musicien chante la dispute d'Achille et d'Ulysse, Agamemnon se réjouissant de les voir ainsi aux mains, à cause que l'oracle lui avoit prédit que la ruine de Troie seroit proche alors :

Τότε γάρ ῥα κυλίνδετο πήματος ἀρχὴ
Τρωσί τε καὶ Δαναοῖσι, Διὸς μεγάλου διὰ βουλάς. [Vers 81 et 82.]

Cela fait venir les larmes aux yeux d'Ulysse, et il fait comme son fils faisoit chez Menelaüs : il met sa robe devant ses yeux :

Κάλυψε δὲ καλὰ πρόσωπα·
Αἴδετο γὰρ Φαίηκας, ὑπ' ὀφρύσι δάκρυα λείβων. [Vers 85 et 86.]

Quand le musicien cesse de chanter, il se découvre le visage ; et prenant un verre, [il[4]] boit en l'honneur des Dieux ; mais sitôt que le musicien recommençoit, car on se plaisoit à l'entendre, et on le faisoit recommencer souvent, Ulysse se

---

1. *Iliade*, livre IX, vers 186-191.
2. *Ibidem*, vers 194.
3. *Énéide*, livre I, vers 460.
4. Il y a *et*, au lieu de *il*, dans le manuscrit.

cachoit encore pour pleurer. Personne n'y prenoit garde ; mais Alcinoüs, qui étoit auprès de lui, s'en aperçoit et l'entend soupirer. Il fait donc cesser, et dit qu'il faut aller s'exercer aux jeux, afin que l'étranger puisse réciter à ses amis combien les Phéaques sont excellents à la lutte, au combat de main, à la danse et à la course. Tout le monde va donc pour voir les jeux, et le héraut, prenant le chantre par la main, l'amène avec les autres. Toute la jeunesse, dont Homère conte les noms, s'apprête à combattre, et entre autres trois enfants d'Alcinoüs, Halius, et Clytoneus, et le beau Laodamas, qui étoit le mieux fait de tout le peuple. On commence par la course :

Τοῖσι δ' ἀπὸ νύσσης[1] τέτατο δρόμος· οἱ δ' ἅμα πάντες
Καρπαλίμως ἐπέτοντο κονίοντες πεδίοιο. [Vers 121 et 122.]

Clytoneus passe les autres de beaucoup. Ensuite on joue aux trois autres jeux, et Laodamas est vainqueur aux poings[2], *pugilatu ;* et il dit à ses amis qu'il faut demander à l'étranger s'il sait quelqu'un de ces jeux, y étant assez propre de son corps, soit pour les cuisses et les jambes, les mains et le cou robuste, et outre cela étant encore dans la force de la jeunesse, si ce n'est que ses travaux ne l'aient beaucoup affoibli : Car, dit-il, je ne crois pas que rien affoiblisse plus un homme que la mer, si fort qu'il soit. Euryalus, le vaillant, loue son dessein. Ainsi Laodamas vient prier Ulysse de montrer son adresse : Car, dit-il, il n'y a point de plus grande gloire à un homme que d'être adroit des pieds et des mains. Et en cela il parloit sans doute comme un jeune homme qui n'est jamais sorti de son pays. Aussi Ulysse lui répond qu'il le prie de l'excuser :

Κήδεά μοι καὶ μᾶλλον ἐνὶ φρεσὶν, ἤπερ ἄεθλοι[3]. [Vers 154.]

Et maintenant que je suis ici pour obtenir le secours dont j'ai besoin, il me siéroit mal de me jouer et de combattre contre vous autres. Euryalus lui dit incivilement qu'il n'a point l'apparence

1. *A carcere.* (*Note de Racine.*) — 2. Dans le manuscrit : *poins.*
3. En tête de la page 89 du manuscrit, qui commence par ce vers, et où se trouve le passage grec suivant (vers 169-173), sur l'homme éloquent, Racine a écrit : « N^a. Éloquence. »

d'un galant homme ; mais que c'est sans doute quelque marchand qui ne sait que trafiquer sur mer, puisqu'il ne sait pas les exercices des honnêtes gens. Ulysse se sentant piqué, lui répond qu'il parle un peu trop en étourdi :

> Οὕτως οὐ πάντεσσι Θεὸς χαρίεντα δίδωσιν
> Ἀνδράσιν, οὔτε φυὴν, οὔτ' ἄρ φρένας, οὔτ' ἀγορητύν·
> Ἄλλος μὲν γάρ τ' εἶδος ἀκιδνότερος πέλει ἀνήρ,
> Ἀλλὰ Θεὸς μορφὴν ἔπεσι στέφει· οἱ δέ τ' ἐς αὐτὸν
> Τερπόμενοι λεύσσουσιν· ὁ δ' ἀσφαλέως ἀγορεύει
> Αἰδοῖ μειλιχίῃ, μετὰ δὲ πρέπει ἀγρομένοισιν,
> Ἐρχόμενον δ' ἀνὰ ἄστυ, θεὸν ὣς, εἰσορόωσιν·
> Ἄλλος δ' αὖ εἶδος μὲν ἀλίγκιος Ἀθανάτοισιν·
> Ἀλλ' οὔ οἱ χάρις ἀμφιπεριστέφεται ἐπέεσσιν. [Vers 167-175.]

On voit bien que Dieu ne donne pas ses grâces à tout le monde, ni le bon naturel, ni l'esprit, ni l'éloquence ; car l'un n'aura point de beauté sur le visage, et Dieu en donne à ses discours ; tout le monde l'écoute et le regarde avec plaisir ; et lui, parle avec assurance, et néanmoins avec une modestie charmante, et il fait ce qu'il veut de son assemblée ; et lorsqu'il va par la ville, on le regarde comme un dieu. Cet endroit est admirable sans mentir, et l'éloquence ne sauroit pas être mieux décrite. Surtout cette belle pensée : ὁ δ' ἀσφαλέως ἀγορεύει Αἰδοῖ μειλιχίῃ..., qui montre bien qu'il faut toujours parler avec confiance, mais néanmoins avec une agréable modestie qui gagne les cœurs. Au contraire, d'autres ont fort bonne mine ; mais ils n'ont point de grâce dans leurs discours. Vous êtes de ceux-là, dit-il ; car vous êtes beau et bien fait, mais vous n'êtes pas assez sage : θυμοδακὴς γὰρ μῦθος[1], car vos discours sont offensants. Cependant je suis plus habile que vous ne pensez, et, tout fatigué que je suis, je ne laisserai pas de vous le montrer. Disant cela, il prend un palet[2], et le jette extrêmement loin. Pallas, déguisée en homme, y met une marque, afin qu'on le voie, et l'assure de la victoire. Ulysse s'en réjouit, étant bien aise d'avoir là trouvé un homme qui lui fût favorable.

> Καὶ τότε κουφότερον μετεφώνεε Φαιήκεσσι. [Vers 201.]

---

1. Vers 185. — 2. Racine a écrit : *un palais*.

Il dit qu'il combattra à toute sorte de jeux contre qui voudra, excepté contre Laodamas, parce qu'il est son hôte. Et qui voudroit, dit-il, se battre contre son ami? ce seroit une sottise, et ce seroit brouiller toutes ses affaires. Pour les autres, il n'en refuse pas un, et croit être plus vaillant que pas un homme de son temps.

Ἀνδράσι δὲ προτέροισιν ἐριζέμεν οὐκ ἐθελήσω. [Vers 223.]

Cela montre le respect qu'on doit [avoir] pour les anciens. Et il ajoute qu'il ne voudroit pas disputer à la course, parce que la mer a affoibli ses genoux.

Alcinoüs prend la parole, et dit qu'on ne trouve point à redire à ce qu'il dit de lui-même, parce qu'il a été injustement attaqué, et qu'il se loue avec raison. Mais il lui dit de trouver bon que ces jeunes gens dansent devant lui, afin qu'il en puisse faire quelque jour le récit à ses amis ; car nous autres, dit-il, nous ne mettons pas toute notre étude aux combats et aux exercices pénibles.

Αἰεὶ δ' ἡμῖν δαίς τε φίλη, κίθαρίς τε χοροί τε,
Εἵματά τ' ἐξημοιβὰ, λοετρά τε θερμὰ καὶ εὐναί.
Ἀλλ' ἄγε, Φαιήκων βητάρμονες, ὅσσοι ἄριστοι,
Παίσατε. [Vers 248-251.]

Alors on va querir un luth[1] pour Démodocus ; on élit neuf juges pour mettre l'ordre à la danse ; on nettoie la place, et on la fait spacieuse. Démodocus se met au milieu avec son luth ; et les jeunes gens, πρωθῆβαι[2], c'est-à-dire qui entroient en adolescence, se mettent autour de lui.

Πέπληγον δὲ χορὸν θεῖον ποσίν· αὐτὰρ Ὀδυσσεὺς
Μαρμαρυγὰς θηεῖτο ποδῶν, θαύμαζε δὲ θυμῷ. [Vers 264 et 265.]

Cependant le musicien chantoit les amours de Mars et de Vénus, qui ont été tant chantés par tous les poëtes. Lucrèce les a décrits en cinq ou six vers, au commencement de son poëme :

Belli fera munera Mavors
Armipotens regit, in gremium qui sæpe tuum se

---

1. Racine écrit : *lut*. — 2. Vers 263.

Rejicit, æterno devinctus vulnere amoris :

. . . .

Pascit amore avidos inhians in te, Dea, visus;

. . . .

*Hunc tu, Diva, tuo recubantem corpore sancto
Circumfusa super* [1], *etc.*

Il y a apparence qu'Homère, que Pline appelle le père de l'antiquité, *antiquitatis parens* [2], l'a été aussi de cette fable. Le musicien chante donc :

Ἀμφ' Ἄρεος φιλότητος, ἐϋστεφάνου τ' Ἀφροδίτης,
Ὡς τὰ πρῶτα μίγησαν ἐν Ἡφαίστοιο δόμοισι
Λάθρῃ· πολλὰ δ' ἔδωκε, λέχος δ' ᾔσχυνε καὶ εὐνὴν
Ἡφαίστοιο ἄνακτος. [Vers 267-270.]

Cela montre que c'est depuis longtemps que les femmes se laissent aller aux présents. Le Soleil, qui les avoit vus lorsqu'ils se divertissoient, en porte la nouvelle à Vulcain.

Ἥφαιστος δ' ὡς οὖν θυμαλγέα μῦθον ἄκουσε,
Βῆ ῥ' ἴμεν ἐς χαλκεῶνα, κακὰ φρεσὶ βυσσοδομεύων. [Vers 272 et 273.]

Cela exprime bien la rage couverte d'un homme jaloux. Il vint dans sa boutique.

Κόπτε δὲ δεσμοὺς
Ἀρρήκτους, ἀλύτους, ὄφρ' ἔμπεδον αὖθι μένοιεν. [Vers 274 et 275.]

Après qu'il eut forgé cette machine, il alla dans la chambre où étoit son lit, et répandit ces filets par tout le lit, les attachant aux quatre piliers, et il en attache encore plusieurs au ciel du lit,

Ἠΰτ' ἀράχνια λεπτά, τά κ' οὔ κέ τις οὐδὲ ἴδοιτο,
Οὐδὲ Θεῶν μακάρων· πέρι γὰρ δολόεντα τέτυκτο. [Vers 280 et 281.]

Ensuite il feignit d'aller à Lemnos, qui étoit la ville où il se plaisoit le plus; et Mars ne fut pas endormi :

Οὐδ' ἀλαοσκοπιὴν εἶχε χρυσήνιος Ἄρης. [Vers 285.]

Mais sitôt qu'il crut Vulcain parti, il vint à son logis,

Ἰσχανόων φιλότητος ἐϋστεφάνου Κυθερείης. [Vers 288.]

---

1. Livre I, vers 33-40. — 2. Livre XXV, chapitre v.

Elle ne faisoit que de revenir de chez Jupiter, son père; et elle étoit assise lorsque Mars entra.

Ἔν τ' ἄρα οἱ φῦ χειρί, ἔπος τ' ἔφατ', ἔκ τ' ὀνόμαζε·
Δεῦρο, φίλη, λέκτρονδε τραπείομεν εὐνηθέντε.
Οὐ γὰρ ἔθ' Ἥφαιστος μεταδήμιος, ἀλλά που ἤδη
Οἴχεται ἐς Λῆμνον, μετὰ Σίντιας ἀγριοφώνους.
Ὣς φάτο. Τῇ δ' ἀσπαστὸν ἐείσατο κοιμηθῆναι·
Τὼ δ' ἐς δέμνια βάντε κατέδραθον. [Vers 291-296.]

Ce mot ne signifie pas là *dormir*, comme il y a dans la version[1], car ils n'en eurent pas le loisir; mais il veut dire *se coucher*.

Ἀμφὶ δὲ δεσμοί
Τεχνήεντες ἔχυντο πολύφρονος Ἡφαίστοιο·
Οὐδέ τι κινῆσαι μελέων ἦν, οὐδ' ἀναεῖραι.
Καὶ τότε δὴ γίνωσκον, ὅτ' οὐκέτι φυκτὰ πέλονται. [Vers 296-299.]

Vulcain ne tarda guère à venir, car le Soleil avoit fait sentinelle pour lui, et l'avoit averti. Il vint dans la chambre; et cette vue le fâcha fort :

Ἔστη δ' ἐν προθύροισι, χόλος δέ μιν ἄγριος ᾕρει·
Σμερδαλέον δ' ἐβόησε, γέγωνέ τε πᾶσι Θεοῖσιν· [Vers 304 et 305.]

Venez, ô Jupiter, et vous autres, Dieux immortels, venez voir des choses honteuses et qui ne sont pas supportables. C'est ainsi que Vénus m'outrage à cause que je suis boiteux, et qu'elle aime le cruel Mars :

Οὕνεχ' ὁ μὲν καλός τε καὶ ἀρτίπος, αὐτὰρ ἔγωγε
Ἠπεδανὸς γενόμην· ἀτὰρ οὔτι μοι αἴτιος ἄλλος,
Ἀλλὰ τοκῆε δύω. [Vers 310-312.]

Je voudrois qu'ils ne m'eussent point mis au monde. Je ne crois pas qu'ils puissent aisément dormir ensemble, quelque amour qu'ils aient, et peut-être ne voudront[-ils] plus y reve-

---

1. Racine parle peut-être de la traduction latine de Van Giffen (*Giphanius*), donnée par plusieurs des anciennes éditions de l'*Iliade*, et où le vers 296 est ainsi rendu : *In lectulum ut conscenderunt, dormierunt.*

nir; mais je les tiendrai renfermés[1] jusqu'à ce que Jupiter me rende tout le douaire de sa fille :

Ὅσσα οἱ ἐγγυάλιξα, κυνώπιδος εἵνεκα κούρης,
Οὕνεκά οἱ καλὴ θυγάτηρ· ἀτὰρ οὐκ ἐχέθυμος. [Vers 319 et 320.]

Ainsi parla-t-il ; et tous les Dieux accoururent à sa maison. Neptune y vint, et l'agréable Mercure, et l'adroit Apollon y vint aussi.

Θηλύτεραι δὲ θεαὶ μένον αἰδοῖ οἴκοι ἑκάστη. [Vers 324.]

Les Dieux vinrent donc à la porte de la chambre :

Ἔσταν δ' ἐν προθύροισι Θεοὶ, δωτῆρες ἑάων·
Ἄσβεστος δ' ἄρ' ἐνῶρτο γέλως μακάρεσσι Θεοῖσι,
Τέχνας εἰσορόωσι πολύφρονος Ἡφαίστοιο. [Vers 325-327.]

Et chacun disoit à son voisin : Les mauvaises actions ne réussissent point bien, et quelquefois le foible attrape le plus fort :

Οὐκ ἀρετᾷ κακὰ ἔργα· κιχάνει τοι βραδὺς ὠκύν·
Ὡς καὶ νῦν Ἥφαιστος, ἐὼν βραδὺς, εἷλεν Ἄρηα,
Ὠκύτατόν περ ἐόντα Θεῶν οἳ Ὄλυμπον ἔχουσι,
Χωλὸς ἐὼν, τέχνῃσι. Τὸ καὶ μοιχάγρι' ὀφέλλει [vers 329-332],

c'est-à-dire qu'il est coupable d'adultère manifeste, ayant été pris en flagrant délit. Ainsi se parloient-ils les uns aux autres ; et Apollon interrogea Mercure :

Ἑρμεία, Διὸς υἱὲ, διάκτορε, δῶτορ ἑάων,
Ἦ ῥά κεν ἐν δεσμοῖσι θέλοις κρατεροῖσι πιεσθεὶς
Εὕδειν ἐν λέκτροισι παρὰ χρυσῇ Ἀφροδίτῃ ; [Vers 335-337.]

Et Mercure lui répondit :

Αἲ γὰρ τοῦτο γένοιτο, ἄναξ ἑκατηβόλ' Ἄπολλον·
Δεσμοὶ μὲν τρὶς τόσσοι ἀπείρονες ἀμφὶς ἔχοιεν,
Ὑμεῖς δ' εἰσορόῳτε, Θεοὶ, πᾶσαί τε Θέαιναι·
Αὐτὰρ ἐγὼν εὕδοιμι παρὰ χρυσῇ Ἀφροδίτῃ. [Vers 339-342.]

Tous les Dieux se prirent à rire ; mais Neptune n'en rit

---

1. En tête de la page 94, qui commence ici, et de la suivante, Racine a écrit : « Mars et Vénus. »

point du tout : au contraire, il prioit toujours Vulcain de les délier, et s'engageoit à lui payer tout ce qu'il faudroit. Mais Vulcain le prioit de ne lui en parler point, et qu'il n'étoit pas meilleur que les autres :

Δειλαί τοι δειλῶν γε καὶ ἐγγύαι ἐγγυάασθαι. [Vers 351.]

Et comment vous pourrois-je attraper dans mes filets, si Mars s'en étoit une fois fui sans rien payer?

Mais Neptune l'en pressa tellement, et en répondit de telle façon, que Vulcain les délia. Mais pourquoi Neptune étoit-il le seul qui s'empresse pour leur délivrance, vu que Jupiter, le père de l'un et de l'autre, n'en dit pas un mot? Je crois que c'est à cause que Neptune étoit le plus sérieux d'entre les Dieux, et le moins enjoué; c'est ce que Lucien fait dire à Momus dans le *Jupiter tragique*[1] : Ô Dieu! dit-il, Neptune, que vous êtes ruste[2] et grossier! Aussi l'on voit qu'il n'y a rien de plus ruste que ces sortes de gens qui sont toujours sur la mer[3], outre que la mer est le plus farouche de tous les éléments. Enfin ils sortent de ces filets :

Τὼ δ' ἐπεὶ ἐκ δεσμοῖο λύθεν, κρατεροῦ περ ἐόντος,
Αὐτίκ' ἀναΐξαντε, ὁ μὲν Θρῄκηνδε βεβήκει,
Ἡ δ' ἄρα Κύπρον ἵκανε φιλομμειδὴς Ἀφροδίτη,
Ἐς Πάφον. Ἔνθα δέ οἱ τέμενος, βωμός τε θυήεις.
Ἔνθα δέ μιν Χάριτες λοῦσαν καὶ χρῖσαν ἐλαίῳ
Ἀμβρότῳ, οἷα θεοὺς ἐπενήνοθεν αἰὲν ἐόντας.
Ἀμφὶ δὲ εἵματα ἕσσαν ἐπήρατα, θαῦμα ἰδέσθαι. [Vers 360-366.]

Après cela[4], Alcinoüs fit danser deux de ses enfants, qui

---

1. Voyez au § 25 de ce dialogue. Racine cite de mémoire. Dans les éditions de Lucien que nous avons vues, ce n'est pas Momus, mais Jupiter qui taxe Neptune de grossièreté, et encore dans de tout autres termes que ceux que lui prête ici notre auteur.

2. Racine a écrit *ruste*, et non *rustre;* ce n'est point par inadvertance; ce mot est ici deux fois, et nous le retrouverons plus loin dans une lettre que Racine écrivait vers le même temps.

3. *Stetitque in limine barbis horrentibus nauta.* PETR. (*Note de Racine.*) Voyez le chapitre XCIX du *Satyricon* de Pétrone.

4. En tête de la page 96, qui, dans le manuscrit, commence par ces mots, Racine a écrit : « Réconciliation. »

excelloient sur tous les autres. L'un jetoit une balle bien haut en l'air, et l'autre, s'élevant de la terre, la prenoit avant que de retomber. Après ils dansèrent, et tout le monde leur applaudissoit. Ulysse prend occasion de flatter Alcinoüs, et lui dit qu'il avoit raison de vanter leurs danseurs, et qu'il étoit tout étonné de les voir.

Ὡς φάτο· γήθησεν δ' ἱερὸν μένος Ἀλκινόοιο. [Vers 385.]

Ce mot μένος est ordinaire dans Homère pour dire la personne, ou l'esprit, ou le courage. Il met ici ἱερὸν μένος, parce que les rois sont des personnes sacrées. Alcinoüs exhorte les douze principaux d'entre eux de lui donner chacun un talent et quelque vêtement riche, et de l'apporter chez lui, et dit à Euryalus de se réconcilier avec lui de paroles et par présent. Chacun loue le discours d'Alcinoüs, et envoie son présent par un héraut.

Euryalus fait présent à Ulysse de son épée, en lui disant :

Χαῖρε, πάτερ ὦ ξεῖνε· ἔπος δ' εἴπερ τι βέβακται
Δεινὸν, ἄφαρ τὸ φέροιεν ἀναρπάξασαι ἄελλαι. [Vers 408 et 409.]

Ulysse lui répond généreusement :

Καὶ σὺ φίλος, μάλα χαῖρε, Θεοὶ δέ τοι ὄλβια δοῖεν·
Μηδέ τί τοι ξιφεός γε ποθὴ μετόπισθε γένοιτο. [Vers 413 et 414.]

Cette forme de réconciliation est fort belle et fort honnête; et il semble qu'Homère a voulu donner des exemples de toutes les actions civiles dans l'*Odyssée*, comme de militaires dans l'*Iliade*; car la querelle d'Achille et d'Agamemnon, et leur réconciliation, est une idée des querelles des grands, et celle-ci des particuliers, qui sont bien plus faciles à terminer. On porte les présents chez Alcinoüs, lequel dit à sa femme de lui faire aussi le sien comme les autres, et de mener Ulysse au bain, afin qu'il en soupe de meilleur cœur ; et il lui donne aussi sa coupe d'or, afin qu'il se souvienne de lui lorsqu'il fera des libations en l'honneur des Dieux. Aussitôt Arété, sa femme, commande à ses femmes de mettre de l'eau sur le feu, ce qu'il exprime ainsi :

Γάστρην μὲν τρίποδος πῦρ ἄμφεπε, θέομετο δ' ὕδωρ. [Vers 437.]

Cependant elle fait apporter une belle cassette, où elle enferme tous les présents qu'on a faits[1] à Ulysse, et lui dit de la bien fermer lui-même, afin qu'on ne lui dérobe rien dans le vaisseau, tandis qu'il dormira. Alors Ulysse ferme le couvercle, et y fait un nœud difficile, ποικίλον[2] que Circé lui avoit appris. Ensuite il va au bain, et on a soin de lui comme d'un dieu :

Τόφρα δέ οἱ κομιδή γε, θεῷ ὥς, ἔμπεδος ἦεν. [Vers 453.]

Lorsqu'il revient dans la salle, ἄνδρας μέτα οἰνοποτῆρας[3], la belle Nausicaa l'arrête à l'entrée, et lui dit : Bonjour, étranger; souvenez-vous de moi quand vous serez de retour chez vous, puisque je vous ai sauvé la vie :

Ὅτι μοι πρώτῃ ζωάγρι' ὀφέλλεις. [Vers 462.]

Ulysse lui répond fort civilement; et puis il se va seoir auprès du Roi, et se met à table. Le héraut amène l'aimable musicien Démodocus, qui étoit honoré des peuples, et le fait asseoir au milieu de tous les conviés. Ulysse lui envoie un grand quartier de fesse de porc, c'est-à-dire, ce me semble, d'un cochon de lait, et force sauce autour, θαλερὴ δ' ἦν ἀμφὶς ἀλοιφή[4]. Donnez cela, dit-il, à Démodocus, et dites-lui que je . . . .[5], tout triste que je suis[6] :

Πᾶσι γὰρ ἀνθρώποισιν ἐπιχθονίοισιν ἀοιδοὶ
Τιμῆς ἔμμοροί εἰσι καὶ αἰδοῦς, οὕνεχ' ἄρα σφέας
Οἴμας Μοῦσ' ἐδίδαξε· φίλησε δὲ φῦλον ἀοιδῶν. [Vers 479-481.]

Démodocus est fort réjoui de la bonne volonté d'Ulysse; et sur la fin du souper, Ulysse lui dit :

Δημόδοκ', ἔξοχα δή σε βροτῶν αἰνίζομ' ἁπάντων·

---

1. *Fait*, sans accord, dans le manuscrit.
2. Vers 448. — 3. Vers 456.
4. Vers 476.
5. Il y a une lacune dans le manuscrit ; les mots *que je* terminent une page ; et *tout triste* commence la suivante.
6. En tête de la page 98, qui commence par ces mots, Racine a écrit : « Musique. — Femme qui pleure son mari. »

Ἤ σέ γε Μοῦσ' ἐδίδαξε, Διὸς παῖς, ἤ σέ γ' Ἀπόλλων·
Λίην γὰρ κατὰ κόσμον Ἀχαιῶν οἶτον ἀείδεις. [Vers 487-489.]

Mais, dit-il, poursuivez, et chantez ce qu'ils firent dans ce cheval de bois qu'Ulysse amena dans le château de Troie. Si vous chantez cela comme il faut, je dirai à tout le monde :

Ὡς ἄρα τοι πρόφρων Θεὸς ὤπασε θέσπιν ἀοιδήν. [Vers 498.]

Ainsi parla Ulysse.

Ὁ δ' ὁρμηθεὶς θεοῦ ἤρχετο [vers 499],

ce qu'il chante fort bien, et loue principalement Ulysse d'avoir combattu comme un Mars, et d'avoir vaincu par l'assistance de Pallas ; ainsi chantoit-il excellemment.

Αὐτὰρ Ὀδυσσεὺς
Τήκετο· δάκρυ δ' ἔδευεν ὑπὸ βλεφάροισι παρειάς [vers 521 et 522] ;

et il ajoute cette belle comparaison, qui est sans doute un des endroits les plus achevés d'Homère :

Ὡς δὲ γυνὴ κλαίῃσι φίλον πόσιν ἀμφιπεσοῦσα,
Ὅς τε ἑῆς πρόσθεν πόλιος λαῶν τε πέσῃσιν,
Ἄστεϊ καὶ τεκέεσσιν ἀμύνων νηλεὲς ἦμαρ·
Ἡ μὲν τὸν θνῄσκοντα καὶ ἀσπαίροντ' ἐσιδοῦσα,
Ἀμφ' αὐτῷ χυμένη, λίγα κωκύει· οἱ δέ τ' ὄπισθεν
Κόπτοντες δούρεσσι μετάφρενον, ἠδὲ καὶ ὤμους,
Εἴρερον εἰσανάγουσι, πόνον τ' ἐχέμεν καὶ ὀϊζύν·
Τῆς δ' ἐλεεινοτάτῳ ἀχεϊ φθινύθουσι παρειαί. [Vers 523-530.]

Le Roi s'aperçoit des larmes d'Ulysse, et ayant peur que le chant ne lui plaise pas, il le fait cesser : Car, dit-il, nous ne nous réjouissons ici que pour divertir l'étranger ; car un étranger tient lieu de frère à un homme sage. Il prie Ulysse de lui dire son nom : Car, dit-il, il n'y a point d'homme au monde, bon ou mauvais, qui n'ait son nom, vu que les pères et mères en donnent toujours un à leurs enfants d'abord qu'ils sont nés. Dites-nous aussi votre pays, afin que nos navires le sachant, elles[1] vous y mènent ; car elles n'ont point besoin de matelots, et n'ont point de gouvernail comme les

1. Voyez le *Lexique*, au mot NAVIRE.

autres; car elles savent elles-mêmes l'intention des hommes, et connoissent tous les pays et toutes les villes, et passent fort vite les eaux de la mer, sans qu'il leur arrive jamais aucun danger, car elles sont couvertes de nuages et d'obscurité : de quoi Neptune étant jaloux a prédit qu'un jour un de nos vaisseaux, revenant de conduire quelqu'un, se changeroit en montagne devant cette ville, et lui boucheroit le chemin de la mer. Homère prépare déjà cet incident, qu'il doit faire arriver à l'occasion d'Ulysse. Enfin il demande à Ulysse pourquoi il pleure sitôt qu'il entend parler du siége de Troie, que les Dieux ont voulu ruiner, afin qu'elle serve de chanson aux siècles futurs. N'y avez-vous point perdu quelque parent, ou quelque gendre, ou quelque beau-père, lesquels nous sont les plus chers après ceux de notre sang, ou bien quelque ami savant ou sage, et d'agréable humeur ?

Ἤ τίς που καὶ ἑταῖρος ἀνὴρ κεχαρισμένα εἰδὼς
Ἐσθλός· ἐπεὶ οὐ μέν τι κασιγνήτοιο χερείων
Γίνεται, ὅς κεν, ἑταῖρος ἐὼν, πεπνύμενα εἰδῇ. [Vers 584-586.]

LIVRE IX.

Ulysse commence le récit de ses voyages, comme Énée fait à Didon; mais au lieu que le récit d'Énée ne tient que deux livres, celui d'Ulysse en tient quatre. Il répond à Alcinoüs sur ce qu'il avoit fait cesser le musicien : Grand prince, dit-il, il est toujours beau d'entendre les musiciens, surtout celui-ci qui chante d'une voix égale aux Dieux; car, dit-il, je ne crois pas qu'il y ait rien de plus beau au monde que de se réjouir dans les festins et dans les concerts, lorsque le peuple cependant est en repos et réjouissances :

Οὐ γὰρ ἔγωγέ τί φημι τέλος χαριέστερον εἶναι,
Ἢ ὅταν εὐφροσύνη μὲν ἔχῃ κάτα δῆμον ἅπαντα,
Δαιτυμόνες δ' ἀνὰ δώματ' ἀκουάζωνται ἀοιδοῦ,
Ἥμενοι ἐξείης· παρὰ δὲ πλήθωσι τράπεζαι
Σίτου καὶ κρειῶν· μέθυ δ' ἐκ κρητῆρος ἀφύσσων
Οἰνοχόος φορέῃσι καὶ ἐγχείῃ δεπάεσσιν.
Τοῦτό τί μοι κάλλιστον ἐνὶ φρεσὶν εἴδεται εἶναι. [Vers 5-11.]

Il dit son nom et son pays. Je suis Ulysse, dit-il :

Εἴμ' Ὀδυσεὺς Λαερτιάδης, ὃς πᾶσι δόλοισιν
Ἀνθρώποισι μέλω, καί μευ κλέος οὐρανὸν ἵκει. [Vers 19 et 20.]

Δόλος se prend là en bonne part, pour adresse, prudence. Je suis bienvenu de tout le monde, à cause de mes adresses; et ma gloire est répandue partout.

Sum pius Æneas,... fama super æthera notus[1].

Il décrit la situation d'Ithaque : Elle est rude, dit-il; mais elle est bonne pour élever des enfants, τρηχεῖ', ἀλλ' ἀγαθὴ κουροτρόφος[2]. C'est peut-être à cause de cette rudesse même; car il n'y a rien qui soit moins propre à l'éducation de la jeunesse qu'un pays mol et délicieux. Enfin, dit-il, je ne vois rien de plus charmant que mon pays; et c'est en vain que Calypso, grande déesse, et Circé, tout de même, m'ont voulu retenir dans leurs grottes, souhaitant que je fusse leur mari. Elles n'ont jamais pu me fléchir de ce côté-là :

Ὣς οὐδὲν γλύκιον ἧς πατρίδος οὐδὲ τοκήων
Γίνεται, εἴπερ καί τις ἀπόπροθι πίονα οἶκον
Γαίῃ ἐν ἀλλοδαπῇ ναίει ἀπάνευθε τοκήων. [Vers 34-36.]

Il commence le récit de ses voyages :

Ἰλιόθεν με φέρων ἄνεμος Κικόνεσσι πέλασσεν,
Ἰσμάρῳ. [Vers 39 et 40.]

Il pilla cette ville, prit force butin, et vouloit s'en aller; mais ses compagnons se mirent à boire et à faire grand chère. Cependant les Cicons allèrent appeler leurs voisins, Κίκονες Κικόνεσσι γεγώνευν[3]; et ils vinrent charger en grand nombre les gens d'Ulysse, autant qu'il y a de feuilles et de fleurs au printemps. Ils se battirent jusqu'au soir :

Ἦμος δ' ἠέλιος μετενίσσετο βουλυτόνδε. [Vers 58.]

Alors les gens d'Ulysse eurent du dessous : il en périt plusieurs, et le reste gagna les vaisseaux, non sans avoir appelé

1. Virgile, *Énéide*, livre I, vers 378 et 379.
2. Vers 27. — 3. Vers 47.

par trois fois chacun de leurs compagnons qui leur manquoient. Quand ils furent en haute mer, la tempête vint; ils furent obligés de prendre terre et d'attendre le vent durant deux jours et deux nuits :

Κείμεθ' ὁμοῦ καμάτῳ τε καὶ ἄλγεσι θυμὸν ἔδοντες. [Vers 75.]

Au troisième jour, il se remit en mer, et le vent le poussa, à la fin, à la terre des Lotophages; il envoya quelques-uns de ses compagnons pour savoir quels peuples c'étoient. Les Lotophages ne leur firent point d'autre mal que de leur faire manger de leur fruit. Ce pays est une île devers l'Afrique, appelée ainsi à cause d'un fruit qu'elle porte, que les Grecs appellent *lotos*. Il est si délicieux que cela a donné lieu à la fable de dire que ceux qui en avoient une fois mangé ne se souvenoient plus de leur pays. Il y a en Égypte une herbe qui porte le même nom, et qu'Homère met au nombre de celles qui naissent pour le plaisir des Dieux, à ce que dit Pline, l. 22, c. 21. En effet, Homère, au [livre] 14. de l'*Iliade*, parlant de Jupiter et de Junon, dit ces paroles :

Τοῖσι δ' ὑπὸ χθὼν δῖα φύεν νεοθηλέα ποίην,
Λωτόν θ' ἑρσήεντα, ἰδὲ κρόκον, ἠδ' ὑάκινθον
Πυκνὸν καὶ μαλακόν, ὃς ἀπὸ χθονὸς ὑψόσ' ἔεργε [1].

Mais en cet endroit de l'*Odyssée*, c'est un arbre qui portoit ce fruit merveilleux, qui fait oublier toutes choses à ceux qui en mangent, de sorte qu'ils veulent demeurer avec les Lotophages. Ulysse fut obligé de ramener par force ses compagnons, qui pleuroient, et de les lier dans leurs vaisseaux; et faisant rentrer tous les autres de peur qu'ils ne mangeassent de ce fruit, ils s'en allèrent devers l'île des Cyclopes, qu'il appelle des tyrans et des gens sans lois, lesquels, dit-il, se fiant aux Dieux immortels, ne plantent et ne labourent point de leurs mains :

Οἵ ῥα Θεοῖσι πεποιθότες ἀθανάτοισιν,
Οὔτε φυτεύουσιν χερσὶν φυτὸν, οὔτ' ἀρόωσιν. [Vers 107 et 108.]

On dit que la Sicile fut autrefois habitée par des gens cruels

---

1. *Iliade*, livre XIV, vers 347-349.

et barbares, qui ont donné lieu à la fable des Cyclopes. Et s'il dit ici qu'ils se fioient aux Dieux immortels, c'est à dire à la nature et à la bonté du territoire; car on voit bien ensuite qu'ils se moquoient des Dieux. Aussi il dit que tout y venoit sans être semé ni cultivé, comme le blé, l'orge et le vin, auxquels la pluie donne de l'accroissement; mais pour eux, ils n'ont aucunes lois ni aucune police :

Τοῖσιν δ' οὔτ' ἀγοραὶ βουληφόροι, οὔτε θέμιστες·
Ἀλλ' οἵγ' ὑψηλῶν ὀρέων ναίουσι κάρηνα,
Ἐν σπέσσι γλαφυροῖσι· θεμιστεύει δὲ ἕκαστος
Παίδων ἠδ' ἀλόχων, οὐδ' ἀλλήλων ἀλέγουσι. [Vers 112-115.]

Et assez près de là il y a une petite île, toute couverte d'arbres, et pleine de biches et de chevreuils, qui ne sont point troublés par les chasseurs, qui se travaillent et se peinent[1] en courant sur le faîte des montagnes, ni par les bergers, ni par les laboureurs. Mais cette île n'étant point cultivée, est déserte d'hommes, et n'est habitée que par des chèvres; car les Cyclopes n'ont point de navires peintes, μιλτοπάρῃοι[2], ni d'ouvriers qui leur en puissent bâtir, afin de voyager sur la mer, comme font les autres hommes; car ils cultiveroient cette île, qui de soi n'est point mauvaise, et qui porteroit de chaque chose en sa saison :

Φέροι δέ κεν ὥρια πάντα·
Ἐν μὲν γὰρ λειμῶνες ἁλὸς πολιοῖο παρ' ὄχθας
Ὑδρηλοί, μαλακοί· μάλα κ' ἄφθιτοι ἄμπελοι εἶεν.
Ἐν δ' ἄροσις λείη· μάλα κεν βαθὺ λήϊον αἰεὶ
Εἰς ὥρας ἀμῷεν, ἐπεὶ μάλα πῖαρ ὑπ' οὖδας. [Vers 131-135.]

Elle a [un] port fort commode, et où il n'est besoin ni de câble ni d'ancre, mais on y peut[3] demeurer tant qu'on veut et y attendre le vent; et là, sous une grotte, il y a une claire fontaine entourée d'aunes : c'est là où aborda Ulysse.

Καί τις θεὸς ἡγεμόνευε
Νύκτα δι' ὀρφναίην· οὐδὲ προὐφαίνετ' ἰδέσθαι·
Ἀὴρ γὰρ περὶ νηυσὶ βαθεῖ' ἦν, οὐδὲ σελήνη

---

1. Dans le manuscrit : *penent*. — M. Aimé-Martin a mis : « et se paissent. »

2. Vers 125. — 3. Racine a écrit par mégarde : « on n'y peut. »

Οὐρανόθεν προὔφαινε· κατείχετο γὰρ νεφέεσσιν.
Ἔνθ' οὔτις τὴν νῆσον ἐσέδρακεν ὀφθαλμοῖσιν,
Οὔτ' οὖν κύματα μακρὰ κυλινδόμενα ποτὶ χέρσον
Εἰσίδομεν, πρὶν νῆας ἐϋσσέλμους ἐπικέλσαι. [Vers 142-148.]

Virgile a imité cette description d'une nuit obscure, lorsqu'il fait aussi aborder Énée à l'île des Cyclopes :

Ignarique viæ Cyclopum allabimur oris....
Nam neque erant astrorum ignes, nec lucidus æthra
Siderea polus ; obscuro sed nubila cœlo ;
Et lunam in nimbo nox intempesta tenebat [1].

Mais celle d'Homère paroît beaucoup plus achevée, et entre plus dans le particulier ; car la description de Virgile peut aussi bien venir sur la terre que sur la mer ; mais celle d'Homère revient parfaitement à une nuit sur la mer. Ce qui rend celle de Virgile fort belle, c'est ce grand bruit du mont Etna qu'on entendoit durant la nuit, sans pouvoir discerner ce que c'étoit :

Nec quæ sonitum det causa videmus [2].

Quand il est jour, Ulysse prend terre dans cette île, et en admire la beauté. Les Nymphes lui suscitent des chevreuils pour le dîner de ses gens. Aussitôt ils prennent leurs arcs et leurs haches et courent après ; et Dieu leur donne une fort belle chasse. Il avoit douze vaisseaux, et il départit neuf chevreuils à chacun, et on lui en donne dix pour le sien. Ils demeurent là jusqu'au soir à faire grand'chère [3] ; car ils avoient encore beaucoup de vin de réserve, qu'ils avoient pris au pillage d'Ismare, ville des Cicons. Il jette la vue sur l'île des Cyclopes, et il voit la fumée qui en sort, et il entend le bruit des chèvres et des brebis. Il attend encore la nuit et le lendemain au matin, et il fait demeurer là le reste de ses vaisseaux, et s'en va avec le sien pour voir qui sont les habitants de cette île. Quand ils sont arrivés au bord, ils voient une grande grotte ombragée de lauriers, et là dormoient grand nombre de brebis et de chèvres, et attenant [4] de cette grotte

---

1. *Énéide*, livre III, vers 569-587. — 2. *Ibidem*, vers 584.
3. Ici Racine a mis une apostrophe. D'ordinaire il n'en met point après *grand*, pris ainsi au féminin.
4. Il y a dans le manuscrit : *entenant*, en un seul mot.

étoit bâtie une espèce de grande salle, où étoit couché un homme prodigieusement grand, lequel habitoit loin du voisinage des autres, car il étoit fort méchant; et c'étoit une chose étrange combien il étoit grand; et il ne ressembloit pas à un homme qui mange du pain, c'est-à-dire à un homme commun, ἀνδρί γε σιτοφάγῳ[1], mais plutôt à une haute montagne séparée des autres. Ulysse commande à ses gens de l'attendre, et en ayant pris douze avec lui, il s'y en alla, après avoir pris un vaisseau de vin noir, μέλανος[2], et fort délicieux, que lui avoit donné Maron, prêtre d'Apollon, à cause qu'il avoit sauvé lui, sa femme et ses enfants; car il demeuroit à Ismare, dans un bois sacré à Apollon. Il fit de beaux présents à Ulysse, sept talents d'or travaillé, une coupe d'argent, et douze vaisseaux d'un vin doux et sans mélange, ou incorruptible,

Ἡδὺν, ἀκηράσιον, θεῖον ποτόν [vers 205];

et pas un de ses valets ni de ses servantes ne savoit qu'il l'eût; et il n'y avoit que lui:

Ἀλλ' αὐτός τ', ἄλοχός τε φίλη, ταμίη τε μί' οἴη [vers 207];

et ce vin-là étoit si puissant qu'on y mettoit vingt mesures d'eau sur une de vin:

Τὸν δ' ὅτε πίνοιεν μελιηδέα οἶνον ἐρυθρὸν,
Ἓν δέπας ἐμπλήσας, ὕδατος ἀνὰ εἴκοσι μέτρα
Χεῦ'· ὀδμὴ δ' ἡδεῖα ἀπὸ κρητῆρος ὀδώδει,
Θεσπεσίη. Τότ' ἂν οὔτοι ἀποσχέσθαι φίλον ἦεν. [Vers 208-211.]

Et Pline dit que ce n'est point une fable, l. 14, ch. 4: *Durat etiam vis eadem in terra generi vigorque indomitus: quippe cum Mutianus ter consul* (c'est sans doute ce grand capitaine qui fit Vespasien empereur), *ex his qui nuperrime prodidere, sextarios singulos octonis aquæ misceri compererit, præsens in eo tractu; esse autem colore nigrum, odoratum, vetustate pinguescere.* Et on l'appeloit *vinum maroneum. Vino antiquissima claritas maroneo*[3]. Et il ajoute qu'Aristée fut le

---

1. Vers 191. — 2. Vers 196.
3. Cette dernière phrase est un peu avant les précédentes dans

SUR L'ODYSSÉE D'HOMÈRE. 147

premier, en ce pays-là, voisin de la Thrace, qui mêla le miel avec le vin, *suavitate præcipua utriusque naturæ sponte provenientis*. Cela montre qu'Homère n'a rien dit sans fondement; et on voit bien qu'il étoit instruit de tout ce qu'il y a de beau dans la nature. Ulysse en prit donc un petit vaisseau avec quelques vivres, et son grand courage l'excita à aller trouver cet homme :

Ἄνδρ' ἐπελεύσεσθαι, μεγάλην ἐπιειμένον ἀλκὴν,
Ἄγριον, οὔτε δίκας εὖ εἰδότα, οὔτε θέμιστας. [Vers 214 et 215.]

Ils entrèrent dans l'antre de ce Cyclope, et ils ne le treuvèrent pas. Homère ne dit pas son nom; mais les autres poëtes, comme Théocrite, Virgile et Ovide, l'ont appelé Polyphème. Ils trouvèrent dans son antre des vaisseaux tout pleins de lait, et les étables remplies d'agneaux et de boucs[1], séparés les uns des autres : les agneaux[2] à part, les plus jeunes ailleurs, et en un autre endroit ceux qui ne faisoient que de naître. On voyoit nager le lait clair sur tous les vases; et tous ceux qui servoient à traire le lait étoient tout prêts. Les compagnons d'Ulysse le prioient bien fort de prendre force[3] fromages, et de chasser dans leur vaisseau tout ce qu'ils pourroient d'agneaux et de cabris; et il eût bien fait.

Οὐδ' ἄρ' ἔμελλ' ἑτάροισι φανεὶς ἐρατεινὸς ἔσεσθαι. [Vers 230.]

Ils s'amusèrent donc à manger quelques fromages, en attendant; et il vint bientôt, portant une charge de bois, qu'il jeta à la porte pour faire cuire son souper. Ce bois fit grand bruit en tombant, et ils se retirèrent tout effrayés jusqu'au fond de l'antre. Le Cyclope fit entrer toutes les chèvres et les brebis pour tirer le lait, et laissa les mâles à la porte. Et étant entré, il ferma son antre avec une pierre si grosse que vingt-deux chariots à quatre roues ne l'auroient jamais pu bouger de là; et il dit un peu après que cette boîte[4] fermoit son

---

ce même chapitre IV de Pline (ailleurs chapitre VI) que Racine vient de citer.

1. On lit en interligne, au-dessus de *boucs* : « cabris. »
2. Le mot *jeunes* a été effacé devant *agneaux*.
3. Ici encore il y a *forces*. Voyez ci-dessus, p. 102, note 1.
4. En termes de métiers, le mot *boîte* a quelques emplois voisins

antre, comme qui fermeroit un carquois ou un étui de son couvercle :

Τόσσην ἠλίβατον πέτρην ἐπέθηκε θύρῃσιν [vers 243];

et s'étant assis,

Ἤμελγεν ὄϊς καὶ μηκάδας αἶγας,
Πάντα κατὰ μοῖραν, καὶ ὑπ' ἔμβρυον ἦκεν ἑκάστῃ. [Vers 244 et 245.]

Après quoi, il fit prendre avec la présure[1] la moitié de son lait, et le mit bien proprement sur des claies d'osier, et mit le reste dans des pots pour boire à son souper.

Homère a voulu décrire le ménage des champs en la personne de Cyclope[2], et tous les poëtes l'ont suivi en faisant un berger de Polyphème : témoin la belle églogue de Théocrite[3], qu'Ovide a copiée dans le [livre] 13. de ses *Métamorphoses*[4]. Après qu'il eut ainsi tout disposé, il alluma du feu, et vit Ulysse et ses compagnons, et leur demanda qui ils étoient, si c'étoit des marchands ou des pirates. Dès qu'ils l'ouïrent, ils pensèrent mourir de peur à l'effroyable ton de sa voix :

Δεισάντων φθόγγον τε βαρὺν αὐτόν τε πέλωρον. [Vers 257.]

Ulysse pourtant lui répondit qu'ils étoient Grecs et soldats d'Agamemnon, dont la gloire étoit répandue partout :

Τόσσην γὰρ διέπερσε πόλιν, καὶ ἀπώλεσε λαοὺς
Πολλούς [vers 265 et 266];

et il le prie, au nom de Jupiter, vengeur des suppliants et des étrangers, d'avoir pitié d'eux en leur donnant quelque chose, et de respecter les Dieux. Le Cyclope lui répondit : Vous

---

de celui que Racine en fait ici en le prenant dans le sens de couvercle, ou d'objet qui ferme en s'emboîtant.

1. Racine a écrit *pressure*.
2. Tel est bien le texte du manuscrit. Racine a-t-il écrit *de* pour *du*, ou omis *ce*, ou mis (en ce seul endroit, ce qui est peu probable) *Cyclope*, sans article, comme nom propre ?
3. L'*idylle* xi.
4. Vers 789 et suivants. Toutefois Ovide a moins copié que défiguré son modèle.

êtes bien sot, mon ami, et vous venez de bien loin, puisque vous me dites de craindre ou de respecter les Dieux :

Νήπιός εἰς, ὦ ξεῖν', ἢ τηλόθεν εἰλήλουθας. [Vers 273.]

Car les Cyclopes ne se soucient point de votre Jupiter, nourri d'une chèvre, ni de tous les Dieux ; car nous valons bien plus qu'eux ; et je ne t'épargnerai ni toi ni les tiens en considération de Jupiter, si ce n'est que je le fasse de mon bon gré. Mais dis-moi si tu as ici près quelque vaisseau.

Ὣς φάτο πειράζων· ἐμὲ δ' οὐ λάθεν εἰδότα πολλά. [Vers 281.]

Et il lui répondit que son vaisseau s'étoit échoué contre leur île. A cela, cette âme farouche ne répondit rien, et il jeta les mains sur deux de ses compagnons, qu'il brisa contre terre comme de petits chiens ; la cervelle couloit par terre et la rendoit humide : et les ayant coupés par morceaux, il les apprêta pour son souper, et les dévora comme un lion nourri sur les montagnes, mangeant tout jusqu'aux intestins, les chairs et la moelle des os.

Ἡμεῖς δὲ κλαίοντες ἀνασχέθομεν Διὶ χεῖρας,
Σχέτλια ἔργ' ὁρόωντες· ἀμηχανίη δ' ἔχε θυμόν. [Vers 294 et 295.]

Et après qu'il eut rempli son grand ventre, μεγάλην ἐμπλήσατο νηδύν[1], de chair humaine, et de lait, qu'il buvoit par-dessus, il se coucha tout de son long parmi ses brebis, et s'endormit. Ulysse eut envie de lui fourrer son épée dans le cœur :

Οὐτάμεναι πρὸς στῆθος, ὅθι φρένες ἧπαρ ἔχουσιν,
Χεῖρ' ἐπιμασσάμενος [vers 301 et 302],

c'est-à-dire de la fourrer jusqu'aux gardes dans un si grand corps ; mais il songea que s'il le tuoit, ils fussent aussi bien morts là dedans, leur étant impossible de reculer cette horrible pierre qui bouchoit l'antre. Ils attendirent donc en gémissant le retour du jour ; et quand il fut venu, le Cyclope fit de même que le soir, et prit aussi deux des compagnons d'Ulysse pour son dîner, après lequel il mena paître son troupeau et ferma sa caverne. Ulysse demeura là :

1. Vers 296.

Κακὰ βυσσοδομεύων,
Εἴ πως τισαίμην, δώη δέ μοι εὖχος Ἀθήνη. [Vers 316 et 317.]

Il aperçut contre la muraille une grande branche d'olivier, que le Cyclope avoit coupée pour en faire son bâton quand elle seroit sèche. Elle étoit aussi grande que le mât d'un vaisseau chargé, à vingt rames. Il en coupa la longueur d'une toise, qu'il donna à ses compagnons, pour l'amenuiser par le bout, et la mit après dans le feu, pour la mieux ajuster. En suite de quoi, il la cacha sous le fumier, qui étoit là en grande abondance. Il jeta au sort pour prendre quatre de ses compagnons qui l'aidassent à lui crever l'œil quand il dormiroit, et le sort tomba sur ceux qu'il eût voulu choisir lui-même. Sur le soir, le Cyclope revient et fait rentrer dans son antre tout son troupeau, mâles et femelles, soit qu'il le fît exprès, ou que Dieu le voulût ainsi. Homère prépare une invention pour faire sortir Ulysse. Et après qu'il eut fermé encore son antre, et fait le reste à son ordinaire, il prit encore deux des compagnons d'Ulysse. A ce compte-là, il y en eut six de mangés, et il n'en restoit plus que six autres avec Ulysse. Cependant Virgile n'en compte que deux, et mal, ce me semble, car Homère en compte trois fois deux, au souper du premier jour, et au dîner et au souper du lendemain. C'est au [livre] 3ᵉ de l'*Énéid*.[1], où il imite parfaitement Homère. Ovide en parle, en passant, au [livre] 14. des *Métam[orphoses]*[2]. Enfin Ulysse, tenant une coupe pleine de ce vin délicieux, lui dit[3] :

Κύκλωψ, τῆ, πίε οἶνον. [Vers 347.]

Je crois que de ce mot de τῆ, qui signifie *prends*, vient le même mot que nous disons aux chiens[4]. Voyez, lui dit-il, quel vin étoit dans notre vaisseau. Je vous en donnerai encore un coup, afin que vous me renvoyiez[5].

1. Vers 623 et suivants. — 2. Vers 205 et 206.
3. Dans le manuscrit : « et lui dit. »
4. Le monosyllabe *té* ou *tè*, dont parfois on fait usage en s'adressant aux chiens, à d'autres bêtes, même aux petits enfants, nous paraît être un substitut diminutif de l'impératif *tiens*, et en venir. C'est remonter bien haut que d'en aller chercher l'étymologie dans l'*Odyssée*.
5. Racine a écrit : *renvoyez*.

Σὺ δὲ μαίνεαι οὐκ ἔτ' ἀνεκτῶς. [Vers 350.]

Comment voulez-vous que personne vous vienne jamais voir, puisque vous êtes si cruel? Il prit le vin et le but :

"Ἥσατο δ' αἰνῶς
Ἡδὺ ποτὸν πίνων, καὶ μ' ᾔτεε δεύτερον αὖτις·
Δός μοι ἔτι πρόφρων, καί μοι τεὸν οὔνομα εἰπέ [vers 353-355],

afin que je te fasse quelque présent; car nous avons de bon vin parmi nous ; mais celui-là semble être écoulé du nectar et de l'ambrosie. Ulysse lui en donne par trois fois, et il en but inconsidérément par trois fois. Et quand le vin eut un peu occupé son esprit, Ulysse lui parla d'une façon flatteuse, et lui dit qu'il s'appeloit Οὖτις, *Personne*. Le Cyclope lui répondit brutalement:

Οὖτιν ἐγὼ πύματον ἔδομαι μετὰ οἷς ἑτάροισι. [Vers 369.]

Il s'endormit là-dessus, καδδέ μιν ὕπνος Ἥρει πανδαμάτωρ[1] : son gosier exhaloit le vin et la chair humaine. Alors Ulysse, ayant pris son levier tout ardent, et ayant fortifié ses gens, αὐτὰρ θάρσος ἐνέπνευσεν μέγα Δαίμων[2], ils le fichèrent dans son œil, Ulysse s'appuyant dessus pour l'enfoncer, comme on enfonceroit un vilebrequin dans une pièce de bois. Son œil grilloit et petilloit comme un fer chaud qu'un forgeron baigne dans l'eau pour le renforcer. Le Cyclope fit un cri horrible, qui les écarta tous. Les Cyclopes accoururent, et lui demandèrent si quelqu'un l'assassinoit; il répondit :

Ὦ φίλοι, Οὖτίς με κτείνει δόλῳ, ἠδὲ βίηφι [vers 408];

et ils lui répondirent qu'il prît donc patience s'il sentoit du mal, et qu'il priât son père Neptune. Ulysse rit de son erreur.

Κύκλωψ δὲ στενάχων τε καὶ ὠδίνων ὀδύνῃσι,
Χερσὶ ψηλαφόων. [Vers 415 et 416.]

Il ouvrit son antre, se mit à la porte pour voir si quel-

---

1. Vers 372 et 373. — 2. Vers 381.

qu'un sortiroit parmi les brebis ; car il croyoit Ulysse si sot que cela.

Πάντας δὲ δόλους καὶ μῆτιν ὕφαινον,
Ὥστε περὶ ψυχῆς· μέγα γὰρ κακὸν ἐγγύθεν ἦεν. [Vers 422 et 423.]

C'est ce que Virgile a fort bien imité :

Oblitusve sui est Ithacus discrimine tanto[1].

Il lia chacun de ses gens sous trois béliers, dont celui du milieu en portoit un ; et lui se mit hardiment sous un grand bélier, s'attachant à sa laine violette. Le Cyclope fit sortir tout son troupeau le matin ; les brebis étoient chargées de lait, crioient ; et lui les manioit tous sur le dos. Le bélier sortit le dernier, chargé de sa laine et d'Ulysse. Polyphème lui tient un discours tout à fait beau et déplorable[2]. Quand Ulysse est sorti, il délie ses gens, et ils s'en vont à leur vaisseau. Ulysse lui insulte de loin. Il lui jette un gros rocher, qui rapproche son vaisseau près du bord. Ulysse, en remontant, lui insulte encore malgré tous ses compagnons, et lui dit son nom. Le Cyclope s'écrie que le devin Telemus lui avoit prédit qu'Ulysse lui crèveroit l'œil.

Νῦν δέ μ' ἐὼν ὀλίγος τε καὶ οὐτιδανὸς καὶ ἄκικυς[3]. [Vers 515.]

Il jette un plus gros rocher, et invoque Neptune qu'il tourmente Ulysse, lequel sacrifie son bélier à Jupiter.

Ὁ δ' οὐκ ἐμπάζετο ἱρῶν [vers 553] ;

mais il méditoit leur perte.

---

1. *Énéide*, livre III, vers 629.
2. Après ces derniers mots, Racine a écrit : « Voyez devant, page 48. » En effet, à la page 48 du manuscrit, sur le verso du même feuillet, dont le recto nous a fourni la note 2 de notre page 110, Racine a copié les vers 447-460 du IX{{e}} livre de l'*Odyssée* : Κριὲ πέπον.... κ. τ. λ., en tête desquels il a écrit : « Polyphème à son bélier. V. (*voyez*) p. 111 ; » c'est-à-dire qu'il renvoie ici.
3. La citation de ce vers, après lequel le sens reste suspendu, et que ne suit aucune explication, ne se comprend pas bien. Racine a sans doute omis ici quelque chose.

LIVRE X.

Ulysse, continuant ses voyages, va en Éolie ; il y avoit sept îles qu'on appeloit de ce nom, toutes proches l'une de l'autre. Elles furent appelées ainsi à cause de cet Éole qui y régnoit du temps du siége de Troie. On l'a fait roi des vents, à cause qu'il fut le premier qui les remarqua, ou bien à cause d'une montagne ou deux qui sont dans ces îles qui jetoient du feu ; et à la fumée les habitants conjecturoient quels vents souffleroient. Celle où Éole demeuroit et où Ulysse aborde s'appeloit Strongyle. Elles sont assez près de la Sicile, à douze milles d'Italie. Ce prince étoit donc le roi des vents, et il l'appelle φίλος ἀθανάτοισι Θεοῖσι[1]. C'est lui à qui Junon fait une si belle harangue au [livre] 1. de l'*Énéide*[2]. Il avoit, dit Homère, douze enfants, six garçons et six filles ; il les maria les uns avec les autres, si bien qu'ils demeuroient tous auprès de leur père et de leur mère.

> Οἱ δ' αἰεὶ παρὰ πατρὶ φίλῳ καὶ μητέρι κεδνῇ
> Δαίνυνται· παρὰ δέ σφιν ὀνείατα μυρία κεῖται·
> Κνισσῆεν δέ τε δῶμα περιστεναχίζεται αὐλῇ
> Ἤματα, νύκτας δ' αὖτε παρ' αἰδοίοις ἀλόχοισιν
> Εὕδουσ', ἔν τε τάπησι καὶ ἐν τρητοῖς λεχέεσσι. [Vers 8-12.]

Cela représente parfaitement bien une maison paisible et commode, et qui n'est troublée d'aucune division. Ulysse y fut fort bien reçu, et Éole le retint un mois durant, lui demandant toutes les particularités du siége de Troie ; et lorsqu'Ulysse le pria de le renvoyer, il lui donna tous les vents enfermés dans une peau de bœuf, qu'il lia dans son vaisseau avec une chaîne d'argent, afin que pas un n'échappât :

> Ἵνα μήτι παραπνεύσῃ ὀλίγον περ. [Vers 24.]

Il n'enferma point le Zéphyr :

> Αὐτὰρ ἐμοὶ πνοιὴν Ζεφύρου προέηκεν ἀῆναι,

---

1. Vers 2. — 2. Vers 65-75.

Ὄφρα φέροι νῆάς τε καὶ αὐτούς· οὐδ' ἄρ' ἔμελλεν
Ἐκτελέειν· αὐτῶν γὰρ ἀπωλόμεθ' ἀφραδίῃσιν. [Vers 25-27.]

Ce passage se peut appliquer aux mauvais chrétiens, à qui Dieu donne des grâces pour les conduire au salut; mais ils périssent par leurs propres fautes.

En effet, après avoir navigué neuf jours, et qu'au dixième ils voyoient leur patrie,

Καὶ δὴ πυρπολέοντας ἐλεύσσομεν, ἐγγὺς ἐόντας [vers 30],

et que ceux qui portoient les flambeaux étoient déjà proches (je crois que c'étoit quelque fanal qui étoit au port d'Ithaque, comme il y en avoit en plusieurs endroits), alors Ulysse s'endormit de fatigue; car il ne quittoit jamais le gouvernail :

Αἰεὶ γὰρ πόδα νηὸς ἐνώμων· οὐδέ τῳ ἄλλῳ
Δῶχ' ἑτάρων, ἵνα θᾶσσον ἱκοίμεθα πατρίδα γαῖαν. [Vers 32 et 33.]

Cela montre que les hommes intelligents font tout eux-mêmes, et qu'ils ne s'en rapportent point à leurs compagnons. Et il en prit mal à Ulysse de n'avoir pas pu continuer; car ses compagnons s'allèrent imaginer que cette peau étoit sans doute pleine d'or et d'argent, et ils disoient entre eux :

Ὢ πόποι, ὡς ὅδε πᾶσι φίλος καὶ τίμιός ἐστιν
Ἀνθρώποις, ὅτεών τε πόλιν καὶ γαῖαν ἵκηται. [Vers 38 et 39.]

Il s'en va tout chargé de butin, et nous revenons les mains vides; mais voyons ce qu'Éole lui a donné.

Ὣς ἔφασαν· βουλὴ δὲ κακὴ νίκησεν ἑταίρων. [Vers 46.]

Ils délièrent cette peau, et tous les vents en sortirent aussitôt : si bien qu'un tourbillon les enleva, tout pleurants, bien loin de leur pays. Ulysse, s'étant éveillé, délibéra en lui-même s'il se jetteroit dans la mer,

Ἢ ἀκέων τλαίην, καὶ ἔτι ζωοῖσι μετείην.
Ἀλλ' ἔτλην καὶ ἔμεινα· καλυψάμενος δ' ἐνὶ νηῒ
Κείμην. [Vers 52-54.]

Les vents les repoussèrent en Éolie, et Ulysse s'en alla chez Éole, prenant avec lui un héraut et un de ses compagnons. Ils le trouvèrent à table avec sa femme et ses enfants.

Ils furent fort surpris de le revoir, et lui en demandoient la cause ; il leur dit d'un ton fort triste :

Ἄασάν μ' ἕταροί τε κακοί, πρὸς τοῖσί τε ὕπνος
Σχέτλιος· ἀλλ' ἀκέσασθε, φίλοι· δύναμις γὰρ ἐν ὑμῖν....
Οἱ δ' ἄνεῳ ἐγένοντο· πατὴρ δ' ἠμείβετο μύθῳ. [Vers 68-71.]

Vous diriez que ces enfants n'osassent parler devant leur père, lequel prit la parole et lui dit :

Ἔρρ' ἐκ νήσου θᾶσσον, ἐλέγχιστε ζωόντων.
Οὐ γάρ μοι θέμις ἐστὶ κομιζέμεν οὐδ' ἀποπέμπειν
Ἄνδρα τὸν, ὅς κε Θεοῖσιν ἀπέχθηται μακάρεσσιν.
Ἔρρ', ἐπεὶ ἄρα Θεοῖσιν ἀπεχθόμενος τόδ' ἱκάνεις.
Ὣς εἰπὼν, ἀπέπεμπε δόμων βαρέα στενάχοντα. [Vers 72-76.]

Tel étoit le respect que les païens portoient aux Dieux, vu qu'ils n'eussent pas voulu assister un homme qui paroissoit ennemi des Dieux, de peur de les offenser. Ulysse s'en alla donc, et au septième jour il arriva au pays des Lestrigons. Pline dit[1] que c'étoit une ville qui depuis a été appelée Formia, assez près du port de Caiète, aujourd'hui Nole dans la Campanie. Homère nomme la ville de Lamus ; c'étoit le père d'Antiphates, fils de Neptune, d'où est descendue la famille patricienne d'Ælius Lamia. Horace, liv. 3, *od*. 17.

Ulysse entra dans le port, qui étoit fort propre et fort paisible :

Λευκὴ δ' ἦν ἀμφὶ γαλήνη. [Vers 94.]

Il appelle peut-être le calme *blanc*, à cause que l'eau paroît blanche lorsqu'elle n'est point agitée. Il vit de la fumée assez loin de là, et il envoya deux de ses compagnons pour savoir quel pays c'étoit. Ils treuvèrent la fille d'Antiphates qui alloit puiser de l'eau à une fontaine hors la ville. Elle leur enseigna la maison de son père, qui étoit roi de ce pays-là. Ils y furent, et ils y treuvèrent sa femme, aussi haute qu'une montagne, et ils en eurent peur :

Τὴν δὲ γυναῖκα
Εὗρον ὅσην τ' ὄρεος κορυφὴν, κατὰ δ' ἔστυγον αὐτήν [vers 112 et 113] ;

---

[1]. Livre III, chapitre v.

et elle fit venir[1] son mari à la place, lequel leur préparoit un fort mauvais traitement ; car d'abord qu'il les vit, il en prit un pour son souper, et les deux autres s'en coururent de toute leur force vers leur vaisseau. Antiphate appela les autres citoyens, qui vinrent en grand nombre, plus semblables à des géants qu'à des hommes ; et prenant de grosses pierres, ils vinrent fondre sur leurs navires ; et alors il tomba dessus une grêle horrible, et il s'éleva un grand fracas d'hommes qui périssoient et de vaisseaux qui se brisoient ; et embrochant les hommes comme des poissons, ils se les gardoient pour leur souper. Ulysse, tirant son épée, coupa le câble de son vaisseau, et faisant ramer ses compagnons, s'éloigna au plus vite.

Ἀσπασίως δ' ἐς πόντον ἐπηρεφέας φύγε πέτρας
Νηῦς ἐμή. [Vers 131 et 132.]

Mais tous les autres périrent. Il s'en alla donc bien marri de la perte de ses compagnons, mais bien aise d'avoir évité la mort.

Πλέομεν, ἀκαχήμενοι ἦτορ,
Ἄσμενοι ἐκ θανάτοιο, φίλους ὀλέσαντες ἑταίρους. [Vers 133 et 134.]

Il arriva à l'île Æée, autrement dite île de Circé. Pline dit[2] que c'étoit autrefois une île, mais que la mer s'étant retirée, elle avoit été attachée à la terre ferme. Circé étoit fille du Soleil et de Persée, et sœur d'Æetas, roi de Colchos et père de Médée, aussi grande enchanteresse que Circé. Cette ville est dans la Campanie, et les Latins l'appeloient *Circes domus*. Ulysse demeura deux jours au port de cette île, fort affligé à son ordinaire ; et le troisième, prenant sa javeline et son épée, il alla faire la découverte de l'île. Il monta sur un tertre vert, d'où il vit sortir de la fumée au travers des arbres, et il s'en retourna vers son vaisseau pour y envoyer quelques-uns de ses compagnons après le dîner ; et en chemin quelque dieu eut pitié de lui. Il envoya devers lui un grand cerf,

---

1. Racine avait écrit : « alla querir. » Au-dessus de ces mots, et sans les effacer, il a mis dans l'interligne : « fit venir. »
2. Livre III, chapitre v.

ὑψίκερων[1], qui sortoit d'un bois pour venir boire à un fleuve, car il se sentoit pris de la chaleur du soleil :

Δὴ γάρ μιν ἔχεν μένος ἠελίοιο. [Vers 160.]

Il le frappa de sa javeline sur l'épine du dos, et elle entra bien avant. Il tomba sur la poussière en gémissant.

Κὰδ δ' ἔπεσ' ἐν κονίῃσι μακών, ἀπὸ δ' ἔπτατο θυμός. [Vers 163.]

Ulysse retira sa javeline de la plaie, et l'ayant mise à terre, il coupa des branches d'osier, et ayant fait un lien d'une aune de long, il en lia le cerf par les pieds ; et il descendit vers son vaisseau, le traînant sur ses épaules, et s'appuyant sur sa javeline : Car c'étoit, dit-il, une fort puissante bête ; et l'ayant jeté devant son vaisseau, il appela ses compagnons[2], et leur parla à chacun avec des paroles fort caressantes : Mes amis, nous ne mourrons pas encore cette fois-ci, jusqu'à ce que le jour destiné arrive ; mais, courage ! tandis que nous avons des vivres, ne nous laissons pas mourir de faim.

Ils sortirent sur le rivage[3], et admirèrent ce beau cerf :

Μάλα γὰρ μέγα θηρίον ἦεν.
Αὐτὰρ ἐπεὶ τάρπησαν ὁρώμενοι ὀφθαλμοῖσιν [vers 180 et 181],

ils lavèrent les mains, et se mirent à manger et à boire jusques au soir ; et quand le soleil fut couché, ils s'endormirent sur le rivage. Le matin Ulysse les assembla, et leur dit :

Ὦ φίλοι, οὐ γάρ τ' ἴδμεν ὅπῃ ζόφος, οὐδ' ὅπῃ ἠώς,
Οὐδ' ὅπῃ ἠέλιος φαεσίμβροτος εἶσ' ὑπὸ γαῖαν,
Οὐδ' ὅπῃ ἀννεῖται [vers 190-192];

et il leur dit qu'il faut de nécessité aller voir en quel pays ils sont.

Τοῖσιν δὲ κατεκλάσθη φίλον ἦτορ [vers 198],

---

1. Vers 158.
2. Racine, par inadvertance, a écrit : « son compagnon. »
3. En tête de la page 120, qui commence ici, Racine a écrit : « Circé ; » et il a répété ce mot au haut des deux pages suivantes.

se souvenant de la barbarie d'Antiphate et du Cyclope; et ils pleuroient tous amèrement; mais cela ne servoit de rien :

Ἀλλ' οὐ γάρ τις πρῆξις ἐγίνετο μυρομένοισιν. [Vers 202.]

Il divisa ses compagnons en deux bandes, et il étoit le chef de l'une, et Eurylochus de l'autre. Il jeta le sort de chacun dans un casque, et celui d'Eurylochus vint; il s'en alla donc avec vingt-deux autres, tout en pleurant, et [ils] laissèrent les autres, qui pleuroient aussi de leur côté. Ils treuvèrent la maison de Circé dans un vallon, bien bâtie, et dans un lieu assez éminent, ou bien dans un lieu avantageux. Elle étoit environnée de loups champêtres et de lions, qu'elle avoit apprivoisés par des breuvages malfaisants. Ces loups et ces lions n'étoient pas des hommes métamorphosés, mais des loups en effet, ὀρέστεροι[1], sauvages, qu'elle avoit rendus privés; et ils ne se ruèrent point sur les gens d'Ulysse, mais ils vinrent au-devant d'eux en les caressant de leurs longues queues; tout de même que des chiens caressent leur maître quand il revient de quelque festin, car il leur apporte d'ordinaire quelques friandises, ainsi ces loups et ces lions les caressoient :

Ὡς δ' ὅταν ἀμφὶ ἄνακτα κύνες δαίτηθεν ἰόντα
Σαίνωσ' (αἰεὶ γάρ τε φέρει μειλίγματα θυμοῦ),
Ὡς τοὺς ἀμφὶ λύκοι κρατερώνυχες, ἠδὲ λέοντες
Σαῖνον [vers 216-219];

et ils eurent peur, voyant de si grosses bêtes. Ils vinrent à la porte de cette déesse aux beaux cheveux, et ils l'entendirent qui chantoit : voyez au 5. livre, p. 52[2]. Polites, le meilleur et le plus sage des amis d'Ulysse, dit aux autres que c'étoit quelque femme ou quelque déesse qui chantoit, et qu'il falloit appeler au plus vite : ce qu'ils firent; et Circé leur vint ouvrir la porte, et les pria d'entrer. Ils la suivirent tous imprudemment, excepté Eurylochus, qui demeura à la porte, soupçonnant quelque trahison. En effet, d'abord qu'ils

---

1. Vers 212.

2. Racine renvoie à la page 52 de son manuscrit (page 98 de ce volume), où il a cité les vers 221-223 du livre X de l'*Odyssée*, et les vers 12-14 du livre VII de l'*Énéide*, sur Circé.

furent entrés, elle les fit asseoir sur de beaux siéges, et leur fit un mélange de fromage, de farine, de miel frais et de vin, et mêla dans le pain des venins malfaisants, afin qu'ils oubliassent leur pays. Homère, ce semble, ne fait pas mettre le poison de Circé dans les breuvages, mais dans le pain, ἀνέμισγε δὲ σίτῳ Φάρμακα λύγρ'[1]. Ovide, au contraire, qui, au reste, a suivi Homère mot à mot, lui fait mettre ce suc empoisonné dans le breuvage, au [livre] 14. *Métam.*[2]. Homère nomme ici le vin Pramnien, qui étoit encore fameux du temps de Pline[3], et qui naissoit à l'entour de Smyrne, dans l'Asie. Après donc qu'elle leur eut donné à boire, elle[4] les frappa d'une baguette, et les renferma dans un toit à cochon; et ils prirent tous la figure de cochon, la tête, la voix, le corps et le poil. Néanmoins leur esprit étoit toujours ferme et entier comme auparavant :

Αὐτὰρ νοῦς ἦν ἔμπεδος, ὡς τὸ πάρος περ. [Vers 240.]

Ceux qui se sont mêlés d'expliquer les fables ont dit que cette métamorphose des compagnons d'Ulysse en cochons signifioit que ces gens-là, s'étant abandonnés au vin et à la bonne chère, étoient devenus comme des cochons. Cependant cela ne revient pas bien au sens d'Homère, qui dit que leur esprit étoit aussi entier qu'auparavant; car il est bien certain que l'ivrognerie et la crapule gâtent l'esprit tout le premier; et on peut dire des gens qui y sont adonnés que ce sont des cochons sous la figure humaine, au lieu que ceux-ci étoient des hommes sous la figure de cochons. Néanmoins tout le monde l'entend en ce sens-là; et Horace, parlant d'Ulysse :

Sirenum voces et Circes pocula nosti,
Quæ si cum sociis stultus cupidusque bibisset,
Sub domina meretrice fuisset turpis et excors,
Vixisset canis immundus, vel amica luto sus[5].

---

1. Vers 235 et 236.
2. Vers 273-276.
3. Voyez Pline, livre XIV, chapitre IV (ou VI).
4. *Il*, dans le manuscrit.
5. *Épître* II du livre I, vers 23-26.

Elle leur donne donc des glands à manger, et autres telles viandes propres aux cochons :

Οἷα σύες χαμαιευνάδες αἰὲν ἔδουσιν. [Vers 243.]

Eurylochus, qui avoit été sage, s'en vint droit à Ulysse, pour lui apporter cette nouvelle; mais il ne pouvoit parler, de tristesse :

Κῆρ ἀχεϊ μεγάλῳ βεβολημένος· ἐν δέ οἱ ὄσσε
Δακρυόφιν πίμπλαντο, γόον δ' ὠίετο θυμός. [Vers 247 et 248.]

Il lui conte donc comme ses compagnons sont tous entrés, et qu'il n'en est pas sorti un seul. Ulysse prend son épée, et dit à Eurylochus de le conduire. Eurylochus se jette à ses pieds, et le prie de n'y point aller, parce qu'il n'en reviendra point. Ulysse lui dit qu'il demeure donc à boire et à manger; mais que, pour lui, il est obligé d'y aller :

Κρατερὴ δέ μοι ἔπλετ' ἀνάγκη. [Vers 273.]

Assez près de la maison de Circé, il rencontre Mercure à la verge d'or, χρυσόρραπις[1], ressemblant à un jeune homme à qui le poil ne fait que de naître :

Τοῦπερ χαριεστάτη ἥβη. [Vers 279.]

Mercure l'arrête, et lui apprend l'état de ses compagnons; et afin qu'il n'y tombe pas, il lui donne un remède puissant pour rendre inutiles les breuvages de Circé. C'est une herbe que Mercure arrache de la terre et en montre la nature à Ulysse :

Ῥίζῃ μὲν μέλαν ἔσκε, γάλακτι δὲ εἴκελον ἄνθος. [Vers 304.]

Les Dieux, dit-il, l'appellent *moly;* il est difficile à déraciner[2] aux hommes, mais tout est possible aux Dieux. Pline, au livre 25., c. 4, l'appelle *laudatissimam herbarum.* Il dit qu'elle croissoit vers la montagne de Cyllène, en Arcadie, *radice rotunda nigraque magnitudine cæpæ, folio scillæ;*

1. Vers 277.
2. Racine a écrit *déraciner* en interligne, au-dessus de *treuver*, qu'il avait d'abord mis.

effodi autem difficulter. Les Grecs dépeignent sa fleur noire, quoique Homère la décrive blanche. Quelques médecins croient qu'il en vient aussi dans la Campanie ; et Pline dit qu'on lui en avoit apporté[1] une sèche, qu'on avoit treuvée dans la Campanie, et que sa racine étoit de trente pieds de long. Il dit en un autre endroit[2] qu'elle est excellente contre la magie. Mercure la donne donc à Ulysse, et lui dit que quand, après avoir mangé, Circé lui donnera un coup de sa baguette, il tire son épée comme pour la tuer : Et alors, dit-il, elle aura peur, et vous invitera à coucher avec elle. Cela montre que pour surmonter la volupté il faut du courage et de la tempérance; car Socrate entend cette vertu par l'herbe moly[3]. Mercure dit à Ulysse qu'il ne refuse point de coucher avec elle, afin d'obtenir la délivrance de ses compagnons; mais qu'il la fasse jurer auparavant le grand serment des Dieux, qu'elle ne lui fera point de mal ni d'affront :

Μή σ' ἀπογυμνωθέντα κακὸν καὶ ἀνήνορα θείη. [Vers 301.]

Mercure s'envole, et Ulysse poursuit son chemin, roulant bien des choses dans son esprit :

Πολλὰ δέ μοι κραδίη πόρφυρε κιόντι. [Vers 309.]

1. Dans le manuscrit : *apportée.*
2. Livre XXV, chapitre x. C'est le chapitre LXXIX dans d'autres éditions, où le chapitre IV, cité plus haut, est le VIII.
3. Nous ne trouvons aucun passage des anciens où cela soit dit expressément; mais peut-être l'interprétation que Racine prête à Socrate lui aura-t-elle paru, à lui ou à quelque commentateur, résulter de ce que dit Xénophon au livre I de ses *Dits mémorables* (chapitre III, § 7) : Οἴεσθαι δ' ἔφη ἐπισκώπτων καὶ τὴν Κίρκην ὗς ποιεῖν τοιούτοις πολλοῖς δειπνίζουσαν· τὸν δὲ Ὀδυσσέα Ἑρμοῦ τε ὑποθημοσύνῃ καὶ αὐτὸν ἐγκρατῆ ὄντα..., διὰ ταῦτα οὐ γενέσθαι ὗν. « Je crois, disait-il en plaisantant, que Circé changeait les hommes en pourceaux par cette abondance de mets qu'elle leur présentait; mais qu'Ulysse avait dû aux conseils de Mercure, et à sa propre tempérance,... de n'avoir pas subi cette métamorphose. » Sur l'assistance de Mercure, on voit que Socrate est d'accord avec Homère ; mais il ne parle pas, comme lui, de l'herbe moly. Comme antidote contre la grande chère de Circé, il ne reconnaît que la tempérance, donnant à entendre que le poëte dans sa fiction a voulu désigner cette vertu.

Il entre donc chez Circé ; elle le traite comme ses compagnons ; mais quand elle lui voit tirer l'épée, elle s'écrie, et lui embrassant les genoux, lui dit : Qui êtes-vous qui ne ressentez point la force de ce breuvage que personne n'a jamais pu éviter? N'êtes-vous point cet Ulysse, si adroit, que Mercure m'a toujours prédit devoir venir ici? Mais remettez votre épée, et couchons ensemble, afin que nous ayons plus de confiance l'un à l'autre. Il lui répond qu'il n'en fera rien, jusqu'à ce qu'elle lui jure de ne lui point faire mal ; et alors ils se mettent au lit. Ils sont servis par quatre servantes, qui étoient nées des fontaines, des arbres et des fleuves. L'une couvre les siéges de tapis de pourpre par haut, et par le bas, de lin ; les dossiers étoient revêtus de pourpre, et le reste de lin, pour être plus mollement. L'autre dresse des tables d'argent, et les couvre de vaisselles[1] d'or. L'autre verse d'un vin excellent dans un vase d'argent, et prépare des coupes d'or ; et la dernière apporte de l'eau, et allume du feu sous un trépied ; elle fait chauffer l'eau, et ensuite lave Ulysse, et lui verse doucement cette eau le long de la tête et des épaules,

Ὄφρα μοι ἐκ κάματον θυμοφθόρον εἵλετο γυίων [vers 363],

afin de soulager la lassitude de ses membres. Θυμοφθόρον, parce que le travail du corps abat l'esprit. Après qu'on l'a frotté d'huile, on le met à table, et Homère le fait servir selon sa coutume. Mais Ulysse ne vouloit point manger, songeant à d'autres choses, et étant toujours affligé :

Ἀλλ' ἤμην ἀλλοφρονέων. [Vers 374.]

Circé s'en met en peine, et tâche de le rassurer ; mais il lui dit : Ô Circé, quel homme juste et raisonnable voudroit manger avant que de voir sortir ses compagnons de l'état où ils sont? Faites-les-moi voir donc, si vous voulez que je mange. Elle s'en va à l'étable avec sa baguette, et en fait sortir ses compagnons, qui étoient comme des porcs de neuf ans ; et les frottant d'une drogue contraire à la première, le poil de cochons leur tombe, et ils deviennent des hommes,

1. Il y a bien *vaisselles*, au pluriel, dans le manuscrit.

plus jeunes encore et plus beaux à voir qu'auparavant. Cela se pourroit appliquer à des débauchés, qui, sortant une fois de leurs débauches, sont plus sages que jamais :

Καὶ πολὺ καλλίονες καὶ μείζονες εἰσοράασθαι. [Vers 396.]

Ils se jettent tous au cou d'Ulysse, et se mettent tous à pleurer; toute la maison en retentit, et Circé même en est émue de pitié. Alors elle dit à Ulysse d'aller à son vaisseau, de le tirer à terre, et de mettre leurs provisions et leurs armes dans quelque caverne, et puis de revenir chez elle avec tous ses compagnons. Ulysse lui obéit, et s'en va à son vaisseau, où il treuve tout son monde affligé, et désespérant de le revoir. Il décrit la joie qu'ils eurent pour lors, et la compare à la joie que de jeunes veaux ont de revoir leurs mères, qui viennent de paître.

Cette comparaison est fort délicatement exprimée, car ces mots de veaux et de vaches ne sont point choquants dans le grec[1], comme ils le sont en notre langue, qui ne veut presque rien souffrir, et qui ne souffriroit pas qu'on fît des églogues de vachers, comme Théocrite, ni qu'on parlât du porcher d'Ulysse comme d'un personnage héroïque; mais ces délicatesses sont de véritables foiblesses :

'Ὡς δ' ὅταν ἄγραυλοι πόρτιες περὶ βοῦς ἀγελαίας
Ἐλθούσας ἐς κόπρον, ἐπὴν βοτάνης κορέσωνται,
Πᾶσαι ἅμα σκαίρουσιν ἐναντίαι· οὐδ' ἔτι σηκοὶ
Ἴσχουσ', ἀλλ' ἁδινὸν μυκώμεναι ἀμφιθέουσι
Μητέρας. [Vers 410-414.]

Ainsi les compagnons d'Ulysse l'embrassèrent en pleurant, et il leur sembloit qu'ils étoient de retour à Ithaque et dans leur logis. Ils lui demandent que sont devenus les autres, et il leur dit qu'ils les viennent voir eux-mêmes buvant et mangeant, après qu'ils auront tiré leur vaisseau à terre. Les autres lui obéissoient; mais Eurylochus les en détournoit à toute force. On voit par là que quand ces esprits médiocres ont

1. On peut rapprocher ce passage de ce que Racine bien plus tard, en 1693, écrivait à Boileau au sujet d'un endroit de Denys d'Halicarnasse, et de la *Neuvième réflexion critique sur Longin*.

une fois réussi en quelque chose, ils en deviennent fiers, et veulent qu'on croie tout ce qu'ils disent pour des oracles. Aussi Ulysse, tout en colère, le vouloit tuer, quoiqu'il fût son parent; mais les autres l'apaisèrent, et le prièrent de le laisser là tout seul; mais il aima mieux suivre les autres, craignant la colère d'Ulysse[1].

1. Les *Remarques sur l'Odyssée*, comme nous l'avons dit dans la *Notice*, ne vont pas, dans le manuscrit de Racine, au delà du livre X.

LIVRES ANNOTÉS

NOTICE.

Lorsque nous avons donné dans le volume précédent, et au commencement de celui-ci, quelques courtes notes de Racine, connues sous le nom de *Fragments historiques*, ses *traductions*, même celles de sa première jeunesse, ses *Remarques sur les Olympiques* et *sur l'Odyssée*, nous n'avons fait que suivre, dans cette édition, l'exemple de nos devanciers, chez qui l'on n'avait pas, ce nous semble, désapprouvé le soin scrupuleux avec lequel ils avaient recueilli jusqu'aux moindres lignes d'une telle plume. Il fallait cependant ou ne pas les imiter, dans la crainte qu'ils n'eussent été plus complets que ne le demandait la curiosité du public, ou, pour être conséquent avec nous-même, ajouter quelque chose à leur travail, en faisant connaître les annotations nombreuses dont Racine a chargé les marges de ses livres; car ce sont là des études analogues à celles que nous venons de rappeler, et intéressantes au même titre et au même degré. Si ce n'est qu'elles ont été écrites, à peu près toutes, non sur des cahiers à part, mais sur les livres mêmes, ces annotations diffèrent peu des *Remarques* manuscrites *sur Homère* et *sur Pindare*. Quant aux fragments de traduction de la *Poétique* d'Aristote, publiés déjà par Geoffroy et par Aimé-Martin, ils sont réellement, comme nous l'avons dit, des notes marginales. Au surplus, nous savions que M. Gail et M. Félix Ravaisson ayant chacun de leur côté, et en différents temps, publié des notes de Racine sur les tragiques grecs, un très-bon accueil avait été fait à ces publications; et qu'on avait aussi jugé intéressant le travail, beaucoup plus étendu, mais malheureusement bien moins exact, de M. de la Rochefoucauld, dont les *Études littéraires et morales* ne sont pour la plupart qu'un recueil des annotations marginales de Racine. Nous avions donc quelque raison de croire que, dans une édition complète des *OEuvres de Racine*, bien des personnes eussent regretté de ne pas trouver ce qui avait paru ailleurs digne d'attention, et, jusqu'ici, n'avait été donné tantôt que très-partiellement, tantôt sans ordre, sans preuve d'authenticité, sans indication des sources, et avec de très-graves altérations.

Ce que nous avons déjà eu l'occasion de dire des fortes études de Racine, et des habitudes laborieuses qu'il eut si jeune, devient plus incontestable et plus frappant encore lorsqu'on a passé en revue, comme nous mettons le lecteur à même de le faire, ceux des livres annotés par lui dont nous avons pu avoir connaissance. Indépendamment de cette valeur, comme renseignement biographique, les notes de Racine peuvent être lues avec plaisir et profit. Non-seulement elles nous donnent un exemple d'une excellente méthode de travail; mais s'il y en a bon nombre qui, prises isolément, sont nécessairement insignifiantes dans leur brièveté, il y en a beaucoup aussi de remarquables par la finesse, par la justesse des jugements, ou par le bonheur de l'expression.

Aux personnes qui ne trouveraient pas suffisamment justifiée par ces raisons la grande place donnée ici à de simples notes qui n'avaient pas été écrites pour être publiées, nous en soumettrons une autre qui ne nous semble pas sans force. Ces mêmes notes ayant déjà été publiées dans un livre assez répandu, où elles sont reproduites inexactement, et présentées dans un ordre arbitraire qui en change le sens et la valeur, il importait de couper court à des erreurs sur des travaux, quels qu'ils soient, de Racine; et si elles devaient être rectifiées quelque part, c'est assurément dans une édition de ses œuvres qu'on s'est efforcé d'établir suivant les règles d'une sévère critique. Nous avons tout à l'heure nommé l'ouvrage de M. de la Rochefoucauld Liancourt, intitulé : *Études littéraires et morales de Racine*. Dans une note que l'on trouvera à la page 205 de notre tome V, nous avons dit que nous expliquerions ailleurs avec quelque détail les raisons que nous avions eues de ne pas faire usage des renseignements que nous offrait ce livre. Ces explications que nous avions promises ont ici leur place.

Dans la *Seconde partie* du livre de M. de la Rochefoucauld, qui porte le titre d'*Études morales*, on trouve, de la page 12 à la page 90[1], une suite de pensées détachées, dont chacune porte un numéro d'ordre; elles ont été partagées en dix sections, composées chacune de cent numéros. Le lecteur se trouve induit à croire que ces pensées, dont les unes sont exprimées en latin, les autres en français, avaient été écrites dans ce même ordre par Racine, soit dans des cahiers, soit sur des feuilles volantes que l'éditeur aurait eues sous les yeux. M. de la Rochefoucauld dit, à la page 3, qu'il a recueilli « sur les nombreuses feuilles volantes qui ont été employées par Racine à son instruction, les observations morales qu'il a faites, les sentiments de piété qu'il a émis. » Voici réellement ce qui en est, ce que nous a fait reconnaître un examen attentif de ces *Études morales*. Presque toutes les phrases détachées dont elles se composent ont été recueillies sur les marges des différents volumes annotés par Racine; quelques-unes ont été tirées des feuillets manuscrits (*Remarques sur Athalie*, *Extrait des 9mes difficultés*, *Extrait des Alnetanæ quæstiones*, etc.), dont nous nous sommes occupé dans notre tome V; il y en a aussi qui ont été prises dans les *Remarques* manuscrites *sur Pindare* et *sur Homère*. Non-seulement M. de la Rochefoucauld ne dit point où il a trouvé ces fragments, mais il ne met pas même les uns à la suite des autres ceux qui appartiennent à un même volume annoté, ou à un même cahier manuscrit : il les donne pêle-mêle, le sacré à côté du profane, une note sur un prosateur latin à côté d'une note sur un poëte grec, un verset de la *Bible*, immédiatement après une pensée de Plutarque, une phrase extraite des écrits polémiques d'Arnauld, à la suite de l'explication d'un passage de Pindare. Au milieu de ces rapprochements bizarres, il s'en est, par un effet du hasard, rencontré quelques-uns d'assez piquants, où quelques personnes ont cru découvrir une intention remarquable de Racine. Aux notes de celui-ci, des phrases latines tirées des textes commentés par lui sont mêlées par M. de la Rochefoucauld; et l'on ne

---

[1]. Nous citons d'après la seconde impression, *Paris, imprimerie de Mme Vᵉ Dondey-Dupré*, 1856.

sait pourquoi elles se trouvent là. D'autres phrases latines, que Racine a citées quelque part, sont accompagnées d'une traduction qu'il n'en a pas donnée ; ou bien encore, pour faire mieux comprendre le sens d'une de ses notes, on y joint un commentaire, un développement qu'on lui attribue, et dont il n'est nullement l'auteur. Veut-on un exemple? Dans la section III des *Études morales*, sous les numéros 57, 58 et 59, on lit : « La leçon de Chiron au jeune Achille est d'honorer les Dieux et son père. — N'est-ce point de même que dans la religion du Christ? — *Deum cole, parentes honora.* » Cela est tiré des notes marginales de Racine sur la VI⁰ *Pythique*, qui sont données par nous ci-après. Racine, comme on le verra, a seulement écrit : « Leçon de Chiron au jeune Achille : *Honora Deum et parentes ;* » et en tête de la page où est cette note : *Deum cole, parentes honora.* Il pensait évidemment à un rapprochement avec les livres saints; mais il l'a sous-entendu. Il serait facile de signaler, dans un bien grand nombre d'autres passages, de semblables additions, ou des retranchements, enfin des altérations de toutes sortes, soit qu'on ait prétendu éclaircir ce que Racine a écrit, soit qu'on ait cru utile de le rajeunir, soit qu'on ait, par distraction, laissé passer, dans la transcription, les plus singulières erreurs. Et lors même que tout eût été copié plus fidèlement, il aurait été impossible encore que toutes ces phrases, prises on ne sait où, et se suivant dans un ordre si arbitraire, ou plutôt dans un tel désordre, ne donnassent pas une idée très-fausse de ces *Études* de Racine. Ainsi que veulent dire ces phrases italiennes, qui dans la section x sont rangées, les unes après les autres, sous les numéros 24 et suivants jusqu'à 30? Pourrait-on y deviner une citation faite par Racine du livre de Balthasar Castiglione, à la marge du traité de Plutarque *de Adulatore et Amico?* C'est également dans les notes sur Plutarque que M. de la Rochefoucauld a rencontré cette phrase (numéros 6 et 7 de la section v) : « Les Romains parloient du cœur, — et les Grecs des lèvres; » sur laquelle il dit dans une note : « On est étonné de trouver ce mot sous la plume de Racine, *etc.*, » donnant par là un exemple des méprises auxquelles il exposait non-seulement ses lecteurs, mais lui-même tout le premier, au milieu de cet étrange farrago de fragments, dont il n'indique pas, dont il avait oublié l'origine. Un mot de Caton l'ancien, cité par Plutarque dans la *Vie* de ce vieux Romain, et dont Racine s'est borné à donner une traduction à la marge, devient une pensée qui lui est propre, dont il est responsable, et que l'on regarde comme un inexplicable blasphème du poëte redevable aux Grecs de tant de belles inspirations.

A la suite des *Études morales* on trouve, dans la même *Seconde partie*, une *Étude sur le commencement de l'histoire de France*, et des *Études sur le règne de Louis XIV*. Ceux qui auront la curiosité de comparer ces pages avec la partie correspondante des *Fragments historiques* dans notre tome V, compléteront l'idée qu'il faut se faire du parti que M. de la Rochefoucauld Liancourt a tiré des papiers de Racine. Dans les *Études sur le règne de Louis XIV*, nous avons remarqué, à la page 139, ce passage : « M. de Luxembourg étoit quelque chose de plus qu'humain, volant partout, et même s'opiniâtrant à continuer les attaques, etc. » Il se trouve mot à mot dans la lettre de Racine à Boileau en date du 6 août 1693. Et même ce n'est pas tout à fait le texte exact de la lettre autographe, mais celui que les éditeurs de Racine ont un peu arrangé. Comment s'est-il ainsi glissé parmi les notes manuscrites et inédites de Racine?

La conclusion à tirer de tout cela, c'est que M. de la Rochefoucauld avait en différents temps pris des notes, souvent peu exactes sans doute, sur les manuscrits de son auteur, sur les livres annotés par lui, et même sur ses œuvres imprimées, sans bien savoir ce qu'il en ferait; qu'il y avait mêlé çà et là quelques réflexions ou explications qui n'appartiennent qu'à lui-même; et que beaucoup plus tard, sans pouvoir remettre de l'ordre dans ces notes éparses, et sans retrouver dans son souvenir d'où il avait tiré chacune d'elles, il les a rassemblées suivant un classement arbitraire, lorsqu'il a voulu les publier. Lui-même, dans sa parfaite sincérité, en faisait l'aveu. Nous avons sous les yeux une lettre qu'il écrivait à une personne fort instruite qui lui avait soumis quelques doutes et quelques objections. « Ma méthode, dit-il, n'était pas bonne. Je copiais et voilà tout. Je copiais le plus souvent des copies, et j'entassais tout pêle-mêle dans des cahiers d'écolier. » Nous eussions voulu ne pas nous croire obligé de critiquer le travail entrepris, dans une excellente pensée, par un homme à qui beaucoup de respect est dû; mais il fallait bien dire pourquoi l'on trouvera si souvent le texte que nous donnons en désaccord avec celui de M. de la Rochefoucauld, et surtout pourquoi nous n'avons pu lui emprunter quelques parties de son travail dans lesquelles nous avons remarqué un petit nombre de notes qui ont échappé à nos recherches, et qu'il avait, à ce qu'il semble, recueillies dans des feuilles manuscrites ou sur les marges de livres que nous n'avons pas eus, comme lui, sous les yeux.

Nous n'avons parlé que de la *Seconde partie* du livre de M. de la Rochefoucauld. Dans la *Première partie*, intitulée : *Études littéraires*, se trouvent les *Études de Racine sur l'Iliade*, et les *Études sur les Tragédies grecques*. C'est un travail qui donnerait lieu à beaucoup moins de critiques. Les notes de Racine y ont été laissées à leur place, et, par conséquent, y sont bien plus faciles à comprendre ; malheureusement elles n'ont pas beaucoup plus échappé, que celles de la *Seconde partie*, aux altérations, aux retouches.

En recueillant les notes marginales des livres de Racine, il ne nous a été ni possible de pousser le scrupule jusqu'à transcrire le moindre mot, ni facile de décider quels retranchements seraient sans inconvénient. Bien des personnes sont disposées à dire que, si l'on a pris sur soi de supprimer quelque chose, rien ne prouve que ce ne soit pas bien souvent ce qui, au jugement d'un autre, eût offert quelque intérêt. C'est une raison pour être circonspect, jusqu'à la timidité, dans les suppressions, mais non cependant pour aller chercher sur les marges des livres annotés un nom propre, traduit du texte, un petit mot servant à marquer seulement de quoi l'auteur parle, un intitulé de chapitre. On verra que nous avons été bien loin encore dans notre exactitude. Non-seulement nous avons conservé avec fidélité toutes les observations critiques de Racine, mais encore, dans tout ce qui n'est que traduction, paraphrase ou résumé du texte, les notes qui peuvent indiquer ce qui l'a particulièrement frappé dans ses lectures, celles où l'on peut chercher sa manière de s'exprimer en quelque temps de sa vie que ce soit. Parmi ses annotations, on en trouvera de fort curieuses, dont les unes attestent avec quel goût délicat, avec quelle vivacité il sentait les beautés des anciens, et les autres quelles pensées, quels sentiments, quels souvenirs d'événements, de personnages ou d'idées modernes, le préoccupaient au moment où il s'appliquait à ces études. Il en est cependant qui, nous l'avons déjà dit, paraîtront, si l'on ne s'attache pas à l'ensemble du travail, très-peu significatives. Racine, la plupart du temps, ne songeait qu'à rendre par ce travail les livres de sa bibliothèque commodes pour son propre usage, à fixer son attention sur ses lectures, à se préparer des répertoires utiles d'idées, de connaissances, et de lieux communs. La manière dont en général il annotait les volumes de ses auteurs ne lui était d'ailleurs pas particulière. Des hommes studieux ont souvent chargé les marges de leurs livres de notes manuscrites du même genre. Il y en a aussi d'imprimées, dont il avait pu rencontrer plus d'un exemple sur les marges de quelques ouvrages. Le Plutarque traduit par Amyot en a qu'il peut être intéressant de comparer à celles de Racine sur le même auteur. L'édition d'Homère donnée à Bâle en 1567 est enrichie d'un semblable travail, que le titre annonce : *Homeri opera græco-latina,... locis communibus ubique in margine notatis.*

Nous faisons précéder les études de Racine sur chacun des livres annotés par de petites notices, pour lesquelles nous réservons ce qu'il y a particulièrement à en dire.

Si l'écriture de Racine, un peu différente en différents temps de sa vie, les changements dans son orthographe, les progrès dans son jugement critique ou dans son style, avaient suffi pour nous faire reconnaître la date plus ou moins ancienne de ces études, nous les aurions classées suivant l'ordre des temps auxquels elles eussent paru se rapporter ; mais les moyens d'arriver à ce discernement ne nous ont point paru assez sûrs : nous avons donc adopté un autre ordre, dont on comprendra facilement les raisons, et qui a aussi son avantage.

La bibliothèque de Racine, qui était sans aucun doute très-nombreuse, s'est naturellement dispersée de bien des côtés. Beaucoup de ses livres annotés se trouvent à la Bibliothèque impériale et à la Bibliothèque de Toulouse ; mais il y en a aussi dans plus d'une bibliothèque particulière. De quelques-uns de ceux-ci nous avons pu retrouver la trace, et ils nous ont été communiqués avec une obligeance dont nous sommes très-reconnaissant. D'autres nécessairement nous sont restés inconnus ; ou, si nous savons qu'ils existent, nous ignorons quels en sont aujourd'hui les possesseurs ; nous aurons ci-après à mentionner quelques-uns de ceux-là. Un travail tel que celui que nous avons entrepris est toujours condamné à être incomplet. Du reste, les notes que nous avons pu recueillir paraîtront bien suffisantes pour se former une juste idée de la direction que Racine donnait à ses études et à ses lectures.

Elles font connaître en même temps une partie de sa bibliothèque, sur laquelle il ne sera peut-être pas inopportun d'ajouter ici quelques autres renseignements, sans avoir la prétention de la reconstituer dans son ensemble. Outre les livres annotés par Racine, il s'est conservé un certain nombre de volumes qui portent seulement sa signature. Nous allons dire, autant que nous l'avons pu savoir, ceux qui sont signalés dans divers catalogues ; nous supprimerons seulement ici, pour éviter les répétitions, la mention de ceux dont nous avons recueilli les notes manuscrites, et de ceux dont nous parlons dans les notices particulières sur ces volumes annotés. C'est là qu'on pourra chercher quels exemplaires, à notre connaissance, Racine a possédés de la Bible, d'Homère, de Pindare, des tragiques grecs, de Platon, d'Aristote, de Plutarque, de Lucien, d'Horace, de Cicéron, de Tite-Live, de Tacite, de Quintilien, des deux Plines, de Quinte-Curce, de l'historien moderne Jean de la Barde.

Le Quérard, Archives d'histoire littéraire, etc., *deuxième année,* Paris,

1856 (p. 394-396), a donné, sous le titre de *Bibliothèque de Racine*, la liste suivante de ses livres :

Aristophane, à la Bibliothèque impériale [1].

Idem. Paris, 1540, in-folio, porté au *Catalogue de la Bibliothèque d'un amateur* (M. Renouard), 1819, tome II, p. 213. (Cet exemplaire a des notes sur trois comédies [2].)

Idem. Leyde, 1625, in-12. Catalogue Sensier, n° 613. Exemplaire, avec la signature de Racine, et quelques notes grecques qui lui sont attribuées.

Bixi (Jacques de Bie) *Numismata imperatorum Romanorum*. Anvers, 1617, in-folio (avec signature). Catalogue G. Duplessis, n° 1341.

Bossuet. Discours sur l'histoire universelle. Paris, 1681, in-4° (avec notes marginales). Catalogue J. L. D. (Merlin, 1834), n° 1952.

Callimachus. Anvers, Plantin, 1584, in-16 (avec signature). Catalogue Lefèvre d'Allerange, n° 516.

Charron. La Sagesse. Elzevir, 1662 (avec signature). Catalogue Renouard, 1829, n° 1395.

Claudianus. Elzevir, 1650 (avec signature). Catalogue Guillaume de Besançon, n° 274.

Demosthenes, græce. Paris, 1570, in-folio (avec notes nombreuses). Catalogue Aimé-Martin, n° 323 [3].

Excerpta ex tragœdiis et comœdiis græcis, emendata et latinis versibus reddita ab H. Grotio, 1626, in-4° (avec signature et notes sur plusieurs feuillets). Catalogue d'un amateur (*Renouard*), tome II, p. 195.

Hesiodus. Leyde, 1650 (avec signature et notes). Il a été vendu à Londres, dans une des ventes que M. Renouard y fit faire.

Josèphe. Histoire des Juifs, traduite par Arnauld d'Andilly, 1676. Exemplaire dont le tome II porte la signature de Racine. Catalogue Montaran, n° 18.

---

1. Le *Quérard*, qui d'ordinaire désigne les éditions, ne donne ici aucune indication ; or nous avons en vain cherché à la Bibliothèque impériale un *Aristophane* portant la signature de Racine. Nous y avons trouvé divers exemplaires du comique grec chargés de notes manuscrites. Il y en a un sur les marges duquel on trouve beaucoup de ces notes écrites en grec, et qui sont de différentes mains. Un petit nombre d'entre elles, une par exemple qui est à la première page, nous a rappelé l'écriture grecque de Racine, mais non avec certitude. Cet exemplaire a pour titre : *Aristophanis facetissimi Comœdiæ undecim. Ex officina Plantiniana, apud Christophorum Raphelengium, Academiæ Lugduno-Batav. typographum. M.DC.*

2. Il est ainsi désigné dans ce *Catalogue* : « *Aristophanis facetissimi Comœdiæ undecim, græce*, Parisiis, Wechel, 1540, in-4°, v. f. ancien. Avec notes de la main de Jean Racine sur toutes les marges de *Plutus*, sur la plus grande partie de la pièce des *Nuées*, et sur dix feuillets de *Ecclesiazusæ*. » — Dans le *Catalogue* Renouard (2° édition, Paris, L. Potier, etc., 1854, n° 1048), le nom du libraire, *Wechel*, est suivi des dates 1537-1540, et la description se termine par ces mots : « Avec la signature de J. Racine sur le titre, et de nombreuses notes de sa main. Elles sont de la belle écriture du temps de sa jeunesse. »

3. Au numéro indiqué ici, le catalogue de la bibliothèque de M. Aimé-Martin (Paris, chez Techener, 1847) décrit en effet ce volume. On y lit : « Il (*Racine*) paraîtrait, d'après une note de quatre pages, qui se trouve à la page 37, donner des instructions pour une édition de Démosthène. »

Martial, 1644, in-12 (avec signature). Catalogue Debure, 1853, n° 537.
Morus, l'Utopie, traduite par Sorbière, 1643 (avec signature). Même catalogue, n° 537.
Divi Paulini opera. Anvers, Plantin, 1622, in-8° (avec signature). Catalogue van Hulthem, n° 992.
Regnier. Elzevir, 1642 (avec signature et notes). Catalogue Aimé-Martin, n° 434[1].
Sallustius, 1665, in-24 (avec signature). Vente J. L. D.
Scholæ Salernitanæ de conservanda valetudine opusculum. Paris, 1555, in-16 (avec signature et quelques notes). Catalogue Parison, n° 495.
Sainte Thérèse. Traité du chemin de la perfection, traduit par Arnauld d'Andilly. Paris, 1659, in-8° (avec signature). Catalogue Feyrrat, 1844, n° 67.
Xenophontis opera, Paris, 1625, in-folio (avec signature). Catalogue de M. Tross, 1852.

A ces indications, tirées du *Quérard*, nous pouvons en joindre quelques autres.

Nous trouvons dans le Catalogue Villenave, Paris, chez Charavay, 1850, sous le numéro 940 : *Nouvelle méthode pour apprendre facilement et en peu de temps la langue espagnole*. 1 vol. in-18, relié en veau (avec signature de Racine sur le titre).

Dans un autre Catalogue de la bibliothèque de M. Villenave, Paris, Chimot, 1848, sous le numéro 548 : *OEuvres de Scarron, suivant la copie imprimée à Paris*, Elzevir, à la Sphère, 1668, petit in-12, 2 part., relié en veau brun (avec signature de Racine sur le titre).

La *Vie de Salomon, par l'abbé de Choisy*, Paris, 1687, in-8°, avec des notes manuscrites de Racine, a été achetée en 1855 par M. Chauveau fils, qui ignore dans quelles mains cet exemplaire se trouve aujourd'hui, après plusieurs ventes successives. Nous tenons de M. Chauveau que les notes de ce volume ont quelque étendue. M. Édouard Fournier (*Notes de Racine à Uzès*, p. 103) en signale plusieurs, celles des pages 5, 7, 8, 15, 17 et 28, comme étant d'un caractère assez différent de celui qu'on pourrait supposer à la date où elles ont été écrites, et où Racine était dans de grands sentiments de piété ; mais comme il n'en cite pas le texte, il ne met pas ses lecteurs à même d'en juger.

Nous avons sous les yeux une *Notice de livres contenant des notes manuscrites de Jean Racine et de ses deux fils, Jean-Baptiste et Louis Racine*. Elle a été extraite du *Bulletin universel des sciences et de l'industrie*, VIIe section, 2e cahier, 1825, art. 229. Les ouvrages qui y sont mentionnés avaient passé par héritage entre les mains de Mlle des Radrets, petite-fille de Louis Racine. Voici quels sont ceux qui, d'après cette *Notice*, avaient appartenu à Jean Racine :

C. Sallustius Crispus cum veterum historicorum fragmentis, editio novissima. Amstelodami..., 1669 [2], avec le nom de Racine, et des notes marginales, les unes du grand poëte, les autres de son fils aîné.

---

1. Le Catalogue Aimé-Martin, qui décrit en effet, sous le numéro 434, cet exemplaire de Regnier (petit in-12, v. f.), ne parle point de notes de Racine, mais seulement de « plusieurs corrections de sa main. »

2. Dans le Catalogue de M. L. D. (Merlin, 1834), il est dit que ce même

LIVRES ANNOTÉS.

Collecta divi Gregorii Nazianzeni plurima poemata, in latinum conversa, etc. Parisiis, apud J. B. Brocas, 1718. Jean Racine a écrit des notes marginales sur le texte, des remarques grammaticales à la fin de l'ouvrage, et sur les feuilles blanches qui précèdent le titre, une *Liste des bons dictionnaires, pour bien apprécier la langue grecque*.

Discours sur l'histoire universelle, par Bossuet, Paris, Seb. Mabre Cramoisy, 1681, in-8°, avec des notes marginales de Jean Racine et de Mlle des Radrets[1].

Dans les *Archives historiques et statistiques du département du Rhône* (tome VII, Lyon et Paris, 1827), une lettre signée *Parelle* fait connaître (p. 32 et 33), comme étant alors en la possession du signataire, les livres suivants :

Le *Sulpice Sévère* de Racine, 1574, in-12. « Les deux livres d'histoire (de l'*Histoire sacrée*), dit M. Parelle, sont annotés en latin, depuis la première jusqu'à la dernière page. L'historien y est souvent rectifié, et l'autorité de Jansénius fréquemment invoquée. »

Une des éditions originales de *Boileau*, Paris, 1674, in-4° : volume « ayant appartenu à Racine, qui a transcrit, en marge des satires, les passages d'Horace, de Perse et de Juvénal, imités par Boileau. »

Un *Abrégé de la Grammaire grecque de Port-Royal*, Paris, 1655, in-8° : « au commencement et à la fin duquel se trouve un supplément relatif à la syntaxe et à la ponctuation, formant cinquante pages environ, écrites entièrement de la main de Racine. »

Les *Sentences de P. Syrus*, grecques-latines, Paris, 1612, in-8°, avec deux lignes seulement de Racine à la page 4.

M. Feuillet de Conches, dans ses *Causeries d'un curieux*, parle de plusieurs volumes annotés par Racine, entre autres (à la page 518 de son tome III) d'un *Platon*, qui est vraisemblablement celui que l'on conserve à la Bibliothèque impériale, et dont on trouvera les notes ci-après. Parmi les livres qu'il nomme, il y en a que lui seul nous a fait connaître. « J'ai vu, dit-il (à la page 519 du même tome), deux volumes des *Essais de Nicole* et un d'*Antoine Arnauld* (M. Feuillet de Conches ne désigne pas autrement ce dernier ouvrage), chargés, aux marges, de notes du grand Racine. Ces notes, fort nombreuses et d'une écriture très-menue, m'ont semblé avoir été rédigées pour l'éducation de ses filles, car leur nom y était glissé. J'ai eu également sous les yeux un certain nombre d'autres livres..., annotés de sa main. Un *Dexter*[2] était noirci de ses notes critiques, à côté d'un *Davila*[3] commenté de sa plume.

---

exemplaire (1 vol. in-24, veau brun) est de 1665. Il y a probablement une erreur dans l'un et dans l'autre catalogue. Cette édition est de 1667, d'après la *Liste chronologique* des éditions de Salluste que Dotteville a donnée en 1763, à la fin de sa traduction de cet historien.

1. C'est probablement le même exemplaire, mentionné dans le *Quérard* : voyez ci-dessus, p. 172.

2. La *Chronique* de Dexter, imprimée plusieurs fois au commencement du dix-septième siècle, est regardée comme apocryphe.

3. Son *Histoire* (*Storia delle guerre civili di Francia*) fut publiée pour la première fois à Venise, en 1630, in-4°. Au temps de Racine, les éditions de ce livre étaient déjà très-nombreuses.

Il y avait aussi des feuillets d'extraits grecs des Pères sacrés, surtout de *saint Chrysostome* et de *saint Basile* [1]. »

La Bibliothèque de Toulouse possède une trentaine de volumes qui portent la signature de Racine, et que le Franc de Pompignan avait achetés après la mort du second fils du grand poëte. La ville de Toulouse en fit elle-même l'acquisition en 1787, trois ans après la mort de le Franc de Pompignan. M. Pont, aujourd'hui bibliothécaire à Toulouse, nous en a communiqué la liste avec une extrême obligeance. Nous allons transcrire, d'après lui, cette liste, après en avoir retranché, comme nous l'avons fait pour les catalogues déjà cités, les ouvrages qui seront mentionnés dans les notices particulières sur les livres annotés.

Huberti Goltzii Numismata. Bruges, 1573-1576, 4 vol. in-folio.

OEuvres de Clement Marot. Lyon, Guillaume Roville, 1561, in-16.

Epigrammatum græcorum libri septem (avec les notes de Jean Brodeau). Francfort, 1600, in-folio.

Stephanus Byzantii, de Urbibus et Populis (gr.-lat.). Amsterdam, 1678, in-folio.

Apollonii Rhodii Argonauticon, libri IV (gr.-lat.). Leyde, Elzevir, 1641, 2 vol. in-8°.

Gisberti Cuperi Apotheosis vel Consecratio Homeri. Amsterdam, 1683, in-4°.

Polybii, Diodori Siculi, Nicolai Damasceni, etc. Excerpta (gr.-lat.). Paris, 1634, in-4°.

Ludovici Nonnii Commentarius in Huberti Goltzii Græciam, insulas, etc. Anvers, 1620, in-4°.

Hesiodi quæ exstant (gr.). *Ex officina Plantiniana Raphelengii,* 1603, in-4°.

Herodiani Historiarum libri VIII (gr.-lat.). Henri Estienne, 1581, in-4°.

J. Crispini Lexicon græco-latinum. Vignon, 1595, 2 vol. in-4°.

Theocriti, Moschi, Bionis, Simmii quæ exstant (gr.-lat.). *Ex bibliopolio Commeliniano,* 1604, in-4°.

Les volumes annotés par Racine qui sont mentionnés dans la *Copie exacte de l'état des livres que Monsieur Racine* (Louis) *a remis à la Bibliothèque du Roi,* forment la plus grande partie de ceux dont nous donnons ci-après les notes. Nous les avons tous trouvés à la Bibliothèque impériale, à l'exception d'un qui a échappé à nos recherches; c'est celui qui a pour titre : *Veterum Comicorum sententiæ,* « avec plusieurs de ses notes à la marge, » dit la *Copie exacte.*

A la même Bibliothèque impériale, il y a un *Pétrone* dont nous devons parler, quoiqu'il n'y ait point de preuves suffisantes qu'il ait, comme on le croit, appartenu à Racine. Cet exemplaire a pour titre : *Titi Petronii Arbitri.... Satyricon. Parisiis, apud Claudium Audinet.... M.DC.LXXVII,* 1 vol. in-12. Sur le feuillet de garde, on lit cette note de M. Capperonnier, qui était, au siècle dernier, bibliothécaire à la Bibliothèque du Roi : « Cet exemplaire de Pétrone est infiniment précieux. Les notes marginales sont du grand Racine, et ont été écrites sous sa dictée par un de ses fils, qui a signé au bas du titre. »

---

1. De ces *Extraits* nous n'avons trouvé à la Bibliothèque impériale que les derniers, si ce sont bien les mêmes qu'a vus M. Feuillet de Conches.

Nous avons lu ces notes marginales, qui sont de l'écriture si correcte et si élégante du fils aîné de Racine. Elles sont très-abondantes, très-érudites, plus érudites que ne l'étaient généralement celles de Racine. Quoique l'annotateur n'ait évidemment étudié le livre licencieux de Pétrone qu'avec les plus doctes préoccupations, cependant il a çà et là expliqué quelques passages des plus scabreux avec une singulière crudité d'expression, dont on ne trouverait d'exemple dans aucun des écrits de son père, de quelque date qu'ils soient. Comment pourrait-on se représenter Racine, dans les dernières années de sa vie, non-seulement sortant ainsi de ses habitudes de langage et écrivant de telles énormités, mais les dictant à son fils, à un fils qui, lorsqu'il perdit son père, n'avait pas vingt et un ans? M. Capperonnier aura donc été abusé par quelque tradition, dont on peut s'étonner qu'il n'ait pas reconnu la fausseté. Jean-Baptiste Racine avait-il trouvé ce *Pétrone* dans la bibliothèque de son père? Il se peut, mais rien ne l'atteste.

Un bibliophile distingué de la ville de Toulouse, M. le docteur Desbarreaux-Bernard, possède deux ouvrages qui ont appartenu à Racine, un *Pline*, dont nous parlerons en son lieu, et un exemplaire de l'édition des *Poetæ græci gnomici*, donnée en 1569 par Crespin (*Crispinus*), 1 vol. petit in-12, qui porte la signature de Racine. La reliure est en vélin, avec tranches dorées.

M. Saint-Marc Girardin, dans une note de son édition des *OEuvres de Racine*, tome I, p. 215, nous apprend qu'il a vu « à Hyères, dans la bibliothèque de M. Denys, ancien député, un *Pétrarque*, où Racine avait noté et traduit quelques expressions. »

Une vente toute récente (1er mars 1869 et jours suivants) nous a fait connaître un volume annoté par Racine, qui est ainsi décrit sous le n° 5405, dans le *Catalogue des livres rares composant la bibliothèque de M. Victor Luzarche* (Paris, A. Claudin, 1869) : « *Relation des troubles arrivez dans la cour de Portugal en l'année* 1667 *et en l'année* 1668 (par Blouin de la Piquetierre), Paris, 1674, in-12, veau fauve. Exemplaire ayant fait partie de la bibliothèque de Jean Racine, avec sa signature et notes autographes. » Le catalogue cite cette note, qui est au bas de la page 169 : « La Reine, en ce temps-là, manda à Mme la duchesse de Vendôme qu'elle se croyoit grosse. Celle-ci envoya la lettre au marquis de Saint-Maurice, afin qu'il mandât la nouvelle en Portugal. » On trouve une note presque semblable dans les *Fragments historiques* de Racine : voyez notre tome V, p. 163.

LA BIBLE. — LE LIVRE DE JOB.

On ne peut douter que, parmi les études auxquelles s'est appliqué Racine, et dont nous cherchons ici les traces dans les volumes qui lui ont appartenu, celle de l'Écriture sainte n'ait, à différentes époques, tenu une des premières places. Il y fut certainement initié dès le temps de son éducation à Port-Royal. Elle devint pour lui un indispensable devoir à Uzès, lorsque, se préparant à l'état ecclésiastique, il mêlait des travaux théologiques à des occupations littéraires, dont quelques-unes étaient d'un caractère bien différent. Beaucoup plus tard, au temps où il composa *Esther*, *Athalie* et les *Cantiques sacrés*, le soin extrême avec lequel il étudiait la *Bible* nous est attesté par ces belles œuvres poétiques; et toutefois c'était alors comme chrétien, plus encore que comme poète, qu'il sentait le besoin de puiser sans cesse à cette source sacrée. Dans le manuscrit de ses *Remarques sur Athalie* (voyez notre tome V, p. 205 et suivantes), nous avons vu que les commentateurs de la *Bible* lui étaient familiers; on reconnaît aisément, lorsqu'il y cite Lightfoot et le *Synopsis*, qu'il n'a pas ouvert ces gros livres seulement pour le besoin du moment et pour y trouver quelques remarques d'une importance très-secondaire, mais qu'il était de longue main versé dans ces savants écrits. Nous avons pu offrir d'autres exemples des mêmes études dans les *Réflexions pieuses sur quelques passages de l'Écriture sainte*, qui ont été recueillies par Louis Racine, et dans les extraits des livres saints rassemblés sous le titre de *Port-Royal et Filles de l'Enfance* (voyez le même tome V, p. 201 et suivantes, et p. 212 et suivantes).

Mais ces différentes notes, écrites sur des feuillets volants, ne sont-elles pas une faible partie seulement de celles que Racine avait recueillies sur la *Bible*, et qu'il avait très-probablement écrites sur les marges de plus d'un exemplaire des livres sacrés, ayant toujours eu l'habitude de ces annotations marginales? Nos recherches de ce côté n'ont pas été aussi fructueuses qu'il nous semblait permis de l'espérer : ce qu'on peut attribuer à la difficulté de retrouver les volumes d'une bibliothèque dispersée. Quoi qu'il en soit, il est naturel de supposer que la bibliothèque de Racine était très-riche en éditions diverses des livres saints et des commentateurs dont ils ont été l'objet. En voici quelques-unes que nous savons lui avoir appartenu.

Dans la *Notice de livres contenant des notes manuscrites de Jean Racine et de ses deux fils, Jean-Baptiste et Louis Racine*[1], on mentionne un *Nouveau Testament* en grec (*Novum Testamentum ex Bibliotheca regia. Lutetiæ, ex officina Rob. Stephani, typis regiis*, 1549, maroquin noir, filets, doré sur

---

[1]. Voyez ci-dessus, p. 173.

tranche), et un *Livre des Psaumes*, également en grec (*Davidis regis ac prophetæ Psalmorum liber. Ad exemplar Complutense*, d'après l'édition d'Alcala, *Antverpiæ, ex officinis Christ. Plantini*, 1584), ces deux livres portant le nom de Racine. C'est probablement le même exemplaire du *Psautier* d'Anvers (1584), avec la signature, qui est placé dans la *Bibliothèque de Jean Racine*, par les auteurs du recueil que nous avons déjà cité sous le nom du *Quérard*. Ce même *Quérard* nomme aussi, parmi les livres ayant appartenu à Racine, un autre *Psautier* (*Psalterium Davidis*, Paris, 1546), avec signature, d'après le Catalogue Nodier (1829); un *Testamentum Novum* in-16 (Paris, Robert Estienne, 1549), également avec signature, d'après le Catalogue Pont-la-Ville (1850); enfin, d'après le Catalogue Séguier de Saint-Brisson, n° 706, l'ouvrage de Van der Driesche, qui a pour titre : *I. Drusii Observationum libri XII. Antverpiæ, M.D.LXXXIV* (in-8°). Ces observations très-savantes du célèbre hébraïsant sont, quoique toutes grammaticales, d'un très-grand secours pour l'intelligence des livres sacrés. L'exemplaire, qui porte la signature de Racine, est aux armes de de Thou. Le *Catalogue des livres rares et curieux composant la bibliothèque de M. J. d'O**** (Joseph d'Ortigue), *Paris, L. Potier*, 1862, fait mention, à la page 1, d'une *Histoire critique du Vieux Testament, par le R. P. Richard Simon, prestre de la Congregation de l'Oratoire*, 1680, in-4°, qui porte sur le titre la signature de Jean Racine. C'était un livre que sans doute Racine, à l'âge où il put le lire, ne consultait qu'avec défiance, car il avait été jugé dangereux et supprimé. L'auteur était d'ailleurs ennemi des théologiens de Port-Royal et imbu de principes tout contraires aux leurs. On ne signale aucune note manuscrite de notre poëte sur les marges de ce volume, non plus que sur celles des précédents.

Racine nous apprend lui-même (voyez sa lettre à Jean-Baptiste Racine en date du 24 septembre 1694) qu'il avait « les *Psaumes latins de Vatable*, à deux colonnes et avec des notes, in-8°. »

La Bibliothèque de Toulouse possède, parmi les livres ayant appartenu à Racine, un *Nouveau Testament* en grec, de Robert Estienne, d'une édition différente de celle dont nous avons parlé plus haut. Il est divisé en deux parties, reliées dans le même volume in-8°. La première partie contient les Évangélistes; elle porte sur le titre la date de 1569 (*Lutetiæ, ex officina Roberti Stephani, typographi regii, typis regiis. M.D.LXIX*). La seconde partie a la date de 1568. L'exemplaire dont nous parlons, et qui a fait partie de la bibliothèque de Racine, dont la signature est sur le feuillet de titre, est en maroquin rouge, avec filets dorés sur les plats, et tranche dorée.

La même Bibliothèque conserve aussi le *Nouveau Testament* de Mons (Gaspar Migeot, 1667, 2 vol. in-8°), qui a appartenu à Racine, et porte sa signature sur le feuillet de titre du Ier volume. Cet exemplaire est relié en maroquin rouge, tranche dorée.

Un exemplaire très-précieux de la *Bible* latine publiée, en 1651 et 1652, à Paris, chez Antoine Vitré (*Biblia sacra vulgatæ editionis*, 8 tomes in-12), se trouve à la Bibliothèque impériale. Il a été divisé par le relieur en dix-sept volumes, dont un, le III°, manque aujourd'hui. Sur le feuillet de garde du Ier volume, Louis Racine a écrit cette note : « Cette Bible qui appartenoit à mon père, avoit appartenu à M. le Maître, et les volumes suivants sont chargés de notes de sa main. » En effet, à l'exception du Ier volume, dont la reliure n'est pas semblable à celle des autres, et qui tient évidemment la place d'un volume perdu, tous ceux dont se compose maintenant cet exemplaire incomplet portent des notes de le Maistre, les unes en latin ou en grec, les autres en français : toutes les marges en sont couvertes, ainsi que les feuillets blancs intercalés. C'est une annotation très-savante, où les Pères, saint Augustin surtout, sont sans cesse cités, et où les réflexions édifiantes tiennent une grande place. Nous y avons fréquemment remarqué ces *Nota* (ou souvent, par abréviation, *N.*) qui servaient à Racine aussi dans tous les livres qu'il a annotés, pour fixer le souvenir des passages qu'il jugeait les plus importants. Il n'est pas sans intérêt de trouver quelque ressemblance entre la manière de travailler qui était familière à Racine et celle qu'il avait pu observer chez un des plus illustres instituteurs de sa jeunesse.

On pouvait espérer qu'en examinant attentivement tous les volumes de cette *Bible* de Vitré, on y trouverait aussi des notes de Racine, quoique son fils, Louis Racine, n'en eût point parlé. Nous avons cru un moment reconnaître l'écriture de Jean Racine à côté de celle de le Maistre, sur les marges de deux volumes, l'un de l'*Ancien*, l'autre du *Nouveau Testament;* mais nous n'avons pas tardé à voir que nous nous trompions. Les notes manuscrites que nous avions crues de sa main, et qui se rapportent aux douze premiers chapitres du livre I des *Rois*, et aux cinq premiers chapitres de l'*Évangile de saint Matthieu*, sont de la main de Jean-Baptiste Racine. Lorsqu'on n'est pas assez sur ses gardes, l'écriture du fils aîné, très-soignée, fine et élégante, peut être confondue avec celle du père, telle surtout qu'elle fut au temps de sa jeunesse. En outre, ce qui rendait l'erreur plus facile, Jean-Baptiste, quelques changements qu'eût déjà subis l'orthographe, nous a paru ne pas les avoir adoptés : il restait fidèle à celle que l'on trouve dans les plus anciens écrits de son père. Enfin, pour certaines particularités, son annotation rappelle beaucoup celle dont notre poëte avait l'habitude : il s'était évidemment formé sur ce modèle. Cependant il faut dire qu'en général les notes de Jean-Baptiste Racine sur la *Bible* ont un caractère plus marqué d'érudition, qu'on retrouve d'ailleurs dans les autres notes qui nous restent de lui, par exemple dans celles du *Petrone* dont nous avons parlé ci-dessus, aux pages 175 et 176. Ce qui nous a d'abord mis en défiance contre notre première erreur, c'est que l'annotateur, citant assez fréquemment le texte hébreu, se sert, pour en transcrire des mots, de caractères hébraïques, qu'il trace d'une main sûre et exercée. On a, nous l'avons dit ailleurs [1], des notes de Jean-Baptiste sur la grammaire hébraïque : il était donc hébraïsant. Si son père se fût livré à la même étude, nous en aurions trouvé des traces quelque part. Du reste, une fois notre attention éveillée sur la nécessité de nous mieux rendre compte des caractères distinctifs des deux écritures, nous l'avons fait de manière, non-seulement à ne conserver aucun doute sur l'auteur des notes mêlées à celles de le Maistre, mais aussi à ne plus être exposé à quelque autre méprise de ce genre.

La Bibliothèque impériale possède un autre volume de la *Bible* de Vitré, ayant également appartenu à Racine, et qui, à la différence de ceux dont nous venons de parler, a des notes manuscrites dans lesquelles son écriture se reconnaît sans le moindre doute. Ce volume ne fait point partie de l'exemplaire de le Maistre. Il n'a aucune note de la main de celui-ci, et est relié en par-

1. Voyez la *Notice biographique sur Jean Racine*, p. 165.

chemin : ceux qui viennent de la bibliothèque de le Maistre sont reliés en veau brun. Quoique le tome annoté par Racine soit le IIIe de la *Bible* de Vitré, il faut écarter toute idée d'un volume destiné à remplacer celui qui, nous l'avons dit, manque à l'exemplaire de le Maistre; car celui-ci ne se trouve le IIIe que par suite de la division adoptée pour la reliure de cet exemplaire, et est réellement la première partie du tome II, contenant le livre de *Josué*, et celui des *Juges*, tandis que le tome III dont Racine s'est servi pour ses notes forme, dans cette même division, le Ve volume, et contient les deux livres des *Paralipomènes*, les deux livres d'*Esdras*, les livres de *Tobie*, d'*Esther* et de *Job*.

Le *Livre de Job* est le seul que Racine ait annoté. Dans les autres on remarque seulement des passages soulignés, soit au crayon, soit à la plume : ce qui montre qu'ils avaient aussi été lus attentivement. On ne remarque point une étude plus particulière du *Livre d'Esther* : les endroits marqués d'une accolade ou soulignés y sont même très-rares. Au livre II des *Paralipomènes* quelques noms sont indiqués à la marge : *Ézéchias, Manassès, Josias, Joachaz, Joachin, Sédécias*, etc. Les chapitres xxii et xxiii de ce même livre, qui ont fourni à Racine le sujet d'*Athalie*, n'ont pas d'annotation.

Les notes marginales de Racine sur le *Livre de Job*, les unes en latin, les autres en français, sont tantôt des gloses, tantôt des sommaires, des paraphrases, des traductions.

Ce travail est très-souvent fondé sur le texte hébreu; mais il est facile de reconnaître où a été puisée l'érudition qu'il suppose. Au bas de la page 561, Racine a écrit cette note sur le verset 26 du chapitre xix : « Hebr. *Postquam circumdederint* hoc *cute mea.* Hoc, i. (id est) *ce misérable corps. Circumdederint,* i. *le Père, le Fils et le Saint-Esprit.* Vatab. » La note est en effet de Vatable. Cela nous a mis sur la trace des emprunts continuels que Racine a faits au docte commentaire qu'il avait sous les yeux; il s'est, en général, borné à en extraire ce qui lui a paru le plus instructif; et ses traductions, aussi bien que ses remarques, seraient presque inintelligibles, si on voulait les rapporter au texte seul de la *Vulgate*, qui est celui que donne la *Bible* de Vitré. La *Bible* dite *de Vatable*, dont Racine a fait usage, est celle que Robert Estienne a donnée en 1545 (2 vol. in-8°), celle que les théologiens catholiques avaient condamnée. L'édition donnée en 1557 par le même Robert Estienne, et celle de Commelin (2 vol. in-folio, 1599) ont, à côté de la *Vulgate*, la traduction latine de Sante-Pagnino : or il est visible que Racine s'est servi de celle qui est connue sous le nom de Zurich; et c'est celle-là qui se trouve avec la *Vulgate* dans l'édition de 1545[1]. Nous avons examiné aussi la *Bible de Vatable* publiée à Salamanque (2 vol. in-folio, 1584), qui a également la traduction de Zurich; mais nous avons trouvé que, parmi les notes de Racine, il y en a qui s'accordent bien mieux avec les notes de l'édition de 1545 qu'avec celles de l'édition de Salamanque, notamment la note sur le verset 24 du chapitre xv : « Comme on environne un homme qui va combattre en champ clos *dans un tournoi.* »

Les notes latines sont nombreuses dans cette étude de Racine. Il était d'au-

---

1. Dans cette traduction de Zurich, le *Livre de Job* a été traduit par Bibliander.

tant moins utile de les recueillir, que pour la plupart il les a copiées, avec une fidélité presque littérale, dans le commentaire de la *Bible* de 1545. Nous avons dû nous borner à la citation des notes françaises, dont un grand nombre sont des traductions ou des paraphrases de la version de Zurich. Nous indiquons au bas des pages les emprunts que Racine a faits à cette version, et ceux qu'il a faits au commentaire. Nous désignons ainsi le commentaire : Vat. (*Vatable*), et la version : Trad. Z (*traduction de Zurich*).

CHAPITRE II, verset 9. Tu n'as qu'à bénir Dieu, et tu mourras aussitôt [1].

CHAPITRE IV. Les amis de Job disputent contre lui, et prétendent lui prouver que Dieu l'afflige parce qu'il l'a offensé, étant persuadés, comme le vulgaire, que les afflictions ne doivent point tomber sur le juste [2].

— verset 9. [*Spiritu iræ.*] Au moindre souffle de sa colère [3].

— versets 12 et suivants. Éliphaz prétend que Dieu lui a révélé que Job étoit un pécheur qui a mérité son malheur [4].

CHAPITRE V, verset 27. Voilà ce que j'ai remarqué, et cela est ainsi.

CHAPITRE VI, versets 9 et 10. Il demande à mourir tout d'un coup [5], afin qu'il ne s'impatiente point. — Qu'il étende sa main pour m'exterminer, *nec sim in Deo blasphemus* [6].

— versets 15 et suivants. Ils (*les torrents*) font bien du ravage, mais ils s'évanouissent bientôt. — Les voyageurs les ont vus, et ont espéré qu'ils y puiseroient longtemps de l'eau; mais ils sont déchus de leur espérance et les ont trouvés à sec. Vous ressemblez à ces torrents [7].

— verset 24. Prouvez-moi mon crime.

---

1. *Benedic Deo, et morere, i.* (id est) *morieris.... Etiamsi benedicas Deo, et ipsum laudes, tamen morieris.* Vat.
2. *Ex afflictionibus Job nititur Eliphaz probare eum esse impium communi omnium carnalium argumento.* Vat.
3. *I.* (id est) *si vel paululum irascatur.* Vat.
4. *Divina revelatione prædictum est Eliphazi, cogitanti de rebus Jobi, quod ob peccata sit miser.* Vat.
5. *Morte repentina perdi optat.* Vat.
6. *Non fuerim in eum blasphemus.* Vat.
7. *Inconstantes amicos torrentibus comparat, qui.... magno impetu feruntur, æstate exarescunt, ad quos mercatores sitibundi, accurrentes spe potus, falluntur.* Vat. — *Ejusmodi mihi torrentem plane exhibetis.* Trad. Z.

Chapitre vi, verset 28. Continuez pourtant de m'examiner, et voyons si vous me convaincrez mieux que vous n'avez fait.

Chapitre ix, verset 33. Il n'y a point d'arbitre entre nous pour nous accommoder[1].

— verset 35. Car je ne suis pas un méchant, comme vous autres prétendez me le prouver[2].

Chapitre x, verset 1. C'est fait de moi : c'est pourquoi je ne contraindrai point ma douleur, et je me veux plaindre en liberté[3].

— verset 8. [*Et plasmaverunt me totum.*] Et m'ont fait tout ce que je suis[4].

Chapitre xii. Vous êtes des modèles de sagesse.

— verset 16. Il permet que nous soyons trompés par les faux prophètes[5].

Chapitre xiii, verset 8. Est-ce que vous croyez lui faire plaisir[6] (à Dieu)?

— verset 19. Car vous me condamnez sans m'entendre[7].

— verset 22. Ou je te répondrai, ou je t'interrogerai.

Chapitre xiv, verset 6. Cesse de l'affliger[8].

— verset 11. Comme les eaux qui séchant ne reviennent plus[9].

— verset 14. [*Immutatio mea*] *vicissitudo mea.* J'attends que tu me fasses changer en mieux.

Chapitre xv, verset 4. Vous détruisez la Providence, et qui est-ce qui priera Dieu s'il n'y a point de Providence[10]?

— verset 7. Vous qui nous reprochez d'être jeunes[11].

— verset 11. Est-ce qu'ils n'ont pas assez d'esprit pour vous consoler? et en savez-vous plus qu'eux[12]?

1. *Non enim esset inter nos arbiter, qui controversiam nostram dirimeret.* Trad. Z.

2. *Non sum talis qualem me esse putatis.* Vat.

3. *Actum est de vita mea; quare.... mihi permittam mussitationem.* Trad. Z.

4. *Ac me fecerunt quantus quantus sum.* Trad. Z.

5. *Permittit nos errare et decipi per pseudoprophetas.* Vat.

6. *An illi gratificari vultis?* Trad. Z.

7. *Nam vos me indicta causa damnastis.* Vat.

8. *Noli eum affligere.* Vat.

9. *Ut aquæ relinquunt alveum arentem, nunquam reversuræ : sic homo moritur....* Vat.

10. *Tu videris tollere Dei providentiam, qua ablata, quis illum timebit, aut illum in afflictione deprecabitur?* Vat.

11. *Quod scilicet toties exprobres meis juventutem.* Vat.

12. Hebr. « *An parum sint tibi consolationes istorum, et an res secreta sit*

CHAPITRE XV, verset 13. Que vous osiez prendre Dieu à partie[1].

— versets 17-19. Je vous dirai ce que j'ai ouï dire à des sages qui ont gouverné des États[2].

— verset 22. Et il voit de loin l'épée[3].

— verset 23. Il tombera dans la nécessité, et sera en danger de mourir de faim[4].

— verset 24. .... L'environneront comme on environne un homme qui va combattre en champ clos dans un tournoi[5]. — Ou bien comme un homme qu'on va jeter dans l'eau, pieds et poings liés[6].

— verset 27. Il n'a songé qu'à la bonne chère[7].

— verset 28. Il a rebâti les maisons qui tomboient en ruine[8].

— verset 29. Mais il ne verra pas la fin de ses bâtiments[9].

— verset 30. Il séchera, et il ne faudra qu'un souffle pour le renverser[10].

— verset 31. Il n'aura point recours à Dieu dans son malheur[11].

— verset 33. Il verra mourir ses enfants tout jeunes, à la fleur de leur âge[12].

CHAPITRE XVII, verset 12. Tout ce qui est jour me paroit nuit; et l'aurore même me paroit ténèbres[13].

— verset 16. Mes espérances mourront avec moi, i. (c'est-à-

---

apud te? » Ac si dicat : An minores sunt consolationes istorum quam ut te consolari possint? An est aliquid secreti quod illapsum sit in animum tuum? Vat.

1. Quæ, inquit, dementia cepit te,... quod tam constanter audeas pro voluntate tua sive arbitrio tuo Deo respondere? Vat.
2. Tibi recensebo quod sapientes homines retulerunt.... quibus solis permissa fuit rerum publicarum gubernatio. Trad. Z.
3. Et e specula prospectat gladium. Trad. Z.
4. Recidet in summam paupertatem, ita ut cogatur.... quærere ubinam invenire possit panem quo vivat. Vat.
5. Instar regis præparati ad bellum quod dicitur chidor. Quidam existimant esse genus præludii quod nos Galli Tournay (sic) dicimus. Vat.
6. Ut rex prævalet illi cui, ut demergatur, caput cum pedibus ligatur.
7. Dedit operam deliciis. Vat.
8. Curavitque instaurari domos quæ collapsuræ erant. Vat.
9. Non absolvet.... ædificia illa. Vat.
10. Veniet ad eam tenuitatem.... ut flatu loco suo moveri possit. Vat.
11. Non fidet Deo quum felicitas ejus in contrarium mutatur. Trad. Z.
12. Filios intelligit per botros, et pueros per florem. Vat.
13. Cogitationes meæ verterunt diem ipsum in noctem..., verterunt etiam in noctem lumen propinquum, i. auroram. Vat.

dire) je vois bien que ma mort est proche : qu'ai-je donc à espérer davantage[1]?

CHAPITRE XVIII, verset 15. Des gens qui ne lui étoient de rien[2]. Ou bien *Hebr.* : Il sera toujours en crainte dans sa maison, parce qu'elle ne lui appartient pas, qu'elle est mal acquise[3].

CHAPITRE XIX, verset 3. Vous m'outragez en me voulant faire passer pour impie[4].

— verset 4. J'ai péché, de quoi vous mêlez-vous? J'en porte la peine[5].

— verset 6. Si Dieu n'affligeoit que les pécheurs, il ne m'affligeroit pas maintenant[6].

— verset 9. [*Gloria mea*] *i.* ses biens. [*Coronam*] *i.* ses enfants[7].

— verset 12. [*Latrones ejus*] ses soldats, *i.* (c'est-à-dire) les afflictions. — Ils ont si souvent passé sur moi qu'ils en ont fait un chemin frayé[8].

— verset 16. Je prie mon valet.

— verset 19. [*Consiliarii mei.*] Ceux à qui je disois tous mes secrets[9].

— verset 20. Je n'ai que la peau sur les os.

— verset 22. N'êtes-vous pas contents de m'avoir insulté comme vous avez fait[10]?

— verset 28. Vous direz un jour: Pourquoi le persécutions-nous? le fondement du salut étoit en lui[11].

CHAPITRE XX. Sophar, en décrivant la punition des impies, veut insinuer à Job qu'il est puni pour ses crimes.

---

1. *Ego, et spes meæ simul morientur. Frustra igitur sperem quicquam a Deo, cum sim periturus.* Vat.

2. *Habitabit in tabernaculo ejus nulla propinquitate attingens eum.* Trad. Z.

3. Hebr. « *Habitabit in tentorio ejus* [sub. *timor*] *eo quod non sit ipsius.* » *Id est : perpetuo timebit, eo quod tentorium illud factum sit rebus non pertinentibus ad ipsum, sed ex rapina.* Vat.

4. *Sæpius conati estis.... me confundere, et ostendere impium.* Vat.

5. *Si peccaverim, quid ad vos ? Ego ipse luam pœnas.* Vat.

6. *Si solos peccatores affligeret, ut dicitis, inique et perverse mecum ageret, affligendo me, quum sim justus.* Vat.

7. Gloriam *suam vocat opes suas.* — (Coronam) *i. liberos suos.* Vat.

8. *Copiæ ejus, i. exercitus tribulationum.... Tam frequentes invaserunt me tribulationes ut viam quasi tritam reddiderint me.* Vat.

9. *Quotquot olim erant mihi a secretis.* Vat.

10. *Abunde calumniati estis me; jam desinite, obsecro.* Vat.

11. *Nam* [olim] *dicetis : Cur eum persequebamur, in quo fundamenta negotii* [salutis] *deprehendebantur?* Trad. Z.

CHAPITRE XX, verset 3. Je réponds pour deux raisons : 1° parce que vous m'avez attaqué ; 2° parce que je me sens assez de savoir pour vous répondre [1].

— verset 6. S'il est élevé en dignité [2].

— verset 10. Ses enfants seront obligés de faire la cour aux gens de la plus basse fortune ; et il sera contraint de rendre tout ce qu'il a volé [3].

— verset 11. Ses vices l'accompagneront jusqu'au tombeau [4].

— verset 12. Et qu'il le retient longtemps sous son palais, comme quelque chose de savoureux [5].

— versets 15 et 16. Tous ses biens mal acquis le perdront [6].

— verset 17. Il ne sera plus dans l'abondance [7].

— verset 18. Il rendra tout ce qu'il a pris, sans s'en être servi, comme des choses empruntées [8].

— verset 19. Il a ruiné la maison qu'il n'avoit point bâtie [9].

— verset 20. Il ne jouira de rien de ce qu'il avoit acquis [10].

— verset 22. Il se trouvera dans le travail au milieu de l'abondance [11].

— verset 23. — Quand même il parviendroit à être content, Dieu le perdra lui et sa richesse [12]. — Il semble que Sophar entende parler de Job sur lequel Dieu a fait pleuvoir sa colère.

— verset 25. Il sera si malheureux que dès qu'un homme tirera

---

1. *Duabus causis.... cogor tibi respondere : partim propter ignominiam qua me affecisti...; partim etiam doctrina illa mea me cogit, quod existimem me satis habere doctrinæ et eruditionis ut tibi respondeam.* Vat.

2. *Si quando in summa dignitate constituatur.* Vat.

3. *Liberi ejus placabunt pauperes, et manus illius restituent opes per vim ademptas.* Trad. Z.

4. *Eumque comitantur* (vitia) *ad* [*sepulcrum*] *pulverem.* Trad. Z.

5. *Si dulce fuerit in ore ejus malum, et absconderit illud sub lingua sua, ut scilicet occultare solemus res dulces sub lingua nostra.* Vat.

6. *Cogetur tandem restituere res furto ablatas; et tandem male peribit.* Vat.

7. *In magna rerum copia egebit.* Vat. (Sens un peu différent de celui que donne Racine.)

8. *Quæ labore acquisivit reddet..., velut merces permutatorias, nec illis gaudebit.* Trad. Z.

9. *Diripuitque domum quam non ædificaverat.* Vat.

10. *Privabitur labore suo..; nec quippiam eorum quæ habet in deliciis servabit sibi.* Vat.

11. *Quum habebit quod sufficiat ei ad vitam tuendam, incidet tamen in angustias.* Vat.

12. *Esto autem ut impleat ventrem suum,* [*Deus tamen*] *immitet ei furorem iræ suæ.* Trad. Z.

l'épée du fourreau, il en sera percé[1], *i. (c'est-à-dire)* tout se tournera contre lui.

Chapitre xx, verset 26. A cause de ses crimes secrets tous les maux tomberont sur lui[2]. — [*Qui non succenditur.*] Qui non follibus excitatur, qui ne s'éteint jamais et qu'il ne faut point souffler[3]. — Tous ceux qui seront avec lui seront enveloppés dans sa ruine[4].

— verset 28. Sa postérité s'évanouira[5].

Chapitre xxi, verset 2. Écoutez-moi, et cela me tiendra lieu de consolation[6].

— verset 4. Puisque Dieu ne me répond pas[7]. — Ou bien : N'est-ce pas à Dieu même que je parle, et aurois-je l'assurance de mentir devant lui[8]?

— verset 6. Quand je me souviens de tout ce qui m'est arrivé[9].

— versets 7-13. Bonheur des impies.

— verset 12. Ils dansent au son du tambour, etc.[10].

— verset 16. Cette félicité ne leur dure guère, n'est point en leur pouvoir.

— verset 21. [*Post se.*] Quand il sera mort.

— verset 25. Qui n'a jamais eu de joie[11].

— versets 27 et 28. Je sais ce que vous pensez de moi. Où est, dites-vous, le palais de Job? Ou bien : Où sont les palais des princes qui n'ont point connu Dieu? C'est-à-dire : vous me prétendez soutenir que Dieu ne punit que les impies[12].

— verset 30. Dieu laisse prospérer l'impie jusqu'au jour de sa perte[13].

1. *Adeo.... infelix erit ut, quum primum extraxerit quis sagittam e pharetra, feriatur ea sagitta.... Alii de ense, non de sagitta exponunt.* Vat.
2. *Omnia mala eum manent propter occulta peccata ejus.* Vat.
3. *Devorabit eum ignis divinus qui non follibus excitatur.* Vat.
4. *Quicquid est residuum in domo ipsius, malo involvitur.* Trad. Z.
5. *Germen domus ejus, i. posteritas ejus, alio demigrabit.* Vat.
6. *Attente me audite, et hoc vestrum silentium erit mihi vice magnæ consolationis.* Vat.
7. *Quum Deum alloquar, nec mihi respondeat.* Vat.
8. *Si ita est ut Deum alloquar, non hominem,... quomodo auderem Deo præsente falsa loqui ?* Vat.
9. *Nam cogitatione obiens quæ mihi acciderunt.* Trad. Z.
10. *Ad tympanum et citharam ducunt choros.* Trad. Z.
11. *Qui nunquam lætus comedit.* Trad. Z.
12. *Videmini dicere pios non timere.... Novi cogitationes vestras, quia dicitis : Ubinam est domus principis? i. mea. Ubinam est tentorium impiorum?* Vat.
13. *Etenim pravis parcitur ad diem perniciei.* Trad. Z.

Chapitre XXI, verset 31. Et qui osera lui reprocher sa mauvaise vie dans la fortune où il est?

— verset 32. [*In congerie mortuorum.*] Sous une pyramide, ou bien : parmi un tas de morts. — [*Vigilabit.*] Sera toujours mort [1].

Chapitre XXII, verset 2. Est-ce qu'un homme prudent est de quelque utilité à Dieu [2]?

— verset 4. Est-ce qu'il a peur de l'impie quand il le punit [3]?

— versets 7 et 8. *Hebr.* Tu ne donnes rien à l'indigent, et tu donnes à celui qui est puissant [4].

— verset 12. Regarde combien les étoiles sont élevées [5].

— verset 13. Il y a un chaos entre lui et nous [6].

— verset 15. Veux-tu être comme on étoit au temps du déluge, où l'on nioit la Providence [7]?

— verset 17. Et qu'est-ce que le Tout-Puissant nous peut faire [8]?

— verset 21. Accoutume-toi à lui et à ses préceptes [9].

— verset 24. Tu auras des montagnes d'or, et tu le fouleras comme la terre sous tes pas [10].

— verset 25. Et tes richesses seront Dieu, c'est-à-dire infinies. Les Hébreux mettent le nom de Dieu quand ils veulent exagérer [11].

— verset 26. Tu mettras alors ton plaisir en Dieu [12].

— verset 28. Et Dieu te favorisera en tout [13].

— verset 30. L'innocent sauve tout un pays [14].

Chapitre XXIII, verset 2. Et mon mal est au-dessus des plaintes et des paroles [15].

---

1. *Tantum vult dicere eum esse mortuum.* Vat.
2. *Num aliquid utilitatis accedet Deo, si vir prudens consulat suæ utilitati et saluti?* Vat.
3. *An, quod timeat sibi ab operibus malis, statim corripit impios?* Vat.
4. *Pauperes non dignaris pane, at potentibus possessiones tuas offers.* Vat.
5. *Spectato enim verticem stellarum, quam sublimes sunt.* Trad. Z.
6. *An propterea quod tantum chaos sit inter nos et Deum...?* Vat.
7. *Visne tueri opinionem illam antiquorum, tempore diluvii, qui omnes censebant tollendam esse divinam Providentiam?* Vat.
8. *Et quid Optimus Maximus faceret nobis?* Trad. Z.
9. *Quapropter accommoda te illi.* Trad. Z.
10. *Non pluris facies aurum quam lapides. Alii : Habebis tantum auri ut æquare possis montem.* Vat.
11. *Et aurum tuum erit Omnipotens, i. multum et ingens. Ita enim res exaggerant Hebræi addito nomine Dei.* Vat.
12. *Tunc enim in Optimo Maximo te oblectabis.* Trad. Z.
13. *Favebit tibi Deus.* Vat.
14. *Innocens servare solet totam regionem.* Vat.
15. *Mea calamitas superat gemitus meos.* Trad. Z.

Chapitre XXIII, verset 7. Lorsqu'il me donnera la force de paroître devant lui, il me renvoyera innocent[1].

— verset 8. Dieu se trouve difficilement quand on le cherche avec un esprit humain[2].

— verset 9. [*Ad sinistram.*] Au septentrion, qui est à la gauche, quand on est tourné vers le levant[3].

— verset 12. Et ses paroles m'ont été plus chères que ma propre vie[4].

— verset 13. Il fait ce qu'il a de coutume de faire[5].

— verset 17. Car je n'ai point été frappé d'un mal qu'on puisse ignorer[6].

Chapitre XXIV. Job fait semblant de nier la Providence[7] et embarrasse ses amis par ses raisonnements.

— verset 1. Vous dites que rien n'est caché à Dieu. Pourquoi donc les méchants prospèrent-ils[8] ?

— verset 4. Ils réduisent le pauvre à se cacher dans des cavernes[9].

— verset 5. Les autres sont comme des bêtes sauvages qui vivent de rapines[10].

— verset 9. Ils pillent l'orphelin dès la mamelle[11].

— verset 10. Ils enlèvent au pauvre le peu d'épis qu'il avoit glanés.

— verset 11. Ils le font travailler, et ne lui donnent pas seulement à boire[12].

— verset 12. Et vous dites que Dieu ne laisse point le méchant impuni.

— verset 15. (*L'œil de l'adultère*) attend le soir.

---

1. .... *Quum scilicet dederit mihi vires subsistendi cum illo. Et liberabo me ipsum in perpetuum a judicante me.* Vat.
2. *Dicit Deum consilio humano non inveniri.* Vat.
3. *Ad septentrionem (qui respiciendo ad Orientem est in sinistra).* Vat.
4. *Cariora mihi fuerunt præcepta Dei quam id quo anima fovetur.* Vat.
5. *Et quum perpetuo sui similis sit.* Trad. Z.
6. *Non enim excisus sum malo improviso.* Trad. Z.
— *Neque texit [Deus] afflictionem meam.* Vat.
7. *Hic Job personam ejus induit qui providentiam Dei non agnoscat.* Vat.
8. *Vos dicitis Deo nihil esse absconditum, et ego quæro a vobis quomodo illi tempora.... non sunt abscondita, quum videamus impios homines libere grassari in innocentes.* Vat.
9. *Qui pauperes pellunt ex via, ita ut in latebras abdantur.* Trad. Z.
10. *Illi sunt feri et crudeles more ferarum...; furto et rapto vivunt.* Vat.
11. *Pupillum deprædantur ab ubere.* Vat.
12. *Pauperes exprimunt oleum istorum impiorum; nec eos potu dignantur.* Vat.

CHAPITRE XXIV, verset 16. Ils percent de nuit la maison, à l'endroit qu'ils ont marqué de jour[1].

— verset 17. Et ils se croient morts, si on les connoit[2].

— verset 18. Ils se retirent dans les lieux déserts, et n'osent marcher par le grand chemin[3].

— verset 19. Ils meurent aussi doucement que la neige est fondue par le soleil[4].

— verset 20. Ils ne souffrent point en mourant, et les vers les mangent en très-peu de temps[5]; ils tombent comme un arbre sec.

— verset 21. Ils n'ont jamais eu pitié de personne.

— verset 22. Ils attaquent tout ce qu'il y a de plus fort, et personne ne leur peut résister[6].

— verset 23. Les gens de bien leur font des présents pour les apaiser; mais bientôt ils recommencent à les persécuter[7].

— verset 24. Ils tuent ceux qui leur ont fait des présents, comme ceux qui ne leur en ont point fait. Ils ferment la bouche à ceux qu'ils égorgent, afin qu'on ne les entende pas crier[8].

— verset 25. Si cela n'est pas ainsi, qu'on me convainque de mensonge.

CHAPITRE XXV. Baldad prétend convaincre Job qu'il est méchant[9].

— verset 2. Dieu ne peut point être injuste, car il est tout-puissant[10]. — Les cieux marchent toujours d'un pas réglé[11].

— verset 6. [*Vermis.*] Qui n'est qu'un ver de terre.

CHAPITRE XXVI, versets 1 et 2. Job se moque des arguments fri-

---

1. *Perfodiunt domos noctu, quas interdiu sibi notarunt.* Trad. Z.
2. *Si quis enim cognoscat eos, affert terrores densissimæ caliginis.* Trad. Z.
3. *Se.... recipiunt in loca.... arentia et inculta, nec recedunt via regia, ne agnoscantur.* Vat.
4. [*Utque*] *terra torrida et calor absumunt aquas nivales,* [*ita*] *infernus eos.* Trad. Z.
5. *Nihil a morte sentit doloris; celerrime absumunt eum vermes.* Vat.
6. *Tantis pollet viribus ut fortissimos robore vincat.* Vat.
7. *Solent boni dare illis munera, ut confidenter habitent inter illos; ac postea insidiantur illis a quibus munera acceperunt.* Vat.
8. *Humiliantur illi, ut alii a quibus improbi munera non acceperunt. Obturantur ora eorum ab improbo, ne clament, et occiduntur.* Vat.
9. *Nititur Baldad.... improbum Job comprobare.* Vat.
10. *Fieri non potest, inquit, ut Deum dicamus injustum,... sumpto argumento a potentia.* Vat.
11. *Facit ut corpora cœlestia sine ullo dissidio.... moveantur.* Vat.

voles de Baldad, comme s'il disoit : N'as-tu point de meilleures raisons pour prouver la Providence[1]? Il enchérit sur Baldad.

Chapitre XXVI, versets 3 et 4. Crois-tu parler à un homme sans esprit[2]?

— verset 5. Dieu a formé les métaux qui sont au-dessous de la mer et des poissons[3].

— verset 6. Il voit à plein le centre de la terre, et l'abîme ne lui est point caché[4].

— verset 9. Qui soutient l'air, lequel est au devant de son trône, i. (c'est-à-dire) du ciel[5].

— verset 10. [*Usque dum finiantur lux et tenebræ.*] Jusqu'à la fin du monde[6].

— verset 12. Et il réprime l'orgueil de la mer[7].

— verset 14. Voilà le peu que nous connoissons de lui. Combien le reste est-il encore au-dessus de nous!

Chapitre XXVII, verset 7. [*Inimicus meus.*] Celui qui n'est pas de mon avis.

— verset 8. Ne sais-je pas que le méchant a beau prospérer, et que sa fin sera malheureuse[8]?

— verset 18. [*Et sicut custos.*] Comme celui qui garde un jardin[9].

— verset 21. [*Ventus urens.*] Hebr. *ventus orientalis.* C'étoient les grands vents en Judée.

— verset 23. Celui qui lui verra arriver tout cela[10].

---

1. *Job ridet quodam modo argumenta Baldad.... In qua re, inquit, adjuvisti sententiam tuam de Providentia Dei particulari...?* Vat.

2. *Cuinam sermonem enarras? — Putasne te sermonem facere cum homine imperito?* Vat.

3. *Res emortuæ [a Deo] formantur sub aquis.* Trad. Z. — *Quæ vitæ expertia sunt, nascuntur sub aquis, sub habitatoribus earum. De metallis loquitur.* Vat.

4. *Nudus ante illum extat infernus, neque interitus habet velamentum.* Trad. Z. — *Infernum intelligit centrum terræ.* Vat.

5. *Qui construxit faciem solii.* Trad. Z. — *I.* (id est) *aerem et vaporem existentem in media regione sublimi, qui est ante faciem solii ejus, hoc est cœli.* Vat.

6. *Quamdiu erit mundus.* Vat.

7. *Sua potentia scindit mare, et intelligentia sua compescit [ejus] ferociam.* Trad. Z.

8. *Quamvis ego dixerim impios feliciter agere, non tamen laudo sortem et conditionem eorum; nam malus eos manet exitus.* Vat.

9. *Utque custos [hortorum].* Trad. Z.

10. *Quicumque, inquit, audierit talia accidisse impiis....* Vat.

CHAPITRE XXVIII. Il prouve que le monde est sujet au changement, et qu'il arrive tous les jours quelque chose de nouveau[1].

— verset 5. (*La terre*) est devenue sèche[2].

— versets 6 et 7. Il y a des pays qui étoient d'une fertilité extraordinaire : chaque motte de terre étoit de l'or et des diamants; et puis ils deviennent déserts, et les oiseaux mêmes n'y passent plus[3].

— verset 8. *Filii superbiæ*, les bêtes sauvages[4].

— verset 10. Il inonde toutes les richesses d'un pays[5].

— verset 11. Après il sèche les fleuves et découvre aux yeux le pays qui étoit inondé[6].

— verset 12. Il n'y a que la sagesse de solide[7].

— verset 15. [*Aurum obrizum*] le plus pur. — Elle ne se donne point pour de l'or.

— verset 22. La matière dit, etc. Ou bien : L'homme qui n'est que mort et que perdition[8].

— verset 26. En prescrivant des lois et des mesures à la pluie et au tonnerre.

CHAPITRE XXIX, verset 3. [*In tenebris.*] Dans les temps difficiles, *in ærumnis*[9].

— verset 6. Quand j'étois dans une extrême abondance[10].

— verset 22. Ils se le redisoient les uns aux autres[11].

— verset 25. J'étois écouté et respecté d'eux, comme un homme qui vient consoler des affligés[12].

---

1. *Hic Jobus docet cur idem probis et improbis eveniat : nempe quia mundus subjectus est mutationibus. His versiculis ostendit quotidie aliquid novi accidere.* Vat.
2. *Arescit, et fit infœcunda.* Vat.
3. *Postea regio illa deseritur, et fit inhabitabilis ipsis etiam avibus.* Vat.
4. *Non calcabunt eam filii superbiæ.... Filios superbiæ vocat belluas truces et immanes.* Vat.
5. *Facit exundare totam regionem, ita ut aquis subvertatur : quum tamen quicquid pretiosum esset, cerneretur in ea regione.* Vat.
6. *Postea efficit ne rupes flumina effundant; et reddit regionem obrutam aquis, aridam et subjectam oculis omnium.* Vat.
7. *Ostendit tandem felicitatem quæ solis probis contingit, quæ æterna est, sita in sola in Deum fiducia.* Vat.
8. *Materia ipsa informis ostendit...*, etc. *Ita Hebræi exponunt. Alii melius : Perditio et mors, i. homo perditus et corruptus....* Vat.
9. *Tenebras, rerum difficultates et tribulationes intelligit.* Vat.
10. *Dum adesset mihi summa copia rerum omnium.* Vat.
11. *Id quod dixeram, alter alteri renuntiabat.* Vat.
12. *Habitabam inter illos sicut qui consolatur lugentes, qui pendere solent ab ore consolatoris.* Vat.

Chapitre xxx, verset 2. Qui ne pouvoient pas même me rendre service[1].

— verset 12. Dès que je me lève, les jeunes gens me poussent pour me faire tomber[2].

— verset 13. Ils renversent tous mes desseins[3].

— verset 17. [*Et qui me comedunt*] *vermes*. Ou bien : Et mes artères battent avec la même force durant la nuit[4].

— verset 18. [*Et quasi capitio tunicæ*....] Les robes étoient toutes cousues, et il n'y avoit d'ouverture que pour passer la tête; c'est de cette ouverture qu'il entend parler.

— verset 24. Et alors les prières ne servent plus de rien, *i.* (c'est-à-dire) dans le temps de la mort[5].

— verset 29. J'ai gémi, *sicut draco*[6]. — [*Struthionum*[7].] Des hiboux.

Chapitre xxxi, verset 27. Si j'ai mis toute ma confiance en moi-même, et si j'ai regardé le ciel avec audace[8]. Ou : Si j'ai baisé ma main en signe d'adoration pour le soleil et pour la lune[9].

— verset 30. Je n'ai point ouvert la bouche pour le maudire[10].

— verset 31. Mes domestiques étoient si fatigués de mon hospitalité qu'ils souhaitoient ma mort[11]. Ou bien : Quoique mes domestiques, indignés des insolences de mes ennemis, leur eussent voulu manger le cœur.

— verset 38. [*Si adversum me terra mea clamat*] ou faute de l'avoir payée ou chargée de trop d'impôts[12].

---

1. *Opera eorum ad quid mihi utilis fuisset?* Vat.
2. *Et adolescentes ad dextrum* [*latus*] *insurgunt, meosque pedes subvertunt.* Trad. Z.
3. *Impedimento mihi sunt quominus assequar quod cupio.* Vat.
4. *Nec quiescunt* [*vermes*] *digredientes a me.* Trad. Z. — *Et arteriæ meæ non conquieverunt.* Vat.
5. *Sane precatio non porriget manum.... Tunc certe non proderunt preces ad Deum.* Vat. — *Clamant aliqui post obitum suum?* Trad. Z.
6. *Naturam draconum sum imitatus; semper emisi vocem lugubrem.* Vat.
7. *Vox hebræa significat genus avis deserta incolentis, cujus cantus est lugubris.* Vat.
8. Ce premier sens, que Racine n'a pas tiré de la *Bible de Vatable*, pourrait faire croire qu'il avait sous les yeux quelque autre commentaire encore.
9. *Si, quum vidi solem, deceptus fui ut suspicarer illum esse Deum, et in signum reverentiæ posui manum meam ad os meum.* Vat.
10. *Quum ne habenas quidem laxarim ori meo, ut de illo maledicerem.* Vat.
11. *Verba sunt domesticorum Jobi, quos nimium fatigabat in tractandis hospitibus.* Vat.
12. Les notes de Racine s'arrêtent après le chapitre xxxi, à la page 591 du volume; on ne trouve plus ensuite que des passages soulignés.

SAINT BASILE.

A la suite des notes de Racine sur un des livres de la *Bible*, nous pouvons, afin de ne pas séparer ce qui appartient à l'antiquité sacrée, parler de quelques notes qu'il a écrites sur plusieurs morceaux extraits de saint Basile. Ce n'est pas sur les marges d'un livre imprimé qu'on les trouve, mais sur celles d'un manuscrit qui est de la main de notre poëte, et qui a pour titre : *Extraits de saint Basile le Grand*. Les cahiers de Racine renferment d'autres études du même genre, qui nous ont paru devoir, comme celle-ci, être placées parmi les *Livres annotés*, en considération de l'analogie du travail. Mais comme les notes peu nombreuses, mêlées à ces extraits manuscrits, qui sont tous du temps où Racine était encore écolier, sont en général très-brèves et de peu d'intérêt, il suffira d'en donner quelque idée, sans les recueillir scrupuleusement.

Les *Extraits de saint Basile* sont écrits sur un cahier in-4°, relié dans un cartonnage blanc [1]. Jean-Baptiste Racine a écrit sur le premier feuillet : « De 1655 à 1658; » et Louis Racine, sur la couverture : « *Extraits de saint Basile*, par Jean Racine, pendant qu'il étudioit à Port-Royal, en 1656. » Nous ignorons si ces deux notes sont simplement des conjectures; en tout cas, la date qu'elles indiquent est vraisemblable. Les *Extraits* ont 84 pages.

En voici les titres tels que Racine les a donnés lui-même, tantôt en français, tantôt en latin : « *Excerpta ex Divi Basilii Magni Sermone, de Abdicatione rerum*. — *Ex ejusdem Sermone* περὶ Ἀσκήσεως. — *Omissa ex de Abdicatione rerum*. — *Ex Divi Basilii Magni Moralibus* (Racine a tiré de cet ouvrage soixante-dix-sept sentences détachées; il les a numérotées). — Extrait de quelques lettres de saint Basile le Grand. — Extrait II des lettres de saint Basile le Grand. — *Ex. S. Basilii Magni Regulis fusius disputatis*. — *Ex D. Basilii Magni de Institutionibus monasticis Sermone primo*. — *Ex ejusdem de Institutionibus monasticis Sermone II*. — *Ex ejusdem Proœmio in Regulas fusius disputatas*. » — Racine a souligné, comme dignes d'attention, de nombreux passages de ces *Extraits*. Les notes marginales qu'il y a jointes ne font qu'indiquer, à la façon d'un sommaire, de quoi il est question, par exemple : « Qualités d'un véritable directeur. — Amis. — Comparaison de ceux qui vomissent dans un petit vaisseau aussi bien que dans un grand. — Comparaison de l'œil. » — Parmi ces notes, une seule nous a paru avoir quelque intérêt. Racine a écrit le mot *Grâce* à côté de ce passage, qu'il cite sous le numéro LXXVII, dans l'*Extrait II des lettres de saint Basile* : τὸ δὲ Ἡμεῖς ὅταν εἴπω, οὐκ εἰς τὴν ἀνθρωπίνην ἀναφέρω δύναμιν, ἀλλ' εἰς τὴν τοῦ Θεοῦ χάριν, τοῦ ἐν τῇ ἀσθενείᾳ τῶν ἀνθρώπων τὸ δυνατὸν ἑαυτοῦ δεικνύντος. C'est-à-dire : « Mais

[1]. Bibliothèque impériale, Fonds français, n° 12889.

quand je dis *Nous*, ce n'est pas que j'attribue à la puissance de l'homme ce qui doit être attribué à la grâce de Dieu, lequel manifeste sa puissance dans la faiblesse de l'homme. » On verra plus loin, dans les notes de Racine sur Plutarque, combien il s'est attaché à relever tous les passages qui lui rappelaient ces questions de la grâce et du libre arbitre. Ces dernières notes étant des années 1655 et 1656, il y aurait là, au besoin, un indice de plus que les fils de Racine ne se sont pas trompés en datant les *Extraits de saint Basile* du même temps, qui était celui où leur père étudiait à Port-Royal, « dans ce lieu par la Grâce habité. »

HOMÈRE.

NOTES SUR L'*ILIADE*.

Le *Quérard*, que nous avons déjà cité (voyez ci-dessus, p. 171-173 et p. 178), place dans la bibliothèque de Racine un *Homère*, Elzévir, 1656, 2 vol. in-4°, avec des notes attribuées à notre poëte, d'après le Catalogue Cramayel, 1826, n° 581; et une *Iliade*, texte grec, Bâle, 1561, in-folio, avec quelques notes, d'après le Catalogue Parison, n° 786.

Si le titre de ce dernier volume est donné exactement, il diffère de celui que la *Notice de livres* extraite du *Bulletin universel des sciences et de l'industrie* mentionne de la manière suivante : *Homeri Opera græco-latina, quæ quidem nunc exstant, omnia. Basileæ. Nic. Brylinger*, 1561, 1 vol. in-folio. « J. B. Racine, et peut-être aussi le poëte tragique, ont, dit cette même *Notice*, entièrement couvert de notes les marges de ce livre. »

La Bibliothèque de Toulouse possède une *Iliade* (gr.-lat.), in-8°, imprimée à Strasbourg, en 1572, par Théodore Rihel, qui porte la signature de Racine.

On trouve à la Bibliothèque impériale, outre les *Remarques manuscrites sur l'Odyssée*, que nous avons données aux pages 56 et suivantes de ce tome VI, une *Iliade* de Turnèbe, avec des annotations marginales de Racine (*Homeri Ilias, id est, de Rebus ad Troiam gestis. Typis regiis, Parisiis, M.D.LIIII. Apud Adr. Turnebum...*, in-8°). Au-dessous du titre est la signature de Racine. Au commencement du volume, sur le feuillet de garde, on a collé un petit papier de l'écriture de notre poëte, sur lequel on lit : « La durée est de quarante-sept jours, dont il n'y a que cinq de combats, neuf de peste, onze pendant que les Dieux sont en Éthiopie; et pendant ce temps les Grecs se guérissent; onze accordés pour les funérailles d'Hector, onze pour les funérailles de Patrocle.

« Des cinq mêmes (*c'est-à-dire des cinq jours de combat*), un jour de trêve pour enterrer les morts.

« Virgile, en Italie, deux mois et demi. »

Cette petite note ne peut pas être du même temps que les notes marginales du volume; car, à la différence de celles-ci, elle est d'une écriture qui rappelle celle des manuscrits qui sont des derniers temps de la vie de Racine. Mais nous allons voir que, dans l'annotation marginale, Racine s'est beaucoup occupé pareillement de déterminer la durée de l'action de l'*Iliade* et d'en noter les journées.

A l'annotation de l'*Iliade* écrite sur les marges d'un livre, Racine ne pouvait donner les mêmes développements qu'à son manuscrit des *Remarques sur l'Odyssée*. C'est par cela même un travail d'un moindre intérêt. De ces notes marginales quelques-unes sont purement philologiques, d'autres se bornent à des indications très-sommaires et semblables à celles d'une table des matières, par exemple : « Calchas. Prophète. — Paris se retire. — Discours d'Iris à Hélène, etc. » Nous ne transcrirons que les notes plus significatives, et celles qui appartiennent plus en propre à Racine.

Nous venons de dire que les notes sur l'*Iliade* étaient un travail moins intéressant que les *Remarques sur l'Odyssée*, parce qu'il est moins étendu. Toutefois on y trouvera autant de goût, et un sentiment aussi juste des beautés d'Homère. Comme on y rencontre fort peu de tours et d'expressions qui aient vieilli, et qu'on y est frappé de la maturité du jugement, nous croirions volontiers qu'elles n'ont pas été écrites au temps de la première jeunesse, mais quelques années plus tard, probablement dans celles où Racine composait ses premières tragédies. En général, nous ne prétendons pas déterminer exactement la date d'un travail de Racine par l'écriture de ses manuscrits. Cette écriture, dans les dernières années du poëte, était devenue très-différente de ce qu'elle avait été dans sa jeunesse; mais elle a dû longtemps rester la même : nous n'avons pu constater les différences qu'entre les deux termes extrêmes de son âge.

Nous indiquons à quels vers de l'*Iliade* se rapporte chacune des remarques ou notes qui suivent; mais nous nous contentons en général de donner le numéro de ces vers, sans en citer le texte. Quelquefois seulement il a fallu, par exception, rappeler quelques mots du passage annoté, lorsque autrement la note de Racine n'eût pas été intelligible.

M. de la Rochefoucauld Liancourt, dans ses *Études sur Racine* (1re partie, *Études littéraires*, p. 5-42), a donné, avant nous, les mêmes notes sur l'*Iliade*, mais très-inexactement, suivant son habitude, et en y introduisant beaucoup de changements. Quelques-uns des passages ajoutés par lui sont évidemment de son propre cru; mais il y en a qui sembleraient avoir été recueillis sur les marges d'un autre exemplaire de l'*Iliade* que Racine aurait également annoté, et que nous n'avons pas vu, peut-être un de ceux que nous venons de mentionner plus haut.

LIVRE I.

Vers 26-32. Discours superbe d'Agamemnon.

Vers 85-91. Discours d'Achille, qui marque sa fierté.

Vers 594. (Ἔνθα με Σίντιες ἄνδρες....) On appeloit ainsi les Lemniens, à cause que c'étoient des pirates, ou à cause qu'ils avoient inventé les armes.

(*Au bas de la page* 21, *où finit le livre I.*) Il se passe douze jours dans le I. livre, depuis l'assemblée des Grecs, c'est-à-dire depuis la querelle d'Achille et d'Agamemnon, qui est proprement le commencement de l'*Iliade;* car la peste, et l'outrage fait à Chrysès est récité comme une chose qui s'est passée devant l'action.

LIVRE II.

Vers 48. (Ἠὼς μέν ῥα θεὰ....) Treizième aurore.

Vers 109. Agamemnon veut tenter l'armée. La raison de cette feinte d'Agamemnon, c'est que, comme c'étoit pour lui et pour son frère Ménélas que les Grecs avoient déjà tant souffert, il n'ose leur proposer de son chef de s'aller encore exposer à un assaut, et il aime mieux que ce conseil leur soit donné par d'autres. Il fait donc semblant de leur proposer de s'enfuir, mais il le fait en termes si artificieux, qu'il leur représente en même temps cette fuite comme la chose du monde la plus honteuse, espérant que d'eux-mêmes ils aimeront mieux s'exposer à tous les périls plutôt que de consentir à cette infamie, ou, au moins, que les princes de l'armée prendront la parole et exhorteront le peuple à combattre, ce qui fera plus d'effet venant de bouches qui ne sont intéressées que pour l'honneur général de la patrie. Que si cette feinte ne réussit point d'abord, et si Agamemnon est pris au mot, c'est que le succès ne répond pas toujours à nos intentions. Et peut-être le poëte a voulu marquer qu'il vaut mieux aller plus rondement, sans tant de finesse.

Vers 114 et 115. Il fait un mensonge, et le poëte a fait que ce mensonge ne réussit pas.

Vers 183-186. Il (*Ulysse*) jette son manteau, et Eurybate le ramasse. — Il prend le sceptre d'Agamemnon pour parler avec plus d'autorité.

Vers 190. (Δαιμόνι', οὔ σε ἔοικε κακὸν ὣς δειδίσσεσθαι.) Comme il parle aux honnêtes gens.

Vers 200. (Δαιμόνι', ἀτρέμας ἧσο, καὶ ἄλλων μῦθον ἄκουε.) Comme il parle à la populace.

Vers 212-215. Thersite. Médisant et grand parleur, toujours envieux des honnêtes gens, et cherchant à faire rire le peuple.

Vers 239. Il loue maintenant Achille pour blâmer Agamemnon.

LIVRE III.

Vers 8-14. Les Grecs marchent en silence, comme un brouillard épais.

Vers 16-20. Description du beau Paris.

Vers 39-57. Discours merveilleux d'Hector à Paris. N^a (*Nota*).

Vers 59-75. Réponse honnête de Paris.

Vers 75. Paris a raison d'appeler la Grèce καλλιγύναικα.

Vers 105 et 106. Ménélas veut que Priam vienne. Car les jeunes gens sont sans foi, et gâtent tout.

Vers 121. Iris va faire venir Hélène aux blanches épaules.

Vers 125-127. Hélène brodoit dans un voile les combats des Grecs et des Troyens.

(*En tête de la page* 58, *où se trouve le vers* 153.) Homère a trouvé moyen de mettre Priam et les vieillards sur le rempart, afin que par les questions qu'ils font à Hélène, le lecteur apprenne agréablement qui sont les principaux des Grecs.

(*Au bas de la même page, avec renvoi au mot* ἦκα, *dans le vers* 155 : Ἦκα πρὸς ἀλλήλους ἔπεα πτερόεντ' ἀγόρευον.) N^a. *Tout bas à l'oreille*, et parce qu'ils étoient honteux d'être touchés à leur âge de la beauté d'Hélène, et pour rendre la louange qu'ils lui donnent moins suspecte, n'étant point donnée en face. *Eustath*[1]. — Grande louange de la beauté d'Hélène par les vieillards troyens.

(*En tête de la page* 59, *commençant au vers* 160.) Eustath. dit qu'Homère fait Hélène respectueuse et craintive (*voyez le vers* 172), et parce qu'elle se sent coupable, et parce qu'elle sait qu'elle est haïe. C'est cette pudeur et cette crainte qui la sauve de la haine des Troyens.

Vers 162-164. Priam la fait asseoir auprès de lui. — Ce n'est point vous qui êtes la cause de mes malheurs.

Vers 172-175. Hélène se confesse coupable de tout. — Elle ne nomme point son mari devant Priam, comme étant amoureuse de Paris, son fils. *Eust.*

Vers 182. (Ὦ μάκαρ Ἀτρείδη....) Exclamation qui sied bien à un roi comme Priam. *Ipse hostis Teucros*, etc.[2] — Eustath. loue la structure de ce vers (*du vers* 182), qui commence par un monosyllabe, suivi d'un disyllabe, et ensuite d'un trisyllabe, et qui finit par un mot de cinq syllabes. — Eustath. dit que les gens qui souffrent un long siége louent volontiers la bravoure de leurs ennemis, comme pour s'excuser de ce qu'ils ne leur ont pas fait lever le siége.

Vers 205 et suivants. Anténor éloquent loue l'éloquence d'Ulysse, comme Priam guerrier loue Agamemnon sur la guerre. *Eustath.* — Homère, dans cette description des Grecs, diversifie la figure : tantôt Priam parle, tantôt Anténor; Hélène interrogée, et Hélène sans attendre qu'on l'interroge. *Eust.*

---

1. Racine, comme on le verra dans ce qui suit, a fait de fréquents emprunts au commentaire d'Eustathe, dont ordinairement il abrège le nom de l'une de ces manières : *Eustath.*, *Eustat.*, ou *Eust.*

2. Virgile, *Énéide*, livre I, vers 625.

Vers 211. (Ἄμφω δ' ἑζομένω, γεραρώτερος ἦεν Ὀδυσσεύς.) Eustath. dit que la phrase de ce vers est un solécisme, qui fait une élégance, comme si la chose étoit dite sur-le-champ, le vers commençant d'une façon et finissant de l'autre.

Vers 214. (Παῦρα μὲν, ἀλλὰ μάλα λιγέως.) Caractère d'un Lacédémonien et d'un homme jeune.

Vers 222. Abondance de discours comparée à la neige qui tombe.

Vers 262. Homère fait accompagner Priam par Anténor, Agamemnon par Ulysse. Cependant ces deux orateurs ne disent mot. Homère est le premier qui a introduit des personnages muets. *Eustath.*

Vers 276. Serment ou prière d'Agamemnon. Eustath. remarque qu'il n'y a pas dans Homère une seule prière juste qui ne soit exaucée.

Vers 305-307. Priam s'en retourne pour ne point voir combattre son fils.

Vers 324. Hector tire au sort à qui des deux lancera son dard le premier.

Vers 365. (Ζεῦ πάτερ, οὔτις σεῖο Θεῶν ὀλοώτερος ἄλλος.) Les malheureux sont toujours prêts à s'emporter contre les Dieux. *Eustat.*

Vers 394. Vous diriez qu'Alexandre revient du bal.

Vers 399 et suivants. Hélène refuse d'aller retrouver Paris. Demeurez vous-même avec lui, et renoncez au ciel[1]. — Cette résistance d'Hélène la justifie un peu, et fait croire que Vénus est coupable de toutes ses fautes.

Vers 427. Hélène lui parle (*à Paris*) en détournant les yeux ailleurs, parce qu'elle le veut quereller, et qu'elle sent bien qu'elle sera amoureuse si elle le regarde.

Vers 428 et suivants. Vous voilà donc revenu de la guerre. — *N^a.* Beaucoup d'amour et peu d'opinion de sa valeur.

Vers 438 et suivants. Réponse de Paris. Il redouble d'amour pour réparer son peu de valeur. — L'amour de Paris se renflamme, parce qu'il s'y mêle de la jalousie, et qu'il craint qu'on ne rende Hélène à Ménélas victorieux. *Eust.*

LIVRE IV.

Vers 31-47. Jupiter reproche à Junon sa colère contre les Troyens. Vous les voudriez manger tout vifs. — Il aimoit Troie sur toutes les villes du monde.

---

1. Ce sont les paroles d'Hélène à Vénus.

Vers 141. Ivoire taché de pourpre.

Vers 234 et suivants. Discours vif d'Agam[emnon].

Vers 257-260. (*Autre discours d'Agamemnon*) à Idoménée. Vous êtes brave et à table et à la bataille.

Vers 274. Un nuage d'infanterie.

Vers 275 et suivants. Comp[araison] d'une grosse nuée.

Vers 293-302. Nestor. Il range ses troupes en batailles (*sic*).

Vers 303. Le poëte le fait parler tout d'un coup.

Vers 339 et suivants. Reproche d'Agamemnon à Ulysse. — Bataille ardente[1], καυστειρῆς. Vous êtes toujours les premiers que j'invite à souper. Et vous êtes ici les derniers.

Vers 370 et suivants. Reproche d'Agamem[non] à Diomède. Il lui étale les louanges de son père, pour le piquer d'émulation.

Vers 399 et 400. Voilà quel étoit Tydée; son fils est moins brave et plus beau parleur.

Vers 401. Diomède se tait, parce qu'il est jeune, et parce qu'on l'appelle parleur. — Diomède ne se défend point, parce qu'il se sent brave, et que ses actions ne parlent pas encore pour lui. Mais il le prend bien d'un plus haut ton au 9ᵉ livre[2], et fait ressouvenir Agamemnon du reproche qu'il lui avoit fait.

Vers 403-405. Sthenelus, fils de Capanée, plus impatient, répond à Agamemnon. — Nous valons beaucoup mieux que nos pères.

Vers 413-417. Diomède dit qu'Agamemnon a raison d'exhorter les Grecs. L'honneur et la honte le regarde.

Vers 429-436. Les Grecs vont au combat en silence, comme des troupes bien réglées et aguerries; les Troyens marchent avec de grands cris, comme un troupeau de brebis.

Vers 521. (Λᾶας ἀναιδής.) Pierre impudente.

Vers 523. Homme qui meurt en tendant les mains à ses amis.

Vers 539-544. Tous faisoient bien leur devoir. Un homme qui auroit pu être spectateur du combat, et que Minerve auroit mené partout, n'auroit rien trouvé à reprocher aux uns et aux autres.

LIVRE VI[3].

Vers 119. Homère introduit Glaucus avec Diomède, et prolonge

---

1. Au-dessus du mot *ardente*, Racine a écrit *cuisante*.
2. Vers 32 et suivants.
3. La plupart des notes du livre V sont de simples gloses, des explications de mots. Rien ne nous y a paru intéressant à recueillir.

ILIADE D'HOMÈRE.

leur entretien, pour donner à Hector le temps de rentrer dans la ville, et pour empêcher le lecteur de trouver mauvais qu'Hector laisse les Troyens dans un si grand besoin.

Vers 237 et suivants. (Ἕκτωρ δ' ὡς Σκαιάς τε πύλας καὶ φηγὸν ἵκανεν.) Homère jette cette entrée d'Hector dans la ville et tout ce qui passe[1] pour délasser son lecteur de tant de carnage et de tant de récits de guerre.

Vers 239-241. Les femmes demandent à Hector des nouvelles de leurs parents ou de leurs maris ; et lui, leur dit pour toute réponse de prier les Dieux.

Vers 266-268. Hector n'ose pas prier Jupiter avec ses mains sanglantes.

> *Me bello e tanto digressum et cæde recenti*
> *Attrectare nefas*[2].

Vers 281 et 282. Imprécation d'Hector contre Paris. — Hector est en colère contre Paris, qu'il ne voit pas. Mais quand il le voit, il lui parle sans aigreur : ce qui marque bien le caractère d'un brave homme, d'épargner ceux qui sont au-dessous de lui.

Vers 296. *Interea ad templum non æquæ Palladis ibant*
Crinibus Iliades passis, peplumque ferebant[3].

Vers 305-310. Vœu des femmes. Il est fort beau.

Vers 307. (Πρηνέα δὸς πεσέειν.) Πρηνέα, couché sur le ventre, c'est-à-dire en fuyant, afin qu'il n'ait pas même l'honneur de mourir en combattant.

Vers 321. Il (*Hector*) trouve Paris qui nettoie ses armes.

Vers 326-331. Hector lui parle doucement. Il feint même d'attribuer sa retraite à sa mauvaise humeur contre les Troyens.

Vers 337. Paris a soin de justifier Hélène devant Hector.

Vers 341. (Ἦ ἴθ', ἐγὼ δὲ μέτειμι.) Cela sent bien son homme qui demeure le plus qu'il peut près de sa maîtresse.

Vers 344-353. Hélène se condamne la première, et condamne aussi Paris, pour montrer que ce n'est pas elle qui le retient. — On remarque la différence qu'il y a entre l'amour de Paris et d'Hélène, et l'amour d'Hector et d'Andromaque. Paris est ici auprès d'Hélène, qui est contrainte de lui prêcher son devoir : au lieu qu'Andromaque fait ce qu'elle peut pour arrêter Hector et pour l'empêcher de se perdre. *Eustath.*

---

1. Voyez ci-dessus, p. 57, note 1.
2. Virgile, *Énéide*, livre II, vers 718 et 719.
3. *Ibidem*, livre I, vers 479 et 480

Vers 352. En condamnant Paris, elle ne laisse pas d'en paroître amoureuse.

Vers 357 et 358. On parlera de nous éternellement.

Vers 363. Hector dit à Hélène de porter Paris à faire son devoir.

Vers 367. Hector dit qu'il ne sait s'il reverra plus sa femme.

Vers 371. Hector ne trouve point Andromaque au logis. Cela se fait pour réveiller l'attention du spectateur, qui se fâche qu'Hector trouve Hélène qu'il ne cherche pas, et ne trouve point Andromaque. *Eust.* — Leur conversation même devient plus tragique et plus noble; elle se passe à la porte de la ville, par où Hector va sortir pour n'y plus rentrer. — V. (*voyez*) Plutarque dans la *Vie de Brutus*. Porcie et Brutus.

Vers 389. (Μαινομένῃ εἰκυῖα.) Cela fait plaisir à Hector, à qui on apprend l'amour d'Andromaque.

Vers 390-394. Hector ne cherche plus sa femme; mais elle court à sa rencontre [1].

Vers 398. (Τοῦπερ δὴ θυγάτηρ ἔχεθ' Ἕκτορι χαλκοκορυστῇ.) Elle étoit possédée par Hector, à la différence d'Hélène, dont Paris dépend. *Eust.* (*Les vers* 400-402 *sont réunis par une accolade, et Racine a écrit à la marge N^a.*)

Vers 402 et 403. Hector modeste avoit nommé simplement son fils du nom du fleuve Scamandre; mais les Troyens l'appelèrent Astyanax, parce que son père défendoit leur ville.

Vers 404 et 405. (Ἤτοι ὁ μὲν μείδησεν, etc.) Image admirable. Silence et sourire d'Hector. Larmes d'Andromaque.

Vers 407. (Δαιμόνιε, φθίσει σε τὸ σὸν μένος.) Ce δαιμόνιε est fort tendre. — Entretien divin d'Hector et d'Andromaque.

Vers 410. (Πάντες ἐφορμηθέντες.) Tous les Grecs ensemble; car elle croit qu'il ne faut pas moins que cela pour venir à bout de son mari.

Vers 414. Elle lui ramène devant les yeux les malheurs de sa maison, pour le toucher davantage. — Homère a soin de parler d'Achille partout.

Vers 425. (Μητέρα δ', ἣ βασίλευεν.) Reine, et non point une concubine.

Vers 431-439. Andromaque veut lui donner un conseil. Cela convient bien à une femme inquiète, et qui a l'esprit tout plein de la guerre à cause du péril de son mari.

Vers 441. Le discours d'Hector est grave et passionné.

Vers 446. Hector a soin de louer son père.

---

1. Au-dessous de cette note, Racine a écrit en caractères plus gros : ANDROMAQUE, et de même, un peu plus bas : ASTYANAX.

Vers 447-449. Hector prévoit que Troie sera prise quelque jour. Cela excite plus de compassion que s'il étoit sûr de la victoire. Néanmoins, comme ce malheur lui paroit encore fort éloigné, cela ne décourage point le lecteur.

Vers 450 et suivants. Il rend la pareille à Andromaque, et comme elle n'aime que lui, il ne craint pour personne tant que pour elle.

Vers 466-470. (Ὣς εἰπὼν οὗ παιδὸς ὀρέξατο.) Tableau divin. — (*En tête de la page* 138.) Adieu d'Hector et d'Andromaque. — (*Au bas de cette même page*.) Artifice admirable d'Homère d'avoir mêlé le rire, les larmes, la gravité, la tendresse, le courage, la crainte, et tout ce qui peut toucher.

Vers 476-481. Prière d'Hector sur son fils.

Vers 496. (Ἐντροπαλιζομένη.) Regardant encore derrière elle, pour voir Hector. — Quand elle est chez elle, elle s'abandonne aux larmes.

Vers 500. (Αἱ μὲν ἔτι ζωὸν γόον.) Elles pleuroient Hector vivant.

Vers 506 et 507. Cheval qui a rompu son lien, et qui échappe de l'écurie.

Vers 521-523. Paroles honnêtes d'Hector à Paris. Vous êtes brave, mais vous êtes négligent. — Homère a soin de ne point rendre Paris trop odieux, et il en fait un homme qui est vaillant, mais trop abandonné aux plaisirs.

Vers 528. *N^a*. Κρητὴρ ἐλεύθερος[1].

LIVRE VII.

Vers 4-7. Hector et Paris paroissent aux Troyens comme un vent favorable à des matelots lassés de ramer.

Vers 62. Image des troupes, *quæ armis horrebant*.

Vers 63 et 64. Comp[araison] des flots que soulève doucement un Zéphir.

Vers 67 et suivants. Hector parle aux Grecs, et fait son défi.

Vers 87-90. Quelqu'un passant un jour le long du bord de l'Hellespont, dira : « Voilà le tombeau d'un brave qui fut tué par Hector. »

Vers 124 et suivants. Discours pathétique de Nestor.

Vers 125. O que Pélée gémira bien, lorsqu'il saura la honte des Grecs !

---

1. Racine était frappé de la beauté et de la hardiesse de cette expression : *le cratère libre*, c'est-à-dire le cratère qui servira aux libations que nous ferons aux Dieux pour célébrer notre indépendance sauvée.

Vers 136 et suivants. Nestor raconte un combat qu'il a fait en sa jeunesse.

Vers 381. (Ἠῶθεν δ' Ἰδαῖος ἔβη.) Voici le quatorzième jour de l'*Iliade*. Car il ne s'est passé qu'un jour depuis le réveil d'Agamemnon, qui est au commencement du second livre, jusqu'au combat d'Hector et d'Ajax, qui sont séparés par la nuit.

Vers 433. (Ἦμος δ' οὔτ' ἄρ πω ἠώς.) Voici la quinzième journée.

Vers 465. (Δύσσετο δ' ἠέλιος.) Nuit du 15ᵉ jour.

LIVRE VIII.

Vers 1. (Ἠὼς μὲν κροκόπεπλος.) La 16ᵉ journée. — Κροκόπεπλος, lorsqu'elle tient encore de la nuit; ῥοδοδάκτυλος, quand le jour se fait plus grand.

Vers 16. Il croyoit la terre le centre du monde, et le ciel et l'enfer aux extrémités.

Vers 19. (Σειρὴν χρυσείην ἐξ οὐρανόθεν.) Cette chaîne d'or est prise allégoriquement, ou pour l'assemblage des éléments liés ensemble, ou pour le soleil, dont tout descend et où tout revient, ou pour la suite et l'enchaînement des planètes, depuis Saturne jusqu'à la Lune, [suivant] d'autres pour les exhalaisons de la mer et de la terre. D'autres enfin l'entendent de la monarchie.

Vers 60-65. Eustath. remarque que ces six vers sont déjà dans le 4ᵉ chant[1], mais qu'Homère ne craint point de redire la même chose, quand il ne la sauroit plus mieux dire.

Vers 77-81. La frayeur saisit les Grecs. Nestor seul demeure à cause que son cheval est blessé.

Vers 80. (Νέστωρ δ' οἶος ἔμιμνε.) On remarque qu'il s'est servi de l'imparfait, pour exprimer la foiblesse du vieux Nestor.

Vers 82. (Δῖος Ἀλέξανδρος, Ἑλένης πόσις.) Hélène semble être nommée là inutilement, mais Eustath. dit qu'Homère aime à se souvenir d'elle.

Vers 130. (Ἔνθα κε λοιγὸς ἔην....) Car la prudence étoit jointe avec la valeur, Nestor avec Diomède.

Vers 485. (Ἐν δ' ἔπεσ' Ὠκεανῷ λαμπρὸν φάος.) Nuit du 17ᵉ jour.

Vers 551-555. Nuit claire et sereine.

---

1. Vers 446-451.

LIVRE IX[1].

(*En tête de la page* 180, *où commence le* IX⁰ *chant.*) Tout ce chant, qui contient la négociation d'Ulysse dans la tente d'Achille, et le dixième, qui contient la mort de Dolon et de Rhésus, se passe en une nuit, qui est la nuit du 16⁰ jour de l'*Iliade*.

Vers 32. Diomède parle ici plus fièrement à Agamemnon qu'au 4⁰ chant[2], car il a fait de grandes actions qui lui élèvent le cœur.

LIVRE X.

Vers 8. ('Ἡέ ποθι πτολέμοιο μέγα στόμα....) Cicéron, *pro Archia*[3] : *Urbem ex totius belli ore et faucibus ereptam.* — *In ore gladii*[4].

LIVRE XI.

Vers 1. ('Ἠὼς δ' ἐκ λεχέων....) Le 17⁰ jour.
Vers 385-395. Raillerie généreuse de Diomède. — Κέρα ἀγλαὲ, ou à cause que les arcs étoient faits de corne, ou à cause qu'il avoit de beaux cheveux; κέρας signifie souvent le crin des animaux, et quelquefois la chevelure d'un homme.

LIVRE XII.

Vers 278 et 279. Neige. — V. (*voyez*) Eustath., p. 903.
Vers 279. (Ἤματι χειμερίῳ.) Jour d'hiver, parce que c'est là où

---

1. Ce chant IX et ceux des chants suivants où nous n'avons eu presque aucune note de Racine à recueillir, n'ont guère que de courtes gloses, soit en français, soit en latin. Un assez grand nombre de passages y ont été soulignés.
2. Voyez ci-dessus, p. 200, remarque sur le vers 401 du livre IV.
3. Chapitre ix.
4. Racine ne dit point d'où il a tiré cette dernière expression. C'est de l'Écriture sainte où elle est extrêmement fréquente, et se trouve ordinairement jointe au verbe *percutere* ou *cadere*. Voyez, entre autres passages des livres saints, *Josué*, chapitre x, versets 28, 30, 32 et 35, et *Saint Luc*, chapitre xxi, verset 24.

sont les grandes neiges. — C'est Jupiter lui-même, ce n'est point une neige passagère et de hasard.

Vers 281. (Κοιμήσας δ' ἀνέμους....) Les vents dorment; car les vents dispersent la neige.

Vers 283. (Καὶ πεδία λωτεῦντα καὶ ἀνδρῶν πίονα ἔργα.) C'est-à-dire les terres en friche et les terres labourées.

Vers 286. (Ὅτ' ἐπιβρίσῃ Διὸς ὄμβρος.) Quoique la neige soit légère, ce mot (ἐπιβρίσῃ) marque qu'elle tombe épaisse, et qu'elle pèse en quelque façon.

LIVRE XV.

Vers 53-77. Voyez dans Eustath. la critique de cette prédiction. Les uns la tiennent d'Homère, les autres non. Ils disent que cela ressemble à un prologue d'Euripide.

Vers 77. (Ἀχιλλῆα πτολίπορθον.) Ils disent que cet épithète [1] n'est donné à Achille qu'en ce seul endroit.

LIVRE XVI.

Vers 97. (Αἲ γάρ, Ζεῦ τε πάτερ....) Souhait digne de la colère d'Achille.

LIVRE XVII.

Vers 670. (Νῦν τις ἐνηείης Πατροκλῆος δειλοῖο Μνησάσθω.) Souvenir d'un mort.

Vers 694-696. Douleur d'Antilochus.

LIVRE XVIII.

Vers 176 et 177. Il excuse par avance la fureur d'Achille contre Hector.

Vers 203-206. Appareil terrible dont il accompagne Achille.

Vers 207-213. Compar[aison]. — *Per diem in columna nubis, et per noctem in columna ignis.* Exod. [2].

---

1. Racine fait *épithète* du masculin. Voyez le *Lexique*.
2. *Exode*, chapitre XIII, verset 21.

Vers 241. ('Ήέλιος μὲν ἔδυ....) Nuit du 17ᵉ jour. — La 17ᵉ journée contient sept chants et la moitié d'un ; c'est-à-dire depuis le commencement du onzième livre jusqu'au milieu du dix-huitième.

Vers 593. (Παρθένοι ἀλφεσίβοιαι.) Ἀλφεσίβοιαι, c'est-à-dire qui trouvent facilement à se marier, parce qu'anciennement la richesse consistoit en troupeaux, et les présents de noces étoient des bœufs, etc.

LIVRE XIX.

Vers 1. ('Ήὼς μὲν κροκόπεπλος....) La 18ᵉ journée.
Vers 14-18. Ardeur d'Achille en voyant les armes de Vulcain. Les autres en tremblent et n'osent les regarder.
Vers 45. Tout le monde court à l'assemblée, parce qu'Achille y va.
Vers 59. Achille voudroit que Briséis fût morte, plutôt que d'avoir causé cette querelle.
Vers 79. ('Εσταότος μὲν καλὸν ἀκουέμεν....) Agamemnon parle assis, ou parce qu'il a honte des paroles trop humbles qu'il va tenir à Achille, ou à cause de la fable qu'il va raconter, et qu'on ne doit point conter debout, ou à cause qu'il est blessé. — On dit qu'il faut ἐσταότως, c'est-à-dire tranquillement, sans tumulte, parce que les partisans d'Achille, ou même la plupart des Grecs, font trop de bruit et empêchent Agamemnon de parler.
Vers 85. Il ne veut pas redire ce que lui disoient les Grecs pour ne se pas donner trop de tort.
Vers 87. Agamemnon rejette tout sur les Dieux.
Vers 149. Achille veut combattre sans rien attendre.
Vers 155 et 156. Ulysse ne veut pas que les Grecs combattent à jeun.
Vers 182 et 183. Il est juste qu'un roi apaise celui qu'il a offensé le premier.
Vers 212. (Κεῖται ἀνὰ πρόθυρον τετραμμένος.) Mort tourné vers la porte.
Vers 216-233. Ulysse à Achille : Vous êtes plus brave que moi, mais j'ai plus d'expérience que vous. Il ne faut point pleurer à jeun. Il faut enterrer le mort, le pleurer un jour, et du reste se mettre en état de combattre. — Les gens de guerre ne doivent point trop s'attendrir pour les morts.
Vers 362. Lueur des armes. Γέλασσε δὲ πᾶσα περιχθών[1].
Vers 375. Feu qu'on découvre de dessus la mer.

---

[1]. Racine a transcrit ainsi cette fin du vers 362, où il avait remarqué la beauté de l'image.

208 LIVRES ANNOTÉS.

Vers 384. Achille s'éprouve dans ses armes.
Vers 396. Achille monte dans son char.

LIVRE XX.

Vers 25-27. On a remarqué que si les Troyens ne sont pas assez forts tout seuls pour soutenir Achille, ils ne le seront pas davantage avec le secours des Dieux; puisque les Dieux des Grecs l'emportent de beaucoup sur ceux des Troyens. Et ainsi les choses demeurent dans l'état ou elles étoient.

Vers 32-40. Dieux contre les Dieux. — Tout l'univers est ébranlé et s'intéresse, maintenant qu'Achille revient au combat.

Vers 76. Achille ne cherche qu'Hector.

Vers 158-173. Eustathius dit qu'Achille auroit pu commencer par quelque chose de plus terrible que par un combat où il n'y a que des paroles, et où il n'y a point de sang répandu; mais qu'Homère aime à surprendre le lecteur, et qu'il fait les plus grandes choses lorsqu'on s'y attend le moins. Mais il me semble qu'Achille cherchant principalement Hector, comme Homère le vient de dire, il dédaigne de s'échauffer contre d'autres que lui. Et il faut qu'il s'irrite peu à peu. De là vient la comparaison du lion.

Vers 178. Achille ne daigne pas presque frapper Énée : ce n'est pas là l'ennemi qu'il cherche. Il veut même le faire retirer. Ainsi il l'interroge et lui laisse tout le temps de parler.

Vers 206-209. *On dit* que vous êtes fils de Thétis, et moi *je suis* le fils de Vénus.

Vers 215. On dit que Dardanus, dans le déluge de Deucalion, s'étoit sauvé dans une peau de bouc, et étoit abordé au pied du mont Ida.

Vers 242. (Ζεὺς δ' ἀρετὴν ἄνδρεσσιν ὀφέλλει τε μινύθει τε.) C'est pour s'excuser de ce qu'il a fui auparavant.

Vers 307 et 308. Prédiction des successeurs d'Énée.

Et nati natorum et qui nascentur ab illis[1].

— Eustathius dit qu'Homère avoit pu lire cette prédiction dans les livres de la Sibylle, ou qu'il l'a faite[2] de son chef, comme poëte.

Vers 367. Je combattrois de paroles contre les Dieux.

---

1. Virgile, *Énéide*, livre III, vers 98.
2. Racine a écrit *fait*.

Vers 371. (Τοῦ δ' ἐγὼ ἀντίος εἶμι....) Cela sent un homme qui tâche à s'encourager lui-même.

Vers 403 et 404. Quand le taureau se taisoit, c'étoit signe que Neptune étoit irrité; quand la victime mugissoit, c'étoit signe qu'il acceptoit le sacrifice.

Vers 407. (Ἀντίθεον Πολύδωρον.) Euripide et Virgile mettent ce Polydore dans la Thrace, et le font survivre à Priam. — Homère se plaît à exciter la compassion pour les enfants de Priam, ici pour Polydore, et dans le chant suivant pour Lycaon.

Vers 498-502. Char d'Achille tout sanglant.

LIVRE XXI.

Vers 68 et suivants. Lycaon aux pieds d'Achille.

Vers 99. Réponse d'Achille.

Vers 106 et 107. Meurs; mon ami Patrocle est bien mort, qui valoit mieux que toi.

Vers 151. (Δυστήνων δέ τε παῖδες ἐμῷ μένει ἀντιόωσι.) Les enfants des malheureux s'offrent à mon épée.

Vers 195-197. Océan, d'où toutes les eaux prennent leurs sources.

Vers 464-466. Hommes sont comme des feuilles.

Vers 489-492. Junon frotte Diane.

Vers 498 et 499. Mercure ne veut point avoir de querelle avec les maitresses de Jupiter.

Vers 505-508. Vénus ne vient point en pleurant quand elle a été blessée; mais Diane, qui est une fille, pleure. — Diane s'enfuit dans les genoux de Jupiter. — Homère représente en Diane l'ingénuité d'une honnête fille.

LIVRE XXII.

Vers 38. Discours de Priam à Hector. — Priam a tout le temps de dire à Hector tout ce qu'il lui dit; car Achille est encore loin.

Vers 98. Hector consulte en lui-même.

Vers 111-125. Il doute s'il traitera d'accord avec Achille.

Vers 126 et 127. Il n'est pas temps de raisonner avec lui, comme un jeune homme avec une jeune fille.

Vers 148. Deux sources du Scamandre.
Vers 154 et 155. (.... Ὅθι εἵματα σιγαλόεντα Πλύνεσκον.) Là où les Troyennes venoient laver leurs[1] robes.
Vers 256-259. Hector veut composer avec Achille pour le corps de celui qui sera tué.
Vers 261-269. Achille n'entend à aucune composition. — Souviens-toi maintenant d'être brave.

LIVRE XXIII.

Vers 58. (Οἱ μὲν κακκείοντες ἔβαν.) Nuit du 18e jour.
Vers 109. (Φάνη ῥοδοδάκτυλος Ἠώς.) La dix-neuvième journée[2].
Vers 226. (Ἦμος δ' Ἑωσφόρος εἶσι.) 20e journée.
Vers 820-822. Il paroit bien qu'Homère n'a point supposé qu'Ajax ne pût être blessé que par le côté, puisque les Grecs ont peur que Diomède ne le blesse au cou.

LIVRE XXIV.

Vers 1-3. Nuit du 20e jour.
Vers 12. (Οὐδέ μιν Ἠώς....) Le 21e jour.
Vers 31. (Ἀλλ' ὅτε δή ῥ' ἐκ τοῖο δυωδεκάτη γένετ' Ἠώς.) Il se passe ici onze jours sans action. — Le 32e jour.
Vers 160-165. État déplorable de Priam.
Vers 163. (Ἐντυπὰς ἐν χλαίνῃ κεκαλυμμένος....) Enveloppé de telle sorte qu'on voyoit toute la figure de son corps. Ses habits étoient attachés à son corps, parce qu'il avoit passé plusieurs nuits sans se coucher.
Vers 198 et 199. Priam veut aller.
Vers 201 et suivants. Discours d'Hécube. Elle est timide comme sont les femmes. Fureur de mère.
Vers 218-227. Priam inébranlable. Quand je devrois mourir, je mourrai en embrassant mon fils, et le pleurant tout mon saoul.
Vers 237-240. Priam chasse les Troyens d'autour de lui. N'avez-vous pas à pleurer chez vous, vous qui me venez consoler?

---

1. Dans le manuscrit : *leur*, sans accord. Voyez tome V, p. 538, note 2.
2. Racine avait d'abord écrit « la vingtième. » Les chiffres de la plupart des journées précédentes et ceux des journées suivantes ont également des surcharges.

Vers 253 et 254. Il querelle ses enfants. Plût aux Dieux que vous fussiez tous morts au lieu d'Hector!

Vers 284-286. Hécube lui présente du vin au devant du chariot.

Vers 363. (Νύκτα δι' ἀμβροσίην....) Ceci se passe durant la nuit du 32ᵉ jour.

Vers 385. Mercure prend occasion de lui parler de son fils.

Vers 408. Priam ne songe d'abord qu'à son fils.

Vers 448-456. Tente d'Achille.

Vers 462-464. Mercure s'en va. Les Dieux ne se communiquent pas si aisément aux hommes.

Vers 475 et 476. Achille venoit de souper. Il étoit encore à table.

Vers 478 et 479. Priam baise les mains d'Achille.

Vers 510-512. Priam et Achille pleurent.

Vers 515. Achille relève Priam.

Vers 629-632. Priam et Achille s'admirent l'un l'autre.

Vers 643-646. Achille fait préparer un lit pour Priam.

Vers 695. ('Ἠὼς δὲ κροκόπεπλος....) Le 33ᵉ jour.

Vers 700. Cassandre aperçoit Priam.

Vers 707-709. Troie sort au-devant d'Hector.

Vers 725. (Ἄνερ, ἀπ' αἰῶνος νέος ὤλεο....) Paroles divines d'Andromaque sur le corps d'Hector. Tout cela marque la jeunesse de l'un et de l'autre. La séparation en est plus douloureuse. — Ἀνὴρ est un mari qu'on aime et dont on est aimée, et c'est un nom amoureux. Πόσις, au contraire, est un nom froid; et c'est un mari quand même il seroit séparé de sa femme. Sophocle fait dire à Déjanire jalouse[1] :

.... Φοβοῦμαι μὴ πόσις μὲν Ἡρακλῆς
Ἐμὸς καλῆται, τῆς νεωτέρας δ' ἀνήρ.

Vers 785. (Ἀλλ' ὅτε δὴ δεκάτη ἐφάνη φαεσίμβροτος Ἠώς....) Il se passe encore onze jours aux funérailles d'Hector. — Ainsi toute l'action de l'*Iliade* se passe en quarante-quatre jours, dont il y en a trente-quatre dont le détail n'est point raconté : savoir douze depuis la querelle d'Achille jusqu'à ce que Thétis monte dans le ciel; onze durant lesquels Achille outrage le corps d'Hector; et onze qui se passent aux funérailles d'Hector[2].

---

1. *Trachiniennes*, vers 550 et 551.
2. On voit que le calcul de Racine n'est pas ici tout à fait le même que dans la petite note citée ci-dessus, p. 195.

PINDARE.

Nous avons dit ci-dessus, p. 6, que Racine avait annoté les *Odes de Pindare* sur les marges d'un exemplaire de l'édition de Jean Benoît, et que ces annotations sont vraisemblablement de date postérieure à ses *Remarques sur les Olympiques*, pour lesquelles il ne paraît pas avoir eu le secours de cette utile édition.

Voici le titre du volume dont nous allons mettre quelques notes sous les yeux du lecteur : ΠΙΝΔΑΡΟΥ ΠΕΡΙΟΔΟΣ. *Pindari Olympia, Pythia, Nemea, Isthmia. Johannes Benedictus.... totum authorem innumeris mendis repurgavit, etc. Salmurii, ex typis Petri Piededii, anno M.DC.XX* (in-4°). Au-dessus du mot *Salmurii*, Racine a signé son nom.

Les notes marginales de cet exemplaire, qui appartient à la Bibliothèque impériale, ne sont ni très-nombreuses ni très-remarquables. Nous en omettrons plusieurs, qui sont entièrement insignifiantes, et étaient seulement destinées à faire retrouver à Racine les passages qui fixaient son attention.

OLYMPIQUE I.

Vers 1-4. L'eau à cause d'Empédocle ; l'or à cause que Pindare l'aimoit.

Vers 21-26. Roi qui aime la poésie.

Vers 48-52. Grâce de la poésie.

Vers 53 et 54. Postérité sage témoin.

Vers 55-57. L'homme doit parler bien des Dieux.

Vers 58-68. Il (*Pindare*) conte la véritable histoire de Pélops.

Vers 76. Voisins envieux.

Vers 84 et 85. Le médisant est souvent puni [1].

Vers 85. Si les Dieux ont honoré quelqu'un, c'étoit Tantale.

Vers 88. (Μέγαν ὄλβον.) Insolence dans la prospérité.

Vers 159-162. Il n'y a point de plus grand bien que celui dont on jouit tous les jours.

Vers 181 et 182. (Τὸ δ'ἔσχατον κορυφοῦται βασιλεῦσι.) Excellence de la royauté.

---

1. Au dessus de ces mots, Racine a écrit ἀκέρδεια.

PINDARE.

OLYMPIQUE II.

Vers 1. Hymnes maîtresses des instruments.
Vers 19-21. Bonheur qui suit la vertu.
Vers 29-33. Ce qui a été fait bien ou mal ne peut point n'avoir point été fait.
Vers 41-43. La douleur est effacée par de plus grands biens.
Vers 56 et 57. Heure de la mort incertaine.
Vers 59. Jour enfant du soleil.
Vers 61-64. Joie et tristesse attachée à la vie.
Vers 93 et 94. Victoire après le combat.
Vers 96 et 97. Richesses jointes avec la vertu.
Vers 106-108. Châtiments de l'autre vie.
Vers 109 et suivants. Champs Élysiens. — Vie douce.
Vers 113-115. Ils (*les Bienheureux*) ne tourmentent ni la terre ni la mer à force de bras.
Vers 128. Iles des Bienheureux.
Vers 141. [*Saturne*] qui a son trône plus haut qu'aucun des Dieux.
Vers 149-154. Sa poésie (*la poésie de Pindare*) est pour les honnêtes gens, mais elle a besoin d'interprète pour le vulgaire.
Vers 154-157. Le génie l'emporte sur l'art.

OLYMPIQUE III.

Vers 9. (Δωρίῳ φωνὰν ἐναρμόξαι πεδίλῳ.) Cothurne[1].
Vers 13 et 14. Harmonie. La lyre à plusieurs sons, la flûte et la cadence des vers.
Vers 24. (Κόσμον ἐλαίας.) C'étoit une branche d'olivier sauvage.
Vers 35 et 36. (Διχόμηνις.... Μῆνα.) Pleine lune.
Vers 40. Plaine sans arbres.
Vers 56. Régions hyperborées.
Vers 77-79. Perfection. On ne passe point les colonnes d'Hercule.

---

1. Benoît traduit πεδίλῳ par *cothurno*.

OLYMPIQUE IV.

(*En tête de l'argument de cette ode qui est adressée à Psaumis de Camarine.*) Ce Psaumis étoit déjà un peu avancé en âge. Voilà pourquoi il lui rapporte l'histoire qui est à la fin.

Vers 3. C'est-à-dire les quatre années sont échues où les jeux se doivent célébrer.

Vers 7-9. Les honnêtes gens se réjouissent aux nouvelles des prospérités de leurs amis.

Vers 26. Homme qui a des sentiments paisibles.

OLYMPIQUE V.

Vers 15 et 16. (Μοναμπυκία τε.) *Celeti*, à un seul coureur, qui n'a point d'autre harnois qu'une bride.

PYTHIQUE VI.

Vers 10 et 11. Pluie, armée de l'affreuse nue.

Vers 21-27. Leçon de Chiron au jeune Achille : *Honora Deum et parentes*[1].

Vers 24. Jupiter, maître des éclairs et des foudres.

Vers 38. Antilochus fameux dans la postérité pour avoir voulu mourir pour son père.

Vers 47 et 48. *Jeune homme sage.* Il use de ses richesses avec prudence, et ne passe point une jeunesse insolente et superbe.

Vers 50. Neptune qui a inventé l'art de conduire les chevaux.

Vers 52-54. La douceur de son esprit, et sa conversation à table passe le miel des abeilles.

PYTHIQUE VII.

Vers 19 et 20. Envie qui suit les belles actions.

---

1. Racine a également écrit en tête de la page 405, où se trouvent ces vers 21-27 : *Deum eole, parentes honora.*

PYTHIQUE VIII.

Vers 1. Paix. Apostrophe à la Paix.

Vers 103-111. Quand on voit un homme riche en peu de temps, plusieurs insensés le croient habile homme, et pensent qu'il a augmenté ses biens par sa bonne conduite. Mais cela ne dépend point de l'homme. La Fortune fait tout.

Vers 119-123. N^a. Honte des vaincus.

Vers 126-131. N^a. Joie et triomphe des vainqueurs.

Vers 131-134. La joie des mortels s'élève et tombe facilement.

Vers 135 et 136. ('Επάμεροι· τί δέ τις;...) Hommes d'un jour, c'est-à-dire qui ne durez qu'un jour. Qu'est-ce que quelqu'un? C'est à dire un homme de conséquence. Qu'est-ce que personne? C'est à dire un homme de rien. Les hommes ne sont que le songe d'une ombre, *i.* (*c'est-à-dire*) moins qu'une ombre.

Vers 136-139. Mais quand Dieu répand ses faveurs sur quelqu'un, il est dans l'éclat, et sa vie est douce.

NÉMÉENNE III.

(*En tête de l'argument de cette ode.*) Louanges de Pélée et d'Achille.

Vers 1-9. O Muse, on t'attend sur les bords d'Asopus.

Vers 11-13. L'hymne est la compagne la plus agréable de la victoire.

Vers 16-19. Commence une hymne digne de plaire à Jupiter; et moi, je la communiquerai aux lyres et aux discours des autres.

Vers 29. La victoire est un remède agréable pour les blessures.

Vers 32-34. Il (*Aristoclidas*) est beau, et fait de belles actions il n'y a point de bonheur qui aille au delà.

Vers 45-47. Mon esprit, dans quelle navigation étrangère t'engages-tu?

Vers 54 et 55. Ta matière est assez belle.

Vers 69-74. N^a. Vertu, génie naturel, opposé à l'art.

Vers 72-74. L'art veut goûter de tout, et n'a jamais le pied ferme.

Vers 75-78. Enfance d'Achille. Enfant, il jouoit en faisant de grandes choses.

Vers 79. (Βραχυσίδαρον.) Il veut dire un petit dard propre pour un enfant.

Vers 80-84. Enfance d'Achille. Il tuoit les lions et les sangliers, et les rapportoit tout palpitants à Chiron.

Vers 85-87. Diane et Pallas étoient épouvantées de le voir.

Vers 88-90. Il tuoit les cerfs sans chiens et sans filets, car il les devançoit à la course.

Vers 93-100. Chiron éleva encore dans son antre Jason et Esculape, et il maria Pélée à Thétis, et nourrit leur enfant.

Vers 95 et 96. Chirurgie.

Vers 97. Thétis qui avoit le dedans de la main beau, ἀγλαόκαρπος.

Vers 125-127. Jeune avec les jeunes, homme avec les hommes, vieillard avec les vieillards.

Vers 128 et 129. Vivre selon son âge.

Vers 134-137. Il compare son hymne à un breuvage de lait et de miel, mêlé de rosée.

Vers 138-144. Les aigles volent de loin à la proie; mais les geais paissent la terre. — Sublime. — Bas.

NÉMÉENNE IV.

(*En tête de la page* 528, *où commence cette ode.*) Louanges. Excellence de la poésie, quand elle part d'un beau génie[1].

Vers 1-3. La joie est un excellent médecin.

Vers 6-9. Un bain d'eau chaude délasse moins que la louange.

Vers 10-13. Les actions vivent moins que les discours, surtout quand le discours part d'un esprit profond, et que les Grâces s'en mêlent.

Vers 21-26. Si ton père étoit encore échauffé du soleil, il joueroit tes louanges sur sa lyre.

Vers 52. Il est juste qu'on souffre ce qu'on a fait souffrir.

Vers 64 et 65. Envieux rêve dans les ténèbres.

Vers 68. Il (Pindare) reconnoît qu'il doit aux Dieux son génie.

Vers 92. (Δάμαρτος Ἱππολύτας.) V. (*voyez*) l'ode suivante (*vers* 48-62), où il est parlé plus au long de l'accusation de cette Hippolyte.

Vers 98-104. Chiron sauva Pélée, et surmonta ensuite toutes les formes que prenoit Thétis, le feu et les ongles de lions.

Vers 112-115. (Γαδείρων τὸ πρὸς ζόφον....) Métaphore. On ne va point au delà de Gadès, et on revient en Europe. On ne passoit point alors au delà des colonnes d'Hercule, et lorsqu'on étoit arrivé jusque-là, on s'en revenoit en Europe.

1. Cette note se rapporte à la strophe 1, vers 1-13.

Vers 131 et 132. Ses vers sont une colonne plus blanche que le marbre de Paros.

Vers 133. (Ὁ χρυσὸς ἑψόμενος.) L'or dans le feu.

Vers 135-138. L'hymne égale un vainqueur aux rois.

Vers 143. (Κορινθίοις σελίνοις.) L'apy[1] étoit la couronne des jeux Isthmiques.

Vers 148. On chante mieux ce qu'on a vu.

Vers 153-156. Poëte ou orateur invincible. — Doux à ses amis, terrible à ses ennemis.

NEMÉENNE V.

Vers 30 et 31. La vérité n'est pas toujours bonne à dire.

Vers 48-56. Hippolyte, femme d'Acaste, voulut persuader Pélée de coucher avec elle; et étant refusée, elle l'accusa auprès de son mari de l'avoir voulu violer.

NÉMÉENNE VIII.

Vers 60-62. Vie dans l'innocence, et bonne renommée après sa mort[2].

---

1. Racine a ainsi francisé le nom latin *apium*, sorte de *persil* (en grec ἄπιον, mot synonyme de σέλινον ou ayant un sens très-voisin). Le vrai correspondant français d'*apium* est *ache*.

2. Celles des odes de Pindare qui sont ici omises n'ont pas été annotées par Racine. Il s'est contenté d'y souligner çà et là des passages. Dans les *Isthmiques*, quelques vers de l'ode II ont été marqués d'accolades au crayon rouge; les autres n'ont gardé aucune trace de l'étude que Racine en a pu faire.

ESCHYLE.

Un intérêt particulier s'attache aux notes de Racine sur les tragiques grecs, à quelque temps de sa vie qu'on les rapporte, soit à celui où, s'inspirant si souvent de ces grands modèles, il pratiquait leur art sur la scène française, soit à celui où sa jeunesse ne faisait encore que se préparer à cet art par de fortes études. La question de date n'est pas tout à fait indifférente; mais nous avons déjà dit que, pour la plupart des volumes annotés, elle ne nous paraît pas pouvoir être résolue avec certitude. Si l'on fait attention toutefois que les exemplaires des tragiques grecs qui ont à la marge des notes de Racine rédigées en français ne nous offrent pas dans ces notes les mêmes archaïsmes d'expressions et d'orthographe que les *Remarques* manuscrites qui sont du temps d'Uzès; que, par exemple, Racine y écrit toujours *trouver* et non *treuver*, *Ménélas* et non *Menelaüs*, ne regardera-t-on pas comme probable que ces annotations marginales sont des années où le poëte produisait ses premières œuvres théâtrales? Nous disons les premières, parce que l'écriture semble être encore celle de sa jeunesse.

Des poëtes tragiques de la Grèce, Eschyle est celui que Racine paraît avoir le moins étudié, peut-être celui qu'il goûtait le moins. S'il en était ainsi, on n'aurait pas le droit de s'en étonner. Longtemps le génie du vieux poëte, moins régulier, plus naïf et plus audacieux dans son inexpérience, que celui de ses successeurs, a dérouté, dans nos âges modernes, et plutôt étonné que satisfait les plus grands et les plus pénétrants esprits. Dans la seule pièce où Racine ait fait choix d'un sujet qu'Eschyle avait lui-même traité, il a mieux aimé suivre les traces d'Euripide, de Stace, et surtout celles de Rotrou, que celles du plus ancien de ses devanciers; et l'on n'est pas bien sûr que, dans sa *Thébaïde*, il ait emprunté à celui-ci une seule expression poétique. Il n'en est pas moins intéressant de constater que, dans le cercle très-étendu de ses études sur la poésie grecque, une lecture attentive d'Eschyle avait trouvé place. Racine, avec tout son siècle sans doute, pouvait le regarder comme un génie inculte, dont les productions marquaient l'enfance de l'art; mais il avait trop bien le sentiment de la grande poésie pour n'être pas au moins frappé de tant de traits sublimes, de grandes pensées et de magnifiques images. Quoiqu'il ne l'ait pas imité, Eschyle est donc un des poëtes dont il s'est nourri, et sans doute avec profit. Ne le rayons pas entièrement de la liste de ses maîtres.

Le Quérard (voyez ci-dessus, p. 171) cite deux *Eschyle* annotés par Racine, à savoir un exemplaire de l'édition de Stanley (1663), et un exemplaire de l'édition de 1552, imprimée à Paris. Nous avons vu l'un et l'autre, et nous allons rendre compte de l'annotation qu'on y trouve.

Nous serons très-bref sur l'édition de 1552. En voici le titre : Αἰσχύλου Προμηθεὺς δεσμώτης, Ἑπτὰ ἐπὶ Θήβας..., etc. *Parisiis, ex officina Adriani*

ESCHYLE

Turnebi.... M.D.LII. *Typis regiis* (in-8°). L'exemplaire annoté par Racine appartient aujourd'hui à Mgr le duc d'Aumale, qui a bien voulu nous en permettre l'examen. Les marges de deux tragédies seulement, celles de *Prométhée* et celles des *Sept chefs*, sont couvertes de notes de la main de notre poëte. Ces notes sont toutes explicatives, toutes en grec. De ces gloses, souvent assez développées, que Racine avait très-vraisemblablement empruntées pour la plupart aux anciennes scolies, nous n'avons rien à transcrire ici. Nous devons nous contenter d'y faire remarquer une preuve de plus de son application sérieuse à l'étude de la langue grecque. Placer la date d'un travail de ce genre à une époque très-voisine des leçons de Port-Royal nous paraît une conjecture très-probable.

C'est évidemment un peu plus tard que Racine a annoté l'*Eschyle* de Stanley, cette édition étant de 1663. A supposer même qu'il ait travaillé sur ce texte au moment où la publication en était toute récente, il venait d'entrer déjà dans la carrière du théâtre.

L'exemplaire de 1663 sur lequel on trouve des notes de Racine est à la Bibliothèque de Toulouse. C'est un in-folio de 886 pages, relié en veau, avec plats dorés. Il a pour titre : Αἰσχύλου τραγῳδίαι ἑπτά. *Æschyli Tragœdiæ septem, cum scholiis græcis omnibus, deperditorum dramatum fragmentis, versione et commentario Thomæ Stanleii. Londini....* MDCLXIII. Au-dessus du mot *Londini* est la signature de Racine. La tragédie des *Choéphores* a seule des annotations; elles ne vont pas plus loin que le vers 623, avec une interruption commençant au vers 149. M. Félix Ravaisson les a transcrites en 1841, et cette transcription a été insérée dans la *Nouvelle Revue encyclopédique*, livraison d'octobre 1846. M. Gail les avait précédemment publiées en 1819, avec quelques différences fort légères, dans le tome VI du journal *le Philologue*, p. 118-121. Une copie des mêmes annotations que M. Dulaurier a bien voulu nous communiquer est conforme à celle qu'avait donnée M. Ravaisson, dont le nom suffisait d'ailleurs pour garantir l'exactitude des notes qu'il avait recueillies. On trouve çà et là toutefois quelques mots que M. Ravaisson avait omis, peut-être à dessein, à cause de leur peu d'importance, et que nous devons à la transcription de M. Dulaurier, qui nous a communiqué également les notes, sur les deux autres tragiques grecs, écrites par Racine sur des volumes appartenant à la Bibliothèque de Toulouse.

NOTES SUR *LES CHOÉPHORES.*

Vers 1. (Ἑρμῆ χθόνιε....) Oreste commence et vient au tombeau de son père.

Vers 3. (.... Κατέρχομαι.) Se dit des bannis qui retournent dans leur pays.

Vers 6. (.... Πλόκαμον Ἰνάχῳ θρεπτήριον.) Les anciens avoient deux manières de se couper les cheveux; la première fois, ils les consacroient au fleuve de leur pays; enfin ils les coupoient sur le tombeau de leurs proches.

Vers 8. (.... Τίς ποθ' ἥδ' ὁμήγυρις...;) Chœur de femmes habillées de noir.

Vers 14. (.... Καὶ γὰρ Ἠλέκτραν δοκῶ.) Electra est à leur tête.

Vers 16. (.... Ὦ Ζεῦ, δός με τίσασθαι μόρον.) Oreste fait entendre pourquoi il vient. Il prie Jupiter de lui aider à venger son père.

Vers 18. (Πυλάδη, σταθῶμεν....) Pylade est avec Oreste.

Vers 20. (Ἰαλτὸς ἐκ δόμων ἔβην.) Le chœur est de femmes qui sont au service de Clytemnestre. Il dit qu'il a été envoyé par Clytemnestre au tombeau d'Agamemnon, avec des présents pour l'apaiser.

Vers 22. (Πρέπει παρηῒς φοίνισσα μυγμοῖς.) Joues déchirées.

Vers 24. (Δι' αἰῶνος δ' ἰυγμοῖσι βόσκεται κέαρ.) Mon cœur se nourrit de gémissements.

Vers 25 et 26. (Λινοφθόροι δ' ὑφασμάτων....) Cela veut dire qu'elles se déchiroient leurs robes.

Vers 30 et 31. (Τορὸς γὰρ φόβος ὀρθόθριξ, Δόμων ὀνειρόμαντις....) La crainte qui fait dresser les cheveux. Songe terrible.

Vers 33. (Μυχόθεν ἔλακε περὶ φόβῳ.) Un songe étoit venu troubler Clytemnestre, et les devins lui disoient que les mânes d'Agamemnon étoient en colère.

Vers 40-44. (Τοιάνδε χάριν ἄχαριν.... Δύσθεος γυνά.) Voilà pourquoi Clytemnestre les envoie à son tombeau. Δύσθεος γυνά, *cette femme impie*. Le chœur dit tout bas cette parole.

Vers 46. (Τί γὰρ λύτρον πεσόντος αἵματος πέδῳ;) Car quel prix peut valoir le sang qu'elle a versé ?

Vers 52-57. (Σέβας δ' ἄμαχον....) Au lieu du respect qui retenoit les peuples du temps d'Agamemnon, c'est maintenant la frayeur qui les retient.

Vers 57 et 58. (Τὸ δ' εὐτυχεῖν Τόδ' ἐν βροτοῖς θεός τε....) Être heureux, c'est être Dieu et quelque chose de plus parmi les hommes.

Vers 59-62. (Ῥοπὴ δ' ἐπισκοπεῖ δίκας....) Les crimes sont punis tôt ou tard.

Vers 64 et 65. (Δι' αἷμά τ' ἐκποθὲν ὑπὸ χθονός....) Le sang que la terre a bu est un vengeur qui ne s'écoule point.

Vers 66 et 67. (Διαλγὴς ἄτη διαφέρει....) Un crime remplit l'âme du coupable de maladies qui ne lui laissent pas de repos.

Vers 69. (Οἴγοντι δ' οὔ τι νυμφικῶν ἑδωλίων....) La fleur de la virginité ne se rend point.

Vers 73-81. (Ἐμοὶ δ' ἀνάγκαν γὰρ ἀμφίπτολιν....) Le chœur dit qu'il est contraint de louer les plus forts et de cacher son aversion, mais qu'il pleure dans son âme.

Vers 79. (Δακρύω δ' ὑφ' εἱμάτων.) Je pleure sous cape.

Vers 82. (Δμωαὶ γυναῖκες....) Cette scène est très-belle. — Electra demande au chœur ce qu'elle doit dire en répandant les libations que sa mère envoie à son père.

Vers 91 et 92. (Ἢ τοῦτο φάσκω τοὔπος....) Le prierai-je, selon la coutume, d'envoyer des biens à ma mère pour les maux qu'elle lui a faits?

Vers 93. (Δόσιν τε τῶν κακῶν ἐπαξίαν.) Il fait une surprise, au lieu de καλῶν.

Vers 94. ("Η σῖγ' ἀτίμως....) Ou plutôt jetterai-je ce vase par terre en détournant les yeux ailleurs, comme ceux qui jettent des ordures?

Vers 98 et 99. (Τῆς δ' ἔστε βουλῆς, ὦ φίλαι, μεταίτιαι· Κοινὸν γὰρ ἔχθος....) Conseillez-moi, car nous avons une haine commune.

Vers 122. (Ἑρμῆ χθόνιε, κηρύξας ἐμοί....) Prière d'Electra en faisant les libations sur le tombeau de son père.

Vers 125 et 126. (Καὶ Γαῖαν αὐτήν....) Terre qui produit, qui nourrit tout, et qui le reprend ensuite.

Vers 137 et 138. (Καὶ σὺ κλῦθί μου, πάτερ, Αὐτῇ τέ μοι δὸς....) Écoutez-moi, mon père, donnez-moi d'être plus chaste que ma mère, et d'avoir les mains plus saintes que les siennes.

Vers 144. (Τήνδε τὴν κακὴν ἀράν....) Imprécation en suite de la prière.

Vers 148 et 149. (Ὑμᾶς δὲ κωκυτοῖς....) Elle fait les effusions, et exhorte le chœur à les accompagner de gémissements.

Vers 323. (Πυρὸς ἡ μαλερὰ γνάθος.) *Sicut devorat stipulam lingua ignis.* - Isaïe, cap. 5 (verset 24).

SOPHOCLE.

On ne peut guère douter que Racine ait étudié Sophocle non-seulement plus qu'Eschyle, mais autant qu'Euripide, quoiqu'il ait fait beaucoup plus d'emprunts à celui-ci, et qu'il ait de préférence choisi plusieurs de ses tragédies, pour les transporter sur notre théâtre, vraisemblablement, comme on l'a dit, parce qu'il jugeait désespérante la perfection de Sophocle. Les exemplaires des œuvres de ce poëte annotés par Racine sont plus nombreux peut-être que nous n'avons pu le savoir. Nous en avons trois à citer.

C'est encore à la Bibliothèque de Toulouse qu'appartient l'un d'eux; il est de l'édition donnée en 1603 par Paul Estienne (*Sophoclis Tragœdiæ septem, una cum omnibus græcis scholiis.... Excudebat Paulus Stephanus, anno M.DC.III*, in-4°). Sur cet exemplaire, les notes sont très-rares et n'offriraient pas d'intérêt. Racine y a voulu particulièrement marquer de quelle manière les personnages se tenaient en scène. Par exemple, à la marge du vers 641 d'*Électre*, il a écrit, parlant de Clytemnestre : « Devant la porte, elle prie à voix basse. » A la fin du volume, près du titre d'une dissertation sur les mètres employés par Sophocle (Δημητρίου τοῦ Τρικλινίου περὶ μέτρων οἷς ἐχρήσατο Σοφοκλῆς), il a donné cette explication sur les mouvements du chœur : « Strophe, lorsque les danseurs alloient de la droite à la gauche, ce qui exprimoit le mouvement du ciel, qui se meut de l'orient à l'occident. — Antistrophe, lorsque les danseurs alloient de la gauche à la droite, ce qui marquoit le mouvement des planètes, qui vont du couchant au levant. — Épode. Les danseurs demeuroient immobiles, ce qui exprimoit l'immobilité de la terre. »

La Bibliothèque impériale possède deux autres exemplaires de Sophocle, qui viennent du don fait par Louis Racine, et sont mentionnés ainsi dans la *Copie exacte de l'état des livres remis par Monsieur Racine à la Bibliothèque du Roi*, copie dont nous avons déjà eu l'occasion de parler : *Sophocle grec, édition d'Alde*, in-8°, *avec ses notes* (les notes de Jean Racine) *sur trois tragédies. — Autre Sophocle, typis regiis*, in-4°, *avec ses notes sur l'Ajax et l'Électre.*

L'annotation que Racine a faite sur ces deux éditions mérite que nous nous y arrêtions plus que sur celle de l'édition de Paul Estienne.

L'édition in-8° d'Alde, dont il vient d'être question (*Sophoclis Tragœdiæ septem, cum commentariis*), est de l'année 1502, comme on le voit à la fin du volume où on lit : *Venetiis, in Aldi Romani Academia, mense Augusto M.D.II.* On a cru quelque temps que l'exemplaire donné par Louis Racine à la Bibliothèque du Roi était celui qui porte l'estampille de la *Bibliothèque A. A. Renouard*. Ses marges sont chargées de variantes et de gloses en grec et de quelques notes en latin; mais aucune de ces notes n'est de la main de Racine[1]. Un autre exemplaire, appartenant, comme celui-là, à la Bibliothèque impériale, était désigné dans l'ancien Catalogue de cette Bibliothèque comme ayant appartenu à M. Varine (*Domini Varini*). On y avait mal lu la signature *Racine*, qui est au bas du premier feuillet, du feuillet de titre. C'est bien de cet exemplaire-là que parle l'*État des livres donnés par M. Racine*. L'annotation marginale y est de cette belle écriture de Racine dont le caractère n'exclut que les dernières années de sa vie, et que nous retrouvons dans toutes ses annotations marginales des anciens classiques. Les trois pièces annotées qu'annonce l'*État des livres* y sont l'*Ajax*, l'*Électre* et l'*OEdipe roi*. Racine y souligne un grand nombre de vers, et traduit fréquemment, soit en latin, soit en français, des mots du texte. Mais nous n'avons dû relever que les notes qui sont plus significatives. Celles de l'*Ajax* sont les moins nombreuses et les moins développées. Au tome VI du *Philologue*, où nous avons dit ci-dessus que se trouvaient les notes sur l'*Électre* d'Eschyle, on a également donné (p. 129-148) celles que nous allons reproduire sur trois des tragédies du *Sophocle* d'Alde. Nous y avons remarqué un petit nombre d'erreurs ; mais, en général, la transcription est exacte.

NOTES SUR *AJAX*.

Vers 55. (Ἔνθ' εἰσπεσών....) Fureur d'Ajax.

Vers 77. (Ἐγὼ γὰρ ὀμμάτων ἀποστρόφους....) Pallas empêche Ajax de voir Ulysse.

Vers 79. (Οὐκοῦν γέλως ἥδιστος....) Il est doux de rire aux dépens de ses ennemis.

Vers 121. (Ἐποικτείρω δέ νιν....) Ulysse a pitié d'Ajax.

Vers 137. (Σὲ δ' ὅταν πληγὴ Διός....) Il (*le chœur*) se plaint des bruits qu'Ulysse fait courir contre Ajax.

Vers 154. (Τῶν γὰρ μεγάλων ψυχῶν....) La médisance ne s'attache qu'aux grands hommes.

Vers 284. (Κεῖνος γὰρ ἄκρας νυκτός....) Récit de la folie d'Ajax.

Vers 342. (.... Ἐγὼ δ' ἀπόλλυμαι.) Ajax déplore sa folie.

Vers 429. (Νῦν γὰρ πάρεστι καὶ δὶς αἰάζειν ἐμοί.) Jeu sur son nom d'Ajax.

Vers 482. (Ὦ δέσποτ' Αἴας....) Tecmesse veut consoler Ajax.

Vers 547 et 548. (Ὦ παῖ, γένοιο....) *Disce, puer, virtutem ex me*[2], etc.

---

1. Cet exemplaire, dont on avait à tort attribué les notes à Racine, serait-il celui qu'on trouve ainsi décrit, sous le n° 1034, dans le *Catalogue de M. Antoine-Augustin Renouard*, Paris, chez L. Potier, 1854? « *Sophoclis Tragœdiæ septem.... Venetiis, in Aldi Romani Academia*, 1502, in-8°, avec de très-nombreuses notes de la main de Jean Racine.... A la Bibliothèque impériale est conservé un second exemplaire du Sophocle d'Alde, aussi annoté par Racine, mais dans lequel les notes sont beaucoup plus rares. »

2. Virgile, *Énéide*, livre XII, vers 435 et 436.

Vers 644. (Κοὐκ ἔστ' ἄελπτον οὐδέν....) Ajax trompe le chœur et feint de vouloir vivre.

Vers 654. (Κρύψω τόδ' ἔγχος τοὐμὸν....) Il dit que son épée lui porte malheur, et qu'il la va cacher; mais c'est à dessein de se tuer.

Vers 691. (Ὦ Πάν, Πάν....) Il (*le chœur*) se réjouit du changement d'Ajax.

Vers 714. (Ἄνδρες φίλοι....) Teucer envoie un homme pour empêcher Ajax de sortir, étant retenu lui-même par les Grecs.

Vers 715. (Τεῦκρος πάρεστιν....) Un messager annonce le retour de Teucer et la prophétie de Calchas sur Ajax.

Vers 799. (Καὶ σπεύσαθ' οἱ μὲν Τεῦκρον....) Ils se séparent pour aller chercher Ajax.

Vers 810. (Ὁ μὲν σφαγεὺς ἕστηκεν....) Ajax seul. Il se vient tuer.

Vers 814. (Πέπηγε δ' ἐν γῇ....) Son épée est appuyée contre terre.

Vers 859. (Ὕστατον θροεῖ.) Il se tue.

Vers 861. (Πόνος πόνῳ πόνον....) Le chœur partagé en deux bandes.

Vers 864. (Κοὐδεὶς ἐπίσταται....) Il revient, n'ayant point trouvé Ajax.

Vers 891. (Αἴας ὅδ' ἡμῖν....) Tecmesse découvre Ajax.

Vers 956. (Θανόντ' ἂν οἰμώξειαν....) On regrette un grand homme après sa mort.

Vers 982. (Οὐχ ὅσον τάχος....) Teucer demande le fils d'Ajax[1].

NOTES SUR *ÉLECTRE*.

Vers 1. Acte 1er, scène 1re. Le Pédagogue explique le lieu de la scène, le temps et le sujet même.

Vers 10. (Δῶμα Πελοπιδῶν τόδε.) La scène est devant la porte du palais d'Agamemnon.

Vers 16. (Πυλάδη.) Pylade est présent.

Vers 18. (Ἑῷα κινεῖ φθέγματ' ὀρνίθων σαφῆ.) Lever du soleil.

Vers 25. (Ὥσπερ γὰρ ἵππος εὐγενής....) Vieux cheval qui a du courage.

Vers 29. (Τοίγαρ τὰ μὲν δόξαντα δηλώσω.) Oreste explique tout le sujet qui le fait venir.

---

1. Après le vers 982, Racine n'a plus écrit à la marge de cette pièce que la division en actes et en scènes, et les noms des personnages. Ces indications ont été notées par lui avec soin, dans tout le cours de la tragédie; il suffit d'en avertir ici. On sait du reste que la division en actes, que Racine a supposée, n'était pas indiquée dans les tragédies grecques.

SOPHOCLE.

Vers 36. (Ἄσκευον αὐτὸν....) Oracle. — Oreste rapporte le commandement de l'oracle pour préparer le spectateur à n'avoir pas tant d'horreur de tout ce qu'il vient faire.

Vers 45. (Φωκεὺς, παρ' ἀνδρὸς Φανοτέως....) Nœud de la fable.

Vers 77. (Ἰώ μοί μοι δύστηνος....) Scène 2. Electra vient seule, et ils s'en vont pour n'être point vus. — Il introduit dans Electra une femme affligée, constante dans son affliction, qui n'aspire qu'à la vengeance, qui aime son frère Oreste, qui est intrépide, et qui se résout de venger elle-même la mort de son père, quand elle croit que son frère est mort.

Vers 88. (Πολλὰς μὲν θρήνων ᾠδάς.) Pleurs continuels.

Vers 108. (Ἐπὶ κωκυτῷ....) Elle rend raison pourquoi elle vient pleurer hors du logis.

Vers 112. (Σεμναί τε Θεῶν παῖδες....) Elle invoque les Furies.

Vers 120. (Ἰὼ παῖ, παῖ....) Scène 3ᵉ. Chœur de filles qui viennent pour la consoler. — Le Chœur est de filles d'Argos, qui approuvent la douleur d'Electra, qui détestent comme elle le crime de sa mère, mais qui sont plus timides qu'elle, et qui n'osent parler librement.

Vers 137. (Ἀλλ' οὔ τοι τόν γ' ἐξ Ἀΐδα.) Les larmes ne font point revivre les morts.

Vers 146. (Ἀλλ' ἐμέ γ' ἁ στονόεσσ' ἄραρε....) Exemples de celles qui pleurent toujours.

Vers 156. (Οἷς ὁμόθεν εἶ....) Exemples de ses sœurs, qui pleurent moins.

Vers 164. (Ὃν ἔγωγ' ἀκάματα προσμένουσ'....) Elle se plaint de ce qu'Oreste ne vient pas.

Vers 176. (Ὦ τὸν ὑπεραλγῆ χόλον νέμουσα.) Laisser à Dieu sa vengeance.

Vers 188. (Ἇς φίλος οὔτις ἀνὴρ ὑπερίσταται.) Elle dit qu'elle est seule et abandonnée de tout le monde.

Vers 213. (Φράζου μὴ πόρσω φωνεῖν.) Le Chœur l'avertit de dissimuler sa douleur.

Vers 223. (Ἀλλ' ἐν γὰρ δεινοῖς οὐ σχήσω.) Elle s'excuse de sa douleur.

Vers 241 et 242. (Ἐκτίμους ἴσχουσα πτέρυγας Ὀξυτόνων γόων.) Arrêter les ailes de ses soupirs.

Vers 246. (Ἔρροι τ' ἂν αἰδώς....) Adieu la piété, si Agamemnon n'est pas vengé.

Vers 251. (Αἰσχύνομαι μὲν, ὦ γυναῖκες....) Description de sa misère, et de l'état de sa famille.

Vers 298. (Ἴδω δὲ τούτων....) Belle image de l'état où est la maison d'Agamemnon.

Vers 305 et 306. (Ἀλλ' ἐν τοῖς κακοῖς Πολλή γ' ἀνάγκη....) Le mal porte au mal.

Vers 307. (Φέρ' εἰπὲ, πότερον....) Le Chœur timide se demande si Égisthe est absent.

Vers 317. (Φιλεῖ γὰρ ὀκνεῖν....) Les grandes choses demandent du temps.

Vers 325. (Τίν' αὖ σὺ,....) Scène 4_ème_. Chrysothemis vient. — Chrysothemis est la sœur d'Electra; mais plus foible qu'elle, elle s'accommode au temps, et garde des mesures avec sa mère, vivant pourtant honnêtement avec sa sœur. — Elle sort pour aller porter des offrandes au tombeau d'Agamemnon.

Vers 341. (Κείνης διδακτὰ....) Vous ne dites rien de vous-même, c'est de votre mère.

Vers 349. ('Επεὶ δίδαξον....) Raisons pourquoi elle (*Electra*) veut toujours pleurer.

Vers 358 et 359. (Σοὶ δὲ πλουσία Τράπεζα....) Elle reproche à sa sœur qu'elle est dans l'abondance.

Vers 362. (Νῦν δ' ἐξὸν πατρὸς....) Qu'au lieu d'être la fille de son père, elle veut l'être de sa mère.

Vers 366 et 367. (Ὡς τοῖς λόγοις Ἔνεστιν ἀμφοῖν κέρδος....) S'entendre l'un l'autre.

Vers 376. (Μέλλουσι γάρ....) Supplice que l'on prépare à Electra.

Vers 384. ('Αλλ' ἐξίκοιτο....) Elle le souhaite.

Vers 387. (Ὅπως πάθης τί χρῆμα;...) Dispute des deux sœurs.

Vers 412. (Πολλά τοι σμικροὶ λόγοι....) Une parole fait bien du mal ou du bien.

Vers 414. (Λόγος τις αὐτήν ἐστιν....) Songe de Clytemnestre. — Ce songe de Clytemnestre vient bien au sujet, pour envoyer Chrysothemis au tombeau d'Agamemnon, où elle trouve des cheveux d'Oreste, qui y a été aussi : ce qui fait un fort bel incident.

Vers 425. (Πρός νυν Θεῶν σε λίσσομαι [1]....) Electra détourne sa sœur de porter les offrandes de sa mère.

Vers 446. (Τεμοῦσα κρατὸς βοστρύχων....) Elle coupe de ses cheveux pour les envoyer au tombeau.

Vers 451-455. (Ἡμῖν ἀρωγὸν αὐτὸν....) Elle prie son père.

Vers 463. (Δράσω.) Chrysothemis se rend.

Vers 466. (Σιγὴ παρ' ὑμῶν....) Elle demande le silence.

Vers 467. (Ὡς εἰ τάδ' ἡ τεκοῦσα....) Caractère timide.

Vers 469. Chœur tout seul. — Il semble pourtant qu'il adresse sa parole à Electra, qui ne rentre point dans la maison durant toute la prière; et il y a apparence qu'elle se promène devant la porte, sans s'en éloigner, comme on peut voir par le premier vers

---

1. L'édition de 1502, sur laquelle Racine écrivait ces notes, met ce passage dans la bouche d'Electra; dans d'autres éditions, c'est Chrysothemis qui parle.

de Clytemnestre (*vers* 511). — Il (*le Chœur*) raisonne sur le songe de Clytemnestre.

Vers 484. (Ἥξει καὶ πολύπους....) Vengeance divine.

Vers 511. (Ἀνειμένη μὲν....) Acte 2. Clytemnestre vient. — C'est une femme qui, dans sa bonne fortune, craint toujours dans le cœur et n'est point en repos. Elle souffre avec chagrin les plaintes d'Electra.

Vers 512. (Οὐ γὰρ πάρεστ' Αἴγισθος....) L'absence d'Égisthe est ce qui donne à Electra la liberté de venir se plaindre dans la place qui est devant le palais.

Vers 526. (Τὴν σὴν ὅμαιμον....) Elle accuse Agamemnon pour se justifier.

Vers 529. (Εἶεν, δίδαξον δή με....) Elle cherche de mauvaises raisons pour s'excuser à elle-même.

Vers 537. (Ἦ τῶν ἐμῶν Ἅδης....) La mort demandoit-elle plutôt mes enfants que ceux d'Hélène?

Vers 549. (Ἀλλ' ἢν ἐφῇς μοι....) Electra lui demande la permission de parler.

Vers 553. (Καὶ δὴ λέγω σοι....) Elle justifie son père. Belle réponse d'Electra.

Vers 577. (Εἰ γὰρ κτενοῦμεν ἄλλον ἀντ' ἄλλου....) Si vous avez dû tuer mon père, on vous doit tuer.

Vers 582. (Ἥτις ξυνεύδεις τῷ παλαμναίῳ....) Est-ce pour venger ma sœur que vous couchez avec Egisthe?

Vers 592. (Καὶ σ' ἔγωγε δεσπότιν....) Vous êtes moins ma mère que ma maîtresse.

Vers 599. (Καὶ τόδ' εἴπερ ἔσθενον....) Sa colère s'augmente.

Vers 603. (Εἰ γὰρ πέφυκα....) Si je suis méchante, je ne dégénère point de vous.

Vers 605. (Ὁρῶ μένος πνέουσαν....) Le Chœur feint d'être neutre.

Vers 609. (Καὶ ταῦτα τηλικοῦτος....) Que seroit-ce si elle étoit plus puissante?

Vers 611. (Εὖ νυν ἐπίστω τῶνδέ μ' αἰσχύνην ἔχειν.) Electra dit qu'elle en a honte elle-même, mais qu'elle y est forcée. — Caractère honnête d'Electra au milieu de son emportement. Elle s'en excuse sur son malheur.

Vers 620. (Τὰ δ' ἔργα τοὺς λόγους εὑρίσκεται.) C'est vos actions qui parlent en moi.

Vers 623. (Ὁρᾷς; πρὸς ὀργὴν ἐκφέρῃ....) Vous vous fâchez, après m'avoir permis de parler.

Vers 625. (Οὔκουν ἐάσεις....) Clytemnestre lui dit de la laisser sacrifier en paix.

Vers 627 et 628. (Ἐῶ, κελεύω, θῦε....) Electra lui dit qu'elle ne parlera plus.

Vers 633. (Κεκρυμμένην μου βάξιν....) *A parte.* Prière secrète de Clytemnestre.

Vers 647. (Φίλοισί τε ξυνοῦσαν....) Elle n'ose nommer Égisthe.

Vers 648. (Καὶ τέκνων ὅσων ἐμοί....) Elle exclut Electra.

Vers 652. (Τὰ δ' ἄλλα πάντα καὶ σιωπώσης ἐμοῦ....) Le reste, ὸ Dieu, vous le savez, sans que je vous le dise.

Vers 655. (Ξέναι γυναῖκες....) Scène 2de. *Pédagogue.* — Le gouverneur d'Oreste vient faire un faux récit de sa mort, pour surprendre Égisthe et Clytemnestre, et pour découvrir en même temps ce qui se passe.

Vers 669. (Οἲ 'γὼ τάλαιν'....) Electra s'écrie.

Vers 676. (Κεῖνος γὰρ ἐλθὼν....) Il fait ce récit long et dans le détail, pour mieux persuader.

Vers 702. (Ἀθηνῶν τῶν θεοδμήτων ἄπο.) Pour plaire aux Athéniens[1].

Vers 725. (Ναυαγίων.... ἱππικῶν....) Naufrage de chevaux.

Vers 738. (Ἔπειτα, λύων ἡνίαν....) Chute feinte d'Oreste.

Vers 746. (Οἷ' ἔργα δράσας....) Mort d'un grand homme.

Vers 754. (Φέρουσιν ἄνδρες....) Ces hommes-là sont Oreste et Pylade.

Vers 761. (Ὦ Ζεῦ, τί ταῦτα....) Clytemnestre doute si elle doit s'affliger ou se réjouir.

Vers 765 et 766. (Δεινὸν τὸ τίκτειν ἐστίν....) Mère.

Vers 770 et suivants. (Ὅστις τῆς ἐμῆς ψυχῆς γεγὼς....) Enfin elle s'en réjouit.

Vers 781. (Ψυχῆς ἄκρατον αἷμα....) Electra boit le plus pur de son sang, c'est-à-dire la désespère.

Vers 786. (Οὔ τοι σύ....) Clytemnestre insulte à sa fille, ne craignant plus Oreste.

Vers 791. (Οὐχ ὅπως σε παύσομεν.) Elle entend parler de sa conscience[2].

Vers 794. (Οὐκοῦν ἀποστείχοιμ' ἄν....) Il (*le Pédagogue*) feint de s'en vouloir aller, afin qu'on le retienne.

Vers 797. (Ἀλλ' εἴσιθ' εἴσω....) Elle le fait entrer.

Vers 799. Scène 3e. Electra demeure avec le Chœur.

Vers 800. (Δεινῶς δακρῦσαι....) Raillerie amère.

Vers 803. (Ὀρέστα φίλταθ' ὥς....) Electra pleure Oreste.

Vers 812. (Ἀλλ' οὔτι μὴν ἔγωγε....) Elle veut mourir.

Vers 818. (Ποῦ ποτε κεραυνοὶ....) Où est le tonnerre, si ces crimes ne sont punis?

1. C'est-à-dire, Sophocle a mis ce vers dans sa pièce pour plaire aux Athéniens.

2. Racine paraît n'avoir pas bien entendu ce passage.

Vers 822. (Ὦ παῖ, τί δακρύεις;) Pleurs bien passionnés.

Vers 832. (Οἶδα γὰρ ἄνακτ' Ἀμφιάρεων....) Qui mourut aussi par l'infidélité de sa femme Ériphile.

Vers 837. (Ἒ ἔ, ἰώ.) Elle l'interrompt.

Vers 838. (Πάμψυχος ἀνάσσει.) Mort glorieux.

Vers 843. (Οἶδ', οἶδ'· ἐφάνη γάρ....) Il eut un vengeur. Ce fut son fils Alcméon.

Vers 858-861. (Πᾶσι θνατοῖς....) Ch. Tous les hommes meurent El. Et meurent-ils dans des courses de chariots?

Vers 868. (Ὑφ' ἡδονῆς τοι....) Acte 3ᵉ, scène 1ᵉʳᵉ. Elle (*Chrysothemis*) vient en courant. — Au milieu de la douleur d'Electra et des regrets qu'elle fait sur la mort d'Oreste, Chrysothemis vient lui dire qu'il est venu. Cela fait un fort bel effet. Car les regrets d'Electra sont interrompus, et sa douleur n'en devient que plus violente. Ainsi la pitié va toujours en s'augmentant.

Vers 885. (Θάλπῃ τῷδ' ἀνηκέστῳ πυρί.) Joie excessive.

Vers 895. (Μή πού τις ἡμῖν ἐγγύς....) La timidité de Chrysothemis est toujours exprimée.

Vers 898. (Νεωρῆ βόστρυχον τετμημένον.) Elle a vu des cheveux d'Oreste.

Vers 906. (Τῷ γὰρ προσήκει...;) Elle prouve qu'ils sont d'Oreste.

Vers 908. (Οὐδ' αὖ σύ· πῶς γάρ;...) Electra ne peut pas s'éloigner de la maison.

Vers 913 et 914. (Τοῖς αὐτοῖσί τοι....) La Fortune n'afflige pas toujours les mêmes.

Vers 917. (Φεῦ, τῆς ἀνοίας....) Electra a pitié de sa sœur.

Vers 931. (Ὦ δυστυχής....) Chrysothemis pleure Oreste.

Vers 940. (Τλῆναί σε....) Electra lui propose de l'aider à tuer Égisthe.

Vers 942. (Ὅρα, πόνου τοι χωρὶς....) Elle l'y prépare.

Vers 944. (Ἄκουε δή νυν....) Beau discours d'Electra à sa sœur.

Vers 948. (Ἐγὼ δ' ἕως μὲν τὸν κασίγνητον....) Elle n'en a point parlé (*de tuer Égisthe*), tant que son frère a vécu.

Vers 960. (Καὶ τῶνδε μέντοι....) Égisthe se gardera bien de nous marier.

Vers 972. (Τίς γάρ ποτ' ἀστῶν ἢ ξένων....) Tout le monde nous admirera.

Vers 983-986. (Ἀλλ', ὦ φίλη, πείσθητι....) Conclusion pathétique.

Vers 987. (Ἐν τοῖς τοιούτοις....) Le Chœur est toujours craintif.

Vers 992. (Ποῖ γάρ ποτ' ἐμβλέψασα....) Chysothemis la veut détourner.

Vers 994. (Γυνὴ μὲν οὐδ' ἀνὴρ ἔφυς.) Nous sommes des femmes.

Vers 996. (Δαίμων δὲ τοῖς μὲν εὐτυχής....) Ils sont heureux.

Vers 1004 et 1005. (Οὐ γὰρ θανεῖν....) Nous ne mourrons pas quand nous voudrons.

Vers 1009. (Ἄῤῥητ' ἐγώ σοι....) Elle lui promet le secret.

Vers 1012. (Πείθου....) Le Chœur est de son avis.

Vers 1016. (Ἀλλ' αὐτόχειρί μοι....) Electra dit qu'elle l'entreprendra elle seule.

Vers 1018-1054. Dispute des deux sœurs. — Leur caractère paroît bien ici. L'une est intrépide et fière, l'autre timide, mais honnête, et sans perdre le respect.

Vers 1024. (Ζηλῶ σε τοῦ νοῦ....) J'aime votre esprit, mais je hais votre timidité.

Vers 1030. (Ἐλθοῦσα, μητρὶ....) Allez tout redire à votre mère.

Vers 1031. (Οὐδ' αὖ τοσοῦτον ἔχθος....) Je ne vous veux pas tant de mal.

Vers 1049. (Ἀλλ' εἴσιθ'....) Electra lui dit de rentrer.

Vers 1055. (Τί τοὺς ἄνωθεν....) Scène 2. Chœur. Electra. — Le Chœur parle seul. — Le Chœur déplore le désordre de la maison de ses rois, la dissension des deux sœurs, et admire Electra.

Vers 1062. (Δαρὸν οὐκ ἀπόνητοι.) Il n'ose nommer personne.

Vers 1077. (Διδύμαν ἑλοῦσ' Ἐρινύν....) Il y a apparence qu'Electra est dans un coin du théâtre, ne prenant point de part à ce que dit le Chœur.

Vers 1084. (Τὸ μὴ καλὸν καθοπλίσασα....) Vous armant contre ce qui n'est pas honnête.

Vers 1087. (Ζώης μοι....) Vœux pour Electra.

Vers 1095. (Ἆρ', ὦ γυναῖκες....) Acte 4e. Oreste. Electra. Le Chœur. — Oreste vient lui-même, apportant le vase où il dit que sa cendre est enfermée. Il s'adresse à Electra. C'est le dernier période de sa douleur (*de la douleur d'Electra*), et où le poëte s'est épuisé pour faire pitié. Il n'y a rien de plus beau sur le théâtre que de voir Electra pleurer son frère mort en sa présence, qui en étant lui-même attendri, est obligé de se découvrir.

Vers 1120. (Δόθ' ἥτις ἐστὶ προσφέροντες....) Il parle à Pylade.

Vers 1123. (Ὦ φιλτάτου μνημεῖον....) Electra prend la cendre d'Oreste. — Belles plaintes d'Electra sur Oreste.

Vers 1140. (Οἴμοι τάλαινα τῆς ἐμῆς....) Elle raconte devant Oreste tout ce qu'elle a fait autrefois pour lui.

Vers 1146-1150. (Νῦν δ' ἐκλέλοιπε....) Plainte bien passionnée.

Vers 1162. (Τοιγὰρ σὺ δέξαι....) Elle veut mourir avec lui.

Vers 1167. (Τοὺς γὰρ θανόντας....) Les morts ne sont point malheureux.

Vers 1168. (Θνητοῦ πέφυκας πατρὸς, Ἠλέκτρα....) Le Chœur nomme Electra pour la faire connoître.

SOPHOCLE.

Vers 1171 et suivants. Oreste attendri. — Oreste plaint sa sœur. Beaux mouvements.

Vers 1197. (Μόνος βροτῶν....) Vous êtes le premier qui m'ayez plainte.

Vers 1188 et suivants. Reconnoissance d'Oreste. Cette reconnoissance est merveilleusement pathétique et bien amenée de parole en parole, en se répondant tous deux fort naturellement et tendrement.

Vers 1200. (Ἐγὼ φράσαιμ' ἄν....) Il demande s'il peut s'assurer sur le Chœur.

Vers 1202 et 1203. (Μέθες τόδ' ἄγγος νῦν....) Il lui veut faire quitter cette urne, et elle ne veut point.

Vers 1224. (Σφραγῖδα πατρός....) Il lui montre l'anneau de son père.

Vers 1227. (Ὦ φθέγμ', ἀφίκου;...) O voix de mon frère!

Vers 1229. (Ἔχω σε χερσίν;...) Joie d'Electra.

Vers 1239. (Ἀλλὰ σῖγ' ἔχουσα πρόσμενε.) Oreste lui veut imposer silence.

Vers 1243-1252. (Τόδε μὲν οὔ ποτ' ἀξιώσω....) Beaux mouvements. — El. Je ne crains point des femmes. Or. Cependant elles sont à craindre. — Il la fait ressouvenir de la mort de son père. — Il (Sophocle) représente dans Electra une joie aussi immodérée que sa douleur étoit excessive. Elle ne craint personne, elle s'abandonne à ses transports avec la même intrépidité qu'elle s'abandonnoit à son affliction.

Vers 1253-1257. (Ἀλλ' ὅταν παρουσία....) Or. Nous y songerons une autre fois. El. J'y veux songer à toute heure.

Vers 1262. (Τίς οὖν ἂν ἀξίαν...;) Et qui pourroit se taire en vous voyant si inopinément?

Vers 1275-1281. (Ἰὼ χρόνῳ μακρῷ....) Elle le prie de ne la point empêcher de se réjouir.

Vers 1286 et 1287. (Ἔσχον ὀργὰν ἄναυδον....) Je crois qu'elle veut dire qu'on ne lui permettoit pas de crier en apprenant la mort de son frère, et qu'elle en étoit au désespoir, mais que maintenant elle est libre.

Vers 1291. (Τὰ μὲν περισσεύοντα....) Oreste songe à ne perdre point de temps.

Vers 1297. (Σήμαιν' ὅπου φανέντες....) Il lui demande où il se placera.

Vers 1301. (Ἀλλ' ὡς ἐπ' ἄτῃ....) Il lui commande de paroître toujours affligée.

Vers 1305 et 1306. (Ἐπεὶ τὰς ἡδονὰς....) Amitié d'Electra.

Vers 1312-1316. (Ἢν σὺ μὴ δείσῃς ποθ' ὡς....) Ne craignez point que ma mère me voie joyeuse : je la hais trop. Et je pleurerai encore de joie.

Vers 1327. (Εἴσιτ', ὦ ξένοι.) Elle les traite d'étrangers, parce qu'elle entend sortir quelqu'un.

Vers 1330. (Ὦ πλεῖστα μῶροι....) Scène 2de. Le gouverneur d'Oreste leur reproche leur imprudence, et leur dit qu'on les auroit surpris sans lui. — Sophocle a voulu marquer l'imprudence des jeunes gens, qui ne peuvent se contenir dans leurs passions, et afin que le spectateur ne trouve point étrange qu'on ne les a point entendus de la maison, il fait que ce vieillard, plus sage qu'eux, a fait sentinelle à la porte.

Vers 1336. (Πάλαι φυλάσσων....) Ainsi il sauve toutes les apparences.

Vers 1346. (Εἷς τῶν ἐν Ἅδου....) Chacun vous croit mort.

Vers 1348. (Τελουμένων εἴποιμ' ἄν....) Il ne veut point s'amuser.

Vers 1353. (Οὐκ οἶσθ' ὅτῳ....) Oreste fait reconnoître son gouverneur à Electra.

Vers 1360. (Ὦ φίλτατον φῶς....) Reconnoissance d'Electra envers lui.

Vers 1368. (Ἴσθι δ' ὡς μάλιστα....) Vous êtes l'homme du monde que j'ai le plus haï et aimé en un même jour.

Vers 1374. (Νῦν καιρὸς ἔρδειν....) Le Gouverneur les avertit qu'il est temps de commencer.

Vers 1380. (Πατρῷα προσκύσανθ' ἕδη.) Oreste adore en passant les dieux de la porte de son père.

Vers 1382. (Ἄναξ Ἄπολλον....) Prière passionnée d'Electra.

Vers 1390. (Ἴδεθ' ὅπου....) Electra entre un moment dans la maison pour les introduire. Chœur tout seul.

Vers 1393. (Μετάδρομοι κακῶν....) Furies qui courent derrière les crimes.

Vers 1404. (Ὦ φίλταται γυναῖκες....) Acte 5e, scène 1re. Electra sort pour n'être pas présente à la mort de sa mère. — Elle dit ce que l'on fait en dedans.

Vers 1407 et 1408. (Ἡ μὲν ἐς τάφον λέβητα κοσμεῖ....) Raison pourquoi Clytemnestre est dans la maison. Elle prépare ce qu'il faut pour les funérailles d'Oreste.

Vers 1410 et 1411. (Φρουρήσουσ' ὅπως....) Il rend raison pourquoi Electra sort. — Pour empêcher qu'Égisthe ne les surprenne.

Vers 1414. (Βοᾷ τις ἔνδον....) Cris de Clytemnestre qu'on tue. — Il fait entendre les cris de Clytemnestre, afin que, sans voir cette mort, le spectateur ne laisse pas d'y être comme présent, et pour épargner un récit.

Vers 1415 et 1416. (Ἤκουσ' ἀνήκουστα....) Le Chœur frémit de l'entendre tuer.

Vers 1426. (Παῖσον, εἰ σθένεις, διπλῆν.) Ce vers est un peu cruel pour une fille ; mais c'est une fille depuis longtemps enragée contre sa mère.

Vers 1433. (Φοινία δὲ χείρ....) Mains sanglantes.

Vers 1435. ('Ορέστα, πῶς κυρεῖ;) Scène 2ᵈᵉ. Oreste et les autres reviennent.

Vers 1437. ('Απόλλων εἰ καλῶς ἐθέσπισεν.) Il se justifie en rejetant tout sur Apollon.

Vers 1440-1442. (Παύσασθε, λεύσσω γάρ....) Le Chœur aperçoit de loin Égisthe. — Electra les fait cacher derrière la porte.

Vers 1448. (Τάδ' ὡς πάλιν....) Il n'achève pas son discours, pour marquer la diligence de l'action. — Ils se cachent.

Vers 1453. (Δι' ὠτὸς ἂν παῦρα....) Electra veut tromper Égisthe en lui parlant plus doucement que de coutume.

Vers 1458. (Τίς οἶδεν ὑμῶν....) Scène 3ᵉ. Égisthe revient, ayant su l'arrivée de ces étrangers qui ont annoncé la mort d'Oreste.

Vers 1461. (Σέ τοι, σὲ κρίνω....) Il s'adresse à Electra, comme y ayant plus d'intérêt.

Vers 1464. ('Έξοιδα. Πῶς γὰρ οὐχί;...) Electra parle toujours à double sens.

Vers 1474-1487. (Σιγᾶν ἄνωγα....) Égisthe commande qu'on ouvre les portes. — Les portes s'ouvrent, et on voit le corps enveloppé. — Oreste veut qu'il le découvre lui-même, pour se jeter en même temps sur lui. — Ce commandement d'Égisthe (*vers* 1474-1479) marque un homme insolent qui ne craint plus rien et qui veut que tout lui obéisse; et en même temps cela prépare aux spectateurs le plaisir de la surprise d'Égisthe, qui, au lieu du corps d'Oreste, découvre le corps de sa femme.

Vers 1491. (Οἴμοι, τί λεύσσω;...) Égisthe se voit perdu.

Vers 1496. (Ζῶν τοῖς θανοῦσιν....) Oreste se fait connoitre à lui.

Vers 1500 et 1501. ('Αλλά μοι πάρες....) Égisthe veut encore parler pour mourir le plus tard qu'il pourra.

Vers 1504. (Τί γὰρ βροτῶν....) Que gaigne un homme qui doit mourir, de différer sa mort d'un moment?

Vers 1507. (Ταφεῦσιν....) Je crois qu'elle entend parler des chiens.

Vers 1510. (Χωροῖς ἂν εἴσω....) Oreste le fait rentrer pour ne le pas tuer sur la scène.

Vers 1514. (Χώρει δ' ἔνθαπερ κατέκτανες....) Il en rend la raison en même temps, qui est de le tuer où son père est mort.

Vers 1519. ('Αλλ' οὐ πατρῴαν....) Égisthe parle et dispute le plus qu'il peut pour tirer en longueur. — Toutes ces disputes d'Égisthe marquent le caractère d'un poltron qui veut toujours différer sa mort.

Vers 1527. (Χρῆν δ' εὐθὺς εἶναι....) Punir les violences.

NOTES SUR *OEDIPE ROI*.

Vers 1. (*Ὦ τέκνα, Κάδμου*....) 1. acte, scène 1ère. — Cette ouverture de la scène est magnifique : tous ces prêtres suppliants qui viennent implorer le secours d'OEdipe.

Vers 15. (Ὁρᾷς μὲν ἡμᾶς....) Belle image de l'état funeste de la ville.

Vers 26. (Φθίνουσα δ' ἀγέλαις....) Peste.

Vers 33. (Ἀνδρῶν δὲ πρῶτον....) En louant OEdipe, ils le font connoitre.

Vers 46. (Ἴθ', ὦ βροτῶν ἄριστ'....) Ils le supplient tendrement de les sauver encore une fois.

Vers 58. (Ὦ παῖδες οἰκτροί....) Il représente en OEdipe un prince qui aime ses peuples, afin qu'il fasse plus de pitié.

Vers 70. (Κρέοντ' ἐμαυτοῦ γαμβρὸν....) Il attend le retour de Créon, qu'il a envoyé à l'oracle.

Vers 79. (Κρέοντα προστείχοντα....) Scène 2ᵉ. Créon arrive.

Vers 97. (Μίασμα χώρας....) L'oracle a commandé que la mort de Laïus soit expiée.

Vers 112. (Πότερα δ' ἐν οἴκοις....) OEdipe se fait conter cette mort.

Vers 130. (Ἡ ποικιλῳδὸς Σφίγξ....) Raison pourquoi on ne la vengea point dans le temps.

Vers 138. (Ἀλλ' αὐτὸς αὑτοῦ....) Les Rois se vengent en vengeant leurs pareils.

Vers 221. (Αἰτεῖς....) Scène 1. [*de l'acte II*].

Vers 229. (Ὅστις ποθ' ὑμῶν Λάϊον....) OEdipe commande au peuple qu'on déclare le meurtrier de Laïus.

Vers 241. (Τὸν ἄνδρ' ἀπαυδῶ τοῦτον....) Imprécations d'OEdipe contre le meurtrier de Laïus. — Bel artifice du poëte, qui fait qu'OEdipe s'engage lui-même dans d'effroyables imprécations.

Vers 264 et 265. (Ἔχων μὲν ἀρχὰς....) Doubles raisons de le venger. Il a succédé à son empire et à son lit.

Vers 266. (Εἰ κείνῳ γένος....) Les autres enfants de Laïus étoient morts.

Vers 290. (Μάλιστα Φοίβῳ Τειρεσίαν....) Le Chœur lui conseille de consulter Tirésie.

Vers 293. (Ἔπεμψα γὰρ Κρέοντος εἰπόντος....) OEdipe dit qu'il l'a mandé par le conseil de Créon. Il prépare les soupçons qu'il doit avoir contre Créon.

Vers 305. (Ὦ πάντα νωμῶν....) Scène 2. Tirésie vient.

Vers 309. (Σωτῆρά τ', ὦ'ναξ....) OEdipe prie Tirésie, avec beaucoup d'humilité, de sauver la ville en déclarant le meurtrier de Laïus.

Vers 325. (Ἄφες μ' ἐς οἴκους....) Tirésie le prie de le renvoyer.

Vers 327. (Οὔτ' ἔννομ' εἶπας....) OEdipe s'irrite peu à peu du refus de Tirésie.

Vers 339. (Οὐκ, ὦ κακῶν κάκιστε....) OEdipe l'injurie. — OEdipe, en querellant Tirésie, l'engage à lui dire des vérités qu'il prend pour des calomnies. — Bel artifice d'instruire le spectateur, sans éclaircir l'acteur. — Dispute violente d'OEdipe et de Tirésie, et néanmoins toujours pleine de majesté.

Vers 364. (Ποῖον λόγον; λέγ' αὖθις....) OEdipe se le fait redire pour avoir plus de sujet de le quereller.

Vers 376. (Τυφλὸς τά τ' ὦτα....) OEdipe lui reproche son aveuglement.

Vers 377. (Σὺ δ' ἄθλιός γε....) Vous serez plus aveugle que moi.

Vers 383. (Κρέοντος, ἢ σοῦ....) Jalousie qui prend à OEdipe contre Créon. Il croit que c'est lui qui fait parler Tirésie, pour se faire roi, après l'avoir fait chasser. — Cette mauvaise humeur d'OEdipe ne le rend point odieux, parce que l'intérêt public le fait parler; mais elle le rend digne de compassion, parce qu'il veut forcer un homme à lui dire des choses qui doivent retomber sur lui.

Vers 387. (Ὅσος παρ' ὑμῖν ὁ φθόνος....) Grandeurs enviées.

Vers 392. (Ὑφεὶς μάγον τοιόνδε....) Créon m'a envoyé cet imposteur, ce misérable, qui ne voit clair que pour gaigner.

Vers 396. (Πῶς οὐχ, ὅθ' ἡ ῥαψῳδὸς....) Où étois-tu quand je sauvai la ville du Sphinx?

Vers 413. (Εἰ καὶ τυραννεῖς....) Tout roi que vous êtes, je prétends vous pouvoir répondre; car je suis au dieu Apollon, et non pas à vous. — Privilége de la prêtrise.

Vers 420. (Ἆρ' οἶσθ' ἀφ' ὧν εἶ;...) Tirésie lui prédit obscurément tous ses malheurs.

Vers 435-442. (Οὐκ εἰς ὄλεθρον;...) OED. Ne t'en iras-tu pas au plus vite? — TIRÉS. Je ne serois pas venu, si vous ne m'eussiez appelé. — OED. Je ne prévoyois pas que tu me dirois des folies. — TIRÉS. Je vous parois fou; mais votre père m'a trouvé sage. — OED. Quel père? arrête. — Cette inquiétude d'OEdipe est admirable; Tirésie le laisse sans l'éclaircir.

Vers 452-467. (Εἰπὼν, ἄπειμ', ὧν οὔνεκ' ἦλθον....) TIRÉS. Je m'en vais, mais je vous avertis que celui que vous cherchez est ici, etc. Si je mens, croyez que je n'entends rien dans les prédictions.

Vers 517. (Ἄνδρες πολῖται....) Acte 3e, scène 1. Créon se vient plaindre des soupçons d'OEdipe.

Vers 536. (Οὗτος σὺ, πῶς δεῦρ' ἦλθες;...) Scène 2. OEdipe le vient trouver.

Vers 540. (Φέρ', εἰπὲ πρὸς Θεῶν....) M'avez-vous cru si stupide que de ne pas reconnoître que c'est vous qui faites parler Tirésie?

Vers 548. (Ἴσ' ἀντάκουσον....) Créon le prie de l'entendre.

Vers 552. (Τοῦτ' αὐτὸ μή μοι φράζ'....) OEdipe ne veut point écouter. Belle image d'un homme en colère.

Vers 559. (Ἔπειθες, ἢ οὐκ ἔπειθες;...) C'est vous qui m'avez fait mander Tirésie.

Vers 566 et 567. (Τότ' οὖν ὁ μάντις....) Pourquoi Tirésie ne parla-t-il point de moi dans le temps que Laïus fut tué?

Vers 596. (Πῶς δῆτ' ἐμοὶ τυραννίς....) Créon lui montre honnêtement qu'il est plus heureux d'être son beau-frère que d'être roi.

Vers 600. (Νῦν πᾶσι χαίρω....) Tout le monde m'aime, tout le monde a besoin de moi.

Vers 615. (Φίλον γὰρ ἐσθλὸν ἐκβαλεῖν....) Il vaut autant renoncer à la vie qu'à un bon ami.

Vers 618 et 619. (Χρόνος δίκαιον ἄνδρα....) Le temps seul fait connoître un homme de bien; mais il ne faut qu'un jour pour découvrir un méchant homme.

Vers 622 et 623. (Ὅταν ταχύς τις....) Il faut une prompte résistance contre une prompte conspiration[1].

Louis Racine (voyez ci-dessus, p. 222) avait aussi fait don à la Bibliothèque du Roi d'un *Sophocle* in-4°, édition *typis Regiis*, avec des notes, dit l'*État des livres*, sur l'*Ajax* et sur l'*Électre*. Il ne semble pas douteux que l'exemplaire ainsi désigné ne soit celui que la Bibliothèque impériale possède aujourd'hui encore de l'édition qui a pour titre : ΣΟΦΟΚΛΕΟΥΣ ΤΡΑΓῼΔΙΑΙ.... *Typis Regiis, Parisiis, M.D.LIII. Apud Adrianum Turnebum, typographum regium* (in-4°). Il n'est cependant pas exact que l'*Ajax* et l'*Électre* y soient les seules tragédies annotées. Si l'on n'a voulu tenir compte que des pièces sur lesquelles Racine a donné dans ce volume des notes nombreuses, il fallait plutôt nommer l'*Ajax* et les *Trachiniennes*. La première surtout de ces tragédies, que nous avons vue très-brièvement annotée dans l'édition d'Alde, a été de la part de Racine l'objet d'une étude plus approfondie dans l'édition de Turnèbe. Aussi ce second travail, où nous croyons trouver plus de marques encore d'un goût exercé que dans le premier, nous paraît-il lui être postérieur en date. Quant à l'*Électre*, Racine s'est contenté d'écrire quelques lignes sur les premiers vers de cette pièce; il en a fait à peu près autant pour l'*OEdipe à Colone* et pour le *Philoctète*. Nous allons transcrire l'annotation de cet exemplaire de 1553. Il ne porte point sur la page de titre la signature de Racine; mais les

---

1. Racine n'a pas été plus loin, dans son annotation de l'édition d'Alde, que le vers 623 de l'*OEdipe roi*. Il n'a pas annoté l'*Antigone*, l'*OEdipe à Colone*, les *Trachiniennes*, le *Philoctète*.

SOPHOCLE.

notes y sont bien de son écriture; et cette écriture est encore celle de sa première manière. Le volume a une reliure en parchemin vert, qui rappelle celle des cahiers de *Remarques sur l'Odyssée* et *sur les Olympiques*. En tête du volume, après une épître en grec d'Adrien Turnèbe au président Aimar de Ranconet, est une *Vie de Sophocle*, également en grec (Γένος Σοφοκλέους, καὶ βίος). Racine, dans des notes marginales, en a donné ce sommaire : « Sophocle. — Plus jeune de dix-sept ans qu'Eschyle, plus âgé qu'Euripide de vingt-quatre ans. — Il fut le premier qui ne joua point lui-même ses tragédies, à cause de sa voix trop foible. — Il fit le chœur de quinze, au lieu qu'il n'étoit que de douze. — Il étoit de mœurs douces, et se faisoit aimer de tout le monde. — Il ne voulut jamais quitter Athènes, quoique appelé par plusieurs rois. — Il étoit dévot. — Sa mort. — Ou d'un grain de raisin qu'un comédien lui avoit envoyé. — Ou d'une période d'*Antigone* qu'il voulut dire tout d'une haleine. — Ou de joie d'avoir été déclaré vainqueur. — Admirable dans les caractères, et seul imitateur d'Homère. — Qualités de ses tragédies : parler à propos, élégance, hardiesse, diversité. — Il peint un caractère par un demi-vers. »

NOTES SUR *AJAX*.

Vers 1. Prologue. C'est Minerve invisible qui parle à Ulysse, qui entre en cherchant. — Il introduit Minerve, qui éclaircit le sujet, parce qu'il n'y a qu'elle qui puisse savoir et redire l'intention d'Ajax, qui est sorti tout seul la nuit, et qui alloit tuer Agamemnon, etc., si Minerve elle-même ne lui eût troublé l'esprit.

Vers 3. (Καὶ νῦν ἐπὶ σκηναῖς....) Il établit d'abord le lieu de la scène auprès des tentes d'Ajax, qui sont les dernières du camp des Grecs.

Vers 14. (Ὦ φθέγμ' Ἀθάνας....) Il marque que Minerve est invisible.

Vers 69. (Ἐγὼ γὰρ ὀμμάτων....) Elle promet à Ulysse de troubler la vue d'Ajax, afin qu'il ne le reconnoisse point.

Vers 74. (Τί δρᾷς, Ἀθάνα;...) Le poëte représente Ulysse peut-être un peu trop timide; mais c'est pour relever Ajax, en le rendant plus terrible.

Vers 79. (Οὐκοῦν γέλως ἥδιστος....) C'est un rire agréable que de rire de ses ennemis.

Vers 118. (Ὁρᾷς, Ὀδυσσεῦ, τὴν Θεῶν....) Vous voyez, Ulysse, ce que c'est que l'homme quand il plaît aux Dieux.

Vers 119. (Τούτου τίς ἄν τοι....) Minerve loue Ajax, afin de prévenir le spectateur en sa faveur.

Vers 121. (Ἐγὼ μὲν οὐδὲν οἶδ', ἐποικτείρω δέ νιν.) Sentiment honnête d'Ulysse, qui a compassion d'Ajax. — Ce caractère d'Ulysse est soutenu jusqu'à la fin; car c'est lui qui fait accorder la sépulture à Ajax, quoiqu'il fût celui qu'Ajax haïssoit le plus.

Vers 125. (Ὁρῶ γὰρ ἡμᾶς οὐδὲν....) Nous ne sommes que des ombres.

Vers 127-133. (Τοιαῦτα τοίνυν....) Piété envers les Dieux.

Vers 134. (Τελαμώνιε παῖ....) Le Chœur est de vieillards de Salamine, soldats d'Ajax.

Vers 154. (Τῶν γὰρ μεγάλων ψυχῶν ἱείς.) La médisance est mieux reçue contre les grands.

Vers 201. (Ναὸς ἀρωγοί....) Tecmesse sort, et conte tout ce qui se passe, et tout ce qui s'est passé.

Vers 210. (Παῖ τοῦ Φρυγίου....) Tecmesse, fille du Troyen Téleutante, captive et femme d'Ajax.

Vers 260. (Τὸ γὰρ ἐσλεύσσειν οἰκεῖα πάθη....) Douleur d'Ajax de se voir cause de ses malheurs.

Vers 284. (Ἅπαν μαθήσῃ τοὔργον....) Récit de la fureur d'Ajax.

Vers 317. (Ὁ δ' εὐθὺς ἐξῴμωξεν....) Gémissements d'Ajax.

Vers 328. (Ἀλλ', ὦ φίλοι· τούτων γάρ....) Raison pourquoi elle est sortie sur la scène.

Vers 333. (Ἰώ μοί μοι.) Ajax crie de dedans sa tente.

Vers 340. (Ὤ μοι τάλαιν', Εὐρύσακες....) Elle craint pour son fils Eurysace.

Vers 346. (Ἰδού, διοίγω....) On ouvre sa tente.

Vers 367. (Οἴμοι γέλωτος....) Il songe à la joie de ses ennemis.

Vers 369. (Οὐκ ἐκτός;...) N^a. Le malheur le rend plus sévère.

Vers 382. (Ἦ που πολὺν γέλωθ'....) Ah! qu'Ulysse se réjouit bien à l'heure qu'il est!

Vers 383. (Ξὺν τῷ Θεῷ πᾶς....) L'on pleure, l'on rit, quand il plait aux Dieux.

Vers 384. (Ἴδοιμι δή νιν....) Que plût aux Dieux que je le pusse voir, tout malheureux que je suis!

Vers 389. (Ἰὼ Ζεῦ, προγόνων πάτερ....) O Jupiter auteur de ma race, que ne puis-je exterminer ce méchant fourbe que je hais! que ne puis-je percer le cœur de deux injustes rois, et me tuer moi-même après eux! — Il s'adresse à tout dans la passion, à Jupiter, aux enfers, aux campagnes de Troie.

Vers 394. (Ἰὼ σκότος....) Belle apostrophe aux enfers.

Vers 412. (Πόροι ἁλίρροθοι....) Apostrophe aux campagnes de Troie.

Vers 485. (Ὦ δέσποτ' Αἴας....) Tendre discours de Tecmesse pour le fléchir.

Vers 489. (Νῦν δ' εἰμὶ δούλη....) Maintenant je suis esclave, puisqu'il a plu aux Dieux, et surtout à votre valeur.

Vers 501. (Λόγοις ἰάπτων, ἴδετε....) Tout ceci est imité des paroles d'Andromaque dans Homère, Iliad. Z[1].

---

1. Le souvenir de Racine n'a pas été ici tout à fait exact. Les vers 455 et

SOPHOCLE.

Vers 527. (Καὶ κάρτ' ἐπαίνου τεύξεται....) Nᵃ. Il ne daigne pas caresser ou approuver Tecmesse, dans la douleur où il est.

Vers 530-534. (Κόμιζε νύν μοι παῖδα....) Il demande son fils. — A. Apportez-moi mon fils, que je le voie. — T. Je l'ai caché, dans la frayeur où j'étois. — A. Que craigniez-vous? Que voulez-vous dire? — T. J'ai craint que le pauvre enfant ne tombât et ne mourût entre vos mains. — A. Cela étoit digne du malheur qui me poursuit.

Vers 544. (Καὶ δὴ κομίζει....) On apporte son fils sur la scène.

Vers 545-547. (Αἶρ' αὐτὸν, αἶρε δεῦρο....) Apportez-le, apportez-le ici. Tout ce sang, tout ce carnage ne l'effrayera point, s'il est véritablement mon fils.

Vers 550 et 551. (Ὦ παῖ, γένοιο....)
O mon fils, sois un jour plus heureux que ton père :
Du reste avec honneur tu peux lui ressembler.

Vers 554. (Ἐν τῷ φρονεῖν γὰρ μηδέν....) Il envie le peu de sentiment de son fils.

Vers 563. (Τοῖον πυλωρὸν φύλακα....) Il se confie à Teucer. Voy. *Iliad.* Θ[1] l'amitié d'Ajax pour Teucer.

Vers 568-570. (Κείνῳ τ' ἐμὴν ἀγγείλατ' ἐντολήν....) Il prie les soldats de sa suite de dire ses dernières volontés à Teucer. — Afin qu'il montre son fils à son père et à sa mère.

Vers 573-578. (Καὶ τἀμὰ τεύχη....) En mémoire de l'affront qu'on lui a fait. — Il laisse son bouclier à son fils, et ne veut point que ses armes soient disputées.

Vers 582 et 583. (Πύκαζε θᾶσσον· οὐ πρὸς ἰατροῦ....) Il fait retirer Tecmesse. — Ce n'est pas au médecin à écouter les plaintes quand la plaie demande le fer.

Vers 588-591. (Οἴμ' ὡς ἀθυμῶ....) Tecm. Au nom des Dieux, ne nous abandonnez point. — Ajax. Ne savez-vous pas que je n'ai point d'obligation aux Dieux?

Vers 599 et suivants. (Ὦ κλεινὰ Σαλαμίς....) Le Chœur déplore la malheureuse fortune d'Ajax.

Vers 623. (Ἦ που παλαιᾷ μέν..) Le Chœur déplore le malheur de la mère d'Ajax, quand elle apprendra cette nouvelle.

Vers 651. (Ἅπανθ' ὁ μακρός....) Ajax revient sur la scène, et pour tromper le Chœur et Tecmesse, il feint de s'être rendu à ses prières.

Vers 655. (Κἀγὼ γὰρ, ὃς τὰ δείν'....) Il n'y a rien de si dur que le temps n'amollisse.

---

suivants du livre VI de l'*Iliade*, auxquels certainement il renvoie, sont dans la bouche d'Hector et non d'Andromaque.

1. *Iliade*, livre VIII, vers 267-272, 330 et 331.

Vers 659. (Ἀλλ' εἶμι πρός τε λουτρά....) Il feint de s'aller purifier sur le bord de la mer.

Vers 663. (Κρύψω τόδ' ἔγχος....) Et d'aller enterrer l'épée d'Hector : c'est pour prétexter sa sortie avec une épée. Apparemment les anciens ne marchoient point, sans quelque besoin, l'épée au côté. C'est ainsi qu'Achille, dans l'*Iphigénie* d'Eurip[ide], lui dit qu'il va cacher son épée sous l'autel, afin que, si elle ne veut point mourir, il ait des armes pour la défendre [1].

Vers 670. (Ἐχθρῶν ἄδωρα δῶρα....) Présents des ennemis.

Vers 672 et 673. (Εἴκειν, μαθησόμεσθα δ' Ἀτρείδας σέβειν.... Τί μή;) Il dit qu'il apprendra à respecter les Atrides. Le poëte lui donne des paroles forcées. Τί μή, pour marquer même la violence qu'il se fait en dissimulant.

Vers 684. (Ὅτ' ἐχθρὸς ἥμην....) Aimer comme si l'on devoit haïr, haïr comme si l'on devoit aimer.

Vers 688. (Ἄπιστός ἐσθ' ἑταιρίας λιμήν.) Amitié infidèle.

Vers 691. (Εὔχου τελεῖσθαι....) Il fait rentrer Tecmesse.

Vers 692-697. (Ὑμεῖς θ' ἑταῖροι....) Il donne ordre au Chœur de dire ses dernières volontés à Teucer. — Paroles équivoques qu'il tient au Chœur.

Vers 698. (Ἔφριξ' ἐν ἔρωτι....) Le Chœur danse et exprime sa joie sur le changement d'Ajax.

Vers 703. (Θεῶν χοροποί' ἄναξ...) Pan qui dresse les danses des Dieux. — Il appelle Pan qui dresse les danses des Dieux, et le prie de lui inspirer une danse sur-le-champ.

Vers 705. (Ὀρχήματα αὐτοδαῆ....) Pour excuser la danse d'un chœur de soldats qui ne doit point avoir appris à danser.

Vers 726. (Ἄνδρες φίλοι....) Voici un messager qui vient troubler la joie du Chœur, et qui leur apprend que Calchas a dit [à] Teucer qu'on prenne bien garde à Ajax, et qu'il est menacé de périr ce jour-là. Teucer ne vient pas lui-même, parce qu'il ne sauroit se défaire des Grecs qui l'environnent et se veulent prendre à lui de la fureur d'Ajax.

Vers 740. (Ἀλλ' ἡμῖν Αἴας ποῦ 'στιν....) Le Messager demande où est Ajax.

Vers 745-753. (Βραδεῖαν ἡμᾶς....) LE MESS. Oh! que je crains bien qu'on ne m'ait envoyé trop tard. — LE CHŒUR. Pourquoi? — LE MESS. Teucer recommandoit qu'on ne laissât point sortir Ajax

---

1. Racine a eu en vue les vers 1427 et 1432 d'*Iphigénie en Aulide*. Le sens qu'il a donné, dans ces vers, à l'expression τὰ ὅπλα n'est pas celui qu'adoptent les meilleurs interprètes. Achille, cela ne paraît pas douteux, parle de placer *près de l'autel* ses *soldats armés*.

jusqu'à son retour. — LE CHOEUR. Ajax est allé apaiser les Dieux. — LE MESS. Ces paroles-là sont bien suspectes, si Calchas dit vrai.

Vers 763. (Ἐλᾷ γὰρ αὐτὸν....) Pallas le poursuit aujourd'hui sans miséricorde.

Vers 767-782. (Ἔφασχ' ὁ μέν τις....) Raisons de la colère des Dieux contre Ajax. — Son orgueil, sa confiance sur lui seul, et le mépris de leur secours.

Vers 774. (Πάτερ, Θεοῖς μὲν....) Paroles d'Ajax à son père, qui lui disoit de se confier aux Dieux.

Vers 781. (Ἄνασσα, τοῖς ἄλλοισιν....) Paroles d'Ajax à Pallas : *Allez secourir les autres, et ne vous mettez point en peine de moi.*

Vers 791. (Ὦ δαΐα Τέκμησσα....) Le Chœur appelle Tecmesse, et lui apprend la nouvelle que le Messager apporte.

Vers 812. (Οἱ δ' ἑσπέρους ἀγκῶνας....) Tecmesse exhorte le Chœur à chercher Ajax, les uns à droite, les autres à gauche.

Vers 814. (Ἔγνωκα γὰρ δὴ....) Je vois bien qu'il ne se confie plus à moi, et que j'ai perdu ses bonnes grâces.

Vers 818. (Χωρῶμεν....) Elle sort, et tout le monde sort comme elle. Le Chœur se sépare en deux bandes ; et ainsi le théâtre demeure vide, afin qu'Ajax s'y puisse tuer aux yeux des spectateurs, sans que personne l'en puisse empêcher. — Il n'y a point changement de scène, je veux dire du lieu de la scène. — Voilà le seul endroit des tragédies grecques où le Chœur sort de la scène, depuis qu'il y est entré ; et c'est un bel artifice du poëte, parce que les dernières paroles d'Ajax étoient trop considérables pour les cacher au spectateur.

Vers 822. (Ὁ μὲν σφαγεὺς ἕστηκεν....) Il plante son épée à terre pour se jeter dessus.

Vers 831. (Σὺ πρῶτος, ὦ Ζεῦ....) Il commence ses invocations par Jupiter.

Vers 832-834. (Αἰτήσομαι δέ σ' οὐ μακρὸν....) Je ne demande pas une grande grâce. Fais si bien seulement que la nouvelle de ma mort soit bientôt portée à Teucer.

Vers 839-841. (Πομπαῖον Ἑρμῆν....) Il prie Mercure de lui acorder une mort prompte et sans beaucoup languir.

Vers 844-849. (Σεμνὰς Ἐρινῦς....) Il prie les Furies de venger sa mort sur les Atrides. — Et comme je meurs par mes propres mains, qu'ils meurent par les mains qui leur seront les plus chères.

Vers 853-856. (Ἥλιε, πατρῴαν....) Il prie le soleil d'annoncer sa mort à son père et à sa mère.

Vers 857 et 858. (Ἦ που τάλαινα....) Ah ! que cette malheureuse poussera de longs gémissements lorsqu'elle apprendra cette nouvelle !

Vers 861. (*Ὦ θάνατε, θάνατε....*) Il s'adresse à la mort.

Vers 866. (*Ὦ φέγγος, ὦ γῆς....*) Il s'adresse à tout, et prend congé de tout.

Vers 871 et 872. (*Τοῦθ' ὑμῖν Αἴας....*) Voilà ce qu'Ajax vous dit pour la dernière fois. Le reste, je le dirai là-bas.

Vers 873. (*Πόνος πόνῳ....*) Le Chœur revient de deux côtés différents, et ils se racontent qu'ils n'ont rien trouvé.

Vers 898. (*Τίνος βοή....*) Le Chœur entend Tecmesse qui s'écrie.

Vers 904. (*Αἴας ὅδ' ἡμῖν....*) Elle leur montre Ajax qui s'est tué.

Vers 923-925. (*Οὔ τοι θεατὸς....*) Tecmesse le couvre d'un manteau, parce qu'il n'y a personne qui ait le cœur de le voir en cet état. Artifice pour cacher le sang au spectateur.

Vers 929. (*Ποῖ Τεῦκρος....*) Elle souhaite le retour de Teucer pour défendre Ajax après sa mort.

Vers 931. (*Ὦ δύσμορ' Αἴας, οἷος ὢν οἵως ἔχεις.*) Beau vers.

Vers 953 et 954. (*Οἴμοι, τέκνον....*) Elle craint pour elle et pour son fils.

Vers 966. (*Ὁ πολύτλας ἀνὴρ....*) Joie d'Ulysse.

Vers 974. (*Θανόντ' ἂν οἰμώξειαν....*) Peut-être le pleureront-ils mort, après l'avoir haï vivant.

Vers 978 et 979. (*Ὧν γὰρ ἠράσθη τυχεῖν....*) Comment se moqueront-ils de lui? Il a ce qu'il souhaitoit : il est mort.

Vers 985. (*Ἰώ μοί μοι.*) Arrivée de Teucer.

Vers 997 et 998. (*Δῆτ' αὐτὸν ἄξεις δεῦρο....*) Teucer envoie querir le fils d'Ajax, de peur qu'on ne l'enlève comme le faon[1] d'une lionne. *Iliad.* Σ. (Livre XVIII, vers 318 et 319.)

    .... Ὥσπερ λῖς ἠϋγένειος
Ὧ ῥά θ' ὑπὸ σκύμνους ἐλαφηβόλος ἁρπάσῃ ἀνήρ.

Vers 1007 et 1008. (*Ὦ φίλτατ' Αἴας....*) Pourquoi il n'est pas arrivé plus tôt: c'est qu'il a cherché partout Ajax[2].

Vers 1010. (*Διῆλθ' Ἀχαιοὺς πάντας....*) Le bruit de sa mort a couru bien vite.

Vers 1016. (*Ὅσας ἀνίας μοι....*) Teucer déplore sa malheureuse condition.

Vers 1019. (*Ἦ που Τελαμὼν....*) Que dira ton père et le mien?

Vers 1025-1027. (*Τὸν δειλίᾳ προδόντα....*) Il croira que je t'ai abandonné, que je t'ai peut-être trahi, pour m'emparer de tes biens.

Vers 1028. (*Τοιαῦτ' ἀνὴρ δύσοργος....*) Vieillard colère.

---

1. Racine écrit *fan*.

2. Racine a mis, par mégarde sans doute : « c'est ce qu'il a cherché partout Ajax. »

Vers 1033. (Πολλοὶ μὲν ἐχθροί....) Irai-je à Troie, où je trouverai beaucoup d'ennemis et peu d'amis?

Vers 1040-1046. (Ἕκτωρ μὲν....) Réflexions sur l'épée d'Hector, dont Ajax s'est tué, et sur le baudrier d'Ajax, dont Hector a été trainé. — Les Furies ont forgé cette épée, et l'enfer ce baudrier.

Vers 1053. (Βλέπω γὰρ ἐχθρὸν φῶτα....) Le Chœur est effrayé de voir venir Ménélas.

Vers 1058. (Οὗτος, σὲ φωνῶ....) Ménélas commande à Teucer de ne point ensevelir Ajax.

Vers 1060. (Τίνος χάριν....) Fierté de Teucer.

Vers 1063. (Ὅθ' οὕνεκ' αὐτὸν....) Raisons de Ménélas.

Vers 1078. (Εἰ γὰρ βλέποντος....) Si nous n'avons pu venir à bout d'Ajax vivant, nous voulons en être les maitres après sa mort.

Vers 1084. (Οὐ γάρ ποτ' οὔτ' ἂν ἐν πόλει....) Obéissance aux magistrats et aux chefs.

Vers 1092-1094. (Ὅπου δ' ὑβρίζειν....) Ville où règne la licence, est bientôt abimée.

Vers 1099. (Αἴθων ὑβριστής....) Il étoit insolent, et moi je prétends lui insulter maintenant. V. (*voyez*) la harangue d'Alcibiade dans Thucydide[1].

Vers 1104. (Οὐκ ἄν ποτ' ἄνδρες....) Réponse généreuse de Teucer.

Vers 1118. (Ἀλλ' ὧν περ ἄρχεις, ἄρχε....) Commandez dans Sparte ou à vos sujets. Ajax commandoit aux siens et ne dépendoit point de vous.

Vers 1121. (Θήσω δικαίως....) Je l'ensevelirai malgré vous et malgré votre frère.

Vers 1126. (Σοῦ δ' οὐδὲν....) Il n'étoit point venu ici pour vous; car il n'honoroit point les gens sans mérite.

Vers 1132 et suivants. (Οὐ γὰρ βάναυσον....) Réponses vives de Teucer à Ménélas.

Vers 1153. (Ἤδη ποτ' εἶδον....) J'ai vu un homme fier lorsqu'il étoit loin de l'orage. Dès que la tempête venoit, il se laissoit fouler aux pieds des matelots.

Vers 1161. (Ἐγὼ δέ γ' ἄνδρ' ὄπωπα....) J'ai vu un homme qui vouloit insulter aux malheureux, et un autre homme, tel que moi, qui lui commandoit d'être sage.

Vers 1170. (Ἄπειμι....) Ménélas s'en va pour revenir avec main forte.

---

1. Nous croyons que Racine a eu en vue ce passage de la réponse d'Alcibiade à Nicias, au chapitre XVI du livre VI de *Thucydide* : Ἐν τῷ ὁμοίῳ τις ἀνεχέσθω καὶ ὑπὸ τῶν εὐπραγούντων ὑπερφρονούμενος.

Vers 1175. (Ἀλλ' ὡς δύνασαι, Τεῦκρε....) Le Chœur recommande à Teucer de se hâter d'enterrer Ajax.

Vers 1178. (Καὶ μὴν ἐς αὐτὸν καιρὸν....) Tecmesse et son fils arrivent.

Vers 1182. (Ὦ παῖ, πρόσελθε....) Ceci est fort tendre et fort noble.

Vers 1184 et 1185. (Θάκει δὲ προστρόπαιος....) Teucer met le fils d'Ajax auprès de son père. Il met dans les mains de cet enfant et ses cheveux, et ceux de Tecmesse, et ceux de l'enfant lui-même.

Vers 1188. (Κακὸς κακῶς ἄθαπτος....) Belles imprécations qu'il fait en se coupant les cheveux.

Vers 1194. (Παρέστατ', ἀλλ' ἀρήγεθ'....) Il recommande au Chœur de le bien défendre, tandis qu'il va chercher ce qu'il faut pour l'enterrer.

Vers 1203. (Ὄφελε πρότερον....) Le Chœur déteste celui qui le premier a inventé les armes parmi les Grecs.

Vers 1210-1215. (Κεῖνος οὔτε στεφάνων.) Le Commentaire[1] dit que Sophocle se jette ici dans ce qui est le plus de son génie, c'est-à-dire dans l'agréable. — Plaisirs dont on est privé par la guerre.

Vers 1224. (Νῦν δ' οὗτος ἀνεῖται....) Maintenant qu'Ajax est mort, quelle consolation nous reste ici ?

Vers 1227. (Ἵν' ὑλῶεν ἔπεστι....) Plût aux Dieux que je revoie bientôt Athènes !

Vers 1235. (Σὲ δὴ τὰ δεινὰ....) Discours superbe d'Agamemnon.

Vers 1237. (Σέ τοι τὸν ἐκ τῆς αἰχμαλώτιδος....) Il lui reproche qu'il est fils d'une captive.

Vers 1246. (Ποῖ βάντος....) Qu'a fait Ajax que je n'en aie fait autant que lui ?

Vers 1269. (Οὐδ' εὐρύνωτοι....) Les gens à larges épaules ne sont pas les plus nécessaires, mais les gens sensés.

Vers 1269. (Ἄλλον τιν' ἄξεις ἄνδρα....) Ne m'amènerez-vous pas ici quelque homme libre qui parle pour vous ? car je n'entends pas la langue des barbares.

Vers 1275. (Φεῦ· τοῦ θανόντος....) Teucer répond courageusement, mais pourtant avec un peu plus de respect qu'à Ménélas. — Ah ! qu'on oublie aisément les bienfaits d'un homme après sa mort !

---

1. Racine cite encore plus bas le Commentaire sur le vers 1318. L'édition de Turnèbe n'a cependant pas de commentaires; mais nous avons vu que Racine avait dans sa bibliothèque le *Sophocle* de Paul Estienne (1603), qui donne les scolies grecques. Cette édition était probablement sous ses yeux, tandis qu'il annotait le *Sophocle* de 1553.

Vers 1282. (Οὐ μνημονεύεις....) Il lui remet devant es yeux ce qu'Ajax a fait pour les Grecs.

Vers 1292. (Χὤτ' αὖθις αὐτὸς....) Quand il fallut se battre contre Hector, Ajax mit son nom pour être tiré au sort.

Vers 1294. (Οὐ δραπέτην τὸν κλῆρον....) Il ne chercha point à tromper le sort, *i. (c'est-à-dire)* comme on l'a trompé lorsqu'on a donné les voix dans le jugement des armes d'Achille.

Vers 1300-1312. (Οὐκ οἶσθα σοῦ πατρὸς....) Vous me reprochez que je suis fils d'une barbare. Et quel étoit Pélops, votre aïeul? N'étoit-il pas Phrygien? Et qu'y a-t-il de plus barbare que votre père Atrée, qui a fait manger à son frère ses propres enfants? Votre mère n'étoit-elle pas de Crète? Votre père la surprit avec un adultère, et la fit jeter dans la mer. Et vous me reprochez la honte de ma naissance, à moi qui suis fils de Télamon, le plus vaillant des Grecs, et d'une mère princesse, fille de Laomédon, qu'Hercule lui-même donna à mon père, pour le récompenser de sa valeur.

Vers 1317-1322. (Εὖ νυν τόδ' ἴσθι....) Si vous faites jeter Ajax, faites votre compte qu'il faudra que vous nous jetiez tous trois avec lui; car j'aime bien mieux mourir pour lui que pour votre femme ou pour votre frère. Mais prenez garde qu'en nous voulant outrager, vous ne vous repentiez de votre entreprise.

Vers 1318. (Τρεῖς ὁμοῦ συγκειμένους.) Le Commentaire dit que ces trois ce sont Teucer, Agamemnon et Ménélas; mais je crois que c'est Teucer, Eurysace et Tecmesse.

Vers 1325. (Ἄναξ Ὀδυσσεῦ....) Arrivée d'Ulysse. Le Chœur prie Ulysse en faveur de Teucer. — Ulysse vient faire l'action d'un honnête homme : il détourne Agamemnon de l'outrage qu'il veut faire à la mémoire d'Ajax, et lui dit qu'il faut que leur haine meure avec lui.

Vers 1337. (Ἔξεστιν οὖν εἰπόντι....) Ulysse le prie de l'écouter favorablement.

Vers 1347. (Ἀλλ' αὐτὸν ἔμπας....) Mon inimitié ne m'empêchera point de dire qu'Ajax étoit le plus vaillant des Grecs après Achille.

Vers 1356. (Ἔγωγ'· ἐμίσουν δ' ἡνίκ' ἦν....) Je l'ai haï, tant que j'ai pu le haïr avec honneur.

Vers 1379. (Ἀλλ' εὖ γε μέντοι....) Agamemnon s'en va, cédant à Ulysse, mais se déclarant toujours ennemi d'Ajax.

Vers 1383. (Ὅστις σ', Ὀδυσσεῦ....) Le Chœur loue Ulysse.

Vers 1387. (Καὶ τὸν θανόντα τόνδε....) Ulysse s'offre à Teucer de lui aider à enterrer Ajax.

Vers 1390. (Ἄριστ' Ὀδυσσεῦ....) Teucer loue Ulysse de sa générosité.

Vers 1398. (Τοιγάρ σφ' 'Ολύμπου....) Imprécations de Teucer contre les Atrides.

Vers 1403-1408. (Τάφου μὲν ὀκνῶ....) Mais je n'ose, ô Ulysse, consentir que vous touchiez le corps d'Ajax, de peur que cela ne soit trop odieux à ses mânes ; mais du reste vous et vos amis vous pouvez faire toutes choses pour honorer sa sépulture. — Ulysse s'en va.

Vers 1412. ('Αλλ' οἱ μὲν κοίλην....) Teucer donne les ordres pour la fosse d'Ajax, et pour le bain nécessaire pour le laver.

Vers 1418. (Σὺ δὲ, παῖ τοῦ πατρός....) Il lève son corps pour le transporter, et se fait aider par son fils.

NOTES SUR *ÉLECTRE*.

Vers 1-4. Il explique dès les quatre premiers vers et le nom du principal acteur et le lieu de la scène.

Vers 2. ('Αγαμέμνονος παῖ, νῦν ἐκεῖν'....) Voilà, ô fils d'Agamemnon, ces mêmes lieux que vous avez tant desiré de voir. — Sophocle a un soin merveilleux d'établir d'abord le lieu de la scène. Il se sert ici pour cela d'un artifice très-agréable, en introduisant un vieillard qui montre les environs du palais d'Argos à Oreste, qui en avoit été enlevé tout jeune. Le *Philoctète* commence à peu près de même : c'est Ulysse qui montre à Pyrrhus tout jeune l'île de Lemnos, où ils sont, et par où l'armée avoit passé. L'*OEdipe Colonéen* s'ouvre par OEdipe aveugle qui se fait décrire par Antigone le lieu où il est. Ces trois ouvertures, quoique un peu semblables, ne laissent pas d'avoir une très-agréable diversité et des couleurs merveilleuses [1].

NOTES SUR *OEDIPE A COLONE*.

Vers 570 et suivants. (Ὦ φίλτατ' Αἰγέως παῖ....) OEdipe prédit à Thésée qu'un jour Athènes et Thèbes se brouilleront.

Vers 572-575. (Τὰ δ' ἄλλα συγχεῖ....) Tour admirable qu'il donne à sa pensée.

---

[1]. Dans son *Sophocle* de Turnèbe (1553), Racine n'a pas fait d'autres remarques sur l'*Électre*, qu'il a, comme nous l'avons vu (p. 224-233), longuement annotée ailleurs, dans l'édition d'Alde. Les deux pièces qui suivent dans celle de Turnèbe, et qui sont l'*OEdipe roi* et l'*Antigone*, n'ont point de notes marginales de notre poëte ; il a seulement souligné, dans la première des deux, un petit nombre de vers.

Vers 584 et 585. ("Ἰν' οὑμὸς εὕδων....) Un jour mes cendres froides boiront leur sang chaud.

NOTES SUR *LES TRACHINIENNES*.

Vers 1. (Λόγος μὲν....) Acte 1, scène 1. Déjanire explique le sujet par un monologue. Il semble pourtant que l'esclave qui lui parle ensuite a été présente à son discours.

Vers 9. (Μνηστὴρ γὰρ ἦν μοι....) Acheloüs demandoit Déjanire en mariage.

Vers 22. (Οὐκ ἂν διείποιμ'....) Artifice pour ne lui point faire perdre le temps à décrire le combat d'Hercule et d'Acheloüs.

Vers 28. (Ἀεί τιν' ἐκ φόβου φόβον τρέφω.) Crainte continuelle.

Vers 31-33. (Κἄφυσα μὲν δὴ παῖδας....) Hercule ne voyoit jamais ses enfants : comme un laboureur qui a un champ éloigné qu'il ne voit qu'au temps qu'il le sème et qu'il le moissonne.

Vers 34. (Τοιοῦτος αἰὼν....) Travaux continuels d'Hercule.

Vers 39. (Ἡμεῖς μὲν ἐν Τραχῖνι....) Raison pourquoi la scène est à Trachine : parce qu'Hercule ayant tué Iphitus, avoit été obligé de se retirer.

Vers 44. (Χρόνον γὰρ οὐχὶ βαιὸν....) Il y a quinze mois qu'Hercule est absent.

Vers 47. (Δέλτον λιπὼν....) Il avoit laissé en partant un écrit qui contenoit ses dernières volontés.

Vers 50. (Κατεῖδον ἤδη....) Je vous vois pleurer à toute heure.

Vers 52. (Νῦν δ' εἰ δίκαιον....) Si une esclave ose se mêler de donner des conseils.

Vers 56. (Μάλιστα δ' ὅνπερ εἰκὸς....) Comment n'envoyez[-vous] point Hyllus pour chercher son père ?

Vers 58. (Ἐγγὺς δ' ὅδ' αὐτὸς....) Mais le voici qui vient à propos.

Vers 61-63. (Ὦ τέκνον, ὦ παῖ....) Scène 2. Hyllus, Déjanire, l'esclave. — Un esclave peut quelquefois parler à propos.

Vers 65. (Σὲ πατρὸς οὕτω δαρὸν....) Déjanire dit à Hyllus qu'il y a quelque honte à lui de ne se point mettre en peine de son père.

Vers 67. (Ἀλλ' οἶδα....) Hyllus dit qu'il croit savoir où il est.

Vers 70. (Λυδῇ γυναικί....) Il a servi l'année passée sous une Lydienne.

Vers 74. (Εὐβοῖδα χώραν....) Et maintenant il assiége ou il a pris la ville d'OEchalie en Euboæ (*sic*).

Vers 79. (Ὡς ἢ τελευτὴν τοῦ βίου....) Hercule avoit eu un oracle qui lui prédisoit que s'il survivoit à cette expédition, il vivroit heureux tout le reste de sa vie.

Vers 82. ('Ἐν οὖν ῥοπῇ τοιᾷδε....) Déjanire excite son fils à aller chercher Hercule dans une nécessité si importante.

Vers 86-89. ('Ἀλλ' εἶμι, μῆτερ....) HYLL. Si j'avois su cet oracle, il y a longtemps que je serois parti ; mais la fortune ordinaire de mon père me défendoit de craindre pour lui.

Vers 92. (Καὶ γὰρ ὑστέρῳ....) Il vaut mieux tard que jamais.

Vers 94 et 95. (Ὃν αἰόλα νὺξ....) Le Chœur est de jeunes filles trachiniennes. — O toi que la nuit enfante et éteint.

Vers 96. (Ἅλιον Ἅλιον....) Elles s'adressent au Soleil pour lui demander où est Hercule.

Vers 104-113. (Ποθουμένᾳ γὰρ φρενί....) Raison pourquoi le Chœur vient. Elles ont appris l'affliction de Déjanire. Elles plaignent l'inquiétude continuelle de Déjanire. Elle pleure toujours.

Vers 114. (Πολλὰ γὰρ ὥστ' ἀκάμαντος....) La vie d'Hercule est dans une continuelle agitation.

Vers 121. ('Ἀλλά τις Θεῶν....) Mais toujours quelqu'un des Dieux l'arrache à la mort ; c'est pourquoi, ô Déjanire, je condamne votre crainte, et vous conseille d'espérer.

Vers 128. ('Ἀνάλγητα γάρ....) Car il n'y a personne exempt de douleur.

Vers 131. ('Ἀλλ' ἐπὶ πῆμα καὶ χαρά....) La vie roule sur la joie et sur l'affliction, comme le chariot de l'Ourse roule toujours.

Vers 134. (Μένει γὰρ οὔτ' αἰόλα νύξ.) Rien n'est stable au monde.

Vers 142. (Τίς ὧδε τέκνοισι....) Qui croira que Jupiter n'ait point de soin de ses enfants?

Vers 144. (Πεπυσμένη μέν....) Acte 2, scène 1. Déjanire. Le Chœur[1].

Vers 148. (Χώροισιν αὐτοῦ....) *I.* (*c'est-à-dire*) car la jeunesse ne se soucie guère des affaires des autres, et ne songe qu'à elle. *Métaph*[*ore*] : *Pascitur in suis campis.*

Vers 149. (Οὐδ' ὄμβρος....) Bonheur des jeunes filles bien exprimé.

Vers 152. (Λάθη τ' ἐν νυκτί....) Une nuit change tout.

Vers 158. ('Οδὸν γὰρ ἦμος....) Elle dit qu'Hercule lui a laissé dans des tablettes ses dernières volontés, et qu'il a fait son testament, ce qu'il n'avoit jamais fait en partant pour tous ses autres travaux.

Vers 167. (Χρόνον προτάξας....) Il lui a dit que s'il ne revenoit

---

1. Racine a souligné les vers suivants, 145 et 146 :

. . . . 'Ὡς δ' ἐγὼ θυμοφθορῶ
Μήτ' ἐκμάθοις παθοῦσα, νῦν δ' ἄπειρος εἶ.

Nous le faisons remarquer ici, parce que les vers 867 et 868 d'*Andromaque* en paraissent une imitation. Voyez notre tome II, p. 83, note 4.

dans quinze mois, il ne le falloit plus attendre ; mais que s'il revenoit, il vivroit heureux tout le reste de ses jours.

Vers 175. (Δωδῶνι, δισσῶν....) Les deux colombes de Dodone. Voy. *Hérodote*, l. 2 (*chapitres* LV-LVII) : il (*Hérodote*) dit que c'étoit deux Égyptiennes.

Vers 176. (Καὶ τῶνδε ναμέρτεια....) Voici le terme qu'il a prescrit arrivé.

Vers 183. (Δέσποινα Δηιάνειρα....) Scène 2. Un messager annonce à Déjanire qu'Hercule est vivant, victorieux et de retour.

Vers 191-194. ('Εν βουθερεῖ λειμῶνι....) Il dit qu'il l'a appris de Lichas, et qu'il a couru devant pour gaigner les bonnes grâces de Déjanire par cette bonne nouvelle.

Vers 197. (Κύκλῳ γὰρ αὐτὸν....) Il dit qu'Hercule est arrêté par le peuple, qui est ravi de le voir.

Vers 205. (Φωνήσατ', ὦ γυναῖκες....) Déjanire exhorte tout le Chœur à chanter des actions de grâce, et demeure pourtant sur la scène.

Vers 229. ('Ορῶ, φίλαι γυναῖκες....) Scène 3. Lichas, héraut d'Hercule, amène les captives, et entre autres Iolé, dont Hercule est amoureux. Lichas trompe Déjanire par un faux récit, et lui cache les amours d'Hercule.

Vers 236. (῏Ω φίλτατ' ἀνδρῶν....) L'amour de Déjanire et son impatience.

Vers 239. (Καὶ ζῶντα καὶ θάλλοντα....) Hercule vit et se porte bien.

Vers 246. (Τοῦ ποτ' εἰσὶ καὶ τίνες.) Leur nom, leur père, leur pays.

Vers 252. (Οὐκ, ἀλλὰ τὸν μὲν πλεῖστον....) Faux récit de Lichas. — Il y a déjà dans l'*Electra* un récit qui est faux tout entier, et qui néanmoins est raconté avec beaucoup de soin, et plus au long que celui[-ci]. Je ne sais si ces narrations si longues sont assez dignes de la tragédie, quand elles ne sont pas sincères.

Vers 285. (Κεῖνοι δ' ὑπεργλιδῶντες....) Railleurs punis.

Vers 307. (῏Ω Ζεῦ τροπαῖε....) O Jupiter, que je ne voie jamais mes enfants en cet état.

Vers 311. (῏Ω δυστάλαινα....) Déjanire s'adresse à Iolé, et la plaint beaucoup plus que toutes les autres sans savoir que [c'est] sa rivale.

Vers 324-332. (Εἴπ', ὦ τάλαιν'....) Déjanire interroge encore Iolé ; mais Lichas lui dit qu'elle ne veut point parler, et qu'elle ne fait que pleurer depuis que sa patrie est ruinée. — Lichas, par cette interruption, empêche Iolé d'instruire Déjanire de la vérité.

Vers 333. ('Η δ' οὖν ἐάσθω....) Déjanire les fait entrer, et est arrêtée par ce premier messager.

Vers 339. (Αὐτοῦ γε πρῶτον....) Scène 4. Le Messager, qui étoit demeuré sur la scène, découvre à Déjanire tout le mystère qu'il avoit appris de Lichas lui-même en présence de plusieurs personnes.

Vers 357. (Ταύτης ἕκατι κεῖνος....) Récit véritable de l'amour d'Hercule pour Iolé.

Vers 364. (Τὴν παῖδα δοῦναι, κρύφιον ὡς ἔχοι λέχος.) Hercule ruina OEchalie parce qu'Euryte, père d'Iolé, ne lui voulut pas permettre de coucher avec elle (κρύφιον λέχος). — Cette injustice d'Hercule et son infidélité envers Déjanire sont cause de sa perte, et l'en rendent digne.

Vers 379. (Οἴμοι τάλαινα....) Jalousie de Déjanire.

Vers 397-411. (Τί χρὴ, γύναι....) Scène 5. Lichas sort, et veut s'en retourner vers son maître. Déjanire le retient, et dissimule son inquiétude. Ce sens froid qu'elle affecte et ses interrogations sont très-belles. Lichas continue à déguiser la vérité. — Ami, regardez-moi un peu. A qui pensez-vous parler? — Je parle à Déjanire, l'épouse d'Hercule, et ma maîtresse.

Vers 414. (Τί δῆτα; ποίαν ἀξιοῖς....) Et si vous offensez votre maîtresse, de quelle peine vous jugez-vous digne?

Vers 418 et 420. (Ἄπειμι· μῶρος δ' ἦν.... Λέγ' εἴ τι χρῄζεις....) Ces deux réponses de Lichas ne sont pas assez respectueuses [1].

Vers 421-431. (Τὴν αἰχμάλωτον....) Elle le presse, il dénie.

Vers 439 et 440. (Ἄνθρωπος, ὦ δέσποιν', ἐπιστήτω....) Ceci sort encore un peu du respect. — Un homme sage ne doit point s'amuser à un homme qui n'est pas dans son bon sens.

Vers 442-465. (Μὴ, πρός σε....) Déjanire en vient aux prières. Discours admirable d'une jalouse qui veut apprendre son malheur. — Vous parlez à une femme qui sait excuser les foiblesses des hommes. C'est en vain qu'on veut lutter et s'élever contre l'amour [2]. Je serois une folle si je voulois du mal à mon époux ou à cette pauvre fille d'une chose si peu volontaire. Si vous mentez une fois, on ne vous croira plus quand vous voudrez être sincère. Le mensonge est indigne d'un homme libre. Mille autres me diront la vérité. Le mal n'est rien, pourvu qu'on ne veuille point me le cacher. Hercule n'en a-t-il pas aimé beaucoup d'autres?

---

1. Il faut faire remarquer que, dans l'édition de Turnèbe, Lichas adresse ces réponses à Déjanire, tandis que les éditions plus récentes ont mis avec raison les vers 406, 408, 412-415, 417, 419 dans la bouche du Messager.

2. Cette dernière phrase n'est pas écrite à la marge, avec les phrases au milieu desquelles nous l'avons insérée à sa véritable place; mais elle a été ajoutée au bas de la page 317, qui finit au vers 465.

Vers 466. (Κοὔπω τις αὐτῶν....) Jamais je n'ai dit une parole fâcheuse à aucune de mes rivales.

Vers 469. (Ὤκτειρα δὴ μάλιστα....) Elle feint d'avoir beaucoup de compassion pour sa rivale.

Vers 477. (Ἀλλ', ὦ φίλη δέσποιν'....) Lichas avoue la vérité.

Vers 478. (Θνητὴν φρονοῦσαν θνητά....) Mortelle vous pensez des choses mortelles[1], *i.* (*c'est-à-dire*) vous vous accommodez à votre fortune.

Vers 486. (Ἀλλ' αὐτὸς, ὦ δέσποινα....) J'ai déguisé la vérité, non point par l'ordre d'Hercule, mais de moi-même, pour vous épargner de l'affliction.

Vers 493 et 494. (Ὡς τἆλλ' ἐκεῖνος....) Hercule, invincible en toute autre chose, vaincu par l'amour.

Vers 496. (Κοῦτοι νόσον....) Je ne veux point m'attirer un nouveau malheur en m'opposant au destin.

Vers 497. (Θεοῖσι δυσμαχοῦντες....) Ne point résister aux Dieux, *i.* (*c'est-à-dire*) à l'amour.

Vers 500 et 501. (Κενὸν γὰρ οὐ δίκαιά σε....) Cela est dit avec une raillerie amère.

Vers 502. (Μέγα τι σθένος....) Déjanire rentre, et le Chœur demeure seul. Elle rentre pour charger Lichas et de ses ordres, et de ses présents pour Hercule. Le Chœur chante la puissance de Vénus, qui est invincible, à propos d'Hercule vaincu par l'amour.

Vers 513. (Ὁ μὲν ἦν ποταμοῦ σθένος....) Combat d'Acheloüs et d'Hercule.

Vers 522. (Εὔλεκτρος ἐν μέσῳ Κύπρις....) Vénus étoit au milieu de la carrière, qui jugeoit du combat.

Vers 524-529. (Τότ' ἦν χερός....) Belle description du combat.

Vers 528. (Κλίμακες....) Κλῖμαξ étoit une espèce de lutte où l'on s'embrassoit l'un l'autre ; et les bras enlacés représentoient une échelle.

Vers 530. (Ἁ δ' εὐῶπις....) Déjanire étoit sur la rive, attendant à qui elle devoit être.

Vers 533. (Ἐγὼ δὲ μάτηρ....) J'en parle avec affection, comme si j'étois sa mère.

Vers 536. (Κἀπὸ ματρὸς ἄφαρ....) Enfin elle fut emmenée d'auprès de sa mère, comme une jeune génisse.

Vers 538. (Ἧμος, φίλαι....) Acte 3. scène 1. Déjanire sort, et prend le temps que Lichas parle en secret aux captives. Elle vient

1. Racine se souvenait peut-être de ce vers de Sophocle quand il a fait dire à Œnone dans *Phèdre* (vers 1302) :

Mortelle, subissez le sort d'une mortelle.

déplorer son malheur en présence du Chœur, et en même temps elle lui confie le déssein qu'elle a pris d'envoyer une robe à Hercule.

Vers 544. (Προσδέδεγμαι, φόρτον ὥστε....) Je reçois cette jeune captive, comme un matelot reçoit malgré lui une marchandise, une charge dangereuse.

Vers 547-549. (Τοιάδ' Ἡρακλῆς....) Voilà la récompense que je reçois d'Hercule pour avoir demeuré seule dans sa maison, que j'ai gardée si longtemps avec fidélité.

Vers 554-556. (Ὁρῶ γὰρ ἥβην....) Je vois que ma rivale est en âge de croître en beauté, et moi en âge de décroître. L'œil des hommes court à l'une, et fuit l'autre.

Vers 557 et 558. (Ταῦτ' οὖν φοβοῦμαι μὴ πόσις μὲν Ἡρακλῆς Ἐμὸς καλῆται, τῆς νεωτέρας δ' ἀνήρ.) Je crains bien qu'Hercule ne soit à la vérité mon époux, mais qu'il ne soit le mari de l'autre, *i*. (*c'est-à-dire*) son[1] petit mari. Πόσις, mari, quand même il seroit séparé de sa femme ; ἀνήρ, quand il demeure avec elle. Ce dernier est tendre, l'autre est un titre seulement. Andromaque dit dans Homère (*Iliade*, livre XXIV, vers 725), en prenant la tête d'Hector : Ἄνερ, ἀπ' αἰῶνος νέος ὤλεο[2].

Vers 605. (Τί χρὴ ποιεῖν ;...) Scène 2. Lichas sort, pour s'en retourner auprès d'Hercule.

Vers 640. (Ὦ ναύλοχα καὶ πετραῖα....) Le Chœur demeure seul[3].

1. Racine avait d'abord écrit *mon*, puis il a effacé l'*m*, et mis une *s* au-dessus.
2. Voyez ci-dessus, dans les notes de Racine sur l'*Iliade*, p. 211, une observation semblable sur les mots πόσις et ἀνήρ. Là aussi le passage de Sophocle et celui d'Homère ont été comparés.
3. Après ce vers Racine n'a plus écrit de notes sur la tragédie des *Trachiniennes*; il a seulement continué à marquer les divisions en actes et en scènes.

Le *Philoctète* a cette note unique, écrite en tête de la pièce : « Belle manière d'expliquer le lieu de la scène dès le premier vers. — Cela ressemble un peu à l'ouverture de l'*Electra*. »

EURIPIDE.

L'*État des livres que* M. *Racine* (Louis Racine) *a remis à la Bibliothèque du Roi* indique un « *Euripide* grec, édition d'Alde, in-8°, où se trouvent quelques-unes de ses notes (*des notes de Jean Racine*) sur deux tragédies. » Outre cette édition aldine, le *Quérard* place dans la bibliothèque de Racine un *Euripide* de l'édition de Paul Estienne (1602), appartenant à la Bibliothèque de Toulouse.

Ces deux exemplaires sont les seuls sur les marges desquels nous ayons pu recueillir des notes de Racine; mais c'est pour les tragédies d'Euripide surtout que nous aurions peine à croire qu'il n'y ait pas eu d'autres volumes annotés par lui, qui se sont perdus ou dont l'existence nous a échappé. Le tragique grec que Racine a surtout imité, et qu'il avait par conséquent étudié avec tant de soin, a dû, ce nous semble, être lu plusieurs fois par lui, la plume à la main, et lui fournir plus d'observations critiques qu'on n'en trouve dans les exemplaires susdits des éditions d'Alde et de Paul Estienne. Sur les marges du premier de ces exemplaires, qui est conservé à la Bibliothèque impériale, l'auteur d'*Iphigénie* et de *Phèdre* n'a point laissé de notes sur l'*Iphigénie à Aulis*, et s'est contenté d'en souligner au crayon quelques passages peu nombreux; il s'est un peu plus occupé de l'*Hippolyte porte-couronne;* mais son annotation de cette pièce est bien courte, et ne va pas au delà du *Prologue*. Sur les marges du second, on trouve une seule observation sur un passage de l'*Iphigénie*, deux sur des vers de l'*Hippolyte*. Remarquons aussi que, dans l'un ni dans l'autre exemplaire, l'*Alceste* ni l'*Iphigénie en Tauride* n'ont laissé trace du travail dont ils auraient été l'objet pour Racine. Il avait cependant, on le sait, entrepris, en un temps de sa vie qu'il n'est pas possible de déterminer, d'emprunter aussi à Euripide ces deux sujets de tragédies. Qui ne pensera que Racine, au moment où il préparait les deux *chefs-d'œuvre* qu'il a transportés de la scène grecque sur la scène française, comme aussi à celui où il esquissait le plan d'une *Iphigénie en Tauride* et d'une *Alceste*, a sans doute fait sur quelque exemplaire différent de ceux que nous connaissons, une étude bien plus détaillée de son modèle? Il nous paraît à peu près certain que les notes sur les volumes des deux éditions dont nous avons parlé ont été faites avant ce moment, et lorsque Racine ne songeait encore à traiter aucun de ces sujets. Pour Euripide comme pour Sophocle, nous croyons vraisemblable que la plus ancienne des deux éditions annotées par Racine (celle d'Alde) l'a été la première. C'est d'elle en conséquence que nous parlerons d'abord. Dans l'édition de Paul Estienne, les développements plus longs donnés aux notes sur *les Phéniciennes* qu'aux notes sur les autres pièces, pourraient faire penser que ce travail est du temps où Racine avait déjà formé le projet d'écrire ses *Frères ennemis*. Toutefois aucune de ses remarques sur la tragédie d'Euripide n'est de nature à établir la certitude de cette conjecture.

L'exemplaire de l'édition d'Alde forme deux tomes in-8°, à la fin de chacun desquels on lit : *Venetiis apud Aldum mense februario M.D.III*. Le *Philologue*, que nous avons déjà deux fois cité, a donné au tome VI (p. 121-129), avec une exactitude à peu près irréprochable, les notes que nous avons nous-mêmes recueillies à notre tour sur cet exemplaire. L'annotation y commence à *Médée*, qui est la quatrième tragédie du tome I; les trois tragédies précédentes, *Hécube*, *Oreste* et *les Phéniciennes*, ne sont pas annotées.

NOTES SUR *MÉDÉE*.

Vers 1-45. La nourrice de Médée fait le Prologue. Elle le fait avec passion et explique l'état des affaires.

Vers 1. (Εἴθ' ὤφελ' Ἀργοῦς....) Cicéron cite souvent ce vers[1] :

Utinam ne in nemore Pelio..., etc.

Vers 20. (Μήδεια δ' ἡ δύστηνος....) Description de la douleur de Médée.

Vers 36. (Στυγεῖ δὲ παῖδας....) Il (*Euripide*) prépare le meurtre de ses enfants.

Vers 44. (Δεινὴ γάρ....) Il est dangereux d'offenser Médée.

Vers 49. (Παλαιὸν οἴκων κτῆμα....) Scène 1. Le gouverneur des enfants de Médée les amène sur la scène. — Ainsi tout le sujet est expliqué par une nourrice qui s'entretient avec un pédagogue. Ils s'en acquittent bien et par de beaux vers; mais je doute que Sophocle eût voulu commencer une tragédie par de tels personnages.

Vers 57. (Ὥσθ' ἵμερός μ' ὑπῆλθε....) Elle rend raison pourquoi elle est venue sur la scène.

Vers 68. (Πεσσοὺς προσελθών....) (*Étant venu*) aux lieux où l'on joue aux dés.

Vers 79. (Νέον παλαιῷ, πρὶν τόδ' ἐξηντληκέναι.) Malheur nouveau avant que de s'être fait au premier.

Vers 83. (Ὄλοιτο μὲν μή....) Plainte modeste d'un domestique.

Vers 86. (Ὡς πᾶς τις αὑτὸν τοῦ πέλας μᾶλλον φιλεῖ.) Amour-propre.

Vers 91. (Καὶ μὴ πέλαζε μητρί....) Cachez ces enfants à leur mère.

Vers 92. (Ἤδη γὰρ εἶδον ὄμμα....) Préparation de leur mort.

Vers 96. (Δύστανος ἐγώ....) Scène 2. Médée parle derrière la scène. Elle parle en s'écriant dans la douleur.

Vers 105. (Ἴτε νῦν, χωρεῖθ'....) La Nourrice fait rentrer les enfants.

---

1. Voyez *ad Herennium*, II, 22; *de Inventione*, I, 49; *Topica*, 16; *de Finibus*, I, 2; *de Natura Deorum*, III, 30; *de Fato*, 15. La traduction latine citée par Cicéron est celle d'Ennius.

Vers 109. (Μεγαλόσπλαγχνος, δυσκατάπαυστος.) Beaux mots pour décrire une femme implacable.

Vers 112 et 114. (Παῖδες, ὄλοισθε....) Médée souhaite que tout périsse.

Vers 119-121. (Δεινὰ τυράννων λήματα....) Les rois font de grandes fautes, ils savent mal obéir, et peuvent tout. Leurs colères sont affreuses.

Vers 123. (Ἔμοιγ' οὖν, εἰ μὴ μεγάλως....) Louanges de la vie médiocre.

Vers 131. (Ἔκλυον φωνάν....) Le Chœur est de femmes corinthiennes. Elles viennent plaindre Médée quoique étrangère, parce que son époux lui manque de foi; et sa cause est la cause commune de tout le sexe.

Vers 144. (Αἲ αἲ διά μου κεφαλᾶς....) Médée souhaite la mort.

Vers 160. (Ὦ μεγάλα Θέμι....) Médée invoque Thémis et Diane, qui est la même qu'Hécate.

Vers 173. (Πῶς ἂν ἐς ὄψιν....) Le Chœur demande à voir Médée, pour essayer de la consoler.

Vers 187. (Καίτοι τοκάδος δέργμα λεαίνης....) Chagrin bien exprimé. — Médée est inaccessible à tous ses domestiques dans son chagrin.

Vers 192-197. (Οἵτινες ὕμνους....) On a inventé la musique pour les festins, où il n'y a déjà que trop de joie, et on n'a point songé à en inventer pour calmer les afflictions. — Cette moralité est agréable, mais peu tragique.

Vers 209. (Τὰν Ζηνὸς ὁρκίαν Θέμιν....) Thémis a amené Médée dans la Grèce, parce qu'elle s'est fiée aux serments.

Vers 214. (Κορίνθιαι γυναῖκες....) Scène 1 (*de l'acte II*). Médée sort.

Vers 215-217. (Οἶδα γὰρ πολλοὺς βροτῶν....) Pourquoi cette moralité, au lieu de dire simplement: *Je sors, puisque vous avez souhaité de me voir; et je ne veux pas passer dans votre esprit pour une femme superbe?* — On trouve superbes et ceux qui se cachent, et ceux qui se montrent.

Vers 220. (Ὅστις πρὶν ἀνδρὸς σπλάγχνον....) On hait des hommes sur leur physionomie.

Vers 231. (Γυναῖκές ἐσμεν ἀθλιώτατον φυτόν.) Malheurs des femmes.

Vers 233. (Πόσιν πρίασθαι....) Nous achetons un maître bien cher.

Vers 238-251. (Ἐς καινὰ δ' ἤθη....) Tout cela est plus comique que tragique, quoique beau et bien exprimé.

Vers 244-247. (Ἀνὴρ δ' ὅταν τοῖς ἔνδον....) Quand un homme est chagrin chez soi, il n'a qu'à sortir, ce que nous ne pouvons pas.

Vers 251. (Θέλοιμ' ἂν μᾶλλον ἢ τεκεῖν ἅπαξ.) Péril de l'accouchement.

Vers 252-259. (Ἀλλ' οὐ γὰρ αὐτὸς....) Médée rentre dans le sujet.

Vers 263. (Σιγᾶν....) Médée prie les Corinthiennes de garder le silence, si elle forme quelques desseins contre la vie de leur roi et de leur princesse. Quelle apparence? Euripide justifie cela le mieux qu'il peut par l'intérêt commun des femmes, qui sont toutes offensées en Médée.

Vers 263-266. (Γυνὴ γὰρ τἄλλα μὲν φόβου πλέα.) La femme est craintive, et n'ose souffrir la lueur d'une épée; mais rien n'est plus terrible quand elle se croit offensée dans les droits de sa couche.

Vers 267. (Δράσω τάδε....) Le Chœur lui promet de se taire[1].

NOTES SUR *HIPPOLYTE*.

Vers 1. Vénus fait le Prologue. Elle déclare sa colère contre Hippolyte qui la méprise, et dit qu'elle le va perdre.

Vers 11. (Ἁγνοῦ Πιτθέως παιδεύματα.) Hippolyte avoit été élevé chez le sage Pitthée, père d'Æthra, mère de Thésée.

Vers 12. (Τῆς δὲ γῆς Τροιζηνίας....) La scène est à Trœzène.

Vers 15. (Φοίβου δ' ἀδελφὴν....) Hippolyte ne sert que Diane.

Vers 27. (Ἰδοῦσα Φαίδρα....) Phèdre l'a vu à Athènes, aux sacrés mystères.

Vers 28. (Τοῖς ἐμοῖς βουλεύμασι.) Vénus, pour excuser Phèdre, dit qu'elle l'a fait devenir amoureuse.

Vers 34-36. (Ἐπεὶ δὲ Θησεὺς....) Thésée fuit Athènes pour le meurtre des Pallantides. — Il amène avec lui Phèdre à Trœzène.

Vers 42-48. (Δείξω δὲ Θησεῖ....) Vénus prédit le dénouement.

Vers 45. (Ἄναξ Ποσειδῶν....) Promesse de Neptune à Thésée.

Vers 48-50. (Τὸ γὰρ τῆς δ' οὐ προτιμήσω καλὸν....) Vénus sacrifie Phèdre pour se venger de son ennemi.

Vers 58. (Ἕπεσθ' ἀείδοντες....) Hippolyte entre avec un chœur de chasseurs.

Vers 274. (Πῶς δ' οὔ; τριταίαν....) Phèdre se veut laisser mourir de faim.

Vers 284. (Ἔκδημος ὢν γάρ....) Thésée absent.

Vers 308-312. (Εἰ θανῇ προδοῦσα σοὺς....) Vous laisserez vos enfants esclaves d'Hippolyte[2].

---

1. Les notes de Racine sur *Médée* ne vont pas au delà de ce vers.
2. Là s'arrêtent les notes sur *Hippolyte*. Dans la scène de Phèdre et de la Nourrice (vers 177-361), que Racine a si admirablement imitée, on remarque, outre les trois courtes notes que nous venons de donner, beaucoup de vers soulignés par lui; ce sont généralement ceux que, dans la scène correspon-

NOTES SUR *LES BACCHANTES*.

Vers 1 et suivants. Bacchus dit qu'après avoir parcouru toute l'Asie, il vient en Grèce et commence par Thèbes, son pays, pour y faire reconnoître sa divinité, laquelle est niée par Penthée, le neveu de sa mère, et par les deux sœurs de sa mère, Ino et Agave, et presque par tous les Thébains. Il a pris pour cela la figure d'un jeune homme.

Vers 8. (Ἔτι ζῶσαν φλόγα.) Les fondements de la maison de Sémélé brûloient encore.

Vers 14. (Ἡλιοβλήτους πλάκας.) Champs exposés au soleil.

Vers 23 et 24. (Νεβρίδ' ἐξάψας χροὸς, Θύρσον τε δοὺς ἐς χεῖρα....) Peau de faon de cerf. — *Thyrse*, javelot fait de bois de lierre.

Vers 27. (Σεμέλην δὲ νυμφευθεῖσαν....) Calomnies contre Sémélé.

Vers 35 et 36. (Καὶ πᾶν τὸ θῆλυ....) Bacchus a fait autant de Bacchantes de toutes les Thébaines.

Vers 43-45. (Κάδμος μὲν οὖν....) Cadmus a abandonné l'empire à Penthée, fils de sa fille, ennemi de Bacchus.

Vers 50-52. (Ἢν δὲ Θηβαίων πόλις....) Bacchus dit que si les Thébains s'arment contre lui, il leur opposera une armée de Bacchantes.

Vers 64. (Ἀσίας ἀπὸ γᾶς....) Le Chœur est de Bacchantes de Lydie, qui suivent Bacchus partout où il va.

Vers 72-74. (Ὦ μάκαρ, ὅστις....) Heureux qui est admis aux mystères des Dieux, et qui mène une vie pure.

Vers 101-104. (Ταυρόκερων θεὸν....) Bacchus avoit des cornes de taureau, et étoit couronné de dragons. De là vient que les Bacchantes se couronnent de même.

Vers 109-113. (Καὶ καταβακχιοῦσθε....) Habillement des Bacchantes.

---

dante de sa *Phèdre*, il s'est appropriés, et que nous avons eu à citer dans les notes sur cette tragédie.

Les deux tragédies qui suivent dans l'édition d'Alde, *Alceste* et *Andromaque*, n'ont pas été annotées. Dans *les Suppliantes*, beaucoup de vers sont soulignés au crayon rouge; mais il n'y a qu'une note, sur le passage qui est aux vers 861-867 :

Καπανεὺς ὅδ' ἐστίν.... κ. τ. λ.

« Capanée. Idée d'un véritable homme de bien. » — L'*Iphigénie à Aulis*, l'*Iphigénie en Tauride*, *Rhésus* et *les Troyennes* sont sans notes.

Vers 118. (Ἀφ' ἱστῶν παρά....) Les femmes quittoient la quenouille.

Vers 121. (Ζάθεοί τε Κρῆτες....) Divins Crétois.

Vers 126-129. (Ἀνὰ δὲ βάκχια συντόνῳ....) Instruments des Bacchantes et des hommes pleins de Bacchus. Le tambour de Cybèle, les flûtes et la voix.

Vers 139. (Αἷμα τραγοκτόνον....) Bacchus aimoit le sang des boucs.

Vers 143 et 144. (Ῥέει δὲ γάλακτι πέδον....) Partout où il va, la terre coule de vin, de lait, de miel, et l'encens fume.

Vers 145-150. (Ὁ Βακχεὺς δ' ἔχων....) Bacchus porte un flambeau allumé, et inspire sa fureur par des chants et par des danses, abandonnant ses cheveux au vent.

Vers 149. (Ἰαχαῖς τ' ἀναπάλλων.) Chant de Bacchus pour exciter les Bacchantes.

Vers 156. (Βαρυβρόμων ὑπὸ τυμπάνων.) Tambours de grand bruit.

Vers 160. (Λωτὸς ὅταν εὐκέλαδος....) La flûte donne le signal de la danse.

Vers 170. (Τίς ἐν πύλαισιν....) Acte 1er, scène 1. Tirésias vient appeler Cadmus, pour aller de compagnie sur la montagne de Cithéron se mêler aux Bacchantes.

Vers 177. (Στεφανοῦν τε κρᾶτα....) Ils se couronnoient de lierre.

Vers 186. (Γέρων γέροντα....) Vieillard qui en instruit un autre.

Vers 201 et 202. (Πατρὸς παραδοχὰς..., οὐδεὶς αὐτὰ καταβάλλει λόγος.) Il s'en faut tenir à la religion de ses pères.

Vers 206-209. (Οὐ γὰρ διήρηχ' ὁ Θεὸς....) Dieu n'accepte point les personnes [1].

Vers 215. (Ἔκδημος ὤν....) Scène 2. Penthée sort. Il est superbe et impie, sous prétexte de défendre les bonnes mœurs.

Vers 217-228. Penthée se plaint que toutes les femmes ont abandonné leurs maisons. Il dit que sous prétexte de célébrer les mystères de Bacchus, elles s'abandonnent à Vénus. Il en a fait enfermer une partie, et veut faire arrêter le reste.

Vers 234-236. Il dit qu'il est arrivé un jeune homme enchanteur, beau, et ayant toutes les grâces de Vénus, (*dans les yeux*, ὄσσοις) i. (*c'est-à-dire*) les yeux noirs.

Vers 237. (Ὃς ἡμέρας τε κεὐφρόνας....) Il croit que Bacchus débauche les femmes.

Vers 240. (Παύσω....) Il menace de le faire mourir.

---

1. Racine a voulu rapprocher des vers d'Euripide le *Non est personarum acceptor Deus* de l'Écriture : voyez les *Actes des Apôtres*, chapitre x, verset 34, et beaucoup d'autres passages de l'*Ancien* et du *Nouveau Testament*, où, avec quelque différence dans l'expression, se trouve la même pensée.

Vers 242. (Ἐκεῖνος εἶναί φησι....) Il ne croit point qu'il soit fils de Jupiter.

Vers 249 et 250. (Τειρεσίαν ὁρῶ Πατέρα τε μητρὸς τῆς ἐμῆς....) Il se moque de Cadmus, son grand-père, et de Tirésias.

Vers 268. (Σὺ δ' εὔτροχον μὲν γλῶσσαν....) Grand parleur.

Vers 288-295. (Ἐπεί νιν ἥρπασ'....) Tirésias justifie Bacchus et sa naissance. — Explication de la naissance de Bacchus, et de la cuisse de Jupiter, qui n'est autre chose qu'un endroit de l'air où Jupiter le fit nourrir.

Vers 296 et 297. (Ὄνομα μεταστήσαντες....) Cela est bien tiré par les cheveux [1].

Vers 298 et 299. (Ὁ δαίμων ὅδε· τὸ γὰρ βακχεύσιμον Καὶ τὸ μανιῶδες....) N^a. Façons de parler platoniciennes [2].

Vers 301-305. (Λέγειν τὸ μέλλον....) Qualités de Bacchus. Devin. Guerrier. Furieux.

Vers 311 et 312. (Μηδ', ἢν δοκῇς μὲν....) Mauvaises opinions d'un savant.

Vers 313. (Καὶ σπένδε καὶ βάκχευε....) Tirésias veut persuader Penthée d'honorer Bacchus.

Vers 314-318. (Οὐχ ὁ Διόνυσος....) Il justifie la chasteté des Bacchantes.

Vers 331. (Οἴκει μεθ' ἡμῶν....) Cadmus prie Penthée de se rendre.

Vers 337. (Ὁρᾷς τὸν Ἀκταίωνος ἄθλιον μόρον;) Actéon étoit cousin germain de Penthée.

Vers 341. (Δεῦρό σου στέψω κάρα....) Il veut couronner Penthée, qui le repousse.

Vers 350. (Καὶ στέμματ' ἀνέμοις....) Il (*Penthée*) fait renverser les couronnes et la chaire de Tirésias.

Vers 355. (Κἄνπερ λάβητε....) Penthée donne ordre qu'on arrête Bacchus.

Vers 360. (Ἐξαιτώμεθα....) Tirésias exhorte Cadmus à prier Bacchus pour son petit-fils.

Vers 365. (Γέροντε δ' αἰσχρὸν δύο πεσεῖν....) Deux vieillards qui tombent.

Vers 370-372. (Ὁσία, πότνα Θεῶν....) O sainte et vénérable Thémis qui voles sur la terre avec des ailes d'or. — Le Chœur demande justice à Thémis des paroles injurieuses de Penthée contre Bacchus.

---

1. Cette remarque s'applique au rapprochement de μηρῷ et de ὠμήρευσε.
2. Racine a souligné les mots δαίμων, βακχεύσιμον et μανιῶδες.

Vers 376. (Τὸν παρὰ καλλιστεφάνοις εὐφροσύναις....) Louanges de Bacchus, le père de la joie.

Vers 385. (Ἀχαλίνων στομάτων....) Bouches sans frein.

Vers 388-391. (Ὁ δὲ τᾶς ἡσυχίας....) *Beati mites*[1].

Vers 393. (Τὸ σοφὸν δ' οὐ σοφία....) *N*^a. Ce n'est pas être sage que d'être si fin[2].

L'*Euripide*, de la Bibliothèque de Toulouse, annoté par Racine, a pour titre : ΕΥΡΙΠΙΔΟΥ ΤΡΑΓΩΔΙΩΝ ὅσαι σώζονται. *Euripidis tragœdiæ quæ extant. Cum latina Gulielmi Canteri interpretatione.... Excudebat Paulus Stephanus. Anno M.D.C.II. Coloniæ Allobrogum* (2 tomes in-4° en un volume). Sur le feuillet de titre est la signature de Racine. Il n'y a, dans cet exemplaire, de notes marginales que sur *les Phéniciennes*, l'*Hippolyte*, l'*Iphigénie en Aulide*, l'*Ion* et l'*Électre*, mais elles ne sont un peu nombreuses que sur la première de ces pièces. La *Nouvelle Revue encyclopédique* avait donné ces notes, en 1846, d'après la transcription de M. Félix Ravaisson. On les trouve dans la même livraison d'octobre où sont, comme nous l'avons dit, les notes sur l'*Électre* d'Eschyle. Nous avons, pour l'*Euripide*, comparé la transcription de M. Dulaurier, comme nous l'avions fait pour l'*Eschyle*.

NOTES SUR *LES PHÉNICIENNES*.

Vers 88. (Ὦ κλεινὸν οἴκοις....) Il (*le Pédagogue*) rend raison de sa sortie (*de la sortie d'Antigone*) sur la scène.

Vers 96 et 95. (Πάντα δ' ἐξειδὼς, φράσω Ἅ τ' εἶδον....) Il rend raison pourquoi il connoît tout dans l'armée.

Vers 120. (Τίς οὗτος ὁ λευκολόφας....) Tout ceci n'est point de l'action; mais le poëte a voulu imiter une chose qui est belle dans

---

1. Racine cite les paroles de l'*Évangile de saint Matthieu*, chapitre v, verset 4.

2. Dans les dernières pièces de cette édition, qui sont *le Cyclope, les Héraclides, Hélène, Ion, Hercule furieux*, on ne trouve pas de notes de Racine, si ce n'est une seule sur le vers 575 des *Héraclides* :

Ὥσπερ σύ· μηδὲν μᾶλλον ἀρκέσουσι γάρ.

« *I. (c'est-à-dire)* rien ne les fera plus longtemps durer. » Le sens donné par Racine, d'après un texte mal ponctué, n'est pas le véritable; il paraît avoir vu dans ce passage une idée analogue à cette promesse qui accompagne, dans le *Décalogue*, le quatrième commandement : *Ut longo vivas tempore*. (*Deutéronome*, chapitre v, verset 16.)

Homère, l'entretien d'Hélène et de Priam sur les murs de Troie [1].

Vers 179 et 180. (Ὦ λιπαροζώνου θύγατερ Ἀελίου, Σελαναία....) La Lune fille du Soleil.

Vers 199. (Ὦ Διὸς ἔρνος, Ἄρτεμι.) Diane fille de Jupiter [2].

Vers 201-205. (Ὦ τέκνον....) Raison pourquoi Antigone rentre.

Vers 206-208. (Φιλόψογον γὰρ χρῆμα....) Les femmes aiment à parler.

Vers 210 et suivants. (Τύριον οἶδμα λιποῦσ', ἔβαν....) Le Chœur explique qui il est, et pourquoi il est encore à Thèbes [3].

Vers 218 et 219. (Ἀκαρπίστων Πεδίων Σικελίας....) Petite ile qu'il appelle stérile, pour la distinguer de la grande.

Vers 268. (Τὰ μὲν πυλωρῶν κλεῖθρά μ' εἰσέδεξατο.) Polynice vient tout seul, s'assurant sur la parole qu'on lui a donnée.

Vers 272. (Ὧν οὕνεκ' ὄμμα πανταχῇ διοιστέον.) Il exprime son inquiétude.

Vers 311 et 312. (Ἰώ, τέκνον, χρόνῳ Σὸν ὄμμα μυρίαις τ' ἐν ἀμέραις Προσεῖδον.) Affection d'Iocaste en voyant son fils.

Vers 328. (Ἄπεπλος φαρέων λευκῶν....) Elle est habillée de deuil.

Vers 334. (Ἐπ' αὐτόχειρά τε σφαγάν.) Elle lui apprend l'état où est OEdipe.

Vers 346. (Ἐγὼ δ' οὔτε σοι πυρὸς ἀνῆψα φῶς.) Elle se plaint qu'elle n'a point été présente à ses noces.

Vers 358. (Δεινὸν γυναιξὶν αἱ δι' ὠδίνων γοναί.) I. (*c'est-à-dire*) que les douleurs de l'enfantement redoublent l'amour pour les enfants.

Vers 360. (Μᾶτερ, φρονῶν εὖ κοὐ φρονῶν ἀφικόμαν.) Polynice confesse lui-même son imprudence de venir parmi ses ennemis.

Vers 369 et 370. (Πολύδακρυς δ' ἀφικόμην Χρόνιος Ἰδὼν μέλαθρα....) Tendresse pour les lieux où l'on est né.

Vers 377. (Ὡς δεινὸν ἐχθρά, μᾶτερ, οἰκείων φίλων.) Haine de parents.

Vers 380 et 381. (Τί δὲ κασίγνητοι δύο; Ἦ που στένουσι...;) Il demande des nouvelles de ses deux sœurs. M'ont-elles pleuré?

Vers 390 et 391. (Καὶ δὴ σ' ἐρωτῶ πρῶτον....) Ces interrogations ne sont point nécessaires au sujet ; mais elles sont tendres et du caractère d'une mère.

Vers 394. (Ἓν μὲν μέγιστον, οὐκ ἔχει παρρησίαν.) Misères de l'exil.

Vers 402. (Ἔχουσιν Ἀφροδίτην τιν' ἡδεῖαν θεόν.) Les espérances ont une Vénus.

---

1. Voyez l'*Iliade*, livre III, vers 161-242.
2. Racine a sans doute fait cette note et celle qui précède, parce que cette diversité de filiation de la Lune et de Diane lui a paru digne de remarque.
3. A la marge de la scolie sur le vers 210, Racine a écrit : « Raison pourquoi le Chœur est de femmes étrangères. »

Vers 406. (Τὰ φίλων δ' οὐδὲν, ἤν τις δυστυχῇ.) Amis inutiles aux malheureux.

Vers 408. (Τὸ γένος οὐκ ἔβοσκέ με....) Noblesse inutile.

Vers 411. (Πῶς δ' ἦλθες Ἄργος;...) Ceci est un peu plus du sujet.

Vers 418 et suivants. (Νὺξ ἦν....) Mariages de Polynice et de Tydée.

Vers 434. (Πάρεισι, λυπρὰν χάριν....) Il donne de l'honnêteté à Polynice, en exprimant sa douleur.

Vers 446. (Καὶ μὴν Ἐτεοκλῆς....) Il donne plus de violence à Étéocle.

Vers 450. (Τί χρὴ δρᾶν; ἀρχέτω δή τις λόγου.) Il ne veut pas nommer son frère.

Vers 451 et 452. (Ὡς ἀμφὶ τείχη....) Il marque qu'il a donné ses ordres pour cette entrevue.

Vers 455. (Ἐπίσχες· οὔτι τὸ ταχὺ τὴν δίκην ἔχει.) Les discours si prompts ne produisent rien de bon.

Vers 458. (Οὐ γὰρ τὸ λαιμότμητον εἰσορᾷς κάρα.) Aversion d'Étéocle contre son frère très-bien marquée. Ils ne veulent point [se] regarder.

Vers 467. (Κακῶν δὲ τῶν πρὶν μηδενὸς μνείαν ἔχειν.) Moyen de se réconcilier : c'est d'oublier le passé.

Vers 472 et 473. (Ἁπλοῦς ὁ μῦθος τῆς ἀληθείας ἔφυ, Κοὐ ποικίλων δεῖτ'....) La raison n'a pas besoin de longs discours.

Vers 480. (Δοὺς τῷδ' ἀνάσσειν πατρίδος ἐνιαυτοῦ κύκλον.) Il ne veut point non plus nommer son frère.

Vers 502 et 503. (Εἰ πᾶσι ταὐτὸ καλὸν ἔφυ....) Si tout le monde pensoit les mêmes choses, il n'y auroit point de disputes.

Vers 507. (Ἄστρων ἀνέλθοιμ' ἡλίου πρὸς ἀνατολάς....) Envie de régner.

Vers 524. (Πρὸς ταῦτ' ἴτω μοι πῦρ, ἴτω δὲ φάσγανα....) Fureur de régner.

Vers 531. (Ὦ τέκνον, οὐχ ἅπαντα τῷ γήρᾳ κακά....) Discours d'Iocaste bien convenable à une mère.

Vers 534. (Τί τῆς κακίστης δαιμόνων...;) A Étéocle[1]. — Contre l'ambition.

Vers 546 et 547. (Νυκτός τ' ἀφεγγὲς βλέφαρον, ἡλίου τε φῶς Ἴσον βαδίζειν....) Égalité.

Vers 558 et 559. (Οὔ τοι τὰ χρήματ' ἴδια....) Les biens sont des dépôts que les Dieux retirent quand ils veulent.

---

1. Un peu plus bas, Racine a aussi marqué que le vers 571 : Σοὶ μὲν τάδ' αὐδῶ..., est adressé à Polynice.

Vers 575. (Τροπαῖα πῶς ἀναστήσεις δορός;) Où dresserez-vous vos trophées?

Vers 591. (Μᾶτερ, οὐ λόγων ἔστ' ἀγών....) Violence d'Étéocle.

Vers 599. ('Εγγὺς, οὐ πρόσω βέβηκας. Εἰς χέρας λεύσσεις ἐμάς;) Ceci est extrêmement vif.

Vers 618-620. (Πατέρα δέ μοι δὸς ἰδεῖν.... Ὦ κασίγνηται....) Ceci est fort tendre.

Vers 624. (Ποῦ ποτε στήσῃ πρὸ πύργων;...) Haine, appel.

Vers 697. (Χώρει σὺ....) Cette scène est languissante, et n'est point nécessaire au sujet.

Vers 841. ('Ηγοῦ προπάροιθε....) Cette scène de Tirésias n'est point assez nécessaire pour intéresser.

Vers 949-955. (Σὺ δ' ἐνθάδ' ἡμῖν λοιπὸς εἶ....) Causes trop recherchées pour faire mourir Ménécée. Ce peu de nécessité rend froide une action très-belle.

Vers 965 et 966. (Φοῖβον ἀνθρώποις μόνον Χρῆν θεσπιῳδεῖν....) Il n'appartient qu'aux Dieux de dire la vérité.

Vers 999 et 1000. (Γυναῖκες, ὡς εὖ πατρὸς ἐξεῖλον φόβον Κλέψας λόγοισιν....) Cette action de Ménécée est trop grande pour être faite comme en passant. Cela devroit être préparé avec bien plus d'éclat. — Κλέψας λόγοισιν, cette feinte est belle.

Vers 1026. (Ἔβας, ἔβας....) Le Commentaire marque fort bien [1] que le Chœur s'amuse mal à propos à parler de la Sphinx, lorsqu'il devoit parler de Ménécée.

Vers 1097. ('Επεὶ Κρέοντος παῖς....) Cette mort méritoit d'être racontée plus au long, au lieu de décrire des boucliers.

Vers 1188. (Βάλλει κεραυνῷ Ζεύς νιν....) Description de Capanée foudroyé.

Vers 1215. (Ἔα τὰ λοιπά· δεῦρ' ἀεὶ γὰρ εὐτυχεῖς.) Ceci rentre dans le sujet.

Vers 1265. ('Αλλ' εἴ τιν' ἀλκὴν....) Pourquoi donc avoir fait un si long récit dans un péril si pressant?

Vers 1270. (Ὦ τέκνον, ἔξελθ', 'Αντιγόνη, δόμων πάρος.) Cette petite scène est du sujet, et elle est tendre.

Vers 1290. (Αἶ, αἶ, αἶ, αἶ· τρομερὰν φρίκαν.) Ce Chœur est plus du sujet que les autres.

Vers 1323. ('Εμός τε γὰρ παῖς γῆς ὄλωλ' ὑπερθανών....) Fils qui meurt généreusement.

Vers 1365. (Τὰ μὲν πρὸ πύργων εὐτυχήματα χθονὸς....) Ce récit est fort beau.

---

1. Voyez en effet, à la page 352 de cette édition de Paul Estienne, la scolie qui commence par ces mots : Πρὸς οὐδὲν ταῦτα.

Vers 1378. (Αἴσχιστον αἰτῶ στέφανον, ὁμογενῆ κτανεῖν.) Polynice est toujours honnête.

Vers 1437 et suivants. (Ἐπεὶ τέκνω πεσόντ' ἐλειπέτην βίον....) Ceci est pathétique.

Vers 1460. (Ξυνάρμοσον δὲ βλέφαρά μου τῇ σῇ χερί....) Cela est fort tendre.

Vers 1493. (Οὐ προκαλυπτομένα βοστρυχώδης....) Le reste de la pièce est inutile et même languissant.

Vers 1583. (Οὔκουν σ' ἐάσω τήνδε γῆν οἰκεῖν ἔτι.) Créon est méchant inutilement, lui qui ne l'est point dans le reste de la pièce.

NOTES SUR *HIPPOLYTE*.

Vers 307. (Μὰ τὴν ἄνασσαν ἱππείαν Ἀμαζόνα....) On jure quelquefois par ses ennemis pour leur insulter. *J'en jure par sa poltronnerie, etc.*

Vers 634 et 635. (Ἔχει δ' ἀνάγκην, ὥστε κηδεύσας καλοῖς Γαμβροῖσι, χαίρων σώζεται πικρὸν λέχος.) Comique.

NOTE UNIQUE SUR *IPHIGÉNIE A AULIS*.

Vers 1532 et 1533. (Ὦ Τυνδαρεία παῖ, Κλυταιμνήστρα, δόμων Ἔξω πέρασον....) Cela est bien brusque.

NOTES SUR *ION*.

Vers 758. (Εἴπωμεν ἢ σιγῶμεν;...) Le Chœur trahit le secret qu'on lui a confié.

Vers 989-995. (Ἐνταῦθα Γοργόν' ἔτεκε Γῆ....) L'Égide; sa description.

Vers 1125. (Ξοῦθος μὲν ᾤχετ', ἔνθα πῦρ πηδᾷ Θεοῦ....) Quelle apparence que Xuthus ne soit pas du festin où il a dit lui-même qu'il vouloit assister avec son fils?

Vers 1146-1158. (Ἐνῆν δ' ὑφανταὶ γράμμασιν τοιαῖδ' ὑφαί.) Belle tapisserie.

Vers 1175. (Σμύρνης ἱδρῶτα....) La sueur de la myrrhe.

Vers 1257 et 1258. (Καὶ μὴν οἶδ' ἀγωνισταὶ πικροὶ Δεῦρ' ἐπείγονται ξιφήρεις....) Que deviennent ces satellites dans la suite? Entendent-ils tout ce qui se dit?

NOTES SUR *ÉLECTRE*.

Vers 921-924. ("Ιστω δ', ὅταν τις διολέσας δάμαρτά του.) Beaux vers à contre-temps.

Vers 1177-1180. (Ἰὼ Γᾶ καὶ Ζεῦ.) Repentir trop prompt.

Vers 1213-1215. (Βοὰν δ' ἔλασκε τάνδε πρὸς γένυν ἐμὰν Τιθεῖσα γέρας· τέκος ἐμὸν, λιταίνω.) Horrible.

Vers 1283. (Εἴδωλον Ἑλένης ἐξέπεμψ' εἰς Ἴλιον.) Simulacre d'Hélène.

PLATON.

Jean-Baptiste Racine, dans une note que nous avons reproduite à la page 436 de notre tome V, parle d'un *Platon* et d'un *Plutarque* qui avaient appartenu à son père, et « dont les marges étoient chargées d'apostilles de sa main. » L'exemplaire de Platon qu'il désignait est-il celui de l'édition de Bâle (1534), qui a des notes marginales de Racine et est conservé à la Bibliothèque impériale : *Platonis omnia Opera.... Basileæ, apud Joan. Valderum, mense Martio, anno M.D.XXXIIII* (1 vol. in-folio)? ou bien celui de l'édition de Henri Estienne (1578) que possède la Bibliothèque de Toulouse, et sur lequel on trouve aussi des notes de la même main : *Platonis augustiss. Philosophi omnia quæ extant Opera, græce et latine, ex nova Joannis Serrani interpretatione* (3 vol. in-folio)? Il s'agissait plus probablement du premier, dont l'annotation est beaucoup plus étendue. Louis Racine, dans l'*État des livres*, remis par lui à la Bibliothèque du Roi, mentionne comme ayant appartenu à son père : *Quelques traités grecs de Platon, petit in-folio, où sont quelques-unes de ses notes.* Nous ne pouvons reconnaître dans cette désignation aucune des deux éditions complètes dont nous venons de parler; ce doit être encore un autre volume dont nous n'avons pas retrouvé la trace.

L'exemplaire de l'édition de 1534 qui a appartenu à Racine, et que nous avons eu déjà l'occasion de citer dans quelques-unes des notes sur la traduction du *Banquet*[1], porte sa signature sur le feuillet de titre. Les marges du volume ont un grand nombre de notes de sa main, les unes en latin, les autres en français.

Cette édition de Platon, qui est une des plus anciennes et ne donne que le texte grec, est beaucoup moins belle que celle de 1578; il est vraisemblable qu'elle est la première que Racine ait possédée, au temps sans doute où sa bibliothèque ne pouvait encore être très-riche; et l'étude très-détaillée pour laquelle il s'en est servi semble bien appartenir aux années de sa jeunesse. C'est donc cette étude que nous ferons d'abord connaître, et nous donnerons à la suite les notes peu nombreuses de l'exemplaire de 1578, qui, à l'exception de deux, sont toutes sur le livre VI de la *République*.

Les notes de Racine en latin sont très-multipliées sur les marges de l'exemplaire de Bâle; nous avons dû nous borner à en recueillir quelques-unes, qui suffiront pour indiquer la nature de ce travail; nous avons choisi celles qui sont accompagnées d'un *Nota*, par lequel l'annotateur marquait qu'un passage l'avait particulièrement frappé, et celles dans lesquelles il avait indiqué un rapprochement, soit avec les dogmes chrétiens, soit avec quelque idée ou quel-

---

1. Voyez notre tome V, p. 453, 454, 455, 457 et 458.

que fait moderne. Quant aux notes en rançais, nous n'avons retranché que celles qui nous ont paru tout à fait insignifiantes.

Les trois premiers dialogues, l'*Euthyphron*, l'*Apologie de Socrate*, le *Criton* (p. 1-22), n'ont que des notes latines [1]. Comme celles que nous citons du second et du troisième sont peu nombreuses et éloignées les unes des autres, et qu'il en est de même pour le *Phédon*, qui suit, et qui a quelques notes françaises mêlées aux notes latines, nous indiquons, pour ces premiers dialogues, les passages grecs auxquels se rapporte l'annotation. Dans les autres dialogues, à partir du *Banquet*, nous nous contentons de renvoyer à la page de l'édition de Bâle où elles se trouvent, en joignant au chiffre de cette page les mots par lesquels elle commence, et ceux par lesquels elle finit.

NOTES SUR L'*APOLOGIE DE SOCRATE*.

Page 7, lignes 25 et 26. (Ἀλλ' ἐκεῖνοι δεινότεροι.... οἱ ὑμῶν τοὺς πολλοὺς ἐκ παίδων παραλαμβάνοντες, ἔπειθον.) N^a. Jés. (*Nota. Jésuites.*)

Page 12, ligne 10. (Πείσομαι δὲ τῷ Θεῷ μᾶλλον ἢ ὑμῖν.) N^a. *Obedire Deo magis quam hominibus* [2].

Ibidem, ligne 31. (Οὐ γὰρ οἶμαι θεμιτὸν εἶναι ἀμείνονι ἀνδρὶ ὑπὸ χείρονος βλάπτεσθαι.) N^a. *Neque bono cuiquam mali nocere possunt.*

Ibidem, ligne 41. (Ἀχθόμενοι ὥσπερ οἱ νυστάζοντες ἐγειρόμενοι.) N^a. *Peccantes objurgatorem ferre non possunt, ut dormitantes excitatorem.*

Page 15, ligne 51. (Ἀλλὰ μὴ οὐ τοῦτ' ᾖ χαλεπὸν.... θάνατον ἐκφυγεῖν κ. τ. λ.) N^a. *Mortis fuga facilior quam flagitii. Flagitium enim morte currit velocius.*

Page 16, ligne 9. (Εἰ γὰρ οἴεσθε ἀποκτείναντες ἀνθρώπους ἐπισχήσειν τοῦ ὀνειδίζειν κ. τ. λ.) N^a. *Non interficiendi sunt reprehensores, sed mutatione vitæ ad silentium redigendi.*

NOTES SUR LE *CRITON*.

Page 19, ligne 17. (Οὐκ ἄρα, ὦ βέλτιστε, πάνυ ἡμῖν οὕτω φροντιστέον, ὅτι ἐροῦσιν οἱ πολλοὶ ἡμᾶς....) N^a. *Quid multi dicant non attendamus, sed quid Deus, quid veritas.*

Page 22, ligne 1. (Καὶ ἐκεῖ οἱ ἡμέτεροι ἀδελφοὶ οἱ ἐν Ἅδου νόμοι....) N^a. *Leges divinæ humanarum legum sunt sorores.*

---

[1]. Il y en a aussi quelques-unes, également en latin, sur la *Vie de Platon*, par Diogène de Laërte, qui précède les *Dialogues*.

[2]. *Actes des Apôtres*, chapitre v, verset 29.

NOTES SUR LE *PHÉDON*.

Page 23, ligne 23. (Ὧ ἂν τὸ ἕτερον παραγένηται, ἐπακολουθεῖ ὕστερον καὶ τὸ ἕτερον.) Le plaisir et la douleur sont tellement liés l'un à l'autre qu'ils se suivent toujours de près.

Page 24, ligne 6. (Εἰ τούτοις τοῖς ἀνθρώποις μὴ ὅσιον αὐτοῦ ἑαυτοὺς εὖ ποιεῖν.) Il n'est pas permis aux hommes de se procurer un bien tel que la mort.

Page 36, ligne 2. (Τοὺς μὲν χρηστοὺς καὶ πονηροὺς σφόδρα ὀλίγους εἶναι ἑκατέρους, τοὺς δὲ μεταξὺ πλείστους.) *N^a. Optimi ac pessimi æque pauci sunt.* Les scélérats et les justes sont rares ; mais ceux qui sont entre ces deux excès sont fort communs.

Page 45, ligne 35. (Οἳ μὲν ἂν δόξωσι μέσως βεβιωκέναι κ. τ. λ.) Purgatorium. *Qui mediam veluti vitam duxerunt, purgantur a peccatis, deinde pro meritis remunerantur.*

Ibidem, ligne 40. (Εἰς τὸν Τάρταρον, ὅθεν οὔποτε ἐκβαίνουσιν.) Infernus. *Unde nullus redit impiorum.*

Ibidem, ligne 52. (Εἰς τὴν καθαρὰν οἴκησιν ἀφικνούμενοι.) Paradisus.

NOTES SUR LE *BANQUET*[1].

Page 176. (Δοκῶ μοι — τὸν οὖν Σωκράτη ἑαυτῷ πως προσέχοντα τὸν νοῦν.) Agathon remporta le prix dès sa première tragédie. — C'est cet Agathon qui est cité trois ou quatre fois dans la *Poétique* d'Aristote[2], et qu'Aristophane raille plaisamment en le faisant venir habillé en femme dans le *Jugement des femmes contre Euripide*[3]. Il falloit qu'il fût beau par excellence. — *N^a. Divites philosophos miseros putant ; philosophi vero divites miseros esse optime norunt.*

Page 177. (Κατὰ τὴν ὁδὸν πορεύεσθαι — οὐ γὰρ ἐμὸς ὁ.) Entrée du festin contée agréablement. — Agathon dit à ses valets : « Imaginez-vous que vous nous avez tous priés à souper. »

Page 178. (Μῦθος, ἀλλὰ Φαίδρου τοῦδε — καὶ ἐποίησαν τὸν θάνατον αὐτοῦ.) *N^a. Aristophanes totus erat circa Bacchum et Venerem.*

---

1. Après le *Phédon* et avant le *Banquet*, on trouve dans l'édition de 1534, le *Cratyle*, le *Théétète*, le *Sophiste*, le *Politique*, le *Parménide* et le *Philèbe* (p. 47-175). Sur le premier de ces dialogues, Racine n'a écrit que des notes en latin ; les cinq autres n'ont pas été annotés par lui. Le *Banquet* est aux pages 176-195.

2. Aux chapitres ix, xv, et trois fois au chapitre xviii.

3. Dans la comédie intitulée : Θεσμοφοριάζουσαι.

PLATON.

Page 180. (Οὕτως, οὐ μὲν αἰσχρὸν — οὕνεκα χαρίζεσθαι.) *N^a. Honestum est amanti vilioribus operibus manum admovere. Ferendus non esset qui vel opum vel bonorum gratia ea faceret quæ amoris causa ab amantibus fiunt. — N^a. Pravus et inhonestus amans est ille vulgaris qui corpus magis amat quam animam; ideoque, quum rem amet parum constantem, parum ipse constat. Contra qui virtutem amat, semper amat.*

Page 181. (Οὗτός ἐστιν ὁ τῆς οὐρανίας — ἃ νῦν δὲ ἐγώ.) *Amor per omnia sese diffundit, et ab eo pendent artes omnes : Medicina, Musica, Poesis. Duplex amor in Medicina qualis. In Poesi duplex amor designatur per Uraniam et Polyhymniam. N^a. — N^a. Cœlestis amor est viris honestis placere; vulgaris autem, vulgo placere et multitudini. Prior est Urania, alter vero Polyhymnia.*

Page 182. (Ἔλεγον, τά τε θερμὰ — ἔτεμνε τοὺς ἀνθρώπους.) L'Amour ordonne les saisons. — Les sacrifices sont un commerce entre Dieu et les hommes. — L'impiété vient de ce qu'on ne respecte pas l'Amour. — Tout amour est fort puissant soit en bien, ou en mal; mais le véritable nous approche des Dieux. — Discours du poëte Aristophane. Il invente une fable tout à fait comique, suivant son caractère. — L'Amour est le plus humain des Dieux. — *Belle fable.* Il y avoit autrefois trois genres d'hommes : l'homme, la femme et l'hermaphrodite. Quel étoit ce troisième. Le premier tenoit du soleil, le second de la terre, et le troisième de la lune. — Ces hommes voulurent attaquer les Dieux. — Jupiter les coupe en deux.

Page 183. (Δίχα, ὥσπερ οἱ τὰ ᾠὰ — ἴσως μὲν γὰρ καὶ οὗτοι τούτων.) (*En tête de la page.*) Les hommes ne sont que des moitiés d'hommes. De là vient l'Amour. — Transports des amants. — (*A la marge.*) Apollon les guérit (*les hommes coupés en deux*) et les reforme. Ceux qui étoient tout hommes recherchent les garçons; ceux qui étoient hommes et femmes aiment les femmes; et celles qui étoient toutes femmes n'aiment que les femmes. — Apologie de l'amour des garçons. *N^a*. — Emportements des amants. Ils veulent ardemment, et ignorent ce qu'ils veulent. Si Vulcain leur disoit : « Je vous collerai inséparablement l'un à l'autre, » ils diroient que c'est là ce qu'ils demandent.

Page 184. (Τυγχάνουσιν ὄντες — ἐκ πάντων ὁμολογουμένως.) Discours fleuri du poëte Agathon. — Aimer selon son inclination. — Socrate et Agathon étoient forts sur l'amour. — La grande attente des spectateurs trouble l'acteur. — Confiance d'Agathon. — Le poëte montoit sur le théâtre avec les comédiens. — Je ne suis pas si plein du théâtre que je ne sache que quelques sages sont plus à craindre qu'une foule d'ignorants. — Socrate dit qu'il est dans la foule. — Socrate ne cessera de vous interroger, étant beau surtout. — Discours d'Agathon. Il est fleuri, plein d'épithètes élevés[1], selon le caractère d'un poëte tragique, jeune et amoureux de la poésie. — L'Amour est jeune. — La vieillesse a des ailes. — L'Amour est délicat. — Il marche dans les cœurs. — Il est humide, i. (c'est-à-dire) flexible et accommodant.

Page 185. (Ὁμολογουμένως Ἔρως ἔχει — προὐρήθη γὰρ, ὡς.) (*En tête de la page.*) Épithètes de l'Amour. — Contre les Panégyriques. — (*A la marge.*) Il (*l'Amour*) aime la bienséance. — Il a le teint beau. — Il aime les fleurs. — Il est juste. Il ne souffre point de violence et n'en fait point. — Il est plus vaillant que Mars. — L'Amour est bon poëte. Tout amoureux veut faire des vers. — Il enseigne tous les arts. — Son empire est plus heureux que celui de la Nécessité. — Épithètes de l'Amour. — Son discours (*le discours d'Agathon*) étoit digne de lui et du dieu. — Socrate feint d'être extrêmement embarrassé. Je pensois sottement qu'il suffisoit de dire la vérité. *N*ᵃ. — Il faut louer à tort et à travers, pourvu qu'on loue.

Page 186. (Ἔοικεν ὅπως ἕκαστος ἡμῶν — Καὶ σὲ μέν γε ἤδη ἐάσω.) *Lingua juravit, non mens.* Eurip[ide][2]. — Socrate ne peut louer. — Socrate parle de l'Amour en philosophe, et en interrogeant toujours. — L'Amour desire quelque chose qui lui manque. Le desir ne va point sans l'indigence. On desire ou pour le présent ou pour l'avenir. L'Amour desire la beauté et la bonté : il n'a donc ni l'un ni l'autre. — On peut facilement contredire Socrate, mais non pas la vérité.

Page 187. (Τὸν δὲ λόγον τὸν περὶ τοῦ Ἔρωτος — ἔστι γὰρ δή.) Socrate feint d'avoir été instruit par Diotime, prophétesse, de la nature de l'Amour. Il se fait interroger par elle. — Il y a quelque chose entre la science et l'ignorance : c'est de penser bien, sans en pouvoir rendre raison. — Il y a un milieu entre le beau et le laid. — Entre le divin et l'humain : ce sont les démons ou anges. L'Amour est de cette nature. NATURE DES ANGES. Ils entretiennent le commerce qui est entre les Dieux et les hommes. — Naissance de l'Amour. Il est fils de Porus (*i.* l'Abondance) et de la Pauvreté. — Il a toutes les qualités du père et de la mère. — Il n'est point délicat comme on le fait; au contraire laborieux. — Toujours riche, toujours pauvre. — Tout ce qu'il a lui coule des mains. — L'ignorance est de croire tout savoir et de ne vouloir rien apprendre. — Les philosophes sont entre les sages et les ignorants.

1. Racine fait ici encore le mot *épithète* du genre masculin. Voyez ci-dessus, p. 206, note 1.
2. *Hippolyte*, vers 612.

Page 188. (Τῶν καλλίστων ἡ σοφία — Ἀλλὰ τί μήν;) L'Amour est philosophe. — On prend l'amour pour la chose aimée. — De quelle utilité est l'amour. — Tout le monde aime ce qui le peut rendre heureux. — *Poésie* est ce qui fait quelque chose. Tous les arts sont poésies; et il n'y a que ceux qui font des vers qu'on appelle poëtes. Ainsi tout le monde aime, mais il n'y a qu'une espèce d'hommes qu'on appelle amants. — Et ce n'est point leur moitié qu'ils cherchent, c'est le bien. — L'Amour est de vouloir toujours être bien. — Tous les hommes veulent engendrer, ou du corps ou de l'esprit.

Page 189. (Τῆς γεννήσεως καὶ τοῦ τόκου — καὶ τοὺς ἄλλους ποιητὰς τούς.) — *(En tête de la page.)* Amour de l'immortalité. — *(A la marge.)* Pourquoi tous les animaux aiment avec tant de passion ce qu'ils ont engendré. C'est par l'envie d'être immortels. — L'homme, tant qu'il vit, n'est jamais le même. C'est toujours quelque chose qui s'en va, et quelque autre chose qui revient en sa place. — Ambition. — Desir d'être immortels. — Génération du corps; génération de l'esprit : poésie; législateurs. — Amour des jeunes gens : pour engendrer de beaux sentiments.

Page 190. (Ἀγαθοὺς ζηλῶν — Εἰπόντος δὲ ταῦτα τοῦ Σωκράτους.) *(En tête de la page.)* Amour de Dieu. Connoissance de la véritable beauté. — *(A la marge.)* Vers, enfants du poëte. Lois, enfants de Lycurgue. — On leur a bâti *(aux poëtes et aux législateurs)* des temples pour de tels enfants, et jamais pour des enfants mortels. — Chemin qu'il faut tenir en amour. Aimer un corps, puis tous les corps; ensuite une âme, et de là toutes les âmes. — La suprême beauté. *Dieu.* — Se servir des choses mortelles comme d'échelons pour arriver jusqu'à lui. — Vous oubliez le boire et le manger pour contempler vos amours. Que sera-ce dans la contemplation de cette immortelle beauté?

Page 191. (Τοὺς μὲν ἐπαινεῖν — καὶ κελεύω λέγειν.) Arrivée d'Alcibiade. — Alcibiade aperçoit Socrate.

Page 192. — (Οὐκ ἂν φθάνοιμι — ὥσπερ ἐραστὴς παιδικοῖς.) *(En tête de la page.)* Discours d'Alcibiade à la louange de Socrate. — *(A la marge.)* Socrate semblable aux Silènes, et au satyre Marsyas. — Il étoit railleur. — Force des discours de Socrate. Il n'y avoit point d'âme qui n'en fût émue. Les autres disoient bien; mais ils n'émouvoient pas. — Alcibiade le craignoit et le fuyoit même, à cause qu'il lui disoit des vérités qu'il ne pouvoit pratiquer. Il se laissoit emporter par les honneurs du peuple. Il eût presque souhaité la mort de Socrate. — Alcibiade connoissoit Socrate mieux que personne. Il *(Socrate)* étoit toujours auprès des belles personnes. — Il méprisoit tout ce que les autres estimoient. — Alcibiade se croyoit aimé de Socrate. Il veut éprouver quel étoit cet amour.

Page 193. (Ἐπιβουλεύων — καί ποτε ὄντος τοῦ.) (*En tête de la page.*) Alcibiade loue Socrate. — (*A la marge.*) Alcibiade fait coucher Socrate chez lui. — Ceux qui ont été mordus d'un aspic ne découvrent leur blessure qu'à ceux qui en ont été mordus comme eux. — Fureur philosophique. — Continence de Socrate. — Entretien d'Alcibiade et de Socrate. — La beauté de l'âme est beaucoup au-dessus de celle du corps. — L'âme ne voit bien clair que quand la vue du corps s'affoiblit. — Alcibiade se lève comme s'il avoit couché avec son père. — Alcibiade admire la continence de Socrate. — Socrate étoit aussi invulnérable aux richesses qu'Ajax au fer. — Socrate à l'armée. — On ne l'a jamais vu ivre.

Page 194. (Πάγου οἵου δεινοτάτου — πάνυ γε, φάναι τὸν Σωκράτη.) Valeur de Socrate. — Socrate est original et ne ressemble à personne.

Page 195. (*Fin du dialogue.*) Comédie et tragédie est du même génie.

NOTES SUR *PHÈDRE* [1].

Page 195. (Δεῦρο ὑποκάτω — ἵνα μελετῴη. Ἀπαντήσας.) Préambule extrêmement beau. — Description d'un homme amoureux des beaux ouvrages.

Page 196. (Δὲ τῷ νοσοῦντι περὶ λόγων ἀκοὴν — Ἔτι δὲ οἱ μὲν ἐρῶντες σκοποῦσιν & τε.) Socrate toujours nus pieds. — Fable d'Orithye. — Contre les gens qui raffinent sur les fables. Il aime mieux croire ce qu'on en dit. Je ne me connois pas encore, et j'irois rechercher la connoissance de toutes ces choses! — Description d'un lieu agréable. — Socrate ne sortoit jamais les portes de la ville. Les arbres n'instruisent point. — Discours de Lysias. — Qu'il vaut mieux[2] se donner à un homme qui n'aime point qu'à un amant.

Page 197. (Κακῶς διέθεντο — τοῖς σφόδρα θεομένοις χαρίζεσθαι.) Les amants imputent tous leurs services; les autres n'ont rien à imputer. — Quelque jour ils feront pour d'autres tout ce qu'ils font maintenant pour vous. — Ils disent eux-mêmes qu'ils aiment malgré eux. — Les amants, pour leur honneur, font croire qu'ils sont aimés. — Les amants écartent de vous tous vos amis. — Les amants aiment souvent le corps devant que d'avoir connu l'esprit. — Les amants vous gâtent l'esprit, vous blâmant et vous louant

---

1. Ce dialogue est à la suite du *Banquet* (p. 195-214), dans l'édition de 1534. Racine ne l'a annoté en français que jusqu'à la page 199.
2. Racine a écrit : « qu'il faut mieux. »

selon leurs passions. — Ce qui peut faire durer une amitié. — On ne traite pas ceux qui meurent de faim, mais ceux qui méritent notre amitié.

Page 198. (Ἀλλὰ τοῖς μάλιστα ἀποδοῦναι χάριν — καὶ ὅτι ἐπεθύμει μὲν λέγειν.) Quand vous les aurez contentés (*les amants*), ils chercheront un prétexte pour vous quitter. — Raillerie fine de Socrate. — J'étois enthousiasmé sur votre bonne foi. — Il loue ce discours d'être bien tourné; mais il le blâme de n'avoir pas dit tout ce qu'il faut. — Il dit que Lysias a voulu montrer qu'il pouvoit dire une même chose en plusieurs façons. — Il dit que les anciens ont dit de plus belles choses. — Ami d'un auteur qui prend ses intérêts. — Il (*Phèdre*) dit qu'il lui pourroit rendre sa raillerie pour l'obliger à parler.

Page 199. (Ἐθρύπτετο δέ — ἀπείργοντα καὶ ὠφελίμων.) Phèdre le menace de ne lui plus rien montrer. — Socrate se couvre le visage, de peur, dit-il, de rougir en parlant sur-le-champ. — Il invoque les Muses. — Il suppose une histoire pour faire parler ses personnages.

NOTES SUR L'*ALCIBIADE I*[1].

Page 215. (Ὦ παῖ Κλεινίου — καὶ οὔτ' ἐπίτροπος, οὔτε συγγενὴς, οὔτε.) Socrate demeure le dernier des amants d'Alcibiade. Alcibiade a désespéré tous ses amants. — Alcibiade le plus beau, le plus noble, et un des plus riches d'Athènes. — Périclès étoit son tuteur. — Ambition d'Alcibiade. Socrate la lui fait avouer agréablement. — Vous voulez être le premier homme de la Grèce. Vous ne le sauriez être sans moi.

Page 216. (Ἄλλος οὐδεὶς ἱκανὸς — εἶπε πρῶτον τίς ἡ τέχνη, ἧς τό.) Il prie Alcibiade de souffrir qu'il l'interroge. — Il lui demande en quel temps il a étudié la justice.

Page 217. (Κιθαρίζειν καὶ τὸ ᾄδειν — διδάσκαλοι οἱ πολλοί, καὶ δικαίως.) Montrez-moi le maître qui vous a instruit, afin que je me fasse instruire. — Le public est un bon maître pour le langage, et non pour la vertu.

Page 218. (Ἐπαινοῖντ' ἂν αὐτῶν — οὐ γὰρ ταῦτα οἶμαι τά τε δίκαια καί.) Il fait confesser à Alcibiade qu'il ne sait rien.

Page 219. (Τὰ συμφέροντα — οὐδὲ τῶν αἰσχρῶν.) Alcibiade ne

---

[1]. Ce dialogue est aux pages 215-227 de l'édition de 1534. Il n'a de notes de Racine que jusqu'à la page 220. Dans celles qui suivent, beaucoup de passages sont soulignés.

veut plus être interrogé. Hé bien! interrogez-moi, dit Socrate. Alcibiade dit qu'il ne peut pas.

Page 220. (Καθόσον αἰσχρὸν — Περικλῆς τίνα.) Absurdité où il réduit Alcibiade. — On ne répond au hasard que sur les choses qu'on croit savoir et qu'on ne sait pas. — La vanité de croire savoir ce qu'on ne sait pas est cause de toutes les fautes. — O Alcibiade, oserois-je nommer l'état où vous êtes? Mais nous ne sommes que nous deux : il faut le dire.

NOTES SUR LE *GORGIAS*[1].

Page 303. (Πολέμου καὶ μάχης — ἐπίδειξιν αὐτοῦ τούτου ποιῆσαι τῆς βραχυλογίας.) Gorgias avoue qu'il est rhéteur. — Gorgias promet de répondre en peu de paroles.

Page 306. (Τί δὲ πεπιστευκέναι; — οὔτε τοὺς ἰατροὺς τὴν δόξαν.) Si on abuse de la rhétorique, il ne faut pas s'en prendre à ceux qui la montrent. Exemples.

Page 307. (Ἀφαιρεῖσθαι, ὅτι δύναιντο — ποιήσεις δ' ἐν τοῖς πολλοῖς.) Querelles dans les disputes. — Socrate aimoit à reprendre, et plus encore à être repris.

NOTES SUR L'*ION*[2].

Page 360. (Ῥαψῳδοί.) C'étoit un art. C'étoient des déclamateurs qui expliquoient sur des théâtres le sens d'Homère; et il y avoit des prix pour eux comme pour les poëtes. — Ils disoient ce qu'ils pensoient de beau sur les poëtes.

Page 361. (Εἷς τις ἄριστα λέγῃ — καὶ χρησμῳδεῖν· ἅτε οὖν.) Attache à un seul poëte. — Raillerie fine de Socrate. C'est vous autres, déclamateurs et comédiens, qui êtes les sages; pour moi, je suis un bon homme qui ne sait[3] dire que la vérité. — Peintres. — Il (*So-*

---

1. Les dialogues qui suivent l'*Alcibiade I* jusqu'au *Gorgias*, et qui sont le *second Alcibiade*, l'*Hipparque*, *les Amants*, le *Théagès*, le *Charmide*, le *Lachès*, le *Lysis*, l'*Euthydème* et le *Protagoras*, n'ont pas été annotés. Le *Gorgias* (p. 303-333) a quelques notes sur les premières pages seulement. Nous n'en donnons ici qu'un très-petit nombre, les autres étant de trop courtes indications pour être recueillies.

2. Ce dialogue est aux pages 360-364. Il est précédé du *Ménon* et des deux *Hippias*, sur lesquels on ne trouve pas de notes de Racine.

3. Racine a bien écrit ainsi : *sait*, à la troisième personne.

crate) le convainc (*Ion*) agréablement. — Sculpteurs. Déclamateurs. — Ion convaincu ne sait point rendre d'autre raison, sinon que tout le monde trouve qu'il dit fort bien. — *N*^{a}. Pierre d'aimant. La Muse est comme la pierre d'aimant qui touche les poëtes, lesquels attirent après les comédiens, et les comédiens attirent les spectateurs. — Raillerie des poëtes. Poëtes sont légers. Ils ne font rien s'ils ne sont hors de leur bon sens.

Page 362. (Οὐ τέχνῃ ποιοῦντες — ἐὰν μνησθῶ τὰ ἔπη.) (*En tête de la page.*) Les poëtes ne le sont que par enthousiasme. La poésie est une pierre d'aimant qui attire les poëtes; les poëtes attirent les comédiens; et les comédiens attirent les spectateurs. — (*A la marge.*) S'ils étoient poëtes par art, ils feroient bien toutes sortes de vers. — *Bon ouvrage d'un méchant poëte. N*^{a}. — Les Dieux ont voulu prouver que c'étoit à eux qu'il falloit attribuer tout ce que les poëtes font de bon. — Les déclamateurs sont interprètes des interprètes. — Le comédien doit être aussi hors de lui. — Bon acteur doit pleurer et frémir. — Direz-vous qu'un homme de bon sens pleure en de si beaux habits, et en si belle assemblée? *N*^{a}. — Le comédien rit quand il voit pleurer ses spectateurs, et pleure quand il les voit rire. — *Pierre d'aimant. N*^{a}. — Vous vous réveillez quand le nom d'Homère vous touche.

Page 363. Vers d'Homère touchant l'art de conduire un char [1].

Page 364. (*Fin du dialogue*). Socrate réduit Ion à dire qu'il est excellent général d'armée. Et que ne commandez-vous donc des armées? — Tant d'autres étrangers ont été généraux. Pourquoi Ion ne le seroit-il pas? — Vous m'échappez comme un Protée, pour paroître enfin général d'armée. — Avouez donc que vous expliquez Homère par enthousiasme, et non par art.

NOTES SUR LE *MÉNEXÈNE* [2].

Page 365. (Ἀποθανοῦσι. Ταφὰς γὰρ — ἐν τῇ χώρᾳ ἄλλοθεν.) Raillerie agréable des oraisons funèbres. — Plaisir de s'entendre louer. — *N*^{a}. Galanterie de Socrate. — Je suis plus de trois jours sans me reconnoître, tant je suis fier de leurs louanges. — Il n'est pas difficile de louer les Athéniens dans Athènes. — *Aspasie.* Elle avoit rendu Périclès excellent orateur, et beaucoup d'autres. Elle composoit les discours de Périclès. — Je danserois, si vous me

---

1. Ceci se rapporte aux vers 335-340 du livre XXIII de l'*Iliade*, cités par Platon.
2. Ce dialogue est aux pages 364-370.

l'ordonniez. — *Discours d'Aspasie.* — Oraisons funèbres. Pour louer les morts, exhorter les enfants et les frères à les imiter, et consoler leur père et leur mère. — Naissance, éducation, actions.

Page 366. (Σφῶν ἡκόντων — καὶ τῶν νήσων. Ὡς.) Athènes étoit leur mère, et non leur marâtre. — Les premiers hommes naquirent dans Athènes. — Toute mère a de quoi nourrir son enfant. — La politique est l'éducation des hommes. — Louange de l'aristocratie.

Page 367. (Τε μὴ δὲ ἀξιοῦν — ὅτι ἐπέδειξαν εἴ τις ἄρα.) Toutes les puissances cèdent à la vertu. — Jalousie, et ensuite l'envie. — Guerres civiles. — Combattre contre les Grecs jusqu'à la victoire, et contre les barbares jusqu'à la ruine.

Page 368. (Ἠμφισβήτει — καὶ ὤμοσαν Κορίνθιοι.) Vaincre avec ses alliés, et les vaincre ensuite.

Page 369. (Καὶ Ἀργεῖοι, καὶ Βοιωτοὶ — ἀνδρεῖος καὶ φρόνιμος.) Il fait parler les morts.

NOTES SUR LA *RÉPUBLIQUE*[1].

Livre I, page 371. (Κατέβην χθὲς — καὶ εἶπον· ὦ Κέφαλε.) Sophocle avoit été amoureux.

Page 377. (Ἀλλὰ μὴν, ὦ Θρασύμαχε — ἡμᾶς τοσούσδε ὄντας.) *Justus utilitatem publicam spectat, injustus suam.* Partisans. — *Sententiæ vere tyrannicæ.* Machiavel.

Page 378. (Εὐεργετήσεις. Ἐγὼ γὰρ — τὸ μὴ ἄρχειν, ὥσπερ.) *N^a. In dignitatibus palam lucrifacere mercenarii est, clam vero furis.*

Page 379. (Νῦν τὸ ἄρχειν — ὁ δὲ ἐπιστήμων.) Coupeurs de bourses.

Livre II, page 383. (Μέγα τοῦτο τεκμήριον ἂν φαίη τις — τὰς δρῦς τοῖς δικαίοις τοὺς Θεοὺς ποιεῖν.) *Idea justi hominis et injusti.* — *Justus in crucem agetur. N^a.* Jésus-Christ.

Page 384. (Ἄκρας μέν τε φέρειν — ἀλλὰ γὰρ ἐν Ἅδου.) (*En tête de la page.*) *N^a. In eos qui docent iniquitatis munera Deum placare.*

Page 389, ligne 16. (Sur le passage : Ὑπὸ τῶν ἐπιτυχόντων μύθους πλασθέντας ἀκούειν τοὺς παῖδας.) Il entend peut-être les fables d'Ésope.

Livre III, page 392. (Ψυχὴ δ' ἐκ ῥεθέων — Διομήδης λέγει.) (*En tête de la page.*) Contre les poëmes. Il ne veut pas qu'on introduise de grands hommes pleurants, pas même d'honnêtes femmes, beaucoup moins les Dieux.

---

1. Les notes de Racine sur la *République* (p. 371-473) sont les unes en latin, les autres en français. Nous citons celles-ci; mais des latines, qui sont très-nombreuses, les plus remarquables seulement.

Page 393. (Τέττα σιωπῆ ἦσο — διήγησις οὖσα τυγχάνει.) (*En tête de la page.*) Il accuse Homère d'avoir fait Achille insolent, avare, et impie. Ou n'en faites point des héros; ou, s'ils sont enfants des Dieux, n'en faites point des vicieux. — (*A la marge.*) Contre Jupiter amoureux dans l'*Iliade*.

Page 394. (Ἢ γεγονότων, ἢ ὄντων — τοὺς φύλακας ἡμῖν τῶν.) Le poëte raconte ou imite. Exemple. — Imitation, parce qu'on fait dire à celui qui parle ce qu'il doit dire. — Épique, si le poëte ne se cache point. — Dramatique.

Page 395. (Ἄλλων πασῶν δημιουργιῶν — Ἀληθῆ ἔφη.) C'étoient des hommes qui jouoient les personnages des femmes.

Page 402. (Καλεῖν τούτους μὲν φύλακας — καὶ οὐδὲν προσδέονται.) (*En tête de la page.*) Episcopi. N[a] [1]. — (*A la marge, ligne dernière:* χρυσίον δὲ καὶ ἀργύριον εἰπεῖν αὐτοῖς ὅτι θεῖον παρὰ Θεῶν ἀεὶ ἐν τῇ ψυχῇ ἔχουσι κ. τ. λ.) N[a]. *Aurum principibus spernendum est, quum divinum aliquod aurum in mente gerant.* Évêques [2].

Livre V [3], page 413. (Γίγνεσθαι ἤδη — Καὶ ἐγὼ εἶπον, ὦ.) Ils (*les interlocuteurs de Socrate*) font entrer Socrate en matière pour la génération des enfants. Audience favorable.

Page 417. (Καὶ κύνας — Πῶς διαγνώσονται ἀλλήλων.) (*Au bas de la page* [4].) Il ne bannit pas tout à fait les poëtes de sa république.

Page 418. (Οὐδαμῶς, ἦν δ' ἐγώ — αὐτὸ ὡμολογήσαμεν.) Dixième et septième mois pour l'accouchement. — Il permet aux frères de coucher avec leurs sœurs. — Tout commun. *Meum et tuum* divisent les républiques. Toute la république comme un seul homme. — Noms. Le peuple appellera les magistrats ses *protecteurs*, et les magistrats appelleront le peuple leurs [5] *nourriciers*. Les magistrats se traiteront de pères, de fils et de frères. Les effets suivront les noms.

Page 419. (Ἀγαθὸν, ἀπεικάζοντες — τελεωθέντας δεήσει.) Magistrats. — Les magistrats n'auront ni biens ni maisons particulières. Ils seront nourris à communs frais. — L'avarice en sera bannie (*de la république*), et les procès. — Les jeunes gens respecteront les vieillards. La crainte et la pudeur les retiendra. — Leur union (*l'union des guerriers*) retiendra les autres dans le devoir.

---

1. Voyez la note suivante.
2. C'est une application aux évêques de ce que Platon dit des premières classes de sa *République*.
3. Les notes du livre IV, fort nombreuses, comme celles des livres précédents, sont toutes en latin. Nous passons au livre V, qui en a dans les deux langues.
4. Avec renvoi au passage des lignes 19 et 20 : Καὶ ὕμνοι ποιητέοι τοῖς ἡμετέροις ποιηταῖς.
5. Racine a écrit : « ses nourriciers. »

Page 420. (Δημιουργεῖν — πολλὰ δέ.) (*En tête de la page.*) Récompenses de la valeur. Les braves embrasseront qui ils voudront. Honneurs pour les morts. Canonisation. Martyrs. Saints qui ne sont pas martyrs[1]. — (*A la marge.*) Mener les enfants à la guerre. — Les enfants des artisans regardent faire leurs pères longtemps avant que de travailler. — Les pères combattront mieux en présence de leurs enfants. — Ne les point mener dans le péril évident. — Donner de bons chevaux aux enfants. — Quand un soldat aura abandonné son rang, on en fera un laboureur. — Récompense de la valeur. — Il sera permis aux braves de baiser qui ils voudront. — Ils auront des plats dans les festins par-dessus les autres pour marques d'honneur et pour entretenir leurs forces. — Ceux qui seront morts vaillamment dans les batailles passeront pour des demi-dieux. *Canonisation.* — On demandera à l'oracle comme on les doit traiter. — On honorera leurs tombeaux. — Et même (*on honorera après leur mort*) ceux qui ayant vécu dans la gloire mourront de leur mort naturelle[2]. — On n'aura point d'esclaves grecs.

Page 421. (Ἤδη στρατόπεδα — αὐτῆς ἐκείνης διαφέρειν.) (*En tête de la page.*) Guerre entre gens de même religion combien doit être humaine. — *N*ᵃ. Contre les brûlements. Bombes[3]. — (*A la marge.*) Ne point dépouiller les morts. — Ne point porter aux temples les dépouilles des Grecs. — *Guerre entre chrétiens.* — Dépouiller les fruits de l'année sans autre dégât. — Guerre de Grecs contre les Grecs est une sédition. — Qu'ils se souviennent qu'ils se réconcilieront quelque jour. — Dans les guerres civiles épargner les peuples, et chercher les coupables pour les punir. — Il écrit tout cela parce que les Grecs se traitoient cruellement les uns les autres. — Nouvelle question si cette forme du gouvernement est possible.

Page 422. (Ἀλλὰ πανταχῇ τοιοῦτο εἶναι — συγχωρῶ τοῦ λόγου.) (*En tête de la page.*) Heureux seront les États quand les philosophes régneront ou quand les rois seront philosophes. — On cherche le mieux sans se mettre en peine si ce mieux est possible. — (*A la marge.*) Un peintre imagine le plus beau visage qu'il peut, sans se mettre en peine s'il y en peut avoir un pareil. — Chercher le plus parfait. — Philosophes rois, ou rois philosophes. — Excuse de So-

---

1. La comparaison que fait Racine des honneurs proposés par Platon pour les braves, avec ceux que l'Église rend aux saints, est suffisamment éclaircie dans quelques-unes des notes qu'il a écrites à la suite, sur la même page 420.

2. Voilà les *saints qui ne sont pas martyrs.*

3. Racine, comme à la page précédente, applique à la société moderne et chrétienne les pensées de Platon.

crate sur ce paradoxe. — Quels sont ces philosophes. — Adresse des amants à excuser les défauts de ce qu'ils aiment [1].

Page 423. (Χάριν. Τί δ', ἦν δ' ἐγὼ — εἰς ἐκεῖνο μόνον βλέπω.) Il en est de même de ceux qui aiment le vin et les honneurs. — Le philosophe aime toute la sagesse et non une partie. — Amateurs de musique. Ils semblent avoir loué leurs oreilles aux musiciens. — Différence de celui qui aime le souverain beau, ou de celui qui n'aime que des espèces du beau. L'un veille, l'autre songe. — Opinion tient le milieu entre la science et l'ignorance. — (*Au bas de la page.*) Gens qui aiment le monde, φιλόδοξοι; gens qui aiment Dieu, φιλόσοφοι. Les premiers aiment les fantômes, et les autres ce qui est. — Ainsi ceux qui n'aiment que les espèces du beau, du bon et du juste, sont φιλόδοξοι, aimant les opinions; mais ceux qui aiment le beau même, le bon et le juste, sont φιλόσοφοι.

Page 424. (*Fin du livre V.*) (*En tête de la page.*) Science, opinion, ignorance : l'une, de ce qui est véritablement; l'autre, de ce qui est entre l'être et le néant; et l'ignorance est pour ce qui n'est pas. — (*A la marge.*) Jeu d'enfants : *Vir non vir percusserat lapide non lapide*, i. pumice, *avem non avem*, i. vespertilionem.

Livre VI, page 425. (Οἱ μὲν δὴ φιλόσοφοι — Ἐπιλήσμονα ἄρα ψυχὴν ἐν ταῖς.) (*En tête de la page.*) Le philosophe n'aime que ce qui est toujours, et ne peut faire cas des choses qui passent et ne subsistent point. — (*A la marge.*) Philosophes sont ceux qui s'attachent à ce qui est toujours le même. Les autres ceux qui errent après les choses qui changent. — Ces derniers incapables de bien gouverner. Ils n'ont aucun modèle fixe et assuré. — L'amateur de la sagesse aime tout ce qui appartient à la sagesse; entre autres, la vérité. — Il embrasse tout ce qui est, tous les temps : peut-il donc compter la vie ou la mort pour quelque chose? — Il faut qu'il ait de la mémoire : sans cela pourroit-il aimer l'étude?

Page 426. (Ἱκανῶς φιλοσόφοις — ἐάν τε πλούσιος.) (*En tête de la page.*) Belle image de ce qui se passe dans les républiques. Vaisseau où tous les matelots veulent gouverner, et se battent à qui prendra en main le timon, n'ayant nulle connoissance de la mer, et persuadés même qu'il n'est pas besoin d'en avoir. — (*A la marge.*) Adimante. On ne peut répondre aux inductions de Socrate; et on se trouve à la fin réduit au silence, mais point convaincu. — Qu'y a-t-il de plus inutile à un État que ceux qu'on appelle philosophes? — Socrate en convient et en donne la raison. Il compare ce qui se passe dans les républiques à un vaisseau où tous les matelots veu-

---

[1]. Dans ce dernier passage, sur le mot μελαγχλώρους, au lieu duquel, dans les éditions plus récentes, on lit μελιχλώρους, Racine a fait cette note : « Lucr. (*Lucrèce*, livre IV, vers 1156) dit μελίχροος. »

lent gouverner, sans savoir un mot de la marine. L'inutilité des sages vient de ceux qui ne veulent pas les employer. Iront-ils aux portes des riches les prier de se laisser gouverner par eux?

Page 427. (Ἐάν τε πένης — Θεῶν τύχῃ. Ἦ καὶ σύ.) N'est-ce pas au malade à prier le médecin de le traiter? — Le décri de la dévotion vient des faux dévots [1]. — La première qualité d'un philosophe, c'est d'être vrai. — Il est passionné pour ce qui est, et n'a point de repos qu'il ne l'ait trouvé. — Chœur qui suit la vérité. — Les âmes propres à la philosophie sont rares. — Plus une âme est élevée, plus elle est dangereuse quand elle vient à se dépraver. — Les grands crimes supposent une âme hardie.

Page 428. (Ἡγῇ ὥσπερ οἱ πολλοὶ — κάμπτηται καὶ ἕλκηται.) (*En tête de la page.*) Combien la fréquentation du monde est dangereuse. — On appelle sages ceux qui étudient les inclinations du monde et qui s'y conforment. — C'est un grand animal à qui il faut parler sa langue. — (*A la marge.*) Fréquentation du monde combien dangereuse. — Tout respire dans le monde les maximes du monde : les tribunaux, les théâtres. — *Dieu seul peut empécher que la vertu ne s'y corrompe* [2]. — Le monde est un grand animal qui rue et qui s'effarouche quand on ne lui parle pas sa langue. — Chacun apprend donc cette langue μεγάλου ζώου. Les poëtes, les musiciens parlent tous cette langue. — Le philosophe même s'y corrompra, s'il s'y laisse engager; et il deviendra pire que les autres.

Livre IX [3], page 457. (Οὐκοῦν οὗτος γίγνεται — καὶ παίδων καὶ γυναικός.) Intérieur d'un tyran. — Un tyran est comme un maître qui vivroit dans un désert avec quantité de ses esclaves.

Page 458. (Μὴ ἀπόλοιντο ὑπὸ τῶν οἰκετῶν; — τὴν τοῦ τιμᾶσθαι.) Le tyran est au fond de son palais, comme dans un cachot. — Plein de frayeurs, de tourments et de déplaisirs. V. Tacit. 1 — 6. *Ann.* [4].

Page 459. (Ἡδονὴν — παῦλαν λύπης εἶναι.) (*En tête de la page.*) C'est au philosophe à juger, et de son bonheur et de celui des autres.

Livre X, page 463. (Καὶ μὴν, ἦν δ' ἐγὼ — δοκεῖ μετριώτατ'.) (*En*

---

1. Racine fait aux dévots cette application de ce que Platon dit des philosophes : Πολὺ δὲ μεγίστη καὶ ἰσχυροτάτη διαβολὴ γίγνεται φιλοσοφίας διὰ κ. τ. λ.

2. Racine a souligné cette dernière phrase, qu'il a tirée du passage : Θεοῦ μοῖραν αὐτὸ σῶσαι λέγων, οὐ κακῶς ἐρεῖς.

3. Racine n'a pas annoté les livres VII et VIII.

4. Racine renvoie aux six premiers livres des *Annales*, où est raconté le règne de Tibère.

tête de la page.) Platon revient encore à Homère et à la poésie dramatique, qu'il continue d'exclure de sa république. — (*A la marge*.) Socrate avoue la peine qu'il a à parler contre Homère, le chef, dit-il, et le maître de tous les tragiques.

Page 464. (Ἄν προσαγορεύεσθαι — τοῖς ἐφ' ἑαυτῶν περιστάναι.) (*En tête de la page*.) Le poëte n'est que le troisième ouvrier. Le premier, c'est Dieu; le second, l'homme qui agit sur l'idée de Dieu; le troisième, le poëte qui représente ce qui est fait. — (*A la marge*.) Homère n'a point laissé de disciples, ni de lois, ni république, comme Lycurgue, Solon, etc. — Pythagore. — *Créophile*, nom ridicule. C'étoit un ami d'Homère.

Page 465. (Ἰδίᾳ ξυγγιγνόμενοι — ὑγιεῖ οὐδ' ἀληθεῖ.) Il (*Homère*) n'a pas même été aussi heureux que les sophistes.

Page 466. (Παντάπασιν, ἦ δ' ὅς — οὗτος ὁ ἔπαινος ἔχει, τὸ δρῶντα.) (*En tête de la page*.) La tragédie nourrit et fortifie les passions et affoiblit l'âme. — (*A la marge*.) Imitation. — La raison veut qu'on soit ferme dans le malheur. La tragédie nous accoutume à nous affoiblir. — S'affliger, c'est faire comme les enfants, qui portent la main en pleurant à l'endroit où ils ont été frappés. — La passion fournit à la poésie, mais non point la tempérance, qui seroit un spectacle bien froid pour ceux qui vont au théâtre.

Page 467. (Τοιοῦτον ἄνδρα — ἡμῶν ἡ ψυχὴ, καὶ οὐδέποτε.) La tragédie entretient en nous ce penchant que nous avons à pleurer et à nous plaindre, τὸ πεπεινηκὸς τοῦ δακρῦσαι. — Elle arrose les passions, au lieu qu'il les faudroit dessécher. — Il ne faut permettre à la poésie que les hymnes et les louanges des Dieux. — Ancienne querelle entre la philosophie et la poésie. — Il faut traiter la poésie comme une maîtresse, belle, à la vérité, mais à laquelle il faut renoncer[1]. — Peut-on rien appeler de grand, lorsqu'il est de si peu de durée? — Immortalité de l'âme.

Page 469. (Ἀθάνατον ψυχὴ — πρὸς ἐκείνοις τοῖς ἀγαθοῖς.) Persévérance. — Les gens de bien sont à la fin reconnus pour tels, et récompensés, et les malhonnêtes gens punis.

Page 470. (Οἷς αὐτὴ παρείχετο ἡ δικαιοσύνη — σφονδύλῳ κοίλῳ καὶ.) (*En tête de la page*.) Fable d'un homme ressuscité, qui racontoit ce qu'il avoit vu en l'autre vie. — (*A la marge*.) Er l'Arménien.

---

1. Après cette note, Racine a reproduit à la marge cette phrase du texte grec : Μέγας ὁ ἀγών, ὦ φίλε, μέγας τὸ χρηστὸν ἢ κακὸν γενέσθαι.

NOTES SUR LES *LOIS*[1].

Livre V, page 547. (Ἀκούοι δὴ πᾶς — οὐκ ἐκ τοῦ νῦν παρακελεύματος.) (*En tête de la page.*) Chacun doit honorer, premièrement Dieu, puis son âme, puis son corps. L'âme est quelque chose de divin, plus précieux que toutes choses. — (*A la marge.*) L'âme est, après les Dieux, ce que nous avons de plus divin, et ce que nous devons le plus respecter après eux. — Deux parties en nous, l'une qui doit commander, l'autre obéir. — De quelle manière chacun doit honorer son âme. — On la déshonore en croyant savoir tout, en se permettant tout; — en rejetant ses propres fautes sur les autres; — en cherchant les plaisirs; — en fuyant le travail; — en faisant trop de cas de la vie; — en préférant la beauté du corps à celle de l'âme; — en estimant trop les richesses, car alors il (*l'homme*) vend son âme à trop vil prix. — Quelle plus grande punition à un homme qui laisse la vertu pour suivre le vice, que de se bannir de la compagnie des gens de bien, et de s'attacher aux méchants? — Après l'âme, il faut honorer son corps. — Avantages de la tempérance. — Avantages de la médiocrité dans les richesses. — Laisser à ses enfants un bien qui ne les expose point aux flatteurs, ἀκολάκευτος οὐσία. — Leur laisser plutôt beaucoup de pudeur que beaucoup d'or.

Page 548. (Τοῖς νέοις γιγνόμενον — ἔχων ἀποφυγήν.) Les gens d'âge doivent respecter les jeunes gens. — Exemple plus efficace que les remontrances. — Faire peu de cas des services qu'on rend à ses amis, et beaucoup de ceux qu'on en reçoit. — La plus belle victoire est celle de se conformer aux lois de son pays. — Charité pour les étrangers.

NOTES SUR LES *COMMENTAIRES* DE PROCLUS[2].

Page 383. (*Sur le chapitre :* Τίνες αἰτίαι δι᾽ ἃς ἡ ποίησις ἀναπέμπει θρήνους κἀπὶ τοὺς ἥρωας, καὶ ἐπὶ τοὺς Θεοὺς κ. τ. λ.) Des larmes

---

1. Le *Timée* et le *Critias*, qui suivent la *République*, sont sans notes. Le dialogue de *Minos* (p. 507-510) a quelques notes au crayon, mais très-sommaires et ne présentant rien de remarquable. Les livres I-IV et VI-XII des *Lois* ne sont pas annotés. Nous donnons les notes du livre V.

2. L'*Épinomis*, ou XIII⁰ livre des *Lois*, a quelques notes au crayon rouge, mais trop courtes pour offrir de l'intérêt. — Les dialogues que l'édition de Bâle

des héros et des Dieux. — On représente les héros agissants, et non pas contemplants comme les philosophes. — Les passions suivent l'action.

Page 384. (*Sur le même chapitre.*) Ils font de grandes actions comme héros, et souffrent les passions comme mortels. — Les larmes des Dieux marquent leur providence.

Ibidem. (Sur le chapitre : Τίς αἰτία τοῦ ἐν τοῖς Θεοῖς γενομένου γέλωτος ἐν τοῖς μύθοις κ. τ. λ.) Du rire des Dieux. — Vulcain représente la fabrique du monde. — Et il semble que Dieu se soit voulu jouer dans la construction de l'univers. *Ludebat in orbe terrarum* [1].

NOTES SUR LA *RÉPUBLIQUE*.

(*Tirées de l'exemplaire de* 1578.)

Livre VI [2], page 485. (Οὐκοῦν τοῦτο δὴ λέγωμεν — τόδε δεῖ σκοπεῖν, ὅταν κρίνειν.) Un amant aime tout ce qui appartient à ce qu'il aime. — Le philosophe aime la vérité, qui est proche parente de la sagesse. — Quand on aime quelque chose avec une passion violente, on aime froidement le reste.

Page 486. (Μέλλης φύσιν φιλόσοφόν τε καὶ μή — Ἀναγκαιότατα

donne comme apocryphes, et les *Lettres* de Platon sont sans notes de Racine. — La seconde partie du volume renferme les *Commentaires de Proclus* sur le *Timée* et sur la *République*. Ceux qui se rapportent à la *République* sont aux pages 349-433; Racine y a mis quelques notes, qui sont celles que nous donnons ici.

1. Sur le verso du dernier feuillet de cette seconde partie du volume, Racine a écrit : « Τί γάρ ἐστι Πλάτων ἡ Μωσῆς ἀττικίζων; *Numenii Pythagorici.* » — Cette parole sur Platon : « Qu'est-ce que Platon? sinon un Moïse parlant la langue d'Athènes, » se trouve dans la *Préparation évangélique d'Eusèbe*, livre VIII, chapitre VI, où elle est attribuée au philosophe pythagoricien Numenius d'Apamée. Sur le feuillet de garde, à la suite du précédent, Racine a recueilli, en les traduisant en latin et en renvoyant aux pages d'où il les a tirés, plusieurs passages de Platon qui ont trait à la médecine. Nous avions déjà pu remarquer, en lisant ses notes dans tout le cours de ces dialogues, qu'il avait fait, nous ne savons pourquoi, une attention particulière à tous les endroits où il est question de la médecine, et qu'en tête des pages où se trouvent ces endroits, il écrit ordinairement *medicina*.

2. Dans l'exemplaire de 1578, les livres précédents de la *République* n'ont pas de notes, à l'exception de deux, comme nous l'avons déjà dit à la page 266, dont l'une, en latin, est sur un passage du livre III, et l'autre, en français, sur ce membre de phrase du livre IV, p. 439 : νεκροὺς παρὰ τῷ δημείῳ κειμένους, à la marge duquel Racine a écrit : « comme étoient à Rome les Gémonies. »

μέν.) Le philosophe n'est point intéressé. — Il a toujours ce grand bien devant les yeux. — Tout plein de l'éternité, peut-il compter pour quelque chose la vie présente ? — Il n'est pas possible qu'il soit injuste et de fâcheuse société. — Il a l'esprit aisé, et l'étude ne lui fait point de peine.

Page 487. (Οὖν ἔφη. Ἔστιν οὖν ὅπῃ μέμψῃ — Ἄκουε δ' οὖν τῆς εἰκόνος ἵν'.) Inductions de Socrate. — On associe plusieurs choses, et, au bout du compte, on trouve qu'on n'a plus rien à répondre, sans qu'on soit pourtant persuadé. — Ainsi l'on voit la plupart des philosophes, ou malhonnêtes gens, ou inutiles pour le monde.

Page 488. (Ἔτι μᾶλλον ἴδῃς ὡς γλίσχρως εἰκάζω — ἀδολέσχην καὶ ἄχρηστον σφίσι.) Belle image d'une grande multitude de fous, qui ne veulent pas se laisser conduire, se croyant plus habiles que personne. — Fous qui se veulent conduire eux-mêmes, et qui se battent à qui conduira le vaisseau. — Ils ne louent et ne trouvent raisonnables que ceux qui sont complaisants à leurs passions.

Page 489. (Καλεῖσθαι ὑπὸ τῶν ἐν ταῖς οὕτω κατεσκευασμέναις ναυσὶ — τὸν καλόν τε κἀγαθὸν ἐσόμενον.) Un vrai philosophe est inutile aux gens du monde. — Un bon pilote ne va pas supplier les gens de se laisser conduire par lui. — Et les sages ne vont point aux portes des riches. — Il est difficile de passer pour sage parmi une foule de gens qui suivent des opinions toutes contraires à la sagesse.

Page 490. (Ἡγείτω δ' αὐτῷ, εἰ νῷ ἔχεις — καὶ μετὰ τοῦτο αὖ τὰς μιμουμένας ταύτην.) Le sage cherche la vérité, et non les opinions. — Il veut posséder ce qui est. — Compagnes de la vérité.

Page 491. (Καὶ εἰς τὸ ἐπιτήδευμα καθισταμένας — Ἢν τοίνυν ἔθεμεν.) Les grandes âmes sont plus dangereuses quand elles se portent au mal.

Page 492. (Τοῦ φιλοσόφου φύσιν — ἐν τοιαύτῃ καταστάσει.) Il faut que le juste périsse, et soit chargé d'affronts s'il se montre parmi les hommes. — Il est impossible qu'on ne soit emporté par la foule. — S'ils ne vous convainquent par leurs discours, ils vous tueront, ils vous chargeront d'ignominies. — Il est impossible humainement de se sauver de la corruption des hommes.

Page 493. (Πολιτειῶν, Θεοῦ μοῖραν αὐτὸ σῶσαι λέγων — καὶ μὴ τὰ πολλὰ ἕκαστα, ἔσθ' ὅπως.) (*En tête de la page.*) Le monde est un animal farouche dont on étudie les inclinations. — (*En marge.*) Le commun des philosophes enseigne les choses qui peuvent plaire au commun des hommes. — Monde. C'est une grande bête dont on étudie les inclinations. — On appelle bon ce qui lui plaît, et mauvais ce qui lui déplaît. — On étudie son goût en toutes sortes de professions, poëtes, peintres, musiciens, magistrats.

Page 494. (Πλῆθος ἀνέξεται — δημοσίᾳ εἰς ἀγῶνα καθιστάντας;) Faux philosophes. — On se met sous leur conduite, comme ils ont une apparence de sagesse. — Que si quelqu'un veut convaincre ces faux philosophes, et les ramener à la vérité, on se jette sur lui et on le veut perdre.

Page 495. (Πολλὴ, ἦ δ' ὅς, ἀνάγκη — τοῦ δεσπότου τὴν θυγατέρα μέλλοντος γαμεῖν; οὔ.) Les vrais sages sont obligés de se cacher, et les imposteurs prennent leur place. — La sagesse est une orpheline dont quelque malheureux esclave s'empare, et l'épouse par violence.

Page 496. (Πάνυ, ἔφη, διαφέρει — ἀλλά τοι, ἦ δ' ὅς, οὐ τὰ ἐλάχιστα ἄν.) (*En tête de la page.*) Le philosophe ou le juste est un homme qui vit parmi les bêtes féroces. — (*En marge.*) Il n'y a que le malheur ou la retraite qui sauve le vrai philosophe. — Le juste est un homme tombé au milieu des bêtes farouches; il faut qu'il se taise, s'il ne veut être déchiré. — Il se retire sous un petit toit, d'où il voit les autres couverts de pluie et de boue, bien heureux d'achever sa vie sans être sali.

Page 497. (Διαπραξάμενος ἀπαλλάττοιτο — ἁπτόμενοι μειράκια ὄντα, ἄρτι.) La vertu parmi les hommes, tels qu'ils sont, au lieu de fructifier, s'altère, et prend la nature du terroir où elle est tombée.

ARISTOTE.

NOTES SUR LES *ÉTHIQUES A NICOMAQUE*.

La Bibliothèque impériale possède un exemplaire de l'édition des *Éthiques à Nicomaque*, publiée à Paris en 1560, qui porte sur le premier feuillet la signature de Racine, et où l'on trouve des notes marginales de sa main. I a une reliure en parchemin vert, semblable à celle du *Sophocle* de Turnèbe et des cahiers de *Remarques sur Pindare* et sur *Homère*. C'est un volume in-4°, qui a pour titre : *Aristotelis de Moribus ad Nicomachum, libri decem..... Parisiis, M.D.LX. Apud Guil. Morelium, in græcis typographum regium. Typis regiis.* Avant d'appartenir à Racine, il avait été dans la bibliothèque du médecin Théophile Gelée, mort en 1650; il a en effet ces mots sur le premier feuillet : « *Sum Theophili Gelidi, medici.* »

Racine n'a écrit de notes que sur les quatre premiers livres; mais ces notes sont nombreuses. Nous avons cru qu'il suffisait d'en recueillir quelques-unes. Parmi les notes qui sont en latin (et il y en a très-peu qui ne soient en cette langue [1]), nous citons seulement, comme nous l'avons fait pour les *Dialogues de Platon*, celles qui sont recommandées à l'attention par un *Nota*. Le lecteur jugera peut-être que la plupart des notes françaises, qui vont être mises sous ses yeux, ne sont pas elles-mêmes très-importantes. Il ne regrettera pas cependant, nous le croyons, la très-petite place qu'elles tiennent dans ce volume, et se souviendra que nous avons voulu donner l'idée la plus complète que nous avons pu des studieuses habitudes de Racine, et chercher partout les traces qui en sont restées.

Livre I, chapitre i, § 11 [2], page 15. *N^a (nota). Vir probus sibi semper constat velut* quadratus, τετράγωνος.

Livre II, chapitre i, § 2, page 21. (Οὐδὲ μία τῶν ἠθικῶν ἀρετῶν φύσει ἡμῖν ἐγγίγνεται.) *N^a. Virtutum moralium nulla nobis innata est.*

Ibidem, chapitre ii, § 6, page 23. (Ὁμοίως δὲ καὶ τὰ ποτὰ, καὶ τὰ

---

1. Toutes les notes du livre I et celles du livre IV, à l'exception d'une seule, sont en latin.
2. Nous indiquons ces divisions en chapitres et en paragraphes, pour la commodité du lecteur, d'après l'édition de Tauchnitz (Leipzig, 1832). Elles n'existent pas dans l'édition dont Racine s'est servi; mais nous marquons en même temps les pages de cette édition.

σιτία πλείω καὶ ἐλάττω κ. τ. λ.) *N^a. Cibi vel plures vel pauciores sanitatem destruunt. Mediocritas ipsam parit, auget et servat.*

Livre II, chapitre III, § 1, page 24. (Σημεῖον δὲ δεῖ ποιεῖσθαι τῶν ἕξεων, τὴν ἐπιγινομένην ἡδονὴν ἢ λύπην τοῖς ἔργοις.) *N^a. Voluptas aut mœror in actu signum est habitus.*

Ibidem, chapitre VIII, § 1 et 4, page 33. (Αἱ μὲν γὰρ ἄκραι καὶ τῇ μέσῃ καὶ ἀλλήλαις ἐναντίαι εἰσίν — πλείων ἐναντιότης ἐστὶ τοῖς ἄκροις πρὸς ἄλληλα ἢ πρὸς τὸ μέσον κ. τ. λ.) Les deux extrémités sont contraires au milieu.... Mais elles sont plus contraires l'une à l'autre que non pas au milieu. Quelquefois l'une est plus éloignée que l'autre du milieu.

Ibidem, chapitre IX, § 2, page 34[1]. (Διὸ καὶ ἔργον ἐστὶ σπουδαῖον κ. τ. λ.) Il est bien difficile d'être vertueux et de choisir le milieu.

Ibidem, chapitre IX, § 3 et 4, même page. (Διὸ δεῖ.... πρῶτον μὲν ἀποχωρεῖν τοῦ μᾶλλον ἐναντίου.... Σκοπεῖν δὲ δεῖ πρὸς ἃ καὶ αὐτοὶ εὐκατάφοροί ἐσμεν.) Il faut d'abord fuir les extrémités les plus vicieuses. — Et surtout celles[2] auxquelles nous penchons le plus.

Ibidem, chapitre IX, § 5, même page. (Ὅπερ οἱ τὰ διεστραμμένα τῶν ξύλων ὀρθοῦντες ποιοῦσιν.) Comme on redresse un arbre en lui faisant prendre un pli contraire au sien.

Ibidem, chapitre IX, § 6, page 35. (Ἐν παντὶ δὲ μάλιστα φυλακτέον τὸ ἡδὺ κ.τ.λ.) Se garder principalement de la volupté. Car nous en sommes des juges corrompus.

Ibidem, chapitre IX, § 9, même page. (Ἀποκλίνειν δὲ δεῖ, τότε μὲν ἐπὶ τὴν ὑπερβολὴν κ. τ. λ.) Il faut tantôt prendre une extrémité et tantôt l'autre.

Livre III, chapitre I, § 1-6, page 37. Actions involontaires. Actions forcées. Actions mêlées.

Ibidem, chapitre I, § 9, page 38. (Ἔνια δ' ἴσως οὐκ ἔστιν ἀναγκασθῆναι.) Il y a des actions où l'on ne doit jamais être forcé.

Ibidem, chapitre I, § 11, même page. (Εἰ δέ τις τὰ ἡδέα καὶ τὰ καλὰ φαίη βίαια εἶναι κ. τ. λ.) Le plaisir ne rend point une action forcée.

Ibidem, chapitre I, § 12, page 39. (Ἔοικε δὴ τὸ βίαιον εἶναι, οὗ ἔξωθεν ἡ ἀρχή, μηθὲν συμβαλλομένου τοῦ βιασθέντος.) *Action forcée.* C'est une action dont la cause est externe, et à laquelle celui qu'on force d'agir ne consent point.

Ibidem, chapitre I, § 13-15, même page. (Τὸ δὴ δι' ἄγνοιαν

1. En tête de cette page, Racine a écrit : « Comment on peut parvenir à la vertu. »
2. Racine a, par inadvertance, écrit *de celles,* croyant sans doute avoir mis, au lieu de *fuir,* dans la phrase précédente, *s'éloigner,* ou quelque chose de semblable. Il a aussi écrit *ausquelles.*

χ. τ. λ.) Actions faites par ignorance; quelles elles sont. — Involontaires, si on s'en repent; volontaires, si on n'en a point de regret. — L'ignorance du bien ne rend pas l'action involontaire, mais l'ignorance des circonstances.

Livre III, chapitre I, § 21, page 40. ("Ισως γὰρ οὐ καλῶς λέγεται τὸ ἀκούσια εἶναι τὰ διὰ θυμὸν, ἢ δι' ἐπιθυμίαν.) Les passions ne font point l'action involontaire.

Ibidem, chapitre II, § 2-10, pages 40 et 41. ('Η προαίρεσις κ. τ. λ.) Προαίρεσις, c'est un choix prémédité. — Ce n'est point un desir (§ 4). — Ni même un souhait ou (*une*) volonté (§ 7). — Ni une opinion (§ 10).

Ibidem, chapitre II, § 17, page 42. ('Η γὰρ προαίρεσις, μετὰ λόγου καὶ διανοίας.) Définition du mot προαίρεσις, choix avec délibération.

Ibidem, chapitre III, § 1-7, même page. (Βουλεύονται δὲ πότερα περὶ πάντων...; βουλευόμεθα δὲ περὶ τῶν ἐφ' ἡμῖν πρακτῶν.) Ce choix ne convient pas à tout. Mais il (*ce choix*) est des choses qui dépendent de nous.

Ibidem, chapitre III, § 10, page 43. (Συμβούλους δὲ παραλαμβάνομεν εἰς τὰ μεγάλα.) Demander conseil dans les grandes choses.

Ibidem, chapitre III, § 11, même page. (Βουλευόμεθα δὲ οὐ περὶ τῶν τελῶν, ἀλλὰ περὶ τῶν πρὸς τὰ τέλη.) On délibère des moyens et non pas de la fin.

Ibidem, chapitre III, § 15, même page. ("Εοικε δὴ.... ἄνθρωπος εἶναι ἀρχὴ τῶν πράξεων· ἡ δὲ βουλὴ περὶ τῶν αὐτῷ πρακτῶν· αἱ δὲ πράξεις ἄλλων ἕνεκα.) L'homme est la cause des actions. La délibération est des choses qu'il faut faire. Et l'action se fait pour d'autres choses.

Ibidem, chapitre IV, § 1, page 44. (Δοκεῖ δὲ τοῖς μὲν τἀγαθοῦ εἶναι, τοῖς δὲ τοῦ φαινομένου ἀγαθοῦ.) Savoir si ce choix est du bien ou de ce qui paroît bien.

Livre IV, chapitre I, § 7, page 61. (Τῆς ἀρετῆς γὰρ.... τὰ καλὰ πράττειν μᾶλλον ἢ τὰ αἰσχρὰ μὴ πράττειν.) La vertu consiste plus à faire le bien qu'à ne pas faire le mal.

NOTES SUR LA *POÉTIQUE*.

Nous avons, dans notre tome V, p. 477-489, donné, parmi les *Traductions de Racine*, les notes qu'il a écrites à la marge du volume intitulé : *Petri Victorii Commentarii in librum Aristotelis de Arte poetarum* (1573), parce que ces notes forment une traduction assez suivie de quelques chapitres de la *Poétique* d'Aristote. Une autre annotation marginale sur la *Poétique* d'Aristote, également de la main de Racine, mais beaucoup plus courte et qui se

ARISTOTE.

borne à quelques indications, se trouve dans un volume qui a pour titre : *Dan. Heinsii de Tragœdiæ constitutione liber...*, *cui et Aristotelis de Poetica libellus.... accedit. Lugd. Batav. Ex officina Elseviriana. M.DC.XLIII* (in-12). Au bas du feuillet de titre est la signature de Racine.

Notre poëte a souligné un certain nombre de passages de l'opuscule d'Heinsius par lequel commence ce volume, et il a quelquefois marqué, soit en tête, soit au bas des pages, les sujets qui y sont traités : « De la purgation des passions. — Définition de la tragédie, etc. » A la page 187, où Heinsius donne une ancienne version en vers ïambiques latins d'une partie de l'*Électre* de Sophocle, Racine a écrit à la marge : *Impertinente version*.

A la page 233 du volume, commence le texte grec de la *Poétique* d'Aristote, avec une traduction latine en regard. Voici les notes marginales de Racine. On y remarquera, comme dans ses notes sur l'édition de Pierre Vettori, qu'il s'est attaché à ce qui regarde le théâtre. Outre les pages de l'édition d'Heinsius, nous avons indiqué les chapitres, suivant la division que cet éditeur a adoptée, et qui lui est quelquefois particulière.

Chapitre III, page 239. (Οὗτοι μὲν γὰρ κώμας κ. τ. λ.) Nom de la comédie.

Chapitre IV, même page. (Ἐοίκασι δὲ γεννῆσαι μὲν ὅλως τὴν ποιητικὴν κ. τ. λ.) Origine de la poésie.

Ibidem, page 240. (Τῷ χαίρειν τοῖς μιμήμασι πάντας.) L'homme aime l'imitation.

Ibidem, page 241. (Διεσπάσθη δὲ κατὰ τὰ οἰκεῖα ἤθη ἡ ποίησις.) Chacun a choisi le genre de poésie qui convenoit à son naturel.

Ibidem. (Ψόγους ποιοῦντες.... Τῶν μὲν οὖν πρὸ Ὁμήρου κ. τ. λ.) Satires. — Homère a commencé. — Il avoit fait *Margitès*, qui avoit du rapport avec la comédie.

Ibidem, page 242. (Τὰ τῆς κωμῳδίας σχήματα πρῶτος ὑπέδειξεν.) On doit à Homère le genre de la comédie.

Ibidem, page 243. (Καὶ πολλὰς μεταβολὰς μεταβαλοῦσα ἡ τραγῳδία.... σκηνογραφίαν Σοφοκλῆς.) Naissance et accroissement de la tragédie. — Sophocle a inventé la décoration.

Ibidem, page 244. (Μάλιστα γὰρ λεκτικὸν τῶν μέτρων τὸ ἰαμβεῖόν ἐστι.) Vers ïambe est propre à la conversation.

Chapitre V, page 244. (Ἡ δὲ κωμῳδία ἐστὶν.... ἀλλὰ τοῦ αἰσχροῦ ἐστι τὸ γελοῖον μόριον.) Comédie ; imitation de choses basses et vicieuses. Ridicule.

Ibidem, page 245. (Τὸ μὲν οὖν ἐξ ἀρχῆς ἐκ Σικελίας ἦλθε.) Naissance de la comédie.

Ibidem, page 246. (Ἡ μὲν καὶ ὅτι μάλιστα πειρᾶται ὑπὸ μίαν περίοδον ἡλίου εἶναι κ. τ. λ.) Temps de la tragédie et du poëme épique. — Tour d'un soleil.

Chapitre VI, page 247. (Ἔστιν οὖν τραγῳδία μίμησις κ. τ. λ.) Définition de la tragédie.

Chapitre vi, page 248. (Ἀνάγκη οὖν πάσης τραγῳδίας μέρη εἶναι ἕξ.) Six parties de la tragédie.

Ibidem, page 249. (Μέγιστον δὲ τούτων ἐστὶν ἡ τῶν πραγμάτων σύστασις.... ἄνευ δὲ ἠθῶν γένοιτ' ἄν.) La fable est la principale partie. L'action n'est pas pour les mœurs. — La tragédie peut être sans mœurs et non pas sans action.

Ibidem, page 250. (Ἔτι ἐάν τις ἐφεξῆς θῇ ῥήσεις ἠθικάς.... δεύτερον δὲ τὰ ἤθη.) La constitution est plus difficile que l'exécution. — Peripétie. *Agnitio.* — Fable est l'âme de la trag[édie]; après, les mœurs.

Ibidem, page 251. (Εἰ γάρ τις ἐναλείψειε τοῖς καλλίστοις φαρμάκοις χύδην κ. τ. λ.) Comp[araison] d'un tableau.

Ibidem, même page. (Οἱ μὲν γὰρ ἀρχαῖοι πολιτικῶς κ. τ. λ.) Les anciens faisoient parler politiquement, et les modernes rhétoriquement.

Ibidem, page 252. (Τῶν δὲ λοιπῶν πέντε ἡ μελοποιια.... ἄνευ ἀγῶνος καὶ ὑποκριτῶν.) Représentation. — Musique. — La tragédie peut être sans acteurs.

Chapitre xvii, page 280. Quatre espèces de tragédie. *Implexa. Pathetica. Morata*[1].

Chapitre xviii, pages 282 et 283. (Περὶ δὲ τὰ ἤθη τέτταρά ἐστιν κ. τ. λ.) Quatre choses à observer dans les mœurs. *Boni, convenientes, similes, æquales.*

Ibidem, page 284. (Ἢ τὸ ἀναγκαῖον, ἢ τὸ εἰκός.... ἀλλὰ μηχανῇ χρηστέον ἐπὶ τὰ ἔξω τοῦ δράματος, ἢ ὅσα πρὸ τοῦ γέγονεν κ. τ. λ.) Vraisemblable ou nécessaire. — Le dénouement doit sortir du sein de la fable. On peut se servir de machine dans ce qui précède l'action.

Ibidem, pages 284 et 285. (Μίμησίς ἐστιν ἡ τραγῳδία βελτιόνων κ. τ. λ.) Il faut rendre meilleurs en rendant semblables[2].

---

[1]. Racine a omis la dernière, *fabulosa*, suivant l'expression employée dans la traduction d'Heinsius.

[2]. La *Poétique* et les *Éthiques à Nicomaque* sont les seuls ouvrages d'Aristote sur lesquels nous ayons trouvé des notes de Racine. Parmi les livres de sa bibliothèque qui sont aujourd'hui à la Bibliothèque de Toulouse, il y a un volume de la *Rhétorique* d'Aristote : *Aristotelis de Rhetorica. Londini, ap. Griffinum,* 1619, in-4°.

PLUTARQUE.

NOTES SUR LES *VIES PARALLÈLES*.

Les notes de Racine sur Plutarque sont très-nombreuses. On les trouve sur les marges de deux volumes in-folio qui renferment le texte grec, l'un des *Vies parallèles*, l'autre des *OEuvres morales*. Tous deux sont conservés à la Bibliothèque impériale. La date des annotations que nous avons jusqu'ici mises sous les yeux des lecteurs nous est inconnue. Nous avons au contraire la date des notes sur Plutarque certifiée de la main même de Racine : c'est l'année 1655 pour les *Vies parallèles*; l'année 1656 pour les *OEuvres morales*. Ce double travail est donc du temps où Racine étudiait à Port-Royal, et nous y trouvons ainsi une des preuves les plus frappantes et du solide enseignement qu'il y recevait, et de l'ardeur avec laquelle il le mettait à profit. A l'âge de seize et de dix-sept ans, avoir lu d'un bout à l'autre, la plume à la main, et avoir annoté avec tant de détail tous les écrits de Plutarque, n'est-ce pas un fait très-digne d'être remarqué, et qui donne une haute idée aussi bien des maîtres habiles de Racine que de leur jeune élève?

Nous allons d'abord faire connaître les notes sur les *Vies parallèles*.

Le volume in-folio dont ces notes couvrent les marges est de l'édition de Philippe Junta (Florence, 1517[1]), et porte en tête une épître en latin de Junta à Marcelle Virgile, secrétaire de la république de Florence. Au bas de cette épître, on lit de la main de notre poëte : *Joannes Racine*, 1655.

Il n'y a pas une des *Vies* écrites par Plutarque que Racine n'ait annotée. Reproduire entièrement ce travail serait passer les justes bornes. Une grande partie de ces notes n'est en quelque sorte qu'une table des matières très-développée. Citons, pour servir d'exemple, les premières notes de ce volume, qui sont sur le commencement de la *Vie de Thésée* : « Voleurs. — Noblesse. — Courage. — Beaux faits[2] de Thésée, qui tâche d'imiter Hercule, son cousin. — Médée. — Thésée est reconnu de son père Égée. — Fable du Minotaure expliquée. Tribut d'Athènes à Minos. — Ariadné. — Mort d'Égée, père de

---

[1]. Le *Catalogue de la bibliothèque de M. Aimé-Martin*, Paris, Techener, 1847, indique, sous le n° 1093, un autre exemplaire de la même édition des *Vies* de Plutarque, avec la signature et des notes de Racine. Le *Quérard* le signale également, comme porté au *Catalogue* de la quatrième vente *de MM. Debure frères, supplément*, n° 57; et en outre les *OEuvres de Plutarque* (*Plutarchi Opera*, Paris, 1624, 2 vol. in-folio), avec la signature de Racine, d'après le *Bulletin du bibliophile*, de Techener, 1845, n° 493.

[2]. Racine écrit en un seul mot : *beaufaicts*.

Thésée. — Institution de la république d'Athènes. — Mort funeste d'Égée. — Thésée établit la république d'Athènes et quitte la monarchie. »

Il y avait, on le voit, beaucoup à retrancher pour ne pas tomber dans une minutieuse exactitude qui nous aurait conduit trop loin. Nous avons dû faire un choix des notes les plus intéressantes. On pouvait surtout regarder comme telles, à ce qu'il nous a semblé, celles qui, rapprochées les unes des autres, se trouvent former comme un résumé de la sagesse de Plutarque, une collection de ses maximes et de ses plus sages pensées. C'est, en effet, un des caractères les plus frappants de cette annotation de Racine, que le soin particulier qu'il a pris d'extraire de son auteur les réflexions générales, et, comme on dit dans la langue de la rhétorique, les *lieux communs*. C'était, il est permis de le croire, une provision qu'il voulait faire, et dont il sentait qu'il pourrait tirer un jour parti, comme orateur ou comme poëte. Peut-être aussi, sans qu'il songeât à cette utilité littéraire, était-il frappé des enseignements moraux que Plutarque tire sans cesse des faits, plus encore qu'il ne l'était de ces faits mêmes; et ce n'était pas mal connaître le biographe qu'il étudiait, que de chercher surtout le moraliste en lui.

Nous nous sommes donc à peu près borné à donner les maximes que Racine a tirées des *Vies parallèles*, qu'il les y ait trouvées expressément ou d'une manière implicite; nous y avons joint cependant un petit nombre de notes qui n'ont pas ce caractère, mais dont l'expression nous a paru mériter d'être remarquée. Ne voulant pas multiplier, sans nécessité, dans ce volume, les citations grecques, nous ne mettrons pas le texte grec en regard des traductions plus ou moins libres de Racine. On pourra, si l'on veut, le trouver, au moyen de l'indication que nous donnons de chacune des *Vies* auxquelles les notes se rapportent.

Vie de Romulus. Ne condamner sans avoir écouté l'accusé. — Il falloit que l'origine de Rome fût aussi étrange que sa puissance a été depuis. — Le haut du pavé accordé aux femmes [1]. — Prospérités rendent orgueilleux. — Nécessité rend généreux. — Princes. Ne se rendre méprisables, ni trop formidables. — Ne se rendre trop populaire ni trop tyrannique.

Vie de Solon. L'esprit est sujet à aimer autant qu'à penser et à songer. — Solon condamnoit ceux qui dans une sédition ne se mettent d'aucun parti. — Accommoder les lois au temps, et non le temps aux lois. — Il faut secourir la nécessité des pauvres, et non entretenir leur lâcheté. — Ne couronner ceux qui combattent encore. — Félicité. La perte en est plus sensible que la possession.

Vie de Publicola. Plus on se rabaisse, et plus on est élevé. — N'être trop sévère ni trop doux.

---

1. Racine a ainsi traduit l'expression de Plutarque : ἐξίστασθαι μὲν ὁδοῦ βαδιζούσαις (chapitre xx). — L'édition dont Racine a fait usage n'ayant pas de divisions de chapitres, nous indiquons ces divisions, quand il y a lieu, d'après celle de Tauchnitz (Leipzig, 1829).

Vie de Thémistocle. La hardiesse et confiance est le commencement de la victoire. — Chercher en mariage plutôt un homme sans argent que de l'argent sans homme.

Vie de Camille. Vaincre par justice plutôt que par force.

Vie d'Aristide. Aimer mieux être vertueux que de le paroitre. — Ne regarder son intérêt dans les jugements. — Obéir aux capitaines savants. — Folie des princes qui aiment mieux se faire renommer par leur puissance que par leur vertu. — La vertu nous rend divins et le vice brutaux. — *N. (nota.)* La vertu est haïe des ignorants. — Ne point considérer son intérêt particulier pour le public. — Il n'importe en quel lieu on fasse bien. — Faire plutôt de belles actions que de louer celles de ses ancêtres. — N'examiner trop un crime en un temps dangereux, lorsqu'il y a plusieurs complices. — Peu souffrent bien la pauvreté.

Vie de Caton l'ancien. Caton ménager. — Choses inutiles sont toujours trop chères. — Paroles font reconnoitre plutôt que le visage. — Peuples moutons. — Ne refuser de l'argent aux alliés dans les combats. — Distribuer aux soldats plutôt que se réserver. — Les Romains parlent du cœur et les Grecs des lèvres. — Ménage de Caton. — Se marier pour donner de bons citoyens à son pays. — Servir le public jusqu'à la mort. — Louer les bons, ne blâmer les méchants.

Vie de Cimon. Ne louer faussement. — Ne trop s'arrêter aux vices. Il n'y a point d'homme parfait. — Inimitiés particulières doivent céder au bien public. — Faire la guerre aux ennemis légitimes.

Vie de Lucullus. Ne refuser tout ce qu'on présente dans les ambassades. — Luculle aime mieux sauver un Romain que de vaincre tous ses ennemis. — Ne quitter la bête pour aller à son gîte. — Reine misérable[1]. — Trop grande félicité trouble le jugement. *Fortuna dulcis inebriat. Hor.* od. 37, lib. I. — Les plaisirs sont aussi peu convenables à un vieillard que les grands emplois. — *Lucullus Xerxes togatus.* — C'est une chose digne d'un grand capitaine ou d'un grand magistrat, de passer sa vieillesse dans les études. — Il vaut mieux être vertueux en sa vieillesse qu'en sa jeunesse.

Vie de Périclès. Cette vie est une idée admirable d'un bon gouverneur et d'un bon prince. — Contre ceux qui s'amusent à des singes ou à des chiens. — Apprendre des choses agréables et utiles. — On admire l'ouvrage, et on méprise l'ouvrier. On admire la vertu

---

1. Nous donnons cette note, parce que Racine y a marqué le malheur de Monime, à l'occasion de ce passage du chapitre XVIII : καὶ ἀπεθρήνει τὴν τοῦ σώματος εὐμορφίαν, qu'il a cité dans sa *Préface* de la tragédie de *Mithridate*. Voyez notre tome III, p. 19.

et celui qui en est doué. — Ne se soucier des calomnies ni des menaces lorsqu'il s'agit du bien du public. — Belle parole de Périclès sur ce que personne n'étoit mort de mort violente sous son gouvernement. — Contre les rêveries des poëtes touchant les Dieux.

Vie de Fabius Maximus. S'instruire par ses fautes.

Vie de Nicias. C'est bassesse d'esprit que de vouloir disputer aux autres la gloire d'écrire mieux. — Le peuple veut être craint. — Nicias faisoit également ses libéralités aux méchants et aux bons. — Ne demander aux ennemis les morts de son parti pour les enterrer. — Ne laisser à ses ennemis aucune occasion de s'acquérir de la gloire. — Les riches, les vieillards et les laboureurs aiment la paix. — Trêves font desirer la paix. — Aimer mieux mourir par les mains de ses citoyens que de les voir mourir avec soi. — Fortunes de la guerre incertaines. — Bien user de sa victoire.

Vie de Crassus. Contre ceux qui aiment à bâtir. — Le maître doit avoir soin de ses serviteurs. — C'est beaucoup que d'avoir ce qui suffit pour vivre. — Ne violer la justice pour de petites choses.

Vie de Coriolan. C'est une chose plus louable de bien manier de l'argent que de bien manier des armes. — La solitude est la compagne de l'arrogance. — Ce n'est pas une chose digne d'un homme d'honneur de se ressouvenir des injures.

Vie d'Alcibiade. Éloigner la guerre le plus qu'on peut de soi. — Les jeunes gens changent facilement le jeu en insolence. — Orgueil des victorieux. — Contre ceux qui flattent le peuple.

Vie de Démosthène. Ne point s'abandonner à la douleur dans les afflictions. — Danger qu'il y a de se mêler des affaires publiques.

Vie de Cicéron. Avocats qui crient à pleine tête. — Idée d'un bon gouverneur. — Naturel gaillard de Cicéron. Gravité de Démosthène.

Vie de Pyrrhus. Princes avares ne peuvent demeurer en paix. — Rois, par leurs[1] infidélités, donnent mauvais exemple à leurs sujets. — Vaincre l'ennemi à force ouverte. — Superbe de Pyrrhus. — N'insulter à ses ennemis.

Vie de Marius. Préférer la gloire de son pays à la sienne. — Contre ceux qui renoncent à la vertu pour acquérir de la puissance. — Faire le bien lorsqu'il y a du danger. — N'être trop exact à garder la justice. — Actions de grâce de Platon à Dieu. — Contre ceux qui ne se contentent de leurs[2] biens présents.

---

1. Racine a écrit ici *leur* sans *s*. De même, dans la *Vie de Marius*, on lit de lui cette note : « Capitaines qui travaillent avec *leur* soldats. » Voyez ci-dessus, p. 210, note 1.

2. Ici encore, et à la ligne suivante, Racine a écrit *leur*.

Vie d'Aratus. Contre ceux qui se vantent de la vertu de leurs ancêtres. — Combien il sert d'avoir de bons capitaines et que la discipline militaire soit bien réglée. — Avantages de l'union et de la concorde. — N'avoir autre but dans ses amitiés et inimitiés que le bien public. — Rendre sa fuite illustre par quelque belle action. — La dissimulation que la crainte nous fait prendre se découvre lorsque nous sommes en sûreté.

Vie d'Artaxerxe. On se souvient plutôt des injures que des faveurs. — Roi doit se rendre agréable à ses sujets. — Les sujets peuvent parler et les rois faire. — Il est indigne d'un roi de craindre les dangers. — La vérité est dans le vin. — La lâcheté ne provient de la volupté. — Tyrans lâches sont cruels. Les généreux sont doux. — *N. (nota.)* Les mauvais conseils sont plutôt suivis que les bons.

Vies d'Agis et de Cléomène. Belle application de la fable d'Ixion aux ambitieux. — Contre ceux qui flattent le menu peuple. — Combien un homme de bien a besoin de gloire. — Ambition dangereuse à ceux qui commandent. — N'obéir à ceux que nous gouvernons. — Ceux qui sont enveillis dans la corruption. — Quand on ne peut vaincre les autres en richesses, les vaincre en vertus. — Obéir aux plus anciens. — Ne se repentir du bien qu'on a fait pour la mort même. — Roi que de nom. — Cléomène rétablit la réformation de Lycurgue. — Craindre le vice et non les malheurs. — Il est impossible de remédier à des corruptions enveillies, sans violence. — Combien sert la douceur dans les princes. — Table de Cléomène. Augmenter l'ordinaire quand on reçoit des étrangers. — N'abandonner une république quand elle est en danger. — Un homme n'est jamais parfait, quoique très-vertueux. Foiblesse humaine [1]. — Combien la réformation de Cléomène servit à Sparte. — Ne se soucier des murmures. — L'argent nerfs [2] de la guerre.

Vies de Tibérius et de Caïus Gracchus. La vertu plus honorable que les dignités et les triomphes. — Combien l'union est puissante. — Vierges criminelles ne sont plus vierges. — Nourriture de ces quatre grands hommes (*Caïus et Tibérius Gracchus, Agis et Cléomène*). — Il ne faut point user de violence, sinon à l'extrémité.

Vie de Lycurgue. Contre les lieux superbes et magnifiques où l'on

---

1. Une feuille qui a été collée intérieurement sur la couverture, à la fin du volume, a également cette note de Racine, avec renvoi au même passage, et ainsi développée : « Foiblesse humaine. La nature humaine est si foible qu'elle ne sauroit produire d'elle-même aucune vertu qui ne soit souillée de quelque vice, même dans les plus parfaits. »

2. Racine a ainsi mis *nerfs*, au pluriel.

tient les assemblées. — Moins un roi est absolu, plus il est en sûreté. — Mort ne doit être inutile.

Vie de Lysandre. Grands esprits mélancoliques. — Belle parole sur l'ambition et la jalousie des grands capitaines. — Agésilas roi que de nom.

Vie de Sylla. Sylla vide les temples des Grecs. — *Honores mutant mores.* — Il faut regarder quel est un prince, et non quels ont été ses pères. — Lysandre fit plus de mal à Sparte, l'emplissant d'argent, que Sylla à Rome en la vidant de celui qu'elle avoit. — Sylla étant méchant rendit ses citoyens bons, et Lysandre rendit ses citoyens pires que lui. — Combats auprès des murs, dangereux.

Vie de Phocion. Comment il faut gouverner une république. — Il y a des vertus qui sont différentes d'elles-mêmes. — Peu de mots, mais beaucoup de sens. — Quelle est l'autorité d'un homme de bien. — Ne faire compte des médisants et des opiniâtres. — Ne point faire de feux de joie pour la mort d'un prince ennemi. — Discours qui sont éloquents et ne font point de fruit. — Ne point avoir des capitaines trop jeunes. — Donner des charges à des hommes modestes, non à des séditieux.

Vie de Caton le jeune. Ce que l'on a de la peine à apprendre, on le retient mieux. — Ne point parler en public avant que s'y être longtemps préparé. — Ne rougir que des choses véritablement déshonnêtes. — S'instruire bien du devoir d'une charge devant que de la prendre. — Parler fortement quand la douceur est méprisée. — Ne point résister à ce que tout le monde a ordonné, quoique injuste. — Le trop grand amour engendre la haine.

Vie de Dion. Peu de soldats, mais bons. — Gens qui font le danger plus grand qu'il n'est, pour excuser leur fuite. — N'être trop passionné dans une histoire. — Belles paroles de Dion touchant la clémence.

Vie de Brutus. Brute suit le parti de Pompée, quoiqu'il eût fait mourir son père. *N. (nota.)* — Ne fléchir aux prières injustes. — Ne se rendre trop familier aux tyrans. — Femmes ne sauroient retenir un secret. — Amnestie [1]. — Brute et Cassius rejoignent leurs troupes ensemble. — *Mortuus non mordet.* — Ne point souffrir d'injustice dans ses amis, comme dans les autres. — Parlement [2] de Cassius et de Brute.

Vie de Paul Émile. Choisir les bonnes choses et rejeter les mauvaises. — Suivre l'exemple de ses ancêtres. — Des petites fautes

---

1. Racine a écrit ce mot ainsi. Richelet, dans son *Dictionnaire* (1680), donne les deux formes : *amnistie* et *amnestie*.

2. *Parlement*, c'est-à-dire *conférence, conseil de guerre.*

on vient aux grandes. — Peuple romain maître du monde et soumis à la vertu. — Acheter les prospérités par l'argent, et non rechercher l'argent dans les prospérités. — Montrer de la gaieté à ses soldats. — Dieu n'exauce point les prières des injustes. — Les ennemis ont compassion des hommes courageux, lorsqu'ils sont vaincus; mais les lâches passent pour des infâmes, quoique vainqueurs. — Les prospérités font craindre les adversités. — On connoît la vertu d'un capitaine lorsqu'il gaigne de grandes victoires avec de mauvais soldats. — Laisser le jugement des capitaines à ceux qui connoissent la guerre. — Les prospérités sont toujours mêlées de quelque adversité. — Être généreux contre les hommes et contre la fortune.

Vie de Timoléon. Ne rien faire sans une résolution ferme et constante, et sans y avoir bien songé. — Le repentir rend même les bonnes actions mauvaises. — On supporte plus facilement les malheurs que les injures. — Contre les scrupuleux.

Vie de Sertorius. La fortune ne peut changer les naturels véritablement vertueux. — Barbares sujets à la superstition. — Il faut qu'un prince généreux préfère l'honnêteté à la victoire et à sa propre vie.

Vie d'Eumène. Les adversités font paroître la véritable vertu. — Ne demander la vie à son ennemi.

Vie de Philopœmen. Lire les livres utiles. — Armes bien parées. — Vue des superfluités excite à la volupté. — Ne corrompre les amis et les gens de bien, mais les méchants. — Maladies diminuent avec les forces.

Vie de Flamininus. Quitter facilement sa colère et conserver toujours son amour. — *Satius dare quam accipere.* — Soldat devant qu'être capitaine. — Prudence et douceur nécessaires à un capitaine. — Bien user de la victoire. — Ceux qui reçoivent un bienfait sont cause de la louange de ceux qui le leur ont fait. — Être aimé vaut mieux qu'être honoré. — Ne se soucier des Barbares, quoique en grand nombre. — Ne protéger des parents injustes. — Ambition se découvre dans les hommes âgés. — Vieillesse ôte la force, et non les inclinations. — Mort est la fin des changements. — Commander aux lois, quand il le faut. — Plus facile de faire plaisir aux foibles que [de] résister aux puissants.

Vie de Pélopidas. Les maux font mépriser la mort. — Un général d'armée ne doit se hasarder trop. — En quel temps il doit se hasarder. — Joindre ensemble les hommes généreux. — Il faut que les princes sauvent les autres. — *Servator servati dominus est.*

Vie de Marcellus. Suivre la tradition. — Dieu conduit les capitaines. — Courage inhumain des Romains. — Contre ceux qui remplissent leurs[1] villes de pièces rares et magnifiques. — Finir les guerres plutôt par prudence et douceur que par force. — Il est plus glorieux d'être honoré par les ennemis que par les amis.

Vie d'Alexandre. Contre ceux qui s'amusent à décrire des guerres et des combats par le menu. — Le naturel d'un homme se reconnoît plutôt dans une petite action que dans beaucoup d'autres grandes. — Donner de bons précepteurs aux jeunes rois. — Ne point flatter les rebelles. — Ne croire trop tôt les calomnies. — C'est une chose plus digne d'un roi de surmonter ses passions que de vaincre ses ennemis. — Danger des gens de bien dans la cour. — Dieu est le père de tous, et adopte pour fils tous les hommes de bien. — C'est une grande consolation d'être vaincu par un prince vertueux. — Ne se soucier du butin dans un combat. — Alexandre ne déroboit point la victoire[2]. — L'affection avec laquelle on donne rend le don plus agréable. — Larmes de mère[3]. — C'est une chose digne de la grandeur d'un roi, de souffrir qu'on parle mal de lui lorsqu'il fait bien. — Rien d'imprenable à la hardiesse. — Tâcher de se vaincre en bienfaits, et non en forces. — Les rois ne doivent trop s'éloigner du milieu de leur royaume.

Vie de César. Vieillesse donne de l'assurance. *Extrema senecta liber.* Tacite (*Annales, livre XIII, chapitre* XLII). — Récompenser bien les vaillants soldats. Ne prendre rien (*du butin*) pour soi plus que les autres. — Se servir de l'occasion. — On éloigne les gens de bien quand on veut faire quelque mauvais dessein. — Le plus grand bien que César tiroit de sa victoire, étoit de sauver ses ennemis.

Vie d'Agésilas. Ambition excessive dangereuse. — Tromper ses alliés est un crime, et ses ennemis une grande vertu. — Il vaut mieux avoir un bon cheval dans une armée qu'un mauvais homme. — Ne regarder ses intérêts particuliers en une chose publique. — Quitter tout pour l'utilité de son pays. — N'empêcher ses ennemis de semer. — Rois ne doivent avoir d'amitié particulière. — Ne combattre souvent contre les mêmes ennemis. — Ne faire rien hors de son temps.

Vie de Pompée. Les grands bonheurs sont toujours mêlés de quel-

---

1. Ici encore il y a *leur* sans *s*.

2. Cette note est écrite en marge du passage : οὐ κλέπτω τὴν νίκην, que nous avons cité (tome I, p. 572, note 1) sur le vers 1062 de la tragédie d'*Alexandre le Grand* :

   Jamais on ne m'a vu dérober la victoire.

3. Cette note se rapporte à ce passage du chapitre XXXIX : ἀγνοεῖν εἶπεν Ἀντίπατρον ὅτι μυρίας ἐπιστολὰς ἓν δάκρυον ἀπαλείφει μητρός.

que adversité. — Ne tuer aucun citoyen romain qu'en bataille rangée. — Ne céder pour les injures, et ne flatter les malades. — Cornélie. Ses pleurs à Pompée [1]. — Préférer la gloire de l'éternité à celle d'une journée.

Vie d'Othon. Princes doivent assister aux combats. — Plus de morts dans les guerres civiles. — Prince. Mourir pour le repos de son royaume.

Vie de Galba. Ne faire mourir sans forme de procès. — Pauvreté marque de bonté en un prince.

Pour achever de faire connaître le travail de Racine sur les *Vies parallèles*, il est bon d'ajouter que les rapprochements empruntés aux auteurs anciens, très-présents évidemment au jeune écolier de Port-Royal, sont fort nombreux dans ses notes. Il y cite des passages de Cicéron, de Salluste, de Tacite, de Quintilien, de Pline le jeune, de Virgile, d'Horace, de Lucain, de Varron, de Polyen. Mais ce que nous devons encore moins omettre, ce que nous avons réservé dans cette annotation pour le recueillir à part, comme en étant la partie la plus curieuse, ce sont les comparaisons qui se sont offertes à l'esprit de Racine entre quelques personnages ou quelques idées qu'il a rencontrés dans Plutarque, et des personnages ou des idées modernes. Les pensées religieuses l'ont beaucoup frappé, et plus particulièrement celles où, avec quelque préoccupation, il croyait trouver la *grâce*. Cela est à remarquer, surtout à cause de la date. Du Fossé, voulant disculper les maîtres des petites écoles du reproche « d'y nourrir de leurs sentiments ceux qui étoient instruits, » a dit dans ses *Mémoires :* « Jamais on ne parle moins de ces sortes de matières théologiques que dans nos écoles. » Quelle que fût cette sage réserve, à laquelle nous voulons bien croire dans une certaine mesure, il est visible cependant que quelque chose de tout cela arrivait aux oreilles, très-ouvertes sans doute, du jeune Racine. Nous en avons déjà trouvé un autre indice dans ses vers *ad Christum*, imprimés aux pages 208-210 de notre tome IV : voyez surtout les vers 35 et 36.

Nous allons donner, cette fois avec l'indication des passages qui y correspondent dans le texte, les notes de Racine que nous venons d'annoncer.

Vie de Romulus, chapitre VII. Θεοῦ συμπαρόντος καὶ συνεπευθύνοντος ἀρχὰς μεγάλων πραγμάτων. GRACE.

Ibidem, chapitre XXVII. Σέβεσθαι Ῥωμύλον, ὡς ἀνηρπασμένον εἰς Θεούς, καὶ Θεὸν εὐμενῆ γενησόμενον αὐτοῖς ἐκ χρηστοῦ βασιλέως. SAINT LOUIS.

Vie de Solon, chapitre XXVII. Ἕλλησιν.... πρός τε τἆλλα μετρίως ἔχειν ὁ Θεὸς ἔδωκε. GRACE.

---

1. Cette note est sur ce passage du chapitre LXXIV : ὁρῶ σε, εἶπεν, ἄνερ κ. τ. λ.

Vie de Caton. Comparaison d'Aristide et de Caton, chapitre II. Κάτων.... πρόβλημα τοῦ βίου, καὶ δραστήριον ὄργανον ἔχων τὸν λόγον· ᾧ δικαιότερον ἄν τις, ἢ τύχῃ καὶ δαίμονι τοῦ ἀνδρὸς, τὸ μηδὲν παθεῖν παρ' ἀξίαν ἀνατιθείη. *N^a*. Grace suffisante.

Vie de Coriolan, chapitre XXIII. Τοσούτῳ βέλτιον ὑπὲρ ὑμῶν πολεμήσοντος, ἢ πρὸς ὑμᾶς, ὅσῳ πολεμοῦσι βέλτιον οἱ γινώσκοντες τὰ παρὰ τοῖς πολεμίοις τῶν ἀγνοούντων. M. le Prince[1].

Ibidem, chapitre XXXII. Τὰ μὲν εἰκότα καὶ συνήθη κατὰ λόγον περαινόμενα τῷ ἐφ' ἡμῖν ἀποδίδωσι. De libero arbitrio[2].

Ibidem. Ἐν δὲ ταῖς ἀτόποις καὶ παραδόλοις πράξεσι κ. τ. λ.[3] Cela est semi-pélagien[4].

Vie d'Alcibiade, chapitre XXII. Θεανὼ.... φάσκουσαν εὐχῶν, οὐ καταρῶν ἱέρειαν γεγονέναι. Voeu de Caen[5]. Je suis consacrée aux Dieux pour faire des vœux pour le bien des hommes, et non pas des imprécations contre eux.

Ibidem, chapitre XXIII. Δόντων δὲ τῶν Σπαρτιατῶν καὶ δεξαμένων, παραγενόμενος προθύμως.... καὶ οἰκοφθόρησε τὴν πόλιν. M. le Prince[6].

Vie d'Aratus, chapitre XV. Ἀντίγονος δ' ὁ βασιλεὺς, ἀνιώμενος ἐπ' αὐτῷ, καὶ βουλόμενος ἢ μὲν ἄγειν ὅλως τῇ φιλίᾳ πρὸς αὐτὸν, ἢ διαβάλλειν κ. τ. λ. Card[inal] de Richelieu[7].

---

1. Au temps où Racine écrivait ces notes (1655), le grand Condé, allié aux Espagnols contre la France, jouait le rôle de Coriolan.

2. En tête de la page où ce passage se trouve, Racine a écrit aussi : *Libre arbitre.*

3. Jusqu'à la fin du chapitre.

4. Racine avait d'abord écrit : « Cela est pélagien. » Il a ensuite ajouté *semi* dans l'interligne.

5. Le vœu de Caen est aussi mentionné dans les notes sur les *Questions romaines* (ci-après, p. 318), et en outre sur la feuille dont nous avons parlé ci-dessus, p. 295, note 1, on trouve encore écrit, avec renvoi à ce même passage de la *Vie d'Alcibiade* : « Voeu de Caen. Jés. (*Jésuites*). Je suis prêtre, non pas pour maudire les hommes, mais pour les bénir. » — Le vœu des PP. Jésuites de Caen, imprimé sous la date du mois de juin 1653, et ayant pour titre : *Ad B. Virginem votum*, est en vingt vers latins. On y demande que ceux qui ressuscitent les erreurs de Jansénius (*dogma Leerdanum*) soient seuls exceptés de la rédemption apportée par Jésus-Christ à tous les hommes. Voyez dans les *Enluminures du fameux Almanach*, la XVe enluminure. Racine a voulu mettre le vœu des Jésuites en contraste avec les belles paroles d'une prêtresse païenne.

6. Voyez ci-dessus, note 1 de cette même page.

7. Il ne nous revient pas en mémoire à quel acte du cardinal de Richelieu Racine fait allusion, lorsqu'il le compare ainsi à Antigone cherchant, pour s'attacher Aratus par une amitié exclusive, à le perdre dans l'esprit de Ptolémée. Nous voyons bien seulement qu'il a voulu le représenter comme ayant

Vie d'Agis, chapitre VII. Κατεσχέθησαν οἷον ἐπιπνοίᾳ πρὸς τὸ καλόν. Grace.

Vie de Cléomène, chapitre XXVII. Ἡ τὰ μέγιστα τῶν πραγμάτων κρίνουσα τῷ παρὰ μικρὸν τύχη. Providence.

Vie de Lycurgue, chapitre V. Οἷον ἕρμα τὴν τῶν γερόντων ἀρχὴν κ. τ. λ. Parlements.

Ibidem, chapitre XXIV. Ἡ γὰρ τῶν ἐφόρων κατάστασις οὐκ ἄνεσις ἦν, ἀλλ' ἐπίτασις τῆς πολιτείας κ. τ. λ. Parlement [1].

Vie de Caton le jeune, chapitre IV. Περὶ πᾶσαν μὲν ἀρετὴν ὥσπερ ἐπιπνοίᾳ τινὶ κατάσχετος γεγονώς. Grace [2].

Vie de Brutus, chapitre XLVII. Ὁ Θεὸς ἐξάγειν καὶ μεταστῆσαι τὸν μόνον ἐμποδὼν ὄντα τῷ κρατεῖν δυναμένῳ βουλόμενος. Providence de Dieu.

Vie de Timoléon, chapitre XVI. Τῷ φυλάττοντι δαίμονι τὸν Τιμολέοντα πάθος ἔχρησε δίκαιον. Providence.

Vie de Flamininus. Comparaison de Flamininus et de Philopémen, chapitre II. Ὁ δὲ μυρίας μάχας κατορθώσας.... ὥστε τοῦ μὲν ἴδιον, τοῦ δὲ κοινὸν ἔργον εἶναι τὸ κατορθούμενον. Grace suffisante [3].

Vie de Marcellus, chapitre XXX. Οὐδὲν ἄρα δυνατὸν γενέσθαι ἄκοντος Θεοῦ. Puissance de Dieu.

Vie d'Agésilas, chapitre IV. Οἱ δὲ γέροντες διὰ βίου ταύτην ἔχουσι τὴν τιμήν, ἐπὶ τῷ μὴ πάντα τοῖς βασιλεῦσιν ἐξεῖναι συνταχθέντες. Parlement.

Vie de Pompée, chapitre XXVII. Ἐφ' ὅσον ὢν ἄνθρωπος οἶδας, ἐπὶ τοσοῦτον εἶ θεός. Humilité.

Ibidem, chapitre LXXV. Ἐμέμψατο καὶ συνδιηπόρησε βραχέα περὶ τῆς προνοίας.... Ἐπεὶ τὸ μὲν ἐρέσθαι τὸν Πομπήϊον ἦν ὑπὲρ τῆς προνοίας κ. τ. λ. Providence.

été jaloux de ceux qui cherchaient une autre faveur que la sienne, et capable de les desservir perfidement.

1. Racine, dans ces notes, nomme le *Parlement* avec une faveur évidente. Louis Racine (voyez notre tome I, p. 209) raconte que son père étant au collége de Beauvais, guerroya, dans une bataille d'écoliers, pour un des deux partis qui divisaient alors la France. Il était probablement du côté des Frondeurs.

2. Sur la feuille mentionnée ci-dessus, p. 295, note 1, Racine, citant ce même passage, depuis ὥσπερ, a de nouveau écrit grace, et ajouté cette traduction : « Caton aimoit tellement la vertu qu'il sembloit y être poussé par une inspiration divine. »

3. Il n'est pas très-facile, ce nous semble, de comprendre par quelle subtilité Racine a trouvé la *grâce suffisante* dans ce passage, qui est certainement l'objet de sa note. Peut-être se rapporte-t-elle uniquement aux derniers mots, et moins au sens qu'ils ont dans Plutarque, qu'à l'application qu'on en pourrait faire.

NOTES SUR LES *OEUVRES MORALES*.

L'ANNOTATION de Racine sur les *OEuvres morales* de Plutarque est tout à fait du même genre que son annotation sur les *Vies parallèles*, comme elle est aussi à peu près du même temps. Il n'a pu manquer toutefois de faire une moisson de maximes plus abondante encore dans ces écrits où Plutarque a été exclusivement moraliste ; et par conséquent nous avons eu, tout en suivant la même règle que dans la transcription des notes des *Vies parallèles*, à retrancher beaucoup moins dans celles des *OEuvres morales*. Nous avons seulement omis ce qui, dans sa brièveté, eût été trop insignifiant. Le volume sur les marges duquel nous avons recueilli l'annotation manuscrite que nous allons donner a pour titre : *Plutarchi...., varia scripta, quæ* Moralia *vulgo dicuntur. Basileæ, per Eusebium Episcopium et Nicolai, Fr. hæredes. M.D.LXXIIII*, in-folio. Sur le feuillet de titre, Racine a écrit : *Joannes Racine. Cœptum 29 maii* 1656.

Nous citons chacun des traités de Plutarque sous le titre latin qu'il porte dans l'édition de Tauchnitz, Leipzig, 1829 (ce titre est en grec dans celle dont Racine s'est servi); et quand nous renverrons aux chapitres, nous suivrons, comme pour les *Vies parallèles*, la division adoptée dans cette même édition de Leipzig.

DE LIBERIS EDUCANDIS. Ne se marier qu'à des personnes très-honnêtes. — Combien l'infamie des pères nuit aux enfants. — Nature inutile sans travail. — Force du travail et de l'exercice. — Nourriture. Les mères doivent tâcher de nourrir elles-mêmes leurs[1] enfants. — Bonnes nourrices. — Les enfants plus faciles à instruire. — Valets et compagnons. — Condition des maîtres. — Contre les mauvais maîtres. — Bassesse des biens corporels. — Vieillesse augmente le jugement. — *N. (nota.)* On ne peut plaire au peuple sans déplaire aux hommes sages. — Ne rien dire sans y avoir bien pensé. — Former le corps aux enfants. — Ne fouetter les enfants. — Comment il faut louer et reprendre. — Ne trop charger les enfants. — Travail et repos. — Les pères doivent visiter souvent leurs enfants. — Rien n'a plus de pouvoir pour rendre un cheval gras que la vue de son maître. — Céder facilement dans les disputes. — Surmonter la colère. — Il vaut mieux savoir bien se taire que bien parler. — La jeunesse a plus besoin de maîtres que l'enfance. — Compagnons d'école vicieux. — Les parents ne doi-

---

1. Racine a écrit *leur* : voyez ci-dessus, p. 294, notes 1 et 2. — Son orthographe variait alors pour ce mot. Lorsqu'on trouvera ici *leurs* sans que nous avertissions qu'il y a *leur* dans le manuscrit, c'est que Racine a écrit suivant l'usage qui pour nous est aujourd'hui la règle.

PLUTARQUE. 303

vent [être] trop rudes. — Ne prendre des femmes plus riches que soi.

DE AUDIENDIS POETIS. Les discours moins sérieux plaisent plus aux enfants. — Il ne sert de rien de fermer toutes les autres portes d'une ville, si les ennemis entrent par une. — La poésie bonne et mauvaise. — *Tragédie. N. (nota*[1]*.)* — Ne retrancher la poésie. — Poëtes sont menteurs. — Fable bien racontée. — Il n'y a point de poésie où il n'y a point de fables. *N. (nota.)* LUCAIN. — Artifice d'Homère dans sa description des enfers. — Dieu auteur des maux[2]. — Poésie peinture parlante. — Belle représentation d'une chose laide. — Ce qu'on dit étant en colère n'est jamais bon[3]. — Contrariétés des poëtes. — Si Dieu fait quelque mal, il n'est pas Dieu. — Ne tuer son ennemi. — Les méchants ne vivent que pour boire et pour manger, et les bons ne boivent et mangent que pour vivre. — Contre ceux qui rendent le mal pour le mal. — Bien remarquer la force des mots dans les auteurs. — Mauvais effets des mauvais conseils. — Les biens nuisent à ceux qui n'en peuvent user. — Pauvreté don de Dieu. — La poésie garde toujours le vraisemblable. — Stoïques disoient que les vertueux n'avoient aucun vice. — Ne croire aucun homme parfait. — Contre ceux qui imitent les vices des grands hommes. — N'estimer les discours qui paroissent fins. — Ne se laisser abattre par les malheurs. — Les vérités sont cachées dans la multitude des fables. — Prudence vertu civile. Hardiesse barbare. — Prier ses ennemis est une chose barbare. — Il est plus louable de prévenir sa colère que de l'apaiser. — Comp[araison] des abeilles, qui tirent le meilleur miel des fleurs les plus aigres. — Ne quitter les affaires pour les pleurs. — C'est un malheur d'acquérir ce que nous desirons, si cela est injuste. — Malheur de ceux qui connoissant la vertu, ne la pratiquent pas. — Nous enseignons plus par nos mœurs que par nos discours. — Il n'y a que les méchants et les ingrats à qui la connoissance de Dieu donne de la crainte. — Compar[aison] des médecins, qui accommodent les mêmes drogues à des maux semblables. — Contre les nobles qui ne sont vertueux. — Contre les biens dont la possession peut arriver aux ingrats. — Contre ceux qui se glorifient des biens corporels. — Ne reprocher les défauts du corps. — Il n'y a rien

---

1. Il s'agit de ce passage du chapitre I : Γοργίας δὲ τὴν τραγῳδίαν εἶπεν ἀπάτην, ἣν ὅ, τε ἀπατήσας δικαιότερος τοῦ μὴ ἀπατήσαντος, καὶ ὁ ἀπατηθεὶς σοφώτερος τοῦ μὴ ἀπατηθέντος.

2. Cette note est sur les vers cités au chapitre II :

Θεὸς μὲν αἰτίαν φύει βροτοῖς κ. τ. λ.

3. Racine avait d'abord écrit : « ne vaut rien. »

de si doux que de bien supporter les injures. — Compar[aison]. Comme, lorsqu'on fouette un homme sur ses habits, on ne blesse point son corps, ainsi, quand on nous reproche nos malheurs, on ne touche point à notre esprit. — Mauvais conseil pernicieux à son auteur. — Les grands travaux ne durent point. — La vertu seule mérite de la gloire. — Belle comparaison. Comme ceux qui sortent de quelque grande obscurité ne peuvent tout d'un coup supporter l'éclat de la lumière du soleil, mais il faut qu'ils s'y accoutument peu à peu en regardant quelque lueur bâtarde et sombre : ainsi la splendeur des vérités chrétiennes nous éblouit, si nous ne passons auparavant par les petites lumières des païens. *Basil. Magn. de Lect. profan.* [1]. (*Basilius Magnus, de Lectionibus profanis.*)

De recta ratione audiendi. Ceux qui se croient en liberté étant délivrés de précepteurs, sont dominés par des maîtres bien plus fâcheux, qui sont leurs[2] passions. — Langue bonne et mauvaise. — Nous sommes naturellement sujets aux vices et aux passions. — Apprendre à bien écouter. — La nature nous a donné deux oreilles et une langue. — Être exempt d'orgueil et d'envie. — Combien l'envie nuit à ceux qui écoutent. — Il est inutile de reprendre son prochain, si on ne se donne de garde des vices qu'on reprend en lui. — Louer facilement et croire avec grande circonspection. — Ne considérer le prédicateur, mais ses discours. — Contre ceux qui ne tâchent qu'à plaire en leurs discours[3]. — Regarder plus le sens que les paroles. — Comp[araison]. Quand on vient de nous faire le poil, nous le[4] regardons en un miroir. Quand on sort d'un sermon, s'examiner soi-même. — Comp[araison]. On regarde la beauté des vases, quand on s'est rempli de ce qui y étoit. — Comment il faut faire des questions. — N'interroger les personnes que sur ce qu'ils savent bien. — Comp[araison]. Fendre du bois avec une clef et ouvrir une porte avec une coignée. — Ne cacher son ignorance. — Philosophes quand ils sont dans leurs[5] chaires. — Contre ceux qui n'osent louer les autres. Ils estiment les louanges comme de l'argent, et que plus ils en donnent, moins ils en ont. — Ils[6] vont

---

1. Racine ne renvoie à saint Basile que pour la dernière phrase. Le reste est tiré de Plutarque, chapitre xiv. — Νόθῳ φωτί a été traduit par Amyot : « quelque clarté *bâtarde*, » et avec la même exactitude littérale par Racine.

2. Racine a écrit *leur*.

3. Il y a : *leur discours;* mais on peut supposer, en remontant à la phrase précédente, que Racine a entendu mettre *discours* au pluriel.

4. *Le* est ajouté au-dessus de la ligne.

5. Racine a écrit *leur*.

6. Ceux qui ne veulent prendre aucune peine en écoutant

aux sermons comme à des festins. Ils n'y veulent point travailler. — Comp[araison]. Il faut que celui qui reçoit la balle se remue selon celui qui la jette. — Ils[1] font tort à ceux mêmes qu'ils louent, comme s'ils avoient besoin de louanges si excessives. — Ne se moquer et ne se rire, quand on est repris. — Contre ceux qui ne peuvent souffrir d'être repris. — Comp[araison]. Ils s'enfuient après avoir reçu la coupure du médecin, sans attendre qu'il l'ait reliée[2]. — Souffrir quand on est injustement repris. — Il y a de la difficulté au commencement de chaque chose — Contre ceux qui disent aussitôt, qu'ils comprennent ce qu'on leur dit. — Saint Thomas[3]. Ceux qui ont de la peine à comprendre retiennent mieux. — Souffrir les railleries de ses compagnons. — Compar[aison]. Ils[4] vont querir du feu chez leur voisin, et y en trouvant un bon, ils y demeurent.

De adulatore et amico[5]. Ceux qui aiment les flatteurs se flattent eux-mêmes les premiers. — Vérité source de tous les biens. — Le flatteur est un ver qui ne s'attache qu'aux bons arbres. — Les flatteurs sont comme les poux qui quittent les corps qui n'ont plus de sang. — Bien expérimenter ceux qu'on veut prendre pour amis. — Flatteurs ressemblent à la fausse monnoie. — Ceux qui louent volontiers ne reprennent qu'à regret. — Hypocrisie. C'est la dernière méchanceté que de vouloir paroître vertueux, ne l'étant pas. — Il n'y a point d'ivraie[6] plus dangereuse que celle qui ressemble le plus au bled. *Hérétiques déguisés*[7]. — La ressemblance des mœurs produit

---

1. Ceux qui applaudissent inconsidérément. — 2. Il y a *relié*, sans accord.

3. Racine a ajouté le nom de saint Thomas à ceux de Cléanthe et de Xénocrate, cités par Plutarque dans ce passage du chapitre xviii : Ὥσπερ ὁ Κλεάνθης καὶ ὁ Ξενοκράτης, βραδύτεροι δοκοῦντες εἶναι τῶν συσχολαστῶν.... On sait que les condisciples de saint Thomas d'Aquin, à l'école d'Albert le Grand, l'appelaient *le bœuf muet*, ou *le grand bœuf de Sicile*.

4. Ceux qui se contentent d'écouter pour leur plaisir.

5. Au bas de la page 30, où commence ce traité, Racine a écrit : « *Si e trovato trà gli antichi sapienti chi ha scritto libri in qual modo possa l'huomo conoscere il vero amico dall' adulatore : ma questo che giova, se molti, anzi infiniti son quelli che manifestamente comprendono esser adulati, e pur amano chi gli adula, e hanno in odio chi dice lor il vero?* Corteg. liv. I. » Cette citation est tirée du livre qui a pour titre : *Il libro del Cortegiano del conte Baldasar Castiglione*. On la trouve à la page 42 du livre I, dans l'édition in-folio d'Alde (non paginée), 1528.

6. L'orthographe de Racine est : *yuroye*.

7. Quoique nous donnions plus loin à part, comme pour les notes des *Vies parallèles*, les rapprochements d'idées modernes et d'idées chrétiennes, nous avons laissé cette phrase à côté de la maxime de Plutarque, dont elle est une application. — Nous avons fait de même en quelques rares endroits :

l'amitié. — Les vieillards se plaisent avec les vieillards. — Flatteur, comme l'eau, s'accommode à toutes sortes de vases. — Les vrais amis n'imitent que les vertus dans leurs amis. Les flatteurs imitent les vices. — Ils n'ont garde de reprendre ce qu'ils imitent. — Folie des courtisans qui imitent les défauts corporels. — Les flatteurs découvrent leur secret, afin d'avoir ceux des autres. — Parasite marche par les dents. — Flatteurs. Ils tâchent de ne point surpasser les autres, sinon en vices. — Flatteur se rend agréable faisant tout ce qui peut plaire; et l'ami déplait quelquefois faisant ce qu'il faut faire. — Médecin tantôt doux, tantôt rude. — Il ne faut pas se soucier si on déplait à son ami, faisant ce qui lui est utile. — Le flatteur ne tâche qu'à plaire. — Être rude aux méchants. — Comment on peut reconnoître un flatteur. — On ne veut être repris ayant mal fait, et on veut être loué. — Flatteurs dangereux, donnant de beaux noms à des vices. — Flatteurs sont cause des vices de ceux qu'ils flattent. *Lucian. in Nigr.* (*Lucianus in Nigrino*, chapitre XXIII.) — Flatteurs qui se blâment eux-mêmes. — Ils demandent conseil à ceux qui se vantent pour leur esprit. — Louanges dissimulées. — Ils honorent les riches, et non les gens de bien. — Les enfants des grands seigneurs ne peuvent apprendre qu'à monter à cheval. — Les louanges nuisent aux hommes vicieux. — Liberté feinte des flatteurs[1]. — Corrections des flatteurs. Ils ne reprennent que les moindres défauts. — Artifice des flatteurs. Ils appellent un avare comme un prodigue. — Le flatteur pousse aux voluptés. — Discours véritable est simple. Différence de l'ami et du flatteur dans les salutations et les compliments. — Dans les services. *Na.* — Dans les promesses. — Amis qui [ne] cèdent facilement aux mauvais desseins. — Le flatteur ressemble aux ombres qui suivent le corps. — Il veut paroître fort officieux. — L'ami est comme l'œuf, qui ne fait rien paroître au dehors. — Dieu se plait à bien faire aux hommes, souvent sans qu'ils le sachent. — Il n'y a rien de plus insupportable que quand on nous reproche un bienfait. — Un bienfait est agréable quand il n'est point augmenté par des paroles. — Ne servir ses amis en des choses mauvaises. — Compar[aison] du flatteur au singe. — Le flatteur ne peut souffrir les vrais amis. — Calomnies laissent toujours quelque soupçon. — Les grands esprits

---

ainsi plus haut pour une citation de saint Basile, ailleurs pour la mention de saint Thomas d'Aquin, etc.

1. Racine a ajouté ici fort à propos la citation de deux passages de Tacite : « *Vid. Tac. init.* 1. *Ann.* (*Vide Tacitum, initio libri I Annalium, cap.* VIII) : *Ea sola species adulandi supererat. Et fin.* 3 (*Et fine libri III, cap.* LXX) : *Intellexit hæc Tiberius ut erant magis quam ut dicebantur.* »

sont facilement trompés. — Se connoître soi-même. — Peu qui sachent reprendre comme il faut. — Ne reprendre trop sévèrement. — Ne reprendre des fautes qu'on fait contre nous. — Être entièrement exempt d'intérêt particulier dans les répréhensions. — Ne se moquer quand on reprend, ni faire parade de la subtilité de son esprit, comme un chirurgien ne doit faire de la légèreté de sa main. — Ne reprendre qu'à temps. — Ne reprendre un homme ivre. — Le vin excite la colère. — N'épargner ses amis dans leurs[1] prospérités. — Il y a peu de personnes heureuses et sages tout ensemble. — Ne reprendre les malheureux, mais les consoler. — Comp[araison]. On ne fouette les enfants qui se laissent tomber qu'après qu'ils sont relevés. — Flatteurs dans les prospérités foulent aux pieds dans les adversités. — Exemple de ceux qui reprochent les[2] fautes dans les adversités. — Reprendre dans les autres des vices dont on veut corriger son ami. — Ne reprendre devant les autres. — On rend une personne insensible quand on le reprend trop. — Ceux qui sont souillés des vices dont ils reprennent les autres. — Se reprendre soi-même avec les autres. — Louer ceux qu'on reprend et leur faire souvenir de leurs[3] vertus passées. — Ne louer les autres devant ceux qu'on reprend. — Sinon les pères. — Ne reprendre en même temps ceux qui nous reprennent. — Contre ceux qui reprennent jusqu'aux moindres défauts. — Louer aussi bien que reprendre. — Ne convaincre trop fort, et recevoir les excuses. — Détourner des vices avec force. — Il faut avoir ou de bons amis ou de méchants ennemis qui nous disent nos vérités. — Adoucir celui qu'on a repris.

De profectibus in virtute. On ne devient parfait en un moment. — Comment on peut reconnoître son avancement dans la vertu. — Ne faire aucune pause. Il faut avancer ou reculer. — Ne donner aucune trêve aux passions. — Comp[araison] des roseaux à ceux qui étant bien ardents d'abord, se relâchent ensuite. — Rompre tous les empêchements. — On reconnoît son amour en l'absence de ce qu'on aime. — Il faut non-seulement se plaire aux sermons, mais pratiquer ce qu'on y apprend. — Les commencements sont difficiles. — Quitter le monde. — Repousser les tentations. — Ne se laisser détourner voyant ses amis bien riches et bien venus dans la cour. — On ne peut bien mépriser le monde si on n'aime parfaitement la vertu. — Contre ceux qui s'amusent à considérer l'éloquence dans les discours, et qui ne les pratiquent point. — Contre

---

1. Il y a *leur*, sans accord.
2. *Les* est biffé.
3. Il y a encore ici *leur*, sans *s*.

ceux qui ne regardent que l'élégance des auteurs. — Faire profit de tout. — Ne se soucier si on est écouté de beaucoup de monde ou non. — Pourquoi Homère a laissé son premier vers défectueux. — Être content du témoignage de sa conscience. — Contre la vaine gloire. — Comp[araison]. Il vaut mieux que les épis soient courbés que droits. — Quand on a l'âme pleine de vertus, il faut que les vices en sortent. — Découvrir ses fautes. — Plus on cache ses vices, plus on est vicieux. — Il n'y a point de pauvres qui soient plus dans la pauvreté que ceux qui veulent paroître riches. — Comparer les passions présentes aux anciennes. — C'est peu de chose d'admirer les grands personnages, si on ne les imite. — Imiter les grands hommes et les aimer. — Et principalement quand ils sont persécutés. — Ne cacher ses actions devant les hommes de bien. — Ne négliger ses fautes, et ne les croire petites, telles qu'elles soient.

DE CAPIENDA EX INIMICIS UTILITATE. On n'a point d'amis sans ennemis. — On se défend des bêtes et on s'en sert. — Si les bêtes manquoient à l'homme, il deviendroit tout sauvage. — Les ennemis, comme les oiseaux carnassiers, ne voient que ce qui est mauvais. — Comp[araison] des villes qui se réforment par les guerres. — On craint plus de faire mal devant son ennemi que devant son ami. — Se venger de son ennemi, ne lui ressemblant pas. — Être exempt des vices dont on reprend les autres. — Il sert d'être calomnié. — Fille qui parle librement à des hommes, mauvaise marque. — Nos malheurs nous doivent rendre sages. — Les amis sont aveugles aux défauts de leurs amis [1]. — Continence dans le parler. — Ne rendre mal pour mal. — Tout le monde a de la jalousie. — Il faut avoir des ennemis. — Tâcher de surpasser ses ennemis.

DE AMICORUM MULTITUDINE. Le désir qu'on a d'avoir plusieurs amis empêche d'en avoir un bon. — L'amitié va de compagnie, et non par troupe. — Amitié divisée. Fleuves divisés en plusieurs ruisseaux. — Il y a plusieurs flatteurs dans la cour des princes, et beaucoup de mouches dans leur cuisine. — Bien examiner ceux qu'on prend pour amis. — Contre la pluralité d'amis. — L'oubli est pardonnable, et non le mépris. — Il faut servir plusieurs, si on veut se servir de plusieurs. — Inimitiés doivent être légères. — Les adversités des amis nuisent. — Amitié ferme est rare.

DE FORTUNA. Bêtes mieux pourvues de tout que l'homme, hormis de la raison. — N'attendre pas tout de Dieu, mais travailler. — Un insensé ne doit régner. — Les prospérités sont cause des adversités à ceux qui n'en savent pas user.

1. Il y a : *leur amis*.

De virtute et vitio. Comp[araison] des vêtements aux biens temporels. — La vertu rend bonnes les adversités, et le vice trouble[1] les prospérités. — Vice ne donne aucun repos. — Une âme ne peut être véritablement gaie si elle n'est vertueuse. — Les malades trouvent mauvais ce qui est bon. — La vertu est indifférente à toutes fortunes.

Consolatio ad Apollonium. Les consolations ne servent de rien au même temps que[2] les malheurs viennent. — Contre ceux qui sont insensibles à la perte de leurs amis. — Foiblesse de la nature humaine. — Il n'y a rien de plus foible que l'homme. — Comparaison de l'homme aux feuilles. — On n'est pas toujours heureux. — Le partage de l'homme sont les douleurs et les maux. — État de ceux qui sont abandonnés de Dieu. — Les larmes sont inutiles. — Comparer son malheur à ceux des autres. — Louange de la mort. — Il n'y a rien d'étrange si ce qui est mortel meurt. — La vie nous est prêtée par le sort. — Incertitude de la mort, utile. — Personne ne sait si il[3] doit vivre encore demain. — Le sommeil est le frère de la mort. — La mort est utile à l'âme. — Empêchements du corps. — Contre ceux qui craignent la mort. — La mort est le plus grand des biens. — La mort afflige ceux qui ne la sentent point. — Bien user de la vie et de la mort. — Contre les longues maladies. — Pour les morts imprévues et avant les temps. — Ce n'est pas la longueur de la vie, mais la bonté qu'il faut regarder. — Nous ne vivons pas pour ordonner de la vie et de la mort, mais pour obéir aux lois de la Providence. — Les pleurs montrent l'amour-propre. — Dieu des pleurs. — Il vaut mieux finir au plus tôt ses pleurs. — Être prêt à toutes sortes d'accident[4]. — Il n'appartient qu'aux femmes de pleurer. — Contre ceux qui meurent de douleur. — Il est meilleur de mourir que de vivre. — Nous tenons la vie et les biens comme par emprunt. — Constance en la perte des siens. — La douleur trouve assez de sujet pour pleurer. — Contre ceux qui louent et n'imitent point. — Celui que Dieu aime, il le retire bientôt du monde. — Honorer les vieillards comme ses pères. — Récompense et punition des bons et des méchants après la mort. — Beaux de corps et difformes dans l'âme.

De tuenda sanitate præcepta. Médecine séparée de la philosophie. Médecine jointe à la philosophie. — S'accoutumer aux viandes des malades lorsqu'on est en santé. — N'aller aux festins sans avoir faim. — Contre la pudeur de ceux qui s'enivrent pour

---

1. Racine avait d'abord mis *gâte*, au lieu de *trouble*.
2. C'est-à-dire, « dans le temps même où. »
3. Racine a écrit ainsi, sans élision : *si il*.
4. Il y a bien *accident* au singulier.

contenter ceux qui les traitent. — Ne manger de quoi que ce soit si on n'a faim. — Contre la vanité de ceux qui mangent des choses rares. — Cupidités qui naissent de l'esprit. — Contre ceux qui mangent plus chez autrui que chez eux. — Santé est la meilleure des sauces. — Travaux sont de bons assaisonnements. — Contre ceux qui ont honte d'avouer leur intempérance. — Contre ceux qui ne se veulent tenir au lit. — Ceux qui veulent manger des choses agréables, étant malades. — Songes étranges signes de maladie. — Visiter ses amis malades et s'enquérir de leur mal. — Ne feindre de lire en compagnie, étant à rien faire. — S'abstenir de viande le plus qu'on peut. — Vin. Le bien tremper dans l'eau. — Lecture contraire à la gourmandise. — Lecture durant le dîner. Quelle elle doit être. — Ne dormir aussitôt après le manger. — Ne travailler à des choses qui bandent l'esprit, après les repas. — Contre les pilules et le vin émétique[1]. — Ne vivre toujours d'une seule façon. — Ne s'embarrasser en de petites choses. — L'âme paye bien sa demeure[2] au corps. — Contre les travaux et les récréations excessives. — N'avoir besoin de médecin en santé. — Ne tuer son corps par des études excessives.

CONJUGALIA PRÆCEPTA. *Primum præceptum.* Ne quereller. — II. Douceur dans les paroles. — III. Supporter les premières querelles. — IIII. Amour doit venir de la vertu. — V. Contre les philtres. — Aimer les hommes sages. — VI. Ne trop rabaisser la femme, pour en être le maître. — VII. Femme. Se cacher en l'absence de son mari. — VIII.... — IX. Le mari doit agir principalement. — X. Douceur plus puissante que la force. — XI. Ne reprendre publiquement. — XII. Égalité d'humeurs. — XIII. Divertissements libres. — XIIII. Femme suit les vices du mari. — XV.... — XVI. N'avoir de religion particulière. — XVII. Biens communs. — Vin mêlé d'eau s'appelle vin. — XVIII. Vices cachés et petits. — Beauté. — XIX. N'épouser que pour la vertu. — XX. Vertu augmente la beauté. — XXI.... — XXII. Contre la colère. — XXIII. Femme. N'être trop sévère. — Familiarité honnête. — XXIV.... — XXV. Femme. Ne parler librement. — XXVI. Agir par le moyen du mari. — XXVII. Femme doit être sujette à son mari. — XXVIII.... — XXVIIII. Belle-mère n'avoir de jalousie. — XXX. *N. (nota.)* Les pères aiment les filles, les mères les garçons. — Aimer les parents de son mari. — XXXI. Silence quand le mari est en colère. — ....

---

1. Racine fait application à la médecine de son temps du passage de Plutarque (chapitre xx de ce traité) : Ἴδιον δὲ τῷ μὲν ἐμέτῳ κακὸν πρόσεστι κ. τ. λ.

2. Racine avait d'abord écrit : « son louage. »

— XXXVII. Magistrats. Avoir leurs maisons bien réglées. — .... — XLI. Faire soi-même ce qu'on commande. — .... — XLIII. Femmes doivent aimer les belles-lettres. — XLIV. Vertu coûte moins que les bagues.

Septem sapientium convivium. — Rendre son règne doux et agréable. — On aime à semer de faux bruits touchant les hommes sages. — Ce que doit faire un prince. — Il ne faut pas regarder le dedans des maisons. — Comment une maison est bien réglée. — Il est bon d'avoir besoin de manger. — Dieu voit tout. — Ne croire trop ni trop peu. — Qui répond, paye.

De superstitione. Superstition craint tout. — On ne craint point les tremblements de terre dans la France. — On ne sauroit fuir Dieu en aucun lieu. — Contre ceux qui croient que tous les maux viennent de Dieu. — Dieu est l'espérance de la vertu, et non de la lâcheté. — Aller à Dieu. — Il vaut mieux n'être point qu'être mauvais. — Contre ceux qui n'aiment Dieu. — Superstition cause de l'athéisme. — Fuir d'un excès à un autre.

Regum et imperatorum apophthegmata. Pays mol. — *N.* (*nota.*) Donner plutôt son argent que de faire une injustice. — Humanité dans les rois. — *N.* (*nota.*) Contre les médisances. — N'obéir à l'injustice. — Obvier à la colère. — La vérité ne va guère jusqu'aux oreilles des rois. — Se sacrifier à l'utilité de son pays. — Nous étions perdus, si nous n'eussions été perdus.

Apophthegmata laconica. Roi doit agir comme un père envers ses sujets. — De rien faire quelque chose. — Parler librement à ses amis. — Contre la rhétorique. — Ne donner des enfants en otage. — Contre la comédie.

De mulierum virtutibus[1]. Femmes ne doivent faire parler d'elles. — Les mêmes vertus s'exercent différemment. — Femmes assistoient aux assemblées parmi les Gaulois. — Amour de femmes envers leur mari. — Fille doit craindre la moindre infamie plus que la mort. — Otages ne doivent fuir de ceux à qui ils sont donnés. — Virginité. Souffrir plutôt la mort que de la perdre. — Hommes maîtres des femmes. — Lâcheté que tuer une femme. — Diane principale déesse des Gaulois.

Aquæ et ignis comparatio. Nations sans feu. — Feu est plus pour les riches que pour les pauvres. — Utilité de la navigation. — Mouvement entretient tout. — Utilité du feu pour les veilles.

Quæstiones Romanæ. Femme doit être chaste. — On portoit cinq flambeaux aux noces. — Ceux qui reviennent de loin, ayant été crus morts. — Femmes baisoient les parents au visage. — On

---

1. Au-dessus du titre, Racine a écrit : « Ce traité est extrêmement beau. »

n'épousoit autrefois les cousines. — Femmes ne recevoient point de présent de leurs maris[1]. Ni les gendres n'en faisoient à leurs beaux-pères. — Ils (*les Romains*) se couvroient en priant Dieu. — Vérité n'est point cachée. — Le temps père de la vérité. — Les terres des premiers Romains n'avoient point de bornes. — Mars étoit autrefois le premier des mois. — Pourquoi Janus avoit deux visages. — Vénus déesse de la mort et de l'amour. — Les Kal[endes], les Non[es] et les Id[es] étoient fêtées avec le premier jour qui les suivoit. — Dispute de la fête avec son lendemain. Fable de Thémist[ocle][2]. — Ne se mêler dans les affaires aussitôt après les fêtes. — Deuil. Habits noirs superflus. — Détourner les enfants de jurer facilement. — On portoit l'épousée sur le seuil de la porte. — Femme. Ne quitter facilement son ménage. — Paroles qu'on disoit aux noces. — On jetoit des statues, au mois de mai, dans l'eau. — Ils menoient autrefois leurs[3] petits enfants au festin. —Pères doivent donner bon exemple. — On ne gardoit longtemps les dépouilles. — Contre les trophées. — Ceux qui avoient passé le temps ordonné de la milice ne pouvoient combattre sans permission. — *Ne tuer de sa propre autorité.* — On ne mangeoit d'aucun fruit d'automne devant que d'en avoir permission. — Pontife ne pouvoit s'absenter plus de trois nuits. — Contre les danses. — Pontife n'osoit jurer[4]. — Il est de l'intérêt public qu'il n'y ait point de méchants prêtres. — Il faut être sobre les jours de fêtes. — Veuves plus malheureuses que les vierges. — Autrefois les pères enseignoient eux-mêmes leurs enfants. — Tempérance. Ne tout prendre ce qui est sur la table. — Prêtres doivent avoir la conscience nette. — Ils doivent avoir toutes les parties du corps. — Ne mépriser les moindres affaires. — Ne tuer les bêtes innocentes. — Donner le superflu. — Lune. La lune est un exemple de l'instabilité des choses humaines. — Elle est l'image de l'obéissance et de la dépendance. — Tribunat. N'est pas une magistrature. — Modestie est puissante. — Tribun accessible à tout le monde. Sa maison toujours ouverte. — Plus nous nous rabaissons extérieurement, plus on nous élève en effet. — Pourquoi on commençoit le jour à minuit. — Les femmes ne se mêloient anciennement de la cuisine. — Les Romains ne se marioient au mois de mai. — Contre

---

1. Au lieu de *maris*, que veut le grec, Racine a, par mégarde, écrit *amis*.

2. Ces mots : « Fable de Thémist[ocle], » sont écrits au-dessus de la ligne. L'apologue raconté par Thémistocle aux généraux qui lui avaient succédé est rapporté au chapitre xxv des *Questions romaines*.

3. Racine a écrit *leŭr*, sans accord.

4. Immédiatement après ces mots vient la note de Racine que nous avons ci-après citée à part, p. 318, lignes 7 et 8.

les deux mariages. — Ne se marier aux parents. — Prêtre ne doit être ivrogne. — Il n'étoit permis aux prêtres d'être dans les magistratures.

De defectu oraculorum. Il n'y avoit plus que deux oracles qui répondissent. — Profanation des temples. — Pureté qu'il y faut apporter. N^a (nota). — Parole de Dieu. — Il (*Plutarque*) ne croit pas qu'Apollon parlât par la bouche des prophètes. — Le grand Pan est mort. Cela est, ce semble, arrivé vers le temps de la mort de J. C.[1]. — Les stoïciens ne croyoient qu'un Dieu immortel. — Il est impossible d'être méchant et heureux.

Gryllus[2]. Contre la finesse. — Générosité naturelle des bêtes. — Bêtes apprivoisées. — Leurs[3] femelles sont aussi généreuses que les mâles. — Générosité forcée. C'est une timidité prudente. — Comparaison des hommes aux bêtes. — Pauvres, qui ne se contentent de ce qu'ils ont. — Passions déréglées. — Repas barbares des hommes. — Science naturelle des animaux. — Preuve que les bêtes ont de l'esprit. — Différences des esprits. — Elles n'en peuvent avoir n'ayant point la connoissance de Dieu[4].

Non posse suaviter vivi secundum Epicurum. Ne blâmer personne que de ce qu'il a dit par écrit. — Calomniateurs. Envie est seule suffisante de perdre les plus savants. — On ne sauroit vivre heureusement si on ne vit vertueusement. — Criminels ne peuvent jamais avoir de repos. — Peintre emporté par son ouvrage. — Épicuriens ne se mêloient de la république. — Mort. Nous voudrions toujours que la dernière action de notre vie fût bonne. — *Vanité*. Comme quand quelques corps manquent de vivres étant pressés de la faim, ils sont contraints de chercher en eux-mêmes leur nourriture: il arrive de même dans l'esprit des ambitieux que quand ils ne reçoivent point d'honneur des autres, ils cherchent en eux-mêmes leur satisfaction et leur louange. — Livres obscurs par crainte. *N.* (*nota.*) — On n'est couronné qu'après le combat.

De occulte vivendo. Prédicateurs qui font mal et disent bien. — Ne demeurer caché. — On ne cache les maladies du corps au médecin. Pourquoi cachera-t-on celles de l'âme? — *N.* (*nota.*) Découvrir ses défauts les uns aux autres. — Gens de bien ne doivent se retirer. — Bons exemples. — Contre la solitude. — Contre l'oisiveté. — Eaux croupissantes. — Nuit affoiblit l'âme et le corps.

---

1. Plutarque rapporte le fait comme arrivé sous le règne de Tibère.
2. Ce titre latin est le nom d'un des personnages du dialogue intitulé en grec : Περὶ τοῦ τὰ ἄλογα λόγῳ χρῆσθαι.
3. Il y a *leur*, sans accord.
4. Plutarque met dans la bouche d'Ulysse cette objection à ce que Gryllus a dit de l'esprit des bêtes.

— Dieu a créé l'homme afin qu'il le connût. — Pourquoi l'homme est appelé φῶς.

DE AMORE PROLIS. L'amour paternel est désintéressé.

DE ISIDE ET OSIRIDE. Orgueil vient de l'ignorance.

DE SERA NUMINIS VINDICTA. Vengeance et punition aussitôt après le crime. — (Τὸ γενναῖον ὡς ἰσχυρὸν αὐταῖς καὶ οὐκ ἐξίτηλον ἐμπέφυκεν, ἐξανθεῖ δὲ παρὰ φύσιν τὴν κακίαν ὑπὸ τροφῆς καὶ ὁμιλίας φαύλης φθειρόμενον). Voy. p. 25 A, où il dit tout le contraire[1]. — Princes qui sont devenus meilleurs. — Ne désespérer d'une jeunesse vicieuse. — Grands naturels ne sont oisifs. — Tyrans dont Dieu se sert comme de bourreaux. — Quelquefois les mauvais pères ont de bons enfants. — Dieu ne brûle les mauvaises racines qu'après qu'elles ont produit leur bon fruit. — Le châtiment naît avec le péché. — Belle comparaison touchant les grands qui ont fait bien des crimes. — Parole admirable touchant ceux qui vivent longtemps après un grand crime. — Le repentir suit le péché. — Méchanceté infructueuse. — La méchanceté est inconstante. — Les méchants craignent ceux qui les louent. — Les méchants se haïssent eux-mêmes. — Ils n'ont point besoin d'autres bourreaux que d'eux-mêmes. — Satisfaction aux descendants. — Punition différée. — Punition des villes entières. — Villes moins changeantes que l'homme. — Vices descendent jusqu'à la postérité. — On combat en cette vie, et dans l'autre on est récompensé. — Punition des pères dans les enfants. — Remédier aux commencements des maladies. — On ne devient pas méchant quand on fait quelque crime, mais on fait voir qu'on l'est. — Dieu prévient les crimes. — Dissimulation est pire qu'un vice découvert. — La 2. ou la 4. race porte quelquefois les péchés de ses pères. — Pénitence en ce monde.

VIRTUTEM DOCERI POSSE. Il n'y a point d'homme si parfait qui n'ait quelque défaut.

DE SE IPSUM CITRA INVIDIAM LAUDANDO. Être loué et se louer. — Raisons belles contre ceux qui se louent. — Pour ceux qui se louent eux-mêmes. — Comment on peut se louer : I. En se défendant. — Ne fléchir sous la calomnie. — II. Quand on est malheureux. — III. Contre les ingrats. — Grands capitaines sont méprisés en paix.

---

1. Le passage auquel Racine renvoie est celui que, dans le traité *De recta ratione audiendi*, il a traduit ainsi : « Nous sommes naturellement sujets aux vices et aux passions. » (Voyez ci-dessus, p. 304.) Ici Racine n'ayant pas traduit la phrase de Plutarque, où il a noté une doctrine toute contraire, nous avons dû citer le texte grec qui est au chapitre VI, et qu'Amyot a ainsi rendu : « Combien la générosité est en elle (*dans l'âme humaine*) forte et puissante..., et que c'est *contre sa propre nature* qu'elle produit des vices, par être trop à son aise ou par contagion de hanter mauvaise compagnie. »

— IV. Pour justifier ses actions. — Louer les exécuteurs de nos conseils. — V. En louant nos semblables. — Contre ceux qui blâment leurs semblables. — VI. Attribuant aux Dieux. — On aime mieux paroître vaincu en fortune qu'en vertu. — VII. En ne voulant être loué des biens externes, mais des intérieurs. — VIII. Par modestie, voulant être loué raisonnablement. — IX. En mêlant quelque blâme. — X. En exhortant les autres. — XI. En voulant rabaisser les orgueilleux. — XII. Encourageant les timides. — XIII. En réfutant ceux qui se vantent de leurs[1] vices. — Il semble par là[2] que les Athéniens ne faisoient point d'oraisons funèbres à ceux qui mouroient dans leur pays, ou d'une mort paisible. — Occasions où l'on peut tomber dans ce vice (*de se louer soi-même*) : I. En voyant louer les autres. — II. En racontant ses actions. — III. En rapportant les caresses qu'on nous a faites. — IV. En reprenant les autres. — Contre ceux qui recherchent leur gloire dans l'infamie des autres. — V. Étant loué par d'autres. — Il n'y a rien de plus insupportable qu'un homme qui se loue soi-même. — Les autres nous blâment lorsque nous nous louons.

DE COHIBENDA IRA. Revoir ses ouvrages de temps en temps. — Correction aussitôt après le mal n'est pas si utile. — Comp[araison] de la colère à un homme qui se brûle avec sa maison. — Comp[araison]. Se préparer à la tentation comme à un siége de ville. — Comp[araison]. La colère est une tyrannie qui veut être détruite par elle-même. — Contre ceux qui se fâchent à tous moments. — Arrêter la colère lorsqu'elle commence. — Prov[erbe]. Qui n'entretient point le feu, l'éteint. — Les discours augmentent la colère. — Socrate. Sa sagesse pour adoucir sa colère. — Larmes adoucissent la douleur. — Colère s'étend sur tout. — Un homme colère est haï et méprisé. — Changement de visage signe de grande colère. — Contre les injures qu'on dit étant en colère. — Avoir la langue douce dans la colère plutôt que dans la fièvre. — Comp[araison] de la colère au vin. — Vices semblables aux vertus. — Colère est lâche. — La colère est une marque de foiblesse. — Femmes sont colères. — Ne railler si on ne veut être raillé. — La colère est dangereuse dans les États. — Causes de la colère : I. On croit qu'on est méprisé. — II. Amour propre. — III. Amour particulier de quelques choses rares. — Colère peste de l'amitié. — Quand il faut éviter la colère. — Colère source de passions. — Maison d'un homme colère. — Pardonner facilement. — Contre les cen-

---

1. Il y a *leur*, sans accord.
2. C'est-à-dire par cette parole de Phocion, à qui on demandait quel bien il avait fait à la république : « Quand j'avais le commandement, vous n'avez jamais fait d'oraisons funèbres. » (Chapitre XVII.)

seurs vicieux. — Contre la trop grande exactitude. — Secours de Dieu. — ('Επὶ πᾶσι τοίνυν τὸ μὲν τοῦ Ἐμπεδοκλέους κ. τ. λ.) Amyot croit que ce reste n'est pas de Plutarque[1].

De curiositate. Vices qu'on peut changer en vertu. — Examiner ses défauts et non ceux d'autrui. — Ne lire les affiches. — Ne regarder même choses permises. S'éprouver en s'abstenant même des choses permises. — Lettres. Ne les décacheter si tôt. — Belle action du grand Rustique, dont parle Tac. *in Agric.* (Tacite dans la Vie d'Agricola, *chapitres* ii *et* xlv). — Mouchards[2]. Délateurs. — Infamie de la curiosité.

De tranquillitate animi. Ne faire le mal ne suffit pas. — Inconstance des naturels. — Vouloir ce que Dieu veut. — Disgrâces qui font quitter le monde. — Ne s'affliger avec les affligés. — Se consoler de ses pertes dans ce qu'on n'a pas perdu. — S'examiner. — Se contenter de sa condition. — Embrasser la vie dont on est capable. — Contre ceux qui songent à leur malheur plutôt qu'à leur bonheur. — Attache excessive à quelque chose. — Être préparé à tout. — Maux en nos biens. — Maux corporels. — Mort des méchants et des justes. — S'exercer dans les moindres choses. — Pureté de conscience.

De vitioso pudore. Vice approchant de la vertu. — Libéralité juste. — Maux de la mauvaise honte. — N'avoir de honte pour le bien. — Comment il faut refuser les demandes injustes.

De fraterno amore. Trois corps séparés peuvent plus que trois corps joints. — Ceux qui cherchent d'autre amitié que la fraternelle. — Contre ceux qui appellent les autres leurs frères, et n'aiment point leurs véritables. — Il est difficile que des frères se réconcilient. — Toute inimitié est fâcheuse. — Sauver plutôt son frère que ses enfants. — Ne vouloir plus être en l'esprit de son père que ses frères. — Reprendre son frère en secret. — Partage des biens. — Oter ces mots de *mien* [et de *non mien*]. — Pour ceux qui ont quelque avantage sur leurs frères. — Leur céder et les consulter même. — Pour les moins parfaits. — Jalousie des frères. — Il ne faut point que les frères soient comme les balances, dont une partie s'abaisse quand l'autre s'élève, mais comme les nombres, dont les moindres s'augmentent à mesure qu'ils sont joints avec les plus grands. — Il est bon qu'ils n'aient pas les mêmes emplois. — *N.* (*nota.*) Exercer une même profession est aussi dangereux

---

1. Nous avons recueilli cette note, parce qu'elle fait connaître que Racine avait sous les yeux la traduction d'Amyot. Celui-ci dit en effet sur cette fin du chapitre xvi et dernier : « Ce reste semble auoir esté aiousté par quelque Chrestien, et n'est point du style de l'auteur. »

2. Racine écrit *moucharts*.

qu'aimer une même personne. — Un frère riche et puissant vaut mieux que les richesses et la puissance mêmes.—Aînés. Ne prendre trop d'autorité sur les cadets. — Amour de Plutarque envers son frère. — Frères qui s'accoutument à disputer ensemble. — Réconciliation avant le soleil couchant. — Les amis doivent avoir les mêmes amis. — Il faut que les amis soient communs entre les amis [1].

DE GARRULITATE. Le trop parler est un mal incurable.

DE FORTUNA ROMANORUM. Temple de la Fortune dans Rome aussi ancien que Rome même.

REIPUBLICÆ GERENDÆ PRÆCEPTA. Ne se mettre dans les affaires que par bonne raison. — N'avoir point pour but de s'enrichir.

Les autres *traités* n'ont pas de notes, ou n'en ont que de très-courtes et qu'il eût été sans intérêt de recueillir.

Comme dans ses notes sur les *Vies parallèles*, Racine, dans celles qu'il a écrites sur les *OEuvres morales*, cite assez fréquemment des auteurs anciens, tels que saint Basile, Horace, Tacite, Sénèque, Quintilien, Pline le jeune, dont il lui revient des passages en mémoire. Les deux études qui, nous l'avons dit, sont à peu près du même temps, se ressemblent encore en ceci, que le jeune écolier de Port-Royal y a pris le même soin de faire application de quelques endroits de Plutarque à des choses ou à des hommes de nos temps chrétiens, et particulièrement de signaler tout ce qui lui rappelait la question de la Grâce. Afin de mieux faire ressortir cette partie intéressante de ses notes, nous les avons détachées des autres, comme nous avons déjà fait pour les *Vies parallèles*, et nous les citons ici en finissant.

DE AUDIENDIS POETIS, chapitre VI. Ζεὺς δ' ἀρετὴν ἄνδρεσσιν ὀφέλλει τε μινύθει τε. GRACE.

Ibidem, chapitre VIII. Ἀλλά τις ἀθανάτων παῦσε[ν] χόλον.... GRACE.

CONSOLATIO AD APOLLONIUM, chapitre VI. Τοῖος γὰρ νόος ἐστὶν ἐπιχθονίων ἀνθρώπων, Οἷόν ἐπ' ἦμαρ ἄγῃσι πατὴρ ἀνδρῶν τε Θεῶν τε. GRACE. Les hommes n'ont point d'autres bons sentiments que ceux que Dieu leur donne.

Ibidem, chapitre XXXI. Τίς γὰρ οἶδεν εἰ ὁ Θεὸς πατρικῶς προειδὼς.... PROVIDENCE.

SEPTEM SAPIENTIUM CONVIVIUM, chapitre XXI. Ἡ ψυχὴ τὰ μὲν ὑφ' ἑαυτῆς κινουμένη πράττει, τὰ δὲ τῷ Θεῷ παρέχει χρωμένῳ κατευθύνειν καὶ

---

[1]. De ces deux traductions de la même idée, l'une est en tête de la page 332, l'autre à la marge de cette même page.

τρέπειν ἑαυτὴν κ. τ. λ. Grace. L'âme est conduite de Dieu partout où il veut.

Apophthegmata laconica. (Παιδαρήτου π.) Οὔτε ἄνδρας γυναιξὶν ὁμοίους ὄντας ἐπαινεῖν δεῖ, οὔτε γυναῖκας ἀνδράσιν, ἐὰν μὴ τὴν γυναῖκα χρεία τις καταλάβῃ. *N.* (*nota.*) Reine de S. (*Christine, reine de Suède*[1].)

Quæstiones Romanæ, chapitre xliv. Οὐδ' ἄλλοις ἐπαρᾶσθαι νομίζεται τοὺς ἱερεῖς. Vœu de Caen[2]. Il n'étoit permis aux prêtres de maudire personne.

Ibidem, chapitre lxi. Πάντας ὑπὸ τῶν πολιτῶν τοὺς θεοὺς τιμᾶσθαι. Honorer tous les saints en général.

Non posse suaviter vivi secundum Epicurum, chapitre xxi. Δεδιότες γὰρ ὥσπερ ἄρχοντα χρηστοῖς ἤπιον,... ἧττον ταράττονται κ. τ. λ. Crainte de Dieu.

Ibidem, chapitre xxii. Καὶ τὸν θεοφιλῆ μή τι εὖ πράττειν, ἢ θεοφιλῆ μὴ εἶναι τὸν σώφρονα καὶ δίκαιον, ἀδύνατόν ἐστιν. Amour de Dieu.

Ibidem, chapitre xxv. Λυσιτελεῖ γὰρ αὐτοῖς τὰ μετὰ τὸν θάνατον φοβουμένοις μὴ ἀδικεῖν κ. τ. λ. Attrition.

De occulte vivendo, chapitre ii. Γνώσθητι, σωφρονίσθητι, μετανόησον,... μὴ μείνῃς ἀθεράπευτος. Confession.

De Iside et Osiride, chapitre i. Πάντα μὲν.... δεῖ τἀγαθὰ τοὺς νοῦν ἔχοντας αἰτεῖσθαι παρὰ τῶν θεῶν. Grace.

Virtutem doceri posse, chapitre ii. Τί τὴν ἀρετὴν λέγοντες ἀδίδακτον εἶναι, ποιοῦμεν ἀνύπαρκτον; Εἰ γὰρ ἡ μάθησις γένεσίς ἐστιν κ. τ. λ. Pour les catéchismes.

Ibidem, même chapitre. Ἀμαθίαν γὰρ Ἡράκλειτός φησι κρύπτειν ἄμεινον. Orgueil du paganisme.

De se ipsum citra invidiam laudando, chapitre xi. Ἐπειδὴ τὸν [δ'] ἄνδρα θεοὶ δαμάσασθαι ἔδωκαν. Grace. Dieu auteur des belles actions.

Ibidem, chapitre xii. Ὅτι δι' αὐτὸν οὐδεὶς Ἀθηναίων μέλαν ἱμάτιον ἀνείληφε. Saint Louis. — Bon roi.

Ibidem, chapitre xvi. Οὐ μόνον ἔφη τοῖς πολλῶν κρατοῦσιν ἐξεῖναι μέγα φρονεῖν, ἀλλὰ καὶ τοῖς περὶ θεῶν δόξας ἀληθεῖς ἔχουσι. Théologie.

De cohibenda ira, chapitre ii. Δεῖν ἀεὶ θεραπευομένους βιοῦν τοὺς σώζεσθαι μέλλοντας. Pénit. contin. (*Pénitence continuelle.*) *N.* (*nota.*) L'homme a toujours besoin de remède.

De curiositate, chapitre xii. Ἐθιζώμεθα θύραν παριόντες ἀλλοτρίαν

---

1. On s'occupait beaucoup, en 1656, des singularités de cette reine, qui vint cette année-là en France. Il est difficile de savoir si Racine entendait faire en sa faveur l'exception que Pédarète admet à la fin de son apophthegme. Cette interprétation de sa note est cependant la plus probable, les deux derniers membres de phrase étant soulignés au crayon rouge.
2. Voyez ci-dessus, p. 300, note 5, et p. 312, note 4.

μὴ βλέπειν εἴσω κ. τ. λ. Ne regarder en monast. (*monastère*) de filles [1].

De tranquillitate anim, chapitre v. Τῇ δεξιᾷ τοὺς λόγους ὀρέγοντος αὐτοῦ, τῇ ἀριστερᾷ δέχεσθαι τοὺς ἀκροωμένους. Préoccup. Jés. (*Préoccupation, Jésuites* [2]).

Ibidem, chapitre x. Τί ἄλλο, ἢ συλλέγοντα προφάσεις ἀχαριστίας ἐπὶ τὴν τύχην; Ingrat envers Dieu.

Ibidem, même chapitre. Ὅτι μυρίων μυριάκις ἐν τοσούτοις εὐσχημονέστερον ζῇ καὶ βέλτιον, ὑμνῶν τὸν ἑαυτοῦ δαίμονα. Grace.

Ibidem, chapitre xi. Ἑκάστῳ τι, ἔφη, ἡμῶν κακόν ἐστιν. Péché originel.

Ibidem, chapitre xvii. Ἀποκτεῖναι μὲν Ἄνυτος καὶ Μέλιτος δύνανται, βλάψαι δὲ οὐ δύνανται. Martyre.

Ibidem, chapitre xviii. Ἀλλ᾽ ἔστιν εἰπεῖν ζῶντα· τοῦτο οὐ ποιήσω, οὐ ψεύσομαι.... τοῦτο γὰρ ἐφ᾽ ἡμῖν κείμενον. Grace suffisante.

De fraterno amore, chapitre i. Ἀρίσταρχος.... ἐπισκώπτων τὸ πλῆθος τῶν σοφιστῶν, ἔλεγε πάλαι μὲν ἑπτὰ σοφιστὰς μόλις γενέσθαι, τότε δὲ μὴ ῥᾳδίως ἂν ἰδιώτας τοσούτους εὑρεθῆναι. Chev. (*chevaliers*) de l'ordre [3]. Dignités multipliées.

1. Il faut se rappeler que ces notes étaient écrites à Port-Royal. On pourrait conjecturer que Racine avait à se reprocher quelque regard curieux « dans ce chaste paradis

> Où règne en un trône de lis
> La virginité sainte; »

et que le passage de Plutarque l'avertissait de son indiscrétion.

2. Racine veut dire que, dans leurs préventions, les Jésuites prenaient à contre-sens les paroles de leurs adversaires, les accusant d'hérésie, comme on accusait d'athéisme Théodore de Cyrène, dont Plutarque rapporte ici les plaintes contre ses auditeurs inintelligents.

3. De l'ordre du Saint-Esprit.

LUCIEN.

Nous avons donné, dans notre tome V (p. 493-499), l'*Extrait du traité de Lucien : Comment il faut écrire l'histoire*. C'est ce même traité que Racine a annoté sur les marges d'un exemplaire des *OEuvres de Lucien*, conservé à la Bibliothèque de Toulouse, et qui a pour titre : *Luciani Samosatensis philosophi Opera omnia quæ extant.... Lutetiæ Parisiorum, apud Julianum Bertault.... M.DC.XV* (in-folio).

Il n'y a pas de notes de sa main sur les autres écrits de Lucien qui sont dans ce même exemplaire. Cela suffirait déjà pour rendre très-probable que les notes sur le traité : *Comment il faut écrire l'histoire*, sont du même temps que l'*Extrait*, et se rattachent à la même étude, par laquelle sans doute Racine se proposait surtout, comme nous l'avons dit, de se bien pénétrer des préceptes qu'il avait à pratiquer dans sa tâche d'historiographe. Mais il y a quelque chose de plus décisif encore à l'appui de cette opinion : si le lecteur compare les passages traduits dans l'un et l'autre travail, le plus souvent il n'y remarquera que de légères différences. Les notes marginales que nous allons donner paraissent donc être tout simplement une première préparation de l'*Extrait*. Ces notes, dont l'encre a pâli, sont encore lisibles, mais bientôt elles auront entièrement disparu.

Nous indiquons les pages de l'édition de 1615, et en même temps les paragraphes de l'édition Lehmann, auxquels nous avions déjà renvoyé dans l'*Extrait*.

Page 346, § 1 (*de l'édition Lehmann*). Les Abdérites prirent une fièvre chaude en voyant représenter l'*Andromède* d'Euripide par un temps chaud.

Page 347, § 2. La guerre engendre beaucoup de maux, entre lesquels sont le grand nombre d'historiens.

Ibidem, § 3. Diogène rouloit son tonneau, pour être en action comme les autres.

Page 350, § 7. Le panégyrique et l'histoire sont éloignés comme le ciel l'est de la terre.

Ibidem, § 8. Différence du poëte et de l'historien. — Le poëte a besoin de tous les Dieux pour peindre son Agamemnon.

Page 351, § 9. L'utilité est le principal but de l'histoire; le plaisir la suit comme la beauté suit la santé.

Ibidem, § 10. Le lecteur est rigoureux comme un changeur qui examine la bonne et la mauvaise monnoie.

Page 352, § 12. Alexandre jeta dans la rivière le livre d'un historien flatteur.

Page 354, § 14. Achille seroit moins grand s'il n'eût vaincu que Thersite.

Ibidem, § 15. Historien impertinent qui commençoit son histoire en mettant son nom, comme Thucydide.

Page 355, § 16. Un autre écrivoit le détail comme l'auroit fait un soldat ou un manœuvre qui auroit travaillé dans l'armée.

Page 356, § 19. Description impertinente des armes du général.

Page 357, § 20. Quand ils viennent dans les grandes affaires, ils sont neufs comme un valet que son maître a fait son héritier. — Ils décrivent de grandes blessures et des prodiges.

Ibidem, § 21. Ils changent des noms latins et en font des noms grecs.

Ibidem, et page 358, § 22. Ils se servent de phrases poétiques. — Et tout d'un coup ils tombent dans des expressions[1].... — C'est un homme qui a un pied chaussé d'un cothurne, et l'autre d'une sandale.

Page 358, § 23. Prologues magnifiques d'une très-petite histoire. — Le casque est d'or, et la cuirasse de méchants haillons. — D'autres entrent d'abord en matière sans prologue, croyant imiter Xénophon, dont le prologue n'a point l'air de prologue.

Page 359, § 24. Ignorance dans la géographie.

Ibidem, § 26. Ridicules imitateurs de Thucydide : ils font une oraison funèbre parce qu'il en a fait une.

Page 360, § 27. Contre ceux qui écrivent au long de petites choses, et passent les grandes légèrement. — Ils décrivent le piédestal et négligent la statue.

Pages 361 et 362, § 29. Un autre, qui n'avoit jamais sorti de Corinthe, commençoit ainsi : *Visa narro*. — Ignorance des termes de guerre.

Page 362, § 31. Un autre faisoit un prologue prophétique.

Pages 363 et 364, § 34. Deux qualités principales d'un historien : un bon sens pour les choses du monde et la facilité de s'ex-

---

1. Un mot est sans doute resté au bout de la plume. Dans ses *Extraits*, Racine a ainsi traduit ce passage : « et tombent tout à coup dans de basses expressions. »

primer. — Les préceptes ne sont que pour les gens qui ont déjà de grands talents, ou naturels, ou acquis.

Pages 364 et 365, § 37. Il faut qu'un historien soit lui-même capable d'agir; — et qu'il ait vu beaucoup de choses; — qu'il ait été dans un camp.

Page 365, § 38. Qu'il n'espère et qu'il ne craigne.

Ibidem, et page 366, § 39. Qu'il dise les choses comme elles sont. — Il faut sacrifier à la seule vérité; songer à la postérité.

Page 366, § 40. Souhaits d'Alexandre.

Page 367, § 43. Vices du style. — Vertus (*du style*). Netteté et images.

Ibidem, § 44. Que tout le monde l'entende, et que les savants le louent.

Ibidem, et page 368, § 45. De la poésie dans les batailles. — Il faut pourtant tenir la bride.

Page 368, § 46. Style ni trop dur ni trop harmonieux.

Ibidem, § 47. Bons mémoires.

Ibidem, et page 369, § 49. Porter les yeux de tous côtés. — Comme il faut décrire une bataille. — Que l'historien ne soit d'aucun parti.

Page 369, § 51. Que son esprit soit un miroir qui reçoive toutes les formes des affaires. — C'est aux Athéniens à lui fournir la matière, soit d'or, soit d'ivoire, et à lui de la tailler.

Page 370, § 53. Prologue. — Exciter l'attention du lecteur par les grandes choses qu'on a à lui dire.

Ibidem, § 55. Narration vive. — Que les choses non-seulement se suivent, mais encore se tiennent ensemble.

Page 371, § 56. Négliger les petites choses.

Ibidem, § 57. Brièveté dans les descriptions. — Imiter Homère, qui a tant évité de belles descriptions à faire. — Thucydide, dans la peste, n'a dit que le nécessaire. — Il fuit (*les choses*), mais les choses l'arrêtent.

Ibidem, § 58. Il est permis d'être orateur dans les harangues.

Ibidem, § 59. Jugements, soit en bien ou en mal, doivent être courts et circonspects. — Non pas comme Théopompe, qui semble plus un accusateur qu'un historien.

Page 372, § 60. Conter les choses peu vraisemblables, sans les appuyer.

Ibidem, § 61. Songer toujours à ce que la postérité dira de vous, bien plus qu'à des espérances pour le temps présent, qui sont courtes.

Ibidem, § 62. L'architecte du Phare songeoit à l'avenir, et non pas à son siècle.

VIRGILE.

Si, dans les études de Racine, les poëtes grecs semblent avoir tenu la première place, les poëtes latins cependant ne peuvent pas avoir été négligés. Le premier en date de ses chefs-d'œuvre tragiques, *Andromaque*, a été inspiré par quelques vers de Virgile. Dans plusieurs des passages les plus passionnés et les plus tendres de *Bajazet* et de *Berénice*, il s'est souvenu du quatrième livre de l'*Énéide*. N'y a-t-il pas d'ailleurs une incontestable parenté entre le poëte de Louis XIV et celui d'Auguste, ces deux génies harmonieux, élégants, doux et purs, dont le cygne est resté l'emblème? Que Racine ait aussi goûté particulièrement Horace et Térence, et se soit nourri de leurs écrits, on n'en saurait douter. Térence, qu'il aime tant à citer dans ses lettres, Térence, si bien fait pour lui plaire par la vérité et la finesse de ses peintures, par sa profonde connaissance du cœur humain, était, il nous l'apprend lui-même[1], le modèle qu'il eût suivi de préférence, si, dans la comédie, il ne se fût pas borné à un seul essai. Le sel piquant, l'enjouement aimable, l'*urbanité* d'Horace dans ses *Épîtres* et ses *Satires*, ne devaient pas moins le charmer. Dans les *Odes* du même poëte, il trouvait une imitation des Grecs à la fois savante et inspirée, comme celle qu'il pratiquait lui-même, et il y reconnaissait sans doute et y goûtait fort l'élégance exquise, la perfection de langage, l'heureuse expression poétique, la hardiesse pleine de goût, qui furent au nombre des plus remarquables dons de son propre génie.

Les trois poëtes latins que nous venons de nommer ont donc été très-vraisemblablement annotés plus d'une fois par lui, suivant sa méthode ordinaire de travail. Nous n'avons cependant point rencontré de *Virgile* ni de *Térence* chargés de ses notes manuscrites. La Bibliothèque de Toulouse possède un *Virgile* qui a appartenu à Racine et porte sa signature. C'est un volume in-4° qui a pour titre : P. VIRGILIUS, *cum veterum omnium commentariis et selectis recent. notis.... Ex offic. Abr. Commelini....* 1646. Mais ce volume n'est pas annoté.

Voici la seule trace que nous ayons rencontrée des études de Racine sur Virgile. Il a fait quelques extraits de ce poëte au commencement du même cahier d'où nous avons tiré les *Remarques sur les Olympiques de Pindare* (voyez ci-dessus, p. 1-55). Les *Extraits* de Virgile ont été pris dans les livres I, III et IV des *Géorgiques*. Dans les dix-neuf pages dont ils se composent, on ne trouve pas, à proprement parler, de notes, mais seulement quelques titres qui précèdent les citations, tels que : « Astres. — Dieux champêtres. — César. Dieu nouveau prince. — S'accommoder au terroir. — Deucalion. — Été. — Pavots. — Diversité, etc. »

---

1. *Préface* des *Plaideurs.* Voyez notre tome II, p. 141.

HORACE.

A la suite des *Extraits de Virgile*, six pages du même cahier dont nous venons de parler renferment des *Extraits d'Horace*, qui sont accompagnés de brèves indications du même genre, parmi lesquelles il nous a paru qu'il n'y avait rien à recueillir. Ils appartiennent à seize des vingt-deux premières *odes* du livre I. Les vii⁰, viii⁰, x⁰, xviii⁰, xx⁰ et xxi⁰ n'ont fourni aucun extrait.

Dans une *Lettre sur quelques notes de Voltaire à la marge d'un exemplaire de Virgile*, que Fontanes fit insérer dans le tome I du *Mercure de France* (16 messidor an VIII), il parle d'un *Horace* annoté par Racine, sans désigner d'ailleurs l'édition. Nous n'avons pas rencontré l'exemplaire qu'il a eu en vue; nous devons donc nous borner à transcrire le passage de sa lettre (p. 94) où il en fait mention : « J'ai lu quelques-unes de ses notes (*des notes de Racine*) à la marge d'un *Horace*, qui avait passé entre les mains de son fils et de le Franc de Pompignan. On voit que le plus parfait des poëtes ne l'était devenu qu'en méditant sans cesse, et dans ses moindres détails, tous les secrets du style poétique.

« Il avait marqué plusieurs expressions d'Horace, comme propres à passer dans la poésie française. A côté de celle-ci : *nigrum pulvere* (*ode* vi *du livre* I, *vers* 14 *et* 15), il avait écrit *noir de poussière*, et ajoutait : « Cette expression « peut se transporter avec succès dans notre langue. » C'est dans ce même exemplaire qu'à la marge du passage si connu d'Horace (*ode* xix *du livre* I, *vers* 9 *et* 10) :

> *In me tota ruens Venus*
> *Cyprum deseruit...*,

on trouvait ce vers admirable de *Phèdre* (*vers* 306) :

> C'est Vénus toute entière à sa proie attachée. »

Des deux notes citées par Fontanes, la première nous semble un peu sortir des habitudes de Racine; mais la seconde surtout nous étonne. Il est bien difficile de croire qu'il ait pu l'écrire avant la tragédie de *Phèdre*, et qu'il ait ainsi, quand il travailla à cette pièce, été chercher sur la marge de son *Horace* ce beau vers que prépare si bien celui qui précède :

> Ce n'est plus une ardeur dans mes veines cachée.

Il faudrait donc plutôt penser qu'il a annoté l'exemplaire d'Horace dont on nous parle en un temps de sa vie où de telles études sont peut-être moins vraisemblables; et qu'il a pris plaisir à se citer lui-même, ce que nous ne voyons pas qu'il ait fait nulle part ailleurs. Le témoignage de Fontanes, qui avait vu de ses yeux cet exemplaire, n'est cependant pas récusable. Cet *Horace* annoté a existé, et existe sans doute encore. Tiré de la bibliothèque de le Franc de Pompignan, son origine mérite toute confiance. Mais est-il impossible qu'on se soit trompé en attribuant à Racine des notes qui seraient d'un de ses fils? Nous n'affirmons rien, n'ayant pas nous-même vu le livre.

En un temps que nous n'avons aucun moyen de déterminer, mais que nous croirions volontiers n'avoir pas été fort éloigné de celui où Racine, dans le cahier mentionné ci-dessus, recueillait les *Extraits d'Horace* en y joignant un petit nombre d'indications sommaires, il écrivait des notes, dont la plupart ne sont guère plus développées, sur les marges d'un exemplaire des *OEuvres* du même poëte. Le volume dont nous parlons est un petit in-8° d'une édition elzévirienne. Il a pour titre : QUINTUS HORATIUS FLACCUS. *Daniel Heinsius ex emendatissimis editionibus expressit, et repræsentavit. Editio nova. Ludg. Batav. Ex officina Elseviriorum, Acad. Typograph. M.DC.LIII.* A la fin du volume, au-dessus du mot *Finis*, Racine a signé son nom. M. de Margency, gentilhomme ordinaire du Roi, a écrit sur le feuillet de garde : « Ce livre a été l'*Horace* du grand Racine; les notes sont de sa main. Il m'a été donné par son fils. » M. de Margency a lui-même ajouté quelques notes, mais elles se rapportent seulement à la 1ʳᵉ *épître* du livre I. Toutes les autres sont de Racine. Ce précieux volume appartient aujourd'hui à M. le duc de Broglie, qui a bien voulu nous en donner communication. Un grand nombre de vers y sont soulignés, et il y a certainement quelque intérêt à voir quels passages avaient surtout frappé Racine; mais il faut avoir sous les yeux le livre même, pour y chercher ainsi jusqu'aux moindres traces de l'étude que le poëte en avait faite. Dans tous les volumes annotés par Racine, nous avons dû négliger l'indication des vers soulignés. Les notes écrites à la marge de l'*Horace* paraîtront, nous l'avons déjà dit, bien courtes, et quelquefois peu significatives. Nous en avons omis quelques-unes qui ne sont rien de plus qu'un seul mot, ou un nom propre. On trouvera que nous avons encore poussé l'exactitude assez loin; mais nous ne pouvions éviter de ce côté quelque excès, dès que nous voulions donner une idée de la méthode de travail suivie par Racine.

LIVRE I DES ODES. — *Ode* IV, vers 19 et 20. Beauté fragile.
Ode V, vers 1. Femme volage.
Ibidem, vers 13-16. Sage après le naufrage.
Ode VI, vers 1-4. Il n'ose chanter des choses hautes.
Ode VII, vers 15-18. Se réjouir quelquefois.
Ode VIII, vers 3 et 4. Amant oisif.
Ode IX, vers 15-24. Plaisirs de la jeunesse.
Ode XI, vers 1-8. Ne point songer au lendemain.
Ode XIII, vers 4. Jalousie.
Ode XVI, vers 15 et 16. Colère.
Ode XIX, vers 5-8. Amour[1].

---

1. Dans cette même *ode*, le vers 9 : *In me tota ruens Venus*, est non-seu-

Ode xxv, vers 13-15. Amour de vieille.
Ode xxx, vers 5-8. Compagnie de Vénus[1].
Livre II. — *Ode* viii, vers 1 et suivants. Parjures des belles.
Ibidem, vers 5-8. Le parjure l'embellit (*Barine*).
Ibidem, vers 17-20. Belle fille. *N^a* (*nota*).
Ode ix, vers 9. Larmes continuelles.
Ode xiii, vers 1. Arbre funeste.
Ibidem, vers 13-20. La mort est imprévue.
Ibidem, vers 30-32. Le peuple aime mieux les choses grandes en vers.
Ode xiv, vers 1 et 2. Les ans fuient.
Ibidem, vers 10-20. La mort ne s'évite point.
Ibidem, vers 21-24. Il faut tout quitter.
Ode xv, vers 1 et 2. Abondance de bâtiments.
Ibidem, vers 10-20. Anciens Romains.
Ode xvi. Cette ode est toute admirable.
Ibidem, vers 17. Pourquoi de si grands desseins?
Ibidem, vers 33-40. Les richesses ne donnent point le repos.
Ode xvii, vers 2 et 3. Il ne veut point survivre à Mécénas.
Ibidem, vers 21 et 22. Leurs astres s'accordent.
Ibidem, vers 30-32. Sacrifices inégaux.
Ode xviii, vers 1 et 2. Il est content de ce qu'il a.
Ibidem, vers 31-33. Mort égale.
Ode xix, vers 1-4. Bacchus enseignant.
Ibidem, vers 25-27. Plus propre aux jeux qu'à la guerre.
Ode xx, vers 9-12. Il devient cygne.
Ibidem, vers 21-24. Honneurs de la sépulture inutiles.
Livre III. — *Ode* iii, vers 1-8. Constance.
Ibidem, vers 17 et suivants. Junon se réconcilie avec les Romains.

lement un de ceux que Racine a soulignés, mais il a écrit à la marge : *N.* (*nota.*) Voyez ce que nous avons dit ci-dessus, p. 324, du vers 306 de *Phèdre*, que ce passage d'Horace lui a inspiré, et qu'il aurait, dit-on, cité à la marge d'un autre exemplaire.

1. Les huit *odes* suivantes, par lesquelles finit le livre I, sont sans notes; mais on voit par le grand nombre de vers qui y sont soulignés qu'elles ont été, comme les précédentes, étudiées avec beaucoup de soin. Parmi tous ces vers que Racine a ainsi recommandés à son souvenir, nous avons remarqué dans l'ode xxxiii, *ad Albium Tibullum*, les vers 5-12, qui l'avaient peut-être assez frappé pour qu'il en ait fait son profit dans la conception de son plan d'*Andromaque* :

> *Sic visum Veneri, cui placet impares*
> *. . . . . animos sub juga ahenea*
> *Sævo mittere cum joco.*

HORACE.   327

Ode III, vers 40-42. Ruines de Troie. N^a (*nota*).
Ibidem, vers 53-56. Étendue de l'empire romain.
Ibidem, vers 70-72. Muse trop élevée.
Ode IV, vers 9 et suivants. Enfance d'Horace.
Ibidem, vers 20. Enfant hardi.
Ibidem, vers 25-28. Les Muses l'ont protégé.
Ibidem, vers 65. Forces sans conduite.
Ibidem, vers 79 et 80. Amour puni.
Ode V, vers 1 et 2. Le tonnerre fait croire en Dieu.
Ibidem, vers 29 et 30. La vertu ne revient point.
Ibidem, vers 41-44. Constance de Régulus.
Ibidem, vers 48. Illustre exilé.
Ode VI, vers 5. Humilité.
Ibidem, vers 17-20. Adultère, source de tous les désordres.
Ibidem, vers 23 et 24. Jeunesse lascive.
Ode VII, vers 19 et 20. Histoires scandaleuses.
Ibidem, vers 29-32. Conseil à une femme.
Ode IX. Renouement [1].
Ode X, vers 1-4. Reproches de cruauté.
Ibidem, vers 14. Pâleur des amants.
Ode XI, vers 9-12. Fille intraitable.
Ibidem, vers 13 et suivants. Puissance de Mercure.
Ode XII, vers 3-5. Amour fait tout oublier [2].
Ode XIV, vers 14-16. Siècle tranquille.
Ibidem, vers 25-28. L'âge adoucit les esprits.
Ode XV, vers 1 et suivants. Vieille doit se retirer.

LIVRE IV. — *Ode* III, vers 1-9. Les poëtes ne sont bons qu'à leur métier.
Ibidem, vers 13-15. On l'estimoit (*Horace*) à Rome.
Ibidem, vers 17-24. Action de grâce aux Muses.
Ode IV, vers 5 et 6. Aiglon qui sort de son nid.
Ibidem, vers 25-32. Bonne naissance.
Ibidem, vers 33 et 34. Bonne éducation.
Ibidem, vers 49. Il fait parler Annibal.
Ibidem, vers 57. Chêne battu.
Ibidem, vers 65-68. Rome devient plus forte, plus elle est attaquée.
Ode V, vers 5-8. Présence du prince.
Ibidem, vers 9-13. Mère qui prie pour le retour de son fils.
Ibidem, vers 17-24. Règne heureux.

---

1. C'est-à-dire *réconciliation*. C'est l'ode : *Donec gratus eram*.
2. Voyez dans *Phèdre* les vers 548-550, que l'on pourrait regarder comme un souvenir des vers d'Horace.

Ode VII, vers 9-16. Les saisons reviennent, et non pas la vie.
Ode VIII, vers 13-22. Poëtes donnent l'immortalité.
Ode IX, vers 9. Poésies délicates.
Ibidem, vers 37 et 38. Juge sévère.
Ode X, vers 1-8. Aimer tandis qu'on est jeune.
Ode XIII, vers 1 et 2. Belle devenue vieille.
Ibidem, vers 9-12. L'amour fuit les vieilles.
Ibidem, vers 17-22. Belle changée.
Ode XIV, vers 22-24. Vaillant capitaine.
Ibidem, vers 41 et 42. Auguste est craint partout.
Ode XV, vers 4-9. Siècle heureux.
Ibidem, vers 25-32. Oisiveté bien heureuse.

LIVRE DES ÉPODES. — *Ode* I, vers 17 et 18. On craint moins de loin.

Ibidem, vers 31-34. Il (*Horace*) est trop riche.

LIVRE I DES SATIRES. — *Satire* I, vers 1 et suivants. Inconstance des hommes. — Chacun est mécontent de sa condition.
Ibidem, vers 28-32. Chacun dit qu'il cherche le repos.
Ibidem, vers 51. Grand monceau d'or.
Ibidem, vers 65. Riche vilain.
Ibidem, vers 84-87. Avare haï.
Satire II, vers 1-6. Prodigue et avare.
Ibidem, vers 11. Divers avis.
Ibidem, vers 24. Fuir les excès.
Ibidem, vers 53 et 54. Admirateur de soi-même.
Ibidem, vers 86-89. Acheter un cheval et lui couvrir la tête.
Ibidem, vers 127-133. Pris sur le fait.
Satire III, vers 1-3. Chantres incommodes.
Ibidem, vers 4-9. Homme inégal.
Ibidem, vers 23. On se pardonne à soi-même.
Ibidem, vers 25-27. Excuser les défauts de ses amis.
Ibidem, vers 29 et 38. Homme prompt n'est pas propre à la raillerie.
Ibidem, vers 33 et 34. Bel esprit malpropre.
Ibidem, vers 38-40. On aime les défauts de sa maîtresse.
Ibidem, vers 43 et 44. Déguiser ceux de ses amis.
Ibidem, vers 96-98. Contre l'égalité des péchés.
Ibidem, vers 105. Origine des lois.
Ibidem, vers 124 et 125. Sage des stoïques.
Satire X, vers 81-83. Plaire seulement aux honnêtes gens.

LIVRE II DES ÉPÎTRES. — *Épître* II, vers 65-75. Vie de Rome.

CICÉRON.

Nous avons dit précédemment (p. 3) que le cahier des *Remarques sur Pindare* renferme, dans ses premières pages, des *Extraits de Virgile, d'Horace, de Pline l'ancien* et *de Cicéron*. Ces derniers *Extraits*, qui sont aux pages 44-50 de la première partie du cahier, appartiennent aux livres I et II des *Lettres à Atticus*. A la marge des passages cités, on trouve quelques indications sommaires, telles que celles-ci : « Homme inutile. — Amitiés pompeuses. — Vrai ami. — Effort d'esprit. — Gens intéressés. — Caton. — Homme de néant, etc. » Louis Racine, dans une note sur la lettre que son père écrivait à Jean-Baptiste Racine, le 4 octobre 1692, dit, en parlant des *Lettres à Atticus :* « C'étoit son livre favori, et le compagnon de ses voyages. » L'exemplaire de ce livre dont il est question dans la même lettre, étant en plusieurs tomes, ne sauroit être celui dont nous trouvons la description suivante dans la *Notice de livres ayant appartenu à Mlle des Radrets*[1] : « *M. Tullii Ciceronis Epistolæ ad Atticum, ad M. Brutum, ad Quintum fratrem.... Paulus Manutius Aldi F. Venetiis*, 1540, 1 vol. in-8°, relié en veau. Louis Racine a écrit cette phrase sur le feuillet blanc qui précède immédiatement le titre : *Cet exemplaire, sur lequel mon père avoit mis quelques notes, a été ensuite rempli de celles de mon frère.* J. B. Racine a écrit sur la couverture 70 noms de Romains dont Cicéron parle dans ces lettres. Après cette table est écrit : *Joannes Racine decimo quinto Cal. Jan.* 1689. Sur la feuille de titre est aussi écrit : *Joannes Racine.* Le volume est ensuite rempli de notes marginales des deux Racine ; ces notes se composent de réflexions, de commentaires, d'explications, relatifs aux faits racontés dans ces lettres ou aux mœurs de ce temps, ou à l'interprétation d'expressions particulières ou obscures. » Ce même exemplaire est aussi mentionné dans le *Querard*, et par M. Feuillet de Conches, à la page xxxiv du tome I de ses *Causeries d'un curieux*.

Nous avons pu recueillir quelques notes de Racine dans deux volumes des *Traités de rhétorique* de Cicéron, appartenant à des éditions différentes. L'un de ces volumes est à la Bibliothèque impériale. C'est le tome I de l'édition qui a pour titre : *M. Tullii Ciceronis Opera. Ex Petri Victorii castigationibus. Lugduni. Apud Seb. Gryphium*, 1540 (in-8°). Sur la page de titre est la signature de Racine. Les IV *Livres à Herennius* qui sont en tête du volume n'ont pas été annotés. A la page 128 commencent les notes de Racine. Elles se rapportent au traité *de l'Invention,* au livre I des *Dialogues de l'Orateur* (*de Oratore*), et à l'*Orateur* (*Orator*).

L'autre volume a fait partie, en 1868, d'une vente de livres faite par

---

[1]. Voyez ci-dessus, p. 173.

M. Brunet, libraire. Il porte le n° 158 dans la première partie de son Catalogue. C'est le tome II des *Traités de rhétorique* de Cicéron dans une édition de Sébastien Gryphe, différente de celle dont nous venons de parler. En voici le titre : *M. Tullii Ciceronis Rhetoricorum secundus tomus. Apud Seb. Gryphium, Lugduni*, 1546. Ce volume in-16 a une reliure ancienne en maroquin rouge, avec tranches dorées. Il porte la signature de Racine, qui y a annoté quelques rares passages des livres I et II des *Dialogues de l'Orateur*. Il y a aussi, dans ce même exemplaire, quelques notes sur le *Brutus*.

Nous commencerons par mettre sous les yeux du lecteur les notes de l'exemplaire in-8° de 1540.

De Inventione. — Livre I, chapitre II[1]. L'éloquence a rassemblé les hommes. — De maître devenir égal.

Chapitre III. Comment la philosophie s'est séparée de l'éloquence.

Chapitre IV. Excellence de l'éloquence.

Chapitre V. Aristote a servi à la rhétorique.

Chapitre VI. C'est peu de donner des règles, il faut les savoir pratiquer.

Chapitres XIV, XV et XVI. Parties de l'oraison. — Exorde. — Moyens de gaigner la bienveillance des juges.

Chapitre XVII. Moyens de s'insinuer. — Commencer par quelque fable ou par quelque chose de surprenant.

Chapitre XVIII. Exorde grave et sérieux. — Point d'élégance ni de fleurs affectées. — Défauts de l'exorde. Exordes vicieux.

Chapitre XIX. Plusieurs sortes de narrations.

Chapitre XX. Narration courte, claire et vraisemblable. Brèveté[2]. — Plusieurs sont longs qui pensent être courts. — Clarté de la narration.

Chapitre XXI. Vraisemblance. — Il faut quelquefois couper la narration, comme quand elle est odieuse. — Il faut faire la narration à son avantage.

Chapitres XXII et XXIII. Partition. — Parties de la division, *Brevitas. Absolutio, i.* (c'est-à-dire) comprendre tout ce qu'on dira. *Paucitas, i.* ne pas confondre les espèces avec le genre. Subdivision. — Exemple de la partition dans l'*Andrienne*.

Chapitre XXIV. Matières des arguments. Les personnes ou les affaires.

Chapitre XXV. Arguments tirés de la personne.

Chapitre XXVI. Matière d'arguments tirée des choses.

---

1. Nous indiquons les divisions de chapitres d'après l'édition Lemaire (*Collection des classiques latins*).
2. « MM. de Port-Royal voulaient qu'on dît *brèveté*. » (*Dictionnaire* de M. Littré, au mot Brièveté.)

Chapitre xxxi. Induction. — Exemple de l'induction. — Socrate ne prouvoit que par induction.

Chapitre xxxii. Cacher la fin de l'induction.

Chapitres xxxiv et xxxv. Raisonnement. — Cinq parties du raisonnement. — Socrate a pratiqué l'induction, et Aristote le raisonnement.

Chapitre xxxix. [Être] trompé [est] 1º fâcheux, 2º fou, 3º honteux.

Chapitre xl. Il faut toujours conclure l'argument, quelque clair qu'il soit.

Chapitre xli. Diversifier les arguments.

Chapitre lv. Comment on excite la pitié : par l'intérêt commun. — S'adresser à des choses même inanimées. — Constance fait souvent plus de pitié que la consternation. — Les larmes sèchent bientôt.

Livre II, chapitre i. Zeuxis excelloit à peindre les femmes. — Zeuxis choisit cinq filles pour faire le portrait d'Hélène. — Tout ne se peut trouver en un seul.

Chapitre ii. Choisir le bon de chaque auteur, et ne s'attacher à aucun. — Tisias premier rhéteur. — Rhétorique d'Aristote. — Isocrate.

Chapitre iii. Modestie de Cicéron. Chacun peut se tromper.

Chapitre iv. Fin du genre judiciel, démonstratif et délibératif.

Chapitres v et vi. Lieux communs pour les causes de conjecture. — Les conjectures se prennent ou de la cause, ou de la personne, ou de l'action même. — Il y a deux causes d'une action : *impulsio*, *ratiocinatio*. — Comment l'accusateur doit pousser les conjectures de l'impulsion ou du raisonnement. — Comment il faut amplifier la force de l'impulsion et du raisonnement.

Chapitre vii. Ne pas considérer le succès, mais l'espérance du succès. — Montrer qu'aucun autre n'a dû ou n'a pu commettre l'action.

Chapitre viii. Comment le défenseur les doit diminuer (*l'impulsion et le raisonnement*). — S'accommoder au fond du cœur de ses auditeurs.

Chapitres ix et x. Conjectures tirées de la personne : du nom ; de la nature ; de la manière de vivre ; de sa fortune ; de l'habitude ; des inclinations ; du dessein ; des actions, et des paroles. — Regarder si la vie passée convient à l'action ; s'il (*l'accusé*) a des vices approchants de celui qu'on lui impute. — Si sa vie est innocente, l'accuser d'hypocrisie ; ou bien dire qu'il y a commencement à tout.

Chapitre xi. Devoir du défenseur pour la personne. — Le défenseur doit appuyer beaucoup sur la vie passée, si elle est bonne.

— S'il y a quelques taches, les excuser. — Si elle est criminelle, dire qu'il s'agit d'une action, et non pas du passé.

Chapitre XII. Conjectures tirées de l'action. — Lieu, temps, occasion. — Qualité de l'action. — Événement, comme la crainte ou la joie. — Suite de l'action.

Chapitre XIII. Conjectures communes à la personne et à l'action. — Ce qui a précédé l'action. — Dans l'action. — Après l'action.

Chapitre XV. Lieux communs. — S'en servir rarement. — Ils sont permis après une exacte discussion de quelque endroit de la cause, pour réveiller l'auditeur. — Les remplir d'éloquence. — Ils ne sont pas propres à toutes les causes ni à tous les orateurs.

Chapitre XVI. Quels lieux communs peuvent tomber dans une cause de conjectures [1].

DIALOGI DE ORATORE. — LIVRE I, chapitre XXIV. Brigue.

Chapitre XXV. Qualités d'esprit. Prompt à imaginer, fécond à expliquer, ferme à se ressouvenir. — Qualités du corps. Physionomies rudes. Physionomies heureuses. — On remarque bien plus le mal que le bien.

Chapitre XXVI. On est difficile pour le plaisir. — On souffre plus facilement un méchant avocat qu'un méchant comédien. — Timidité de l'orateur. — On est impudent si l'on n'est timide. — Un méchant orateur est toujours impudent, quoiqu'il rougisse. — Pâleur et crainte de Crassus.

Chapitre XXVII. On ne réussit pas toujours. — On excuse dans les autres arts, mais non pas l'orateur. — Roscius n'a pas voulu jouer ; ou il se trouvoit mal. — Sévérité que l'on a pour les fautes d'esprit.

Chapitre XXVIII. Un maître renvoyoit ses écoliers, quand il ne leur trouvoit point de naturel. — Qualités de l'orateur. *N*ᵃ (*nota*). — Roscius. Il n'a jamais pu trouver de disciple qu'il pût souffrir. — On appeloit *Roscius* tous ceux qui excelloient dans leur art.

Chapitre XXIX. Le principal est de plaire ; et c'est ce qui ne se montre point. — Raillerie honnête.

Chapitre XXX. Passion pour sa profession. — Étude de Crassus.

Chapitre XXXI. Trouver, disposer, orner, retenir, prononcer.

Chapitre XXXIII. Mauvais exercice. — Le principal est de bien écrire. — On en parle plus éloquemment. — On en parle mieux sur-le-champ. Comparaison.

Chapitre XXXIV. Traduire. — Action. — Imiter les bons acteurs. — Mémoire locale. — Parler en public de bonne heure. — Lire

---

1. Le reste du traité *de l'Invention* est sans notes, ainsi que les *Topiques*, et le dialogue *de la Partition oratoire*.

les poëtes et les historiens, et tous les bons auteurs. — Lieux communs. — Apprendre l'urbanité. C'est le sel[1].

ORATOR. — Chapitres XII et XIII. Hérodote et Thucydide. — Fleurettes. — Isocrate.
Chapitre XV. Esprit et étude. — Exordes.
Chapitre XVI. Discours étendu, et coupé. — Discours sec.
Chapitre XVII. Action est l'éloquence du corps. — Bonne grâce.
Chapitre XVIII. Voix. — Se la perfectionner. — Gestes. — Visage.
Chapitre XIX. Philosophes éloquents. Platon. — Différence de leur éloquence. — Déclamateurs.
Chapitre XX. Histoire. — Harangues d'histoire. — Platon est plus poëte que les comiques. — Comédie. — Éloquence des poëtes.
Chapitre XXI. Prouver, plaire, emporter. — *Decorum*.
Chapitre XXVI. Fautes dans le plaisant.

DIALOGI DE ORATORE (*de l'édition in-16, 1546*). — LIVRE I, chapitre V. Bons comédiens rares.
Chapitre VIII. Avantages de l'éloquence.
Chapitre XIV. On ne peut bien dire ce qu'on ne sait point.
Chapitre XVIII. Éloquence des philosophes.
Chapitre XXI. Cicéron se prédit.
Chapitre XXV. Parler en public.
Chapitre XXVI. Difficulté des arts qui sont faits pour le plaisir. — Pudeur des méchants auteurs. — Pudeur, modestie.
Chapitre XXVII. Raison de cette crainte des grands hommes.
Chapitre XXVIII. Excellence de Roscius. Il n'a pu avoir de disciple qu'il approuvât.
Chapitre XXX. Amour de son art.
LIVRE II, chapitre LIV. Bons mots.
Chapitre LX. — (En marge de la phrase : *Risum quæsivit, qui est, mea sententia, vel tenuissimus ingenii fructus.*) N^a (*nota*).
Chapitre LXIV. Surprise.

BRUTUS (*de la même édition de 1546*). — Chapitre XII. L'éloquence vient de Sicile.
Chapitre XVI. Oraisons funèbres.
Chapitre XXIV. Ne point publier ses harangues.

---

1. Ce qui suit du livre I de ce dialogue, et les livres II et III sont sans notes. Le *Brutus* n'a que deux petites notes qui n'ont pas d'intérêt.

TITE-LIVE.

Nous avons parlé à la page 103, note 2, de notre tome V, d'un très-petit nombre de notes manuscrites sur Tite-Live. Elles sont d'une écriture qui n'est pas celle de la jeunesse de Racine; et comme d'ailleurs on les trouve sur un des feuillets de ses *Fragments historiques*[1], elles paraissent être du temps où il écrivait ces *Fragments*. Elles peuvent faire conjecturer (et c'est le seul intérêt qu'elles offrent) que Racine, lorsqu'il s'occupait de ses travaux d'historiographe, relisait les historiens anciens, pour étudier leur style, comparer, par exemple dans l'expression des choses militaires, leur langue à la nôtre, recueillir quelques pensées à son usage, peut-être préparer certains rapprochements. Il indique lui-même dans ses notes deux des pages de l'édition dont il se servait, et cette indication se rapporte à une édition de Francfort-sur-le-Mein (*Francoforti ad Mœnum, apud Joannem et Sigismundum Feyerabendt, M.D.LXXVIII*[2]). Les quelques expressions et les quelques faits qu'il a notés étant tirés de sept pages seulement de cette édition (400-406), on peut croire que nous n'avons là qu'un fragment d'extraits nombreux qu'il faisait alors du même historien. Nous ne nous exagérons pas l'intérêt d'un si court fragment, mais précisément parce qu'il est fort court, nous croyons pouvoir le reproduire : « *Moratores aut palantes*. Tit. Liv.[3]. C'est ce que nous appelons traîneurs[4]. — *Intra bina castra*[5], en deux jours de marche. — *Obsidionem sine certamine solvit*[6], fit lever le siége sans donner de combat. — *Gens nata instaurandis reparandisque bellis*[7]. — *Munierunt Romana imperia*[8]. — Quæs-

---

1. Au feuillet 197 recto du tome II des manuscrits de Racine conservés à la Bibliothèque impériale.
2. Cette édition est, dit-on, la répétition exacte de celle de 1568, publiée également à Francfort, chez les mêmes libraires. Racine a donc pu se servir de l'une ou de l'autre de ces éditions.
3. Page 400. Livre XXIV, chapitre xli. Nous citons la page d'après l'édition de Francfort, mais le chapitre d'après l'édition Lemaire, le *Tite-Live* in-folio de 1578 n'étant pas divisé en chapitres.
4. A la suite de *traîneurs*, on peut lire, bien qu'ils soient effacés, les mots : « marauds de grande route. » Il y a dans le texte de Tite-Live : *aut moratorum* (qui peut venir ou de *morator* ou de *moratus*) *aut palantium*. Le latin *morator* est une des étymologies qu'on a proposées pour expliquer l'origine du français *maraud*. Est-ce pour cela que Racine avait rapproché les deux mots?
5. Page 400. Livre XXIV, chapitre xli. — 6. *Ibidem*.
7. Page 401. Livre XXIV, chapitre xlii.
8. Page 401. Livre XXIV, chapitre xliv. La leçon ordinaire est *Romanum imperium*; mais elle est douteuse : il faudrait, ce semble, un sujet pluriel à *munierunt*. On a proposé de lire *Romani*, au lieu de *Romanum imperium*.

tus ex alieno errore facilis, quem velut ex concessæ artis usu exercebant. Devineresses, p. 405¹. — Partisans fameux², p. 406. On ménageoit les gens d'affaires, *ibid.* »

1. Livre XXV, chapitre I. C'est ici, et dans la citation suivante, que Racine a lui-même indiqué les pages qui se rapportent à l'édition de 1578.
2. Livre XXV, chapitre III.

TACITE.

Parmi les cahiers de Racine que possède la Bibliothèque impériale, on en trouve un qui contient des *Extraits de Tacite*[1]. Il est de format in-4° comme celui des *Extraits de saint Basile*, et a été relié dans un cartonnage semblable. Sur la couverture, Louis Racine a écrit cette note : « Extraits écrits par Jean Racine des auteurs latins qu'il lisoit à Port-Royal en 1656. Il avoit alors environ quinze ans. » Il eût fallu dire : « Il avoit environ dix-sept ans. » L'écriture de ces *Extraits* est très-belle, et comme moulée; celle des notes qui les accompagnent est plus courante et aussi plus fine. La date que donne Louis Racine à ce travail n'est pas de sa part une simple conjecture. On lit en tête des *Extraits* ce titre, qui est de la main de Racine lui-même : *Taciti sententiæ illustriores. Excerptæ anno* 1656. *R.* (*Racine.*) Il y a des passages tirés de chacun des douze livres qui nous restent des *Annales* (livres I-VI, et XI-XVI) et des cinq livres des *Histoires*. Après les *Extraits* des *Histoires*, Racine a écrit : *Nihil de Germania et Agricolæ vita excerpsimus, quia omnia in illis miranda, excerpenda et ediscenda.* Les notes qui sont à la marge de ces *Extraits* ne sont que des espèces de têtes de chapitres, ou les pensées même de Tacite brièvement résumées. Quelques-unes sont en français, mais la plupart en latin. Ainsi dans les trois premiers chapitres du livre I des *Annales* : *Adulatio ingenia deterit.* — *Metus et odium historiæ pestes.* — *Principatus affectatio.* — *Adulatores.* — *Tuta incertis præferenda.* — *Legum pestes.* — *Filii regum subsidia dominationis, etc.* Ces notes latines sont en général très-élégantes; celles que nous venons de transcrire suffisent pour faire voir que, dans cette étude, Racine s'attachait surtout à faire ressortir les lieux communs. Nous avons remarqué, dans le livre XIV des *Annales*, qu'il a très-fortement souligné ce passage du chapitre L : *Libros exuri jussit, quæsitos lectitatosque, donec cum periculo parabantur : mox licentia habendi oblivionem attulit;* et qu'il a écrit à la marge : « Livres défendus, » seule note que l'on trouve sur les extraits de ce livre. Si Racine paraît avoir été particulièrement frappé de ce passage sur les précautions, plus dangereuses qu'utiles, des brûleurs de livres, ne serait-ce pas qu'il le transcrivait dans le temps où Lancelot avait deux fois jeté au feu, plus qu'inutilement, le roman d'*Héliodore*? Les *Extraits* des *Annales* ont 141 pages, ceux des *Histoires* 68 pages.

1. *Fonds français*, n° 12888.

QUINTILIEN.

Le même cahier où Racine a recueilli des *Extraits de Tacite*, renferme, dans sa seconde partie, des *Extraits de Quintilien*, qui remplissent 255 pages. Ici encore la date du travail est donnée par Racine lui-même dans ce titre : *Quintiliani sententiæ illustriores. Excerptæ anno* 1656. *R.* (*Racine.*) Ces extraits appartiennent à l'épître *Au libraire Triphon* et aux douze livres des *Institutions oratoires*. Les notes marginales sont du même genre que celles des *Extraits de Tacite*. Elles sont en latin, à l'exception de quelques-unes sur le livre X, qui sont en français. Une seule d'entre celles-ci nous a paru assez curieuse par le rapprochement littéraire dont Racine y a trouvé l'occasion. A la marge de ce passage du livre X (chapitre 1) : *Ennium, sicut sacros vetustate lucos, adoremus, in quibus grandia et antiqua robora jam non tantam habent speciem, quantam religionem*, Racine a écrit : « Ronsard. Du Bartas. » En comparant ces deux poëtes du seizième siècle au vieil Ennius, Racine ne les traitait pas trop mal. Cela pourrait faire croire que, tout en les jugeant surannés, il les goûtait un peu plus que bientôt après Boileau ne l'eût trouvé bon.

Ce qu'il y a de plus digne peut-être d'être remarqué au sujet de ces *Extraits de Quintilien* et *de Tacite*, c'est qu'étant bien authentiquement du temps de Port-Royal, ils nous apprennent qu'en 1656, Racine, écolier depuis un an à peine dans cette studieuse maison, y avait déjà lu tout entiers, la plume à la main, deux auteurs que d'ordinaire au collége on ne connaît guère que par quelques fragments.

PLINE L'ANCIEN.

Racine, dans ses *Remarques sur l'Odyssée* (voyez ci-dessus, p. 56-164), a plusieurs fois cité l'*Histoire naturelle* de Pline. Nous avons dit qu'il faisait usage alors de l'édition in-folio de Lyon, 1563. Sa signature se trouve aussi sur un exemplaire que possède M. le docteur Desbarreaux-Bernard, de Toulouse, et qui est d'une autre édition. C'est un Elzévir de Leyde (1635), en trois petits volumes in-12. Cet exemplaire n'est pas annoté; mais le soin avec lequel il a été lu par Racine est attesté par les corrections qu'il a faites lui-même d'un assez grand nombre de fautes typographiques.

Nous avons parlé ailleurs (p. 3 de ce volume) d'*Extraits de Pline l'ancien* que le cahier des *Remarques sur Pindare* renferme dans sa première partie, à la suite des *Extraits de Virgile* et d'*Horace*, et avant les *Extraits de Cicéron*. Racine a recueilli ces passages de Pline dans la *Préface à Vespasien* et dans les livres II, III, IV, V et VII. Il les a accompagnés de quelques notes, dont plusieurs ne sont que des indications sommaires, par exemple, dans la *Préface* : « Cicéron. — Caton le jeune. — Écrits. — Esprit agissant. — Veilles. — Citer ses auteurs. — Pédant orgueilleux. » Nous remarquons surtout, parmi les passages cités par Racine, celui où Pline parle des Esséniens (livre V, chapitre XVII[1]) : *Esseni... gens sola... Tam fœcunda illis aliorum vitæ pœnitentia est*. Ces *Extraits* sans doute sont à peu près du temps où Racine traduisait quelques pages de Josèphe et de Philon sur ces mêmes Esséniens (voyez notre tome V, p. 532-558); il devait être alors curieux de tout ce qui avait été anciennement écrit sur ces solitaires.

Nous omettons quelques notes très-brèves; il suffit d'en recueillir un petit nombre qui sont un peu moins sommaires. Racine traduit çà et là des passages, et mêle à ses traductions quelques lambeaux du texte latin.

Livre VII, chapitre II. Pyrrhus avoit un pouce, au pied droit, dont l'attouchement guérissoit les malades de rate; il ne put être brûlé avec le reste de son corps. — Il y a dans l'Inde des arbres si hauts qu'on ne les sauroit passer avec une flèche, et des figues si grosses, *ut sub una ficu turmæ condantur equitum*.

Ibidem, chapitre VII. De l'infirmité humaine. — C'est une pitié,

---

1. Racine indique lui-même ce chapitre d'après la division qui est celle des anciennes éditions, notamment de celle de Lyon (1563). Dans les indications de chapitres qu'on trouvera ci-après, nous continuerons à suivre cette même édition.

et même c'est une honte, de voir combien est vile l'origine du plus superbe des animaux, vu que l'odeur seule d'une lampe éteinte fait avorter. *His principiis nascuntur tyranni....* *Tu qui te deum credis, aliquo successu tumens, tanti perire potuisti.* Et même vous pouvez périr encore à moins, et par la morsure d'un petit serpent, ou, comme le poëte Anacréon, d'un grain de raisin sec, ou, comme le sénateur Fabius, d'un poil avalé avec du lait.

Ibidem, chapitre XXIII. De la patience. — Lyonne....[1] n'a jamais découvert parmi les tortures Armodius et Aristogiton. Anaxarchus étant à la question pour un semblable sujet, se coupa la langue avec les dents, et la jeta au visage du tyran.

---

1. *Leænæ meretricis*. Racine a traduit le mot *meretrix* par une expression que nous avons dû passer, mais qui choquait moins alors qu'aujourd'hui, puisqu'on la trouve dans l'*Amphitryon* de Molière.

PLINE LE JEUNE.

Un exemplaire des *OEuvres* de Pline le jeune, portant sur les marges des notes manuscrites de Racine, appartient aujourd'hui à Mgr le duc d'Aumale, qui a bien voulu nous en permettre l'examen, comme il nous avait gracieusement permis celui de son *Eschyle*. Voici le titre de ce précieux exemplaire : *C. Plinii Cæcilii Secundi Epistolæ et Panegyricus, editio nova. Marcus Zuerius Boxhornius recensuit et passim emendavit. Lugd. Batav. Apud Joannem et Danielem Elsevir. M.DC.LIII.* Sur le feuillet de titre est le nom de le Maistre, et au bas de la dernière page du volume celui de Racine.

Une note sur cet exemplaire se trouve, sous le n° 2267, dans le Catalogue de M. Cicogne, qui l'a possédé dans sa bibliothèque : « Le nom de M. le Maistre, y est-il dit, semble indiquer que Racine tenait ce volume d'un des deux solitaires de Port-Royal de ce nom, Antoine le Maistre, ou le Maistre de Saci. » Il s'agit vraisemblablement d'Antoine le Maistre, qui paraît avoir légué à son ancien élève quelques-uns des livres de sa bibliothèque[1].

Les notes du volume ne sont pas toutes de la main de Racine. Quelques-unes, particulièrement celles qui sont au crayon, sont d'une autre écriture, probablement de celle de le Maistre. Les unes et les autres sont fort courtes. Nous n'avons à reproduire ici que celles qui sont de Racine, en omettant les plus insignifiantes. Le *Panégyrique de Trajan*, dont quelques passages ont été soulignés, n'est pas annoté. Tout ce qui suit se rapporte donc aux *Lettres*.

Livre I. *Lettre* ii. *Libelli quos emisimus dicuntur in manibus esse*, etc. Il aimoit que son livre fût vendu.

Lettre viii. *Ii vero qui benefacta sua verbis adornant*, etc. Bienfaits reprochés.

Lettre ix. *Satius est.... otiosum esse, quam nihil agere.* Il vaut mieux être de loisir que de ne rien faire.

Lettre x. *Vitæ sanctitas summa, comitas par. Insectatur vitia, non homines*, etc. Honnête dévot.

Ibidem. Illiteratissimas literas. Lettres d'affaires.

Ibidem. Adfirmat etiam esse hanc philosophiæ, et quidem pulcherrimam, partem, agere negotium publicum, etc. C'est être philosophe que de faire sa charge.

---

1. Voyez ci-dessus, p. 178. Antoine le Maistre mourut en 1658 ; Isaac le Maistre (M. de Saci) seulement en 1684. C'est bien avant cette dernière date que Racine a dû posséder l'exemplaire de *Pline*.

Lettre XIII. (*En tête de la lettre.*) Poëtes qui récitoient.

Ibidem. Sed tanto magis laudandi probandique sunt, quos a scribendi recitandique studio hæc auditorum vel desidia vel superbia non retardat. Boy. (Boyer[1]).

Lettre XIV. *Est illi facies liberalis, etc.* Beau mari.

Lettre XVI. *Neque.... debet operibus ejus obesse, quod vivit.* Nᵃ (*nota*). Grand personnage vivant.

Lettre XX. (Τὸ κέντρον ἐγκατέλιπε τοῖς ἀκροωμένοις.) Il laisse un aiguillon à ses auditeurs.

Lettre XXIV. *Nam mala emptio, etc.* Acheter trop cher.

Livre V. *Lettre* XIII. (*En tête de la lettre.*) Lire ses ouvrages à ses amis.

Lettre XVI. (*En tête de la lettre.*) Mort d'une jeune fille.

Ibidem. O triste plane acerbumque funus! Mort précipitée.

Ibidem. Pietatis totus est. Dévotion.

Lettre XVII. (*En tête de la lettre.*) Jeune seigneur qui se plaît à la poésie.

Ibidem. Gratulatus et fratri, qui ex auditorio illo non minorem pietatis gloriam, etc. Amitié de frère.

Livre VI. *Lettre* XV. (*En tête de la lettre.*) Poëte qui récite ses vers.

Lettre XXIV. (*En tête de la lettre.*) Affection d'une femme envers son mari.

Lettre XXVII. *Facilis inventio, non facilis electio.* Il est aisé de trouver, et non de choisir.

Livre IX. *Lettre* XXIII. *Exprimere non possum, quam sit jucundum mihi, etc.* Tendresse d'auteur.

Lettre XXVI. *Nihil peccat, nisi quod nihil peccat.* Médiocre.

Ibidem. Sæpe accedere ad præceps, etc. Sublime.

Ibidem. Maxime periculosa. Hardiesses.

Ibidem. Sed vide quanto major sit qui reprehenditur ipso reprehendente. Celui qui pèche ainsi est plus grand que celui qui le reprend.

---

1. Tel est le nom que désigne, avec une vraisemblance qui n'est pas loin de la certitude, l'abréviation *Boy*. Cette malice de Racine s'explique fort aisément. Boyer avait très-peu d'auditeurs pour ses sermons, comme pour ses pièces de théâtre; mais ses mauvais succès ne le décourageaient pas : il les interprétait à sa manière, comme le prouve l'épigramme attribuée par quelques personnes à Racine (voyez notre tome IV, p. 249):

> Quand les pièces représentées
> De Boyer sont peu fréquentées, etc.

LA BARDE.

Les notes marginales de Racine sur l'*Histoire* de la Barde, qui est écrite en latin, sont, comme ses *Fragments historiques*, du temps où il rassemblait des matériaux pour son *Histoire du règne de Louis XIV*. Elles n'ont pas le même caractère que celles dont il chargeait les marges des classiques anciens. Il ne s'agissait plus d'un travail littéraire, d'une étude de style, d'une provision à faire de belles pensées et de lieux communs. Comme dans Siri, dans Nani et autres historiens de la même époque, Racine recueillait dans la Barde les renseignements dont il se proposait de faire usage. Le soin avec lequel il a annoté ce livre semble, aussi bien que plusieurs de ses *Fragments historiques*, une preuve que le plan de son *Histoire* était assez vaste, et qu'il voulait y donner de longs développements, non-seulement à la partie du règne de Louis XIV dont il pouvait parler comme témoin oculaire, mais aussi au temps de la Régence et aux troubles de la Fronde, qui sont le sujet du livre de la Barde. Ce livre a pour titre : *Johannis Labardæi Matrolarum ad Sequanam marchionis, Regis ad Helvetios et Rhætos extra ordinem legati, de Rebus Gallicis Historiarum libri decem, ab anno 1643 ad annum 1652. Parisiis, apud Dionysium Thierry.... M.DC.LXXI* (1 volume in-4°). L'exemplaire, relié en veau, sur lequel Racine a écrit ses notes, appartient aujourd'hui à M. Dubrunfaut, à qui nous devons exprimer notre gratitude pour l'obligeance qu'il a eue de le laisser plusieurs jours entre nos mains. Il porte la signature de Racine sur le feuillet de titre, au-dessous de la vignette. Onze pages manquent.

L'auteur de cette histoire, Jean de la Barde, marquis de Marolles-sur-Seine, fut envoyé de France au congrès d'Osnabruck, puis ambassadeur en Suisse. Il parle de lui-même aux pages 189, 190 et 193 de son *Histoire*.

Racine ne s'est pas contenté de noter sur les marges les noms et les principaux faits qu'on trouve dans ce livre, comme on l'eût pu faire dans un sommaire ou dans une table des matières. S'il en avait été ainsi, rien de cette annotation manuscrite ne vaudrait la peine d'être cité. Mais il complète les renseignements de l'historien, donnant souvent des dates plus précises; il le critique et le juge quelquefois. Il signale les sources où il a puisé, ou renvoie à d'autres auteurs. On apprend ainsi qu'il prenait fort au sérieux son devoir d'historiographe, ne négligeant aucune des histoires, aucun des mémoires de cette époque. Ses notes ont encore un autre genre d'intérêt. Lorsque Racine y traduit la Barde, il le fait dans un style précis, retrouvant avec une grande facilité la véritable expression française sous les circonlocutions du texte latin; et, dans plus d'un endroit, ces traductions méritent d'être recueillies pour l'histoire de la langue. En général, lorsque les notes qu'on trouve ici n'ont rien de remarquable par l'expression, nous les avons recueillies par la seule raison que les faits, les dates, ou les détails géographiques qu'elles renferment, n'ont pas été donnés par la Barde, mais ajoutés par Racine. Voilà les diverses considérations qui nous ont guidé dans le choix que nous avons dû faire entre des notes trop nombreuses pour être toutes reproduites ici. Nous indiquons les pages où se trouvent les notes que nous donnons, et nous citons du texte de la Barde ce qui est indispensable pour les rendre intelligibles.

Livre I (1643), pages 3 et 4. *Armando Brezæo Clara-Clementia soror erat, Ludovico Borbonio Angiano nupta, cui ab Richelio avunculo per nuptiarum pacta dos satis ampla dicta.... Sed homini.... ab ipso Rege.... coli atque observari sueto.... ea affinitas haud tanti quam par erat visa.* Le cardinal de Richelieu ne prétendoit pas que le mariage du duc d'Anghien lui eût fait plus d'honneur que de merveille.

Page 7. *Chavignius operam dabat uti cum eo nihil de solita familiaritate.... remitteret. Id vero quanto gravius animadvertebat Mazarinus, etc.* Chavigny ne vouloit point changer d'air avec le Cardinal, ce qui lui déplaisoit.

Page 19. *Rediit Regi ad memoriam Nucerium Richelio plane deditum fuisse.* Le Roi disoit que si le Cardinal se fût fait Turc, des Noyers auroit aussitôt pris le turban. *Siri* [1].

Page 26. *In eo principe* (Ludovico XIII) *nullam magis virtutem quam celeritatem laudaverim, qua sæpius....* (hostes) *oppressi.... Re infecta discedere impatiens animus properabat.* Il (*Louis XIII*) alloit fort vite opprimer [2] ses ennemis, mais il s'ennuyoit bientôt aussi.

Page 51. *Prima hostium munitio ordo palorum fuit, ab terra in majorem humana altitudinem prominentium*; dein ab his leniter acclive ad oppidi fossam versus spatium**, id quoniam ad glaciei speciem politum est,* glaciarium *appellant.* * Palissade. — ** L'auteur se trompe et ne connoit point ce que c'est que le glacis [3].

Livre II (1644), page 78. *Visum.... administris, qui locupletiores in urbe erant, ab iis grandem pecuniam fœnore sumere.* On veut contraindre les aisés de prêter de l'argent au Roi.

Page 106. *Hoc* (Nucerio) *aula pulso nuper, Mottæus nihil postea operæ pretii fecit.* La Motte n'avoit plus rien fait qui vaille depuis la disgrâce de [des] Noyers.

Livre III (1645), page 134. *Sed ut æstivorum tempus in Hispania maturum est..., etc.* Tout ceci est pris mot à mot d'un petit traité qu'on appelle : *Conjuration sur la ville de Barcelone* [4].

---

1. Cette note est une de celles où Racine ne traduit pas le texte, mais y ajoute quelque chose. Plus haut déjà, à la page 5, il renvoie également à Siri.
2. On trouve ce latinisme dans *Andromaque*, vers 1209. Voyez notre tome II, page 101, note 1.
3. Cette note se lit sous les ratures, malgré le soin avec lequel elle a été effacée, sans doute par Racine lui-même.
4. Nous n'avons pas trouvé cet écrit.

Page 136. *Igitur Pralinoplessius.... circumquaque oppidum castra ponit....* Siége de Roses. Voir les *Mémoires* du maréchal du Plessy [1].

Page 139. *Noguera amnis*, qui propius Camaras** Sicorim subit.*
**Noguera Pallaresa*, à la différence d'une autre rivière appelée *Noguera Ribagorçana*, qui se décharge encore dans la Sègre, entre Lerida et Balaguer, au lieu que celle-ci se décharge entre Balaguer et Camaras. — **Camaras sur la Sègre, proche de l'embouchure de la Noguère.

Ibidem. Nostri, superato ab equitibus vado, jam uno agmine ad Camaras contendere. Camaras avait été pris par Saint-Aunay peu de jours auparavant; mais les ennemis avoient brûlé une arche du pont, de l'autre côté de la rivière [2].

Page 144. *Sed quæ dudum Cæsar Choiseulius Pralinoplessius...*, etc. Le Plessy Praslin est fait maréchal de France, 14 juillet (1645).

Page 146. Tout cela [3] est trop long et sent le gazetier.

Page 155. *Id per hyemem fiebat, rem majoribus nostris insolitam, sed hac tempestate ab Suecis factitatam, queis ad septentrionem agitantibus remissiora in Germania frigora videntur.* Les Suédois ont inventé de faire la guerre en hiver, parce que leur pays les a accoutumés à de plus grands froids.

Pages 158 et 159. Défaite de M. de Turenne à Mariendal, le 4ᵉ mai (1645). — Toute cette relation est copiée de l'*Extraordinaire* de la *Gazette*.

Page 163. Bataille de Norlingue, le 3ᵉ août (1645). — Tout ceci est pris de l'*Extraordinaire* de la *Gazette*.

Page 168. *Turena.... quid ex copia rerum optimum factu sit semper agitans.* Turenne va toujours au bien.

Page 177. Mort [de] des Noyers. Le 20ᵉ octobre (1645).

Livre IV (1646), page 180. Les états de l'Empire s'opposoient à la satisfaction de la France. V[oyez] Siri, tome VI.

Page 182. *Fabius Chigius, Innocentii X. Pontificis nuntius, et Ludovicus Contarinus Venetorum legatus....* Chigi, nonce d'Innocent X à Munster, étoit un peu favorable aux Espagnols, et Contarin, ambassadeur de Venise, n'étoit guère pour les François.

Page 204. Le cardinal Mazarin se fait surintendant de la conduite et gouvernement du Roi, et de Monsieur [4].

---

1. *Mémoires des divers emplois et des principales actions du maréchal du Plessy.* Paris, C. Barbin, 1676, in-4°.
2. Ceci n'est point dans la Barde, dont Racine complète le récit.
3. Il s'agit du récit que fait la Barde du passage de la Colme en Flandre (1645) par l'armée du duc d'Orléans.
4. Racine avait d'abord écrit : « surintendant de l'éducation du Roi et de Monsieur. »

Page 211. Tranchée ouverte devant Orbitelle. 15 mai (1646). — L'armée navale d'Espagne est auprès de Cagliari, en Sardaigne.

Page 216. Tranchée ouverte devant Courtray. 14 juin (1646).

Page 222. La Reine avoit retenu pour elle la charge de Brézé. — Le 16 juillet (1646), furent registrées au Parlement les lettres patentes en faveur de la Reine, pour la surintendance générale du commerce et de la navigation de France.

Page 227. *Eo Rupiguidonus ac Flexius comites*, *eo Teminius* (le marquis de Temine), *eo Nemerosius* (le duc de Nemours) *et ipse Anguianus graviter vulnerati*. La Rocheguyon, Flex et le chevalier de Fiesque, tués devant Mardick, à une sortie (ajoutez-y le prince de Marsillac). Le duc d'Anguien blessé à la main.

Page 241. Turenne passe le Rhin à Vesel et se joint aux Suédois. Cette jonction se fait le 7 août (1646). — Il (*la Barde*) ne parle point de deux mille cavaliers qui abandonnèrent M. de Turenne, et se retirèrent dans l'armée de Wrangle. V[oyez] *Mémoires* de Chanut [1].

Page 242. *Rhainum Arcem*. Rhain, sur la rivière d'Acha, assez près du lieu où le Leck se décharge dans le Danube.

Page 243. *Hoc anno mortem obiit Gaspar Colinius Castillonus equitum tribunus*. Mort du maréchal de Chastillon, dès le 4 janvier (1646).

LIVRE V (1647), page 245. Ce sont eux (*il s'agit de* Paw *et de* Knuitz, *députés des Provinces-Unies*) qui avoient fait le traité d'alliance entre Louis XIII et les états, et ils n'avoient dès lors pour but que de forcer l'Espagne à faire la paix avec eux, et de se tirer d'affaire dès qu'ils pourroient.

Page 246. (*En tête de la page.*) Voir un petit traité : *Motifs de la guerre d'Allemagne* [2]. — (*En marge.*) Le cardinal de Richelieu avoit eu de la répugnance à s'engager dans cette guerre; et ce fut Charnacé et le P. Joseph qui, pour leurs intérêts particuliers, l'y engagèrent.

Page 247. (*En tête de la page.*) Les ambassadeurs de France prennent pour interpositeurs entre la France et l'Espagne les dé-

---

1. Les *Mémoires et négociations de M. Chanut, depuis l'an* 1645 *jusqu'en* 1655, ont été publiés à Paris, en 1676, 3 volumes in-12.

2. *Motifs de la France pour la guerre d'Allemagne, et quelle y a été sa conduite*. Ce petit écrit, qui semble avoir émané de quelque source officielle, est une apologie de la politique de la France contre ceux qui l'accusaient d'avoir dans les guerres d'Allemagne trahi les intérêts de la religion catholique. Nous l'avons trouvé imprimé aux pages 402-487 du *Recueil de plusieurs pièces servant à l'histoire moderne*, à Cologne, chez Pierre du Marteau, M.DC.LXIII, 1 volume in-12. Aux pages 458-460, on raconte les faits dont il est question dans l'*Histoire de la Barde* (p. 245 et 246), le traité signé avec l'Espagne par les ambassadeurs de Hollande, Paw et Knuitz.

putés hollandois, qui les trahissent. — (*En marge.*) Chigi et Contarin, suspects aux plénipotentiaires de France, qui prennent les ambassadeurs de Hollande pour interpositeurs entre eux et les Espagnols. — Paw et Knuits les trompent, et en font plus tôt leur traité. — L'un étoit député de Hollande et d'Amsterdam; l'autre de Zélande, et gagné par la princesse d'Orange. — Tous deux ayant été choisis pour interpositeurs, donnoient avis de tout aux Espagnols, et retardoient notre traité pour mieux avancer le leur.

Page 248. Toute cette harangue (*la harangue aux états, à la Haye, que la Barde attribue à Servien*) est tirée de plusieurs articles que Servien présenta aux états, et qui sont imprimés [1].

Page 252. [*Brunus*] *ingenio populari, aptissimoque fuco plebi faciundo.* Portrait de Brun (*ambassadeur d'Espagne*), homme propre pour mettre le peuple de son côté.

Ibidem. Mémoire de Brun aux états. — Tout cela est imprimé, aussi bien que la réponse de Servien, dans le petit livre appelé *la Pierre de touche* [2].

Page 259. *Servianum inter et Brunum.... privatæ fuere simultates, hunc illo spernente, quod in æquo legationis jure cum Penneranda, sicut ipse cum Longavilla non esset.* Servien haïssoit Brun, et le traitoit de haut en bas, parce qu'il n'alloit pas de pair avec Pegneranda, comme lui avec Longueville.

Ibidem. Huic omnia nobilia, magnifica, excelsa fuere; Bruno vero vulgaris ac popularis omnis ratio. Servien étoit haut; Brun réussissoit mieux auprès du public, et avoit les rieurs pour lui.

Page 265. Servien conclut le traité de garantie avec les Hollandois. — Traité de garantie avec les états, conclu et signé le 29 juillet (1647).

Page 269. Bavière [3] rend Hailbron au Roi, Meminghen et Uberlingue aux Suédois, et on lui rend Raïn et Donavert, vers la fin de mars (1647).

Page 280. Condé assiége Lérida. — Il ouvre la tranchée le 27 mai (1647).

---

1. En une pièce in-4° (s. l. n. d.), qui commence ainsi : *Le 22 mai de l'an present 1647, fust communiqué à MM. les estats generaux des Provinces Unies des Pays-Bas, par M. de Servient, le memoire et escrit contenant dix-neuf articles, rapporté ci-aprez.* On les trouve aussi dans la seconde édition du livre dont il est parlé dans la note suivante.

2. *La Pierre de touche des veritables interests des Provinces Unies des Pays-Bas, et des intentions des deux couronnes de France et d'Espagne, sur les traitez de paix à Munster....* (s. l.) M.DC.L. Les deux lettres de Brun sont données aux pages 27-39, et la réponse de Servien aux pages 40-80.

3. C'est-à-dire Maximilien, duc de Bavière.

Page 291. *Hic* (Guisius), *amori deditus ab natura, huic ita obsecutus est, uti nuptiarum sanctitatem ludibrio habuerit.* Il (*Guise*) épousoit pour se démarier aussitôt après. — Comtesse de Bossut[1]. — Il vouloit se démarier pour en épouser une autre, Mlle de Pons.

Page 292. Il (*Michel Mazarin*) est fait cardinal, — non point à la nomination de Pologne, mais du propre mouvement du Pape.

Page 298. Arrivée de Guise dans Naples. — Il va chez Gennaro Anese. V[oyez] les *Mémoires* de Guise[2], d'où tout cela est tiré.

Page 307. Les Allemands de son armée (*de l'armée de Turenne*) se mutinent et ne veulent point le suivre. — 25 juillet (1647). Il fait mettre Rose en prison. — 5 août (1647). Turenne fait charger les mutins et en tue trois cents. Le reste s'enfuit.

Page 314. Prétentions du Parlement. — De pouvoir corriger ou supprimer les édits. — On en avoit vérifié un à la cour des aides. Le Parlement ordonne qu'il lui soit apporté. — C'étoit l'*édit du tarif*, qui étoit une imposition générale sur toutes les marchandises et denrées qui entroient dans Paris. Voyez un petit livre intitulé : *Histoire des dernières guerres civiles*[3], d'où tout cela est tiré mot à mot.

Pages 316 et 317. *In urbe ædes permultæ Regi vectigales sunt*[4],

1. Guise l'avait épousée en Belgique, comme le raconte la Barde.
2. *Mémoires de feu M. le duc de Guise*, Paris, E. Martin, et S. Mabre-Cramoisy, 1668, in-4°. Ils ont été plusieurs fois réimprimés dans le format in-12, à Cologne et à Paris, en 1668, 1669 et 1681.
3. Le livre dont parle Racine, et qui n'est pas un si *petit livre*, puisqu'il a 542 pages de format in-8°, pour la première partie, et 352 pour la seconde, n'a pas pour titre : *Histoire des dernières guerres civiles*, mais : *l'Histoire du temps, ou le Véritable recit de ce qui s'est passé dans le Parlement de Paris, depuis le mois d'août* 1647, *jusques au mois de novembre* 1648 (s. l.), M.DC.XLIX. L'auteur est du Portail. Il est difficile d'expliquer comment Racine a donné à ce livre un titre qui n'est, à notre connaissance, celui d'aucune des éditions qui en ont été faites : à moins qu'on ne conjecture qu'il avait trouvé ce titre au dos de la reliure de l'exemplaire qu'il avait sous les yeux. Il est très-certain d'ailleurs qu'il ne s'agit pas d'un autre ouvrage. C'est bien à celui-ci que se rapportent les diverses citations que Racine fait de l'*Histoire des dernières guerres civiles*. Elles sont tirées toutes de la première partie. Le passage qu'il indique sur les prétentions du Parlement et sur l'*edit du tarif* est aux pages 4 et 5 de l'*Histoire du temps*. Un peu plus loin, il renvoie aux pages 82 et 147 pour des passages que nous trouvons aux pages 81 et 144 (1re partie) de l'*Histoire du temps* : voyez plus bas les notes 1 et 3 de la page 349. Il s'est donc trompé, mais, comme on le voit, bien peu, dans l'indication des pages; peut-être s'est-il servi d'une édition différente de celle dont nous avons donné le titre. Cependant toutes les éditions que nous avons pu comparer à celle-ci s'éloignent encore plus, pour la pagination, des indications qu'il donne.
4. Dans la censive du Roi. (*Note de Racine.*)

quarum videlicet in solo suo ædificandarum ipse aut majores ejus oppidanis facultatem dedere, ea lege ut annuatim perexiguum quidpiam pecuniæ, censum appellant, *huic penderent, etc.* C'étoit une déclaration par laquelle le Roi mettoit en franc alleu toutes les maisons qui étoient dans sa censive, moyennant une année du loyer et du revenu qui lui seroit payée par les propriétaires.

Page 318. MONSIEUR a la petite vérole. — Et puis le Roi, qui est très-malade. — On craignoit que le duc d'Orléans ne se rendit maître de la personne de MONSIEUR, s'il venoit faute du Roi.

LIVRE VI (1648), page 321. *Is* (senatus) *non sua magis quam reipublicæ causa sibi administrorum consiliis.... obsistendum est arbitratus.... At viri principes, et quæ hos sectabatur nobilium turba, ea vero, more suo, commodis suis studebat....* Le Parlement songeoit au bien public ; et les princes à leurs affaires.

Page 324. Toutes ces harangues [1] sont tirées de l'*Histoire des dernières guerres civiles*, où elles sont mieux qu'ici.

Page 335. *Sed in omnibus rebus ferme nimii homines sunt, quod tamen in ulciscendo quam in ignoscendo minus offensionis habet; nam quos ultus fueris, ab iis nihil amplius mali metuas; quorum vero vitæ peperceris, iis tuæ insidiari copia est.* Méchante maxime.

Page 338. Le Plessis attaque le retranchement des Espagnols. V[oyez] ses *Mémoires*.

Page 340. Le marquis de Ville attaque près de Dertone, en chemin faisant.

Page 347. *Adversum quos* (Gallos) *tamen Maximilianus remittebat bellum gerere, si forte eo pacto Ludovicum pacatum habere posset.* V[oyez] l'*Extraord.* (l'*Extraordinaire* de la *Gazette*), p. 293.

Ibidem. Igitur Turenam copias Rhenum traducere et cum Suecis conjungere jubet (Rex Ludovicus). Cette jonction se fait le 18 février (1648).

Page 354. Les édits sont portés à la chambre et à la cour des aides. — V[oyez] ces harangues [2] dans l'*Histoire des guerres civiles*.

Page 355. *Ibi administri sensere quantum offendissent, ubi Rationum et Vectigalium Curiis atque ipsi Magno Consilio novam annuæ pecuniæ solvendæ conditionem tulerant; nam ut his hujus rei facultas in*

---

1. Les harangues du chancelier Seguier, du premier président Molé et de l'avocat général Talon (p. 324 et 325 de la Barde). A la page 325, Racine souligne un membre de phrase dans la harangue de Talon, et écrit à la marge : « Cela n'est pas dans le françois. » — Voyez ces harangues dans l'*Histoire du temps*, p. 34-45.

2. Celles qui furent prononcées à la chambre et à la cour des aides par les premiers présidents Nicolaï et Amelot. Voyez-les aux pages 65-74 de l'*Histoire du temps*.

proximum novennium foret, uniuscujusque magistratus stipendia, aut partem horum Rex sibi retinere decreverat, qua re maxime exasperati harum Curiarum animi quæ diximus ea designaverunt. Sed istuc corrigere visum. Quamobrem Rex edixit, etc. L'*Histoire des G. C.* (*des dernières guerres civiles*) prétend, au contraire, qu'ils publièrent cette déclaration par malice, pour empêcher l'effet de l'arrêt du Parlement, puisqu'on rendoit aux Compagnies leurs gages, en révoquant le droit annuel[1]. V[oyez] p. 82.

Page 359. Harangue de Molé (*à la Reine*). Voyez-la dans l'*Hist.* (l'*Histoire des dernières guerres civiles*[2]).

Page 360. On vouloit châtier le Parlement; mais il falloit en venir à la violence. — On aime mieux leur permettre de s'assembler.— L'*Hist.* (l'*Histoire des dernières guerres civiles*) dit qu'on espéroit qu'il arriveroit des inconvénients dans leurs assemblées. (Page) 147[3].

Ibidem. Les traitants étoient ceux qui avançoient leur argent au Roi, pour lequel on leur abandonnoit les tailles et les autres impôts. — On appeloit cela emprunt, et beaucoup de gens du Parlement étoient intéressés avec eux, parce qu'ils faisoient valoir leur argent à gros intérêt.

Page 374. *Sub vesperam.... inter duces consultatum. In cornu dextro novem equitum turmæ alæ fuere...,* etc. Disposition de son armée (*de l'armée de Condé*). — Cette relation (*de la bataille de Lens*) est tirée mot à mot de la *Gazette*.

Page 379. [*Gondius*] *homo potentiæ avidus, cui adipiscendæ perturbatam quam pacatam rem publicam malebat.* Homme séditieux.

Ibidem. Longolio senatore. Longueil (*président de Maisons*). On l'appeloit *Domine Petre.*

---

1. On lit à la page 81 de l'*Histoire du temps :* « Ils commencèrent par un artifice et une adresse subtilement inventée, pour empêcher l'exécution de l'arrêt et pour le rendre inutile. Ils firent pour cela une déclaration.... par laquelle ils firent révoquer le droit annuel qui avoit été donné aux compagnies souveraines, prenant pour prétexte que le Roi ne vouloit forcer personne d'accepter cette grâce, et qu'ayant retranché les gages aux trois compagnies souveraines, Grand conseil, Chambre des comptes et Cour des aides, au lieu du prêt qu'ils avoient accoutumé de payer, sa pensée n'avoit point été de les obliger à des conditions qu'ils trouvoient trop rigoureuses; et qu'ainsi il les mettoit dans les mêmes termes qu'ils étoient auparavant, [en révoquant] le droit annuel qu'il leur avoit voulu donner. »

2. Pages 136-142 de l'*Histoire du temps.*

3. « Ils (*les ministres*) crurent qu'il seroit plus à propos de plier,... espérant que dans l'exécution des arrêts d'union, ils trouveroient sans doute des moyens pour embarrasser les compagnies. » (*Histoire du temps,* p. 144.)

Livre VII (1649), page 405. Condé et le maréchal de la Meilleraye vouloient que le Roi se retirât dans l'Arsenac.

Page 414. Le Parlement s'empare de l'Arsenac et de la Bastille.

Page 454. La survivance de Normandie promise à Longueville, avec le Pont de l'arche et le Ponteau de mer.

Livre VIII (1650), page 500. *Gondius vero ac Nigromonasterius*[1].... *noctu ad Mazarinum ventitabant.... Gondius mutabat vestem, ac versicolore sagulo militariter ornatus erat.* Siri : en chausses grises et en manteau d'écarlate galonné d'or, l'épée au côté. — Monsieur le Prince pensa les surprendre tous trois avec le Cardinal, comme ils formoient le projet de son emprisonnement[2].

1. Racine ajoute à la marge : « et Laigues. » Aussi dit-il plus bas : « tous trois (*Gondi, Noirmoustier et Laigues*). »

2. Les notes de Racine finissent à la page 513 de l'*Histoire* de la Barde. Il n'y en a aucune sur les livres IX et X. A la fin du volume, il y a un *Errata*, que Racine a complété, en relevant quelques fautes d'impression qui n'y sont pas corrigées. Cela montre avec quel soin il avait lu cette *Histoire*.

LA PRATIQUE DU THÉATRE

DE L'ABBÉ D'AUBIGNAC.

Racine a écrit quelques notes sur les marges d'un exemplaire de la première édition de *la Pratique du Théâtre* (Paris, chez Antoine de Sommaville, M.DC.LVII, 1 volume in-4°). Cet exemplaire est à la Bibliothèque de Toulouse. Les plus intéressantes de ces notes ont été recueillies par M. Félix Ravaisson, et publiées dans la livraison de novembre 1846 de la *Nouvelle Revue encyclopédique*. Quelques erreurs de l'abbé d'Aubignac sont réfutées par Racine. On remarquera surtout la critique qu'il fait d'un passage de *la Pratique du Théâtre* sur la *Rodogune* de Corneille. Nous reproduisons ici ces notes, en faisant précéder chacune d'elles du texte à la marge duquel elles ont été écrites, et que nous imprimons entre guillemets.

Page 145. « J'ai su d'un homme très-savant aux belles choses, et qui avoit assisté à la représentation du *Pastor fido*, en Italie,... que ce poëme dont la lecture ravit, parce qu'on peut la quitter quand on veut, n'avoit donné que des dégoûts insupportables.... Nous voyons que les tragédies (*des anciens*) n'étoient environ que de mille vers, et encore de vers bien plus courts que nos héroïques. » — Comment peut-il dire que la lecture du *Pastor fido* ravit? Il dit dans cette page que les tragédies des anciens n'étoient environ que de mille vers, et, dans la page suivante, il dit, avec bien plus de raison, qu'elles ont été jusqu'à seize cents vers. L'*OEdipe colonéen* de Sophocle en marque jusqu'à dix-huit cent soixante.

Pages 167 et 168. « Il (*Corneille*) fait mourir Cléopatre par un poison si prompt, que Rhodogune en découvre l'effet, auparavant qu'Antiochus ait prononcé dix vers. Véritablement que Cléopatre ait été assez enragée pour s'empoisonner elle-même..., cela est assez préparé dans tous les actes précédents...; mais que l'effet du poison soit si prompt que, dans un espace de temps qui suffit à peine pour prononcer dix vers, on l'ait pu reconnoître, c'est, à mon advis, ce qui n'est pas assez préparé, parce que, la chose étant fort rare, il falloit que Cléopatre elle-même, quand elle espère que le poison la délivrera d'Antiochus et de Rhodogune, expliquât la force de ce poison, et qu'elle en conçût de la joie : vu que par ce moyen elle eût préparé l'événement sans le prévenir, etc. » — L'embarras ne seroit pas moindre. Car quelle apparence que cette Cléopatre, après avoir dit que le poison fera mourir sur-le-champ celui qui le prendra, se puisse résoudre à en prendre elle-même la moitié, afin de porter son fils et Rhodogune à prendre le reste? Elle aura lieu de supposer qu'elle mourra avant qu'ils aient le temps de boire le reste de son poison. Ainsi on ne pourra plus dire ce vers :

> Pour vous perdre après elle, elle a voulu périr[1];

et elle mourra bien plus légèrement qu'elle ne fait. C'est bien assez qu'elle se fasse mourir de gaieté de cœur, sans y être forcée (comme elle l'est dans l'histoire avec bien plus de vraisemblance), elle qui se doit fier sur l'amitié de son fils, et réserver sa vengeance à une autre occasion.

Page 186. « Cette espèce de poëme (*le poëme dramatique nommé satyre*) ne fut point reçu des Latins. »

> *Silvis deducti caveant, me judice, Fauni*[2], *etc.*

Ne semble-t-il pas, par ce vers et les suivants, que les Latins avoient quelques poëmes semblables à la *satyre* ou *pastorale* des Grecs?

Page 224. « Sophocle qui naquit dix ou douze ans après la mort d'Eschyle. » — Comment peut-il dire que Sophocle est né dix ou douze ans après la mort d'Eschyle? Sophocle tout jeune a remporté le prix sur Eschyle, qui étoit déjà vieux; et ce fut pour cela qu'Eschyle sortit d'Athènes. Il a pu lire que Sophocle étoit plus jeune de dix ou douze ans.

---

1. *Rodogune*, acte V, scène IV, vers 1809.
2. Horace, *Art poétique*, vers 244.

VAUGELAS.

TRADUCTION DE QUINTE-CURCE.

Aux feuillets 84-87 du tome II des manuscrits de Racine, conservés à la Bibliothèque impériale, se trouvent des *Extraits* des livres III et X du *Quinte-Curce de Vaugelas*. Racine a fait de courtes remarques sur quelques-unes des phrases qu'il a recueillies dans cette traduction, si célèbre alors, et regardée comme un modèle de bon langage. Lors même que les citations ne sont accompagnées d'aucune note, il est facile de se rendre compte de ce qu'il y a jugé digne d'attention, surtout lorsqu'il souligne, comme il le fait presque toujours, les mots de la phrase qui l'ont frappé. C'est une étude sur la langue française qui a quelque analogie avec celle des *Lexiques* de notre *Collection*. Tout ce que Racine a écrit montre quelle science il avait des nuances les plus délicates de notre langue; il est curieux de surprendre ici quelque chose du travail auquel il devait une telle science. Les secrets du génie restent cachés; mais ce que le génie doit au travail, se révèle plus facilement.

Racine a trouvé ces phrases de Vaugelas dans la première édition du *Quinte-Curce*, publiée après la mort du traducteur en 1653 (*Quinte-Curce* [1], *de la vie et des actions d'Alexandre le Grand, de la traduction de M. de Vaugelas.... A Paris, chez Augustin Courbé. M.DC.LIII*, 1 volume in-4°). Une 3ᵉ édition de ce livre, très-différente de celle de 1653, fut publiée en 1659, dans le même format, et chez le même libraire, *sur vne nouuelle copie de l'autheur qui a esté trouuee depuis la premiere et la seconde impression*. Patru ayant cette fois revu le travail de Vaugelas, il est impossible de savoir quelle part il faut faire à celui-ci dans les nombreux changements qu'on y remarque. Ces changements ont fait disparaître de la nouvelle édition une partie des locutions et des tours que Racine avait relevés. Rien n'indique cependant qu'il ait voulu noter d'un blâme ces divers passages, qui ont fini par donner des scrupules à Vaugelas ou à Patru; mais, comme il s'est attaché surtout à ce qui lui paraissait insolite ou très-hardi, il n'est pas étonnant que les corrections de 1659 aient si souvent modifié les extraits mêmes qu'il avait choisis.

Nous avons imprimé en italique les mots soulignés par Racine. Le chiffre des pages est indiqué par lui dans son manuscrit; il se rapporte à l'édition de 1653, et non à celle de 1659, dont la pagination n'est pas tout à fait la même.

---

1. *Quinte-Curce* est l'orthographe du nom de l'historien latin, dans le titre que nous citons. Racine a écrit en tête de ses extraits : *Quinte-Curse de Vaugelas*. Voyez notre tome I, p. 516, note 2.

On trouvera en note, au bas des pages, les changements de l'édition de 1659 qui portent sur les expressions signalées par Racine.

Livre III, p. 207. Ce fleuve venant à *s'épandre* dans la plaine.

Page 208. Ils ne faisoient pas *même* jugement que lui de la place. — Au jour *préfix*.

Page 209. Réduire *en* son obéissance.

Page 214. *C'est merveille comme* la fortune gâte et pervertit la nature.

Page 215. Le plus salutaire conseil qu'on lui *eût su* donner.

Page 222. Ce fleuve n'est pas si renommé pour la grandeur de *son canal* que, etc. — Il *s'épand dans un lit* de gravier fort pur.

Page 223. Car outre que c'étoit un défilé, *il se rencontroit* que, etc. — Le chemin étoit rompu par *l'affluence* des ruisseaux qui *descendent du* pied des montagnes [1].

Page 226. Ayant fait entrer *ses familiers* [2] et ses médecins. — Provoquer au combat. — Une mort prompte *m'est meilleure* qu'une tardive guérison.

Page 228. Ces lettres le mirent en une étrange *perplexité*.

Page 229. Philippe, après l'avoir *toute lue*, i. (*c'est-à-dire*) la lettre.

Page 230. Il lui présenta la main *en signe* de confiance [3].

Page 233. *Ayant été* mis en délibération [4] si..., etc.

Page 234. *Il n'y* eut pas grand'peine à faire approuver un avis si raisonnable [5]. — Il étoit des premiers dans sa confiance. — Que cela le mettroit en haute estime.

Page 235. Il différoit de jour en jour, attendant de rencontrer l'occasion à propos [6]. — Un revers de fortune.

Page 236. Et qui l'étoient *venus* servir [7]. — En matière de guerre, la réputation fait tout.

Page 237. De téméraire, devenu sage tout à coup. — Tout cela n'étoit que paroles jetées en l'air avec plus *de pompe* que de vérité [8].

Page 239. Cette armée, grande et mal ordonnée comme elle

---

1. *Édition de* 1659 : par la chute des torrents qui descendent des montagnes.

2. *Ibidem :* ses confidents.

3. Les mots « en signe de confiance » ont été retranchés dans l'édition de 1659.

4. *Édition de* 1659 : On mit là en délibération.

5. *Ibidem :* Il n'eut pas grand'peine à persuader cela.

6. *Ibidem :* Il différoit toujours, attendant l'occasion.

7. *Ibidem :* Et qui l'avoient suivi sur sa foi. — Dans l'édition de 1653, il y a *venu*, sans accord, à cause de l'infinitif qui suit le participe.

8. *Ibidem :* Ces paroles étoient magnifiques, s'il y eût ajouté les effets.

étoit, tenoit une étendue de pays *infinie*. — Alexandre *assit son camp* et se retrancha au même endroit.

Page 240. Où faisant allumer *force* flambeaux.

Page 241. La fortune plus puissante que la raison *ni* la bonne conduite[1].

Page 242. Il est *force* que..., etc.

Page 243. Nicanor menoit l'aile droite, renforcé de Cenus, de Perdiccas, etc.

Page 244. Il déploya ses bataillons, lorsque peu à peu les montagnes vinrent à s'ouvrir. — Et la *réverbération* du cri dans les vallons, etc. — Alexandre faisoit *à tous coups* signe de la main[2], etc.

Page 246. La cavalerie des Perses *se mit* à charger *furieusement* l'aile gauche[3].

Page 247. Il se jette *au fort de la mêlée*. — Se voyant donc forcés de combattre de plus près, les voilà tous l'épée à la main[4].

Page 248. On se battoit *corps à corps*. — Ils combattoient de pied ferme et *main à main*, comme en un combat singulier. — Tout *recrus* et harassés.

Page 249. Ils enfoncent cet escadron et en font une cruelle boucherie.

Page 250. Tant la peur est une passion insensée, *de craindre même*[5]..., etc.

Page 251. Les Thessaliens faisant manier leurs chevaux à toutes mains d'une grande vitesse..., etc. — Cette *poignée* de gens les alloit chassant *devant soi*, comme des troupeaux de moutons. — Amyntas, autrefois lieutenant d'Alexandre, et alors du parti contraire, s'étoit tiré de la mêlée[6]..., etc.

Page 252. Non *certes* en gens qui fuyoient[7], mais faisant une retraite honorable.

Page 254. Tant il eut bon marché d'une si grande et si mémorable victoire.

Page 258. La fortune n'avoit pas encore gagné le dessus de son esprit[8].

1. *Édition de* 1659 : La fortune plus puissante que toute la prévoyance de ce prince.
2. *Ibidem* : Faisant signe de sa main. — Les mots « à tous coups » ont été supprimés.
3. *Ibidem* : La cavalerie des Perses chargea furieusement l'aile gauche.
4. *Ibidem* : Etant donc forcés de combattre de près, ils mirent tous l'epée a la main.
5. *Ibidem* : Tant la peur est insensée de craindre même....
6. *Ibidem* : Amyntas s'étant détaché des autres, s'étoit retiré.
7. *Ibidem* : Non pas en gens qui fuyoient.
8. *Ibidem* : La fortune ne s'étoit pas encore emparée de son esprit.

Page 259. Personne ne fut *si osé* de s'émanciper en la moindre chose[1].

Page 260. Ce petit enfant se mit à l'embrasser *avec les deux mains*, dont le Roi se sentit touché, et admirant son *assurance*[2]..., etc.

Page 261. Parménion se confiant en la bonne fortune de son roi. — Des paysans lui montrèrent le chemin *et le rendirent* le quatrième jour devant la ville.

Page 262. Ce malheureux prince en étoit *venu à ce point* que jusqu'aux plus vils et aux plus abjects des hommes se donnoient la licence de violer sa dignité.

Page 263. Ces sommes immenses d'or et d'argent, destinées pour *l'entretènement* de cette effroyable multitude de gens de guerre[3], etc.

Page 264. Il n'y avoit pas *assez de mains* pour ravir un si ample butin.

Page 265. L'argent monnoyé *se trouva* monter à [4]..., etc. — Ayant encore en quelque révérence la majesté du Prince.

Livre X, page 727. *Si grand peur.* Ils eurent si grand peur..., etc.

Page 728. *Ce fut des clameurs*[5] par tout le camp. — *Deux participes actifs tout de suite, dans un sens tout différent :* « Et étant assemblés, ... prenant un truchement il leur parla..., etc. »

Page 730. *Ni* pour tout cela il n'y eut point d'émeute. — Les soldats *furent* par brigades trouver leurs capitaines.

Page 732. On eut *grand'* peine. *Abl.* (Ablancourt[6]) dit aussi : « à grande peine. » — Il y avoit là des ambassadeurs de tous les *coins* du monde.

Page 734. Ils *furent* au Palais tout *espleurés* (*et ailleurs*[7] : « esplorée »). — Et faisant approcher ses *familiers*[8].

Page 735. A la fleur de son âge et *de sa fortune.*

Page 737. *Naguères* leur ennemi. — Ils le *regrettoient* d'un véritable *regret*[9].

---

1. *Édition de* 1659 : Il eut un soin extrême d'empêcher qu'il ne se passât rien qui lui pût déplaire.
2. *Ibidem :* Ce petit enfant, sans s'étonner, l'embrassa, de sorte que le Roi, touché de son assurance....
3. *Ibidem :* Des richesses immenses éparses çà et là par la campagne, tout l'or et l'argent destiné pour le payement d'une si grande armée....
4. *Ibidem :* L'argent monnoyé monta à....
5. *Ibidem :* Ce furent des clameurs.
6. Vaugelas avait pris pour un de ses modèles la traduction d'Arrien par Perrot d'Ablancourt.
7. A la page 737. — 8. *Édition de* 1659 : ses confidents.
9. *Édition de* 1659 : Ils (*le*) pleuroient sans feinte.

Page 738. Après avoir perdu Darius, elles avoient trouvé qui les avoit recueillies. — Et *certes*.

Page 739. Un courage incomparable, non-seulement à l'égard des rois, mais * de ceux même qui n'ont excellé qu'en cela [1]. (* *Il n'a point répété :* à l'égard.) — Cela étoit pardonnable à un jeune prince, *et qui* faisoit de si grandes choses. (*Il n'a point dit :* à un prince jeune, et qui....) — Venger [2]. — Judicieux plus que ne portoit son âge. — Voici ce que sa fortune lui avoit apporté, *de* s'égaler aux Dieux.

Page 740. Il semble avoir eu la fortune en son pouvoir et à son commandement. — Elle a borné sa vie au période * de sa gloire. (* *Ablancourt met* « au comble. ») — *Navigé* [3] (*et Ablanc. aussi*).

Page 742. Mais *que* d'attendre un roi..., etc., c'étoit...,. etc. — Le fils de Roxane ou * de Barsine, lesquels..., etc. (* *Il n'a point répété :* le fils).

Page 744. Une *urgente* nécessité. — *A quoi faire* en venir aux armes (*pour* « à quoi bon »)?

Page 745. Si vous cherchez un roi comme Alexandre, c'est ce que vous ne trouverez jamais; si le plus proche à succéder,... etc. (*Il ne répète point :* vous cherchez, *et cela est mieux*).

Page 746. *Il n'est* point de mer qui excite plus d'orages.

Page 748. Ne cessoit d'*inciter* le Roi à faire mourir Perdiccas.

Page 749. *Courre fortune* (*pour dire* « être en péril »).

Page 750. Ils se défioient les uns des autres à un point qu'on n'eût osé parler ensemble, ni s'être accosté [4] de personne.

Page 751. Et s'il ne tient qu'à cela que les affaires *ne* s'accommodent.

Page 753. *Bon Dieu* [5] (*exclamation assez étrange en traduisant Q. Curse*)! — Les Dieux *béniront* cette maison *d'une* postérité..., etc. — Prendre au dépourvu [6].

Page 754. Dans l'espace *d'entre-deux*.

Page 755. Ils furent *en branle* de regagner la ville. — Il perdit et jugement et courage tout à la fois.

---

1. *Édition de* 1659 : Sa vaillance a passé non-seulement la vaillance des autres rois, mais de ceux-là même qui n'ont excellé qu'en cette vertu.

2. Racine a noté cette orthographe; lui-même écrivait *vanger*. Dans l'édition de 1659, on est revenu à « vanger. »

3. Voyez ci-dessus, p. 20, note 2. — Au lieu de « et *navigé* jusques sur la mer Océane, » on lit dans l'édition de 1659 : « et porté ses armes jusques sur l'Océan. »

4. Dans l'édition de 1659 : « ni s'accoster; » un peu avant : « et à un point. »

5. Cette exclamation a été supprimée dans l'édition de 1659.

6. *Édition de* 1659 : Surprendre au dépourvu.

Page 757. Perdiccas se tiendroit auprès du Roi, lieutenant général de ses armées[1] (*Il n'a point dit :* « avec la qualité ou le titre »).

Page 758. Les chaleurs y font mourir plusieurs animaux qu'elles surprennent *en rase campagne*.... D'ailleurs l'eau y est fort rare, *et encore* les habitants la cachent..., etc. — Les Égyptiens qui avoient charge de l'embaumer à leur *façon*.

Page 760. *En* Alexandrie.

Une note, d'un autre caractère que les précédentes, a été écrite par Racine sur un exemplaire du *Quinte-Curce* de Vaugelas, publié en 1664, à Paris, chez Thomas Jolly (1 volume in-12). Cette édition est, aussi bien que l'édition de 1659, désignée sur le titre comme étant la *troisième*. Elle n'est en effet qu'une réimpression du texte de 1659. L'exemplaire qui a fait partie de la bibliothèque de Racine appartient aujourd'hui à M. Léon Duval, qui a eu la bonté de nous le communiquer. La note unique de Racine est sur ce passage du livre VI, p. 313 : « Et Mégalopolis dans l'Arcadie demeura ferme dans le parti de la Macédoine. » Racine a écrit à la marge : « Ceci n'est point de Quinte-Curce, et il y a de l'erreur; car il est dit après, p. 317, que les Mégalopolitains furent condamnés à payer six vingt talents. Comment auroient-ils été condamnés, s'ils fussent demeurés fidèles? »

---

1. *Édition de* 1659 : Perdiccas demeureroit à la cour, et commanderoit l'armée qui accompagnoit le Roi.

REMARQUES

SUR L'ORTHOGRAPHE FRANÇOISE.

L'Académie françoise, au temps où Racine venait d'y entrer, avait fait imprimer, et distribuer évidemment à tous ses membres, une petite brochure in-4° de 61 pages, intitulée : *Cahiers de Remarques sur l'orthographe françoise pour estre examinez par chacun de Messieurs de l'Academie*[1] (s. l. n. d.). A la dernière page de l'exemplaire qui paraît avoir été destiné à Racine, et qui est aujourd'hui conservé à la Bibliothèque impériale, on a écrit, à côté du mot *fin* : « M. Racine. » L'écriture de Racine se reconnaît dans quelques petites corrections typographiques, et aussi dans deux observations qu'on trouve sur les marges de cet exemplaire. Nous allons transcrire ces observations. Elles sont assurément de peu d'importance; cependant l'orthographe a son histoire; et, dans les éditions de cette collection, on a coutume de signaler ce qu'elle offre de remarquable chez les grands écrivains.

Page 7. *Quand dans la composition du mot la preposition* A *est suivie d'vn* G *ou d'vne* M, *ces consones*[2] *ne se doublent point.... Exceptez, pour le* G, *les mots où il est déjà double en latin, comme* AGGREGER, AGGRES-

---

[1]. M. Marty-Laveaux a publié en 1863 ces *Cahiers de Remarques* (Paris, Jules Gay, 1 volume petit in-12), d'après la seconde édition. C'est aussi sur un exemplaire de la seconde que Racine a écrit ses notes. Elle a, comme nous le disons, 61 pages; la première en a 71. C'est l'historien Mézeray qui avait été chargé par l'Académie de rédiger ce traité. Son manuscrit est à la Bibliothèque impériale (fonds français, n° 9187); il avait été soumis à plusieurs des plus illustres membres de la Compagnie, Bossuet, Pellisson, etc., qui y ont mis leurs observations. L'époque où l'Académie s'est occupée de ce travail sur l'orthographe est ainsi indiquée au haut du troisième feuillet : « Cet ouurage a esté commencé un lundy 14. d'aoust, et finy un jeudy 12. d'octobre 1673. » Racine avait été reçu le 12 juillet précédent. Est-ce parce qu'il était encore si nouveau à l'Académie que son nom ne se trouve pas sur la liste des membres (treize en tout) auxquels on avait demandé leur avis sur le projet de Mézeray? Cette liste est en tête du manuscrit, sur le feuillet qui précède le titre.

[2]. Dans ces deux extraits des *Cahiers de Remarques* et dans les observations qui les accompagnent, nous reproduisons l'orthographe de l'ancienne impression et celle de Racine.

SEUR, AGGRAVER, EXAGGERER. — Je ne voudrois qu'un G à *exagerer;* et je sens quelque difference dans la prononciation d'*aggreger*, et des autres où on prononce en quelque façon le double G, au lieu qu'il me semble qu'on ne le prononce point du tout dans *exagerer*[1].

Pages 7 et 8. *Toute autre consone que le G ou l'M se double aprés la preposition A. Exemple* : ABBATRE, ABBONNER, ABBREUVER, ABBREGER, ABBREVIATION, ABBRUTIR, *etc.* — Je mettrois tousjours *abreger*, avec un B simple[2].

---

1. Bossuet, dans une observation qu'il a faite sur le manuscrit dont il est parlé dans la note 1 de la page précédente, dit, comme Racine, qu'il ne met qu'un g à *exagerer*, et qu'il en met deux à *aggresseur, aggraver*. Voyez l'édition de M. Marty-Laveaux, *Introduction*, p. xx.

2. Bossuet, dans l'observation que nous venons de citer, ne parle point d'*abréger*, mais il dit au sujet d'un autre de ces doubles *b* : « *abattre*, quoy que nous fassions, l'emportera contre *abbattre*. »

NOTICE.

Quelque vrai et quelque facile à prouver qu'il soit que, dans toutes les précédentes éditions des *OEuvres de Racine*, sa correspondance a subi d'innombrables mutilations et des altérations de toute sorte, nous éprouvons un certain embarras à emprunter pour le dire le langage même de nos devanciers. Ceux-ci en effet, si étrangement inexacts, malgré tous les moyens qu'ils avaient, aussi bien que nous, de transcrire fidèlement les lettres autographes, ont épuisé avant nous toutes les formules pour annoncer qu'enfin et pour la première fois le lecteur allait avoir sous les yeux un texte qui méritait toute confiance. C'est ce que nous avons déjà fait remarquer aux pages ii, xv et xvi de l'*Avertissement* qui est en tête de notre tome I.

La première publication des lettres de Racine est due à son fils Louis. En livrant à l'impression, à laquelle elle n'était pas destinée, la correspondance intime de son père, évidemment Louis Racine a pensé que non-seulement son droit, mais son devoir était d'en retrancher beaucoup de passages, de corriger, de retoucher tout ce qui était ou lui paraissait écrit avec négligence. Des expressions, des tours avaient vieilli : ne fallait-il pas les rajeunir? Ici quelque incorrection avait échappé à la rapidité de la plume : ne devait-elle pas être effacée? Tel détail était sans intérêt pour le public, et faisait longueur : le supprimer rendrait la lecture des lettres plus facile et plus agréable. Quelquefois tout s'arrangerait mieux en rapprochant des fragments de lettres diverses, pour en faire une seule. Dans la correspondance de la première jeunesse, la plume de Racine prenait des licences, et s'il était impossible d'expurger ces lettres de tous les traits de gaieté, il y en avait quelques-uns cependant qui décidément étaient trop vifs, et que les scrupules respectueux d'un fils ne pouvaient y laisser. Voilà, sans nul doute, l'idée que Louis Racine s'était faite de ce qu'exigeait de lui le soin d'une mémoire vénérée. Ajoutons que, parmi les changements qu'il a faits, il y en a beaucoup qui ne s'expliquent pas, et qu'il apportait d'ailleurs quelque négligence à son travail. Son inexactitude, tantôt involontaire, tantôt préméditée, eût été sans remède pour toutes les lettres qu'il a publiées, et qui forment la plus grande partie de celles que nous possédons, s'il n'avait lui-même déposé à la Bibliothèque du Roi les originaux de ces lettres.

Luneau de Boisjermain, lorsqu'il fit son édition de 1768, pouvait rétablir le véritable texte d'après les autographes : il s'est contenté de reproduire le texte donné par Louis Racine.

L'éditeur de 1807, Germain Garnier, comprit que le travail était à refaire : il aimait l'exactitude, et elle lui était ici très-facile, puisqu'il n'avait qu'à transcrire fidèlement les lettres originales qu'il savait où trouver. Dans l'*Avertissement* qu'il a mis en tête des *Lettres de Racine* (tome VII, p. 61-64), il déclare que, dans son édition, ces lettres « paraissent, pour la première fois, telles qu'elles sont, d'après les manuscrits autographes déposés à la Bibliothèque impériale, ou conservés par sa famille. » Cependant son texte, très-infidèle, donne le plus singulier démenti à des promesses si formelles. Comment supposer qu'il ait voulu induire le public en erreur? Voici plutôt ce que nous croyons vraisemblable : au lieu de ne s'en rapporter qu'à lui-même pour la révision des lettres publiées par Louis Racine, il aura chargé de ce travail des personnes qui ne s'en sont pas acquittées avec assez de conscience. Le bénéfice d'une explication semblable doit s'étendre aux éditeurs des temps suivants, dont le texte ne vaut pas beaucoup mieux, et qui, sans doute avec la même bonne foi, ont tour à tour prétendu avoir comblé les lacunes et porté remède aux altérations des publications antérieures. La partie la plus malaisée de la tâche de l'éditeur est celle dont Germain Garnier s'est le mieux acquitté. Il y avait dans la correspondance de Racine beaucoup de passages à éclaircir par des notes : celles que l'on doit à Germain Garnier, sans donner satisfaction sur tous les

LETTRES

points, ont été et seront toujours du plus grand secours pour tous les éditeurs venus après lui; c'est un travail fait avec grand soin, sur des renseignements que lui seul a eus à sa disposition.

Geoffroy, dans la *Préface du Commentateur*, qui est aux pages 43 et suivantes du tome VII de l'édition de 1808, dit (p. 46) : « Nous rétablissons le texte dans toute sa pureté et dans toute son intégrité, d'après des manuscrits originaux de la main même de Racine; » et à la page 49 du même tome, dans une note sur l'*Avertissement* de Louis Racine : « Je me flatte que le public me saura quelque gré de lui faire connoître les lettres de Racine telles qu'il les a écrites. »

Aimé-Martin, au tome VI de son édition de 1844, p. 31, exprime dans une note, comme Geoffroy l'avait fait avant lui, son étonnement du peu de fidélité du texte de Louis Racine, lorsqu'on le confronte avec les manuscrits autographes, et affirme que le véritable texte « est rétabli dans la présente édition, ainsi que l'ordre chronologique. »

On voit que, l'un après l'autre, chacun de ces éditeurs s'est donné pour le premier qui ait complétement reproduit le texte des manuscrits; et cependant de l'édition de 1807 aux suivantes le progrès est assez faible. Dans la dernière de toutes, c'est-à-dire dans celle d'Aimé-Martin, qui a passé pour définitive, les passages des lettres de la jeunesse, qui, cette fois encore, ont été ou défigurés, ou entièrement omis, dépassent en nombre et en étendue ceux qui ont été rétablis pour corriger le texte de Louis Racine. Des phrases, des pages entières, chose à peine croyable, sont restées supprimées. Nous ne craignons pas d'encourir les mêmes reproches; car nous avons nous-même, suivant notre habitude, tout collationné scrupuleusement, et, en outre, soumis notre travail, pour plus de sûreté, au contrôle d'une seconde collation, dont a bien voulu se charger M. Cattant, ancien professeur de l'Université, dont le concours nous a été également utile dans la révision du texte des autres manuscrits de Racine.

La première note de chaque lettre dira où l'on en trouve maintenant, quand nous le saurons, l'original autographe. Ceux qui sont conservés à la Bibliothèque impériale et les deux lettres, l'une de Racine à Boileau, l'autre de Boileau à Racine, qui sont à la bibliothèque du Louvre, ont été revus deux fois, comme nous venons de le dire[1]. La seconde des lettres écrites par Racine à la Fontaine, dont le manuscrit n'est point dans ces bibliothèques, a été corrigée d'après une copie de Louis Racine, que M. Auguste de Naurois a bien voulu nous communiquer. Cette copie contient un assez grand nombre de vers qui étaient demeurés inédits, Louis Racine ayant jugé à propos de les supprimer, lorsqu'il publia cette lettre.

La correspondance entre Racine et Boileau avait été depuis longtemps donnée avec exactitude, particulièrement par M. Berriat-Saint-Prix, dans son excellente édition des *OEuvres de Boileau*. Le texte des lettres de Racine à son fils aîné Jean-Baptiste avait été beaucoup moins altéré que celui des lettres de la jeunesse; il était loin cependant jusqu'ici d'avoir été reproduit dans toute sa pureté.

Trois lettres de Racine avaient été imprimées en 1773 avec une lettre de le Franc de Pompignan à Louis Racine; une seule de ces lettres avait trouvé place dans les précédentes éditions des *OEuvres* de notre auteur; les éditeurs l'avaient prise ailleurs que dans cette impression de 1773 : ils ne connaissaient pas le petit volume où elle avait été publiée, avec les deux autres que nous sommes les premiers à joindre aux *OEuvres;* ceux qui possèdent aujourd'hui les autographes de ces deux dernières, les regardaient eux-mêmes comme inédites.

C'est pour la première fois aussi que, dans une édition des *OEuvres de Racine*, auront été données les lettres que M. l'abbé Adrien de la Roque a publiées en 1862. Son texte, que M. Adolphe Regnier fils est allé revoir sur les autographes qui sont conservés à la Ferté-Milon et à Soissons, dans la famille de Racine, a été trouvé très exactement conforme à ces manuscrits, jusque pour l'orthographe, que M. l'abbé de la Roque a fidèlement reproduite. Nous faisons remarquer ce dernier caractère de son édition, parce qu'elle conserve par là une valeur particulière. Nous avons dû, pour nous, suivre dans le texte de ces lettres, comme dans celui de tous les écrits de Racine, la règle différente que nous nous sommes faite pour l'orthographe de notre édition.

1. Voyez sur les originaux des lettres, comme sur les manuscrits de Racine en général, la *Notice bibliographique*.

En un point, nous nous sommes beaucoup écarté de l'édition de M. l'abbé de la Roque. La manière dont il a suppléé les dates qui manquent à la plupart des lettres publiées par lui nous a fréquemment paru devoir être réformée. Le plus souvent Racine ne datait ses lettres que du jour de la semaine, ou de ce jour, du quantième et du mois, très-rarement de l'année. Dans toute sa correspondance, nous avons étudié avec soin les indices de la véritable date de chaque lettre, sans accepter de confiance celle qu'avaient adoptée nos devanciers. Quand la date que nous proposons peut être contestée, nous ne manquons pas de dire qu'elle est incertaine; pour la plupart des lettres, il ne nous a paru y avoir aucun doute. Toutefois, nous avons toujours enfermé entre crochets les dates qui ne sont pas dans les autographes.

L'annotation de la correspondance de Racine laissait beaucoup encore à désirer dans les précédentes éditions. Nous nous sommes efforcé de donner des éclaircissements sur tous les passages qui en demandaient. Les plus difficiles à expliquer complétement sont ceux où il est question de parents et d'amis qui n'ont laissé aucune trace dans l'histoire. Nous avons pu connaître la plupart d'entre eux par une comparaison attentive des différentes lettres, et par les nombreux actes de baptême, de mariage et d'inhumation que nous avons nous-même relevés sur les registres de la Ferté-Milon, et qui nous avaient été déjà d'un grand secours pour notre *Notice biographique*.

Nous croyons avoir, la plupart du temps, débrouillé cette nombreuse parenté de Racine; quelquefois cependant un peu d'incertitude ne pouvait être évitée : il y a, comme l'on verra, quelque danger de confusion, au milieu de tous ces oncles, tantes, cousins et cousines, qui portaient le même nom.

Louis Racine avait formé des recueils distincts de la correspondance de Racine avec ses amis de jeunesse, puis avec Boileau, puis avec son fils Jean-Baptiste. C'est ainsi qu'on a adopté dans les plus anciennes éditions des lettres de Cicéron, et conservé depuis dans la plupart des réimpressions, certaines divisions auxquelles ont été donnés des titres plus ou moins exacts.

Les éditeurs de 1807 ont partagé la correspondance de Racine en six recueils : 1° ses lettres aux amis de sa jeunesse; 2° sa correspondance avec la Fontaine; 3° sa correspondance avec Boileau; 4° ses lettres à son fils aîné; 5° ses lettres à diverses personnes; le sixième recueil est composé de lettres écrites à Racine, ou à son sujet, par des personnes célèbres de son temps.

Geoffroy et Aimé-Martin ont, à de légers changements près, suivi le même plan.

La correspondance avec la Fontaine, dont il ne reste que trois lettres, n'aurait point dû, ce semble, former de division distincte; mais les lettres de jeunesse ont véritablement un caractère particulier et se classent bien à part par leur date: la séparation même de la correspondance avec Boileau et de celle qui s'adresse à Jean-Baptiste Racine peut sembler assez naturelle, quoique dans l'ordre chronologique elles se trouvent mêlées. Nous aurions donc pu être tenté de nous conformer à un usage depuis longtemps consacré, en nous contentant de le modifier légèrement; mais les lettres publiées par M. l'abbé de la Roque auraient exigé une nouvelle division : de ces lettres les unes appartiennent au temps de la jeunesse de Racine, les autres ont été écrites plus tard, quelques-unes jusque dans les dernières années. Leur classement à part eût peut-être été arbitraire; en général, toutes ces divisions en *Recueils* ont plus ou moins ce défaut. En rangeant d'ailleurs toutes les lettres, sans distinction, dans l'ordre des dates, les éclaircissements qu'elles tirent souvent les unes des autres s'offrent plus aisément. C'est donc dans cet ordre que la fin de ce volume et le volume suivant vont les présenter au lecteur. Nous ne donnerons séparément que quelques lettres qui ne sont ni de Racine, ni adressées à Racine, mais qui ont été écrites à son sujet. Au surplus, nous n'avons fait que suivre la règle adoptée pour toutes les correspondances dans la *Collection des grands écrivains de la France*.

Ce que l'on trouvera ici d'entièrement inédit n'est pas très-considérable. On a lieu de s'étonner qu'outre les lettres qui avaient été conservées dans la famille de Racine, et que M. Adrien de la Roque a publiées, il n'en ait point été découvert un certain nombre depuis les dernières éditions des *OEuvres de Racine*. Sa correspondance a été sans nul doute très-étendue; et parmi ses correspondants il faut vraisemblablement compter beaucoup de personnes illustres de son temps. Il n'est pas croyable que toutes ces lettres aient été détruites ou perdues. Comment se fait-il donc que les familles qui doivent les posséder ne les produisent pas? Il est particulièrement difficile à expliquer que nous n'ayons presque aucune lettre des années qui ont été les plus brillantes de la vie de Racine et ont vu naître tous ses chefs-d'œuvre dramatiques profanes, depuis *Andromaque* jusqu'à *Phèdre* : elles ne seraient certes pas les moins intéressantes pour sa biographie.

Fréron, dans son *Année littéraire* (1758, tome II, p. 19), cite une lettre très-digne d'attention que lui avait adressée, vers 1751 ou 1753, Charles-Louis de la Fontaine, petit-fils du fabuliste, né le 25 avril 1720, mort le 15 novembre 1757. Lorsqu'il écrivait à Fréron, Charles-Louis de la Fontaine était dans le comté de Foix, où il surveillait l'administration des biens du marquis de Bonnac, dont il était le secrétaire et l'ami. « Croiriez-vous, disait-il dans la lettre citée par l'*Année littéraire*, que j'eusse trouvé au pied des Pyrénées des lettres de mon grand-père? J'en ai sur ma table quelques-unes en vers et en prose. Outre cela, j'ai environ *cinq cents lettres de Racine*, quarante de Mme de la Sablière..., enfin des lettres de tous les illustres du règne de Louis XIV, depuis 1676 jusqu'en 1716. » M. Rathery, dans l'*Amateur d'autographes* (15 avril 1862), a signalé cette lettre, qui semblait oubliée depuis longtemps. Il avait lui-même provoqué une enquête, qui pouvait mettre sur la trace d'un trésor un moment entrevu, puis laissé de côté avec tant de négligence. Le petit-fils de la Fontaine, quelque incroyable que puisse paraître un tel nombre de lettres inédites, n'avait pu vouloir en imposer ridiculement, lorsqu'il affirmait les avoir sur sa table. On a moins de peine à croire à l'insouciance héréditaire qui l'aurait laissé s'endormir à côté de ces richesses placées sous sa main. On s'explique très-bien que dans les archives du château de Bonnac, qui est à une lieue de Pamiers, il ait pu trouver des lettres de Racine; car on sait qu'un Bonnac avait été lié avec notre poëte, dont il avait protégé le fils aîné auprès de son oncle M. de Bonrepaux. Encouragé par toutes ces considérations, M. Rathery s'était adressé à l'abbé Santerre, grand vicaire de Pamiers, qui se chargea de faire des recherches dans les archives de Bonnac, de Foix et de Pamiers. Ces recherches ne purent faire découvrir la correspondance qu'avait vue Charles-Louis de la Fontaine. Toutefois la réponse de l'abbé Santerre, que depuis la mort a enlevé, ne paraissait pas à M. Rathery exclure toute espérance. Il pouvait donc y avoir lieu à de nouvelles tentatives : regardant comme un devoir pour nous de les faire, nous avons eu recours à l'obligeance d'une personne qui est particulièrement en état d'en assurer le succès. M. Orliac, archiviste du département de l'Ariége, avait été mis au courant par M. l'abbé Santerre de toutes les investigations déjà commencées ; à notre prière, il a bien voulu les continuer ; et quoiqu'elles n'aient, jusqu'au jour où nous écrivons cette *Notice*, amené aucun résultat, il nous promet de ne point se décourager, mais, il faut l'avouer, sans se flatter beaucoup d'être plus heureux que M. l'abbé Santerre.

Nous avons peine à croire, pour nous, à la perte irrévocable des cinq cents lettres de Racine. Quelques-unes au moins d'entre elles, et d'autres aussi venues d'autre part, reparaîtront peut-être quelque jour, soit (nous voudrions bien l'espérer) avant que nous ayons achevé cette édition, soit plus tard. C'est surtout quand il s'agit d'une correspondance qu'on ne peut jamais prétendre avoir donné une édition complète et définitive.

LETTRES.

1. — D'ANTOINE LE MAISTRE A RACINE[1].   1656

Ce 21 de mars [1656[2]].

Mon fils, je vous prie de m'envoyer au plus tôt l'*Apo-*

Lettre 1 (revue sur l'autographe, conservé à la Bibliothèque impériale). — 1. On a déjà vu ce billet d'Antoine Arnauld aux pages 210 et 211 de notre tome I, dans les *Mémoires sur la vie de Jean Racine;* mais à la note 1 de la page 211, nous avons annoncé que nous en donnerions le texte conforme à l'autographe : il avait été un peu altéré par Louis Racine. L'éditeur de 1807 l'a rétabli exactement.

2. Lorsque, en 1656, Arnauld, contre qui la Sorbonne préparait sa censure, se fut retiré « dans un logis en un quartier de Paris,... M. le Maistre et M. Nicole vinrent aussi s'y renfermer, » dit Fontaine dans ses *Mémoires*, tome II, p. 112. Ce logis était au faubourg Saint-Marceau, chez M. le Jeune (voyez la *Vie de Messire Antoine Arnauld*, par Larrière, tome I, p. 164); et c'est de là que le Maistre écrivit à la Mère Agnès une lettre insérée au *Supplément du Nécrologe de Port-Royal*, p. 268, lettre qui donnerait à croire qu'il ne quitta cette retraite que pour rentrer à Port-Royal. Cependant Louis Racine (*Mémoires*, p. 210 de notre tome I) dit que le billet adressé en 1656 au jeune Racine fut écrit de Bourg-Fontaine, où était une chartreuse, voisine de la Ferté-Milon, qui avait autrefois servi d'asile à quelques-uns des solitaires de Port-Royal, dans les premiers troubles de leur abbaye. Comment Racine aurait-il pu envoyer si loin à M. le Maistre, qui se cachait, tant de gros volumes? Il est permis de douter que Louis Racine parlât d'après de sûres informations.

logie des saints Pères[3] qui est à moi, et qui est de la 1. impression. Elle est reliée en veau marbré, in-4. J'ai reçu les cinq volumes de mes *Conciles*[4], que vous aviez fort bien empaquetés. Je vous en remercie. Mandez-moi si tous mes livres sont au château[5], bien arrangés sur des tablettes, et si tous mes onze volumes de *saint Chrys*. (*Chrysostome*) y sont, et voyez-les de temps en temps pour les nettoyer. Il faudroit mettre de l'eau dans des écuelles de terre où ils sont, afin que les souris ne les rongent pas. Faites mes recommandations à Mme Racine[6] et à votre bonne tante[7], et suivez leurs conseils en tout. La jeunesse doit toujours se laisser conduire, et tâcher de ne point s'émanciper. Peut-être que Dieu nous fera revenir où vous êtes. Cependant il faut tâcher de profiter de cette persécution, et de faire qu'elle nous serve à nous détacher du monde, qui nous paroît si ennemi de la piété. Bonjour, mon cher fils. Aimez toujours votre papa, comme il vous aime. Écrivez-moi de temps en temps. Envoyez-moi aussi mon *Tacite* in-folio.

Suscription : Pour le petit Racine, à Port-Royal.

3. L'*Apologie pour les saints Pères de l'Église, défenseurs de la grâce de Jésus-Christ*, écrite en 1650 par Antoine Arnauld.

4. Le Maistre parle sans doute du recueil qui a pour titre : *Concilia generalia et provincialia....* Cologne, 1605, 5 volumes in-folio.

5. Au château de Vaumurier, que le duc de Luynes avait fait bâtir près de l'abbaye de Port-Royal des Champs.

6. Marie des Moulins, religieuse à Port-Royal, veuve de Jean Racine, grand-père de notre poëte. Voyez la *Notice biographique*, p. 2, 11, 12 et 55.

7. Agnès de Sainte-Thècle Racine, qui avait fait profession en 1648 à Port-Royal. Née au mois d'août 1625, elle mourut en mai 1700. Voyez la *Notice biographique*, p. 4.

2. — DE RACINE A L'ABBÉ LE VASSEUR[1]. 1660

Ce jeudi au matin [1659 ou 1660[2]].

Je vous envoie mon sonnet. C'est à dire un nouveau sonnet; car je l'ai tellement changé hier au soir, que vous le méconnoîtrez. Mais je crois que vous ne l'en approuverez pas moins. En effet, ce qui le rend méconnoissable est ce qui vous le doit rendre plus agréable, puisque je ne l'ai si défiguré que pour le rendre plus beau et plus conforme aux règles que vous lui[3] prescrivîtes hier, qui sont les règles mêmes du sonnet. Vous trouviez étrange que la fin fût une suite si différente du commencement. Cela me choquoit de même que vous. Car les poëtes ont cela des hypocrites, qu'ils défendent toujours ce qu'ils font, mais que leur conscience ne les laisse jamais en repos. J'en étois de même. J'avois fort bien reconnu ce défaut, quoique je fisse tout mon pos-

---

Lettre 2 (revue sur l'autographe, conservé à la Bibliothèque impériale). — 1. Sur l'abbé le Vasseur, voyez la *Notice biographique*, p. 28-32.

2. Cette lettre, dans le recueil de Louis Racine, est ainsi datée : *A Paris, le 8. septembre* 1660; mais seulement : *Ce jeudi au matin*, dans l'autographe. Le 8 septembre en 1660 était un mercredi, et non un jeudi; la date donnée par Louis Racine n'est donc pas exacte, et semble avoir été choisie au hasard. Si le sonnet adressé au cardinal Mazarin célébrait, comme on l'a conjecturé, la paix des Pyrénées, conclue au mois de novembre 1659, la lettre est probablement de la fin de cette même année ou plutôt du commencement de l'année 1660, ce qui y est dit du retour de le Vasseur aux champs permettant difficilement de songer aux premiers mois de l'hiver. A cette lettre Louis Racine en a mêlé une autre (c'est la lettre 7) qu'on trouvera plus loin (p. 387-390), et qui ne peut pas être non plus du 8 septembre, ayant été écrite en carême.

3. Les précédents éditeurs ont substitué *me* à *lui*. — Nous ne relèverons les fausses leçons que lorsque l'altération nous paraîtra, pour une raison ou pour une autre, curieuse à noter, ou lorsque la vraie leçon pourra, comme ici, étonner.

sible pour montrer que ce n'en étoit pas un; mais la force de vos raisons étant ajoutée à celle de ma conscience a achevé de me convaincre. Je me suis rangé à la raison, et y ai aussi rangé mon sonnet. J'en ai changé la pointe, ce qui est de plus considérable dans ces ouvrages. J'ai fait comme un nouveau sonnet. Et quoique si dissemblable à mon premier, j'aurois pourtant de la peine à le désavouer. Ma conscience ne me reproche plus rien, et j'en prends un assez bon augure. Je souhaite qu'il vous satisfasse de même : je vous l'envoie dans cette espérance. Si vous le jugez digne de la vue de Mlle Lucrèce [4], je serai heureux, et je ne le croirai plus indigne de celle de S. É. Retournez aux champs le plus tard que vous pourrez. Vous voyez le bien que cause votre présence.

Suscription : Pour M. l'Abbé.

3. — DE RACINE A MARIE RACINE [1].

A Paris, ce 4. mars [1660].

MA TRÈS-CHÈRE SOEUR,

Je m'attends bien que dans la colère où vous êtes contre moi, vous déchirerez cette lettre sans la lire.

---

4. Il sera souvent parlé de Mlle Lucrèce dans les lettres suivantes. Elle paraît avoir logé dans la même maison que le Vasseur. Peut-être était-elle une parente de Mlle de la Croix, chez qui le jeune abbé demeurait.

LETTRE 3 (revue sur l'autographe, conservé à la Ferté-Milon). — 1. La sœur de notre poëte, Marie Racine, à qui cette lettre est adressée, était née le 24 janvier 1641. Elle épousa, le 30 juin 1676, Antoine Rivière, contrôleur du grenier à sel et médecin à la Ferté-Milon; elle mourut le 17 mai 1734.

C'est pourquoi je ne m'excuse point d'avoir été deux mois sans vous écrire ; car aussi bien vous ne verrez pas mes excuses ; et quand vous les verriez, vous êtes assez entière pour ne les pas croire. Je ne vous dis donc point que j'ai été à la campagne et que j'ai été accablé d'affaires à Paris ; car vous prendrez tout cela pour des contes. D'ailleurs vous ne devez pas, ce me semble, vous plaindre beaucoup : quand je vous aurois écrit, vous n'auriez pas eu le temps de lire mes lettres. Vous étiez aux noces, c'est assez. Je crois que vous vous serez bien divertie. Je suis ravi que ma cousine soit mariée[2] ; je voudrois que vous fussiez à la peine de l'être, mais cela viendra s'il plaît à Dieu. Ma tante Vitart[3] m'a dit qu'elle vous avoit écrit pour votre manchon. Mon cousin Vitart[4] a été cause que je n'en ai pas pris : il me fit revenir comme j'étois déjà dans la rue, en me disant que je ne m'y connoissois pas, et que je vous envoyerois quelque mauvaise marchandise, si bien qu'il dit qu'il falloit que ma tante l'achetât. Mais elle, voyant l'hiver fort avancé, crut qu'il valoit mieux vous demander si vous ne voudriez point quelque autre chose pour l'été. Mandez-lui donc ce que vous voulez

---

2. Cette cousine est probablement Jeanne du Chesne, fille d'Antoine du Chesne et d'Anne Sconin, sœur de la mère de Racine. Le mariage de Jeanne du Chesne avec Louis Parmentier, greffier à Chauny, paraît avoir été de ce temps-là ; mais une lacune (de 1656 à 1668) dans les actes de mariage des registres de la Ferté-Milon ne nous a pas permis d'en constater exactement la date.

3. Claude des Moulins, femme de Nicolas Vitart, greffier et contrôleur de la gabelle à la Ferté-Milon, morte le 11 mars 1668. Elle était grand'tante de Racine. Voyez la *Notice biographique*, p. 2.

4. Antoine Vitart, fils de Nicolas Vitart et de Claude des Moulins. Toutes les fois que Racine dit : « mon cousin Vitart, » nous pensons qu'il s'agit d'Antoine, plutôt que de son frère aîné Nicolas Vitart, intendant du duc de Luynes. Il nommait d'ordinaire l'aîné : *Monsieur Vitart*.

qu'elle vous achète pour deux écus d'or, et vous l'aurez à l'heure même. Je vous écrirai après demain, et je mettrai la lettre dans celle de mon oncle Sconin⁵. Dites-lui, je vous prie, que j'ai été cinq ou six jours hors de Paris, et que je lui écrirai sans faute après demain. Adieu : je suis à vous de tout mon cœur. Ma mère⁶ se recommande à vous, et ma tante⁷ aussi.

RACINE.

Je vous écrirai sans manquer.

Suscription : A Madame Madame Marie Racine, chez M. le Commissaire⁸.

4. — DE RACINE A L'ABBÉ LE VASSEUR.

A Paris, ce dimanche au soir, 5ᵉᵐᵉ sept. [1660¹].

JE vous envoie, Monsieur, une lettre que la Roque² vous écrit, qui vous apprendra assez l'état où sont nos

---

5. Pierre Sconin, avocat, grènetier au grenier à sel de la Ferté-Milon. Il avait épousé Françoise Lefebvre. Il mourut trois mois avant son père, nommé, comme lui, Pierre Sconin. Son acte d'inhumation est daté du 7 janvier 1667.
6. Sa grand'mère, Marie des Moulins. Voyez ci-dessus, p. 372, note 6 de la lettre 1.
7. Agnès de Sainte-Thècle Racine. Voyez ci-dessus, p. 372, note 7 de la lettre 1.
8. Pierre Sconin, commissaire enquêteur et examinateur, président au grenier à sel de la Ferté-Milon, aïeul maternel de Racine. Voyez la *Notice biographique*, p. 8 et 55.
LETTRE 4 (revue sur l'autographe, conservé à la Bibliothèque impériale). — 1. La date de 1660 est certaine : ce fut en cette année que Racine composa et publia son *ode de la Nymphe de la Seine*. Voyez notre tome IV, p. 49-64. Le 5 septembre en 1660 était bien un dimanche.
2. Comédien de la troupe du Marais.

affaires, et combien il seroit nécessaire que vous ne fussiez pas si éloignés³ de nous. Cette lettre vous surprendra peut-être; mais elle nous devoit surprendre bien davantage, nous qui avons été témoins de la première réception qu'il a faite à la pièce⁴. Il la trouvoit toute admirable, et il n'y avoit pas un vers dont il ne parût être charmé. Il la demanda après, pour en considérer le sujet plus à loisir. Et voilà le jugement qu'il vous en envoie. Car je vous regarde comme le principal conducteur de cette affaire. Je crois que Mlle Roste⁵ sera bien plus surprise que nous, vu la satisfaction que la pièce lui avoit donnée. Nous en avons reçu d'elle tout autant que nous pouvions desirer. Et ce sera vous seul qui l'en pourrez bien remercier, comme c'est pour vous seul qu'elle a tout fait. Je ne sais pas à quel dessein la Roque montre ce changement. M. Vitart⁶ en donne plusieurs raisons, et ne désespère rien. Mais pour moi, j'ai bien peur que les comédiens n'aiment à présent que le galimatias, pourvu qu'il vienne d'un grand auteur⁷; car je vous laisse à juger de la vérité de ce qu'il dit sur les vers de l'*Amasie*.

L'ode⁸ est faite, et je l'ai donnée à M. Vitart pour la faire voir à M. Chapelain. S'il n'étoit point si tard, je

---

3. Il y a bien le pluriel dans l'original.
4. Nous ne savons que le titre de cette pièce que Racine espérait alors faire jouer : il dit lui-même un peu plus bas que c'était l'*Amasie*. Il y avait dans le Pont une ville de ce nom. Le sujet de la pièce était-il tiré de la vie d'Ovide, qui fut exilé dans ces contrées? En tout cas, elle est distincte de celle que Racine entreprit l'année suivante. Voyez plus bas la note 4 de la lettre 11.
5. Comédienne de la troupe du Marais.
6. Nicolas Vitart, cousin de Racine. Voyez ci-dessus, p. 375, note 4 de la lettre 3; et, au tome I, la *Notice biographique*, p. 24-28.
7. Racine avait d'abord écrit : « *du* grand auteur. » Voulait-il désigner Corneille?
8. *La Nymphe de la Seine* : voyez la note 1.

vous en ferois présentement une autre copie, pour vous l'envoyer dès demain. Mais il est 10 heures du soir, et j'ai reçu votre billet à 8. D'ailleurs, je crains furieusement le chagrin où vous met votre maladie, et qui vous rendroit peut-être assez difficile pour ne rien trouver de bon dans mon ode. Cela m'embarrasseroit trop; et l'autorité que vous avez sur moi pourroit produire en cette rencontre un aussi mauvais effet, qu'elle en produit de bons en toutes les autres. Néanmoins, comme il y a espérance que cette maladie ne durera pas, je prierai M. Houÿ[9], dès demain, d'en faire une copie, ou j'en ferai une moi-même pour vous l'envoyer. Ce qui est encore à craindre, c'est que vos notes ne reviennent tard : ce qui arrivera sans doute si elles sont dans le chemin autant que votre billet, lequel est daté du jeudi et ne m'a été donné qu'aujourd'hui au soir. Je vous en veux toujours envoyer par avance une stance et demie. Ce n'est pas que je les croie les plus belles, mais c'est qu'elles sont les dernières ou au moins les pénultièmes, et qu'elles sont sur l'entrée. Les voici :

> Qu'il vous faisoit beau voir, en ce superbe jour
> Où, sur un char conduit par la Paix et l'Amour,
> Votre illustre beauté triompha sur mes rives!
> Les Discords après vous se voyoient enchaînés.
>   Mais, hélas! que d'âmes captives
> Virent aussi leurs cœurs en triomphe menés!

>   Tout l'or dont se vante le Tage,
>   Tout ce que l'Inde sur ses bords
>   Vit jamais briller de trésors,
>   Sembloit être sur mon rivage.
> Qu'étoit-ce toutefois de ce grand appareil,
> Dès qu'on jetoit les yeux sur l'éclat nompareil

9. Nous ne connaissons pas d'ailleurs ce personnage, qui paraîtrait avoir eu quelque emploi dans la maison du duc de Luynes.

Dont vos seules beautés vous avoient entourée?
Je sais bien que Junon parut moins belle aux Dieux,
    Et moins digne d'être adorée,
Lorsqu'en nouvelle reine elle entra dans les cieux[10].

Si vous recevez celle-ci avant que de recevoir toutes les autres, vous m'obligerez toujours de m'en écrire votre sentiment. Peut-être en trouverez-vous qui ne vous paroîtront pas moins belles. Cependant il y en a dix toutes entières que vous n'avez pas vues, et c'est de quoi je suis fort marri. Je prierois Dieu volontiers qu'il vous ôtât vos frissons, mais qu'il vous envoyât des affaires en leur place. Vous n'y perdriez pas peut-être, et j'y gaignerois.

Je ne sais si vous aurez eu connoissance en votre solitude de quelques lettres qui font un étrange bruit. C'est de M. le C^{al} de R.[11]. Je les ai vues, mais c'étoit en des mains dont je ne pouvois pas les tirer. Jamais

---

10. Voyez dans notre tome IV, la note 3 de la page 61, et la note 1 de la page 62.

11. Le cardinal de Retz. — Après avoir inutilement écrit, au commencement de 1660, une lettre au Roi, pour le supplier de rendre la paix au diocèse de Paris, le cardinal de Retz écrivit deux autres lettres, qu'il adressa à ses grands vicaires, et dans lesquelles il leur ordonnait « de ne résoudre rien de considérable sans ses sentiments et sans ses ordres. » Il leur annonçait une lettre circulaire « à tous les évêques, prêtres et enfants de l'Église. » Cette lettre circulaire, datée du 24 avril 1660, a été imprimée; elle a 49 pages in-8°. On y entrevoit la menace d'un interdit lancé sur le diocèse de Paris. Dans une ordonnance du Roi, affichée le 7 mars 1661, où tous ceux qui ont intelligence et tiennent correspondance avec l'Archevêque sont menacés de *confiscation de corps et de biens*, il est dit que Sa Majesté est « bien informée que le cardinal de Retz.... écrit des lettres à ceux de sa faction..., reçoit leurs réponses, etc. » Nous devons ces détails à l'obligeance de M. Alphonse Feillet. On les trouvera, plus complets encore, dans l'édition des *OEuvres de Retz*, qu'il prépare pour la collection des *Grands écrivains de la France*.

on n'a rien vu de plus beau, à ce qu'on dit. On craint à Paris qu'il ne vienne quelque chose de plus fort, comme, par exemple, un interdit. Mais cela passe ma portée, et je ne doute pas que vous ne sachiez[12] infiniment plus que moi de tout ce qui se passe dans le monde, tout solitaire que vous êtes. Mais au moins vous ne sauriez trouver de personne qui soit plus à vous que

RACINE.

5. — DE RACINE A L'ABBÉ LE VASSEUR.

Ce lundi au matin, 13ème septembre [1660].

JE crois que vous nous voulez abandonner tout à fait, et ne nous plus parler que par lettres. Est-ce[1] point que vous vous imaginez que vous en aurez plus d'autorité sur nous, et que vous en conserverez mieux la majesté de l'Empire, *cui major ex longinquo reverentia*[2]? Mais croyez-moi, Monsieur, il n'est pas besoin de cette politique. Vos raisons sont trop bonnes d'elles-mêmes sans que vous les appuiez[3] par ces secours étrangers. Votre présence seroit beaucoup plus utile que votre absence en cette saison. Au moins elle l'auroit été; car l'*ode* étant presque imprimée, vous arriveriez maintenant trop tard. Cependant je m'étois fié sur la

---

12. Racine avait commencé par écrire : « que vous n'en sachiez. »

LETTRE 5 (revue sur l'autographe, conservé à la Bibliothèque impériale). — 1. Comme nous l'avons déjà fait remarquer ailleurs (p. 67, note 1), Racine écrivait *esce*.

2. C'est, comme l'on sait, la pensée que Tacite (*Annales*, livre I, chapitre XLVII) prête à Tibère : *Majestate salva, cui major e longinquo reverentia*, « sans compromettre la majesté suprême, qui de loin impose plus de respect. »

3. Racine a écrit ainsi *appuiez*, sans doubler l'*i*.

lettre de M. Vitart, dans laquelle je croyois qu'il vous pressoit bien fort de revenir pour un jour ou deux. Au moins il m'avoit promis de le faire. Mais, à ce que je vois, il ne fait pas tout ce qu'il dit, ou bien vous ne faites pas tout ce qu'il vous demande. La raison de cette nécessité que nous avions de votre présence, c'est qu'il est bien vrai que l'ode a été revue ; mais comme on avoit marqué quelques changements à faire, je les ai faits, et j'étois le plus embarrassé du monde pour savoir si ces changements n'étoient point eux-mêmes à changer. Je ne savois à qui m'adresser. M. Vitart est rarement capable de donner son attention à quelque chose. M. l'Avocat[4] n'en donne pas beaucoup non plus à ces sortes de choses. Il aime mieux, ce me semble, ne voir jamais une pièce, pour belle qu'elle soit, que de la voir une seconde fois. Si bien que j'étois près de consulter, comme Malherbe, une vieille servante qui est chez nous, pour assurer mon jugement, si je ne m'étois aperçu qu'elle est janséniste comme son maître[5], et qu'elle pourroit me déceler : ce qui seroit ma ruine entière, vu que je reçois encore tous les jours lettres sur lettres, ou, pour mieux dire, excommunications sur excommunications, à cause de mon triste sonnet. Ainsi j'ai été obligé de me rapporter à moi seul de la bonté

4. Voici encore un personnage souvent mentionné dans les premières lettres de Racine, et qui nous est inconnu. Louis Racine ne savait rien sur lui. « Ce M. l'Avocat, dit l'éditeur de 1807, était un jeune pédant de leurs amis. » Pour un ami, on le raillait beaucoup. Nous conjecturons qu'il était moins un ami qu'un parent, un parent de l'abbé le Vasseur, peut-être son frère; il devait lui tenir de très-près, comme porte à le croire un passage de la lettre du 28 mars 1662, où Racine témoigne à l'abbé un déplaisir très-sensible d'une maladie de M. l'Avocat.

5. Le duc de Luynes. Ce passage indique que Racine demeurait alors dans la maison de ce duc, près de Nicolas Vitart, qui en était l'intendant.

de mes vers. Voyez combien un jour de votre présence m'auroit fait de bien. Mais puisqu'il n'y a plus de remède pour l'avenir, il faut que je vous rende compte[6] de tout ce qui s'est passé. Je ne sais seulement si je le devrois faire, puisque vous vous y êtes si peu intéressé. Mais en vérité je suis si accoutumé à vous faire part de mes fortunes, bonnes ou mauvaises, que je vous punirois moins que moi-même en vous les taisant.

M. Chapelain a donc revu l'ode avec la plus grande bonté du monde, tout malade qu'il étoit. Il l'a retenue trois jours durant, et en a fait des remarques par écrit, que j'ai fort bien suivies. M. Vitart ne se vit jamais si aise qu'après cette visite. Il me pensa confondre de reproches, à cause que je lui avois un peu reproché la longueur de M. Chapelain. Je voudrois que vous eussiez vu la chaleur et l'éloquence avec laquelle il me querella. Mais cela soit dit en passant. Au sortir de chez M. Chapelain, il alla voir M. Perrault[7], contre notre dessein, comme vous savez. Il ne s'en put empêcher, et je n'en suis pas marri à présent. M. Perrault lui dit aussi de fort bonnes choses, que M. Vitart mit par écrit, et que j'ai encore toutes suivies, à une ou deux près, où je ne suivrois pas Apollon même, comme est la comparaison de Vénus et de Mars, qu'il récuse à cause que Vénus est une prostituée. Mais vous savez que quand les poëtes parlent des Dieux, ils les traitent en divinités, et par conséquent comme des êtres parfaits, n'ayant même jamais parlé de leurs crimes comme s'ils eussent été des crimes; car aucun ne s'est jamais avisé d'appeler Jupiter ni Vénus incestes ou adultères. Et si cela étoit, il ne faudroit plus introduire les Dieux dans la poésie, vu qu'à regarder

---

6. L'orthographe de Racine est *conte*.
7. Charles Perrault.

leurs actions, il n'y en a pas un qui ne méritât pour le moins d'être brûlé, si on leur faisoit bonne justice. Mais, en un mot, j'ai Malherbe, qui a comparé la reine Marie à Vénus, avec quatre vers aussi beaux qu'ils me sont avantageux, puisqu'ils renferment aussi la prostitution[8] :

> Telle n'est point la Cythérée
> Quand, d'un nouveau feu s'allumant,
> Elle sort pompeuse et parée
> Pour la conquête d'un amant[9].

Voilà ce qui regarde leur censure. Je ne vous dirai rien de leur approbation, sinon que M. Perrault a dit que l'ode valoit dix fois la comédie. Et voilà les paroles de M. Chapelain, que je vous rapporterai comme le texte de l'*Évangile*, sans y rien changer. Mais aussi *c'est M. Chapelain*, comme disoit à chaque mot M. Vitart. « L'ode est fort belle, fort poétique, et il y a beaucoup de stances qui ne se peuvent mieux. Si l'on repasse ce peu d'endroits marqués, on en fera une fort belle pièce. » Il a tant pressé M. Vitart de lui en nommer l'auteur, que M. Vitart veut me le faire voir à toute force. Cette vue nuira bien sans doute à l'estime qu'il en avoit déjà conçue. Ce qu'il y a eu de plus considérable à changer, ç'a été une stance entière qui est celle des Tritons. Il s'est trouvé que les Tritons n'avoient jamais logé dans les fleuves,

---

8. Racine a biffé le mot *adultère*, qui était d'abord venu sous sa plume, et l'a remplacé par celui de *prostitution*. — C'est un des nombreux passages qu'ont adouci les précédents éditeurs, à commencer par Louis Racine. Au reste cette lettre, si on compare notre texte à celui des impressions antérieures, peut presque suffire à montrer à quel point, et de combien de façons, on s'est permis d'altérer les lettres de Racine.

9. C'est le commencement de la strophe 4 de l'*Ode à Marie de Médicis sur sa bienvenue en France.* Voyez le *Malherbe* de M. Lalanne, tome I, p. 46.

mais seulement dans la mer. Je les ai souhaités bien des fois noyés, tous tant qu'ils sont, pour la peine qu'ils m'ont donnée. J'ai donc refait une autre stance. Mais

Poi che da tutti i lati ho pieno il foglio[10].

---

6. — DE RACINE A L'ABBÉ LE VASSEUR.

A Babylone[1], ce 26. janvier [1661].

Tout éloigné que je suis de Paris, je ne laisse pas de savoir tout ce qui s'y passe. Je sais l'état qu'on y fait de moi, et en quelle posture je suis près des uns et des autres. Je sais que M. l'Avocat me voulut venir voir hier, et que Monsieur l'Abbé ne voulut pas seulement ouïr cette proposition. En effet, vous étiez en trop belle compagnie pour la quitter, et ce n'est pas votre humeur de quitter les dames pour aller voir des prisonniers. Monsieur, Dieu vous garde jamais de l'être! Je jure par toutes les divinités qui président aux prisons (je crois qu'il n'y en a point d'autres que la Justice, ou Thémis en termes

---

10. « Puisque de tous les côtés j'ai la feuille pleine. » C'est un vers de l'*Arioste*, l'avant-dernier du XXXIIIe chant de l'*Orlando furioso*, qui finit ainsi :

Poi che da tutti i lati ho pieno il foglio,
Finire il canto, e riposar mi voglio.

Louis Racine, après la citation du vers, a ajouté : « Adieu. Je suis, etc. » Mais dans l'original la lettre finit au mot *foglio*. Le reste est sous-entendu.

Lettre 6 (revue sur l'autographe, conservé à la Bibliothèque impériale). — 1. Cette lettre est datée de Babylone, nom que donnait Racine au château de Chevreuse, où il feignait, en plaisantant, de se regarder comme exilé et captif. On voit, par la lettre du 27 mai suivant, que l'année où il passa quelque temps dans le château du duc de Luynes, pour y surveiller des travaux, est l'année 1661.

de poëtes) : je jure donc par Thémis que je n'aurai jamais le moindre mouvement de pitié pour vous, et que je me changerai en pierre, comme Monsieur le Marquis² et Niobé, afin d'être aussi dur pour vous, que vous l'avez été pour moi. Vous m'accusiez d'avoir plus de correspondance avec M. l'Avocat qu'avec vous. Je vous fais juge vous-même de la différence que je dois mettre entre vous et lui. Aussi, après un témoignage d'amitié comme celui-là, je vous proteste que M. l'Avocat ne sera pas plus tôt dans un des plus noirs cachots de la Bastille (car un homme de sa conséquence ne sauroit jamais être prisonnier que d'État) : il n'y sera pas sitôt, en vérité, que je m'irai enfermer avec lui, et croyez que ma reconnoissance ira de pair avec mon ressentiment.

Vous vous attendez peut-être que je m'en vais vous dire que je m'ennuie beaucoup à Babylone, et que je vous dois réciter les lamentations que Jérémie y a autrefois composées. Mais je ne veux pas vous faire pitié, puisque vous n'en avez pas déjà eu³ pour moi. Je veux vous braver au contraire, et vous montrer que je passe fort bien mon temps. Je vas au cabaret deux ou trois fois le jour. Je commande à des maçons, à des vitriers et à des menuisiers, qui m'obéissent assez exactement, et me demandent de quoi boire quand ils ont fait leur ouvrage. Je suis dans la chambre d'un duc et pair : voilà ce qui regarde le faste. Car dans un quartier comme celui-ci, ou il n'y a que des gueux, c'est grandeur que d'aller au cabaret. Tout le monde n'y peut pas aller. Mais j'ai des⁴

---

2. Le jeune marquis de Luynes, depuis duc de Chevreuse, né en 1646. Racine l'accuse de dureté, sans doute parce qu'il était aussi un de ceux qui avaient refusé de venir le voir.

3. Dans l'original : *eue*.

4. « Mais j'ai des » est écrit au-dessus des mots suivants effacés . « Si vous voulez savoir mes.... »

divertissements plus solides, quoiqu'ils paroissent moins. Je goûte tous les plaisirs de la vie solitaire. Excepté cinq ou six heures du jour, je suis tout seul, et je n'entends pas le moindre bruit. Il est vrai que le vent en fait beaucoup, et même jusqu'à faire trembler la maison. Mais il y a un poëte qui dit :

O quam jucundum est recubantem audire susurros
Ventorum, et somnos, imbre juvante, sequi[5] *!*

Ainsi, si je voulois, je tirerois ce vent à mon avantage; mais je vous assure que je ne m'y accoutume pas, et que ce vent-là m'empêche de dormir toute la nuit, tant il est horrible. Je crois que le poëte vouloit parler de ces Zéphirs flatteurs,

Che dibattendo l'ali
Lusingano il sonno de' mortali[6].

Je lis des vers, je tâche d'en faire. Je lis les aventures d'Arioste, et je ne suis pas moi-même sans aventure. Une dame me prit hier pour un sergent. Je voudrois qu'elle fût aussi belle que Doralice ; je lui aurois fait les offres que Mandricard fit à cette belle quand il congédia toute sa suite pour l'emmener :

Io mastro, io balia, io le sarò sergente
In tutti i bisogni suoi[7].

---

5. « Oh! qu'il est agréable d'entendre, couché, le murmure du vent, et de chercher le sommeil au bruit de la pluie qui le favorise! » On reconnaît facilement dans cette citation un passage de Tibulle (livre I, *élégie* I, vers 45-48), que Racine a fort altéré, soit qu'il n'en eût qu'une mémoire imparfaite, soit peut-être qu'il l'eût ainsi appris à Port-Royal dans quelque livre expurgé.

6. « Qui en agitant les ailes caressent le sommeil des mortels. » (*La Jérusalem délivrée*, chant XIV, stance 1.) Racine a cette fois encore un peu modifié la citation :

E i venticelli dibattendo l'ali
Lusingavano il sonno de' mortali.

7. « Je serai son maître, sa nourrice, son sergent et serviteur dans tous ses besoins. » (Arioste, *Orlando furioso*, chant XIV,

LETTRES. 387

Mais je ne me suis pas trouvé assez échauffé pour lui faire cette proposition. Voilà comme je passe mon temps à Babylone. Je ne vous prie plus d'y venir après cela. Il me semble que vous devez assez vous hâter pour prendre des divertissements de cette nature. Nous irons au cabaret ensemble. On vous prendra pour un commissaire, comme on me prend pour un sergent, et nous ferons trembler tout le quartier. Faites donc ce que vous voudrez; au moins ne faites rien par pitié, car je ne vous en demande pas le moins du monde. Pour M. l'Avocat, c'est une autre affaire : je lui écrirai par le premier messager ; car voilà les maçons qui arrivent, et je suis obligé d'aller voir à ce qu'ils doivent faire. Je vous prie cependant de remercier M. l'Avocat, et de faire votre profit des reproches que je vous fais. S'il étoit de bonne grâce à un prisonnier de faire le galant, je vous supplierois de présenter à Mlle Lucrèce mes respects, et de lui témoigner que je suis son très-humble sergent et prisonnier. Elle le prendra en quel sens il lui plaira.

Suscription : A Monsieur Monsieur l'abbé le Vasseur, à Paris. (Deux cachets bruns, portant : J. RAC. (*Jean Racine*), avec une soie verte.)

7. — DE RACINE A L'ABBÉ LE VASSEUR.

Ce jeudi [février ou mars 1661 [1]].

JE n'ai pu passer tantôt chez vous, comme je vous avois

stance LIV.) Le texte original est, au second vers : *In tutti i suoi bisogni*. — Mandricard, fils d'Agrican, roi de Tartarie, dit ces paroles, après avoir enlevé Doralice, fille du roi de Grenade.

LETTRE 7 (revue sur l'autographe, conservé à la Bibliothèque impériale). — 1. Les derniers mots de cette lettre prouvent qu'elle a été écrite pendant le carême. On l'avait jusqu'ici datée de l'année

promis, à cause du mauvais temps. Ainsi je vous écris ce billet, afin de vous faire souvenir de la proposition que M. l'Avocat vous fit hier d'aller aux machines [2]. Je vous prie de me mander le jour que vous irez. M. Vitart se laissera peut-être débaucher pour y aller avec nous. Ainsi, si ma compagnie vous est indifférente, la sienne ne vous le sera pas peut-être. J'ai reçu aujourd'hui réponse de Daphnis [3], qui me fait de grands reproches à cause de son épitaphe, et qui me menace de me faire bientôt rétracter, et de me montrer que la croix ne fut jamais un partage qu'il voulût embrasser tout seul [4].

1660; mais Racine y parlant d'aller *aux machines* (voyez la note suivante), nous croyons qu'elle est de 1661.

2. « L'année 1661, dit de Léris (dans son *Dictionnaire portatif, historique et littéraire des Théâtres*, p. xvi), fut l'époque de la construction du grand théâtre des machines des Thuilleries, qui fut élevé sous la conduite et sur les dessins de Vigarani, Italien, pour servir à la représentation des ballets et des comédies que Louis XIV vouloit faire exécuter. » Voyez aussi le *Parallèle des principaux théâtres modernes*, par Joseph de Philippi (2 volumes in-folio), tome I, p. 9 et 10. C'est, nous le croyons, cette salle des machines des Tuileries que Racine se proposait de visiter. Blondel l'a décrite aux pages 89 et 90 du tome IV de son *Architecture françoise* (1756). Construite pour remplacer la salle du Petit-Bourbon, qui avait servi aux ballets et aux fêtes de la cour, et qu'on avait démolie en 1660, elle offrait, suivant Philippi, « la plus vaste scène qu'on eût encore vue de ce côté des Alpes. » Quelques personnes ont pensé, avec peu de vraisemblance, selon nous, que les machines dont parle Racine étaient celles de *la Toison d'or* de Corneille sur le théâtre du Marais. Les premières représentations à Paris de cette pièce à grandes machines sont aussi du commencement de 1661.

3. Ainsi que nous l'avons dit dans une note sur le *Sonnet pour célébrer la naissance d'un enfant de Nicolas Vitart* (tome IV, p. 204), Daphnis paraît être le surnom que Racine donnait à Nicolas Vitart dans ses badinages poétiques. Il est vrai que deux lignes plus haut il le désigne sous son vrai nom; mais ici il s'agit sans doute de quelque réponse en vers faite par Vitart, sous le nom de *Daphnis*, à une épitaphe satirique.

4. Nous n'avons pas la clef de ces badinages.

J'ai déjà lu toute la *Callipédie*⁵, et je l'ai admirée toute entière. Il me semble qu'il ne se peut pas faire de plus beaux vers latins. Balzac diroit qu'ils sentent tout à fait l'ancienne Rome et la cour d'Auguste, que le cardinal du Perrone⁶ les auroit lus⁷ de fort bon cœur. Mais moi, qui ne sais pas si bien quel étoit⁸ le goût de ce cardinal, et qui m'en soucie fort peu aussi, je me contente de vous en dire mon sentiment. Vous vous fâcherez peut-être de voir tant de ratures⁹; mais vous les devez pardonner à un homme qui sort de table. Vous savez que ce n'est pas le temps le plus propre du monde pour concevoir les choses bien nettement, et je puis dire avec autant de raison que M. Quillet, qu'il ne se faut pas mettre à travailler sitôt après le repas :

> *Nimirum crudam si ad læta cubilia portas*
> *Perdicem, incoctaque agitas genitalia cœna,*
> *Heu tenue effundes semen*¹⁰.

Mais il ne m'importe de quelle façon je vous écrive,

---

5. Poëme latin de Cl. Quillet, dont la 1ʳᵉ édition fut publiée en 1655.

6. Le cardinal du Perron (Racine écrit *Perrone*), né en 1556, mort en 1618.

7. L'original porte *lu* (*lû*), sans accord.

8. *Quel etoit* a été ajouté au-dessus de la ligne.

9. Il n'y a pourtant jusqu'ici dans l'original que deux corrections, l'addition que mentionne la note 8, et un *que* effacé après *Rome*. Dans la suite, il y a plusieurs ratures avant les vers latins, une après.

10. Louis Racine a retranché de la citation tout ce qui suit le mot *Perdicem*, après lequel il s'est contenté de mettre un *etc*. Le texte cité par Racine est celui de la 1ʳᵉ édition de la *Callipédie*, publiée sous ce titre : *Calvidi Leti Callipædia.... Lugduni Batavorum. Veneunt Parisiis, apud Thomam Jolly*, 1 volume in-4°, MDCLV. Voyez à la page 16 de cette édition, les vers 20-22 du livre II. Dans l'édition de 1656 (à Paris, chez le même Thomas Jolly), où l'auteur (Cl. Quillet) n'a plus déguisé son nom, les vers cités, qui sont devenus les 46ᵉ et suivants du livre II, ont été un peu changés :

> *Nimirum crudum si ad læta cubilia portas*
> *Ventre cibum....*

pourvu que j'aie le plaisir de vous entretenir : de même qu'il me seroit bien difficile d'attendre après la digestion de mon souper si je me trouvois à la première nuit de mes noces. Je ne suis pas assez patient pour observer tant de formalités. Cela est pitoyable de fonder un entretien sur 3 ou 4 ratures, mais je ne suis pas le seul qui fais des lettres sur rien. Il y a bien des beaux esprits qui sont sujets à faire des lettres à quelque prix que ce soit, et à les remplir de bagatelles. Je ne prétends pas en être pour cela du nombre. Mais M. Vitart monte à cheval. Je vous écrirai plus au long quand j'aurai plus de choses à vous mander. *Vale et vive*[11]; car le carême ne le défend pas.

RACINE.

Suscription : A Monsieur Monsieur l'abbé le Vasseur. (Deux cachets bruns : J. RAC., avec une soie jaune.)

8. — DE RACINE A L'ABBÉ LE VASSEUR.

A Paris, le lendemain de l'Ascension [27 mai] 1661.

Vous avez beau dispenser vos faveurs le plus libéralement du monde, vous n'avez pas laissé de faire des malcontents. Mlles de la Croix [1], Lucrèce, Madelon,

---

11. « Portez-vous bien et vivez. »

LETTRE 8 (revue sur l'autographe, conservé à la Bibliothèque impériale). — 1. C'était chez Mlle de la Croix, rue Galande, que demeurait l'abbé le Vasseur, comme on le voit par la suscription de quelques-unes des lettres de Racine. Sur les registres de baptême de la Ferté-Milon nous avons trouvé des de la Croix alliés, en 1653, aux Vitart. Mais ce que nous savons de plus certain sur cette famille nous est fourni par l'acte suivant tiré des registres de la paroisse Saint-Séverin, à laquelle appartenait la rue Galande. La signature de le Vasseur au-dessous de celle de trois demoiselles de la Croix ne laisse pas douter que l'une d'elles ne soit celle dont parle Racine : « Le lundi, 24º jour dudit mois (*mars* 1659), furent épou-

LETTRES.   391

Thiennon, Marie-Claude et Vitarts² ; MM. l'Avocat, d'Aigreville, du Binart, de Monvallet, Vitart, etc., se tiennent, à ce qu'on m'a dit, fort obligés à votre souvenir. Pour moi, je n'ai garde de m'en plaindre. Cependant cette grande foule de lettres ne vous a pas exempté des querelles que vous vouliez éviter en satisfaisant également tout le monde³. En effet, il falloit pousser la galanterie⁴ jusqu'au bout, et contenter M. de la Charles⁵ aussi bien que les autres. Vous n'auriez pas sur les bras le plus dangereux ennemi du monde, ou plutôt nous-mêmes n'en serions pas accablés comme nous sommes. Il a été averti de tout ce qui se passoit, et commença hier une harangue qui ne finira qu'avec sa vie si vous n'y donnez ordre, et que vous ne lui fermiez la bouche par une grande⁶ lettre d'excuses, qui fasse le même effet que cette miche dont Énée ferma la triple gueule de Cerbère.

.... *Ille fame rabida tria guttura pandens,*
*Corripit*⁷....

sés.... Messire Jacques Tulloue, procureur au Parlement, et damoiselle Catherine de la Croix, tous deux de cette paroisse, en présence, du côté.... d'elle, de M. Jean de la Croix, prieur de Chalmaison-en-Brie, son frère, et de Geneviefve, de Germaine et de Suzanne de la Croix, ses sœurs. »

2. Si ce n'est point par un *lapsus* que Racine a mis ici au pluriel le nom de Vitart, il n'a pu, ce nous semble, vouloir désigner que la mère et la femme de Nicolas Vitart. A cette époque, Antoine Vitart, son frère, n'était pas encore marié. Les noms de cette même phrase sur lesquels nous ne disons rien sont ceux de personnes qui nous sont restées inconnues.

3. Il y avait d'abord : « à tout le monde ; » *à* est effacé, mais nous ne savons par quelle main il l'a été.

4. Racine avait d'abord écrit : « la générosité. »

5. Nous ignorons quel est ce M. *de la Charles*.

6. Les mots *grande*, et, à la ligne suivante, *triple*, ont été ajoutés après coup dans l'interligne.

7. « Celui-ci, dans sa faim furieuse, ouvrant son triple gosier, saisit (le gâteau). » (Virgile, *Énéide*, livre VI, vers 421 et 422.)

Pour moi, dès que je le vis commencer, je n'attendis pas que l'exorde de la harangue fût fini. Je crus que le seul parti que je devois prendre, étoit de m'enfuir après m'être contenté de dire : « Monsieur a raison, » pour ne pas tomber dans cet inconvénient où me jeta autrefois le dur essai de sa meurtrière éloquence.

J'étois à l'hôtel de Babylone quand M. l'Avocat y apporta vos lettres, qui de part et d'autre furent reçues avec toute la joie possible. Néanmoins, pour ne vous rien cacher de tout ce qui s'y passa, il y eut deux endroits dans celle de Mlle Vitart[8] qui produisirent deux effets assez plaisants. Le premier fut que Mlle Vitart, lisant que vous alliez prendre les eaux, ne put s'empêcher de crier comme si vous étiez déjà mort, et de dire que cela vous tueroit infailliblement. Elle dit cela avec chaleur, et M. Vitart s'en aperçut bien. Mais quand elle vint à lire que c'étoit pour l'aborder plus librement, et pour vous guérir de cette secrète incommodité dont elle seule s'étoit aperçue,

S'attonito restasse e mal contento[9],

vous n'en devez nullement douter. Il prit la lettre, et ayant cherché cet endroit, après s'être frotté les yeux,

Tre volte, e quattro e sei lesse lo scritto[10],

et ayant regardé ensuite Mlle Vitart, il lui demanda *con il ciglio fieramente inarcato*[11], ce que tout cela vouloit

---

8. Marguerite le Mazier, fille d'un procureur au Parlement, mariée en 1658 à Nicolas Vitart, intendant du duc de Luynes, morte le 29 novembre 1693. Voyez la *Notice biographique*, p. 26.

9. « S'il demeura étonné et mécontent. » (*Orlando furioso*, chant XXVIII, stance XXII.)

10. « Trois, quatre et six fois il lut l'écrit. » (Arioste, *Orlando furioso*, chant XXIII, stance CXI.)

11. « Avec un sourcil froncé et menaçant. » Si c'est une citation, nous ignorons à quel auteur Racine l'a empruntée.

dire. Ce fut à M. l'Avocat et à moi de nous taire cependant, car nous ne trouvions point là le mot pour rire. Mlle Vitart tâcha de détourner la chose. Enfin elle fut obligée de lui dire quelque chose à l'oreille, que nous n'entendîmes point. Cela le satisfit peut-être. Quoi qu'il en soit, il n'en dit plus mot, et se mit à parler d'autres choses. Nous fûmes promener ensuite tous trois le reste de l'après-dînée. J'avois eu le loisir d'entretenir Monsieur le Marquis [12] une heure ou deux, comme j'ai fait encore dimanche, avec tous les témoignages de son amitié. Je vous en entretiendrai une autre fois; car je m'imagine bien que vous me voulez mal dans le cœur de laisser là votre lettre et votre poésie, pour vous entretenir de bagatelles qui ne vous touchent pas tant. J'ai tort, je l'avoue, et je devois considérer qu'étant devenu poëte, vous êtes sans doute devenu impatient, qui est une qualité inséparable des poëtes aussi bien que des amoureux [13], qui veulent qu'on laisse toutes choses pour ne leur parler que de leur passion et de leurs ouvrages. On croit ici que vous êtes l'un et l'autre ; et c'est Mlle Lucrèce qui le croit, et, à ce qu'elle dit, pour de bonnes raisons. Mais consolez-vous. On peut être amant et poëte, sans renoncer à l'honnête homme. M. l'Avocat n'en sait rien. Cela suffit ; car tous les autres ne vous seront pas si rigoureux que lui. Je ne vous parlerai point de votre amour. Un homme aussi délicat que vous ne sauroit manquer d'avoir fait un beau choix, et je suis persuadé que la belle mignonne de quatorze ans mérite les adorations de tous tant que nous sommes, puisque

12. Le jeune marquis de Luynes. Voyez ci-dessus, p. 385, la note 2 de la lettre 6.
13. On voit par quelques ratures de l'original que Racine avait d'abord voulu écrire : « inséparable de la poésie aussi bien que de l'amour. »

vous l'avez jugée digne des vôtres, jusqu'à devenir poëte pour elle. Cela me confirme de plus en plus que l'Amour est celui de tous les Dieux qui sait mieux le chemin du Parnasse. Croyez-le, Monsieur, puisqu'il vous y a su si bien mener. Avec un si bon conducteur, vous n'avez garde de manquer d'y être bien reçu. D'ailleurs, les Muses vous connoissoient déjà assez de réputation, et sachant que vous étiez si bien venu parmi toutes les autres dames, il ne faut point douter qu'elles ne vous aient fait le plus obligeant accueil du monde. On en peut juger par vos vers,

Utque viro Phœbi chorus assurrexerit omnis[14].

Et ils en sont une belle marque. Ils ne sont pas seulement amoureux : la justesse y est toute entière. Néanmoins, si j'ose vous dire mes sentiments sur deux ou trois mots, celui de *radieux* est un peu trop antique pour un homme tout frais sorti du Parnasse ; j'aurois tâché de mettre *impérieux* ou quelque autre mot. J'aurois aussi retranché ces deux vers : *Ainsi, si comme nous*, et le suivant, ou je leur aurois donné un sens ; car il me semble qu'ils n'en ont point. Vous m'accuserez peut-être de trop d'inhumanité de traiter si rudement les fils aînés de votre Muse et de votre Amour : je ne veux pas dire les fils uniques ; la Muse et l'Amour n'en demeureront pas là, s'il plaît à Dieu. Mais au moins cela vous doit faire voir réciproquement que je n'ai rien de caché pour vous, et que ce n'est point par flatterie que je vous loue, puisque je prends la liberté de vous censurer. *Scito eum pessime dicere, qui laudabitur maxime*[15]. En effet, quand

---

14. « Et comment tout le chœur de Phébus se leva devant le poëte. » (Virgile, *églogue* VI, vers 66.)
15. « Sachez que celui-là parle le plus mal, à qui l'on donnera le plus de louanges. » (Pline le jeune, livre II, *lettre* XIV.)

une chose ne vaut rien du tout, c'est alors qu'on la loue démesurément, et qu'on n'y trouve rien à redire, parce que tout y est également à blâmer. Il n'en est pas de même de vos vers. Croyez, je vous prie, que, hormis ces deux petits défauts, je n'y en trouve point du tout. Ils sont aussi naturels qu'on le peut desirer, et vous ne devez point plaindre le sang qu'ils vous ont coûté. Ne vous amusez pas pourtant à vous en épuiser les veines pour continuer à faire des vers, si ce n'est qu'à l'exemple de la femme de Sénèque, vous ne vouliez témoigner la grandeur de votre amour, *ore ac membris in eum pallorem albentibus, ut ostentui esset multum vitalis spiritus egestum*[16]. Mais je ne crois pas que les beaux yeux qui vous ont blessé soient si sanguinaires, et que ces marques de votre amour leur fussent[17] plus agréables qu'une santé forte et robuste, qui vous rendroit plus capable de la servir *in tutti i suoi bisogni*[18], comme le *gaillardo*[19] *Mandricardo*. Croyez que si ce galant homme se fût amusé à perdre tout son sang pour Doralice, elle ne se fût pas levée le matin si gaie, et qu'elle n'eût pas remercié si fort ce bon berger

Che nel suo albergo le havea fatto honore[20],

c'est-à-dire qui l'avoit logée avec Mandricard. Mais

---

16. « La pâleur de son visage et la blancheur de ses membres montraient combien la force vitale s'était épuisée en elle. » (Tacite, *Annales*, livre XV, chapitre LXIV.)

17. Racine avait d'abord écrit : « leur soient. »

18. Voyez ci-dessus, p. 386.

19. Racine a ainsi écrit, suivant l'orthographe française du mot *gaillard*, au lieu de *gagliardo* (vaillant).

20.   *E Doralice ringraziò il pastore*
      Che nel suo albergo le avea fatto onore.

« Et Doralice remercia le berger qui dans son logis lui avait fait honneur. » (*Orlando furioso*, chant XIV, stance LXIII.)

l'heure me presse, et je dois songer que ma lettre est peut-être la 15 ou 16° de celles que vous en recevrez avec elle. Je suppose que vous aurez réponse de tous ceux à qui vous avez écrit. Je ne quittai hier au soir Mlle Lucrèce qu'après qu'elle se fut engagée de parole à le faire, et je lui exposai la commission que vous m'avez donnée d'y tenir la main. Elle voulut me gaigner afin que je ne lui fusse pas si sévère; mais je lui ai dit que j'étois trop ennemi des traîtres pour en devenir un, et qu'il falloit qu'elle vous écrivît ou qu'elle me vît toujours à ses talons pour la presser inexorablement de s'acquitter envers vous. Je me suis acquitté de même des autres commissions. M. du Chesne[21] est votre serviteur, et M. d'Houÿ est ivre[22], tant je lui ai fait boire de santés, et moi je suis tout à vous.

Suscription : A Monsieur Monsieur l'abbé le Vasseur, à Bourbon[23]. (Deux cachets bruns : J. RAC., avec une soie amarante.)

21. C'était un cousin germain de Racine, fils d'Antoine du Chesne, que nous trouvons, dans un acte, qualifié « bourgeois de Soissons », et d'Anne Sconin. Voyez ci-dessus, p. 375, la note 2 de la lettre 3. Nous pensons qu'il s'agit ici, non de l'oncle de Racine, mais de son cousin, parce que nous verrons dans la lettre 12, p. 409, que celui-ci quittait Paris pour retourner à la Ferté-Milon, trois mois environ plus tard.
22. Racine avait commencé par écrire : « est ivre des santés que je...; » puis il a effacé ces quatre derniers mots.
23. Le Vasseur était alors aux eaux de Bourbon, près de Moulins.

9. — DE RACINE A L'ABBÉ LE VASSEUR. 1661

[A Paris, ce 2 ou 3ème juin 1661[1].]

M. l'Avocat me vient d'apporter une de vos lettres, et il a bien voulu prendre cette peine; car il veut absolument que nous soyons réconciliés ensemble. Je gaigne trop à cette réunion pour m'y opposer. Aussi bien, comme les choses imparfaites recherchent naturellement de se joindre avec les plus parfaites, je ferois un monstre dans la nature si, étant creux comme je suis, je refusois de me joindre et de m'attacher au solide, tandis que ce même solide tâche d'attirer à lui[2] ce même creux,

*Quod quoniam per se nequeat constare, necesse est
Hærere*[3].

C'est de Lucrèce qu'est cette maxime, et c'est de lui que j'ai appris qu'il falloit me réunir avec M. l'Avocat; et il faut bien que vous l'ayez lu aussi, car il me semble que la lettre que vous avez écrite à ce grand partisan du solide, est toute pleine des maximes de mon auteur. Il dit, comme vous, qu'il ne faut pas que tout soit tellement solide qu'il n'y ait un peu de creux parmi :

*Nec tamen undique corporea stipata tenentur
Omnia natura; namque est in rebus inane*[4].

LETTRE 9 (revue sur l'autographe, conservé à la bibliothèque du Louvre). — 1. Cette date, d'une encre plus noire, semble avoir été ajoutée après coup, et n'être pas de la main de Racine.

2. Racine a substitué *lui* à *soi* (*soy*), effacé.

3. « Qui n'ayant point par lui-même de consistance, doit nécessairement chercher où s'accrocher. » C'est une citation, légèrement altérée, de Lucrèce (livre I, vers 608 et 609):

*Quæ quoniam per se nequeunt constare, necesse est
Hærere....*

4. « Et cependant tout n'est pas condensé en une masse corporelle sans interstice; car il y a du vide dans la nature. » (Lucrèce, livre I, vers 330 et 331.)

1661

Mais sortons de cette matière, qui elle-même est trop solide, et mêlons-y un peu de notre creux.

Au moins [5] vous reconnoîtrez bien de là que j'ai lu la lettre de M. l'Avocat et qu'il ne l'a pas déchirée, comme vous témoignez l'appréhender.

Au reste ne vous allez pas imaginer que je ne vous aurois pas écrit si je n'eusse reçu une lettre de vous, à cause que j'ai passé mardi sans le faire. Ce n'étoit point là du tout mon dessein. Je vous aurois écrit infailliblement aujourd'hui et je l'aurois fait mardi, n'eût été qu'il me fallut passer toute l'après-dînée à l'hôtel de Babylone. Je crois néanmoins que depuis votre lettre écrite vous en aurez déjà reçu une autre de moi. Vous ne devez donc pas vous en plaindre [6]; mais encore bien moins de Mlle Lucrèce. Elle a fait pour vous tout ce qu'elle devoit en bonne justice. Car il ne faut point vous flatter; et je ne suis point traître, comme vous savez. Elle vous a écrit la semaine passée, comme vous lui aviez écrit, une lettre pour une lettre. Elle ne vous en doit point davantage, tant que vous en demeurerez là. Mais il semble que vous vous soyez oublié, et au lieu de lui écrire à elle, et de laisser là tous les autres, vous vous amusez à vous plaindre d'elle dans toutes les lettres que vous écrivez aux autres, et [à [7]] presser tout le monde, afin qu'on lui mette de force le papier à la main et qu'on l'oblige de vous écrire. Je m'attendois bien d'aller ce soir chez elle pour la conjurer de me donner une lettre pour vous; car je supposois que vous lui auriez écrit. Cependant vous n'en avez rien fait; car

---

5. Tout ce passage, depuis : « Au moins vous reconnoîtrez, » jusqu'à : « Avouez, Monsieur, que vous êtes pris (p. 400), » a été omis par Louis Racine et par tous les éditeurs qui sont venus après lui.

6. Racine avait d'abord écrit : « vous plaindre de moi. »

7. Racine a écrit *de* par inadvertance.

je m'en suis enquis à M. l'Avocat. Je n'oserois donc y
aller. En effet, avec quel front lui demanderois-je qu'elle
écrivît à une personne qui ne lui écrit qu'une lettre durant un voyage d'un mois? Voyez-vous? ce procédé
n'est point du tout soutenable, et vous tenez un peu
trop de l'humeur de ce gentilhomme qui, à ce que dit
la reine Marguerite[8], ne se soucioit point de faire des
querelles[9] avec ses maîtresses, parce qu'il s'assuroit sur
ses belles qualités qui le faisoient courir de tout le
monde. Je veux bien qu'on vous coure comme lui,
mais il ne faut pas lasser les gens en les laissant courir
tout seuls : il est de la civilité d'aller au-devant d'eux.
Je vous parle avec chaleur, comme vous voyez, et je
vous fais des remontrances. Mais il y va de mon intérêt, aussi bien et plus encore que du vôtre. Car je ne
subsiste que par vous auprès de Mlle Lucrèce, et je
participerai assurément à vos disgrâces, au lieu qu'il
m'est plus incertain[10] si j'aurai part à votre faveur. Quoi
qu'il en soit, je vous excuse dans le fond[11], et comme les
lettres que vous écrivez à la charmante Parthénice[12] sont

---

8. Marguerite de Valois, reine de Navarre, sœur de François 1er.
— Voici le seul passage de l'*Heptaméron* qui ait quelque rapport,
mais d'un peu loin, avec ce qui était resté dans la mémoire de Racine. Il est dans la *nouvelle* LVIII : « Il n'y avoit gentil-homme en
la cour qui menast plus la guerre aux dames que cestuy-là : et estoit
tant aimé et estimé d'un chacun que l'on n'eust voulu pour rien se
trouver au danger de sa mocquerie. » (Voyez à la page 681, dans
l'édition de Loys Cloquenin. Lyon, 1681, 1 volume in-16.)

9. Nous donnons cette phrase telle qu'elle est dans l'autographe.
Racine n'a pas écrit : « de se faire des querelles. »

10. Il y avait d'abord : « incertain de savoir si...; » *de savoir* a
été biffé.

11. Racine écrit *fonds*.

12. On voit par ce passage que *Parthénice* était le nom poétique
donné à Mlle Lucrèce, ainsi que nous l'avons dit dans la *Notice* sur
les *Stances à Parthénice*, tome IV, p. 44.

des affaires d'importance pour vous, sans doute que vous n'oseriez vous y appliquer si souvent qu'aux autres, pour ne pas contrevenir aux ordres de vos médecins.

D'ailleurs je vois bien que votre Aurore ne vous a pas donné peu d'occupations : vous vous en souvenez trop souvent pour ne me pas faire croire que vous êtes bien avant dans ses belles chaînes. Car quoique je ne sache pas précisément quelles elles sont, je sais assez qu'il n'y en eut jamais de laides. C'est un quolibet que je déguise [13]. Il seroit pourtant à souhaiter que tous les quolibets fussent aussi beaux que celui-là. Il n'y auroit point d'empêchement qui privât les quolibetiers du bénéfice du jubilé [14] : ce que je puis dire des bagateliers, si toutes les bagatelles étoient aussi belles que les vôtres.

Pour revenir à vos amours, avouez, Monsieur, que vous êtes pris, et que vous laisserez bientôt votre pauvre cœur à Bourbon, puisque vous en devez si tôt partir, si vous n'en êtes déjà parti. Je vois bien que ces eaux ont la même force que ces fameuses eaux de Baie : c'est un lac célèbre dans l'Italie, quand il ne le seroit que par les louanges d'Horace et des autres poëtes latins. On y alloit en ce temps-là, et peut-être y va-t-on encore, comme vos semblables vont à Bourbon et à Forges. Ces eaux sont chaudes comme les vôtres, et il y a un auteur qui en rapporte une plaisante raison. Je voudrois, pour votre satisfaction, que cet auteur fût ou vénitien [15] ou espagnol ; mais la destinée a voulu encore que celui-ci

---

13. Le *quolibet*, ou proverbe que Racine a déguisé, doit être celui-ci : « Il n'y a pas de belles prisons ni de laides amours. »

14. « Le 29 (*du mois de mai*) se fit ici (*à Paris*) l'ouverture du jubilé qui a été accordé par Sa Sainteté, pour obtenir l'assistance du ciel en la guerre des princes chrétiens contre les infidèles. » (*Gazette* du 4 juin 1661, p. 532.)

15. *Vénitien* est écrit à la suite d'*italien*, effacé. L'original a, dans les lignes précédentes, diverses autres traces de tâtonnements.

fût latin[16]. Il parle donc du lac de Baie, et voici ce qu'il en dit à peu près[17] :

C'est là qu'avec le dieu d'amour
Vénus se promenoit un jour.

Enfin, se treuvant un peu lasse,
Elle s'assit sur le gazon,
Et voulut aussitôt faire seoir Cupidon;
Mais ce mauvais petit garçon,
Qui ne peut se tenir en place,
Lui répondit : « Çà, Votre Grâce,
Je ne suis point las comme vous. »
Vénus se mettant en courroux,
Lui dit : « Petit fripon, vous aurez sur la joue[18]. »
Il fallut donc qu'il filât doux,
Et vînt s'asseoir à ses genoux.

16. Nous ne croyons pas douteux que Racine n'ait eu en vue Regianus, à qui l'on attribue cette épigramme :

Ante bonam Venerem gelidæ per litora Baiæ.
Illa natare lacus cum lampade jussit Amorem.
Dum natat, algentes cecidit scintilla per undas.
Hinc vapor ussit aquas : quicumque natavit, amavit.

« Avant la bonne Vénus, sur les rives de Baïes les eaux étaient froides. La Déesse ordonna à l'Amour de nager sur le lac en tenant sa torche. Pendant qu'il nage, une étincelle tombe dans les ondes glacées. Depuis lors une chaleur ardente pénétra ces eaux; quiconque y nagea, s'enflamma d'amour. » P. Pithou (*Epigrammata et poematia vetera*, 1 volume in-12, Paris, 1590) a donné l'épigramme sur les eaux de Baïes, à la page 73 de son livre II, comme étant de Regianus; de même Burmann, dans son *Anthologie latine* (tome I, p. 476, épigramme XXVIII du livre III), mais ce dernier avertit, dans une note, que l'auteur est nommé *Regilianus* par Saumaise.

17. Racine avait, comme on va le voir, beaucoup développé les quatre vers du poëte latin. De son imitation très-libre nous n'avons que le commencement, la fin de sa lettre s'étant perdue.

18. Le vers qui devait rimer avec celui-ci a été omis dans l'autographe. Quelques éditeurs ont ajouté avant le vers qui suit :

Tout en faisant un peu la moue.

Cependant tous ses petits frères,
Les Amours qu'on nomme vulgaires,
Peuple qu'on ne sauroit nombrer,
Passoient le temps à folâtrer.

Ce seroit le perdre à crédit, que m'amuser à vous faire le détail de tous leurs jeux et de toutes leurs postures : vous vous imaginez bien quels peuvent être les passe-temps d'une troupe d'enfants qui sont abandonnés à leur caprice.

Vous jugez bien aussi que les Jeux et les Ris,
Dont Vénus fait ses favoris,
Et qui gouvernent son empire,
Ne manquoient pas de jouer et de rire[19].

---

10. — DE RACINE A L'ABBÉ LE VASSEUR.

[1661.]

. . . .
. . . . . . qu'elle[1] ne peut pas faire faire la débauche à des paysans, fussent-ils de l'âge d'or ou de Normandie.

Le plus bel esprit du hameau
Doute si le Duc est un homme.

19. La lettre s'arrête ici dans l'autographe, comme dans le texte qu'en a donné Louis Racine. M. Aimé-Martin l'a continuée à tort par une partie du fragment que nous donnons immédiatement à la suite. Il est clair que le récit poétique commencé par Racine n'est pas achevé, comme nous l'avons fait remarquer déjà, et que la fin de la lettre nous manque. — Au bas d'une des pages de cette lettre, Racine a écrit, comme une sorte de *post-scriptum*, qu'il a enfermé entre parenthèses : « Nous sommes fort bien avec Daphnis. » Sur *Daphnis*, voyez ci-dessus, p. 388, note 3 de la lettre 7.

LETTRE 10 (revue sur l'autographe, conservé à la Bibliothèque impériale). — 1. Il n'en reste que ce fragment, que M. Aimé-Martin a publié le premier, sans lui assigner de date. Comme au verso

Les pyrrhoniens ont fait autrefois ce doute ; et c'étoit leur force d'esprit qui le leur faisoit faire ; mais d'en douter par bêtise, je ne crois pas qu'un homme le puisse jamais faire, si brute qu'il puisse être. Les deux derniers vers font passer ce prêtre plutôt pour un athée qui se pique d'esprit fort que pour un ignorant. Voilà de la matière, si vous voulez exercer votre bel esprit ; car je crois qu'il y a bien à dire que mes sentiments ne soient les vôtres ; et je ne les prends aussi que pour des sentiments erronés, que vous détruirez[2] au moindre souffle dont vous les voudrez attaquer.

J'avois vu[3] l'épitaphe de *la bella Monbazon* dans le *Recueil des poésies choisies*[4], et je vous l'avois même

de l'unique feuillet qui le compose, on lit cette suscription : *A Monsieur, Monsieur l'abbé le Vasseur, à Bourbon*, il n'est pas douteux qu'il ne soit de 1661, et à peu près du même temps que la lettre précédente et que la suivante. La lettre était fermée par deux cachets bruns : J. RAC., et par une soie bleue. — Nous aurions voulu pouvoir, malgré la lacune, expliquer le commencement du fragment. Les deux vers cités auraient pu nous mettre sur la voie; mais nous les avons vainement cherchés dans les poésies de ce temps. Il semble, et c'est tout ce que nous pouvons dire, que les vers critiqués ici par Racine étaient du goût de l'abbé le Vasseur.

2. Racine avait mis d'abord : « que vous me ferez quitter. »

3. M. Aimé-Martin a fait de tout ce qui suit la fin de la lettre précédente. Voyez ci-dessus, p. 402, note 19 de la lettre 9.

4. L'épitaphe dont parle Racine est dans la *quatrième partie* des *Poésies choisies*, publiée en 1658, à Paris, chez Charles Sercy. La voici, telle qu'elle y est donnée à la page 95 :

ÉPITAPHE DE MADAME LA DUCHESSE DE MONTBAZON.

Sotto quel' duro marmo,
Dal' velo mortal' sciolta,
La bella Monbazon giace sepolta.
Le donne festeggin', piangono gli Amori,
E liberi hogghi mai vadano i cuori.

Elle est signée du nom de *l'abbé Butti*. L'éditeur de 1807, dans une note sur cette lettre de Racine, a dit que l'épitaphe de Mme de Montbazon est « un quatrain italien de Regnier Desmarais. » Son dit⁵ par cœur, il y a longtemps, non pas en italien, mais en françois. Et pour le distique du statuaire⁶ (il y a le mot de *pictor* dans le latin), il⁷ mériteroit assurément une bonne place dans le *Recueil des épigrammes*⁸, si on n'y avoit eu plus d'égard aux pointes qu'aux beaux sentiments. Voilà un billet d'une assez belle longueur, ce me semble. Si M. l'Avocat le voyoit, il ne pourroit jamais s'empêcher de se pendre, et la rage qu'il auroit de voir tant de creux le porteroit sans doute à quelque résolution violente. C'est pourquoi je lui veux épargner cette peine, en lui épargnant celle de vous envoyer ma lettre. Aussi bien est-il chez M. de Villers⁹.

erreur a passé dans les notes des éditions qui ont suivi la sienne. Dans les poésies italiennes de Desmarais, on en trouve une qui a pour titre : *Epitaphio di bella dama*. C'est peut-être cette petite pièce (qui d'ailleurs n'est pas un quatrain, mais a douze vers) qu'on aura voulu citer, d'après un souvenir confus.

5. Le mot *épitaphe* était alors employé tantôt au féminin, tantôt au masculin. Voyez le *Lexique*.

6. Ce distique est-il en français? est-il en italien, comme l'épitaphe dont Racine vient de parler ? Nous n'avons pu le trouver. Il paraît qu'il était imité du latin. L'*Anthologie* de Burmann donne, au tome I, p. 696, une épigramme de six vers dans laquelle le poëte s'adresse à un peintre (*pictor*) :

  Pinge, precor, pictor, tali candore puellam, etc.,

et qui finit par ce trait :

  . . . . *miseri suspiria pinge.*

Il pourrait sembler téméraire de supposer que le *distique du statuaire* en fût une imitation.

7. Dans l'original, *il* est au-dessus de *elle*, effacé.

8. Nous ne connaissons de ce temps que l'*Epigrammatum delectus* (1 volume in-12, Paris, chez Savreux, 1659), que l'on devait à Nicole; mais il ne donne que des épigrammes latines.

9. Ce M. de Villers est encore nommé au commencement d'une autre lettre de Racine à le Vasseur (voyez ci-après, p. 502). Ce second passage pourrait donner à penser qu'il était en relation d'affaires avec le duc de Luynes.

11. — DE RACINE A L'ABBÉ LE VASSEUR.

[Juin 1661[1]].

. . . .
. . . cette langue[2] que l'on conserve encore dans la Moscovie. Mais il ne songe pas que j'ai voulu[3] pourvoir à son établissement sur toutes choses, que j'ai fait un beau plan de tout ce qu'il doit faire, et que ses actions étant bien réglées, il lui sera aisé après cela de dire de belles choses. Car M. l'Avocat me le disoit encore ce matin, en me donnant votre lettre : il faut du solide, et un honnête homme ne doit faire le métier de poëte que quand il a fait un bon fondement pour toute sa vie, et qu'il se peut dire honnête homme à juste titre. C'est donc l'avis que j'ai donné à Ovide, ou, pour parler plus humainement (car ce langage sent un peu trop le poëte), j'ai fait, refait et mis enfin dans sa dernière perfection tout mon dessein. J'y ai fait entrer tout ce

LETTRE 11 (revue sur l'autographe, conservé à la Bibliothèque impériale). — 1. Ce fragment de lettre, qui manque dans le recueil de Louis Racine, est naturellement sans date, le commencement n'en ayant pas été conservé ; mais ce qui y est dit des événements qui venaient de se passer à Port-Royal donne la date approximative que nous avons proposée, à l'exemple des précédents éditeurs.

2. Racine travaillait alors à une pièce où il mettait Ovide en scène, et dont les vers étaient à peine commencés. Si nous entendons bien la phrase incomplète par laquelle débute ce fragment, l'idée qu'elle termine est une objection qu'il suppose lui être adressée par le poëte latin lui-même, inquiet de la façon dont le jeune auteur le ferait parler. Ovide demandait sans doute si on n'allait pas mettre dans sa bouche cette langue barbare des Scythes dont il avait horreur, *cette langue que l'on conserve encore dans la Moscovie*. Racine répond, pour le rassurer, qu'il n'a encore donné ses soins qu'au plan de sa comédie, et qu'il tâchera ensuite de ne pas faire parler le héros de sa pièce d'une manière trop indigne de lui.

3. Il y avait d'abord : « que j'ai songé. »

que m'avoit marqué Mlle de Beauch.[4], que j'appelle la seconde Julie d'Ovide, dans la lettre que je lui ai écrite hier par M. Armand, qui va à la cour; et quand vous verrez ce dessein, il vous sera malaisé de le reconnoître. Avec cela, j'ai lu et marqué tous les ouvrages de mon héros, et j'ai commencé même quelques vers. Voilà l'état où en est cette affaire. Au reste, je suis si peu inquiété du temps que j'ai employé pour ce dessein, que je n'y aurois pas plaint encore quinze autres jours. M. Vitart, qui considère cette entreprise du même œil que celle de l'année passée[5], croit que le premier acte est fait pour le moins, et m'accuse d'être réservé avec lui; mais je crois que vous me serez plus juste. Il reçut hier une nouvelle qui lui est bien plus sensible que cette affaire, comme elle le doit être en effet, et comme elle me l'est à moi-même. C'est qu'il a appris que mon cousin son frère[6] est à Hédin, frais et gaillard, portant le mousquet dans cette garnison aussi gaiement que le peut faire la Prairie et la Verdure. Je ne vous en puis mander d'autres particularités, parce que je ne sais cette nouvelle que par M. l'Avocat, qui l'apprit hier de M. Vitart; et vous savez que M. l'Avocat est toujours fort au-dessus des petites circonstances dont nous au-

---

4. Mlle de Beauchâteau, comédienne de l'Hôtel de Bourgogne. L'éditeur de 1807, dans une note sur ce passage, dit que la pièce destinée par Racine à l'Hôtel de Bourgogne était *les Amours d'Ovide*. Peut-être devait-il la connaissance de ce titre à quelqu'une des notes manuscrites de Jean-Baptiste Racine qu'il a eue entre les mains.

5. Ce passage confirmerait, s'il en était besoin, la date de 1660, c'est-à-dire de l'année précédente, que nous avons donnée à la lettre 4, où Racine parle de son *Amasie* (p. 377).

6. Ce frère de Nicolas et d'Antoine Vitart était peut-être Pierre Vitart, dont nous avons trouvé sur les registres de la Ferté-Milon l'acte de baptême en date du 30 juillet 1639.

tres hommes⁷ sommes plus curieux : aussi avons-nous
plus de pente pour le creux et la bagatelle. Je vous en
instruirai plus au long dans ma première lettre, à moins
que M. Vitart ne me prévienne. Je vas dès cette après-
dînée en féliciter Madame sa sainte mère⁸, qui se
croyoit incapable d'aucune joie depuis la perte du saint
père⁹, ou, comme disoit M. de Gomberville¹⁰, de son
futur époux. En effet, il n'est plus dessus le trône
de saint Augustin, et il a évité, par une sage retraite, le
déplaisir de recevoir une lettre de cachet par laquelle on
l'envoyoit à Kimper. Le siége n'a pas été vacant bien
longtemps. La cour, sans avoir consulté le saint Esprit,
à ce qu'ils disent, y a élevé M. Bail¹¹, sous-pénitencier
et ancien confrère du Bailli¹² dans la société des bourses des Cholets¹³. Vous le connoissez sans doute, et

7. Le mot *hommes* est écrit en abrégé (*hões*), dans l'interligne.
8. Racine avait d'abord mis : « Madame notre sainte tante. »
Claude des Moulins, mère de ces Vitart, était sa grand'tante. Voyez
ci-dessus, p. 375, la note 3 de la lettre 3.
9. Les mots « du saint » sont écrits au-dessus de ceux-ci : « de
son cher », que Racine a effacés. — Le *saint père* est Antoine Singlin, supérieur de la maison de Port-Royal, « qui se retira le
8 mai 1661, pour prévenir un ordre de la cour qui l'exiloit en
Bretagne. » (*Histoire générale de Port-Royal*, tome IV, p. 50.) Singlin se retira dans une petite maison du faubourg Saint-Marceau,
qui appartenait à Mme Vitart.
10. Marin le Roy de Gomberville, qui était entré à l'Académie
française au moment de sa formation (1634), fut un des amis de
Port-Royal. Nous ne savons en quelle circonstance il se servit de
l'expression que lui prête Racine. Mais, de sa part, on suppose-
rait difficilement une intention de raillerie contre la pieuse veuve.
11. « M. Bail fut nommé le 14 mai, et présenté le 17 par les
grands vicaires à l'Abbesse. » (*Histoire générale de Port-Royal*,
tome IV, p. 50.)
12. Pierre Sellyer, bailli de Chevreuse, beau-frère de Nicolas
Vitart. Il avait épousé Agnès Vitart, née le 18 septembre 1632, fille
de Mme Vitart (Claude des Moulins).
13. Le collége des Cholets, sur la montagne Sainte-Geneviève.

peut-être est-il de vos amis. Tout le consistoire a fait schisme à la création de ce nouveau pape, et ils se sont retirés de côté et d'autre, ne laissant pas de se gouverner toujours par les monitoires de M. Singlin, qui n'est plus considéré que comme un antipape. *Percutiam pastorem, et dispergentur oves gregis*[14]. Cette prophétie n'a jamais été plus parfaitement accomplie, et de tout ce grand nombre de solitaires à peine reste-t-il M. Guays et maître Maurice [15].

avait été fondé en 1291 par les exécuteurs testamentaires du cardinal Jean Cholet. Il avait eu d'abord seize boursiers, choisis parmi des jeunes gens des diocèses de Beauvais et d'Amiens. Plus tard, le nombre des bourses fut augmenté.

14. Il est remarquable que, dans le récit des mêmes événements, la même citation de l'*Évangile de saint Matthieu*, chapitre xxvi, verset 31, est faite (il n'est pas besoin de dire que c'est dans un tout autre esprit) par Fontaine dans ses *Mémoires* (tome II, p. 196) : « Ils voyoient la vérité de cette parole : *Je frapperai le pasteur, et le troupeau sera dispersé.* »

15. Sur le frère Florent Guais, mort à l'abbaye de Saint-Cyran, le 21 février 1675, voyez le *Nécrologe de Port-Royal*, p. 93. « Il fut, dit M. Sainte-Beuve, plus de vingt ans au service du monastère en qualité de pourvoyeur. C'était lui qui achetait toutes les provisions de la maison.... C'était un des plus humbles et des moins comptés entre tous ces Messieurs, et Racine met une certaine ironie à le nommer comme le seul restant. » (*Port-Royal*, tome VI de l'édition de 1867, p. 97.) — Nous ne trouvons nulle part le nom de Maurice dans les listes des solitaires de Port-Royal. Maître Maurice n'était peut-être pas précisément un des Messieurs, mais quelque ouvrier au service du monastère, ou le cuisinier, ce qui expliquerait le titre de *maître*. — L'éditeur de 1807 fait remarquer justement que « Racine a raconté les mêmes événements sur un ton fort différent de celui-ci dans son *Histoire de Port-Royal*. » Voyez notre tome IV, p. 503-506. On comprend sans peine que Louis Racine n'ait rien donné d'une lettre où les douleurs de Port-Royal étaient traitées si légèrement.

12. — DE RACINE A MARIE RACINE.

[1661¹.]

Ma très-chère soeur,

J'ai manqué jusques ici d'occasion pour vous écrire. En voici Dieu merci une assez belle, par le moyen de mon cousin du Chesne² qui s'en va. Je n'en manquerai pas une de toutes celles qui se présenteront. Mon cousin Vitart doit aller encore bientôt à la Ferté : je lui donnerai aussi une lettre. Plût à Dieu que vous fussiez dans la même disposition que moi, et que vous me voulussiez écrire quand vous le pouvez! Mais on voit bien que vous manquez plus de bonne volonté que d'autre chose. Car je vous ai déjà mandé mon adresse si je m'en souviens, et il est assez aisé de me faire tenir vos lettres. Au moins j'en espérois une de vous tous les mois. Mais je vois bien que vous êtes toujours en colère, et que vous me voulez punir de ce que je n'ai pas été, ce vous semble, assez diligent pour vous voir, tandis que j'étois à la Ferté. Je n'y veux plus retourner de ma vie. Car je n'y ai pas fait encore un voyage qui ne m'ait mis mal avec vous. Et en cela je suis le plus malheureux du monde, puisque c'étoit plus pour vous que j'y allois que pour quelque chose que ce fût.

Mais c'est temps perdu à moi de vous en parler : vous n'oubliez pas si aisément votre colère. Il n'y auroit rien pourtant que je ne fisse pour vous apaiser. Mandez-moi ce qu'il faut faire, et s'il ne faut que vous écrire

---

Lettre 12 (revue sur l'autographe, conservé à Soissons). — 1. Au mois de juillet ou d'août, très-vraisemblablement, et peu de temps avant le départ pour Uzès. Cette date se conclut de ce qui est dit, dans un endroit de la lettre, du prochain accouchement de Mlle Vitart et de la canonisation très-prochaine aussi de M. de Saci. Voyez à la page suivante les notes 7 et 8.
2. Voyez ci-dessus, p. 396, la note 21 de la lettre 8.

tous les huit jours, et faire un serment que quand j'irai à la Ferté, ce qui ne sera de longtemps, je ne bougerai d'avec vous, je ferai tout cela du meilleur cœur du monde.

Je vous écris même avec du papier doré, tout exprès, afin que cela puisse³ faire ma paix ou aider à la faire. Pour vous, quand vous me devriez écrire du plus gros papier qui se vende chez M. de la Mare⁴, je le recevrai aussi bien que si la lettre étoit écrite en lettres dorées.

Ma mère⁵ s'est trouvée mal, et ne se porte pas encore fort bien. Vous passez ce temps-là plus à votre aise que moi. Quand vous m'écrirez, si vous le faites, mandez-moi comment je suis dans l'esprit de mon grand-père⁶, et si ce voyage-ci ne m'aura point nui autant que l'autre. Mlle Vitart accouchera bientôt⁷, et on canonisera bientôt M. de Sacy⁸. Je souhaite que vous vous

3. Racine avait mis d'abord : « afin que si cela pouvoit.... »

4. Ce M. de la Mare était sans doute un parent de Racine. Claude Sconin, fille de Pierre Sconin et de Claude Joly, par conséquent sœur consanguine de la mère de Racine, avait épousé un Jean de la Mare.

5. Sa grand'mère, Marie des Moulins. Voyez, p. 372, la note 6 de la lettre 1.

6. Pierre Sconin.

7. Mlle Vitart (Marguerite le Mazier, femme de Nicolas Vitart, eut, en 1661, un enfant, Anne-Charlotte, qui fut baptisée le 23 août. Ce que Racine dit ensuite de M. de Saci ne nous paraitrait pas s'expliquer, si l'on entendait qu'il s'agit de l'accouchement de l'année précédente, c'est-à-dire de la naissance de Marie-Charlotte Vitart, qui avait été baptisée le 17 mai 1660.

8. Antoine de Saci, avocat au Parlement, avait épousé Nicole-Madeleine Vitart, sœur, comme Mme Sellyer, de Nicolas Vitart. Il mourut, fort jeune encore, le 18 août 1661, ainsi que nous l'apprennent les *Mémoires* de Fontaine, dans sa petite maison du faubourg Saint-Marceau, où était alors réfugié M. Singlin (voyez ci-dessus, p. 407, la note 9 de la lettre 11). Racine a dû écrire cette lettre peu de temps avant la mort de M. de Saci, dont on vantait la sainteté, et lorsque sa maladie faisait prévoir sa fin prochaine. L'accouche-

divertissiez très-bien avec mon cousin du Chesne. Il a bonne intention de le faire. Je ne ferai pas cette lettre plus longue, afin de garder de quoi en faire bientôt une autre. Mais, au nom de Dieu, écrivez-moi, et adressez votre lettre à moi-même, à l'Image Saint-Louis, près de Sainte-Geneviève[9]. Je vous le répète encore, afin que vous n'ayez point d'excuse. Je vous promets une entière exactitude de mon côté. Adieu : je vous donne le bonsoir ; je puis bien vous le donner, car j'entends minuit qui sonne. Adieu donc, ma chère sœur, et pardonnez-moi toutes mes négligences, vous assurant que je serai à vous[10] toute ma vie.

RACINE.

Je vous manderai tout ce que je ferai. Ne croyez rien de moi que je ne vous le mande.

Suscription : A Madame Madame Marie Racine, à la Ferté-Milon.

ment de Mlle Vitart et la mort d'Antoine de Saci ayant eu lieu à peu de jours de distance, notre interprétation de ce passage est, nous le croyons, très-vraisemblable.

9. Dans la *Notice biographique*, p. 23, nous avons dit que Racine demeurait à l'Image Saint-Louis au commencement de 1660 ; et un peu avant (note 2 de la page 22), nous avions expliqué pour quelle raison nous assignions cette date à la lettre dont nous nous occupons ici. D'après la conjecture mieux établie que nous avons proposée dans la note précédente pour justifier la date de 1661, ces deux passages sont à corriger. — Racine, dans sa lettre à la Fontaine du 11 novembre 1661 (voyez ci-après, p. 413), rappelle le temps où il avait demeuré dans le quartier Sainte-Geneviève.

10. Racine avait commencé par écrire : « que je vous serai. »

13. — DE RACINE A LA FONTAINE.

A Usez, ce 11. novembre 1661[1].

J'AI bien vu du pays, et j'ai bien voyagé,
Depuis que de vos yeux les miens prirent congé.

Mais tout cela ne m'a pas empêché de songer toujours autant à vous que je faisois, lorsque nous nous voyions[2] tous les jours,

Avant qu'une fièvre importune
Nous fît courir même fortune,
Et nous mît chacun en danger
De ne plus jamais voyager.

Je ne sais pas sous quelle constellation je vous écris présentement ; mais je vous assure que je n'ai point fait encore tant de vers depuis ma maladie. Je croyois même en avoir tout à fait oublié le métier. Seroit-il possible que les Muses eussent plus d'empire en ce pays, que sur les rives de la Seine? Nous le reconnoîtrons dans la suite. Cependant je commencerai à vous dire en prose que mon voyage a été plus heureux que je ne pensois. Nous n'avons eu que deux heures de pluie depuis Paris jusqu'à Lyon. Notre compagnie étoit gaie, et assez plaisante : il y avoit trois huguenots, un Anglois, deux Italiens, un conseiller du Châtelet, deux secrétaires du Roi

---

LETTRE 13. — 1. Cette lettre a été publiée pour la première fois au tome III (p. 322-326) des *OEuvres diverses de M. de la Fontaine, de l'Académie françoise* (à Paris, chez Didot, M.DCC.XXIX), 3 volumes in-8º, dont l'éditeur est l'abbé d'Olivet. Nous avons suivi avec plus de fidélité que nos devanciers le texte de cette édition, que Louis Racine a désignée inexactement sous le titre d'*OEuvres posthumes*. — Sur le départ de Racine pour Uzès, voyez la *Notice biographique*, p. 41-43.

2. Dans l'édition de 1729, comme sans doute aussi dans l'original : *voyons*, sans *i*.

et deux de ses mousquetaires ; enfin, nous étions au nombre de neuf ou dix. Je ne manquois pas tous les soirs de prendre le galop devant les autres, pour aller retenir mon lit ; car j'avois fort bien retenu cela de M. Botreau, et je lui en suis infiniment obligé : ainsi j'ai toujours été bien couché, et quand je suis arrivé à Lyon, je ne me suis senti non plus fatigué que si du quartier de Sainte-Geneviève j'avois été à celui de la rue Galande[3].

A Lyon je ne suis resté que deux jours avec deux mousquetaires de notre troupe, qui étoient du Pont-Saint-Esprit. Nous nous embarquâmes, il y a aujourd'hui huit jours, dans un vaisseau tout neuf et bien couvert, que nous avions retenu exprès avec le meilleur patron du pays ; car il n'y a pas trop de sûreté de se mettre sur le Rhône qu'à bonnes enseignes ; néanmoins comme il n'avoit point plu du tout devers Lyon, le Rhône étoit fort bas, et avoit perdu beaucoup de sa rapidité ordinaire.

> On pouvoit, sans difficulté,
> Voir ses nayades toutes nues,
> Et qui, honteuses d'être vues,
> Pour mieux cacher leur nudité,
> Cherchoient des places inconnues.
> Ces nymphes sont de gros rochers,
> Auteurs de mainte sépulture,
> Et dont l'effroyable figure
> Fait changer de visage aux plus hardis nochers.

Nous fûmes deux jours sur le Rhône, et nous couchâmes à Vienne et à Valence. J'avois commencé dès Lyon à ne plus guère entendre le langage du pays, et à n'être

---

3. Dans la lettre précédente, adressée à Marie Racine, on a vu que Racine, en 1661, demeurait près de Sainte-Geneviève, à l'Image Saint-Louis. Son ami le Vasseur avait son logement rue Galande, chez Mlle de la Croix. La Fontaine sans doute connaissait bien l'une et l'autre maison, où il allait voir les deux jeunes amis.

plus intelligible moi-même. Ce malheur s'accrut à Valence, et Dieu voulut qu'ayant demandé à une servante un pot de chambre, elle mit un réchaud sous mon lit. Vous pouvez vous imaginer les suites de cette maudite aventure, et ce qui peut arriver à un homme endormi qui se sert d'un réchaud dans ses nécessités de nuit. Mais c'est encore bien pis en ce pays. Je vous jure que j'ai autant besoin d'interprète, qu'un Moscovite en auroit besoin dans Paris. Néanmoins je commence à m'apercevoir que c'est un langage mêlé d'espagnol et d'italien; et comme j'entends assez bien ces deux langues, j'y ai quelquefois recours pour entendre les autres, et pour me faire entendre. Mais il arrive souvent que j'y perds toutes mes mesures, comme il arriva hier, qu'ayant besoin de petits clous à broquette pour ajuster ma chambre, j'envoyai le valet de mon oncle en ville, et lui dis de m'acheter deux ou trois cents de broquettes : il m'apporta incontinent trois bottes d'allumettes [4]. Jugez s'il y a sujet d'enrager en de semblables malentendus. Cela iroit à l'infini si je voulois vous dire tous les inconvénients qui arrivent aux nouveaux venus en ce pays comme moi. Au reste, pour la situation d'Usez, vous saurez qu'elle est sur une montagne fort haute, et cette montagne n'est qu'un rocher continuel : si bien qu'en quelque temps qu'il fasse, on peut aller à pied sec tout autour de la ville. Les campagnes qui l'environnent sont toutes couvertes d'oliviers, qui portent les plus belles olives du monde, mais bien trompeuses pourtant; car j'y ai été attrapé moi-même. Je voulus en cueillir quelques-unes au

---

4. Dans le *Dictionnaire languedocien-françois*, par M. L. D. S. (Lacroix de Sauvages), imprimé à Nimes en 1785, on trouve le mot *broukéto*, traduit par *allumettes*, ce qui explique l'erreur du valet. Le même *Dictionnaire* donne le mot *broucó*, signifiant *broquette*, *petite espèce de clous*.

premier olivier que je rencontrai, et je les mis dans ma
bouche avec le plus grand appétit qu'on puisse avoir;
mais Dieu me préserve de sentir jamais une amertume
pareille à celle que je sentis. J'en eus la bouche toute
perdue plus de quatre heures durant, et l'on m'a appris
depuis qu'il falloit bien des lessives et des cérémonies
pour rendre les olives douces comme on les mange.
L'huile qu'on en tire sert ici de beurre, et j'appréhendois bien ce changement; mais j'en ai goûté aujourd'hui
dans les sauces⁵, et sans mentir il n'y a rien de meilleur.
On sent bien moins l'huile qu'on ne sentiroit le meilleur
beurre de France. Mais c'est assez vous parler d'huile,
et vous me pourrez reprocher, plus justement qu'on ne
faisoit à un ancien orateur, que mes ouvrages sentent
trop l'huile⁶. Il faut vous entretenir d'autres choses, ou
plutôt remettre cela à un autre voyage pour ne vous pas
ennuyer. Je ne me saurois empêcher pourtant de vous
dire un mot des beautés de cette province. On m'en
avoit dit beaucoup de bien à Paris; mais sans mentir on
ne m'en avoit encore rien dit au prix de ce qui en est, et
pour le nombre et pour leur excellence. Il n'y a pas une
villageoise, pas une savetière qui ne disputât de beauté
avec les Fouillous et les Menevilles⁷. Si le pays de soi
avoit un peu plus de délicatesse, et que les rochers y
fussent un peu moins fréquents, on le prendroit pour

---

5. Dans l'édition de 1729, comme dans l'autographe probablement : *sausses*.

6. C'était le reproche que l'orateur Pythéas faisait à Démosthène. Voyez le traité de Plutarque intitulé *Préceptes d'administration publique*, chapitre vi.

7. Mlle du Fouilloux (Bénigne de Meaux), qui épousa le marquis d'Alluye au mois d'octobre 1661, et Mlle de Meneville, étoient toutes deux filles d'honneur de la Reine. Elles figurèrent l'une et l'autre dans le *Ballet des Saisons*, donné à Fontainebleau en 1661. Leur beauté était célèbre.

un vrai pays de Cythère. Toutes les femmes y sont éclatantes, et s'y ajustent d'une façon qui leur est la plus naturelle du monde; et pour ce qui est de leur personne,

Color verus, corpus solidum et succi plenum[8].

Mais comme c'est la première chose dont on m'a dit de me donner de garde, je ne veux pas en parler davantage : aussi bien ce seroit profaner une maison de bénéficier comme celle où je suis, que d'y faire de longs discours sur cette matière. *Domus mea domus orationis*[9]. C'est pourquoi vous devez vous attendre que je ne vous en parlerai plus du tout. On m'a dit : « Soyez aveugle. » Si je ne le puis être tout à fait, il faut du moins que je sois muet ; car, voyez-vous? il faut être régulier avec les réguliers, comme j'ai été loup avec vous et avec les autres loups vos compères. *Adiousias*.

RACINE.

14. — DE RACINE A M. VITART.

A Usez, ce 15. nov. [1661].

Il y a aujourd'hui huit jours que je partis du Pont-Saint-Esprit, et que je vins à Usez, où je fus reçu de mon oncle[1] avec toute sorte d'amitié. Il ne m'attendoit que deux jours après, parce que mon oncle Sconin[2] lui avoit mandé que je partirois plus tard que je n'ai fait.

---

8. « Un teint naturel, un embonpoint ferme et dru. »
(Térence, *Eunuque*, acte II, scène IV, vers 318.)

9. « Ma maison est une maison de prière. » (*Isaïe*, chapitre LVI, verset 7; *saint Luc*, chapitre XIX, verset 46.)

LETTRE 14 (revue sur l'autographe, conservé à la Bibliothèque impériale). — 1. Le R. P. Antoine Sconin, vicaire général à Uzès. Voyez la *Notice biographique*, p. 41.

2. Pierre Sconin, frère du vicaire général. Voyez ci-dessus, p. 376, la note 5 de la lettre 3.

Sans cela il eût envoyé au Saint-Esprit son garçon et son cheval. Il m'a donné une chambre tout auprès de lui, et il prétend que je le soulagerai un peu dans le grand nombre de ses affaires; car je vous assure qu'il en a beaucoup. Non-seulement il fait toutes celles du diocèse, mais il a même l'administration de tous les revenus du chapitre, jusqu'à ce qu'il ait payé quatre-vingt mille livres de dettes où le chapitre s'est engagé. Il a pris pour cela un terme de six ans. Il s'y entend tout à fait, et il n'y a point de dom Cosme[3] en son affaire. Avec tout cet embarras, il a encore celui de faire bâtir ; car il fait achever une fort jolie maison qu'il a commencée, il y a un an ou deux, à un bénéfice qui est à lui, à une demi-lieue d'Usez. J'en reviens encore tout présentement. Elle est toute faite déjà; il n'y a plus que le jardin à défricher. C'est la plus régulière et même la plus agréable de tout Usez. Elle est tantôt toute meublée. Mais il lui en a coûté de l'argent pour la mettre en cet état : c'est pourquoi il ne faut pas demander à quoi il a employé ses revenus. Il est fort fâché de ce que je n'ai point apporté de démissoire[4]; mais c'est la faute de M. Sconin[5]. Je l'ai pressé le plus que j'ai pu pour cela, et lui-même lui en écrit, mais j'appréhende furieusement sa longueur.

Il m'auroit déjà mené à Avignon pour y prendre la tonsure; et la raison de cela est que le premier bénéfice

---

3. Dom Cosme, qui, selon l'éditeur de 1807, était un religieux bénédictin, est un des frères d'Antoine Sconin : c'est ce que dit expressément Racine dans sa *Lettre à M. Vitart*, du 16 mai 1662. Voyez, sur ce dom Cosme, la *Notice biographique*, p. 45 et 46.

4. Un *démissoire*, ou, forme plus ordinaire et plus correcte, *dimissoire*, est une lettre par laquelle un évêque consent qu'un de ses diocésains soit consacré par un autre évêque.

5. Ce M. Sconin paraît être le même que Racine désigne plus haut sous le nom de dom Cosme.

qui viendra à vaquer dans le chapitre est à sa nomination. L'Évêque[6] a nommé, et le Prévôt aussi; c'est maintenant son tour. Quand ce temps-là viendra, je vous en manderai des nouvelles. Cependant si vous pouviez me faire avoir un démissoire, vous m'obligeriez infiniment. Monsieur le prieur de la Ferté vous donnera aisément mon extrait baptistère, et vous n'auriez qu'à l'envoyer à quelqu'un de votre connoissance à Soissons : on auroit le démissoire aussitôt. Mais ce sera quand vous y pourrez songer sans vous détourner le moins du monde. Au reste, nous ne laisserons pas d'aller à Avignon quelqu'un de ces jours; car mon oncle veut m'acheter des livres, et il veut que j'étudie. Je ne demande pas mieux, et je vous assure que je n'ai pas eu encore la curiosité de voir la ville d'Usez, ni quelque personne que ce soit. Il est bien aise que j'apprenne un peu de théologie dans saint Thomas, et j'en suis tombé d'accord fort volontiers. Enfin, je m'accorde le plus aisément du monde à tout ce qu'il veut. Il est d'un naturel fort doux, et il me témoigne toutes les tendresses possibles. Il reconnoît bien que son affaire d'Anjou a été fort mal conduite, mais il espère que Monsieur d'Usez raccommodera tout. En effet, il lui a mandé qu'il le feroit. Il me demande tous les jours mon *ode* de la paix[7], car il a donné à Monsieur l'Évêque celle que je lui envoyai ; et non-seulement lui, mais même tous les chanoines m'en demandent, et le Prévôt surtout. Ce prévôt[8] est le doyen du chapitre ; il est âgé de 75 ans, et le plus honnête homme du monde.

---

6. L'évêque d'Uzès était Jacques Adhémar de Grignan, oncle du gendre de Mme de Sévigné. Voyez la *Notice biographique*, p. 41.
7. L'*ode* de *la Nymphe de la Seine :* voyez ci-dessus, p. 377-379.
8. Thomas Thiboult, qui fut prévôt du chapitre d'Uzès de 1658 à 1666. Il avait été chanoine de Saint-Lô. Voyez le *Gallia christiana*, tome VI, p. 652.

Enfin c'est le seul que mon oncle m'a bien recommandé d'aller voir : ils sont grands amis. Son bénéfice vaut cinq mille livres de rente ; il est des anciens, et il n'est pas réformé. Il a beaucoup d'esprit et d'étude. Ainsi, si vous avez encore quelque ode, je vous prie d'en faire bien couper toutes les marges, et de me l'envoyer ; j'avois négligé d'en apporter. On me fait ici force[9] caresses à cause de mon oncle. Il n'y a pas un curé ni un maître d'école qui ne m'ait fait le compliment gaillard, auquel je ne saurois répondre que par des révérences, car je n'entends pas le françois de ce pays, et on n'entend pas le mien : ainsi je tire le pied fort humblement ; et je dis, quand tout est fait : *Adiousias*. Je suis marri de ne les point entendre pourtant ; car si je continue davantage à ne leur pouvoir répondre, j'aurai bientôt la réputation d'un incivil ou d'un homme non lettré. Et je suis perdu si cela est ; car en ce pays les civilités et les cérémonies sont encore plus en usage qu'en Italie. Je suis épouvanté tous les jours de voir des villageois, pied-nus[10] ou ensabotés (ce mot doit bien passer, puisque *encapuchonné* a passé), qui font des révérences comme s'ils avoient appris à danser toute leur vie. Outre cela, ils causent des mieux, et pour moi j'espère que l'air du pays me va raffiner de moitié, pour peu que j'y demeure ; car je vous assure qu'on y est fin et délié plus qu'en aucun lieu du monde. Pour les jours, ils y sont les plus beaux du monde. Tous les arbres sont encore aussi verts qu'au mois de juin, et aujourd'hui que je suis sorti à la campagne, je vous proteste que la chaleur m'a tout à fait incommodé : jugez ce que ce peut être en été. Je n'ai plus de papier que pour assurer Mlle Vitart de mes

9. Il y a dans l'original *forces*, au pluriel : voyez p. 102, note 1.

10. Dans l'autographe : *piednus*, en un seul mot.

très-humbles respects, et [pour[11]] souhaiter à vos deux infantes[12] tout ce que les poëtes s'en vont prédire de bien au Dauphin[13].

J'oubliois à vous prier[14] d'adresser mes lettres à M. Symil, chirurgien à Usez, et, au dedans, à mon illustre personne chez le R. P. Sconin, vicaire général et official de Monseigneur d'Usez. Je salue M. d'Houÿ de tout mon cœur, et le prie d'avoir quelque peu de soin de mes livres, dont je plains fort la destinée s'il ne s'en mêle un peu; car je serois honteux de vous en parler dans la multitude de vos affaires. Excusez même si j'ai fait cette lettre longue. J'ai cru qu'il falloit vous instruire une fois en gros de tout ce qui se passe ici; une autre fois j'abuserai moins de votre loisir.

15. — DE RACINE A L'ABBÉ LE VASSEUR.

[Usez, novembre 1661.]

.... Si[1] vous prenez la peine de m'écrire, je vous prie, ou de donner vos lettres à M. Vitart, ou de me les

11. Racine, par mégarde, a écrit *de*, au lieu de *pour*.
12. Marie-Charlotte et Anne-Charlotte Vitart. Voyez ci-dessus, p. 410, la note 7 de la lettre 12.
13. Né le 1er novembre 1661.
14. Racine avait d'abord mis *dire*, qu'il a ensuite remplacé par *prier*.
LETTRE 15 (revue sur l'autographe, conservé à la Bibliothèque impériale). — 1. Le commencement de cette lettre manque, et par conséquent la date. M. Aimé-Martin l'a datée d'Uzès, le 15 novembre 1661, comme la précédente. Il est probable qu'elle a été en effet écrite ce jour-là, ou le lundi 14; car Racine faisait souvent ses lettres la veille du courrier. Le *Te Deum*, dont il est parlé dans la lettre, avait été chanté évidemment avant le 18 (probablement le dimanche 13 novembre), comme on doit le conclure d'un passage de l'article que Racine envoya à la *Gazette*, et que nous donnons plus loin, p. 430, dans la dernière note de la lettre 17.

adresser chez le P. Sconin, vicaire général, et official de Monsieur d'Usez, avec une enveloppe adressante à M. Symil, chirurgien à Usez. On m'a dit d'user de ces précautions pour la sûreté des lettres qu'on m'envoyera de Paris. Je vous prie de me mander des nouvelles de nos anciennes connoissances, et de m'instruire un peu de ce qui se passe de beau dans Paris; et moi je prendrai le soin de vous mander ce qui se passera de beau dans le Languedoc. Nous savons la naissance du Dauphin : c'est pourquoi je vous exempte de me l'apprendre. J'aurois peut-être chanté quelque chose de nouveau sur cette matière si j'eusse été à Paris; mais ici je n'ai pu chanter² rien que le *Te Deum*, qu'on chanta hier ici en grande cérémonie. Mandez-moi, s'il vous plaît, qui aura le mieux réussi de tous les chantres du Parnasse. Je ne doute pas qu'ils n'emploient tout le crédit qu'ils ont auprès des Muses, pour en recevoir de belles et magnifiques inspirations. Surtout si elles continuent à vous favoriser, comme elles avoient commencé à Bourbon, faites quelque chose, et envoyez-moi tout ce que vous aurez fait.

Incipe, si quid habes : et te fecere poetam
*Pierides*³.

Suscription : A Monsieur Monsieur l'abbé le Vasseur, à Paris. (Deux cachets rouges : J. RAC., avec une soie jaune.)

---

2. Racine avait commencé par mettre : « je n'ai pu faire autre chose. »

3. « Commence, si tu sais quelque chose; toi aussi, les Muses t'ont fait poëte. » (Virgile, *églogue* IX, vers 32 et 33.) — Dans le premier de ces vers, Racine a substitué *te* à *me*.

16. — DE RACINE A L'ABBÉ LE VASSEUR.

A Usez, ce 24ᵈᵐᵉ novembre [1661].

Je ne me plains pas encore de vous; car je crois bien que c'est tout au plus si vous avez maintenant reçu ma première lettre; mais je ne vous réponds pas que dans huit jours je ne commence à gronder si je ne reçois point de vos nouvelles. Épargnez-moi donc cette peine, je vous supplie, et épargnez-vous à vous-même de grosses injures, que je pourrois bien vous dire dans ma mauvaise humeur :

Nam contemptus amor vires habet[1].

Je vous aurois écrit mardi passé par l'ordinaire, n'étoit que j'étois allé faire un tour à Nîmes : ainsi je me sers aujourd'hui de l'extraordinaire, qui part les vendredis. Mais puisque j'ai commencé à vous parler de ce voyage, il faut que je vous en entretienne un peu. Nîmes est à trois lieues d'ici, c'est-à-dire à sept ou huit bonnes lieues de France. Le chemin est plus diabolique mille fois que celui des diables à Nevers, et la rue d'Enfer, et tels autres chemins réprouvés; mais la ville est assurément aussi belle et aussi *polide*, comme on dit ici, qu'il y en ait dans le royaume. Il n'y a point de divertissements qui ne s'y treuvent :

Suoni, canti, vestir, giuochi, vivande,
Quanto può cor pensar, può chieder bocca[2].

LETTRE 16 (revue sur l'autographe, conservé à la Bibliothèque impériale). — 1. « Car l'amour méprisé est fort. » (Pétrone, *Satyricon*, chapitre CVIII, vers la fin.) — Au commencement du vers Racine a substitué *nam* à *sed*, qui est dans le texte de Pétrone.

2. « De la musique, des chants, des parures, des jeux, des festins, autant que l'esprit en peut imaginer, la bouche en demander. » (*Orlando furioso*, chant IV, stance XXXII.)

On m'avoit dit tout cela devant que j'y allasse, mais je n'en voulois rien croire. Vous ne voudrez pas m'en croire aussi. Cependant je n'en dis pas la moitié de ce qu'on en pourroit dire. J'y allois pour voir le feu de joie³ qu'un homme de ma connoissance avoit entrepris. Il en a coûté deux mille francs à la ville. Il étoit fort beau sans doute. Les jésuites avoient fourni les devises, qui ne valoient rien du tout : ôtez cela, tout alloit⁴ bien. Mais je n'y pris pas assez bien garde pour vous en faire le détail ; j'étois détourné par d'autres spectacles : il y avoit tout autour de moi des visages qu'on voyoit à la lueur des fusées, et dont vous auriez bien eu autant de peine à vous défendre, que j'en avois. Il n'y en avoit pas une à qui vous n'eussiez bien voulu dire ce compliment d'un galand du temps de Néron : *Ne fastidias hominem peregrinum inter cultores tuos admittere: invenies religiosum, si te adorari permiseris*⁵. Mais pour moi, je n'avois garde d'y penser ; je ne les regardois pas même en sûreté ; j'étois en la compagnie d'un R. Père de ce chapitre, qui n'aimoit pas trop à rire :

E parea, più ch' alcun fosse mai stato,
*Di coscienza scrupulosa e schiva*⁶.

3. « *De Nîmes....* 8 décembre 1661. — Le chapitre de notre cathédrale s'étant dignement acquitté de son devoir, en l'absence de notre évêque, par les grâces solennelles qu'il a rendues pour l'heureuse naissance de Monseigneur le Dauphin, nos consuls et habitants de l'une et l'autre religion en firent pareillement, le 22 du passé, des feux, qui furent accompagnés de concerts, de festins, et de toutes les marques d'une extraordinaire réjouissance. » (*Gazette* du 17 décembre 1661, p. 1323.)

4. Racine avait d'abord écrit : *tout étoit ;* et, deux lignes p us loin : *attaché*, au lieu de *détourné*.

5. « Ne dédaignez pas de recevoir un étranger parmi ceux qui vous rendent un culte : vous le trouverez plein de ferveur, si vous voulez bien vous laisser adorer. » (Pétrone, *Satyricon*, chapitre cxxvii.)

6. « Et il sembloit être, plus que personne ne le fut jamais,

Quoi qu'il en soit, il falloit être sage avec lui, ou du moins le faire. Voilà ce que vous auriez treuvé de beau dans Nîmes; mais j'y treuvai encore d'autres choses qui me plurent fort, surtout les Arènes. Vous en avez sans doute ouï parler. C'est un grand amphithéâtre, un peu en ovale, tout bâti de prodigieuses pierres, longues de deux toises, qui se tiennent là, depuis plus de seize cents ans, sans mortier et par leur seule pesanteur. Il est tout ouvert en dehors par de grandes arcades, et en dedans ce ne sont tout autour que de grands siéges de pierre, où tout le peuple s'asseyoit pour voir les combats des bêtes et des gladiateurs. Mais c'est assez vous parler de Nîmes et de ses raretés : peut-être même trouverez-vous que j'en ai trop dit. Mais de quoi voulez-vous que je vous entretienne? Il ne se passe rien en ce pays qui mérite qu'on le mande de si loin. Car de vous dire qu'il y fait le plus beau temps du monde et qu'il n'a fait ni froid ni pluie depuis que j'y suis, vous ne vous en mettez guère en peine. De vous dire tout de même qu'on doit cette semaine créer des consuls ou des *conses*, comme on dit, cela vous touche fort peu. Cependant c'est une belle chose de voir le compère cardeur et le menuisier gaillard avec la robe rouge, comme un président, donner des arrêts et aller les premiers à l'offrande. Vous ne voyez pas cela à Paris. A propos de consuls, il faut que je vous parle d'un échevin[7] de Lyon, qui doit l'emporter sur les plus fameux quolibetiers du monde. Je l'allai voir[8] avec un autre de notre troupe, quand nous voulûmes sortir de Lyon, pour avoir un billet de sortie pour notre bateau; car sans billet les chaînes du Rhône ne se lèvent point.

---

d'une conscience scrupuleuse et sévère. » (*Orlando furioso*, chant II, stance XIII.)

7. Avant *échevin*, il y a *grand*, effacé.
8. Racine avait d'abord écrit : « Je fus le voir. »

Il nous fit nos dépêches fort gravement, et après, quittant un peu de cette gravité magistrale qu'on doit garder en donnant de telles ordonnances, il nous demanda :
« *Quid novi*⁹? Que dit-on de l'affaire d'Angleterre¹⁰? »
Nous lui dîmes qu'on ne savoit pas encore à quoi le Roi se résoudroit. « Le Roi, dit-il, fera la guerre assurément ; car il n'est pas parent du P. Souffren¹¹. » Nous lui fîmes lors la révérence et je fis bien paroître¹² que je ne l'étois pas non plus; car je le regardai avec un froid qui montroit bien la rage où j'étois de voir un si grand quolibetier impuni. Je n'ai pas voulu en enrager tout seul ; j'ai voulu que vous me tinssiez compagnie, et c'est pourquoi je vous fais part de cette marauderie. Enragez donc, et si vous ne trouvez point de termes assez forts pour faire des imprécations, dites avec l'emphasiste Brébeuf :

A qui, Dieux tout-puissants, qui gouvernez la terre,
A qui réservez-vous les éclats du tonnerre¹³?

Si vous ne vous hâtez de m'écrire, je vous ferai enrager tous les voyages par de semblables nouvelles. Écrivez-moi donc si vous m'en croyez, et faites¹⁴ de ma part à Mlle Lucrèce le compliment latin dont je vous ai parlé, mais que ce soit en beau françois.

9. « Quoi de nouveau? »
10. Cette affaire d'Angleterre est l'insulte faite le 10 octobre 1661 par le baron de Batteville, ambassadeur d'Espagne, au comte d'Estrades, ambassadeur de France, à l'occasion de l'entrée à Londres de l'ambassadeur de Suède. Voyez à la page 364, note 3, de notre tome IV.
11. Louis Racine et les éditeurs venus après lui ont corrigé *Souffren* en *Souffrant*. — Le P. Suffren, jésuite, mort en 1641, avait été confesseur de Louis XIII. On prononçait son nom *Souffrant* : de là le *quolibet*.
12. Racine écrit *parestre* ; d'autres fois *paroître*.
13. *La Pharsale*, chant VII, vers 713 et 714.
14. *Faites* est écrit au-dessus de *dites*, effacé.

Suscription : A Monsieur, Monsieur l'abbé le Vasseur, à Paris. (Deux cachets rouges : J. RAC., avec une soie jaune.)

17. — DE RACINE A L'ABBÉ LE VASSEUR.

A Usez, le 26ème décembre 1661.

Dieu merci, voici une de vos lettres. Que vous en êtes devenu grand ménager ! J'ai vu que vous étiez plus libéral, et il ne se passoit guère de semaines, lorsque vous étiez à Bourbon, que vous ne m'écrivissiez une fois ou deux, et non-seulement à moi, mais à des gens mêmes à qui vous n'aviez presque jamais parlé, tant les lettres vous coûtoient peu. Maintenant elles sont plus clair-semées, et c'est beaucoup d'en recevoir une en deux mois. J'étois le plus en peine du monde d'où pouvoit venir ce changement. Je croyois que vous étiez retombé malade, ou du moins que vous nous aviez cassés aux gages. J'enrageois de voir qu'une si belle amitié se fût ainsi évanouie pour n'avoir été que deux mois hors de Paris. *En dextra fidesque*[1] ! m'écriois-je, *e 'l cor pien di sospir' parea un Mongibello*[2], lorsque heureusement votre lettre m'est venue tirer de toutes ces inquiétudes, et m'a appris que la raison pourquoi vous ne m'écriviez pas, c'est que mes lettres étoient trop belles. Qu'à cela ne tienne, Monsieur : il me sera fort aisé d'y remédier ; et il m'est si

---

Lettre 17 (revue sur l'autographe, conservé à la Bibliothèque impériale). — 1. « Voilà donc la foi promise ! » (Virgile, *Énéide*, livre IV, vers 597.)

2. « Et le cœur plein de soupirs paroissoit un Etna, un volcan. » Cette phrase italienne est sans doute une réminiscence de ce passage de l'Arioste (*Orlando furioso*, chant I, stance XL) :

Sospirando piangea, tal ch' un ruscello
Parean le guance, e 'l petto un Mongibello.

naturel de faire de méchantes lettres, que j'espère, avec 1661 la grâce de Dieu, venir bientôt à bout de n'en faire pas de trop belles. Vous n'aurez pas sujet de vous plaindre à l'avenir, et j'attends dès à présent des réponses par tous les ordinaires. Mais parlons plus sérieusement. Avouez que tout au contraire vous croyez les vôtres trop belles pour être si facilement communiquées à de pauvres provinciaux comme nous. Vous avez raison, sans doute, et c'est ce qui me fâche le plus ; car il ne vous est pas aisé, comme à moi, de faire de mauvaises lettres, et ainsi je suis fort en danger de n'en guère recevoir. Après tout, si vous saviez la manière dont je les reçois, vous verriez qu'elles ne sont pas profanées pour tomber entre mes mains ; car, outre que je les reçois avec toute la vénération que méritent les belles choses, c'est qu'elles ne me demeurent pas longtemps, et elles ont le vice dont vous accusez les miennes injustement, qui est de courir un peu trop les rues, et vous diriez qu'en venant en Languedoc elles se veulent accommoder à l'air du pays. Elles se communiquent à tout le monde, et ne craignent point la médisance : aussi savent-elles bien qu'elles en sont [à] couvert ; chacun les veut voir, et on ne les lit pas tant pour apprendre des nouvelles, que pour voir la façon dont vous les savez débiter. Continuez donc, s'il vous plaît, ou plutôt commencez tout de bon à m'écrire, quand ce ne seroit que par charité. Je suis en danger d'oublier bientôt le peu de françois que je sais ; je le désapprends tous les jours, et je ne parle tantôt plus que le langage de ce pays, qui est aussi peu françois que le bas breton.

Ipse mihi videor jam dedidicisse latine;
Nam didici getice sarmaticeque loqui[3].

3. « Il me semble que déjà j'ai désappris à parler latin ; car j'ai

J'ai vu qu'Ovide vous faisoit pitié quand vous songiez qu'un si galand homme que lui étoit obligé à parler scythe lorsqu'il étoit relégué parmi ces barbares : cependant il s'en faut beaucoup qu'il fût si à plaindre que moi. Ovide possédoit si bien toute l'élégance romaine, qu'il ne la pouvoit jamais oublier; et quand il seroit revenu à Rome après un exil de vingt années, il auroit[4] toujours fait taire les plus beaux esprits de la cour d'Auguste : au lieu que, n'ayant qu'une petite teinture du bon françois, je suis en danger de tout perdre en moins de six mois, et de n'être plus intelligible si je reviens jamais à Paris. Quel plaisir aurez-vous quand je serai devenu le plus grand paysan du monde? Vous ferez bien mieux de m'entretenir toujours un peu dans le langage qu'on parle à Paris. Vos lettres me tiendront lieu de livres et d'Académie.

Mais à propos d'Académie, que le pauvre Pélisson[5] est à plaindre, et que la Conciergerie est un méchant poste pour un bel esprit! Tous les beaux esprits du monde[6] devroient-ils pas faire une solennelle députation au Roi pour demander sa grâce? Les Muses elles-mêmes devroient-elles pas se rendre visibles afin de solliciter pour lui?

*Nec vos, Pierides, nec stirps Latonia, vestro
Docta sacerdoti turba tulistis opem*[7] !

appris à parler gète et sarmate. » (Ovide, *Tristes*, livre V, *élégie* xii, vers 57 et 58.)

4. Racine avait d'abord mis *eût*.

5. Pellisson était en prison depuis le mois de septembre 1661.

6. *Ne* a été ajouté au-dessus de la ligne, devant *devroient;* mais peut-être pas de la main de Racine. Voyez la phrase suivante.

7. « Ni vous, Piérides, ni vous, fils de Latone, vous n'avez, ô troupe savante, porté secours à votre prêtre. » (Ovide. *Tristes*, livre III, *élégie* ii, vers 3 et 4.

Mais on voit peu de gens que la protection des Muses ait sauvés des mains de la justice. Cependant il eût mieux valu pour lui qu'il ne se fût jamais mêlé que de belles choses, et[8] la condition de roitelet, en laquelle il s'étoit métamorphosé[9], lui eût été bien plus avantageuse que celle de financier. Cela doit apprendre à M. l'Avocat que le solide n'est pas toujours le plus sûr, puisque M. Pélisson ne s'est perdu que pour l'avoir préféré au creux; et sans mentir, quoiqu'il fasse bien creux sur le Parnasse, on y est pourtant plus à son aise que dans la Conciergerie. Après tout, il n'y a point[10] de plaisir d'avoir place dans les histoires tragiques, dussent-elles être écrites de la main de M. Pélisson lui-même.

Je baise les mains de tout mon cœur à M. l'Avocat, et je diffère encore ce voyage de lui écrire, afin de laisser un peu passer ce reste de mauvaise humeur que sa maladie lui a laissée, et qui lui feroit peut-être maltraiter les lettres que je lui envoyerois. Quoi qu'il en soit, il n'y a point de plaisir d'écrire à des gens qui sont encore dans les remèdes, et c'est trop exposer des lettres. Je salue très-humblement toute votre maison, où est compris l'illustre M. Botreau ; *ipsa ante alias pulcherrima Dido*[11] : vous savez de qui j'entends parler.

J'écrirai à Mlle Vitart, et j'avois dessein de lui écrire bien devant que d'avoir reçu votre lettre. Je vous prie

---

8. Après *et*, il y a : *à voir*, effacé.
9. Plusieurs petites pièces du *Recueil de pièces galantes en prose et en vers de Mme la comtesse de la Suze et de M. Pelisson* (Paris, chez Quinet, M.DC.LXIV) roulent sur cette métamorphose. On voit par la lettre de Racine qu'elles étaient connues avant la publication du *Recueil*.
10. *Du tout* a été rayé après *point*.
11. « Didon elle-même, la plus belle de toutes. » Cette phrase est tirée en partie du vers 60 du livre IV de l'*Énéide*.

de me remettre dans ses bonnes grâces, si je suis si malheureux que de les avoir perdues; sinon, je vous prie de m'y entretenir toujours, et de penser un peu à mes affaires en faisant les vôtres; surtout *scribe et vale*[12]. Mandez-moi des nouvelles de tout, et entre autres d'un petit mémoire[13] que j'envoyai pour la *Gazette* il y a huit jours.

Suscription: A Monsieur Monsieur l'abbé le Vasseur, à Paris. (Deux cachets rouges : J. RAC., avec une soie jaune.)

12. « Écrivez, et portez-vous bien. »
13. Ce *petit mémoire*, qui n'avait jamais encore été cité dans les OEuvres de Racine, est certainement l'article sur le feu d'artifice allumé par les consuls d'Uzès, à l'occasion de la naissance du Dauphin; il est imprimé dans la *Gazette* du 31 décembre 1661, p. 1372, sous la rubrique : *D'Usez, le 25 décembre* 1661. Il devrait cependant avoir une date un peu antérieure. Le voici, tel que la *Gazette* le donne, après l'avoir peut-être abrégé : « Outre les réjouissances qui se sont ici faites par l'ordre de notre évêque, pour la naissance de Monseigneur le Dauphin, nos consuls voulants aussi en signaler leur joie, firent le 18 courant allumer un feu dont le succès répondit des mieux à la beauté du dessein. Après que la Renommée, qui étoit élevée sur un piédestal, eut fait sonner trois fois un cor chargé de pétards, qu'elle avoit en sa main, une colombe partit d'un autre côté, toute en feu, qui tenant à son bec un rameau d'olive, vint allumer l'artifice. En même temps on ouït un grand bruit de bombes et de pétards, et l'air se couvrit d'une épaisse fumée, à laquelle succéda une grande clarté, qui découvrit un rocher fort élevé, vomissant des flammes de toutes parts, au sommet duquel paroissoit la Paix, avec une corne d'abondance en l'une de ses mains, et s'appuyant de l'autre sur un dauphin; ayant à ses pieds les Vertus cardinales qui jetoient quantité de fusées, comme elle en épanchoit grand nombre, qui alloient semer en l'air une infinité d'étoiles : tellement que cette machine parut des plus industrieusement inventées. »

18. — DE RACINE A MADEMOISELLE VITART[1].

A Usez, le 26ème décembre 1661.

Je pensois bien me donner l'honneur de vous écrire il y a huit jours, mais il me fut impossible de le faire : je ne sais pas même si j'en pourrai bien venir à bout aujourd'hui; car vous saurez, s'il vous plaît, que ce n'est pas à présent une petite affaire pour moi que de vous écrire. Il a été un temps que je le faisois assez aisément, et il ne me falloit pas beaucoup de peine pour faire une lettre un peu passable. Mais ce temps-là est passé pour moi : il me faut suer sang et eau pour faire quelque chose qui mérite de vous l'adresser; encore sera-ce un grand hasard si j'y réussis. La raison de cela, c'est que je suis un peu plus éloigné de vous que je n'étois lors. Quand je songeois seulement que je n'étois qu'à quatorze ou quinze lieues de vous, cela me mettoit en train, et c'étoit bien autre chose quand je vous voyois en personne : c'étoit alors que les paroles ne me coûtoient rien, et que je causois d'assez bon cœur. Au lieu qu'aujourd'hui je ne vous vois qu'en idée; et quoique je songe assez fortement à vous, je ne saurois pourtant empêcher qu'il n'y ait cent cinquante lieues entre vous et votre idée. Ainsi il m'est un peu plus difficile de m'échauffer; et quand mes lettres seroient assez heureuses pour vous plaire, que me sert cela? J'aimerois mieux recevoir un soufflet ou un coup de poing de vous, comme cela m'étoit assez ordinaire, qu'un grand merci qui viendroit de si loin. Après tout, il vous faut écrire, et il en faut revenir là. Mais que vous mander? Sans mentir, je n'en sais rien pour le présent. Faites-

LETTRE 18 (revue sur l'autographe, conservé à la Bibliothèque impériale). — 1. L'original de ce billet, peut-être incomplet, ne remplit que les deux pages d'un même feuillet. La suscription manque.

moi une grâce, donnez-moi temps jusqu'au premier ordinaire pour y songer, et je vous promets de faire merveille. J'y travaillerai plutôt jour et nuit : aussi bien n'ai-je plus qu'un demi-quart d'heure à moi, et vous-même avez maintenant bien d'autres affaires. Vous n'avez pas à déloger[2] seulement, comme on m'a mandé ; mais vous avez même à préparer les logis au Saint-Esprit[3], qui doit venir dans huit jours à l'hôtel de Luynes. Travaillez donc à le recevoir comme il mérite, et moi je travaillerai à vous entretenir comme vous méritez. Comme ce n'est pas une petite entreprise, vous treuverez bon que je m'y prépare avec un peu plus de loisir. Cependant je souhaite que tout le monde se porte bien chez vous, que vos deux infantes vous ressemblent, et que vous ne soyez point en colère contre moi de ce que j'ai tant tardé à m'acquitter de ce que je vous dois. C'est bien assez que je sois si loin de votre présence, sans me bannir encore de votre esprit. Ainsi soit-il.

Vous me permettrez d'assurer ici Monsieur le Marquis[4] de mes très-humbles respects. Je gagerois qu'il recevra cette assurance de fort bon cœur, non pas en ma considération, mais pour la vôtre. Je n'écris pas à mon cousin, car on m'a mandé qu'il étoit à la campagne ; et puis c'est lui écrire que de vous écrire.

2. Le duc de Luynes, qui demeurait alors rue du Bac, allait habiter son nouvel hôtel de la rue de la Butte (depuis rue Saint-Guillaume) sur la paroisse Saint-Sulpice.

3. Le duc de Luynes avait été créé chevalier de l'ordre du Saint-Esprit dans le chapitre tenu par le Roi le 3 décembre 1661 ; il fut reçu le 1er janvier 1662.

4. Le jeune marquis de Luynes.

19. — DE RACINE A MARIE RACINE.

A Usez, le 3eme janvier 1662.

MA TRÈS-CHÈRE SOEUR,

Je reçus hier votre lettre avec beaucoup de joie; mais j'en aurois encore davantage, si vous m'écriviez un peu plus souvent. Vous n'avez qu'à donner librement vos lettres à mon oncle Sconin [1], comme je vous l'ai déjà mandé. Il prend la peine de m'écrire presque tous les quinze jours, et il prendra bien celle d'envoyer votre lettre avec les siennes. Mandez-moi tout ce qui se passe à la Ferté, comme vous avez commencé, mais faites-le un peu plus au long que vous n'avez fait. Quand on écrit de si loin, il ne faut pas écrire pour une page. J'ai vu que vous m'écriviez de si belles lettres quand j'étois à Paris : il ne se passoit rien à la Ferté que je ne susse par votre moyen. Assurez-vous que je ne saurois avoir plus de plaisir que lorsque vous vous donnerez cette peine pour moi. En récompense, lorsque je treuverai l'occasion de vous envoyer quelque chose de ce pays, je ne la laisserai pas passer. Mais il faut un peu attendre. Je ne fais encore qu'arriver, et je n'ai pas eu le loisir de reconnoître ce qu'il y a de beau. Ma mère m'écrivit, il y a huit jours; elle avoit en effet encore de la fièvre comme vous me mandez, mais elle espéroit d'en être bientôt dehors. Je reçois assez souvent des nouvelles de Paris; il n'y a que vous qui êtes une paresseuse. Vous direz peut-être que vous avez encore la fièvre; mais vous avez bien vu que quand je l'avois encore, je ne laissois pas de vous écrire. Après tout, je suis bien marri que vous l'ayez, et que vous la gardiez si

---

LETTRE 19 (revue sur l'autographe, conservé à Soissons). —
1. Voyez ci-dessus, p. 376, la note 5 de la lettre 3.

longtemps. J'en ai eu quelques accès la semaine passée; mais elle m'a quitté, Dieu merci.

Quant à ce que vous me mandez que ma cousine Parmentier[2] est encore malade, je vous puis assurer que j'y prends grande part, et qu'elle me touche toujours d'aussi près qu'elle a fait. Je suis marri que mon cousin son frère ait rompu avec moi, comme il a fait à cause de mon voyage, et je vois bien qu'il n'est pas aussi bon ami que je le suis envers lui. Quand il seroit venu ici au lieu de moi, je ne lui en aurois pas voulu mal[3] pour cela. Il ne sait pas les raisons qui m'ont obligé d'y venir. Cependant je sais assez que lui et mon oncle du Chesne ont fait bien du bruit pour cela, à cause que j'y étois venu sans lui, comme si cela dépendoit de moi. Quoi qu'il en soit, je suis marri d'être mal dans son esprit; mais je ne lui en ai pas donné de sujet. Il est vrai que je ne lui ai pas écrit depuis ma maladie, parce qu'étant encore à Paris, je ne pouvois presque écrire à personne, et depuis que je suis ici, je n'ai pas su par quelle voie lui écrire, aussi bien qu'à d'autres personnes qui peut-être m'en voudront mal. Je vous dis tout cela parce qu'il n'y a rien que je haïsse tant que d'être mal avec une personne comme lui, avec qui j'ai toujours été si bien. Si l'occasion s'en présente et qu'il vous parle de moi, dites-lui ces raisons, s'il vous plaît, et faites mes baisemains à ma cousine sa sœur. Je vous en prie de tout mon cœur. Vous savez combien je l'ai toujours honorée, et je l'honore toujours de même.

Après tout, il ne faut pas s'étonner si mon oncle Sconin ne s'est pas employé pour le faire venir[4], parce que vous savez bien la manière dont mon oncle du

2. Voyez ci-dessus, p. 375, la note 2 de la lettre 3.
3. *Mal* a été ajouté dans l'interligne.
4. Racine avait d'abord mis simplement : « pour lui. »

Chesne a vécu avec lui. Mais je n'en veux pas parler davantage. Ne montrez point ma lettre, et mandez-moi toutes choses comme elles se passent. C'est toute la prière que je vous fais, de m'écrire souvent et de vous souvenir de moi. N'oubliez pas aussi de faire vos recommandations à mon oncle quand vous m'écrirez. Je salue mon oncle Racine[5] et ma cousine Cathau[6]. Adieu, ma très-chère sœur.

Suscription : A Madame Madame Marie Racine, chez M. le Commissaire à la Ferté-Milon. (Cachet : J. R., avec une soie bleu clair.)

20. — DE RACINE A M. VITART.

[A Usez,] du 17ᵉ janvier [1662[1]].

Je ne fais qu'arriver d'une lieue et demie d'ici, où j'étois allé promener; car il est impossible de demeurer longtemps dans la chambre par le beau temps qu'il fait en ce pays. Les plus beaux jours que vous donne le printemps ne valent pas ceux que l'hiver nous laisse,

5. Claude Racine, contrôleur au grenier à sel de la Ferté-Milon, né en 1620.
6. Catherine Sconin, fille de Pierre Sconin, dont il est parlé quelques lignes plus haut, sous le nom de *l'oncle Sconin*, et de Françoise Lefebvre. Elle épousa, au commencement de 1667, Antoine Vitart, et fut mariée en secondes noces, en 1687, à Joseph de Malortique. Elle mourut en 1716, âgée de soixante-douze ans.
Lettre 20. — 1. Nous n'avons pas l'autographe de cette lettre, mais nous l'avons revue sur une copie de Louis Racine, que nous a communiquée M. Auguste de Naurois. Cette copie diffère du texte que Louis Racine a fait imprimer, en l'altérant beaucoup, suivant sa coutume. On verra plus loin que, commencée le 17 janvier, la lettre a été continuée le 24.

et jamais le mois de mai ne vous paroît si agréable, que l'est ici le mois de janvier.

> Le soleil est toujours riant,
> Depuis qu'il part de l'Orient
> Pour venir éclairer le monde,
> Jusqu'à ce que son char soit descendu dans l'onde.
> La vapeur des brouillards ne voile point les cieux;
> Tous les matins, un vent officieux
> En écarte toutes les nues :
> Ainsi nos jours ne sont jamais couverts;
> Et dans le plus fort des hivers,
> Nos campagnes sont revêtues
> De fleurs et d'arbres toujours verts.
>
> Les ruisseaux clairs et murmurants
> Ne grossissent point en torrents :
> Ils respectent toujours leurs rives,
> Et leurs nayades fugitives,
> Sans sortir de leur lit natal,
> Errent paisiblement, et ne sont point captives
> Sous une prison de cristal.
>
> Nos oiseaux ne sont point forcés,
> De se cacher ou de se taire,
> Et leurs becs n'étant pas glacés,
> Ils chantent à leur ordinaire,
> Et font l'amour en liberté
> Autant l'hiver comme l'été.
>
> Enfin, lorsque la nuit a déployé ses voiles,
> La lune, au visage changeant,
> Paroît sur un trône d'argent,
> Tenant cercle avec les étoiles :
> Le ciel est toujours clair tant que dure son cours,
> Et nous avons des nuits plus belles que vos jours.

J'ai fait une assez longue pause en cet endroit, parce que, lorsque j'écrivois ces vers il y a huit jours, la chaleur de la poésie m'emporta si loin, que je ne m'aperçus pas que le temps se passoit et qu'il étoit trop tard pour porter mes lettres à l'ordinaire. Je recommence aujourd'hui, 24. de janvier, à vous écrire; mais il est arrivé un assez plaisant changement; car en relisant mes vers, je reconnois qu'il n'y en a pas un de vrai : il ne cesse de pleuvoir depuis trois jours, et l'on diroit que le temps a juré de me faire mentir. J'aurois autant de sujet de faire une description du mauvais temps, comme j'en ai fait une du beau; mais j'ai peur que je ne m'engage encore si avant, que je ne puisse achever cette lettre que dans huit jours, auquel temps peut-être le ciel se sera remis au beau : je n'aurois jamais fait. Cela m'apprend que cette maxime est fort vraie :

La vita al fin, il di loda la sera[2].

Nous ne sommes qu'à quatre lieues de Marnas, et nous avons ici près un gentilhomme d'Avignon qui se fait fort d'être parent de M. de Luynes. Il s'appelle.... Je viens de l'oublier : je vous le manderai une autre fois. C'est peut-être lui qui a profité de cette succession dont j'ai ouï parler autrefois; mais comme vous dites, il faut attendre que j'aie été à Avignon. J'irai ce carnaval. Je vous remercie de la peine que vous avez prise pour notre feu de joie [3]. Messieurs d'Usez en sont fort glorieux et vous en remercient en corps. C'est bien la plus maudite ville du monde. Ils ne travaillent à autre chose qu'à se tuer tous tant qu'ils sont, ou à se faire pendre les uns et les autres. Il y a toujours ici des commissaires : cela est cause que je n'y veux faire aucune connoissance, parce qu'en faisant un ami, je m'attire-

2. « Louez la vie à la fin, et le jour le soir. » (Pétrarque, *Rime*, parte I, canzone I, *Nel dolce tempo*, vers 31, édition de Venise, 1741.)
3. Sans doute parce qu'il en avait fait insérer la description dans la *Gazette*. Voyez ci-dessus, p. 430, note 13 de la lettre 17.

1662 rois cent ennemis. Ce n'est pas qu'on ne m'en ait pressé plusieurs fois, et qu'on ne [me] soit venu solliciter, moi indigne, de venir dans les compagnies; car on a trouvé mon *ode* chez une dame de la ville, et on est venu me saluer comme auteur; mais tout cela ne sert de rien, *mens immota manet*⁴. Je n'aurois jamais cru être capable d'une si grande solitude, et vous-même n'aviez jamais espéré cela de ma vertu.

Je passe tout le temps avec mon oncle, avec saint Thomas et avec Virgile; je fais force extraits de théologie, et quelques-uns de poésie : voilà comme je passe le temps, et ne m'ennuie pas, surtout quand j'ai reçu quelque lettre de vous : elle me sert de compagnie pendant deux jours.

Mon oncle a toute sorte de bons desseins pour moi; mais il n'en a point encore d'assuré, parce que les affaires du chapitre sont encore incertaines. J'attends toujours un démissoire. Cependant il m'a fait habiller de noir depuis les pieds jusqu'à la tête. La mode de ce pays est de porter un drap d'Espagne qui est fort beau, et qui coûte vingt-trois livres. Il m'en a fait faire un habit; j'ai maintenant la mine d'un des meilleurs bourgeois de la ville. Il attend toujours l'occasion de me pourvoir de quelque chose, et ce sera alors que je tâcherai de payer une partie de mes dettes si je puis; car je ne puis rien faire avant ce temps. Je me remets devant les yeux toutes les importunités que vous avez reçues de moi; j'en rougis à l'heure que je vous parle : *erubuit puer, salva res est*⁵. Mais mes affaires n'en vont

---

4. « Mon âme demeure inébranlable. » (Virgile, *Énéide*, livre IV, vers 449.)

5. « L'enfant a rougi, tout est sauvé. » (Térence, *Adelphes*, acte IV, scène v, vers 647.) — Racine a ajouté *puer*, qui n'est pas dans le texte.

pas mieux, et cette sentence est bien fausse, si ce n'est que vous vouliez prendre cette rougeur pour reconnoissance de tout ce que je vous dois, dont je me souviendrai toute ma vie.

21. — DE RACINE A MADEMOISELLE VITART.

A Usez, le 24ᵉ janvier [1662].

Ce billet n'est qu'une continuation de promesse et une nouvelle obligation. Je m'étois engagé l'autre jour [1] de vous écrire une lettre raisonnable, et après 15 jours d'intervalle je suis si malheureux que de n'y pouvoir satisfaire encore aujourd'hui, et je suis obligé malgré moi de remettre à l'autre voyage. Mais toutes ces remises ne sont pour moi qu'un surcroît de dettes, dont il me sera fort difficile de m'acquitter; car vous vous attendez peut-être de recevoir quelque chose de beau, puisque je prends tant de temps pour m'y préparer. Vous me ferez charité de perdre cette opinion, et de vous attendre plutôt à être fort mal payée; car je vous ai déjà avertie que je suis devenu un très-mauvais payeur. Quand je n'étois pas si loin de vous, je vous payois assez bien, ou du moins je le pouvois faire; car vous me fournissiez assez libéralement de quoi m'acquitter envers vous. J'entends de paroles; car vous êtes trop riche, et moi trop pauvre pour vous pouvoir payer d'autre chose. Quoi qu'il en soit, cela veut dire

Que j'ai perdu tout mon caquet,

Lettre 21 (revue sur l'autographe, conservé à la Bibliothèque impériale). — 1. Voyez ci-dessus, dans la lettre 18, datée du 26 décembre 1661, les premières lignes de la page 432.

Moi qui savois fort bien écrire[2]
Et jaser comme un perroquet.

Mais quand je saurois encore jaser des mieux, il faut que je me taise à présent. Le messager va partir, et on m'arrache la plume des mains. Vous me permettrez donc de finir. Il ne faut pas faire attendre un messager de grande ville comme est Usez. Pardonnez donc, et attendez encore huit jours.

Suscription : A Mademoiselle Mademoiselle Vitart. (Deux cachets rouges : J. RAC., avec une soie jaune.)

---

22. — DE RACINE A MADEMOISELLE VITART [1].

A Usez, le 31ème janvier 1662.

Que votre colère est charmante,
Belle et généreuse Amarante!
Qu'il vous sied bien d'être en courroux!
Si les Grâces jamais se mettoient en colère,
Le pourroient-elles faire
De meilleure grâce que vous?

Je confesse sincèrement
Que je vous avois offensée;
Et cette cruelle pensée
M'étoit un horrible tourment.
Mais depuis que vous-même en avez pris vengeance,
Un si glorieux châtiment
Me paroît une récompense.

---

2. Racine avait d'abord ainsi tourné ce vers :
Et que moi qui savois écrire.

Lettre 22. — 1. Revue sur l'autographe, conservé à la Bibliothèque impériale.

> Les reproches mêmes sont doux
> Venant d'une bouche si chère :
> Mais si je méritois d'être loué de vous,
> Et que je fusse un jour capable de vous plaire,
> Combien ferois-je de jaloux ?

Je m'en vas donc faire tout mon possible pour venir à bout d'un si grand dessein. Je serai heureux si vous pouvez vous louer de moi avec autant de justice que vous vous en plaignez; et je ferois de mon côté un fort bel ouvrage si je savois dire vos vertus avec autant d'esprit que vous dites les miennes. Je ne vous accuserai point de me flatter : vous les représentez au naïf. S'il en est de même de la passion de Monsieur l'Abbé, je tiens qu'il n'est pas mal partagé. Et quand le portrait de Mlle Lucrèce auroit été fait par le plus habile peintre du monde, il ne sauroit sans doute égaler celui que vous faites d'un amoureux en sa personne.

> Je me l'imagine en effet
> Tout languissant et tout défait,
> Qui gémit et soupire aux pieds de cette image.
> Il contemple son beau visage,
> Il admire ses mains, il adore ses yeux,
> Il idolâtre tout l'ouvrage.
> Puis, comme si l'Amour le rendoit furieux,
> Je l'entends s'écrier : « Que cette image est belle !
> Mais que la belle même est bien plus belle qu'elle !
> Le peintre n'a bien imité
> Que son insensibilité. »

Ainsi il ne faut pas s'étonner s'il a voulu donner une hydropique à M. d'Houÿ. Ce n'est pas qu'il ait aucune mauvaise volonté pour lui : il auroit grand tort. Mais il est si fortement possédé de l'idée de Mlle Lucrèce, que tout le reste des choses lui est entièrement indifférent. J'ai même de la peine à croire que vous ayez assez de puissance pour rompre ce charme, vous qui aviez accoutumé de le charmer lui-même autrefois, aussi bien que beaucoup d'autres. Ce n'est pas qu'il pourroit avoir eu une pensée qui l'obligeoit de procurer ce mariage. Il vouloit sans doute marier l'eau avec le vin, en mariant M. d'Houÿ à une hydropique. Mais je suis bien certain que M. d'Houÿ s'y sera fortement opposé; car, comme dit la chanson, ni le vin ni lui ne veulent point d'eau. Outre qu'il aime mieux soupirer toute sa vie auprès de vous [au] hasard d'en être quelquefois battu, et de faire tous les jours la prière.

On m'a mandé que ma tante Vitart étoit allée à Chevreuse pour Mlle Sellyer[2]; mais je crois qu'elle n'y sera pas longtemps, et qu'elle sera[3] bientôt nécessaire au fauxbourg Saint-Germain[4]. Elle ne manquera pas de pratique[5], s'il plaît à Dieu, et elle ne se reposera de longtemps si elle attend que vous vous reposiez toutes. Peut-être qu'autrefois je n'en aurois pas tant dit impunément, mais je suis à couvert des coups. Vous pouvez néanmoins vous adresser à mon lieutenant M. d'Houÿ : il ne tiendra pas cette qualité à déshonneur, puisqu'il a bien passé pour mon recors[6].

---

2. Agnès Vitart, fille de Claude des Moulins (*ma tante Vitart*), et mariée à Pierre Sellyer, bailli de Chevreuse. Voyez ci-dessus, p. 407, la note 12 de la lettre 11.

3. Racine avait commencé par écrire : « et qu'il faudra. »

4. C'est-à-dire auprès de Mlle Vitart, à qui cette lettre est adressée. Claude-Auguste Vitart naquit quelques mois après. Son acte de baptême est du 21 octobre 1662. — Si l'éditeur de 1807 s'est uniquement fondé sur ce passage, et sur celui qu'on trouvera plus bas, dans la *lettre à Mlle Vitart* du 15 mai 1662, pour avancer que Mme Vitart exerçait la profession de sage-femme, il est clair que rien ne justifie son assertion. Il est d'ailleurs vrai que ses informations étaient d'ordinaire puisées à bonne source. Voyez la *Notice biographique*, p. 40.

5. *Pratique* est ainsi au singulier dans l'autographe.

6. Sans doute le jour où une dame prit Racine lui-même pour

Vous m'avez mis en train, comme vous voyez, et vos lettres ont sur moi la force qu'avoit autrefois votre vue; mais je suis encore obligé de finir plus tôt que je ne voudrois : j'ai quatre ou cinq lettres à écrire. Monsieur l'Abbé me mandoit un jour qu'il en avoit douze ou treize à faire, et qu'il n'avoit plus qu'une demie heure de temps. Je crus en ce temps-là qu'il disoit vrai, et je le crois encore. Aussi j'espère que vous ne me refuserez pas la même grâce, et que vous me donnerez, en vertu de mes cinq lettres, la permission de finir, et en vertu de la soumission et du respect que j'ai pour vous, la permission de me dire votre passionné serviteur.

Vous m'excuserez si j'ai plus brouillé de papier à dire de méchantes choses, que vous n'en aviez employé à écrire les plus belles choses du monde.

Suscription : A Mademoiselle Mademoiselle Vitart, à Paris. (Deux cachets rouges : J. RAC., avec une soie jaune.)

23. — DE RACINE A L'ABBÉ LE VASSEUR.

A Usez, le 3ᵉ février 1662.

Quoique vous ne soyez pas le plus diligent homme du monde quand il s'agit de répondre à une lettre, je m'assure que vous ne laisserez pas de vous formaliser beaucoup de ce que ma réponse ne vient que huit ou dix jours après votre lettre. Vous attribuerez sans doute ce retardement à un desir de vengeance : elle seroit juste après tout[1] ; mais je n'y ai pas pensé néanmoins. Je m'é-

---

un sergent. Voyez ci-dessus la lettre 6, du 26 janvier 1661, à la page 386. — Racine écrit *records*.

Lettre 23 (revue sur l'autographe, conservé à la Bibliothèque impériale). — 1. Il y avoit d'abord : « quand cela seroit. »

tois préparé à vous écrire les deux derniers voyages, et j'en ai été malheureusement détourné. Mais à quoi bon m'excuser pour un délai de huit jours? Vous ne faites pas tant de cérémonies quand vous avez été deux bons mois sans songer seulement si je suis au monde. C'est assez pour vous de dire froidement que vous avez perdu la moitié de votre esprit depuis que je ne suis plus en votre compagnie. Mais à d'autres! il faudroit que j'eusse perdu tout le mien si je recevois de telles galanteries en payement. Dieu merci, je sais à présent ce qui vous occupe si fort, et ce qui vous fait oublier de pauvres étrangers comme nous. *Amor non talia curat*[2]. Oui, c'est cela même qui vous occupe, et j'en sais des nouvelles.

Amor che solo i cor leggiadri invesca[3].

Et je ne m'étonne pas qu'un cœur si tendre que le vôtre, et si disposé à recevoir les douces impressions de l'amour, soit devenu amoureux d'une si charmante personne. Bien d'autres que vous auroient succombé à la tentation:

> Socrate s'y trouveroit pris,
> Et malgré sa philosophie,
> Il feroit ce qu'a fait Pâris,
> Et le feroit toute sa vie.

Vous l'aviez tous les jours devant vos yeux, et vous aviez tout le loisir de considérer ses belles qualités, *e le sue fattezze*[4], comme disent les Italiens. Et ainsi, selon le passage que citoit hier notre prédicateur: *Mutuo conspectu mutui crescebant amores*[5]. Pour moi, loin d'y

---

2. « L'amour n'a pas de tels soucis. » (Virgile, *églogue* x, vers 28.)
3. « L'Amour qui seul charme les nobles cœurs. » (Pétrarque, *Rime*, *parte I*, sonnet cxxxi, *Come 'l candido piè*, vers 5.)
4. « Et ses beaux traits. »
5. « En présence l'un de l'autre croissait l'amour qu'ils avaient

trouver à redire, je vous loue d'un si beau choix et d'aimer avec tant de discernement, s'il peut y avoir du discernement en amour. Il ne faut pas demander si c'est là l'espagnol qui vous tient; l'amour est ce porteur d'eau dont vous aimez tant la compagnie, et qui vous apprend si bien à parler toutes sortes de langues : *et mentem Venus ipsa dedit*[6]. Il ne me fait pas tant d'honneur, quoique j'aie assez besoin de compagnie en ce pays; mais j'aime mieux être seul que d'avoir un hôte si dangereux. Ne m'accusez pas pour cela d'être un farouche et un insensible :

> Vous savez bien que les déesses
> Ne sont pas toutes des Vénus;
> Et vous savez que les belles, non plus,
> Ne sont pas toutes des Lucrèces.

A propos de belles, j'avois déjà vu les vers du *Ballet des Saisons*[7], et on me les avoit apportés lorsque j'étois encore malade. Je suis ravi qu'il ne reste aucune apparence de blessure sur le beau front d'Angélique. Elle n'est pas la seule beauté qui ait souffert de si douloureuses aventures : *et Veneris violata est vulnere dex-*

---

l'un pour l'autre. » Dans l'édition de 1808 on a imprimé *mutus*, au lieu de *mutuo*; ce qui n'était pas une raison pour que l'éditeur (Geoffroy) traduisît : « Muet à son aspect, je sentais mon amour croître dans le silence. » Il est fort étonnant que M. Aimé-Martin ait conservé cette traduction.

6. « Et c'est de Vénus elle-même qu'est venue l'inspiration. » (Virgile, *Géorgiques*, livre III, vers 267.)

7. Le *Ballet des Saisons* fut dansé pour la première fois, le 26 juillet 1661, à Fontainebleau (voyez la *Gazette* du 30 juillet 1661, p. 727). Les vers sont de Benserade; Racine a sans doute en vue particulièrement ceux que le poëte a mis dans la bouche de Mlle de Montbazon (Anne de Rohan), laquelle devint quelques mois après la duchesse de Luynes. Voyez ces vers dans les *OEuvres de Monsieur de Benserade*, Paris, M.DC.XCVII (in-12), tome II, p. 219.

*tra*⁸; et peut-être bien que qui auroit considéré l'endroit où elle tomba, il y auroit vu naître des roses et des anémones pareilles à celles qui sortirent du sang de Vénus; mais il est trop tard pour y aller voir. Et quand il y seroit venu des roses, l'hiver les auroit fort maltraitées; elles auroient été plus en sûreté en ce pays, où nous voyons dès le mois de janvier

> *Schietti arboscelli e verdi frondi acerbe,*
> *Amorosette e pallide viole* ⁹.

On m'a assuré même qu'il y avoit un jardin tout plein de roses, mais de roses toutes fleuries, à une lieue d'ici, et cela ne passe pas même pour une rareté.

La nouvelle que vous me mandez sur la fin de votre lettre m'a d'abord surpris étrangement; mais je suis entré peu à peu dans vos sentiments, que cela n'étoit qu'un soulagement et un avantage pour M. Vitart¹⁰. Je ne lui en ai rien témoigné pourtant, et je ne le ferai pas que je n'en sois informé de sa part ou de quelque autre que de vous. Mais que vous avez raison d'accuser l'autre d'une infidélité si noire! Il est capable des plus lâches trahisons :

> *Ille horridus alter*
> *Desidia, latamque trahens inglorius alvum* ¹¹.

8. « La main de Vénus elle-même a été profanée par une blessure. » Racine a un peu arrangé ce vers de Virgile (*Énéide*, livre XI, vers 277) :

> .... *Et Veneris violavi vulnere dextram.*

9. « De tendres arbrisseaux, un jeune et vert feuillage, d'amoureuses et pâles violettes. » (Pétrarque, *Rime*, *parte I*, sonnet CXXVIII, *Lieti fiori*, vers 5 et 6.)

10. Le bailli de Chevreuse (*Pierre Sellyer*) avoit cherché à nuire à M. Vitart, et l'avoit supplanté dans une partie des attributions de son emploi. (*Note de l'édition de 1807.*)

11. « L'autre hideux dans sa paresse, et traînant sans gloire son large ventre. » (Virgile, *Géorgiques*, livre IV, vers 93 et 94.)

A votre avis, Virgile ne sait-il pas aussi bien faire le portrait d'un traître, que d'un héros? Je n'ai pas peur que vous vous lassiez de voir tant de vers dans une seule lettre, *quoniam*[12] *te amor nostri poetarum amantem reddidit*[13]. Pour vous, soit latin, soit espagnol, soit turc si vous le savez, écrivez-moi, je vous prie. Je suis confiné dans un pays qui a quelque chose de moins sociable que le Pont-Euxin : le sens commun y est rare, et la fidélité n'y est point du tout. On ne sait à qui se prendre. Il ne faut qu'un quart d'heure de conversation pour vous faire haïr un homme, tant les âmes de cette ville[14] sont méchantes et intéressées : ce sont tous baillis[15]. Aussi, quoiqu'ils me soient venus quérir cent fois pour aller en compagnie, je ne me suis point encore produit nulle part. Enfin il n'y a ici personne pour moi[16]. *Non homo, sed littus, atque aer et solitudo mera*[17]. Jugez si vos lettres seroient bien reçues. Mais vous êtes attaché ailleurs.

Il cor preso ivi, come pesce a l'hamo[18].

12. *Quoniam* est ajouté au-dessus de la ligne.
13. « Puisque votre amour pour moi vous a fait aimer les poëtes. » — C'est une phrase de Cicéron que Racine a un peu modifiée. On la lit ainsi dans la *lettre* xiii du livre I *à Atticus* : *Liber tibi mittetur, quoniam te amor nostri* φιλορήτορα *reddidit*. Racine a substitué l'*amour des poëtes* à l'*amour des orateurs* ou *de la rhétorique*.
14. Une première rédaction était *hommes*, au lieu d'*âmes*, et *pays*, au lieu de *ville*.
15. Allusion au bailli de Chevreuse, dont il vient de maudire la trahison.
16. Racine avait commencé par écrire : « Je ne vois personne. »
17. « Pas un homme, mais seulement un rivage, l'air, et une pure solitude. » (*Lettre* xviii du livre I *à Atticus*.)
18. « Le cœur est pris là comme un poisson à l'hameçon. » (Pétrarque, *Rime, parte I*, sonnet ccxviii, *In quel bel viso*, vers 5.)

448 LETTRES.

1662 *Adiousias* : je salue tout le monde, et M. du May [19].

Suscription : A Monsieur Monsieur l'abbé le Vasseur.
(Deux cachets rouges : J. RAC., avec une soie verte.)

24. — DE RACINE A L'ABBÉ LE VASSEUR.

[A Usez, 21 mars 1662[1].]

.... Je dis à la françoise, car nous appelons ici la France tout le pays qui est au delà de la Loire ; celui-ci passe comme une province étrangère. Aussi c'est à ce pays, ce me semble, que Furretière a laissé le galimatias en partage[2], en disant qu'il s'étoit relégué dans les pays de delà la Loire[3]. Cela n'empêche pas, comme je vous ai dit, qu'il n'y ait quelques esprits bien faits. Je n'explique pas non plus Cypassis[4], qui est digne de n'être fille de chambre que des déesses, *solas pectere*

---

19. M. du May, qui nous est inconnu, comme M. d'Houy, était peut-être aussi de la maison du duc de Luynes.

LETTRE 24 (revue sur l'autographe, conservé à la Bibliothèque impériale). — 1. Le commencement de la lettre manque. Pour la date, qui manque naturellement aussi, voyez ci-après la note 8.

2. Racine avait mis d'abord : « pour partage. »

3. Voyez la *Nouvelle allegorique ou Histoire des derniers troubles arrivez au royaume d'Eloquence.... à Paris, chez Guillaume de Luyne*, M.DC.LIX (in-12. Cette édition est la seconde ; la première est de 1658, et de format in-8°). Furetière y raconte la grande guerre que le prince *Galimatias* déclara à la *Rhétorique*, reine de l'Éloquence, et qui finit par un traité de pacification, dont l'article v (p. 96) est ainsi conçu : « Que pareillement il seroit permis à *Galimatias* de courir les provinces, et y faire telles conquêtes que bon lui sembleroit, particulièrement celles au delà de la Loire, qui étoient abandonnées à sa discrétion. »

4. Il l'explique ci-après (p. 457) dans sa lettre du 30 avril 1662.

digna Deus[5]. Je réserve à l'autre voyage de vous dire les sentiments qu'on a eus ici de l'*ode* de M. Perraut[6], et je vous dirai, pour finir par l'endroit qui m'a le plus réjoui de votre lettre, que je n'ai pas moins pris de part à la paix de votre famille que Monsieur le Surintendant[7] en prendroit au recouvrement de la bonne volonté du Roi; et pour ne parler point par hyperbole, je vous assure que quand je serois réconcilié avec mon propre père si j'en avois encore un, je n'aurois pas été plus aise qu'en apprenant que vous étiez remis parfaitement avec M. le Vass[eur], parce que je sais fort bien que vous vous en estimez parfaitement heureux. Adieu, Monsieur : je vous écrirai sans faute dans huit jours[8]. Je vous prie aussi de vous souvenir de moi. M. Vitart m'a merveilleusement oublié. Vous ne l'imiterez pas, comme je crois.

Suscription : Monsieur Monsieur le Vasseur. (Deux cachets rouges : J. RAC., avec une soie violette.)

---

5. « Seule digne de coiffer les Déesses. » — Racine a un peu altéré le vers d'Ovide (*Amores*, livre II, *élégie* VIII, vers 2) qui est :

    Comere sed solas digna, Cypassi, Deas.

6. Son *Ode au Roy sur la naissance de Monseigneur le Dauphin*. Voyez le *Recueil de divers ouvrages en prose et en vers. Par Monsieur Perrault de l'Académie françoise. Seconde édition*, à Paris, M. DC. LXXVI (1 volume in-12), p. 173-178.

7. Le surintendant Foucquet avait été arrêté le 5 septembre 1661. Depuis ce temps il était retenu en prison.

8. Voyez ci-après, p. 452, la lettre 26. C'est de cette lettre 26, datée du 28 mars (mardi), que nous avons pu conclure que celle-ci est du 21 mars. Les éditeurs précédents, depuis 1807, la dataient, sans donner le quantième, de mars 1662.

25. — DE RACINE A MADEMOISELLE VITART.

[A Usez, mars 1662[1].]

.... Si vous vous offensez de cette façon de parler, vous en devez accuser le quolibet, qui ne s'est pas énoncé plus civilement. M. Vitart m'a mandé le retour de ma tante sa mère, et le succès de son voyage de Chevreuse[2], qui, pour vous dire vrai, m'a bien surpris. Je croyois qu'il se préparoit[3] quelque chose de bien grand dans le château de Chevreuse : j'avois ouï autrefois toutes les grandes promesses de Monsieur le Bailli, et je croyois même que tout le monde étoit en haleine chez vous pour savoir ce qui en arriveroit, car depuis deux ou trois mois je n'ai pas reçu une lettre. Enfin, je m'attendois qu'il sortiroit de ce château quelque géant, ou du moins un enfant aussi puissant que Joseph du Pin[4], et il n'est venu qu'une fille. Ce n'est pas qu'une fille soit peu de chose; mais M. Sellyer parloit bien plus haut que cela. Cela lui apprend à s'humilier; car, voyez-vous? j'ai ouï dire à un bon prédicateur, que Dieu changeroit plutôt un garçon en fille avant qu'il soit né, pour humilier un homme qui s'en fait accroire[5]. Ce n'est pas qu'il y ait eu du miracle en l'affaire de M. Sellyer, et je crois fort bonnement qu'il n'a eu que ce qu'il a fait.

Lettre 25 (revue sur l'autographe, conservé à la Bibliothèque impériale). — 1. Le commencement de cette lettre manque, et, par suite, la date. La naissance d'une fille de M. Sellyer, les nouvelles reçues à Uzès du ballet où Mme de Luynes avait figuré, rendent probable la date de mars 1662, déjà proposée dans l'édition de 1807.

2. Voyez la lettre du 31 janvier 1662, à la page 442.

3. Racine avait d'abord écrit : « qu'il se tramoit. »

4. Frère du docteur Louis Ellies du Pin. Tous deux étaient fils de Marie Vitart, sœur, comme Mme Sellyer, de M. Vitart.

5. Racine a écrit : « qui s'en fait à croire »

Si je pouvois vous envoyer des roses nouvelles et des pois verts, je vous en envoyerois en abondance; car nous en avons beaucoup ici. Le printemps est déjà fort avancé. Nous avons vu ici Mme de Luines dans le récit du *Ballet*⁶, et je ne doute point que vous ne l'y ayez vue⁷ paroître dans tout son éclat. Je crois que tout le monde se porte bien maintenant chez M. le Mazier⁸; car mon cousin ne m'en mande plus de nouvelles, et j'aime mieux qu'il ne m'en mande point, que de m'en mander de fâcheuses. Je prendrai la liberté de les assurer tous ici de mes très-humbles obéissances, qui vous sont particulièrement dévouées, comme à la personne du monde que j'honore avec plus de passion.

Suscription : A Mademoiselle Mademoiselle Vitart, à Paris. (Deux cachets rouges, avec une soie amarante. Les cachets ont un écusson portant deux étoiles au chef, trois barres horizontales et une étoile en bas.)

---

6. Ce ballet n'est pas, comme l'a cru l'éditeur de 1807, celui *des Saisons*, dont il a été question dans la lettre à l'abbé le Vasseur du 3 février 1662, p. 445. Lorsque celui-ci fut dansé à Fontainebleau, Mlle de Montbazon n'était pas encore duchesse de Luynes. Racine parle évidemment du *Ballet royal d'Hercule amoureux*, dansé pour la première fois à Paris le 7 février 1662. Le *récit* de ce ballet est peut-être celui qu'on trouve dans la *Gazette* du 11 février 1662, p. 147 et 148, et où la duchesse de Luynes est nommée. La *Gazette* donne au ballet le titre de *Mariage d'Hercule avec la Beauté;* il a celui d'*Hercule amoureux* dans les *OEuvres de Monsieur de Bensserade*, tome II, où sont à la page 259 les *Vers pour la duchesse de Luynes*.

7. Racine a écrit *vu*, sans accord.

8. Sans doute Claude le Mazier, frère de Mlle Vitart.

26. — DE RACINE A L'ABBÉ LEVASSEUR.

A Usez, le 28. mars 1662.

Je ne veux pas manquer à la parole que je vous ai donnée[1] de vous écrire aujourd'hui, mais aussi je ne vous entretiendrai pas longtemps. L'incertitude où je suis de la santé de M. l'Avocat fait que je ne sais de quelle façon vous parler ou comme à un homme triste, ou comme à un homme de bonne humeur; et l'idée que j'ai toujours présente de la tristesse qui paroissoit dans votre dernière lettre m'empêche de vous en faire aucune qui soit tant soit peu enjouée. J'en ai reçu une de M. Vitart cette semaine, et je viens[2] de lui écrire aussi. Il m'a envoyé une *Lettre* de M. de Luines pour les pairs[3], que nous avions déjà vue en ce pays, et je suis toujours des derniers à savoir les nouvelles, quoique j'aie une correspondance aussi bonne que la vôtre. On ne parle en cette ville que de la merveilleuse conduite du Roi, du grand ménage de Colbert[4], et du procès de M. Fouquet, qu'on dit avoir été interrogé par

---

Lettre 26 (revue sur l'autographe, conservé à la Bibliothèque impériale). — 1. Voyez ci-dessus la lettre 24, à la page 449.

2. Racine avait commencé par écrire : « et je lui viens. »

3. Cette lettre, que nous ne connaissons pas, avait trait probablement à des difficultés semblables à celles qui s'étaient élevées en 1660, et qui avaient été l'objet d'un écrit attribué au duc de Luynes, et intitulé : *Relation de ce qui se passa à l'entrée du roi Louis XIV en 1660. Au sujet des rangs de Messieurs les Ducs et Pairs.* On le trouve imprimé à la suite d'une autre pièce qui a pour titre : *État présent d'Espagne.... A Villefranche, chez Étienne le Vray* (1 volume in-12, M.DCC.XVII). Nous pensons qu'il ne faut pas confondre la *Lettre* du duc de Luynes avec sa *Relation*, qui, en 1662, ne pouvait plus être une nouveauté.

4. Racine écrit *Collebert*. En général, nous conservons aux noms propres l'orthographe des originaux ; mais ici le lecteur eût pu trouver l'altération par trop choquante.

trois fois depuis peu de jours⁵. Et cependant, vous qui êtes des premiers instruit des choses, ne m'en mandez rien du tout. Mais, pour vous dire le vrai, ce n'est pas cela qui m'inquiète : j'aime mieux que vous me mandiez de vos nouvelles particulières et de celles de nos connoissances. Vous serez le plus cruel homme du monde si vous ne m'en faites savoir au moins de M. l'Avocat, dans la maladie ou dans la santé duquel je m'intéresse sensiblement.

J'ai eu tout le loisir de lire l'*ode* de M. Perraut⁶. Aussi l'ai-je relue⁷ plusieurs fois, et néanmoins j'ai eu bien de la peine à y reconnoître son style, et je ne croirois pas encore qu'elle fût de lui, si vous et M. Vitart ne m'en assuriez. Il m'a semblé que je n'y treuvois point cette facilité naturelle qu'il avoit à s'exprimer; je n'y ai point vu, ce me semble, aucune trace d'un esprit aussi net que le sien m'a toujours paru, et j'eusse gagé que cette ode avoit été taillée comme à coups de marteau par un homme qui n'avoit jamais fait que de méchants vers. Ç'a été le sentiment et les termes⁸ de quelques gens qui l'ont vue ici. Mais je crois que l'esprit de M. Perraut est toujours le même, et que le sujet seulement lui a manqué; car, en effet, il y a longtemps que Cicéron a dit que c'étoit une matière bien stérile, que l'éloge d'un enfant en qui l'on ne peut louer que l'espérance⁹; et toutes ces espérances sont telle-

---

5. Les interrogatoires de Foucquet commencèrent le 4 mars 1662.
6. Voyez ci-dessus, p. 449, la note 6 de la lettre 24.
7. Racine a écrit *relu*, sans accord.
8. « Et les termes » a été ajouté après coup, dans l'interligne.
9. Si Racine a fait allusion à ce passage de l'*Orator* (chapitre xxx) : *Adolescentis non tam re et maturitate, quam spe et exspectatione, laudati*, il n'a eu qu'un souvenir un peu vague de ce passage, qui ne contient pas toute la pensée qu'il prête ici à Cicéron. S'il a eu en vue un autre endroit, nous n'avons pu le trouver.

ment vagues, qu'elles ne peuvent fournir de pensées solides. Mais je m'oublie ici, et je ne songe pas que je dis cela à un homme qui s'y entend mieux que moi. Vous me devez excuser de cette liberté que je prends. Je vous parle avec la même franchise que nous nous parlions dans votre cabinet ou le long des galeries de votre escalier, et si j'en juge mal et que mes pensées soient éloignées des vôtres, remettez cela sur la barbarie de ce pays et sur ma longue absence de Paris, qui, m'ayant séparé de vous, m'a peut-être entièrement privé de la bonne connoissance des choses.

Je vous dirai pourtant encore qu'il y a un endroit où j'ai reconnu M. Perraut : c'est lorsqu'il parle de Josué [10], et qu'il amène là l'Écriture sainte. Je lui dis une fois qu'il mettoit trop la *Bible* en jeu dans ses poésies; mais il me dit qu'il la lisoit fort, et qu'il ne pouvoit s'empêcher d'en insérer quelque passage. Pour moi, je crus que la lecture en étoit fort bonne, mais que la citation étoit mieux séante à un prédicateur qu'à un poëte.

Vengez-vous, Monsieur, de toutes mes impertinences sur la pièce que je vous envoie [11]. Ce n'est pas une pièce, ce semble, tout à fait nouvelle pour vous; mais vous la trouverez pourtant toute nouvelle. Je l'avois mise en l'état qu'elle est huit jours devant ma maladie, et je l'avois même montrée [12] à deux personnes seulement, dont l'un [13] étoit fort grand poëte, et ils étoient tous deux amoureux du dessein et de la conduite de

10. Voyez la strophe xi de l'*Ode sur la naissance de Monseigneur le Dauphin*. Nous avons cité ce passage à la note 2 de la page 63 de notre tome IV.

11. C'est la pièce dont Racine parle dans la lettre suivante, et qu'il y nomme *les Bains de Vénus*.

12. *Montré*, sans accord, dans l'autographe.

13. Il y a bien *l'un*, et ensuite *ils*, dans l'autographe, et de même, six lignes plus loin, *il*. Voyez le *Lexique*.

cette fable. Je vous la voulois donner, mais ma maladie survint, qui me fit perdre absolument toutes ces idées. Je n'y avois plus songé depuis; mais il y a environ deux mois qu'en ayant dit quelques endroits à une personne de cette ville, il me conjura de lui dicter toute la pièce. Je le fis : il la montra à d'autres, et ils crurent qu'elle étoit fort belle. Je n'ose dire qu'elle l'est que vous ne me l'ayez mandé, et que vous ne m'en ayez envoyé[14] l'approbation de Mlle Lucrèce et de quelques autres experts avec vous. Mais mandez-moi tout par le détail, ce que vous jugerez des Grâces, des Amours, et de toute la cour de Vénus qui y est dépeinte. Si le titre ne vous plaît, changez-le : ce n'est pas qu'il m'a paru[15] le plus convenable. Si vous le donnez, ne dites point l'auteur : mon nom fait tort à tout ce que je fais. Mais montrez-moi en cette occasion ce que c'est qu'un ami, en me découvrant tout votre cœur. Je prends intérêt à cette pièce à cause qu'elle fut faite pour vous, et à cause de l'opinion que vous eûtes d'abord de ce dessein. Adieu : je salue tout le monde, et M. l'Avocat surtout. Si cette galanterie vous plaît, j'en pourrai faire d'autres : il y a assez de sujet en ce pays. Brûlez l'original, si vous l'avez encore, je vous en conjure.

Suscription : A Monsieur Monsieur l'abbé le Vasseur. (Deux cachets rouges : J. RAC., avec une soie verte.)

14. Racine avait mis d'abord : « et que vous ne m'envoyez. »
15. C'est-à-dire : « changez-le, bien que ce soit là le titre qui m'a paru le plus convenable. »

27. — DE RACINE A L'ABBÉ LE VASSEUR.

A Uzés¹, le 30. avril 1662.

Je ne vous demandois pas des louanges quand je vous ai envoyé ce petit ouvrage des *Bains de Vénus*²; mais je vous demandois votre sentiment au vrai, et celui de vos amis. Cependant vous vous êtes contenté de dire, comme ce flatteur d'Horace : *Pulchre, bene, recte*³; et Horace dit fort bien qu'on loue ainsi les méchants ouvrages, parce qu'il y a tant de choses à reprendre, qu'on aime mieux tout louer que d'examiner les beaux et les mauvais endroits. Vous m'avez traité de la sorte, Monsieur, et vous me louez comme un vrai demi-auteur, qui a plus de bons endroits que de mauvais⁴. Soyez un peu plus équitable, je vous prie, ou plutôt ne soyez pas si paresseux; car je crois que c'est là ce qui vous tient. Vous auriez mille bonnes choses à me dire; mais vous avez peur de tirer une lettre en longueur. Vous avez cent autres personnes à satisfaire, tantôt le maître du luth, tantôt des chartreux, tantôt des beaux esprits, et quelquefois aussi la belle Cypassis. N'êtes-vous pas admirable dans votre lettre sur le sujet de cette Cypassis? Vous faites semblant de ne la pas connoître, et vous m'allez jeter le chat aux jambes⁵. Ce quolibet passera, mais pour n'y plus revenir. Je

---

Lettre 27 (revue sur l'autographe, conservé à la Bibliothèque impériale). — 1. Racine écrit tantôt *Usez*, tantôt *Uzés* ou *Uzès*.

2. Nous n'avons pas cette pièce, dont il est déjà parlé dans la lettre précédente.

3. « Beau! bon! parfait! » (*Art poétique*, vers 428.)

4. Racine a écrit ainsi; mais il doit s'être trompé, et sans doute il a voulu écrire « plus de mauvais endroits que de bons, » comme ont imprimé les précédents éditeurs, excepté Geoffroy (1808), qui donne, de même que nous, le texte du manuscrit.

5. C'est-à-dire : « vous allez chercher à m'embarrasser. »

vous en avois parlé en passant, sur ce que vous m'aviez mandé que vous aviez lié quelque amitié avec une demoiselle⁶ d'Angélique, et pour déguiser cette histoire j'avois pris le nom de Cypassis, qui fut autrefois la demoiselle de Corinne. Relisez ma lettre, si vous l'avez encore, et cela vous sautera aux yeux. Mais n'en parlons plus, et croyez au reste que, si j'avois reçu quelque blessure en ce pays, je vous la découvrirois naïvement, et je ne pourrois pas même m'en empêcher. Vous savez que les blessures du cœur demandent toujours quelque confident à qui on puisse s'en plaindre, et si j'en avois une de cette nature, je ne m'en plaindrois jamais qu'à vous. Mais, Dieu merci, je suis libre encore, et si je quittois ce pays, je reporterois mon cœur aussi sain et aussi entier que je l'ai apporté. Je vous dirai pourtant une assez plaisante rencontre à ce sujet. Il y a ici une demoiselle⁷ fort bien faite et d'une taille fort avantageuse. Je ne l'avois guère vue que de cinq ou six pas, et je l'avois toujours trouvée fort⁸ belle. Son teint me paroissoit vif et éclatant, les yeux grands et d'un beau noir, la gorge et le reste de ce qui se découvre assez librement en ce pays, fort blanc. J'en avois toujours quelque idée assez tendre et assez approchante d'une inclination ; mais je ne la voyois qu'à l'église ; car, comme je vous ai mandé, je suis assez solitaire et plus que mon cousin ne me l'avoit recommandé. Enfin je voulus voir si je n'étois point trompé dans l'idée que j'avois d'elle, et j'en trouvai l'occasion fort honnête. Je

6. Racine écrit *démoiselle*, non-seulement ici, mais deux fois encore quelques lignes plus bas, dans cette même lettre.

7. M. Édouard Fournier, dans les notes de sa comédie de *Racine à Uzès*, p. 79, dit que l'on montre à Uzès un portrait qui passe pour être celui de cette demoiselle. Mais ce qu'on lui a raconté à l'appui de cette tradition nous parait bien peu concluant.

8. *Fort* est écrit au-dessus de *plus*, effacé.

m'approchai d'elle et lui parlai. Ce que je vous dis là m'est arrivé il n'y a pas un mois, et je n'avois point d'autre dessein que de voir quelle réponse elle me feroit. Je lui parlai donc indifféremment, mais sitôt que j'ouvris la bouche et que je l'envisageai, je pensai demeurer interdit. Je treuvai sur son visage de certaines bigarrures, comme si elle eût relevé de maladie, et cela me fit bien changer mes idées[9]. Néanmoins je ne demeurai pas[10], et elle me répondit d'un air fort doux et fort obligeant; et pour vous dire la vérité, il faut que je l'aie prise en quelqu'un de ces jours fâcheux et incommodes où le sexe est sujet; car elle passe pour fort belle dans la ville, et je connois beaucoup de jeunes gens qui soupirent pour elle du fond de leur cœur; elle passe même pour une des plus sages et des plus enjouées. Enfin je fus bien aise de cette rencontre, qui me servit du moins à me délivrer de quelque commencement d'inquiétude; car je m'étudie maintenant à vivre un peu plus raisonnablement, et à ne me laisser pas emporter à toute sorte d'objets. Je commence mon noviciat, mais je souhaiterois qu'on me le fît achever à Ouchie[11]. Je vois bien que vous êtes disposés, vous et mon cousin, à travailler pour moi de ce côté-là, et je passerai volontiers par-dessus toutes ces considérations d'habit noir et d'habit blanc qui m'inquiétoient autrefois, et dont vous me faisiez tous deux la guerre. Aussi il n'y a plus d'espérance en ces quartiers. On a reçu

9. Au lieu de : « comme si elle eût relevé de maladie, etc. », on lit encore sous les ratures : « comme si elle eût changé de peau, qui me firent bien changer d'idée. »

10. C'est-à-dire : « je ne m'arrêtai pas, je poursuivis l'entretien sans retard. »

11. Le P. Sconin songeait alors à faire obtenir à son neveu le prieuré d'*Ouchie* (Oulchy ou Aulchy-le-Château), dans le Soissonnais. Voyez la *Notice biographique*, p. 32.

nouvelle aujourd'hui que l'accommodement étoit presque [12] fait avec les Pères de Sainte-Geneviève [13]. Ainsi je ne puis plus prétendre ici qu'à quelque chapelle de vingt ou vingt-cinq écus. Voyez si cela vaut la peine que je prends. Néanmoins je suis tout résolu de mener toujours le même train, et d'y demeurer jusqu'à ce que mon cousin m'en retire pour quelque meilleure espérance. Je gagnerai cela du moins que j'étudierai davantage, et que j'apprendrai à me contraindre, ce que je ne savois point du tout. Je vous prie de communiquer à mon cousin cette nouvelle, qui est certaine, et que Monsieur l'archev[êque] d'Arles a mandée aujourd'hui à Monsieur d'Uzès [14]; car ce sont eux deux qui ont fait ce beau dessein sans en parler à personne. Enfin, comme je mandois à M. Vitart, il semble que je gâte toutes les affaires où je suis intéressé. Je ne sais si mon malheur nuira encore à la négociation que mon cousin entreprend pour Ouchie. Quoi qu'il en soit, croyez que, s'il en vient à bout, *urbem quam statuo, vestra est* [15]. Je pourrois être le seul titulaire ; mais nous serons bien quatre bénéficiers. Vous n'y serez point M. Thomas [16] ; mais vous

12. *Presque* a été ajouté après coup, dans l'interligne.

13. L'évêque d'Uzès, qui avait eu des différends avec la congrégation de Sainte-Geneviève, était sur le point d'entrer en accommodement en cédant à cette congrégation la nomination aux bénéfices vacants dans le chapitre de son diocèse. Voyez la *Notice biographique*, p. 44.

14. Ils étaient frères. Le premier, François Adhémar de Monteil de Grignan, fut archevêque d'Arles de 1643 à 1689 ; le second, Jacques Adhémar de Monteil de Grignan (voyez, p. 418, la note 6 de la lettre 14), fut évêque d'Uzès de 1660 à 1674.

15. « La ville que je fonde est vôtre. » (Virgile, *Énéide*, livre I, vers 573.)

16. Ce M. Thomas était alors sous-prieur d'Oulchy. On trouve en 1660, 1661 et 1662 les actes de baptême, de mariage et d'inhumation signés de lui sur les registres d'Oulchy. Racine veut donc

serez Monsieur l'Abbé ou Monsieur le Prieur; car je crois que M. Vitart et M. Poignant[17] vous en céderont bien facilement l'autorité. Écrivez-moi tout, je vous prie, et fût-ce pour me blâmer, ne soyez point du tout réservé. Conservez-moi quelque petite part dans les bonnes grâces de Mlle Lucrèce. Entretenez-moi auprès de M. l'Avocat, et soyez toujours le même à mon égard. L'été est fort avancé ici. Les roses sont tantôt passées, et les rossignols aussi. La moisson avance, et les grandes chaleurs se font sentir.

Suscription : A Monsieur Monsieur l'abbé le Vasseur, chez Mlle de la Croix, rue Galande, à Paris. (Deux cachets rouges : J. RAC.)

28. — DE RACINE A MADEMOISELLE VITART[1].

A Uzés, le 15. mai 1662.

Encore n'avez-vous pas oublié mon nom : j'en avois bien peur pourtant, et je croyois être tout à fait disgracié auprès de vous, vu que, depuis plus de trois mois, vous n'avez pas donné la moindre marque que vous me connussiez seulement. Mais enfin Dieu a voulu que vous ayez écrit un dessus de lettre, et cela m'a un

---

dire : « vous ne serez pas seulement sous-prieur. » Voyez la *Notice biographique*, p. 45, note 1.

17. Antoine Poignant, fils de Jeanne Chéron, qui était la tante maternelle de la mère de Racine. Voyez la *Notice biographique*, p. 37 et 38. Poignant était, comme on sait, un des plus intimes amis de la Fontaine. Voyez l'*Histoire de la vie et des ouvrages de J. de la Fontaine* par Walckenaer, p. 14 (4e édition).

Lettre 28. — 1. Revue sur l'autographe, conservé à la Bibliothèque impériale.

peu remis. Jugez quelle reconnoissance j'aurois pour une lettre toute entière! Je ne sais pas ce qui me prive d'un si grand bien, et pour quelle raison votre bonne volonté s'est sitôt éteinte. Je fondois ma plus grande consolation sur les lettres que je pourrois quelquefois recevoir de vous, et une seule par mois auroit suffi pour me tenir toujours dans la meilleure humeur du monde; et dans cette belle humeur je vous aurois écrit mille belles choses. Les vers ne m'auroient rien coûté du tout, et vos lettres m'auroient inspiré un génie tout extraordinaire. C'est pourquoi, si je ne fais rien qui vaille, prenez-vous-en à vous-même, et croyez que je ne suis paresseux que parce que vous l'êtes toute la première : j'entends lorsqu'il s'agit d'écrire ; car en d'autres choses vous ne l'êtes pas, Dieu merci. Vous faites assez d'ouvrage, vous deux M. Vitart, et j'avois bien prédit que Mme Vitart treuveroit de l'occupation à son retour de Chevreuse[2]. On m'a mandé que vous ne laisseriez pas pour cela de faire un tour à la Ferté, et que ce voyage qu'on médite depuis si longtemps s'accompliroit à la Pentecôte[3]. J'enrage de n'y être pas, et vous n'en doutez pas, comme je crois, quoique vous ne vous en mettiez guère en peine[4], et peut-être ne songerez-vous pas une seule fois à la triste vie que je mène ici, pendant que toute votre compagnie se divertira fort à son aise. Il ne faut pas demander si Monsieur l'Abbé fait l'entendu à présent. Nous mènerons, dit-il, Mlle Vitart à la campagne avec M. et Mlle le

---

2. Mme Vitart avait été, au mois de janvier précédent, à Chevreuse, pour l'accouchement de Mlle Sellyer. Voyez la *lettre à Mademoiselle Vitart*, du 31 janvier 1662, et la note 4 de cette lettre, p. 442.

3. La Pentecôte, en 1662, était le 28 mai.

4. Racine avait d'abord écrit : « quoique vous ne vous en souciez guère. »

Mazier⁵. On voit bien que cela lui relève bien le cœur, et qu'il se prépare à passer les fêtes bien doucement. Je ne m'attends pas de les passer si à mon aise.

> J'irai parmi les oliviers,
> Les chênes verts⁶ et les figuiers,
> Chercher quelque remède à mon inquiétude :
> Je chercherai la solitude,
> Et ne pouvant être avec vous,
> Les lieux les plus affreux me seront les plus doux.

Excusez si je ne vous écris pas davantage; car en l'état où je suis, je ne vous saurois écrire que pour me plaindre de vous, et c'est un sujet qui ne vous plairoit pas peut-être. Donnez-moi lieu de vous remercier, et je m'étendrai plus volontiers sur cette matière. Aussi bien je ne vous demande pas des choses trop déraisonnables, ce me semble, en vous priant d'écrire une ou deux lignes par charité. Vous écrivez si bien et si facilement, quand vous le voulez. Il n'y a donc que la volonté qui vous manque, et tout iroit bien pour moi si vous me vouliez autant de bien que vous m'en pourriez faire : comme, au contraire, je ne puis pas vous témoigner le respect que j'ai pour vous autant que je le voudrois bien.

Suscription : A Mademoiselle Mademoiselle Vitart, à Paris. (Deux cachets rouges : J. RAC., avec une soie jaune.)

5. Claude le Mazier, conseiller d'État, ancien avocat au Châtelet, et Marguerite Charpentier sa femme, frère et belle-sœur de Mlle Vitart. Voyez ci-dessus, p. 451, la note 8 de la lettre 25. Claude le Mazier et Mlle Vitart étaient enfants de François le Mazier, procureur au Parlement, et de Marguerite Passart. Cela résulte d'actes que nous avons vus à l'étude de M. Defresne, notaire à Paris.

6. Il y a dans l'autographe : *Les cheneverds*, en un seul mot. Racine veut parler de cette espèce de chênes, qu'on appelle *yeuses*.

29. — DE RACINE A M. VITART[1].

A Usez, le 16ème mai [1662].

Vous aurez sans doute reçu mes lettres, qui étoient du même jour que votre dernière. Je vous suis infiniment obligé de la peine que vous avez prise de m'envoyer un démissoire. Je ne l'aurois jamais eu si je ne l'eusse reçu que de D. Cosme[2]. Il y a deux mois qu'il ne nous a point écrit, ni à mon oncle ni à moi. Nous n'en savons pas le sujet, et nous ignorons tout de même à quoi en est le bénéfice d'Anjou[3]. Mon oncle est tout prêt de vous l'abandonner, puisque aussi bien il n'en espère plus rien. Mais j'ai bien peur que D. Cosme ne veuille point lâcher les papiers qu'il a en main. Il n'y a que Blandin, le procureur, dont on puisse savoir l'état de l'affaire, et puis il ne faut qu'une lettre pitoyable de D. Cosme pour faire pitié à mon oncle[4], qui laissera perdre cette affaire entre ses mains. Comme, la dernière fois qu'il m'écrivit, il me mandoit que son âme ne tenoit plus qu'à un filet, tant il avoit pris de peine, jugez si cela ne toucheroit pas son frère. Au reste, je vous prie très-humblement de m'acquitter d'un grand merci envers Monsieur le prieur de la Ferté et M. du Chesne[5]. Je reconnois beaucoup la bonne volonté qu'ils ont tous deux témoignée pour moi. Si je savois où demeure M. du Chesne le fils, je lui écrirois ; car je serois hon-

LETTRE 29. — 1. Revue sur l'autographe, conservé à la Bibliothèque impériale.

2. Voyez ci-dessus, p. 417, la note 3 de la lettre 14.

3. Ce bénéfice d'Anjou est très-probablement le prieuré de l'Épinay, que Racine obtint plus tard. Voyez la *Notice biographique*, p. 47-49.

4. Après *mon oncle*, Racine avait d'abord continué ainsi : « et pour.... »

5. Son oncle. Voyez ci-dessus, p. 375, note 2 de la lettre 3.

teux de vous charger de tant de lettres. Je souhaite que votre second[6] voyage de la Ferté vous soit aussi agréable que le premier, et qu'il me soit aussi utile, s'il ne peut pas l'être davantage. Je ne vous renouvelle point mes protestations d'être honnête homme, et d'être reconnoissant : vous avez assez de bonté pour n'en douter plus. J'écris à M. Piolin, et je l'assure que sa dette lui est infaillible, mais qu'il me donne quelque temps pour le satisfaire ; je l'entends néanmoins à raison d'une pistole par mois. Voici le mémoire de mes livres, que vous avez eu la bonté de me demander. J'ai reçu avant-hier une lettre de Monsieur l'Abbé, et je lui écrirai aujourd'hui. Il m'a mandé que Mlle Vitart étoit disposée d'aller à la Ferté, quelque empêchement que vous y ayez voulu mettre. Vous vous doutez bien quel est cet empêchement-là, et je m'en réjouis autant que du voyage même. Je tâcherai d'écrire cette après-dînée à ma tante Vitart et à ma tante la religieuse[7], puisque vous vous en plaignez. Vous devez pourtant m'excuser si je ne l'ai pas fait, et elles aussi ; car que puis-je leur mander ? C'est bien assez de faire ici l'hypocrite, sans le faire encore à Paris par lettres ; car j'appelle hypocrisie d'écrire des lettres où il ne faut parler que de dévotion, et ne faire autre chose que se recommander aux prières. Ce n'est pas que je n'en aie bon besoin ; mais je voudrois qu'on en fît pour moi sans être obligé d'en tant demander. Si Dieu veut que je sois prieur, j'en ferai pour les autres autant qu'on en aura fait pour moi.

Monsieur notre évêque est allé faire sa visite, et il attend bientôt Monsieur l'archev[êque] d'Arles, qui a

---

6. *Second* est écrit au-dessus de la ligne.
7. Agnès de Sainte-Thècle Racine.

mandé qu'on ne lui écrivît plus à Paris. Cela différera peut-être l'entière conclusion de leur accommodement; mais c'est tout un, puisque la chose est faite, aux signatures près. Monsieur d'Usez treuvera plus d'obstacles qu'il ne pense. Il s'attend que le Prévôt et tout le monde signera son concordat, et il est fort trompé. Imaginez-vous si le Prévôt, qui a la collation de douze chanoinies de deux ou trois mille francs chacune[8], renoncera à ce droit-là pour complaire à Monsieur l'Évêque, dont il ne se soucie point du tout, à ce qu'on dit. Mais il ne reviendra de tout cela que des procès, et les réformés[9] feront rage.

On me vient voir ici fort souvent, et on tâche de me débaucher pour me mener en compagnie. Quoique j'aie la conscience fort tendre de ce côté-là, et que je n'aime pas à refuser, je me tiens pourtant sur la négative, et je ne sors point. Mon oncle m'en sait fort bon gré, et je m'en console avec mes livres. Comme on sait que je m'y plais, il y a bien des gens dans la ville qui m'en apportent tous les jours. Les uns m'en donnent des grecs, les autres d'espagnols, et de toutes les langues. Pour la composition, je ne puis m'y mettre. *Sic enim sum complexus otium ut ab eo divelli non queam. Itaque aut libris me delecto, quorum habeo festivam copiam, aut te cogito. A scribendo prorsus abhorret animus*[10].

---

8. *Chacune* a été ajouté dans l'interligne.

9. Les chanoines réformés de l'église cathédrale d'Uzès : voyez notre tome I, p. 179 et 180, où nous avons donné un *Extrait* du *Gallia christiana* (tome VII, p. 794-796). Il y est parlé des différends de ces réformés avec l'évêque d'Uzès. — Racine avait d'abord écrit : « la réforme. »

10. « Car je me suis tellement attaché à l'oisiveté que je ne puis en être arraché. Ou bien donc je m'amuse avec mes livres, dont j'ai une agréable provision, ou bien je pense à vous. J'ai la plus grande répugnance à écrire. » (Cicéron, *Lettres à Atticus*, livre II,

1662 Cicéron mandoit cela à Atticus; mais j'ai une raison particulière de ne point composer, qui est que je suis trop embarrassé du mauvais succès de mes affaires, et cette inquiétude sèche toutes les pensées de vers ou de galanterie que je pourrois avoir. Je ne sais même où j'en serois, n'étoit la confiance que j'ai en vous, puisque vous voulez bien que je l'aie. Je me réjouis que Mlle Manon[11] soit si gaillarde, et je la voudrois bien voir en cet état, et je voudrois aussi voir ce beau garçon[12] que vous avez fait depuis peu, aussi avancé qu'elle.

J'espérois bientôt pouvoir écrire à ma tante Vitart; mais on m'a malheureusement détourné cette après-dînée, et je suis obligé de remettre cela au premier voyage. Je ne vous prie pas de vous souvenir de moi quand vous serez à Ouchie : vous y êtes assez porté; car vous serez toujours le plus généreux homme du monde, et je tâcherai de mon côté d'être parfaitement reconnoissant. Je salue très-humblement toute votre famille et celle de M. le Mazier. Je ne puis non plus écrire à ma mère[13], et je remets cela au premier voyage.

---

lettre VI.) — Racine a substitué, dans cette citation, *aut te cogito* à *aut fluctus numero*.

11. Marie-Charlotte Vitart, l'aînée des filles de M. Vitart.

12. Cette lettre est très-certainement du 16 mai 1662, et Claude-Auguste Vitart ne naquit qu'au mois d'octobre suivant : voyez ci-dessus, p. 442, note 4 de la lettre 22. Racine supposait, pour plaisanter, que l'enfant dont on attendait la naissance, ne pouvait être qu'un « beau garçon. » La prophétie s'accomplit. Dans les vers qui terminent ci-après la lettre 31, p. 474, on remarquera que Racine parle encore du

. . . . beau petit mignon
Qui va bientôt venir au monde.

13. A sa grand'mère Mme Racine (Marie des Moulins).

30. — DE RACINE A L'ABBÉ LE VASSEUR.

A Uzés, le 16. mai 1662.

Je vous écrivis par le dernier ordinaire[1], et ainsi ne faites pas tant valoir l'obligation que je vous ai de ce que vous m'avez écrit deux fois de suite; car, Dieu merci, aucune de vos lettres n'est demeurée sans réponse; et quand cela seroit arrivé cette fois-ci, je crois que je ne vous en devrois pas beaucoup de ce côté-là : vos lettres n'ont pas toujours suivi les miennes de si près. Après tout, je vous suis tout à fait obligé de toutes les nouvelles que vous m'avez mandées de la province qui est vers la Marne[2]. Ce n'est pas que je sois si sot que de croire tout ce que vous dites à mon avantage. Vous me mettez sans doute en meilleure posture que je ne suis dans les esprits de ce pays-là. Quand je dis cela, je n'entends pas parler de M. Poignant; car après les marques qu'il a données de l'affection qu'il avoit pour moi, il ne me siéroit pas bien d'en douter. Vous m'en avez mandé des particularités trop assurées, et vous ne sauriez croire *con quanto contentamiento acabe de leer esta carta, y quantas vezes, en aquella hora mesma, la bolvi a leer*[3]. Je puis dire que ce témoignage de son amitié m'a touché plus que toutes les choses du monde. Vous croyez bien que ce n'étoit pas quelque

---

Lettre 30 (revue sur l'autographe, conservé à la Bibliothèque impériale). — 1. La lettre dont parle Racine s'est perdue, si toutes les précédentes sont bien datées.

2. Racine avait d'abord écrit : « sur la Marne. » Cette « province vers la Marne » est celle où se trouve la Ferté-Milon et Château-Thierry. Racine veut plus probablement parler de Château-Thierry.

3. Cette fin de phrase espagnole signifie littéralement : « avec quelle satisfaction j'ai achevé de lire cette lettre, et que de fois, dans cette même heure, je me suis remis à la lire. »

intérêt bas qui me dominoit[4]; mais cela m'a fait reconnoître qu'une belle amitié étoit en effet ce qu'il y avoit au monde de plus doux; et il me semble que cette connoissance que je suis aimé d'une personne me consoleroit dans toutes les plus cruelles disgrâces. Ce n'est pas que je souhaite le moins du monde qu'on en vienne à de si tristes effets, et je me flatte même que l'amitié que vous et M. Vitart avez pour moi, n'est pas moins forte que celle de M. Poignant, parce que je sens bien en moi-même que je vous suis très-fortement attaché, et le quolibet m'assure de ce côté-là : *Si vis amari, ama*[5]. Je suis ravi que vous ayez fait une si belle connoissance avec lui, parce qu'il est bon que vous vous connoissiez l'un l'autre; et il n'en est pas des amis comme des maîtresses; car bien loin d'avoir la moindre jalousie, au contraire, ce m'est bien de la joie que vous soyez aussi bons amis l'un avec l'autre, comme je crois l'être avec vous deux.

Quoique je me plaise beaucoup de causer avec vous, je ne le puis pas faire néanmoins fort au long; car j'ai eu cette après-dînée une visite qui m'a fait perdre tout le temps que j'avois envie de vous donner. C'étoit un jeune homme de cette ville, fort bien fait, mais passionnément amoureux. Vous saurez qu'en ce pays-ci on ne voit guère d'amours médiocres : toutes les passions y sont démesurées, et les esprits de cette ville, qui sont assez légers en d'autres choses, s'engagent plus fortement dans leurs inclinations qu'en aucun autre pays

---

4. Poignant aimoit beaucoup Racine, et disoit sans cesse qu'il lui laisseroit tout son bien. Il le fit en effet son héritier, mais à sa mort tout le bien se trouva mangé; Racine, par reconnoissance, acquitta les frais de la maladie et ceux de l'enterrement. (*Note de l'édition de* 1807.)

5. « Si tu veux être aimé, aime. »

du monde. Cependant, ôtez trois ou quatre personnes qui sont belles assurément, on n'y voit presque[6] que des beautés fort communes. La sienne est des premières, et il me l'a montrée tantôt[7] à une fenêtre, comme nous revenions de la procession[8], car elle est huguenote, et nous n'avons point de belle catholique. Il m'en est donc venu parler fort au long, et m'a montré des lettres, des discours, et même des vers, sans quoi ils croient que l'amour ne sauroit aller. Cependant j'aimerois mieux faire l'amour en bonne prose, que de le faire en méchants vers ; mais ils ne peuvent s'y résoudre, et ils veulent être poëtes, à quelque prix que ce soit. Pour mon malheur, ils croient que j'en suis un, et ils me font juge de tous leurs ouvrages. Vous pouvez croire que je n'ai pas peu à souffrir ; car le moyen d'avoir les oreilles battues de tant de méchantes choses, et d'être obligé de dire qu'elles sont bonnes? Encore je suis si heureux que j'ai un peu appris à me contraindre et à faire beaucoup de révérences et de compliments à la mode de ce pays-ci. Voilà donc à quoi mon après-dînée s'est passée. Il m'a mené à une de ses métairies proche d'ici ; il m'y a fait goûter des premières cerises de cette année ; car quoique nous en ayons depuis huit jours, je n'y avois pourtant pas songé encore ; car c'est de bonne heure, comme vous voyez. Mais tout est étrangement avancé en ce pays, et on fera la moisson devant un mois. Pour revenir à mon aventure, j'étois en danger de revenir plus tard ; mais le ciel s'est heureusement couvert, et nous avons ouï des coups de tonnerre, qui nous ont fait songer à éviter la pluie, et à revenir chez nous. Je n'ai eu

---

6. Racine avait écrit « presque point, » puis il a effacé *point*.
7. *Tantôt* a été ajouté dans l'interligne.
8. Le 16 mai, jour de la date de la lettre, était cette année le mardi des Rogations. (*Note de l'édition de* 1807.)

le temps, depuis cela, que de vous faire cette lettre et d'écrire deux mots à Mlle Vitart. Adieu donc : faites votre voyage de la Pentecôte aussi heureusement que celui de Pâques, et gardez-moi la même fidélité à m'en faire le récit. Je salue M. l'Avocat, et je vous prie d'assurer de mes respects Mlle Lucrèce, dont je trouve fort étrange que vous ne me parliez plus du tout, comme si je ne méritois pas d'en ouïr parler. Croyez que je la révère infiniment, et ménagez-moi toujours quelque petite place dans son souvenir. Soyez-moi encore fidèle de ce côté-là, et je vous garderai fidélité entière dans toutes les occasions qui pourroient jamais arriver, et, comme dit l'espagnol, *antes muerto que mudado*[9].

Suscription : A Monsieur Monsieur l'abbé le Vasseur, à Paris. (Deux cachets rouges : J. RAC., avec une soie verte.)

31. — DE RACINE A M. VITART[1].

A Uzés, le 30. mai 1662.

Je crois que cette lettre vous trouvera de retour, si vous avez été à la Ferté ; je ne la ferai pas bien longue, parce que je n'ai qu'un moment de loisir. Nous nous préparons à traiter Monsieur d'Usez après demain au matin, parce qu'il doit faire sa visite à un bénéfice qui dépend de la sacristie, et qui appartient par conséquent à mon oncle. C'est là où il a bâti un fort beau logis assurément, et il veut traiter son évêque avec grand appareil. Il est allé cette après-dînée à Avignon, pour acheter ce qu'on ne

9. « Plus tôt mort que changé. »
Lettre 31. — 1. Revue sur l'autographe, conservé à la Bibliothèque impériale.

pourroit treuver ici, et il m'a laissé la charge de pour- 1662
voir cependant à toutes choses. J'ai de fort beaux emplois, comme vous voyez, en ce pays-ci, et je sais quelque chose de plus que manger ma soupe, puisque je la
sais bien faire apprêter. J'ai appris ce qu'il faut donner
au premier, au second et au troisième service, les en-
tremets qu'il y faut mêler, et encore quelque chose de
plus; car nous prétendons faire un festin à quatre services, sans compter le dessert. J'ai la tête si remplie
de toutes ces belles choses-là, que je vous en pourrois
faire un long entretien; mais c'est une matière trop
creuse sur le papier, outre que, n'étant pas tout à fait
bien confirmé dans cette science, je pourrois bien faire
quelque pas de clerc, si j'en parlois encore longtemps.

Je ne vous prie plus de m'envoyer des *Lettres provinciales*[2] : on nous les a prêtées ici; elles étoient entre
les mains d'un officier de cette ville, qui est de la religion. Elles sont peu connues, mais beaucoup estimées
de ceux qui les connoissent. Tous les autres écrits de
cette nature sont venus pour la plupart en ce pays,
jusques aux *Nouvelles méthodes*[3]. Tout le monde a les
Plaidoyers de M. le Maistre[4]. Enfin on est plus cu-

2. Louis Racine a mis : « Je vous prie de m'envoyer les *Lettres
provinciales* », et retranché tout ce qui suit jusqu'aux mots : « Nos
moines » (p. 472). On s'explique aisément de sa part cette suppression d'un passage où il est dit que les *Provinciales* et les autres écrits
de Port-Royal n'étaient à Uzès qu'entre les mains des huguenots.
Louis Racine a également supprimé plus bas ce qui est dit du
P. Meynier.

3. Les *Nouvelles méthodes* de Lancelot, *pour apprendre la langue
latine* (1644), *pour apprendre la langue grecque* (1655), *pour apprendre la langue italienne* (1660), *pour apprendre la langue espagnole* (1660).

4. Ils avaient été publiés pour la première fois à Paris, en 1657
(in-folio).

rieux que je ne croyois pas. Ce ne sont pourtant que des huguenots; car pour les catholiques, ôtez un ou deux de ma connoissance, ils sont dominés par les jésuites. Nos moines sont plus sots que pas un, et, qui plus est, de sots ignorants, car ils n'étudient point du tout. Aussi je ne les vois jamais, et j'ai conçu une certaine horreur pour cette vie fainéante de moines, que je ne pourrois pas bien dissimuler. Pour le P. Sconin, il est, sans mentir, fort sage et fort habile homme, peu moine et grand théologien. Nous avons ici le P. Meynier, jésuite, qui passe pour un fort grand homme. On parle de lui dans la *Seizième lettre au provincial*[5]. Il n'a pas mieux réussi à écrire contre les huguenots, que contre M. Arnaud. Il y avoit ici un ministre assez habile, qui le traita fort mal. M. le prince de Conty[6] se fie à lui, à ce qu'on dit, et il lui a donné charge d'examiner tous les prêches qui seroient depuis l'édit de Nantes, afin qu'on les démolît. Le P. Meynier a fait donner indiscrètement assignation à trois prêches de ce quartier; et on nous dit hier que les commissaires avoient été obligés de donner arrêt de confirmation en faveur de ces prêches. Cela fait grand tort au P. Meynier et aux commissaires. Je vous conte tout cela, parce qu'on ne parle d'autre chose en cette ville. Il y a un évêque de cette province que les jésuites ne peuvent souffrir : c'est Monsieur d'Aleth[7], que vous connoissez assez[8] de réputation.

5. Voyez notre tome IV, p. 437, note 1.
6. Armand de Bourbon, prince de Conti, né en 1629, mort à Pézenas en 1666, était alors gouverneur du Languedoc. Voyez sur ce prince notre tome IV, p. 477, note 1.
7. Nicolas Pavillon, évêque d'Aleth de 1639 à 1677; il mourut le 8 décembre de cette dernière année. Voyez, à la page 520 de notre tome IV, ce que Racine dit de ce prélat dans son *Abrégé de l'histoire de Port-Royal*.
8. *Assez* a été ajouté au-dessus de la ligne.

Il est adoré dans le Languedoc, et Monsieur le Prince va faire toutes ses Pâques chez lui.

Je vous dirai une autre petite histoire, qui n'est pas si importante; mais elle est assez étrange. Une jeune fille d'Usez, qui logeoit assez près de chez nous, s'empoisonna hier elle-même et prit une grosse poignée d'arsenic, pour se venger de son père, qui l'avoit querellée fort rudement. Elle eut le temps de se confesser, et ne mourut que deux heures après. On croyoit qu'elle étoit grosse, et que la honte l'avoit portée à cette furieuse résolution. Mais on l'ouvrit toute entière, et jamais fille ne fut plus fille. Telle est l'humeur des gens de ce pays-ci, et ils portent les passions au dernier excès.

Je crois que vous aurez la bonté de me mander quelque chose de votre voyage, qui se sera sans doute passé encore plus doucement que le premier, puisque la compagnie devoit être si belle. Je ne sais si vous y aurez vu M. Sconin[9]; il nous écrivit avant-hier de Paris. Dans ma lettre, il se plaignoit fort de vous et de M. du Chesne. Je dissimule tout cela à cause de son frère; mais s'il continue davantage sur cette matière, je ne pourrai pas toujours me tenir, et j'éclaterai. Ne lui en témoignez pourtant rien, je vous prie : cela est infiniment au-dessous de vous. Je salue très-humblement Mlle Vitart. J'écrirai, un autre voyage, à Monsieur l'Abbé; je suis trop occupé aujourd'hui.

Je suis fort serviteur de la belle Manon
    Et de la petite Nanon,
      Car je crois que c'est là le nom
    Dont on nomma votre seconde;

---

9. Racine parait ici désigner ce frère du vicaire général d'Uzès, qu'il nomme ailleurs dom Cosme. Dans la lettre suivante on verra qu'il lui donne indifféremment l'un ou l'autre nom.

Et je salue aussi ce beau petit mignon
  Qui va bientôt venir au monde [10].

Suscription : A Monsieur Monsieur Vitart, à Paris. (Deux cachets bruns : J. RAC.)

---

32. — DE RACINE A M. VITART.

A Uzés, le 6. juin 1662.

Quoique je vous aie écrit par le dernier ordinaire, toutes vos lettres me sont trop précieuses pour en laisser une seule sans réponse. Croyez que c'est le plus grand soulagement que je reçoive en ce pays-ci, parmi tous les sujets de chagrin que j'y ai. Mon oncle est encore malade, et cela me touche sensiblement; car je vois que ses maladies ne viennent que d'inquiétude et d'accablement : il a mille affaires, toutes embarrassantes; il a payé plus de trente mille livres de dettes, depuis que je suis ici, et il s'en découvre tous les jours de nouvelles : vous diriez que nos moines avoient pris plaisir à se ruiner, tant ils se sont endettés. Cependant, quoique mon oncle se tue pour eux, il reconnoît de plus en plus la mauvaise volonté qu'ils ont pour lui : il en reçoit tous les jours des avis, et avec tout cela il faut qu'il dissimule tout. Il traita splendidement Monsieur d'Usez la semaine passée, et Monsieur d'Usez témoigne toute sorte de confiance en lui; mais il n'en attend rien. Il[1] a des

---

10. Voyez ci-dessus la note 12 de la lettre 29, p. 466.
Lettre 32 (revue sur l'autographe, conservé à la Bibliothèque impériale.) — 1. L'évêque d'Uzès. Les éditeurs précédents ont corrigé l'équivoque en substituant les mots *cet évêque* au pronom *il*.

gens affamés à qui il donne tout. Mon oncle est si lassé de tout cet embarras-là, qu'il me pressa beaucoup avant-hier pour recevoir son bénéfice par résignation. Cela me fit trembler, voyant l'état où sont les affaires, et je lui sus si bien représenter ce que c'étoit que de s'engager dans des procès, et au bout du compte demeurer moine sans titre et sans liberté, que lui-même est tout le premier à m'en détourner, outre que je n'ai pas l'âge, parce qu'il faut être prêtre; car quoiqu'une dispense soit aisée, ce seroit nouvelle matière de procès; et je serois traité de Turc à More par les réformés. Enfin il en vint jusque-là qu'il voudroit treuver un bénéficier séculier qui voulût de son bénéfice à condition de me résigner celui qu'il auroit; mais il est difficile qu'on en trouve. Vous voyez par là si je l'ai gagné, et s'il a de la bonne volonté pour moi. Il est résolu de me mener un de ces jours à Nîmes ou à Avignon, pour me faire tonsurer, afin qu'en tout cas, s'il vient quelque chapelle, il la puisse impétrer; car dès que les réformés seront rétablis, vous êtes assurés[2] qu'ils ne me verront pas volontiers avec lui; et son bénéfice se treuve malheureusement engagé pour trois ans, si bien qu'il n'en peut jouir, car il l'a engagé lui-même, pour donner exemple aux autres. S'il venoit à vaquer quelque petite chose dans votre détroit[3], souvenez-vous de moi, sauf les droits de Monsieur l'Abbé, que je consens de bon cœur que vous préfériez aux miens. Je crois qu'on n'en murmureroit pas à P. R.[4], puisqu'on voit bien que je suis ici dévoué à l'Église. Mon oncle est résolu d'écrire à son frère qu'il remette entre vos mains l'affaire d'Anjou;

---

2. Il y a ainsi le pluriel dans l'original.
3. Louis Racine a substitué la forme plus moderne *district* à *détroit*, qui, dans ce sens, n'était plus usité de son temps.
4. A Port-Royal.

mais j'y prévois bien de la répugnance de la part de D. Cosme. Je voudrois savoir auparavant votre sentiment là-dessus. Il vous aura peut-être dépeint l'affaire plus difficile qu'elle n'est. Cependant croyez que l'aumônier de Monsieur d'Usez l'a consultée[5] à Paris, et que M. Couturier lui a dit que c'étoit une bagatelle. Les provisions de mon oncle sont onze ou douze jours en date devant celles que sa partie a eues en cour de Rome. L'affaire étoit incontestable, et on ne l'a disputée que sur ce que, dans la copie des provisions, on avoit mis simplement *testibus nominatis*[6], sans y ajouter *signatis*[7]. Cependant il est dans l'original, et j'en ai envoyé moi-même une autre copie collationnée par-devant notaire; et M. Couturier même prétendoit que quand cela auroit été oublié, il suffit que le collateur ait signé lui-même. Ce que M. Sconin nous oppose, c'est qu'il dit que toute la famille de Bernay[8] sollicite contre nous. Je n'en sais rien; mais en tout cas vous connoissez ces Messieurs-là. Et par un admirable raisonnement, il me mandoit, il y a huit jours, que les blés sont gâtés en Anjou pour trois ans, et qu'il valoit mieux qu'il tirât son argent, et qu'il laissât le bénéfice. Au contraire, il me semble que les autres seront bien plus aises de s'accommoder, puisqu'ils n'ont rien à prendre de trois ans; et ils avoient déjà fait l'an passé porter parole qu'on les remboursât des frais, et qu'ils désisteroient[9]. Mais D. Cosme, à ce qu'il

---

5. C'est-à-dire : « a consulté l'affaire, a pris conseil sur l'affaire. » M. Aignan a changé *consultée* en *consulté*, ce qui détruit le véritable sens.

6. « Les témoins étant nommés. »

7. « [Les témoins] étant signés (ayant signé). »

8. Huault de Bernay, famille très-ancienne dans la magistrature de Paris, et actuellement éteinte. (*Note de l'édition de* 1807.)

9. Les précédents éditeurs ont mis : « se désisteroient. » Mais *se* n'est point dans le manuscrit, et ce n'est pas un lapsus. Voyez le

dit, fut bien fin, car il leur dit : « Remboursez-moi, et je 1662 vous laisse le titre. » Son frère est assez scandalisé de cette conduite. Excusez si je vous importune tant : vous y êtes assez accoutumé.

Je ne saurois [10] écrire à personne aujourd'hui, j'ai l'esprit trop embarrassé, et je suis en état de ne parler que de procès. Cela scandaliseroit peut-être ceux à qui j'ai accoutumé d'écrire. Tout le monde n'a pas la patience que vous avez pour souffrir mes folies : outre que mon oncle est au lit, et je lui suis fort assidu. Il vous baise les mains de tout son cœur, et vous remettroit tous ses intérêts plus sûrement et plus volontiers qu'entre les mains de son frère. Il est tout à fait bon, je vous assure, et je crois que c'est le seul de sa famille [11] qui a l'âme tendre et généreuse; car ce sont tous de francs rustes [12], ôtez le père, qui en tient pourtant sa part. Je n'en dirois pas tant, n'étoit la colère où je suis du vilain tour qu'ils vous ont joué. Je n'en ai encore osé parler à mon oncle : cela viendra dans son temps. Acquittez-moi envers Mlle Vitart et toute votre famille et la sienne. Je lui écrirai, et à Monsieur l'Abbé, lorsque j'aurai quelque intervalle un peu plus enjoué. J'écrirai en même temps à ma mère : je vois bien qu'elle est tout à fait inquiétée de la pièce qu'on vous a faite à mon sujet; j'en suis au

---

Lexique. — Louis Racine a fort abrégé cette lettre et retranché tout ce morceau. Voyez la note suivante.

10. Tout ce qui suit, jusqu'à la fin de la lettre, a non-seulement été fort altéré par ceux de nos devanciers qui l'ont donné, mais aussi mis par la plupart d'entre eux hors de sa place. Louis Racine l'a réuni, en l'abrégeant beaucoup, à la lettre du 25 juillet 1662 (notre *lettre* 36), et M. Aimé-Martin l'a donné à part, comme un fragment de date incertaine.

11. Louis Racine, et les éditeurs qui sont venus après lui, ont substitué *de sa communauté* à *de sa famille*.

12. Racine a écrit *rustes*, et non *rustres*. Voyez ci-dessus, p. 137, note 2.

désespoir sitôt que j'y songe ; et je vous puis protester que je ne suis pas ardent pour les bénéfices, mais que je n'en souhaite que pour payer au moins quelque méchante partie de tout ce que je vous dois. Je meurs d'envie de voir vos deux infantes ; et je salue M. Houÿ de tout mon cœur.

33. — DE RACINE A M. VITART.

A Uzés, le 13. juin 1662.

J'ATTENDS avec empressement des nouvelles de votre voyage, et votre absence de Paris m'ennuie déjà autant que si j'étois à Paris même, à cause que je n'ai point reçu de vos lettres depuis que vous en êtes sorti. J'écrivis la semaine passée à D. Cosme pour le disposer à vous abandonner le bénéfice, ou à quelqu'un de vos amis qui lui fût moins suspect, puisqu'il a pour vous des sentiments si injustes ; et mon oncle approuva ma lettre par une apostille ; car il a tout de bon envie de me le donner, et m'a dit même de traiter avec l'aumônier de Monsieur d'Uzés, qui a grande envie sur ce bénéfice, pour voir s'il me voudroit donner en échange un prieuré simple de cent écus qu'il a en ce pays. Je ne lui en ai point parlé, et j'attends de vos nouvelles. Il seroit fort disposé à cet échange, pourvu que le bénéfice lui fût assuré ; car il ira l'hiver prochain à Paris avec son maître, et ce bénéfice seroit fort à sa bienséance, parce que le fermier est le même [à] qui son maître a arrêté Saint-George[1]. Mais il seroit du moins autant à ma

LETTRE 33 (revue sur l'autographe, conservé à la Bibliothèque impériale). — 1. Saint-Georges-sur-Loire, dans le diocèse d'An-

biensèance qu'à la sienne, si vous pouviez être assuré
du succès de l'affaire; car je n'aurois pas grande inclination de faire séjour en ce pays-ci. Conseillez-moi donc,
et je verrai après en quelle disposition il sera. Il me
parle toujours du bénéfice de mon oncle, et il enrage
de l'avoir². Mais la méchante condition que d'avoir
affaire à D. Cosme! Je crois que cet homme-là est né
pour ruiner toutes mes affaires.

Je souhaite que vous ayez une aussi belle récolte à
vos deux fermes, que nous avons en ce pays-ci. La moisson est déjà fort avancée, et elle se fait fort plaisamment ici au prix de la coutume de France; car on lie les
gerbes à mesure qu'on les coupe; on ne laisse point
sécher le blé sur la terre, car il n'est déjà que trop sec,
et dès le même jour on le porte à l'aire, où on le bat
aussitôt. Ainsi le blé est aussitôt coupé, lié et battu.
Vous verriez un tas de moissonneurs rôtis du soleil, qui
travaillent comme des démons, et quand ils sont hors
d'haleine, il[s] se jette[nt] à terre au soleil même, dorment un *miserere*³ et se relèvent aussitôt. Pour moi,
je ne vois cela que de nos fenêtres, car je ne pourrois
pas être un moment dehors sans mourir: l'air est à peu
près aussi chaud qu'un four allumé, et cette chaleur continue autant la nuit que le jour; enfin il faudroit se résoudre à fondre comme du beurre, n'étoit un petit vent
frais qui a la charité de souffler de temps en temps; et
pour m'achever, je suis tout le jour étourdi d'une infinité de cigales qui ne font que chanter de tous côtés,
mais d'un chant le plus perçant et le plus importun du

---

gers, dont l'évêque d'Uzès fut abbé de 1654 à 1674 : voyez notre tome I, p. 48, note 1.

2. Il a un violent désir de l'avoir.

3. C'est-à-dire : « le temps de dire un *miserere*. »

monde. Si j'avois autant d'autorité sur elles qu'en avoit le bon saint François, je ne leur dirois pas, comme il faisoit : « Chantez, ma sœur la cigale [4]; » mais je les prierois bien fort de s'en aller. faire un tour jusqu'à Paris ou à la Ferté, si vous y êtes encore, pour vous faire part d'une si belle harmonie.

Monsieur notre évêque ne se découvre encore à personne sur le beau projet de réforme qu'il a fait faire à Paris, et pour vous dire ce qu'on en pense ici, il est plus irrésolu que jamais. Il appréhende furieusement d'aliéner tous les esprits de cette province. Sur le simple bruit qui courut que l'affaire étoit conclue, il se voit déjà désert, à ce qu'on dit, et cela le fâche ; car il ne hait pas de voir le monde chez [lui], mais il reconnoît bien déjà qu'on ne fait la cour en ce pays-ci qu'à ceux dont on attend du bien. Il en a témoigné son étonnement il y a quelques jours, et ce n'est rien encore pourtant ; car s'il établit une fois la réforme, on dit qu'il sera abandonné même de ses valets. Chacun avoit de belles prétentions sur ce chapitre. Le mal est qu'on lui impute

---

4. Cette histoire de saint François d'Assise et de la cigale se lit au folio xxxi de la *Légende* de saint François, imprimée en 1509 par Philippe Junta (in-8°) sous ce titre : *Aurea Legenda major beati Francisci, composita per sanctum Bonaventuram.* Voici le passage : *Apud sanctam Mariam de Portiuncula, juxta cellam viri Dei super ficum cicada residens et decantans, quum servum Domini qui etiam in parvis rebus magnificentiam Creatoris admirari didicerat, ad divinas laudes cantu suo frequentius excitaret, ab eodem quadam die vocata, velut edocta cœlitus, super manum volavit ipsius. Cui quum dixisset :* « *Canta, soror mea cicada, et Dominum creatorem tuo jubilo lauda;* » *sine mora obediens canere cœpit, nec destitit donec jussu Patris ad locum proprium revolavit. Mansit autem per octo dies ibidem, quolibet die veniendo..., ejus jussa perficiens. Tandem vir Dei ait ad socios :* « *Demus jam sorori nostræ cicadæ licentiam; satis nimirum nos suo cantu lætificans ad laudes Dei octo dierum spatio excitavit.* » *Et statim ab eo licentiata recessit; nec ultra ibidem apparuit, ac si mandatum ipsius non auderet aliquatenus præterire.*

d'aimer beaucoup à dominer, et qu'il aime mieux avoir dans son Église des moines dont il prétend disposer, quoique peut-être il se trompe, que non pas des chanoines séculiers qui le portent un peu plus haut. Cependant ceux qui font les politiques en ces sortes d'affaires disent que les particuliers sont plus maniables qu'une communauté, et les moines n'ont pas toute sorte de déférence pour les évêques. Avant-hier[5], il arriva une chose par où il montra bien qu'il avoit envie d'être le maître. Nous avons un religieux qu'on dit être un janséniste couvert. Je connois le bon homme, et je puis dire, sans le flatter, qu'il ne sait pas encore seulement l'état de la question. Son sous-prieur[6] le défera à Monsieur l'Évêque, lequel appela mon oncle, et lui dit, avec beaucoup d'empressement, qu'il vouloit l'interroger, et en être le juge seul sans que le Prévôt ni le chapitre s'en mêlât. Mon oncle lui dit froidement qu'il l'interrogeât, mais que ce bon religieux ne savoit pas seulement, comme je vous ai dit, ce que c'étoit du jansénisme. Voilà toutes les nouvelles que je vous puis mander : il ne se passe rien de plus mémorable en ce pays-ci. Le blé est enchéri, quelque belle que soit la récolte, à cause qu'on en transporte en vos quartiers. Le beau blé, qui ne valoit que quinze livres, en vaut vingt et une livres la salmée[7]. On l'appelle ainsi, et cette me-

---

5. Louis Racine a supprimé ce morceau sur le religieux qui passait pour janséniste. Nous notons cette suppression, parmi tant d'autres, parce que l'intention en est évidente : voyez ci-dessus la note 2 de la lettre 31, p. 471. A la suite de ce morceau, toute la fin de cette lettre 33 a été omise par Louis Racine.

6. Racine écrit *souprieur*.

7. La *salmée*, qui est de douze hémines, est égale à un septier et un quart de septier de Paris. Les 21 livres d'alors contenaient autant d'argent qu'en contiennent 39 fr. 50 c. de notre monnaie actuelle. (*Note de l'édition de 1807.*)

sure contient environ dix minots ou dix pichets[8] ou un peu plus. Pour le vin, on ne saura du tout qu'en faire. Le meilleur, c'est-à-dire le meilleur du royaume, se vend deux carolus le pot[9], mesure de Saint-Denys. J'aurai de quoi boire à votre santé à bon marché ; mais j'aimerois mieux l'aller boire là-bas avec du vin de la montagne de Reims.

Je baise très-humblement les mains à Mlle Vitart, à vos deux mignonnes, et universellement à toute la famille. Je m'avise toujours un peu tard d'écrire : cela est cause que je ne saurois presque écrire qu'à vous. J'ai pourtant écrit [à] ma mère, et je remets Monsieur l'Abbé à jeudi prochain ; il lui en coûtera un port de lettre de ce retardement, car je ne pourrai pas vous l'adresser comme les autres fois. Je voudrois qu'il m'en fît coûter plus souvent qu'il ne fait pas; il est grand ménager de ses lettres et de la bourse de mon oncle. Je suis tout à lui, et uniquement à vous.

Suscription : A Monsieur Monsieur Vitart, à Paris. (Deux cachets bruns : J. RAC.)

---

8. [Le *pichet* ou *bichet* est une] mesure qui contient environ trente livres de froment, poids de marc. (*Note de l'édition de* 1807, à la lettre du 25 juillet 1662.)

9. Le pot de vin de Languedoc pèse une livre et demie, poids de marc. Le *carolus*, qui est une monnaie de compte en usage parmi le peuple, vaut deux blancs ou dix deniers tournois. Ainsi trois *carolus* sont la même valeur que *six-blancs* ou trente deniers. (*Note de l'édition de* 1807.)

34. — DE RACINE A L'ABBÉ LE VASSEUR. 1662

A Uzés, le 4. juillet 1662[1].

QUE vous tenez bien votre gravité espagnole ! Il paroît bien qu'en apprenant cette langue, vous avez pris un peu de l'humeur de la nation. Vous n'allez plus qu'à pas comptés, et vous écrivez une lettre en trois mois. Je ne vous ferai pas davantage de reproches, quoique j'eusse bien résolu ce matin de vous en accabler. J'avois étudié tout ce qu'il y a de plus rude et de plus injurieux dans les cinq langues que vous me donnez ; mais votre lettre est venue à midi, qui m'a fait perdre la moitié de ma colère. N'êtes-vous pas fort plaisant avec vos cinq langues ? Vous voudriez justement que mes lettres fussent des Calepins[2], et encore des lettres galantes. Je vous trouve, sans mentir, de fort belle humeur. Il y a assez de pédants au monde sans que j'en augmente le nombre. Si Mlle Lucrèce a besoin de maîtres en ces cinq langues, j'en ai vu souvent trois ou quatre autour de vous. Donnez-lui celui-là qui avoit tant à démêler avec M. Lancelot[3] : c'étoit une assez bonne figure. Aussi bien ne croyez pas que ma bibliothèque

LETTRE 34. — 1. Revue sur l'autographe, conservé à la Bibliothèque impériale.

2. Ce mot, qui maintenant signifie d'ordinaire un *agenda*, un recueil de notes, d'extraits, etc., veut dire ici un dictionnaire en plusieurs langues. L'édition la plus complète du *Dictionnaire* d'Ambroise Calepin est en onze langues (Bâle, 1590 ou 1627, in-folio).

3. Dans une note de l'édition de 1807 sur ce passage, il est dit que Claude Lancelot avait été, dans les écoles de Port-Royal, le maitre, non-seulement, comme on sait, de Racine, mais aussi de l'abbé le Vasseur. Nous ignorons si ce renseignement est exact. Si l'on devait croire que le professeur « qui avoit tant à démêler avec M. Lancelot » fût le P. Labbe, ce fameux détracteur des *hellénistes* de Port-Royal, le Vasseur aurait reçu au contraire des leçons des jésuites ; mais nous ne pouvons rien dire ici de certain.

soit fort grosse eu ce pays-ci : le nombre de mes livres est fort borné ; encore ne sont-ce pas des livres à conter fleurettes : ce sont des sommes de théologies latines, méditations espagnoles, histoires italiennes, Pères grecs, et pas un françois. Voyez où je pourrois trouver quelque chose de revenant à Mlle Lucrèce. Tout ce que je pourrai faire sera de lui donner de mon françois, tel qu'il pourra être. Aussi bien il y a longtemps que j'avois envie de lui écrire, mais vous me mandiez toujours qu'elle étoit à la campagne, et je croyois que cela vouloit dire que vous n'aviez rien de bon à me dire de sa part et qu'elle me donnoit mon congé. Je n'avois pas envie de le prendre pour cela, et j'étois trop attaché à l'idée que j'ai toujours d'elle, pour n'y plus songer. Croyez que vous m'avez mis bien au large par cette proposition que vous me faites[4], et que, si Dieu m'assiste, je lui ferai de belles et grandes lettres. Ce ne sera pas encore d'aujourd'hui ; car j'ai reçu votre lettre trop tard. Cependant entretenez-la bien dans cette humeur de souffrir de mes lettres ; car j'ai bien peur qu'elle ne retourne à la campagne, c'est-à-dire qu'elle ne me laisse là, sitôt qu'elle en aura vu une. *Porque mis razones no deven ser manjar para tan subtil entendimiento como el suyo*[5]. Donnez-lui toujours ce passage en attendant, et assurez-la de tous mes respects.

Je savois déjà depuis longtemps que M. Poignant n'aimoit pas à écrire beaucoup, et lorsque je lui ai écrit, c'étoit sans espérance de réponse ; et c'est dans cette pensée que je lui écrirai toujours, quand j'aurai quelque chose de bon à lui mander.

M. de la Fontaine m'a écrit et me mande force nou-

4. « Que vous me faites » a été ajouté au-dessus de la ligne.
5. « Parce que mes raisonnements ne sauraient être un mets pour un entendement aussi délicat que le sien. »

velles de poésies, et surtout de pièces de théâtre. Je m'étonne que vous ne m'en disiez pas un mot. N'est-ce point que ce charme étrange qui vous empêchoit d'écrire, vous empêchoit aussi d'aller à la comédie? Quoi qu'il en soit, il me portoit à faire des vers[6]. Je lui récris aujourd'hui, et j'envoie sa lettre[7] décachetée à M. Vitart. S'il en fait retirer copie, ayez soin, je vous prie, que la lettre ne soit point souillonnée, et qu'on ne la retienne pas longtemps. Mandez-moi surtout ce qui vous en semble, et ne me payez pas d'exclamations: autrement je ne vous envoyerai jamais rien. Je ne suis pas content de ce que vous avez ainsi traité mes *Bains de Vénus*. Croyez-vous que je les envoyasse seulement pour vous divertir un quart d'heure? Je prétends que vous me payez[8] en raisons. Vous en avez tant de bonnes pour vous justifier d'un silence de trois mois. Faites des vers un peu pour voir, et vous verrez si je ne vous en manderai pas au long tout ce que j'en pourrai dire. Au moins ayez la bonté de donner ces *Bains* à quelqu'un pour les copier, afin que mon cousin les envoie à M. de la Fontaine.

Il ne se passe rien de nouveau en ce pays, et je ne vois pas que mes affaires s'y avancent beaucoup. Cela me fait désespérer. Je ne sais si M. Vitart ne songe plus du côté d'Ouchie.

Je cherche quelque sujet de théâtre, et je serois assez disposé à y travailler; mais j'ai trop de sujet d'être mélancolique en ce pays-ci, et il faut avoir l'esprit plus libre que je ne l'ai pas. Aussi bien ce me seroit une

---

6. Parmi les lettres perdues, de la Fontaine à Racine, celle-ci nous semble particulièrement regrettable.

7. C'est-à-dire la lettre à lui adressée, ma réponse. C'est la lettre que nous donnons après celle-ci.

8. Il y a bien *payez* dans l'original: à la suite, Racine avait d'abord écrit: « de raisons. »

gêne de n'avoir pas ici une personne comme vous, à qui je pusse tout montrer à mesure que j'aurois fait quelque chose. Et s'il faut un passage latin pour vous mieux exprimer cela, je n'en saurois trouver un plus propre que celui-ci : *Nihil mihi nunc scito tam deesse quam hominem eum quicum omnia quæ me ad aliqua afficiunt una communicem, qui me amet, qui sapiat, quicum ego colloquar, nihil fingam, nihil dissimulem, nihil obtegam. Non homo, sed littus, atque aer, et solitudo mera. Tu autem qui sæpissime curam et angorem animi mei sermone et consilio levasti tuo, qui mihi in rebus omnibus conscius et omnium meorum sermonum et consiliorum particeps esse solebus, ubinam es*[9]? Quand Cicéron eût été à Uzès, comme j'y suis, et que vous eussiez été en la place d'Atticus son ami, eût-il pu parler autrement?

Mais adieu : en voilà assez pour aujourd'hui. Écrivez-moi plus souvent, et ne me parlez plus de charme ni d'autres empêchements; mais souvenez-vous toujours de moi, et m'en donnez quelques marques. L'exemple de

---

9. « Sachez que rien ne me manque tant en ce moment qu'une personne à qui je puisse m'ouvrir de tout ce qui me cause quelque inquiétude, une personne qui m'aime, qui pense sagement, avec qui j'ose m'entretenir en toute liberté, sans déguisement, sans réserve. Ici pas un homme, mais seulement un rivage, l'air, et une pure solitude. Mais vous, qui très-souvent, par votre entretien et vos conseils, avez soulagé mes peines et mes tourments, vous qui, en toutes circonstances, étiez habitué à recevoir toutes mes confidences, à entrer dans tous mes projets, où êtes-vous? » (*Commencement de la* lettre xviii *du livre I* à Atticus.) Nous avons déjà vu plus haut une phrase de ce même passage, dans la lettre 23 (p. 447). Racine cite de mémoire; il y a dans Cicéron, à la seconde ligne : *quæ me cura aliqua afficiunt;* quelques mots sont omis, à dessein, devant *Non homo;* et vers la fin, le vrai texte de la lettre latine est : *qui mihi et in publica re socius, et in privatis omnibus conscius.... particeps esse solebas,* etc.

M. Poignant n'est pas bon pour tout le monde, et surtout pour ceux qui écrivent si facilement que vous.

Je salue M. l'Avocat de tout mon cœur.

Suscription : A Monsieur Monsieur l'abbé le Vasseur, à Paris. (Deux cachets rouges : J. RAC., avec une soie rose.)

35. — DE RACINE A LA FONTAINE[1].

[A Usez, le 4 juillet[2] 1662.]

Votre lettre[3] m'a fait grand bien, et je passerois assez doucement mon temps, si j'en recevois souvent de pareilles. Je ne sache rien qui me puisse mieux consoler de mon éloignement de Paris : je m'imagine même être au beau milieu du Parnasse, tant vous décrivez agréablement tout ce qui s'y passe de plus mémorable ; mais je m'en trouve fort éloigné, et c'est se moquer de moi que de me porter, comme vous faites, à y retourner. Je n'y ai pas fait assez de voyages pour en retenir le chemin ; et ne m'en souvenant plus, qui pourroit m'y remettre en ce pays-ci? J'aurois beau invoquer les Muses : elles sont trop loin pour m'entendre ; elles sont toujours occupées auprès de vous autres Messieurs de Paris. Il arrive rarement qu'elles viennent dans les provinces : on dit

---

Lettre 35 (revue sur la copie de Louis Racine, appartenant à M. Auguste de Naurois). — 1. Louis Racine, dans son *Recueil*, l'a donnée comme étant adressée à M. Vitart. Cette erreur, comme le fait remarquer l'éditeur de 1807, est venue de ce que la lettre est sans suscription, et se trouvait renfermée dans la précédente. Le même éditeur dit fort bien qu'une lecture un peu attentive de la lettre aurait suffi pour avertir Louis Racine de sa méprise.

2. Louis Racine a, dans sa copie, comme dans son *Recueil* imprimé, daté cette lettre du 9 juillet. D'autres éditeurs l'ont datée du 6. Mais elle doit être du 4, comme la précédente.

3. Voyez ci-dessus la note 6 de la lettre précédente.

mème qu'elles ont fait serment de n'y plus revenir, depuis la violence que leur voulut faire Pirénée. Je ne sais si vous vous souvenez de cette histoire [4] :

> C'étoit un fameux homicide ;
> Il avoit conquis la Phocide,
> Et faisoit des courses, dit-on,
> Jusques au pied de l'Hélicon.
>
> Un jour, les neuf savantes sœurs
> Qu'on adore en cette montagne,
> S'amusant à cueillir des fleurs,
> Se promenoient par la campagne.
>
> Tout d'un coup le ciel se couvrit ;
> Un épais nuage s'ouvrit :
> Il plut à grands flots, et l'orage
> Les mit en mauvais équipage.
>
> Le barbare assez près de là
> Avoit établi sa demeure ;
> Il les vit, et les appela.
> Elles y vinrent tout à l'heure [5].
>
> Sitôt qu'elles furent dedans,
> Il ferma la porte sur elles,

4. Racine en a emprunté quelques traits à Ovide, *Métamorphoses*, livre V, vers 276-293.

5. Ce vers et les neuf couplets qui suivent jusqu'au vers :

> Lorsqu'elles furent de retour,

sont imprimés ici pour la première fois. Ils avaient été retranchés dans le *Recueil* de Louis Racine, et remplacés par ces lignes de prose : « Vous savez la suite, vous savez que ce malheureux Pyrénée voulut faire violence aux Muses, et que pour les en garantir, les Dieux leur donnèrent des ailes ; et elles revolèrent aussitôt vers le Parnasse. » Nous ne notons pas les nombreuses corrections que la copie de Louis Racine nous a fournies, et qui nous ont permis de rétablir le véritable texte des vers qu'il n'a pas supprimés dans son *Recueil*.

Et sans dissimuler longtemps,
« Je vous tiens, leur dit-il, mes belles. »

Il est à croire que les Muses
Eurent sujet d'être confuses.
Un si farouche compliment
Les étourdit étrangement.

« Hélas! disoient-elles entre elles,
Nous ne serons donc plus pucelles. »
Elles essayèrent d'abord
De lui donner horreur d'une action si noire,
Lui promettant que sa mémoire
Vivroit longtemps après sa mort.

« Je me moque de vos leçons,
Leur dit-il, et de vos chansons :
Je ne prétends pas avoir place
Dans les registres du Parnasse. »

Les Muses, qui jugeoient bien
Qu'elles n'obtiendroient jamais rien
Sur une âme si mal instruite,
Gagnèrent toutes au plus vite
Jusques au faîte du balcon
D'où l'on découvroit l'Hélicon;

Et choisissant plutôt un glorieux trépas
Que de se voir déshonorées,
Les pauvres Muses éplorées
S'alloient précipiter en bas.

Mais les Dieux, qui ne dormoient point,
Leur envoyèrent bien à point
A chacune une paire d'ailes,
Qui d'un si grand péril garantirent ces belles.

Leur persécuteur aveuglé
Prétendoit voler sur leurs traces :

Mais son dos n'étant point ailé,
Sa chute punit son audace :
Les Muses cependant voloient sur le Parnasse.

Le mauvais temps étoit passé,
Et ce fut un bonheur pour elles;
Car si l'orage n'eût cessé,
La pluie auroit gagné leurs ailes,
Et c'étoit fait des neuf pucelles.

Lorsqu'elles furent de retour,
Considérant le mauvais tour
Que leur avoit joué cet infidèle prince,
Elles firent serment que jamais en province
Elles ne feroient leur séjour.

En effet, se trouvant des ailes sur le dos,
Elles jugèrent à propos
De s'en aller, à la même heure,
Vers la ville où Pallas [avoit fait⁶] sa demeure.

Elles y [rest]èrent⁷ longtemps;
Mais lorsque les Romains devinrent éclatants,
Et qu'ils eurent conquis Athènes,
Les Muses se firent Romaines.

Enfin, lorsqu'il plut au Destin
Que Rome allât en décadence,
Les Muses au pays latin
Ne firent plus leur résidence.

6. Dans la copie, au lieu de *avoit fait*, que nous avons donné par conjecture, il y a *faisoit*. Le vers étant faux ainsi, il y a un lapsus évident. Peut-être Racine a-t-il voulu écrire : « faisoit lors. » Dans l'édition de Louis Racine, les deux derniers vers de la strophe sont :

> De s'en aller, à la même heure,
> Où Pallas faisoit sa demeure.

7. Au lieu de *restèrent*, il y a *demeurèrent* dans la copie et dans l'édition de Louis Racine. C'est encore un vers faux, et par conséquent une inadvertance de l'auteur ou du copiste.

Paris, le siége des amours,
Devint aussi celui des filles de Mémoire;
Et l'on a grand sujet de croire
Qu'elles y logeront toujours.

Quand je parle de Paris, j'y comprends tout le beau pays d'alentour; car quelque serment qu'elles aient fait de ne s'éloigner jamais des bonnes villes, cela n'empêche pas qu'elles n'en sortent de temps en temps pour prendre l'air de la campagne :

Tantôt Fontainebleau les voit
Le long de ses belles cascades;
Tantôt Vincennes les reçoit
A l'ombre de ses palissades.

Elles vont souvent sur les eaux,
Ou de la Marne, ou de la Seine;
Elles étoient toujours à Vaux⁸,
Et ne l'ont pas quitté sans peine.

Ne croyez pas pour cela que les provinces manquent de poëtes; elles en ont en abondance : mais que ces Muses sont différentes des autres! Il est vrai qu'elles leur sont égales en nombre, et elles se vantent même d'être presque aussi anciennes : au moins sont-elles depuis longtemps en possession des provinces. Vous êtes peut-être en peine de savoir qui elles sont. Vous n'avez qu'à vous souvenir des neuf filles de Piérus : leur histoire est connue au Parnasse⁹, d'autant que les Muses prirent leurs noms après les avoir vaincues, comme les

8. Vaux-le-Vicomte, bien plus connu par les vers de la Fontaine, que par toutes les magnificences de Foucquet. Racine passe ici en revue les lieux que la Fontaine fréquentait le plus habituellement. (*Note de l'édition de 1807.*)

9. Voyez les *Métamorphoses* d'Ovide, livre V, vers 300 jusqu'à la fin du livre.

fameux Romains prenoient les noms des pays qu'ils avoient conquis :

> Ces filles[10] étoient savantes,
> Coquettes et bien disantes,
> Au reste fort suffisantes.
>
> Elles furent si hautaines
> Que de disputer le prix
> Aux Muses qui sont les reines
> Des arts et des beaux esprits.
>
> Mais il leur coûta bien cher
> D'avoir été si hardies :
> Les filles de Jupiter
> Les firent devenir pies.
>
> Être agaces leur parut
> Une fort vilaine chose,
> Et pas une ne se plut
> A cette métamorphose.
>
> Toutefois cette figure
> Avoit grande liaison
> Avec leur démangeaison
> De parler outre mesure.
>
> Elles partirent de là,
> Battant les ailes de rage,
> Et craignant outre cela
> Qu'on ne les retînt en cage.
>
> Ces oiseaux, plus importuns
> Mille fois que les chouettes,
> Sont cause que les poëtes
> Se sont rendus si communs.

10. Ce couplet et les cinq suivants sont inédits. Louis Racine les avait remplacés dans son *Recueil* par cette phrase : « Les filles de Piérus furent changées en pies. »

Dessus les bords des étangs[11]
Moins de grenouilles s'amassent,
Et moins de corbeaux croassent
Présageant le mauvais temps.

Tous ces petits avortons
Jasent comme leurs maîtresses;
Et la plupart sont larrons
Comme elles sont larronnesses.

Vous savez que toutes pies
Dérobent fort volontiers :
Celles-ci, comme harpies,
Pillent les livres entiers.

On dit même qu'à Paris
Ces fausses Muses font rage,
Et force menus esprits
Se font à leur badinage.

Pour réprimer leur audace,
Les Muses ont des chasseurs
Qui, sous les noms de censeurs,
Leur donnent souvent la chasse.

Lorsqu'elles sont attrapées,
Les ailes leur sont coupées,
Et leurs larcins confisqués;

Et pour finir cette histoire,
Tels oiseaux sont relégués
Delà les rives de Loire.

C'est où Furetière relègue leur général Galimatias[12], et il est bien juste qu'elles lui tiennent compagnie. Mais

11. Ce couplet et le suivant sont aussi imprimés ici pour la première fois.
12. Voyez ci-dessus, p. 448, note 3 de la lettre 24.

je ne songe pas que vous me condamnerez peut-être moi-même à cette peine et à y demeurer comme elles, puisque je m'y suis transporté. En effet, j'ai bien peur que ceci n'approche fort de leur style, et que vous n'y reconnoissiez plutôt le caquet importun des pies, que l'agréable facilité des Muses. Je vous prie de me renvoyer cette bagatelle des *Bains de Vénus;* ayez la bonté de mander ce qu'il vous en semble; jusque-là je suspends mon jugement : je n'ose rien croire bon ou mauvais que vous n'y ayez pensé auparavant. Je fais la même prière à votre Académie de Château-Thierry, surtout à Mlle de la Fontaine. Je ne lui demande aucune grâce pour mes ouvrages : qu'elle les traite rigoureusement, mais qu'elle me fasse au moins celle d'agréer mes respects et mes soumissions.

36. — DE RACINE A M. VITART[1].

A Uzés, le 25. juillet [1662].

Depuis vous avoir adressé la lettre que j'écrivois à M. de la Fontaine, j'en ai reçu deux des vôtres, dont la dernière m'a extrêmement consolé, voyant que vous preniez quelque part à l'affliction où j'étois de la trahison de D. Cosme. Nous n'avons point encore reçu de ses nouvelles, au moins mon oncle; car pour moi, je n'en attends plus de lui, étant bien résolu de ne lui plus écrire de ma vie. Son silence étonne son frère, qui attendoit de merveilleux effets de sa conduite pour l'affaire d'Ouchie. Je lui montrai une partie de votre lettre,

---

Lettre 36. — 1. Revue sur l'autographe, conservé à la Bibliothèque impériale.

et il fut assez surpris de voir que M. Sconin eût tant fait de bruit pour rien. Néanmoins je n'ai pas encore osé lui reparler d'une résignation, parce que j'ai peur qu'il ne me croie intéressé. Cependant il devroit bien s'imaginer que je ne suis pas venu si loin pour ne rien gaigner; mais je lui ai tant témoigné jusqu'ici de soumission et d'ouverture de cœur, qu'il a cru que je voudrois vivre longtemps avec lui de la sorte sans avoir aucune intention sur son bénéfice, et je voudrois bien qu'il eût toujours cette opinion-là de moi. J'épie tous les jours les occasions de lui faire faire quelque chose en ma faveur. Pour Monsieur l'Évêque, il n'y a rien à faire auprès de lui : il donne à ses gens le peu de bénéfices qui vaquent ici, et mon oncle auroit de la peine à lui en demander le moindre. Depuis quelques semaines, le bruit avoit couru en ce pays que Monsieur d'Uzés seroit archevêque de Paris, et j'ai vu une de ses lettres où il mandoit lui-même à mon oncle que le Roi avoit jeté la vue sur lui, et en avoit parlé en des termes fort obligeants; mais nous avons su que c'étoit Monsieur de Rhodez[2]. On dit que le jansénisme est étrangement menacé.

Je suis fort alarmé de votre refroidissement avec Monsieur l'Abbé. Quoiqu'il ne m'en eût rien mandé dans ses lettres, j'avois pourtant bien reconnu quelque changement. Cela m'affligeroit au dernier point, si je ne savois bien que votre amitié est trop forte pour demeurer longtemps refroidie, et que vous êtes trop généreux l'un et l'autre pour ne pas passer par-dessus de petites choses qui pourroient avoir causé cette mésintelligence. Je souhaite ardemment que cet accord se fasse au plus tôt.

2. Hardouin de Beaumont de Péréfixe, évêque de Rhodez depuis l'année 1648, fut nommé archevêque de Paris le 30 juin 1662. Son prédécesseur, Pierre de Marca, était mort la veille (29 juin). Voyez notre tome IV, p. 532.

1662 Ayez la bonté de m'en mander la nouvelle, dès que vous le pourrez faire ; car je mourrois de déplaisir si vous rompiez tout à fait, et je pourrois bien dire comme Chimène :

> La moitié de ma vie a mis l'autre au tombeau[3].

Mais vous n'en viendrez pas jusqu'à cette extrémité : vous êtes trop pacifiques tous deux.

Il m'a témoigné qu'il souhaitoit que j'écrivisse à Mlle Lucrèce, et qu'elle-même m'en sauroit quelque gré. D'abord, j'ai eu peur que vous ou Mlle Vitart ne m'en voulussiez mal dans ce méchant contre-temps ; mais comme je ne crois pas votre querelle de longue durée, je le satisferai au premier voyage. D'ailleurs, j'ai bien de la peine à croire que Mlle Vitart ait la moindre curiosité de voir quelque chose de moi, puisqu'elle ne m'en a rien témoigné depuis plus de six mois. Vous savez bien vous-même que les meilleurs esprits se trouveroient embarrassés s'il leur falloit toujours écrire sans recevoir de réponse ; car à la fin on manque de sujet.

Je vous aurois écrit les deux derniers voyages ; mais j'ai toujours accompagné mon oncle, qui alloit voir faire la moisson dans toutes leurs terres.

Je me réjouis beaucoup que vous en ayez une si belle à Moloy[4] ; mais je m'attriste déjà de ce que vous y allez, dans l'appréhension où je suis de ne recevoir que bien rarement de vos nouvelles ; car si je n'en recevois point, je languirois étrangement ici. Vos lettres me donnent courage et m'aident à pousser le temps par l'épaule, comme on dit en ce pays. La moisson a été belle,

---

3. *Le Cid*, acte III, scène III, vers 800.
4. Dans un acte du 20 mai 1672, où Racine est partie, nous avons trouvé la mention de la *ferme de Moloy, paroisse de Saint-Vaast de la Ferté-Milon.*

mais pas tant qu'on s'étoit imaginé. Le blé sera cher, c'est-à-dire qu'il vaudra environ trente-quatre ou trente-cinq [sous][5] le pichet. Nous en mangeons déjà du nouveau. Les raisins commencent à être mûrs, et on fera la vendange sur la fin du mois prochain. Les chaleurs sont grandes et difficiles à passer.

M. le prince de Conty est à trois lieues de cette ville, et se fait furieusement craindre dans la province. Il fait rechercher les vieux crimes, qui y sont en fort grand nombre. Il a fait emprisonner bon nombre de gentilshommes et en a écarté beaucoup d'autres. Une troupe de comédiens s'étoit venue établir dans une petite ville proche d'ici : il les a chassés, et ils ont passé le Rhône pour se retirer en Provence. On dit qu'il n'y a que des missionnaires et des archers à sa queue. Les gens de Languedoc ne sont pas accoutumés à telle réforme; mais il faut pourtant plier.

Je n'ai pas vu M. Arnaud; et son maître[6] n'est pas

5. Les 35 sous d'alors étaient le même poids d'argent que 3 fr. 30 cent. de notre monnaie actuelle. (*Note de l'édition de 1807.*)

6. L'éditeur de 1807 dit ici en note : « Les persécutions suscitées contre Arnauld l'avaient forcé de s'éloigner de Paris, et il fut alors attaché pendant quelque temps à l'archevêque d'Arles.... » — Quoique cet éditeur n'ait fait d'ordinaire usage que de renseignements dignes de confiance, qu'il avait souvent tirés des papiers de Jean-Baptiste Racine, il est difficile de ne pas élever contre ce qu'il avance ici de très-fortes objections. Le grand Arnauld au service d'un *maître!* Et ce maître est l'archevêque d'Arles, qui aurait ainsi publiquement accordé sa protection à un proscrit, tel qu'Arnauld, lorsque rien cependant ne nous apprend, ni dans les lettres de Mme de Sévigné, ni dans la correspondance d'Arnauld, ni ailleurs, que l'oncle du comte de Grignan eût pris parti pour les hommes de Port-Royal! Depuis l'année 1656 jusqu'à la paix de l'Église (1668), Arnauld vécut dans les lieux les plus retirés. « Il fuyoit de tous côtés, nous dit Fontaine (*Mémoires*, tome II, p. 403), pour ne se point laisser voir. » Et le voilà attaché ouvertement à l'archevêque d'Arles! Ce M. *Arnaud*, dont parle Racine, nous parait être

venu à Uzés. Monsieur d'Uzés l'a été recevoir à Grignan[7], où ils passeront l'été : ainsi je ne crois pas voir M. Arnaud de longtemps. Mais je n'espère plus rien des affaires du chapitre : je crois seulement qu'elles tireront en longueur, et au bout du compte la réforme subsistera.

Tâchez de m'écrire de Moloy, je vous en prie, ou faites-moi écrire par quelqu'un. Souvenez-vous de me mettre en bonne posture dans l'esprit de mon oncle d'Ouchie. Je baise très-humblement les mains à Mlle Vitart, à vos petites, à M. le Mazier et à tout le monde.

Suscription : A Monsieur Monsieur Vitart, à Paris. (Deux cachets rouges : J. RAC., avec une soie violette.)

37. — DE RACINE A MARIE RACINE.

A Paris, le 23. juillet [1663[1]].

Ma très-chère soeur,

Je suis infiniment obligé à la bonté de mon père[2] qui a pris la peine de m'écrire, je vous assure que je n'ai

quelque personne aujourd'hui inconnue, qui remplissait des fonctions auprès de l'Archevêque, peut-être celles d'aumônier (voyez ci-dessus les quatre dernières lignes de la page 478).

7. Le château de Grignan, dans la ville et le comté de ce nom, non loin de Saint-Paul-Trois-Châteaux et de Montélimar, était alors en Provence, dans les terres dites adjacentes.

Lettre 37 (revue sur l'autographe, conservé à Soissons.) —
1. Cette lettre et la suivante, que M. l'abbé de la Roque a datées de 1662, sont évidemment de 1663. Le *Nécrologe de Port-Royal* fixe, il est vrai, au 12 août 1662 la mort de Marie des Moulins; mais l'erreur ne peut être regardée comme douteuse. Voyez notre tome I, p. 55, note 1.

2. Son grand-père, Pierre Sconin.

eu jamais tant de joie au monde, et que je garde sa lettre comme un trésor. Je l'en remercierai au premier jour. Cependant je vous prie de le faire pour moi, et de lui dire que j'ai été voir ma tante Suzanne[3], qui m'a reçu avec bien de l'amitié, et qui est assurément une fort bonne personne. J'irois la voir plus souvent n'étoit que son quartier est fort éloigné du nôtre, et qu'avec cela il a fait fort sale à Paris tous ces jours passés. Et puis, lorsque j'ai un moment de loisir, je vais à Port-Royal, où ma mère est maintenant. Elle est malade à l'extrémité, et il n'y a pas d'apparence qu'elle en revienne. Je ne vous saurois dire combien j'en suis affligé, et il faudroit que je fusse le plus ingrat du monde, si je n'aimois une mère qui m'a été si bonne, et qui a eu plus de soin de moi que de ses propres enfants. Elle n'a pas eu moins d'amitié pour vous, quoiqu'elle n'ait pas eu l'occasion de vous le témoigner.

On vous aura dit peut-être que le Roi m'a fait promettre[4] une pension[5]; mais je voudrois bien qu'on n'en eût point parlé jusqu'à ce que je l'aie touchée. Je vous en manderai des nouvelles. Et cependant n'en parlez à personne; car ces choses-là ne sont bonnes à dire que quand elles sont toutes faites. Écrivez-moi, je vous prie; car vos lettres me sont[6] les plus agréables du monde. Ma tante Vitart est bien aise aussi quand vous lui écrivez.

---

3. Suzanne Sconin, fille de Pierre Sconin. D'après un ancien tableau généalogique, elle fut, nous ne savons à quelle date, religieuse à la Ferté-Milon. M. l'abbé de la Roque a pensé qu'il s'agissait de Suzanne des Moulins, sœur de la grand'mère de Racine et de la mère de Nicolas Vitart. Mais Suzanne des Moulins, religieuse à Port-Royal, était morte en 1647.

4. Racine avait d'abord écrit : « m'a promis. »

5. Il s'agit probablement des six cents livres accordées à Racine sur la liste du 22 août de l'année suivante (1664).

6. *Sont* est au-dessus de *semblent*, effacé.

Témoignez-lui que la maladie de ma mère vous met en peine; car je ne doute pas qu'elle ne vous en fasse en effet, et elle le lui redira. Adieu, ma chère sœur. Je vous ai envoyé ce que vous m'aviez demandé par mon cousin Fournier[7], et à mon cousin du Chesne[8] aussi.

Suscription : A Madame Madame Marie Racine, chez M. le Commissaire. (Un petit fragment de cachet : J. R.)

38. — DE RACINE A MARIE RACINE.

A Paris, le 13. d'août [1663].

MA TRÈS-CHÈRE SOEUR,

Tout affligé que je suis, je crois être obligé de vous mander la perte que vous avez faite avec moi de notre bonne mère[1]. Je ne doute point que vous n'en receviez beaucoup d'affliction, quoique vous ne l'eussiez vue depuis longtemps; car je vous assure qu'elle vous aimoit tendrement, et qu'elle vous auroit traitée comme ses propres enfants, si elle avoit pu faire quelque chose pour vous. Je vous prie de la recommander aux prières de mon grand-père[2]. Nous n'avons plus que lui maintenant, et il nous tient lieu de père et de mère tout ensemble. Nous devons bien prier Dieu qu'il nous le conserve. Je

---

7. Jacques Fournier, baptisé à la Ferté-Milon le 12 mars 1638, fils de Jacques Fournier, notaire, président au grenier à sel de la Ferté, et d'Élisabeth Sconin, tante de Racine.
8. Voyez ci-dessus, p. 396, la note 21 de la lettre 8.
LETTRE 38 (revue sur l'autographe, conservé à la Ferté-Milon). — 1. Marie des Moulins, leur grand'mère paternelle, dont la maladie était annoncée dans la lettre précédente. Elle était morte la veille, 12 août 1663. Voyez, p. 498, la note 1 de la lettre 37.
2. Pierre Sconin.

vous supplie de lui dire que je mets toute ma confiance
et tout mon recours à lui, et que j'aurai toujours pour
lui toute l'obéissance et l'affection que j'aurois pu avoir
pour mon propre père. Je crois que vous savez bien
qu'il vous faut faire habiller de deuil. Je suis bien marri
de n'avoir point reçu encore l'argent qu'on m'avoit promis. J'aurois de tout mon cœur contribué à la dépense
qu'il vous faudra faire. Je demanderai³ demain à ma tante
Vitart⁴ ce qu'elle jugera à propos que vous fassiez.
Mandez-moi vous-même toutes vos pensées là-dessus,
et si vous vous adresserez à mon père⁵ pour cela. Adieu,
ma chère sœur : j'ai trop de douleur pour songer à autre chose qu'à l'extrême perte que j'ai faite. Mon oncle
Racine⁶ ne manquera pas sans doute de faire tout ce
qu'il faudra pour le service de ma mère. Adieu donc :
la mort de ma mère nous doit porter à nous aimer
encore davantage, puisque nous n'avons plus tantôt
personne. Vous devez espérer beaucoup d'assistance
en la personne de ma chère tante Vitart : elle vous aime
beaucoup, et elle nous servira de mère à l'un et à
l'autre.

RACINE.

Suscription : A Madame Madame Marie Racine, chez
Monsieur le Commissaire, à la Ferté-Milon. (Cachet noir :
J. RAC.)

3. Racine avait d'abord mis : *je parlerai*.
4. Claude des Moulins, sœur de la grand'mère que Racine venait
de perdre.
5. C'est-à-dire, comme toujours, à mon grand-père Sconin.
6. Claude Racine, contrôleur au grenier à sel de la Ferté-Milon,
fils de Mme Racine (Marie des Moulins) qui venait de mourir. Né
en 1620, il était de cinq ans plus jeune que son frère Jean Racine,
père de notre poëte.

39. — DE RACINE A L'ABBÉ LE VASSEUR.

[A Paris, novembre 1663[1].]

Si M. Vitart étoit ici tandis que votre laquais y est, je lui ferois donner absolument ce bail que vous demandez; car il ne me l'a point encore donné, et il s'obstine à le vouloir faire transcrire pour en donner la copie à M. de Villers. Je vous proteste que je l'en ai horriblement persécuté, et que je ferai tout mon possible pour faire donner demain au matin ce papier à votre laquais avant qu'il parte. Je n'aime pas à manquer de parole quand j'ai promis de m'employer pour quelqu'un : c'est ce qui fait que j'ai de grands reproches à vous faire pour cette sauvegarde[2] que j'avois promis de faire obtenir par votre moyen, et je ne vais à l'hôtel de Liancour qu'en enrageant, quoique je sois obligé d'y aller presque tous les jours, parce que c'est là où sont mes plus grandes affaires. C'est pourquoi je vous conjure de faire tout votre possible pour mettre ma conscience en repos de ce côté-là, et de donner des ordres, du lieu où vous êtes, aux gens que vous m'avez promis d'employer auprès de Monsieur le Comte; car je peste tous les jours contre vous, et je serois bien aise, quand je songe à vous, de n'y point songer avec ces sortes de scrupules.

Pour ce qui regarde *les Frères*[3], ils ne sont pas si avancés qu'à l'ordinaire. Le 4ᵉ étoit fait dès samedi;

LETTRE 39 (revue sur l'autographe, conservé à la Bibliothèque impériale). — 1. Cette date est donnée par la mention qui est faite vers la fin de la lettre de la cérémonie qu'on devait célébrer le dimanche suivant à Notre-Dame. Voyez ci-après, p. 504, note 9.

2. On appelait ainsi des lettres que l'on obtenait pour être exempt de loger les gens de guerre.

3. La tragédie des *Frères ennemis*, ou *la Thébaïde*, qui ne fut jouée qu'au mois de juin de l'année suivante.

mais malheureusement je ne goûtois point, ni les autres non plus, toutes les épées tirées : ainsi il a fallu les faire rengainer, et pour cela ôter plus de deux cents vers, ce qui est malaisé.

La Renommée⁴ a été assez heureuse. M. le comte de Saint-Aignan⁵ l'a trouvée fort belle. Il a demandé mes autres ouvrages, et m'a demandé moi-même. Je le dois aller saluer demain. Je ne l'ai pas trouvé aujourd'hui au lever du Roi; mais j'y ai trouvé Molière, à qui le Roi a donné assez de louanges, et j'en ai été bien aise pour lui : il a été bien aise aussi que j'y fusse présent.

Pour mon affaire de chez M. de Bourzeis⁶, elle est fort⁷ honnête et bien avancée; mais on m'a surtout recommandé le secret, et je vous le recommande.

M. de Bellefont⁸ est premier maître d'hôtel depuis

4. *La Renommée aux Muses.* Voyez notre tome IV, p. 71-78.

5. François de Beauvilliers, comte, et depuis duc de Saint-Aignan, à qui Racine dédia sa première tragédie. Ce fut au mois de décembre 1663 que la terre de Saint-Aignan fut érigée en duché-pairie. Voyez sur ce protecteur du jeune Racine notre tome I, p. 389, note 2.

6. L'abbé de Bourzeis était alors à la tête de la *petite Académie* (plus tard l'*Académie des inscriptions et belles-lettres*), que Colbert réunissait dans sa bibliothèque. Mais il ne pouvait être question de faire entrer Racine, comme l'ont dit ici quelques-uns de ses éditeurs, dans cette compagnie naissante, pour laquelle il n'avait à cette époque aucun titre, et où il ne fut admis que vingt ans plus tard. Peut-être cette « affaire de chez M. de Bourzeis » est-elle la gratification que Racine espérait obtenir de Colbert. Il avait pu connaître Bourzeis à l'hôtel Liancourt, dont cet abbé était un des familiers.

7. *Fort*, et, deux lignes plus bas, *depuis*, ont été ajoutés au-dessus de la ligne.

8. La *Gazette* du 17 novembre 1663 (p. 1120) annonce, sous la date du 11 novembre, la mort de Louis de Cominges, marquis de Vervins, premier maître d'hôtel du Roi. Le marquis de Bellefonds lui succéda dans cette charge; il avait en 1663 un commandement en Italie; il fut fait maréchal de France en 1668.

1663 aujourd'hui. Le Roi a été à Versailles. Les Suisses iront dimanche à Notre-Dame[9], et le Roi a demandé la comédie pour eux à Molière : sur quoi Monsieur le Duc[10] a dit qu'il suffisoit de leur donner *Gros-René*[11] bien enfariné, parce qu'ils n'entendoient point le françois. Adieu. Vous voyez que je suis à demi courtisan; mais c'est à mon gré un métier assez ennuyant[12].

Suscription : A Monsieur Monsieur l'abbé le Vasseur. (Deux cachets noirs : J. RAC.)

40. — DE RACINE A L'ABBÉ LE VASSEUR.

[A Paris, 1663[1].]

Le mauvais temps m'a empêché de sortir depuis quatre jours : c'est ce qui fait que je n'ai point été chez Mlle de la Croix pour y porter des lettres pour vous[2], et que je n'ai point été ailleurs non plus. Ainsi ne vous

---

9. La cérémonie du renouvellement de l'alliance des Suisses se fit à Notre-Dame, le dimanche 18 novembre 1663. Voyez la *Muse historique* de Loret du 25 novembre, et la *Gazette* du 24 novembre de cette même année, p. 1144. Ainsi la date de la lettre est entre le 12 et le 17 novembre.

10. Henri-Jules de Bourbon, né en 1643, fils du grand Condé.

11. Le comédien du Parc, connu au théâtre sous le nom de *Gros-René*. Il mourut en 1664.

12. Sur la page où est cette lettre, Louis Racine a mis : « Lettres écrites par mon père pendant sa jeunesse. »

Lettre 40 (revue sur l'autographe, conservé à la Bibliothèque impériale). — 1. Les éditeurs de Racine ont daté cette lettre du mois de décembre; elle peut aussi bien être de la fin de novembre; on voit par son contexte qu'elle a été écrite peu de temps après la précédente.

2. L'abbé le Vasseur était alors à Crône. Voyez la lettre suivante.

attendez pas d'apprendre de moi aucunes nouvelles, sinon de ce qui s'est passé dans l'étendue de l'hôtel de Luynes; car quoique j'aie vu tout ce qui s'est passé à Notre-Dame avec Messieurs les Suisses, je n'ose pas usurper sur le gazetier l'honneur de vous en faire le récit. Je crois que M. Vitart vous envoie le bail que vous attendiez. Je n'ai pas encore été à l'hôtel de Liancour pour ôter à mon homme l'espérance que je lui avois donnée de sa sauvegarde, et je suis assez embarrassé comment je m'y prendrai. Je n'ai point vu l'Impromptu³ ni son auteur depuis huit jours : j'irai tantôt. J'ai tantôt achevé ce que vous savez⁴, et j'espère que j'aurai fait dimanche ou lundi. J'y ai mis des stances qui me satisfont assez. En voilà la première; car je n'ai guère de meilleure chose à vous écrire :

> Cruelle ambition, dont la noire malice
>   Conduit tant de monde au trépas,
> Et qui, feignant d'ouvrir le trône sous nos pas,
>   Ne nous ouvres qu'un précipice :
>   Que tu causes d'égarements!
> Qu'en d'étranges malheurs tu plonges tes amants!
>   Que leurs chutes sont déplorables!
> Mais que tu fais périr d'innocents avec eux!
>   Et que tu fais de misérables
>   En faisant un ambitieux⁵!

C'est un lieu commun qui vient bien à mon sujet; mais ne le montrez à personne, je vous en prie, parce que,

---

3. *L'Impromptu de Versailles*, de Molière, avait été joué pour la première fois, à Versailles, sur le théâtre de la cour, le 14 octobre 1663, et à Paris, le 4 novembre suivant, sur le théâtre du Palais-Royal.

4. *La Thébaïde*.

5. Voyez notre tome I, p. 467, note 2. Racine se décida à retrancher ces vers, qui faisaient partie des stances récitées par Antigone au commencement de l'acte V de *la Thébaïde*.

si on[6] l'avoit vu, on s'en pourroit souvenir, et on seroit moins surpris quand on le récitera.

La déhanchée fait la jeune princesse. Vous savez bien, je crois, et qui est cette déhanchée[7], et qui sera cette princesse. Adieu : je suis marri d'avoir si peu de bonnes choses à vous mander. Je souhaite que ma stance vous tienne lieu d'une bonne lettre. Le Bailli[8] a été tous ces jours passés ici avec sa femme ; ils s'en vont à l'heure que je vous parle, et je ne leur dis point adieu. Monfleury[9] a fait une requête contre Molière, et l'a donnée au Roi. Il l'accuse d'avoir épousé la fille, et d'avoir autrefois couché avec la mère[10]. Mais Monfleury n'est point écouté à la cour. Adieu : ne laissez point, s'il vous plaît, revenir votre laquais sans m'écrire ; vous avez plus de temps que moi.

Suscription : A Monsieur Monsieur l'abbé le Vasseur. (Deux cachets noirs : J. RAC.)

6. Racine avait d'abord tourné autrement : « parce que ceux qui.... »

7. Mlle de Beauchâteau, comédienne de l'Hôtel de Bourgogne, devait jouer le rôle d'Antigone.

8. Pierre Sellyer. Voyez ci-dessus, p. 407, note 12 de la lettre 11.

9. Comédien de l'Hôtel de Bourgogne.

10. Louis Racine, pour corriger la crudité de l'expression, a ainsi changé la phrase, qu'il comprenait mal : « Il accuse Molière d'avoir épousé sa propre fille. » Il n'a pas songé qu'il aggravait beaucoup ainsi ce qu'il voulait atténuer, et qu'il ferait accuser son père d'avoir rapporté, sans la repousser avec indignation, une si odieuse calomnie. Voyez la *Notice biographique*, p. 60.

41. — DE RACINE A L'ABBÉ LE VASSEUR. 1663

[A Paris, décembre 1663¹.]

Nous étions prêts à partir, lorsque M. Vitart s'aperçut qu'il n'avoit point de bottes, et qu'il les avoit prêtées. Cela fut d'abord capable d'ébranler sa résolution, et Mlle Vitart acheva ensuite de l'en détourner, en lui représentant qu'il auroit huit lieues de chemin à faire cette journée-là, qu'il seroit obligé de revenir fort tard, et qu'il étoit malheureux. Il demeura donc, et il fallut que je demeurasse avec lui, mais dans le dessein de m'en aller² moi seul dans quatre ou cinq jours si vous êtes encore à la campagne tant que cela. Je n'ai pas de grandes nouvelles à vous mander. Je n'ai fait que retoucher continuellement au cinquième acte³, et il n'est tout achevé que d'hier. J'en ai changé toutes les stances avec quelque regret. Ceux qui me les avoient demandées s'avisèrent ensuite de me proposer quelque difficulté sur l'état où étoit ma princesse, peu convenable à s'étendre sur des lieux communs. J'ai donc tout réduit à 3 stances⁴, et ôté celle de l'*ambition*⁵, qui me servira peut-être ailleurs.

LETTRE 41 (revue sur l'autographe, conservé à la Bibliothèque impériale.) — 1. Cette date n'est point dans l'autographe; elle n'a pas été donnée non plus par Louis Racine, mais pour la première fois dans l'édition de 1807. Elle est vraisemblable; car en comparant cette lettre à la lettre 40, qui précède, on reconnaît qu'elle doit avoir été écrite peu de jours après. Or, dans la lettre 40, la mention de la cérémonie célébrée récemment à Notre-Dame avait donné à peu près la date.

2. Racine avait mis d'abord : « d'y retourner. »

3. De *la Thébaïde*.

4. M. Aimé-Martin a mis: « à cinq stances »; et nous avons nous-même admis ce texte dans une note de notre tome I (p. 467, note 2). Mais c'est bien plutôt un 3 qu'un 5 qu'on lit dans l'autographe. Louis Racine a lu *trois*; et c'est aujourd'hui le nombre de ces stances.

5. Celle qui est citée dans la lettre précédente.

1663 On promet depuis hier *la Thébaïde* à l'Hôtel⁶; mais ils ne la promettent qu'après trois autres pièces. Je n'ai pas été depuis longtemps à l'hôtel de Liancour. On m'a envoyé redemander depuis quatre jours le papier qu'on m'avoit donné pour faire signer, et que je vous ai donné aussi. Tâchez de vous souvenir où il est. Je viens de parcourir votre belle et grande lettre, où j'ai trouvé assez de difficultés qui m'ont arrêté, et d'autres sur lesquelles il seroit aisé de vous regagner. Je suis pourtant fort obligé à l'auteur des remarques⁷, et je l'estime infiniment. Je ne sais si il⁸ ne me sera point permis quelque jour de le connoître. Adieu, Monsieur : votre

6. A l'Hôtel de Bourgogne. Elle n'y fut pas jouée cependant. La première représentation fut donnée sur le théâtre du Palais-Royal, le 20 juin 1664. Voyez au tome I la *Notice* qui est en tête de *la Thébaïde*.

7. Cet endroit est remarquable : il parle des critiques sur son *ode de la Renommée*, faites par Boileau, à qui M. le Vasseur avoit montré cette ode. Ces critiques lui inspirèrent de l'estime pour Boileau, et une grande envie de le connoître. M. le Vasseur le mena chez Boileau; et dans cette première visite commença leur fameuse et constante amitié. (*Note de Louis Racine.*) — Si Louis Racine ne dit rien dans cette note dont il n'ait été bien informé, il n'y a point de doute à opposer à son témoignage ; mais si c'est de la lettre seule qu'il a conclu que les remarques communiquées à Racine par le Vasseur avaient été faites sur l'*ode de la Renommée*, on peut regarder comme plus vraisemblable qu'elles avaient pour objet *la Thébaïde*. Quant à l'auteur des remarques, il serait difficile de ne pas admettre qu'il s'agit de Boileau. La suscription de la lettre nous montre que le Vasseur était alors à Crône, petit village près de Villeneuve-Saint-Georges. Le père de Boileau avait eu à Crône une maison, où il passait le temps des vacances du Palais (voyez les *Mémoires* de Louis Racine, tome I, p. 221 et 222). Après sa mort, en 1657, cette maison était sans doute restée dans sa famille. Ce fut probablement à Crône que l'abbé le Vasseur, comme le dit ici, dans une note, l'éditeur de 1807, fit la connaissance de Boileau ; et les deux illustres poëtes durent ainsi à ce tiers les premières relations qui s'établirent entre eux et devinrent bientôt si étroites.

8. Il y a bien *si il* dans l'autographe.

laquais attend, et il est cause que je ne lis pas plus posément votre lettre, et que je n'y réponds pas plus au long dans celle-ci.

Suscription : A Monsieur Monsieur l'abbé le Vasseur, à Crosne. (Deux cachets noirs : J. RAC.)

42. — DE LA SŒUR AGNÈS DE SAINTE-THÈCLE[1]
A RACINE.
[1663[2].]

Gloire à Jésus et au Très-Saint Sacrement.

Ayant appris que vous aviez dessein de faire ici un

Lettre 42. — Cette lettre a été imprimée pour la première fois dans l'édition de 1807 des *OEuvres de Racine*. L'éditeur ne dit point s'il a eu l'autographe entre les mains ; et nous ignorons si le texte de la lettre a été exactement suivi. — 1. Voyez ci-dessus, p. 372, la note 7 de la lettre 1. La tante de Racine était alors cellérière à Port-Royal. Son neveu reçut d'elle sans doute bien des lettres semblables. Dans sa lettre du 13 septembre 1660, Racine, on s'en souvient, parle (p. 381) des *excommunications* qu'il recevait de Port-Royal. Vers la fin de sa vie, il écrivait à Mme de Maintenon : « C'est elle (*la Mère Agnès de Sainte-Thècle*) dont Dieu s'est servi pour me tirer de l'égarement et des misères où j'ai été plongé pendant quinze années. »

2. L'éditeur de 1807 a, par conjecture, daté cette lettre de 1665 ou 1666. Il nous semble probable qu'elle est antérieure à la querelle avec Nicole, et même aux débuts de Racine dans la carrière du théâtre (juin 1664), puisqu'il ne s'y trouve aucune allusion ni à l'un ni à l'autre de ces faits. On pourrait faire remonter la date plus haut encore que 1663, les lettres de Racine écrites en 1660 nous apprenant que dès lors il fréquentait les comédiens. Cependant sa tante lui reproche de les *fréquenter plus que jamais :* il n'était donc pas alors au commencement de ses liaisons avec eux. Il peut sembler aussi que la lettre a été écrite après la mort de la grand'-mère de Racine, qui n'y est pas nommée, du moins expressément. En deux passages cependant la sœur de Sainte-Thècle dit *nous,* et,

voyage, j'avois demandé permission à notre Mère de vous voir, parce que quelques personnes nous avoient assurées que vous étiez dans la pensée de songer sérieusement à vous, et j'aurois été bien aise de l'apprendre par vous-même, afin de vous témoigner la joie que j'aurois, s'il plaisoit à Dieu de vous toucher. Mais j'ai appris, depuis peu de jours, une nouvelle qui m'a touchée sensiblement. Je vous écris dans l'amertume de mon cœur, et en versant des larmes que je voudrois pouvoir répandre en assez grande abondance devant Dieu pour obtenir de lui votre salut, qui est la chose du monde que je souhaite avec le plus d'ardeur. J'ai donc appris avec douleur que vous fréquentiez plus que jamais des gens dont le nom est abominable à toutes les personnes qui ont tant soit peu de piété, et avec raison, puisqu'on leur interdit l'entrée de l'église et la communion des fidèles, même à la mort, à moins qu'ils ne se reconnoissent. Jugez donc, mon cher neveu, dans quel état je puis être, puisque vous n'ignorez pas la tendresse que j'ai toujours eue pour vous, et que je n'ai jamais rien desiré, sinon que vous fussiez tout à Dieu dans quelque emploi honnête. Je vous conjure donc, mon cher neveu, d'avoir pitié de votre âme, et de rentrer dans votre cœur, pour y considérer sérieusement dans quel abîme vous vous êtes jeté. Je souhaite que ce qu'on m'a dit ne soit pas vrai; mais si vous êtes assez malheureux pour n'avoir pas rompu un commerce qui vous déshonore devant Dieu et devant les hommes, vous ne devez pas penser à nous venir voir; car vous savez bien que je ne pourrois pas vous parler, vous sachant dans un état si déplorable et si contraire au christianisme. Cependant

---

si ce pluriel peut s'entendre dans plusieurs sens, il peut signifier aussi : « votre grand'mère et moi. » Au résumé, nous devons reconnaître que la date de cette lettre est fort incertaine.

je ne cesserai point de prier Dieu qu'il vous fasse miséricorde, et à moi en vous la faisant, puisque votre salut m'est si cher.

43. — DE RACINE A MARIE RACINE.

A Paris, le 9ᵉ janvier [1664¹].

MA TRÈS-CHÈRE SOEUR,

J'étois à la campagne² lorsque votre dernière lettre est venue, et ce voyage a été cause que j'ai été un peu longtemps sans vous écrire. Vous pouvez croire que je n'ai pas laissé de penser à vous durant tout ce temps-là. Je voudrois pouvoir vous le témoigner bien autrement que je ne le fais, et ne vous pas envoyer pour si peu de chose; mais il faut un peu attendre que mes affaires se fassent, comme j'espère qu'elles se feront tôt ou tard; et je n'aurai jamais de bonne fortune que vous ne vous en ressentiez, si je puis, aussi bien que moi. Je ne m'étonne pas que mon oncle³ ne vous ait rien dit de moi. Il

---

LETTRE 43 (revue sur l'autographe, conservé à Soissons). —
1. Cette lettre est antérieure à l'année 1667, qui fut celle de la mort de Pierre Sconin, chez qui elle est adressée. Nous la croyons de 1664. Le cachet noir qu'on y remarque conviendrait à ce temps où Racine devait porter encore le deuil de sa grand'mère Marie des Moulins.
2. Au commencement de la lettre 41 (p. 507), qui est de la fin de 1663, Racine parlait d'un très-prochain voyage qu'il allait faire. C'est une indication de plus en faveur de la date qui nous a paru probable pour cette lettre-ci.
3. Il est assez difficile de savoir de quel oncle il s'agit; mais nous sommes porté à croire que c'est de Claude Racine (voyez ci-dessus, p. 501, la note 6 de la lettre 38). Le compte sur lequel, d'après un passage de cette lettre, on était en désaccord, semblerait être un compte de partage après la mort de Marie des Moulins, mère de Claude Racine.

s'en est allé fort en colère : non pas que je lui en aie donné du sujet, car je l'ai traité avec tout le respect possible ; mais je ne crois pas qu'il ait beaucoup d'affection pour moi. Il me voulut reprocher que j'avois mangé tout son bien ; je ne lui répondis rien, mais mon cousin [4] le querella [5] de belle manière, et le fit bien repentir de ce beau langage. J'en étois assez honteux pour lui. Et le lendemain il s'en alla sans nous dire adieu. Ne dites pas un mot de tout cela à personne ; car cela est un peu de conséquence. Mon cousin lui remontra encore combien il s'abusoit pour notre compte. Je crois qu'on le terminera bientôt, et j'y ferai tout mon possible, quoiqu'il ne nous importe guère qu'il se termine si tôt. Mandez-moi, je vous prie, des nouvelles de ma cousine Hennequin [6] ; j'en suis fort en peine. Faites aussi mes baisemains à ma cousine sa sœur [7]. Mlle Vitart vous baise les mains. J'écrirai demain au P. Adrien [8],

4. Vraisemblablement Nicolas Vitart.

5. Racine a mis, par mégarde, le subjonctif : *querellast*.

6. Françoise Sconin, qui avait épousé le 12 février 1652 Adam Nicolas Hennequin, grènetier au grenier à sel de la Ferté-Milon. Elle était fille de Pierre Sconin, oncle maternel de Racine (voyez ci-dessus, p. 376, note 5 de la lettre 3), qu'il ne faut pas confondre avec son père Pierre Sconin (M. le Commissaire) chez qui cette lettre est adressée, et de Françoise Lefèvre. La cousine Hennequin, dont la santé causait des inquiétudes à Racine, lorsqu'il écrivit cette lettre, approchait alors de la fin de sa vie. Nous ne savons pas précisément à quelle date elle mourut, mais ce fut avant son père. Dans le partage de la succession de Pierre Sconin, fait le 10 février 1667, elle est représentée par ses enfants. Elle était née en janvier 1631.

7. Catherine Sconin. Voyez ci-dessus, p. 435, la note 6 de la lettre 19.

8. Le P. Adrien Sconin, jésuite. Il était fils de Pierre Sconin et de Claude Joly, et par conséquent frère consanguin d'Antoine Sconin, vicaire général à Uzès, et de Jeanne Sconin, mère de Racine, enfants l'un et l'autre de Pierre Sconin et de Marguerite Chéron. Son acte de baptême est du 1er octobre 1638.

qui m'a écrit une fort belle lettre et bien obligeante. Adieu, ma chère sœur : je ne vous dis point que vous me demandiez les choses dont vous aurez besoin ; car je vous l'ai dit déjà plusieurs fois, et je crois que vous n'y manquerez pas. Écrivez-moi le plus tôt que vous pourrez.

Assurez, je vous prie, Monsieur le Procureur[9] de mes très-humbles respects.

Suscription : A Madame Madame Marie Racine, chez M. le Commissaire. (Cachet noir, dont l'empreinte est effacée.)

---

44. — DE RACINE A MARIE RACINE.

Ce mercredi 19eme août [1665[1]].

MA TRÈS-CHÈRE SOEUR,

J'ai vu ma cousine de Sacy[2], par qui j'ai appris de vos

---

9. Jean Sconin, procureur du Roi au grenier à sel de la Ferté-Milon ; c'était un des frères de la mère de Racine. Il mourut au mois de mai 1673.

LETTRE 44 (revue sur l'autographe, conservé à Soissons). —
1. Parmi toutes les années où cette lettre peut avoir été écrite, il n'y a que l'année 1665 où le 19 août soit un mercredi. La mention qui y est faite de la cousine de Saci et de la cousine du Chesne (voyez les deux notes suivantes) ne nous semble pas une raison suffisante de supposer une erreur de jour ou de quantième, et de dater cette lettre de 1658 ou de 1659, comme l'a fait M. l'abbé de la Roque. — L'original porte : *mecredy*.
2. Nous ne savons s'il s'agit de Nicole-Madeleine Vitart, veuve d'Antoine de Saci, mort en 1661, et qui mourut elle-même en 1670 : voyez ci-dessus, p. 410, la note 8 de la lettre 12. Était-ce bien elle qui faisait ainsi des voyages de Paris à la Ferté-Milon? Il n'est peut-être pas vraisemblable que, depuis son veuvage, elle se soit éloignée de Port-Royal. Il se peut qu'entre la famille des Saci et

nouvelles; car il n'y a pas moyen d'en apprendre autrement. Je ne sais pas ce que je vous ai fait pour vous dépiter de telle sorte contre moi. J'ai vu le temps que les lettres ne vous coûtoient pas si cher. Il ne vous coûteroit pas beaucoup de m'en écrire au moins une en trois mois; cependant il y a bien cela que je n'en ai reçu aucune de vous. Mandez-moi pourquoi vous êtes fâchée contre moi, et je tâcherai de vous apaiser; car vous êtes assez souvent d'humeur à croire les choses autrement qu'elles ne sont. Quoi que c'en soit, mandez-moi ce que vous avez contre moi.

J'ai quelques petites choses à vous envoyer; mais j'attendrai que ma cousine du Chesne[3] ou ma cousine de Sacy s'en aille. J'ai rendu au marchand la dentelle qu'elle vous avoit achetée, et elle vous en doit acheter d'autre. Si vous voulez la moindre chose, vous n'avez que[4] me le mander sans faire de façons. Je n'ai pas si peu de crédit que je ne vous puisse contenter, quelque opinion que vous ayez de moi. Surtout écrivez-moi, je vous prie; et je vous en écrirai moi-même plus souvent. J'ai su toutes les brouilleries de Logeois[5]

---

celle des Racine il y ait eu d'autres alliances dont nous n'avons pas retrouvé la trace; ou encore que Racine ait donné le nom de cousine à une belle-sœur de Nicole-Madeleine Vitart.

3. C'était probablement une fille d'Antoine du Chesne et d'Anne Sconin (voyez ci-dessus, p. 375, la note 2 de la lettre 3); mais nous ne pensons pas que ce fût Jeanne du Chesne, qui était déjà mariée à Louis Parmentier. Racine l'eût sans doute appelée « ma cousine Parmentier. »

4. Racine a écrit ainsi.

5. Un Martin Logeois ou Laugeois avait épousé en 1638 Antoinette Racine, qui mourut en 1692, et dont la parenté avec notre poëte ne nous est pas connue. Dans l'acte de mariage de Marie Racine (voyez notre tome I, p. 187) nous trouvons parmi les témoins un Philippe Laugeois et une Antoinette Racine.

et de M⁶ Nanon⁶, et celles de M. de Sacy⁷ et de Monsieur le Procureur⁸. Faites-moi savoir de vos nouvelles, et aimez-moi toujours.

RACINE.

Suscription : A Madame Madame Marie Racine, à la Ferté-Milon.

---

45. — DE RACINE AU P. BOUHOURS¹.

[1676²].

JE vous envoie les quatre premiers actes de ma tra-

6. Cette Mme ou Mlle Nanon (l'original porte *M⁶*) est peut-être Anne-Marie Racine, tante de Jean Racine, qui fut mariée à François Moufflard le 10 juillet 1635.
7. Vraisemblablement Adrien de Saci, substitut du procureur du Roi à la châtellenie de la Ferté-Milon, et que nous croyons frère d'Antoine de Saci, mort en 1661, dont nous avons déjà plusieurs fois parlé comme d'un cousin de Racine.
8. Voyez ci-dessus, p. 513, la note 9 de la lettre 43.

LETTRE 45 (revue sur l'autographe, appartenant à M. Jules Boilly). — 1. Cette lettre ne se lit dans aucune des précédentes éditions des *OEuvres de Racine*. Elle n'est cependant pas inédite : on la trouve imprimée à la page 82 de l'opuscule qui a pour titre : *Lettre à M. Racine sur le théâtre en général et sur les tragédies de son père en particulier. Par M. L. F. de P**** (le Franc de Pompignan). *Nouvelle édition. Suivie d'une pièce de vers du même auteur et de trois lettres de Jean Racine qui n'avoient point été imprimées. A Paris, chez de Hansy. M.DCC.LXXIII* (84 pages in-8⁰). Le texte de cette première impression ne diffère de celui de l'autographe que par *enverrai*, pour *envoierai*.

2. La lettre est sans date. Celle que nous proposons par conjecture a, nous le croyons, beaucoup de vraisemblance. Racine, dans sa lettre, nomme le P. Bouhours « un des plus excellents maîtres de notre langue. » Cela ne donne-t-il pas à penser qu'elle a été écrite non-seulement après la publication des *Doutes sur la langue françoise* (1674), mais même après celle des *Remarques nouvelles sur la langue françoise* (1675)? La tragédie envoyée au P. Bouhours

gédie, et je vous envoierai le cinquième, dès que je l'aurai transcrit. Je vous supplie, mon Révérend Père, de prendre la peine de les lire, et de marquer les fautes que je puis avoir faites contre la langue, dont vous êtes un de nos plus excellents maîtres.

Si vous y trouvez quelques fautes d'une autre nature, je vous prie d'avoir la bonté de me les marquer sans indulgence. Je vous prie encore de faire part de cette lecture au Révérend Père Rapin, s'il veut bien y donner quelques moments.

Je suis votre très-humble et très-obéissant serviteur,

RACINE.

46. — DE RACINE A *** [1].

A Paris, le 28. [octobre 1678[2]].

JE vous suis bien obligé, Monsieur, de la promptitude avec laquelle vous avez bien voulu me faire réponse. Je

serait donc *Phèdre*, que Racine achevait en 1676. Quant aux deux tragédies sacrées, il ne saurait en être question ici, puisque Racine prie le P. Bouhours de faire part de la lecture de sa pièce au P. Rapin, qui mourut en 1687. Cela nous dispense de faire remarquer que la tragédie sur laquelle notre poëte désirait avoir les observations critiques du célèbre jésuite ne pouvait être *Esther*, qui n'a que trois actes.

LETTRE 46 (copiée sur l'autographe, appartenant à M. Boutron-Charlard). — 1. La familiarité de ce billet pourrait donner à croire qu'il est adressé à Boileau. L'authenticité en est-elle bien certaine? Nous ne nous en portons nullement garant, quoique l'écriture semble bien être celle de Racine. Ces quelques lignes sont d'ailleurs assez insignifiantes pour que la lettre ait pu sans peine être fabriquée.

2. La réception de l'abbé Colbert ayant eu lieu le 31 octobre 1678, nous avons complété la date de la manière que nous croyons la plus vraisemblable.

ne mets pas moins d'empressement moi-même à vous renvoyer le commencement de la réponse que je dois prononcer à la réception de M. l'abbé Colbert, dont la feuille s'est égarée. Je vous conjure de m'envoyer votre sentiment sur tout ceci. Je suis entièrement à vous³.

RACINE.

47. — DE RACINE A MADEMOISELLE RIVIÈRE¹. 1681

A Paris, ce 10ᵉ septembre 1681.

JE vous envoie, ma très-chère sœur, une lettre de mon oncle Racine par laquelle il me prioit de donner quelque argent à mon cousin son fils². Je lui ai donné trente-trois livres, comme vous verrez par le reçu de mon

---

3. A la suite de ce billet est la transcription du commencement de la harangue jusqu'aux mots : « Vous n'avez guère tardé à exciter notre admiration. » Voyez notre tome IV, p. 351 et 352 : nous y renvoyons le lecteur, la transcription jointe au billet étant exactement semblable au texte donné par le recueil de Coignard. On peut voir cependant par les variantes que nous avons citées au bas des pages indiquées ci-dessus, que Racine, avant l'impression du discours, y avait fait plusieurs corrections. Il n'a plus trouvé à en faire, après avoir consulté l'Aristarque dont il sollicitait les avis. Là encore il y a quelque chose qui nous met en défiance.

LETTRE 47 (revue sur l'autographe, conservé à Soissons). — 1. Nous cessons de donner à la sœur de Racine le nom de Marie Racine. Elle avait épousé Antoine Rivière le 30 juin 1676. Voyez ci-dessus, p. 374, la note 1 de la lettre 3.

2. Nous ne saurions dire si ce cousin est Nicolas Racine, né en 1657, fils de Claude Racine et de Geneviève Castel, qui devint notaire et procureur à la Ferté-Milon, et épousa en 1683 Anne Regnault. L'oncle Claude Racine eut aussi d'autres enfants; trois avaient reçu au baptême le nom de Claude; le dernier né de ces trois Claude fut baptisé le 24 octobre 1655. Les deux autres étaient sans doute morts en bas âge.

cousin. Je vous prie, à mesure que vous aurez besoin d'argent pour faire les petites charités dont vous avez bien voulu vous charger, d'en demander à mon oncle. Ne le pressez pas néanmoins. Dites-lui seulement l'intention qui vous obligera de lui en demander. J'en avancerai à mon cousin son fils, tant que mon oncle voudra, sur un simple mot d'écrit de lui. Je vous prie de lui faire beaucoup d'honnêtetés de ma part.

Vous avez eu tort de me vouloir du mal de ce que je n'ai point été vous voir à mon voyage de Brenne[3]. J'avois pris mes mesures pour repasser par la Ferté. Mais le baptême de M. de la Fontaine[4], auquel je ne m'attendois pas, nous obligea de revenir à Villers-Cotterets. Nous aurions grande envie, ma femme[5] et moi, de vous aller voir, et peut-être irons-nous dès cette année. Je baise les mains à M. Rivière et à mon cousin et à ma cousine Vitart[6]. Adieu, ma chère sœur : je suis tout à vous.

Je vous recommande toujours ma mère nourrice.

---

48. — DE RACINE A ANTOINE RIVIÈRE.

A Paris, ce 27. octob. [1682].

Je vous suis fort obligé, Monsieur, de l'honneur que vous me faites de vouloir que je tienne votre enfant[1].

---

3. Très-probablement, comme le fait remarquer M. l'abbé de la Roque, Braisne-sur-Veyle, à quatre lieues de Soissons.

4. Quelque baptême sans doute où la Fontaine tint un enfant sur les fonts.

5. Racine était marié depuis le 1er juin 1677. Voyez la *Notice biographique*, p. 94.

6. Antoine Vitart et Catherine Sconin, sa femme.

Lettre 48 (revue sur l'autographe, conservé à Soissons.) — 1. La

Je me rendrai pour cela à la Ferté-Milon², dès que j'aurai su que ma sœur est accouchée. Je pars demain pour aller à Fontainebleau³, où je ne serai que sept ou huit jours. Je vous prie de faire mes compliments à ma cousine Vitart, et de lui témoigner la joie que j'ai d'être son compère⁴. Si le temps le permet le moins du monde, je mènerai ma femme, qui aussi bien a une grande envie de voir sa fille⁵. Je suis bien obligé à mon cousin Regnaut⁶ de la bonté qu'il a d'avoir quelque égard pour notre nourrice dans les passages de gens de guerre. Je vous prie de lui dire que je la lui recommande de bon cœur, et que j'aurai une extrême reconnoissance de ce qu'il fera pour elle. Pour vous, si on vous incommodoit sur ce sujet, je vous prie de me le mander; car je n'épargnerai ni mes pas ni mes soins pour vous exempter

seconde fille de M. Rivière, Marie-Catherine, née le 21 novembre 1682. La date de cette lettre est certaine.

2. Racine ne put tenir sa promesse. Il ne se rendit à la Ferté-Milon que l'année suivante. L'enfant, qui avait été ondoyé le jour de sa naissance, fut baptisé le 5 octobre 1683 : voyez notre tome I, p. 187 et 188.

3. En 1682, le Roi et la Reine arrivèrent à Fontainebleau le 15 octobre, et retournèrent à Versailles le 16 novembre. Voyez la *Gazette* du 17 octobre et du 21 novembre 1682.

4. Ce fut en effet avec sa cousine Vitart (Catherine Sconin, femme d'Antoine Vitart) que Racine tint sur les fonts la fille de sa sœur. L'acte de baptême le constate.

5. Nanette (Anne Racine), née le 29 juillet de cette même année 1682. Elle avait été confiée à Mme Rivière pour être nourrie sous ses yeux à la Ferté-Milon.

6. François Regnault, qui avait épousé Jeanne Sconin, fille de Jean Sconin, oncle maternel de Racine. Il était père d'Anne Regnault, qui en 1683 épousa, comme nous l'avons dit ci-dessus, p. 517, note 2 de la lettre 47, Nicolas Racine. François Regnault et sa femme furent inhumés le même jour, 24 novembre 1694, âgés l'un de soixante-deux ans, l'autre de soixante. Dans un acte de baptême du 7 juin 1686, et dans l'acte de son inhumation, François Regnault est qualifié procureur du Roi au grenier à sel de la Ferté.

tout autant que je pourrai. Il y a des villes où le médecin[7] est toujours exempt, en qualité de médecin de l'hôpital. Informez-vous tout doucement de cela, et sans en faire de bruit; car peut-être je pourrois vous faire donner cette exemption pour toujours en cette qualité. Sachez comme on fait ou à Château-Thierry ou à Crespy. Adieu, Monsieur : je souhaite à ma sœur un heureux accouchement. Ma femme lui baise les mains, et à vous aussi. Elle mène demain ses enfants[8] à Melun, où elle demeurera quatre ou cinq jours, tandis que je serai à Fontainebleau. Nos enfants vous remercient de vos alouettes. Ç'a été une grande réjouissance pour eux; mais je voudrois que vous ne nous envoyassiez point tant de biens à la fois.

Je suis de tout mon cœur votre très-humble et très-obéissant serviteur,

RACINE.

Ma femme demande si ma sœur a songé à compter à la nourrice sa couverture de 3^{lt} 10^s.

Suscription : A Monsieur Monsieur Rivière, conseiller du Roi, contrôleur au grenier à sel, à la Ferté-Milon.

7. Antoine Rivière était médecin à la Ferté-Milon.
8. Jean-Baptiste, né le 11 novembre 1678, et Marie-Catherine, née le 16 mai 1680.

49. — DE RACINE A MADEMOISELLE RIVIÈRE.

1683

Ce mardi, 28. septembre [1683 [1]].

Je vous écris ce mot, ma chère sœur, pour vous avertir que je me prépare à partir demain pour vous aller voir avec ma femme et mes enfants. Nous prétendons souper jeudi au soir avec vous. Je vous plains de l'embarras que nous vous allons donner, mais je ne vous pardonnerai point si vous faites la moindre façon pour nous. Commencez dès le premier jour à ne nous point faire de festin : nous sommes gens à qui il ne faut pas grand chose pour faire bonne chère. J'espère coucher demain au soir à Nanteuil. Je vous donne le bon[jour][2], et à M. Rivière aussi. Nos enfants [sont] dans la plus grande joie du monde [de vous] aller voir. Racine couchera avec nous. Pour la petite, si vous lui pouvez trouver une manne ou un berceau, nous vous serons obligés. Pour nos gens, ne vous en mettez en aucune peine.

Suscription : A Mademoiselle Mademoiselle Rivière, à la Ferté-Milon. (Reste d'un cachet connu par d'au-

---

Lettre 49 (revue sur l'autographe, conservé à la Ferté-Milon).
— 1. M. l'abbé de la Roque a daté cette lettre de 1680, mais elle ne paraît pouvoir être que de 1683, année où le 28 septembre était un mardi, tandis qu'en 1680 cette même date était un samedi. Nous avons d'ailleurs dit, à la note 2 de la lettre précédente, que Racine se trouvait à la Ferté-Milon le 5 octobre 1683, et ici il annonce son départ pour le 29 septembre. Il est évident qu'en 1680 Racine n'aurait pu écrire : « Nos enfants sont dans la plus grande joie du monde de vous aller voir. » Le 28 septembre 1680 les deux aînés de ses enfants avaient l'un dix-huit mois, l'autre quatre mois seulement.

2. Les mots de cette lettre que nous avons mis entre des crochets se trouvaient sur une partie du papier qui a été arrachée ; ils sont faciles à suppléer.

tres lettres et dont l'écu, portant un cygne, a pour support deux oiseaux de proie posés sur leurs serres.)

---

50. — DE M. DE GUILLERAGUES A RACINE[1].

Au Palais de France, à Péra, le 9. de juin 1684.

J'ai été sensiblement attendri et flatté, Monsieur, de la lettre que vous m'avez fait l'honneur et le plaisir de m'écrire. Vos œuvres, plusieurs fois relues, ont justifié mon ancienne admiration. Éloigné de vous, Monsieur, et des représentations qui peuvent en imposer, dégoûté de ces pays fameux, vos tragédies m'en ont paru encore plus belles et plus durables. La vraisemblance y est merveilleusement observée, avec une profonde connoissance du cœur humain dans les différentes crises des passions. Vous avez suivi, soutenu et presque toujours enrichi les grandes idées que les anciens ont voulu nous donner, sans s'attacher à dire ce qui étoit. Dieu me préserve de traiter la respectable antiquité comme Saint-Amant a traité l'ancienne Rome[2]; mais vous savez mieux que moi

---

Lettre 50. — 1. Elle a été donnée, mais très-incomplétement et avec beaucoup d'altérations par Louis Racine, à la page 252 du *Recueil des lettres de Jean Racine*. L'éditeur de 1807 en a rétabli le texte sur l'original, qui était entre les mains de M. Jacobé de Naurois. — Gabriel-Joseph de Lavergne, comte de Guilleragues. Ambassadeur de France à Constantinople en 1679, il mourut dans cette ville en 1685 (voyez de Hammer, *Histoire de l'Empire ottoman*, traduction de Hellert, tome XII, p. 189). Il était lié d'amitié avec Racine. Boileau lui a adressé sa v[e] *épître*, qui commence ainsi :

    Esprit né pour la cour, et maître en l'art de plaire,
    Guilleragues, etc.

2. Dans son petit poëme burlesque, intitulé : *la Rome ridicule*. Voyez au tome II, p. 391-424 des *OEuvres complètes de Saint-Amant*, publiées par M. Ch.-L. Livet, dans la bibliothèque elzévirienne (Paris, 1855).

que, dans tout ce qu'ont écrit les poëtes et les historiens, ils se sont plutôt abandonnés au charme de leur brillante imagination, qu'ils n'ont été exacts observateurs de la vérité. Pour vous et M. Despréaux, historiens du plus grand roi du monde, la vérité vous fournit une matière tellement abondante que, pouvant même vous accabler et vous rendre peu croyables à la postérité, elle me laisse en doute si vous êtes, à cet égard, ou plus heureux, ou plus malheureux que les anciens.

Le Scamandre et le Simoïs sont à sec dix mois de l'année : leur lit n'est qu'un fossé. Cidaris et Barbisès[3] portent très-peu d'eau dans le port de Constantinople. L'Hèbre est une rivière du quatrième ordre. Les vingt-deux royaumes de l'Anatolie[4], le royaume de Pont, la Nicomédie donnée aux Romains, l'Ithaque, présentement l'île de Céphalonie, la Macédoine, le terroir de Larisse et celui d'Athènes ne peuvent jamais avoir fourni la quinzième partie des hommes dont les historiens font mention. Il est impossible que tous ces pays, cultivés avec tous les soins imaginables, aient été fort peuplés. Le terrain est presque partout pierreux, aride et sans rivières : on y voit des montagnes et des côtes pelées, plus anciennes assurément que les plus anciens écrivains. Le port d'Aulide, absolument gâté, peut avoir été très-bon ; mais il n'a jamais pu contenir un nombre approchant de deux mille vaisseaux ou simples barques. Sdile ou Délos est un misérable rocher ; Cerigue[5], et Paphos, qui est dans l'île de Chypre, sont des lieux affreux. Cerigue est une petite île des Vénitiens, la plus

---

3. *Cydaris* ou *Cicus* et *Barbycès* ou *Barbyssus* sont les anciens noms de deux rivières de Thrace.
4. Dans le texte de Louis Racine : « la Natolie. »
5. *Cerigue* ou *Cerigo*, nom moderne de l'île et de la ville de Cythère.

désagréable et la plus infertile qui soit au monde. Il n'y a jamais eu d'air si corrompu que celui de Paphos, lieu absolument inhabité. Naxie ne vaut guère mieux. Les divinités ont été mal placées : il en faut demeurer d'accord. Je croirois volontiers que les historiens se sont imaginé qu'il étoit plus beau de faire combattre trois cent mille hommes que vingt mille, et vingt rois plutôt que vingt petits seigneurs. Les poëtes avoient des maîtresses dans les lieux où ils ont fait demeurer Vénus ; mais en vérité la beauté ravissante de leurs ouvrages justifie tout. Linières et tant d'autres ne pourroient pas aussi impunément consacrer Senlis [6] ou la rue de la Huchette, quand même ils y seroient amoureux. Dans le fond, les grands auteurs, par la seule beauté de leur génie, ont pu donner des charmes éternels, et même l'être aux royaumes, la réputation aux nations, le nombre aux armées, et la force aux simples murailles. Ils ont laissé de grands exemples de vertu comme de style, fournissant ainsi leur postérité de tous ses besoins ; et si elle n'en a pas toujours su profiter, ce n'est pas leur faute. Il n'importe guère de quel pays soient les héros ; il n'importe guère aussi, ce me semble, si les historiens et les grands poëtes sont nés à Rome ou dans la cour du Palais [7], à Athènes ou à la Ferté-Milon [8]. Je vous observerai, Monsieur, avant de finir cet article, qu'il y a deux mille évêchés en Grèce seulement, nommés dans l'his-

---

6. Le poëte Linières, que Boileau, au vers 89 de son *épître* VII, nomme *de Senlis le poëte idiot*, avait une maison de campagne près de Senlis ; mais Senlis n'était pas sa patrie, comme le dit en note l'éditeur de 1807 ; il était né à Paris en 1628. Nous ignorons si à Paris il logeait rue de la Huchette, ou quel autre poëte y avait sa demeure.

7. Allusion à Boileau, né dans une ancienne maison canoniale, voisine de la cour du Palais.

8. Lieu de naissance de Racine.

toire ecclésiastique, qui ne peuvent avoir eu deux paroisses chacun.

J'ai appris avec un sensible déplaisir la mort de M. de Puymorin⁹. Je l'ai tendrement regretté ; je remercie Dieu de tout mon cœur de lui avoir fait l'importante grâce de songer à son salut avant sa mort.

Les témoignages de votre souvenir, Monsieur, m'ont été et me seront toujours fort chers : j'eusse voulu que vous souvenant aussi de l'attachement que j'ai pour tout ce qui vous touche, vous m'eussiez écrit quelque chose de votre famille et de vos affaires. Je crois le petit Racine¹⁰ bien vif, et il n'est pas impossible qu'à mon retour je ne l'interroge, et je ne le tourmente sur son latin : peut-être m'embarrassera-t-il sur le grec littéral ; mais je saurai un peu mieux le grec vulgaire, langue aussi corrompue et aussi misérable que l'ancienne Grèce l'est devenue.

Adieu, mon cher Monsieur. Je vous conjure de penser quelquefois à notre ancienne amitié, de m'écrire encore, quand même vous devriez continuer à m'appeler *Monseigneur*, et d'être bien persuadé de l'extrême passion et de l'estime sincère et sérieuse avec laquelle je serai toujours votre très-humble et très-obéissant serviteur.

Je ne vous ai jamais rien appris, et vous m'avez appris mille choses : cependant vous êtes obligé de demeurer d'accord (vous qui me donnez libéralement quelque part à vos tragédies, quoique je n'y en aie jamais eu d'autre que celle de la première admiration) que je

---

9. Pierre Boileau, sieur de Puymorin, frère consanguin de Boileau Despréaux ; il était mort le 11 décembre 1683 : voyez au tome I, p. 226, note 3.

10. Jean-Baptiste Racine avait alors six ans, à deux jours près, étant né le 11 juin 1678.

vous ai découvert qu'un trésorier général de France [11] prend le titre de chevalier, et qu'il a la satisfaction honorable d'être enterré avec des éperons dorés; qu'ainsi il ne doit pas légèrement prodiguer le titre de *Monseigneur*.

Vous ne m'avez pas mandé si vous voyez souvent M. le marquis de Seignelay. Adieu, Monsieur.

Suscription: A M. Racine, trésorier général de France, à Paris.

51. — DE RACINE AU P. BOUHOURS.

[Janvier 1685[1].]

Je vous envoie, mon Révérend Père, trois exem-

---

11. Nous avons dit, à la page 97 de la *Notice biographique*, que la charge de trésorier de France en la généralité de Moulins appartenait à Racine dès avant son mariage (1677); mais nous n'avions pu alors fixer plus précisément la date de sa nomination à cette charge. La pièce suivante, qui depuis nous a été communiquée, la fait remonter à l'année 1674: *Du samedi matin, 27 octobre 1674.* — *M⁰ Jean Racine, avocat en parlement, a été reçu au serment de l'office de conseiller du Roi, trésorier de France et général des finances de Moulins, au lieu de Antoine Prieur, sur lui vendu, après qu'il a été ouï, et trouvé suffisant et capable, et fait les affirmations et soumissions portées par le règlement du 23 novembre 1658, à la charge d'observer les ordonnances et arrêts concernant les foi et hommage.* M. DE LA CROIX, RAPPORTEUR.

LETTRE 51 (revue sur l'autographe, appartenant à M. Rathery). — 1. Cette lettre a été imprimée, en 1773, à la page 81 de l'opuscule de le Franc de Pompignan que nous avons déjà cité p. 515, à la note 1 de la lettre 45, également adressée au P. Bouhours. Comme celle-ci, elle est restée inconnue aux précédents éditeurs des *OEuvres de Racine*. — Les *Harangues académiques*, dont cette lettre annonce l'envoi au P. Bouhours, ne peuvent être que celles qui furent prononcées le 2 janvier 1685 à la réception de Thomas Corneille et de Bergeret, et imprimées la même année chez Pierre le

plaires de nos harangues académiques. Je vous prie de tout mon cœur d'en vouloir donner un au R. P. Rapin, et un au R. P. de la Baune². J'ai bien peur que vous ne trouviez sur le papier bien des fautes, que ma prononciation vous avoit déguisées ; mais j'espère que vous les excuserez un peu, et que l'amitié que vous avez pour moi aidera peut-être autant à vous éblouir que ma déclamation l'a pu faire. Je suis de tout mon cœur

Votre très-humble et très-obéissant serviteur,

RACINE.

52. — DE RACINE A MADEMOISELLE RIVIÈRE¹.

A Paris, ce 27 février [1685²].

M. Rivière vous aura dit, ma chère sœur, tous les

Petit (voyez à la page 349 de notre tome IV). La harangue de Racine à la réception de l'abbé Colbert en 1678 ne se trouve pas dans le recueil de Coignard, ainsi que nous l'avons dit à la page 342 du même tome : elle n'avait donc pas été imprimée, et ne saurait être celle dont il s'agit ici. L'impression du beau discours académique de 1685 a dû suivre de près la séance où il fut prononcé. En datant du mois de janvier la lettre au P. Bouhours, nous croyons ne pas nous écarter de la vraisemblance.

2. Jacques de la Baune, jésuite, auteur de poésies et de harangues latines, né le 15 avril 1649, mort le 21 octobre 1726.

LETTRE 52. — 1. M. Aimé-Martin a le premier donné cette lettre dans sa cinquième édition des OEuvres de Racine, tome VI, p. 423, où il avertit qu'elle a été copiée sur l'original, sans nous dire où il a trouvé cet original ; mais l'authenticité de la lettre ne peut paraître douteuse.

2. M. Aimé-Martin n'a pas essayé d'indiquer l'année. La date de 1685 est une conjecture que nous proposons, et que nous croyons assez vraisemblable. La lettre n'a pas pu être écrite après 1687, année où mourut Antoine Vitart, dont elle fait mention comme étant encore vivant. Nous verrons même plus loin, dans une lettre de Racine du 31 janvier 1687, que son cousin Vitart était déjà fort

soins que je prends pour vous faire rétablir, et l'expédient qu'on m'avoit proposé pour lui, qui lui seroit bien plus avantageux que la charge qu'il avoit. J'ai reçu ce matin une lettre de Monsieur l'Intendant, qui est au désespoir de n'avoir pas seulement su que M. Rivière m'appartient le moins du monde. Il se trouve d'assez grandes difficultés pour la chose que j'ai entreprise, et je ne vous puis pas en dire les raisons, de peur que ma lettre ne soit vue de quelque autre que de vous. Cependant si cette affaire-là ne réussit pas, je vois de grandes apparences de faire rétablir M. Rivière à la Ferté-Milon. Monsieur l'Intendant en fait son affaire; car outre l'amitié qu'il a pour moi, il me mande que ce M. Gressier qu'on a fait contrôleur est un banqueroutier qui n'a payé ni prêt ni paulette, et qui n'a été ni reçu ni installé. Il me mande qu'il a su tout cela de M. Vitart et de M. Regnaud[3], et

---

malade à ce moment. Le commencement de l'année 1686 serait donc la dernière limite. Pour trouver celle en deçà de laquelle il faut nous arrêter, nous ne pouvons remonter plus haut que l'année 1678 : le mariage de Marie Racine est de juin 1676, et l'établissement de Racine à la cour de 1677. Dans les neuf années entre lesquelles il reste ainsi à faire un choix, l'année 1685 nous a paru la plus probable en raison du passage où Racine dit qu'il se propose d'aller sous deux jours visiter le contrôleur général, mais qu'il ne le pourra faire que lorsqu'il sera habillé de deuil. Il ne sauroit être question, ce nous semble, que d'un deuil de cour; et ce deuil, pour lequel l'habillement de l'historiographe du Roi n'était pas encore prêt, devait être tout récent. Nous ne trouvons qu'en 1685 un semblable deuil au mois de février. C'est celui qui fut porté pour la mort de Charles II, arrivée le 16 de ce même mois, et dont un courrier de Londres apporta la nouvelle à Paris le 19. La cour prit le deuil pour trois mois, comme l'annonce la *Gazette* du 24 février 1685.

3. Antoine Vitart, procureur du Roi des eaux et forêts du duché de Valois, et François Regnault, procureur du Roi au grenier à sel de la Ferté-Milon, tous deux cousins de Racine. Voyez ci-dessus, p. 375, note 4 de la lettre 3, et p. 519, note 6 de la lettre 48.

qu'il leur a ordonné de s'opposer à l'enregistrement. De
là l'affaire sera portée au Conseil, et renvoyée à Monsieur l'Intendant, qui fera supprimer ce Gressier, et rétablir M. Rivière. J'aurai soin en ce cas que M. Rivière
soit rétabli dans sa charge de grènetier. Monsieur l'Intendant me mande aussi que M. Rivière a été supprimé
comme contrôleur alternatif, et qu'il a appris de moi qu'il
étoit grènetier ancien. J'ai vite fait partir un laquais pour
avertir de tout Monsieur le Contrôleur général[4], en attendant que je sois habillé de deuil pour y aller aprèsdemain. Ainsi, ma chère sœur, je crois que vous pouvez
avoir l'esprit en repos. Vos affaires, s'il plaît à Dieu, iront
bien; du moins vous pouvez vous assurer que je n'ai jamais eu rien si fort à cœur. Il me paroît par la lettre de
Monsieur l'Intendant que mon cousin Vitart n'a point
tant de tort que je pensois, puisqu'il a été lui-même le
trouver pour lui donner avis de tout cela. Ainsi ne vous
brouillez point. Au contraire, que M. Rivière le père et
M. Regnaud se hâtent de faire leur opposition à l'enregistrement, comme il leur a ordonné. Monsieur l'Intendant me mande qu'il a songé à me faire plaisir en faisant
conserver mon oncle Racine[5]. Jugez ce qu'il auroit fait
pour vous. On ne peut pas avoir plus de torts que vous en
avez, vous et M. Rivière, de ne m'avoir pas averti qu'on
alloit à Monsieur l'Intendant. Cependant ayez soin de ne
vous point chagriner et de n'avoir point de querelle avec
personne surtout. J'aurai soin de vos intérêts. Que M. Rivière me mande tout ce qu'il sait. Adieu, ma chère sœur.

---

4. Si cette lettre, comme nous l'avons cru, doit être datée de
1685, le contrôleur général était alors Claude le Pelletier, qui avait
succédé à Colbert, mort le 6 septembre 1683.

5. Claude Racine, contrôleur au grenier à sel de la Ferté-Milon.
Voyez ci-dessus, p. 435, note 5 de la lettre 19.

53. — D'ANTOINE ARNAULD A RACINE.

Ce 7. avril [1685[1]].

J'AI à vous remercier, Monsieur, du *Discours* qu'on m'a envoyé de votre part. Rien n'est assurément plus éloquent, et le héros que vous y louez en est d'autant plus digne de vos louanges, que l'on dit qu'il y a trouvé de l'excès. Mais il est bien difficile qu'il n'y en ait toujours un peu : les plus grands hommes sont hommes, et se sentent toujours par quelque endroit de l'infirmité humaine. On auroit bien des choses à se dire sur cela, si on se parloit; mais c'est ce qu'on ne voit pas lieu d'espérer de pouvoir faire. Il faudroit pour cela avoir dissipé un nuage, que j'ose dire être une tache dans ce soleil. Ce ne seroit pas une chose difficile, si ceux qui le pourroient faire avoient assez de générosité pour l'entreprendre; mais j'avoue qu'il y en a peu qui aient tous les talents nécessaires pour cela, entre lesquels on doit compter celui que les pères appellent *talentum familia-*

LETTRE 53 (revue sur l'autographe, conservé à la Bibliothèque impériale). — 1. En tête de l'autographe, Louis Racine a écrit : « Antoine Arnauld à Racine. 1678. Après le 30 octobre. » Il s'est trompé très-certainement. La lettre d'Arnauld a été écrite au sujet du discours académique dont Racine, dans la lettre 51 (p. 526), annonçait l'envoi au P. Bouhours, c'est-à-dire de celui qu'il prononça le 2 janvier 1685, à la réception de Thomas Corneille et de Bergeret : voyez notre tome IV, p. 357. Ce fut à l'occasion de ce discours que le Roi trouva de l'excès dans les louanges de Racine, comme le rappelle ici Arnauld, et comme Racine l'a raconté lui-même dans ses *Fragments historiques* (voyez notre tome V, p. 124). Les éditeurs des OEuvres d'Arnauld n'ont pas commis une moindre erreur, lorsque, dans leur tome II, p. 413, ils ont intitulé cette lettre : *Lettre de M. Arnauld à M. Jean Racine, au sujet du discours de ce dernier au Roi sur la Prise de Namur. Juillet* 1692. La date dans l'autographe est : *Ce* 7. *avril.* Dans les éditions précédentes des OEuvres de Racine, on a ajouté avant cette date : *De Bruxelles.* Ces mots ne sont pas dans la lettre originale.

ritatis. Cependant je vous assure que les pensées que j'ai sur cela ne sont point intéressées; que ce qui me peut regarder me touche fort peu, et que ce [que je] considère ² principalement, est les biens infinis que pourroit faire à l'Église un prince si accompli, si cet obstacle étoit levé.

Celui, Monsieur, qui vous rendra cette lettre est un ami qui demeure avec moi depuis quinze ans ³, et qui a pour moi tant d'affection, que je ne puis pas que je ne lui en sois très-obligé. Il a un frère qui est fort honnête homme, et capable de s'acquitter d'un emploi, comme seroit d'avoir soin des affaires dans une grande maison, avec beaucoup d'application et de fidélité. Si vous pouviez, Monsieur, lui en procurer quelqu'un, je vous ⁴ en aurois une grande obligation.

Je suis tout à vous et à votre incomparable ami ⁵.

2. Au lieu de : « ce [que je] considère », Arnauld a écrit par inadvertance : « ce qui considère. »

3. François Guelphe. C'était un protégé de la duchesse de Longueville, qu'elle avait placé, comme copiste, auprès de Nicole et d'Arnauld. Lorsque ce dernier fut forcé de sortir de France, Guelphe le suivit, et s'attacha constamment à son sort. Ce fut lui qui se chargea d'apporter à Port-Royal le cœur de son maître et son ami. (*Note de l'édition de* 1807.)

4. Arnauld avait écrit *lui*. La leçon *vous*, que veut le sens, y a été substituée, par une surcharge en encre plus noire.

5. Boileau. (*Note de l'édition de* 1807.)

54. — DE RACINE A MADEMOISELLE RIVIÈRE[1].

A Paris, ce 16. août [1685[2]].

Je ne vous écris qu'un mot par Mme de Passy[3], pour vous prier, ma chère sœur, de ne me point envoyer d'argent pour le surtout de M. Rivière, que je lui enverrai la semaine prochaine. J'en ai besoin dans le pays où vous êtes. Donnez quatre ou cinq pistoles, selon que vous le jugerez à propos, à cette des Fossés[4] que

Lettre 54. — 1. Cette lettre a été publiée pour la première fois par M. Aimé-Martin dans sa cinquième édition des OEuvres de Racine, tome VI, p. 425. Elle lui avait été communiquée par M. Feuillet de Conches, possesseur de l'autographe.

2. Racine s'est occupé en d'autres temps encore des affaires du grenier à sel, dans lesquelles il y avait à défendre les intérêts de son beau-frère. Cependant il nous a semblé probable que cette lettre est de la même année que la lettre 52, où il est dit (p. 529) que « l'affaire sera portée au Conseil. » Dans celle-ci nous lisons qu'elle est au greffe du Conseil. Cela paraît assez bien se rapporter.

3. Mme de Passy doit être cette demoiselle Vitart à qui Racine a adressé plusieurs des lettres de sa jeunesse. En 1685, elle était veuve, depuis deux ans, de Nicolas Vitart, seigneur de Passy (Passy en Valois, canton de Neuilly-Saint-Front). Nous avons eu sous les yeux un acte du 18 août 1684, qu'elle a signé : *Marguerite le Mazier de Passy.*

4. Nous ne savons si cette des Fossés est la même que Racine, dans deux lettres qu'on trouvera au tome suivant, datées de 1697, nomme « ma cousine des Fossés, » et « la pauvre cousine des Fossés. » Il y eut une cousine germaine de Racine, Agnès Racine, fille de Claude Racine, et de Geneviève Castel, qui épousa d'abord Jean Scart, officier chef de paneterie chez la feue Reine, et, en secondes noces, le chevalier des Fossés, capitaine des chasses au comté de Nanteuil. Voilà certainement une cousine des Fossés. Mais, née en 1664, elle avait vingt et un ans en 1685 : ce n'est donc point la femme « fort âgée » dont Racine parle ici. Quoique nous n'ayons pu savoir à quelle époque se fit son second mariage, il ne paraît pas non plus que ce puisse être « la pauvre cousine » des lettres de 1697. Les des Fossés étaient sans doute alliés aux Racine avant le mariage du capitaine des chasses de Nanteuil avec la fille de Claude Racine.

vous dites fort âgée et fort incommodée avec son mari. 1685
Est-ce la fille qui fut mariée à Neuilly, il y a deux ans,
qui est maintenant veuve[5]? Mandez-le-moi ; car si elle
est dans le besoin, je tâcherai encore de l'assister. Je
vous enverrai[6] de l'argent tant que vous en jugerez à propos. Je me repose sur vous de tout cela. J'espère que
les affaires du grenier à sel seront bientôt terminées. On
dit que cela est au greffe du Conseil. Adieu, ma chère
sœur : je suis tout à vous.

55. — DE RACINE A MADEMOISELLE RIVIÈRE.

A Paris, ce 4ᵉ septembre [1685[1]].

JE donnai hier votre argent à M. de Sacy[2], et je vous
envoie son reçu. Je suis bien en colère contre M. Rivière
de ce qu'il s'est tant hâté de vendre son blé, malgré
toutes les exhortations que je lui fis pour l'en empêcher.
Je voudrois que vous en eussiez encore une grande
quantité : vous seriez riche, et cela me feroit un fort

---

5. M. Aimé-Martin a mis : « qui est maintenant venue. » Nous
n'avons pas l'autographe sous les yeux, comme lui-même l'a eu ;
mais il nous paraît fort vraisemblable, pour ne pas dire plus, que
le mot *veuve*, écrit par Racine *veuue*, aura été lu à tort *venue*. Le
sens exigeait, ce nous semble, notre correction.

6. Probablement l'original, ici et plus haut, porte : *envoierai*.

LETTRE 55 (revue sur l'autographe, conservé à la Ferté-Milon).
— 1. Le *post-scriptum* de cette lettre en fixe la date. Louis Racine
en effet dit dans ses *Mémoires* (voyez notre tome I, p. 335) : « Lorsqu'en 1685 il (*Racine*) eut contribué à une somme de cent mille
livres, que le bureau des finances de Moulins avoit payée en conséquence de la déclaration du 28 avril 1684, il avoit obtenu du
Roi une ordonnance sur le trésor royal pour y aller reprendre sa
part, qui montoit environ à quatre mille livres. »

2. Voyez ci-dessus, p. 515, la note 7 de la lettre 44.

grand plaisir. Vous avez bien fait de nous en acheter. Si vous trouvez occasion de nous en acheter encore à peu près au même prix, j'en serai fort aise; mais je ne crois pas qu'il y revienne de long temps.

Pour ce qui est de l'argent que vous avez à nous, je vous prie de le garder pour les occasions, et surtout d'en assister tous ceux de nos pauvres parents que vous croirez en avoir besoin dans ce temps de cherté. Si vous connoissez même quelques autres pauvres qui vous paroissent en grand besoin, je vous prie de ne leur en point refuser. Je me repose sur vous de tout cela, et je ne vous accuserai point d'avoir trop donné.

La petite Nanette[3] a été bien tourmentée de deux grosses dents qui lui sont percées; mais il me semble qu'elle commence à revenir. Elle a l'humeur bien jolie, et ne manque point d'esprit, quoiqu'elle ne parle pas plus que quand vous nous l'avez renvoyée.

Vous ne mandez point à ma femme des nouvelles de sa toile. Elle vous salue, et M. Rivière aussi. Adieu, ma chère sœur : je suis tout à vous.

RACINE.

Je ne sais si je vous ai mandé que le Roi m'a remis ma taxe de trésorier en France, qui montoit à quatre ou cinq mille francs.

Suscription : A Mademoiselle Mademoiselle Rivière, à la Ferté-Milon. (Cachet au cygne.)

---

3. Nanette (Anne Racine), née le 29 juillet 1682, avait alors trois ans et un mois.

LETTRES. 535

56. — DE LA FONTAINE A RACINE[1]. 1686

Du 6. juin 1686.

Poignan, à son retour de Paris, m'a dit que vous preniez mon silence en fort mauvaise part : d'autant plus qu'on vous avoit assuré que je travaillois sans cesse depuis que je suis à Château-Thierry, et qu'au lieu de m'appliquer à mes affaires, je n'avois que des vers en tête. Il n'y a de tout cela que la moitié de vrai : mes affaires m'occupent autant qu'elles en sont dignes, c'est-à-dire nullement ; mais le loisir qu'elles me laissent, ce n'est pas la poésie, c'est la paresse qui l'emporte. Je trouvai ici le lendemain de mon arrivée une lettre et un couplet d'une fille âgée seulement de huit ans ; j'y ai répondu : ç'a été ma plus forte occupation depuis mon arrivée. Voici donc le couplet, avec le billet qui l'accompagne :

Sur l'air de Joconde.

Quand je veux faire une chanson
   Au parfait la Fontaine,
Je ne puis rien tirer de bon
   De ma timide veine.
Elle est tremblante à ce moment,
   Je n'en suis pas surprise.
Devant lui un[2] foible talent
   Ne peut être de mise.

« Je crois, en vérité, que je ne serois jamais parvenue à faire une chanson pour vous, Monsieur, si je n'a-

---

Lettre 56. — 1. Le texte que nous donnons est conforme à celui qui est dans les *OEuvres diverses de la Fontaine* (tome III, p. 317-321), publiées en 1729 par l'abbé d'Olivet. C'est là que cette lettre a été imprimée pour la première fois, aussi bien que la lettre 13 : voyez ci-dessus, p. 412, note 1.

2. Pour supprimer l'hiatus, l'éditeur de 1807, et après lui Aimé-Martin, ont remplacé *un* par *mon*.

vois en vue de m'en attirer une des vôtres. Vous me l'avez promise, et vous avez affaire à une personne qui est vive sur ses intérêts. Songez que je vous assassinerai jusqu'à ce que vous m'ayez tenu votre parole. De grâce, Monsieur, ne négligez point une petite Muse qui pourroit parvenir, si vous lui jetiez un regard favorable. »

Ce couplet et cette lettre, si ce qu'on me mande de Paris est bien vrai, n'ont pas coûté une demi-heure à la demoiselle, qui quelquefois met de l'amour dans ses chansons, sans savoir ce que c'est qu'amour. Comme j'ai vu qu'elle ne me laisseroit point en repos que je n'eusse écrit quelque chose pour elle, je lui ai envoyé les trois couplets suivants. Ils sont sur le même air.

> Paule, vous faites joliment
>   Lettres et chansonnettes;
> Quelques grains d'amour seulement,
>   Elles seroient parfaites.
> Quand ses soins au cœur sont connus,
>   Une Muse sait plaire.
> Jeune Paule, trois ans de plus
>   Font beaucoup à l'affaire.

> Vous parlez quelquefois d'amour,
>   Paule, sans le connoître;
> Mais j'espère vous voir un jour
>   Ce petit dieu pour maître.
> Le doux langage des soupirs
>   Est pour vous lettre close.
> Paule, trois retours de zéphirs
>   Font beaucoup à la chose.

> Si cet enfant, dans vos chansons,
>   A des grâces naïves,
> Que sera-ce quand ses leçons
>   Seront un peu plus vives
> Pour aider l'esprit en ces vers

Le cœur est nécessaire.
Trois printemps sur autant d'hivers
Font beaucoup à l'affaire.

Voyez, Monsieur, s'il y avoit là de quoi vous fâcher de ce que je ne vous envoie pas les belles choses que je produis. Il est vrai que j'ai promis une lettre au prince de Conti[3]; elle est à présent sur le métier : les vers suivants y trouveront leur place.

Un sot plein de savoir est plus sot qu'un autre homme :
 Je le fuirois jusques à Rome ;
 Et j'aimerois mille fois mieux
 Un glaive aux mains d'un furieux,
 Que l'étude en certains génies.
 Ronsard est dur, sans goût, sans choix,
Arrangeant mal ses mots, gâtant par son françois
Des Grecs et des Latins les grâces infinies.
Nos aïeux, bonnes gens, lui laissoient tout passer,
Et d'éruditions ne se pouvoient lasser.
C'est un vice aujourd'hui : l'on oseroit à peine
En user seulement une fois la semaine.
Quand il plaît au hasard de vous en envoyer,
Il faut les bien choisir, puis les bien employer,
Très-sûrs qu'avec ce soin l'on n'est pas sûr de plaire.
Cet auteur a, dit-on, besoin d'un commentaire.
On voit bien qu'il a lu ; mais ce n'est pas l'affaire :
Qu'il cache son savoir, et montre son esprit.
Racan ne savoit rien : comment a-t-il écrit ?
Et mille autres raisons, non sans quelque apparence.
Malherbe de ces traits usoit plus fréquemment.
Sous lui la cour n'osoit encore ouvertement
 Sacrifier à l'ignorance.

Puisque je vous envoie ces petits échantillons, vous

---

3. François-Louis de Bourbon, prince de la Roche-sur-Yon, puis prince de Conti après la mort de son frère aîné, Louis-Armand de Bourbon (9 novembre 1685). Né le 30 avril 1664, il mourut le 21 février 1709. Voyez au tome I, p. 320, note 4.

en conclurez, s'il vous plaît, qu'il est faux que je fasse le mystérieux avec vous. Mais, je vous en prie, ne montrez ces derniers vers à personne; car Mme de la Sablière ne les a pas encore vus.

57. — DE RACINE A MADEMOISELLE RIVIÈRE.

A Paris, ce 4e novembre [1686[1]].

Je ne vous écris qu'un mot, ma très-chère sœur, pour vous dire que je n'ai point reçu de vos nouvelles, depuis une lettre où vous me parliez du procès qu'on fait à la ville pour les reliques de saint Vulgis[2]. Comme j'étois alors en Picardie, je ne vous fis point de réponse. Si j'avois été à Paris, j'aurois sollicité de bon cœur avec Monsieur le procureur du Roi[3]. Depuis ce temps, j'ai été à Fontainebleau. Je suis maintenant de retour à Paris, et nous sommes logés dans une maison où apparemment nous demeurerons longtemps : c'est dans la rue des Maçons[4], près de la Sorbonne. Ainsi, lorsque vous m'écrirez, je vous prie de m'adresser vos lettres simplement dans la rue des Maçons. Vous ne m'avez point mandé si vous aviez reçu celle où je vous envoyois une promesse

---

Lettre 57 (revue sur l'autographe, conservé à la Ferté-Milon). —
1. La date de 1686 est donnée par la mention que Racine fait, dans cette lettre, de son récent établissement dans la rue des Maçons et de l'accouchement prochain de sa femme. Jeanne-Nicole-Françoise, née le 29 novembre 1686, est le premier de ses enfants qui ait été baptisé dans l'église Saint-Séverin, paroisse de la rue des Maçons. Voyez son acte de baptême, tome I, p. 185.
2. Saint Vulgis était le patron de la Ferté-Milon.
3. François Regnault, cousin de Racine. Voyez ci-dessus, p. 519. la note 6 de la lettre 48.
4. Racine a écrit : « des Massons. »

de cent francs de mon oncle Racine. Faites, je vous prie, nos baisemains à M. Rivière, et chez mon cousin Vitart, et mandez-nous de vos nouvelles. Ma femme croit accoucher vers la fin de ce mois. Nous prendrons une nourrice à Paris, l'hiver n'étant pas une saison propre pour envoyer un enfant à la campagne. Nanette[5] crève de graisse, et est la plus belle de nos enfants. Je vous donne le bonjour, ma chère sœur, et suis tout à vous.

RACINE.

Suscription : A Mademoiselle Mademoiselle Rivière, à la Ferté-Milon. (Reste du cachet J. RAC.)

---

58. — DE RACINE A MADEMOISELLE RIVIÈRE.

A Paris, ce 12e novembre [1686[1]].

JE vous remercie, ma chère sœur, des excellents fro-

---

5. Anne Racine. Elle avait alors quatre ans. Voyez ci-dessus, p. 519, la note 5 de la lettre 48.

LETTRE 58 (revue sur l'autographe, conservé à Soissons). — 1. Nous donnons à cette lettre la date de 1686, parce qu'il y est dit que Mme Racine était « dans l'embarras des nourrices. » M. l'abbé de la Roque l'a datée de 1684, conjecturant qu'il s'agissait de chercher une nourrice pour Élisabeth Racine, née le 31 juillet de cette année. Mais il eût été tard au mois de novembre pour prendre ce soin ; et s'il fallait entendre qu'on s'occupait d'un changement de nourrice, il serait étonnant que rien dans la lettre ne l'expliquât. Il est bien plus vraisemblable que le 12 novembre 1686, attendant la naissance très-prochaine d'un enfant, on cherchât déjà celle qui devait le nourrir (voyez la lettre précédente). Le chiffre 2, que, dans l'autographe, on lit au bas de la suscription, signifie-t-il que la lettre était la seconde adressée par Racine à Mlle Rivière au mois de novembre? La précédente est en effet du 4 de ce même mois.

mages que vous nous avez envoyés : je n'en ai jamais vu de si bons. Il n'y a pas jusqu'à nos petits enfants qui les aiment mieux que tout autre dessert. Ma femme est dans l'embarras des nourrices. Elle a bien de la peine à en trouver une, à Paris, qui l'accommode. Si la saison n'étoit pas si rude, je me serois bien vite adressé à vous pour nous en trouver une; car, à tout prendre, Nanette est celle de nos enfants que je crois qui a été le mieux nourrie.

Vous me parlez d'un fils de Mme d'Acy[2]; mandez-moi, je vous prie, s'il est tout seul, quel âge il a, et s'il pourroit bientôt apprendre quelque métier; car je crois que c'est ce qui vaut mieux pour ces gens-là qu'un bon métier, au lieu qu'en apprenant à lire et à écrire, ils se font tout au plus de misérables sergents et deviennent de fort grands fainéants : surtout tous les enfants de ce côté-là, dont il n'y en a pas eu qui se soit voulu tourner au bien. Je me chargerois volontiers de mettre celui-ci en métier, s'il est en âge de cela. Sinon, mandez-moi ce qu'on peut faire pour lui.

« Ma chère tante, je vous baise bien les mains et à mon oncle et à ma cousine.

« RACINE[3]. »

Racine vous a voulu faire ses baisemains, et vous a écrit sur mon genou; car il écrit mieux que cela. Je suis bien aise que ma nièce se porte bien. C'est tenir des enfants bien jeune[4]. On est plus scrupuleux à Paris, et je crois qu'on a raison.

2. Nous n'avons pu découvrir si cette dame d'Acy était alliée à la famille de Racine.
3. Cette signature et les deux lignes qui précèdent sont de Jean-Baptiste Racine, qui avait alors huit ans. Au lieu de *cousine*, sa main inexpérimentée avait d'abord écrit *coune*, qui a été effacé.
4. On doit entendre par là que la nièce de Racine venait d'être

Adieu, ma chère sœur : faites, s'il vous plaît, nos baisemains à M. Rivière et à mon cousin Vitart.

Suscription : A Mademoiselle Mademoiselle Rivière, à la Ferté-Milon. 2. (Cachet : J. R.)

---

59. — DE RACINE A MADEMOISELLE RIVIÈRE.

A Paris, ce 31. janvier [1687[1]].

J'avois reçu, ma très-chère sœur, les lapins que M. Rivière a eu la bonté de nous envoyer, qui se sont trouvés excellents. Mais je ne vous en ai point remerciés[2] à cause d'un grand mal de gorge qui me tient depuis trois se-

marraine. Mais quelle nièce? Marie-Antoinette Rivière était née le 25 juillet 1677. A Paris, on n'était pas scrupuleux jusqu'à ne pas permettre de tenir, à l'âge de neuf ans, des enfants sur les fonts : Jean-Baptiste et Marie-Catherine Racine furent en 1688 parrain et marraine de leur sœur Madeleine; l'un avait alors neuf ans et demi, l'autre un peu moins de huit ans. La nièce dont parle Racine doit donc être Marie-Catherine Rivière, qui, au mois de novembre 1686, avait quatre ans seulement. Il est à remarquer d'ailleurs que Racine, dans ses lettres, ne parle jamais que d'une de ses nièces, de Marie-Catherine, sa filleule; et Jean-Baptiste Racine, dans son petit billet, ne parait connaître qu'une cousine. Marie-Antoinette était-elle morte en bas âge? Nous n'avons pas rencontré l'acte de son décès; mais le silence de Racine et de son fils sur elle paraît significatif. Nous savons d'ailleurs que Marie-Catherine Rivière a seule laissé une postérité.

Lettre 59 (revue sur l'autographe, conservé à la Ferté-Milon). — 1. Cette lettre, où il est parlé, comme dans la précédente, du jeune d'Acy, semblerait par cela même avoir été écrite à peu près dans le même temps. Il y a une autre raison de regarder comme vraisemblable la date de 1687. Dans sa lettre à Boileau du 24 mai 1687, comme dans celle-ci, Racine parle de son mal de gorge, « qui va toujours son même train : » voyez ci-après, p. 550.

2. Dans l'original : *remercié*, sans accord.

maines et qui m'a extrêmement incommodé. Je vous prie donc de m'excuser, et de faire aussi mes excuses à mon cousin Regnaud[3], que je n'ai point encore remercié d'un panier de fromage qu'il m'a envoyé. J'attends à m'acquitter envers lui que je puisse lui aller choisir un baril d'olives pour son carême. Je voulois aussi envoyer quelque chose à mon cousin Vitart; mais votre lettre m'a donné bien du déplaisir en m'apprenant l'état fâcheux où il se trouve[4]. Je vous prie, au nom de Dieu, de lui bien témoigner la part que je prends à sa maladie, et d'assurer aussi ma cousine, sa femme, qu'on ne peut pas s'intéresser plus que je fais à son déplaisir. Je voudrois de [tout] mon cœur être en état de les so[igner] l'un et l'autre. Mandez-moi de ses nouvelles quand vous le pourrez[5].

J'approuve tout ce que vous faites à l'égard de ce petit Dassy[6], et comme le temps est fort rude, je vous prie de faire de mon argent toutes les charités que vous croirez nécessaires. Je vous écrirai, s'il plaît à Dieu, avant la fin de la semaine prochaine.

3. Voyez ci-dessus, p. 538, la note 3 de la lettre 57. Dans la lettre 48, Racine a écrit *Regnaut* le nom de ce cousin.

4. Il est évident que ce fut la dernière maladie d'Antoine Vitart, et qu'il mourut fort peu de temps après, puisque le second mariage de sa veuve est de cette même année 1687. Voyez ci-dessus, p. 435, la note 6 de la lettre 19. Nous avons déjà eu plusieurs occasions de parler de ce frère de M. Vitart, intendant du duc de Luynes. Dans des actes de différentes dates, Antoine Vitart est qualifié, tantôt avocat au Parlement, procureur du Roi des eaux et forêts de Valois, tantôt conseiller du Roi et de son Altesse Royale Monsieur le duc d'Orléans.

5. Racine avait d'abord écrit : « le plus tôt que vous pourrez. » — Dans la phrase précédente, *tout* et la fin de *soigner* ont été enlevés avec le cachet.

6. C'est le même dont Racine, dans la lettre précédente, écrit le nom d'*Acy*.

Mon mal de gorge est un peu diminué depuis hier. Ma femme et nos enfants vous saluent, et M. Rivière. Je suis de tout mon cœur, ma chère sœur,

Votre très-humble et très-obéissant serviteur,

RACINE.

Je vous prie de me mander le jour où mon père et ma mère moururent, afin que je fasse prier Dieu ces jours-là pour eux. Il me semble que c'est vers ce temps-ci que nous perdîmes feue ma mère [7].

Adieu, ma chère sœur : j'embrasse ma petite nièce [8], qu'on dit qui est la plus jolie du monde.

Suscription : A Mademoiselle Mademoiselle Rivière, à la Ferté-Milon. (Cachet : J. RAC.)

---

60. — DE RACINE A MADEMOISELLE RIVIÈRE.

A Paris, ce 10ᵉ mai [1687[1]].

JE pars ce matin, ma chère sœur, pour aller en Flandres. Mais ne soyez point en inquiétude pour votre commission. J'allai hier prendre congé de M. Lhuillier,

---

7. La mère de Racine était morte en effet au mois de janvier. Elle avait été inhumée le 29 janvier 1641. Son père était mort au commencement de février 1643. Voyez notre tome I, p. 175 et 176.
8. Marie-Catherine Rivière. Voyez ci-dessus, p. 540, la note 4 de la lettre 58.

LETTRE 60 (revue sur l'autographe, conservé à la Ferté-Milon). — 1. Il y avait d'abord 7 *mai*. Le 7 a été corrigé en 10. La date de l'année est bien 1687. Le Roi partit le 10 mai 1687 pour la Flandre, où il allait visiter les fortifications de Luxembourg. Racine l'accompagna dans ce voyage, comme on le voit ci-après (p. 549), dans sa lettre à Boileau du 24 mai 1687.

qui est proprement celui de qui vous la tenez. Il m'a promis d'avoir soin de vos intérêts, et que tout iroit bien. Faites mes baisemains à M. Rivière. Je suis tout à vous.

Dites à mon oncle Racine que j'ai parlé pour une dispense en faveur de M. le Moine son gendre[2], et que je me suis adressé à M. de Harlay[3], conseiller d'État, gendre de Monsieur le Chancelier, auprès duquel il a tout pouvoir. Il a demandé la dispense; mais elle lui a été refusée, parce que Monsieur le Chancelier s'est fait une loi de n'en point donner de cette nature, à cause des conséquences. Mais il m'a dit qu'on fermoit les yeux sur ces sortes de choses, quand il ne s'agit que de petites charges comme celle-là, et qu'on n'inquiétoit personne. Voilà tout ce que j'ai pu faire.

Suscription : A Mademoiselle Mademoiselle Rivière, à la Ferté-Milon. (Restes d'un cachet dont l'empreinte représente deux oiseaux de proie posés sur leurs serres, et qui servent de support à l'écu sur lequel est un cygne.)

2. Jean le Moine, avocat au Parlement, avait épousé Agnès-Thérèse Racine, une des filles de Claude Racine, qui est l'oncle de Racine dont il est parlé ici, et de Geneviève Castel. Agnès-Thérèse Racine, baptisée le 27 février 1667, mourut au mois de novembre 1694.
3. Nicolas-Auguste de Harlay, seigneur de Bonneuil, gendre du chancelier Boucherat, cousin par alliance de Bussy Rabutin. Voyez les *Lettres de Mme de Sévigné*, tome II, p. 433, note 2; et tome VII, p. 472, note 3.

61. — DE BOILEAU A RACINE[1].

1687

A Auteuil, 19e mai [1687].

Je voudrois bien vous pouvoir mander que ma voix

Lettre 61 (revue sur l'autographe, appartenant à M. le marquis de Biencourt). — 1. Cette lettre, qui manque dans le *Recueil* de Louis Racine, a été publiée pour la première fois par Cizeron-Rival au tome III, p. 55, de ses *Lettres familières de MM. Boileau Despréaux et Brossette* (Lyon, 1770, 3 volumes in-12). — Les précédents éditeurs des *OEuvres de Racine* ont donné les lettres que Boileau adressait à son ami, non point telles que celui-ci les a reçues, mais conformes au texte des copies corrigées par Boileau. Usant d'un droit incontestable, Boileau ne voulait paraitre devant le public qu'après avoir effacé les négligences échappées à la rapidité de sa plume. On voit par la lettre qu'il écrivait à Brossette, en date du 4 mars 1703, qu'il se proposait de soumettre les lettres de Racine à une semblable révision. Dans une édition des *OEuvres de Boileau*, il est nécessaire de tenir compte des deux rédactions, de celle des lettres originales, comme de celle des copies corrigées, quelle que soit d'ailleurs celle qu'on donne comme texte et celle qu'on indique dans les variantes. Pour nous, dont les lettres écrites par Racine sont le principal objet, nous ne pouvions hésiter à choisir le texte des lettres originales de Boileau, qui est celui de la correspondance des deux amis. En outre, les lettres de Racine n'ayant pas été remaniées et refaites après coup, il importait que tout restât égal de part et d'autre. Nous avons même pensé que ce n'était pas ici la place de citer comme variantes les corrections de Boileau. Le texte de la plupart de ses lettres a été revu par nous sur les autographes conservés à la Bibliothèque impériale, au tome I des manuscrits de Racine, où ils ont été réunis aux lettres de celui-ci. Nous avons aujourd'hui cinquante-deux lettres de la correspondance de Racine et de Boileau, sans y comprendre la lettre que Racine écrivit à Boileau en lui envoyant le *Banquet* de Platon, et qu'il eût été superflu de répéter ici : nous l'avons donnée dans notre tome V, p. 451 et 452. Des cinquante-deux, quarante-sept ont été publiées dans le *Recueil* de Louis Racine. Il avait déposé à la bibliothèque du Roi les originaux de ces quarante-sept lettres. Aujourd'hui, sur ce nombre, quatre manquent à cette bibliothèque : elles sont de Boileau; nous avons trouvé ailleurs les manuscrits originaux de deux d'entre elles; quant aux deux autres, il est à remarquer que, dans les notes qu'il y a jointes, Berriat-Saint-Prix, éditeur des *OEuvres de Boileau*,

est revenue, mais la vérité est qu'elle est au même état que vous l'avez laissée, et qu'elle n'est haussée ni baissée d'un ton. Rien ne peut la faire revenir, et mon ânesse y a perdu son latin, aussi bien que tous les médecins, à la réserve que son lait m'engraisse et que leurs remèdes me desséchoient. Ainsi, mon cher Monsieur, me voilà aussi muet et aussi chagrin que jamais. J'aurois bon besoin de votre vertu, et surtout de votre vertu chrétienne, pour me consoler ; mais je n'ai pas été élevé, comme vous, dans le sanctuaire de la piété, et, à mon avis, une vertu moliniste ne sauroit que blanchir contre un aussi juste sujet de s'affliger qu'est le mien. Il me faut de la grâce, et de la grâce la plus efficace, pour m'empêcher de mourir de déplaisir. Car, entre nous, quelque chose qu'on me puisse dire, j'ai peur de ne me retrouver jamais en l'état où j'ai été. Cela me dégoûte fort de toutes les choses du monde, sans me donner néanmoins (ce qui est de plus fâcheux) un assez grand goût de Dieu. Quelque détaché pourtant que je sois des choses de cette vie, je ne suis pas encore indifférent pour la gloire du Roi. Vous me ferez donc plaisir de me mander quelques particularités de son voyage[2], puisque tous ses pas sont

en cite le manuscrit aussi bien que celui de toutes les autres lettres. Il a donc eu ce manuscrit sous les yeux, et nous avons suivi son texte avec confiance ; car toutes les fois que nous avons pu contrôler son travail, si nous y avons de loin en loin découvert quelques petites inexactitudes, elles sont fort légères. Nous avons d'ailleurs, pour une des lettres, dont l'autographe nous manque, comparé le texte de Berriat-Saint-Prix avec celui qu'a publié M. Laverdet dans sa *Correspondance entre Boileau Despréaux et Brossette* (Paris, Techener, 1858), d'après une copie qui est de la main de Jean-Baptiste Racine, et sur laquelle Boileau avait fait ses corrections.

2. La réponse de Racine, qui est écrite de Luxembourg, fait connaître de quel voyage Boileau parle ici, et détermine la date de 1687 que tous les éditeurs ont donnée à cette lettre. Le Roi était parti le samedi 10 mai 1687 pour aller visiter les fortifications de

historiques, et qu'il ne fait rien qui ne soit digne, pour
ainsi dire, d'être raconté à tous les siècles. Je vous aurai
aussi beaucoup d'obligation, si vous voulez en même
temps m'écrire des nouvelles de votre santé. Je meurs de
peur que votre mal de gorge ne soit aussi persévérant que
mon mal de poitrine. Si cela est, je n'ai plus l'espérance
d'être heureux, ni par autrui, ni par moi-même. On me
vient dire que Furetière[3] a été à l'extrémité, et que, par
l'avis de son confesseur, il a envoyé querir tous les aca-
démiciens offensés, et qu'il leur a fait une amende
honorable dans les formes, mais qu'il se porte mieux
maintenant. J'aurai soin de m'éclaircir de la chose, et je
vous en manderai le détail. Le P. Sovennin[4] a dîné aujourd'hui chez moi, et m'a fort prié de vous faire ses
recommandations. Je vous les fais donc, et en récompense, je vous conjure de faire bien les miennes au cher
M. Félix[5]. Pourquoi faut-il que je ne sois point avec lui
et avec vous, ou que je n'aie pas du moins une voix
pour crier contre la fortune qui m'a envié ce bonheur ?
Dites bien aussi à M. le marquis de Termes[6] que je

1687

Luxembourg, place que Créqui avait prise en 1684. Il arriva à
Luxembourg le 21 mai au soir. Voyez le *Journal* de Dangeau, à
cette dernière date.

3. Antoine Furetière ne mourut que l'année suivante (14 mai
1688). On connaît ses démêlés avec l'Académie, son exclusion de
cette compagnie le 22 janvier 1685, et ses *Factum*, dont les deux
premiers avaient été imprimés lorsque Boileau écrivait cette lettre,
l'un en 1685, l'autre en 1686.

4. Il étoit Génovéfain, et parent de Racine. (*Note de Cizeron-
Rival.*) — Cizeron écrit *Souvenin*.

5. Charles-François-Félix de Tassy. Il succéda à son père, en 1676,
dans la charge de premier chirurgien du Roi : voyez au tome IV,
p. 470, note 1. Il était lié d'amitié avec Racine et Boileau dès le
temps de leur jeunesse. Ce fut lui qui fit au Roi l'opération de la
fistule, le 21 novembre 1686. Il mourut le 25 mai 1703.

6. Roger de Pardaillan de Gondrin, marquis de Termes, mort
en 1704. Boileau le nomme au vers 54 de son *épître* XI.

songe à lui malgré mon infortune, et qu'encore que je sache assez combien les gens de cour sont peu touchés des malheurs d'autrui, je le tiens assez galant homme pour me plaindre. Maximilien[7] m'est venu voir à Auteuil, et m'a lu quelque chose de son *Théophraste*. C'est un fort bon homme, et à qui il ne manqueroit rien si la nature l'avoit fait aussi agréable qu'il a envie de l'être. Du reste, il a du savoir et du mérite. Je vous donne le bonjour et suis tout à vous.

Despréaux[8].

Suscription : A Monsieur Monsieur Racine, en cour.

7. Cizeron-Rival avertit que c'est la Bruyère qui est ainsi désigné. M. Édouard Fournier (*la Comédie de la Bruyère*, xxxix, p. 512 et 513) croit que par ce sobriquet de *Maximilien*, Boileau fait allusion à la liaison de la Bruyère avec la femme de Maximilien Belleforière, marquis de Soyecourt. — Boileau sans doute pensa plus tard que la façon dont il parle ici de l'illustre auteur des *Caractères* pourrait étonner. Il fit donc quelques changements dans sa copie corrigée. Au lieu de : « un fort bon homme, » il mit : « un fort honnête homme ; » et avant les mots : « du savoir et du mérite, » il ajouta : « de l'esprit. »

8. Dans le recueil, ci-dessus mentionné, de M. Laverdet, où cette lettre est une de celles qui ont été données d'après les copies écrites par Jean-Baptiste Racine, il y a à la fin un post-scriptum que les éditeurs précédents n'ont pas connu ; il n'est pas non plus dans l'autographe appartenant à M. de Biencourt. On s'explique avec peine que Boileau ait pu faire après coup une addition de ce genre. Quoi qu'il en soit, voici ce post-scriptum : « Nous (*Maximilien*, c'est-à-dire *la Bruyère*, *et moi*) parlons quelquefois de vers, et il ne me parle point sottement. Il m'en lut l'autre jour un assez grand nombre de très-méchants qui ont été faits l'année passée dans Bourbon même, à l'occasion des eaux de Bourbon. Il me parut qu'il étoit aussi dégoûté de ces vers que moi, et pour vous montrer que je ne suis encore guéri de rien, c'est que je ne pus m'empêcher de faire sur-le-champ, à propos de ces misérables vers, cette épigramme que j'adresse à la fontaine même de Bourbon :

> Oui, vous pouvez chasser l'humeur apoplectique,
> Rendre le mouvement au corps paralytique,

62. — DE RACINE A BOILEAU. 1687

A Luxembourg, ce 24. mai [1687].

VOTRE lettre m'auroit fait beaucoup plus de plaisir si les nouvelles de votre santé eussent été un peu meilleures. Je vis M. Dodart[1] comme je venois de la recevoir, et la lui montrai. Il m'assura que vous n'aviez aucun lieu de vous mettre dans l'esprit que votre voix ne reviendra point, et me cita même quantité de gens qui sont sortis fort heureusement d'un semblable accident. Mais, sur toutes choses, il vous recommande de ne point faire d'effort pour parler, et, s'il se peut, de n'avoir commerce qu'avec des gens d'une oreille fort subtile ou qui vous entendent à demi-mot. Il croit que le sirop d'abricot vous est fort bon, et qu'il en faut prendre quelquefois de pur, et très-souvent de mêlé avec de l'eau, en l'avalant lentement et goutte à goutte; ne point boire trop frais, ni de vin que fort trempé; du reste vous tenir l'esprit toujours gai. Voilà à peu près le conseil que M. Menjot[2] me donnoit autrefois[3].

> Et guérir tous les maux les plus invétérés;
> Mais quand je lis ces vers par votre onde inspirés,
>   Il me paroît, admirable fontaine,
> Que vous n'eûtes jamais la vertu d'Hippocrène. »

Ces vers sont donnés par Berriat-Saint-Prix, au tome II des OEuvres de Boileau, p. 460, parmi les *épigrammes* (n° XVIII). Il ne dit pas qu'ils soient extraits d'une lettre à Racine.

LETTRE 62 (revue sur l'autographe, conservé à la Bibliothèque impériale). — 1. Denis Dodart, né en 1634, mort le 5 novembre 1707. Il était médecin de la princesse de Conti, fille du Roi. On sait qu'il fut lié d'amitié avec Racine, Antoine Arnauld et tous les solitaires de Port-Royal. Saint-Simon (*Mémoires*, tome XV, p. 319) l'appelle « très-savant et fort saint homme. » Son fils Claude-Jean-Baptiste Dodart fut premier médecin de Louis XV.

2. Antoine Menjot, né vers 1615, mort en 1696, docteur de l'école de Montpellier. Il eut une charge de médecin du Roi.

3. Il (*Racine*) racontoit, quand il vouloit rire, qu'un médecin lui

M. Dodart approuve beaucoup votre lait d'ânesse, mais beaucoup plus encore ce que vous dites de la vertu moliniste. Il ne la croit nullement propre à votre mal, et assure même qu'elle y seroit très-nuisible. Il m'ordonne presque toutes les mêmes choses pour mon mal de gorge, qui va toujours son même train, et il me conseille un régime qui peut-être me pourra guérir dans deux ans, mais qui infailliblement me rendra dans deux mois de la taille dont vous voyez qu'est M. Dodart lui-même[4]. M. Félix étoit présent à toutes ces ordonnances, qu'il a fort approuvées, et il a aussi demandé des remèdes pour sa santé, se croyant le plus malade de nous trois. Je vous ai mandé qu'il avoit visité la boucherie de Châlons. Il est, à l'heure que je vous parle, au marché, où il m'a dit qu'il avoit rencontré ce matin des écrevisses de fort bonne mine. Le voyage est prolongé de trois jours, et on demeurera ici jusqu'à lundi prochain[5]. Le prétexte est la rougeole de M. le comte de Toulouse ; mais le vrai est apparemment que le Roi a pris goût à sa conquête, et qu'il n'est pas fâché de

ayant défendu de boire du vin, de manger de la viande, de lire et de s'appliquer à la moindre chose, ajouta : « Du reste, réjouissez-vous. » (*Note de Louis Racine.*)

4. Il étoit extrêmement maigre. (*Note de Louis Racine.*)

5. Jusqu'au lundi 26 mai. Ce fut en effet ce jour-là que le Roi partit de Luxembourg. Voyez le *Journal* de Dangeau, à la date du lundi 26 mai 1687. Berriat-Saint-Prix dit ici, dans une note, que ce passage montre « que la lettre a été écrite au moins trois jours avant celui qu'on avait fixé pour le départ du Roi.... Il est donc clair, ajoute-t-il, qu'elle est non du 24, mais du 22. » Berriat se trompe : la date écrite de la main de Racine sur l'autographe n'est pas, comme il le croit, fautive. Racine dit que « le voyage est prolongé de trois jours, » parce qu'on avait d'abord annoncé le départ pour le 23. On lit dans le *Journal* de Dangeau : « *Vendredi*, 23 (mai 1687), *à Luxembourg*. M. le comte de Toulouse a la rougeole, et le Roi ne partira que lundi. Il est bien aise de voir la place à loisir. »

l'examiner tout à loisir. Il a déjà considéré toutes les 1687
fortifications l'une après l'autre, est entré jusque dans
les contre-mines du chemin couvert, qui sont fort belles,
et surtout a été fort aise de voir ces fameuses redoutes
entre les deux chemins couverts, lesquelles ont tant
donné de peine à M. de Vauban. Aujourd'hui le Roi va
examiner la circonvallation [6], c'est-à-dire, faire un tour
de sept ou huit lieues. Je ne vous fais point ici le détail
de tout ce qui m'a paru ici de merveilleux : qu'il vous
suffise que je vous en rendrai bon compte quand nous
nous verrons, et que je vous ferai peut-être [7] concevoir
les choses comme si vous y aviez été. M. de Vauban a
été ravi de me voir, et, ne pouvant pas venir avec moi,
m'a donné un ingénieur qui m'a mené partout. Il m'a
aussi abouché avec M. d'Espagne [8], gouverneur de
Thionville, qui se signala tant à Saint-Godard [9], et qui
m'a fait souvenir qu'il avoit souvent bu avec moi à l'auberge de M. Poignant [10], et que nous étions, Poignant
et moi, fort agréables avec feu M. de Bernage, évêque

6. « *Samedi* 24, *à Luxembourg*. Le Roi fit le tour des lignes de circonvallation que le maréchal de Créqui avoit fait faire durant le siége. » (*Journal de Dangeau.*) — Nous avons là une preuve irrécusable que Racine a daté sa lettre très-exactement. Voyez la note précédente.

7. Racine a écrit *ferai peut-être* au-dessus de *dépeindrai*, qu'il a effacé.

8. Ce M. d'Espagne servait (*à Saint-Gothard*), comme major, dans le régiment de la Ferté, infanterie. (*Note de l'édition de* 1807.) — Suivant une note de Cizeron-Rival, c'était un « célèbre officier dans le corps du génie. »

9. La *Gazette* de 1664 suit partout pour ce nom la même orthographe que Racine : *Saint-Godard*, au lieu de *Saint-Gothard*. — Le combat de Saint-Gothard (petite ville de la basse Hongrie) fut livré le 1ᵉʳ août 1664. Les Impériaux, grâce aux Français qui combattaient à côté d'eux comme auxiliaires, y défirent les Turcs.

10. Voyez ci-dessus, p. 460, la note 17 de la lettre 27.

de Grasse[11]. Sérieusement ce M. d'Espagne est un fort galant homme, et il m'a paru un grand air de vérité dans tout ce qu'il m'a dit de ce combat de Saint-Godard. Mais, mon cher Monsieur, cela ne s'accorde ni avec M. de Montecuculli, ni avec M. de Bissy, ni avec M. de la Feuillade[12], et je vois bien que la vérité qu'on nous demande[13] tant est bien plus difficile à trouver qu'à écrire. J'ai vu aussi M. de Charüel[14], qui étoit intendant à Gigeri. Celui-ci sait apparemment la vérité; mais il se serre les lèvres tant qu'il peut[15] de peur de la dire, et j'ai eu à peu près la même peine à lui tirer quelques mots de la bouche, que Trivelin en avoit à en tirer de Scaramouche, musicien bègue. M. de Gourville arriva hier[16], et tout en arrivant me demanda de vos nouvelles.

11. Antoine de Bernage, successeur du célèbre Antoine Godeau, était mort en 1675. (*Note de l'édition de* 1807.)

12. Le maréchal de la Feuillade, n'étant encore que comte de la Feuillade et maréchal de camp, avait commandé les Français à Saint-Gothard, où Montecuculli commandait les troupes impériales. Claude de Thyard, comte de Bissy, baron de Pierre, s'y était très-distingué. On voit quels soins Racine se donnait pour se procurer des renseignements exacts sur l'histoire qu'il était chargé d'écrire. (*Note de l'édition de* 1807.)

13. Racine avait d'abord mis : « que nous demandons. »

14. Dans l'édition de 1807 des OEuvres de *Racine*, et dans quelques éditions des OEuvres de *Boileau*, on a substitué le nom de *Charvil* à celui de *Charüel*, qui est dans l'autographe. Germain Garnier, dans une note sur ce passage, dit que « le chevalier de Charvil dirigeait l'expédition » de Gigeri. Nous croyons qu'il y a quelque confusion avec le chevalier de Clerville, qui se distingua à la prise de Gigeri, où il servait comme aide de camp du duc de Beaufort. Quant à Charuel, c'était un des intendants qui avaient le mieux su mériter la confiance de Louvois : voyez l'*Histoire de Louvois* par M. Rousset, tome I, p. 492. — Gigeri, près d'Alger, fut pris le 22 juillet 1664 par François de Vendôme, duc de Beaufort

15. « Tant qu'il peut » est ajouté, dans l'interligne. — De même, six lignes plus loin : « tous les jours. »

16. Dangeau dit qu'il arriva le 22, c'est-à-dire un jour plus tôt

Je ne finirois point si je vous nommois tous les gens qui m'en demandent tous les jours avec amitié : M. de Chevreuse[17] entre autres, M. de Noailles[18], Monseigneur le Prince[19], que je devois nommer le premier, surtout M. Moreau[20] notre ami, et M. Rose[21], ce dernier avec des expressions fortes, vigoureuses, et qu'on voit bien en vérité qui partent du cœur. Je fis hier grand plaisir à M. de Termes de lui dire le souvenir que vous aviez de lui. Monsieur l'archevêque d'Ambrun[22] est ici, toujours mettant le Roi en bonne humeur[23], Monsieur de Rheims[24],

que Racine ne le mande ici à Boileau. « *Jeudi 22, à Luxembourg.* Gourville rejoignit le Roi, venant d'Aix-la-Chapelle, où il avoit été pour négocier avec M. le duc d'Hanovre, qui y prenoit les eaux. » — Jean Hérault de Gourville, né en 1625, mort en 1703. On sait qu'il était attaché à la maison de Condé. Racine et Boileau, fort en faveur tous deux dans cette maison, se trouvèrent souvent en relation avec Gourville. Mgr le duc d'Aumale a ce petit billet de lui, adressé au grand Condé, en date du 3 septembre 1684 : « Je feray les complimens de V. A. S. à M. Racine, ainsi qu'elle me l'ordonne. » La date de ce billet peut faire conjecturer que Condé avait donné l'ordre de complimenter Racine au sujet de la naissance d'un de ses enfants (Élisabeth Racine, née le 31 juillet 1684).

17. Le duc de Chevreuse, que Racine, dans ses lettres à l'abbé le Vasseur, nomme *Monsieur le Marquis.* Voyez la note 2 de la lettre 6, p. 385.

18. Anne-Jules duc de Noailles, né le 5 février 1650, mort le 2 octobre 1708. Il avait pris rang de lieutenant général en 1682, et avait, en 1684, secondé le duc de Créqui dans le siége de Luxembourg. Il fut fait maréchal de France le 27 mai 1693.

19. Henri-Jules de Bourbon, né en 1643, mort en 1709. Il était Monsieur le Prince depuis la mort du grand Condé son père (10 décembre 1686).

20. Chirurgien ordinaire du Roi.

21. Toussaint Roze, président à la chambre des comptes, secrétaire du Roi. Il était entré à l'Académie française en 1675.

22. Charles Brûlart de Genlis, archevêque d'Embrun, de 1668 à 1714 : voyez au tome V, p. 123, note 7.

23. « Toujours mettant le Roi, etc., » est encore une addition au-dessus de la ligne.

24. Charles-Maurice le Tellier, né en 1642, mort en 1710, arche-

554 LETTRES.

1687 M. le président de Mesmes [25], M. le cardinal de Furstemberg [26]; enfin plus de gens trois fois qu'à Versailles, la presse dans les rues comme à Bouquenon [27], une infinité d'Allemands et d'Allemandes qui veulent [28]....

63. — DE BOILEAU A RACINE [1].

A Auteuil, le 26. mai [1687].

JE ne me suis point hâté de vous répondre [2], parce

vêque de Reims depuis l'année 1671 : voyez au tome V, p. 146, note 3.

25. Jean-Jacques de Mesmes, comte d'Avaux, président à mortier au Parlement, né en 1640, mort le 9 janvier 1688. Il était entré à l'Académie française en 1676.

26. Guillaume Egon, évêque de Strasbourg. La *Gazette* du 31 mai 1687 dit qu'il arriva le 23 mai à Luxembourg, en même temps que le comte Ferdinand de Furstemberg, premier ministre et envoyé extraordinaire de l'archevêque de Cologne.

27. Saar-Bockenheim, petite ville du comté de Saar-Werden, aujourd'hui dans le département du Bas-Rhin. — On voit par la *Gazette de France* que ce nom s'écrivait en effet *Bouquenon*, et que Louis XIV, lors d'un voyage qu'il fit, en 1683, en Alsace, s'arrêta quelques jours (30 juin à 5 juillet) dans ce lieu. (*Note de Berriat-Saint-Prix.*)

28. La fin de la lettre manque. Quelques éditeurs, après le mot *veulent*, ont ajouté : « voir le Roi. » Il est dit dans l'édition de 1807 que la suscription de cette lettre est : « A M. Despréaux, chez M. l'abbé de Dreux, cloître Notre-Dame, à Paris. » Nous ne trouvons pas cette adresse sur l'original.

LETTRE 63. — 1. Publiée par Cizeron-Rival. Elle manque dans le *Recueil* de Louis Racine. Nous avons suivi le texte de Berriat-Saint-Prix, qui a été revu par lui sur l'autographe.

2. Si Boileau a écrit cette lettre le 26 mai, il s'est au contraire hâté de répondre, comme le fait bien remarquer Berriat-Saint-Prix. Pour résoudre la difficulté, il propose une de ces deux conjectures : que Racine s'est trompé sur la date de sa lettre, et qu'il a par mégarde écrit *le 24 mai*, au lieu du 22; ou que Boileau lui-

que je n'avois rien à vous mander que ce que je vous avois déjà écrit dans ma dernière lettre. Les choses sont changées depuis. J'ai quitté au bout de cinq semaines le lait d'ânesse, parce que non-seulement il ne me rendoit point la voix, mais qu'il commençoit à m'ôter la santé en me donnant des dégoûts et des espèces d'émotions tirant à fièvre. Tout ce que vous a dit M. Dodart est fort raisonnable, et je veux croire sur sa parole que tout ira bien; mais, entre nous, je doute que ni lui, ni personne connoisse bien ma maladie ni mon tempérament. Quand je fus attaqué de la difficulté de respirer, il y a vingt-cinq ans, tous les médecins m'assuroient que cela s'en iroit, et me rioient au nez quand je témoignois douter du contraire. Cependant cela ne s'est point en allé, et j'en fus encore hier incommodé considérablement. Je sens que cette difficulté de respirer est au même endroit que ma difficulté de parler, et que c'est un poids fort extérieur que j'ai sur la poitrine, qui les cause l'une et l'autre. Dieu veuille qu'elles n'aient pas fait une société indissoluble! Je ne vois que des gens qui prétendent avoir eu le même mal que moi et qui en ont été guéris; mais outre que je ne sais au fond s'ils disent vrai, ce sont pour la plupart des femmes ou de jeunes gens qui n'ont point de rapport avec un homme de cinquante ans; et d'ailleurs, si je suis original en quelque chose, c'est en infirmités, puisque mes maladies ne ressemblent jamais à celles des autres. Avec tout ce que je vous dis, je ne me couche point que je n'espère le lendemain m'éveiller avec une voix sonore; et quelquefois même, après mon réveil, je demeure longtemps sans parler, pour m'entretenir

même a daté sa réponse du 26, croyant écrire le 29. La seconde pourrait seule être admise : voyez les notes 5 et 6 de la lettre précédente, p. 550 et 551.

dans mon espérance. Ce qui est de vrai, c'est qu'il n'y a point de nuit que je ne recouvre la voix en songe; mais je reconnois bien ensuite que tous les songes, quoi qu'en dise Homère³, ne viennent pas de Jupiter, ou il faut que Jupiter soit un grand menteur. Cependant je mène une vie fort chagrine et fort peu propre aux conseils de M. Dodart, d'autant plus que je n'oserois m'appliquer fortement à aucune chose, et qu'il ne me sort rien du cerveau qui ne me tombe sur la poitrine et qui ne me ruine encore plus la voix. Je suis bien aise que votre mal de gorge vous laisse au moins plus de liberté, et ne vous empêche pas de contempler avec M. de Vauban les merveilles de Luxembourg. Vous avez raison d'estimer comme vous faites M. de Vauban. C'est un des hommes de notre siècle, à mon avis, qui a le plus prodigieux mérite, et pour vous dire en un mot ce que je pense de lui, je crois qu'il y a plus d'un maréchal de France qui, quand il le rencontre, rougit de se voir maréchal de France⁴. Vous avez fait une grande acquisition en l'amitié de M. d'Espagne, et c'est ce qui me fait encore plus déplorer la perte de ma voix, puisque c'est vraisemblablement ce qui m'a fait aussi manquer cette acquisition. J'écris à M. de Flamarens⁵. Je veux croire que notre cher Félix est le plus malade de nous trois; mais si ce que vous me mandez est véritable, l'affliction qu'il en a est une affliction à la *Puimorine*⁶, je veux dire fort dévorante, et qui ne lui a pas

3. *Iliade*, livre I, vers 63.
4. Vauban ne devint lui-même maréchal de France qu'en 1703, à l'âge de soixante-dix ans. Il mourut quatre ans après, en 1707.
5. François Agésilan de Grossoles, chevalier, comte de Flamarens, premier maître d'hôtel du duc d'Orléans, frère de Louis XIV. Il mourut à Paris, le 9 février 1710. Voyez le *Dictionnaire* de Moréri.
6. C'est une plaisanterie de Boileau sur son frère, Boileau de Puymorin, mort depuis un peu plus de trois ans. Voyez ci-dessus.

fait perdre la mémoire des soles et des longes de veau. Faites-lui bien mes baisemains, aussi bien qu'à M. de Termes, à M. de Nyert⁷ et à M. Moreau. Adieu, mon cher Monsieur : aimez-moi toujours, et croyez que je vous rendrai bien la pareille.

64. — DE RACINE AU P. RAPIN.

A Paris, ce 10ᵉ juin [1687[1]].

Je me suis acquitté, mon Révérend Père, de la commission dont vous avez bien voulu me charger. J'ai lu moi-même votre ouvrage à Monseigneur le Prince[2]. Il m'a commandé de vous dire qu'il le trouvoit très-beau, et qu'il vous étoit fort obligé du zèle que vous témoigniez pour la mémoire de feu Monsieur son père[3]. Vous trouverez à la marge plusieurs remarques qu'il a faites, et que j'ai écrites par son ordre. Si vous croyez qu'il soit

---

p. 525, la note 9 de la lettre 50. Cizeron-Rival dit ici en note : « Il aimoit fort les plaisirs de la table, et mangeoit prodigieusement. »

7. Louis de Nyert ou de Niel, mort en 1719. Il avait eu la survivance de la charge de son père, François de Nyert, premier valet de chambre de Louis XIII, puis de Louis XIV.

Lettre 64 (imprimée pour la première fois d'après l'autographe, appartenant à M. Dubrunfaut). — 1. La date de 1687 ne peut être douteuse, le grand Condé étant mort le 11 décembre 1686, et le P. Rapin le 27 octobre 1687. L'ouvrage que Racine renvoyait au P. Rapin avec cette lettre fut imprimé en 1687 (voyez ci-après la note 3). Le *permis d'imprimer* est daté du 14 juin 1687, quatre jours après que l'approbation de Monsieur le Prince avait été transmise par Racine à l'auteur.

2. Voyez ci-dessus, p. 553, note 19 de la lettre 62.

3. L'ouvrage du P. Rapin a pour titre : *Le Magnanime, ou l'Éloge du Prince de Condé premier prince du sang. Par un Père de la Compagnie de Jésus. A Paris, chez la veuve de Sébastien Mabre-Cramoisy....* M.DC.LXXXVII (1 volume in-12, de 112 pages).

besoin que je vous explique plus au long sa pensée sur ces remarques, vous n'avez qu'à prendre la peine de me mander le jour et l'heure où il vous plaira que je vous aille trouver. Pour moi, mon Révérend Père, je ne saurois assez vous remercier de cette marque si honorable que vous m'avez donnée de votre confiance. Vous ne pouviez assurément vous adresser à un homme qui eût plus de vénération pour votre mérite, et plus d'amour, si je l'ose dire, pour votre personne. Je vous demande pardon si vous n'avez pas eu plus tôt de mes nouvelles. Son Altesse Sérénissime m'a fait un peu attendre après l'audience que je lui demandois. Vous trouverez même votre livre un peu frippé, parce que j'ai été obligé de le porter plusieurs jours[4] dans ma poche. Je suis de tout mon cœur,

Mon Révérend Père,

Votre très-humble et très-obéissant serviteur,

RACINE.

65. — DE BOILEAU A RACINE.

A Bourbon, 21e juillet[1] [1687].

DEPUIS ma dernière lettre, j'ai été saigné, purgé, etc., et il ne me manque plus aucune des formalités préten-

---

4. Racine avait d'abord écrit : « plusieurs fois. » Il a biffé le mot *fois*.

LETTRE 65 (revue sur l'autographe, appartenant à M. Boutron-Charlard). — 1. Dans la copie faite par Jean-Baptiste Racine, que M. Laverdet a publiée, il y a 20e, au lieu de 21e *juillet*. La même copie à la ligne 7, au lieu de : « C'est demain que se doit commencer, » porte : « C'est demain, Monsieur, que je dois commencer. » Il n'y a pas d'autres différences avec l'autographe, que nous avons suivi.

dues nécessaires pour prendre des eaux. La médecine
que j'ai prise aujourd'hui m'a fait, à ce qu'on dit, tous
les biens du monde; car elle m'a fait tomber quatre ou
cinq fois en foiblesse, et m'a mis en état[2] qu'à peine
je me puis soutenir. C'est demain que se doit commencer le grand chef-d'œuvre, je veux dire que je dois
demain commencer à prendre des eaux[3]. M. Bourdier,
mon médecin, me remplit toujours de grandes espérances. Il n'est pas de l'avis de M. Fagon[4] pour le
bain, et cite même des exemples de gens, non-seulement qui n'ont pas recouvert la voix, mais qui l'ont
même perdue pour s'être baignés. Du reste, on ne peut
pas faire plus d'estime de M. Fagon qu'il en fait, et il
le regarde comme l'Esculape de ce temps. J'ai fait connoissance avec deux ou trois malades qui valent bien
des gens en santé. J'en ai trouvé un même avec qui
j'ai étudié autrefois, et qui est fort galant homme. Ce
ne sera pas une petite affaire pour moi que la prise des
eaux, qui sont, dit-on, fort endormantes, et avec lesquelles néanmoins il faut absolument s'empêcher de
dormir. Ce sera un noviciat terrible; mais que ne fait-
on point pour avoir de quoi contredire M. Charpentier[5]?

2. Tel est bien le texte; il n'y a ni *tel*, ni *un tel*, devant *état*.
3. Cizeron-Rival, dans ses *Récréations littéraires*, p. 115, rapporte
ces paroles de Boileau, sur l'effet de son séjour à Bourbon : « En
1687, je fus attaqué d'un asthme et d'une extinction de voix. Les
principaux médecins de Paris, après avoir essayé sur moi toutes
sortes de remèdes sans aucun succès, m'envoyèrent aux eaux de
Bourbon-l'Archambaud, d'où je revins comme j'y étois allé. Un
rhume violent avoit causé mon indisposition, et je n'en fus guéri
que par un autre rhume qui me survint l'année après. »
4. Gui-Crescent Fagon, qui avait alors le titre de premier médecin de la feue Reine. En 1693, il devint premier médecin du
Roi.
5. François Charpentier, confrère de Racine et de Boileau à
l'Académie française et à l'Académie des médailles.

1687 Je n'ai pas encore eu de temps pour me remettre à l'étude, parce que j'ai été assez occupé des remèdes, pendant lesquels on m'a défendu surtout l'application. Les eaux, dit-on, me donneront plus de loisir, et pourvu que je ne m'endorme point, on me laisse toute liberté de lire, et même de composer. Il y a ici un trésorier de la Sainte-Chapelle[6], grand ami de M. de la Moignon[7], qui me vient voir fort souvent; il est homme de beaucoup d'esprit, et s'il n'a pas la main si prompte à répandre les bénédictions que le fameux Monsieur de Coutances[8], il a en récompense beaucoup plus de lettres et beaucoup plus de solidité. Je suis toujours fort affligé de ne vous point voir; mais franchement le séjour de Bourbon jusqu'ici ne m'a pas paru si horrible que je me l'étois imaginé. J'ai un jardin pour me promener, et je m'étois préparé à une si grande inquiétude, que je n'en ai pas la moitié de ce que j'en croyois avoir. Celui qui doit porter cette lettre à Moulins me presse fort : c'est ce qui fait que je me hâte de vous dire que je n'ai pas mieux conçu combien je vous aime, que depuis notre triste séparation. Mes recommandations au cher M. Félix, et je vous supplie, quand même je l'aurois oublié dans quelqu'une de mes lettres, de supposer toujours que je vous aie parlé de lui, parce que[9] mon

---

6. Dans une lettre à Mme Manchon, datée du 31 juillet de la même année, Boileau dit : « J'ai lié, depuis que je suis ici (*à Bourbon*), une étroite connoissance avec M. l'abbé de Sales, trésorier de la Sainte-Chapelle de Bourbon. »

7. Chrétien-François de Lamoignon, alors avocat général au Parlement, depuis président à mortier; né le 26 juin 1644, mort le 7 août 1709. C'est à lui qu'est dédiée l'*épître* VI de Boileau.

8. Claude Auvry, le héros du *Lutrin* de Boileau, évêque de Coutances en 1646, trésorier de la Sainte-Chapelle en 1653. Il venait de mourir le 9 juillet 1687, âgé de quatre-vingts ans.

9. Cette fin de la phrase a été ajoutée par Boileau, en interligne.

cœur l'a fait si ma main ne l'a pas écrit. Je vous embrasse de tout mon cœur.

DESPRÉAUX.

---

66. — DE RACINE A BOILEAU.

A Paris, ce 25e juillet [1687].

Je commençois à m'ennuyer beaucoup de ne point recevoir de vos nouvelles, et je ne savois même que répondre à quantité de gens qui m'en demandoient. Le Roi, il y a trois jours, me demanda à son dîner comment alloit votre extinction de voix. Je lui dis que vous étiez à Bourbon. Monsieur prit aussitôt la parole, et me fit là-dessus force[1] questions, aussi bien que Madame[2], et vous fîtes l'entretien de plus de la moitié du dîner. Je me trouvai le lendemain sur le chemin de M. de Louvois, qui me parla aussi de vous, mais avec beaucoup de bonté, et me disant, en propres mots, qu'il étoit très-fâché que cela durât si longtemps. Je ne vous dis rien de mille autres qui me parlent tous les jours de vous; et quoique j'espère que vous retrouverez bientôt votre voix toute entière, je doute que vous en ayez jamais assez pour suffire à tous les remerciements que vous aurez à faire. Je me suis laissé débaucher par M. Félix pour aller demain avec le Roi à Maintenon.

Lettre 66 (revue sur l'autographe, conservé à la Bibliothèque impériale). — 1. Ici encore Racine a écrit *forces*. Voyez la note 1 de la page 102. Nous y avons parlé des exemples de cette irrégularité d'orthographe qui se trouvent dans les lettres de la jeunesse de Racine; mais on voit ici que beaucoup plus tard il écrivait encore de même.

2. Élisabeth-Charlotte de Bavière, seconde femme de Monsieur, et mère du duc d'Orléans, alors duc de Chartres, et depuis régent.

C'est un voyage de quatre jours[3]. M. de Terme nous mène dans son carrosse, et j'ai aussi débauché M. Hessin[4] pour faire le quatrième. Il se plaint toujours beaucoup de ses vapeurs, et je vois bien qu'il espère se soulager par quelque dispute de longue haleine; mais je ne suis guère en état de lui donner contentement, me trouvant toujours assez[5] incommodé de ma gorge dès que j'ai parlé un peu de suite. Cela va pourtant mieux que quand vous êtes parti, mais je ne suis pas encore hors d'affaire. Ce qui m'embarrasse, c'est que M. Fagon et plusieurs autres médecins très-habiles m'avoient ordonné, comme vous savez, de boire beaucoup d'eau de Sainte-Reine[6] et des tisanes de chicorée; et j'ai trouvé chez M. Nicole un médecin qui me paroît fort sensé, qui m'a dit qu'il connoissoit mon mal à fond, et qu'il en a guéri plusieurs gens en sa vie, et que je ne guérirois jamais tant que je boirois ni eau ni tisane; que le seul moyen de sortir d'affaire, c'étoit de ne boire que pour la seule nécessité, et tout au plus[7] pour détremper les aliments dans l'estomac. Il m'a appuyé cela de quelques raisonnements qui m'ont paru assez solides. Ce qui est arrivé de là, c'est que présentement je n'exécute ni son ordonnance ni celle de M. Fagon. Je ne me noie plus d'eau comme je faisois[8]; je bois à ma soif, et vous jugez bien

---

3. « Le 26 du mois dernier (*juillet*), le Roi alla à Maintenon, et Sa Majesté en revint le 30, après y avoir visité les travaux de l'aqueduc, et fait la revue des troupes qui y sont employées. » (*Gazette* du 2 août 1687.)

4. M. Hessein, leur ami commun, et frère de Mlle de la Sablière, avoit beaucoup d'esprit et de lettres; mais il aimoit à disputer et à contredire. (*Note de Louis Racine.*) — Pierre Hessein était secrétaire du Roi. On écrit quelquefois son nom *Hesselin*.

5. *Assez* est écrit au-dessus de : *un peu*, effacé.

6. Alise-Sainte-Reine, près de Semur, en Bourgogne.

7. « Tout au plus » a été ajouté, en interligne.

8. Tout ce membre de phrase est aussi écrit au-dessus de la ligne.

que, par le temps qu'il fait, on a toujours assez soif. 1687
C'est à dire, à vous parler franchement, que je me suis
remis dans mon train de vie ordinaire, et je m'en trouve
assez bien. Ce même médecin m'a assuré que, si les
eaux de Bourbon ne vous guérissoient pas, il vous gué-
riroit infailliblement. Il m'a cité l'exemple d'un chantre
de Notre-Dame (je crois que c'étoit une basse), à qui
un rhume avoit fait perdre entièrement la voix. Cela lui
avoit duré six mois, et il étoit sur le point de se retirer.
Le médecin que je vous dis l'entreprit, et avec une
tisane d'une herbe qu'on appelle, je crois, *erisimum*[9],
le tira d'affaire en trois semaines : en telle sorte que,
non-seulement il parle, mais il chante très-bien, et a la
voix aussi forte qu'il l'ait jamais eue. Ce chantre a, dit-
il, quelque quarante ans. J'ai conté la chose aux médecins de la cour; ils avouent que cette plante d'*erisimum* est très-bonne pour la poitrine ; mais ils disent
qu'ils ne lui croyoient pas la vertu que dit mon médecin. C'est le même qui a deviné le mal de M. Nicole; il
s'appelle M. Morin[10], et il est à Mlle de Guise[11]. M. Fagon en fait un fort grand cas. J'espère que vous n'aurez pas besoin de lui; mais toujours cela est bon à savoir, et si le malheur vouloit que vos eaux ne fissent
pas tout l'effet que vous souhaitez, voilà encore une
assez bonne consolation que je vous donne. Je ne vous

9. Ou plutôt *erysimum* (comme écrit Boileau), que MM. Quiche-
rat et Daveluy, dans leur *Dictionnaire*, traduisent par « cresson d'hiver, » et par « vélar, herbe aux chantres » (avec un point d'inter-
rogation).

10. Louis Morin, né au Mans le 11 juillet 1635, mort le 1er mars
1715. Reçu docteur vers 1662, il fut nommé associé botaniste de
l'Académie des sciences en 1699. Il était fort lié avec M. Dodart.

11. Marie de Lorraine, duchesse de Guise et de Joyeuse, dite
Mlle de Guise, née le 15 août 1615, morte le 3 mars 1688. En elle
s'éteignit la maison des Guise.

manderai point cette fois-ci d'autres nouvelles que celles qui regardent votre santé et la mienne. Je vous dirai seulement que j'ai encore mes deux chevaux sur la litière.

J'ai[12]....

67. — DE BOILEAU A RACINE[1].

A Bourbon, 29⁰ juillet [1687].

Votre lettre[2] m'a tiré d'un fort grand embarras; car je doutois que vous eussiez[3] reçu celle que je vous avois écrite, et dont la réponse est arrivée fort tard à Bourbon. Si la perte de ma voix ne m'avoit fort guéri de la vanité, j'aurois été très-sensible à ce que vous m'avez mandé de l'honneur que m'a fait le plus grand prince de la terre, en vous demandant des nouvelles de ma santé; mais l'impuissance où ma maladie me met de répondre par mon travail à toutes les bontés qu'il me témoigne, me fait un sujet de chagrin de ce qui devroit faire toute ma joie. Les eaux jusqu'ici m'ont fait un fort grand bien, selon toutes les règles, puisque je les rends de reste, et qu'elles m'ont pour ainsi dire tout fait sortir du corps, excepté la maladie pour laquelle je les prends. M. Bourdier, mon médecin, soutient pourtant que j'ai la voix plus forte que quand je suis arrivé, et M. Baudière, mon apothicaire, qui en est encore meilleur juge que lui puisqu'il est sourd, prétend aussi

12. La fin de la lettre manque.

Lettre 67. — 1. Revue sur l'autographe, conservé à la Bibliothèque impériale. Cette lettre ne s'y trouve pas, comme les autres lettres de Boileau à Racine, réunie aux manuscrits de celui-ci. C'est une des pièces que la Bibliothèque a mise en montre.

2. C'est la lettre précédente.

3. Boileau avait d'abord écrit *ayez*, qu'il a effacé

la même chose; mais pour moi, je suis persuadé qu'ils me flattent, ou plutôt qu'ils se flattent eux-mêmes; et à ce que je puis reconnoître en moi, je tiens que les eaux me soulageront plutôt la difficulté de respirer que la difficulté de parler. Quoi qu'il en soit, j'irai jusqu'au bout, et je ne donnerai point occasion à M. Fagon et à M. Félix de dire que je me suis impatienté. Au pis aller, nous essayerons cet hiver l'*erysimum*. Mon médecin et mon apothicaire, à qui j'ai montré [l'endroit] de votre lettre où vous parlez de cette plante, ont témoigné tous deux en faire un fort grand cas; mais M. Bourdier prétend qu'elle ne peut rendre la voix qu'à des gens qui ont le gosier attaqué, et non pas à un homme comme moi, qui a tous les muscles de la poitrine embarrassés. Peut-être[4], si j'avois le gosier malade, prétendroit-il que l'*erysimum* ne sauroit guérir que ceux qui ont la poitrine attaquée. Le bon de l'affaire est qu'il persiste toujours dans la pensée que les eaux de Bourbon me rendront la voix, plus tôt même qu'on ne sauroit s'imaginer. Si cela arrive ainsi, il se trouvera, mon cher Monsieur, que ce sera à moi à vous consoler, puisque de la manière dont vous me parlez de votre mal de gorge, je doute qu'il puisse être guéri si tôt, surtout si vous vous engagez en de longs voyages avec M. Hessein. Mais laissez-moi faire : si la voix me revient, j'espère de vous soulager dans les disputes que vous aurez avec lui, sauf à la perdre encore une fois pour vous rendre cet office. Je vous prie pourtant de lui faire bien des amitiés de ma part, et de lui faire entendre que ses contradictions me seront toujours beaucoup plus agréables que les complaisances et les applaudissements fades de

---

4. La phrase commençait d'abord ainsi : « Peut-être que; » mais le *que* a été barré.

la plupart des amateurs de beaux esprits. Il s'est trouvé ici, parmi les capucins, un de ces amateurs, qui a fait des vers à ma louange. J'admire ce que c'est que des hommes : *vanitas, et omnia vanitas*⁵. Cette sentence ne m'a jamais paru si vraie qu'en fréquentant ces bons et crasseux Pères. Je suis bien fâché que vous ne vous soyez point encore habitué à Auteuil, où

*Ipsi te fontes, ipsa hæc arbusta vocabant*⁶;

c'est-à-dire, où mes deux puits⁷ et mes abricotiers vous appeloient.

Vous faites très-bien d'aller à Maintenon avec une compagnie aussi agréable que celle dont vous me parlez, puisque vous y trouverez votre utilité et votre plaisir. *Omne tulit punctum*⁸....

Je n'ai jamais pu deviner la critique que⁹ peut faire M. l'abbé Tallemant¹⁰ sur l'endroit de l'épitaphe¹¹ que vous m'avez marqué. N'est-ce point qu'il prétend que ces termes, *il fut nommé*, semblent dire que le Roi Louis XIII. a tenu M. le Tellier sur les fonts de baptême, ou bien que c'est mal dit, que le Roi le *choisit pour remplir la charge, etc.*, parce que c'est la charge

---

5. « Vanité, et tout est vanité. »
6. « Les sources mêmes, ces arbustes mêmes vous appelaient. » (Virgile, *églogue* 1, vers 46.)
7. Il n'avoit pas d'autres eaux dans cette petite maison dont il faisoit ses délices. (*Note de Louis Racine.*)
8. « Il a obtenu tous les suffrages (celui qui a joint l'utile à l'agréable). » (Horace, *Art poétique*, vers 343.)
9. *Vous* a été effacé devant *peut*.
10. Paul Tallemant, né le 18 juin 1642, mort le 30 juillet 1712. Il devint l'un des quarante de l'Académie française en 1666. Il fut secrétaire de l'Académie des médailles, de 1694 à 1706.
11. De l'épitaphe de Michel le Tellier : voyez au tome V, p. 12 et 13. Voyez aussi au même tome la *Notice sur les épitaphes de Racine*, p. 3 et 4.

qui a rempli M. le Tellier, et non pas M. le Tellier qui a rempli la charge : par la même raison que c'est la ville qui entoure les fossés, et non pas les fossés qui entourent la ville? C'est à vous à m'expliquer cet[12] énigme.

Faites bien, je vous prie, mes baisemains au P. Bouhours et à tous nos autres amis quand vous les rencontrerez; mais surtout témoignez bien à M. Nicole la profonde vénération que j'ai pour son mérite, et pour la simplicité de ses mœurs, encore plus admirable que son mérite. Vous ne me parlez point de l'épitaphe de Mlle de la Moignon[13]. Voilà, ce me semble, une assez longue lettre pour un homme à qui on défend surtout les longues applications, et qu'on presse d'ailleurs de donner cette lettre pour la porter à Moulins. J'ai appris par la *Gazette* que M. l'abbé de Choisi étoit agréé à l'Académie[14]. Voici encore une voix que je vous envoie pour lui, si trente-neuf ne suffisoient pas. Adieu : aimez-moi toujours, et croyez que je n'aime rien plus que vous. Je passe ici le temps, *sic ut quimus, quando ut volumus non possum*[15].

Adieu encore une fois. Dites à ma sœur[16] et à M. Man-

12. Boileau avait écrit *cette*, mais il paraît avoir effacé *te*.
13. Voyez cette épitaphe au tome V, p. 13 et 14. Voyez aussi la *Notice sur les épitaphes de Racine*, p. 3-6 du même tome.
14. « Le 24 de ce mois, l'Académie françoise élut l'abbé de Choisy, pour remplir une des quarante places, vacante par le décès du duc de Saint-Aignan. » (*Gazette* du 26 juillet 1687.)
15. « Comme je peux, puisque ce ne peut être comme je voudrais. » C'est une citation, un peu altérée, des vers 805 et 806 de l'*Andrienne* de Térence (acte IV, scène VIII) :

Sic
Ut quimus, aiunt, quando ut volumus non licet.

16. Geneviève Boileau, née le 27 avril 1632, mariée le 7 janvier 1651 à Dominique Manchon, commissaire examinateur au Châtelet, morte le 17 juillet 1720.

1687 chon[17] que je ne manquerai pas de leur écrire par la première commodité. J'ai écrit à M. Marchand[18].

68. — DE M. DE BONNAFAU[1] A RACINE.

A Luxembourg, ce 31e de juillet [1687].

Monsieur,

Les voyages que Mgr de Louvoy m'a fait faire en divers endroits de la frontière m'ont empêché de vous adresser plus tôt le plan de l'attaque de Luxembourg[2] que je vous ai promis. Je vous l'aurois envoyé plus proprement dessiné, si je n'avois pas eu peur de vous faire trop attendre. Je souhaiterois, Monsieur, vous pouvoir être utile à quelque autre chose en ces quartiers, ayant

---

17. Jérôme Manchon, fils de Geneviève Boileau (voyez la note précédente). Ce neveu de Boileau prenait alors la qualité d'ecclésiastique et de bachelier en théologie de la faculté de Paris. Plus tard, vers la fin de 1692, il fut commissaire des guerres. Né en 1661, il mourut après 1711.

18. Antoine Petit-Jean Marchand, pourvoyeur de Monsieur, frère du Roi. Il était ami de Boileau et son voisin à Auteuil. Voyez les *OEuvres de Boileau* (édition de Berriat-Saint-Prix), tome IV, p. 207, note 4.

Lettre 68 (copiée sur l'autographe, appartenant à M. Dubrunfaut; cette lettre inédite était intercalée dans l'exemplaire de l'*Histoire* de la Barde, où sont les notes de Racine, dont nous avons donné ci-dessus des extraits, aux pages 343-350). — 1. M. de Bonnafau était un ingénieur attaché, dans les années antérieures à 1687, à la place de Longwy. Nous devons ce renseignement à l'obligeance de l'historien de Louvois, M. Camille Rousset, qui seul aujourd'hui sans doute pouvait savoir quelque chose sur cet officier très-oublié.

2. Racine, dans la lettre suivante qu'il adressait quatre jours plus tard à Boileau, parle de ce plan qu'il vient, dit-il, de recevoir.

beaucoup de passion de vous marquer que j'ai l'honneur d'être, Monsieur,

Votre très-humble et très-obéissant serviteur

De Bonnafau.

69. — DE RACINE A BOILEAU.

A Paris, ce 4. août [1687].

Je suis ravi des bonnes espérances que l'on continue de vous donner, et du soulagement que vous ressentez déjà à votre poitrine. Je ne doute pas que la difficulté de parler ne soit encore plus aisée à guérir que la difficulté de respirer. Je n'ai point encore vu M. Fagon depuis que j'ai reçu de vos nouvelles, oui bien M. Daquin[1], qui trouve fort étrange que vous ne vous soyez pas mis entre les mains de M. des Trapières[2]. Il est bien en peine même qui peut vous avoir adressé à M. Bourdier. Je jugeai à propos, tant il étoit en colère[3],

---

Lettre 69 (revue sur l'autographe, conservé à la Bibliothèque impériale). — 1. Antoine d'Aquin, premier médecin du Roi, prédécesseur de Fagon dans cette charge.

2. On verra plus loin (p. 594), dans la lettre de Boileau du 23 août suivant, qu'il finit par demander quelques conseils à ce médecin, peut-être pour ne pas mécontenter M. d'Aquin. — Vicq d'Azir, dans la *Suite des Éloges* (imprimée en l'an vi, in-4°), viie cahier, parle d'un Guillaume-Martin Destrapières, doyen du collége de médecine à la Rochelle, né en avril 1712, à Bourbon-l'Archambauld, de Jean-François Destrapières, lieutenant général du bailliage de la même ville. « L'un de ses aïeux, dit-il, était le premier médecin de Gaston, frère de Louis XIII. » Si le Destrapières dont parle ici Racine n'est pas ce dernier (il eût été assez vieux en 1687), c'est assurément du moins un médecin de la même famille.

3. Ce membre de phrase a été ajouté par Racine, au-dessus de la ligne.

de ne lui pas dire un mot de M. Fagon. J'ai fait le voyage de Maintenon [4], et suis fort content des ouvrages que j'y ai vus : ils sont prodigieux et dignes, en vérité, de la magnificence du Roi. Il y en a encore, dit-on, pour deux ans [5]. Les arcades qui doivent joindre les deux montagnes vis-à-vis de Maintenon sont presque faites : il y en a quarante-huit ; elles sont fort hautes et bâties pour l'éternité. Je voudrois qu'on eût autant d'eau à faire passer dessus, qu'elles sont capables d'en porter. Il y a là près de trente mille hommes qui travaillent [6], tous gens bien faits, et qui, si la guerre recommence, remueront plus volontiers la terre devant quelque place sur la frontière, que dans les plaines de Beausse. J'eus l'honneur de voir Mme de M. [7], avec qui je fus une bonne partie d'une après-dînée, et elle me témoigna même que ce temps-là ne lui avoit point duré. Elle est toujours la même que vous l'avez vue, pleine d'esprit, de raison, de piété, et de beaucoup de bonté pour nous. Elle me demanda des nouvelles de notre travail : je lui dis que votre indisposition et la mienne, mon voyage de Luxembourg et votre voyage de Bourbon nous avoient un peu reculés, mais que nous ne perdions pas cependant notre temps. A propos de Luxembourg, j'en viens de recevoir un plan, et de la place et des attaques [8], tout cela dans la dernière exactitude.

Je viens aussi tout à l'heure de recevoir une lettre de Versailles, d'où l'on me mande une nouvelle fort surprenante et fort affligeante pour vous et pour moi :

4. Voyez ci-dessus, p. 562, la note 3 de la lettre 66.
5. L'ouvrage fut abandonné en 1688.
6. « Qui travaillent » est en interligne.
7. Mme de Maintenon.
8. C'est celui que lui avait envoyé M. de Bonnafan : voyez la lettre précédente.

c'est la mort de notre ami M. de Saint-Laurent⁹, qui a été emporté d'un seul accès de colique néphrétique, à quoi il n'avoit jamais été sujet en sa vie. Je ne crois pas qu'excepté Madame, on en soit fort affligé au Palais-Royal : les voilà débarrassés d'un homme de bien.

Je laissai volontiers à la *Gazette* à vous parler de l'abbé de Choisy : il fut reçu sans opposition ; il avoit pris tous les devants qu'il falloit auprès des gens qui auroient pu lui faire de la peine. Il fera le jour de saint Louis¹⁰ sa harangue, qu'il m'a montrée. Il y a quelques endroits d'esprit ; je lui ai fait ôter quelques fautes de jugement. M. Bergeret¹¹ fera la réponse : je crois qu'il y aura plus de jugement. Je suis bien aise que vous n'ayez pas conçu la critique de l'abbé Tallemant : c'est signe qu'elle ne vaut rien. La critique tomboit sur ces mots : *Il en commença les fonctions ;* il prétendoit qu'il falloit dire nécessairement : *Il commença à en faire les fonctions.* Le P. Bouhours ne le devina point, non plus que vous ; et quand je lui dis la difficulté, il s'en moqua.

Je donnai l'épitaphe de Mlle de la Moignon à M. de la Chapelle¹² en l'état que nous en étions convenus à Montgeron. Je n'en ai pas ouï parler depuis.

9. « Le sieur Nicolas-François Parisot de Saint-Laurent, sous-gouverneur et précepteur de M. le duc de Chartres, et ci-devant sous-introducteur des ambassadeurs auprès de Monsieur, mourut le 3 de ce mois à Versailles, âgé de soixante et quatre ans. » (*Gazette* du 9 août 1687.) — Voyez ce que dit de cet homme de bien Saint-Simon, dans ses notes sur le *Journal* de Dangeau, tome I, p. 235 et 236, et dans ses *Mémoires*, tome I, p. 19 et 20.

10. L'abbé de Choisy fut en effet reçu à l'Académie le 25 août 1687.

11. Voyez notre tome IV, p. 345, et p. 363, note 2.

12. Henri de Bessé (ou Besset), marié à Charlotte Dongois, nièce de Boileau. Il était contrôleur des bâtiments du Roi, et, en cette qualité, adjoint, comme secrétaire, à l'Académie des médailles. Il mourut en 1694.

1687

M. Hessin n'a point changé. Nous fûmes cinq jours ensemble. Il fut fort doux les quatre premiers jours, et eut beaucoup de complaisance pour M. de Termes, qui ne l'avoit jamais vu, et qui étoit charmé de sa douceur. Le dernier jour, M. Hessin ne lui laissa pas passer un mot sans le contredire, et même, quand il nous voyoit fatigués de parler ou endormis, il avançoit malicieusement quelque paradoxe qu'il savoit bien qu'on ne lui laisseroit point passer. En un mot, il eut contentement : non-seulement on disputa, mais on se querella ; et on se sépara sans avoir trop d'envie de se revoir de plus de huit jours. Il me sembla que M. de Termes avoit toujours raison ; il lui sembla aussi la même chose de moi. M. Félix témoigna un peu plus de bonté pour M. Hessin, et nous gronda tous plutôt que de se résoudre à le condamner. Voilà comme s'est passé le voyage. Mon mal de gorge est beaucoup diminué, Dieu merci ; mais il n'est pas encore fini : il me reste de temps en temps quelques âcretés vers la luette, mais cela ne dure point. Quoi qu'il en soit, je n'y fais plus rien. Mes chevaux marcheront demain pour la première fois depuis votre départ ; celui qui avoit le farcin est, dit-on, entièrement guéri : je n'ose encore trop vous l'assurer. M. Marchand me vint voir il y a trois jours, un peu fâché de ce que vous n'avez pas pris à Bourbon le logis qu'il vous avoit dit. Il doit mener à Auteuil sa fille, qui est sortie de religion, pour lui faire prendre l'air. Cela ne m'empêchera pas d'y aller passer des après-dînées, et même d'y aller dîner avec lui. Adieu, mon cher Monsieur : mandez-moi au plus tôt que vous parlez ; c'est la meilleure nouvelle que je puisse recevoir en ma vie.

70. — DE RACINE A BOILEAU.

A Paris, ce 8ᵉ août [1687].

Mme Manchon[1] vint avant-hier me chercher, fort alarmée d'une lettre que vous lui avez écrite[2], et qui est en effet bien différente de celle que j'ai reçue de vous. J'aurois déjà été à Versailles pour entretenir M. Fagon; mais le Roi est à Marly depuis quatre jours, et n'en reviendra que demain au soir : ainsi je n'irai qu'après-demain matin, et je vous manderai exactement tout ce qu'il m'aura dit. Cependant je me flatte que ce dégoût et cette lassitude dont vous vous plaignez n'auront point de suite, et que c'est seulement un effet que les eaux doivent produire quand l'estomac[3] n'y est pas encore accoutumé. Que si elles continuent à vous faire mal, vous savez ce que tout le monde vous dit en partant, qu'il falloit les quitter en ce cas, ou tout du moins les interrompre. Si par malheur elles ne vous guérissent pas, il n'y a point lieu encore de vous décourager, et vous ne seriez pas le premier qui, n'ayant pas été guéri sur les lieux, s'est trouvé guéri étant de retour chez lui. En tout cas, le sirop d'*erisimum* n'est point assurément une vision. M. Dodart, à qui j'en parlai il y a trois jours, me dit et m'assura en conscience que ce M. Morin qui m'a parlé de ce remède est sans doute le plus habile médecin qui soit dans Paris, et le moins charla-

---

Lettre 70 (revue sur l'autographe, conservé à la Bibliothèque impériale). — 1. Voyez ci-dessus, p. 567, note 16 de la lettre 67.

2. Cette lettre, datée de Bourbon, 31 juillet 1687, à Mme Manchon, se trouve au tome IV des OEuvres de Boileau (édition Berriat-Saint-Prix), p. 23-26. Boileau y dit que les eaux lui « ont causé de fort grandes lassitudes dans les jambes, » qu'il « demeure toujours sans voix, avec très-peu d'appétit et une assez grande foiblesse de corps. »

3. Racine écrit *estomach*.

tan. Il est constant que pour moi, je me trouve infiniment mieux depuis que, par son conseil, j'ai renoncé à tout ce lavage d'eaux qu'on m'avoit ordonnées, et qui m'avoient presque gâté entièrement l'estomac sans me guérir mon mal de gorge. Je prierai aussi M. de Jussac d'écrire à Madame sa femme à Fontevraud, et de lui mander l'embarras de ce pauvre paralytique, qui étoit, sans vous, sur le pavé⁴.

M. de Saint-Laurent est mort d'une colique de *miserere*, et non point d'un accès de néphrétique, comme je vous avois mandé. Sa mort a été fort chrétienne, et même aussi singulière que le reste de sa vie. Il ne confia qu'à Monsieur de Chartres qu'il se trouvoit mal, et qu'il alloit s'enfermer dans une chambre pour se reposer, conjurant instamment ce jeune prince de ne point dire où il étoit, parce qu'il ne vouloit voir personne. En le quittant, il alla faire ses dévotions : c'étoit un dimanche, et on dit qu'il les faisoit tous les dimanches ; puis il s'enferma dans une chambre jusqu'à trois heures après midi, que Monsieur de Chartres, étant en inquiétude de sa santé, déclara où il étoit. Tancret y fut, qui le trouva tout habillé sur un lit, souffrant apparemment beaucoup, et néanmoins fort tranquille. Tancret ne lui trouva point de pouls; mais M. de Saint-Laurent lui dit que

---

4. Dans la lettre à Mme Manchon que nous avons citée ci-dessus (note 2), Boileau racontait qu'il était arrivé depuis quelques jours à Bourbon un pauvre homme, paralytique de la moitié du corps, avec une recommandation de Mme de Montespan pour être reçu à la Charité qui y était établie, recommandation écrite et signée par Mme de Jussac, dame attachée à Mme de Montespan. Cependant le paralytique ne fut pas reçu, malgré l'offre que faisait Boileau de se charger de toute la dépense. Boileau lui fit alors donner une chambre dans la maison qu'il occupait. Il recommandait à Mme Manchon d'en parler à Racine, « afin, disait-il, que dans l'occasion il témoigne à M. et à Mme de Jussac que leur nom n'a pas peu contribué en cette rencontre à exciter ma piété. »

cela ne l'étonnât point, qu'il étoit vieux, et qu'il n'avoit pas naturellement le pouls fort élevé. Il voulut être saigné, et il ne vint point de sang. Peu de temps après, il se mit sur son séant, puis dit à son valet de le pencher un peu sur son chevet, et aussitôt ses pieds se mirent à trépigner contre le plancher, et il expira dans le moment même. On trouva dans sa bourse un billet par lequel il déclaroit où l'on trouveroit son testament. Je crois qu'il donne tout son bien aux pauvres. Voilà comme il est mort, et voici ce qui fait, ce me semble, assez bien son éloge. Vous savez qu'il n'avoit presque d'autre soin auprès de Monsieur de Chartres, que de l'empêcher de manger des friandises; qu'il l'empêchoit le plus qu'il pouvoit d'aller aux comédies et aux opéra; et il vous a conté[5] lui-même toutes les rebuffades qu'il lui a fallu essuyer pour cela, et comme toute la maison de Monsieur étoit déchaînée contre lui, gouverneur, sous-précepteur[6], valets de chambre[7]. Cependant on a été plus de deux jours sans oser apprendre sa mort à ce même Monsieur de Chartres; et quand Monsieur enfin la lui a annoncée, il a jeté des cris effroyables, se jetant non point sur son lit, mais sur le lit de M. de Saint-Laurent, qui étoit encore dans sa chambre, et l'appelant à haute voix comme s'il eût encore été en vie : tant la vertu, quand elle est vraie, a de force pour se faire aimer. Je suis assuré que cela vous fera plaisir, non-seulement pour la mémoire de M. de Saint-Laurent, mais même pour Monsieur de Chartres. Dieu veuille qu'il persiste longtemps dans de pareils sentiments!

5. Racine a écrit *compté*.
6. Le gouverneur était le duc de la Vieuville, qui mourut en 1689, et le sous-précepteur l'abbé Dubois.
7. Les mots : « gouverneur, etc., » ont été ajoutés au-dessus de la ligne.

Il me semble que je n'ai point d'autres nouvelles à vous mander. M. le duc de Roannez⁸ est venu ce matin pour me parler de sa rivière, et pour me prier d'en parler. Je lui ai demandé s'il ne savoit rien de nouveau; il m'a dit que non; et il faut bien, puisqu'il ne sait point de nouvelles, qu'il n'y en ait point; car il en sait toujours plus qu'il n'y en a. On dit seulement que Monsieur de Lorraine⁹ a passé la Drave, et les Turcs la Save : ainsi il n'y a point de rivière qui les sépare. Tant pis apparemment pour les Turcs : je les trouve merveilleusement accoutumés à être battus.

La nouvelle qui fait ici le plus de bruit, c'est l'embarras des comédiens, qui sont obligés de déloger de la rue de Guénégaud, à cause que Messieurs de Sorbonne, en acceptant le collége des Quatre-Nations, ont demandé, pour première condition, qu'on les éloignât de ce collége¹⁰. Ils ont déjà marchandé des places dans cinq ou six

---

8. Le maréchal de la Feuillade (François d'Aubusson, vicomte de la Feuillade, devenu en 1666 duc de Roannez). Voyez ci-dessus, p. 552, la note 12 de la lettre 62. On a vu dans cette dernière lettre que Racine cherchait à se renseigner exactement sur le combat de Saint-Gothard, dont sans doute alors il préparait le récit pour son histoire de Louis XIV. Dans ce combat, la Feuillade, à la tête des volontaires, avait précipité les Turcs dans le Raab, qui est, ce semble, la rivière dont il était venu parler à Racine.

9. Charles V duc de Lorraine. Quatre jours après cette lettre écrite, c'est-à-dire le 12 août 1687, il défit à Mohacz les Turcs commandés par Kara Mustapha.

10. Le 17 juin 1687, Louvois écrivait au lieutenant de police la Reynie : « Le Roi ne jugeant pas que la représentation des comédies dans la rue Guénégaud puisse compatir avec l'exercice qui va s'établir au collége des Quatre-Nations, Sa Majesté m'a commandé de vous écrire d'avertir les comédiens de chercher à se mettre ailleurs entre ci et le mois d'octobre prochain. » Voyez l'*Histoire de Louvois* par M. C. Rousset, tome I, p. 417, à la note. Les comédiens français furent en effet avertis par la Reynie. Repoussés de tous les côtés, un arrêt du 1ᵉʳ mars 1688 leur permit, après bien des

endroits; mais partout où ils vont, c'est merveille d'entendre comme les curés crient. Le curé de Saint-Germain de l'Auxerrois a déjà obtenu qu'ils ne seroient point à l'hôtel de Sourdis[11], parce que de leur théâtre on auroit entendu tout à plein les orgues, et de l'église on auroit entendu parfaitement bien les violons. Enfin ils en sont à la rue de Savoie, dans la paroisse Saint-André. Le curé a été aussi au Roi, lui représenter qu'il n'y a tantôt plus dans sa paroisse que des auberges et des coquetiers; si les comédiens y viennent, que son église sera déserte. Les grands Augustins ont aussi été au Roi, et le P. Lembrochons, provincial, a porté la parole. Mais on dit que les comédiens ont dit à S. M. que ces mêmes Augustins qui ne veulent point les avoir pour voisins sont fort assidus spectateurs de la comédie, et qu'ils ont même voulu vendre à la troupe des maisons qui leur appartiennent dans la rue d'Anjou, pour y bâtir un théâtre, et que le marché seroit déjà conclu si le lieu eût été plus commode. M. de Louvois a ordonné à M. de la Chapelle de lui envoyer le plan du lieu où ils veulent bâtir dans la rue de Savoie : ainsi on attend ce que M. de Louvois décidera[12]. Cependant l'alarme est grande dans le quartier, tous les bourgeois, qui sont

1687

---

tribulations, de s'établir dans le jeu de paume de l'Étoile, rue des Fossés-Saint-Germain des Prés (depuis rue de l'Ancienne-Comédie). Ils y restèrent jusqu'en 1770.

11. Cet hôtel, où, suivant quelques-uns, mourut Gabrielle d'Estrées, était attenant au cloître Saint-Germain l'Auxerrois. Voyez Sauval, *Histoire et Recherches des antiquités de la ville de Paris*, tome , p. 307.

12. Nous trouvons à la page de l'*Histoire de Louvois* qui est citée dans la note 10, ce second billet de Louvois à la Reynie : « C'est à M. de Seignelay que vous devez envoyer les mémoires qui contiendront ce que vous devez représenter au Roi concernant la permission que les comédiens ont eue de s'établir dans la rue de Savoie. »

gens de palais, trouvant fort étrange qu'on vienne leur embarrasser leurs rues. M. Billard[13] surtout, qui se trouvera vis-à-vis de la porte du parterre, crie fort haut; et quand on lui a voulu dire qu'il en auroit plus de commodité pour s'aller divertir quelquefois, il a répondu fort tragiquement : « Je ne veux point me divertir. »

Adieu, Monsieur. Je fais moi-même ce que je puis pour vous divertir, quoique j'aie le cœur fort triste depuis la lettre que vous avez écrite à Madame votre sœur. Si vous croyez que je puisse vous être bon à quelque chose à Bourbon, n'en faites point de façon, mandez-le-moi : je volerai pour vous aller voir.

71. — DE BOILEAU A RACINE.

A Bourbon, 9e août [1687].

Je vous demande pardon du gros paquet que je vous envoie; mais M. Bourdier mon médecin a cru qu'il étoit de son devoir d'écrire à M. Fagon sur ma maladie. Je lui ai dit qu'il falloit que M. Dodart vît aussi la chose : ainsi nous sommes convenus de vous adresser sa relation, avec un cachet volant, afin que vous la fissiez voir à l'un et à l'autre. Je vous envoie un compliment pour M. de la Bruyère[1]. J'ai été sensiblement affligé de

---

13. Germain Billard, avocat renommé; il avait marié une de ses filles à Jérôme Bignon, qui fut prévôt des marchands de la ville de Paris en 1708; l'autre à Louis Chauvelin, père du garde des sceaux. (*Note de l'édition de 1807.*)

Lettre 71 (revue sur l'autographe, conservé à la Bibliothèque impériale). — 1. Germain Garnier veut que ce compliment soit « sur son livre des *Caractères*, qui venait, dit-il, de paraître. » Mais c'est une erreur. Le privilége pour l'impression de ce livre ne fut

la mort de M. de Saint-Laurent. Franchement, notre siècle se dégarnit fort de gens de mérite et de vertu ; et sans ceux qu'on a étouffés sous prétexte de J.[2], en voilà un grand nombre que la mort a enlevés depuis peu. Je plains fort le pauvre M. de Sainctot[3].

Je ne vous dirai point en quel état est ma poitrine, puisque mon médecin vous en écrit tout le détail : ce que je vous puis dire, c'est que ma maladie est de ces sortes de choses *quæ non recipiunt magis et minus*[4], puisque je suis environ au même état que j'étois lorsque je suis arrivé. On me dit pourtant toujours, comme à Paris, que cela reviendra, et c'est ce qui me désespère, cela ne revenant point. Si je savois que je dusse être sans voix toute ma vie, je m'affligerois sans doute, mais je prendrois ma résolution, et je me trouverois peut-être moins malheureux que dans un état d'incertitude qui ne me permet pas de me fixer, et qui me laisse toujours comme un coupable qui attend le jugement de son procès. Je m'efforce pourtant de traîner ici ma misérable vie du mieux que je puis, avec un abbé très-honnête homme, qui y est trésorier d'une Sainte-Chapelle[5], mon médecin et mon apothicaire. Je passe le temps avec eux à peu près comme don Guichot[6] le

obtenu que le 8 octobre 1687, et la première édition fut publiée seulement en 1688 : voyez les *OEuvres de la Bruyère*, édition de M. Servois, tome I, p. 91 et 92.

2. On a généralement imprimé *jansénisme*. Boileau s'est contenté de l'initiale.

3. Nicolas de Sainctot, maître des cérémonies, plus tard introducteur des ambassadeurs ; mort en 1713, âgé de quatre-vingt-cinq à quatre-vingt-six ans. Il était sans doute lié d'amitié avec Saint-Laurent.

4. « Qui n'admettent pas le plus et le moins. »

5. L'abbé de Sales : voyez ci-dessus, p. 560, la note 6 de la lettre 65.

6. Telle est ici l'orthographe du manuscrit, et de même un peu

passoit *en un lugar de la Mancha*[7] avec son curé, son barbier et le bachelier Sanson Carasco. J'ai aussi une servante : il me manque une nièce; mais de tous ces gens-là celui qui joue le mieux son personnage, c'est moi, qui suis presque aussi fou que lui, et qui ne dirois guère moins de sottises, si je pouvois me faire entendre. Je n'ai point été surpris de ce que vous m'avez mandé de M. Hessein :

Naturam expellas furca, tamen usque recurret[8].

Il a d'ailleurs de très-bonnes qualités; mais, à mon avis, puisque je suis sur la citation de don Guichot, il n'est pas mauvais de garder avec lui les mêmes mesures qu'avec Cardenio[9]. Comme il veut toujours contredire, il ne seroit pas mauvais de le mettre avec cet homme que vous savez de notre assemblée, qui ne dit jamais rien qu'on ne doive contredire[10] : ils seroient merveilleux ensemble. Adieu, mon cher Monsieur. Conservez-moi toujours une amitié qui fait ma plus grande consolation.

J'ai déjà formé mon plan[11] pour l'année 1667, où je vois de quoi ouvrir un beau champ à l'esprit; mais à ne vous rien déguiser, il ne faut pas que vous fassiez un grand fonds sur moi tant que j'aurai tous les matins

---

plus bas, si ce n'est qu'au lieu de *don*, Boileau cette seconde fois écrit *dom*.

7. « Dans une bourgade de la Manche. »
8. « Chassez le naturel avec une fourche; toujours cependant il reviendra au galop. » (Horace, livre I, *épître* x, vers 24.)
9. Voyez le *Don Quichote*, partie I, chapitres XXIII et suivants.
10. Charpentier. Voyez ci-dessus la lettre 65, p. 559, et la note 5 de cette même page.
11. Il parle de l'histoire du Roi, dont ils étoient tous deux continuellement occupés. (*Note de Louis Racine.*)

à prendre douze verrées d'eau, qu'il coûte encore plus à rendre qu'à avaler, et qui vous laissent tout étourdi le reste du jour, sans qu'il soit permis de sommeiller un moment. Je ferai pourtant du mieux que je pourrai, et j'espère que Dieu m'aidera. Vous faites bien de cultiver Mme de Maintenon ; jamais personne ne fut si digne qu'elle du poste qu'elle occupe, et c'est la seule vertu où je n'ai point encore remarqué de défauts. L'estime qu'elle a pour vous est une marque de son bon goût. Pour moi, je ne me compte pas au rang des choses vivantes.

Vox quoque Mœrim
Jam fugit ipsa : lupi Mœrim videre priores[12].

Suscription : A Monsieur Monsieur Racine. (Fragment d'un cachet rouge.)

---

72. — DE BOILEAU A RACINE.

A Moulins, 13ᵉ août [1687].

Mon médecin a jugé à propos de me laisser reposer deux jours, et j'ai pris ce temps pour venir voir Moulins, où j'arrivai hier au matin, et d'où je m'en dois retourner aujourd'hui au soir. C'est une ville très-marchande et très-peuplée, et qui n'est pas indigne d'avoir un trésorier de France comme vous[1]. Un M. de Cham-

---

12. « Voici que la voix elle-même aussi manque à Mœris : les loups ont vu Mœris les premiers. » (Virgile, *églogue* ix, vers 53 et 54.)

Lettre 72 (revue sur l'autographe, conservé à la Bibliothèque impériale). — 1. Racine était trésorier de France en la généralité de Moulins depuis l'an 1674. Voyez ci-dessus, p. 526, la note 11 de la lettre 50.

blain, ami de M. l'abbé de Sales [2], qui y est venu avec moi, m'y donna hier à souper fort magnifiquement. Il se dit grand ami de M. de Poignant, et connoît fort votre nom, aussi bien que tout le monde de cette ville, qui s'honore fort d'avoir un magistrat de votre force, et qui lui est si peu à charge [3]. Je vous ai envoyé, par le dernier ordinaire, une très-longue déduction de ma maladie, que M. Bourdier mon médecin écrit à M. Fagon : ainsi vous en devez être instruit à l'heure qu'il est parfaitement. Je vous dirai pourtant que, dans cette relation, il ne parle point de la lassitude de jambes et du peu d'appétit : si bien que tout le profit que j'ai fait jusqu'ici à boire des eaux, selon lui, consiste à un éclaircissement de teint, que le hâle du voyage m'avoit jauni plutôt que la maladie ; car vous savez bien qu'en partant de Paris je n'avois pas le visage trop mauvais, et je ne vois pas qu'à Moulins, où je suis, on me félicite fort présentement de mon embonpoint. Si j'ai écrit une lettre si triste à ma sœur, cela ne vient point de ce que je me sente beaucoup plus mal qu'à Paris, puisqu'à vous dire le vrai, tout le bien et tout le mal mis ensemble, je suis environ au même état que quand je partis; mais dans le chagrin de ne point guérir, on a quelquefois des moments où la mélancolie redouble, et je lui ai écrit dans un de ces moments. Peut-être dans une autre lettre verra-t-elle que je ris : le chagrin est comme une fièvre, qui a ses redoublements et ses suspensions.

La mort de M. de Saint-Laurent est tout à fait édifiante : il me paroît qu'il a fini avec toute l'audace d'un philosophe et toute l'humilité d'un chrétien. Je suis persuadé qu'il y a des saints canonisés qui n'étoient

2. Voyez ci-dessus, p. 560, note 6 de la lettre 65; et p. 579, note 5 de la lettre 71.
3. Parce qu'il n'y alloit jamais. (*Note de Louis Racine.*)

pas plus saints que lui : on le verra un jour, selon toutes les apparences, dans les litanies ; mon embarras est seulement comment on l'appellera, et si on lui dira simplement saint Laurent ou saint Saint-Laurent. Je n'admire pas seulement Monsieur de Chartres [4], mais je l'aime, j'en suis fou. Je ne sais pas ce qu'il sera dans la suite ; mais je sais bien que l'enfance d'Alexandre ni de Constantin n'ont [5] jamais promis de si grandes choses que la sienne, et on pourroit beaucoup plus justement faire de lui les prophéties que Virgile, à mon avis, a fait [6] assez à la légère du fils de Pollion [7].

Dans le temps que je vous écris ceci, M. Amyot [8] vient d'entrer dans ma chambre. Il a précipité, dit-il, son retour à Bourbon pour me venir rendre service. Il m'a dit qu'il avoit vu, avant que de partir, M. Fagon, et qu'ils persistoient l'un et l'autre dans la pensée du demi-bain, quoi qu'en pussent dire MM. Bourdier et Baudière. C'est une affaire qui se décidera demain à Bourbon. A vous dire le vrai, mon cher Monsieur, c'est quelque chose d'assez fâcheux que de se voir ainsi le jouet d'une science très-conjecturelle [9], et où l'un dit blanc et l'autre noir; car les deux derniers ne soutiennent pas seulement que le bain n'est point bon à mon mal, mais ils prétendent qu'il y va de la vie, et citent sur cela des exemples funestes. Mais enfin me voilà livré à la médecine, et il n'est plus temps de reculer. Ainsi ce que je demande à Dieu, ce n'est pas

---

4. Voyez ci-dessus, p. 575, la lettre 70.
5. Il y a bien *ont* dans l'original, comme si les mots précédents étaient : « l'enfance d'Alexandre ni celle de Constantin. »
6. Boileau a ainsi écrit *fait*, sans accord.
7. Virgile, *églogue* IV, vers 7 et suivants.
8. Médecin de Bourbon. (*Note de l'édition de* 1807.)
9. Boileau a écrit ainsi ; les éditeurs de Racine et de Boileau ont substitué *conjecturale* à *conjecturelle*.

qu'il me rende la voix, mais qu'il me donne la vertu et la piété de M. de Saint-Laurent, ou de M. Nicole, ou même la vôtre, puisque, avec cela, on se moque des périls.

S'il y a quelque malheur dont on se puisse réjouir, c'est, à mon avis, de celui des comédiens. Si on continue à les traiter comme on fait, il faudra qu'ils s'aillent établir entre la Villette et la porte Saint-Martin : encore ne sais-je s'ils n'auront point sur les bras le curé de Saint-Laurent [10].

Je vous ai une obligation infinie du soin que vous prenez d'entretenir un misérable comme moi. L'offre que vous me faites de venir à Bourbon est tout à fait héroïque et obligeante ; mais il n'est pas nécessaire que vous veniez vous enterrer inutilement dans le plus vilain lieu du monde, et le chagrin que vous auriez infailliblement de vous y voir, ne feroit qu'augmenter celui que j'ai d'y être. Vous m'êtes plus nécessaire à Paris qu'ici, et j'aime encore mieux ne vous point voir, que de vous voir triste et affligé [11]. Adieu, mon cher Monsieur. Mes recommandations à M. Félix, à M. de Termes et à tous nos autres amis.

10. La paroisse de Saint-Laurent s'étendait jusque-là. (*Note de Berriat-Saint-Prix*.)

11. L'offre si cordiale, et évidemment si sincère, que Racine avait faite à Boileau, et les raisons que donne celui-ci pour ne pas l'accepter, font trop bien connaître, non-seulement l'amitié des deux poëtes, mais plus particulièrement le caractère de Racine, pour que nous n'appelions pas ici l'attention du lecteur.

73. — DE RACINE A BOILEAU.

A Paris, ce 13e août [1687].

Je ne vous écrirai aujourd'hui que deux mots ; car outre qu'il est extrêmement tard, je reviens chez moi pénétré de frayeur et de déplaisir. Je sors de chez le pauvre M. Hessin[1], que j'ai laissé à l'extrémité : je doute qu'à moins d'un miracle je le retrouve demain en vie. Je vous conterai sa maladie une autre fois, et je ne vous parlerai maintenant que de ce qui vous regarde. Vous êtes un peu cruel à mon égard, de me laisser si longtemps dans l'horrible inquiétude où vous avez bien dû juger que votre lettre à Mme Manchon me pouvoit jeter[2]. J'ai vu M. Fagon, qui, sur le récit que je lui ai fait de ce qui est dans cette lettre, a jugé qu'il falloit quitter sur-le-champ vos eaux. Il dit que leur effet naturel est d'ouvrir l'appétit, bien loin de l'ôter. Il croit même qu'à l'heure qu'il est vous les aurez interrompues, parce qu'on n'en prend jamais plus de vingt jours de suite. Si vous vous en êtes trouvé considérablement bien, il est d'avis qu'après les avoir laissées pour quelque temps, vous les recommenciez ; si elles ne vous ont fait aucun bien, il croit qu'il faut les quitter entièrement. Le Roi me demanda avant-hier au soir si vous

---

Lettre 73 (revue sur l'autographe, conservé à la Bibliothèque impériale). — 1. Une lettre de la Fontaine à M. de Bonrepaux, qui est de la même date que celle-ci, fait aussi mention de cette maladie de M. Hessein. (*Note de l'édition de* 1807.) — Dans l'édition de M. Walckenaer, cette lettre de la Fontaine est datée (nous ne savons si c'est par erreur) du 31 et non du 13 août. L'état de M. Hessein y est présenté comme bien moins grave que Racine ne le dit ici. On y lit : « Il n'y a nul mauvais accident dans sa maladie. »

2. On voit par là que Racine n'avait pas encore reçu la lettre de Boileau en date du 9 août (*lettre* 71). Il y répond dans la lettre suivante.

étiez revenu : je lui répondis que non, et que les eaux jusqu'ici ne vous avoient pas fort soulagé. Il me dit ces propres mots : « Il fera mieux de se remettre à son train de vie ordinaire; la voix lui reviendra lorsqu'il y pensera le moins. » Tout le monde a été charmé de la bonté que S. M. a témoignée pour vous en parlant ainsi, et tout le monde est d'avis que, pour votre santé, vous ferez bien de revenir. M. Félix est de cet avis, le premier médecin et M. Moreau[3] en sont entièrement. M. du Tartre[4] croit qu'absolument les eaux de Bourbon ne sont point bonnes pour votre poitrine, et que vos lassitudes en sont une marque. Tout cela, mon cher Monsieur, m'a donné une furieuse envie de vous voir de retour. On dit que vous trouverez de petits remèdes innocents qui vous rendront infailliblement la voix, et qu'elle reviendra d'elle-même quand vous ne feriez rien. M. le maréchal de Bellefont[5] m'enseigna hier un remède dont il dit qu'il a vu plusieurs gens guéris d'une extinction de voix : c'est de laisser fondre dans sa bouche un peu de myrrhe, la plus transparente qu'on puisse trouver; d'autres se sont guéris avec de la simple eau de poulet, sans compter l'*erisimum;* enfin, tout d'une voix, tout le monde vous conseille de revenir. Je n'ai jamais vu une santé plus généralement souhaitée que la vôtre. Venez donc, je vous en[6] conjure, et à

---

3. « Et M. Moreau » est dans l'interligne.

4. Chirurgien-juré du parlement de Paris; il fut ensuite chirurgien ordinaire du Roi. (*Note de l'édition de* 1807.)

5. Mme de Sévigné, dans une lettre à Mme de Coulanges, du 5 juillet 1694, raille le maréchal de Bellefonds sur ce qu'il se mêlait un peu de médecine. (*Note de l'édition de* 1807.) — Voyez les *Lettres de Mme de Sévigné*, tome X, p. 168, où l'on remarquera que la lettre n'est pas adressée à Mme de Coulanges, mais à Coulanges, son mari.

6. Racine a ajouté *en*, dans l'interligne.

moins que vous n'ayez déjà un commencement de voix qui vous donne des assurances que vous achèverez de guérir à Bourbon, ne perdez pas un moment de temps pour vous redonner à vos amis, et à moi surtout, qui suis inconsolable de vous voir si loin de moi, et d'être des semaines entières sans savoir si vous êtes en santé ou non. Plus je vois décroître le nombre de mes amis, plus je deviens sensible au peu qui m'en reste. Et il me semble, à vous parler franchement, qu'il ne me reste presque plus que vous. Adieu. Je crains de m'attendrir follement en m'arrêtant trop sur cette réflexion. Mme Manchon pense toutes les mêmes choses que moi, et est véritablement inquiète sur votre santé.

Suscription : Moulins. A Monsieur Monsieur Despréaux, chez M. Prevost, maître chirurgien, à Bourbon. (Un reste de cachet rouge.)

---

74. — DE RACINE A BOILEAU.

A Paris, ce 17. août [1687].

J'ALLAI hier au soir à Versailles, et j'y allai tout exprès pour voir M. Fagon, et lui donner la consultation de M. Bourdier. Je la lus auparavant avec M. Felix, et je la trouvai très-savante, dépeignant votre tempérament et votre mal en termes très-énergiques; j'y croyois trouver en quelque page : *Numero Deus impari gaudet*[1]. M. Fagon me dit que du moment qu'il s'agis-

---

LETTRE 74 (revue sur l'autographe, conservé à la Bibliothèque impériale). — 1. « La Divinité aime le nombre impair. » (Virgile, *églogue* VIII, vers 75.) Racine a bien écrit *impari*, au lieu de *impare*. — « On peut présumer, dit Berriat-Saint-Prix dans une note sur

soit de la vie et qu'elle pouvoit être en compromis, il s'étonnoit qu'on mît en question si vous prendriez le demi-bain. Il en écrira à M. Bourdier, et cependant il m'a chargé de vous écrire au plus vite de ne point vous baigner, et même, si les eaux vous ont incommodé, de les quitter entièrement, et de vous en revenir. Je vous avois déjà mandé son avis là-dessus, et il y persiste toujours. Tout le monde crie que vous devriez revenir, médecins, chirurgiens, hommes, femmes.

Je vous avois mandé qu'il falloit un miracle pour sauver M. Hessin[2] : il est sauvé, et c'est votre bon ami le quinquina qui a fait ce miracle. L'émétique l'avoit mis à la mort ; M. Fagon arriva fort à propos, qui, le croyant à demi mort, ordonna au plus vite le quinquina. Il est présentement sans fièvre : je l'ai même tantôt fait rire jusqu'à la convulsion, en lui montrant l'endroit de votre lettre où vous parlez du bachelier, du curé et du barbier[3]. Vous dites qu'il vous manque une nièce. Voudriez-vous qu'on vous envoyât Mlle Despréaux[4]? Je m'en vais ce soir à Marly. M. Félix a demandé permis-

la lettre de Boileau en date du 23 août 1687, que Bourdier insistait sur les *jours intercalaires* (les 3e, 5e, 9e, 13e, 19e....), jadis si accrédités en médecine. »

2. Racine, d'ordinaire, écrit *Hessin;* mais ici, et dans la suite de cette même lettre : *Hessins.* Boileau écrit toujours *Hessein.*

3. Voyez la lettre 71 ci-dessus, p. 579 et 580.

4. Petit trait de raillerie. Il n'aimoit pas beaucoup cette nièce. (*Note de Louis Racine.*) — Cette nièce était Marie-Charlotte Boileau Despréaux, née en 1649, morte après 1718, fille de Jérôme Boileau, greffier au Parlement. Germain Garnier dit que la femme de Jérôme Boileau « avait l'humeur la plus bizarre et la plus acariâtre, » que « la fille tenait la mère, » et que « toutes deux avaient beaucoup tourmenté Boileau, lorsqu'il demeurait chez son frère. » Berriat-Saint-Prix doute que ces assertions soient fondées. Toutefois la malicieuse proposition que fait ici Racine montre assurément que Boileau craignait un peu la société de Mlle Despréaux.

sion au Roi pour moi, et j'y demeurerai jusqu'à mécredi prochain.

M. le duc de Charost⁵ m'a tantôt demandé de vos nouvelles d'un ton de voix que je vous souhaiterois de tout mon cœur. Quantité de gens de nos amis sont malades, entre autres M. le duc de Chevreuse et M. de Chanlay⁶ : tous deux ont la fièvre double-tierce. M. de Chanlay a déjà pris le quinquina; M. de Chevreuse le prendra au premier jour. On ne voit à la cour que des gens qui ont le ventre plein de quinquina. Si cela ne vous excite pas à y revenir, je ne sais plus ce qui vous peut en donner envie. M. Hessin ne l'a point voulu prendre des apothicaires, mais de la propre main de Chmith⁷. J'ai vu ce Chmith chez lui; il a le visage ver-

---

5. Armand de Béthune, duc de Charost. Ses lettres ne furent vérifiées que trois ans après la date de cette lettre. Il était gendre du ministre Foucquet. (*Note de l'édition de* 1807.)

6. Racine écrit ainsi, au lieu de *Chamlay*. — Maréchal des logis des armées dès le temps de Turenne. A la mort de Louvois, en 1691, Chamlay refusa le ministère de la guerre.... Il mourut en 1719.... Sa liaison avec Boileau et Racine.... résulte encore de ce billet inédit, adressé par le dernier au premier, et qui existe en original dans les papiers de Brossette : « M. de Chamlay se doit trouver avec moi ce matin à neuf heures; vous nous feriez plaisir à l'un et à l'autre de vous y trouver aussi. Je vous donne le bonjour. RACINE. Ce 15. août. » (*Adresse :* à Monsieur Monsieur Despréaux.) Il est probable que l'entrevue où Boileau était appelé avait pour but des éclaircissements que l'emploi de Chamlay le mettait à portée de donner sur la guerre à nos deux historiographes. Il est par conséquent postérieur à 1677. (*Note de Berriat-Saint-Prix, sur un passage de la lettre de Racine à Boileau, en date du* 9 *juin* 1693.)

7. L'éditeur de 1807, corrigeant l'orthographe de ce nom, a substitué *Smith* à *Chmith*. Mme de Sévigné (voyez le tome VI de ses *Lettres*, p. 28) écrit *Schemit* le nom de ce même personnage; elle associe son nom à celui du fameux chevalier Tabord ou Talbot, qui vendit à Louis XIV la recette du quinquina. Voyez à la même page 28 des *Lettres de Mme de Sévigné*, la note 11 de la lettre 737.

meil et boutonné, et a bien plus l'air d'un maître cabaretier que d'un médecin. M. Hessin dit qu'il n'a jamais rien bu de plus agréable, et qu'à chaque fois qu'il en prend[8], il sent la vie descendre dans son estomac. Adieu, mon cher Monsieur. Je commencerai et finirai toutes mes lettres en vous disant de vous hâter de revenir.

Suscription : A Monsieur Monsieur Despréaux, chez M. Prevost, maître chirurgien. A Bourbon. (Cachet rouge, au cygne.)

75. — DE BOILEAU A RACINE.

A Bourbon, 19e août [1687].

Vous pouvez juger, Monsieur, combien j'ai été frappé de la funeste nouvelle que vous m'avez mandée de notre pauvre ami[1]. En quelque état pitoyable néanmoins que vous l'ayez laissé, je ne saurois m'empêcher d'avoir toujours quelque rayon d'espérance, tant que vous ne m'aurez point écrit : « Il est mort; » et je me flatte même qu'au premier ordinaire j'apprendrai qu'il est hors de danger. A dire le vrai, j'ai bon besoin de me flatter ainsi, surtout aujourd'hui que j'ai pris une médecine qui m'a fait tomber quatre fois en foiblesse, et qui m'a jeté dans un abattement dont même les plus agréables nouvelles ne seroient pas capables de me relever. Je vous avoue pourtant que, si quelque chose pouvoit me rendre la santé et la joie, ce seroit la bonté qu'a Sa Majesté

---

8. « Qu'il en prend » est ajouté au-dessus de la ligne.
LETTRE 75 (revue sur l'autographe, conservé à la Bibliothèque impériale). — 1. Hessein. Voyez ci-dessus, p. 585, la lettre 73.

de s'enquérir de moi toutes les fois que vous vous présentez devant lui². Il ne sauroit guère rien arriver de plus glorieux, je ne dis pas à un misérable comme moi, mais à tout ce qu'il y a de gens plus considérables à la cour; et je gage qu'il y en a plus de vingt d'entre eux qui, à l'heure qu'il est, envient ma bonne fortune, et qui voudroient avoir perdu la voix, et même la parole à ce prix. Je ne manquerai pas, avant qu'il soit peu, de profiter du bon avis qu'un si grand prince me donne, sauf à desobliger M. Bourdier mon médecin et M. Baudière mon apothicaire, qui prétendent maintenir contre lui que les eaux de Bourbon sont admirables pour rendre la voix. Mais je m'imagine qu'ils réussiront dans cette entreprise, à peu près comme toutes les puissances de Europe ont réussi à lui empêcher de prendre Luxembourg et³ tant d'autres villes. Pour moi, je suis persuadé qu'il fait bon suivre ses ordonnances en fait même de médecine. J'accepte l'augure qu'il m'a donné, en vous disant que la voix me reviendroit lorsque j'y penserois le moins. Un prince qui a exécuté tant de choses miraculeuses est vraisemblablement inspiré du ciel, et toutes les choses qu'il dit sont des oracles. D'ailleurs, j'ai encore un remède à essayer, où j'ai grande espérance, qui est de me présenter à son passage dès que je serai de retour; car je crois que l'envie que j'aurai de lui témoigner ma joie et ma reconnoissance me fera trouver de la voix, et peut-être même des paroles éloquentes⁴. Cependant je vous dirai que je suis aussi muet que jamais, quoique inondé d'eaux et de remèdes. Nous attendons la réponse de M. Fagon sur la relation que M. Bourdier lui a en-

2. Boileau avait d'abord écrit : *à lui.*
3. Devant *tant*, il y a *trente*, effacé.
4. Tout ce passage a certainement été écrit dans la pensée que Racine montrerait cette lettre au Roi.

voyée. Jusque-là je ne puis rien vous dire sur mon départ. On me fait toujours espérer ici une guérison prochaine; et nous devons tenter le demi-bain, supposé que M. Fagon persiste toujours dans l'opinion qu'il me peut être utile. Après cela, je prendrai mon parti. Vous ne sauriez croire combien je vous suis obligé de la tendresse que vous m'avez témoignée dans votre dernière lettre : les larmes m'en sont presque venues aux yeux, et quelque résolution que j'eusse fait[5] de quitter le monde, supposé que la voix ne me revînt point, cela m'a entièrement fait changer d'avis : c'est-à-dire, en un mot, que je me sens capable de quitter toutes choses, hormis vous. Adieu, mon cher Monsieur. Excusez si je ne vous écris pas une plus longue lettre. Franchement je suis fort abattu; je n'ai point d'appétit; je traîne les jambes plutôt que je ne marche; je n'oserois dormir, et suis toujours accablé de sommeil. Je me flatte pourtant encore de l'espérance que les eaux de Bourbon me guériront. M. Amyot est homme d'esprit et me rassure fort. Il se fait une affaire très-sérieuse de me guérir, aussi bien que les autres médecins. Je n'ai jamais vu de gens si affectionnés à leur malade, et je crois qu'il n'y en a pas un d'entre eux qui ne donnât quelque chose de sa santé pour me rendre la mienne. Outre leur affection, il y va de leur intérêt, parce que ma maladie fait grand bruit dans Bourbon. Cependant ils ne sont point d'accord, et M. Bourdier lève toujours des yeux très-tristes au ciel quand on parle de bain. Quoi qu'il en soit, je leur suis obligé de leurs soins et de leur bonne volonté; et quand vous m'écrirez, je vous prie de me dire quelque chose qui marque que je parle bien d'eux. M. de la Chappelle[6] m'a écrit une lettre fort obligeante, et m'en-

---

5. *Fait* est ainsi écrit, sans accord.
6. Voyez ci-dessus, p. 571, la note 12 de la lettre 69.

voie plusieurs inscriptions sur lesquelles il me prie de dire mon avis. Elles me paroissent toutes fort spirituelles; mais je ne saurois pas lui mander cette fois ce que j'y trouve à redire : ce sera pour le premier ordinaire. M. Boursaut[7], que je croyois mort, me vint voir il y a cinq ou six jours, et m'apparut le soir assez subitement : il me dit qu'il s'étoit détourné de trois grandes lieues du chemin de Mont-Luçon, où il alloit et où il est habitué, pour avoir le bonheur de me saluer. Il me fit offre de toutes choses, d'argent, de commodités, de chevaux. Je lui répondis avec les mêmes honnêtetés, et voulus le retenir pour le lendemain à dîner; mais il me dit qu'il étoit obligé de s'en aller dès le grand matin : ainsi nous nous séparâmes amis à outrance. A propos d'amis, mes baisemains, je vous prie, à tous nos amis communs. Dites bien à M. Quinaut[8] que je lui suis infiniment obligé de son souvenir, et des choses obligeantes qu'il a écrites de moi à M. l'abbé de Sales[9]. Vous pouvez l'assurer que je le compte présentement au rang de mes meilleurs amis, et de ceux dont j'estime le plus le cœur et l'esprit. Ne vous étonnez pas si vous recevez quelquefois mes lettres un peu tard, parce que la poste n'est point à Bourbon, et que souvent,

7. Boursault étoit alors receveur des fermes à Mont-Luçon, d'où, à l'occasion de son emploi, il écrivit une lettre assez connue. Boileau l'avoit attaqué dans ses *satires*. Boursault, pour s'en venger, fit imprimer contre lui une comédie intitulée : *Satire des satires*. Cependant, quand il sut Boileau malade à Bourbon, il alla le voir, et lui offrit sa bourse. Boileau, sensible à ce trait de générosité, ôta, dans la suite, de ses *satires* le nom de Boursault. (*Note de Louis Racine*.)

8. Celui même que Boileau avait autrefois si maltraité dans ses *satires*. Il mourut l'année d'après la date de cette lettre. (*Note de l'édition de* 1807.)

9. Voyez ci-dessus, p. 560, la note 6 de la lettre 65.

faute de gens pour envoyer à Moulins, on perd un ordinaire. Au nom de Dieu, mandez-moi, avant toutes choses, des nouvelles de M. Hessein.

76. — DE BOILEAU A RACINE[1].

A Bourbon, 23e août [1687].

On me vient d'avertir que la poste est de ce soir à Bourbon : c'est ce qui fait que je prends la plume à l'heure qu'il est, c'est-à-dire à dix heures du soir, qui est une heure fort extraordinaire aux malades de Bourbon, pour vous dire que, malgré les tragiques remontrances de M. Bourdier, je me suis mis aujourd'hui dans le demi-bain par le conseil de M. Amyot, et même de M. des Trapières, que j'ai appelé au conseil. Je n'y ai été qu'une heure. Cependant j'en suis sorti beaucoup en meilleur état que je n'y étois entré, c'est-à-dire, la poitrine beaucoup plus dégagée, les jambes plus légères, l'esprit plus gai ; et même mon laquais m'ayant demandé quelque chose, je lui ai répondu un *non* à pleine voix, qui l'a surpris lui-même, aussi bien qu'une servante qui étoit dans la chambre, et pour moi j'ai cru l'avoir prononcé par enchantement. Il est vrai que je n'ai pu depuis rattraper ce ton-là ; mais, comme vous voyez, Monsieur, c'en est assez pour me remettre le cœur au ventre, puisque c'est une preuve que ma voix n'est pas entièrement perdue, et que le bain m'est très-bon. Je m'en vais piquer de ce côté-là, et je vous manderai le succès. Je ne sais pas pourquoi M. Fagon a

LETTRE 76. — 1. Revue sur l'autographe, conservé à la Bibliothèque impériale.

molli si aisément sur les objections très-superstitieuses de M. Bourdier². Il y a tantôt six mois que je n'ai eu de véritable joie que ce soir. Adieu, mon cher Monsieur. Je dors en vous écrivant. Conservez-moi votre amitié, et croyez que si je recouvre la voix, je l'emploierai à publier à toute la terre la reconnoissance que j'ai des bontés que vous avez pour moi, et qui ont encore accru de beaucoup la véritable estime et la sincère amitié que j'avois pour vous. J'ai été ravi, charmé, enchanté du succès du quinquina; et ce qu'il a fait sur notre ami Hessein m'engage encore plus dans ses intérêts que la guérison [de ma fièvre³] double-tierce.

77. — DE RACINE A BOILEAU.

A Paris, ce 24. août [1687].

JE vous dirai, avant toutes choses, que M. Hessin, excepté quelque petit reste de foiblesse, est entièrement hors d'affaire, et ne prendra plus que huit jours du quinquina, à moins qu'il n'en prenne pour son plaisir; car la chose devient à la mode, et on commencera bientôt, à la fin des repas, à le servir comme le café et le chocolat. L'autre jour, à Marly, Monseigneur¹, après un fort grand déjeuner avec Mme la princesse de Conty² et d'autres dames, en envoya querir deux bou-

2. Voyez ci-dessus, p. 587 et 588, la note 1 de la lettre 74.
3. Le papier est déchiré à cet endroit.
LETTRE 77 (revue sur l'autographe, conservé à la Bibliothèque impériale). — 1. Le Dauphin. — Racine a ajouté *à Marly*, après coup, en interligne.
2. Anne-Marie de Bourbon, dite Mademoiselle de Blois, fille de Louis XIV et de Mlle de la Vallière. Elle était veuve alors, depuis un peu moins de deux ans, de Louis-Armand de Bourbon, prince

teilles chez les apothicaires du Roi, et en but le premier un grand verre : ce qui fut suivi par toute la compagnie, qui, trois heures après, n'en dîna que mieux. Il me sembla même que cela leur avoit donné un plus grand air de gaieté. Ce jour-là[3], et à ce même dîner, je contai au Roi votre embarras entre vos deux médecins, et la consultation très-savante de M. Bourdier. Le Roi eut la bonté de me demander ce qu'on vous répondoit là-dessus, et s'il y avoit à délibérer. « Oh ! pour moi, s'écria naturellement Mme la princesse de Conty, qui étoit à table à côté de S. M., j'aimerois mieux ne parler de trente ans, que d'exposer ainsi ma vie pour recouvrer la parole. » Le Roi, qui venoit de faire la guerre à Monseigneur sur sa débauche de quinquina, lui demanda s'il ne voudroit point aussi tâter des eaux de Bourbon. Vous ne sauriez croire combien cette maison de Marly est agréable : la cour y est, ce me semble, toute autre qu'à Versailles; il y a peu de gens, et le Roi nomme tous ceux qui l'y doivent suivre. Ainsi tous ceux qui y sont, se trouvant fort honorés d'y être, y sont aussi de fort bonne humeur. Le Roi même y est fort libre et fort caressant. On diroit qu'à Versailles il est tout[4] entier aux affaires, et qu'à Marly il est tout à lui et à son plaisir. Il m'a fait l'honneur plusieurs fois de me parler, et j'en suis sorti à mon ordinaire, c'est-à-dire fort charmé de lui et au désespoir contre moi; car je ne me trouve jamais si peu d'esprit que dans ces moments où j'aurois le plus d'envie d'en avoir.

de Conti, mort le 9 novembre 1685. Voyez, au tome V, la note 1 de la page 186.
3. Les éditeurs précédents, sans en excepter Berriat-Saint-Prix, ont mis : « un plus grand air de gaieté ce jour-là; et, à ce même dîner, je contai.... »
4. *Tout* est écrit au-dessus de la ligne.

Du reste, je suis revenu riche de bons mémoires[5]. J'y ai entretenu tout à mon aise les gens qui pouvoient me dire le plus de choses de la campagne de Lille[6]. J'eus même l'honneur de demander cinq ou six éclaircissements à M. de Louvois, qui me parla avec beaucoup de bonté. Vous savez sa manière, et comme toutes ses paroles sont pleines de droit sens et vont au fait. En un mot, j'en sortis très-savant et très-content. Il me dit que, tout autant de difficultés que nous aurions, il nous écouteroit avec plaisir. Les questions que je lui fis regardoient Charleroy et Douay. J'étois en peine pourquoi on alla d'abord à Charleroy, et si on avoit déjà nouvelles que les Espagnols l'eussent[7] rasé; car en voulant écrire, je me suis trouvé arrêté tout à coup, et par cette difficulté, et par beaucoup d'autres que je vous dirai. Vous ne me trouverez peut-être, à cause de cela, guère plus avancé que vous : c'est-à-dire beaucoup d'idées et peu d'écriture. Franchement je vous trouve fort à dire, et dans mon travail, et dans mes plaisirs. Une heure de conversation m'étoit d'un grand secours pour l'un, et d'un grand accroissement pour les autres.

Je viens de recevoir une lettre de vous[8]. Je ne doute pas que vous n'ayez présentement reçu celle où je vous mandois l'avis de M. Fagon[9], et que M. Bourdier n'ait aussi reçu des noûvelles de M. Fagon même, qui ne serviront pas peu à le confirmer dans son avis. Tout ce que vous m'écrivez de votre peu d'appétit et de votre

---

5. Pour l'histoire du Roi.
6. La campagne de 1667. — Racine a écrit *Lisle*, et, huit lignes plus loin, *Charle Roy*.
7. Il a substitué *eussent* à *avoient*; et, six lignes plus loin, *mes* à *mon*.
8. La lettre 72, datée de Moulin, 13 août 1687.
9. La lettre 73, datée de Paris, même jour.

grand abattement est très-considérable, et marque toujours de plus en plus que les eaux ne vous conviennent point. M. Fagon ne manquera pas de me répéter encore qu'il les faut quitter, et les quitter au plus vite; car, je vous l'ai mandé, il prétend que leur effet naturel est d'ouvrir l'appétit et de rendre les forces : quand elles font le contraire, il y faut renoncer. Je ne doute donc pas que vous ne vous remettiez bientôt en chemin pour revenir. Je suis persuadé, comme vous, que la joie de revoir un prince qui témoigne tant de bonté pour vous, vous fera plus de bien que tous les remèdes. M. Rose m'avoit déjà dit de vous mander de sa part qu'après Dieu le Roi étoit le plus grand médecin du monde, et je fus même fort édifié que M. Rose voulût bien mettre Dieu devant le Roi : je commence à soupçonner[10] qu'il pourroit bien être en effet dans la dévotion. M. Nicole a donné depuis deux jours au public deux tomes de *Réflexions sur les Épîtres et sur les Évangiles*[11], qui me semblent encore plus forts et plus édifiants que tout ce qu'il a fait. Je ne vous les envoie pas, parce que j'espère que vous serez bientôt de retour, et vous les trouverez infailliblement chez vous. Il n'a encore travaillé que sur la moitié des épîtres et des évangiles de l'année ; j'espère qu'il achèvera le reste, pourvu qu'il plaise à Dieu et au Révérend Père de la Ch.[12] de lui laisser encore un an de vie.

Il n'y a point de nouvelles de Hongrie que celles qui sont

10. Racine avait d'abord écrit : « cela m'a fait soupçonner; » ce qui était un peu moins fin. — On s'aperçoit bien que les lettres qui allaient à Bourbon n'avaient pas les mêmes chances d'être lues à Versailles que celles qui venaient de Bourbon.

11. C'est une continuation des *Essais de morale*. Il en parut deux autres tomes l'année suivante 1688. (*Note de l'édition de* 1807.)

12. Le P. de la Chaise. Louis Racine a supprimé les mots : « et au Révérend Père de la Ch. »

dans la *Gazette*. Monsieur de Lorraine[13], en passant la Drave, a fait, ce me semble, une entreprise de fort grand éclat, et fort inutile. Cette expédition a bien de l'air de celle qu'on fit pour secourir Philisbourg[14]. Il a trouvé au delà de la rivière un bois, et au delà de ce bois les ennemis retranchés jusqu'aux dents. M. de Termes est du nombre de ceux que je vous ai mandé qui avoient l'estomac farci de quinquina. Croyez-vous que le quinquina, qui vous a sauvé la vie, ne vous rendroit point la voix? Il devroit du moins vous être plus favorable qu'à un autre, vous qui vous êtes enroué tant de fois à le louer. Les comédiens, qui vous font si peu de pitié, sont pourtant toujours sur le pavé, et je crains, comme vous, qu'ils ne soient obligés de s'aller établir auprès des vignes de feu Monsieur votre père[15]. Ce seroit un digne théâtre pour les œuvres de M. Pradon : j'allois

13. Voyez ci-dessus, p. 576, la lettre 70, et la note 9 de cette lettre.

14. En 1676, tandis que le duc de Luxembourg s'était porté dans la basse Alsace pour recueillir un renfort, le duc de Lorraine investit Philisbourg, qu'il prit le 13 septembre. Le 1er août, Luxembourg promettait de livrer bientôt bataille, et de vaincre. Le 12, dans une dépêche datée de Landau, il avoua qu'il n'avait pu secourir Philisbourg; on avait marché à l'ennemi; mais lorsqu'on était arrivé en vue du camp, on s'était trouvé masqué sur la droite par un bois, qui rompait tout l'ordre de bataille : il avait fallu se retirer. Voyez l'*Histoire de Louvois*, tome II, p. 262 et 263. Mme de Sévigné, dans une lettre du 19 août 1676 à Mme de Grignan (tome V, p. 23), se plaint de ce « diable de bois inconnu sur la carte,... qui obligea d'abandonner Philisbourg à la brutalité des Allemands. » De même ici Racine parle d'un bois au delà duquel Monsieur de Lorraine, en 1687, trouva les ennemis fortement retranchés. Cela explique le rapport qu'il croyait trouver entre deux expéditions qui eurent une issue si différente.

15. Le père de Boileau avait eu des vignes du côté de Pantin, près du lieu où l'on transportait les immondices de Paris. (*Note de l'édition de 1807.*)

ajouter de M. Boursault, mais je suis trop touché des honnêtetés que vous avez tout nouvellement reçues de lui. Je ferai tantôt à M. Quinaut celles que vous me mandez de lui faire. Il me semble que vous avancez furieusement dans le chemin de perfection. Voilà bien des gens[16] à qui vous avez pardonné.

On m'a dit, chez Mme Manchon, que M. Marchand partoit lundi prochain pour Bourbon. *Hui! vereor ne quid Andria apportet mali*[17]. Franchement j'appréhende un peu qu'il ne vous retienne : il aime fort son plaisir. Cependant je suis assuré que M. Bourdier même vous dira de vous en aller. Le bien que les eaux vous pouvoient faire est peut-être fait : elles auront mis votre poitrine en bon train. Les remèdes ne font pas toujours sur-le-champ leur plein effet, et mille gens qui étoient allés à Bourbon pour des foiblesses de jambes, n'ont recommencé à bien marcher que lorsqu'ils ont été de retour chez eux. Adieu, mon cher Monsieur. Vous me demandez pardon de m'avoir écrit une lettre trop courte, et vous avez raison de le demander; et moi je vous le demande d'en avoir écrit une trop longue, et j'ai peut-être raison aussi.

---

78. — DE BOILEAU A RACINE[1].

A Bourbon, 28e août [1687].

JE ne m'étonne point, Monsieur, que Mme la prin-

---

16. Racine avait d'abord écrit : « bien des offensés. »
17. « Hélas! je crains que l'Andrienne n'apporte quelque mal. » (Térence, *Andrienne*, acte I, scène I, vers 73.)
LETTRE 78. — 1. Revue sur l'autographe, conservé à la Bibliothèque impériale.

cesse de Conti soit dans le sentiment où elle est. Quand elle auroit perdu la voix, il lui resteroit encore un million de charmes pour se consoler de cette perte, et elle seroit encore la plus parfaite chose que la nature ait produite depuis longtemps[2]. Il n'en est pas ainsi d'un misérable qui a besoin de sa voix pour être souffert des hommes, et qui a quelquefois à disputer contre M. Charpentier. Quand ce ne seroit que cette dernière raison, il doit risquer quelque chose, et la vie n'est pas d'un si grand prix qu'il ne la puisse hasarder pour se mettre en état d'interrompre un tel parleur. J'ai donc tenté l'aventure du demi-bain avec toute l'audace imaginable, mes valets faisant lire leur frayeur sur leurs visages, et M. Bourdier s'étant retiré pour n'être point témoin d'une entreprise si téméraire. A vous dire vrai, cette aventure a été un peu semblable à celle des maillotins[3] dans *Don Guichot* : je veux dire qu'après bien des alarmes, il s'est trouvé qu'il n'y avoit qu'à rire, puisque non-seulement le bain ne m'a point augmenté la fluxion sur la poitrine, mais qu'il me l'a même fort soulagée, et que s'il ne m'a rendu la voix, il m'a du moins en partie rendu la santé. Je ne l'ai encore essayé que quatre fois, et M. Amyot prétend le pousser jusqu'à dix. Après quoi, si la voix ne me

2. Voici encore un passage qui ne laisse pas douter que Boileau ne sût fort bien que ses lettres seraient montrées. Voyez ci-dessus, p. 591, note 4 de la lettre 75. On voit d'ailleurs par la lettre de Racine, datée du 5 septembre 1687 (p. 608), que celle-ci fut communiquée par lui aux P.P. Rapin et Bouhours. Il dut aussi la faire lire à la cour.
3. Par l'aventure des *maillotins* il désigne probablement celle des *moulins à foulon* (*Don Quichote*, partie I, chapitre XXIX), moulins qui, dans les traductions anciennes, telles que celles de 1620 et 1668, sont désignés par les mots *maillets à foules* ou *à foulon*, correspondants aux mots du texte original, *maços de batan*. (*Note de Berriat-Saint-Prix*.)

revient, il m'assure qu'il me donnera mon congé. Je conçois un fort grand plaisir à vous revoir et à vous embrasser; mais vous ne sauriez croire pourtant tout ce qui se présente d'affreux à mon esprit quand je songe qu'il me faudra peut-être repasser muet par ces mêmes hôtelleries, et revenir sans voix dans ces mêmes lieux où l'on m'avoit tant de fois assuré que les eaux de Bourbon me guériroient infailliblement. Il n'y a que Dieu et vos consolations qui me puissent soutenir dans une si juste occasion de désespoir. J'ai été fort frappé de l'agréable débauche de Monseigneur chez Mme la princesse de Conti. Mais ne songe-t-il point à l'insulte qu'il a fait par là à tous Messieurs [4] de la Faculté? Passe pour avaler le quinquina sans avoir la fièvre; mais de le prendre sans s'être préalablement fait saigner et purger, c'est une chose qui crie vengeance, et il y a une espèce d'effronterie à ne se point trouver mal après un tel attentat contre toutes les règles de la médecine. Si Monseigneur et toute sa compagnie avoient, avant tout, pris une dose de séné dans quelque sirop convenable, cela lui auroit à la vérité coûté quelques tranchées, et l'auroit mis, lui et tous les autres, hors d'état de dîner; mais il y auroit eu au moins quelques formes gardées, et M. Bachot [5] auroit trouvé le trait galant, au lieu que,

4. Boileau a écrit ainsi, et non « à tous ces Messieurs, » comme la plupart des éditeurs le lui font dire.

5. Étienne Bachot, médecin et poëte latin, né à Sens, mort à Paris, le 18 mai 1688. Il reste de lui plusieurs écrits, les uns en français, les autres en latin, où il a exposé ses doctrines médicales. C'était un grand partisan de la saignée, un véritable Tomès, et, comme l'étaient alors tous les phlébotomisants, un docteur orthodoxe, qui faisait la guerre à l'émétique, à la médecine nouvelle, à la médecine chimique, un sévère gardien des formes. Voyez particulièrement son *Apologie ou Defense pour la saignée contre ses calomniateurs* (1 volume in-8º, à Paris, chez Sébastien Cramoisy, M.DC.XLVI), où, dans un style digne des médecins de Molière, il

de la manière dont la chose s'est faite, cela ne sauroit jamais être approuvé que des gens de cour et du monde, et non point des véritables disciples d'Hippocrate, gens à barbe vénérable, et qui ne verront point assurément ce qu'il peut y avoir eu de plaisant à tout cela. Que si personne n'en a été malade, ils vous répondront qu'il y a eu du sortilége. Et en effet, Monsieur, de la manière dont vous me peignez Marly, c'est un véritable lieu d'enchantement. Je ne doute point que les fées n'y habitent. En un mot, tout ce qui s'y dit et ce qui s'y fait me paroît enchanté; mais surtout les discours du maître du château ont quelque chose de fort ensorcelant, et ont un charme qui se fait sentir jusqu'à Bourbon. De quelque pitoyable manière que vous m'ayez conté la disgrâce des comédiens, je n'ai pu m'empêcher d'en rire. Mais, dites-moi, Monsieur, supposé qu'ils aillent habiter où je vous ai dit, croyez-vous qu'ils boivent du vin du cru? Ce ne seroit pas une mauvaise pénitence à proposer à M. de Chammeslé[6] pour tant de bouteilles de vin de Champagne qu'il a bues, vous savez aux dépens de qui. Vous avez raison de dire qu'ils auront là un merveilleux théâtre pour jouer les pièces de M. Pradon; et d'ailleurs ils y

---

invective contre « la racaille, » qui traite les maladies « chimiquement, empiriquement, et jamais raisonnablement; » et où il défend *mordicus* les remèdes les plus *méthodiques*, « bien que le succès ne réponde pas toujours à la fin que l'on s'étoit proposée. » Par là s'explique ce que Boileau dit ici de lui. L'année même où fut écrite cette lettre de Boileau, c'est-à-dire en 1687, Bachot publia un autre écrit pour la défense de la saignée (celui-ci en latin), que nous n'avons pu voir, mais qui pourrait bien être celui auquel Boileau fait allusion. Berriat-Saint-Prix a eu raison, on le voit, de dire que Bachot était un médecin, plutôt qu'un apothicaire, comme l'avait cru Saint-Surin.

6. Le mari de la Chammeslé, grand ivrogne. (*Note de Louis Racine.*)

auront une commodité, c'est que quand le souffleur aura oublié d'apporter la copie de ses ouvrages, il en trouvera infailliblement une bonne partie dans les précieux dépôts qu'on apporte tous les matins en cet endroit. M. Fagon n'a point écrit à M. Bourdier. Faites bien des compliments pour moi à M. Rose. Les gens de son tempérament sont de fort dangereux ennemis; mais il n'y a point aussi de plus chauds amis, et je sais qu'il a de l'amitié pour moi. Je vous félicite des conversations fructueuses que vous avez eues avec Mgr de Louvois, d'autant que j'aurai part à votre récolte. Ne craignez point que M. Marchand m'arrête à Bourbon. Quelque amitié que j'aie pour lui, il n'entre point en balance avec vous, et l'Andrienne n'apportera aucun mal[7]. Je meurs d'envie de voir les *Réflexions* de M. Nicole, et je m'imagine que c'est Dieu qui me prépare ce livre à Paris pour me consoler de mon infortune. J'ai fort ri de la raillerie que vous me faites sur les gens à qui j'ai pardonné : cependant savez-vous bien qu'il y a à cela plus de mérite que vous ne croyez, si le proverbe italien est véritable, que *chi offende non perdona*[8]? L'action de Monsieur de Lorraine ne me paroît point si inutile qu'on se veut imaginer, puisque rien ne peut mieux confirmer l'assurance de ses troupes, que de voir que les Turcs n'ont osé sortir de leurs retranchements, ni même donner sur son arrière-garde dans sa retraite ; et il faut en effet que ce soit[9] de grands coquins pour l'avoir ainsi laissé repasser la Drave. Croyez-moi, ils seront battus, et la retraite de Monsieur de Lorraine a plus de rapport à la retraite de César quand il décampa devant Pom-

7. Voyez ci-dessus, p. 600, le vers de Térence que Racine avait cité.
8. « Qui offense ne pardonne pas. »
9. Il y a bien *soit*, au singulier, dans l'original.

pée, qu'à l'affaire de Philisbourg. Quand vous verrez M. Hessein, faites-le ressouvenir que nous sommes frères en quinquina, puisqu'il nous a sauvé la vie à l'un et à l'autre. Vous pensez vous moquer; mais je ne sais pas si je n'en essayerai point pour le recouvrement de ma voix. Adieu, mon cher Monsieur. Aimez-moi toujours, et croyez qu'il n'y a rien au monde que j'aime plus que vous. Je ne sais où vous vous êtes mis en tête que vous m'aviez écrit une longue lettre, car je n'en ai jamais trouvé une si courte.

79. — DE BOILEAU A RACINE[1].

A Bourbon, 2e septembre [1687].

NE vous étonnez pas, Monsieur, si vous ne recevez pas les réponses à vos lettres aussi promptes que peut-être vous souhaitez, parce que la poste est fort irrégulière à Bourbon, et qu'on ne sait pas trop bien quand il faut écrire. Je commence à songer à ma retraite. Voilà tantôt la dixième fois que je me baigne, et à ne vous rien celer, ma voix est tout au même état que quand je suis arrivé. Le monosyllabe que j'ai prononcé n'a été qu'un effet de ces petits tons que vous savez qui m'échappent quelquefois quand j'ai beaucoup parlé, et mes valets ont été un peu trop prompts à crier miracle. La vérité est pourtant que le bain m'a renforcé les jambes

---

LETTRE 79. — 1. Cette lettre est une de celles dont l'autographe ne se trouve plus à la Bibliothèque impériale, qui l'a possédé autrefois (voyez ci-dessus, p. 545 et 546, la note 1 de la lettre 61.) Nous avons suivi le texte donné par Berriat-Saint-Prix, d'après le manuscrit. Nous avons eu sous les yeux aussi le texte de M. Laverdet, publié sur la copie de Jean-Baptiste Racine.

et fortifié la poitrine; mais pour ma voix, ni le bain ni la boisson des eaux ne m'y ont de rien servi. Il faut donc s'en aller de Bourbon aussi muet que j'y suis arrivé. Je ne saurois vous dire quand je partirai : je prendrai brusquement mon parti, et Dieu veuille que le déplaisir ne me tue pas en chemin! Tout ce que je vous puis dire, c'est que jamais exilé n'a quitté son pays avec tant d'affliction que je retournerai au mien. Je vous dirai encore plus, c'est que, sans votre considération, je ne crois pas que j'eusse jamais revu Paris, où je ne conçois aucun autre plaisir que celui de vous revoir. Je suis bien fâché de la juste inquiétude que vous donne la fièvre de Monsieur votre jeune fils [2]. J'espère que cela ne sera rien. Mais si quelque chose me fait craindre pour lui, c'est le nombre de bonnes qualités qu'il a, puisque je n'ai jamais vu d'enfant de son âge si accompli en toutes choses. M. Marchand est arrivé ici samedi. J'ai été fort aise de le voir; mais je ne tarderai guère à le quitter. Nous faisons notre ménage ensemble; il est toujours aussi bon et aussi méchant homme que jamais. J'ai su par lui tout ce qu'il y a de mal à Bourbon, dont je ne savois pas un mot à son arrivée. Votre relation de l'affaire de Hongrie [3] m'a fait un très-grand plaisir, et m'a fait comprendre en très-peu de mots ce que les plus longues relations ne m'auroient peut-être pas appris. Je l'ai débitée à tout Bourbon, où [4] il n'y avoit qu'une relation d'un

2. Il parle de mon frère aîné. (*Note de Louis Racine.*) — Jean-Baptiste Racine, né le 11 novembre 1678, avait alors près de neuf ans.
3. Cette relation que Racine avait faite de la victoire du duc de Lorraine, Charles V, à Mohacz, se trouvait probablement dans une lettre écrite à Boileau depuis celle du 24 août, et qui n'a pas été conservée.
4. *Où* manque dans le texte donné par M. Laverdet; mais il est probable qu'il est bien dans l'original, et qu'une correction de Boileau l'a plus tard fait disparaître, à cause de l'autre *où* qui suit.

commis de M. Jacques⁵, où, après avoir parlé du grand visir, on ajoutoit entre autres choses, que *ledit visir voulant réparer le grief qui lui avoit été fait*, etc. Tout le reste étoit de ce style. Adieu, mon cher Monsieur. Aimez-moi toujours, et croyez que vous êtes ma seule consolation⁶.

Je vous écrirai en partant de Bourbon, et vous aurez de mes nouvelles en chemin. Je ne sais trop le parti que je prendrai à Paris. Tous mes livres sont à Auteuil, où je ne puis plus désormais aller les hivers. J'ai résolu de prendre un logement pour moi seul. Je suis las franchement d'entendre le tintamarre des nourrices et des servantes⁷. Je n'ai qu'une chambre et point de meubles au cloître où je suis⁸. Tout ceci soit dit entre nous; mais cependant je vous prie de me mander votre avis. N'ayant point de voix, il me faut du moins de la tranquillité. Je suis las de me sacrifier au plaisir et à la commodité d'autrui. Il n'est pas vrai que je ne puisse

---

5. Entrepreneur des vivres dans l'armée du duc de Lorraine. (*Note de l'édition de* 1807.)

6. Le texte de cette lettre s'arrête ici dans le livre de M. Laverdet, qui après le mot *consolation* donne la signature : *Despréaux*.

7. Ceci annonce qu'il demeurait, au moins pendant le jour, dans la maison de son neveu Dongois, cour du Palais. Mme Gilbert de Voisins, fille de celui-ci et habitant avec lui, avait alors deux fils âgés seulement, l'un de deux et l'autre de trois ans. (*Note de Berriat-Saint-Prix.*)

8. La suscription de quelques lettres adressées à Boileau montre qu'il logeait au cloître Notre-Dame, chez l'abbé de Dreux, chanoine de l'église de Paris. — Boileau avait pris cette chambre (*au cloître Notre-Dame*) au mois d'octobre 1683, comme nous l'apprenons par une lettre que lui écrivit Maucroix le 2 novembre suivant, et qui est dans les manuscrits de Brossette. Dongois l'engagea sans doute à conserver en même temps un appartement chez lui, et à y vivre, de sorte que, selon toute apparence, la chambre du cloître ne lui servait que pour la nuit. (*Note de Berriat-Saint-Prix.*)

bien vivre et tenir seul mon ménage : ceux qui le croient se trompent grossièrement. D'ailleurs je prétends désormais mener un genre de vie dont tout le monde ne s'accommodera pas. J'avois pris des mesures que j'aurois exécutées, si ma voix ne s'étoit point éteinte. Dieu ne l'a pas voulu. J'ai honte de moi-même, et je rougis des larmes que je répands en vous écrivant ces derniers mots.

80. — DE RACINE A BOILEAU.

A Paris, ce 5. septembre [1687].

J'avois destiné cette après-dînée à vous écrire fort au long; mais un cousin, abusant d'un fâcheux parentage[1], est venu malheureusement me voir, et il ne fait que de sortir de chez moi. Je ne vous écris donc que pour vous dire que je reçus avant-hier une lettre de vous[2]. Le P. Bouhours et le P. Rapin étoient dans mon cabinet quand je la reçus. Je leur en fis la lecture en la décachetant, et je leur fis un fort grand plaisir. Je regardai[3] pourtant de loin, à mesure que je la lisois, s'il n'y avoit rien dedans qui fût trop janséniste. Je vis vers la fin le nom de M. Nicole[4], et je sautai bravement ou, pour mieux dire, lâchement par-dessus. Je n'osai m'exposer à troubler la grande joie et même les éclats de rire que leur causèrent plusieurs choses fort plaisantes que vous me mandiez. Nous aurions été tous trois les plus contents du

Lettre 80 (revue sur l'autographe, conservé à la Bibliothèque impériale). — 1. Allusion à un vers de Boileau (vers 46 de l'*épître* vi à *M. de la Moignon*).

2. C'est la lettre 78, datée du 28 août.

3. Les précédents éditeurs, sans en excepter Berriat-Saint-Prix, ont mis : « je regardois. »

4. Voyez ci-dessus, p. 604.

monde si nous eussions trouvé à la fin de votre lettre que vous parliez à votre ordinaire, comme nous trouvions que vous écriviez avec le même esprit que vous avez toujours eu. Ils sont, je vous assure, tous deux fort de vos amis, et même fort bonnes gens. Nous avions été le matin entendre le P. de Villiers[5], qui faisoit l'oraison funèbre de Monsieur le Prince, grand-père de Monsieur le Prince d'aujourd'hui. Il y a joint a[ussi] les louanges du dernier mort, et il s'est enfoncé jusqu'au cou dans le combat de saint Antoine[6], Dieu sait combien judicieusement. En vérité il a beaucoup d'esprit; mais il auroit bien besoin de se laisser conduire. J'annonçai au P. Bouhours un nouveau livre, qui excita fort sa curiosité. Ce sont les *Remarques* de M. de Vaugelas, avec les notes de Thomas Corneille[7]. Cela est ainsi affiché dans Paris depuis quatre jours. Auriez-vous jamais cru voir ensemble M. de Vaugelas et M. de Corneille le jeune donnant des règles sur la langue?

J'eusse bien voulu vous pouvoir mander que M. de Louvois est guéri, en vous mandant qu'il a été malade; mais ma femme, qui vient de voir Mme de la Chapelle[8], m'apprend qu'il a encore de la fièvre. Elle étoit

---

5. Il était alors jésuite; mais il quitta cette société deux ans après (*et devint cluniste*). Il a fait un poëme sur l'*Art de prêcher*, et, entre autres ouvrages en prose, un *Entretien sur les tragédies*. L'oraison funèbre dont il s'agit ici est celle de Henri de Bourbon (II), prince de Condé, mort en 1646. *Le dernier mort* est le grand Condé, fils de celui-ci, et qui était mort l'année précédente, 1686. (*Note de l'édition de 1807.*)

6. Cette journée du faubourg Saint-Antoine, dans laquelle Condé avait combattu contre l'armée royale commandée par Turenne, est celle du 2 juillet 1652.

7. *Remarques sur la langue françoise de M. de Vaugelas. Nouvelle édition, revue et corrigée, avec des notes de Thomas Corneille.* Paris, 1697 (2 volumes in-12).

8. Charlotte Dongois, nièce de Boileau, née en 1638, morte en

d'abord comme continue, et même assez grande; elle n'est présentement qu'intermittente⁹, et c'est encore une des obligations que nous avons au quinquina. J'espère que je vous manderai lundi qu'il est absolument guéri. Outre l'intérêt du Roi et celui du public, nous avons, vous et moi, un intérêt particulier à lui souhaiter une longue santé. On ne peut pas nous témoigner plus de bonté qu'il nous en témoigne; et vous ne sauriez croire avec quelle amitié il m'a toujours demandé de vos nouvelles. Bonsoir, mon cher Monsieur. Je salue de tout mon cœur M. Marchand. Je vous écrirai plus au long lundi¹⁰. Mon fils est guéri.

1719, femme de Henri Bessé de la Chapelle (voyez ci-dessus, p. 571, note 12 de la lettre 69). — La place de contrôleur des bâtiments mettait son mari en relation avec Louvois, qui en était surintendant. (*Note de Berriat-Saint-Prix.*)

9. *Ne.... que* a été ajouté après coup.

10. La lettre que Racine annonce nous manque. Après la lettre du 5 septembre, nous n'en avons plus de lui qui soit datée de 1687.

TABLE DES MATIÈRES

CONTENUS DANS LE SIXIÈME VOLUME.

REMARQUES SUR LES OLYMPIQUES DE PINDARE ET SUR L'ODYSSÉE D'HOMÈRE..................	1
Notice...	3
Remarques sur les Olympiques de Pindare.........	9
Remarques sur l'Odyssée d'Homère...............	56
LIVRES ANNOTÉS....................................	165
Notice...	167
La Bible. — Le livre de Job......................	177
Saint Basile.....................................	193
Homère. Notes sur l'Iliade.......................	195
Pindare...	212
Eschyle...	218
Sophocle..	222
Euripide..	253
Platon..	266
Aristote..	286
Plutarque...	291
Lucien..	320
Virgile...	323
Horace..	324
Cicéron...	329

TABLE DES MATIÈRES.

Tite-Live	334
Tacite	336
Quintilien	337
Pline l'ancien	338
Pline le jeune	340
La Barde	342
La Pratique du théatre de l'abbé d'Aubignac	351
Vaugelas. Traduction de Quinte-Curce	353
Remarques sur l'orthographe françoise	359
LETTRES	361
Notice	363
1. D'Antoine le Maistre à Racine	371
2. De Racine à l'abbé le Vasseur	373
3. De Racine à Marie Racine	374
4. De Racine à l'abbé le Vasseur	376
5. Du même au même	380
6. Du même au même	384
7. Du même au même	387
8. Du même au même	390
9. Du même au même	397
10. Du même au même	402
11. Du même au même	405
12. De Racine à Marie Racine	409
13. De Racine à la Fontaine	412
14. De Racine à M. Vitart	416
15. De Racine à l'abbé le Vasseur	420
16. Du même au même	422
17. Du même au même	426
18. De Racine à Mlle Vitart	431
19. De Racine à Marie Racine	433
20. De Racine à M. Vitart	435
21. De Racine à Mlle Vitart	439
22. Du même à la même	440
23. De Racine à l'abbé le Vasseur	443

TABLE DES MATIÈRES.

24. De Racine à l'abbé le Vasseur.................. 448
25. De Racine à Mlle Vitart...................... 450
26. De Racine à l'abbé le Vasseur.................. 452
27. Du même au même.......................... 456
28. De Racine à Mlle Vitart...................... 460
29. De Racine à M. Vitart....................... 463
30. De Racine à l'abbé le Vasseur................. 467
31. De Racine à M. Vitart....................... 470
32. Du même au même.......................... 474
33. Du même au même.......................... 478
34. De Racine à l'abbé le Vasseur................. 483
35. De Racine à la Fontaine..................... 487
36. De Racine à M. Vitart....................... 494
37. De Racine à Marie Racine.................... 498
38. Du même à la même......................... 500
39. De Racine à l'abbé le Vasseur................. 502
40. Du même au même.......................... 504
41. Du même au même.......................... 507
42. De la sœur Agnès de Sainte-Thècle à Racine.... 509
43. De Racine à Marie Racine.................... 511
44. Du même à la même......................... 513
45. De Racine au P. Bouhours.................... 515
46. De Racine à ***............................ 516
47. De Racine à Mlle Rivière (*Marie Racine*)........ 517
48. De Racine à Antoine Rivière.................. 518
49. De Racine à Mlle Rivière..................... 521
50. De M. de Guilleragues à Racine................ 522
51. De Racine au P. Bouhours.................... 526
52. De Racine à Mlle Rivière..................... 527
53. D'Antoine Arnauld à Racine................... 530
54. De Racine à Mlle Rivière..................... 532
55. Du même à la même......................... 533
56. De la Fontaine à Racine..................... 535
57. De Racine à Mlle Rivière..................... 538
58. Du même à la même......................... 539
59. Du même à la même......................... 541

TABLE DES MATIÈRES.

60. De Racine à Mlle Rivière	543
61. De Boileau à Racine	545
62. De Racine à Boileau	549
63. De Boileau à Racine	554
64. De Racine au P. Rapin	557
65. De Boileau à Racine	558
66. De Racine à Boileau	561
67. De Boileau à Racine	564
68. De M. de Bonnafau à Racine	568
69. De Racine à Boileau	569
70. Du même au même	573
71. De Boileau à Racine	578
72. Du même au même	581
73. De Racine à Boileau	585
74. Du même au même	587
75. De Boileau à Racine	590
76. Du même au même	594
77. De Racine à Boileau	595
78. De Boileau à Racine	600
79. Du même au même	605
80. De Racine à Boileau	608

FIN DE LA TABLE DES MATIÈRES.

10515. — IMPRIMERIE GÉNÉRALE DE CH. LAHURE
Rue de Fleurus, 9, à Paris

www.ingramcontent.com/pod-product-compliance
Lightning Source LLC
Chambersburg PA
CBHW060402230426
43663CB00008B/1362